A HISTORY OF MALTA

[*Frontispiece.*

MALTA AND GOZO.
(1803.)

A HISTORY OF MALTA

DURING THE PERIOD OF THE FRENCH AND BRITISH
OCCUPATIONS, 1798—1815

BY THE LATE
WILLIAM HARDMAN
OF VALETTA

EDITED
WITH INTRODUCTION AND NOTES BY
J. HOLLAND ROSE, Litt.D. (Cantab.)

The Naval & Military Press Ltd

Published by

The Naval & Military Press Ltd
Unit 5 Riverside, Brambleside
Bellbrook Industrial Estate
Uckfield, East Sussex
TN22 1QQ England

Tel: +44 (0)1825 749494

www.naval-military-press.com
www.nmarchive.com

In reprinting in facsimile from the original, any imperfections are inevitably reproduced and the quality may fall short of modern type and cartographic standards.

PREFATORY NOTE

BY THE LATE MR. HARDMAN

This work makes no pretension to be anything more than a collection of English and foreign documents referring to events in the history of Malta which occurred during the years from 1792 to 1815. These documents, if presented in their entirety and without comment, unless when absolutely necessary, will serve to remove misunderstandings, and will allow the student of history to form a correct appreciation of the action of Great Britain with regard to Malta during the memorable years 1798–1815; for they describe in a concrete form, not only the circumstances which led to the attack and capture of the Islands by the French Republic, but also the subsequent naval and military operations of the British and Maltese forces, aided by the Portuguese and Neapolitan allies, which resulted in Great Britain obtaining and securing the possession of Malta and its dependencies.

Contemporary official documents, and other sources of information, having of late years become accessible to the public, both in London and Paris, they have materially aided the effort to elucidate certain controversial points, more particularly with reference to the capture of Valetta and the Three Cities from the French garrison. Owing to the want of such official information in the past authors have in many instances wandered from the truth. They have given their opinions or conjectures as history, influenced or biassed according to their nationality.

CONTENTS

CHAP.		PAGE
	INTRODUCTION	ix
I.	THE SOCIAL CONDITION OF THE MALTESE PEOPLE AT THE CLOSE OF THE EIGHTEENTH CENTURY	1
II.	BONAPARTE'S PLAN OF SEIZING MALTA (1797)	7
III.	POUSSIELGUE'S REPORT ON HIS MISSION TO MALTA	19
IV.	THE PREPARATIONS IN FRANCE FOR THE EXPEDITION TO MALTA AND EGYPT	29
V.	THE DEPARTURE OF THE FRENCH EXPEDITION AND ARRIVAL OFF MALTA	32
VI.	THE BRITISH PREPARATIONS FOR THE CONFLICT	35
VII.	ATTACK AND CAPTURE OF MALTA BY THE FRENCH	44
VIII.	THE FRENCH GOVERNMENT OF MALTA	74
IX.	THE INTERVENTION OF THE BRITISH FLEET	107
X.	THE BRITISH BLOCKADE—1798	125
XI.	THE BRITISH BLOCKADE—1799	161
XII.	THE BRITISH BLOCKADE—1799	202
XIII.	THE BRITISH BLOCKADE—1799–1800	242
XIV.	THE BRITISH BLOCKADE—1800	276
XV.	THE BRITISH BLOCKADE UP TO THE CAPITULATION OF VALETTA	307
XVI.	CORRESPONDENCE (FROM NOVEMBER 1800 TO JULY 1801)	336
XVII.	RUSSIA'S CONNEXION WITH THE ORDER OF ST. JOHN	361
XVIII.	THE PRELIMINARY TREATY OF PEACE BETWEEN ENGLAND AND FRANCE	396
XIX.	THE MISSION OF THE MALTESE DEPUTIES TO ENGLAND	405

CONTENTS

CHAP.		PAGE
XX.	The Treaty of Amiens	432
XXI.	Discussions and Correspondence relating to Malta	440
XXII.	Discussions and Correspondence relating to Malta	474
XXIII.	The British Administration of Malta up to the 30th May 1814	494
XXIV.	A Retrospect and Comparison	535

APPENDICES

I.	The Financial Condition of the Order of St. John and the Revenue of the Islands in 1798	547
II.	Report on the Revenue of Malta, with some Observations	550
III.	General Vaubois' 'Journal of the Siege of Malta' (Parts I—IV)	556
IV.	Note by the late Mr. Hardman on Maltese Histories	643
Index		649

ILLUSTRATIONS

Malta and Gozo (1803) . . . . *Frontispiece*

Valetta (1803) . . . . *To face p.* 1

INTRODUCTION

I

THE late Mr. William Hardman, of Valetta, with most praiseworthy zeal and assiduity collected the following series of documents relating to the fortunes of the island with which he had so long been associated. He also connected them by an explanatory narrative. Death supervened before he could entirely prepare them for the Press; and his executors applied to the present editor to revise the whole of the MS., and add to it an Introduction and footnotes.

The editor has felt it to be his duty to keep the narrative and general arrangement of the work, so far as was possible, in the state in which Mr. Hardman left it. At the same time he was empowered by the executors, in accordance with instructions left by the deceased, to curtail or amend the MS. where it was found necessary to do so. He has felt it necessary to restrict the narrative and documents at several points, especially where they covered ground that had already been traversed in other works, such as the 'Nelson Dispatches,' M. de la Jonquière's 'l'Expédition d'Egypte,' the 'Paget Papers' (in part), &c. But even in those cases he has retained enough of the MS. to form the continuous and ample description which Mr. Hardman desired to give to the world.

The history of Malta in the eventful years 1798-1803 is of so much interest and importance in the career of Napoleon, and in the development of the British Empire, that it seems in every way desirable to present a detailed picture of the incidents which centred in the siege of Valetta, and in the diplomatic campaign of the years 1802-3, which resulted in the greatest war that Europe has ever known. Students of naval history will also be grateful to Mr. Hardman for throwing fuller light on the careers of Nelson and of his doughty lieutenants, Troubridge and Ball. The figures of Sir Charles Stuart, General Sir Thomas Graham (Lord Lynedoch), and others, also come out in sharper outline than before; and the staunchness of the French defenders of Valetta, especially of General Vaubois and Rear-Admiral Villeneuve, has never been so clearly set forth. Finally, the questions connected with the fall of the Order of St.

John, the designs of the Czar Paul I on Malta, the fluctuating policy of Great Britain, and the censure which the Maltese have never ceased to bestow on her for her method of acquisition of the island, lend to the mass of documents here published an interest which ought to carry many readers to the end of what is a complex but interesting story.

At some points these documents do not give the wider light which is necessary for the full illumination of the Maltese question. The editor, therefore, seeks in this Introduction to present other aspects of it which are needful for a complete understanding of the issues that are involved. The fate of Malta depended, not on the Maltese, not on the Knights of St. John, but on the mighty forces that were set in motion by the will of Bonaparte, and were thwarted ultimately by the mistress of the seas. It will be well, then, to supplement the information given in the early chapters of this work by the following sketch of the salient points in the Oriental policy of Bonaparte.

II

In the course of the Italian campaign of 1797 the young conqueror struck southwards into the Papal States and occupied Ancona. There he gazed over the waters of the Adriatic, and pondered on the possibilities which might accrue from the possession of that excellent harbour. 'Ancona' (so he wrote to the Directory at Paris, on February 10, 1797) 'is the only good port on the Adriatic on this side of Venice. It is, in all points of view, very essential for our dealings with Constantinople. Macedonia is only twenty-four hours from here.'[1] In these sentences we have a sign of those plans which ripened into the Egyptian expedition of the following year.

The eastward trend of the young warrior's thoughts had always been strong ever since the days when he conversed with the *savant*, Volney, author of 'Les Ruines'; and now the fortune of war brought these glowing visions of Eastern conquest almost within the sphere of actuality. For along with that same letter he was able to forward to the Directory dispatches which had been taken from a Russian envoy passing through Ancona, addressed to the Grand Master of the Order of the Knights of St. John at Malta. He added that, if sent to the French ambassador at Constantinople, they might prove to be of great service.[2] The weakness of the Turkish Empire, and the desire of the new Czar, Paul I, to cultivate close relations with the Knights of St. John, were facts already known to the diplomatic world. And the strange chance which called the attention of Bonaparte to the importance of Malta, at the very time when he was meditating on

---

[1] *Correspondance de Napoléon I*, vol. ii. p. 318.
[2] *Ibid.* For Bonaparte's description of this treaty, see the details given in chap. viii of this volume, taken from *Corres. de Nap. I*, vol. iv. p. 164.

INTRODUCTION

the weakness of Turkey, probably led him to focus his plans more clearly, and to suggest to him as their basis the island of Malta.

Certain it is that from this time he thought more and more about the Orient, and therefore about Malta. (See Chapter II for details.) He bent his energies to the task of ending the campaign against Austria, and on terms not utterly repugnant to her, provided that France gained the Venetian fleet and the Ionian Isles (Corfu, Zante, &c.). His insistence on the latter condition was very marked during the long negotiations which preceded the Peace of Campo Formio (October 17, 1797). In the highly suggestive letter which, on the following day, he wrote to Talleyrand, Minister for Foreign Affairs under the French Directory, he laid stress on the importance of those islands for France, and on the need of having peace on the Continent in order to wage war more effectually against England. 'Let us concentrate all our activity on our navy, and destroy England. That done, Europe is at our feet.'[1]

Corfu, then, was a pawn in the great game which was to end in the destruction of 'the modern Carthage.' Malta was another pawn. It is the fate of points of vantage like these—and to them we may add Copenhagen, Gibraltar, Egypt, and Panama—to be bandied about in strifes in which they have no concern. If the Power that holds the key of a sea be strong, it can impose a toll on all who pass by. If it be weak, it falls a prey to stronger States which struggle for the mastery of that sea. The story, set forth in detail in this volume, centres, not in the interests of the Maltese, but in the world-policy of Bonaparte and Great Britain. That cyclone of colonial strife, far vaster than that of the age of Louis XIV, trended towards Calcutta; but its starting-point was Valetta. Bonaparte soon came to see the essential importance of Malta, as the documents printed in this volume amply prove. Corfu sank to a secondary place in his thoughts; and the mission of Poussielgue to Malta at the close of 1797 shows the forethought of the great commander in using beforehand all possible means for weakening the defence of the Knights of St. John. The official account of that mission here given amplifies our knowledge of the secret negotiations conducted by Poussielgue at Valetta which facilitated the French conquest in June 1798; and it must enhance our admiration of the manner in which Bonaparte put in practice the old adage: *Divide et impera*.

III

The policy of Great Britain, on the other hand, was tentative and halting. Perhaps this lay in the nature of things. The Cabinet of London had suffered terrible shocks. The monarchical coalition

---

[1] *Corres. de Nap. I*, vol. iv. p. 392.

of 1793 went to pieces in the spring of 1795. Spain and Prussia made peace with France, and the former Power accepted the French alliance in the following year. This untoward event led to the evacuation of the Mediterranean by the British fleet in November 1796. This in its turn weakened the resistance of Austria to Bonaparte, and was alleged by that Power as part cause of her surrender to France in the autumn of 1797. And not only was England deprived of her allies: her own fighting power for some months declined owing to the mutinies at Spithead and the Nore. Fortunately the crisis soon passed; and the victory at Camperdown restored the prestige of the islanders on the high seas.

Nevertheless, to a daring nature like Bonaparte's it seemed practicable to keep the Union Jack out of the Mediterranean by threats of an invasion of Ireland. The naval forces of France, Holland, and Spain seemed equal to the task of covering a landing in that island, in which case the British Ministry must concentrate all its efforts on the suppression of the national rising that would undoubtedly take place. Therefore, as soon as news of the great armament at Toulon came to the ears of Pitt and his colleagues, they naturally inferred that its objective was Ireland. The instructions sent on May 21 by Lord St. Vincent to Nelson, who was then in the Mediterranean scouting with three ships-of-the-line and five smaller vessels, pointed to the Neapolitan coast, or that of Spain (with a view to the conquest of Portugal) or of Ireland, as the aim of the French; and in these conjectures he was fully warranted by the news which had reached him from the British Admiralty.[1] Nelson was also bidden to exact supplies for his squadron (now to be strengthened by the addition of ten battleships) either from Tuscan, Neapolitan, Turkish, *Maltese*, or Austrian harbours. This is the only mention of Malta at this time in the British official dispatches; and it is clear that the Pitt Cabinet did not in the least foresee Bonaparte's attack on Malta and Egypt.

Here, then, as in so many parts of the Anglo-French struggle for empire, it was the active, far-seeing and ambitious statecraft of France which opened up new arenas of strife, while Britons followed, doubtfully at first, but in the long run doggedly. Bonaparte was unconsciously acting in the way in which Dupleix, Montcalm, and many others had acted. He precipitated a conflict which was ultimately to turn to the aggrandisement of the Sea Power.

The information brought together by Mr. Hardman in Chapter VI of this volume shows the many speculations as to the destination of Bonaparte's armada, two of which, those of General Acton at Naples, and Mr. Udney, our consul at Florence, were correct. Very interesting is it to observe the motives which induced our Government, on or

---

[1] *Nelson Dispatches*, vol. iii. p. 26.

just before April 20, 1798, to order a part of Lord St. Vincent's fleet, cruising off Cadiz, to enter the Mediterranean. They sprang, not only from the appeals of the Neapolitan Court, which Mr. Hardman cites, but also from those of the Court of Vienna. The Hapsburgs were cut to the quick by the many insults heaped upon them by the French during the Congress of Rastadt and the carrying out of the terms of peace. It was soon apparent that Austria intended to draw the sword at the first favourable opportunity, and that she was resolved to prevent by force the overthrow of the Kingdom of the Two Sicilies (Naples), which seemed to be the natural sequel to the recent occupation of Rome by the French. On March 17, 1798, Thugut, the Austrian Chancellor, urged his ambassador in London, Count Stahremberg, to find out whether England would loyally support the Hapsburg Power against 'a fierce nation irrevocably determined on the total subversion of Europe, and rapidly marching to that end'; also whether the British Government would send a fleet into the Mediterranean, and would continue the struggle in the year 1799, if need arose.[1]

England had no less interest than Austria in the preservation of the Kingdom of the Two Sicilies; for, if the French overran the south of Italy, they could, with the help of the Sicilian Jacobins, conquer Sicily and dominate the whole of the Mediterranean. These disasters could be averted only by the operations of an Austrian army acting from the strong base, Venetia, and by the advent of a British fleet into the Mediterranean. The immediate aim in view, then, was the preservation of the Kingdom of the Two Sicilies; but the appeal which the Emperor Francis II had made on March 9 to the Czar Paul, to mediate between France and the German States with respect to disputes then pending, opened up the prospect of a European league against France; and the sending of a British fleet into the Mediterranean was a potent means of furthering its formation. This appears in the important dispatch of April 20, 1798, from Lord Grenville to Sir Morton Eden, British ambassador at Vienna. He urged that Austria and Prussia should be persuaded to lay aside their jealousies, should frame a plan of pacification for the Holy Roman Empire, and present it to France:

> Then (he continues), if the French accept it, Russia and Prussia will become bound to defend the neutrality of the Empire, and Austria be (*sic*) left at liberty to turn her attention to Italy. If they refuse it, there seems great ground to hope that the two Powers above named will concur in active measures against France, or will at least take upon them the

[1] F. O. Austria, No. 51. I lay stress on the dispatches in our Austrian archives, because Mr. Hardman relied chiefly on those of Naples; and it is clear that the promised help of Austria decided Pitt and Grenville to risk the sending of a fleet into the Mediterranean..

defence of the Rhine while Austria acts in Italy. And as this course of events may lead immediately to the *casus foederis* of the new alliance, it will then become necessary immediately to settle the quotas of the different Powers. If Prussia and Russia charge themselves with the defences of the German frontier, Austria will find in Italy many resources of every sort for the maintenance of her army.[1]

Further particulars show that the movements of Austria all turned on the dispatch of a British fleet to the succour of Naples. This appears in the dispatch of Eden to Lord Grenville (May 7), describing the answer of Francis II to Baptiste, a special envoy from Naples:

The answer of the Emperor to M. Baptiste's instances was that he could not march an army in support of Naples till the [British] fleet arrived, but that then he would decidedly carry into execution the assurances which he had given, if it became necessary: and that he would order special instructions to be given to Count Cobenzl,[2] peremptorily to insist on the French withdrawing their troops from the Roman State, and on their ceasing to molest the Court of Naples.[3]

For reasons which need not be detailed here, Austria did not as yet draw the sword. The Czar Paul also for the present failed to make good his promises of armed support both by sea and land, and Prussia played a waiting game at Rastadt, with results that were profitable at the time but ruinous for the future. England alone made good her promises; and hence came about the entry of a British fleet into the Mediterranean, with results startlingly different from those which Pitt and Grenville expected. They had in view the protection of the Kingdom of the Two Sicilies, or Ireland or Portugal. In point of fact their action led on to events which ensured the ruin of Bonaparte's Egyptian expedition and the expulsion of the French from Malta.

The reader who peruses the following documents with an eye to the wider issues of events and the subtle ironies of history will not fail to notice the more general causes of this wholly unexpected finale. It is clear that Bonaparte himself was too eager for the immediate start of his expedition. Secrecy doubtless was an important factor contributing to success, and personal and political motives also prescribed speed in sailing; but it was perilous to risk so much until France, along with her allies, Spain, Holland, and the Genoese Republic, had gained a decided maritime supremacy over England. Such a supremacy might have been assured in a year or two; and the conquest of Egypt and Malta might have developed into permanent possession.

[1] F. O. Austria, No. 51.
[2] Austrian envoy to the Congress of the Powers at Rastadt.
[3] F. O. Austria, No. 51.

Instead of that, Bonaparte pushed on the preparations with a speed which in some respects impaired the efficiency of his armada.[1] And what was even worse, the French Directory, not content with the plunder of Swiss cantonal treasuries and of Rome, wounded Austria in her German interests, and threatened the overthrow of the Neapolitan dynasty, with which the Hapsburgs were closely related.[2] Thus, at the very time when the Directory should have obeyed Bonaparte's advice and concentrated their energies on their fleet, they irritated neighbouring States by raids and other provocations, with the result that a new coalition against France began to be discussed, and England took the very step (albeit in the dark) which proved to be fatal to Bonaparte's designs. The Nemesis which waits on overweening pride and reckless action has rarely appeared in more singular guise than at this crisis; for the British Government, though having in view only the security of Naples, Ireland, or Portugal, dispatched the admiral who was best fitted to ensure the ruin of Bonaparte's plans for the ascendancy of France in the Mediterranean and the Orient.

IV

It is impossible within the limits of this Introduction to discuss the details of the French attack upon Malta. Very noteworthy is the statement in Poussielgue's report (Chapter III) of the losses sustained by the Order of the Knights of St. John by the confiscation of its property in France, and still more so is his suggestion that the Court of Madrid, then allied to France, should be induced to take the same step towards its possessions in Spain. The plan of depleting the funds of the Order, so as to ensure its ruin, was to be carried out in Spain, with results which appeared in 1802-3 during the discussions with France relative to the future destinies of the island.

The documents which follow show the Grand Master of the Knights, Hompesch, in a light far more favourable than usual; and there seems good reason for agreeing with the conclusion of Mr. Hardman (at the end of Chapter VII, as also in Chapter XVII), that the blame for the surrender of Valetta must rest, not upon Hompesch, but upon certain of the Knights, especially Bosredon de Ransijat, and those who acted with him. The behaviour of some renegade Knights who were with the French also contributed to the surrender; but, as the documents abundantly prove, it was the uprising of the civil population which very largely led to that singular result. The hatred

[1] See the chapter by Mr. H. W. Wilson (No. XX) in the *Camb. Mod. History* (vol. viii) on this point.
[2] Maria Carolina, a daughter of Maria Theresa (and therefore a sister of Marie Antoinette), had married Ferdinand IV of Naples.

felt by the populace for the Knights was greater than their repugnance towards the French. When we consider the damning indictment brought against the Knights Hospitallers in Chapter I of this volume, we cannot be surprised at this. The vice, luxury, and greed of the quondam Crusaders were matters known to every islander; the reputation of France as a liberator from oppression had not been wholly lost, even amidst the rapacious actions of the Directory and its satraps in Switzerland, Italy, and the Rhineland. Probably to the mass of the Maltese the policy of plunder then favoured at Paris was scarcely known. In any case the islanders at that time preferred the rule of the French to that of the Knights. The awakening was soon to come. But for the present the Maltese sided with the invaders, and must therefore bear the chief share of responsibility for the events which followed.[1]

The documents setting forth the administrative reforms and monetary exactions of the French sufficiently explain the disappointment and anger of the islanders at the new order of things now thrust upon them. The Arabic strain in the blood of the Maltese, together with their remoteness from the main current of European thought, predisposed them to superstition, as Bonaparte and his officers speedily observed. Yet little care was taken to avoid giving offence to the natives in this all-important particular. The plunder of the churches of Valetta and Citta Vecchia for the benefit of the army-chest and the making up of the sum of 500,000 francs, which was accorded to the officers on June 18 as a *gratification d'embarquement*,[2] would by itself have severely strained the allegiance of the islanders. But far more dangerous than this was the suppression of all monasteries, except one of each Order, and the sale of their buildings, lands, and possessions for the behoof of the new centralised administration. In the words of General Vaubois (quoted in Chapter X of this work), 'Malta was nothing but a vast monastery'; and 'many persons lived on the gifts of the Order.' It was the sale of Carmelite and other monastic possessions at Citta Vecchia on September 2, 1798, which furnished the occasion for the revolt against French rule.

It is indeed strange that the experience of the revolutionists in France itself, and still more in Italy, should not have taught them the need of caution in dealing with fervently Roman Catholic communities. Bonaparte, indeed, at a later time, showed far more

---

[1] As I pointed out in my *Life of Napoleon*, vol. i. (p. 184, note), the British consul at Malta, Mr. Williams, believed that the Maltese had decided the surrender of Valetta. He wrote (June 30, 1798) : ' I do believe the Maltees (*sic*) have given the island to the French in order to get rid of the Knighthood ' (F. O. Malta No. 1).

[2] *Corres. de Nap. I*, vol. iv. p. 177. See, too, the *Note sur Malte* of General Vaubois, printed in Chapter X of this work, where he states that Bonaparte took away to Egypt all the money that was in the Maltese exchequer, and left behind only the silver taken from the churches.

statesmanlike restraint than other French commanders; but in 1798 his conduct at Malta was scarcely less provocative than that of the satraps of the Directory who wounded the feelings of the Romans, Swiss, and Rhinelanders. In all these quarters the seeds, which bore fruit in the anti-French reaction of the years 1798, 1799, were scattered broadcast.[1]

In Malta there were especial reasons why the reaction should come almost as quickly as was the case in Switzerland. Both peoples were naturally impatient of control by a foreigner; and their surroundings encouraged them to a daring and activity which were impossible for dwellers in plains. The Maltese were fretted by a multitude of new regulations, some of which were singularly fussy. Apart from those which are quoted by Mr. Hardman, we may call attention to this one: 'As the divisional general controls the general police of the island and of the port (Valetta), no vessel may enter or leave except in pursuance of his order.'[2] And, again, this: 'The general commanding the island will have solely the right to control and undertake the administration of the country.'[3] The Maltese might well inquire whether their last state was not worse than their first; for the rule of the French commander, General Vaubois, and his civilian advisers, was not less autocratic than that of the Grand Master of the Knights, and it certainly entailed heavier financial burdens than the islanders could bear.

As may be seen by reference to Appendix I, in which Mr. Hardman has dealt with the finances of the Order of St. John, the condition of the island was most unsatisfactory after the year 1792, when the possessions of the Order in France were confiscated. That act swept away a revenue of about £50,000 a year. Incredible as it may seem, the revenues of the Order had fallen from £136,417 in 1788 to £34,663 14s. 2d. in 1798. This latter sum was altogether inadequate to support the extravagances of the Knights and the heavy charges entailed by the maintenance of a small navy and a first class fortress. Thus, the French entered upon a virtually bankrupt possession; and Bonaparte, probably not realising the extent of the financial difficulty and the poverty of the island, inaugurated a fiscal system which implied commercial activities of no mean order. His enactment of June 18, 1798 (No. 2,694 of the *Correspondance*), provided for the establishment at the earliest possible time of a system of dues which should produce 720,000 francs (£28,800) a year.

[1] It seems highly probable that Bonaparte became a Freemason at Malta. Mr. H. M. Broadley, in his *History of Freemasonry in Malta* (London, 1880), has proved that there was a lodge in Malta, and that de Rohan was a member. As Bonaparte was a Freemason after the Eastern expedition, and as there was no lodge then in Egypt, it is nearly certain that he was initiated at Malta. But no proof of this can be alleged.
[2] *Corres. de Nap. I*, vol. iv. p. 170.
[3] *Ibid.* p. 171.

This was a very hopeful estimate. It could have been fulfilled only in a time of peace and prosperity, and by the exercise of the most resolute economy. But the programme set before the new Government of Malta was no less ambitious than that which Bonaparte undertook in Egypt. It is clear that in both cases he far outran the resources of those new colonies. The letters which General Kléber sent to the Directory, after the departure of Bonaparte from Egypt, supply a curious commentary upon the state of affairs in Malta. On October 8, 1799, Kléber affirmed that there was a deficit of 10,000,000 francs, or more than a whole year's revenue; and that the commander-in-chief had not left a sou behind in the exchequer.[1] The effect of Napoleon's administrative energy, suddenly brought to bear on a poor and backward community, was almost as marked in Malta as in Egypt; and, speaking generally, one may say that his administrative triumphs were achieved in lands such as France, North Italy, and the Rhineland, where the natural resources were great and only needed skilful development; but that his schemes were too vast and rigid, and their application too abrupt, to lead to success in the case of poor and stationary peoples. Certainly his first efforts, those in Malta and Egypt, had not the beneficent results which have often been claimed for them. He pointed out the way in which progress might be made; but the pace which he set in the year 1798 was so rapid as to cause a breakdown.

Moreover, he had not calculated on the effects soon to be produced by the presence of Nelson. Quietly but irresistibly, as if it were the oncoming of an eclipse, the shadow of the Sea Power drew itself over Bonaparte's plans; and even before the great seaman had ruined them at the Battle of the Nile, the three frigates, which by a series of strange mishaps failed to join him in Sicilian waters,[2] had spread dismay among the French vessels sent from Malta to obtain provisions in Sicily or South Italy. The letter of Regnaud de St. Jean d'Angely, of date July 21, 1798, quoted near the end of Chapter VIII of this volume, announcing the passage of Nelson's fleet through the Straits of Messina, and the mischief subsequently done by the three frigates, contains the significant sentence: 'Ainsi, environné d'ennemis, nous ne sommes pas sans inquiétude sur les approvisionnements.' This sentence, and indeed the whole letter, deserve careful attention, as illustrating the influence of naval affairs on the tenure of Malta. Even

[1] *Kléber et Menou en Égypte* (Documents publiés pour la Société d'Histoire Contemporaine, par M. François Rousseau, Paris, 1900), pp. 76-79; with a good note by M. Rousseau.
[2] In my *Napoleonic Studies*, pp. 350, 351, I have printed letters of Captain Hope (the senior officer of the three frigates), which explain how he came to miss Nelson off Sicily, and then again near Crete. The letters collected by Mr. Hardman show that Captain Hope's cruise was far from useless.

before the Battle of the Nile—that is, in the time when French ascendancy in the Mediterranean was only challenged and not yet shattered—the French governor of Malta felt his position most difficult. The dependence of that island on other lands for a large part of its supplies of food caused its fortunes to rise or fall according as friends or foes held the sea.

Viewing the question more broadly, one may remark on the singular good fortune which enabled a comparatively weak body like the Knights of St. John to hold their own for so long in an essentially precarious position. Indeed, this can be explained only on the ground of the exceeding tolerance accorded to small and weak States in the old order of things in Europe—a tolerance which allowed the survival of a hundred or more little States or Free Cities in the plains of Germany, which were certain to disappear as soon as reverence for the *ancien régime* vanished. Similarly, it was respect for the Knights of St. John that had secured them from aggression in the Mediterranean wars, which, moreover, had of late turned mainly on the possession of Gibraltar, the Balearic Isles, and Corsica, or other points of vantage near to the coasts of Spain, France, or Northern Italy.

All at once the will of Bonaparte turned the course of affairs towards the Orient, and forthwith the rule of the Knights of St. John collapsed as speedily as that of dozens of German princelings before the breath of the French Revolution. But the age-long immunity of the Knights from serious attack had almost hidden from them and their subjects the disagreeable truth that in reality they existed on sufferance, and that if any one of the Western Powers of Europe sought to dominate the Levant it must almost of necessity seize Malta. A half-perception of this truth probably led the Grand Masters, first Rohan and then Hompesch, to seek the protection of Russia as a safeguard against possible pressure from the west.[1] But, in view of the anti-British contentions of a later date, it is needful to point out that, up to the years 1798–1801, the native Maltese had had no recent experience of the irresistible effect of sea power on the fortunes of a small island. Since the decline of the Turkish navy they had been in no great danger, and now, of a sudden, Malta became one of the storm centres of the world.

The tidings of a reverse sustained by Brueys' fleet at Aboukir on August 1, 1798, were set forth in vague and not very reassuring terms by General Vaubois and Commissary Regnaud de St. Jean d'Angely, in a proclamation to the garrison and citizens of Malta, dated August 29. It must be considered as a main cause of the rising of the Maltese at Citta Vecchia on September 2, though the

[1] See de la Jonquière, *l'Expédition d'Egypte*, vol. i. p. 637.

sale of monastic property was the immediate occasion of the revolt. The Journal of General Vaubois published in the Appendices of this volume shows that the Maltese were encouraged to rise by the knowledge that 'nous (i.e. les Français) serions longtems réduits à la faible garnison qui occupait la ville.'

V

The details of the rising of the Maltese on September 2, 1798, as given in Chapter IX, reflect great credit on the islanders for their dash and bravery, but the statements of Vaubois in his Journal show that the outbreak at Citta Vecchia was premature, and that, had the Maltese matured their plans, they might possibly have seized Valetta itself. It is also clear that quite early in their struggle they received no small help in munitions of war from Captain (afterwards Admiral) Sir James Saumarez during his short stay off the island; and it is curious to note that, as happened at St. Jean d'Acre, most of the arms which were sent on shore came from the French prizes which he was convoying to Gibraltar. But the first successes gained by the Maltese over isolated bodies of French in the open did not seriously compromise the position of Vaubois and his main force in Valetta. The Maltese naturally appealed to Great Britain and to Naples for help, but at that time the fate of the Neapolitan Bourbons was trembling in the balance. The dispatch of a single column of French veterans sufficed in the year 1799 to overturn that dynasty, and in the autumn of 1798 it dragged on its miserable existence for a few weeks solely by virtue of Nelson's victory at the Nile. To rely on Ferdinand IV of Naples was to lean upon the weakest of reeds, and the details supplied in Chapter X of this work show that the Maltese very early discovered the fact.

In truth, the destiny of Malta depended on the larger question of the mastery of the Mediterranean. If Great Britain had had sufficiently large naval forces to ensure a complete and continuous blockade of the island, the position of Vaubois would before long have been utterly untenable. The evidence on this topic contained in Chapter X may be reinforced from evidence which, by the kindness of Mr. A. M. Broadley, the editor has been able to procure from a new source, namely, a letter from Rear-Admiral Villeneuve to Admiral Bruix, Minister of Marine at Paris. It is dated *à Malte, à bord du Guillaume Tell* (one of the two battleships which escaped from Aboukir), 22 Fructidor, An 6 (6th September 1798), and begins with the statement that that disaster was due to the want of proper equipment and the defective condition of the French ships. With respect to the present situation at Malta, he adds: 'On paroit désirer ici que cette division y reste; mais si le gouvernement ne vient pas à son secours d'une manière bien efficace elle y sera bientôt fort à charge. Il m'est impossible de t'envoyer par cette occasion un état de notre situation, mais ce sera par la première qui se présentera. Elle n'est pas satisfaisante . . .'[1]

Equally significant is the dispatch of Vaubois to the Directory, of 18th September 1798. In that urgent request for succour he very naturally painted his situation in the darkest colours (see Chapter X *ad init.*). He stated that he had only 2,200 men wherewith to defend the long line of walls; but on December 21, 1798, he admitted that he had 3,822 present under arms, exclusive of 172 sick (see Chapter X *ad fin.*). We may also note in passing, as a sign of the singular discrepancies on these essential matters, that the Maltese credited the French with having 3,000 men, even after they (the Maltese) had inflicted on them the loss of 1,500 men, with only ten Maltese killed! As to his provisions, Vaubois asserts that they were limited to bread and water. He adds that the heat had exhausted the soldiery, and that they urgently need reinforcements and provisions in order to maintain themselves in that 'position cruelle.'

Still more important is his statement near the beginning of his 'Note sur Malte' (Chapter X), that if all the soil of the islands of Malta and Gozo were to produce grain, the crops would provide sufficient food for only one-third of the population. That there is exaggeration in this statement appears from the far more careful estimate of the French Commissary Doublet that the corn crops of the islands would not suffice to support one-third of the garrison and population. But this, again, proves that the defence of Malta depended mainly on food supply. In view of the urgent importance of this question for Great Britain in the event of war with naval Powers, the details presented in this volume acquire a new significance.[2] Up to that time there had never been, since the days of the old Roman Empire, a State so dependent for its very existence on food brought from over the sea, as Malta. When this fact is firmly grasped, it will be seen that the details of fighting along the walls of Valetta are less essential to the fate of that island than the unseen but irresistible agencies that make for mastery at sea.

The reader who does not know the particulars of the naval war in the Mediterranean and of British policy at that time, might naturally infer that the return of Nelson after the Battle of the Nile to Sicilian waters was prompted by a resolve to blockade Malta. But it is quite clear that his return to Southern Italy resulted from the orders first issued to him by Lord St. Vincent (emanating, of course, from the British Government), which directed him to concern

---

[1] In Mr. Broadley's extra-illustrated edition of his work, *Nelson's Hardy.*
[2] I have treated the larger question at issue in an essay, 'Britain's Food Supply in the Napoleonic Wars,' in my *Napoleonic Studies* (G. Bell & Sons).

himself with the defence of Naples against the expected inroad of the French from Rome. These instructions were doubtless repeated in 'most secret orders,' which reached him on August 16 off Aboukir.[1]

In truth the blockade of Malta formed no part of the original design of the British Ministry, simply because its capture by the French had not been anticipated. Not until October 3, the day after the receipt of the news of Nelson's victory at London, did the Ministry issue any orders respecting the blockade of Valetta. By that time the situation in the Mediterranean had become clearer. Yet (despite the friendly assurances of the Neapolitan Court regarding the future ownership of Malta) Lord Grenville penned the very suggestive and noteworthy sentence : ' His [Britannic] Majesty does not entertain any idea of acquiring the sovereignty of Malta to himself, or of any of the Venetian Islands.'[2] All that Great Britain desired at this time, and for many months afterwards, was the restoration of the *status quo ante bellum,* provided that there were sufficient safeguards for its maintenance both in Malta and elsewhere. The dispatch from the Admiralty to the Earl of St. Vincent, dated 3rd October 1798, specifies the following as the duties of the British squadron in the Mediterranean :—

1. 'The protection of the coasts of Sicily, Naples, and the Adriatic, and in the event of war being renewed in Italy, an active co-operation with the Austrian and Neapolitan armies.
2. 'The cutting off of all communication between France and Egypt, that neither supplies nor reinforcements may be sent to the army at Alexandria.
3. 'The blocking up of Malta, so as to prevent provisions being sent into it.
4. 'The co-operating with the Turkish and Russian squadrons which are to be sent into the Archipelago.'

Further instructions call attention to the first of these objects as the most important of all.[3] It is clear, then, that the blockade of Malta was only a subsidiary aim of British naval policy; and this fact, together with the comparative smallness of the force left to Nelson for the fulfilment of these extensive aims, explains the inadequacy of the measures which could at first be taken against the French garrison at Valetta. Nelson's ships at Naples urgently needed repair, and but for the work done by the Portuguese squadron, together with the *Alexander, Terpsichore, Bonne Citoyenne,* and *Incendiary,* detached from Nelson's squadron, the place would have been open to a relieving squadron from Toulon or Marseilles. As

---

[1] *Nelson Dispatches,* III. p. 105.

[2] Nearly the whole of this important dispatch is quoted in Chapter X of this work.

As will presently appear, the British Ministry soon came to the decision to allow the Czar Paul I to have the predominant influence in Malta when it was recaptured from the French. See *Dropmore Papers,* IV. p. 419.

[3] Clarke and McArthur, II. p. 111 (4vo. edit.).

it was, however, the blockade was sufficiently close to prevent the arrival of any news, still less supplies, either from France or from Bonaparte himself. Regnaud de St. Jean d'Angely in his letter of November 23, 1798, to the Directory states that they had heard nothing for five months. This is an exaggeration, as the Portuguese squadron did not close in on Malta till about September 20; but after that time the blockade was effective. Vaubois states in his letter of November 27 to the Directory that only one of the five *avisos* (dispatch-boats) sent off from Toulon to Valetta had reached its destination up to that date.

The same letter, however, bears testimony to the valuable nelp given by the crews of the ships that sought refuge at Valetta after the Battle of Aboukir—the *Guillaume Tell, Diane,* and *Justice*. But for the arrival of these ships Vaubois confesses that he would not have been able to man 'l'ouvrage immense de la Côte Noire' or the forts Manoel, Ricasoli, St. Elmo, and St. Ange. The letters published in Chapter XI (especially those of Villeneuve and Menard) show, however, that some small vessels were able to slip into Valetta during the storms and long nights of December 1798—January 1799, and that the provisions which they brought to the garrison were of the utmost importance.

Vaubois' 'Journal of the Siege of Valetta,' now printed for the first time in the Appendix to this volume, will be found to contain a mine of information on everything connected with that event. Very noteworthy is his statement (Part I): 'L'insurrection des habitans fournit au Général des moyens de subvenir aux frais de l'habillement de la troupe, à ceux des effets de casernement, à la solde, et aux dépenses qu'exigoient les rafraichissemens qu'il se procurait malgré le blocus de Sardaigne et de Barbarie, en attendant que le gouvernement [français] peut [*sic*] venir à son secours.' The last phrase of course refers only to the early days of the siege; but the extract is of interest as showing that Vaubois derived some benefit from the revolt of the Maltese. He could now exact forced loans, &c., from the people of Valetta, and so meet expenses which could not have been defrayed by legal measures from an obedient populace.

As regards the state of the besiegers, the most authentic account for the early part of the blockade of Valetta is probably that which is contained in their petition to the King of the Two Sicilies, which was handed to Nelson on October 25, to be forwarded to Naples (see Chapter X). The trust which the Maltese still felt in the government of Ferdinand IV, despite the fact that he had sent them no help and had shut the Sicilian ports against their vessels, is there pathetically expressed. They confess their 'extreme penury of munitions of war,' and mention gratefully the gift of 1,300 muskets and several barrels of powder from the squadron of Saumarez. What is even more noteworthy, they assert that, as most of the corn was in Valetta, at the disposal of the enemy's garrison, they themselves are 'totally unprovided with the means of subsistence,' and beg that corn from Sicily may be furnished to them on credit, as they have no money. Still more emphatic is the description of the hunger, penury, and despair of the Maltese at the end of January, after the failure of the plot for opening the gates of Valetta. The petition to Nelson, dated 26th January 1799 (see Chapter XI), shows that the islanders had been cowed by the stern reprisals of the French, and reduced to privation by the lack of provisions and stores. The sentence, 'Our desolation is complete and the urgency is inexpressible,' tells its own tale. As at that time Naples was in the hands of the French,[1] the fortunes of the Maltese turned almost entirely on the amount of succour procurable by means of the British naval forces, as appears in the further statement: 'Our only hope, my Lord, is in the protection of Your Excellency and the great Britannic nation.'

In the letter of Vincenzo Borg to Captain Ball, dated 4th February 1799, comes the first suggestion that the island should be placed under British protection: 'La plus part de nous en très-grand nombre se proteste ouvertement qu'il ne désire rien autant que de ne voir l'Isle dominée que par les Anglais et Maltais et gouvernée par le Commandant Ball.' The rest of the letter (Chapter XI) shows that fear of Russian schemes for the domination of the island played no small part in the formation of this desire. The abortive plot of January 1799, headed by Lorenzi, was to have led to the hoisting of the Russian colours; but the islanders in general seem greatly to have disliked the thought of Russian ascendancy, rumours of which now began to circulate. Ball in his letter to Nelson, of date 4th February 1799, states that the adherents of the Russians were merely a few persons who had previously held places under the Grand Master, Hompesch. Ball adds that he sought to attach the Maltese to the Neapolitan connexion, and whenever Valetta capitulated, he would grant a passage to Maltese deputies who desired to consult Lord Nelson. As is well known, Nelson was then strongly of opinion that Malta ought to belong to the King of Naples; and he urged Captain Ball, who was then conducting the blockade, to do everything in his power, short of the use of actual force, to prevent a Russian squadron from doing anything which might invalidate the sovereign rights of His Sicilian Majesty. A most awkward situation would have arisen had the Russians arrived before instructions came to hand from Whitehall couched in a contrary sense. The question did not arise.

---

[1] See *Camb. Mod. History*, vol. viii. pp. 654, 655.

VI

We must at this point retrace our steps in order to throw fuller light on the arrangements which had been framed between Great Britain and Russia respecting Malta; for the character of the Czar Paul was destined to exert a curious influence on the fate of Malta and the policy of the Great Powers. Already in this, the second year of his reign, his vain, impulsive, and passionate nature was beginning to be known. Nevertheless, the desire of the Pitt Cabinet to form a new coalition against France in order to set bounds to her aggressions in the Rhineland, Switzerland, and Italy led it to take steps for bringing Russia into the new league. This proved to be far from easy. The Czar plumed himself on reversing the policy of his mother, Catharine II, at all points. As she was warlike, he was resolved to be peaceful; and but for the Eastern expedition of Bonaparte, it is probable that he would long have held aloof from the politics of the West. That event, however, and especially the seizure of Malta, completely altered his feelings. Sir Charles Whitworth, British ambassador at St. Petersburg, wrote to Lord Grenville on August 6, 1798: 'The loss of Malta has affected the Czar deeply.'[1]

As has been shown, and will appear more in detail in Chapter XVII of this work, Paul I had framed a compact with the Order of St. John; and it was natural that many of the expelled Knights should seek refuge in Russia and appeal to their august champion. They received a warm welcome. Patronage of so ancient and august an Order in the days of its misfortune was consonant with the Czar's chivalrous and fantastic nature. The Knights skilfully played upon his foibles. In the forged letter of 21st June, 1798, purporting to come from the bailli de Tigné, the Grand Master, Hompesch, was accused of cowardice and treason in surrendering Valetta to the French; and though de Tigné publicly repudiated the letter, the slanders were believed, especially in Russia, where the Knights had every reason for blackening the character of Hompesch in order to quicken the zeal of their imperial protector.

The ruse was eminently successful. On November 13, 1798, the autocrat accepted the Grand Mastership of the Order, which the Knights in Russia had offered to him three weeks before; and for some months its insignia were the most precious of decorations. He bestowed them on Whitworth, on Nelson, and on Lady Hamilton. Ill did it betide any courtier or diplomatist who seemed to slight the Order. The confiscation of the estates of the Order by Bavaria cost the envoy of that Electorate his post: he was summarily dismissed, and conducted to the frontier by the police in

[1] Foreign Office Records, Russia, No. 40.

the depth of winter. The Spanish ambassador was driven away with scarcely less of rigour. As Whitworth phrased it, 'The rock of Malta is that on which all the sufferers split.'[1]

Even before the Czar's acceptance of the new dignity, Whitworth reported the fear of the autocrat that the British would keep Malta, and his desire for the re-establishment of the Order at Valetta.[2] Those fears were groundless. The British Government inclined strongly towards the restoration of the *status quo ante* in Europe. Lord Grenville stated this decisively to Whitworth in a dispatch of November 16, 1798, and urged the need of framing a compact with Russia, Austria, and Prussia, 'the basis of which should be the employment of their united efforts to reduce France within her ancient limits —an object of evident and pressing interest to the future tranquillity and independence of Europe.' All possible means were to be taken to induce Russia to act as a 'principal' in the formation of this league; and Whitworth was allowed a certain latitude in the choice of means, the end being more especially the deliverance of Holland, and parts of Germany, and Italy from French control.[3]

In truth, nothing but the pressure of Russian diplomacy and Russian arms was likely at that juncture to end the vacillations of the Austrian and Prussian Courts.[4] In short, the Czar had to be coaxed in order to induce or compel those Powers to adopt measures which Pitt and Grenville believed to be essential for the preservation of the European system.

To acquiesce in the Czar's plans respecting Malta seemed to be the readiest means of infusing a steady driving-power into his policy. On December 13, the day after the public proclamation of the Emperor Paul as Grand Master, Whitworth reported to Grenville that 'the views of His Imperial Majesty on the subject of the reorganisation of the Order are perfectly conformable to those of His [Britannic] Majesty.' And on December 24, after an interview with the Czar, he reported that the autocrat expressed his resolve to restore peace to Europe on the basis described above. For that purpose Russia would form an alliance with England, and would engage to furnish 45,000 men for the support of Prussia, and 8,000 for the succour of Naples. Further, he (Paul) would spare 'neither arguments nor threats' to compel Austria 'to do her duty.' Corfu was to be independent, but under the protection of Turkey, with which Power Russia was then in alliance. As to Malta (proceeded Whitworth), the Emperor Paul saw 'no impropriety in the island being garrisoned by Neapolitan troops, should it fall into the hands of the Allies, and should that manner [*sic*] be found most convenient, but merely as a Depôt, and subject to the dispositions which may be taken by the

[1] F. O. Russia, No. 41. See too *Paget Papers*, vol. i. pp. 144-46.
[2] F. O. Russia, No. 41. Whitworth to Grenville, October 3, 1798.
[3] *Ibid.*
[4] See the *Camb. Mod. History*, vol. viii. pp. 643-45.

Allies, as well with regard to the government of the island as to the reorganisation of the Order.' In a postscript he added that the Emperor Paul desired to see Malta garrisoned by Russian, British, and Neapolitan troops, and that his ardour respecting the Order of St. John was unabated. This last arrangement respecting Malta was embodied in the treaty which Whitworth signed with the Russian Chancellor on December 29, 1798.[1]

On January 2, 1799, Whitworth reported that Russia would send 3,000 troops via the Black Sea and the Dardanelles in order to assist in the siege of Valetta; but six days later he expressed his surprise that an officer high in the Russian service had been appointed to command *at Malta*. When he pointed this out to the Chancellor, the latter replied that the phrase should have been 'to command the Russian troops at Malta.'[2] The British Government evidently suspected that Russia's designs were to gain absolute possession of Malta; but on January 25, Whitworth assured Grenville that any suspicion of that nature was 'unwarrantable.' On March 5 he qualified this expression, and admitted that the recognition of the Czar as Grand Master would be hazardous. On April 16 he urged Grenville to do so, as the Czar must be humoured. If Malta fell into the hands of the British, he said, the situation would be most difficult. Nevertheless it would be well to recognise Paul as Grand Master owing to his keen susceptibility on that topic.

With all his rashness on points of detail, Paul was cautious on larger matters. Not until April 30, when the British ratification of the convention of December 29 arrived, was the order given to the Russian forces to begin their march westward.[3] I have now cited enough evidence to show that the Maltese question entered largely into the motives which led Russia to declare war against France, and commence the ever-memorable campaign of Suvóroff in Italy and Switzerland, and, somewhat later, the ill-concerted efforts of the Anglo-Russian forces in Holland. These events, in their turn, were to affect the future of Malta, as the sequel will show.

VII

While the British Government, for diplomatic reasons, was about to consign Malta to the Knights and to their imperial Grand Master, public opinion began to run strongly in a contrary direction. The first definite suggestion from a British official that Malta ought to belong to Great Britain came from Captain Ball, in his letter of 9th February 1799, to Lord Nelson (see Chapter XI). He pointed out that the

---

[1] F. O. Russia, No. 41. For the general terms of the treaty, see *Camb. Mod. History*, vol. viii. pp. 648, 649.
[2] F. O. Russia, No. 42.
[3] *Ibid.*

Maltese alone could never be strong enough to defend their islands, and that the cost of a garrison of 2,000 British soldiers would amply be repaid by the advantages which the island conferred on the navy and commerce of Great Britain.

On the following day he commented on the extreme penury of the Maltese levies, and the need of taking them into our pay, as they disliked and distrusted the Neapolitan Government, and were inspirited when Ball allowed them to hoist British colours by the side of those of Naples. The recent flight of the Neapolitan Bourbons to Palermo, where they owed their protection and maintenance almost solely to Nelson's squadron, added point to these representations. It was inevitable in this state of things that the Maltese should look for help either to Great Britain or to Russia; and their distrust of the Czar Paul, as Grand Master of the Order of St. John, strongly inclined them to look solely to Nelson and his Government. This appears in the petition and the covering letter of 31st March 1799 (see Chapter XII), which begged the British admiral, in the event of the King of Naples approving, to set forth the desire of the Maltese for the sovereignty of Britain. It is noteworthy that Vincenzo Borg and others who afterwards opposed Captain Ball signed this petition along with the deputies and notables of the island. This decision was doubtless due to the necessities of the Maltese as well as to their dislike of Russia. It may be taken as certain that Captain Ball had not influenced this decision, which bears every mark of spontaneity. On or before April 6, 1799, the Congress of Maltese deputies urged that the island should belong to Great Britain, and sent a petition to the King of the Two Sicilies to that effect. Equally noteworthy is the statement of Captain Ball, in his letter of 12th April 1799, to Lord Nelson, that the Maltese wished to have no connexion whatever with the Order of St. John, and, above all, to live at peace with Turkey and the Barbary States.

Nevertheless, so weak and disheartened were the Maltese troops at that time that Ball expressed his satisfaction at the news that Russian troops were coming to help in the reduction of Valetta. He believed, and very naturally, that the French garrison, reduced as it was to miserable straits by sickness and want of food (see Vaubois' letters of this date in the Appendix, Part II), would seize the opportunity to compel Vaubois to surrender.

VIII

But now the whole situation was suddenly to change owing to the operation of causes far remote yet potently effective. On April 25, 1799, the French Admiral Bruix managed to elude the vigilance of Hood (now Lord Bridport) at Brest; and though he failed to rally the Spanish squadron held in Cadiz by the bold seamanship of Lord Keith, yet his entrance into the Mediterranean carried perplexity and dismay to the scattered British squadrons at Minorca, Naples, Palermo, and Malta. Fortunately the Earl of St. Vincent, who started in pursuit, was as efficient a leader as Bruix was incompetent. The French admiral, crippled by the incompetence of his crews both in seamanship and gunnery (witness the failure of his ships to hit an Algerian corsair in 900 rounds![1]), succeeded in achieving the impossible. Having every advantage in numbers and position, he failed to take a single British ship; and his only feat was that of relieving the wants of the French garrison then besieged by the Austrians at Genoa. Even after his junction with sixteen Spanish ships at Cartagena on June 29, he did nothing more than retrace his steps, enter the Atlantic, and cast anchor at Cadiz, whence, on July 21, he made sail for Brest. The inner reasons for this ludicrous failure do not concern us here; but if we can picture Nelson in the place of Bruix, we can imagine the results that would have accrued—Duckworth's squadron snapped up at Port Mahon; the British ships driven off from, or caught, either at Naples or Valetta, and the ascendancy of the enemy in the Mediterranean summarily ended.

Even as it was, the promenade of Bruix into the Mediterranean altered the whole state of affairs at Malta. The documents quoted in Chapter XII of this volume are unfortunately somewhat scanty, owing to the enforced withdrawal of that excellent correspondent, Captain Ball, from his station off Valetta; but even those which are there given will enable the discerning reader to appreciate the advantages reaped by the beleaguered garrison in regaining for several days the command of the sea and replenishing their scanty supplies. During the gales of February 1799, a French frigate and smaller vessels had managed to slip in; and Vaubois states in his letter of February 17, 1799, that they brought in supplies for some months (see his Part II of Journal in Appendix). Other letters of the besieged, however, state that these ships brought comparatively little except a large consignment of putrid salt meat. This is scarcely credible.

As appears from Lieutenant Vivion's letter of May 31, 1799, the French managed to send five or six Maltese *speroneras* over to the coast of Sicily, and also captured several boats belonging to the besiegers. Evidently the departure of Captain Ball for the purpose of effecting the much-needed concentration of force was a turning-point in the siege, which must otherwise have come to a speedy end.

The dissensions which broke out among the Maltese at this time further complicated the situation, and it speaks well for Lieutenant

---

[1] Mahna, *Influence of Sea Power on the French Revolution and Empire*, vol. i. p. 307, note.

Vivion, who took the place of Captain Ball, that he managed to keep the semblance of order among the discouraged besiegers, and to save the lives of some of the native leaders who were accused, and perhaps rightly, of treachery. Why the French did not attempt a sortie at this time it is difficult to say. But the letter of Vaubois to Villeneuve of November 21, 1799, shows that the local conditions did not favour a sortie (see the letter in Vaubois' 'Journal of the Siege,' Part III, in Appendix). Further, the French were too weak in numbers to risk anything. It is also possible that they were during that time (June—July 1799) ready to mutiny (as Vivion was informed), or else they expected Bruix to appear and utterly discomfit the besiegers. This last supposition acquired credibility from the report that they were busy in making good the defects of their ships, the *Guillaume Tell*, &c., which apparently were not then in a condition to risk the chance of meeting a British squadron. However that may be, it is certain that the garrison of Valetta, both soldiers and sailors, lost their chance of routing the besiegers and of putting to sea with their squadron. Thus Vivion was able to hold on; and the siege was ultimately pressed forward once more, though under conditions which indefinitely postponed a capitulation.

The only means of overpowering the brave Vaubois was that suggested by Captain Ball to Colonel Thomas Graham (afterwards Lord Lynedoch), who then commanded the British troops holding the citadel of Messina. It was that he should come with some 1,100 British soldiers and infuse vigour into the attack. Colonel Graham warmly favoured the scheme, but had to refer it to his superior at Port Mahon. Owing to perplexing changes in that command, long delays took place, as will appear by reference to Chapter XII. Thus was lost a good opportunity of attacking the French with vigour while they were depressed by the failure of Bruix to bring them succour.

There is one curious episode which finds no place among the papers collected by Mr. Hardman, namely, that the Maltese sent to Captain Ball an urgent request that he would become their governor. The letter of August 3, 1799, in which he named this affair to William Augustus Miles, has not been recovered, but the letter which Miles sent in reply on September 20, 1799, shows that Ball acted with great self-restraint and delicacy of feeling. I quote the following passages:—

It may be your duty to acquiesce in the prayer in consideration that it represents the desire of almost an entire people. With respect to Sicily and its monster of a King—for he is everything but a man—the less you have to do with his Court and Government the better. I do not suppose that Malta will be in any way under the control of His Neapolitan Majesty. You will have a difficult card to play with the [Maltese] Congress, of which you are a President, if France, now that Bonaparte is no longer formidable to the Turk, should make her peace with the Porte. Should any private agreement with the Court of Petersburg hereafter appear, by which it has been stipulated by our Cabinet to cede Malta to the Emperor Paul, I feel no difficulty in saying that, if the public virtue of this country bears any proportion to the delinquency of such an arrangement, the Minister will be impeached. . . .[1]

That a Russian fleet should enter the Mediterranean, *in defence of Turkish interests*, was strange enough; but it could not have been prevented at that time. The action of the Russians at Corfu and on the neighbouring coasts, especially the Cattaro, soon revealed the presence of wider plans, which proved ultimately to be as formidable to the Turkish Empire as the Oriental policy of Bonaparte had been.

In face of the warnings which Captain Ball had sent to Lord Nelson of the immense value of Malta to Great Britain, it is difficult to see why the latter should have expressed an opinion exactly the contrary in his letter, dated Palermo, the 6th April 1799, to Earl Spencer, First Lord of the Admiralty [2] :

. . . To say the truth, the possession of Malta by England would be an useless and enormous expense; yet any expense should be incurred rather than let it remain in the hands of the French. . . . The poor islanders have been so grievously oppressed by the Order that many times we have been pressed to accept of the island for Great Britain; and I know, if we had, His Sicilian Majesty would have been contented. But, as I said before, I attach no value to it for us.[3]

This extraordinary pronouncement must, of course, be viewed in relation to the events of that time, when Minorca was once more in our hands, and was deemed by Nelson a far better base of operations against Toulon than Malta. The reduction of the French army in Egypt was also thought to be merely a matter of time, as proved to be the case. Still, even when full allowance is made, the statement quoted above must be considered as most extraordinary. Certainly it must have produced an impression at the Admiralty, and therefore, presumably, on the Pitt Ministry.[4]

The need of Russian support, both at Naples, in North Italy, and in Holland, served to keep the British Government true to the convention of December 29, 1798, as the documents quoted in Chapter XII abundantly prove. It is therefore practically certain that, if the Emperor Paul had been faithful to his allies and had remained on the throne, the island would have passed into his hands. All the evidence seems to show that, so long as the Anglo-Russo-Austrian

---

[1] *Correspondence of W. A. Miles on the French Revolution*, vol. ii. pp. 299–301.
[2] *Nelson Dispatches*, vol. iii. p. 315.
[3] At that time Nelson urgently wished for the arrival of the 10,000 Russian troops now promised to assist in the recovery of Naples (see his letter of April 5 to Whitworth, in *Nelson Dispatches*, vol. iii. p. 314).
[4] Nelson altered his views, and on June 28, 1803, pronounced Malta 'a most important outwork to India' (*Nelson Dispatches*, vol. v. p. 507).

Alliance held good, this would have been the solution of the Maltese problem.

As a matter of fact, the Russian force, which was at Naples in the autumn of 1799, did nothing towards the fulfilment of Nelson's hope that it would very materially help in the reduction of Valetta; and it is interesting to observe that the British admiral twice referred to Bonaparte's escape from Alexandria to Corsica, and thence to Fréjus, as being directly due to the failure of the Russians to discharge their part of the onerous duties off Malta, which therefore fell upon the small British squadron and prevented the patrolling of the sea between Malta and Cape Bon, which would otherwise have been carried out.[1] So much, then, depended on the loyal and punctual fulfilment of the expectations which Nelson and the British Government placed in Russia, for which they were ready to waive their own pretensions and those of the Neapolitan Bourbons respecting Malta.

IX

Meanwhile Vaubois had fortunately been quiescent at Valetta. The hardships of the siege had reduced the number of Maltese blockading the fortress to 1,500, though 1,000 more might, it was thought, be relied on to help in case of an assault. When the 30th and 89th Regiments, under the command of Brigadier-General Sir Thomas Graham, landed in Malta on December 10, the British forces amounted to 800 regular troops and 400 marines—so Colonel Lindenthal reported to General Fox on that day (see Chapter XII). He considered the defences of Valetta to be so strong as to render an assault quite impracticable. He added: 'I do not suppose there will ever be sent here an army provided with the necessary artillery, stores, and provisions requisite for a regular siege.' It is clear, then, that the fortress was as strong as ever, despite the puny efforts of the besiegers; and Lindenthal expected that famine alone would compel the French to surrender. He estimated that this might happen in two or three months; but, as the event proved, Vaubois, thanks to the cessation of the blockade in part of May and June, had been able to lay in stores sufficient to defy the blockaders for nine months from that date. Lindenthal frankly recognised the excellence of the work done by the Maltese; but his report can leave no doubt on the mind of every unprejudiced reader that the fate of Valetta depended on an effective and rigorous blockade kept up both by land and sea. A perusal of Chapters XII and XIII will also show that, had not the Marquis de Niza disobeyed the orders from Lisbon and continued with the squadron off Valetta, the siege would have been ineffective. As it was, he held on and gave the services of several

[1] *Nelson Dispatches*, vol. iv. pp. 145, 153.

marines of his squadron on shore—a matter of the utmost moment in the anxious weeks before Graham's contingent arrived. It is worth noting that Captain Ball, in his letter of September 3, 1799, to Nelson, estimated the total number of armed Maltese fit for duty at 1,500, but of these only 600 were fit to take part in an attack. As the French were also depressed by dearth and sickness, the whole affair speedily assumed the aspect of a stalemate.

It is needless to dwell on the details of the siege during the close of the year 1799 and the early part of 1800. The acute distress borne by the Maltese, the eager efforts of Ball and Troubridge to induce Nelson, then at Palermo, to press the Neapolitan Government to send supplies of corn, the difficulties in which that admiral found himself placed owing to the lack of the stipulated pecuniary succour from London, the failure of the Russians to co-operate, and the grave risk attending Graham's force in case Vaubois attempted a sortie—all this, and much besides, receives valuable illustration from the dispatches cited in this volume. Among them, perhaps the most important, as bearing directly on the siege of Malta, are the reports of Brigadier-General Graham to his superior, General Fox, at Minorca, of date December 28, 1799, and of Lieutenant-Colonel Lindenthal, of December 31, 1799 (see Chapter XIII).

It will be more suitable to refer here to the wider questions connected with the naval supremacy in the Mediterranean, on which the fate of Malta almost entirely depended. The diffusion of the naval strength of Great Britain over that sea had for some time prevented the needed concentration of effort at Malta; but on February 5 Keith and Nelson were able to set sail from Palermo with 1,200 Neapolitan troops, and on the 15th they cast anchor at Marsa Scirocco, the bay on the east side of Malta, and landed the troops. Scarcely was this operation completed before Nelson was called off by the exciting news that a French relief expedition had been sighted off the west of Sicily. As the documents cited by Mr. Hardman are somewhat scanty at this point, it will be well to call attention here to the extraordinary good fortune of Nelson. He had not been at Malta since October 1798, and now immediately on his arrival, which was largely due to Keith's orders, the French ships were reported. As Ball wrote with some bitterness to Lady Hamilton: 'We have been carrying on the blockade of Malta sixteen months, during which time the enemy never attempted to throw in great succours. His Lordship arrived off here the day they were within a few leagues of the island, captured the principal ships, dispersed the rest, so that not one has reached the port [Valetta].' If we look into details, Nelson's good fortune appears in even stronger colours; for while his ship, the *Foudroyant*, had a long stern chase of the chief French ship *Le Généreux*, the British frigate *Success* appeared, cut in in front of the latter, and as she came on raked her heavily, mortally wounding her commander, Rear-Admiral Perrée. *Le Généreux* struck her colours after the second shot from the *Foudroyant*, the *Northumberland* being now near at hand. One of the French transports was afterwards captured, but the rest of their squadron made off to the north.[1] As they were conveying about 4,000 French troops to Valetta, the thwarting of this effort was the decisive event of the whole siege. This appears very forcibly in the despairing terms in which Vaubois wrote to the Minister of War on the 3rd of March 1800 : ' Voilà donc Malte compromis, et le fruit de dixhuit mois de siège et de blocus peutêtre perdu sans resource ' ('Journal du Siège de Malte,' Part III, in Appendix of this volume). The rest of the letter is written in a sentimental and unmanly spirit, that contrasts most unfavourably with the firm and decided tones in which Admiral Villeneuve referred to the same event in his letter of March 4, quoted at length in Chapter XIV. The first thought of the admiral seems to have been to make ready the fine battleship, *Guillaume Tell*, in the hope that she might fight her way through to Toulon, and carry the necessary news concerning the critical state of the garrison.

Meanwhile the condition of the besiegers also caused grave concern to their commanders. The documents quoted in Chapter XIII show how precarious was the position of Sir Thomas Graham and his motley forces. It was not materially improved by the arrival of 1,200 untrustworthy Neapolitans. A sortie of the French, if strengthened by the arrival of 4,000 fresh troops, must have reduced Graham to the necessity of embarking in haste in face of a victorious enemy, or even of surrendering. His letters cited near the end of Chapter XIII of this work prove that that officer, who showed his dauntless will and power of swift resolve at Barossa in March 1811, was far from easy in his mind, even after the capture of *Le Généreux* and one of her consorts. His letter of February 24, 1800, to General Fox, commanding in Minorca, gives some interesting details of that event, his own forecast of the future, and his evident reliance on help from the Russians (then at Corfu) or from England.

After the failure of the effort made by *Le Généreux*, desertions from Valetta became for a few days more frequent. In the account of the siege given in 'Les Victoires et les Conquêtes de l'Armée française ' (vol. xiii. p. 142), it is stated that at this time prices ruled as follows in the beleaguered city—a fowl, 16 francs ; a rabbit, 12 francs ; an egg, 20 sous ; a lettuce, 18 sous ; a rat, 40 sous ; and fish, 6 francs the pound. Typhus was raging among the troops, and there were few means of combating this deadly foe or of restoring to health the sick in the hospitals ; but the scarcity must have been to some extent relieved by the French corvette which managed to elude Nelson's blockade on March 4.

---

[1] Jurien de la Gravière, *Guerres maritimes* (Paris, two vols.), vol. i. pp. 314–16 ; Mahan, *Life of Nelson*, vol. ii. pp. 27–32 ; James, *Naval History*, vol. ii. pp. 438–40.

X

The besiegers were beset by perplexities of diverse kinds. The progress of the Austrians in the north-west of Italy, and the evident need of supporting them in the blockade of General Masséna's force at Genoa, compelled Lord Keith, as commander-in-chief in the Mediterranean, to turn his attention to that quarter. The Russian squadron under Admiral Ouchakoff, which ought to have assisted the Austrians in the blockade of Genoa, had retired to Corfu, and there was little hope that it would do anything for the Allies.

A problem of a very exceptional order now confronted Keith. If he went to Genoa, he must leave the blockade of Malta to Nelson; and it was notorious that the infatuation of that brave seaman for Lady Hamilton was clouding his vision, sapping his energies, and turning his thoughts to the present abode of the siren—Palermo. This was, in part, the reason why Keith ordered that Syracuse, and not Palermo, should be the rendezvous for the ships blockading Malta; and this decision, also called for by geographical considerations, was deeply resented by Nelson. Keith had to content himself with giving precise orders to this effect, and on February 25, just before he set sail from Malta, he wrote to Sir William Hamilton the following hitherto unpublished letter:—

[Off Malta] 25 *Feb.* 1800.

DEAR SIR W[ILLIAM],—I am still here, and I hardly know how to quit it, Lord Nelson and Troubridge are so unwell. The French know the fate of the intended succour, and desert, some every day; they are preparing their ships to push out. Had we a thousand straightforward men we should have it [Valetta] presently; they are sickly and discontented. Anything which may come for me should go to Leghorn, where I ought to have been ere now, but we cannot do all we wish, and I do all I can. Assure the Royal Family their commands will honor me at all times, remember me to our friends at Palermo, and make my best regards acceptable to Lady Hamilton.—Ever yours,   KEITH.[1]

As has been shown by Mr. Allardyce in the 'Life of Lord Keith,' and by Captain Mahan in the 'Life of Nelson,' the behaviour of the commander-in-chief to his brilliant second in command was as considerate as possible; but it must be admitted that the conduct of Nelson was peevish and unmanly. After his success in capturing *Le Généreux* he seems to have relapsed into a kind of torpor, which would have had serious consequences but for the unremitting attention to duty of his subordinates, Troubridge and Ball. A French corvette managed to slip into Valetta on the night of March 4–5—a fact partly attributable, perhaps, to slight repairs needed by the *Foudroyant*. There is a suggestion of reproach in Ball's letter of

[1] From Mr. A. M. Broadley's collection of MSS.

March 5, 1800, announcing that event (Chapter XIV). It is also clear from the dispatch of Villeneuve which follows, that the arrival of that corvette enabled the garrison to hold out for three months longer than had previously been deemed possible.

The general situation also called for the utmost watchfulness and energy on the part of the blockaders. There were good grounds for believing that the great Franco-Spanish fleet at Brest would find means to elude their blockaders during the gales of February or March, and make a raid into the Mediterranean, with results more effective than in the previous year. Bruix had every reason for striving to restore French ascendancy in that sea. The French army in Egypt needed succour, the garrison of Valetta was nearing the end of its resources, and Masséna was beleaguered in Genoa by the Austrians. Further, the British fleet was widely dispersed, owing to the need of guarding Minorca, of helping in the siege of Genoa, of closely watching Valetta, and of intercepting supplies from France to Egypt. On the squadrons detailed for these very diverse duties the great fleet of Bruix might have fallen with crushing effect.

This was the chief concern of the besiegers of Valetta. Vaubois was fast losing his striking-power; but Bruix, had he got away from Brest, might have overpowered the squadron which formed the only base of Graham's operations, and reduced that officer to surrender. It is clear that Nelson felt the strain of this unseen and therefore doubly terrible menace. 'The French ships here' (wrote Nelson off Valetta on February 25 to Hamilton) 'are preparing for sea; the Brest fleet, Lord Keith says, may be daily expected; and with all this I am very unwell.[1] . . . The first moment which offers with credit to myself I shall assuredly give you my company. . . . Lord Keith is commander-in-chief, and I have not been kindly treated.' That Nelson, in the face of the facts above described, should have longed to get away from Malta to be with the Hamiltons at Palermo, is highly discreditable. Troubridge begged him most urgently not to leave his duty at Malta until the place and the three ships of Bruix's fleet sheltering there alike surrendered to him.[2] But all was in vain. On March 10 he sailed on the *Foudroyant* to Palermo. Fortunately his flagship returned to her proper station in time to take part in the chase of the *Guillaume Tell*.

As Graham had foretold, the French ships in Valetta had long been preparing to escape, and now one of the finest ships in their Navy came forth to fight her way to Toulon. Shortly before midnight of March 30, Rear-Admiral Decrès and Captain Saulnier slipped out of Valetta harbour on that 80-gun ship. She was soon sighted

---

[1] Those who saw him at this time describe his indisposition as of the mental, not of the bodily, order.

[2] Mahan, *Life of Nelson*, vol. ii. p. 29; also Clarke and McArthur, pp. 246, 247, 253. On March 31 he wrote to the Pasha of Egypt that there was no cause for alarm even if Bruix entered the Mediterranean; but this was not his real belief (see *ibid.* p. 246).

by H.M.S. *Penelope* (36 guns), which gave chase and several times raked her from astern, finally damaging her topmasts and sails so that H.M.S. *Lion* (64) and *Foudroyant* (80) were able successively to bear up and finally overpower the defence, which will ever rank among the most brilliant ever made against superior force. It afterwards transpired that the *Guillaume Tell* carried 1,220 men—a number in excess of her rating.[1] This fact, together with the desperate nature of the defence, shows the determination of the crew to reach France. That Vaubois and Decrès overmanned the ship in order to lessen the number of mouths in Valetta appears decisively from the interesting dispatch of Villeneuve of March 4, 1800, cited in Chapter XIV, and that of Vaubois of April 2, cited in the Appendix, Part IV, of his 'Journal of the Siege.' The account of the conflict given in Chapter XIV from the log of the *Foudroyant*, and the official report of Captain Dixon, of H.M.S. *Lion*, will be found the most circumstantial ever published.

The critical situation of the besiegers on land may be seen in the long letter written by Sir Thomas Graham to Sir William Hamilton, of May 19, 1800 (see Chapter XIV), in the hope that he would speedily lay it before the authorities in London. At that time the Hamiltons (it is needful to use the plural) were being recalled home in thinly veiled disgrace;[2] and it does not appear that Sir William took any special means of forwarding the letter home. As is well known, Nelson withdrew from Malta in order to escort the King and Queen of Naples and the Hamiltons from Palermo to Leghorn (June 10–15, 1800), and thereby materially weakened the strength of the blockade at Valetta. By great good fortune no serious effort was made by the French at that time to relieve the fortress; but, as we shall see, a French brig got in on June 8. As Nelson acted in direct contravention of the orders of his superior, Lord Keith, we can imagine the annoyance of the latter at this dereliction of duty. It finds expression in his letter, dated Leghorn, July 16, 1800, in the following unpunctuated sentence: 'The Queen, Nelson and —— left Florence two or three days ago, after embarking and landing repeatedly. I was so displeased by the withdrawing of the Ships from Malta and with other proceedings that Her Majesty did not take any notice of me latterally [*sic*] which had no effect on my attention to her Rank, what a clamour to [?] letting in the Ships to Malta will occasion, I assure you nothing has given me more real

---

[1] James, vol. ii. p. 443 (edit. of 1902), says only 919 men; but the official reports in Clarke and McArthur (pp. 249, 251) give 1,220 men, and a loss of 200 to the *Guillaume Tell*. The discrepancy is explained by the resolve formed at the court-martial of March 1, 1800, cited in Chapter XIV of this work, to send away the sick and all who were useless to the defence of Valetta. Some of the British reports assign to her 86 guns; but six of these were probably carronades mounted on the upper deck.

[2] See Lord Grenville to Paget (*Paget Papers*, vol. i. pp. 237, 238); also *ibid.* pp. 246–48, for Hamilton's intrigues against Paget at Palermo.

concern, it was so near exhausted.'¹ The last statement refers to the successful blockade-running accomplished by the brig *La Marguerite*, which entered Valetta under close pursuit by the *Penelope* on June 8. As was pointed out by Villeneuve in his letter of June 14, this event caused great joy among the besieged, as it assured to them a supply of provisions for three months longer. That this incident resulted from Nelson's anxiety for the safety of Their Sicilian Majesties and Lady Hamilton can scarcely be denied. This was the opinion of Lord Keith, who was best qualified to pass judgment. He gave it as follows in his letter of July 23 to Paget: 'Had not Nelson quitted it [Malta] and taken the ships off the station it would have fallen about this time.'² In view of the documents printed in this volume, the conclusion is inevitable that Nelson was responsible for the prolongation of the siege by two months. We may hazard the statement that, had any other officer than Nelson behaved as he did, the result must have been a sharp censure.

The letters of Villeneuve and Vaubois, of the months June and July [?] 1800 (see Chapters XIV., XV, and Vaubois' 'Journal du Siège de Malte,' Part IV), prove conclusively that the defence of Valetta turned essentially on the question of food supply. 'Recevons de quoi subsister, et Malte est à la République.' Such is the burden of the letters and appeals of Vaubois.³ Even after the arrival of *La Marguerite* and two smaller vessels, the garrison stood in urgent need of flour, biscuits, oil, lard, rice, beans, and, to a less extent, of wine and brandy. At that season of calms and short nights it was unlikely that the vigilance of the British cruisers would again be eluded; but both officers pressed for the dispatch of isolated vessels or feluccas, as one of them might possibly slip in if several were sent. At that time dysentery, scrofula, and verminous disorders were weakening the garrison, which could scarcely subsist on bread and water, and needed better nutriment to withstand the wear and tear of the siege. The letters of Vaubois in his Journal give a terrible description of the misery of the populace of Valetta.

Meanwhile, the presence of the Franco-Spanish fleet of forty-eight sail of the line at Brest (blockaded though it was by the Earl of St. Vincent with from twenty-four to thirty sail of the line) had been paralysing the energies of British officials. On July 23, Keith

---

¹ *Paget Papers*, vol. i. p. 253. See, too, his letter of June 20 at Genoa: 'I must go to Leghorn ... to be bored by Lord Nelson for permission to take the Queen [back] to Palermo and princes and princesses to all parts of the globe: to every request I have said my duty to the Nation forbids it.' Nelson's conduct appears the worse in the light of his admission to Troubridge on May 22 (see *Nelson Dispatches*, vol. iv. p. 239), that the *Northumberland* was the only really effective ship of the line off Valetta. Keith's statement as to *ships* getting into Valetta is incorrect; only one brig, *La Marguerite*, got in. See Villeneuve's letter of June 18, 1800 (Chapter XIV).

² *Paget Papers*, vol. i. p. 256.

³ Letter of July 18, 1800, to the Commissaire ordonnateur de Marine à Toulon. See *Journal du Siège*, Part IV, in Appendix.

INTRODUCTION

complained to Paget that the British Admiralty was so entirely occupied with the blockade of Brest as to forget Mediterranean affairs.[1] Still more deadening was the influence of that fleet upon General Fox, commanding the British forces in Minorca. He was so beset by scruples and fears as not to allow any men to be removed from that island. Keith wrote from Genoa on June 20 to Paget: 'There are 14,000 men on Minorca which cannot be used by reason there is no general, and Fox has not the nerves to send a man on.'[2] In this particular case Keith was referring to his proposed attempt to hold Genoa by a British force, despite its having been ceded to the French by the precipitate action of Melas in the Convention of June 15. But these words are also applicable to the previous action of Fox with regard to Malta. Either from fear of officials at home, or from nervous apprehensions about Bruix, he declined to allow any of his troops to proceed to Malta, though he could well have spared enough to have decided the fate of Valetta. Not until the arrival of Sir Ralph Abercromby did the 2nd Battalion of the 35th Regiment set sail from Minorca, namely, on the 23rd of June.

The arrival of this succour enabled the besiegers to press the French more closely and hasten the surrender, as is evident from the letters of Vaubois and Villeneuve to the Minister of Marine, cited in the middle of Chapter XV. Among other items of interest is the fact that the besiegers' batteries were now brought up so as to sweep the Marsamuscet, or Quarantine Harbour, where the garrison had previously been able to procure fish. But the tightening of the blockade by land would have been of little avail had not the British ships been able to cruise close inshore, or even to anchor, during the calms or light airs of the summer weather. The difficulty of blockade-running now became insuperable. Two or three feluccas were caught by the British cruisers; and it is said that in all ten small vessels were dispatched from French ports to the relief of Valetta without success. Villeneuve, foreseeing the end drawing near, took the magnanimous resolve of saving to the Republic the two fine frigates, *La Diane* and *La Justice*, which now were the sole survivors of the disaster of Aboukir. The letters in which he announced his determination, and the arguments whereby he overcame the reluctance of Vaubois, will serve to raise the esteem which students of history have long felt for one of the most valiant, and certainly the

---

[1] This should have absolved Keith from the censure of Captain Mahan (*Life of Nelson*, vol. ii. p. 38), that he (Keith) was too nervous and preoccupied about what the Brest fleet might do. Captain Mahan, in his *Influence of Sea Power on the French Revolution and Empire*, vol. i. pp. 366–70), gives an excellent account of the blockade of Brest, first by Lord Bridport, and then by his far more efficient successor, the Earl of St. Vincent. In point of fact, the whole naval situation, and therefore the fate of Malta, turned on the blockade of Brest, as was the case in 1803–5.

[2] *Paget Papers*, vol. i. p. 232.

most unfortunate, of French admirals. The result was the escape of *La Justice* and the capture of *La Diane*, which was towed back dismasted within view of Valetta. This further misfortune (and the uncertainty for the present whether *La Justice* had escaped) probably weighed heavily on the garrison, and the council of war held on September 2 decided on negotiating with a view to surrender. It is, however, to be observed that among their reasons for taking this step the want of food was first and foremost. It is there also stated that, as the besiegers had taken the precaution of keeping possession of all the corn in the country districts, a sortie would be useless. General Pigot, in his letter of September 5, 1800 (see Chapter XV), asserts that the capitulation was accelerated by Graham's refusal to allow any more Maltese to be sent out from Valetta by Vaubois' orders. There is no mention whatever of any damage done to the fortifications by the besiegers.

The conclusion is therefore inevitable that, as a fortress, Valetta was still absolutely intact. The garrison surrendered, on September 4, owing to the privations which they had undergone and the near approach of absolute famine. And as Signor Miège has pointed out, if Vaubois had had to feed all the Maltese (as he must have done if they had remained loyal to the French connexion), the surrender to the British fleet must have taken place far earlier. It was most fortunate for him that the Maltese did revolt. They did no damage to his fortifications, and enabled him to husband his food supply.

In truth, no one can peruse the evidence (much of which is now for the first time published) without perceiving the fact that Valetta fell, not because of the bombardment and demonstrations made against it on land, but because of the constricting grip of the British Navy, especially during the summer months of 1800. An apology is due to students of naval history for insistence on this fact, which ought to be obvious in the case of a small island dependent on foreign food; but, inasmuch as it has been denied by some of the Maltese, Mr. Hardman resolved to establish it beyond reach of cavil by reference to the final court of appeal, viz. the documents of besiegers and besieged. That this has now been done must be clear to any person who will take the trouble to peruse the dispatches contained in this volume.

The evidence is of interest, however, for far wider reasons. It throws light on the careers of distinguished men—Nelson, Keith, Sir Thomas Graham, Sir Alexander Ball, Sir Thomas Troubridge, Sir William Hamilton, and the Hon. A. Paget. It tends to deprive Nelson of the credit which, on very slender grounds, was accorded to him, of having directly brought about the fall of Malta. Except in so far as his victory at the Nile was an indispensable preliminary to its capture, he deserves very little credit. It has been amply shown that his connexion with Lady Hamilton, his pique against Keith, and his excessive deference to the King and Queen of Naples, betrayed him into acts of disobedience to his superior, which compromised the efficiency of the blockade and tended to prolong the defence of Vaubois. The care and forethought of Keith, on the contrary, appear in a very favourable light; and too much praise cannot be accorded to Ball, Troubridge, and Graham, as also to Lieutenant Vivion for the courage and energy which he displayed at the time when the besiegers' fortunes were at their lowest.

Respecting the services of Captain Ball, Alexander Macaulay wrote to a friend on June 24, 1800 : ' Until he resigned the military command to General Graham, who came here from Messina with two English regiments about four months ago, he blocked up a garrison of veterans in one of the strongest fortresses of Europe with only the ill-disciplined, half-naked, but faithful Maltese.'[1] This judgment leaves out of count the fact which we now know, that the French had no good reason for making sorties.

It is noteworthy that, after the surrender of Genoa, and after Nelson's withdrawal to Leghorn, Ancona, and Vienna (where his behaviour inexpressibly pained all his friends and admirers),[2] the blockade gained in consistency and vigour. Further, the conduct of General Fox, commanding the British troops at Minorca, was weak and dilatory. Had he possessed the courage to spare two more regiments from his garrison, possibly Valetta might have been taken by assault in the month of July, when the garrison was enfeebled by privations and disease. As it is, the honours on land certainly rested with Vaubois and his brave garrison. It is somewhat singular that every historian of this period has sung the praises of Masséna for his fine defence of Genoa during two months, while few have noticed the far more remarkable exploit of Vaubois in holding out at Valetta for fully two years. All things considered, his defence ought to reckon among the most memorable on record. The most brilliant episode of all was the attempted escape of the *Guillaume Tell*, and thereafter that of the frigates *La Diane* and *La Justice*. Seeing that they had been cooped up in harbour for eighteen months or more, those attempts shed glory on the French Navy, and on Admirals Villeneuve and Decrès, who adopted that heroic resolve.

XI

The Maltese have always felt sore because their levies assisting in the blockade of Valetta were in no wise recognised in the negotiations for the surrender. But it is proved conclusively by the

---

[1] C. O. R. Malta No. 1.

[2] Fitzharris, son of the Earl of Malmesbury, wrote at Vienna: 'Lord Nelson and the Hamiltons dined here the other day: it is disgusting to see her with him' (Earl of Malmesbury's *Memoirs*, vol. ii. p. 24).

documents given in Chapter XV that General Vaubois would on no account have recognised them or their governor, Captain Ball.[1] The latter had been appointed to the governorship by the suzerain, the King of Naples, and by the Congress of the Maltese. But the French recognised neither of these authorities in the present question. It is therefore incorrect to state, as is sometimes done, that the Maltese made a free gift of the island to Great Britain. True, the Maltese Congress made that offer, when the fortunes of the besiegers were at a low ebb; but the whole question turned on the possession of Valetta, and as has been shown, that fortress fell to the British navy and to a less extent to the land forces. Besides, as the sequel will show, the independence of Malta was impossible so soon as three great Powers (France, Great Britain, and Russia) discerned its strategic importance.

For the present we note that there was good reason why Great Britain should reconsider its resolve to admit the sovereignty of the King of Naples. His mainland possessions were now practically at the mercy of the French, and it was natural that he should come to terms with them. His weak and indolent nature, and the proneness of his Queen towards intrigue (she was at that time bargaining with the Hapsburgs in Vienna), rendered it highly probable that he would barter away to the First Consul his sovereignty over Malta as the price of his security at Naples. In fact, he came to terms with the French in the armistice of February 17, 1801, agreeing to close his ports to British ships, a provision which was ratified in the Treaty of Florence, of March 28, 1801. Russia was unable to do anything for Naples. It is well known that her plenipotentiary, Kalicheff, went to Paris in order to secure the interests of Sardinia and Naples. The Czar hoped to gain this boon by offering to the First Consul that France and Russia should pledge themselves never to make peace with England until Malta were handed over to Russia. Talleyrand waived this matter aside, and hastily pressed terms of peace on Naples, which made that kingdom a mere satrapy of France.

The relations of Russia to Malta now claim attention. As has been stated above, and will appear more fully in Chapter XVII of this work, the Czar had in November 1798 accepted the Grand Mastership of the Order of St. John, which the Knights had most unjustly forced Hompesch to resign. Thereafter the affairs of the Order held the first place in the thoughts of the Czar, and all diplomatists and favourites had to humour this latest whim of that most untrustworthy of rulers.

---

[1] The British Government seems to me to have acted very shabbily in refusing to allow to the Maltese levies a share in the prize-money. See Captain Ball's letter of 6th March 1801 (Chap. xvi.).

The dispatches and secret letters printed in the new volume of the 'Dropmore Papers' (MSS. of J. B. Fortescue, Esq.) show that our Ministers held to the compact of December 1798, whereby Malta was to be occupied during the war against France by British, Russian, and Neapolitan troops conjointly. The Pitt Ministry was also still bent on reinstating the Order of St. John. Nevertheless, Dundas in his letter to Grenville of April 20, 1800, added the significant words: 'I hope in God you will be able to make such an arrangement with Russia as may secure to us, *as a naval Power*, all the advantages which Malta possesses. . . . To France its value is incalculable.'[1] Grenville evidently thought less highly of Malta, for in his reply of April 23 he expressed a doubt whether it was of much importance either to England or to France, *seeing that a naval war between the two Powers was not likely to occur again in the Levant*. Minorca, he added, was of far higher value to us. He concluded thus: 'As for arrangements with Russia I own that I despair, and when you read the dispatches you will probably do likewise, of being able to conclude anything with that Court just now, but especially on the very point on which the Emperor is most sore. My opinion therefore clearly is to leave the thing as it is: to satisfy ourselves with the advantage of having Malta rather in the hands of Russia than of France; and not to attempt to open any fresh negotiations at St. Petersburg on the subject.'[2]

Matters were left in that state. The Russian troops did not sail from Naples to Malta, as was expected; and the events of the Marengo campaign led to their recall to Corfu and the abandonment of the King of Naples by the Czar. The Anglo-Russian convention was therefore of no effect, owing to the peevish and perverse action of Paul I. On October 17 Grenville wrote to Paget, our envoy at the Neapolitan Court, then at Palermo: 'The Russian troops and ships, wherever employed, have been withdrawn, the Emperor's forces have in no degree contributed to the reduction of the Island of Malta, nor has he during the present campaign afforded to the Allies the smallest aid against the common enemy.'[3]

A few days later the rupture with Russia was complete: and it is well known that the offer to cede Malta to the Czar, which Bonaparte skilfully made in July 1800, contributed materially to this event. The facts connected with the British expedition into the Baltic under Parker and Nelson, the assassination of the Czar Paul, and the accession of his son, Alexander I (March 1801), do not concern us here, save in so far as they brought to power a ruler who was far from hostile to Great Britain, and felt less concern about the

---

[1] *Dropmore Papers*, vol. vi. p. 199.
[2] *Ibid.* p. 200. This refutes the statement of Alison (chap. xxxiii), that 'it was easy to anticipate that the English Cabinet would not readily part with that important fortress.'
[3] *Paget Papers*, vol. i. p. 274.

possession of Malta. As is shown near the end of Chapter XVII of this work, Alexander I accorded his protection to the Order of St. John, but in other respects his cool treatment of the Maltese question was in signal contrast to the captious fussiness of his father.

It is, therefore, not surprising that the opinions of the British Government also underwent a change. The Addington Ministry, which succeeded that of Pitt in March 1801, soon proved to be weak in its handling of foreign affairs; but there are signs which show that, for some time at least, it intended to retain Malta. As will be seen by reference to Chapter XVI of this volume, the long dispatch of May 14, 1801, sent by Lord Hobart, Minister for War and the Colonies, to Mr. Charles Cameron, the Civil Commissioner for Malta, who succeeded Captain Ball, seems to imply that the British Government had at that time resolved to retain the island. The Neapolitan troops had retired, and it ought to have been possible to persuade the Czar, Alexander I, to waive his claim to protect the Knights of St. John. His policy was at very many points in direct opposition to that of his father. He cared little for expansion in the Mediterranean. Moreover, his interest in the projected reforms of the social and political system of Russia,[1] and his championship of the interests of the German princes against Bonaparte's interventions, should have afforded the means to bind him to England, and acquiesce in her retention of Malta.

The recent publication of Volume VI of the 'Dropmore Papers' enables us to see the views of some of our officers and diplomatists respecting Malta. As will further appear by reference to the documents published in this volume, Sir Charles Stuart felt very keenly the need of retaining Malta; and we now know that his refusal to comply with the instructions issued to him in the early spring of 1800, for allowing the Russians to garrison it conjointly with British and Neapolitan troops, led to the resignation of his command in the Mediterranean, and to the refusal of the Rt. Hon. Henry Dundas, Minister at War, to employ him again, at least for the present ('Dropmore Papers,' vol. vi. p. 207). Dundas, as we have seen already, felt strongly on the question of retaining a hold upon Malta; and Grenville, who at first valued Minorca more than Malta, seems to have come round owing to letters which he received from General Graham at Malta, the Earl of Carysfort at Berlin, and William Wickham at Vienna, urging on him the extreme importance of holding that island (*ibid.* vol. vi. pp. 248, 249, 371, 421, 430). The last-named, in his letter of January 21, 1801, said: 'With Malta in your hands, you will still be gods even at Vienna, in spite of Buonaparte. It opens a prospect at Vienna which, in the present state of things, has no bounds.' The Earl of Carysfort also wrote (November 1, 1800) that to hand

[1] See the *Memoirs of Prince Czartoryski*, I. pp. 272–79 (Eng. edit.).

Malta over to the Order, which would be equivalent to ceding it to Russia, would be 'a serious misfortune to all Europe.'

Grenville appears to have been convinced by these arguments, for he sharply criticised the Preliminary Treaty of London, assented to by the Addington Cabinet on October 1, 1801, largely because we gave up both Minorca and Malta, and thereby yielded to France complete predominance in the Mediterranean. Dundas certainly wanted to keep Malta. Indeed, as the rupture with Russia had annulled the Anglo-Russian convention of December 29, 1798, the members of the Pitt Cabinet were perfectly free to press for the retention of the island by the Power which had almost singly effected its reduction. The opinion of Pitt is not easy to fathom. He felt himself in honour bound to support his successors, so far as he conscientiously could; and his speech in Parliament was in complete contrast to that of Grenville. Pitt sought to persuade members that the gain of Ceylon, Trinidad, and Mysore (the last-named was a question which did not directly concern France) was more glorious than that of Canada and Florida by the Seven Years' War. He, however, admitted that the giving up of Malta was a very regrettable fact.

It seems probable, then, that the continuance of the Pitt Ministry in power would have implied the retention of Malta. We may also observe that, had the news of the surrender of General Menou in Egypt arrived in London two days earlier (namely, on September 30), even the Addington Cabinet might have felt an accession of confidence sufficient to empower it to make that a *sine quâ non* of peace.[1] The last claims to be surrendered by the Addington Ministry were those relating to Malta and Tobago. The evidence contained in the British Archives (C.O.R. Malta No. 4.) shows that the Cabinet considered several plans for the adjustment of the Maltese Question. Among the *Projects* for a Maltese constitution is an undated one by Prince Alexander Vorontzoff (Woronzow), somewhat on the lines finally adopted, which was handed in to our ambassador, Sir John Borlase Warren, at St. Petersburg. Signs are not wanting that the final plan of reinstating the Order of St. John was due to more general considerations. This is stated in the British Foreign Office dispatch of September 17, 1801, to Lord St. Helens at St. Petersburg (F.O. Russia, No. 49) :—'The future situation of the Island of Malta has given rise, as might be expected, to much discussion; but the importance of endeavouring to secure by a general peace the integrity of the Turkish Empire and of the Kingdoms of Portugal and Naples have (*sic*) induced His Majesty to consent to withdraw the British forces from that Island and to agree that it should be placed in a state of independence either on (*sic*) Great

[1] For some details of the negotiations which led up to the Preliminary Treaty, see Rose, *Life of Napoleon I*, vol. i. chap. xiii. *ad init.*

Britain or France, provided the French Government would consent to a suitable arrangement for the East and West Indies.' Thus British interests at Malta were sacrificed to the wider considerations just noticed, which were deemed to further the cause of peace and national security. Certain it is that in giving way on Malta this pacific Cabinet left the door open for disputes which were the final cause of the war of 1803. There is every reason to believe that a firm attitude towards Napoleon in 1801 would at least have prolonged the time of peace.

XII

The British Government soon began to feel concern respecting Malta. For in the instructions issued on October 27, 1801, to the Marquis Cornwallis, on whom devolved the task of reducing the Preliminaries of London to the definitive treaty signed at Amiens on March 27, 1802, Article V runs as follows :—

The Fourth Article [of the Preliminaries of Peace] respecting Malta is of the greatest importance and will demand your most serious attention. It is hereby stipulated that the island shall be restored to the Order of St. John; but that, to render it independent of either of the contracting parties, it shall be placed under the guaranty and protection of a third Power. The first point which it will be necessary to determine is—Where is the Order, and who are to be considered as composing it ? We are ready to acknowledge as the Order those Knights who, in consequence of the Declaration of the 28th of August last of the Emperor of Russia, shall proceed to the election of a Grand Master, and the person so elected as Grand Master. As a consequence of this acknowledgment the island should be considered as under the protection and guaranty of the Emperor of Russia.

Although the supreme authority both civil and military must necessarily be vested in the Order, it appears to be highly just and expedient that the condition of the natives and inhabitants of Malta should be meliorated [sic], and that for this purpose admission to the Order and such privileges and immunities should be granted and secured to them, as may not be inconsistent with or derogatory from, the supreme authority of the Knights. With respect to the defence and security of the island, it is indispensable that a garrison, to be composed in part at least of the troops of the Emperor of Russia or of some other Power, should be provided. In order to defray the expense of such a garrison, the most practicable and equitable mode appears to be that of opening the ports of Malta to the commerce and navigation of all nations on their paying equal duties, and that the amount of those duties should be applied, in the first instance, to the payment of the expenses of the garrison.[1]

This document, which has not been printed before, is of value as

[1] F. O. France, No. 59.

showing that the British Government had resolved to safeguard the interests of the Maltese, even before it received the long and urgent 'Representation' drawn up by them and handed in to Commissioner Cameron on October 19, 1801. It is noteworthy that the first impression produced on the Maltese by the news of the reinstatement of the Order of St. John was that this would be but a stepping-stone to the acquisition of the island by France. Their 'Representation' to Mr. Cameron (printed in Chapter XIX *ad init.*) is well worthy of attention as showing their attachment to Great Britain and their keen forecast of the probable course of events should they be handed over once more to a weak and discredited Order.[1] The services of the Maltese levies are ludicrously overestimated in this document, as those of the British fleet and land forces are belittled; but in other respects the Maltese shrewdly interpreted the action of France, and showed how easily she could dispose of a guarantee which any third Power might give. This document may have opened the eyes of the somewhat purblind statesmen and officials at Downing Street. That the Maltese deputies knew very well the paramount importance of the services rendered by the British fleet and soldiery appears in the following sentence of their letter of April 2, 1802, to Lord Hobart, Secretary of State for War and the Colonies: 'In transmitting to our descendants the story of our Revolution, we shall tell them that without the assistance of Great Britain our ruin would have been inevitable.'[2] Had all the Maltese, at that time and at a later date, been as frank in acknowledging their indebtedness to Great Britain, much of the friction which has since occurred would have been averted.

On the other hand, it is difficult, except on the score of political expediency, to justify the action of the British Government in handing over to the Order of St. John a population which detested that Order and demanded to be part of the British Empire. The Maltese very naturally resented such conduct; but it may be pleaded in excuse of the Addington Cabinet that the First Consul showed himself most exacting on this point, while the Czar Alexander would have been offended by any other solution of the difficulty. There had been signs of a possible Franco-Russian *entente*. Thus, as had happened so often of late, Malta was sacrificed to the wider diplomatic questions of that time.[3]

[1] The Porte took the same view. In F. O. Turkey, No. 35, is a dispatch of Lord Elgin, our ambassador at Constantinople, to Lord Hawkesbury, which contains similar statements: 'The Porte considers her interests and tranquillity secure [i.e. in Egypt] while England possesses Malta; but not so after our abandoning it.' He adds that, as Turkey had sworn perpetual peace with the Order of St. John, it now had no *raison d'être*.

[2] See chap. xix of this work; also *Papers relative to the Discussion with France in 1802 and 1803* (Papers presented to Parliament 1803), p. 325.

[3] See *The Cornwallis Correspondence*, vol. iii, *Paget Papers*, vol. ii. *ad init.* and Rose, *Life of Napoleon I*, vol. i. pp. 333-40, for these questions.

Nevertheless, the efforts of the Maltese to procure some alleviation of their lot were not wholly fruitless. The British Government resisted the effort of the Czar to exclude commoners from the proposed Maltese Langue. Article X, section 3, of the Treaty of Amiens contained the following provision: 'No proofs of nobility shall be necessary for the admission of Knights into the said Langue; they shall be competent to hold every office and to hold every privilege in the like manner as the Knights of the other Langues.'

The documents collected by Mr. Hardman in Chapters XXI, XXII, show more fully than has been done before the perverse policy of the Czar Alexander at this time and during the disputes respecting Malta in 1802-3. In the first place, his punctiliousness about the affairs of the Order of St. John enhanced the difficulties of a settlement, and that, too, though the British Government had offered that he should undertake the defence of the island. For a time in the summer of 1801 he favoured the proposal; but on the resignation of his Minister, Count Panin, he veered round and declared that a Russian garrison at Malta would be expensive and compromising. The offer itself, however, is a proof that the Cabinet of St. James sincerely desired a complete and lasting settlement of the Maltese Question on terms favourable to Russia; and the strife that ensued may be traced to the vacillations of Alexander, not to the Addington Ministry.[1]

Other things besides the shifts and turns of the young Czar gave cause for alarm. Even before the signature of the Peace of Amiens, rumours flew about that Bonaparte meant to acquire Malta. Italinsky, the Russian envoy at the Neapolitan Court, reported on February 20, 1802, [that the first Consul was known to be set on securing complete supremacy in the Mediterranean and juggling the English out of Malta, as a preliminary to the re-conquest of Egypt and the driving them out of India.[2] These reports gained in credibility when Bonaparte dispatched Colonel Sebastiani on a mission to the Levant and published his very threatening report in extenso in the *Moniteur*.

When we further remember that much of the property of that Order on the Continent had been sequestrated before the Peace of Amiens, that the Spanish Government shortly afterwards confiscated its lands in Spain, and that Russia and Prussia withheld their guarantees to the terms of that treaty respecting Malta (though that guarantee was required by the terms of Article X of the treaty), we see that on technical grounds the British Government had a good case for not withdrawing its troops.

The real reason for that course of conduct was that the recent acquisitions of France, namely, Piedmont, Parma, Piacenza, and Elba, not to speak of the control of Switzerland by the French and their refusal to evacuate the fortresses of Holland, constituted a most serious menace to the safety of Great Britain. M. Coquelle in his

[1] *Paget Papers*, vol. ii. p. 24.   [2] *Ibid.* p. 42.

work, 'Napoleon and England,' which is founded on a careful study of the French archives, has pointed out the importance of securing the actual neutrality of the Dutch Republic. His argument would have acquired more strength had he pointed out that a French expedition set sail from Brest for the East Indies on March 6, 1803, which touched at the Cape of Good Hope, and was instructed (so we now know) to use that Dutch possession as a *point d'appui* in case of a rupture with England.[1] The secret instructions issued by the First Consul to the commander of the expedition, General Decaen, prove that measures were to be undertaken in India in order to strengthen French interests, with a view to an ultimate conflict with England; and the date, September 1804, is referred to in this connexion as one that might witness the outbreak of war.

These plans were unknown to the British Government; but it is clear that the departure of the French expedition to India aroused its anxiety respecting the means of communicating with the Orient. Lord Whitworth, British ambassador at Paris, mentioned that event in his dispatches of March 24 and 31, 1803, to Lord Hawkesbury; and it is significant that in his reply of April 4 (which contained the British proposal for the retention of Malta, as a counterpoise to the gains of France in Italy) Lord Hawkesbury stated that the whole question must now be brought to a definite issue. There was every reason why the British Government should seek to clear up a situation which was becoming more dangerous than open war. If Bonaparte were allowed to keep his hold on Holland, to strengthen his grip on Italy, to fortify Elba, to threaten the reconquest of Egypt and the Ionian Isles, and to mature his plans for India (whatever they might be), he would in that case soon be able to contest with England the mastery of the high seas, to drive her from the Mediterranean, and to take up once more the Oriental designs which had been interrupted by Nelson's victory at the Nile.

The researches of M. Coquelle have thrown light on the interesting condition of affairs at the end of March and beginning of April. He shows that on March 28 the French ambassador, General Andréossy, handed to Lord Hawkesbury, Minister for Foreign Affairs in the Addington Cabinet, a note demanding the cession of Malta to Naples, a weak State which France could at all times coerce and overbear. Andréossy thereupon informed the First Consul and Talleyrand in letters, which will be found quoted in Chapter XX, that the British Ministry, though distressed by the late demand, still desired peace, and that it rested with him, the First Consul, to assure its continuance. In Andréossy's letter of April 4 to Bonaparte occurs a phrase which Mr. Hardman did not cite, but which deserves

[1] For the actions of Decaen at Cape Town, see my article in the *Eng. Historical Rev.* of January 1900.—J. H. R.

quotation: 'Everybody [in England] wants peace. By preserving the peace of Europe you will crush this country without appealing to the arbitrament of the mailed fist.'[1]

This was so. Bonaparte only had to wait in order to gain an accession of strength which, if wisely wielded, must overbear Great Britain when the fit time came for throwing down the gauntlet. That he resolved to do so can admit of little doubt.[2] His plans of aggrandisement in Europe, especially the control which he kept over the maritime resources of Holland and Italy, revealed the presence of grandiose designs which could not but be perilous for the Island Power.

Let us seek to realise the position of England at that juncture. She had recently evacuated the Cape of Good Hope and Egypt, and therefore had no means of barring the road eastwards to the First Consul save by holding on to Malta. If that island went to a moribund Order, or to the weak and vacillating Government at Naples, its independence would never be worth a month's purchase; and when the tricolour floated at Valetta, there was nothing to prevent the re-occupation of Egypt by the French. By this time everyone had come to see the importance of Malta. Nelson, revising the strange opinion as to its uselessness which he had earlier expressed, now termed it 'a most important outwork to India.'[3] That phrase was repeated by Ministers in Parliament, who grounded their determination to keep Malta on the urgent danger to which Egypt was exposed by the openly avowed designs of Bonaparte.[4]

In this connexion it should be noticed that the French Government had recognised the reasonableness of the British demand for territorial compensation as a set-off to the great gains of France in recent months. It had used the following terms: 'Cependant on reconnoit que les grands événemens survenus en Europe, et les changemens arrivés dans les limites des grands États du Continent peuvent autoriser une partie des demandes du Gouvernement Britannique.'[5] The only question, then, was—What land should Great Britain acquire as 'compensation'? She claimed Malta, because her interests in the Orient were seriously menaced. Bonaparte resisted, and accepted war rather than allow Malta to be the compensation. The inference is inevitable, that he had determined on schemes which would be checked or thwarted by the sovereignty of Great Britain at Valetta.

[1] Coquelle, *op. cit.* p. 56 (Eng. edit.).
[2] See *inter alia* the able articles by Professor Philippson in the *Revue Historique* for March, June 1901.
[3] *Nelson Dispatches*, vol. v. p. 507.
[4] Alison, chap. xxxvi (pp. 279 *et seq.* in 9th edit. 1854).
[5] O. Browning, *England and Napoleon*, p. 7; Lord Hawkesbury to Lord Whitworth, November 14, 1802. See, too, pp. 73, 121, 149, 161, 163, 170, for proofs that the British Government never ceased to press the First Consul to give effect to the principle of compensation as formally admitted by him.

XIII

The Foreign Office Records for the months May–July, 1803, reveal the complexity of the Maltese Question. For, on the news of the rupture, the Emperor of Russia offered to arbitrate on that matter. As I have shown in my 'Life of Napoleon I' (ch. xviii), the British Government viewed his action with some suspicion, and decided to accept his mediation only if it concerned all the causes in dispute—a condition which he accepted and Napoleon refused. That Alexander strongly desired to have a voice in the disposal of Malta appears in his insistence on its abandonment by England during the discussions for an Anglo-Russian alliance in the spring and summer of 1805. The Pitt Ministry decided at all costs ' to preserve the rock which is the cause of all existing difficulties.'[1] This fact, among many others, proves that the fate of Malta was essentially an international question, and that England had to reckon not only with France, but also with Russia. Her title to Malta was not decided solely by the events of the years 1798–1803: in the main it turned on the fortunes of the Great War. The pressing need of British help felt by Alexander in 1812 furnished the opportunity for eliminating the Russian claims. Those of Napoleon lapsed with his fall.

It is needless to review the facts which find their place in the last chapter of Mr. Hardman's work. As is well known, the years of Napoleon's Continental System (1806–13) formed a time of great prosperity for Malta. It became one of the *points d'appui* for the Sea Power in its struggle against the master of the Continent. Heligoland, the Channel Islands, Portugal, Cadiz, Sicily, Malta, and for a time Ischia and Corfu, were stations from which British commerce carried on its war of pin-pricks against the Continental System; and even the mighty will and energy of Napoleon failed to keep the Continent hermetically sealed against the efforts of enterprising seamen ever striving at these diverse points to puncture that tense and artificial System. There was something of retributive justice in the events of these years, which poured back into Malta the wealth of which Bonaparte and Vaubois had drained her in 1798–1800.

The collapse of Napoleon's power in 1813–14 brought about the return of more normal conditions; and in the meantime Russia had recognised the complete sovereignty of Great Britain in Malta. By the treaty of alliance with her in 1812, the Czar, Alexander I, surrendered all his pretensions to the championship of the Order of St. John at Malta. Here, again, we may notice that this resulted

[1] '*Memoirs of Prince Czartoryski*,' vol. ii. ch. viii, also p. 186 (Eng. edit.).

from his rupture with Napoleon, which in its turn was mainly due to the acute friction brought about by the Continental System.

In the end, then, Malta came to England. It is not very reassuring to recollect that she might have acquired it outright in 1801–2 by that best of all titles, the almost universal assent and desire of the islanders themselves. Whether a firm handling of the Maltese problem at that time might have postponed, or even averted, war with Napoleon in 1803 it is futile to inquire. What is certain is that the vacillation of British policy on that topic brought about a situation in which the rupture was well-nigh impossible to avoid. The excess of the evil finally brought about the solution which was most natural; but that fact does not justify the Addington Cabinet for its weak treatment of the matter in the years 1801–2.

The statistics published in Mr. Hardman's last chapter sufficiently illustrate the material progress of the Maltese in the long years of peace which followed after Waterloo. In this connexion it should be remembered that the naval demonstration of Lord Exmouth at Tripoli, Tunis, and Algiers, together with the bombardment of the last-named city on August 27, 1816, dealt a blow to slavery in the Barbary States from which it never recovered. On that one day England did more to free the Mediterranean from the Barbary rovers than the Knights of St. John had done, or indeed could have done, in their whole career. The influence of this expedition on Mediterranean commerce, and therefore on the prosperity of Malta, can scarcely be overrated.

Many narratives of travellers might be cited in proof of the benefits resulting from British rule in the ensuing period; but I limit myself to short extracts from the work of Friedrich von Raumer, 'Italy and the Italians' (Eng. edit., Lond., two vols., 1840). The evidence of that cultured and much-travelled German may be taken as that of an unprejudiced witness. Visiting Valetta in the middle of August 1839, he thus records his impressions, in contrast with Sicily and North Italy, which he had recently left:

Owing to the circumstance that England obtained possession of the island, it has become an intermediate point between the East and the West, and the opposition formerly kept up has been changed into a cordial accommodation. Look at those tall, fair, ruddy descendants of Germans, striding with stately step; they appear like a totally different race of men, a race destined to command. . . .

The greatest activity prevails in every branch of agriculture; thus, at Syracuse, I had Maltese potatoes set before me, professedly because Sicily produces no good ones!

Wherever the English come, idleness is driven away; but then they bring political views and parties along with them. Thoughtless, passive obedience cannot maintain itself as the sole foundation of human society; among a variety of new errors are also developed new and grand truths, and while the one assumes, or at least strives to gain, a higher position

INTRODUCTION

the whole at last moves upward. Hence at this moment in Malta so many questions concerning the rights of the inhabitants, municipal regulations, appointment of natives and foreigners, grants of taxes, &c. Many may wish to consider the English as merely a voluntarily admitted garrison of their fortress, but in other respects to maintain complete independence. England can and will neither grant everything nor refuse everything: without England, Malta would retrograde in every respect.

I have traversed the city in all directions. It is regular, clean, full of signs of activity, and of (apparently) increasing prosperity, only street beggary prevails to the same extent as in Italy.

Subsequent events, namely, the disputes concerning Syria and Egypt, the Crimean War, and the opening of the Suez Canal, enhanced the value of Malta to Great Britain, and served to confirm the decision which was rendered inevitable by the events of the years 1798–1812. So soon as the mighty will of Bonaparte re-opened the Eastern Question in a novel and acute phase, the fate of the island was certain to link it with the naval Power that could gain command of the Mediterranean. As has been shown in this Introduction, British Ministers came slowly and reluctantly to this resolve. In the years 1800–1, Pitt and Grenville, Addington and Hawkesbury, regarded the Egyptian Question as settled, and looked with equanimity to the re-establishment of the Order of St. John under the suzerainty of the Czar or (finally) under the guarantee of the Great Powers. A careful survey of the events of the years 1802–3 must convince every unprejudiced student that it was the renewal of Bonaparte's schemes in the Mediterranean lands and in India which brought the Addington Cabinet to the determination to hold on to Malta as an 'outwork of India.' In a very real sense, then, it was the First Consul who compelled us to keep the Union Jack flying at Valetta. In that vast and complex game Malta was a serviceable pawn, able to do much within a restricted area, but always at the mercy of the heavier pieces, and fated ultimately to fall to the Queen of the Sea.

It only remains to thank Sir John Knox Laughton and Mr. William Carr for their valuable help and advice respecting this Introduction, and Mr. A. M. Broadley for permission to reproduce the contemporary map of Malta and plan of Valetta which are in his possession.

J. HOLLAND ROSE.

December, 1908.

ABBREVIATIONS USED IN THE REFERENCES TO THE CHIEF WORKS QUOTED IN THIS VOLUME.

Alison	Alison, Sir A., 'History of Europe during the French Revolution,' 10 vols. (Edinburgh, 1833–42).
Arch. Nat.	Archives Nationales, Paris.
Azopardi	Azopardi, Giornale della Presa di Malta.
Botta	C. G. G. Botta, 'Storia d'Italia' (1789–1814) 4 vols. (Paris, 1832).
Brit. Mus. Add. MSS.	British Museum, Additional Manuscripts (MS. Department).
C. O. R.	Colonial Office Records.
Corres. de Nap. I	'Correspondance de Napoléon I,' 32 vols. (Paris, 1859–1870).
De la Jonquière (or 'Jonquière')	C. E. L. M. de T. de la Jonquière, 'L'Expédition d'Egypte,' 3 vols. (Paris, 1899).
Dropmore Papers	Report on the MSS. of J. B. Fortescue, Esq., preserved at Dropmore, 6 vols. (London, 1892-1908; Historical MSS. Commission).
F. O. R.	Foreign Office Records.
James	W. James, 'The Naval History of Great Britain' (1793–1820), 6 vols. (London, 1902).
Mahan	Capt. A. T. Mahan, 'Influence of Sea Power upon the French Revolution and Empire,' 2 vols. (London, 1893).
Miège	Miège, 'History of Malta.'
M. P. L.	Malta Public Library (MSS. preserved in).
Paget Papers, The	Diplomatic and other Correspondence of the Right Hon. Sir A. Paget, G.C.B., 1794–1807, 2 vols. (London, 1896).
Pettigrew	Pettigrew, T. J., 'Memoirs of the Life of Lord Nelson,' 2nd edit., 2 vols. (London, 1849).
Rose, 'Life of Nap.'	Rose, J. H., 'Life of Napoleon I,' 3rd edit., 2 vols. (London, 1903).
Thiers	L. A. Thiers, 'Histoire de la Révolution Française' (translated by F. Shoberl) 5 vols. (London, 1881).

VALETTA.
(1803.)

CHAPTER I

THE SOCIAL CONDITION OF THE MALTESE PEOPLE AT THE CLOSE OF THE EIGHTEENTH CENTURY

[NOTE.—The narrative of this chapter and the following chapters is that of Mr. Hardman. The foot notes are also his, except in cases where the editor's initials (J. H. R.) are added.]

BEFORE referring to the object of the French expedition to the East, there are two points in connexion with the capture of Malta which it is necessary should be defined, inasmuch as they both materially contributed to the result, namely, the social and moral condition of the inhabitants, and the financial difficulties of the Government, culminating in 1792, when, by an edict of the French Convention, the Order of St. John was abolished within the borders of France, and its territorial possessions therein were confiscated.

With regard to the social and moral condition of the inhabitants during the latter period of the Knights' rule : it is not surprising that the arrogance, tyranny, and oppression of this nobility had created such discontent that it finally rendered the islands an easy prey to the ambitious designs of Bonaparte. The development of these characteristics in the members of the Order was due to the fact that Mohammedism had become no longer the dreaded enemy of the Christian Powers. By the close of the eighteenth century Turkey was no longer a formidable Sea Power, and after the destruction of the Algerian, Tunisian, and Tripolitan corsairs, the fleet of the Order of St. John of Jerusalem was, according to Doublet, used only

'for carrying treasure collected from their various bailiwicks, extending from Lisbon to Syracuse. Their cruising area had also been restricted by France, and the Venetian Republic. France had found it necessary to adopt this measure, owing to retaliation which had been exercised against her subjects resident in Turkish territory, for acts committed by the Order; which resulted in a prohibition to the latter, from making captures within two leagues of Ottoman territory.'

Cruising in the Adriatic was likewise interdicted. Instead, therefore, of recounting feats of daring, Doublet goes on to say:

'It was deeds of gallantry, of hunting, or of sport, which upon their return they had to relate.'[1] Consequently the necessity of maintaining the Order as a Military Power and barrier to Mussulman aggression, which had been required during the Middle Ages for the safety of Christendom, no longer existed. With their *raison d'être* gone, the three hundred Knights led a life of idleness which afforded them time, opportunity, and free scope for the gratification of their unbridled passions. Their vows of chastity and obedience were completely ignored.

In considering the various causes which contributed to the ruin of the Order, a distinction must be drawn between the people and the Knights. With a *celibate* Order, recruited from, and supported entirely by foreigners, there could not possibly be any amalgamation between the two classes. Thus, at the close of the eighteenth century, there existed in Malta an oligarchy, despotic and arrogant in the extreme, without the slightest sympathy for the ruled, with nothing to their credit but the military reputation which their valiant predecessors of the sixteenth century had bequeathed them. Furthermore, the immorality of the Knights now placed an impassable barrier to any assimilation between the governing and governed classes. The secretary of the last Grand Master stigmatised the Knights in the following words [2]:—

They made no secret of keeping mistresses, generally married women and mothers of a family, a practice which became so general, that neither age, nor ministers of the Gospel [*sic*], dissolute like the rest, blushed at the fact. Instances were known to have happened where a Maltese married to an attractive wife had been exiled, owing to the influence of rich and immoral Knights, and if the banishment of husbands, on account of their wives, or of fathers on account of their daughters, was not more frequent, it was not because these crimes of seduction were few, but from dread of the consequences which would surely follow any resistance, owing to the protection which the Government afforded the Knights.

This picture of depravity does not appear to have been exaggerated, for within six years after the emancipation of the Maltese from this terrible condition of slavery and thraldom, the poet and essayist, S. T. Coleridge, who had been private secretary to Sir Alexander John Ball, the first British Governor or Commissioner of Malta, made the following lamentable statement:—

The very existence for so many generations of an Order of lay celibates in that Island, who abandoned even the outward shows of adherence to their vow of chastity, must have had pernicious effects on the morals of the inhabitants. But when it is considered too, that the Knights of Malta had

---

[1] See the description of the habits of the Knights and their neglect of their lands in Malta, in a 'Report on Malta,' of June 16, 1800, in the *Dropmore Papers*, vol. vi. pp. 248, 249.—J. H. R.
[2] Doublet, *Mémoires*, p. 14.

been for the last fifty years or more a set of idlers, generally illiterate, for they thought literature no part of a soldier's excellence; and yet effeminate, for they were soldiers in name only; when it is considered that they were, moreover, all of them aliens, who looked upon themselves, not merely of a superior rank to the native Nobles, but as beings of a different race (I had almost said species) from the Maltese collectively; and finally that these men possessed exclusively the government of the Island, it may be safely concluded that they were little better than a perpetual influenza, relaxing and diseasing the hearts of all the families within their sphere of influence. Hence the peasantry, who fortunately were below their reach, notwithstanding the more than childish ignorance in which they were kept by their priests, yet compared with the middle and higher classes, were in mind and body as ordinary men compared with dwarfs.

Every Knight attached himself to some family as their patron and friend, and to him the honour of a sister, or a daughter, was sacrificed as a matter of course. But why should I disguise the truth? Alas! in nine instances out of ten, this patron was the common paramour of every female in the family.[1]

Whether Doublet's assertion, that the immorality ascribed to the Knights in their latter degenerate days had extended to the priesthood, is correct or not, must remain in doubt; but the fact remains, that within a few weeks after Bishop Labini took possession of the diocese, one of his first acts, if not the first, was to fulminate an 'Edict against Cohabitation of Women with Priests.'

Bishop Labini, a native of Bitonto, near Bari, landed in Malta on the 7th September 1780, and on the 29th of the following month the edict in question was issued. Nor does this step appear to have been sufficient to suppress the evil, for His Grace, on the 25th October 1784, by a second edict on the same subject, had to 'express his sorrow that his former orders had not been faithfully observed, and called for an immediate and exact obedience to his spiritual commands, under the threat of increased pains and penalties.'[2]

Bosredon Ransijat, treasurer of the Order, gives his testimony on this subject in the following words: 'The Maltese shut their eyes to the seductions of their wives and daughters, but this applied only to the citizens, not to the country people, who kept themselves free from this corruption.'[3]

The evidence of Lieutenant Anderson, of the 40th Regiment, quartered in Malta from November 1800 to November 1801, is to the same effect:

Though all ranks of people are devotees, and minutely attentive to the Church ordinances, yet chastity does not appear to maintain its due rank among their virtues. It certainly is not to be found in the Island, while prostitution, from the familiar and open manner in which it is carried on, both by married as well as single women, and with the knowledge of their

---

[1] Coleridge, *The Friend*, p. 352.   [2] Malta Public Library, MSS. 261.
[3] B. Ransijat, *Journal du Siège de Malte* (Paris, 1801), p. 83.

husbands and relations, is not, unless attended with some peculiar degree of enormity, considered as a crime.[1]

Or again, Dr. Davy, in his work entitled 'Notes and Observations on the Ionian Islands and Malta,' published in 1842, whose residence of eleven years (1824–35) made him fully conversant with the history of the islands during the early part of last century, says:[2]

I have seen an 'M.S.' [sic] written by an individual of the name of Doublet which was in the possession of the late Sir F. Ponsonby, then Governor of Malta, 1827–1836, and from this account, the Knights appear then (1798) to have been, with a few exceptions, completely sunk in profligacy and dissipation, and to have lost very much even the sense of shame, *and what I have heard related by old persons who remember their doings, was much in accordance.*

Other authorities may be mentioned, such as Miège,[3] who says: 'The expulsion of the Order left in Malta a great number of natural children, the result of adulterous intercourse, and the licentious lives of the Knights'; and Dr. Gauci,[4] who adds: 'For in later times Valetta became a brothel, nor did a family remain which was not dishonoured.'

These facts are fully confirmed in the petition prepared for presentation to the British throne by the Maltese deputies, dated the 22nd October 1801 (hereafter referred to), wherein they protest against the re-establishment of the Order in the island, pleading, among other reasons, ' that their families might be saved from dishonour or ruin, whenever the caprice of a Knight had selected his victim.'

Justification of the people's dread of the restoration of the Order to the possession of Malta is eloquently given by Lieutenant-General Sir Charles Stuart, commander-in-chief of the British military forces in the Mediterranean, as well as by General Graham, when relinquishing his command in Malta, fourteen days after the fall of Valetta, both dispatches being addressed to the Minister for War, the Right Honourable H. Dundas. The former, under date of the 22nd April 1800, writes:[5]

... My feelings of honour and humanity render it impossible for me to obey the particular instructions concerning the introduction of a Russian force (preparatory to the restoration of the Order), for after having been a witness to the long and arduous effort of the Maltese, in conjunction with Captain Ball and the Navy, to reduce the French, I could not engage their services by such fallacious hopes, and afterwards prove instrumental in replacing them under the tyranny of the most corrupt, hypocritical and cowardly vagrants that ever were fostered, or what is worse, rivetting their chains by subjecting all they held dear to the oppression of a despotic sovereign.[6]

[1] Anderson, *Journal Secret Expedition*, p. 183.   [2] Davy, *op. cit.* vol. i. p. 40.
[3] Miège, *History of Malta*, vol. iii. p. 172.
[4] Gauci, *Capture of Malta by the French*, p. 13.
[5] Colonial Office Records, Malta, No. 1.
[6] As I pointed out in the Introduction, Stuart's refusal to obey this order cost him his command in the Mediterranean. See Dundas's letter of April 25, 1800, in *Dropmore Papers*, vol. vi. p. 207.—J. H. R.

THE SOCIAL CONDITION OF THE MALTESE

Whilst Graham, under date of the 19th September 1800, says : [1]
. . . There cannot be a doubt in the mind of anyone who has had the opportunity or the inclination of inquiry, that a very considerable part of the richer Maltese favoured the French invasion. The same causes which have all over Europe (Britain excepted) inclined that middling class to destroy the galling distinctions which the arrogance of a tyrannical nobility had created, operated in a much stronger degree in Malta than elsewhere. Every Knight was a sovereign and tyrant, their oppressions were mutually supported for the honour of the Order, and the idleness and the luxury in which so many young men were destined to spend their days by this monastic institution, naturally led to the severest outrages against the feeling and honour of every family in a country where the climate and character seem to have made jealousy an universal characteristic. No man's wife or daughter could be defended against the attacks of these privileged despoilers, those of independent spirit and circumstances were found to bow to the strong hand of power, while an universal depravity of morals pervaded the remainder, who sought their own advancement in the prostitution of their nearest relations. This is noticed as one, and the strongest, among many causes of discontent, which that separation of classes occasioned in Malta, and is more than sufficient to account for a numerous party in favour of the French, or of any change.

With regard to the arrogance of the Knights, it may be mentioned that the inhabitants were prohibited from promenading on the two Baraccas, except on one day in the year, and if attending the opera house, built by Grand Master Manoel, they were, according to Poussielgue's report, relegated to back seats. [2]

Referring to this prohibition of promenading in public places, Regnaud St. Jean d'Angely (the civil governor), in his speech delivered on the occasion of celebrating the French national festival on the 14th July 1798, made the following remark : 'The free use of the public promenades was prohibited to you, and your insolent and despotic rulers punished the pacific citizen who transgressed, but who now can tread the same pavement on which your former Rulers paraded their presumptuous pride.' [3]

To the sufferings of an oppressed people, as already described, there must be added that of the despotic power which, for a long time previously, the Grand Master and the Order had usurped and exercised, reducing the people to a condition of servitude and degradation which could scarcely be paralleled in Europe. According to Bosredon Ransijat, than whom no better authority could be cited, corruption had permeated all branches of the Order, chiefly through briefs, pecuniary grants, and appointments to lucrative posts or benefices.

[1] Colonial Office Records, Malta, No. 1.
[2] De la Jonquière, *l'Expéd. d'Egypte*, vol. i. p. 127.
[3] Azopardi, *Presa di Malta*, p. 57.

Briefs were originally intended to procure a dispensation in the administration of the law, in cases where unforeseen circumstances rendered it impracticable, but such eventually were granted by the Grand Masters to their favourites and partisans as rewards for their past services or to purchase them for the future. By the abuse of this prerogative, Knights were dispensed from the obligation of residing in convent!! others from the necessity of attending a portion, if not all, of the *Carovane*,[1] others from the obligation of paying the fee to the Treasury when acquiring a *Commenda*, others again from the loss of seniority, when so liable for misdemeanours committed, in a word to dispense from the fulfilment of their various duties, provided they showed submission and subserviency to the authority who distributed these gifts directly, or through favourites.

Moreover, by means of such briefs, pensions were charged on *Commende*, to the great injury of future occupants. Pecuniary grants and appointments to lucrative posts, although in many instances provided for by statute, were only intended to be enjoyed by those who had deserved well of the Order, but as in process of time opportunities for testing their valour and sacrifice in the defence of Christianity against the Turks became less frequent, so gradually what had been intended for the reward of virtue, became the patrimony of intrigue and baseness.

Although rules and regulations existed in the statutes of the Order to moderate the abuse of absolute power, yet towards the close of the eighteenth century they had become obsolete and of no effect, in fact the Grand Master had not only become law maker, but had also usurped the prerogatives of the Council, and nominated the judges, who thus became his servants, disposing of the property and lives in accordance with the will of their patron. In civil appeal cases it was feasible for the appellant to obtain from the Grand Master a third trial, provided he was 'protected,' and in the event of the decision being again unfavorable, to procure such a delay of time in its execution, that justice virtually miscarried. . . .

A debtor, provided he possessed the 'protection' of a Knight in authority, could obtain by petition a delay of five years in the presentation of any suit by his creditors, at the expiration of which term it could be extended for an indefinite number of similar periods. At a meeting of creditors, those who were so 'protected' could obtain by an express order from the Grand Master the entire payment of their claim, leaving the balance to be divided among the remainder.

When to all these circumstances there was to be added that of the jealousy which existed between the various 'Langues,'[2] we have the conditions ready to hand for a catastrophe which not even the maintenance of its financial resources in a flourishing state could prevent.

[1] i.e. sailings on board of the squadrons of the Order, of which the statute required four, for all Knights desirous of becoming eligible to a commandery.
[2] The Langues were the divisions of the members of the Order according to nations. —J. H. R.

CHAPTER II

BONAPARTE'S PLAN OF SEIZING MALTA (1797)

The French military successes in Italy, and the propaganda of Republican ideas, had no slight influence in directing political affairs in Malta, where so large a number of the Knights were French, culminating at last in sedition and intrigue. During the early months of 1797, the Republican party in Malta, which for some time had been in existence, acquired additional strength, both in the number and influence of its adherents. Traitorous Knights and disaffected Maltese joined in the conspiracy. Vassallo,[1] the Maltese historian, states that amongst the former there were Ransijat, Bordonenche, Fay, St. Priest, and Toussard; whilst among the Maltese there were Caruson, Eynaud, Poussielgue (captain of the port), Guido, Doublet, Vassalli, and Vincent Barbara, with many others.[2]

Capefigue[3] adds Picault de Mornas, an ex-Knight of the Order, and captain in the Engineers, who had deserted and joined Bonaparte two years previously.

The suspicions of the Maltese Government having been aroused, Vassalli and Vincent Barbara, who took a leading part in the events which followed (as will hereafter be seen), were arrested, and arraigned on the charge of high treason.[4] The investigation which followed disclosed the fact that many members of the Order were implicated, and it was consequently thought advisable to quash further proceedings, and be satisfied with the banishment of several of the accused.[5]

It would appear that Vincent Barbara, upon landing in Italy, made his way to Milan, and there reported to Bonaparte the unsettled state of Malta, the disaffection of many of the Knights to the existing government, and the desire of many of the inhabitants to welcome French intervention, for on the 26th May 1797, Bonaparte, as the result of the information he had received, wrote to the Executive Directory as follows :—

[1] Vassallo, pp. 728, 730.
[2] De la Jonquière, l'Expéd. d'Egypte, vol. i. pp. 598, 599.
[3] Capefigue, l'Europe pendant le Consulat et l'Empire, vol. i. p. 65.
[4] De la Jonquière, vol. i. p. 599.
[5] Vassallo, p. 730.

'The Island of Malta for us is of great importance — the Grand Master is dying, and it would appear that a German will be his successor. It would require from 500,000 to 600,000 francs to place a Spaniard in his place. Is it impossible to induce the Prince of the Peace[1] to occupy himself in this matter, which is most important? Valetta has 37,000 inhabitants extremely well disposed towards the French—there are no more English in the Mediterranean.[2] Why should not our fleet (or that of Spain), on its way to the Atlantic, pass in that direction, and capture it? The Knights are only 500, and the regiment of the Order counts only 600 men. If we do not adopt these means, Malta will fall into the hands of the King of Naples. This small island is priceless for us.'[3]

Bonaparte's prediction with regard to the approaching demise of the Grand Master, as reported in his dispatch to the Executive Directory from Milan, under date of the 26th May, was verified. De Rohan died on the 13th July, and a German in the person of Ferdinand Hompesch, Bailiff of Brandenburg and Minister for Germany, was elected as his successor in the magistracy of Malta. This election took place on the 17th July, when Hompesch, knowing too well from what direction danger threatened his Order, addressed the following propitiatory letter to the French Government:—

[Translation.]

Malta, the 17*th July* 1797.[4]

CITIZEN DIRECTORS,—I perform a duty in acquainting you with the death of the Grand Master Emmanuele de Rohan, and that the suffrages of all the Nations (Langues) which compose the Order of Malta have unanimously, in the election of his successor, been declared in my favour. I have had the flattering satisfaction of seeing all classes of the Maltese Nation displaying the sincerest joy, and lavishing upon me, in a spirit of universal emulation, the most touching marks of their love and fidelity.

Nothing further is required, Citizen Directors, to complete my extreme happiness, than the possession of a proof, that you will participate in these feelings towards me, and will accept with interest my assurance and promise, to imitate and excel, if it be possible, my Predecessors in their attachment and due deference to the French Nation, and [desire] for the prosperity of her commerce—for I am persuaded, that on your side you will desire to treat the Government which has been confided to me, with that equity, loyalty, and kindness, which characterises the French Republic.

I have desired Monsieur Cibon, our *chargé d'affaires* with you, Citizen Directors, to have the honour of presenting you this letter. I beg you will favourably receive him on all occasions when the needs of our service may

---

[1] The statesman Godoy, styled the Prince of the Peace, directed Spanish affairs; he was very Gallophile. Spain was allied to France.—J. H. R.
[2] It should be remembered that, owing to the declaration of war by Spain against England, the British fleet in the Mediterranean was withdrawn from that sea in November 1796, and Corsica was evacuated.—J. H. R.
[3] *Correspondance de Nap. I*, vol. iii. p. 65.
[4] Archives Nationales, Paris.

require him to appeal in my name to your justice and support. My gratitude will equal the profound respect with which I am, &c.
(Signed) FERDINAND HOMPESCH.

Immediately after Hompesch's election he was made aware that France had cast her eyes upon Malta, as the following incident proves.

Upon receipt of Bonaparte's letter of the 26th May, addressed to the Executive Directory, that body readily acquiesced in his views; but before proceeding to extremities it made an effort to obtain it by barter; for on the 16th August 1797, the British Minister at Vienna, Sir Morton Eden, informed Lord Grenville[1] that General Herbenstein, the Minister of the Order at Vienna, when delivering to him a letter from the new Grand Master (Hompesch), to be forwarded to King George III, had stated that he had been charged to communicate to him for Lord Grenville's information, that the Grand Master had received intelligence from France of its being the intention of the French Directory to propose to the Order to exchange the island of Malta for some other island in the Mediterranean.[2]

In what spirit Hompesch's letter of the 17th July, announcing his election, was received by the Executive Directory, may be further gathered from Talleyrand's dispatch dated two months later, namely, on the 23rd September, quoted later on. The entry of this Minister on the scene, and its importance on the events which followed, make it necessary to refer to the rôle which he undertook in advocating the conquest of Malta and Egypt. In subsequent years, much controversy arose in France as to who was responsible for engaging the nation in an expedition which ended so disastrously. Whilst the moral responsibility no doubt rested upon the Executive Directory, then composed of Barras, Rewbel, La Revellière-Lépaux, Merlin, and François de Neufchâteau, it would appear that the initiative must be placed to the charge of Bonaparte and Talleyrand, and that the accusation made by the member, Briot, at a meeting of the 'Five Hundred,' held on the 29th August 1799, denouncing the latter 'as having been its principal promoter, instigator, and supreme dictator,' must be held partly justified.[3]

It should be remembered that Talleyrand during his stay in America had seen sufficient to encourage him in the belief that France had sadly neglected her colonies, and in the then distracted condition of his native country he considered a panacea for many

---

[1] William Wyndham Grenville was cousin of Pitt and was born in the same year, 1759. He became joint Paymaster of the Forces. In 1789 he was Speaker of the House of Commons for a short time, after which he was raised to the Peerage, and in 1791 became Minister for Foreign Affairs in the Pitt Cabinet, a post which he held till its resignation early in 1801. He died in 1834.—J. H. R.
[2] Foreign Office Records, Austria, 50.
[3] De la Jonquière, *Expéd. d'Egypte*, vol. i. p. 9.
See the Introduction to this work for other proofs of Bonaparte's interest in Malta during his stay at Ancona early in 1797.—J. H. R.

evils might be found in colonisation. Immediately upon his return from exile he was elected a member and appointed secretary of the National Institute, and upon the 3rd July 1797 delivered a lecture therein, 'On the Advantages to be derived from Colonial Expansion,' which made a profound impression, not only in Government circles, but also upon the general public.

An interval of comparative political calm reigned at this time, owing to Bonaparte's utter defeat of the Austrian armies and the negotiations for peace between these two nations which followed, commencing with the preliminary Treaty of Leoben, signed on the 18th April, and the subsequent definitive Treaty of Campo Formio, concluded on the 17th October. The sequel to Talleyrand's lecture was his appointment, thirteen days later, to the Ministry of Foreign Affairs, in succession to Delacroix (16th July 1797).

As soon as the news of Talleyrand's nomination to the direction of foreign affairs reached Bonaparte, then at Milan, he felt assured of that Minister's support in the project of colonisation which he entertained—a project which would not only gratify Talleyrand by the acquisition of an important colony, but would also, by threatening England in one of her most vulnerable points, coincide with the aspirations of the Directory. Accordingly, on the 16th August he wrote to the Government:[1] 'The time is not far distant when we shall find that the only way to destroy England is by occupying Egypt.'

Fearing a resumption of hostilities on the part of Austria, notwithstanding the preliminaries of peace signed at Leoben, Bonaparte on the 4th August ordered Admiral Brueys to move up with his fleet from Corfu to Venice as promptly as possible, promising to see him soon after his arrival.[2] Meanwhile he transferred his headquarters to Passeriano, to be near at hand to Venice, and not far from Udine, where the peace negotiations with Austria would for the future be conducted.[3]

To Bonaparte's dispatch of the 16th August, which would reach the Directory about the 21st, Talleyrand replied on the 23rd:[4] 'The Directory approves your action with regard to the occupation of Zante, Corfu, and Cephalonia'; adding: 'Nothing is more important to us than obtaining a good footing in Albania, Greece, Macedonia, and other provinces of the Turkish Empire in Europe, and other shores washed by the Mediterranean, particularly Egypt, which some day may be of great utility to us.'

The first conference at Udine was held on the 31st August, but owing to the subsequent removal of Carnot and Barthelemy, and the

[1] *Corres. de Nap. I*, vol. iii. p. 235.
[2] Admiral Brueys was destined to command the French fleet sailing to Egypt, and to perish at the Battle of the Nile.—J. H. R.
[3] De la Jonquière, vol. i. p. 28. *Corres. de Nap. I*, vol. iii. p. 221.
[4] De la Jonquière, vol. i. p. 30.

BONAPARTE'S PLAN OF SEIZING MALTA

substitution of Merlin and François de Neufchâteau in the Directory (the result of the *coup d'etat* of the 18th Fructidor—the 4th September), the French Government became more exacting in their terms. During the consequent delay which followed, as well as in that which was occurring at Lille in the negotiations with England, Bonaparte on the 13th September addressed Talleyrand as follows, repeating what he had written to the Directory on the 26th May :—

Passeriano, 13*th September* 1797.[1]

... Why should we not take possession of Malta ? Admiral Brueys might easily anchor there and capture it ; 400 Knights, and at the most a regiment of 500 men, are the only defence of Valetta. The inhabitants, more than 100,000 (!) in number, are all for us, and are very disgusted with their Knights, who are dying of hunger. I have purposely confiscated all their property in Italy. With the Islands of St. Pierre (ceded to us by Sardinia), Malta, Corfu, &c., we shall be masters of the Mediterranean.

If when a treaty of peace is concluded with England we have to surrender the Cape of Good Hope, we ought to take Egypt.[2]

That country has never belonged to a European Power, the Venetians have had a certain preponderance there for many centuries, but such has only been precarious. We might leave this with 25,000 men, taken from Northern Italy, escorted by eight or ten Venetian ships of the line, or frigates, and possess ourselves of it. Egypt no longer belongs to the Grand Signor ; I desire, Citizen Minister, that you will make inquiries and inform me what effect an expedition to Egypt might have at the Porte.

Admiral Brueys reached Venice on the 6th September, and from the correspondence which passed it is evident that Bonaparte was most anxious to obtain a personal interview with the admiral. The conferences then being held at Udine, however, prevented Bonaparte leaving Passeriano, and accordingly on the 17th September he invited Brueys to join him there, 'if only for thirty-six hours.'[3]

From the following extract from a dispatch of Brueys to the Minister of Marine and Colonies, dated Venice, the 3rd October 1797, it would appear that this interview took place on the 21st and 22nd September, when the *petite expédition* (projected capture of Malta), based upon Barbara's (the Maltese) information, was discussed. The dispatch says : 'The last letter that I wrote to you was dated from Head Quarters at Passeriano, where I passed two days at the solicitation of General Bonaparte ; I left Venice on the 4th Complémentaire (20th September 1797), at night.' Barbara was then taken on board the fleet pending developments, and in order that he should possess an official position, he was subsequently appointed to the two-decker *Dubois* (taken from the Venetians), under Captain

---
[1] *Corres. de Nap. I*, vol. iii. p. 293.
[2] This sentence is a proof that Bonaparte resolved that France should dominate at least one of the highways to India.—J. H. R.
[3] *Corres. de Nap. I*, vol. iii. p. 307.

Le Joille, with the rank of 'Enseigne de Vaisseau.'[1] On the 23rd September, Admiral Brueys with his fleet sailed for Corfu, where he arrived on or about the 12th November, having had orders to call at Ragusa *en route*.[2]

To Bonaparte's dispatch of the 13th September Talleyrand replied on the 23rd as follows[3]:—

... The Directory approves of your ideas with regard to Malta. Since that Order has elected Monsieur de Hompesch as Grand Master the suspicions of the Directory are confirmed, based upon previous information, that Austria is desirous of gaining possession of that Island. She is anxious to become a maritime Power in the Mediterranean; it was for that purpose that, at the preliminaries at Leoben, she demanded before all else that portion of the Italian coast. Again, her haste to possess herself of Dalmatia, all which is further proved by her avidity in taking Ragusa. Besides all this, the Neapolitan Government is entirely under her influence.[4] Malta for her would have a double advantage, it would serve to attract to her all the products of Sicily. It is not only on commercial grounds that she is desirous of retiring from the centre of Italy towards its coast line, but in view of contemplated conquests; she is in truth arranging the means of attack on Turkish territory where Albania and Bosnia join her own, so that in concert with Russia she could attack these said provinces in the rear in the event of the Russian fleet entering the Archipelago.[5] It is to our interests that such maritime extension on the part of Austria be stopped, and the Directory accordingly desires that you will take the necessary steps to prevent Malta falling into her hands.

With regard to Egypt, your views in this respect are grand, and their utility must be recognised. I shall write to you more fully on this subject later on. ... Egypt as a colony would soon compensate for the loss of the Antilles[6] and open a road to us for obtaining the trade of India.

This dispatch of Talleyrand's crossed another of the same date (23rd September) from Bonaparte, still at Passeriano, addressed to the Directory, worded as follows[7]:—

'... Finally, if we have peace (with Austria) your Fleet in leaving the Adriatic on its return to France might carry some troops, and in passing place 2,000 as a garrison in Malta, an island which sooner or later will fall into the hands of the English if we are so foolish as not to anticipate them. ... I demand, therefore, that you issue an official order authorising me to *cultivate the correspondence that I already possess with Malta*, and that I may, when I consider the time propitious, capture it and place a garrison therein.'

[1] Arch. Nat. BB⁴ 115; Jonquière, vol. i. p. 262.
[2] *Corres. de Nap. I*, vol. iii. p. 328; Jonquière, vol. i. p. 50.
[3] Jonquière, vol. i. p. 36.
[4] Maria Carolina, consort of the King of Naples, was both aunt and mother-in-law of Francis II of Austria.—J. H. R.
[5] This would have revived the Austro-Russian schemes of 1787-1790 for the partition of Turkey.—J. H. R.
[6] Captured by the British in 1794.
[7] *Corres. de Nap. I*, vol. iii. p. 331.

BONAPARTE'S PLAN OF SEIZING MALTA

On the 27th September, Talleyrand gave Bonaparte more explicit instructions with regard to Malta, as follows[1] :—

The Directory considers it necessary that I should write to you in more positive terms regarding your proposal to acquire Malta. It is advisable to anticipate the action of Austria, England, and Russia on this point. From recent information which has come into possession of the Directory it confirms their opinion, which they have had for a long time, that this island has become a nest for Austrian, Russian, and English intrigue, and being governed by an Austrian Grand Master is on the eve of falling under the power of the Emperor and his allies.

The possession of this island, joined to that of Istria and Dalmatia, would make Austria a maritime Power capable of causing anxiety to France and the Cisalpine Republic, of which latter it is easy to believe she could not be other than her enemy. Malta from its geographical position would give her the means of troubling the navigation of the entire Mediterranean. There is also the danger that this island might fall into the possession of the English and the Russians.

After due consideration the Directory gives you full power to put into execution the plan you have proposed in your dispatch of the 13th September, and authorises you to convey to Admiral Brueys the necessary orders to obtain possession of Malta with the object of preventing Austria acquiring it, as she has done in the case of Ragusa. Her appropriation of Ragusa gives us a legitimate right to possess ourselves of Malta. . . . I enclose some letters of the greatest importance, which had better be forwarded in advance by a sure and certain route to Malta. You will understand that it is necessary to prepare public opinion there for any change which may take place.

And on the 8th October he added:

I am sending you three letters which it will be advisable to forward to Malta on successive occasions; they are intended to facilitate the expedition which you have projected.[2]

Talleyrand's instructions of the 27th September were confirmed by the Directory on the 3rd October, to the following effect[3] :—

The details contained, Citizen General, in your letter of the 23rd September, and the copy of that which you had written to Rear-Admiral Brueys on the 22nd September, have satisfied the Government. You will have already received instructions relative to the necessity of seeing that the Island of Malta should not be occupied by the English, or any other of the enemies of the Republic. All your arrangements and views are approved, and the orders which you ask for are being given to the Minister of Marine.

The treaty of peace with Austria having at last been signed at Campo Formio on the 17th October, Bonaparte dispatched his step-son, Eugène de Beauharnais, on the following day to Venice,

[1] Jonquière, vol. i. p. 39.
[2] Bonaparte, *Lettres inédites*, vol. ii. p. 282; Jonquière, vol. i. p. 38.
[3] Jonquière, vol. i. p. 37.

with orders to sail at once after Brueys with two letters, dated the 6th and 18th October, containing instructions regarding the *petite expédition* or capture of Malta.[1]

Beauharnais sailed from Venice in the brig *Alerte* on the 20th October, but having been delayed by contrary winds, it was not until the 12th November that he reached Brueys at Corfu. Soon after the receipt of Bonaparte's instructions Brueys dispatched the frigates *La Justice* and *L'Artémise*, with Barbara on board, on a special mission to Malta, which was to coincide with that of Poussielgue, hereafter referred to.[2]

The dispatch from the Directory of the 3rd October was followed by a second, dated the 21st October, as follows:—

'Clause 21. . . . With regard to the Island of Malta, you will have received orders to take the necessary steps, so that it may not be possessed by any other Power than France. You have informed Citizen Bottot that this possession is to be bought at a price. The Executive Directory attaches great value to its acquisition, and trusts that you will not allow it to escape you.'[3]

Being thus empowered by the Directory to enter into correspondence with the disaffected in Malta, Bonaparte deemed it expedient to dispatch a special messenger, bearer of the treasonable correspondence, and selected for this purpose Monsieur E. Poussielgue, first secretary to the French Legation at Genoa. Poussielgue had come under the favourable notice of Bonaparte whilst at Passeriano, owing to his work entitled 'The History of the Revolution of Genoa,' and this had called from the latter, not only an eulogistic letter, dated the 9th September 1797, but an order for 500 copies of his work, which were to be distributed over Europe.

Poussielgue's instructions were dated the 12th November, and the object of his mission is clearly defined in Bonaparte's dispatch to the Directory, under the same date, as follows: '. . . I have sent Citizen Poussielgue to Malta under the pretext of inspecting and reporting upon the various seaports of the Levant, but in reality to complete our arrangements for the project we have in view regarding that island.'[4]

A similar letter of the same date was addressed to Citizen Caruson, French consul in Malta, by Bonaparte, and copies of both transmitted to Talleyrand on the 14th November. At the interview between Bonaparte and Brueys at Passeriano, already referred to, details were gone into with regard to this projected *coup de main* on Malta, which was described as the *petite expédition*,[5] and on the 14th November Bonaparte further wrote to Brueys from Milan :

---

[1] *Corresp. de Nap. I*, vol. iii. p. 393. [2] Jonquière, vol. i. pp. 50, 137.
[3] Arch. Nat. AF III. 473. [4] Jonquière, vol. i. p. 50.
[5] *Ibid.* p. 138. Brueys informed the Minister of Marine on the 26th December that 'he knew Malta well, having during his thirty-two years of service visited the Island on fifteen different occasions.'

BONAPARTE'S PLAN OF SEIZING MALTA

'I have sent a diplomatic agent to Malta. The 6th demi-brigade, 1,600 strong, sails to-morrow to join you at Corfu. This will enable you to embark 3,000 men for the *petite expédition*, and I will forward you the express orders later on by one of my *aides-de-camp*.' On the 19th December, Brueys, still at Corfu, acknowledged the receipt of this dispatch. He now informed Bonaparte 'that Vincent Barbara had been sent to Malta'—that is, at the same time that Poussielgue was expected to arrive. The dispatch ran as follows:—

Corfu, 19th December 1797.[1]

I have received on the 19th by the frigate *Sensible* the letter which you did me the honour to write under date of the 14th ultimo. I have been waiting to receive funds for payment of the crews, now five months overdue, and for the purchase of victuals, as I am driven to the last extremity in obtaining food for the fleet. . . . The Venetian fleet is in the same condition. . . . At this moment there remain but two months' provisions for the French fleet, which I reserve as precious as my eyes, so as to be enabled to undertake any enterprise which you may order. In the meanwhile you write under the impression that I am abundantly provided with all to undertake the *petite expédition* [the capture of Malta], proceeding thence to the Isles of Saint Peter, and from there to Brest. All this is very brilliant, but the means are wanting, and whilst waiting for such, the time is passing, the remaining victuals are being consumed, and the winter season, favourable to effect the junction you desire, flies. . . . I have sent *La Justice* and *L'Artémise* to cruise off Malta. They will land at that port the Maltese of whom I have spoken to you [Barbara], but under the pretext of obtaining from our Consul some information regarding the corsairs which are cruising in those waters. . . . They will then sail for the south of Sardinia, where it has been reported to me that English corsairs have been seen. On their return to Corfu they will call at Malta to re-embark the man in question, who will be able to give me intelligence as to the disposition of the people.

Three days previously Brueys acquainted the Minister of Marine of his action in a dispatch, of which the following is an extract:—

'J'ai expedie *La Justice* et *L'Artémise* pour Tunis; ma lettre au Consul et mes instructions dont je vous envoie copie, vous instruiront de l'objet de leur mission. Je remplis aussi celui d'être prévenu de l'arrivée des ennemis s'ils envoyoient des forces dans ces parages et de *faire mettre à Malte un homme qui peut nous être fort utile.*'[2]

In due course *La Justice* and *L'Artémise* returned to Corfu, the former bringing another Maltese, whose name is not given, but who is described by Brueys as 'a hot-headed patriot who has abandoned wife, children, and profession in order to offer his services to the French.'[3]

[1] *Ibid.* vol. i. p. 137.   [2] Arch. Nat. BB⁴ 115.   [3] Jonquière, vol. i. p. 144.

La Justice was again dispatched to Malta, bearing the following letter to Monsieur Caruson, the French consular agent at Malta :—

[Translation.]

On board the *Guillaume Tell*, at Corfu,
24th January 1798.

CITIZEN,—Captain Villeneuve, with the frigate *La Justice*, is again leaving this to cruise in your waters. He will anchor at Malta to inquire whether the English corsairs are still there, and whether a prize they have captured, laden with wheat, has been taken into that port. He has handed me the letter which you wrote to me, under date of the 22nd December last, and I have read with pleasure that you have rendered to him all the service which was in your power. I have with me here thirty vessels of war of all sizes, and have need of sailors to make them equally useful if you can collect a few ; you can place them on board *La Justice*, and by so doing you will render me a service. It appears to me that, as such aid has been given to the English corsairs, you have an equal right to obtain the same for us. You will be good enough to inform me of all interesting news which may come to your knowledge.

Greeting and fraternity,
(Signed) BRUEYS.

From this cruise *La Justice* returned to Corfu, bringing with her two prizes which she had captured—namely, the *Cornish Hero* of sixteen guns and the *Fortune* of twenty guns, both British privateers. It is not clear whether Barbara rejoined Brueys on this voyage or the previous one, but in either case he was on board the *Dubois* when the fleet next sailed from Corfu for Malta.[1]

Brueys, despairing of receiving the necessary funds to revictual his fleet at Corfu, where he had been detained since September 1797, decided at last, upon his own responsibility, to return to Toulon, and accordingly, on the 24th February 1798, he set sail from Corfu, arriving off Malta on the 3rd March. Anxious to carry out the views of Bonaparte (if it were possible) he communicated with the island, and the day preceding his arrival, prepared the following letter for Consul Caruson :—

[Translation.]

On board the *Guillaume Tell* at sea,
2nd March 1798.

I have only time to write you one word, my dear Consul, to tell you that the Venetian vessels, which I am taking with me to France, are so badly equipped, that I had no sooner left Corfu than I was signalled that they were leaking, and that repairs were urgently required to their steering apparatus, masts, and yards, and to such an extent that in passing

---

[1] Jonquière, vol. i. p. 144.

BONAPARTE'S PLAN OF SEIZING MALTA

by this Island I have ordered the *Frontin*, which is very badly leaking, to enter the harbour, in order that she may as promptly as possible be put in such a condition as to be able to follow me. I am convinced that you will give all the assistance which depends upon you.

The Venetian vessels are badly manned, and I am unable to make up for this deficiency from my own ships for fear of meeting a superior enemy. If it is possible for you to procure me some sailors, you will render a great service to the nation. I do not enter the harbour with the fleet in order that there should be no fear that I wish to infringe the rights of neutrality. I shall, therefore, wait cruising in the vicinity until the *Frontin* is repaired, which, I trust, will not occupy more than two days. And I shall not enter the port unless compelled, or unless you think I might do so without exciting suspicion.

Greeting and fraternity,
(Signed) BRUEYS.

However feasible the capture of Malta by a *coup de main* appeared to be on paper, it was found to be altogether impracticable; and in justification of his conduct, Brueys, on the 11th March 1798, addressed the following dispatch to Bonaparte, which will be found in the volume of M. de la Jonquière (vol. i. p. 261).[1]

[Translation.]

On board the *Guillaume Tell*,
11th March 1798.

GENERAL,— . . . On the 3rd of March I steered for the city of Valetta, anchoring the *Frontin* and a dispatch vessel off the port, where I with the fleet defiled in line of battle. The weather was superb, and I was near enough, without the aid of glasses, to distinguish the infinite number of people on the ramparts and at the windows. Nothing decisive, therefore, could be done, and I therefore deemed it wise to respond to the tokens of friendship which were made to me, to maintain secrecy, and to give every proof that I had no other object in appearing before Malta than to wait for the completion of the repairs necessary to the *Frontin*. My appearance has had this good result, that it has calmed the apprehensions of the Knights with regard to France; it has convinced me that our partisans in the Island are numerous, and has made me feel certain that France may become mistress of this important port, should it be the intention of the Directory to capture it. The two Maltese are now on board my ship, one of them is the individual you mentioned [Barbara], the other a warm patriot, who broke through the quarantine barriers in order to join the *Justice* on her first voyage to Malta (December 1797), and has abandoned wife and family and his trade in order that he might offer his services to the French. I have left a third officer on shore at Malta as an invalid, whose family is at Corfu, and I believe he will be of service to us. My secret is unknown, except to the Chief of Division, Le Joille, Captain Saunier, commanding the *Frontin*, and the two Maltese.

[1] Owing to its length I am compelled to omit the first part.—J. H. R.

After proposing to Bonaparte that the two Maltese should be sent on to Paris to be interrogated, Brueys closes his report as follows: 'All the fleet believe that I have only remained off the port waiting for the repairs of the *Frontin* to be completed. The Knights must now, therefore, remain under the impression of complete security, and a surprise might at some time be made with success, and if attacked by a force of 4,000 men with means we might capture it by assault, should it be necessary.'

To allay the suspicions and alarm of the Grand Master, which the arrival of so formidable a squadron had excited, Brueys, on the 4th March, sent a letter to the French Consul Caruson, in which he declared that he came to Malta merely because the ship *Frontin* had sprung a leak, and that the French Government intended to remain on the best of terms with the Order of St. John. Brueys then proceeded on his voyage, and arrived with his fleet at Toulon on the 2nd April, to learn that the contemplated invasion of England had been abandoned, and that active preparations were being made for an expedition, the objective being the capture of Malta and the occupation of Egypt; but its destination in the meanwhile was to be kept a profound secret.

CHAPTER III

POUSSIELGUE'S REPORT ON HIS MISSION TO MALTA

POUSSIELGUE, in addition to high administrative qualities and political knowledge, which subsequently secured for him the appointment of 'Comptroller of the Funds and Administrator-General of the Finances of the French Army in Egypt,' had the good fortune to be related to the captain of the port in Malta, of the same name, which circumstance was of great service to him in securing the success of his mission. Being well supplied with money, he entertained, and spent it lavishly, during his eighteen days' stay in the island (24th December 1797 to 11th January 1798).[1]

Caruson reported Poussielgue's arrival in Malta to Bonaparte in the following letter, dated the 25th December 1797 :—

[Translation.]

The citizen Poussielgue, first secretary to the legation at Genoa, arrived in this city yesterday, and has delivered to me the letter dated Milan, the 12th November last, with which you have honoured me.

The duty you have deigned to accord me is flattering in the extreme, and I shall not be better able to justify the confidence you place in me, than by displaying the sincerest zeal (which has always animated me in matters concerning our Republic) in assisting citizen Poussielgue to the best of my ability and knowledge in all which concerns his mission. On the day of his arrival I introduced him to members of this Government, by whom he was favorably received. . . .[2]

On the 11th January 1798, Poussielgue left Malta for Italy, and on the 8th of the following month forwarded to Bonaparte from Milan the following report [3] :—

---

[1] Capefigue, *l'Europe pendant le Consulat et l'Empire*, vol. i. chap. iii. p. 65 ; Hardenberg, vol. v. pp. 457-60.
[2] Jonquière, *l'Expédition d'Egypte*, vol. i. p. 73.
[3] As this report has been published almost in full in M. de la Jonquière's work, *l'Expédition d'Egypte*, vol. i. pp. 126 *et seq.*, I have kept only the most important parts.— J. H. R.

Milan le 20 *Pluviôse* an VI (8 *Février* 1798).

Citoyen Général,—Je suis arrivé à Malte le 4 Nivôse dernier (24 Decr.); c'était la veille des fêtes de Noël, le grand-maître se préparait à renouveler toutes les cérémonies d'étiquette autrefois en usage et que ses prédécesseurs avaient laissées tomber en désuétude. Pendant dix-huit jours que j'ai demeuré à Malte, j'ai eu l'occasion de voir toutes ces cérémonies, qui par leur puérilité ont étonné même les Chevaliers de l'Ordre; ils n'en avaient plus de souvenir.

Il y a en ce moment, à Malte environ six cents Chevaliers dont les deux tiers sont Français. En général les Français composaient la moitié de l'Ordre; presque tous sont à Malte. Ce sont les chevaliers français qui ont élu le nouveau grand-maître Hompesch. Il leur avait promis, lorsqu'il briguait l'élection de leur continuer les secours que Rohan leur donnait. Il leur tient parole et la plus grande partie des places de l'Ordre est occupée par des Français. . . . Le grand-maître est très-populaire et généreux. Il se montre souvent au peuple, et lui jette de l'argent. Il est extrêmement poli et affable avec tout le monde et, quoique d'ailleurs ses connaissances soient très bornées, il juge bien et a su se concilier l'estime et l'amour des Chevaliers de toutes les langues, comme du peuple. Il joint à ces qualités celle d'être discret et de ne point laisser pénétrer son secret. Jusqu'à présent on ne connaît personne qui ait exclusivement sa confiance ou qui puisse se flatter d'exercer sur son esprit une influence étrangère. Enfin pendant mon séjour à Malte je n'en ai entendu dire que du bien et par les Maltais et par les Chevaliers français et étrangers, et par les aristocrates et par les démocrates, et j'ai été le témoin de l'empressement avec lequel le peuple pour jouir un instant du plaisir de le voir, venait de tous les points de l'île environner son Palais. On ne peut avoir une conduite plus politique et mieux entendue que celle du grand-maître relativement aux circonstances dans lesquelles il se trouve placé. Le Conseil de l'Ordre est entièrement dévoué au grand-maître, quoiqu'il n'y ait que deux voix; mais il a la proposition exclusive de toutes les grâces, de tous les emplois, et cet prérogative le rend un des princes les plus absolus de l'Europe, surtout depuis que les langues de France sont tombées entièrement à la charge de l'Ordre.

Parmi les trois à quatre cents Chevaliers français qui sont à Malte on n'en peut compter que quinze à vingt qui soient amis ou très disposés à le devenir de la République française et de son gouvernement. Les autres sont tous des royalistes inabordables. Ils ne s'occupent qu'à dénigrer le Directoire et les Conseils et même les armées. Cependant les Chevaliers patriotes pensent qu'aujourd'hui le plus grand nombre, frappé de l'eclat de la République regrette intérieurement de s'être rangé dans le parti contraire et reviendrait, s'il n'était retenu par une fausse honte à avouer et défendre les principes qu'il a si longtemps niés et combattus : si l'existence de ces Chevaliers est actuellement entièrement à la charge de l'Ordre, en compensation l'Ordre n'a pas de défenseurs plus zélés et plus dévoués, parce qu'ils sont convaincus que, si l'Ordre cessait d'être il ne leur resterait aucune ressource. Le grand-maître le sait et compte beaucoup sur eux pour la défense de la place si elle doit être attaquée. Les Chevaliers des autres nations comptent fort peu à Malte parceque la plupart n'y résident pas. Ils sont, en général, assez indifférents sur la Révolution française. La classe aisée des Maltais et les marins sont secrètement les ennemis de l'Ordre de Malte ; les premiers parce qu'ils sont exclus de toute participation au gouvernement, un Maltais ne pouvant être Chevalier de Malte ; les seconds par rapport au système de guerre contre les Barbaresques qui est l'essence du gouvernement de Malte, système qui prive leur pavillon de l'avantage de pouvoir commercer et qui a l'inconvénient bien plus grave de les exposer toute leur vie à tomber dans un esclavage pire que la mort.

Il n'y a pas de pays où l'aristocratie et le despotisme se fassent plus sentir qu'à Malte. Tout homme qui après une certaine heure du soir, est rencontré sans lumière dans les rues de Malte est mis en prison. Aller *sans lumière* est un privilège qui n'appartient qu'aux Chevaliers. A la comédie les dix à douze premiers bancs du parterre du côté de la scène sont exclusivement destinés aux Chevaliers, aucun Maltais ne peut s'y placer, quand même ils seraient vides. Il faut que les Maltais se contentent des dix à douze bancs de derrière, où ils se trouvent confondus avec les laquais. Ensuite, l'influence de cette aristocratie se fait sentir dans la société et surtout dans les tribunaux, soit dans les causes civiles, soit dans les affaires criminelles. Le grand-maître a même le droit bien abusif de suspendre le cours de justice lorsque par extraordinaire les décisions des tribunaux ne sont point conformes à ses désirs.

Il y a une noblesse à Malte. Le grand-maître fait des Nobles et des Barons pour avoir de l'argent et pour s'attacher les principales familles ; mais comme ces nobles n'acquièrent aucun privilège sur les autres Maltais et qu'ils continuent à être exclus de l'Ordre de Malte ils en deviennent d'autant plus les ennemis qu'étant plus près des distinctions, leur amour-propre souffre davantage d'en être privé.

En arrivant à Malte j'ai trouvé qu'on y était fort inquiet sur les projets de la République française. Quelques journaux de Paris et de Milan annonçaient que la France allait s'emparer de Malte ; deux frégates françaises venaient de mouiller pendant quelques jours dans son port ; enfin ma présence inattendue étaient [*sic*] autant de circonstances propres à alarmer dans un petit pays où depuis le commencement de la guerre on s'est toujours imaginé être le point de mire de toute l'Europe. J'ai été voir le grand-maître le lendemain de mon arrivée et ensuite des baillis, des commandeurs et des chevaliers pour qui j'avais des lettres de recommandation. Le grand-maître m'a reçu avec beaucoup de politesse, mais avec beaucoup de réserve. Les autres m'ont reçu avec curiosité. J'ai aussi beaucoup vu de membres de l'Ordre chez mon cousin Capitaine du Port de Malte où l'on trouve à peu près la seule société qui soit à Malte. Les patriotes s'y voient le matin, les aristocrates le soir. Tous ont le désir de rentrer en France, mais à l'exception de douze à quinze patriotes et de quelques aristocrates modérés, il n'en est aucun qui puisse vaincre assez sa haine ou sa prévention contre la République pour qu'il soit facile de le déterminer à acheter sa réhabilitation par quelque service important. Je n'ai pas tardé apres avoir sondé le terrain à faire sur l'objet de ma mission quelques ouvertures aux personnes qui j'ai reconnues être les patriotes les plus énergiques, et en même temps les mieux instruits. Ces ouvertures ont été reçues avec enthousiasme. Nous avons recherché, examiné et discuté pendant dix à douze séances différentes les moyens de parvenir le plus promptement et avec le moins d'inconvénients à la réunion de Malte à la France.

Le résultat de ces conférences a été de reconnaître qu'il n'y a pas un instant à perdre pour opérer d'une manière quelconque cette réunion afin que Malte ne passe pas à une autre puissance.

Il est évident pour le grand-maître, pour les chevaliers et pour les Maltais, que les moyens qui alimentaient l'Ordre manquent de toutes parts, et qu'ainsi on ne peut se dissimuler sa dissolution prochaine. Il ne serait pas étonnant que dans cet état de choses, le grand-maître pendant qu'il est encore assez fort pour obtenir des conditions avantageuses, ne négociât secrètement la cession de son île à l'Angleterre ou à la Russie ou au roi de Naples.

Les dispositions des Chevaliers et des habitants sont assez prononcées contre les Anglais pour espérer qu'on s'opposera avec succès pendant quelques moments à toutes les tentatives qu'ils ont tenté la voie des négociations, ils ont envoyé exprès un certain Chevalier de Sade qui a fait ouvertement des propositions, et au grand-maître et à quelques-uns des principaux officiers de l'Ordre ; on n'a pas voulu les écouter et de Sade est parti sans avoir rien obtenu.[1]

On n'a rien à redouter de la Russie à cause de son éloignement.

L'Empereur[2] est celui qui donne le plus de craintes, d'abord parce que la possession de Malte rendrait à ses possessions dans l'Adriatique toute la valeur que leur ôtent les îles que nous nous sommes réservées ; ensuite parce que l'Empereur aurait plus de moyens que toute autre puissance de dédommager le grand-maître, qui est Allemand, et d'en faire consentir en sa faveur à une résignation qu'il faut qu'il fasse tôt ou tard.

Les Maltais sont plus disposés en faveur des Français que de toute autre nation ; mais il ne faut pas attendre d'eux qu'ils favorisent un coup de main ; on peut, tout au plus, compter sur leur inertie si les Français attaquent Malte. Il faut absolument renoncer à avoir dans la ville ou dans l'île un parti soit parmi les Chevaliers, soit parmi le peuple, qui veuille agir d'intelligence avec les Français pour livrer Malte, parce que l'Ordre est trop sur ses gardes pour que personne veuille se compromettre.

D'ailleurs le grand-maître a trop bien su gagner tous les cœurs pour n'être pas sur-le-champ instruit de tout projet qui pourrait se diriger contre lui. Malgré le peu de forces qu'a l'Ordre, elles sont, avec l'esprit de surveillance dont on ne s'écarte pas un moment, plus que suffisantes pour empêcher toute surprise et pour résister à une attaque à force ouverte jusqu'à l'arrivée d'un secours étranger.

Si une enterprise à force ouverte ou par surprise échoue nous nous couvrirons de honte aux yeux de toute l'Europe et nous porterons avec l'Angleterre le fardeau de la haine des nations qui naît toujours de la violation du droit des gens, quand le succès ne la justifie pas.

Il sera probablement plus facile d'obtenir Malte par négociation que par force. Il sera encore plus sûr, d'employer simultanément ces deux moyens. Pour réussir dans cette négociation il faut commencer par enlever au grand-maître tout espoir de soutenir l'Ordre ; à cet effet, il serait facile d'engager la Cour d'Espagne à prendre les biens de l'Ordre de Malte et à les affecter aux besoins de l'Espagne.[3] Ces biens formeraient une

---

[1] Elliot, while acting as British Governor of Corsica, sent de Sade (see Jonquière vol. i. p. 657).—J. H. R.

[2] i.e. Francis II, of Austria.—J. H. R.

[3] This was done by Spain after the Peace of Amiens.—J. H. R.

hypothèque propre à remonter le crédit de cette cour. Mais si l'Espagne avait des scrupules trop difficiles à vaincre, ils seraient bientôt enlevés en forçant le Pape à supprimer d'un coup de plume l'Ordre de Malte, suppression qui entrerait dans les intérêts de tous les princes de l'Europe qui, chacun chez soi, convoitent les biens de l'Ordre de Malte.

En même temps qu'on serait prêt à négocier en Espagne et à Rome, le Directoire Exécutif enverrait un Ministre Plénipotentiaire à Malte pour résider publiquement auprès du grand-maître, et traiter secrètement avec lui de la cession de Malte, soit par échange avec une autre île dont on lui abandonnerait la jouissance et la souveraineté, sa vie durant, avec reversibilité à la République Française; soit pour une somme d'argent; soit pour toutes les deux, car le grand-maître tient à ce qu'il paraît à régner, et, d'un autre côté, il a grand besoin d'argent, car il est fort endetté.

On amènera aisement le grand-maître à une négociation. 1° En lui faisant entrevoir la suppression de l'Ordre et la perte de tous ses revenus; 2° en lui démontrant, ce qui est facile aujourd'hui, qu'aucune puissance ne peut lui offrir un dédommagement aussi avantageux et aussi solide que celui que la France lui donnera; que l'Angleterre peut lui faire des offres très-brillantes, mais qu'elle ne les effectuerait pas, dès qu'elle serait Maîtresse de Malte, ou que même il ne dépendrait pas d'elle de les effectuer, en supposant que, pour la première fois, elle fût loyale dans ses promesses; que la Russie ne peut donner que de l'argent; que l'Empereur dans l'état actuel des affaires de l'Allemagne ne pourrait disposer d'aucune souveraineté en échange de Malte, ou que, s'il en disposait, rien ne garantirait cette disposition en faveur du grande-maître.

J'ai examiné les différentes moyens de s'emparer de Malte par surprise, et par force. Par surprise, cela ne se pourrait qu'avec des intelligences dans la ville, et l'on regarde comme impossible d'en pratiquer dans tous les points où il en faudrait, même dans un seul. Les plus déterminés patriotes répugnent à ce moyen; ils ont du courage, mais trop d'honneur pour jamais employer ce qu'ils appellent la *trahison*. D'ailleurs comme je l'ai observé plus haut, il n'y a qu'une quinzaine de patriotes qui aient du pouvoir et parmi eux il n'y en a que trois ou quatre qui aient de l'énergie. Ils se sont cependant prêtés avec grâce à examiner si la surprise était possible ou facile. Il y a plusieurs manières qu'on pourrait tenter ensemble ou séparément.

La première serait de s'emparer à la tombée du jour de la porte d'entrée ordinaire de la ville sur le port. Il faudrait avoir dans le port deux vaisseaux et deux frégates qui auraient à bord 1,500 hommes de troupes.

La porte n'est gardée ordinairement que par 15 à 20 soldats. Je suppose qu'on en mette 30 ou 40 par excès de precaution lorsqu'on verra des vaisseaux français dans le port. On sera très attentif, pendant les cinq ou six premiers jours; on se relâchera ensuite, et il sera facile à 10 à 12 hommes à l'aide d'une rixe excitée, de s'emparer inopinément de la porte, d'empêcher qu'on ne la ferme et de donner le temps aux troupes des vaisseaux d'arriver. Il est vrai qu'il faut réussir, sans cela les vaisseaux et les hommes seraient à l'instant foudroyés par les nombreuses batteries du château Saint-Ange sur lesquelles la mèche est toujours allumée. Mais si l'on peut être maître de la porte, on est maître de la ville, et quand on a la ville, on est maître de l'île. La ville renferme les greniers à blé, une partie des poudres, l'arsenal, le Trésor, le grand-maître et presque tous les

Chevaliers. Une fois maître de la ville, on ferait des offres avantageuses aux Maltais, aux Chevaliers mêmes qui occuperaient tous les postes, et il n'est pas douteux qu'ils ne se rendissent. Dans tous les cas, il faudrait faire soutenir les 1,500 hommes par une escadre qui mouillerait dans le port de Marsa-Musciet. Ces 1,500 hommes s'empareraient facilement du château Saint-Elme, et de toutes les fortifications qui sont à l'ouest, et que la ville domine.

Le second moyen serait d'escalader pendant la nuit la fortification qui est entre le château Saint-Elme, et l'endroit de la Marine, où l'on communique avec les bâtiments en quarantaine. Ce moyen paraît plus sûr d'abord parce qu'il s'emploierait dans une nuit obscure et les vaisseaux seraient moins exposés; ensuite parce que tout vaisseau de guerre étant tenu de faire quarantaine, ce serait un grand obstacle au premier projet de surprendre la porte, tandis que, dans ce projet-ci les vaisseaux se trouveraient placés tout près du lieu qu'il s'agirait d'escalader. Il ne faudrait gagner que deux ou trois gardes de la Santé, ce qui ne serait point difficile. Dans cet endroit, le rempart n'a plus de 12 à 15 pieds d'élévation à cause de décombres qui sont au bas et qui touchent à la mer. On aurait des échelles ou d'autres machines toutes prêtes dans les vaisseaux. Trente hommes parvenus sur ce rempart y protégeraient l'arrivée des autres.

L'autre moyen (et c'est celui des hommes de l'art, qui pensent, qu'il serait trop difficile de s'emparer de la ville, et que, quand on en serait maître, on n'aurait encore rien gagné) l'autre moyen dis-je, serait d'attaquer à la fois et le fort de Ricasoli, et le château Saint-Elme, de faire à cet effet un débarquement de 4 à 5,000 hommes dans le port de Marsa-Scirocco, qui s'empareraient d'abord de la villa Cottonera, et attaqueraient ensuite le fort Ricasoli. Si on parvenait à s'emparer de ce fort et du château Saint-Elme, on serait maître de Malte, parce qu'il ne pourrait y entrer aucun secours.

Mais, pour employer ce dernier moyen, il faut agir à force ouverte. Il serait temps d'y songer lorsqu'on verrait traîner en longueur la négociation entamée avec le grand-maître, ou qu'on verrait l'impossibilité absolue de réussir dans cette négociation.

L'Ordre de Malte, par lui-même, ne peut pas résister plus longtemps à une attaque régulière; il manque de moyens, et surtout d'hommes, car on est généralement persuadé que les Maltais ne se battraient pas pour le défendre.

Voici les forces actuelles:

200 hommes formant la garde du grand-maître; ils sont casernés au château Saint-Elme; chaque jour, il y en a 30 de garde, savoir: 16 au Palais du grand-maître, 4 à la Douane, et 10 au château Saint-Elme.

450 hommes composant le régiment de Malte; il fournit chaque jour 42 hommes de garde aux portes; il y a une réserve de 24 hommes; il fournit aussi la garde des prisons, du quartier et de quelques autres postes; il y a une compagnie de ce régiment qui est caserné e au château Saint-Ange.

300 hommes du corps des galères; il y en a chaque jour 20 de garde au palais du général des galères.

300 soldats des vaisseaux; ils sont casernés à l'île ou cité Victorieuse.

80 hommes aux Ricasoli } Il y a une fondation pour l'entretien de
80 ,, au Fort Manöel } 80 hommes de garnison dans chacun de ces forts.

800 hommes de chasseurs qui ne font de service que dans les cas extraordinaires; ils sont habillés, mais ne sont payés que quand ils servent. Ils restent à la campagne.

C'est donc en tout 2,210 hommes. Il faut y ajouter la garde nationale, ou milice, qu'on évalue à 10,000 hommes. Elle ne fait point de service, et elle est très peu exercée. Parmi tous ces hommes, il n'y a qu'un très petit nombre d'artilleurs très mal instruits et presque point d'officiers. La force principale de Malte, est renfermée dans les 3 à 400 Chevaliers français. Eux seuls provoqueront et soutiendront la résistance, d'abord parce qu'ils sont Français et qu'ainsi ils sont braves, ensuite parce que, n'ayant pas d'autre refuge que Malte, ils se battront en désespérés pour empêcher qu'on ne [la] leur enlève.

La preuve que les Français sont à Malte en nombre bien plus considérable que les autres nations, c'est que le Trésor a payé en argent comptant, pour les tables de tous les Chevaliers qui se sont trouvés à Malte pendant l'année du 1er Mai 1796 au 1er Mai 1797 (V.S.) 18,267 écus dont 10,777 pour les trois langues Françaises, et 7,490 seulement pour toutes les autres langues.

Malte est approvisionée en grains pour huit mois. Il y avait dans les fosses au 1er Janvier 1798 (V.S.) 31,468 salmes de blé, ce qui fait environ 80,000 quintaux, on avait consommée en Decembre 1797 3,946 salmes. Au moment où je suis parti, on manquait totalement de bois et on ne savait comment en faire venir à cause des corsaires barbaresques. On y était réduit à chauffer les fours publics avec des débris de vieux vaisseaux. On ne manque ni de poudre ni d'eau, mais on manque d'artillerie et de boulets de calibre.

Tous les patriotes qui j'ai vus à Malte pensent que, si l'on veut s'emparer de Malte, soit par force, soit par négociation, le premier obstacle le plus fort qu'il faille écarter, ce sont les Chevaliers français; qu'il faut renoncer à leur faire acheter leur rentrée en France par des services, tels que celui de livrer Malte, surtout sans aucune garantie préalable de ce que l'on ferait pour eux ensuite; que le moyen le plus simple et le seul qu'il convienne peut-être d'employer est de les faire rentrer en France, par un décret qui, en statuant définitivement sur les réclamations de l'Ordre de Malte, confirmerait la confiscation sans indemnité des biens de l'Ordre, et déclarerait en même temps que les Chevaliers de Malte, attendu leur affiliation à un Ordre et à une puissance étrangère antérieurement à la Révolution, ayant dès lors suivant l'esprit et le texte même de la Constitution, cessé d'être Français ne seront point considérés comme émigrés, mais seulement comme étrangers, et pourront à ce titre seul rentrer en France, et y jouir des biens qu'ils y possédaient.

Si le Directoire exécutif ne pouvait obtenir ce décret spécial, il trouverait, autant que je puis m'en souvenir, dans les lois existantes des moyens d'y suppléer. L'effet ne serait pas aussi prompt, mais il suffirait, avec le désir qu'ont les Chevaliers de rentrer, et leur habitude de ne doubter de rien, pour les déterminer à prendre sur-le-champ le chemin de la France. Si le Directoire se déterminait à employer la négociation vis-à-vis du grand-maître, ce serait un grand moyen à mettre en avant que de laisser transpirer que la rentrée des Chevaliers français en France, et dans leurs biens, serait une des conditions.

On intéresserait ainsi tous ces Chevaliers à la réussite de la négociation et peut-être à se prononcer d'une manière plus précise encore s'ils voyaient le grand-maître peu disposé à l'accepter.

Pendant mon séjour à Malte, j'ai fait des promesses, j'ai semé des espérances, et en même temps sans trop m'ouvrir pour ne pas me compromettre. J'ai répandu que le Directoire exécutif était instruit des démarches de la Russie et de l'Angleterre; qu'il ne les voyait pas sans inquiétude; que jusqu'à présent les Chevaliers de Malte Français n'étaient pas absolument exclus de leur patrie comme émigrés, puisqu'on avait toujours différé de statuer définitivement sur leur sort; que pour disposer les deux conseils et le Directoire à les traiter favorablement et à accélérer le moment de leur rentrée en France, il fallait qu'ils témoignassent leur attachement au nouveau gouvernement par des services évidents; que c'était à eux de veiller à ce que les Anglais, ennemis de la France et de tous les Français, quelles que soient leurs opinions, ne s'emparassent pas d'un point aussi important que l'est Malte pour la France, et que si le sort de cette île était de cesser d'être indépendante, c'était à eux Français à préparer les voies, de la faire réunir à la France, plutôt qu'à toute autre puissance. J'ai chargé les deux ou trois apôtres que j'avais initiés dans le secret de ma mission de répandre cette doctrine; plusieurs aristocrates l'avaient reçue avec transport et déjà la propageaient.

Je suis persuadé que l'effet en aurait été très prompt si le rapport fait au Conseil des Cinq Cents par le député Laloi sur les réclamations des Chevaliers de Malte et le Décret d'Ordre du jour qui en a été la suite n'étaient arrivés en même temps que moi et n'avaient beaucoup atténué l'effet de mes belles promesses.

Malte est tellement fortifiée qu'avec très peu d'hommes et de moyens on peut résister assez longtemps, et ce n'est point absolument chimère que de regarder cette importante forteresse comme plus qu'à moitié conquise si on parvient à en éloigner les quatre cents Français sur lesquels on se repose principalement du soin de la défendre. Cet avis est celui des patriotes de toutes les nouances que j'ai vus à Malte; ils diffèrent d'opinion en toute autre chose, mais en cela ils sont d'accord et ils pensent qu'il est plus sûr, plus facile et plus prompt de les faire sortir de Malte que de les gagner même avec l'appât de leur intérêt, parce que, se trouvant réunis en espèce de corps, il est presque impossible d'en changer l'esprit, quoique chaque individu isolément puisse faire des vœux conformes à nos désirs.

Peu de jours avant mon départ de Malte, le bruit s'est répandu qu'une flotte de quarante vaisseaux Anglais était entrée dans la Méditerranée, et qu'elle laissait entrevoir que son objet était de s'emparer des îles de Minorque et de Majorque.[1] Le grand-maître a tenu un conseil secret et s'est enfermé pendant plusieurs heures avec le directeur de l'artillerie. On a présumé qu'il avait donné l'ordre de mettre sur-le-champ l'île en état de défense contre l'Angleterre....

Ensuite, sous les rapports politiques, celui qui possède Malte est le maître absolu du commerce de la Méditerranée. Cette île a les ports les plus beaux et les plus sûrs qui existent; elle en a beaucoup de très grands et pour tous les vents. Ses fortifications la rendent imprenable même

---

[1] This report was false. Nelson was not detached from Lord St. Vincent's fleet blockading Cadiz until May 2, 1798. He appeared off Toulon on May 17. Minorca was captured by the British several weeks after the date of Poussielgue's report (Feb. 8, 1798).—J. H. R.

entre les mains d'une puissance de second ordre. C'est un autre Gibraltar. Tous ces avantages et tant d'autres sur lesquels je crois inutile de m'étendre, me persuadent, et je le dis sans hésiter, que l'acquisition de Malte pour la France serait un des plus grands avantages qu'elle aurait retirés de la guerre.

Il n'y a donc pas à balancer pour tenter tous les moyens de l'avoir. S'il faut faire des sacrifices pécuniaires, soit en faveur du grand-maître, soit en faveur des Chevaliers, il ne faut pas qu'ils effrayent.

Revenus du grand-maître: 205,000 écus de Malte,[1] dont 90,000 en biens-fonds à Malte, 85,000 du produit de la douane, 25,000 d'impôts sur le vin, 5,000 du produit des lots et ventes.

Biens nationaux: Les revenus en biens-fonds, de l'évêché, des canonicats, des divers ordres religieux; s'élèvent à 108,000 écus. Les Palais et immeubles divers, possédés par l'Ordre à Malte, peuvent fournir un loyer de 100,000 écus. En y ajoutant les 90,000 écus de rente du grand-maître, le total des revenus en biens-fonds atteint 298,000 écus, soit 715,200 livres tournois, représentant, 'un capital de plus de 15 millions.' On doit y ajouter; les richesses des églises, valant de 4 à 500,000 francs; le matériel naval (2 Vaisseaux, dont un en construction, 2 Frégates, quelques galères et galiotes) le matériel de l'arsenal; l'artillerie etc. L'île n'était assujettie qu'à un petit nombre d'impôts indirectes (droits de douane et autres) rendant annuellement 100 à 115,000 écus (soit de 240 à 250,000 francs).

Ce revenu serait susceptible d'accroissement entre les mains des Français. Quant à la situation financière de l'Ordre, en voici le bilan, *avant la Revolution*. *Recettes*: Revenus des biens de l'Ordre en France 580,406 écus, en Espagne 271,454, en Italie 235,324, en Portugal 91,876, en Allemagne 40,954, en Bavière 2,156, en Pologne 6,016, à Malte 86,500. Total 1,315,296 écus, ou 3,156,710 livres tournois. *Dépenses*: 1,261,860 écus, ou 3,028,464 livres tournois.

Il y avait donc, un excédant annuel de 128,246 livres.

Mais depuis la Révolution, l'Ordre a perdu tous ses revenus de France, une grande partie de ceux d'Allemagne et d'Italie; il doit subvenir à l'entretien des Chevaliers français, privés de leurs commanderies, aussi peut-on évaluer le déficit annuel à 2 millions environ. Il est impossible que cet état de choses subsiste longtemps. Quelques ressources extraordinaires peuvent bien soutenir l'Ordre pendant encore un an; mais il faut qu'ensuite il s'anéantisse sous son propre poids, et c'est à Malte une vérité évidente pour les Maltais, comme pour tous les Chevaliers. . . . J'ai déjà parlé plus haut, des bases d'une négociation avec le grand-maître. En voici d'autres qui pourraient convenir davantage puisqu'elles coûteraient moins; ce serait de profiter de l'affaire de Rome pour négocier en même temps avec Naples et avec le grand-maître des dédommagements à donner à l'un pour sa suzeraineté et à l'autre pour sa souveraineté de l'île de Malte.

Le roi de Naples veut avoir Bénévent[2] qui est enclavé dans ses états. Non seulement on pourrait lui donner Bénévent, mais encore d'autres portions des états du Pape à sa convenance, moyennant qu'il céderait à la

---

[1] A Maltese crown was worth nearly two shillings.—J. H. R.
[2] A papal fief enclaved in the kingdom of Naples.—J. H. R.

France ses droits de suzeraineté sur Malte et qu'il assignerait au grand-maître une principauté en propriété dans la Sicile et lui donnerait en toute souveraineté et sa vie durant, ce qui lui appartient dans l'île d'Elbe.

Poussielgue then suggests other ways for gaining over the Grand Master and the Knights, especially by inducing Spain to confiscate the possessions of the Order in her territory, and so reducing the Order to complete weakness, in which state the Knights would listen to the overtures from Paris.[1]

This report of Poussielgue would reach Paris a few days before the return of Bonaparte to that city from his visit of inspection of the northern coast of France, whence he arrived on the 23rd February—and from its importance would be of the greatest service at the deliberations of the Directory, which took place on the 1st and 2nd of the following month, when it was decided to abandon the expedition to England, and to prepare for that of Malta and Egypt.

---

[1] It is worth noting that this act of confiscation by the Spanish Government after the Peace of Amiens was one of the events which convinced the British Ministry that the existing arrangements for Malta were impracticable.—J. H. R.

CHAPTER IV

THE PREPARATIONS IN FRANCE FOR THE EXPEDITION TO MALTA AND EGYPT

IT is unnecessary to describe here the policy of the French Republic towards the Papacy and Switzerland. The causes of dispute with those States were comparatively slight, and it is now generally recognised that financial motives played no small share in prompting the occupation of Rome and of the Swiss cantons, which took place in the early part of the year 1798. By the Treaty of Tolentino (19th February 1797) the papal treasury had been drained of a sum of £1,200,000, and a further sum of £160,000 had been subsequently exacted. Now, on the occupation of Rome by the French, large sums were levied on the wealthy families and on clerical and monastic property; and Berthier, when sent by Bonaparte to Rome on this mission, said: 'You appoint me treasurer to the English expedition; I will endeavour to fill the chest.' He faithfully fulfilled his promise.

The plunder of several of the cantonal treasuries in Switzerland yielded equally valuable results—in all about 23,000,000 francs.[1] On this whole subject we have the testimony of Bonaparte's general, Marmont, afterwards Duke of Ragusa, who states that at 'Passeriano the expedition to Egypt was first mentioned, and that such was to be provided for with funds to be realised by expeditions to Berne and Rome, whilst the general public was led to believe that it was intended for Portugal or Ireland.'[2] By means such as these were the first funds provided for the Eastern expedition.

On the 2nd March 1798 the Directory abandoned the contemplated invasion of England, and decided to attempt that of Egypt. Three days later the military preparations with that object in view were discussed, when, at the sitting of the Directory, held on the 5th, Bonaparte submitted a note to the following effect: 'To possess ourselves of Egypt and Malta, from 20,000 to 25,000 infantry, and 2,000 to 3,000 cavalry, without horses, would be required'; and he

[1] See *Cambridge Modern History*, vol. viii. pp. 640, 641; Rose, *Life of Napoleon*, vol. i. pp. 178–81.
[2] Marmont, vol. i. p. 296.

further suggested 'that troops for the purpose might be withdrawn from Civita Vecchia, Genoa, Corsica, Marseilles, and Toulon, and that the transport would have to be provisioned for two months, taking water for one month.'[1]

Brueys' arrival at Toulon with his squadron from Corfu and from off Malta on the 2nd April (after his abortive attempt at capture of the latter island) enabled the French Government to push forward without further delay the organisation and details of the expedition. Soon after his arrival Brueys received a letter from Bonaparte, dated the 30th March, informing him that 'his fleet would be of such strength as to enable him to fulfil the brilliant mission for which he was destined,'[2] and ten days after his arrival—namely, on the 12th April—he drew up eight *arrêtés*, which were signed by the Directory, and remained secret.

The first *arrêté* changed the name of the 'Army of England' to that of the 'Army of the East,' and appointed Bonaparte commander-in-chief thereof.

The fifth *arrêté* chiefly concerns us here. It comprises these articles:

Art. 1 authorised Bonaparte to occupy Egypt.

Art. 2 authorised Bonaparte to drive the English out of all possessions in the East, particularly out of their settlements in the Red Sea.

Art. 3 authorised the cutting of the isthmus of Suez and the 'free and exclusive possession of the Red Sea for the French Republic.'[3]

The sixth *arrêté* referred to Malta as follows[4] :—

THE EXECUTIVE DIRECTORY.—Considering that the Order of Malta has by its own action, and since the commencement of the present war, placed itself in hostility towards France, as expressed in a manifesto of the Grand Master, bearing date the 10th October 1794; and that by this insolent document he has declared, that he neither can, nor ought, nor desires to acknowledge the French Republic; that the efforts he has made before, and since, in aid of the coalition of the armed Sovereigns against Liberty have throughout confirmed the same; that quite recently the cup of iniquity has been filled to the brim in his attempts against the Republic, by receiving with open arms, and admitting to the highest dignities, Frenchmen universally known as the bitterest enemies of the country, and for ever disgraced by having carried arms against her; and that appearances lead to the belief that it is his intention to deliver the Islands to one of the Powers still at war with France, through which French trade in the Mediterranean would be paralysed. And as this Order is, to all intents and purposes, in the same position towards the French Republic as all the other Powers with whom, at the time of the establishment of the Constitutional *régime*, France was found in a state of war, they,

[1] De la Jonquière, vol. i. p. 197.
[2] *Corres. de Nap. I*, vol. iv. p. 29.
[3] *Ibid.* pp. 50, 52; Jonquière, vol. i. p. 197.
[4] *Corres. de Nap. I*, vol. iv. p. 53.

without previous declaration on their part, have voluntarily placed themselves in that position.

And as, in consequence, no act of the Legislative Body is necessary to authorise the Executive Directory to adopt such measures as the national honour and interests require, they do hereby order as follows :—

Art. 1. The Commander-in-Chief of the Army of the East is authorised to take possession of the Island of Malta.

Art. 2. He will proceed at once, with the land and sea forces under his command, to the island of Malta.

The seventh *arrêté* was to the following effect :—

Art. 1. The order of this day addressed to General Bonaparte, Commander-in-Chief of 'the Army of the East,' instructing him to take possession of the Island of Malta, is not to be executed, unless it can be accomplished without prejudicing the success of other operations with which he is charged.

The Directory on this point relies completely on his prudence.

These orders having been issued, Brueys was instructed to detach and maintain some of his fast cruisers between Gibraltar and the island of St. Peter, and report any movements of the British fleet, whilst Najac was instructed to supply the fleet with two months' water instead of one.

At Marseilles, 3,900 infantry and 680 cavalry had been collected; at Genoa, 5,419 infantry, 683 cavalry, and 150 artillery; at Civita Vecchia, 5,053 infantry and 799 cavalry; and the main body at Toulon numbered 10,473 infantry, 880 cavalry, and 1,365 artillerymen—making a grand total of 29,402 men.

According to De la Jonquière, this number was eventually increased (by the Corsican contingent and from other sources) to 36,826 men under arms, and 12,782 in the crews of the fleet, making a grand total of 49,608 men.

This vast force was officered as follows: Bonaparte was commander-in-chief; Brueys, vice-admiral, commanded the fleet; Villeneuve, Blanquet-Duchayla, and Decrès were rear-admirals; Ganteaume was chief staff officer.[1]

---

[1] For the names of the ships and their captains, and those of the regiments, see Jonquière, vol. i. pp. 518–38. Besides the combatants there was a company of *savants* celebrated in the various departments of science, art, and learning. But their names do not concern us here.—J. H. R.

CHAPTER V

THE DEPARTURE OF THE FRENCH EXPEDITION AND ARRIVAL OFF MALTA

By virtue of the several decrees issued by the Directory, under date of the 12th April 1798, the 'Army of the East' was organised, its mission authorised, and its command given to Bonaparte. The army was to be composed of five contingents, drawn from Marseilles, Corsica, Genoa, Civita Vecchia, and Toulon. The command of these divisions was given to Reynier, Vaubois, Baraguey d'Hilliers, and Desaix respectively, with Bonaparte in supreme command at Toulon. Admiral Brueys was informed by Bonaparte on the 17th April that the expedition would sail for its destination from Toulon by the western coast of Sardinia, communicating with the island of St. Peter, and that he was to take the necessary precautions by having scouts cruising between that island and the Straits of Gibraltar.

There is no need to describe the departure of the armada, which (after some delays) began at Toulon on May 19. A letter was drafted to the brave and victorious sultan, Tippoo Sahib; another to the King of Ceylon; a third to the sovereign of Tanjore; and seven others were destined for other Oriental potentates whose names were left in blank.[1] These were not sent, owing to the disaster to the fleet at Aboukir; but Bonaparte at Cairo, on the 25th January 1798 wrote a second letter to Tippoo Sahib stating his resolve to come and deliver him 'from the iron yoke of England.' These letters shed an interesting light on the expedition, and prove that the capture of Malta was to be the first step in a mighty enterprise aiming at the entire overthrow of the British power in the East. As regards details of the voyage from Toulon and the Italian ports to Malta, the reader may consult the elaborate work of M. de la Jonquière. Here we may note that orders were sent to the French ships-of-war at the isles of Bourbon (Mauritius) and Réunion to repair to Suez and place themselves under Bonaparte's orders; also that Poussielgue and the renegade Barbara were ordered to accompany the expedition. News of British warships being in the vicinity accelerated the concentration of the French squadron off Malta.

[1] De la Jonquière, vol. i. p. 368.

DEPARTURE AND ARRIVAL OF FRENCH EXPEDITION

At 4 p.m. of the 9th June, 1798, Bonaparte, on the flagship *L'Orient*, arrived off Malta. The rest of Brueys' fleet soon came up. Desaix's squadron from Civita Vecchia was next sighted, and on that same day orders were issued for the troops destined for the attack on Valetta to be landed at three different points in Malta, and one in Gozo.

General Desaix was instructed to sail that same night (the 9th) and land his division at any point he might choose between St. Thomas Bay and Point Wied-is-Sciacca, and arrange so that 300 to 400 men must be on shore before daybreak of the morrow. Duchayla, with four ships of the line, would cover the landing. His troops would then march on the city and endeavour to surprise one of the gates, or scale one of the outworks of Cottonera, which was known to be without a fosse.[1]

Should the enemy be on the alert, or the attempt from other causes be found impracticable, he was to invest Fort Ricasoli and the Cottonera lines, extending his left wing until he communicated with the central Division under General Vaubois.[2]

As this latter Division was to be the permanent garrison of the island, General Vaubois was ordered to leave at 2 a.m. of the 10th, and land between St. Julian's and Maddalena. The troops destined for this service were the 80th Demi-Brigade, the 7th Light Infantry, the 4th Light Infantry, and the 19th of the Line. Generals Marmont and Lannes were placed under his orders. The troops under the former would start 200 to 400 yards in advance of those under Lannes. Marmont would land where he considered most feasible, and take possession of the batteries which might oppose the landing of the entire Division. This accomplished, Marmont would occupy Spinola Palace and garden.[3]

Lannes, in the meanwhile, was to forward a detachment, and possess himself of all the other batteries which threatened Maddalena Bay, as well as Saint Mark's tower.

As soon as the 19th of the Line and 4th Light Infantry arrived, Marmont would blockade Valetta from Pinto city, extending his pickets as far as Casal Nuovo, communicating with General Desaix's left. Vaubois would in the meanwhile blockade Forts Manoel and Tigné, which latter was said to be unfinished. Three companies of the 18th and 32nd of the Line would be reserved as guard to headquarters, which would be established at Gargur. A flying column of the 6th of the Line, or a detachment thereof, would advance upon Casals Lia, Attard, and as far as Citta Vecchia, holding the inhabitants in check.

---

[1] *Corres. de Nap. I*, vol. iv. p. 128.
[2] General Vaubois had done good service in the Italian campaigns of 1796-97, especially at the outposts north of Rivoli. He was to be named Governor of Malta; and his firmness during the siege of 1798-1800 ensured for him the admission to the Senate of France, and the dignity of Count of the French Empire.—J. H. R.
[3] *Corres. de Nap. I*, vol. iv. p. 131.

Simultaneously with these movements in the neighbourhood of the fortress, General Baraguey d'Hilliers, with his troops from Genoa, was ordered to make a descent either on St. Paul's or Melleha Bay, about ten miles distant from Valetta; whilst General Reynier, in command of the troops embarked at Marseilles, consisting partly of the 3rd Company of the Grenadiers and 95th Demi-Brigade, was ordered to land at Ramla in Gozo, under the protection of the frigate *Alceste*, and take possession of the island.[1] These military dispositions being made, no further act of hostility was to occur until authorised by the commander-in-chief. In the meanwhile, General Vaubois would issue a proclamation to the inhabitants stating that the free exercise of their religion would be assured, discipline maintained, and, wherever the people remained tranquil, protection would be afforded them, and that the priests and the nuns would have special protection. The adjoining villages on the Valetta side would supply provisions for Vaubois' troops. Desaix's Division would be supplied with bread and provisions levied on the villages of Zabbar, Zeitun, Gudia, and Tarsiun. The convoys were to be supplied with forage and water, and be ready for sea in three days.

Instructions were also issued on the 9th June to Rear-Admiral Blanquet-Duchayla to anchor a league off Marsa Scirocco, and support the landing of the troops and all subsequent operations.

The detailed orders issued by the commander-in-chief to Brueys, Berthier, Baraguey d'Hilliers, Desaix, Vaubois, and Reynier, under date of the 6th and 9th June, will be found in the volume of M. de la Jonquière, 'l'Expédition d'Egypte,' I. pp. 558 *et seq.*

The instructions regarding Malta were issued at 8 p.m. of the 9th June, whilst those addressed to Reynier at Gozo were dated at 9 p.m. of the 9th June, and were to the following effect: 'Le Général en chef étant décidé à attaquer l'île et les possessions de l'Ordre de Malte, il vous ordonne d'exécuter ponctuellement l'ordre et les dispositions que je vous ai fait passer, et dont l'exécution a été soumise à la réception du présent ordre.'

The other points of attack being nearer at hand, it was only at 10 p.m. that Bonaparte gave orders to Desaix to leave at midnight, and to put into execution the disembarkation in conformity with the dispositions made on the 21st Prairial (9th June).

[1] *Corres. de Nap. I*, vol. iv. p. 129.

CHAPTER VI

THE BRITISH PREPARATIONS FOR THE CONFLICT

The great European coalition against the French Republic having been almost completely destroyed by the Treaty of Campo Formio on the 17th October 1797, England was left entirely dependent upon her own resources, beyond what feeble aid Portugal and the Two Sicilies might render. Spain, as we have seen, had been forced to join the French Republic, Flanders had been incorporated, Holland converted into a Republic and ally, Piedmont crushed, Lombardy revolutionised, the Pope deposed and in exile, and a Roman Republic had been set up. Moreover, Austria had retired from the strife. The Czar Paul was for the present strictly neutral, and the kingdom of the Two Sicilies was lukewarm, or overawed.

Notwithstanding the isolated position in which England now stood, she took every precaution against the impending danger. She had become aware of the great preparations which were being made at various ports in France and Italy, but continued ignorant as to the destination of this formidable expedition. Ireland being deemed its objective, the efforts of the Admiralty were directed to strengthen the fleets off Brest and the Spanish coast.

Bonaparte, referring to the events of this period, when speaking to his aide-de-camp, General Gourgaud, at St. Helena, observed: 'The British Government had prepared for all eventualities, except that of an invasion of Egypt; they felt certain the expedition was intended to join the Spanish fleet at Cadiz, make for Brest, and then land simultaneously in England and Ireland.'

The Government of the Two Sicilies appear to have been equally perplexed, but they were more inclined to believe that the expedition was intended, after all, for that kingdom. In April, Sir William Hamilton wrote to Lord St. Vincent as follows[1]:—

Although this Monarchy is at apparent peace with the French Republic, it is threatened with immediate destruction. . . . Your Lordship will see that the greatest hope this Government entertains of being saved from impending danger, is in the protection of the King's fleet under

---
[1] Clarke and MacArthur, *Life of Nelson*, vol. ii. p. 51.

your Lordship's command. . . . If in consequence of the application of this Government to the Cabinet of St. James, by a messenger sent direct to London six weeks ago, a British fleet should have been ordered into the Mediterranean, it will come and save this country, if not, the only chance of respite from Republicanism is in the Austrian army already in Italy, which, as your Lordship will see, is to be immediately augmented.[1]

The Neapolitan Prime Minister, General Acton,[2] had already acquainted Sir William Hamilton with the latest information that Government had received as to the movements of the French armies, in the following dispatch, dated the 3rd April [3] :—

The troops which the French are bringing to Genoa from their places in Piedmont, and from the Roman States to Civita Vecchia, have the Two Sicilies for their destination—all threatening an invasion, yet with all the demonstration of friendship and good intelligence from the French Government and its Generals. At Rome and Milan they were told that Corsica and Sardinia were the meaning of the expedition, whilst at Genoa the confidential answer has been, that the squadron and troops were directed for Portugal or Gibraltar, if the Spaniards could not sail from Cadiz, but this morning has brought us letters of the 22nd March wherein we are offered Benevento (States of the Church), provided we pay a large sum, sufficient to satisfy the Directory in return for such a present, and we are advised, in case of a refusal, or even of a delay in accepting the proposal, that the former resolution of republicanising all Italy shall take place.

Toulon, Genoa, and Civita Vecchia, are preparing means, as we are told by the Ministry of Foreign Affairs, to put such a project into effect, if we do not find some method to procure a deviation from a resolution so dangerous to this Monarchy.' Acton concluded by urging ' the sending of a dispatch vessel to Lord St. Vincent for help,' adding that ' every exertion would be employed on their part. We shall perish, if such is our destiny, but we hope to sell dear our destruction.'

To the direct appeal which had been made by the Neapolitan Government to the Court of St. James for help, Lord Grenville, on the 20th April, informed Sir William Hamilton

that His Majesty had come to the determination of sending a Fleet into the Mediterranean for the protection of Naples, so soon as it is possible for it to be brought forward without detriment to the indispensable objects of his naval service or imminent hazard to the safety of his dominions . . . for this purpose an augmentation of the British naval establishment will be necessary. This augmentation will be made, and a Fleet sufficient for all the purposes of protection and assistance will sail

---

[1] Brit. Mus. Add. MSS. 34906, p. 384.

[2] General Sir John Acton was the son of a physician, and was born at Besançon in 1737. He served in the public services of Tuscany and Naples, and finally became Prime Minister at the latter Court. French influence brought about his retirement in 1803, and he died a few years later in Sicily.—J. H. R.

[3] Clarke and MacArthur, *Life of Nelson*, vol. ii. p. 52; Brit. Mus. Add. MSS. 34906, p. 386.

for the Mediterranean from this country with the first fair wind after the beginning of June.[1]

Notwithstanding the conflicting information which the British Government received from various quarters as to the destination of the force which was being assembled at Toulon and the western coast of North Italy, they were nevertheless put in possession of what proved to be the exact truth, but too late to be conveyed to Nelson; for on the 29th May, Sir William Hamilton informed Lord Grenville that 'General Acton had told him the day before, that Monsieur Garratt' [sic] (the ambassador extraordinary from the French Republic) 'had assured him seriously, that the grand expedition from Toulon, which was commanded by General Bonaparte' (then ten days out at sea), 'was really destined for Egypt, that they were to establish a colony, and rebuild a city on the spot on which stood ancient Berenice, and that he did not doubt of their being able soon to put in execution the ancient plan of cutting a canal across the isthmus of Suez.'[2] It will be observed, there was not a word said about Malta from Monsieur 'Garratt.'

The British consul at Leghorn, Mr. Udney, appears likewise to have obtained somewhat similar information, for on the 20th April he wrote Admiral Nelson to this effect:[3]

... From what I can hear I feel confident that the expedition is intended first for Malta, then Sicily in order to secure that granary, then Naples, in all which places the French Republic have secured a strong party; then will proceed to Alexandria, Cairo, and Suez. If France intends uniting with Tippoo Saib against our possessions in India, the danger of losing half an army in crossing the desert from Egypt would be no obstacle.[4]

Judging from the admiral's subsequent movements, it is reasonable to suppose that Mr. Udney's dispatch never reached Lord Nelson, or if it did, that it arrived too late to be of any service. In fact Nelson had sailed from Spithead ten days previously to the date of the dispatch, reaching Lord St. Vincent's fleet off Cadiz on the 30th of that month.

Owing to this uncertainty, the First Lord of the Admiralty, Lord Spencer,[5] in April 1798 instructed Lord St. Vincent, commander-in-chief of the British fleet cruising off Spain and Portugal, to discover,

---

[1] Foreign Office Records, Sicily, 11.
See, too, additional information on this affair in my chapter (No. xxi) in the *Cambridge Modern History*, vol. viii; also for the provisional compact between Austria and Naples, signed on May 20, 1798.—J. H. R.
[2] Foreign Office Records, Sicily, 11.
[3] Brit. Mus. Add. MSS. 34906.
[4] In a PS. Mr. Udney adds: 'I forward the above by the way of England.'
[5] Lord Spencer succeeded Lord Chatham (brother of Pitt) as First Lord of the Admiralty in 1794.—J. H. R.

if possible, the object of the immense warlike preparations which were being made in the south of France.

Nelson, as Rear-Admiral of the Blue, with his flag flying on board the *Vanguard*—Captain Edward Berry [1]—then off Cadiz, was accordingly dispatched to the Mediterranean, taking with him the *Orion* (74)—Captain Sir James Saumarez—and *Alexander* (74)—Captain Alexander John Ball.[2]

He was informed that a considerable armament was preparing at Toulon, and a number of transports collecting at Marseilles and Genoa for an embarkation of troops, and he was directed to proceed with such of the squadron as might be at Gibraltar and move up the Mediterranean, and endeavour to ascertain, either on the coast of Provence or Genoa, the destination of that expedition, which, according to some reports, was Sicily and Corfu, and according to others, Portugal or Ireland.

If he found the enemy intending to join a squadron of Spanish ships said to be equipping at Carthagena, he was to dispatch the *Bonne Citoyenne* or *Terpsichore* with the information to Lord St. Vincent, and to continue with the rest of the squadron on that service as long as he might think it necessary. If the enemy's armament should be coming down the Mediterranean, he was to take special care not to allow it to pass the Straits before him, which would impede his joining Lord St. Vincent in time to prevent a junction between it and the Spanish fleet in Cadiz Bay. On the 4th May, Nelson with his limited squadron had arrived at Gibraltar, and after a short detention of four days, occupied in revictualling, he sailed on the 8th, after adding the *Flora*, *Emerald*, *Terpsichore*, and *Bonne Citoyenne* to his force.[3]

Before the 17th May, Nelson had reached Cape Sicie, about ten miles to the west of Toulon, and on that day the *Terpsichore*

---

[1] Berry, Sir Edward (1768–1831), became a lieutenant in the Navy in January 1794. On board the *Agamemnon* (Nelson's ship) he distinguished himself greatly at the Battle of Cape St. Vincent, and gained his captaincy. On the *Vanguard* (Nelson's flagship) he rendered signal service at the Nile (August 1, 1798), for which he received the honour of knighthood. He afterwards assisted in the capture of the *Généreux* and the *Guillaume Tell*. In 1805 he shared in the glories of Trafalgar, and received a baronetcy. In 1821 he became rear-admiral, but afterwards saw little service, owing to declining health.—J. H. R.

[2] Clarke and MacArthur, vol. ii. p. 54.

Ball, Sir Alex. John (1757–1809), came of an old Gloucestershire family, entered the Navy, became lieutenant in 1778, and served under Rodney in the West Indies. In the next French war he served under Murray on the Newfoundland station, and on his return to England in August 1796, was appointed to command the *Alexander* (74), which rendered Nelson in the *Vanguard* signal service by towing the latter when dismasted by a gale off Toulon. Their friendship ripened owing to the signal services of Ball at the Battle of the Nile (August 1, 1798). Ball thereafter undertook the blockade of Malta, and his services in this connexion are amply described in the present volume. They gained for him a baronetcy in 1802; and after Great Britain definitely annexed the island, Ball became the first governor, a position in which he endeared himself to the Maltese.—J. H. R.

[3] Nicolas, *Nelson's Dispatches*, vol. iii. pp. 12, 13.

captured the French corvette *Le Pierre*, of six guns and sixty-five men, which had sailed from Toulon the night previous at 11 p.m. The information Nelson elicited from the officers and crew was mostly false and misleading. It was stated by a portion of the crew that the expedition would be ready to sail in a few days, whilst others affirmed that it would require a fortnight before it could be prepared for sea, whereas it had in reality been ready to start since the early part of the month, and for many days past had been only waiting for a change of wind, and actually weighed anchor on the 19th of May. The crew further added, that although Bonaparte was at Toulon, it was not believed that he would accompany the expedition, nor was its destination known, whereas on the 10th May, seven days previously, Bonaparte, as commander-in-chief, had issued his address to the land and sea forces under his command. They admitted the force to consist of fifteen sail of the line, which were ready for sea; that 12,000 men were already on board, and others daily embarking.[1]

On the following Saturday, the 19th May, whilst the French fleet was leaving Toulon in calm weather, Nelson experienced strong winds from the N.W., causing some damage to the *Vanguard's* rigging. On the 20th the weather moderated, but after dark it began to blow strong again, increasing to a gale, and early on the morning of the 21st, the main-topmast and mizen-mast went overboard, the foremast following soon after, the bowsprit springing in three places. The gale continued to blow hard all day, the *Vanguard* being then about seventy-five miles south of Hyères. The *Alexander*, in command of A. J. Ball, towards evening took the *Vanguard* in tow, and made for the Gulf of Oristano, the wind and currents nearly driving both ships on shore. They eventually reached the island of St. Peter on the 23rd, where, after four days of incessant toil, they equipped jury-masts and were ready for service, sailing on the 27th for their old cruising station off Cape Sicie, where they arrived on the 31st May.[2]

News of this disaster to the *Vanguard* reached Bonaparte by the privateer *Cisalpine* on the 1st June. This vessel had been dispatched from Genoa with the intelligence, and found the French fleet off Cape Carbonaro *en route* to Malta. The message was to the following effect: 'Three English battleships under the command of Nelson have taken shelter at St. Peter's, and sailed again on the 28th May' (it was really the 27th). 'Nelson's ship had lost her foremast.' It is thus seen that in the short space of nine days news of the disaster reached Bonaparte, then in the open sea.

In the meanwhile, the 'most secret' instructions, under date of the

[1] Nicolas, *Nelson's Dispatches*, vol. iii. p. 15.
[2] *Nelson's Dispatches*, vol. iii. pp. 17–24. St. Peter's Island is at the south end of Sardinia.

40 A HISTORY OF MALTA

2nd May, were issued by the Admiralty, reaching Lord St. Vincent on the 19th (the day the French expedition was leaving Toulon), which, after stating that political affairs had rendered it absolutely necessary that the fleet and armament fitting at Toulon should be prevented from accomplishing its object, and that their lordships had in consequence reinforced his fleet with eight sail of the line and two fireships under Rear-Admiral Sir Roger Curtis, proceeded thus:

Having been joined by the Rear-Admiral, and the ships above mentioned, your Lordship is to lose no time in detaching from your Fleet a squadron consisting of twelve sail of the line and a competent number of frigates under the command of a discreet Flag Officer, into the Mediterranean, with instructions for him to proceed in quest of the said armament, and on falling in with it, or any other force belonging to the enemy, to take or destroy it.

Your Lordship is to direct the commanding officer of the abovementioned squadron to remain upon this service so long as the provisions of the said squadron will last, or as long as he may be enabled to obtain supplies from any of the ports in the Mediterranean, and when from want of provisions, or any other circumstance, he shall be no longer able to remain within the Straits, to lose no time in rejoining you.[1]

Five days after receiving these instructions from the Admiralty, Earl St. Vincent was able to dispatch Captain Troubridge[2] of the *Culloden* with strong reinforcements, and with the following orders to join Nelson as promptly as possible:—

Before Cadiz,
(Most secret and confidential.)[3]   24th May 1798.

THE EARL OF ST. VINCENT, K.B., Admiral of the Blue, &c., to CAPTAIN TROUBRIDGE.

You are hereby required and directed to take under your command the ships named in the margin [viz. the *Goliath, Minotaur, Defence, Bellerophon, Majestic, Zealous, Swiftsure, Theseus, Audacious*], their captains being instructed to obey you, and when the signal No. 123 accompanied by that of the detached squadron is made by me you are forthwith to proceed for the Mediterranean, taking His Majesty's ship the *Audacious* (which you will find off Tangier, should the wind be easterly, or in Raccio Bay with a westerly wind) also under your command.

You are then to make the best of your way with the ships before mentioned in quest of Rear-Admiral Sir Horatio Nelson, whose route is

---

[1] Nicolas, *Nelson's Dispatches*, vol. iii. p. 24.
[2] Troubridge, Sir Thomas (1758?-1807), entered the Navy in 1773; he was taken by the French in 1794, but was soon retaken, viz. on June 1, 1794. He commanded the *Culloden* in 1795, and distinguished himself in her at St. Vincent. After the Battle of the Nile, when the *Culloden* grounded, he served at Naples and off Malta. He became a Lord of the Admiralty in 1801-4, and thereafter did good service in the East Indies. He was made baronet in 1799.—J. H. R.
[3] Brit. Mus. Add. MSS. 34906, f. 421.

contained in the enclosed paper and whose orders and instructions herewith delivered are under a flying seal for your more particular information; from which you will learn the serious importance of the proposed expedition, and how essential it is to the success of it, that you should form as early a junction as possible with the Rear-Admiral, and to use every precaution in your power not to suffer him to pass your squadron in the night on his way to Gibraltar. On falling in with him you are to deliver the pacquet bearing his address, and putting yourself with the ships which accompany you under the Rear-Admiral's command follow his orders for your future proceedings.

The following are extracts from Lord St. Vincent's orders to Nelson, dated 21st May 1798, conveyed by Captain Troubridge[1]:—

... I do hereby authorise and require you on being joined by the following ships [as above named], to take them and their captains under your command, in addition to those already with you, and to proceed with them in quest of the armament preparing by the enemy at Toulon and Genoa, the object whereof appears to be either an attack upon Naples and Sicily, the conveyance of an army to some part of the coast of Spain for the purpose of marching towards Portugal, or to pass through the Straits with the view of proceeding to Ireland.

On falling in with the said armament, or any part thereof, you are to use your utmost endeavours to take, sink, burn, or destroy it. ... In any event you are to exact supplies of whatever you may be in want of, from the territories of the Grand Duke of Tuscany, the King of the Two Sicilies, the Ottoman territory, Malta, and *ci-devant* Venetian dominions, now belonging to the Emperor of Germany. You will also perceive by an extract of a letter from Mr. Master, His Majesty's Consul for Algiers, that the Dey is extremely well-disposed towards us—the Bey of Tunis, by the report of Captain Thompson, of His Majesty's ship *Leander*, is also perfectly neutral and good-humoured. From the Bashaw of Tripoli, I have every reason to believe any ships of your squadron having occasion to touch there, will be received in a most friendly manner. In a private letter from Lord Spencer, I am led to believe that you are perfectly justifiable in pursuing the French squadron to any part of the Mediterranean, Adriatic, Morea, Archipelago, or even into the Black Sea, should its destination be to any of those parts. ...

To the above-named ships were subsequently added the *Leander* frigate—Captain Thomas B. Thompson—and the brig *Mutine*—Captain Hardy.[2]

Some animadversions on Nelson's failing to discover the sailing or destination of the French expedition from Toulon have been made, but the fact is forgotten that if Nelson had extended his line of observation to the east of Toulon (which was the eventual route of the fleet), he would not only have exceeded his instructions, but in

---

[1] For the full text see Nicolas, *Nelson's Dispatches*, vol. iii. p. 26.
[2] Two of the ships of Nelson's squadron were defective in the hull, and the rigging of all was far from sound; but the crews were the best and smartest in the Navy. (See Mr. H. W. Wilson's chapter (No. xx) in the *Camb. Mod. History*, vol. viii.).—J. H. R.

all probability his small squadron of three battleships and two cruisers would have been captured or annihilated by Bonaparte's fleet of fifteen battleships and twelve frigates, which for five days previous to Nelson's arrival off Cape Sicie had been ready for sea, and only waiting for a change of wind to sail.

It is now known from Bonaparte's dispatches to General Desaix (which have been lately published), dated from Paris on the 19th April, that it was his original intention to sail for Malta by the western coast of Sardinia, and touching at the island of St. Peter. Providentially, at the last moment this intention was changed, and the day after Bonaparte's arrival at Toulon from Paris, and two days before the expedition was officially declared ready to sail, Bonaparte again advised Desaix on the 10th of May of the altered route, and that the fleet would now sail by the eastern coasts of Corsica and Sardinia, starting on the 12th.

Strong easterly winds prevailed from the 13th to the 18th May, preventing their departure until the morning of the 19th. Had they carried out the original intention, they would have arrived at St. Peter's about, or simultaneously with, the crippled *Vanguard* and her two escorts, in which case the future history of Europe would have been very different.

On the day Nelson arrived off Cape Sicie for the second time, namely, the 31st May, Bonaparte, who had been already joined by the contingents from Genoa and Ajaccio, was sailing southwards between Sardinia and the mainland, making for the north-western point of Sicily, and four days later Desaix's portion of the expedition embarked at Civita Vecchia was seen off Trapani, which fact later on was reported to Nelson.[1]

In the meanwhile, the reinforcements for Nelson under Troubridge were well on their way, and by the 7th June joined Nelson, who at once sailed for Talamone Bay, where he expected to find part, if not all, of the French fleet; but owing to continuous calms, it was only on the 12th that he was able to round Cape Corse and reach off Elba. The brig *Mutine*, Captain Hardy, was then dispatched to Talamone Bay for intelligence, but returned on the following day without any, the fleet in the meanwhile steering between the islands of Monte Cristo and Giglio.

By noon of the 14th Civita Vecchia had been reached, when the *Leander* communicated with a Greek vessel, whose captain reported that he had passed through a French fleet of about 200 sail on the 4th, off the north-west point of Sicily, near Trapani, and steering to the east.[2]

On the 15th the British fleet reached off Ponza Islands, when Nelson determined upon sending Captain Troubridge, of the *Culloden*,

---

[1] *Nelson's Dispatches*, vol. iii. p. 27 (edit. 1845).
[2] *Ibid.* vol. iii. p. 30.

in the brig *Mutine* to communicate with Sir William Hamilton, British ambassador at the Court of Naples, and with General Acton, Prime Minister of that Government, and glean some information regarding the French, expressing as his opinion that if they had passed Sicily, then Alexandria must be their destination, with the ultimate intention of getting troops to India and aiding 'Tippoo Saib.' Troubridge was to implore the help of some frigates or smaller craft from the Neapolitan Government, without which it was impossible to get timely news of the enemy's movements.

The King of Naples, as well as His Majesty's Prime Minister, however, had become so alarmed at the French successes in the vicinity of the frontier, that they feared to declare openly in favour of the British, but a tacit agreement was arrived at, by which stores and provisions were to be obtained when needed at any of the Calabrian or Sicilian ports. Ships-of-war, however, could not be granted.[1]

At 8 a.m. of Sunday, the 17th, the fleet was hove to in the Bay of Naples, and on the following day Troubridge returned with a letter from Sir William Hamilton, dated the 16th, to the following effect: 'That the 1st Division of the Toulon armament had been seen off Trapani on the 5th June, and had been there joined by the 2nd Division on the 7th, making in all sixteen sail of the line, French and Venetian.' That a frigate had been detached near Favignana, on which island an officer had landed, who had acquainted the commandant that Bonaparte had desired him to say 'that the approach of the French fleet need not give any uneasiness to his Sicilian Majesty, with whom the Republic was at perfect peace, and that the armament he commanded had another object in view, not Sicily. Malta, as you know, belongs to Sicily.'[2]

Upon receipt of this intelligence, Nelson made sail immediately for Messina and Syracuse, arriving at the former on the 20th, and at the latter on the 22nd June. Captain Hardy,[3] in the *Mutine*, in the meanwhile boarded a Genoese vessel, which had left Malta on the 21st, and then learned that the French had captured Malta, and sailed again on the 18th with a fresh gale from the north-west, destination *supposed* to be Sicily. From the direction given of the wind, Nelson judged that Alexandria was the destination, and immediately made sail in pursuit.[4]

---

[1] For some new light on the dealings of Nelson with the Neapolitan Government, as well as Sir William and Lady Hamilton, see Mr. W. Sichel's *Emma, Lady Hamilton* (1905), chap. viii.—J. H. R.
[2] Clarke and MacArthur, *Life of Nelson*, vol. ii. p. 64.
[3] Captain Hardy (1769–1839) came of a Dorset family, and his valour largely contributed to the capture of *La Mutine*, brig, in 1797. In 1803 he became captain of H.M.S. *Victory*. See Mr. A. M. Broadley's work, '*Nelson's Hardy*.'—J. H. R.
[4] *Nelson's Dispatches*, vol. iii. p. 39.

CHAPTER VII

ATTACK AND CAPTURE OF MALTA BY THE FRENCH

ALTHOUGH information was received in Malta that a formidable armament had been in preparation at Toulon since the beginning of March, it would appear that Hompesch, the Grand Master of the Order, believed that an attack on Portugal, and eventually on Ireland, was contemplated. On the authority of Porter ('Knights of Malta') it is stated that Hompesch, so late as a few days before the appearance of the French off Malta, informed the German Knights 'that he was persuaded that the French Government had no designs on the Order.' This letter still exists in the archives of the Grand Priory of the Order in Germany.

It has been further stated that the following dispatch in cipher, from the bailli, de Schoenau, the Minister Plenipotentiary of the Order at the Congress then being held at Rastadt, dated the 18/19 May, was received by Hompesch on or about the 4th June:

[Translation.]

MONSEIGNEUR,—I have to acquaint you, that the formidable expedition now preparing at Toulon is intended for the capture of Malta and Egypt. I have this information from the secretary of Monsr· Treilhard, one of the French Republican Ministers at the Congress. You will most assuredly be attacked. Take all necessary steps for your defence. All the Ministers of the various Powers attending this Congress, friends of the Order, have the same intelligence, but they also know that the fortress of Malta is impregnable, or at least capable of resisting a three months' siege. The honour of Your Eminence, and the preservation of the Order, are at stake, and if you surrender without making any defence, you will be dishonoured in the eyes of Europe. Moreover this expedition is regarded here as a disgrace inflicted upon Bonaparte, who has two powerful enemies in the Directory who fear him, and have so arranged that he should now be removed to a distance. These members of the Directory are Rewbell and La Révellière-Lépaux.

It is difficult, however, to believe that a subordinate official would presume to address his sovereign in these terms, or that he would compromise himself by naming the authority from whom he received

ATTACK AND CAPTURE OF MALTA BY THE FRENCH 45

the information, or that such authority, considering the official position that individual held, would be guilty of so great an indiscretion. Moreover, the assertion that at that date (18/19 May) all the Ministers of the various Powers attending the Congress were fully informed of the destination of the expedition is manifestly incorrect, and carries with it its own refutation. The probability is that the document is apocryphal, and was concocted by that portion of the Order which subsequently placed themselves under the protection of Paul I of Russia, for the purpose of discrediting Hompesch.

Returning to an account of the hostilities, we find that on the 6th June, when Desaix's Division had been sighted off Gozo, Hompesch called out the militia, and summoned a council of war. According to Azopardi, the following orders for the defence were issued:—

All men in the four cities and Floriana should be divided into 24 companies of 150 men each, to be commanded by a captain, lieutenant, and sub-lieutenant, all Knights of the Order; 150 of the Grand Master's guard should defend the palace with a company of the Regiment of the Bolla: the remainder of the guard to be located in St. Elmo; 700 men of the chasseurs, of which the colonel and majors were Maltese, should be divided between Manoel, Tigné, and Ricasoli; 250 marines from the galleys, together with such men as might be obtained from the battleships, should defend San Angelo and Cottonera; 1,000 men of the Malta Regiment, and two companies of that of the Bolla, should be distributed on the ramparts of Valetta and Floriana; 250 gunners should occupy the forts, whilst the towns on the coast-line should be defended by the country militia, commanded by Knights belonging to the sea forces of the Order.

The coast-line of defence at Marsa Scirocco was confided to the bailli, Saint Tropez; that of the east, with the tower of Saint Thomas, to the bailli, Tommasi; that of the west to the bailli, La Tour du Pin; and the castle of Gozo to the Chevalier de Mesgrigny.

The French military preparations for landing the troops having been completed, Bonaparte during the afternoon of the 9th dispatched his aide-de-camp, Chief of Brigade Junot, to the Grand Master, asking permission to water the fleet and transports at various anchorages. Referring to this request, General Belliard in his Journal observes: 'I know not whether we shall take in a supply of water at Malta *en passant*, or whether we shall call for a forced loan there, to cover our travelling expenses, for, generally speaking, our visits are not usually disinterested.'[1]

Upon receipt of Bonaparte's message Hompesch convoked a meeting of the Council at 6 p.m., to decide whether the permission should be granted. At this meeting the bailli, de Pennes, reminded the Council of the existence of an old statute of the Order, prohibiting entrance to any of the ports of Malta during hostilities between Christian nations of more than four vessels at a time. All the

[1] De la Jonquière, vol. i. p. 572.

members of the Council, with one exception, were of opinion that this regulation should be enforced.

Spain being at the time in alliance with France, the Spanish bailli, Vargas, considered it incumbent upon him to support Bonaparte's demand. The majority being opposed, a verbal refusal, within the limits of the statute, was delivered to the French consul for conveyance to Bonaparte. 'Water is refused!' said he, upon receiving this message. 'Then we will go and take it.' An ultimatum was accordingly dictated by Bonaparte, but written and signed by Caruson, and forwarded to the Grand Master, as follows [1]:—

[Translation.]

On board *L'Orient*,

22 *Prairial*, An VI (10 *June* 1798).

To the Grand Master of the Island of Malta.

EMINENCE,—Having been called on board the flagship as bearer of the reply which your Eminence had made to the request that permission might be granted to the Fleet to water—the Commander-in-Chief, Bonaparte, is indignant to learn that you will not grant such permission except to four vessels at a time—for in effect, what length of time would be required under such circumstances to water and victual 500 to 600 sail? This refusal has surprised General Bonaparte all the more, as he is aware of the favours shown to the English, and also of the proclamation published by your Eminence's predecessor.

General Bonaparte is resolved to obtain by force that which ought to have been accorded him by virtue of the principles of hospitality, the fundamental rule of your Order. I have seen the considerable forces which are under the orders of General Bonaparte, and I foresee the impossibility of the Order resisting. It would be well, if your Eminence under such extreme circumstances, for the love of your Order, your Knights, and the whole population of Malta, might propose some means of concluding an arrangement.

The General will not on any account permit my returning to a city which henceforth he feels obliged to treat as belonging to an enemy, and which can have no hope, except in the sincerity of General Bonaparte, who has given strict orders, that the religion, the customs, and the property of the Maltese shall be most scrupulously respected. By order of the Commander-in-Chief. (Signed) CARUSON.

On the morning of the 10th June the invading force closed in upon Valetta and the Three Cities. The French military orders issued in anticipation on the 6th and 9th were duly carried out, and the disembarkations made at *four* different points: one (A) at Gozo under Reynier; a second (B) at Saint Paul's Bay and the vicinity under Baraguey d'Hilliers; a third (C) at Saint Julian's and the neighbourhood under Vaubois; whilst the fourth (D), under Desaix, as already recorded, landed at Marsa Scirocco.

[1] *Corres. de Nap. I*, vol. iv. p. 132.

ATTACK AND CAPTURE OF MALTA BY THE FRENCH 47

Taking the reports of the four different attacks seriatim, which in due course were communicated to the commander-in-chief, and commencing with those of General Reynier from Gozo (A), under dates of the 11th and 13th June, we learn that 'Gozo had been defended by 800 militia, one regiment of coastguardsmen numbering 1,200, and one company consisting of 300 regular troops, of whom 30 were mounted, making in all 2,300 men. A point for landing was selected between the New Tower and the first battery of Ramla, called Redum Kbir.

'The whole morning of the 10th had been occupied in preliminary arrangements. Calms and contrary breezes had still further delayed operations; but by 1 p.m. the shore was approached by the 3rd Company of Grenadiers and 95th Demi-Brigade. The heights meanwhile had become crowded with the enemy, who received the French with showers of bullets, Sergeant-Major Bertrand of the Grenadiers in the general's boat, being killed.

'The batteries of Ramla and New Tower then opened fire. The boats of the *Alceste* conveyed Generals Reynier and Fugière, Captains Geoffrey and Sabatier, and the 3rd Company of the Grenadiers, who were the first to land. After a rapid ascent of the heights, notwithstanding the heavy fire, the enemy at last decamped, and the battery of Ramla was taken. The bombards, *Étoile* and *Pluvier*, by their successful fire against the enemy's batteries, were of great assistance.

'The remainder of the troops had landed in the meanwhile, and upon reassembling, the general marched with a portion of the 95th Demi-Brigade upon Fort Chambray, by Casal Nadur, in order that by capturing the fort communication with Malta by way of the port of Migiarro might be cut off. The remainder of the 95th were ordered to march by way of Casal Sciara to the citadel at Rabato, leaving a detachment for occupation of the tower at Marsa-al-forno.

'During the day, Fort Chambray, filled with refugees from the neighbouring villages, surrendered, and at 2 p.m. the terms of the capitulation, laconically expressed in the following words, *Honores, proprietates, et Religionem habebitis majorum*, were duly signed. By night the citadel at Rabato was also occupied. About 116 guns were found, 44 of which were in the citadel, and 22 at Fort Chambray, the remainder in the forts and coast batteries. A large number of muskets were also captured, and three stores full of wheat.'[1]

General Reynier in his report added that he was informed 'that each village had a syndic, subordinate to a Central Administration, residing at Rabato, composed of four jurats, the Governor of the Island being the fifth member, as well as President of the Administration. The population was reckoned at between 13,000 and 14,000.'[2]

Regarding the operations at St. Paul's Bay (B), Baraguey

---

[1] Bonaparte's *Lettres inédites*, vol. i. pp. 153–60.
[2] General Reynier's Journal, referring to these operations, will be found in De la Jonquière's *Expédition d'Egypte*, vol. i. p. 607.

d'Hilliers reported from on board *La Sérieuse* that the troops of his Division had captured all the forts, batteries, and positions which defended the bays of St. Paul and Melleha. The Maltese, he went on to say, ' had defended themselves as far as lay in their power, but all had to cede before the audacity and intelligence of the attack.' [1] In this direction there were no French casualties, whilst that of the Maltese consisted of one Knight and one soldier killed, and 150 prisoners taken, three French Knights being in the number. The forts and batteries captured were armed with about fifty guns.

Of Vaubois' proceedings (C) Marmont gives the following account of that portion of the brigade under his *personal* command :—

Being charged with the landing party of five battalions, three of the 4th Light Infantry, and two of the 19th of the Line, he found a few companies of the Maltese Regiment collected to dispute his landing, but as he approached the shore they retired with a show of little resistance, and being followed by his men, the enemy re-entered Valetta. The city was then invested from the sea to the aqueduct, joining Desaix's corps, who had effected a landing at Marsa Scirocco. When all these arrangements were completed the drawbridge of the city was lowered, and a numerous body of troops came marching towards him. The French troops retired slowly, firing occasionally to retard the advance; then orders were issued to the 2nd Battalion of the 19th, encamped at about gun-shot distance from the city, to place themselves in ambush on the right and left of the route, and to await further orders, which was duly carried out. The Maltese, upon observing the troops retiring, advanced with confidence, when upon coming to close quarters, the 19th rose and met them with a murderous fire, which threw them in great disorder. A general advance was then made, defeating them totally, and following them with the bayonet, he captured with his own hand the flag of the Order carried at the head of the column.

On the morrow, an emissary brought word from a portion of the garrison that if the negotiations already commenced for the surrender of the fortress were concluded, they would be prepared to deliver up St. Joseph's Gate.[2]

[1] Bonaparte, *Lettres inédites*, vol. i. p. 148.
[2] Marmont at a later date stated: ' If the Maltese Government had performed its duty, if the French Knights had not made sorties such as that described, with a Militia undrilled, to meet a numerous and veteran enemy, and had been content to remain behind their ramparts, the strongest in Europe, we should not have gained entrance. The English fleet in our wake would have quickly destroyed ours, or put it to flight, and with the army landed wanting in every necessity, would in a few days have been suffering the pangs of famine, and compelled to surrender. There is no exaggeration in this picture, it is the simple truth, and one trembles to think of such risks, which might so easily have been anticipated, so capriciously encountered by a brave army; but the hand of Providence was guarding us, and preserved us from such a catastrophe.'

Marmont omits to mention, however, that he had under his command the ex-Chevalier Picault de Mornas, captain of Engineers, who had abandoned the Order two years previously for the purpose of joining the Republican forces in Italy. That this traitor directed the landing at St. George's Bay, and that through his treason the tower of St. George, in charge of the Chevalier de Preville, was surrendered, the latter joining his perfidious friend.

Bonaparte's aide-de-camp, Sulkowski, gives the following detailed account of Vaubois' operations :—

Division Vaubois.[1]

. . . Je fus du nombre de ceux qui reconnurent le lieu de débarquement. Le lendemain, il s'exécuta dans quatre endroits. Le général Reynier devait attaquer le Goze ; le général Baraguey d'Hilliers la cale de Saint-Paul, et les généraux Desaix et Vaubois devaient cerner la cité Valette. Le point de jonction de ces deux dernières divisions était l'aqueduc qui conduit dans la forteresse, le seul filet d'eau qui existe dans l'île. . . .

Le général en chef avait partagé en deux la division Vaubois. Le général Lannes avec sept bataillons, avait la tâche de longer le port de Marsa Musceit à la droite de Malte, sans y entrer et de chercher à s'emparer d'un des forts qui commandent l'entrée ; pendant que cinq bataillons, sous les ordres de l'aide de camp Marmont, devaient marcher droit à l'aqueduc et barrer l'isthme qui joint la cité Valette au reste de l'île. Il m'assigna pour mon poste l'avant-garde de cette brigade, composée de plusieurs compagnies de carabiniers que je devais guider.

Nous partîmes, le 22 Prairial, de l'*Orient*, à la pointe du jour. Toutes les chaloupes avaient été rassemblées à l'abri de ce vaisseau. L'ennemi ne défendit que faiblement le débarquement, car il fut surpris, ce n'est qu'une heure plus tard, lorsque nous avions déjà gravi plusieurs coteaux qu'il vint engager une fusillade insignifiante. Lorsque Marmont eut réuni toutes ses forces, il marcha en avant. L'on nous avait avertis que l'ennemi nous attendait ; mais il fut impossible de le reconnaître dans un pays barré par un dédale de murailles sèches, qui contournent chaque champ. Je m'avançais vers les tirailleurs, lorsque je trouvai déjà ceux-ci engagés. Les Maltais s'étaient placés derrière l'aqueduc même, car il domine les alentours ; ils occupaient aussi plusieurs maisons et une muraille leur servait de parapet. Les tirailleurs furent repoussés, et je voyais l'instant où l'ennemi enhardi, aurait prolongé sa défense. Sans attendre le reste de la demi-brigade, je perçai avec les grenadiers par un chemin à demi-couvert ; on les joignit ; une décharge à brûle-pourpoint les déconcerte, et ils fuient en déroute ; l'habitude de sauter des murailles les préserva du trépas ; nous n'en tuâmes qu'une quinzaine, et un drapeau rouge que j'atteignis, moi troisième, [fut] pris. Ce choc fut court mais vif ; nous ne tardâmes pas à en avoir un autre. Marmont, qui pendant ce temps, avait enfoncé la droite des ennemis, plaça ses troupes militairement, et m'envoya reconnaître la ville, en me soutenant d'un bataillon. Je m'approche des portes, et mes tirailleurs s'engagent malgré moi ; allors cinq cents hommes, qui si trouvaient sur le glacis, les serrent et les poussent à leur tour. Ceci enhardit la garnison et elle tenta une sortie. Mon dessein était de feindre une retraite pour les attirer sur le bataillon ; mais l'ardeur des grenadiers ne me permit pas d'exécuter cette manœuvre ; ils ne virent pas plutôt les ennemis à leur portée que, fondant dessus au pas de course, ils les forcèrent de se renfermer dans leurs murailles.

Le soir, les Maltais tâtèrent encore inutilement nos avant-postes, et la

[1] De la Jonquière, vol. i.

nuit, une forte fusillade, du côté de Desaix, nous mit à même de nous convaincre, que ce général avait rempli son but; effectivement, il venait de s'emparer des forts qui commandent la rade de Marsa Scirocco et venait pour cerner la ville de l'autre côté.

Ceci se passait au dehors de la ville, lorsqu'un événement inattendu vint nous livrer cette place formidable.

Les Chevaliers avaient posté l'élite de leurs troupes dans la cité Valette, comme le point le plus menacé. Le seul bataillon des galères devait surveiller les immenses ouvrages au delà du port, ainsi que la vaste enceinte de la Cottonère, construite dans le temps pour contenir tous les habitants de l'île. Ces postes n'étaient donc réellement gardées que par les paysans et surtout par les habitants des faubourgs, tous ennemis jurés de l'Ordre et issus des anciens regnicoles de Malte.

L'insurrection commença dans ces endroits. Un quiproquo, qui fit prendre des individus chargés de couper un pont pour un détachement français, ayant engagé une fusillade, plusieurs Chevaliers quittèrent leur porte. A cette vue, le peuple se met en fureur; il croit qu'on le trahit et demande à être conduit pour marcher contre les ennemis, et de sortir des retranchements. Sur le refus qu'en fit le bailli, qui commandait, il fut massacré, ses compagnons eurent le même sort et la fuite seule préserva les autres Chevaliers du trépas. Cet acte de vengeance fut suivi d'une décharge générale; après quoi le peuple laissant les portes de l'enciente à l'abandon, retourne sur ses pas, et s'empare des faubourgs.

Cette nouvelle désastreuse parvint au grand-maître, Hompesch, dans l'instant même où la sortie de la garnison de la cité venait d'être si vigoureusement repoussée. Ce veillard sexagénaire, digne de combattre pour une meilleure cause, n'en fit que redoubler d'énergie. Il ordonne sur-le-champ, de concentrer dans la cité les munitions et les vivres. Il fait braquer du canon sur les insurgés, il annonce que l'on se défendra jusqu'à la dernière extrémité; il y eut même des individus qui proposèrent de faire sauter la forteresse dans un cas de détresse; mais le peuple de la ville ne partageait pas cette ardeur guerrière. L'attente d'un bombardement effrayait tous les esprits, et l'exemple des faubourgs leur indiquait les moyens de s'en affranchir. A l'issue d'une procession solennelle, par laquelle les chefs avaient espéré de pouvoir électriser les esprits, les citoyens qui gardaient le donjon des Chevaliers s'insurgent, blessent divers membres de la Religion qui s'y trouvent, incarcèrent les autres et font cesser le feu que ce donjon n'avait cessé de faire sur la brigade de Lannes. En même temps, tous les propriétaires, s'assemblent, dressent une requête, choisissent des députés et se présentent le soir devant la congrégation de défense, où présidait le grand-maître. Le contenu de la requête était la demande de la paix, le refus d'exposer leurs vies et leurs propriétés pour la défense de l'Ordre et la menace de livrer la ville aux Français, si on s'obstinait à ne pas traiter avec eux. Cette requête, soutenue par les cris d'un peuple armé et furieux, convainquit le grand-maître qu'il n'avait d'espoir que dans la loyauté de la République française, et il capitula dès le lendemain. . . .

Desaix's movements (D) on the east coast at Marsa Scirocco soon resulted in a successful landing, and in the surrender of Fort Rohan.

ATTACK AND CAPTURE OF MALTA BY THE FRENCH

The defenders abandoned other works in that quarter, and the French convoy was able to put into that bay.[1]

As soon as the landing of the French troops had been effected, Bosredon Ransijat, then Secretary of the Treasury, a Commander and Grand Cross of the Order, and strong partisan of the Republic, concluded that the time had now arrived to throw off the mask, and accordingly addressed the following letter to the Grand Master :—

[Translation.]

YOUR HIGHNESS,—In the extreme affliction in which I am placed, owing to the misfortune, amidst many others, which our Order has now to face, and as a war with France would be a calamity certainly greater than all the others, I consider it my duty to represent to your Highness, with that frankness which I claim to be characteristic, that when I became by vow a member of our Institution, I did not contract any other military obligation beyond that of warring against the Turks, our constitutional enemies. I could never contemplate fighting against my native country, to which, by duty, as well as feeling, I am, and ever shall be, as firmly attached as I am to our Order.

Finding myself, therefore, in this critical and painful dilemma, for on whichever side I declare myself, I shall be considered at fault by the other, I beg your Highness will not take it amiss if I observe the strictest neutrality, and hereby beg you will be pleased to appoint a member of our Order to whom I may deliver the keys of the Treasury, and at the same time assign to me a place of residence. I have the honour, &c.

(Signed) BOSREDON RANSIJAT,
Secretary of the Treasury.

To His Highness
 FRA EMMANUEL HOMPESCH.
 10th June 1798.

This act of treachery on the part of one of the most important officers of the Government was immediately met by placing him in confinement in the castle of St. Angelo.

Whilst the main body of the French troops were encircling Valetta, the flying column, under General Vaubois, advanced upon Citta Vecchia, whither the remainder of the militia, under the bailli, La Tour du Pin, driven from Melleja and St. Paul's Bay by Baraguey d'Hilliers, had retired. A city council then assembled at the bishop's palace, consisting of the capitan di verga (or governor) and three jurists, at which the Bishop Labini assisted, together with one, Romualdo Barbaro, on behalf of the people.

During the meeting a message was received from the renegade Vincenzo Barbara, intimating his approach with Vaubois' troops, and demanding on behalf of Bonaparte an immediate answer whether the French soldiers would be received as friends or foes. As they were

---

[1] These operations not being of the first importance, and having been fully described by De la Jonquière (vol. i. pp. 601-3), omitted.—J. H. R.

unable to make any resistance, it was resolved to surrender the city, provided that the religion of the people, their liberty, and their property be respected, and the safety of the public institutions be guaranteed. These conditions having been granted, capitulation followed, and the keys of the city were delivered to General Vaubois. As these proceedings took place about midday, Vaubois and his staff were invited to dine at the bishop's table, which hospitality they accepted.

In the archives of the cathedral at Citta Vecchia there is to be found a volume of numerous MSS., one of which, numbered 28, is entitled 'Notizie e Ragguaglie sul Blocco, 1798,' containing a copy of the act of capitulation of that city to the French troops under General Vaubois, on the 22nd Prairial, An VI (10th June 1798).

This document was signed in the bishop's palace, and is interesting from the fact that it records the names of the negotiators, viz. :

> Vincenzo Barbara, representing Bonaparte and the French Republic, on the one part,

and the authorities of the city on the other, viz. :

> Gregorio Bonici, the governor of the city.
> Salvadore Manduca ⎫
> Ferdinando Teuma ⎬ the jurists.
> Salvadore Tabone ⎭
> Romualdo Barbaro, on behalf of the people.

Whilst Vaubois was marching on Citta Vecchia he received information that negotiations for the surrender of Valetta were in progress, Bonaparte at the same time expressing a hope that the ancient city and that part of the island would be in his (Vaubois') possession before the day closed, inasmuch as the suspension of hostilities, if arranged, would only have reference to the fortress, unless otherwise declared, and that negotiations were then only pending.

Towards midnight of the 10th, orders were issued by Bonaparte to land two field pieces of 12 calibre, and accessories, at Saint Julian's Bay, also two 6-inch howitzers; whilst General Dommartin, commanding the artillery, was instructed to place them in position before the Tigné batteries at certain specified points, but not to open fire until further orders. All egress from the fort was to be stopped, and the fire of the enemy silenced, as soon as operations were commenced. The commander-in-chief was desirous that these works should be completed as quickly as possible, so as to impress the enemy.

In the meanwhile, the commotion and consternation within Valetta were indescribable. The faction favourable to the French took advantage of the difficulties in which Hompesch was placed. A deputation waited upon His Eminence, insisting upon negotiations being opened with the invader, with a view of arranging terms of peace. Among Hompesch's papers collected by his secretary, Mayer, and now

ATTACK AND CAPTURE OF MALTA BY THE FRENCH

preserved in the Malta Public Library (MS. No. 421), the following statement is to be found:—

> Du milieu du tumulte il sortit une Députation composée des Juges, et de tous les Magistrats du Peuple; voici le discours qu'ils adresserent à leur souverain. Malte est attaquée, l'Ordre ne peut la défendre et vous allez exposer nos personnes et nos biens à la fureur d'un vainqueur irrité. Nous vous declarons au nom de Peuple que nous représentons que si dans l'instant même vous ne vous résolvez pas à demander la paix, le peuple traitera lui même et sans vous.

Not to rely upon *ex parte* statements, we may quote what has been related as to the events which at this moment occurred within Valetta. These authorities, however, with the exception of Boisgelin (1804), have all borrowed their accounts from that of Doublet, who, as secretary to the French section of Hompesch's secretariat, became a prominent assistant in the subsequeut negotiations with Bonaparte. It is, therefore, a fortunate circumstance that a minute detailed account of what happened within the city, and at the palace of the Grand Masters, after the arrival of the French fleet off Valetta harbour, has come down to us from the pen of a protagonist in the proceedings. Doublet's work, entitled 'The Occupation of Malta in 1798,' appears to have been commenced in the year 1805, and completed in 1820, but remained in manuscript (of which there were two copies), and so circulated until the year 1883. One manuscript copy was in the possession of Sir Frederick Ponsonby, Governor of Malta from 1824 to 1835.

The work was eventually published in the year 1883, fifty-nine years after Doublet's death. The book appears to have been written for the purpose of repudiating a charge of treachery towards the Order of St. John, which had been brought against Doublet, for having disclosed to Bonaparte for a consideration the key to the Order's secret code of correspondence.

Although from the tenour of this attempt at vindication some doubts may be entertained as to the reliability of his alleged conversations with the Grand Master, and other authorities of the Order, there seems to be no reason why his statement of occurrences may not be true, and particularly for the reason that they were accepted by writers such as Bargemont-Villeneuve (1829), Panzavecchia (1835), Azopardi (1836), Miège (1840), Davy (1842), and Vassalo (1854), many of whom were contemporaries, and the remainder almost so.

In his work Doublet describes the arrival of the Frence fleet, the refusal of the Grand Master to admit it, and the beginning of hostilities. He then proceeds in the following terms :—

> The consternation which reigned in the city can be imagined. Messengers followed each other quickly from various parts of the country, reporting the progress of the French, yet the Government took no steps to tranquillise

the people. The Grand Master and Council remained assembled, and all the Knights, with the exception of those who commanded inside the fortifications, gathered in various apartments in the Palace, where they discussed the event with such fear and trembling as if the enemy had already attacked the city, whilst nobody thought of calming the apprehensions of the few civilians who remained in town, the greater portion being under arms. The Bishop and clergy, both secular and regular (excepting those of the Order, who were less devout than the others), formed into processions, carrying with them the statue of Saint Paul, offering up prayers to the Divine Majesty, and beseeching His merciful protection. It was scandalous to observe certain young French Knights making jocular remarks on the occasion, showing further disregard by remaining covered, and although the Maltese murmured at such proceedings, they did so in a low tone, for they feared the young Knights.

During the time this procession was taking place in the centre of the city, an unfortunate occurrence took place at the Marina, whereby two Frenchmen of the name of Patot and Eynaud were murdered, on suspicion of being implicated in the threatened attack on the city.

Whilst all this was proceeding, I remained at my post, that is to say, in the secretary's office with all my clerks, where from early morning I awaited the equerry, Rouyer; but at four p.m., surprised at his non-arrival, I proceeded to his residence, and there learned that he had been ordered by the Grand Master to remain at his post as Governor of the Prison, as there was some fear of the slaves rising in revolt. I inquired from my friend why he was so alarmed on my account, when he answered: 'Are you not French, and known to be a friend of Eynaud's; and do you think the assassins will spare you any more than they did him? Take my advice: return to the Palace at once, endeavour to see the Grand Master, and ascertain if it is absolutely necessary for you to remain in the secretary's office the entire night. I trust that he will say no, and that you may be able to reach home before dark.' Whilst believing I had nothing to fear, I yet promised to adopt his advice, and accordingly sought an interview, but as the Council was sitting I was unable to obtain it. The chamberlain, Ligondez, however, promised to ascertain the wishes of His Eminence, and within an hour brought me word that I was to discharge all the clerks, and to remain at home, and not leave until sent for.

From the Palace to my residence there may be the distance from 200 to 300 yards, and arriving at the corner of the Carmelite church, I there found acting as a sentinel the advocate, Torregiani, a neighbour of mine, whom I asked, 'What are you doing there? Are you guarding the Madonna (whose statue was just above him)?' He replied: 'I know what I am doing, but I fear very much that the Grand Master knows not what he is doing. They are firing away; but to what purpose? It can only alarm women and children.

'It would be far better if the Council would consider and verify whether they have sufficient forces to resist an assault which the French are capable of attempting this very night; as for me, I am of opinion that all the Bailiffs and Knights, as well as the Grand Master, lost their heads when they refused water to Bonaparte. The entire country is now in possession of the enemy; what can be worse? Do they wish the city should be taken and sacked, our churches profaned, our wives and daughters violated, and ourselves killed?'

Continuing my route homewards, Torregiani remarked: 'Instead of sighing as you do, it would be better for you to tell me frankly what is your opinion, for I have told you mine, as to what we Maltese should do under these circumstances.' 'To rely with confidence on the operations of the Order, as good and faithful subjects,' I replied.

'What? Sacrifice ourselves for a handful of degenerate and panic-stricken Knights, who know not how to defend, govern, or command us!' 'It is useless,' I replied, 'for you to address these words to me, for I am of no account.' 'To whom, then, should they be addressed?' 'My duty, like yours,' I observed, 'is to respect authority, and to keep silent.'

'Well and good; if you intend to keep silent, I shall not, and from this moment I shall go and seek the Jurists, and ascertain what they are doing.' We thereupon separated, and I retired to my house.'

I obtained but little sleep during the night, and at dawn was informed that two of the forts which defend the entrance to the harbour ('St. Elmo' and 'Ricasoli') had hoisted the white flag. Anxious to ascertain how this had come to pass, I went to the Palace, and there met the chamberlain, Ligondez, who had been with the Grand Master the whole night, and received from him the following account, which was confirmed by the equerry, Rouyer, who not only knew all that had passed in the Council, where he had personally assisted, but also what had happened outside in the city. Upon reaching the top of the Palace staircase, Ligondez addressed me as follows: 'You see we are all lost, for no doubt you have heard that the Grand Master has sent an envoy to demand a suspension of hostilities.' 'But how,' I asked, 'is such suspension asked for? Has the enemy made an attack during the night?' 'No,' he replied; 'but the Maltese, fearing an assault, have begged the Grand Master to ask for a suspension of arms.' 'What Maltese do you mean? Are they those who have taken up arms to defend the place?' 'No,' he answered; 'they were three of the Notables of the city who attend the Council board, and in the name of all the Maltese presented a petition to that effect, signed by about forty individuals.' Not sufficiently satisfied with these particulars, I proceeded towards the Grand Master's apartments, and just as I entered the first ante-chamber, I met the equerry, Rouyer, who asked me if I had heard what had happened during the past night, when I related what Ligondez had told me.

To this Rouyer replied: 'You know only part of our unfortunate history; come, and I will tell you the rest.' I followed him into a corner of the balcony, and there he told me what follows:—

'After the arrival of the first division of the French fleet off the grand harbour, I noticed the great anxiety of the Grand Master, as he feared a revolution in the country, and imagined that the French were in secret communication with traitors in the place. I endeavoured to discover whence he obtained this imaginary belief, and I became persuaded that it was due to his weak and suspicious character.

[1] This conversation which passed between Doublet and Torregiani, and is so suggestive, has been given in detail, owing to the circumstance that the latter took an important part in the negotiations between the Grand Master and the people's deputies later on during that day.

'He also believed that the slaves and prisoners would immediately rise in revolt the moment the Fortress was attacked. "But is your Eminence sure that this attack will take place?" I asked. To which he replied: "No, I cannot say positively, but I believe so."

'You are no doubt also aware, that he had a suspicion that Caruson had been working hard to create a powerful party, among whom there were supposed to be many Knights, and at their head Ransijat, and that those who supplied the list of suspects were anxious that they should be placed under arrest, but that His Eminence had refused, for the reason that most of them occupied the most important offices in the service of the Order, and many of them possessed his intimate confidence.

'The Grand Master, moreover, could not believe the majority capable of such delinquency, although he had doubts about a few of them.

'... I was present' (Rouyer went on to say) ' when Ligondez by order of Rouyer came to ask the Grand Master whether it was necessary for you to stay the whole night in the secretary's office.' I interrupted the equerry at this point in order to repeat the surprising conversation which I had had with the advocate, Torregiani. 'This advocate' (he then observed) 'has played a rôle during the past night, and from the information which I have received from the Batavian Consul, at whose residence part of the events took place, and from the auditor, Schembri, who was one of the Assembly of Notables, I am enabled to relate to you what happened in the order they occurred.

'Torregiani, upon quitting his post, repaired to the University, where ten or twelve Maltese Notables had assembled, to ascertain something of the unfortunate and difficult situation of the place. The ex-auditor, Muscat, and Baron Mario Testaferrata were there, also Guido, son of Donat Guido of the Anglo-Bavarian Langue, who, although of inferior rank, was allowed admission, and subsequently harangued the Assembly with much audacity. For more than two hours Muscat and Guido discoursed without coming to any decision or practical conclusion. Each in turn made proposals, but no one came forward to put them into execution. At ten p.m. Guido then proposed to draft a Petition addressed to the Grand Master and Council, advocating that an envoy be dispatched to the Commander-in-Chief of the French army soliciting a suspension of hostilities, and to ask whether the French were at war with the Order or with the Maltese. Guido offered to be one of those who should be selected to present the Petition to the Grand Master in full council. After a slight modification which was suggested in the wording, and the Petition having been duly drawn up, it was proposed that the Batavian Consul (a Maltese) should present it. The Consul, whilst receiving the deputation politely, and not disapproving of their action, could not, as a foreign Consul accredited to the Grand Master, undertake the presentation, but permitted the registration of the Petition in the archives of the Chancellery, in order that should it not be taken into consideration, there would be proof existing that the Maltese Nation was ignorant of the reason which had caused the French Nation to declare war against them. Thereupon four of the Assembly were selected to present the Petition, the choice falling upon Don Mario Testaferrata, Councillor Bonanni, Torregiani, and Guido. As they were leaving, Schembri, the second auditor, suggested that it would be well to inform the Grand

ATTACK AND CAPTURE OF MALTA BY THE FRENCH 57

Master of the approaching deputation, and its object, so that they might not run the risk of being badly received.

'Schembri's proposal was accepted, and he was requested to undertake this delicate mission, being informed that the deputation would await his return before proceeding further.

'Although objecting, he was at last induced to undertake the duty, but instead of interviewing the Grand Master personally, he called the auditor, Bruno, from the Council, which was then sitting, and informed him of what had occurred, begging him to acquaint His Eminence thereof, and to let him, Schembri, know the result as soon as possible, in order that he might report the same to his comrades, who were waiting.

'Bruno re-entered the Council chamber, but failed to acquaint the Grand Master, Schembri waiting in vain for an answer for fully an hour.

'The deputies, becoming impatient, came on to the Palace, when Schembri informed them what had happened, and then prudently retired to his own home. They then presented themselves at the door of the Council chamber, demanding permission to be introduced, having, so they stated, a Petition to present in the name of the entire Maltese Nation, to His Eminence and sacred Council. Permission after some little time having been granted, the Deputation entered, when Guido addressed the Grand Master and Council as follows: "your Highness and Sacred Council,—Owing to the present critical circumstances, we have been appointed Deputies of the Maltese Nation to present and read to this venerable Council the Petition which I hold in my hand. We therefore ask for the necessary permission, whilst we at the same time declare our most profound respect for the person of Your Highness and the members of this venerable Council." Permission having been granted, the Petition, to the following effect, was then read: "That the Maltese had felt glorified whenever called upon to sacrifice their fortunes, their liberty, nay, even their lives, in the service of the Order and Grand Masters, when it had been a question of fighting against their natural enemies the Mahometans; but to-day they see themselves attacked by a Christian Power without knowing the reason why, and with forces against whom the Order would be powerless to resist, because already the country districts have been invaded by numberless troops who might even this very night take the city by assault, and subject it to pillage.

'"The inhabitants had consequently desired them, their humble deputies, most respectfully to supplicate the Grand Master and sacred Council to prevent this terrible misfortune, by asking the Commander-in-Chief of the French Army for an armistice until we could hear from him for what reason the French Nation, who had always been friends of the Order, and of the Maltese, had declared war against them." He concluded with this special address to the Grand Master: "I appeal to the equity of your Highness, and to your paternal heart, and supplicate with joined hands, that you would deign to look with compassion upon this unfortunate country, which has always prayed for your prosperity and that of the Order."

'The Grand Master assured the deputation that their Petition would be taken into consideration. They were to hand it over to Auditor Bruno and retire, so that the Council might deliberate more freely.

'Upon leaving the Council chamber, Guido remarked that he would wait for the decision of the Council, and convey it to the Assembly, who would be anxiously looking for their return.

'The discussion lasted for more than an hour and a half. Some of the councillors called this action of the Maltese seditious, and blamed the Grand Master for receiving them, desiring their arrest; others considered the step sufficient proof that these individuals were in active communication with the enemy, that consequently they should be arrested, and their papers seized; others, again, recommended the Grand Master and Council to take refuge in one of the cavaliers near Porta Reale, which command the city, as the Palace was no longer safe, from whence these rebels could be brought to reason.

'At last two members of the Maltese deputation, Guido and Bonanni (Testaferrata and Torregiani having left), asked to be readmitted to the Council chamber and learn what had been determined regarding their mission. Whilst all this was happening a report was brought to the Grand Master, that two young Knights at Cottonera had been murdered, and, as a general rising of the people was feared, it was then decided by the members present to ask for a truce. His Eminence then sent me to Monsieur de Fremeaux, the Batavian Consul, to request him to be the bearer of the letter; but he, owing to his age and infirmities, was obliged to decline, permitting, however, one of his official staff, Monsieur Mélan, to take his place, granting him for the occasion the official title of Chancellor of the Consulate.'

Mélan arrived on board *L'Orient* for the purpose of a parley at 9 a.m. of the 11th June, requesting on behalf of the Grand Master a suspension of arms, and by the same opportunity Miari, secretary of the Grand Master, forwarded the following letter addressed to the ex-Knight Dolomieu, one of the *savants* accompanying the expedition [1]:—

[Translation.]

Under the distressing circumstances in which we find ourselves placed, His Highness the Grand Master authorises me to recall myself to your memory.

His Highness being informed how great in former days was the affection you entertained for our Order, and being aware of the constant attachment, even in these later years, which you have preserved for it, notwithstanding that your scientific attainments called you elsewhere, and knowing the friendship and confidence in which you are held by the incomparable General Bonaparte, requests that in the negotiations which the Grand Master and Council are about to open with him, you will be pleased to exercise your good offices for the welfare of this Order, which your past zeal on its behalf encourages them to hope for.

Your knowledge and ability will indicate to you what line of argument would be suitable for this Order to adopt, considering the painful losses and misfortunes which it has suffered during the past nine years. I do not therefore stop to suggest what you might solicit for us from your

[1] Ransijat's *Siege*, p. 119.

famous General. The reliance which the Grand Master, as well as myself, place in you is based in great measure upon your efficiency and zeal, which we trust will obtain from the generosity and loyalty of the French such conditions which you would desire for yourself, if unfortunately you were placed in our position. With the sincere attachment and esteem entertained for you for the past twenty years, I am, &c.,

(Signed) CAVALIERE MIARI,
His Highness's Secretary.

Malta, 11th June 1798.

Mélan returned with a verbal message from General Berthier, chief staff officer, that the commander-in-chief would, about midday, send an official to the Grand Master to arrange for the armistice demanded.

Doublet informs us that about midday he was sent for by the Grand Master and ordered to await the arrival of the envoy from Bonaparte, who soon after appeared in the person of General Junot, accompanied by Poussielgue and ex-Commandeur Dolomieu, followed by a number of Knights, in the midst of whom was Ransijat, a great friend of Dolomieu, who in the meanwhile had been liberated. The Grand Master, with the Bailli des Pennes, the Bailli Tommasi, and two others, Grand Crosses, forming the so-styled State Congregation, sat in council to receive the envoy.

Junot, upon entering the presence, handed the following letter to the Grand Master:—

Liberty—Equality—French Republic.

To His Excellency the Grand Master of St. John of Jerusalem.

In consequence of the demand which your Excellency has made for a suspension of arms, the Commander-in-Chief has ordered his first aide-de-camp, the Chief of Brigade [Junot], to attend upon your Eminence, and has authorised him to conclude and sign a suspension of arms. I beg your Excellency to be assured of the desire I have to proffer to you marks of esteem, which I entertain for you.

(By order of the Commander-in-Chief.)

The Bailli des Pennes then, turning towards the Grand Master, inquired what should be the preamble of this act of suspension of arms, when Junot remarked: 'There is no occasion for a preamble, four lines will be sufficient, and Poussielgue will draw them up,' which was accordingly done in the following words:—

Article I.

A suspension of arms for twenty-four hours is arranged between the French Republican army, commanded by General Bonaparte, represented by the Chief of Brigade Junot, first aide-de-camp, and His Highness and the Order of St. John of Jerusalem, to count from six o'clock this evening, the eleventh of June 1798, to six o'clock to-morrow evening, the twelfth of the same month.

Article II.

During these twenty-four hours, Deputies will be sent on board *L'Orient* to arrange for the capitulation.
Made in duplicate.

(Signed) JUNOT.   (Signed) HOMPESCH.

By order of the commander-in-chief the powers granted to Junot were precise. 'He was only to agree and sign an armistice, if, as a Preliminary, His Eminence consented to negotiate for the surrender of the Fortress.'

Doublet's narrative is now continued :

It was then arranged that Deputies should proceed at once on board *L'Orient*, and, meeting Auditor Bruno, he informed me that the Maltese had requested the Grand Master, when nominating such Deputies who were to accompany Bonaparte's envoy on board for the purpose of executing the act of capitulation, that he would appoint four of the Notables of the Maltese Nation.

That in consequence, Baron Mario Testaferrata, the Auditor Benoît Schembri, the ex-Auditor Muscat, and Dr. F. T. Torregiani, had been chosen for the People, and for the Order, the Bailli Frisari, and the Knight Bosredon Ransijat, to whom was added the Chevalier de Amati. The Advocate Torregiani having been sent on a Mission to calm the excited inhabitants at Burmola, could not be found in time, and the Councillor Bonanni was substituted in his stead. It was then that I (Doublet) also received orders from His Eminence to accompany the Deputation, and render it any assistance that might lie in my power. We accordingly started in company with Junot, his suite, and Giuseppe Guido, proceeding as far as Floriana on foot. There Junot mounted on horseback, and the Deputies entered Calesses, and all proceeded together as far as Porte des Bombes, where we separated, the former joining the French Head-Quarters on the San Giuseppe road, and the latter proceeding by Pietà to St. Julian's, where for want of a conveyance to the flagship we had to remain until 11 p.m. After a rough passage we reached *L'Orient* about midnight, to find that Bonaparte and his staff had retired for the night, but within half an hour the interview was granted. Bonaparte personally drafted the articles, which out of consideration for the honour of the Knights, he desired should be called a Convention. Ex-Auditor Muscat asked for an additional article, to the effect that the exceptions and privileges of his Nation should be guaranteed.

Bonaparte, much amused, declared that 'privileges no longer existed, nor corporations, and that the law was the same for all.' The Bailli Frisari had some scruples in signing the Convention, and requested his colleague Ransijat to be his interpreter with the General. He desired to reserve by a memorandum under his signature the rights of his sovereign the King of Naples on the Isle of Malta, believing that if he did not do so he would be punished, by the confiscation of his commanderies. 'You may,' replied Bonaparte, 'make use of all the reserve you please, we shall be ready to render them null and void by cannon-shot.' The discussion being ended, the following Convention was signed :—

ATTACK AND CAPTURE OF MALTA BY THE FRENCH 61

[Translation.]

On board *L'Orient*,[1]
12th June 1798.

    Convention agreed upon, between the French Republic, represented by the Citizen Bonaparte, Commander-in-Chief, of the one part, and the Order of the Knights of St. John of Jerusalem, represented by the Bailly Torino Frisari, the Commander Bosredon Ransijat, Baron Mario Testaferrata, Dr. Nicolo Muscat, Advocate Benedetto Schembri, and Councillor Bonanni, of the other part—with and through the mediation of His Catholic Majesty, King of Spain, represented by the Knight Felipe de Amati, his *chargé d'affaires* in Malta.

    Art. 1. The Knights of the Order of St. John of Jerusalem will surrender to the French Army the city and forts of Malta. They renounce in favour of the French Republic the rights of sovereignty and ownership which they have over the city, as well as over the Islands of Malta, Gozo, and Comino.

    Art. 2. The French Republic will exercise its influence at the Congress of Rastadt, in order to obtain for the Grand Master during his lifetime a principality equivalent to that which he now loses, and in the meanwhile, it hereby engages itself to pay to him an annual pension of 300,000 francs; two years' pension will also be paid to him as an indemnity for his furniture or private effects; he will retain during the time that he remains in Malta the military honours that he has hitherto enjoyed.

    Art. 3. The French Knights of the Order of St. John of Jerusalem at present in Malta, certified by the Commander-in-Chief, may return to their native land; their residence in Malta shall, however, be considered as if in France. The French Republic will exercise its good offices with the Cisalpine, Roman, Ligurian, and Swiss Republics, in order that this article may have common effect regarding the Knights of such Nations respectively.

    Art. 4. The French Republic will grant a pension of 700 francs during life to French Knights actually in Malta, such pension to be increased to 1,000 francs to Knights above the age of 60. The French Republic will employ its good offices with the Cisalpine, Roman, Ligurian, and Swiss Republics, in order to secure like pensions to the Knights of such Nations respectively.

    Art. 5. The French Republic will endeavour to obtain from the other Powers of Europe the preservation of the properties and legal rights situate in such States belonging to the Knights.

    Art. 6. The Knights shall retain all their private property which they possess in the Islands of Malta and Gozo.

    Art. 7. The inhabitants of Malta and Gozo shall continue to enjoy as in the past the free exercise of the Apostolic and Roman Catholic Religion; they shall preserve their property, and the privileges they now possess. No extraordinary contributions shall be imposed.

    Art. 8. All civil Acts passed under the Government of the Order shall be valid, and be executed accordingly.

[1] *Corres. de Nap. I*, vol. iv. p. 137.

A HISTORY OF MALTA

Signed in duplicate on board *L'Orient*, off Malta, 12th June 1798.
(Signed) BONAPARTE.   (Signed) COMMANDEUR BOSREDON RANSIJAT.
           „ BARON MARIO TESTAFERRATA.
           „ DOTTORE G. NICOLO MUSCAT.
           „ DOTTORE BEN. SCHEMBRI.
           „ THE COUNCILLOR F. T. BONANNI.
           „ BAILLI DI TORINO FRISARI—saving the rights of High Dominions belonging to my sovereign, as King of the Two Sicilies.
           „ CAVALLIERE FELIPE DE AMATI.

CONDITIONS TO BE OBSERVED IN THE EXECUTION OF THE CONVENTION FOR THE SURRENDER OF THE CITY AND FORTRESS OF MALTA TO THE FRENCH.[1]

Art. 1. This day the 12th June 1798, Forts Manoel, Tigné, St. Angelo, Burmola fortifications, Cottonera, and Vittoriosa will be delivered over to the French troops at midday.

Art. 2. To-morrow the 13th June 1798, Forts Ricasoli, St. Elmo, and the works of Valetta and Floriana, and others, will be transferred to the French troops at midday.

Art. 3. French officers will this day attend upon the Grand Master at 10 a.m., and receive his orders to the respective Commanders of the various forts and positions, for the said delivery—they will be accompanied by a Maltese officer. There shall be as many officers as there are forts to be handed over.

Art. 4. The same dispositions as those referred to above, will be applicable for the occupation of the Forts and the works by the French troops, to be delivered to-morrow, 25 Prairial (13th June).

Art. 5. With the Forts and works will also be delivered the artillery, magazines, and papers connected with the Engineers' department.

Art. 6. The troops belonging to the Order of Malta can remain in the barracks they now occupy, until other accommodation is provided.

Art. 7. The Admiral commanding the French fleet will appoint an officer to take possession this day of the vessels of war, galleys, ships, stores, and other naval effects, belonging to the Order of Malta.

(Signed) BONAPARTE.   (Signed) BAILLI DI TORINO FRISARI.
           „ COMMANDEUR BOSREDON RANSIJAT.
           „ BARON MARIO TESTAFERRATA.
           „ DOTTORE G. NICOLO MUSCAT.
           „ DOTTORE BENEDETTO SCHEMBRI.
           „ COUNCILLOR F. T. BONANNI
           „ CABALLERO FELIPE DE AMATI.[2]

Upon the return of the Deputies to Valetta, the terms of the Convention were publicly announced from the Banca dei Giurati. A meeting of the Council was held at the same hour at the Palace, where the greatest agitation existed. Some of the members urged the Grand Master to refuse the ratification.

[1] *Corres. de Nap. I*, vol. iv. p. 138.
[2] In Napoleon's *Correspondance*, vol. iv. pp. 137, 138, the name of the first signatory is given as 'Torio' Frisari, but Mr. Hardman corrected this to TORINO Frisari.—J. H. R.

ATTACK AND CAPTURE OF MALTA BY THE FRENCH

Auditor Bruno, being referred to, represented the futility of opposition, and recommended that for the present the Grand Master should bow to circumstances, and reserve to himself the right at some future time of protesting against such an arbitrary act.

As confirmatory of Doublet's statement regarding the petition presented to the Grand Master and Council, the following so-termed ' Representation ' is taken from a MS. in the Malta Public Library, numbered 269 :—

[Translation.]

In the meanwhile, to add to the Grand Master's difficulties, a declaration was prepared and deposited at the ' Officina Giuratale,' signed by various Maltese families, who may be considered supporters of the French Republic. This declaration, in the preparation of which Messieurs Francesco Dorel and ex-Auditor Muscat took leading parts, was to the following effect :—

' We the undersigned, Jurists and Syndics of the Four Cities, together with some of the principal Ministers and Counsellors of this city of Valetta, being fully persuaded that the garrison of this Fortress is unable to resist an invasion of a warlike people, such as that which now assails us—a people who have always proved themselves to be invincible—have in a body petitioned the reigning Sovereign that he would deign to arrange terms with the Invaders, in some form or other, conformably with the generosity of a Nation which has ever listened to those who ask for peace.

' Our prayer has been benignly granted.

' And that for all future time this document should be a record of our action, we the underwritten have signed this, our Representation, with our own hands, affixing thereto the seal of this University, wherein we are all now assembled, this tenth day of June 1798.

' (Signed)
    GALEA, Jurat.
    DOREL, do.
    DELICATA, do.
    GRUNIET, do.
    GIO. NICOLA MUSCAT, Syndic.[1]
    PIETRO PAOLO TESTAFERRATA.
    BENEDETTO SCHEMBRI.[1]
    GIUSEPPE BORG OLIVIER.
    FRANCESCO BONANNI, Councillor.[1]
    SALVADORE SCIFO, Fiscal Advocate.
    FRANCESCO FIORE.
    SAVERIO MARCHESI.
    GIO. LORENZO TESTAFERRATA.
    ANTONIO VITTORIO REVEAU.
    MARIO TESTAFERRATA.[1]
    PAOLO VARISI (for self and sons).

(Signed)
    BARTOLOMEO SCIFO.
    FRANCESCO GAUCI (for self and sons).
    ISODORO MUSCAT, Chancellor of the University (for self, and the family of Xibberas).
    EMANUELE GAVINO (for Gaetano Labati, absent).
    VINCENZO MARCHESI.
    LUIGI PREZIOSI.
    ALESSANDRO SPITESI.
    GIUSEPPE GUIDO (for self and family).
    TORREGIANI (father and son).
    GIUSEPPE NICOLO ZANUNIT.
    NOTARY MICHAEL ANGELO PORTELLI.

[1] These four persons subsequently formed the Maltese portion of the deputation to Bonaparte, and signed the capitulation.

'In order that this statement may have greater effect, we have ratified it with our oath, and have delivered the document to Francesco Dorel, who in the name of the French Republic has accepted it, and further that it may possess more validity it is registered in the Archives of the Chancery of the Consulate of the Batavian Republic, this tenth day of June 1798. '(Signed) GIO. FRANCO DOREL.

'Presented and registered this tenth day of June 1798, in the Registry of the Chancery of the Consulate of the Batavian Republic in Malta.
'(Signed) B. MELAN, Under-Secretary and Acting Chancellor.'

Knowing the religious feelings of the Maltese, and their devotion to the head of the Church, Bonaparte, upon hearing from Vaubois of the submission of the ancient city of Citta Vecchia, the then episcopal residence, addressed Bishop Labini as follows :—

On board L'Orient,[1]
12th June 1798.

To the BISHOP OF MALTA,—I have observed, my Lord Bishop, with very great pleasure, the satisfactory manner in which you have conducted yourself, and the reception you have given the French troops.

You may assure your diocesans, that the Roman and Apostolic Catholic Religion will not only be respected, but her Ministers specially protected. I know of no character worthy of greater respect, and the veneration of man, than a priest, who, inspired by the true spirit of the Gospel, is persuaded that his duties oblige him to preach obedience to the temporal power, to maintain peace, tranquillity, and union in the midst of a diocese. I desire therefore, my Lord Bishop, that you will at once proceed to the city of Valetta, and by your influence, maintain calmness and tranquillity among the people. I shall also be there present this evening. I further desire that upon my arrival you will present to me all the curates, and other authorities of Valetta and the neighbouring villages.

I beg, my Lord Bishop, that you will be assured of the desire which I possess of giving you proofs of the esteem and consideration which I entertain for your person. (Signed) BONAPARTE.

In accordance with the terms of the Convention, Forts Manoel, Tigné, St. Angelo, the fortifications at Burmola, Cottonera, and Vittoriosa, were occupied by the French troops on the 12th June, and on the day following, Forts Ricasoli, St. Elmo, and the works of Valetta and Floriana were similarly occupied, when the French fleet, headed by the flagship L'Orient, entered the grand harbour, where two line-of-battle ships, one frigate, and four galleys belonging to the Order were found, whilst on the ramparts 1,200 guns, and in store 40,000 muskets and 1,500,000 lb. of powder, were captured.

Upon landing in Valetta, Bonaparte proceeded to the Banca dei Giurati, where he slept the first night, and the next day he, together with his personal staff, took up his quarters at the Palazzo Parisi.

[1] *Corres. de Nap. I*, vol. iv. p. 139.

It has been observed in this narrative that the Bailli Frisari, representing the King of the Two Sicilies, thought proper when signing the Convention to reserve the rights of sovereignty over the island on behalf of that monarch. Bonaparte, therefore, on the day following the capitulation, ordered Monsieur Garat, then Minister of the French Republic at the Neapolitan Court, to acquaint that Government of what had occurred in Malta, and that such alleged rights of sovereignty and property had now been acquired by the French Republic. He was further instructed to add, in that vein of satire in which Bonaparte was so accomplished, 'that so far as regards claim of suzerainty over the Island of Malta, which the King of Sicily advances, it shall not be refused, whenever that Monarch acknowledges the suzerainty of the Roman Republic.'[1]

Bonaparte was of opinion that any rights which the King of Sicily possessed over Malta, if any such existed, were disposed of by the capture; he was also advised by Bosredon Ransijat that such rights could only be exercised by the King of Naples in the event of the Order having *spontaneously* abandoned the island.

Owing to the excitement which existed among the people in the four cities, it was deemed advisable to offer some explanation, if not justification, for the sudden and extreme step of attacking and capturing the island, which the French Republic had resolved upon without any previous direct diplomatic communication between the two Governments.

This was conveyed to the people by a public notice, dated headquarters, 13th June, recapitulating a series of charges which the French Government had to make against the Order, to the following effect:—

EXPOSÉ OF THE CONDUCT OF MALTA TOWARDS FRANCE DURING THE REVOLUTION.[2]

1st. That from 1791 to 1795 the Maltese Government openly authorised and encouraged such of the Knights who were desirous of joining the army of the French *émigrés*.

2nd. That all *émigrés*, refugees in Malta, even when not of the Order, were admitted therein, and among others the Count de Narbonne-Fritzlar, who moreover was received with the greatest distinction.

3rd. That notwithstanding the Decree declaring all property in France, belonging to the Order, national, the Grand Master has not ceased to apportion such chimerical commanderies in France as they became vacant.

4th. That at the time of the Spanish declaration of war against France[3] all vessels of war belonging to the former Nation were permitted openly to recruit seamen, and at the request of the Court of Spain 4,000 muskets were granted to her land forces.

5th. That permission was also granted to the English in 1794 to recruit seamen in the Island, and with such devotion to their cause on the part

---
[1] *Corres. de Nap.* I, vol. iv. p. 140.
[2] *Ibid.* pp. 142, 143.   [3] In March 1793.—J. H. R.

of this government that the penalty of three years' service in the galleys was pronounced against all who violated their engagements.

6th. That Elliot, the English governor in Corsica, requiring gunpowder to preserve his conquest, obtained from the Maltese Government 200 quintals for that purpose.

7th. That up to 1796 all French trading vessels, when entering port, were compelled to lower the French flag.

8th. That in the month of last December, two French frigates, *La Justice* and *L'Artemise*, anchoring in the port, solicited permission, through their consular agent, to recruit sailors, but in vain; whilst at the same time, two English corsairs had every facility in that respect granted.

9th. That all the partisans of the French Revolution have been persecuted, many exiled without any formality, and during the month of May last, a large number were arrested and imprisoned as criminals—Vassallo, one of the most remarkable men of his country for the profound knowledge and acquirements which he possesses, being condemned to imprisonment for life.

10th. That finally, from all these facts, it results that Malta by her own acts has been the enemy of France since the commencement of the Revolution, and in a state of war against her since 1793.

Monsieur Chevalier di Amati, who had been a willing mediator between the Order and Bonaparte, as representing the Republic, and who by virtue of the offensive and defensive treaty concluded between France and Spain at St. Ildefonso on the 19th August 1796, had acted in that capacity, was now courteously dismissed with the following letter, dated the 17th June[1] :—

To the KING OF SPAIN CHARLES IV,—The French Republic has accepted the mediation of your Majesty for the capitulation of the city of Malta.

Monsr. Chevalier di Amati, your Representative in this city, has made himself acceptable to the French Republic as well as to the Grand Master. The occupation of the port of Malta by the Republic, however, necessitates the suppression of the position occupied by Monsr. di Amati.

I recommend to your Majesty, that in the disposal of your favours, you may graciously keep him in remembrance. . . .

(Signed) BONAPARTE.

The successful result of these operations, both military and diplomatic, with details of the movements by which such had been attained, was communicated by General Berthier, chief of the staff, to the French Minister for War, in a dispatch dated the 12th June. As it has been printed in full by M. De la Jonquière in his work, 'l'Expédition d'Egypte' (vol. i. p. 594), and traverses ground which has already been fully covered in this chapter, the reader is referred to the work just named.

Bonaparte on the 13th June had the candour to state in his

[1] *Corres. de Nap. I*, vol. iv. p. 166.

official dispatch to the Directory: 'I did not restrict myself to
military measures, but had recourse to several negotiations, with a
happy result.'[1] This dispatch of Bonaparte's, dated the 13th June,
was discussed at the sitting of the Directory of the 1st July, as
recorded in the 'Procès verbal' of that meeting, from which the
following is extracted:—

L'an sixième de la République Française, une et
indivisible le 13 *Messidor* (1*st July* 1798).[2]

La séance s'ouvre par la lecture d'une lettre du Général en chef
Bonaparte dattée de Malte le 25 Prairial an 6 (13th June 1798), et apportée
par un courrier extraordinaire, dans laquelle ce général annonça au
Directoire que l'armée qu'il commande vient de venger la République de la
longue suite de manœuvres hostiles que le Gouvernement de Malte s'étoit
permises contre elle; que le 21 Prairial (9th June 1798) ayant fait
demander au grand-maître la faculté de faire de l'eau dans les différents
mouillages de l'isle pour les troupes françaises qu'il commande celui-ci
repondit à cette invitation par un refus ironique, qu'en conséquence les
troupes ayant été débarquées, la ville fut cernée et attaquée; que le 24
(12th June 1798) au matin les Chevaliers de l'Ordre de St. Jean de Jérusalem ont remis à la République française la ville et les forts de Malte et
renoncé en sa faveur au droit de souvereineté et de propriété qu'ils exerçoient
tant sur cette isle que sur celle de Gozo et de Comino. Le Directoire se
hate de faire part de cette importante [?] à l'un et à l'autre Conseil du
Corps Législatif par un message qu'il leur expédie de suite.

(Signed) LA REVELLIÈRE LÉPEAUX.
,, TREILHARD.
,, MERLIN.
,, BARRAS.

So fell the institution of the Knights Hospitallers, for, in the
words of De Caro, 'War with religious sentiment had ceased to be
useful, and the Order of St. John of Jerusalem no longer fulfilled the
obligations for which it had been founded, and under which it had
flourished. The fatal stab was not given by Bonaparte's sword, he
only executed the sentence. Its fate was already decreed by the
change which had taken place, not only in opinions, but in the
altered circumstances of the times and the conditions of society.'

Various theories have been advanced as to the cause which rendered Malta so easy a conquest by Bonaparte, or again, as to who
should bear the responsibility for its loss.

These opinions have differed according to the prejudices or nationality of the writers. Whilst Maltese historians have attributed the loss
of the island to the pusillanimous behaviour of the Grand Master and
cowardice of the Knights, it can incontestably be proved that its fall
was due to treachery and intrigue within the Order itself, combined,

[1] *Corres. de Nap. I*, vol. iv. p. 140. [2] Arch. Nat. AF III. 11.

as we have seen, with an imperative demand for a suspension of hostilities, followed by the act of capitulation, which was insisted upon by the Maltese citizens.

It is true that Napoleon (according to Bourrienne) stated at St. Helena that 'Malta had physical, but no moral means of resistance, and that the Knights had done nothing disgraceful'; but Bonaparte's veracity can no more be trusted on this occasion than on many others which refer to his subsequent dealings with regard to Malta. Much light is thrown upon this event by a perusal of original manuscripts which have lately come into possession of the Government of Malta, and are now lodged at the Public Library of that island. These volumes, numbered in the catalogue 417 to 421, were recently purchased in Germany by the Maltese Government, and are credibly believed to have belonged to the family of Baron de Mayer Kornau, Knight of the Order of St. John of Jerusalem, sometime secretary to the Grand Master, Hompesch. But apart from these documents, the authorities are numerous who testify to the fact that the fall of Malta was due to a conspiracy within the fortress, aided and abetted by renegades of the Order, who branded Hompesch with cowardice for the purpose of hiding their own apostasy and treachery; and that it was owing to Russian intrigues, to a schism in the Order which followed, and to the political disturbances of the entire Continent of Europe at the time, that the honour of Hompesch was not then fully vindicated.

Capefigue, in his work entitled 'Europe during the Consulate and Empire of Napoleon,' vol. i. p. 64, informs us that

to accomplish this odious and treacherous design of capturing Malta, certain *felonious Knights*, some time before the expedition to Egypt started, entered into correspondence with the Director Barras, with this object in view. That the ruin of the Order of Malta had been decided upon a long time previously, and that for this purpose Poussielgue was dispatched to Malta, provided with letters of introduction addressed to *disloyal members of the Order*, which were supplied by the *ex-Knights Dolomieu* and *Picault de Mornas*, the latter a captain in the Engineers, who two years previously had deserted the Order, and had joined Bonaparte in Italy.

The letters from Dolomieu, it would appear, were procured by Talleyrand and forwarded to Bonaparte, then at Passeriano, under date of the 8th October 1797, with instructions 'that they should be sent on to Malta, on successive occasions, for the purpose of facilitating the expedition which he (Bonaparte) had projected.'[1] Poussielgue was made the bearer of a *portion* of the letters to Malta, a mission which he faithfully fulfilled; 'for by bribery and promises he succeeded

---

[1] See *Correspondance inédite officielle et confidentielle de Napoléon Bonaparte*, vol. vii. p. 282, and a dispatch from a secret British agent on the same subject, to be found in Capefigue's *l'Europe pendant la Révolution*, vol. iv. p. 120.

in seducing many *unworthy Knights* of their allegiance, amongst others *Bardonenche*, who commanded the artillery.'[1]

It would appear that Poussielgue succeeded in seducing the allegiance not only of certain Knights, but also of several members of the Grand Master's *personal and domestic suite*, namely, his secretary, equerry, and chamberlain, who, as Bonaparte officially acknowledged, 'had supplied him with valuable information during the previous six months.'

By an order (No. 4) of Bonaparte's, issued from head-quarters, Malta, on the 13th June 1798,[2] it was stipulated in Article 3 'that all Knights and inhabitants subjects of a Power at war with France, such as Russia and Portugal, should leave Malta within forty-eight hours'; and by Article 4, 'all Knights being less than sixty years of age should quit the island within three days.' But to this general order an appendix was attached, wherein a list is given of members of the Order of Malta exempted from such expulsion by order of the commander-in-chief, and the reasons therein given, which merit careful attention :—

Ransijat, Secretary of the Treasury; Fay, Commissary of Fortifications, officer of artillery; Breuvart, priest; *Rouyer, chief equerry*; Sandelleau, priest; *Greicher, chamberlain;* Fim, priest; Beaufort, priest; Dacla, *servant d'armes*; Toussard, Engineers; Lascaris, two brothers; Gras, priest; Bœuf, priest; *Doublet, secretary of Grand Master*; Medecis; Stendardi.*

* '*Almost all have furnished me within the last six months useful notes*, or have made patriotic donations towards the expenses incurred for the descent upon England.

'The last two are *Tuscan Knights* who have made patriotic donations towards the expenses incurred for the descent upon England.

(Signed) BONAPARTE.'

A glance at the offices which these members of the Order of St. John filled, or of the trade or profession of the remainder, must leave the *amount* of their patriotic donations very problematical. It would rather appear that these supposititious donations were intended to serve as a screen for the avowed cause of their reward.

In the MS. 421, already referred to, there appears a document amongst De Mayer's papers styled a 'Relation,' which bears the stamp of having been officially drawn up by order of the Grand Master, Hompesch, giving a list, with the rank or position, of the various members therein styled traitors to the Order of St. John. This document is dated Trieste, the 15th September 1798, and goes on to say:

[1] See Capefigue's *l'Europe pendant le Consulat et l'Empire*, vol. i. pp. 64, 65.
[2] *Corres. de Nap. I*, vol. v. pp. 145, 146.

Without fear of contradiction, the first place in the list of Traitors should be given to Commandeur Ransijat, and next, having regard to the importance of their positions, should be named Commandeur Bardonenche, commanding the Artillery; to Commissary de Fay, in charge of the Fortifications and Fountains; to Toussart, commanding the Engineers; to Picault de Mornas; and to Commandeur Dolomieu (the two latter being embarked on board the French fleet), the former at one time commanding the Engineers in the island, and who now recently directed the landing operations of the French troops.

To the above should be added Doublet, first clerk in the French branch of the Secretariat; the French Consul, Caruson, born in Malta; some conventual priests; and Poussielgue, the German Consul, cousin of the envoy of that name. . . . Among the Maltese (it proceeds to say) there should be mentioned Baron Dorrail, the two brothers Schembri, Guido, Herri, Caruana the Bishop's secretary, his Assessor Biagio Bourgeois, Notary Gavino Bonnvita, Sachet, and a number of advocates, at the head of whom should be named the ex-Auditor Muscat, besides nearly all the Maltese Nobility.

Regarding this Bosredon Ransijat, who has been stigmatised by Hompesch as the prime mover and instigator of the machinations which were to result in the destruction of the Order, Parisot has contributed the following sketch in the 'Biographie Universelle,' which also confirms the treasonable action of others implicated:—

Bosredon de Ransijat was born at Combraille, in Auvergne, in 1743, of noble family. When twelve years old he was sent to Malta, and became page to Grand Master Pinto, remaining three years in that capacity. He then returned to his native country in order to complete his education, which had been sadly neglected.

When twenty-four years old he returned to Malta, becoming eventually a Commander and Grand Cross in the Order of St. John, and was finally appointed to the administration of the Finances, and styled Secretary of the Treasury, occupying this post at the time of the French Revolution, by which Government five-eighths of the revenues of the Order were confiscated. Bosredon was less unsympathetic than many of the Knights to the new order of things in France, and showed himself to be a partisan of the Jacobin faction; but this, nevertheless, did not prevent him retaining his credit at the palace of the Grand Masters, the keys of the Treasury, some friends, and many flatterers.

This state of affairs continued during the five years which elapsed between the date of the Decree of the Legislative Assembly, nationalising the Domains of the Order of Malta in France, and the commencement of 1798.

Bosredon, representing the French disaffected, and Bardonenche that of Spain, had for some time been in direct communication with France, through the medium of the French Consul (Caruson), whom the Order tolerated in Malta, and with the Commandeur Dolomieu, their friend, who did not occupy his time exclusively with mineralogy!

Bonaparte sent Poussielgue, under a frivolous pretext, on a mission to

ATTACK AND CAPTURE OF MALTA BY THE FRENCH

Malta early in 1798, but really in order to complete the concoction of a plot which had been devised for the destruction of the Order. The Chevalier de St. Tropez joined also in the conspiracy, together with many other French and Spanish Knights. The Consuls of Holland (De Fremeaux) and Spain (Di Amati) were circumvented in such a manner (both countries being allies of France) that they became not silent witnesses of the events, but rather favoured them.

Upon the Grand Master's refusal to Bonaparte's demand for a supply of water to the Fleet, Bosredon threw off the mask, and declared that, having been born French, he would never fight against his country, and requested to be placed in confinement, and was consequently imprisoned in Fort St. Angelo.

During the negotiations with Bonaparte which followed, the Spanish *chargé d'affaires* (Di Amati) required that Bosredon should be recalled from St. Angelo, and lead the deputation to Bonaparte. Hompesch deemed it advisable to consent, and Bosredon, with two Bailiffs of the Order and four Maltese Notabilities (despite the statutes of the Order, which interdicted them from participating in politics), concluded the capitulation.

Bosredon, after the capitulation of the Island to the British, returned to France, where his services were no longer required. He died about 1812, sixty-nine years old, in an obscure corner of Auvergne. In his last published work he declares very positively that he merited the confidence (protection) of Bonaparte, for he had rendered that great man all the services that it had been in his power to give.

Confirming much of the preceding, there is a 'secret' letter amongst the 'Castlereagh Papers' (vol. i. p. 268), dated Rastadt, 26th July 1798, which says : 'You are doubtless aware that Malta has been obtained and delivered through the medium of French officers (Knights of Malta), who for the price of their good and loyal services! have had their names removed from the list of proscribed emigrants (permitting them to return to France), and have been pensioned.'

There may also be quoted an extract from a MS. in the possession of Sir Gerald Strickland, formerly Chief Secretary to the Malta Government, believed to have been written by an ancestor of his, one of the Scibberas family :—

[Translation.]

At the interview which took place on board *L'Orient* on the 11th June 1798, between Bonaparte and the Maltese Plenipotentiaries, for the purpose of signing the Deed of Convention, Bonaparte informed them that he had that day dined at Nigret, in the village of Zurrico, with the Spanish *chargé d'affaires*, the Chevalier Amati (through whose mediation the Convention was subsequently arranged, and one of the *signatories* thereto), and that he had there met and spoken with certain *other Knights, his adherents*, who had come out from Valetta for that purpose, and had been informed by them that the Fortress was not in a position to hold out.

Although the treachery of members of the Order was the principal factor in the surrender of the fortress to Bonaparte, yet the civil population must bear its share of the responsibility in the premature capitulation of Valetta. The part which the populace took in this occurrence, which has been related by Doublet and confirmed by others, is also corroborated by a MS. in the De Mayer Collection (Vol. 421, Malta Public Library), drawn up in the form of a protest by the exiled Knights who accompanied Hompesch to Trieste. The document is entitled, 'Observations on the Manifest issued by the Priory of Russia,' from which the following extract is taken :—

[Translation.]

In the midst of the tumult, there appeared before the Grand Master and Council a deputation composed of Judges and of all the Magistrates of the People, and this is the discourse which they addressed to their Sovereign ! !

'Malta is attacked; it is impossible for the Order to defend it, and you are about proceeding to expose our lives and our property to the fury of an irritated conqueror. We now declare to you in the name of the People, whom we represent, that if you do not this moment sue for peace, the People will do so without you.'

Another proof of the treason and treachery which prevailed prior to the arrival of the expedition off Malta, as well as during the attack on the fortress, is to be found in Bonaparte's own admission, together with General Caffarelli's observations, which are recorded by Bourrienne.

Bourrienne joined Bonaparte at Leoben on the 19th April 1797, the day after the preliminaries of peace between France and Austria had been signed, and was at once placed by Bonaparte at the head of his Cabinet as private and confidential secretary, and at pages 64 and 65 of vol. ii. of his Memoirs he informs us that 'the fall of Malta was due to treason within the Fortress, *Bonaparte openly declaring* that it was at Mantua, by means of *private correspondence*, that he had captured Malta'; adding further, 'that when Bonaparte and General Maximilian de Caffarelli du Falga, who commanded the Engineers, were inspecting the military works after capitulation, the latter remarked to Bonaparte *in Bourrienne's presence*, "By my faith, General, we have been most fortunate in finding there was *somebody within the city* ready to open the gates for us !"'

That there were many within the city willing to open the gates is also mentioned *officially* by the English consul at Malta, Mr. Williams, who on the 30th June 1798 (eighteen days after the capitulation) informed the British Government 'that Bonaparte had been assured that there were 4,000 Maltese in his favour, and that most of the

ATTACK AND CAPTURE OF MALTA BY THE FRENCH

French Knights were publicly known to be so'; and pertinently added: 'I do believe the Maltese have given the Island to the French, in order to get rid of the Knighthood.'[1]

Nor can it be surprising that such was the case, for if ever there were an instance in which a people was justified in rebelling against their rulers (having regard to what is recorded in Chapter I of this work), it was that of the Maltese against the tyrannical and dissolute reprobates who formed the Government of the Order of St. John.

[1] Colonial Office Records, Malta, No. 1.

CHAPTER VIII

THE FRENCH GOVERNMENT OF MALTA

(From the 12th June 1798 to the 2nd September 1798)

On the day following the capitulation General Berthier was instructed to order citizens Monge and Berthollet[1] to visit the Mint, the treasury of the Church of St. John, and other places where it was thought that precious articles might be found. Their precise instructions were as follows[2]:—

[Translation.]

Head Quarters, 13th *June* 1798.

Citizen Berthollet, Comptroller of the Army, along with a paymaster's clerk, will remove all the gold, silver, and precious stones which may be found in the Church of St. John, and other places, dependencies of the Order of Malta, the silver plate in the Inns, and that of the Grand Master. They will cause to be melted during the course of to-morrow all the gold into ingots, which will be placed in the military chest following the Army. An inventory of all the precious stones will be made by them, and such precious stones shall be placed under seal in the military chest following the Army. They will sell to the merchants of the place silver plate to the extent of 250,000 to 300,000 francs against payment in gold or silver coin, which shall be placed in the military chest following the Army.

The remainder of the silver plate shall be placed in the Paymaster's military chest, who will leave the same at the Mint, there to be coined, and its produce remitted to the Paymaster of the Division, and to be used for its maintenance. It must be specified what such ought to realise, in order that the Paymaster may be held accountable for the same. Such articles as may be necessary for the performance of Divine Service in St. John's, and other Churches, can be left.

(Signed) BONAPARTE.

In compliance with these instructions, the following statement of treasure and money found in St. John's Church, the Palace, and in Gozo was drawn up and furnished to Bonaparte :—

---

[1] Two of the most illustrious of the *savants* accompanying Bonaparte.—J. H. R.
[2] De la Jonquière, *Expédition d'Egypte*, vol. i. p. 622 ; *Corres. de Nap. I*, vol. iv. p. 147.

THE FRENCH GOVERNMENT OF MALTA 75

ÉTAT DES TRÉSORS TROUVÉS À MALTE.[1]

Trésor de l'Église de Saint Jean.

Diamants	Écus de Malte	59,943'00	
Or	,,	97,470'00	
Argent	,,	263,025'00	
	sc.	420,438'00	Equal to livres 1,019,051

Trésor de l'Église de Saint Antoine dépendant de Saint Jean.

Diamants	Écus de Malte	703'00	
Or	,,	550'00	
Argent	,,	7,410'00	
	sc.	8,663'00	Equal to livres 20,786

Matières d'or et d'argent dans le Palais du Grand Maître.

Or	Écus de Malte	2,334'06	
Argent	,,	50,642'02	
	sc.	52,976'08	Equal to livres 127,144

Il existait en outre dans la caisse de la banque juratale de l'île de Gozo
    Écus de Malte 7,578'09   Equal to livres 18,189

                                    Total livres 1,185,170

Soon after the arrival of the expedition in Egypt, a more detailed report of the treasure seized in Malta was forwarded to the Commissaries of the National Treasury in Paris by Paymaster-General Estève, under date of Cairo, 21st September 1798. It amounted in all to 1,227,129 livres or francs.[2]

On the 13th June, Desaix was ordered to evacuate all the forts and positions he had occupied in the cities, which would be replaced by the troops under Vaubois. Those under Desaix were to return to Marsa Scirocco and neighbouring villages, and be ready to embark on the 16th, by which time all the transports and ships of war would be revictualled and watered.[3]

On the 14th, orders were issued for detachments of the 41st

---

[1] De la Jonquière, vol. i. p. 644.
[2] As the full list of the objects seized by the French is given by M. de la Jonquière in vol. iii of his work, I have thought it needless to reprint it here. The silver gates of the Church of St. John in Valetta escaped the French only owing to the fact that they were painted over in time.—J. H. R.
[3] *Corres. de Nap. I*, vol. iv. p. 149.

Regiment to land and join the garrison, as well as the 2nd and 3rd Battalions of the 19th of the Line, whereby the garrison left in Malta was to be composed of the following:—

6th Line	518
7th Light Infantry	900
19th Line (2nd battalion)	700
41st	285[1]
80th Line	650
	3,053

besides five companies of artillerymen.

On the 14th June, two days after the capitulation, General Dugua, for the purpose of obtaining volunteers to accompany the expedition to Egypt, passed in review what remained of the troops belonging to the Order. His report on the various corps shows that the totals were as follows: Guards of the Grand Master, 148; regiment of chasseurs, 434; battalion of the galleys, 106; battalion of the ships of war, 183; Maltese Regiment, 60. The last three were the most soldierly. The men of the chasseurs were small, 'hideous,' and barefooted. Twenty-four men of the Maltese Regiment offered to enter the French service and leave the island.[2]

Bonaparte in his dispatch of the 17th June informed the Directory that 'the original Treaty between the Order of Malta and Russia had been discovered and seized, and was now forwarded to them.' It had been ratified only five days, and the courier engaged to carry it to St. Petersburg proved to be the same who, two years previously, had been arrested on a similar mission at Ancona. Bonaparte sarcastically added that the thanks of the Emperor of Russia were due to France for having occupied the island, whereby his treasury would save 400,000 roubles; and that evidently his [the Czar's] interests were better understood by France than by him himself. Meanwhile, if the Emperor's object had been to prepare the way for establishing himself in the island, His Majesty would have been wiser had he observed a little more secrecy in his proceedings, and not allowed his project to be discovered so easily; but all the same, he concluded, 'be the reasons what they may, we have now in the centre of the Mediterranean the strongest fortress in Europe, and it will cost those dear who dislodge us.'[3]

The *Sensible*, Captain François Bourdé, sailed for Toulon on the 18th; on the 26th, at 4 p.m., she was observed off the island of Marittimo by H.M.S. *Seahorse*, Captain E. J. Foote. A chase of

---
[1] The 41st can have left only a detachment.—J. H. R.
[2] For the full report see De la Jonquière, vol. i. p. 592.—J. H. R.
[3] *Corres. de Nap. I*, vol. iv. p. 163; De la Jonquière, vol. i. p. 646.

twelve hours in the direction of Malta, with a close action of eight minutes, followed, resulting in her surrender. General Baraguey d'Hilliers was taken to England as a prisoner of war.

On the 16th June, Bonaparte informed the Directory that the Fleet had commenced to leave the harbour, that he expected by the 18th all would be under sail for their destination, and that Vaubois, who had charge of the landing, and had conciliated the inhabitants by his wisdom and pleasant manners, would be left in command.[1]

He also stated that the Grand Master was sailing on the morrow for Trieste, that of the 600,000 francs which had been accorded him, 300,000 were retained in discharge of his debts, and that this latter sum would be covered by sale of the lands belonging to the Order in Malta, then in possession of the French. Of the remaining 300,000 francs, 100,000 had been paid in cash, and four drafts of 50,000 francs each had been drawn upon the Treasury.[2]

All the Plate so far discovered, including that of the co-Cathedral (*sic*) Church of Saint John, would not realise, it was believed, more than one million francs. This silver would be left in Malta for the requirements of the Garrison, and the fitting out of the line-of-battle ship *Saint John*, captured from the Order.[3]

During the interval of eighty-two days which elapsed between the occupation of the islands by the French (the 12th June) and the insurrection of the Maltese (the 2nd September), dissensions on the method of government arose between Regnaud de Saint Jean d'Angely, who had been appointed by Bonaparte as commissary in the administration of the civil government, and Vaubois, commander-in-chief of the military forces.

In the official correspondence which passed between Vaubois and the Directory, as well as with Bonaparte, together with that of Doublet with the Directory, there is sufficient evidence to prove that in the opinion of Vaubois the disaffection of the Maltese to the French government of the islands was to be attributed to Regnaud de St. Jean d'Angely's excessive zeal in carrying out Bonaparte's instructions; that he had, further, exceeded the authority deputed to him, and that by the severe measures adopted he had alienated the loyal feelings of the population, which at last culminated in open rebellion.

Bosredon Ransijat, who had been nominated the first President of the Government Commission, than whom no one was better able to form an opinion, has left on record the various reasons which he

[1] *Corres. de Nap. I*, vol. iv. p. 155.
[2] De la Jonquière, vol. i. p. 640.
[3] Bonaparte on June 14, 1798, wrote to General Brune at Corfu that he had captured at Malta—2 sail of the line, 1 frigate, 4 galleys, 1,200 cannon, two million (quintaux?) of powder, and 40,000 muskets (*Corres. de Nap. I*, vol. iv. p. 149).

It was falsely said that Hompesch had been bought by Bonaparte for 300,000 francs, and the promise of a pension to be paid him by France (*Mémoires du Général Baron Desvernois*, pp. 94, 96, notes). For a vindication of him, see Chap. xvii. Hompesch died in the year 1803.—J. H. R.

considered had given rise to the disaffection and revolt of the Maltese.[1] He gives no fewer than thirteen, which may be enumerated as follows:

1stly. That appeals to the Commission of Government for indemnification for depredations, and forced contributions made by the troops, received no redress. Complainants were simply informed that there were 'no grounds for discussion.'

2ndly. The monthly allowances promised to a large number of sailors and soldiers, who had sailed with the French fleet for Egypt, were never paid.

3rdly. The possessors of claims against the Order, such as Bondholders' warrants, orders for payment for articles supplied, in fact all classes of creditors, were unable to obtain payment.

4thly. All pensions, with the exception of a few enjoyed by octogenarians, who received but one month's allowance, were suspended. Daily alms, in the shape of bread to about four hundred indigent women, were stopped.

5thly. Loans advanced by the Monte di Pietà were charged at the rate of 6% interest, instead of $4\frac{1}{8}$%, and all articles pledged above the value of £4 were ordered to be sold within eight days, unless the arrears of interest were in the meanwhile paid.

6thly. Leaseholds granted for three lives were suddenly altered to a fixed term of one hundred years, thus cancelling at once many Leases, and reducing such tenants to poverty. This measure affected so many, not only in the country districts in Malta, but also in Gozo, that great discontent followed.

7thly. Immense loss caused to the people owing to the Grand Master having left the Island in debt to the extent of £40,000, and to the departure of the Knights heavily in debt, most of whom were French. There were also many families in the service of the past Government who were deprived of the means of subsistence.

8thly. Taxes levied for the erection of barracks, &c., created great discontent. The people considered that the terms of the capitulation, which exempted them from any extra contribution, had been violated.

9thly. That Sicily, whence hitherto supplies had been received, was now closed to them, owing to Quarantine, which (for political reasons) had there been established against arrivals from Malta, and further that the presence of British cruisers kept trading vessels in port, which increased the misery.

10thly. The confiscation of the greater portion of the silver plate belonging to the Cathedral at Citta Vecchia, which had been coined into money for payment of the garrison.

11thly. The fact of reducing the number of convents to one of each Order, and consequent closing of many churches.

12thly. The introduction of the form of civil marriage, and registration of births.

13thly. The defeat of the French fleet at Aboukir.

These arguments are more or less substantiated by General Vaubois in the opening chapter of his 'Journal of the Siege of Malta,' a minute record which, after the capitulation of the garrison to the British, Vaubois presented to Bonaparte (then First Consul) on the 10th November 1800.

Between the 13th and 18th June, the dates of Bonaparte's landing

[1] Bosredon Ransijat, *Journal du Siège et Blocus de Malte*, Paris, 1801, pp. 274-79.

in Valetta and approaching departure from Egypt, various 'orders' or enactments were promulgated,[1] embracing a complete reorganisation of the government of the islands, in its civil, military, and ecclesiastical departments, on the lines (according to Monsieur A. V. Arnault) of what had been established at Corfu.[2] A record of these 'orders' is interesting from the fact that to several of them may be traced the cause of public discontent which followed their promulgation, and the subsequent insurrection of the people, which occurred eleven weeks later.

On the 13th June several such 'orders' were issued, which were to have legal effect from that date.[3]

The 1st 'order' appointed a Commission in which was vested the government of the islands.

The 2nd 'order' nominated the *personnel* of the said Commission.

The 3rd 'order' decreed the expulsion of certain Knights, and subjects of nations at war with France.

The 4th 'order' contained a list of exceptions to the decree of expulsion.

The 5th 'order' ordered seals to be placed on all British, Russian, and Portuguese property.

The 6th 'order' appointed Monge and Berthollet to take an inventory of Government plate.

The first 'order' ran as follows:—
Decreed by order of Bonaparte as follows:

Art. 1. The Islands of Malta and Gozo shall be governed by a Commission of nine persons, nominated by the General Commander-in-Chief.

Art 2. Each member of this Commission in rotation shall preside for the period of six months. The Commission shall appoint a Secretary and Treasurer outside its own body.

Art. 3. Attached to this Government Commission there shall be a French Commissary.

Art. 4. This Commission shall be specially charged with the whole administration of the Islands of Malta and Gozo, and the superintendence of the receipts of all contributions (taxes), direct or indirect. It will take the necessary steps for the provisioning of these Islands. The administration of the Health Board (or Office) will be specially under its orders.

Art. 5. The Commissary-General will fix, in conjunction with the Commission, the amount which the latter will subscribe monthly to the military chest.

Art. 6. The Commission will unceasingly occupy itself in organising the Civil and Criminal Courts of Justice, approaching as near as possible to the organisation which at present exists in France. The nomination of

---

[1] *Corres. de Nap. I*, vol. iv. pp. 143–76.

[2] Extract from *Souvenirs d'un Sexagénaire*, vol. iv. p. 135. Monsieur Arnault was one of the scientists of the expedition, and selected by Bonaparte to succeed Regnaud St. Jean d'Angely as commissary; owing, however, to the latter recovering from a severe illness, Arnault returned to France, but being a passenger in the frigate *Sensible*, he was made prisoner of war upon her capture by H.M.S. *Seahorse*.

[3] *Corres. de Nap. I*, vol. iv. pp. 143–76.

Judges will require the approval of the General in command of the Division in Malta. Until such time as these Courts are so organised, the procedure thereof and the administration of the law will continue as in the past.

Art. 7. The Islands of Malta and Gozo will be divided into Cantons, the smallest to possess not less than 3,000 souls. In the city of Valetta there will be two municipalities.

Art. 8. Each Canton will be governed by a municipal body composed of five members.

Art. 9. Each Canton will have a magistrate.

Art. 10. Such magistrate will be appointed by the Commissioner, subject to the approval of the General in command of the Division in Malta.

Art. 11. All the property belonging to the Order of Malta, of the Grand Master, and of the different convents of the Knights belongs to the French Republic.

Art. 12. A Commission will be appointed composed of three members, who will form an Inventory of the said properties, and administer the same, giving an account thereof to the Commissary-General.

Art. 13. The entire body of police will be under the orders of the General in command of the Division, and the various officers under his orders.

In the second 'order' the Commander-in-Chief decrees:

Art. 1. In accordance with the decree of this day relating to the organisation of Government of these Islands, the citizens mentioned below will compose the Government Commission, viz.:

Bosredon Ransijat; Vincent Caruana, secretary to the Bishop; Charles Astor, merchant in Malta; Paolo Ciantar, merchant in Malta; Jean François Dorell, alderman; Grungo, judge in Gozo; Benedetto Schembri, magistrate; Canon Don Saverir Caruana, cotton weaver at Citta Vecchia; Christopher Frendu, notary.

Art. 2. Citizen Regnaud de Saint Jean d'Angely will be the Government Commissary on the said Commission.

Art. 3. Citizens Matthew Poussielgue, Caruson and Roussel will form the Commission created by Article 12 of the order of this date.

Art. 4. General Berthier will call a meeting of these two bodies to-morrow, and after their installation will cause them to take the oath of allegiance to the Republic, drawing up a *procès verbal* of the proceedings.

Art. 5. The Government Commission will within forty-eight hours fix the demarcations of the two city municipalities, and within five days the remainder for the Islands of Malta and Gozo.

The third 'order' requires by Art. 2 the effacing of all escutcheons within twenty-four hours, and the prohibition of wearing livery, or any other mark or title distinctive of nobility.

Art. 3. That all Knights and inhabitants, subjects of a Power at war with France, such as Russia and Portugal, will leave Malta within forty-eight hours.

Art. 4. All Knights under sixty years of age will leave Malta within three days.

The fourth 'order,' specifying the exceptions from the decree of expulsion of certain Knights, has already been referred to at p. 69.[1]

---

[1] For a full list, see *Corres. de Nap.* I, vol. iv. p. 146.—J. H. R.

The fifth 'order.' The General Commander-in-Chief decrees:
Art. 1. That on all merchandise, and on all effects belonging to English, Russian, and Portuguese merchants, seals shall be placed.
Art. 2. The Consul of the Republic is specially charged to put this order into effect.

The sixth 'order,' after requiring the chief of staff, General Berthier, to instruct citizens Monge and Berthollet to visit the mint and treasury of the Conventual Church of St. John, and other places where valuables might be stored, prescribed that an inventory thereof shall be drawn up.

Then followed these enactments, on subsequent dates:

Malta, 16*th June* 1798.

The Commander-in-Chief orders:
Art. 1. All the inhabitants of Malta have henceforth equal rights; their talents, their merit, their patriotism, their attachment to the French Republic, will alone establish any difference amongst them.
Art. 2. Slavery is abolished. All slaves known as 'buonavogli' (vagabonds) are set at liberty, and the '*Contrat*,' dishonourable to the human race, is abolished.
Art. 3. In accordance with the preceding article, all Turks who are slaves, and the property of private individuals, will be brought before the General commanding, and treated as prisoners of war, and having regard to the friendship existing between the Ottoman Porte and the French Republic, they will be sent home whenever the General in command so orders, and whenever he will have had information that the Beys consent to send to Malta all French slaves, or Maltese, who may be in his power.[1]
Art. 4. All the inhabitants of the Islands of Malta and Gozo are obliged to wear the tricolor cockade. No inhabitant of Malta can wear the French national dress, unless he has obtained special permission from the Commander-in-Chief. The Commander-in-Chief will grant the privilege of French citizenship, and permission to wear the French national dress to such inhabitants of Malta who may distinguish themselves, by their attachment to the Republic, through any brilliant act, deed of benevolence, or bravery.
Art. 5. Ten days after the publication of this present order it is prohibited to retain escutcheons either in the interior or exterior of dwellings, to seal letters with armorial bearings, or to use feudal titles.
Art. 6. The Order of Malta being dissolved, it is expressly prohibited to anyone to take the titles of Bailiff, Commander, or Knight.
Art. 7. Ten days after the publication of this present order it is prohibited to wear, under any pretext, the uniform of the corps of the ancient Order of Malta.
Art. 8. In each church will be placed the arms of the French Republic, in place of those of the Grand Master.
Art. 9. The Island of Malta belonging to the French Republic, the mission of the various plenipotentiaries has ceased.

[1] Napoleon in his *Mémoires* dictated at St. Helena (vol. ii. p. 29) states that 700 Turk and Arab slaves were freed at Malta and sent home. Desvernois (*Mémoires*, p. 97) asserts that many of them were taken into the French naval service and sailed with the fleet to Egypt.—J. H. R.

Art. 10. The functions of all foreign Consuls having ceased, they will remove the arms from over their doors, until such time as they may receive from their respective Governments their credentials to serve in the city of Malta, now a port of the Republic.

Art. 11. All foreigners arriving and living in Malta will be obliged to obey this order, be their position or rank what it may.

Art. 12. All transgressors of the above articles will be condemned, for the first offence, to a fine of ⅛ of their income; for the second offence, to three months' imprisonment; for the third, to one year's imprisonment; for the fourth offence, to banishment from the Island of Malta, and the confiscation of half their property. Ten days' interval must elapse between the repetition of the offence.

Malta, 16*th June* 1798.

Art 1. A general disarmament of all the inhabitants of Malta and Gozo will be made. Permission to carry arms will only be granted to men of well-known patriotism, and by the General commanding.

Art. 2. The organisation of the Volunteer Light Infantry in the Islands of Malta and Gozo will be continued, but this body shall be composed of men who can be depended upon, care being taken that it is officered by Patriots.

Art. 3. The signal stations between Gozo point and Malta shall be re-established.

Art. 4. The health laws of Malta shall be neither more nor less rigorous than those existing at Marseilles.

Art. 5. A company of 30 volunteers shall be formed of young men, members of the richest families, from 15 to 30 years old.

Art. 6. The General of Division will select within ten days, and report to the Commission of Government, the names of the members of the said company.

The Commission of Government will notify the same to the members selected, and ten days later they will wear an uniform and carry a sword. They will have the same uniform as the Guides, with the exception that they will carry the *aiguillette*[1] and white button.

Art. 7. Such members who may not attend the review, which will be held ten days later by the General commanding the Division, will be condemned to one year's imprisonment, and the parents holding the family property to a fine of 1,000 crowns.

Art. 8. The Commission of Government will name 60 youths of the age from 9 to 14, belonging to the richest families, who will be sent to Paris to be educated in the colleges of the Government.[2] The parents will be held liable to pay an annual allowance of 800 francs, and 600 francs for the expenses of the journey, but the sea passage will be granted free by vessels of war.

Art. 9. The Commission of Government will forward to the Commander-in-Chief a list of these youths, within twenty days at the latest; they will wear blue trousers and jackets, with red facings and white lines.

---

[1] The *aiguillette* is the shoulder-knot.—J. H. R.
[2] Of course these youths were virtually hostages. Art. 11 shows that some amount of coercion was deemed necessary to get them.—J. H. R.

They will land at Marseilles, where they will receive orders from the Minister of the Interior as to the national schools at which they are to be placed.

Art. 10. The Naval Commissary will give to the Commission of Government the names of six young Maltese belonging to the richest families, to be placed as naval apprentices for their education, and eventual eligibility to all grades of the service.

Art. 11. As education so much affects the prosperity and public safety, the parents of the youths selected as above who refuse their adherence will be condemned to pay 1,000 dollars' fine.

Art. 12. Sailors' classes will be established as in French ports, and whenever the Fleet requires sailors, and sufficient volunteers are not to be found, forced conscription of youths from 15 to 25 years of age will first be taken; if these do not suffice, then from the class of men from 25 to 35; and finally, those from 35 to 45.

Malta, 16th June 1798.

Art. 1. There will be formed in each municipality of the city of Malta, a battalion of National Guards, to consist of 900 men, wearing a green uniform, with red collars and facings, and white pipings. This National Guard will be selected from the richest members of the community, merchants, and such who are the most deeply interested in the preservation of public tranquillity.[1]

Art. 2. They will furnish daily all the police guards and patrols necessary, but never on guard in the forts.

Art. 3. The corps of light infantry will be continued.

Art. 4. The General of Division will issue regulations for the organisation of the National Guard, as well as for the light infantry, and will deliver to both the arms necessary for the service.

Art. 5. Four companies of veterans of all the old soldiers who may have served the Order of Malta, and are now incapable of active service, will be formed. The two first will, so soon as they are organised, be dispatched to hold garrison at Corfu. This present article must be executed, notwithstanding any difficulties which may arise, as my intentions are, that so large a body of men who have been in the service of the Order shall no longer remain in Malta.

Art. 6. Four companies of artillerymen shall be formed on the same footing as those previously existing, who will be employed in the coast batteries. In each company there will be a French officer and sub-officer.

Art. 7. All those individuals who may desire to form a company of 100 light infantry shall be empowered to do so. They and the officers of these companies will be retained, and from the moment they are organised the General of Division will cause them to sail and join the army.

[Another order of this date enacts that the best hospital used by the Knights is to be reserved exclusively for the French.]

---

[1] This was on the model of the National Guards in France, who, after the disturbances of 1794 and 1795, were composed of well-to-do men almost entirely.—J. H. R.

Malta, 16th June 1798.[1]

The Commander-in-Chief orders :

Art. 1. All priests and members of Religious bodies, male and female, of whatsoever nature, who are not natives of the Islands of Malta and Gozo, will be required to leave the Island, at the latest, ten days after the publication of this present order. The Bishop, having regard to his pastoral duties, will be the sole exception to this present order.

Art. 2. All curacies or benefices which by virtue of this order become vacant shall be given to natives of the Islands of Malta and Gozo, as it is unjust that foreigners should enjoy the benefits of the country.

Art. 3. Religious vows before the age of thirty shall henceforth be illegal. It is prohibited to ordain new priests until all those now living are employed.

Art. 4. Only one monastery for each Order can be allowed in Malta and Gozo. The Commission of Government, in concert with the Bishop, will name the houses where the members of the same Order may dwell. All the surplus property, beyond what is necessary for the maintenance of the said monasteries, will be employed in the alleviation of the poor. All private foundations, all houses of secular Orders and penitential corporations, and all collegiate properties, are suppressed. The Cathedral will have fifteen canons resident in the city of Malta (Valetta), and five resident at Citta Vecchia.

Art. 5. It is expressly prohibited to all seculars, unless they be at least deacons, to don the cape and cassock.

Art. 6. The Bishop shall be required to forward to the Government Commissary, ten days after the publication of this order, a list of the priests and a certificate of their birth in the Islands of Malta and Gozo, and a list of those who by virtue of this order will have to leave the Islands. Each chief of an Order is required to send a similar list to the Government Commissary. Every individual who does not obey this present order will be condemned to six months' imprisonment.

Art. 7. The Government Commission, the Government Commissary, and the Divisional General are severally charged, as may concern them respectively, to execute this present order.

Malta, 17th June 1798.

Art. 1. Wives and children of grenadiers of the Grand Master's Guard and Malta Regiment leaving with the French Fleet will receive : the women at the rate of 20 sous every ten days ; the children under ten years of age 10 sous each every ten days.

Art. 2. All boys, sons of the above, over ten years of age, will be shipped as cabin boys on board of vessels belonging to the Republic.[2]

Malta, 17th June 1798.

Art. 1. All Latin priests are prohibited from officiating in the Church belonging to the Greeks.

Art. 2. Masses performed hitherto by Latin priests in the Greek Churches will be performed in other Churches of the place.

---

[1] *Corres. de Nap. I*, vol. iv. pp. 161, 162.
[2] There are four more articles, but they are unimportant.—J. H. R.

THE FRENCH GOVERNMENT OF MALTA

Art. 3. Protection will be granted to Jews who may wish to establish a synagogue.

Art. 4. [Thanks Greeks established in Malta for their good behaviour.]

Art. 5. All Greeks of Malta, Gozo, Ithaca, Corfu, and the Ægean Sea, who may have relations of any nature with Russia, will be condemned to death.

Art. 6. All Greek vessels navigating under the Russian flag whenever captured by French ships will be sunk.[1]

Malta, 18*th June* 1798.

Art. 1. The Commission of Government will be divided into a Bureau and Council.

Art. 2. The Bureau will be composed of three members, including the President.

Art. 3. The Council will nominate every six months one of the two members composing the Bureau.

Art. 4. The Bureau will be in constant active service. Each member will enjoy a salary of 4,000 francs.

Art. 5. The Council will meet once every ten days to take cognisance of the Bureau's proceedings.

Art. 6. To each member of the Council will be paid 1,000 francs per annum.

Art. 7. [Nominates on this first occasion two members for the Bureau for six months, and one for twelve months.]

Art. 8. The Government Commissary will have a salary of 6,000 francs; besides office expenses he will have a *gratification*.

Malta, 18*th June* 1798.

Art. 1. The established taxes or imposts will be provisionally maintained. The Government Commissary and the Administrative Commission will assure their collection.

Art. 2. With the shortest delay, a new system of taxation will be established, so that the total product realised from the customs, wine, registration, stamps, tobacco, salt, on the hire of houses, and domestics, may reach 720,000 francs.

Art. 3. Of this sum, 50,000 francs are to be paid monthly to the military chest of the Army, such first payment not to be made until 3 months after this date, during which interval the National Domain Treasury will make good the amount.

Art. 4. The remaining 120,000 francs will be left for the expenses of administration, justice, &c., according to a statement attached.

Art. 5. This statement shall be definitely decided by the Commission of Government, together with the French Commissary, respecting the organisation of the Tribunals and various administrative services.

Art. 6. The pavement of the towns, the maintenance of cleanliness, and lighting will be paid by the inhabitants.

Art. 7. The maintenance of the fountains, as well as the wages of the employees attached to this service, will be secured by a charge to be established on vessels requiring water.

---

[1] The extraordinary rigour of these two articles shows how very jealous Bonaparte was of any intervention of Russia in Mediterranean affairs.—J. H. R.

Art. 8. A passage toll will be established for the maintenance of the roads.

Art. 9. Public instruction will be paid by the endowments already set apart for that purpose, and in case of insufficiency, with those of suppressed foundations and monasteries, in accordance with the Commander-in-Chief's order.

Art. 10. The pay of health officers, and charges relative thereto, will be recovered by a fee upon vessels and travellers.

Art. 11. The Monte di Pietà will be continued, but under a new organisation to be provided by the Government Commissary.

Art. 12. The establishment called the 'University,'[1] for providing grain for the use of the Island, will be continued, but will close its present form of administration on the 1ᵐ Messidor [19th June], and the Government Commissary is charged to reorganise it in such a manner as to leave no anxiety to the Republic as to the provisioning of the Island.

Art. 13. The hospitals will be organised on a new basis, and their needs obtained from the properties belonging to monasteries or foundations suppressed. The endowments of such hospitals which are so provided for will be maintained.

Art. 14. The Post Office will be organised in such a manner that the expense thereof will be covered by a charge on letters.

Art. 15. The expenses relative to the Army when passing through the Island, and for the provisions furnished it, as well as for those attending the establishment of the new Government, will be charged against the funds remaining disposable during that term of three months when the Government do not contribute towards the expense of the Army.

Art. 16. The Government Commissary is authorised to make provisional arrangements for any unforeseen or unprovided-for case, rendering an account of his procedure to the Commander-in-Chief.

Malta, 18th June 1798.

Art. 1. A central school shall be established, replacing the University and other chairs.

Art. 2. It shall be composed of:

1st. A Professor of Arithmetic and of Stereometry, at a salary of 1,800 francs.
2nd. A Professor of Algebra and Stereometry, at a salary of 2,000 francs.
3rd. A Professor of Geometry and Astronomy, at a salary of 2,400 francs.
4th. A Professor of Mechanics and Physics, at a salary of 3,000 francs.
5th. A Professor of Navigation, at a salary of 2,400 francs.
6th. A Professor of Chemistry, at a salary of 1,200 francs.
7th. A Professor of Oriental Languages, at a salary of 1,200 francs.
8th. A Librarian charged with the teaching of Geography, at a salary of 1,000 francs.

---

[1] Of course 'University' in this sense is equivalent to 'corporation' or 'company.'—J. H. R.

THE FRENCH GOVERNMENT OF MALTA

Art. 3. To the Central School will be attached:
1st. The Library and Cabinet of Antiquities.
2nd. A Museum of National [sic] History.
3rd. A Botanical Garden.
4th. The Observatory.

Art. 4. A sum of 3,000 francs will be devoted to the maintenance of the Central School and its effects.

Art. 5. The Professors as a body will be the Council, which will establish the best means of improving the instruction, and will propose to the Government Commission such measures of administration as they may deem necessary.

Art. 6. The appointment of the Professors, the salary of the employees—to be decided by the Government Commission—and the expenses necessary for the maintenance of the divers establishments, will be charged on the funds formerly appropriated to the maintenance of the University and chair of Oriental languages.

Art. 7. To the Botanical Garden will be appropriated a piece of land 30 acres in extent, which the Commission of Government will select without delay from the most fertile and nearest to the city.

Art. 8. In the hospital of the city a course of Anatomy, of Medicine, and Accouchement will be established, and given by the officers attached to the same.

Malta, 18th June 1798.

Art. 1. Fifteen primary schools will be established in Malta and Gozo.

Art. 2. The masters of these schools will teach their pupils reading and writing in French, the elements of Arithmetic and Pilotage, and the principles of morality and of the French Constitution.

Art. 3. The teachers will be nominated by the Commission of Government.

Art. 4. They will have quarters allowed them in a National building, to which a garden will be attached.

Art. 5. Their salary will be 1,000 francs in silver for the cities, and 800 francs for the villages.

Art. 6. For the payment of each teacher, a sufficient portion will be appropriated out of the properties belonging to the suppressed monasteries.

Art. 7. The distribution of the schools, and the regulations for their management and *régime*, will be confided to the Commission of Government.

Malta, 18th June 1798.[1]

Bonaparte, Commander-in-Chief, orders:

Art. 1. The Bishop shall have no other jurisdiction than that of surveillance over ecclesiastics. All procedure relating to marriage will appertain to the Civil and Criminal Courts.

Art. 2. It is expressly prohibited to the Bishop, the ecclesiastics, and the inhabitants of the Island to receive or pay for the administration of the Sacraments: the duties of the former, and their position, require them to

---

[1] *Corres. de Nap. I*, vol. iv. p. 175.

administer same gratis. Moreover, the fees of the Stole, and such similar charges, are abolished.

Art. 3. No foreign prince shall exercise any power, either in the administration of Religion, or in the Courts of Justice, nor shall any ecclesiastic or inhabitant appeal to the Pope or any metropolitan.

Malta, 18*th June* 1798.

Art. 1. Forty thousand francs annually will be reserved and appropriated for the use of the hospitals, derived from the funds arising from the suppressed monasteries and endowments. Any of these endowments already appropriated for the purpose are to be taken first.

Art. 2. From the national property 300,000 francs will be appropriated for payment of the Grand Master's creditors.

Art. 3. National property to the value of 300,000 francs will be sold to serve for the needs of the garrison and navy.

Art. 4. National property to the value of 300,000 francs will be sold for the purpose of providing provisions in the event of a siege.

Art. 5. The Commission of Government, in concert with the Land Commission, will arrange for the sale of the said properties.

Malta, 18*th June* 1798.

Art. 1. General Vaubois will arrange within forty-eight hours for the transportation to Rome of the English and Russian Consuls.

Art. 2. If these two Consuls are Maltese by birth, this banishment will be of one year's duration, after which they may return, provided the French Republic has had no occasion to complain of them.

Of the many grievances which provoked the people, perhaps those which had most influence in increasing the general discontent were such as affected the religious feelings of the population. Notwithstanding the express terms of the capitulation, Bonaparte on the 16th June ordered all monasteries of the secular Orders (with the exception of one to each) to be closed, and the surplus property belonging to them confiscated, the proceeds of their sale being applied to the needs of education and the relief of the poor. This step, whilst meeting the views of many of the advanced Liberals, created much anxiety and alarm amongst the majority of the people, for it now became evident to them that the provisions of the Act of Capitulation had become a dead letter.

The evil forebodings anticipated by many were soon to be realised, for although it had been stipulated that no extraordinary contributions were to be imposed upon the islands, nevertheless national property of the value of £12,000 sterling was ordered on the 18th June to be sold '*for the needs and requirements of the Garrison and Navy.*'

Discontent and murmurings were naturally caused by such

extortions, and this feeling in the islands was greatly aggravated by another enactment, of the 18th June, limiting the jurisdiction of the bishop, and introducing the form of civil marriage.

These measures, which were so obnoxious to the general public, and naturally still more so to the priests, caused great excitement, but the actual presence of Bonaparte prevented for the moment any open demonstration or protest. In fact the letters which were shortly afterwards addressed to Bonaparte in Egypt, by Vaubois on the 15th, and by Bosredon Ransijat on the 17th and 31st July (which follow), exhibit the false sense of security then prevailing. The subject which more concerned the authorities at this period was their embarrassment with regard to their future supply of food, for on the 15th July Vaubois informed Bonaparte [1] that the difficulty of provisioning the island was great owing to the conduct of the King of the Two Sicilies, yet he hoped to have better success from Barbary. He further mentions that although the Maltese appear to become daily more reconciled to the French occupation, and show attachment to the new order of things, as was testified at a charming *fête* organised for the day preceding,[2] yet they refrain from buying national property, and that consequently funds were badly wanted. He was, however, dissatisfied with the troops, who had shown signs of insubordination, owing to the privations they had endured.

Finally, he added:[3] 'I am generally beloved in the Island, but I see with pain my brethren-in-arms behave badly towards me, although I do my utmost to improve their position. I feel certain that if their pay is long delayed trouble will follow. We may carry on until Fructidor (September), but by then we must have funds.

'The Commission of Government and the municipalities work well. This people are very attractive by their goodness and gentleness; I have observed them closely, and have reason to believe that no signs of machinations exist amongst them.

'All goes well here with the exception of a little misunderstanding with Regnaud de St. Jean d'Angely (the civil governor) on one point. I believe he is in the wrong, for he is alone in his opinion, and if he persists it will be owing to his *amour propre*. It is a subject of the greatest importance, as it is a question regarding the administration of the University (i.e. the corporation provisioning the Island with wheat).

'He wishes to place at the head of the Institution a man against whom much may be said. All the capitalists have the greatest fear. Regnaud has ability, but he is a little imperious, and a little vain. I will not oppose him, except in cases for the public weal, and notwithstanding this little difference in our mode of thinking, the harmony between us shall not be destroyed.'

[1] Bonaparte, *Lettres inédites*, vol. i. p. 287.
[2] The French national festival of July 14, the anniversary of the capture of the Bastille.—J. H. R.
[3] Bonaparte, *Lettres inédites*, vol. i. p. 287.

On the 17th July, Bosredon Ransijat, as President of the Commission charged with the administration of the government of the islands, wrote as follows:—

[Translation.]

Malta, 17th July 1798.

To GENERAL BONAPARTE.[1]—I take the liberty of informing you that the Commission which you appointed to organise the new Government of these Islands pursues its functions with much activity and zeal, to which work it devotes the greatest assiduity.

Besides the motives which cause the members to respond to the confidence you have reposed in them, there exists the satisfaction of perceiving in the Maltese people the happiest disposition to conform to the new Institutions and condition of things, particularly by the inhabitants of the city, who being more enlightened than the country people, are better able to appreciate them, and also because they are now free from the vexations of the Knights, whose departure they have witnessed with great joy. The people show an affectionate disposition towards the French whom you have left behind to guard this Island, and the magnificent *fête* which was celebrated here on the 14th instant, a description of which I shall leave to Regnaud, has furnished touching proofs thereof, for after the great glee which was manifested, and the perfect harmony which prevailed between the Maltese and French, it might be truly said that in Malta there existed on that day but one nation. Although the Maltese in general are steeped in ignorance and superstition more than any other people, they will, I trust, thanks to their natural goodness and docility, soon adopt and scrupulously obey the French Constitution.

They are enchanted with the amiability and goodness of General Vaubois, who is truly an excellent man, and just the one to fulfil the object you had in view. His frank and loyal conduct has gained all hearts, and the Government Commission above all are extremely pleased with him, because he is always ready with zeal and good grace to aid us in any way which will facilitate our work. Thanks indeed are due to you, Citizen General, for having given us so good a man, who by reason of his excellent qualities influences so efficaciously the spirit of the Maltese, and contributes not a little to hasten the time of the submission of these good people to the new laws. I trust, therefore, that by the time you return you will be content with Malta, for by then these inhabitants will have learned to appreciate as they ought the inestimable boon of liberty which you have given them. (Signed) BOSREDON RANSIJAT.

Whilst the authorities so far failed to observe any sign of real danger to their rule from within the island, yet the question of victualling the garrison and inhabitants was one of supreme importance and difficulty so long as the Neapolitan Government continued unfriendly and the British fleet remained mistress of the seas,[2] and

[1] Bonaparte's *Lettres inédites*, vol. i. p. 290.
[2] Mr Hardman here somewhat anticipates events. Not until Nelson's victory of the Nile (August 1, 1798) was British maritime ascendancy assured in the Mediterranean.—J. H. R.

on the 21st July Regnaud de St. Jean d'Angely informed the Executive Directory in the following dispatch of the straits they were likely to be put to :—

À la Cité Valette de l'Isle de Malte le 3 *Thermidor* an 6 (21*st July* 1798).[1]

Le Citoyen Regnaud de Saint-Jean d'Angely, au Directoire exécutif.

CITOYENS DIRECTEURS,—J'ai lieu de craindre que les communications, ne soient interceptées momentanément ou au moins difficiles entre l'armée et l'isle de Malte.

Tout nous confirme le passage de l'escadre Anglaise à Messine le 23 Juin. Un bâtiment venu ici a parlé au pilote qui a guidé leurs vaisseaux dans le détroit.

Il est à supposer qu'elle a fait voile vers le levant à la suite de notre escadre.

Cependant tous les bâtimens venus de ce côté n'annoncent que l'existence de 3 frégates Anglaises et un bâtiment léger qui croisent dans le canal.

L'Escadre Française a été vue la dernière fois vers la Canée [2] ; et ce raport cadre avec un précédent fait par un ragusois qui avait aperçue, le 24 Juin, le convoi et la flotte à la hauteur de Cerigo.

Il y a trois jours est rentré un aviso sorti trois jours avant. Il a trouvé à 20 lieues une frégate Anglaise qui lui a pris ses munitions et vivres, mais a renvoyé l'équipage et le bâtiment.

Ainsi environnés d'ennemis nous ne sommes pas sans inquiétude sur les approvisionnements. Nos allarmes sont d'autant plus grandes que la Sicile, ayant mis, ainsi que vous l'avez sans doute appris déjà par mes précédentes dépêches, tous nos bâtimens en quarantaine, les vivres n'arrivent plus. Nous n'avons pas de nouvelles de deux individus envoyés près du Vice-Roi de Palerme, avec des lettres et instructions dont le Chargé d'Affaires de Naples doit vous avoir donné connaissance. Nous craignons que l'Escadre Anglaise a intercepté les bâtimens que j'avais engagé divers négociants à faire partir, afin de rapporter des provisions que les régences [3] paraissent disposées à nous fournir. D'un autre côté le Général en Chef n'a laissé ici au payeur de la Division que 50,000 [*sic*] environ de numéraire et de l'argenterie à fondre pour 250 à 280,000 [*sic*] suivant le rapport du payeur.[4]

Il n'y avait rien dans la caisse de l'ancien gouvernement voidée [*sic*] dans celle du payeur Estève, avant le départ de l'Escadre. Il y avait, il y a, au contraire des dettes à acquitter, dont quelques unes ne peuvent être retardées, telles que les dépenses des Hôpitaux des Invalides, des Tribunaux, des prisons etc. Le Général en Chef autorise la vente des domaines nationaux jusqu'à concurrence de 600,000.

Mais les gens du pays, peu riches et craintifs n'achètent rien. Les négociants français ne voudraient acheter qu'à des pris auxquels je ne crois pas devoir autoriser la vente. Cependant il existe ici plus de 3,000

---

[1] Arch. Nat., AF III. 73. [2] i.e. Crete.—J. H. R.
[3] i.e. the regencies of Tripoli, Tunis, and Algiers.—J. H. R.
[4] Vaubois in his letter of August 29 (see below) gives these figures as 78,000 francs and 340,000 francs.—J. H. R.

hommes de troupes, trois vaisseaux à armer, dont deux le sont déjà en partie, savoir le Dége et la Carthaginoise; les bâtiments qui passent, à secourir, à ravitailler ; la troupe à habiller suivant un ordre du Général en Chef ; 500 malades de l'Escadre ou de la garnison à pourvoir ; un approvisionnement de siège de 300,000 ordonné par Bonaparte et commandé par la prudence. Enfin les dépenses de l'artillerie, du Génie, de l'Arsenal, du gouvernement civil à assurer.

Ce tableau rapide vous mettra à même de prendre une détermination sur ce que vous croirez devoir faire pour ce poste important.

Il paraît que les Anglais laisseront plutôt les communications libres entre la France et Malte qu'entre Malte et l'Escadre française.

Vous jugerez de l'usage qu'il convient de faire de cette liberté.

Vous déciderez quels secours il est utile de faire passer en bois pour les vaisseaux, s'ils avaient besoin de radoub ; en chanvre ou cordage qui manque; en approvisionnemens de marine de tout genre; en effets d'hôpitaux dans lesquels il n'y a pas *une seule chemise*, en boulets dont l'approvisionnement est peu considérable ; enfin en argent. Vous jugerez des mesures à prendre avec la Cour de Naples si elle persévère à nous fermer les ports de Sicile d'où nous aurions pû, même en présence de nos enemis, tirer de quoi pourvoir aux besoins journaliers de l'Isle au moyen des Bâtimens légers qui ne peuvent être atteints. Salut & respect.

(Signed) REGNAUD DE ST. JEAN D'ANGELY.

A second letter from Bosredon Ransijat to Bonaparte was dispatched on the 31st July, as follows:—

[Translation.]

Malta, 31*st July* 1798.

To GENERAL BONAPARTE,[1]—Since your departure the Commission (of Government) has not forgotten that the Islands of Malta and Gozo owe their liberty to you, and that you have left to us in General Vaubois a Citizen General who has succeeded in conciliating at the same time the confidence of the soldier and the love of the Maltese people. Further, that the French Government Commissary (Regnaud de St. Jean d'Angely), zealous friend of the grand principles (of the Revolution) as well as of your glory, is the flame which guides and directs our steps in the new yet consoling career in which you have placed us—for if we have been able to do any good, it is due, on the one hand, to the support and trust of General Vaubois, and on the other, to the indefatigable zeal of Commissary Regnaud.

Finally, it is in the hope of happy success in your expedition to Egypt, and the incessant desire of again seeing you not only covered with new laurels in the East, if the perfidious English follow you there, but victorious in our own districts, should they have the temerity to attack us, that animates and encourages us to fulfil our duties. The twelve municipalities which you have instituted are in full activity, and we second their efforts as much as we possibly can. The justices of the peace are in full exercise, and their ministry, which had been earnestly waited for, is found more

[1] Bonaparte, *Correspondance inédite*, vol. i. Egypt, p. 430 (translation).

useful than that of the Priests, for it affords security to the laborious villagers. Means are adopted to hasten and superintend their functions, and in such a manner that the people obtain the double advantage of not only detesting the past spirit of chicanery which existed, but also to bless the Republic and Bonaparte, who has delivered them from it. The Civil and Criminal Tribunals will shortly be instituted. The civic guard, established according to your orders, performs regular service, not only for the reserve, but also for the principal constituted authorities.

The numerous monasteries have been reduced to one of each Order, the abusive and anti-social jurisdictions of the Bishop and Inquisitor have been abolished, and the essential portion of their archives has been united with those of the National Archives. The erection of military barracks and officers' lodgings, as well as the assessment of the patriotic tax to provide for them, is on the eve of being accomplished.

A new administration of the University (providing for the supply of wheat), based on regenerating principles, tranquillising capital, which for a moment became alarmed and injured the provisioning of this place, is now going on well, and in such a manner that the Republic will have nothing to fear from English cupidity and corruption. A Tribunal of Commerce is to be established under the name of Consular Tribunal, and the merchants are convoked for a meeting, to elect under the direction of the Government the five Judges which will compose it. A newspaper directed in the best spirit is shortly to appear to fulfil the double duty of worthily celebrating your late and glorious enterprises, and to enlighten the Maltese people on the advantages they obtain by their union with France.

(Signed) BOSREDON RANSIJAT,
President of the Administration of Malta.

On the day preceding the date of Bosredon Ransijat's letter to Bonaparte, describing the working of the Government Commission, the substance of the enactment of the 18th June, which had been issued under martial law by Bonaparte personally, was proclaimed by a decree of the civil authority, as follows:

[Translation.]

Extract from the Registers of the Government Commission Session of the 30th July 1798.[1]

The Commissary of the French Government having forwarded to the Government Commission his decree requiring that it should be transcribed in the *procès verbal* of the sitting of this day, [the Commission] agrees to his demand, and the decree has been registered as follows :—

The Commissary of the French Government, having seen the Order of the General Commander-in-Chief,

That the Bishop of Malta possesses only the surveillance over ecclesiastics ;

That all proceedings relating to matrimony appertain to the Civil and Criminal Codes ;

[1] *Collection of Decrees issued by the French*, p. 151. Printed by order of the Government of Malta, 1840.

That no foreign prince shall have any authority in the administration of Religion, nor in that of Justice;

And consequently no ecclesiastic or inhabitant can have recourse to the Pope, nor to any metropolitan—

Thereby establishes :

1. The acts concerning the civil state, that is to say, of the birth, marriage, and death of individuals, shall provisionally be received by the parish priests.

2. Their registers shall be numbered and countersigned in duplicate by the Judges of each municipality.

3. Every year one of these registers shall be placed in the chancery of the Civil Tribunal.

4. Every certificate of birth or death, every certificate of marriage, which are not recorded in the registers, will be null and void, so far as the civil effects thereof are concerned, and in the eyes of the Law.

5. No one shall be allowed to avail himself either of the dispositions of the Council of Trent, or any ecclesiastical law, in order to declare as valid any marriage celebrated before any priest, unless he happens to be the parish priest of one of the contracting parties, after three publications, with an interval of thirty days' time between each, and with the consent of their fathers, mothers, tutors or guardians, whenever the betrothed are not free to act according to law.

6. No proofs of witnesses, or any other kind, to serve instead of the acts which the present deliberation requires, will be allowed.

7. This decree shall be sent to the Government Commission, and by it to the parish priests, to the bishop, and to the Tribunals, to be transcribed in their respective registers, published, registered, and fulfilled.

Malta, 29th July [sic] 1798.

(Signed) REGNAUD DE SAINT-JEAN-D'ANGELY.

Upon the publication of this decree the irritation of the people became extreme, and many were the signs of their anger. Amongst the number of these indications, cockades, which by the order of the 16th June *all* inhabitants were *compelled to don*, were by many defiantly discarded. To calm the indignation and allay the disquietude of the people which this decree had aroused, the Civil Government requested the intervention of Bishop Labini, who accordingly, on the 13th August, issued the following pastoral letter, which was published in French and Italian :—

[Translation.]

Nos Fra Vincentius Labini, Dei et Sanctæ Sedis Apostolicæ gratia Archiepiscopus Rhodi, Episcopus Melitæ.

We cannot help feeling, my beloved children, with all bitterness of soul, the tribulation you are now experiencing in the fear that the Holy Faith which by special blessing of the Divine Providence has been bestowed upon your forefathers through the medium of our great father apostle Saint Paul should now be assailed by the present Government.[1]

It is certainly not only laudable, but indeed obligatory on every Catholic to be zealous in the preservation of the Holy Faith, for without such it is impossible to please God, as we are taught by the holy minister of the truth, ' Sine fide impossibile est placere Deo.'

But an unreasonable zeal, which disturbs not only the conscience, but also the family repose and public tranquillity, is not laudable.

Our holy Religion is the lover of peace and charity. The character of true Christians, that is to say of the true disciples of Jesus Christ, has been always that of exhibiting perfect tranquillity, in the desire of being good subjects, by respecting the authority which, by Divine Providence, has been placed over them, and by being good citizens advancing the common interests. Such certainly cannot be said of those who amongst you go about disseminating false news, by which they would have you believe that it is intended to abolish our ' Culta,' and to destroy our holy Religion.

We cannot hide from ourselves the fact that we also have felt some uneasiness in reading certain notices issued by the Government, from which it would appear that there was an intention to declare that the sacrament of marriage in certain cases, declared legal by the Catholic Church, was illegal, transferring to the Civil Court all cases connected with the sacrament of marriage, and further that it was intended to prevent all appeal to His Holiness the Pope, and as if we were no longer to acknowledge and venerate that visible head and centre of our Catholic Church.

But we have the pleasure to make known unto you that the Government has solemnly explained that it did not intend to attack on these points our holy Faith, inasmuch as what had been prescribed with regard to marriages had reference only to the civil effects without in any form derogating from the power and authority of the Church with regard to the sacrament of marriage.

And so far as regards His Holiness the Pope, it was not intended to offend our consciences by preventing our recognising him as head of the Church, to whom we might refer when occasion required.

In fact the Government has declared and protested that it leaves to the inhabitants of these Islands freedom to exercise the Roman Catholic Apostolic Religion.

Such being the case, you will clearly understand that if in the Government notices which have been published there are certain expressions which appear equivocal, reason requires that such should be understood and interpreted by you in consonance with the capitulations entered into with Citizen Bonaparte, Commander-in-Chief, and with the clear explanations given by the depositories of public authority. Thus, as every motive causing disquietude has ceased to exist, peace and tranquillity is restored to all reasonable minds. To the further establishing this tranquillity, we assure you that the said depositories of public authority promise, with every safeguard, that the property of your Parish Churches

[1] MS. 261, M.P.L., Vol. of Edicts of Monsignor Labini; Acts in the Bishop's Court.

shall always be preserved and defended, together with the plate and treasures appertaining thereto.

Listen not, then, my beloved children, to those who for their own private ends, or through ignorance, disturb your minds by malicious or idle discourse, but listen rather with holy meekness to our words, with which in the discharge of our duty we acquaint you that the true and sincere zeal of our holy Faith consists principally in so acting that with all diligence our Faith should not be sterile or dead, but living and productive of holy works worthy of eternal life.

One of the principal duties so recommended to us and earnestly required, is certainly that of honouring, respecting, and obeying the authorities constituted by the will of God.

So are we clearly taught by our great apostle St. Paul in the XIII Chapter of his Epistle to the Romans, in the II Chapter of his First Epistle to Timothy, in the XIII Chapter of his Epistle to the Hebrews, and in the III Chapter of his Epistle to Titus.

So also is it recommended by the Prince of Apostles in the II Chapter of his First Epistle.

The same was also diligently practised by the early Christians towards Princes, although Gentiles; as is attested by Tertullian amongst others. 'We,' he says, speaking on behalf of all Christians in his 'Apology,' 'venerate in Emperors the justice of God, to whom he has given the Empire of Nations; and in another place (in Chapter I) he reasons thus : ' The Christian is an enemy to nobody, much less to an Emperor, because he, knowing that he has been constituted as such by the will of his God, cannot do less than love, reverence, honour, and wish him well.'

Let us, then, fulfil, my beloved children, with every exactness, commands so pressing, which our holy Religion imposes upon us, and let us imitate the enlightened examples of our dear forefathers, if we desire with faith to implore, and obtain from the Most High, Giver of all gifts, the fullness of His celestial benedictions, which we, in the amplitude of our heart, desire for you.

These subversive proceedings, so offensive to the religious feelings of the people, were aggravated by others directed against the richer portion of the community. A new system of taxation was ordered to be levied with the shortest delay possible, and in such a form that the total product was to realise £28,800 annually.[1]

Of this sum, no less than £24,000 (£2,000 monthly) *was to be paid to the military chest of the Army*, so that for the luxury of French protection the inhabitants were called upon to contribute five-sixths of their total revenue. The remaining £4,800 per annum was considered sufficient for the expenses of the administration of government, including the law courts. Extraneous expenses were to be defrayed out of other imposts; public instruction, hospitals, &c., supported by the proceeds of suppressed foundations and monasteries.

It was further ordered that the expenses attending the transit of

---

[1] *Corres. de Nap. I*, vol. iv. p. 172.

the army passing by Malta to Egypt, the supply of provisions, &c., should also be paid *out of local funds*.

The feelings of joy which the people at first experienced when rescued from the thraldom of the detested Knights soon gave place to the deepest depression. The liberty acquired was one in name only, and the rights which had been promised and guaranteed them by Article 7 of the capitulations were entirely ignored.

The confidence of the people in their new masters was completely lost, but they were powerless to act. Their redemption could only be obtained through the intervention of and by an act of Divine Providence, which was shortly to come by the destruction of the French fleet.

In the meantime, and within a month of the date of the decree establishing the form of civil marriage, and eleven days after the issue of Bishop Labini's pastoral letter, the municipality, by order of the Government Commissary, under date of the 24th August, revised the provisional decree of the 30th July, as follows :—

[Translation.]

Session of the 24th August 1798.[1]

The Commissary of Government, considering—

That the provisional regulations in force for guaranteeing the civil status of the citizens, which leaves to the priests of the various parishes of Malta the right of proving, might offer difficulties to such who do not profess the religion of which the priests are the ministers :

That whatever the religious opinions of an individual may be, he or she should nevertheless fully enjoy the rights of citizenship, which the law guarantees to them :

That the French law permits perfect religious freedom, but does not acknowledge religious vows, and leaves to all the liberty of conscience, provided the law is conformed to :

That the authorities of the French Government are required to use every exertion to see that every individual residing in Malta, of any religion, and whatsoever opinion they may possess, and whatsoever may have been their former position, profession, country, or habitation, shall enjoy the benefit of this liberty :

Orders

1. All individuals, French, Maltese, and Foreigners, who do not wish to apply to the Parish priests for the certificate or act of civil status, can apply for same to the municipality.

2. For this purpose a triple Register will be opened, each page of which will be numbered, divided into columns, and signed by the President, in which will be entered marriages, births, and deaths.

---

[1] Azopardi, *Giornale della Presa di Malta*, p. 80.

3. To enable citizens to enter into a matrimonial contract it will be necessary.

First, That in the case of minors, the espoused shall have obtained the consent of their father, mother, or guardian.

Secondly, That notice of their reciprocal matrimonial engagement shall be affixed for eight days to the door of the place of sitting of their respective municipalities. If both the parties are of age, no consent of third parties is required.

4. For the proof of birth, the presence of two witnesses, one of either sex, and a certificate from the professor or midwife who has assisted at the birth, will only be required, and to be presented within twenty-four hours, under penalty for non-observance to prohibition to practise their profession, together with a pecuniary fine and imprisonment.

5. For the proof of death, the parents, friends, or neighbours of the deceased, immediately after death, will make the necessary declaration at the municipality.

A municipal officer will then proceed personally and verify the reality of the case.

The Funeral shall not take place until twenty-four hours have elapsed since the death. Two witnesses, parents, friends, or neighbours, with the municipal officer, shall sign the notification of death.

6. The place of burial existing in each municipality shall be common to all religions.

7. The Registers of marriages, births, and deaths shall be kept in duplicate, and at the close of each year deposited, one with the President of the Municipality, and the other with the Parish priest at the Chancery of the Civil Tribunal.

8. The municipality will grant extracts of the Registers, for proof of the civil status of the citizens, to all who may demand them, and no Judge or individual shall refuse recognition thereof, under the penalty of exile for non-conformance.

(Signed) REGNAUD DE ST. JEAN D'ANGELY.

This notification, combined with the suppression of certain monasteries, &c., evidently caused some ebullition of public temper, for, two days later, namely, on the 26th August, Regnaud de St. Jean d'Angely gave the home Government, in the following dispatch, the *first* intimation of what he termed 'a fanatical agitation having shown itself amongst the people':—

À Malte, le 9 *Fructidor* l'an 6 (26th August 1798).[1]

Regnaud de Saint Jean d'Angely, au Directoire Exécutif.

CITOYENS DIRECTEURS,—Depuis mes dernières dépêches notre situation avec la Sicile, loin de s'améliorer, est devenu plus fâcheuse.

Le Bulletin cy-joint vous fera connoître quel est le dernier état des choses.

Manquans icy des Denrées les plus nécessaires au peuple, et du vin en

[1] Arch. Nat., AF III. 73.

particulier, j'ai encouragé le plus possible un espèce de commerce interlope qui nous a procuré quelques ressources.

Mais le vin ne se chargeant qu'à Mascali, qui est un port gardé, est sur le point de manquer icy et l'hôpital n'en est approvisionné que par un envoy que j'ai demandé au Consul Ribaud à Messine et qu'il a effectué.

Je n'entre dans ces détails, minutieux en apparence, que pour fixer plus précisément vos idées sur la position générale de l'isle et de la Div$^{on.}$ et pour que vous puissiès établir par des faits les instructions que vous donnerès à vos agens près la Cour de Naples.

Un Bâtiment Maltais appartenant à Paul Savona, par[ti] sur mes instances, pour Civita-Vecchia, a été pris à la côte d'Avola en Sicile par un Brick Anglais. J'ai écrit au Consul pour le reclamer et il a déjà fait des demarches, jusqu'à présent inutiles malgré leur légitimité.

Au milieu de ces difficultés je me sens occuppé de maintenir et d'activer l'Etablissement appelé l'Université, chargé de l'approvisionnement des grains. Les consommations ont été remplacées et l'isle a encore du bled pour dix mois.

Quelques mouvemens fanatiques étoient prêts d'éclater par suite de la suppression de quelques couvens, fondations, et bénéfices, ordonnés par le Gén$^{l.}$ en Chef. Ils ont été étouffés par quelques mesures de précaution et de prudence, et par la publication d'un mandement de l'Evêque.

Rien n'est égal à l'ignorance profonde des neuf dixièmes des habitans. Les prêtres y règnent conséquemment & la destruction de leur dangereuse influence, sera le résultat de l'Instruction publique.

D'après les ordres du Gén$^{l.}$ en Chef, j'ai rassemblé les moyens d'y pourvoir en réunissant les revenus nécessaires pour payer les instituteurs des écoles primaires, et d'une école centrale.

Il y avait en outre plusieurs hospices appelés Conservatoires, où sont placés les enfants naturels abandonnés au nombre d'environ 500.

Ces établissemens les recoivent à 7 ans des mains des nourrices qui les gardent jusqu'alors à raison de 3 fr. [?] de france par mois et qui en ont environ 400.

J'ai établi dans ces hospices un maître de Français & d'Italien pour enseigner à lire et à écrire à ces enfants abandonnés: ce moyen contribuera à repandre l'usage de la langue française, et assurera l'instruction par la lecture.

L'organisation générale du païs est presque terminée. Dès qu'elle le sera entièrement je vous en adresseray le tableau.

Il manque à l'école centrale un professeur de Chimie et un professeur de Botanique dont l'employ restera vacant jusqu'au moment où il arrivera de France des hommes capables de les remplir.

Vous jugerès peut être convenable, Citoyens Directeurs, de faire dresser icy les sujets necessaires à ces deux places.

Il seroit aussi extrèmement important d'avoir un assortiment de caractères d'imprimerie. Je projettois la redaction d'un petit ouvrage élémentaire pour l'instruction publique: mais il est impossible de l'imprimer sans avoir de nouveaux caractères.

L'aviso *l'Anemone* est parti hier pour Alexandrie avec l'Adjudant Gén$^{l.}$ Camin, malgré quatre Bâtimens de Guerre signalés dans le Canal.

Je confie cette dépêche au C^en. Fournier commandant *l'Assaillante* prise et relaché par les Anglois, et qui va vous rendre compte de sa conduite. Salut & respect.

(Signed) REGNAUD DE ST. JEAN D'ANGELY.

On the same day the Government Commissary, for the purpose of alleviating in some degree the distress which prevailed amongst a certain class, due to the deportation of the Grand Master and many Knights so heavily in debt, made the following proposal to the home Government:—

À Malte le 9 *Fructidor* l'an 6 de la République
(26*th August* 1798).[1]

Regnaud de Saint-Jean d'Angely au Directoire Exécutif.

CITOYENS DIRECTEURS,—Le Grand Maître Hompesch et les Chevaliers partis de Malte ont laissé icy une masse de dettes très considérable.

Hompesch n'en a donné qu'un état incomplet, dont le montant ne peut être payé avec les trois cent mille livres de domaines nationaux que le Gén^al. en Chef Bonaparte a affecté à cet objet.

J'ai chargé un membre du gouvernement de faire un état général de ces dettes que je vous adresserai :

Vous penserès peut être qu'il seroit juste & convenable même aux intérêts de la République, d'acquitter pour le comte du cy-devant Grand Maître Hompesch, toutes ces dettes, en domaines nationaux sur le pied de vingt fois l'évaluation du revenu.

Le montant de la somme ainsi acquittée pourroit être retenu sur les 300,000 que la République doit payer annuellement au cy-devant Grand Maître.

J'attendrai vos ordres à cet égard.

Quant aux dettes des cy-devant Chevalliers ; j'ai fait inviter par une proclamation tous leurs créanciers à se faire inscrire à la Comm^on. de Gouvernement.

Quand l'État sera dressé, il vous sera envoyé, et vous jugerez si vous retiendrès sur la pension des débiteurs une somme pour leur créances, et si au fur et mesure de la retenue, on pourra la leur delivrer icy en domaines nationaux.

Je pense que cet acte de justice, prendroit pour ainsi dire aux yeux des Maltais, le caractère de la Bienfaisance, et produiront un très bon effet.

Four days after publication of the revised decree regarding the forms to be adhered to, respecting births, marriages, and deaths, viz. on the 28th August, the *Guillaume Tell*, the *Diane*, and the *Justice* arrived in Malta Harbour from Aboukir Bay, bringing news of the total defeat of the French fleet. This intelligence was conveyed to the Directory in a joint dispatch of the 29th August, signed by Vaubois and Regnaud de St. Jean d'Angely, as follows :—

[1] Arch. Nat., AF III. 73.

Malthe, 12 *Fructidor* an 6 (29*th August* 1798).

Le Général de Division, Vaubois, au Directoire Exécutif de la Rép.^{que.} française.

CITOYENS DIRECTEURS,—Hier matin 11 Fructidor à 10 heures sont entrés dans le port de Malte, le vaisseau *le Guillaume Tell*, commandé par le Contre Amiral Villeneuve & les frégates *la Diane* et *la Justice*, commandés par les Cap.^{nes.} Decrais & Villeneuve.

Nous ne répéterons pas icy les détails contenus dans le compte que vous rend le Contre Amiral des événements du 15 Thermidor.

Nous joignons icy un exemplaire de la proclamation, par laquelle nous avons cru devoir fixer l'opinion de la Division et du païs.

Nous avons eu, au millieu des sentiments douloureux dont nous avons été agités, la satisfaction de voir que le désir le plus ardent de l'armée et des Maltais est de trouver l'occasion de venger leurs frères d'armes et que le découragement est aussi loin de nous que l'insensibilité.

Après avoir receuilli tous les renseignements sur le combat naval livré devant Alexandrie, nous avons assemblé en conseil de guerre tous les Officiers Généraux, commandant des Corps et Commissaires Ordonnateurs, pour prendre une résolution sur notre position.

Elle est embarrassante sous plus d'un rapport.

La Sicile refuse de laisser sortir aucune espèce de vivres, ainsi que vous le verrès par les pièces cy-jointes qui ont été mise sous les yeux du Conseil.

Les vaisseaux Anglois, au contraire en sont abondamment pourvus et on va jusqu'à leur donner des matelots quand ils en manquent.

Les procédés les plus insultans, les plus contraires au droit des Gens, les violations les plus marquées du traité avec la République, caractérisent chaque jour, la conduite de la Cour de Naples.

Il semble même qu'elle est résolue à la guerre et n'ayant aucune nouvelle de France, n'ayant pu encore recevoir des spéronares envoyés successivement depuis cinq semaines, avec des dépêches pour le C.^{en.} Lachaise, nous ignorons si vous avès [*sic*] arrêté de venger les injures faites à la grande nation ; ou si le Roy de Naples a l'audace de se joindre de lui même à nos ennemis.

Dans cette position le Conseil a unanimement pensé qu'il n'avoit que quatre points de détermination à arrêter.

1° Faire rester icy les trois Bâtiments arrivés d'Egypte, ainsi que les deux qui sont déjà dans le port, *Le Diego* et *la Carthaginoise*.

2° Les employer de tems en tems à repousser de la côte les croiseurs Anglais qui interceptent nos barques, ou en empêcher la sortie &c., assurer par ce moyen, l'entrée à Malte des vivres qui nous manquent.

3° De vous expédier par trois voyes différentes de couriers pour vous instruire de notre position.

4° Enfin d'attendre vos ordres ; soit ceux du Général en Chef Bonaparte et de nous tenir prêts à les exécuter avec tous les moyens qui pourraient se préparer et le dévouement que vous devés attendre des soldats et des Citoyens français.

Vous ne devés pas douter Citoyens Directeurs que si vous avés décidé la guerre avec Naples, les soldats français, les Maltais même ne soyent brûlans du désir de seconder les efforts de l'armée qui attaqueroit par terre.

Tous les cœurs ulcérés accusent la Cour de Naples des pertes que nous avons faites. Si l'Escadre Angloise n'avoit pas trouvé dans tous les ports des raffraîchissements, des vivres, des secours de tous genres, elle ne pouvait tenir la Meditérannée, & profondement convaincus qu'elle n'y peut rester si ces mêmes ports lui sont fermés.[1] Tous les vœux sont pour que vous jugiès conforme aux intérêts de la République d'ordonner à l'armée d'Italie de s'en emparer.

Vous êtes accoutumé à commander la Victoire, comme les armées françaises à l'obtenir.

Dans tous les cas inébranlable dans le poste qui lui est confié, il est inutile de vous dire que la Division le conservera quoiqu'il arrive.

Mais notre devoir est de vous ajouter que Bonaparte n'a laissé icy que 78,000 et pour 340,000 d'argenterie.[2] Vous recevrès sur notre position en finance et en denrées un court exposé du Comm^re. du Gouvernment.

Vous sentirès combien il importe que nous recevions de vous des secours pécuniaires, des secours en denrées, des munitions de marine et de guerre.

Nous réunirons nos efforts pour arriver au tems où nous calculons pouvoir obtenir ce que nous sollicitons de vous des Bâtiments rentrés, partis de Gènes, Livourne, Civita Vecchia, de Marseille même peuvent nous apporter ce qui nous manque et nous n'entrerons pas sur les moyens de les faire arriver, dans des détails inutiles.

Nous finissons en vous renouvellant l'assurance que la Division et tous ceux qui y sont attachés se montreront dignes de garder et de défendre le poste d'honneur qui lui est confié. VAUBOIS.

29th August 1798.[3]

PROCLAMATION

Le Général de Division et le Commissaire du Gouvernement à l'Armée et aux Citoyens de Malte.

Bonaparte et son armée sont descendus à Alexandrie vainqueurs des premiers obstacles, ils ont vu fuir les Mamelucs loin de cette ville qu'ils opprimaient. Bientôt ils ont marché sur le Caire et le 5 Thermidor (July 25, 1798) l'armée victorieuse y a fait son entrée.

Nul échec, nulle perte n'a acheté ce triomphe de l'armée de terre. Elle y est comme dans une terre amie. L'escadre n'a pu entrer dans le port d'Alexandrie dont le mouillage avait trop peu de fond.

Elle a jetté ancre en rade à environ une lieue et demie.

C'est là qu'elle a été attaquée le 15 Thermidor (August 1, 1798), à 5 heures du soir, par l'Escadre Anglaise forte de 15 vaisseaux contre treize dont deux, *le Dubois* et *le Causse*, n'étaient pas armés.

Cependant nos braves marins, commandés par l'Amiral Brueys, faisaient une vigoureuse résistance, quand, au bout d'une heure de combat l'Amiral a été tué d'un coup de canon. Cette perte cruelle a donné le

---

[1] See the new materials on this subject collected by Mr. Sichel in his work, *Emma, Lady Hamilton.*—J. H. R.

[2] These figures, like those of Regnaud in his letter of 21 July (see above), are in francs. The present estimate exceeds the former by about one half.—J. H. R.

[3] Arch. Nat., AF III. 73.

tems à l'ennemi de mettre le vaisseau *Orient* entre deux feux. Il a été embrasé et a sauté.

Ainsi la victoire, fidelle sur terre à nos légions a échappé à nos marins. Mais ils seront vengés. Déjà la perte des ennemis a consolé leurs manes. Les Anglais ont eu, à ce qu'on assure, leur Amiral tué également.[1] Ils avaient cinq à six vaisseaux desemparés de tous leurs mâts, les autres très maltraités.

Les Maltais n'ont pu dans ce jour mémorable, mêler leur sang à celui que les Français ont répandu pour la République.

Les soldats du Régiment de Malte étaient à terre avec les Légions victorieuses de Bonaparte.

La Galère se trouvait dans le port avec le convoi qui n'a pas souffert la moindre atteinte, et les deux demie-galères de Civitta-Vecchia, montées par quelques Maltais, protégeaint l'aiguade de l'embouchure du Nil et n'ont pas été attaquées.

Français, Maltais, payons ensemble un tribut de regrets et de gloire à la mémoire de l'intrepide Brueys et de ses braves compagnons. Ils sont morts au champ d'honneur. Ne les plaignons pas. Ne les pleurons pas. Songeons à les imiter ou à les venger. C'est notre devoir, notre vœu, notre serment. Que ce soit aussi le vôtre.

(Signé) Vaubois.
(„) Regnaud de St. Jean d'Angely.

This dispatch of the 29th August was supplemented by two others of the same date from Regnaud de St. Jean d'Angely to the Executive Directory, complaining of the acts of the Neapolitan Government, and suggesting the best mode of communicating with the island, and covering a report on the position of Malta with regard to its finances and provisions—questions which had become vital owing to the anticipated blockade by the British.

Malte, 12 *Fructidor* an 6 (29*th August* 1798).[2]

Regnaud de Saint Jean d'Angely au Directoire Exécutif.

Citoyens Directeurs,—Au moment où le Citoyen Fournier porteur de mes dépêches avait mis à la voile, est arrivé le premier spéronare que j'avois envoyé à Naples.

Il m'apporte des dépêches qui en confirmant la mauvaise volonté, les intentions perfides du Roy de Naples, ne laissent aucune doute sur les embarras de notre position.

Ribaud, Consul en Sicile, fait ce qu'il peut, mais les ressources qu'il procure sont bien peu considérables & sans celles que j'ai eu de Barbarie nous aurions déjà manqué des premiers besoins. Je serai obligé cependant, d'après l'engagement pris par moy de le faire payer. Je le ferai avec quelques fonds que j'avois avec moi ou avec les crédits que la maison de commerce de mes beaux frères m'ont donné. Mais cette ressource même a un terme et je vous prie de prendre la position de l'Isle en considération.

---

[1] Nelson was slightly wounded.—J. H. R.
[2] Arch. Nat., AF III. 73.

La correspondance la moins difficile sera par Civitta Vecchia. Mes idées et celles du C^en. Lachaise se sont accordées à cet égard.

Une de mes dépêches vous parviendra par cette voye; je ne connais pas de moyen plus sûr pour l'expédition de votre réponse.

Le service sera organisé quand elle arrivera et pourra marcher régulièrement. J'écris à cet effet à vos commissaires à Rome.

Vous pouvès en même tems écrire pour Alexandrie, je me flatte toujours que le moyen d'y arriver par terre sera assuré.

Je joins ici la copie de la lettre du C^en. Lachize et du C^en. Ribbaud. N°. 1 & 2. Salut & respect.

(Signed) REGNAUD DE ST. JEAN D'ANGELY.

À Malte le 12 *Fructidor* an 6 (*29th August* 1798).[1]

Régnaud de Saint Jean d'Angely au Directoire Exécutif.

CITOYENS DIRECTEURS,—Le compte rendu par le Contre Amiral Villeneuve des évènements du 15 Thermidor est adressé par lui au Ministre de la Marine. Je joins icy sous le N°. 1 un apperçu de la position de Malte sous le rapport des approvisionnements et des finances.

J'ai entretenu une correspondence très active avec les Consuls de la République dans les diverses échelles.

J'ai engagé des négociants à faire des expéditions qui jusqu'à présent ont procuré en viande et bois le strict nécéssaire.

Mes instances à Tripoly et celles du Consul Guys au moment de son départ pour la Syrie ont obtenu un chargement de 140 bœufs, entré hier dans le port.

J'en attends un de 100 bœufs de Tunis. Mais il faut de l'argent pour payer les fournisseurs. Malgré trois expéditions successives à Naples je n'en ai reçu encore aucune nouvelle. Le premier spéronare expédié est parti d'ici le 6 Thermidor.

Vous verrès par les pièces que je vous envoye N°s. 2, 3, 4—4 bis qu'elle est la conduite soutenue de la Sicile depuis ma dernière dépêche. Les magasins de bled sont tous réunis à Girgenty comme ceux du vin à Mascaly. Les Maltais voudraient recevoir l'ordre d'aller les enlever. On ne seroit embarrassé que du nombre de ceux qui s'offriraient pour l'Expédition.

Tunis arme une flotille légère contre les Napolitains. Elle sera de 7 à 8 Bâtimens, qui désoleront leur commerce. Un Reis est icy avec une pinque de 20 canons. Il m'a renouvellé de la part du Bey l'assurance du désir qu'il a de fournir à Malte, tout ce que désirera la République.

Nous n'avons aucune nouvelle du vaisseau *le Généreux*, sorti de la Rade des Béquiers avec *le Guillaume Tell*. On espère qu'il est à Corfou.

Le porteur de cette dépêche qui vous sera expédié par triplicata a reçu pour instructions de chercher le convoy de Toulon et de luy faire part des évènemens.

Je vais chercher à établir par Tripoly, le Golfe de la Sidra & la Bombe, puis de là par terre le long de la côte jusqu'à Alexandrie une correspondance avec le Général en Chef Bonaparte. J'espère qu'elle sera prête pour vos premières dépêches. Il est impossible de se dissimuler

[1] Arch. Nat., AF III. 73.

qu'il n'y a que cette voye, ou celle de Constantinople, à moins d'évènemens extraordinaires & imprévus. Toute communication par mer doit être interdite.

Je crains beaucoup pour l'Aviso qui portoit le Général Lamasse [Lanusse ?] et Tallien et pour le dernier qui portoit le brave Adjud. Général Camin.

(Signed) REGNAUD DE ST. JEAN D'ANGELY.

NOTES SUR LES RESSOURCES DE LA DIVISION DE L'ARMÉE ET DU PORT DU MALTE.

Bonaparte a laissé la Division avec 75,000 [francs] et beaucoup de dettes. 340,000 [livres] d'argenterie environ ont été fondues & battues. Les pays n'avoit que des dettes. Celles du Grand Maître envers les particuliers et les Établissemens publics. Celle du Trésor d'environ 700 mille écus. Celles de l'Université ou caisse des subsistances de 1,200,000 écus. Celles faites pour le passage de l'armée. Il y auroit en Recouvrement des Impôts pour 50,000 [écus ?] par mois. Mais la Douane qui donne 25,000 [écus ?] ne produit rien. La ferme du droit sur le vin a produit 300 écus au lieu de 16,000 [écus ?]. La cause est le blocus du port. Les églises n'ont plus d'argenterie ou très peu. Les particuliers sont pauvres. Le pays ne produit d'objet d'exportation que le coton. Il ne peut sortir. On n'assureroit pas son neutre [?] à 25%. Cependant la dépense de la Division de terre est de 150,000 [écus ?]. Il faut pourvoir à un approvisionnement de siège de 273 M. Liv. non compris le bled. Il faut habiller la Troupe. Il faut monter l'Hôpital, où il n'y a pas une chemise, pas de draps, pas de drogues. Il faut fournir à la Marine, au lieu de 25,000 [écus ?] L50,000 par mois, puisque depuis deux mois elle a absorbé ses fonds et fait pour 60,000 [écus ?] de dettes. Il faut fournir aux besoins des équipages et des vaisseaux qui passent. Les 3 arrivés d'Egypte n'ont ni pièces à eau, ni cables, ni ancres, ni provisions d'aucune espèce. Il faudroit armer *l'Athénien* qui n'a que sa coque—encore elle est délabrée. Il faudroit monter un Arsenal de Marine, en mâtures, cordages, ancres, cloux, goudron, voilures &c. Tout manque. Il faudroit avoir des boulets pour l'Artillerie, du bois de charronnage ; du charbon dont il n'y a pas dix quintaux dans le pays. Enfin il faudroit du numeraire puisque dans un païs stérile c'est le seul moyen d'échange & qu'après avoir épuisé le peu qu'a frappé la monnoye, il n'y en aura plus dans l'Isle. Le Directoire jugera des moyens qu'il doit employer. Les communications les plus faciles sont par Barcelone, Gènes & Livourne, si celles de Naples et de Sicile sont interceptées. Des lettres de Change sur ces places se négocieroient ici pour 150 à 200,000 [écus ?] en s'y prenant bien. Mais il faut calculer sur une dépense de 250,000 [écus ?] par mois, des quelles il n'éxiste ici que 50,000 [écus ?] dans la plus heureuse supposition. Le bled seul est abondant, l'Isle en a pour 9 à 10 mois. Si le païs n'est pas secouru sous peu, il ne luy restera que du pain de l'eau et des armes.

(Signed) RÉGNAUD DE ST. JEAN D'ANGELY.

The news of the total defeat of the French fleet at Aboukir soon spread, nor did the proclamation of the 29th August have the desired effect. The people were ripe for revolt, and they did not hesitate to show their delight at the calamity which had overtaken the French. It required but the slightest cause to light the flame of rebellion, and that was to happen four days later, when, on the 2nd September, functionaries were sent from Valetta to Citta Vecchia for the purpose of disposing by public auction of certain articles belonging to the local Carmelite church, and of other churches and monasteries which had been suppressed. Against these measures the country people were determined to make a stand. The officials were met and compelled to return to Valetta, the tocsin was sounded from the church towers, the commanding officer and garrison of the ancient capital were barbarously murdered, and the Valetta garrison defied.[1]

[1] Captain Mahan (*Influence of Sea Power on the French Revolution and Empire,* vol. i. p. 285) wrongly gives the date of the Maltese insurrection as August 26.—J. H. R.

CHAPTER IX

THE INTERVENTION OF THE BRITISH FLEET

It is unnecessary to describe the departure of the French fleet from Malta, its pursuit by Nelson, and the victory gained by the latter at Aboukir on August 1, 1798. Of the French battleships, only two, the *Guillaume Tell* and the *Généreux*, together with the frigates *La Justice* and *Diane*, managed to escape. We are concerned here only with those details of the naval campaign which bear upon the fate of Malta.

By order of Nelson, on Tuesday, the 14th August, Captain Sir James Saumarez in H.M.S. *Orion* (74) sailed from Aboukir for Gibraltar and England with the following sail of the line: *Bellerophon* (74), 590; *Minotaur* (74), 648; *Defence* (74), 590; *Audacious* (74), 590; *Theseus* (74), 590; and *Majestic* (74), 590; each ship of the line having under her special charge one of the prizes lately taken at the Nile, viz. *Le Tonnant* (80), *Franklin* (80), *Le Souverain Peuple* (74), *Conquérant* (74), *Spartiate* (74), and *L'Aquilon* (74).[1] The remainder of the British fleet under Nelson, after refitting (so far as circumstances allowed), viz. the *Vanguard* (74), *Culloden* (74), *Alexander* (74), and *Bonne Citoyenne* (sloop), sailed at 8.30 p.m. of Sunday, the 19th, for Naples, to obtain there a thorough overhaul and repair.

Five days later they fell in with Sir James Saumarez's squadron off Cape Celadonia in Asia Minor. These vessels, owing to their battered condition, and having to tow the prizes, had been unable to make much progress.[2]

This meeting of the two squadrons is referred to in the *Vanguard's* log-book as follows: 'On Friday the 24th August 1798 at 5 a.m. sighted the *Orion*, Sir J. Saumarez, and twelve other ships of the Line; remained in sight of each other until sunset of Friday the 31st August, when *La Bonne Citoyenne* was detached for Sir J. Saumarez.'[3]

It is interesting to observe here that this separation of the two

---

[1] Nicolas' *Nelson's Dispatches*, vol. iii. p. 101.
[2] *Ibid.* vol. iii. p. 107.
[3] Brit. Mus. Add. MSS. 34974.

fleets occurred off the south-west point of Candia, and, with regard to time, within thirty-six hours of the outbreak of the Maltese insurrection; and as from the log-book we gather that the latitude and longitude were then 34° 39′ N. and 26° 48′ E., they were consequently 550 miles distant from that island.

Before sailing from Aboukir Bay, Nelson informed Lieutenant Hoste, of the *Mutine*, who had been sent on six days previously with dispatches, that he intended to make for some point between Cape Passaro and Syracuse, and would there expect to receive all correspondence which might be accumulated.

During the voyage, and when in the waters of Southern Italy, Nelson was informed of the Maltese insurrection, as may be gathered from his dispatch to Captain Hood, of H.M.S. *Zealous*, dated the 8th September. In the meanwhile, the Portuguese admiral, De Niza, who had passed Messina *en route* to Egypt on the 28th August to join Nelson, returned thence, anchoring in that port on the 13th September. On the day previous Nelson had reached the Faro, and being possessed of the information regarding the revolt in Malta, he immediately ordered the cutter *Earl St. Vincent* to proceed with dispatches to the Marquis de Niza, requesting him to sail without delay to that island and blockade Valetta, and endeavour to capture the French two-decker *Le Guillaume Tell* (80), and the two frigates, *Diane* and *La Justice*, which rumour gave as still cruising off Malta. The Portuguese squadron consisted of; he *Principe Real* (74), flagship of Rear-Admiral the Marquis de Niza; *Rainha de Portugal* (74), *St. Sebastien* (74), *Alfonço de Albuquerque* (74), and *Falcao* (brig). These ships had been placed by the Portuguese Government under the orders of Earl St. Vincent, who in the beginning of July dispatched them from Lisbon to reinforce Nelson's fleet, with instructions to proceed via Leghorn and Naples, and thence to Alexandria.[1]

These arrangements had been made by virtue of an old treaty between the Courts of Great Britain and Portugal contracted in 1703, wherein it had been stipulated that the officer of either contracting Power commanding a smaller number of ships should be subordinate to the one who commanded the larger number, without consideration of their respective rank.

This stipulation was duly conveyed to the Marquis de Niza, when ordered on the 2nd July to place himself and squadron under the directions of Nelson, who at that time was sailing in quest of the French expedition.

Continuing his voyage to Naples, and when off Stromboli, Nelson on the 15th September ordered Captain Gage in the *Terpsichore* (who had just joined Nelson with dispatches from Naples) to proceed to

---

[1] Nicolas, *Dispatches of Nelson*, vol. iii. pp. 117, 121. Brit. Mus. Add. MSS. 34963.

THE INTERVENTION OF THE BRITISH FLEET 109

Malta by the northern and western coasts of Sicily, and acquaint the Maltese that Sir Horatio Nelson would come to their relief as soon as he had refitted his squadron at Naples.[1] Gage was able to accomplish this errand by the 22nd September.

Whilst Nelson was proceeding to Naples, Saumarez, with his fleet and captured prizes, called at Augusta, in Sicily, for a supply of water on the 17th September, and after replenishing, which occupied a few days, he sailed again for Gibraltar. Upon rounding Cape Passaro on the 23rd he fell in with De Niza and his squadron, who had been off Malta blockading since the 19th. Saumarez, it would appear, remained three days off Malta, and in communication with De Niza.

During this interval the British admiral was visited by a deputation of Maltese asking for arms and ammunition, and suggesting that a summons to surrender should be sent to General Vaubois in Valetta. De Niza approved of the suggestion. The particulars of their joint summons to the French garrison to surrender are given in Saumarez's dispatch to Nelson, dated the 26th September, as follows[2]:—

> On Sunday (the 23rd September) we fell in with Marquis de Niza's squadron off Malta. The day following we were kept in sight of that Island by light airs and calms, which continued most of Tuesday.
>
> On that morning (the 25th) a deputation from the principal inhabitants came on board this ship (the *Orion*) to solicit a supply of arms and ammunition, at the same time informing me that the French garrison in the town of Valetta were driven to great distress, and that they had good grounds to believe the appearance of the English squadron would induce them to surrender, if they were summoned to that purpose. I waited on the Marquis de Niza, who readily concurred in sending a flag of truce, with the enclosed proposal, dated September the 25th, to the French general.[3]

After three hours' deliberation the latter returned the following laconic answer:—

> [Translation.]
>
> You have without doubt forgotten that Frenchmen are now at Malta. The future of its inhabitants is a matter which does not concern you.
>
> With regard to your summons to surrender, Frenchmen do not understand such style.
>
> The General Commander-in-Chief of the Islands of Malta and Gozo,
>
> (Signed) VAUBOIS.

Upon receipt of this refusal Sir James Saumarez, before proceeding on his voyage to Gibraltar and England with the captured

---

[1] Nicolas, *Dispatches of Nelson*, vol. iii. p. 124.
[2] Brit. Mus. Add. MSS. 34907, f. 294.
[3] Clarke and MacArthur, *Nelson's Letters*, vol. ii. p. 116.

prizes, supplied the Maltese with 1,062 muskets, ball cartridges, cartouche-boxes, and 200 barrels of gunpowder, which were taken out of the French prizes, forwarding the following statement to Nelson :—

AN ACCOUNT OF THE AMMUNITION SUPPLIED BY HIS MAJESTY'S SQUADRON UNDER THE ORDERS OF CAPTAIN SIR JAMES SAUMAREZ TO THE INHABITANTS OF MALTA.[1]

Muskets, 1,062 ; do. ball cartridges, 18,740 ; bayonets, 142 ; cartouche-boxes complete with musket ball cartridges, 4,080 ; cartouche-boxes, 204 ; flints, 1,060 ; wooden cases, 20 ; cartridges filled, 6 [cwts. ?] ; musket balls, 32 pounds.

PS.— Supplied a vessel from Malta off the port of Syracuse with 2,000 ball cartridges and 500 flints.

I hereby certify that the above arms and ammunition have been supplied by my order to the inhabitants of the Island of Malta.

Given on board His Majesty's ship *Orion*, off Malta, 25th September 1798.
(Signed) JAS. SAUMAREZ.

The first official news of the Maltese insurrection reached Syracuse on the 4th September. The authorities there, under that date, informed the Neapolitan Government

that a Maltese fishing boat, under the command of Publio Camilleri, and manned by a crew of nine men, had arrived from Marsa Scala in the Island of Malta, which had been sent by John, chief of the Maltese people in Casal Zeitun, who reported that on Sunday, the 2nd instant, the French went to the old city for the purpose of looting the Church of St. Paul, which action was opposed by the people *en masse*, when the French were obliged to retire to the city of Valetta, and not without some loss of their men.[2]

Nelson arrived at Naples on Saturday, the 22nd September, 11.30 a.m., to find the *Culloden* at Castellamare, and the *Alexander* and *La Bonne Citoyenne* already in Naples Harbour. The delay in Nelson's arrival had been caused by a serious accident to the *Vanguard* on Saturday, the 15th, when during a heavy squall her foremast, head of the main-topmast, and jibboom were carried away, whereby four of her seamen were lost and several wounded. In this disabled condition she had to be towed by the *Thalia*. Immediately upon arrival the Neapolitan Government gave Nelson all the information they had received regarding the outbreak in Malta, namely, such as had been brought to Syracuse by the fishing boat on the 4th, and the substance of Messrs. Briffa and Farrugia's mission, who had been dispatched for that special purpose by the Maltese insurgents, and had arrived at Naples by a Maltese speronara

[1] Brit. Mus. Add. MSS. 34907, f. 296.
[2] Foreign Office Records, Sicily, 11.

by the 9th.[1] The information thus received had already been communicated by General Acton to Sir William Hamilton on the 12th. The following is a synopsis of his letter :—

GENERAL ACTON TO SIR WILLIAM HAMILTON.[2]

12th September 1798.

The people of Malta have risen for the expulsion of the invaders of that Island, which was betrayed by the infamous treason of some Knights of the Order of St. John. . . . They acknowledge their constant and lawful Sovereign, the King of Sicily. This good and faithful people require, as lawful subjects, the protection and power of their King for help in this moment, and desire only muskets, ammunition, and victuals. They have authorised two of their Deputies to express before his Majesty their dutiful dependence.[3]

The French garrison had offered twice to capitulate, but the Maltese want to have them at discretion, in order to punish the heads of this treason and to be free from every sort of condition.

The demands are for some officers and victuals especially, and for arms and ammunition. They want likewise several of our King's colours to hoist for showing their dependence from [sic] his Sicilian Majesty as his true and faithful vassals.

This information was further supplemented by what was termed 'secret intelligence' from Malta (more or less accurate) up to the end of August, and within a few days before the outbreak of the revolution. This report had been received by the Neapolitan Government from one of its emissaries stationed there, and is here given verbatim :—

By secret but sure means, I have been able to discover that the inhabitants of that Island are by no means satisfied with their new Government or Governor-in-Chief, Mons$^{r.}$ de Vaubois, and second in command, Mons$^{r.}$ Bertier [sic], who are Jews by birth, and of that sect.

The contributions imposed on the patriots are enormous, and exacted with the utmost rigour—there is great misery and a general discontent. Massacres of the French are daily committed, both by day and night, with open insults and contempt. The east part of the Island of Gozo, where the towers are situated to guard that part of it, and exactly where the French under Bonaparte suffered some loss on the invasion of Malta, is now abandoned by the French to the inhabitants, after having taken away the greatest part of the artillery—therefore the extent of it, including two or three rows of houses or villages, is entirely independent of the French, and they govern themselves openly as they like, without any notice being taken of them by the French. The garrison, from near 4,000 men it was composed of, is now reduced to 2,000 to 2,500. The orders that are daily given by their provisional Government are frequently

---

[1] Clarke and MacArthur, Nelson, vol. ii. p. 99.
[2] Foreign Office Records, Sicily, 11.
[3] It should be remembered that the King of Naples was the suzerain of Malta.—J. H. R.

in writing and in print, but little observed or obeyed. One was latterly given out to acknowledge no longer the Pope or the Bishop, and that baptism should not be conferred till seven years after birth. That matrimony is no sacrament. They have shut up three convents of monks, and enrolled all the Maltese sailors, and obliged them to be ready for going to sea. On being, however, called to man the ship of the line and frigate which belonged to the Knights of Malta, most of them refused to go, and with great difficulty they united a certain number to send out with the above ships, which, after a short cruise in the Channel, they were obliged to return in port, for want of their full compliment [*sic*] of men. Besides those two vessels, there are in readiness two galleys, which equally belonged to the Knights of Malta, and six transports, all armed, but they have no sailors to man them.

The garrison is composed mostly of a collection of different nations, and so discontented, that a few days ago they posted up at the house of the Commander-in-Chief mottoes with these words: '"*Equality*," "*Equality*"; but where is that equality ?' The chiefs are well lodged, live well, sleep better, and the soldiers die with hunger, and sleep on the ground.

There is a report that Bonaparte is to return soon, having prepared in that expectation lodgings, and constructed a large barrack in the Lazzaretto, in case, on his arrival, it should be found necessary to put him in quarantine.

These are the news I have been able to collect by my secret agents in that Island. I will not, however, answer for the absolute truth of them, considering the Maltese as a corrupted and suspicious people.[1]

On this same day, the 12th September, ten days after the outbreak, the deputies of the Maltese people, assembled at their headquarters at Notabile, addressed to Nelson the following letter :—

[Translation.]

From the City of Notabile,
12th September 1798.

YOUR EXCELLENCY,[2]—The population of the Islands of Malta and Gozo, betrayed by a certain number of the Knights of the Order, and by a few Maltese, their adherents, find themselves assailed by the French Republican Army, which since the 10th of the past June have exercised the most tyrannical government in the Islands. Moreover, not satisfied with the immense property belonging to the Grand Master, and to the Order of St. John, which they seized, they have appropriated all other.

Wearied beyond measure by these innumerable insults, the said people regained their liberty on the 3rd of the current month of September, and by armed force possessed themselves of the city of Notabile, the ancient capital of the Island, the whole of the coast, and, of most importance, the ports of St. Paul and Marsa Scirocco. The French garrison retain only the city of Valetta, its ports, and the fortifications belonging thereto.

Whilst we acknowledge for our ancient Sovereign His Majesty the

---

[1] Brit. Mus. Add. MSS. 34907, f. 233.
[2] *Ibid.* 34942, f. 234.

THE INTERVENTION OF THE BRITISH FLEET

King of the Two Sicilies, who has possessed the high dominion of these Islands, we have, in the capacity of Deputies of the people of these Islands, done ourselves the honour of addressing His Majesty, and have sent two delegates, who sailed on this mission from St. Paul's Bay on the 5th instant.

The French Fleet having been defeated off Alexandria by the Forces of Great Britain, which Your Excellency commands as Admiral in these waters, and this being an opportune moment to blockade the French garrison, which is aided only by a very weak squadron, composed of one line-of-battle ship and two Frigates, the remnant of the defeated fleet at Alexandria, we now address you for the purpose of attaining that object.

The Maltese line-of-battle ship and two Frigates are also in port, but disarmed, and we have now the honour to supplicate Your Excellency, as an ally of His Majesty the King of the Two Sicilies, our Sovereign, immediately to succour us by blockading the Grand Harbour with four ships, in order that a free passage may be afforded to vessels sailing from the ports of St. Paul and Marsa Scirocco to Sicily for procuring provisions for this Island—the more so as the Island is completely denuded of all food, and unprovided with munitions of war.

Under these critical and pressing circumstances, we fervently implore you to accede to our prayer on behalf of the entire Maltese Nation, whom we represent, and who are anxiously desirous of your protection,

We have the honour, &c.,
(Signed) COUNT SALVATORE MANDUCA.
" MARCHESE VINCENZO DE PIRO.
" EMMANUELE VITALE.
" CONTE FERDINANDO TEUMA-CASTELLETTI.

Sir James Saumarez's dispatch to Nelson of the 26th September was conveyed in H.M.S. *Terpsichore,* and delivered on the 29th, when Sir William Hamilton immediately acquainted Lord Grenville with the important intelligence that Valetta, by order of Nelson, was blockaded. The following is a synopsis of his letter:—

SIR WILLIAM HAMILTON TO LORD GRENVILLE.

Naples, 29th Septr. 1798.

Captain Gage in the *Terpsichore* arrived here this morning.

He left Malta on the 26th inst., when Sir James Saumarez, with his squadron, in conjunction with the Portuguese squadron under the command of the Marquis Nizza, had summoned the French to surrender and evacuate Malta, which was refused by Mr Vaubois, the Commander-in-Chief of the Valetta [garrison], and that Sir James Saumarez was proceeding with his squadron and French prizes to Gibraltar, having left the Portuguese to block Malta, and having at the request of the Maltese insurgents supplied them with plenty of ammunition and twelve hundred stand of arms from his French prizes. . . . This Government, as yet, has not (at least openly) given any assistance to the Maltese insurgents to recover an Island which they claim as their own, and the insurgents are fighting under Neapolitan colours—*most extraordinary.*[1]

[1] Foreign Office Records, Sicily, 11.

Of the various accounts of the incidents which occurred in Malta between the 2nd and 5th September (the latter being the date of the first application for assistance presented to King Ferdinand IV of Naples), perhaps those given by Vassallo in his 'History of Malta,' and by Azopardi in his 'Journal of the Capture of Malta and Gozo by the French Republic,' are the most lucid.

On the 2nd September, Notary A. P. Spiteri, G. Spiteri, and another were sent to Rabato, of Notabile, to bring to Valetta certain articles belonging to the suppressed Church of Our Lady of Mount Carmel, but the people there prevented them carrying out their instructions. At that moment a boy rang the church bell, when a crowd assembled, and the three officials had to retire, amidst much whistling, hissing, and signs of derision. The 2nd of September happening to be a Sunday, many of the country folk from the neighbouring villages had congregated at Notabile.[1]

This gathering of the People, and the attitude they bore, offended Masson, the officer then in command of the local garrison, who, accompanied by a Lieutenant and a soldier, proceeded to Rabato, sword in hand, in anger, and full of threats.

The crowd gathered closer, and stones were thrown. Masson took refuge in the house of Notary Bezzina and closed the door; the mob smashed the door and entered, and notwithstanding all his supplications, and the breaking of his sword, Masson was hurled into the street from the balcony, and killed on the spot, the soldier having been previously killed, whilst the Lieutenant escaped to Notabile, the gates then being immediately closed by the garrison of sixty soldiers.

The bells of the churches were immediately set ringing, and messengers dispatched to the various villages, and in a few hours the insurrection spread over the whole Island, as well as Gozo.

Firearms were found at the Palace of Sant Antonio, also at Zebbug, where a small armoury existed, which was seized, killing the head of that municipality, a certain Stanislas l'Hoste, a Maltese by birth.

During that night a rigorous search for firearms and ammunition was made. A correct version of what had happened at Rabato did not reach Vaubois until night, when a council of war was immediately held.

As a result of their debate, a messenger was dispatched to Notabile, promising a reinforcement of 200 men on the morrow, but whilst *en route* he was captured, and taken before Emmanuele Vitale, one of the leaders of the movement.

At dawn of the following day, the crowd, led by Vitale, besieged Notabile, and succeeded in effecting an entrance into the city, when the garrison offered to surrender.

This was accepted, but before the formalities were concluded some of the French fired, killing four of the people, when the whole body of the French were slaughtered, and their bodies carried to the hill of Imtarfa, and there burned; whilst the ancient standard of Malta, white and red, was raised upon the ramparts of the Old City. Aware of reinforcements having been promised to the French garrison at Notabile, the insurgents marched towards Valetta, and met the French troops in the vicinity of

[1] Vassallo, p. 764.

Porte des Bombes, where, after a brisk engagement, they compelled them to take refuge within the city walls, leaving behind a few killed and three wounded, one of the latter being an officer.

So infuriated had the people become, that they spared not the lives of three Maltese officers, by name T. Attard, G. B. Trigance, and Ferroni, who favoured the Republican party, and in like manner (presumably for the same reason) several citizens who happened to be in the country fell victims, among the number the ex-Chevalier Vatanges.

Finding the revolt was becoming so serious, Vaubois decided to send a larger body of men against the insurgents, when news reached the General that an outbreak had also taken place at Cospicua, where many of the peasants had arrived from the southern villages.

The French flag had been lowered, and several street fights had taken place with the military, but, being within the walls, the authorities were able to quell it by fire from Fort St. Michele, and shooting two of the insurgents on the spot. The line-of-battle ship *Dego* was also brought to bear on the city, and the threat of an immediate bombardment quelled the rising there.

After this experience Vaubois decided not to send any expeditions into the country.

Within Valetta, fearing a rising similar to that of Cospicua, all firearms were ordered to be delivered up, and the National Guard was dissolved.

The Government expected an early submission of the country people, but the latter were not to be pacified, and at once assumed the offensive.

On this same 4th of September, various influential citizens assembled at Citta Vecchia for the purpose of proposing the constitution of a National Assembly, which would assist and guide the movement which had so unexpectedly, and perhaps prematurely, occurred.

The motion was received and passed with acclamation.[1]

The notary Emmanuele Vitale was there and then elected General in command of the insurgent troops, and as Representatives of the people, Count Salvatore Manduca, Marquis Vincenzo de Piro, and Count Ferdinand Teuma. To the above was also added by the villages of Zebbug and Siggieu, Canon Don Francesco Saverio Caruana, as General of the forces contributed by them.

The Representatives at their first sitting appointed Lorenzo Bugeja as their secretary; Modesto Sapiano as chief of the Artillery; Giuseppe Azzopardi, registrar of Orders; Giuseppe Abela, storekeeper and purveyor of grain; Gaetano Vitale and Pietro Paolo Bezzina, receivers of grain; Alessio Huereb, courier; Giuseppe Musci, inspector of the towers, and Paolo Galea and Vincenzo Muscat, distributors of bread.

No sooner was Canon Caruana in power, than he represented to the Assembly that the ancient flag of Malta was nothing more than an emblem, recording a domination which had ceased centuries ago, in other words, nothing more than an historical reminiscence, whilst what they required at the present moment was the help and protection of an existing Power; that for reasons of State, as well as to obtain munitions of war and provisions quickly, it would be advisable, in the interests of the people, to place

[1] Azopardi, p. 93.

themselves under the protection of the Sovereign of Sicily, proclaiming him as their Sovereign, and who was then in close alliance with the Powers at enmity with France.

Consequently, one of the first acts of the Representatives was to acquaint His Majesty the King of Naples, in the following letter, what had occurred in Malta, and to solicit His Majesty's protection and immediate aid.

[Translation.]

To His Majesty the King of the Two Sicilies.

SIRE,—The Maltese people at the present time being reduced to the direst extremities, humbly prostrate themselves at the feet of Your Majesty, for the purpose of representing how unable they have been to suffer any longer the tyrannical despotism of the French, who for their misfortune have invaded and occupied their Island for the last four months.

Animated by a sudden and natural impulse, we have risen in revolt, for the purpose of shaking off this unbearable yoke, and in the short space of seventeen hours have succeeded in capturing from them the ancient city of Notabile, and all the outlying towers in the country.

The enthusiasm which the Maltese have shown in their desire to capture the capital and adjacent cities cannot be described; but owing to the strength of their fortifications, it will be a matter of difficulty to successfully storm them. The object in view being their emancipation, all the country proprietors have contributed, and still contribute, provisions and large sums of money, for the necessary maintenance of the poorer classes who have joined the forces.

Whilst the besieged are obstinate, and disinclined to surrender the capital and leave Malta, there is every probability of a siege lasting a long time, with the consequent result that provisions for the inhabitants of the country will constantly decrease, whilst the granaries in the besieged cities are abundantly provided.

We have further to represent, that whilst the funds appertaining to the University,[1] as well as the public banks, as well as those which belong to the wealthy classes, are to be found in the city now occupied by our enemies, the country is thus deprived of all means of subsistence, and whereas no further aid can be obtained from the inhabitants, who at the best of times are not very rich, we shall find ourselves compelled to abandon the enterprise, or die of famine, unless some opportune and adequate assistance is rendered.

As the Maltese, under the existing calamitous circumstances, can have no more loving and tender Father than Your Majesty, they now implore Your Majesty's most powerful protection, and they further pray for Your Majesty's merciful compassion by the granting of permission to obtain from Sicily the necessary grain and all other provisions upon credit, the cost of which will be defrayed at the close of the campaign; and whereas firearms and ammunition are also required, they further take the liberty of asking Your Majesty for this supply of warlike stores.

The particular affection which Your Majesty has always evinced (and

[1] 'University' here, as before, means the corporation for supplying the island with corn.—J. H. R.

on occasions far less pressing than the present) towards this Island, persuades the Inhabitants that if Your Majesty will deign to cast a benign glance upon them, and will take into consideration their miserable and deplorable state, Your Majesty will then not refuse them this desired act of grace, otherwise they will find themselves compelled to perish miserably, unable to continue the effort which they are making to free themselves from a Nation opposed to all the tenets of the Christian religion; an effort which is also made as the first duty of a Government, and likewise on the grounds of public tranquillity.

All the world acknowledges, that amongst the many virtues which adorn a sovereign, the greatest of all is charity; therefore the Maltese cannot doubt but that they will obtain all that they ardently desire from the benign hand of Your Majesty, whose glorious name, under thousands of guises, and particularly for his mercy and compassion, is universally admitted.

May the Almighty inspire in Your Majesty an early and efficacious response to the prayers of your dear Maltese children and subjects, whilst they on their own account, as well as on behalf of their descendants, will ever pray for the prosperity of their beloved Sovereign, and that the Almighty may increase the days and bless Your Majesty with ever continued health.

Your most obliged and most affectionate subjects,

(Signed) CANON D. SAVERIO CARUANA.
,, EMANUELE VITALE.
,, CONTE SALVATORE MANDUCA.
,, MARCHESE VINCENZO DE PIRO.
,, CONTE FERDINANDO TEUMA.

Malta, 5th September 1798.

The circumstances connected with this application of the Maltese deputies, and with their acknowledgment of vassalage to the Neapolitan Government, render it necessary to present here a brief recital of the history of the connexion of these islands, which had been considered as a fiefdom to the kingdom of Sicily from the time of the Norman occupation and their successors, up to the date of the French capture in 1798, which cancelled such rights of sovereignty.

Not to go farther back than 1421, Queen Joanna of Naples in that year adopted as her successor Alfonzo V of Aragon (son of Ferdinand the Just), who in 1435 united Sicily to his dominions, Upon his death in 1458 without legitimate issue, his illegitimate son, Ferdinand, took Naples, and Sicily fell to Alfonzo's younger brother, John. John's son, Ferdinand the Catholic, succeeded to the island of Sicily in 1479, having married Isabella, Queen of Castile, in 1469. In 1504 Ferdinand perfidiously usurped the sovereignty of Naples, uniting Naples and Sicily as provinces of Spain.

Ferdinand having no male heirs, his grandson, son of his daughter Joanna, who had married Philip of Austria, became, upon the death of Ferdinand in 1516, Charles the First of Spain and Fifth of

Germany; and it was under this monarch that Malta was conveyed as a fief to the Knights of St. John, on the 24th March 1530. From the date when Ferdinand acquired the sovereignty of Naples (1504), up to the death of Charles II in 1700, Naples and Sicily, as provinces of Spain, were governed by viceroys.

In 1700 the War of the Spanish Succession broke out, which lasted thirteen years, when at the Peace of Utrecht, in 1713, Naples fell to Austria, and Sicily to Savoy; but in 1720, Austria, under Charles VI, German Emperor, acquired Sicily by surrendering Sardinia in exchange to the House of Savoy.

War having been declared by Spain against the Emperor Charles VI in 1733, it was arranged at the peace which followed that Naples and Sicily should be ceded to Don Carlos of Bourbon, son of Philip V of Spain, with a stipulation that they should never be united to the Spanish Monarchy. Upon the death of his elder brother, Ferdinand VI, this Don Carlos, as Charles III, succeeded to the throne of Spain in 1759. He thereupon, in fulfilment of the above stipulation, abdicated the throne of Naples and Sicily in favour of his third son, Ferdinand IV, who was not of age until 1768.

This monarch reigned (including the regency) from 1759 to 1825 : up to 1806 as King of Naples and Sicily, from 1806 to 1815 as King of Sicily (Joseph Bonaparte and Murat being successively in occupation of the throne of Naples from 1806 to 1815), and from 1815, by the provisions of the Treaty and Congress of Vienna in that year, he was restored to his former patrimony, and assumed the title of Ferdinand I, 'King of the Two Sicilies'; whilst, so far as Malta and Gozo are concerned, this same Congress at the same time *diplomatically* severed their connexion with that kingdom by confirming the sovereignty which Great Britain had already acquired by the right of conquest, and by the Treaty of Paris of the year previous.

We now resume the general narrative.

Whilst waiting for a favourable reply to the petition to the King of Sicily, heavy guns were taken from the towers bordering the seacoast, and planted against Porte des Bombes, at a point called Samra. Trenches were opened at Corradino, others in the neighbourhood of Fort Ricasoli, and others at Ghorgar, a short distance from Fort Manoel. Field-pieces were placed at Casal Zabbar on the road to Casal Luca, and in the vicinity of Tarxien.

The head-quarters were fixed at the Palace of San Giuseppe (St. Antonio), where Vitale and Caruana took up their residence, but pending the arrival of ammunition active hostilities only occasionally occurred.

On the day following the dispatch of this petition to the King of Naples the French military authorities in Valetta held a council of war, whereat, whilst vowing to defend the fortress to the last moment, they informed the Directory that funds for the purchase of victuals were what they chiefly needed.

The *procès verbal* of this meeting was forwarded to the Directory by the same opportunity as a dispatch from Regnaud of the day following, and was to this effect:

À Malte le 20 *Fructidor*, an 6 de la Révolution
(*6th September* 1798).[1]

Le Conseil de Guerre de la Div$^{on.}$ du G$^{al.}$ Vaubois au Directoire Exécutif de la République française.

Lors de l'arriveé du Contre Amiral Villeneuve en ce port, il sembloit difficile que nous eussions des nouvelles plus importantes à vous transmettre, pour la République. Celles que nous avons à vous apprendre ne le sont pas moins.

Nous vivions icy dans une assez grande sécurité. Tous les patriotes pensoient que les Maltais étoient incapables de former aucun projet contre les français. Nous nous reposions d'ailleurs, sur le sentiment de la conduite tenue icy par l'armée et tous les agens la République.

Aucune réquisition n'a eu lieu dans le pays. Aucune contribution n'a été établie. Aucune espèce de propriété n'a cessé d'être respectée. Aucun individu n'a été imprisonné, hors deux Maltais accusés par leur compatriotes mêmes et remis au Tribunal Criminel composé de Maltais.

Cependant les mêmes individus qui avoient calomnié les français pour prolonger leur empire, ont continué leurs impostures pour le recouvrir. Le Dimanche 16 courant (2 Sep$^{re.}$ Vieux Style) étoit le jour indiqué par le Roi de Naples pour faire *lever son peuple contre une nation ennemi du trône et de l'autel*. Il paroit que la même époque étoit fixé pour Malte.

Ce même Dimanche le peuple s'est attroupé dans la plupart des cazaux ou villages, disant qu'ils voulaient garder la maison de Dieu, *d'autres qu'ils vouloient deffendre leurs églises*, ceux cy qu'ils voulaient empêcher qu'on n'enlevât leur argenterie. Deux compagnies de carabiniers furent envoyés dans la nuit du 16 au 17 vers la Cité Vieille pour fortifier le détachement. Arrêtées, cernées par une troupe nombreuse de paysans armés, elles n'ont dû leur salut qu'à l'intelligence & à la bravoure du Cap$^{ne.}$ Busnot du 1$^{er.}$ B$^{on.}$ de la 23$^{me.}$ ½ Brigade, qui, blessé mais intrépide, s'est fait jour à travers les Rebelles avec la bayonnette. Bientôt de nombreux rapports ont appris que dès la veille tout étoit en insurrection dans la campagne, et que des troupes de païsans, ayant des prêtres pour instigateurs et probablement des chefs, étoient en armes sur divers points. On a coupé l'aqueduc qui porte l'eau à la ville.

Les portes de la ville ont été fermées, toutes les mésures de précautions ont été prises, toutes les batteries ont été armées, les Bâtimens de Guerre prévenus de se tenir prêts à séconder la force militaire de la garnison.

La Garde Nationale de la municipalité de l'ouest a été rassemblée, placée au millieu d'un B$^{on.}$ quarré de français et désarmée.

Une proclamation a ordonné à tout habitant de déposer ses armes sous peine d'être fusillé.

[1] Arch. Nat., AF III. 73.

Cependant la partie de la ville qui est au levant et comprend La Sengle, le Bourg, la Victorieuse et Burmola, s'étoit insurgée. Deux Chefs de B$^{on.}$ y ont péri, avec deux officers & plusieurs français. L'Adjudant Général Brouard a reçu ordre de s'y porter. Sa présence, celle d'un B$^{on.}$ de renfort et le canon des Forts St. Elme, Riccazoli et St. Ange, qui menaçoient les habitans ont facilité le désarmement.

De manière, que depuis le 18 nous sommes maîtres de la ville et n'y sommes entourés que d'habitans sans armes, du moins autant que nous avons pû nous en assurer.

Cependant nous n'avons eu aucune nouvelle du Détachement de la Cité Vieille, et les rapports annoncent que, surpris pendant la nuit, il a été massacré.

On craint d'apprendre sur la garnison du Goze, commandée par le Chef de B$^{on.}$ Lochey, des nouvelles aussi fâcheuses.

Grâce à la bravoure, à l'intelligence du Sergent de la 41$^{ème.}$ ½ Brigade Mourey, on a sauvé le Détachement qu'il commandait au fort St. Julien et le Conseil de Guerre l'a élevé au grade de sous-lieutenant dans lequel il vous prie de le confirmer.

Le Conseil de Guerre au surplus considérant la faiblesse de la garnison, comparée à l'étendue des fortifications, et au nombre de points à garder, observant qu'il n'existe presque point de pièces de campagne, et aucun affut, remarquant que la nature du sol, les murailles qui bordent les chemins, et entourent chaque subdivision de propriété, multipliés à l'infini, donnent grand avantage aux naturels du païs, tirailleurs exellens, chasseurs adroits, a pensé qu'il étoit de son devoir de défendre, de conserver la ville contre les attaques des insurgés.

Ce qui l'a fixé encore plus à cette résolution a été la crainte de voir les Anglais, ou de perfides voisins apporter aux Rebelles des secours d'hommes et de munitions.

En ce cas il n'y auroit pas un homme de trop. Il y auroit peut être 2,000 de manque pour le service, et de sacrifier dix même pour en détruire cent, a semblé un calcul irréfléchi.

Notre position en résultat, est donc en ce moment telle que nous allons vous la retracer. Il existe à peu près 3,000 ho$^{es.}$ de garnison pour les armes.

Les Chasseurs Maltais sont dans la campagne et contre nous.

Les païsans se sont armés et sont encore en armes et de garde sur plusieurs points.

Nous avons au plus 200 canoniers.

Ceux qu'on avoit organisés ont été suspendus par une juste défiance.

Nous avons un Général de Div$^{on.}$, un de Brigade, un Adjudant Général et les forts ne peuvent plus être commandés que par des Cap$^{nes.}$

Nous avons 36 mille salmes de bled pezant chacune 4 qu^x. un tiers.

Nous avons un approvisionnement de siège en biscuit & lard, mais l'eau de vie, le vin nous manquent entièrement.

Nous n'avons pas de légumes, presque pas de bois.

Nous avons mis en réquisition 25 M$^{re.}$ de riz, quelques pièces de vin pour les malades, et env$^{on.}$ 4,000 P$^{tes.}$ d'eau de vie.

Nous avons quelques bœufs arrivés de Tunis. L'argent nous manque, pour envoyer en Cephalonie, ou en Dalmatie, prendre du vin et si nous réussisons [*sic*] à envoyer, serons-nous assès heureux pour voir revenir les bâtiments.

Cependant outre la garnison, nous devons pourvoir aux besoins de

5 vaisseaux de guerre, de leur équipage, et de leur garnison, nous devons payer, nourrir les marins qui montent de petits bâtiments envoyés à la côte pour intercepter les communications, les secours de Sicile ou d'ailleurs pour les insurgés.

Dans cette position cependant, la prévoyance n'a rien ôté à l'énergie, le danger a exalté le courage. Tous les français pressés, unis, infatigables quand il s'agit du salut d'un poste important, ne songent qu'à le défendre. Ils en sont comptables à la patrie et ils le défendront.

Le compte que nous vous rendons est pour que vous sachiez que la connoissance de n$^{e.}$ position n'a pu faire noître un moment de decouragement ni de doute : pour que vous sachiez quelle nature de secours nous seroit nécessaire. Mais pour que soyès instruits que nous saurons y suppléer, si la nécessité l'ordonne et que tant que nous pourrons tenir icy, tant qu'il nous restera des forces et de la vie pour nous défendre, Malte sera à la République.

Si vous pouvès venir à notre aide, les trois articles sur lesquels nous insisterons en finissant sont le besoin d'hommes, de canoniers surtout, de boulets, d'argent en piastres, mais avec ou sans secours, nous nous défendrons, nous soutiendrons la gloire du nom français et de nos armées.

Si vous nous envoyez des fonds, comme ils devront servir à payer les étrangers qui nous apporteront des vivres, nous nous répétons qu'il importe de n'envoyer que de la monnoye d'Espagne, piastres ou quadruples. En ce moment encore les gens refusent du lingot et même la monnoye de France.

Cet objet est le plus important et pour vous en convaincre il suffira que vous vous fassiès remettre sous les yeux, le mémoire que vous a envoyé le commissaire du Gouvernement par les dernières dépêches. Salut & respect,

Les Membres du Conseil de Guerre.

(Signed)
L'Adjudant Général BROUARD.
VAUBOIS, Génl. D$^{Iv.}$
CHANEZ, Gén$^{l.}$ de Brigade, Comm$^{t.}$ la place.
Le Chef de Batt$^{n.}$ NOBLOT.
Le Chef de Brigade DEJEAN.
L'Ordonnateur de la Marine MENARD.

Le Chef de Batt$^{n.}$ du Genie BLÉRUS AINÉ.
D'HENNGEL, Gén$^{l.}$ d'Artillerie.
Le Chef de Batt$^{n.}$ GUIPONY.
RÉGNAUD DE ST. JEAN D'ANGELY (*illegible*).
Le Commissaire des Guerres.
F$^{t.}$ f$^{our.}$ d'Ord$^{nce.}$ DOT.

À Malte le 21 *Fructidor* l'an 6 de la République

(*7th September* 1798).[1]

REGNAUD DE SAINT JEAN D'ANGELY au DIRECTOIRE EXÉCUTIF.

La lettre du Conseil de Guerre vous indique notre position, mais n'a pu encore vous la peindre comme elle est.

La population à la campagne insurgée est, tout compris, d'environ 75,000 âmes, elle donne au moins 10,000 païsans et dans le nombre sont les Chasseurs. Tous les Chasseurs du Reg$^{t.}$ imprudemment réarmés et qui ont leurs fusils et leur gibernes.

Independament de ce corps, existant en entier, en armes, les habitans

[1] Arch. Nat., AF III. 73.

de la campagne ont toutes leurs armes en tromblons, fusils, &c., que le Général de Division avoit fait enlever lors du désarmement et que dans un sentiment de confiance, bien mal justifié, il avoit consenté à leur laisser reprendre.

Les païsans ont, en outre toutes les armes qu'ils se sont procurées par des achats faits de longue main, sous prétexte d'aller en Sicile et en sus dans les boutiques de fabricants de Malte. Le nombre de celles-ci ne peut être apprécié au juste mais il doit être considérable. Ils ont les fusils pris à nos malheureux soldats qu'ils ont égorgés à la Cité Vieille.

Enfin ils ont les canons pris dans les petits forts et tours de la cité, avec leurs boulets. La poudre, achetée par eux depuis longtems et 150 barils qu'ils ont enlevé à la Cotonere, où il n'y avait que quatre hommes de garde et qu'ils ont forcée. Les canons pris par eux sont au nombre de plus de 100, à la vérité avec des affuts mauvais.

Ils ont à leur tête les gens aisés des casals, ceux surtout qui ont soufferts de l'arrivée de l'Armée Française, et des Prêtres et des Moines.

Ils ont massaccrés tous les français, même sans armes, qui étoient déhors, et les Maltais suspects d'attachement ou employés pour la République Française.

Cette espèce de conjuration m'avait été annoncée pour le 10 Aoust et on m'avait désigné quelques complices, qui ont été arrêtés quelques jours avant celle cy. J'avais eu par un patriot l'avis détaillé de ce qui est arrivé au moyen d'une confidence faite par un moine, qui a été fusillé ; tout jusqu'au brisement de l'Aqueduc étoit annoncé. Il n'y a que l'arrivée des Anglais qui n'est pas encore réalisé, et que je ne crains pas, mais je crains du secours des Néapolitains pour les insurgés, et le blocus du port.

Nous avons environ 39,000 âmes dans les deux cités, selon les états de population approximatifs.

Mon avis étoit, d'en envoyer sur le champ, 30,000 et d'embarrasser ainsi les Rebelles par l'impossibilité de nourrir tant d'individus qui tous auroient agi pour les ramener au devoir par le désir de rentrer dans leurs maisons.

La mésure a été ajournée.

Cependant j'ai travaillé nuit et jour pour assurer du pain à cette population, qu'un casal appelé *fornaro* ou village des fours, alimente journellement, et j'ai réussi. On n'en a pas manqué, et cette partie de l'approvisionnement journalier est certaine.

Nous aurions besoin de viande et du vin en comestibles. Je voulois envoyer chercher du vin en Cephalonie, mais les fonds nous manquent ; j'espère avoir une petite resource d'un négociant qui partant pour France, laisse 8,000 louis de 48 f^{cos} à prendre sur l'Université, de l'orge pour environ 10,000 louis et du tabac pour 5,000 louis. Total à peu près de 50,000*l*. de France. Si je réussis, je tirerai sur la Trésorerie et je verserai les fonds au payeur de l'armée ; j'en écrirai à Ramel et je vous prie dans l'intérêt de ce malheureux pays, d'assurer le crédit des françois qui y sont en donnant des ordres pour l'acquit de cet engagement. Du reste j'écris à Civitta Vecchia pour qu'on envoye icy des boulets, qui y sont en abondance. C'est au Commissaire à Rome que je m'adresse. J'écris à Brune pour qu'il envoye quelques officiers, adjudant généraux, ou chef de bataillons pour commander les forts ou les postes. Vous savés combien il y en a, et le nombre des officiers supérieurs est presque réduit à rien ; et encore, leur santé et leurs forces, pour les généraux, ne repondent pas à leur volonté. Dans une enceinte de fortifications qui a deux lieues et plus de circuit, où on ne peut aller à cheval.

L'argent aussi seroit bien nécessaire pour payer les cargaisons, qui pourront nous arriver, sans cela nous serons forcés de les laisser sortir, ou de les prendre sans payer—ce qui empêcheroit l'entrée de tous bâtimens et je n'hésite pas, à préférer le 1$^{er.}$ parti.

Enfin vous verrès s'il convient de risquer quelque envoy d'hommes. Nous avons abondament des armes, vous jugerès de ce que, selon mes précédentes, vous devez faire. Nous n'avons aucune nouvelle des généraux. Il est possible que nous recevions de la Sicile, la nouvelle de la guerre, car il est remarquable que depuis le 1$^{er.}$ 7$^{bre.}$ nous n'avons eu aucune barque venant de ce côté, quoiqu'il y en a eu plusieurs de parties, même avec des armes ; elles vont peut être aborder à la côte dans de petits ports appelés Calles. La frégate et des chaloupes canonnières, mises en mer, n'ont pu jusqu'à present en arrêter aucune, quoiqu'il en est paru plusieurs.

Je desire, Citoyens Directeurs, pouvoir bientôt vous donner des nouvelles plus heureuses, mais j'ai cru devoir vous dire la vérité toute entière.

Je ne vous assure pas de la constance de mon zèle et de mes efforts ; j'espère que vous me rendez la justice d'y compter. Salut & respect.

(Signed) REGNAUD DE ST. JEAN D'ANGELY.

It will have been observed that at this council of war, held on the 6th September, Regnaud recommended that 30,000 out of the 39,000 inhabitants of Valetta should be at once expelled ; nevertheless his recommendation was overruled. Had his advice been adopted, how very different might have been the result of the siege ! Martial law having been proclaimed, all authority was removed from the hands of Regnaud, who on the 8th September, disappointed at the loss of power and authority, appealed to the Director Treilhard to remove him from a position in which he was now no longer of service.

À Malte le 22 *Fructidor* an 6 de la République

(8*th September* 1798).[1]

REGNAUD DE ST. JEAN D'ANGELY au CITOYEN TREILHARD, Membre du Direct. Ex.

Tu verras, mon cher Treilhard, par mes diverses dépêches, où nous en sommes en ce moment. Je sens qu'il est inutile de te demander de t'occuper de nous.

Tant que la crise durera, je serai à mon poste, mais si elle finit je ne puis m'empêcher de songer à rejoindre ma femme, mes enfants, ma famille.

Je ne fais rien pour eux et je suis pourtant leur unique ressource.

J'avais apporté avec mois quelques fonds comptant suivre des affaires commerciales. Dévenu, bien malgré moy, Commissaire du Directoire, j'ai cru n'en faire aucune. Je dépense beaucoup plus que mes appointemens

[1] Arch. Nat., AF III. 73.

pour exister honorablement. Ma maison en France est la même, ma femme et ceux auxquels j'y donne azile vivent comme si j'y étois.

* Je dois donc songer à les rejoindre. Je le feray si le calme renaît.

Ton amitié excusera si je te parle ainsi de moy, donnès m'en une preuve en recevant mon beau frère Alph. Buffault qui ira te voir, et reçois mes vœux pour ton répos avec l'assurance de mon attachement.

(Signed) REGNAUD DE ST. JEAN D'ANGELY.

* J'invite le Directoire à me remplacer, j'auray, je crois, payé ma dette et servi avec zèle, activité et courage mon païs au poste où j'étois, j'espère obtenir le témoignage unanime de tout ce qui m'entoure.

PS.—J'engage le porteur de ma lettre à aller te voir pour t'instruire des détails.

CHAPTER X

THE BRITISH BLOCKADE

(From the 18th September to the 21st December 1798)

By the 18th September the divergencies between Vaubois and Regnaud had become so acute that the latter reconsidered his determination to remain at his post until relieved, and volunteered to proceed to France for the purpose of acquainting the Ministry in Paris of the exact situation of the fortress, and to accelerate the dispatch of the necessary succour, in the shape of funds, provisions, and ammunition.

Accordingly Vaubois addressed the Directory, under date of the 18th September, to the following effect :—

Au Quartier Général de Malte le $2^{me.}$ *jour complémentaire* an 6 (18*th September* 1798).[1]

Vaubois, Général de Division.

CITOYENS DIRECTEURS,—Je remets cette lettre au $C^{en.}$ Regnaud de St. Jean d'Angely qui s'est offert pour aller vous rendre compte de notre situation et accélérer l'arriver des secours que nous réclamons, et qui nous sont si nécessaires.

La Révolte des Campagnes se continue ; les Prêtres ont fanatisé les Paÿsans, et comme avant notre venue ils implorent contre nous l'ange exterminateur.

Nous nous sommes tenus dans nos murs pour ne pas compromettre notre faible garnison.

Elle n'est en effectif actuellement, hôpitaux déduits, et d'après nos pertes, que de 2,200 hommes, et qu'est ce que cette poignée de monde pour une immense étendue de Remparts ?[2]

D'un autre côté n'ayant pu rien tirer de la Sicile depuis notre entrée ici, nous avons vécu sur le passé, et nous n'avons plus que du pain et de l'eau.

Dans un païs où le climat brûlant épuise les forces du soldat, il faut autre chose pour en obtenir un service actif.

---

[1] Arch. Nat., AF III. 73.
[2] These figures of Vaubois may be contrasted with those given to Nelson by the deputation of Maltese, who reckoned the French force at about 3,000, after 1,500 had been killed ! See later in this chapter.—J. H. R.

Nous avons donc besoin d'hommes et de vivres.

Le Commissaire du Gouvernement par ses lettres a sonné le tocsin de la nécessité de tous côtés auprès de nos consuls dans les Echelles, dans la Méditerrannée et l'Adriatique. Nous n'avons rien reçu.

Il nous faut de tout pour la marine et pour la terre.

Ecoutès ce que le Citoyen Régnaud vous dira ; il connoît notre position en détail, il a partagé nos efforts pour l'améliorer ; il va en faire ailleurs de nouveaux au lieu de ceux qu'on ne peut plus tenter ici.

Il a la confiance du Conseil et des Officiers qui le composent et son départ est notre unique espérance pour obtenir les moyens de nous maintenir, et de nous deffendre dans notre position cruelle.

Recevez l'assurance de mon dévouement, de ma fidélité, de mon courage et de mon respect. (Signed) VAUBOIS.

The day after Vaubois had confided this dispatch to Regnaud, the Marquis de Niza with his squadron appeared off Valetta, in compliance with Nelson's instructions.[1] Owing to the close blockade which followed, Regnaud, who at first intended to get away in the frigate *La Justice,* was unable to leave until the 9th November, when, accompanied by a Maltese friend, Baron Camillo Scebberras, he left the island in a small craft, under the command of Padron G. Scolaro, and landed at Civita Vecchia on the 22nd November.[2]

This detention enabled Vaubois to supplement his dispatch of the 18th September with a minute and detailed note on the condition and requirements of the fortress, dated the 27th September, as follows :—

NOTE SUR MALTE

6 *Vendém$^{re.}$* an 7 (*27th September* 1798).

La population des isles de Malte et du Goze, s'élève à environ 90,000 âmes ; elle est trois fois plus nombreuse que le sol en pourroit nourrir, s'il étoit totalement cultivé en grains.

Les subsistances sont importées à Malte ; savoir :

LE BLED DU LEVANT.

Les Bâtiments Grecs et Ragusois qui transportent annuellement les bleds de l'Egypte dans les ports de ———, relachent presque tous à Malte ; beaucoup y vendent leurs cargaisons.[3]

Une Commission dite de l'Université est uniquement chargée de l'achat des grains, qu'elle revend ensuite aux habitants à un prix constant. La

---

[1] Private Journal.

[2] From Villeneuve's dispatch to the French Minister of Marine and the Colonies, under date of the 30th November 1798, it would appear that the name of this craft was the *Désirée*, which carried Lieutenant Vathier in supreme command.

[3] The name left blank would enable us better to understand the nature of this little-known trade in Egyptian wheat. Probably its destination was Algeria or Morocco.—J. H. R.

différence du prix d'achat à celui de vente, couvre les frais de magasinage, intérêts des fonds, pertes dans les années diséteuses, &c.

Je crois que les derniers achats ont eu lieu à raison de 10 francs le quintal et que la livre de pain se vend 25 centimes (5 sols).

L'approvisionnement étoit fait pour 8 mois pour la totalité des habitants.

BESTIAUX DE LA SICILE & DES ÉTATS DE TUNIS ET DE TRIPOLI.

Sous l'ancien gouvernement, cet article ne s'importait que de la Sicile. Les entraves que la Cour de Naples y met aujourd'hui le réduisent à peu de chose et il seroit nul sans la contrabande. Tunis & Tripoli fournissent à meilleur compte. Le Grand Maître Pinto, ayant eu quelqu'altercation avec le Roi de Naples relativement à la suzerainété de ce dernier sur l'Isle de Malte, il passa une trève avec les États Barbaresques et en tira toutes les subsistances. Les Maltais disent n'avoir jamais été plus abondamment pourvu, et à aussi bon marché que durant cette trève.

Une cargaison de 140 bœufs a dernièrement été apportée de Tripoli et des marchands Maltais sont partis pour y faire de nouveaux achats. La consommation de la viande n'est pas en raison du nombre des habitants, car beaucoup vivent de poisson mariné, légumes secs &c. On élève à Malte un grand nombre de cochons.

LE VIN DE LA SICILE.

Cet article manque—la proximité de la Sicile et la facilité des transports faisoient négliger les approvisionnements, qui maintenant sont très difficiles. Ils ne peuvent s'effectuer qu'à la dérobée et sur de très petits bateaux.

BOIS À BRÛLER, DES CÔTES DE LA MER ADRIATIQUE.—CHARBON DE CIVITA VECCHIA.

Ces deux articles manquent absolument. La consommation en est moindre à Malte qu'ailleurs. Elle se borne à la préparation des aliments et à l'exercise de quelques métiers. Le charbon est préférable au bois; parcequ'à volume égale il fait beaucoup plus d'usage.

Les revenues de Malte montent annuellement à . . . 1,200ML.
La dépense actuelle est évaluée par mois à cent mille écus et par an à . . . . 3,600ML.
Malte coûte donc en ce moment à la Métropole . . 2,400ML.

Elle coûtera moins à la paix; parceque les Douanes, présentement nulles, rendront beaucoup, parceque les Domaines Nationaux, qui sont très nombreux, rendront pareillement, soit qu'on les loue ou qu'on les vende; en disposer avant cette époque, quelque le mode adopté, se [ce ?] seroit favoriser des agioteurs au dépens de la chose publique.

On trouvera qu'une dépense de 3 millions six cents mille livres est excessive et l'on pensera avec raison que l'Ordre ne dépensoit pas une telle somme pour l'entretien de Malte. Mais il faut observer :—

1°. Que les principaux emplois étoient confiés à de riches commandeurs et ne coûtoient rien à l'État.

2°. Que l'Ordre n'entretenoit point de Troups à l'exception de la garde du Palais et à celles des Forts presque toutes composées de vétérans; le reste n'avoit que le logement nud et ne recevoit de solde que pour les jours de service effectif qui étoient rares.

3°. Que les travaux publics, fortifications &c. étoient éxécutés par des ésclaves ; l'entretien des autres parties de l'administration militaire étoit très négligé ; témoin l'état où nous avons trouvé l'artillerie.

Le Général Bonaparte a emporté tout le numéraire qui étoit dans les caisses publiques. J'en ignore l'approximation. Il n'a laissé pour faire face aux dépenses journalières que l'argenterie des églises ; on s'est occupé de monnoyer celle-ci.[1]

La garnison est sur le pied de l'intérieur, elle ne reçoit que du pain. Le haut prix de la viande et l'incertitude des approvisionnements ont motivé cette mesure, ordonnée par le Général en Chef. Il en résulte que le prêt doit être fait exactement tous les cinq jours.

Pour gagner du temps, on ne paye aux troupes que le courant ; le remboursement de l'arrière a été renvoyé à un temps plus opportun ; delà des murmures.

L'entretien des fortifications est estimé à 60MB par an, celui des biens nationaux doit être considérable ; il y a beaucoup de maisons et de magasins de commerce.

Je crois que c'est tout au plus, si les fonds pour le mois de Vendémiaire, peuvent être faits. L'établissement des Français à Malte a nécessité des dépenses extraordinaires, qui ont absorbé la caisse, telles sont :

Les Informations Militaires.

Tout étoit à créer—l'hôpital excepté. Il n'existoit pas un fort, une caserne, un corps de garde, où il se trouvât un seul des meubles les plus urgents. Sous l'ancien gouvernement tout soldat Maltais portait son ménage à la caserne et y vivoit avec sa famille.

L'Habillement.

Conformément à l'ordre du Général Bonaparte on a fait des achats de toile de coton pour habiller les troupes de la Division.

L'Artillerie.

À peine un tiers des affuts peut servir ; le reste est pourri et le petit nombre de coups de canon que les Maltais ont tiré à nôtre arrivée, a suffit pour démonter les pièces : on travaille à les rétablir.

Lazaretts.

L'ancien Lazareth, suffisant autrefois, ne l'est plus aujourd'hui. Le Général Bonaparte en a ordonné un nouveau destiné aux troupes françaises; il a fallut l'enclore et le meubler.

Secours Individuels.

D'après la reddition de Malte chaque Chevalier a reçu 600 francs pour ses frais de voyage. Sous la domination des Chevaliers cette Isle n'étoit

---

[1] Students will find it interesting to compare the great expenses incurred by a Government of the European type in Malta (that is, over and above those of the old Government) with the similar difficulties resulting from Bonaparte's extensive and ambitious reforms in Egypt. See *Kléber et Menou en Egypte*, passim.—J. H. R.

qu'un vaste monastère. Ainsi que dans toutes les communautés réligieuses beaucoup d'individus vivoient des bienfaits de l'Ordre ; soit en exerçant de petits emplois, soit entièrement de modiques pensions. L'abolition de l'Ordre les a laissés sans pain ; il a fallu venir à leur secours.

Pour le faire avec plus d'économie, on a crée quatre compagnies de vétérans composées de tous les militaires Maltais sexagenaires, 4 compagnies de canoniers pris parmi ceux du ci-devant Ordre et une compagnie d'ouvriers d'Artillerie.

Enfin on ne peut refuser la pain aux femmes et enfants en bas âge des matelots & militaires que Bonaparte a emmenés.

Résumé.

D'après l'exposé ci-dessus ; il est indispensable de faire passer Malte :—
Quelques cargaisons de vin de France, elles s'y vendront bien. Du charbon ; la Côte de *Terracina à Civita Vecchia* en abonde. Je crois qu'un approvisionne[me]nt de viande salée y seroit aussi nécessaire. Du *numéraire*. Quelque moyen que l'on adopte, pour la subsistance de la garnison je n'en connais point de plus assuré et de moins coûteux que le numéraire.

The insurrection of the Maltese had by this time raised the hopes and aspirations of the Order and its chief officials, who, under the protection of the Czar of Russia, trusted to regain possession of the island, and on this point a suggestion to that effect was now made to the British Government.[1]

In the meantime, Lord Grenville on the 3rd October transmitted to Sir William Hamilton, His Britannic Majesty's Ambassador at the Court of Naples, full powers for negotiating and signing a treaty of defensive alliance with that Government, and on the same day wrote to Sir William Dispatch No. 7, of which the following is a synopsis [2] :—

Lord Grenville to Sir Wm. Hamilton.

Dispatch No. 7. *3rd October* 1798.[3]

Among the first objects to which His Majesty's attention would be directed in case of the renewal of the war between Naples and France, would be that of establishing an effective blockade of Malta. . . . If by these measures the Island of Malta should be wrested from the French, it will remain to be considered what future system should be adopted for its defense and government. The communications from the Court of Naples on this head are in the highest degree liberal and friendly. But His

---

[1] In chap. xxi of the *Camb. Mod. History* (vol. viii) I have shown from the reports of our envoy to St. Petersburg (Sir Charles Whitworth) that the Czar, Paul I, attached the highest importance to the possession of Malta, and proposed to send a fleet into the Mediterranean largely for that purpose.—J. H. R.

[2] Foreign Office Records, Sicily, 11.

[3] Strange to say, the news of Nelson's victory at the Nile (August 1) did not reach London until October 2.—J. H. R.

Majesty does not entertain any idea of acquiring the sovereignty of Malta to himself, or of any of the Venetian Islands.[1] He is ignorant how far any such wish is entertained by the Emperor of Russia, or by His Sicilian Majesty, though it does not appear to His Majesty that such an acquisition would be advantageous to either of those sovereigns. He has, however, directed the Court of St. Petersburg to be sounded on the subject—in the meantime, [he] transmits a suggestion which has been made here on the subject of the restoration of the Order as the best means of settling the question.

On the 4th October, Captain Alexander John Ball, whose association with Malta and the Maltese became in the future so intimate, was ordered by Nelson to proceed from Naples in His Majesty's ship *Alexander*, taking under his command the frigate *Terpsichore*, Captain Gage; sloop *Bonne Citoyenne*, Captain Nisbet; and fireship *Incendiary*, Captain Barker; and co-operate with the Portuguese squadron in blockading the Maltese ports, stopping all supplies for the French garrison, and preventing the escape of the French ships of war which had taken refuge there.[2]

These British ships, however, did not get away from Naples until the 6th October.

The early surrender of Valetta being expected, Nelson was given to understand that the Neapolitan Government laid claim to the island, to which he raised no objection, provided that it was agreed that the French warships there sheltered should be delivered up to him, as his legitimate prize, when the time came; and provided, further, that in the eventual fall of the island it should not be ceded to any other Power without the previous consent of His Britannic Majesty.[3]

Vaubois on the 7th and 12th October acquainted the French Government with Saumarez's and De Niza's summons to surrender, and of the difficulties experienced by his troops, for the want of absolute necessities: clothing, food, wine, brandy, bullets, lead, all being urgently required.

Au Quartier Général de Malte le 16ème. *Vendémiaire* an 7
(7th October 1798).[4]

VAUBOIS, Général de Division, au DIRECTOIRE EXÉCUTIF.

Depuis quatre decades nous sommes bloqués dans Malte par terre par tous les habitans de l'isle en insurrection, et par mer par quatre vaisseaux [5] portuguais et deux frégates. Vous pouvez compter sur le

---

[1] This declaration is of great importance. There is no proof that Great Britain desired to keep Malta until the aggressions of Bonaparte in 1802-3 on the Mediterranean States made its tenure by the reconstituted Order of St. John most precarious. See my *Life of Napoleon*, vol. i. ch. xvii.—J. H. R.

[2] Nicolas, *Dispatches of Nelson*, vol. iii. p. 141. [3] *Ibid.* vol. iii. pp. 146-47.

[4] Arch. Nat., AF III. 73.

[5] *Vaisseaux* technically means 'ships of the line.'—J. H. R.

courage des Républicains qui se trouvent enfermés ici, mais nous manquons de tout.

Nous n'avons pas de viande ; nous n'avons point de vin, nous n'avons point d'eau de vie ; tous commestibles en général nous manquent excepté le blé. Nous sommes mal approvisionnés en boulets de 18 et de 24 ; nous n'avons pas de plomb pour faire des balles. Un million de cartouches d'infanterie nous serait nécessaire. Nous n'avons pas assez de troupes à beaucoup près pour garder nos immenses remparts. Le soldat mal nourri est sur les dents.

Nous manquons absolument d'habillements, de tout genre. Les bivouacs souffrent prodigieusement. Il en faudrait non seulement pour les soldats, mais encore pour les matelots des vaisseaux *Le Guillamme Tell, La Diane, La Justice, La Cartaginoise et Le Dégo*. Partie de ces matelots font le service à terre pour nous aider.

Hier 14 du courant j'ai fait une sortie qui a coutté des hommes à l'ennemi, mais nous avons aussi perdu des braves, et nous n'avons rien à perdre ; la fanatisme et la haine qu'on a inspiré aux gens du païs [*sic*] depuis longtems a elevé leur courage à un point extraordinaire ; nous esperons, Citoyens Directeurs, que vous nous ravitaillerés en hommes et en vivres. Comptez sur notre courage qui ne démentira nos actions de huit années.

Malgré le blocus par mer, on peut venir des côtes d'Italie et de France, et entrer aisément quand un vent du Nord Ouest force nos ennemis de dériver sous le vent. Les Anglais ont paru avec les portugais. Nous ne savons pas ce que sont devenu les Anglais.[1] Ils m'ont fait une sommation signé le Marquis de Nizza, contre amiral Portugais et Saumarez chef de division Anglais qui était à la tête de douze vaisseaux dont neuf demâtés. Cette sommation portait de me rendre, qu'on nous reconduirait à Marseille ; de leur livrer les bâtiments de guerre Français et le vaisseau et la frégate du ci-devant ordre de Malte. Ils sommaient en apparence en faveur des Maltais.

Cette sommation était accompagnée d'une lettre signée de deux chefs de révolte de l'isle, *Saverio Carouana* membre de la commission du gouvernement, et *Manuel Vitale* de la Citté Vieille, mandataire du peuple.

Ci-joint ma reponse aux premiers, et rien aux derniers.

'Vous avez oublié sans doute que des français sont dans Malte. Le sort de ses habitants ne doit pas vous regarder. Quant à votre sommation, les français n'entendent pas ce stile.'

Dès notre arrivée ici, le Roi de Naples nous a fermé la Sicile, ce qui cause notre penurie. Notre attention est obligée de se porter aussi sur l'intérieur de la ville où nos ennemis ne manquent pas d'avoir un très grand nombre de partisans. Nous avons un extrême besoin d'argent : Le peu de denrées que l'on trouve a déjà sextuplé de prix. Vous instruire de notre situation est éveiller votre sollicitude qui sûrement viendra à notre secours. Salut, Respect et Dévouement, &c.

(Signed) VAUBOIS.

[1] i.e. the ships of Saumarez's squadron which had sailed for England.—J. H. R.

Au Quartier Général de Malte le 21 *Vendémiaire* an 7.
(12*th October* 1798).[1]

VAUBOIS, Général de Division aux CITOYENS COMPOSANT LE DIRECTOIRE EXÉCUTIF.

Depuis mes premières lettres écrittes, le Citoyen Regnaud, commissaire, contrarié par les vents, n'a pu partir. Il n'a eu que plus de temps pour connoître notre situation. Je réitère mes sollicitations pour un ravitaillement. Non seulement il est indispensable physiquement, mais il doit aussi faire perdre confiance à ces insurgés de l'isle qui comptent au moins autant sur notre pénurie, que sur leur courage. Salut et Respect.

(Signed) VAUBOIS.

From the following document, found amongst Lord Nelson's papers, it would appear that a series of questions had been sent to Malta soon after his arrival at Naples, which in due course were announced on the 12th October:—

STATE OF THE ISLANDS OF MALTA AND GOZO ON THE 12TH DAY OF OCTOBER 1798.[2]

QUESTIONS.	ANSWERS.
1st. What force does the French consist of in the Island of Malta?	1st. Supposed to be 3,000 soldiers and sailors, and not above 1,500 Maltese, of which not scarce 100 will take up arms for the French.
2nd. What posts are they in possession of?	2nd. The whole city and all the posts immediately belonging to it, excepting Corradino, which is in possession of the Maltese, and commands part of the harbour. They have guns *en masque*, but not any works thrown up.
3rd. What quantity of provisions have they got, and of what quality?	3rd. Corn for eighteen months, and mills, plenty of oil, very little cheese; scarce the smallest taste of anything else. The acqueduct is cut off, but they have wells not likely to fail but in summer.
4th. Are they sickly?	4th. At the time of the insurrection there were 700 in the hospital.
5th. How near are the Maltese posts to those of the French, and what is the force and state of the Maltese opposed to them?	5th. Corradino is very near the French posts. The Maltese are about 10,000 in arms, and could drive them out of several posts if of use, but the French could easily retire to St. Elmo.

[1] Arch. Nat., AF III. 73.
[2] Brit. Mus. Add. MSS. 34907, f. 408.

THE BRITISH BLOCKADE—1798

QUESTIONS.	ANSWERS.
6th. Have the Maltese any guns mounted, or any that can command the French posts or the ships in the harbour?	6th. About twelve mounted: two on Corradino, four at Samrat, two or three at each of their camps. There are thirty unmounted of different calibres. No post of theirs commands any part of the harbour but Corradino.
7th. What is the number and state of the French ships of war in the harbour?	7th. Two ships of the Line and three frigates. The *Guillaume Tell* is much damaged, but may put to sea. The *St. Giovanni*, formerly a Maltese 64, ready for sea; very old and in a bad state, and badly manned. *La Diane* and *La Justice*, French frigates, in good order, and ready for sea. The *St. Maria*, formerly a Maltese 40-gun frigate, badly manned, but ready for sea.
8th. Have they any transports or merchant vessels ready for sea?	8th. One cutter and four or five Greek or other merchant ships.
9th. Of what description are they?	9th. Only two of any size.
10th. Have they any galleys or gunboats?	10th. Two galleys and four gunboats.
11th. What are the Maltese most in want of?	11th. Principally bombs and mortars. They also want more powder and muskets, and balls to fit their cannon, but cannot exactly tell their calibre.
12th. What are the number of the Maltese camps, and the troops in each?	12th. *At Samrat 1,000, at St. Joseph 4,000, at St. John's 500, at Corradino 500, at Zabbar 700, and at Zeitun 800.
13th. Are there any Foreign officers arrived from Sicily or Naples to assist the Maltese?	13th. None.

ISLAND OF GOZO.

1st. What force does the French consist of?	1st. Not 50 men, who are all in the castle. They have corn and water, but no mills, wood, or any convenience whatever. Few of the people of Gozo are armed. They have about 60 French prisoners.

REMARKS:—On Saturday (1st September), the day before the Revolution, the French, in addition to their usual professions in the 'Gazette,'

* A Portuguese officer has arranged the distribution of the camps, and can give a more correct account. (Note added to report.)

issued a Manifesto, declaring that they should consider the Plate and riches of the churches as sacred, and promising neither to take nor request.

It was the very next morning, when the churches were opened for Public worship, they began their plunder, and the Maltese, injured and irritated beyond bearing, took upon themselves their own revenge. Among the French whom they put to death was a general officer who had been very active.

On his wife they found a plan for entering all the towns on the Island, murdering the strongest and richest of the inhabitants, and taking possession of the best houses. They also found a paper of the distribution of different classes of people to different employments. In this paper 60 Maltese were destined for burying the dead. The French, when questioned on this subject, said that, as they expected soon to be attacked by the English, and as it was their custom to conceal their loss of men as speedily as possible, they had intended this preparation for it; but the Maltese are fully persuaded these men were destined to bury as quick as possible those of their countrymen who were to have been murdered by the French for the sake of plunder.

In the sortie above 50 of the French threw down their arms and begged to join the Maltese, but they were fired on indiscriminately with the others.[1] All the dead bodies of the French the Maltese could lay hold of they decapitated, and carried the heads about the Island with parsnips in their teeth, in revenge for the French having given out they had no provisions on the Island but parsnips.

By the 13th October Nelson completed the repairs and refitting of his fleet, and on that day acquainted his chief, the Earl of St. Vincent, with his intention to sail for Malta on the following Monday, in accordance with his promise to the Maltese insurgents.

[Extract.]

Naples, *October 13th*, 1798.[2]

To EARL ST. VINCENT.— . . . We sail on Monday morning. When at sea, I shall detach *Audacious* and *Goliath* to join my dear friend Ball off Malta, to whom I shall entrust the blockade.

The Government here are very sanguine about Malta, expecting to get hold of it in a short time. I am not so sanguine. The French have bread and water.

I shall send to the French Commanders a proper letter offering my mediation with the injured and plundered Maltese, but should the French ships escape, in that case I shall not trouble myself either with the capitulation, or in obtaining mercy for the deluded people who have joined them. . . . The Island is certainly the property of the King of Naples. . . .

(Signed) NELSON.[3]

---

[1] This and other statements in these Remarks are incorrect.—J. H. R.
[2] Clarke and MacArthur, *Nelson*, vol. ii. p. 116.
[3] For the whole dispatch see *Nelson Dispatches*, vol. iii. pp. 148, 149. For the causes of the long delay in repairing the fleet, see the previous dispatches, especially that of October 9.—J. H. R.

On Monday, the 15th October, at 10.30 a.m., after being honoured with a visit on board the *Vanguard* from the King of Naples, Nelson sailed for Malta, taking with him the *Minotaur*, *Audacious*, *Goliath*, and *Mutine*, the two former ships having been detached from Sir John Saumarez's fleet. The King of Naples having expressed a desire that Nelson should return to Naples in the first week of November, his projected visit to Egypt, and destruction of French shipping there, was abandoned.

Sailing by the western coast of Sicily, and the fleet being in need of wine, Nelson anchored off Marsala on the evening of the 21st October, and there entered into an agreement for a supply from Mr. John Woodhouse.

On Tuesday, the 23rd, at 4 p.m., he resumed his voyage to Malta, arriving off that island at noon of the 24th, relieving the Portuguese squadron, which sailed for Naples to refit on the 25th.

On this latter day a deputation of Maltese notables, consisting of the Marquis Vincenzo de Piro, Count Ferdinand Theuma-Castelletti, Count Salvadore Manduca, and Canon Caruana, waited upon Nelson, and presented him with a statement of the position of affairs in the island, to the following effect:—

[Translation.]

BRIEF STATEMENT OF THE PRESENT SITUATION OF THE MALTESE.[1]

The Maltese people having happily captured Citta Vecchia (Notabile), the maritime fortresses, and the entire country districts, completely blockading the French in Valetta, and the other three adjacent cities, i.e. Vittoriosa, Senglea, and Cospicua, have thus gained considerable advantages over their enemies.

This will be understood by reflecting on the fact, that although the French, after the defeat they so ignominiously suffered in their first sortie from Valetta, had decided, and with defiant expressions threatened on their second sortie, with the aid of 500 subsidised Greeks and disloyal Maltese, to show no quarter, yet whilst firing against our positions innumerable discharges of shot and shell, they became discouraged, and as they retired our advance guard, closing in, compelled them to take refuge within the walls.

The French troops are well organised, commanded by efficient officers, and furnished with excellent arms; whilst the Maltese troops, on the contrary, are irregulars, with few guns, and those not very good, captained by individuals whom necessity and not profession has made officers.

The number of the French at the commencement of the revolution was about 4,500 in Malta and Gozo. Of these we have captured about 60 prisoners, and about 1,500 have been killed—so that to about 3,000 which remain there may be added 500 Greeks and a few evil-minded Maltese.[2]

---

[1] Brit. Mus. Add. MSS. 34950, f. 188.
[2] Contrast these rough estimates with the total of 2,200 French troops as stated by Vaubois to the Directory on 18th September. See ante.—J. H. R.

From this number, after deducting the number required to man the fortifications and public places of the four cities, which would be about 1,000, there will remain, after allowing for the sick, about 2,000 available, or a trifle more, for any contemplated sortie.

Against this number we are able to occupy our positions with about 3,200 men badly equipped with guns, but no bayonets, and from 6,000 to 7,000 men armed, some with pikes, some with swords, and others with cudgels.

From this number we have lost no prisoners, and on various occasions we have had about ten killed.[1] Such, more or less, is about the state of present affairs as reported to the military.

With regard to food in possession of our enemies, they are well provided with wheat and oil, although wanting in meat and cheese; whilst we, on the contrary, have but a poor supply of wheat.

Of this kind of food we are sending to Sicily for a supply by means of speronare,[2] but this will assist us only in a small degree, and is not sufficient; we require ship-loads to be properly supplied.

Foreign money adapted to trade has become scarce, whilst Maltese money for the greater part is held by the Maltese now within the besieged city. We have money at Barcelona, but the means of bringing it are wanting. The Sicilians might be prevailed upon to sell their wheat upon credit to the Maltese, whose integrity they have always experienced, and who would offer them every guarantee.

At the present moment nothing else makes us anxious but this scarcity of wheat.

We therefore approach your Excellency, with tears in our eyes and with all humility, begging that by your means and protection we may be able to obtain the necessary provisions in wheat and barley, so that we may succeed in triumphing over our common enemy, promising in all sincerity that we shall keep in perpetual memory our warmest gratitude for such particularly great favour by the granting of our petition.

     (Signed) MARCHESE VINCENZO DE PIRO.
        " CONTE FERDINANDO THEUMA-CASTELLETTI.
        " CONTE SALVADORE MANDUCA.
        " CANONICO CARUANA.

To this report was attached the following statement of the expenses incurred for maintaining the insurgents then under arms. They are given in detail, village by village; but for lack of space we can give only the total cost. It amounted to 46,979 scudi, or £3,914 18s. 4d.

Nelson has left on record a 'Memorandum of what passed between himself and the Deputies of the Island of Malta' at this interview, which runs as follows [3]:—

---

[1] The estimate of ten Maltese killed, as against about 1,500 of the French, should be noticed. It throws light on the credibility of this statement.—J. H. R.
[2] The *speronara* is a Maltese small coasting vessel.—J. H. R.
[3] Brit. Mus. Add. MSS. 34902, f. 158. In Nelson's own writing.

On Wednesday, October 24th, I arrived off the Islands of Gozo and Malta. I saw the French colours flying on the castle of Gozo and in the town of Malta. I learned from Captain Ball that the Islanders were using every endeavour to force the French to abandon the Island, and I also learned with astonishment that not the smallest supply of arms or ammunition had been sent from Sicily by the King of Naples. Sure I am his Minister told me that the Governor of Syracuse had orders to supply secretly the inhabitants of Malta with arms and ammunition, and that officers were gone to Malta to encourage the Maltese in their resistance against the French, and when the *Alexander* sailed for Malta I went with Sir William Hamilton to General Acton to offer that the *Alexander* should carry to the Island any supplies the King might wish to send.

The answer was to this effect, that supplies had been (furnished), and that there was nothing necessary to be (sent) from Naples. Conversations and letters on the subject of Malta had frequently taken place between Sir William Hamilton, the (Marquis) de Gallo, and myself, and from them, particularly the conversation on Friday evening, the 12th October, I was led to believe that promises of protection, with supplies of arms, ammunition, and provisions, had been given to the inhabitants of Malta. What must have been my surprise when I found that neither promises of protection, nor the smallest supply of arms, ammunition, or provisions, had been sent to the Island; and that so far from supplies of provisions being granted from Sicily, a quarantine has been laid on the vessels of the good people of Malta, equal to those of the French.

The petition of the Maltese deputies, dated the 5th September, was duly laid before His Majesty the King of Naples, but from what can be gathered from the already quoted letter from General Acton to Sir William Hamilton, of the 12th September, it does not appear to have succeeded in obtaining the *immediate* co-operation of that Government, or any promise that it would be granted.

Accordingly a second petition was prepared, and a copy handed to Nelson through Captain Ball on the 25th October. This petition ran as follows:—

[Translation.]

To His Majesty the King of the Two Sicilies.[1]

The Maltese people, who have always been attached to Your Majesty, have now the honour, with the most profound humility and respect, to represent that they are conscious of the pain which Your Majesty must have experienced in learning of the usurpation by the French Republic of these two Islands of Malta and Gozo, a pain which must have been increased upon hearing of the laws, or more strictly speaking, of the despotical and tyrannical measures enacted by it, culminating at last in their shameful disregard of the agreement which had been established with all formality. Such is the cause which at last has overcome all restraint, and has given occasion for the commencement of what [it] is hoped will be the redemption of these two Islands.

[1] Brit. Mus. Add. MSS. 34942.

In this enterprise the Maltese people have happily succeeded, so far as Citta Vecchia, the sea-board fortresses, and the entire country are concerned, and to such an extent that the French, since the second day of the Revolution, find themselves blockaded in the city of Valetta and the three adjacent cities. The capture of these, and more particularly that of the city of Valetta, by the Maltese people alone, is most difficult, not only on account of their fortifications, but also owing to the abundance of wheat which the enemy possesses.

The providential arrival of the English and Portuguese squadrons, due to Your Majesty's intercession, intercepts all arrivals in aid of the French, whether of men or food.

In the extreme penury of munitions of war in which we find ourselves, they have in their extreme goodness supplied us with about 1,300 muskets and sundry barrels of powder, so that to-day, with this addition, our musketeers are now 3,300. We have also 35 iron cannon distributed in various positions, the greatest calibre of which is 18, but of mortars and bombshells we have none.

We have further to represent to Your Majesty, that as the supply of wheat is preserved in the cities now in possession of the enemy, and as this revolt of the people has taken place most suddenly, we find ourselves totally unprovided with the means of subsistence, and for this reason the Maltese people approach Your Majesty without delay, to represent the state of affairs in Malta, and to humbly present their petitions, in order that they may obtain from the singular beneficence, readiness, and attachment of Your Majesty to these Islands, the necessary aid.

That whereas, owing to the complete suppression of all trade in Malta since the usurpation of the Island by the French, nearly all Foreign money has disappeared, whilst the local money is chiefly possessed by the Maltese now within the beleaguered city, and that consequently the Maltese people are deprived of the means of obtaining a sufficient and constant sustenance, which is the cause of the greatest anxiety.

The People therefore prostrate themselves at the feet of Your Majesty in all humility, beseeching that Your Majesty will order that the necessary beneficent means may be provided to the Maltese from Sicily, even on credit, if they are unable to pay for its value at once in money or effects, and which they will be able to liquidate hereafter, should the war continue for any length of time. Moreover, we are unable to recover, through the want of means, a considerable sum of money which we have at Barcelona, the value of cotton shipped there.

We therefore humbly supplicate Your Majesty's favour to appeal to His Catholic Majesty, in order that the early withdrawal of the aforesaid sum may be facilitated.

In anticipation of Your Majesty's benevolence, we sign ourselves the Deputies of this Population.

(Signed) SALVADORE MANDUCA.
,, FERDINANDO THEUMA-CASTELLETTI.
,, VINCENZO DE PIRO.
,, CANONICO CARUANA.

Endorsed by Nelson in his own writing :
' Delivered to me by Captain Ball, October 25th, 1798.

(Signed) HORATIO NELSON.'

THE BRITISH BLOCKADE—1798

Nelson further issued on the same day the following instructions to Captain Ball [1] :—

25th October 1798.

To CAPTAIN BALL, His Majesty's ship *Alexander*.

You are hereby required and directed to take under your command the ships named in the margin (*Audacious, Goliath, Terpsichore, Incendiary*), their captains having my directions to follow your orders, and to undertake the blockade of the Island of Malta, and to prevent as much as in your power any supplies of arms, ammunition, or provisions getting to the French army, or the port in their possession, and to grant every aid and assistance to the Maltese, and consulting with the Maltese delegates upon the best methods of distressing the enemy, using every effort to cause them to quit the Island or oblige them to capitulate. And relying upon your zeal and abilities in the service, in the event of a capitulation with the enemy, the Island, towns, and forts to be delivered to the Islanders, to be restored to their lawful sovereign, but to insist upon the French ships, *Guillaume Tell, Diane*, and *Justice*, to be delivered up to you, with all the French property in the place; and you are to dispatch the *Terpsichore* to Naples on the 14th November next, with an account of your proceedings to that time.

(Signed) HORATIO NELSON.

In accordance with the desire of the Maltese deputation, Nelson addressed a second summons to Vaubois and Villeneuve to surrender, as follows :—

To the French General and Admiral commanding in the town of Valetta and port of Malta.[2]

His Britannic Majesty's ship *Vanguard*,
Off Malta, 25th October 1798.

GENTLEMEN,—In addressing to you this letter containing my determination respecting the French now in Malta, I feel confident that you will not attribute it either to insolence or impertinent curiosity, but a wish of [having] my sentiments clearly understood.

The present situation of Malta is this : The inhabitants are in possession of all the Island, except the town of Valetta, which is in your possession ; that the Islanders are in arms against you; and that the Port is blockaded by a Squadron belonging to His Britannic Majesty. My objects are to assist the good people of Malta in forcing you to abandon the Island, that it may be delivered into the hands of its lawful Sovereign, and to get possession of *Le Guillaume Tell, Diane*, and *Justice*. To accomplish these as speedily as possible, I offer, that on the delivery of the French ships to me, that all the troops and seamen now in Malta and Gozo shall be landed in France, without the condition of their being prisoners of war; that I will take care that the lives of all those Maltese who have joined you shall be spared, and I offer my mediation with their Sovereign for the restoration of their property. Should these offers be rejected, or the French ships make their

---
[1] Nicolas, *Dispatches of Nelson*, vol. iii. p. 157 (edit. 1845).
[2] *Ibid*. vol. iii. p. 155 (edit. 1845).

escape, notwithstanding my vigilance, I declare that I will not enter or join in any capitulation which the General may hereafter be forced to enter into with the inhabitants of Malta, much less will I intercede for the forgiveness of those who have betrayed their duty to their country. I beg leave to assure this is the determination of a British Admiral, and I have the honour to be, Gentlemen, your most obedient, humble servant,

(Signed) HORATIO NELSON.

To this summons the following reply was received [1] :—

[Translation.]

Valetta, 25*th October* 1798.

SIR,—We have received the letter which you have done us the honour to write.

Jealous of meriting the esteem of our Nation, as you are in that of yours, we are resolved to defend this Fortress to the last extremity.

With regard to the interest you take in the welfare of the country rebels, we have only to say that their perjured conduct will bring them to their ruin—that is all which they will gain by their insensate enterprise.

We sincerely regret that they should have become the dupes of certain ambitious Counsellors, and we are determined to repulse their efforts with all the courage of which men of honour are possessed. We have the honour to be, Sir, (Signed) GENERAL VAUBOIS.

„ REAR-ADMIRAL VILLENEUVE.

Two days later, the 27th October, Captain Ball was ordered to proceed to Gozo in the *Alexander*, and summon the French troops stationed there to surrender.[2]

Lieutenant-Colonel Lochey, with the troops under his command (217 in number), surrendered the day following, the articles of capitulation, which had been prepared by Nelson, being signed on the 28th, when Captain Cresswell, of the Marines, took possession, hoisting His Britannic Majesty's colours. The day following the island was delivered up in form to the local deputies, and His Sicilian Majesty's colours hoisted, he being acknowledged the lawful sovereign of the island.[3] In the castle were found 3,200 sacks of corn, one 18-pounder, two 12-pounders, four 6-pounders, 50 barrels of gunpowder, and a quantity of other ammunition.[4] Gozo, it was then computed, held 16,000 inhabitants.

[1] Arch. Nat., AF III. 73.
[2] Nicolas, *Dispatches of Nelson*, vol. iii. p. 161; Brit. Mus. Add. MSS. 34908, f. 79.
[3] *Annual Reg.*, 1798, p. 158.
[4] Brit. Mus. Add. MSS. 34908, f. 78. 'Memorandum of articles found in the Castle of Gozo, the 28th October, 1798 :—50 barrels powder; 9,000 ball cartridges; 1,000 musket cartridges without ball; 1,700 flints; 38 18-pound cartridges, filled; 140 12-pound cartridges, filled; 450 6-pound cartridges, filled; 268 4-pound cartridges, filled; 25 3-pound cartridges, filled; 88 2-pound cartridges filled; 1 18-pounder gun, good, and 200 shot; 2 12-pounder guns, good, and 990 shot; 4 6-pounder guns, good, and 2,985 shot; 400 hand-grenades filled; 90 pikes and 90 halberts; and 3,200 sacks of corn. Part of these, with the 3,200 sacks of corn, were delivered to the Maltese in arms.'

These prisoners were transferred to the *Vanguard* and *Minotaur*, both vessels sailing for Naples on Wednesday, the 31st, at 6 p.m., where they arrived on the 5th November, the prisoners being eventually sent on to Nice.

Before leaving Malta, Nelson supplied the insurgents, on Saturday, the 27th October, with twenty more barrels of gunpowder—2,800 lb.[1]

Captain Ball was thus again left in command of the blockading squadron, consisting of the *Alexander, Goliath, Audacious, Terpsichore,* and *Incendiary*.

Nelson, upon arrival in Naples, proceeded to Caserta, where the Royal Family was then residing, and on the 6th November presented to His Sicilian Majesty the French flags captured at Gozo, together with the memorial from the inhabitants of Malta.[2]

Before leaving Malta, Nelson acquainted Sir William Hamilton of the timely assistance he had been able to render the Maltese, for on the 6th November Sir William informed Lord Grenville of the valuable aid which had been given to the islanders, as detailed in the annexed extract of his dispatch :—

SIR WM. HAMILTON TO LORD GRENVILLE.[3]

Naples, *6th Novr.* 1798.

Has received a letter from Sir H. Nelson, dated off Malta, 27th October. The Admiral adds, that if it had not been for the supplies of arms, ammunition, and *provisions* afforded them by the King's (British) fleet, those brave Islanders must have long ago bent their necks again to the French yoke.

Nelson's efforts were not limited to personal aid, for at the interview which he had with His Majesty the King of Naples at Caserta, on the 6th November, he pleaded their cause so successfully, that some mortars and artillery were immediately dispatched to Malta, and the Marquis di Gallo was authorised, nine days later, to reply to the petitions in the following words :—

[Translation.][4]

His Majesty our King, sensible of the expressions of fidelity and submission which the Deputies of the Island of Malta, on behalf of that nation, have humbly presented to the Royal Throne, has ordered me to acquaint you with His Royal acceptance and complaisance with which he has received the vows of that People, towards whom his paternal sentiments and Royal beneficence have continued undiminished, notwithstanding the vicissitudes which have happened, and the attempts which have been made against his legitimate and incontestable sovereign rights. Due to these sentiments of commiseration, His Majesty has been moved, in accordance

[1] Brit. Mus. Add. MSS. 34963, f. 32.　[2] Clarke and MacArthur, vol. ii. p. 125.
[3] Foreign Office Records, Sicily, 11.　[4] Azopardi, p. 112.

with your repeated requests, to order the Viceroy of Sicily to accord to His faithful Maltese all the succour, in the shape of victuals, and of other kinds, which they may require, not only in allowing the exportation on their behalf, but also to grant them every facility in making the purchases. On behalf of His Majesty, I have the honour to communicate the above to you, illustrious Sirs, for your information and guidance.

(Signed) MARCHESE DI GALLO.

S. Gennaro, 15th Novr. 1798.

It has been already related that Regnaud, owing to the strict blockade of Valetta Harbour, maintained by Ball, had been unable to leave the island until the 9th November, but no sooner *had he quitted the island* than Vaubois thought proper to inform the Directory that he attributed most of the disasters which had befallen the French to the political errors of his late colleague. This he communicated in the following dispatch :—

Malthe le 29 *Brumaire* (19th *November* 1798).

VAUBOIS au DIRECTOIRE EXÉCUTIF.

Si mes dépêches vous sont parvenues, Citoyens Directeurs, vous savès que nous sommes bloqués depuis trois mois par terre et par mer, sans nouvelles du Gouvernement ni du Général Bonaparte. Les vaisseaux Anglais bloquent le port ; les habitants de l'isle cernent la place ; comptès sur notre courage ; mais des vivres, à tous prix et à tous risques ; des médicamens, des bombes, des boulets de 24.

Donnès des ordres, Citoyens Directeurs, pour qu'on nous expédie de tous les points ; il en arrivera. Nous touchons au mauvais tems pour ce pays. Des vivres, et Malthe sera pour toujours à la République.

Le Citoyen Renaud de St. Jean d'Angely vous est expédié ; il vous mettra au fait de nos besoins, mais ne croyez pas à tout ce qu'il pourra vous dire ; il a fait de grandes fautes politiques, et ces fautes jointes à l'attitude du Roi des deux Siciles, qui nous a tout refusé depuis notre arrivée, sont les causes de notre situation.

Nos dangers sont au dedans aussi pressans. Tous les habitans partagent les sentimens des insurgés. J'en ai déjà fait sortir plus de 10,000 pour notre sûreté.[1]

Malthe sera soutenue jusqu'à qu'il n'y ait plus ni chats ni chiens à manger. Salut and respect. (Signed) VAUBOIS.

Regnaud, upon his arrival in Rome on the 23rd November, prepared the following important and detailed account of the position of affairs in the island, together with the urgent requirements which the garrison needed.

This dispatch was addressed to the Directory, under cover of another to the Foreign Minister, Monsieur Talleyrand, as follows :—

---

[1] This sentence proves that thus early Vaubois saw that the defence turned on the question of food supply.—J. H. R.

Rome, le 3 *Frimaire* an 7 de la République
(23rd November 1798).[1]

Regnaud de St. Jean d'Angely au C^{n.} Talleyrand, Min. des Affaires Étrangères.

J'ai l'honneur de vous adresser, Citoyen Ministre, une dépêche pour le Directoire Exécutif.

Comme elle est ouverte, je n'y ajouteray en ce moment aucuns détails a ceux qu'elle contient.

J'ai taché d'y renfermer dans une rapide analize ce qu'il m'a paru important de faire connoître au Gouvernement.

Sous deux jours j'espère que ma santé delabrée me permettra de me mettre en route, et je me rendray sans m'arrêter au près de vous.

Je donneray alors au Directoire, tous les renseignemens ultérieurs qu'il croira nécessaires.

Je vous prie d'agréer l'assurance de mon attachement sincère.

(Signed) Regnaud de St. Jean d'Angely.

Rome, le 3 *Frimaire* an 7e Rép^{ue.} (23rd November 1798).[2]

Regnaud de St. Jean d'Angely au Directoire Exécutif de la République Française.

Citoyens Directeurs,—Peu après le départ de la lettre que le Conseil de Guerre de la Division de Malte vous a adressée, les membres de ce Conseil desirèrent que la position de l'île pût vous vous [*sic*] être exposée par quelqu'un qui en connût tous les détails.

Je m'offris pour cette mission, et d'après l'arrêté pris par le Conseil, je me disposois à partir, lorsque l'escadre Portugaise parrût devant le port avec 4 vaisseaux et une frégatte.

Peu après l'escadre Anglaise arrivant d'Alexandrie & trainant avec elle ses propres vaisseaux, et ses prises presque razés et semblables à des pontons s'est montrée.

Une sommation de rendre la ville a été faite et a reçue la réponse que vous transmet le Gal. Vaubois.

Les Anglois se sont retirés ne laissant que deux frégates pour assurer le blocus d'avantage, et un vaisseau de ligne.

Trois semaines après l'Amiral Portugais a fait en son nom seul (la 1^{tre.} sommation étoit au nom des escadres combinées) une nouvelle sommation qui a reçue la même réponse que la 1ère.

Deux jours après les Anglois ont paru avec six batimens, dont 4 vaisseaux de 80 & 74, et deux frégates. Ils ont relevés les Portugais, et leurs propres vaisseaux de la station, et le blocus est demeuré établi par les dernières forces seulement y joint une corvette de 24 canons, un bricq, & quelques batimens legers.

Nelson qui commande les forces navales a fait une 3ème. sommation de rendre la ville, le port & les vaisseaux françois, ou pris sur les Maltois, avec ménace de ne plus admettre à aucune capitulation en cas de refus.

Les Généraux Vaubois & Villeneuve à qui cette dernière sommation étoit adressée, ont répondu par un réfus aussi formel que les précédens.

---

[1] Arch. Nat., AF III. 73.   [2] *Ibid.*

Cependant le tems qui s'étoit constamment maintenu au beau, laissoit aux Anglois le moyen de bloquer le port de si près qu'il a été impossible de faire sortir, sans la compromettre, la frégate *la Justice* destinée d'abord à me porter en France.

Une corvette de commerce frétée par le Gouvernement n'a pas été plus heureuse.

Sentant enfin, après la capitulation du Goze que les circonstances devenoit de jour en jour plus pressantes, n'ayant reçu à Malte aucunes nouvelles pendant cinq mois,[1] ni du G$^{al.}$ en Chef, Bonaparte, ni de vous, Citoyens Directeurs, ni de vos ministres, ni des Commissaires de Rome, je me suis décidé à risquer le passage, par une barque plate, ou galiotte, qui peut sortir du port la nuit à rames et sans être vue.

C'est ainsi que le 19 Brumaire (9th November 1798) à 9 h. $\frac{1}{2}$ du soir je suis sorti du port de Malte, et après une navigation pénible et dangereuse, dont je crois devoir vous épargner les détails, je suis venu faire naufrage par un coup de vent des plus violens, sur les plages Romaines à 24 milles de la capitale.

J'y suis arrivé hier, et j'ai vu le Citoyen Maichin[2] ainsi que les Commissaires du Gouvernement ici. Je leur ai donné connoissance de la position de Malte, telle que je vais vous la retracer.

Vous connoissès, parceque je vous en ai dit plus haut, les forces navales qui composent le blocus. J'ignore où s'est rétirée l'escadre portugaise et si elle est à portée de venir promptement les accroître.[3] On m'a dit, mais je n'ay pu vérifier le fait, qu'il existoit des vaisseaux Anglois dans les ports de Naples, Siracuse et Messine.

La position militaire des François à Malte est la même qu'à l'époque où le Conseil de Guerre vous a adressé sa dépêche.

Toutes les fortifications et tous les forts de la ville entière de Malte, et tous les ports sont au pouvoir de la garnison & on n'éprouve aucune crainte de voir la force les leur enlever.

Les assiégeans, si on peut appeler ainsi les hommes armés qui environnent la ville, n'ont de corps réguliers, selon ce qu'on a appris, que l'ancien Régiment des Chasseurs de Malte et quelques Corps de Volontaires : tous les païsans sont la proie ; ils forcent sous peine de mort tous les habitants à marcher, quand le son du tocsin les appelle.

Les Portugais et les Anglois leur ont amené de nouveaux officiers pour les diriger dans leurs travaux, car ils en avoient à ce qu'il paroit d'arrivés avant la révolte.

Ils ont dressé une batterie à St. Joseph, une au Cazal Zabbar, et une 3ème du côté de la Piéta.

Ils ont faits des travaux assez considérables et placé quelques pièces au Couradin [*sic*], vis à vis la partie sud est des fortifications de la ville. Présumant que l'on préparoit dans cet emplacement une batterie de bombes, le G$^{al.}$ a fait inquiéter les travailleurs et jusqu'à présent on n'a rien démasqué.

On ne peut apprécier au juste le nombre d'hommes armés que les

---

[1] This is an exaggeration. The blockade by the Portuguese squadron did not begin till about September 20.—J. H. R.

[2] Otherwise spelt Mechain: see *postea*. He was *chargé d'affaires* at the French Embassy.—J. H. R.

[3] The Portuguese sailed to Naples to refit.—J. H. R.

rebelles pourroient réunir : mais comme on doit penser que les étrangers ne les laisseront pas manquer d'armes, on évalue à 12,000 le nombre de ceux qui peuvent et veulent les porter.

Ce nombre est calculé d'après la mésure adoptée par le G$^{al.}$ de faire sortir de la ville tous les habitans qui lui inspiroient de la défiance afin de ne pas se trouver, dans un moment d'attacque entre les ennemis du dehors et ceux du dedans.

La garnison françoise est diminuée par la perte de vingt cinq à trente hommes tués dans les premières attaques, et dans une seule sortie faite sur le Cazal Zabbar, sans un grand succès, et par le séjour à l'hôpital de 400 malades environ.[1]

Mais elle se trouve fortifiée par la garnison des vaisseaux et des frégates qu'on a employé à la défense des forts et au service militaire.

Le Contre Amiral Decréz a été chargé du Command$^{t.}$ des Forts Manuel & Dragut au Port de Marsamuchetto et du Fort Ricazoli au grand port.

Le Contre Amiral Villeneuve a pris celuy des Forts S$^{te.}$ Ange & St. Elme.

Tous deux ont sous leurs ordres dans chaque fort un officier d'infanterie commandant.

Les canoniers de marine y font le service des batteries, les matelots celui de soldats ; les uns et les autres sont commandés par des officiers de marine.

Les vaisseaux pendant ce tems sont avec la portion d'équipage indispensablement nécessaires. Dans le port des galères, qui a été fermé pour plus grande précaution, en cas de la tentative d'un coup de main, par une forte chaîne qui en défend l'accès [*sic*]. . . .

Ces mesures ont permis d'employer aux batteries des remparts la majeure partie des canoniers de terre qui sont au nombre de 250 environ et à peu près 100 Maltois, débris peu fort d'une compagnie précédemment organisée et que la désertion à réduit à ce nombre et même audessous.

Il existe pourtant encore une compagnie nouvellement formée de citoyens connus, qui apprennent l'exercice du canon, mais qui n'a pu encore faire aucune service et n'est destinée à en faire que par occasion.

Le nombre des habitans renfermés dans l'enceinte des fortifications ainsi gardées est de 20,000 environ tout compris, du moins je l'estime ainsi.

Les ressources que j'ai laissé à cette garnison, plein de courage, d'énergie, de dévouement consistent :—

En Vivres Principaux.

Dans 34,000 salmes environ de bled (la salme pèze 432 poids de marc).

Dans quatre vingt milliers d'huile d'olive, avec des légumes secs en quantité suffisante pour en fournir à la garnison pendant plusieurs mois.

Dans 500 quintaux de ris environ.

Une petite quantité de lard salé, reste de l'approvisionnement extraordinaire heureusement commencé de bonne heure.

12,000 pintes de vins réservés pour les malades, point de vinaigre.

45 bœufs restant de ceux que j'avois fait venir de Tripoli, et destinés exclusivement pour l'hôpital.

[1] Contrast these figures with those of the Maltese deputies, *ante*.—J. H. R.

120 cochons parqués.
Un assès fort approvisionnement de biscuit.
Les citernes ne laissent aucune crainte de manque d'eau.
Vous voyès que le vin, l'eau de vie, la viande manquent entièrement & c'est un des premiers besoins qui appelle votre sollicitude.

En Habillement.

La troupe et les marins manquent des vêtemens et des chemises.
On a pris, en payant à l'estimation, chès les marchands tout ce qui se trouvoit en ce genre. Mais il y a une grande différence entre la masse des besoins et celles des ressources. Il y a encore du cuir, mais en petite quantité.
Tout seroit à envoyer dans cette partie.

En Hôpitaux.

Le linge est audessous des besoins de beaucoup : $1^{o.}$ parceque l'on n'étoit pas dans l'usage de fournir de chemises aux malades ; $2^{e.}$ parceque l'on n'a pour linge à pansement de ressource que les draps vieux, qu'il est impossible de remplacer.
Les drogues, non renouvellées depuis 6 mois, sont épuisées.

En Cazernement.

Il y a des paillasses suffisamment, point de draps, point de couvertures.

En Armes et Munitions.

Il y a de la poudre suffisamment, à ce que je crois, et d'ailleurs on en continue la fabrication.
Il y a un peu de boulets.
Il y a des fusils audessus du besoin, ainsi que des armes blanches. On ne peut armer toutes les batteries existantes.
Les affuts seuls sont en petit nombre, on manque pour en faire de bras, et de bois.
Faute de mieux on supplée aux charpentiers par les menuisiers, à l'orme par l'acajou et le cèdre. Il y a beaucoup de fer encore.
Le charbon de terre est en grande provision, celui de bois est épuisé, et pourtant nécessaire.
Au surplus le $G^{al.}$ d'Artillerie a écrit au Ministre de la Guerre une lettre que je luy envoye, et dont il nous communiquera sans doute les résultats.

Bois et Lumières.

Il n'y a pas une libre de chandelle, l'huile y supplée, et il y en a. Le bois à brûler ordinaire est épuisé.
Mais les bois de rebut de la marine, le déchirage de quelques vieux pontons, ou batimens condamnées, assureroient le service encore pour longtemps.

Pour la Marine.

Puisque tout est équipé le détail des besoins est impossible. Il est présenté par l'ordon$^{r.}$ Minard au Ministre, qui recevra sa lettre par le même courrier, et sans doute vous en rendra compte.

THE BRITISH BLOCKADE—1798

Pour les Fonds.

La solde de terre pour le soldat et l'officier a été faite exactement décade par décade, et mois par mois.

La marine a reçu un à compte.

Un emprunt forcé fait par le Gen$^{al.}$ de Div$^{on.}$ assure encore des ressources pour ce mois et le prochain.

Nulle réquisition d'aucune espèce, n'a été exercée : tout ce qui a été pris à été payé.

Tel est Citoyens Directeurs l'apperçu rapide que je puis vous tracer à la hâte de l'état de Malte.

Il en résulte selon moi la nécessité de porter à ce poste important les plus prompts secours.

J'ai pensé que la première chose à faire étoit de tenter de faire parvenir à la garnison des nouvelles de France et de luy donner la certitude que vous vous êtes occuppés d'elle, que vous vous en occuppés encore avec la plus vive sollicitude et de lui faire part de ce qui a été fait déjà, de ce qu'on va tenter en ce moment même.

Je place cette mésure au premier rang parceque j'ai éprouvé personnellement combien est douloureuse et décourageante l'idée de l'abandon, où on croit être quand cinq mois entiers se sont écoulés sans recevoir une espérance, une promesse, une instruction, un ordre des autorités supérieurs.

Le Citoyen Mechain et les Comm$^{res.}$ icy ont pensé comme moy et en conséquence, ils ont ordonné l'armement et le départ d'un petit bateau qui portera 20,000 pintes d'eau d'$^{e.}$ [1] et des dépêches.

Quant à la manière d'approvisionner, il est extrêmement difficile que de gros batimens faciles à appercevoir à raison de leur force échappent au blocus vigilant des Anglais.

Ils ne quittent le port que lorsque les coups de vents d'est ou de l'ouest, mais les d$^{ers.}$ surtout, plus violens, plus fréquens, les forcent de dériver vers le Maritimo ou le Cap Passaro.

Quand ils restent à leur station, de petits batimens seules peuvent échapper à leur vigilante avidité, à la faveur du vent ou des rames, et de la nuit.

Partant de ces observations, je crois que la manière la plus sûre d'approvisionner Malte est de multiplier les chances en divisant les risques.

On pourroit expédier de Civita Vecchia de petites barques, portant chacune une petite quantité d'eau de vie, vin, vinaigre, viande et charbon, les barques doubleroient le Maritimo, longeroient la Sicile jusqu'à Girgenti; ou Alicata, feroient voile de manière à se trouver à mi-canal quoique hors de vue à la chute du jour, & partant de ce point pourroient entrer sans peine à Malte, en traversant même l'escadre ennemi avant le retour du soleil.

Il y a même dans le dernier port une chance de plus, en ce qu'un seul coup de vent de l'ouest, qui ne permet pas comme je vous l'ai dit, aux Anglois de tenir la station, amène une barque en trente six heures dans le port de Malte.

Vos commissaires adoptant ces idées se proposent d'expédier quatre petites embarcations à la suite de la première et en attendant vos ordres ultérieurs.

[1] Eau de vie.

Enfin on pourroit peutêtre encore faire partir quelques secours de Tripoli de Barbarie.

Le Commiss.^{re} Guye partant pour la Syrie avoit laissé cette échelle sans Consul. J'ai eu l'honneur de vous dire par mes précédentes dépêches que j'avois engagé le C^{re} Beaussier à s'y rendre ; heureusement il l'a fait, et a contribué à maintenir des bonnes dispositions du Pacha en faveur de la France.

Un françois qui étoit allé à Tunis où il n'a pu rien faire pour nous à cause de l'arrivé du chiaoux porteur d'un firman du Grand Seigneur qui sonne le tocsin contre la France, a été accueilli à Tripoli. Le Pacha avoit chargé 92 bœufs pour Malte sur deux bâtimens & à son compte personnel le 1er. Mais les deux bâtimens ont été pris avec les lettres des Com^{res} Devoize & Beaussier pour moy.

Il seroit possible de faire de Tripoli par un vent de l'est ce qu'on feroit de Cagliari par un vent de l'ouest.

Au reste Citoyens Directeurs, je vous esquisse rapidement ce que j'ai connu : je serai sous peu à même de joindre à ces idées, tracées à la hâte, tous les détails qui sont à ma connoissance, et je me borne à vous présenter en ce moment l'hommage de mon respect.

(Signed) REGNAUD DE ST. JEAN D'ANGELY.

The following letters from French officials, which give an interesting account of the situation of the French garrison during this month of November, were intercepted by the British fleet, and were as follows :—

Vaubois to the French Minister of War, Schérer,[1] dated the 26th November 1798.

Vaubois to the Directory, 27th November 1798.

Doublet to the Colonial Minister, 28th November 1798.

Admiral Villeneuve to the Minister of Marine, dated the 30th November 1798.

Malte, le 6 *Frimaire* (*26th November* 1798).

VAUBOIS, Général de Division, au Ministre de la Guerre, SCHERRER [*sic*].[2]

Vous auriez reçu beaucoup de lettres de moi, Citoyen Ministre, si nous n'étions aussi étroitement bloqués par terre et par mer.

Je mandai au Directoire Exécutif tout le détail de notre situation que je n'ose ici mettre en français, crainte que cette lettre ne tombe au pouvoir des Anglais. J'ai écrit il y a quelque tems une lettre au Directoire avec le chiffre que le Ministre de la Marine avait envoyée en 8 au Ministre de France, Caumont à Malte. Je lui écris par cette même occasion avec un autre chiffre dont le Citoyen Cibon chargé des affaires de Malte à Paris a la clef. Je suis obligé d'user de ces resources parcequ'il est difficile d'échapper aux Anglais surtout le temps se soutenant aussi beau.

---

[1] General Schérer had formerly commanded the French forces in Italy, but was superseded by Bonaparte early in 1796. As Minister for War under the Directory he was not successful, and still less in the command of the French army in North Italy in 1799, when he was several times beaten by Suvórof.—J. H. R.

[2] Brit. Mus. Add. MSS. 34943.

Je connais [?] toute la solicitude du gouvernement pour nous, et il peut compter sur la deffense la plus opiniâtre comme il paroît que la guerre va se pousser avec rigueur et que l'on connoît la conduite du gouvernement étranger qui a si horriblement manqué à la nation française. Nous attendons tout de notre gouvernement, et il verra qu'il y a à Malte des enfans dignes de lui. Salut et respect. (Signed) VAUBOIS.

Traduction de la lettre en chiffre du Général Vaubois, Commandant à Malte, addressé au Directoire de la République Française, en date du 7 Frimaire an 7 de la République (27th November 1798).[1]

J'ai eu l'honneur de vous écrire il y a quelques jours avec un chiffre qu'avait ici le Ministre Drace à Malte qui lui fut envoyé en mille sept cent soixante dix huit, espérant qu'on retrouverait la clef de ce chiffre dans les Bureaux, et que je pourrais être lu. Aujourd'hui je me sers d'un chiffre plus récent dont le Citoyen Cibon ci-devant chargé des affaires de Malte à Paris a la clef. Le blocus de Malte par terre et par mer se continue. Comptès sur notre résistance et notre courage. Mais les subsistances, les munitions de guerre de toute espèce s'épuisent.

Je sais par un aviso que vient d'arriver quels sont les moyens que vous prenès pour nous ravitailler. Ce batiment est le seul des cinq expédiés de Toulon qui soit parvenu à sa destination. J'ai cru qu'il était de mon devoir d'associer encore des entreprises aux votres pour rendre notre ravitaillement plus sûr. Ce qui est arrêté venant d'une part se trouve ainsi remplacé par ce qui vient d'une autre, et notre salut en dépend.

J'ai trouvé ici un bon courrier qui s'endosse des lettres de change tirées sur la Trésorerie Nationale pour cent cinquante mille livres.

Je dépêche à Cagliari en Sardaigne et à Tripoli des agentes à qui je crois pouvoir donner ma confiance pour nous expédier de ces endroits des viandes fraîches et des salaisons ce qui nous fera. . . . [illegible] Citoyens Directeurs et ce que je pense fera conserver Malte à la France. Le courage est au dernier point ; mais des vivres, du vin, de l'eau de vie, des bombes de 8 à 12 pouces de 24 liv., et tout ira bien.

Que le Roi de Naples expie les échecs de la Méditerrannée, il fait le sujet de notre misère, pour nous, nous mourrons, s'il le faut, toujours dignes de notre patrie. L'argent nous est très nécessaire, tout est presque épuisé, et le peu qui reste encore est à des prix incroyables.

Après le malheur qu'a éprouvé l'escadre, il est heureux pour nous d'avoir receuilli ici *le Guillaume Tell*, *la Diane* et *la Justice*, sans l'arrivée de ces batiments il m'eut été impossible d'occuper l'ouvrage immense de la Côte Noire, leur garnison et une partie des matelots qui ne cessent de s'exercer aux armes, me défendent le Fort Manoel, le Fort Ricasoli, le Fort St. Elme et celui de St. Ange. J'ai donné des commandemens aux Contre Amiraux Villeneuve et Decrès, on ne peut mettre plus de zèle, d'activité et d'intelligence. Les soldats sont tous sur les remparts et tous sur la paille, ils sont extrêmement fatigués. L'enciente est immense et il faut tout deffendre. Tout est commun pour notre pauvre nourriture, entre la terre et la marine, l'eau est nitreuse—quelle boisson ! Nous prenons le plus grand soin de l'hôpital dont les malades

[1] Brit. Mus. Add. MSS. 34043.

sont nombreux, mais malgré nos épargnes la viande fraîche va nous manquer. Cet état ne nous abbat cependant pas, pensés à nous Citoyens Directeurs et nos regards sont fixés sur la République.

(Signed) V<small>AUBOIS</small>.

Ven aowbilash fa diol akhuha uweewawxal. Viohl dakot Kbuggha Zoedumuke. Wagululmha fheshae gewma Zerewowlamarat dica ut guwlarm Katml.[1]

À Malte le 8 Frimaire l'an 7 (28th November 1798).

Doublet, Commissaire du Gouvernement Français pour les Isles de Malte et du Goze, au Ministre de la Marine et des Colonies.[2]

C<small>ITOYEN</small> M<small>INISTRE</small>,—Après le départ du Citoyen Regnaud de St. Jean d'Angely pour Paris, le Général de Division, Vaubois, Commandant en Chef pour la République en cette isle, m'ayant fait l'honneur de me nommer pour le remplacer comme Commissaire du Gouvernement, j'ai reçu quelques jours après par le Cap^{ne.} Rapon, commandant un aviso venu de Toulon en 13 jours, votre lettre du 13 Fructidor.

La place étant bloquée par terre et par mer et par conséquent en état de siège, le départ précipité de mon prédécesseur, ne lui ayant pas permis de me laisser aucune instruction relative à mes fonctions, et celles qu'il a remplies paraissant devoir, à mon égard, rencontrer icy des difficultés; j'ai cru devoir pour y obvier, et par amour pour la paix intérieure et le bien du service de la République, adopter dès le principe le sistème de ne rien faire que de concert avec le Général et la Commission du Gouvernement. J'ai donc d'après ce sistème communiqué votre lettre au Général, à qui elle a fait, sous tous les rapports, le plus grand plaisir, en voyant les différens ordres émanés du Directoire, et les sages mesures que vous aviès prises pour nous faire parvenir de tous côtés les objets d'approvisionnements, et les munitions que le C^{en.} Regnaud de St. Jean d'Angely paraît vous avoir mandé, Citoyen Ministre, nous être nécessaires.

Le capitaine de l'aviso, Rapon, nous a rapporté qu'il était le 6ème bâtiment expédié de Toulon pour Malte. Il est jusqu'à présent le seul arrivé icy, il n'a pu embarquer que dix barriques d'eau de vie, qui vu le manque presque absolu du vin, servira quelque tems pour l'usage de la troupe, de terre et de mer.

L'ignorance où était le Général Vaubois sur l'arrivée de ses lettres et de celles de mon prédécesseur, en France et le défaut de viande fraîche, et de vin, se faisant chaque jour sentir avec plus de force, surtout aux approches de l'hyvert [hiver] dans un pays où le soldat n'a point de bois de chauffage, il a cru de son devoir, d'envoyer en Sardaigne, et à Tripoli, des négociants, auxquels il a donné le titre d'agents pour la République, avec des traites sur la Trésorerie Nationale, signées de lui seulement, pour nous procurer, s'il est possible, une quantité suffisante de l'un et de l'autre, de ces deux genres de commestibles.

Le négociant qu'il envoye en Sardaigne, partira peut être ce soir sur l'aviso du Capitaine Rapon et se nomme Vital Coste, et paraît être propre à remplir cette commission, dont il s'est chargé sans aucune condition fixe

---

[1] There is no key to this cypher.—J. H. R.   [2] Arch. Nat., AF III. 73.

d'intérêt, laissant au gouvernement de lui décerner la récompense qu'il jugera convenable, lorsqu'il aura pu réussir à lui donner des preuves de son zèle et de son dévouement. Il donne en cela, Citoyen Ministre, une preuve de désintéressement et d'attachment à la République, bien rare dans ce pays cy. On lui donne 7,000*l*. en traites.

L'autre négociant destiné pour se rendre à Tripoli est le C$^{en.}$ Consul, venu de Paris il y a environ 4 mois, et très connu de mon prédécesseur. On se propose de lui donner 8,000 en traites. On l'autorisera à faire, au nom de la République, un cadeau au Pacha du brick sur lequel il s'embarquera, et qui sera armé de 6 canons. On prendra pour plus de sûreté la précaution de passer les traites à l'ordre du Citoyen Beaussier, Consul de France à Tripoli, qui sera chargé de surveiller, et vérifier les achats et de diriger les expéditions d'après les indications qui lui seront envoyées d'icy ; s'en rapportant d'ailleurs à sa prudence et à son zèle éclairé.

On craint de ne pouvoir rien procurer à Tunis, mais on tentera cependant des entreprises sur les villes de cette Régence où les gouverneurs sont bien disposés pour la République.

Je ne puis, Citoyen Ministre, vous en écrire d'avantage aujourd'hui. Incessament j'entrerai dans de plus grands détails. Je vous prie de compter sur mon zèle et mon dévouement à me conformer aux ordres du Directoire et aux vôtres. Salut & respect. (Signed) DOUBLET.

PS.—Depuis que ma lettre est écrite le C$^{en.}$ Coste s'étant consulté à ce qu'il paraît avec le C$^{en.}$ Guis, notre Consul en Syrie, qui se trouve icy depuis quelque tems, s'est ravisé et a demandé dix pour % de commission sur toutes les expéditions qu'il nous fera de Sardaigne. Le Général considérant que ce négociant ne met point de fonds dehors, a réduit sa demande à 8% et il s'en est contenté. J'ai cru de mon devoir, Citoyen Ministre, de vous en informer. Les Anglais nous bloquent chaque nuit plus étroitement que jamais, et d'accord avec les rébelles, ils allument des fanaux sur les différens points de la côte, où il y a de cales, ou des petits ports, pour tromper par là et attirer à eux les bâtiments qui nous viendraient de quelque côté que ce soit. J'en préviens nos différens consuls afin qu'ils en avertissent les capitaines respectifs de ces bâtimens, qui ne seraient jamais venus à Malte, et même tous en général, en leur disant que le fanal de St. Elme qui est le nôtre, est bien plus éclairé et plus élevé que les autres, et que par conséquent, en y faisant attention, il leur sera facile de le distinguer, et d'entrer dans un des deux ports de cette place.

(Signed) DOUBLET.

Contre Amiral Villeneuve, commandant les forces navales stationées à Malte, au Ministre de la Marine et des Colonies, du 10 Frimaire an 7 de la République Française (30th November 1798).[1]

Je vous ai écrit les 16 et 29 Brumaire la première par la galiotte *La Désirée* commandée par l'enseigne de vaisseau Vathier qui a transporté à Cagliari le Commissaire du Gouvernement Regnaud de St. Jean d'Angely et la dernière par le Citoyen Gaivoard enseigne de vaisseau que le Général Vaubois a employé auprès du consul de Cagliari pour l'expédition de subsistance pour Malte et qui est parti d'ici dans la nuit du 1er au 2e de ce mois sur un bateau sarde ; depuis lors (parti) nous avons vu arriver ici

[1] Brit. Mus. Add. MSS. 34943.

l'aviso *L'Assaillante* commandé par le Citoyen Rampon lieutenant de vaisseau provisoire, expédié de Toulon par le Contre Amiral Vence, l'arrivée de cet aviso a porté la joie et l'espérance dans le cœur de toute la garnison mais il n'était porteur d'aucune dépêche du gouvernement relative à notre position.

J'ai conjecturé par le contenu des lettres du Général Vence au commandant des armes dans ce port et par celle de l'Ordonnateur à Toulon au Citoyen Menard Commissaire de la Marine ici, qu'en France l'on me suppose parti pour Corfu. Mes différentes dépêches vous ont annoncé que je n'avois reçu aucun ordre, ni aucune nouvelle du Général Buonaparte, que depuis que je suis ici, nous n'avons vu arriver dans ce port que trois bateaux sardes, que la foiblesse de la garnison et la position de ce pays, ne permet pas au Général Vaubois de se départir d'aucun bâtiment de guerre, dont le secours des équipages lui est absolument nécessaire, que nous avons mis garnison dans les forts Manoel, Ricasoli et St. Ange, que presque tous les marins Maltais ayant étés se joindre aux rebelles, tout le service du port, le passage des troupes est fait par les équipages des vaisseaux, qu'enfin, il ne nous reste bientôt ici pour la subsistance de la garnison que du pain, des fèves et un peu de ris. Dans cette conjoncture l'assurance que nous donne l'aviso *L'Assaillante* des nombreuses expéditions qui doivent se faire dans les ports de France, à Gènes, à Tunis, la sollicitude du Gouvernement à l'égarde de Malte et la position formidable de nos armées en Italie ont produit le meilleur effet; et le courage, la patience, et la persévérance des Républicains dévoués à la défense de Malte est un sûr garant au Gouvernement que ce port important sera conservé à la République. Depuis mes dernières lettres il ne s'est rien passé d'intéressant, les rebelles ont démasqué une nouvelle batterie du côté du Casal Tarscien, ils continuent à travailler au Coradin,[1] on continue à les y chauffer, et j'espère qu'ils ne pourront s'y établir de manière à nous inquiéter beaucoup. Je vous ai fait part dans son tems du besoin de câbles et d'ancres du vaisseau *Le Guillaume Tell* et du mauvais état de son grand mât. J'ai fait fortifier le grand mât par de fortes jumelles, mais si ce vaisseau est destiné à remplir une nouvelle mission il lui devient indispensable d'avoir encore deux câbles et deux ancres. J'écris au commandant des armes à Toulon et à l'ordonnateur de me les faire parvenir s'il se présentoit une occasion asses sûre pour cet objet et je me refère pour tous les autres besoins de ce port à ce que doit vous en écrire le Commissaire de Marine, Menard. Je ré-expédie l'aviso *L'Assaillante* qui doit déposer à Cagliari un nouvel agent de subsistances que le Général Vaubois y envoye; il se rendra de là, à Toulon pour y recevoir de nouveaux ordres. Le Citoyen Rampon lieutenant de vaisseau provisoire qui la commande est entré ici, en essuyant le feu de toutes les batteries de la côte, celui d'un vaisseau de guerre et de plusieurs embarcations détachées à sa poursuite, il s'est fort bien conduit et mérite les grâces du Gouvernement, il se loue beaucoup du Citoyen Venel, enseigne de vaisseau son second, il a eu deux hommes blessés dans cette occasion. Salut et respect.
(Signed) VILLENEUVE.

PS.—Une frégate Napolitaine vient de rallier l'escadre Anglaise qui nous bloque; c'est le premier bâtiment de guerre de cette nation qui ait encore paru sur ce parage. (Signed) VVE.

---

[1] Corradino.—J. H. R.

The incidents of the siege during the month of November, from the besiegers' side, were reported to Nelson by Ball on the 30th of that month, as follows [1] :—

[Extract.]

CAPTAIN BALL TO NELSON.

H.M.S. *Alexander*, off Malta, 30*th November* 1798.[2]

... On the 7th instant about 120 French soldiers made a sortie from La Valette to get some cattle from the country, but they were very soon driven in, with the loss of eighteen men killed. ... I have prevailed on the Maltese to fit out speronaras to assist our guard-boats at night; they are stationed off St. Paul's and Marsa Scirocco. On the 20th, at night, they captured off St. Paul's a French galley called the *Vaubois*, from Sardinia, bound to Valetta with provisions. On the 21st the French made an attack on the post of Corradino with 1,000 men, but were repulsed with the loss of 600 killed and wounded.[3]

The Maltese troops evince great courage and perseverance on all occasions, and are very desirous of storming Valetta whenever it is thought practicable. I have desired them to consult on the best plan for an assault which they have taken into consideration, and are drawing up the plan for my opinion.

This dispatch covered a confidential letter of the same date, deploring the jealousies which reappeared amongst the Maltese leaders—an unfortunate circumstance which became more serious later on. In this dispatch Captain Ball also described, so far as he had been able to gather, the merits and demerits of the leaders of the people. The extract of this letter is as follows :—

EXTRACT OF A LETTER FROM CAPTAIN A. J. BALL TO LORD NELSON, DATED 30TH NOVEMBER 1798.[4]

The Maltese chiefs hurt the general cause by petty jealousies. I have exerted every possible influence to induce them to unite for the common good, and they promise me to act up to my wishes. General Vital has such bad health that he cannot be active, but he is very ambitious and turbulent, and has caused great dissatisfaction in his management of public money. General Caruana possesses much greater abilities, and is allowed to have great integrity. He has the voice of the people. He is accused of assuming too much power. He appears to carry on all the business of the islands, but he has been injudicious in not communicating with the deputies.

[1] It may be noted here that a squadron detached from the Earl of St. Vincent's fleet succeeded in bringing about the reduction of Port Mahon and the island of Minorca on November 15, 1798. At that time Nelson and the British Admiralty attached great importance to the possession of Minorca, and thought little of that of Malta. See *Dispatches of Nelson*, vol. iii. p. 315.—J. H. R.
[2] Brit. Mus. Add. MSS. 34908, f. 209.
[3] Of course this was the estimate of the Maltese. The proportion of killed and wounded is so entirely abnormal that one may be permitted to doubt it.—J. H. R.
[4] Brit. Mus. Add. MSS. 34908, f. 208.

Old Cardon, the Neapolitan colonel, is a very respectable character; he has endeavoured to unite the parties, and has been very forward in encouraging the Maltese at the different posts. He speaks very highly of one of his young officers, Pascal Gauci, a lieutenant in the Neapolitan service, in the regiment of Sannio. (Signed) A. JNO. B.

Although three months had not elapsed since the outbreak of the Maltese insurrection, yet by November European negotiations were already under consideration as to the future destiny of the island, and without any consideration for the welfare or the views of the inhabitants. The Czar of All the Russias having recently accepted the dignity of Grand Master, and taken the Order under his protection (as related hereafter), Austria demurred (Hompesch being an Austrian subject), and considered such a step precipitate, although agreeing that the Order should return and occupy the island. These views of the Austrian Government were communicated to Lord Grenville by the British Minister at the Court of Vienna under date of the 25th and 28th November.

The following is an extract and synopsis of these dispatches :—

SIR MORTON EDEN TO LORD GRENVILLE.

25th November 1798.[1]

[He encloses a protest of the Grand Master against the taking of the island by the French.]

28th November 1798.

Thugut[2] complained of not comprehending the Emperor of Russia's views on the subject of Malta; thought his proclamation of himself Grand Master a precipitate step, as that dignity could only be conferred by the election of all the Langues.

He added, 'that it appeared to him most prudent that the Order should, if possible, be established as it formerly existed; that M. de Hompesch, who was desirous of returning to Malta to head the insurgents and to recover the place, who, though he had acted weakly, had not, in his opinion, acted treacherously, might afterwards, if it were found expedient, resign this dignity. He thought that from the confiscation of the property of the Order in His Sicilian Majesty's dominions, the Court of Naples had in view the acquisition of the island.'

Regnaud, when on his way to Paris, again wrote to the Directory from Milan, under date of the 1st December, forwarding the same under cover of another of the same date, addressed to Talleyrand. This dispatch enclosed a copy of a memorandum, suggesting the best means which Regnaud could conceive for conveying provisions and news to the distressed garrison of Valetta. The memorandum was prepared for the commander-in-chief of the French army in Italy

---

[1] Foreign Office Records, Austria, 53.
[2] Thugut was the Austrian Chancellor.—J. H. R.

(residing at Milan), under whose command the fortress of Malta was then included. The following are copies of the dispatches and memorandum referred to :—

Milan, 11 *Frimaire* an 7 de la Rép. (1*st* *December* 1798).[1]

REGNAUD DE ST. JEAN D'ANGELY au CITOYEN TALLEYRAND, Ministre des Affaires Extérieures.

Je vous adresse, Citoyen Ministre, une lettre pour le Directoire Exécutif.

Je vous prie de la luy transmettre après avoir pris connoissance de son contenu.

Ma première démarche après mon arrivée, que retarde le mauvais état de ma santé sera chès vous ; recevez en attendant l'assurance de mes sentimens sincères d'estime et d'attachement.

(Signed) REGNAUD DE ST. JEAN D'ANGELY.

Milan, 11 *Frimaire* an 7ème (1*st* *December* 1798).

REGNAUD DE ST. JEAN D'ANGELY AU DIRECTOIRE EXÉCUTIF.

CITOYENS DIRECTEURS,—Ayant appris à Rome que le Général en Chef de l'Armée d'Italie avoit le commandement de Malte, j'ai cru devoir me rendre à Milan pour lui donner connoissance de l'État de ce poste important.

À la suite d'une longue conférence, je luy ai remis, avec un mémoire contenant les faits rapportés dans la dernière lettre que j'ai eu l'honneur de vous adresser, la note dont je crois devoir vous envoyer une copie.

Le Général en Chef, le Commissaire des Finances, et l'Ordonnateur en Chef de l'Armée me paroissent décidés à prendre provisoirement & en attendant vos ordres le parti que je leur ai indiqué.

Peut être penserès-vous qu'il est d'autant plus pressant de s'y arrêter que les secours projettés, & qui dévoient partir de Civita Vecchia sont probablement suspendus par les évènements de Rome.[2] Salut & respect.

(Signed) REGNAUD DE ST. JEAN D'ANGELY.

NOTE SUR LA MANIÈRE DE FAIRE PARVENIR DES APPROVISIONNEMENS ET DES NOUVELLES À MALTE.

Le blocus de Malte est fait avec un extrême vigilance : les Anglois ont toujours un ou deux vaisseaux en face du port, les autres sont distribués à l'est et à l'ouest de l'isle ou croisent dans le canal à portée de vue ; enfin des bâtiments légers, tel qu'un brick de 20 canons, une corvette de 32, vont et viennent des calles de St. Paul et de Marsa Scirocco où ils se retirent en Sicile ou à Naples.

Cet ordre habituel n'est interompu que lorsque le gros tems ne permet

---

[1] Arch. Nat., AF III 73.
[2] This refers to the invasion of the Roman territory on November 24, 1798, by the Neapolitan troops, who speedily compelled the French commander, Championnet, to withdraw from Rome. Nelson had sailed from Naples on November 22 for Leghorn in order to raise Tuscany against the French garrisons there. These successes of the Anglo-Neapolitan forces were brief, but they for the time lessened the chance of supplies going from Central Italy to Malta.—J. H. R.

pas aux bâtiments Anglois de rester stationnaires et les forcent [*sic*] de se retirer, pour n'être pas jettés sur les rochers de l'isle, si le vent est nord, ou de dériver si le vent vient de l'ouest ou de l'est vers le Maritimo ou le Cap Passaro.

C'est en profitant particulièrement du vent de l'ouest qu'on peut faire entrer des secours dans le port.

Il faut quand il commence à souffler faire partir de Cagliari de petites embarquations pontées, appelés bateaux sardes, qui tiennent la mer même au gros tems et en vingt quatre heures et même moins elles seront dans le canal de Malte.

Il importe qu'elles viennent dans le canal jusqu'à la hauteur de Malte à peu près, et ne longent pas la côté de l'isle en arrivant pour n'être pas apperçus des bâtiments légers Anglois qui sont quelques fois à la Calle de Saint Paul située entre le grand port et le Goze; et elles doivent éviter de reconnoître cette dernière isle, qui étant au pouvoir de l'ennemi peut faire des signaux le long de la côte.

On pourrait même, en saisissant bien le moment et prenant les précautions indiquées, risquer quelques bâtiments plus forts, et si on vouloit envoyer des secours d'hommes ou d'officiers, généraux ou autres, ils devroient attendre à Cagliari l'occasion favorable.

Un envoy parti d'un autre point et derigé sur Malte par toute espèce de tems ne peut échaper aux ennemis que par une sorte de miracle :

On vient de dire comment par un vent de l'ouest fort, les bateaux sardes peuvent aborder avec une grande probabilité.

Mais ils peuvent entrer encore même en tems ordinaire.

Pour cela ils doivent longer la côte de Sicile jusques à la hauteur de l'Alicata, partir de ce dernier port ou d'un des abris voisines, que la côte de Sicile offre en abondance, de manière de se trouver par un petit vent favorable à un canal avant la nuit, partant ensuite de ce dernier point à la chute du jour, ils peuvent entrer dans le port de Malte avant d'avoir été apperçus.

Les embarquations peuvent même quoique vues de l'ennemi être confondues avec des barques de pêcheurs ou avec des spéronares qui vont sans cesse prendre des vivres en Sicile, et n'éveillant pas l'attention des Anglois, se trouver en position de leur échaper & d'entrer malgré eux. Il y en a eu un exemple par une barque chargée de fromage qui est entrée en plein jour, par un beau tems, sous les yeux des Anglois, et après trois jours de navigation seulement à partir de Cagliari.

Pour assurer le départ de ces barques, l'achat préliminaire des marchandises qu'elles doivent porter et leur chargement, il paroit indispensable de faire partir de Gênes, et d'envoyer à Cagliari avec des fonds et un crédit un homme intelligent et sûr.

Porteur de lettres pour le Consul il devroit se consulter avec lui pour faire commercialement et sans bruit ses petits achats, mettre autant que possible à bord de chaque barque un assortiment des objets qui sont les plus nécessaires à la garnison de Malte ; tels que vin, vinaigre, eau de vie, viande salée, ou même moutons vivants, afin d'avoir un peu de viande fraîche pour les malades, charbon de bois, médicaments principaux, effets d'habillement, enfin ce qui manque absolument d'après l'apperçu donné au Directoire Exécutif.

On ne peut en finissant s'empêcher de rappeler combien il est urgent d'adopter cette mésure, de ne pas laisser plus longtems la garnison de Malte dans l'espèce d'abandon où elle a le droit de se croire et dans le découragement qui en est la suitte presque nécéssaire.

Laissés sur le stéril rocher de Malte, les militaires et agens de toutes les classes, n'ont reçu depuis le 30 Prairial, époque du départ de Bonaparte jusqu'au 19 Brumaire, époque du depart du Commissaire du Pouvoir Exécutif, aucunes lettres, aucunes instructions, aucunes nouvelles de ce qui se passe loin d'eux, de ce qu'on projette ou de ce qu'on exécute pour les secourir ; peut [sic] attiéder le zèle, rendre plus amer le sentiment des privations, et enfin diminuer l'énergie ou la durée de la République.

(Signed) REGNAUD DE ST. JEAN D'ANGELY.

Milan, 11 *Frimaire* an 7.

The guns and ammunition promised Nelson by the Neapolitan Government in the early part of November reached Malta in His Sicilian Majesty's ships *La Sirène* and *Retuza* on the 6th December, when they were ordered to proceed to Marsa Scirocco, and discharge the military stores there.

Captain Ball's dispatch of the 10th December, notifying the arrival of these vessels, was as follows :—

[Extract.]

CAPTAIN BALL TO LORD NELSON.

H.M.S. *Alexander*, off Malta, 10*th December* 1798.[1]

I have the honour to acquaint your Lordship that His Sicilian Majesty's ships, *La Sirène* and *Retuza*, joined me the night of the 6th instant. I directed their captains to go to Marsa Scirocco to deliver the military stores they brought for the Maltese, since which the weather has been so severe that I have not heard of the progress they have made. However, as it is now getting moderate, I hope in a day or two to see shells thrown among the French ships. . . . The Maltese applied for eight mortars and some battering cannon, and they were much disappointed at getting only two mortars and not any cannon. . . . I have directed the Maltese to make false attacks every night to keep the French in constant alarm, and as their garrison is very weak, I think they will soon be induced to capitulate.

A French dispatch-boat lately got into Malta at night in a gale of wind.

My guard-boat wounded three of their men, and would have taken her had the Maltese boats done their duty. She carried the French very bad news, and occasioned much dejection among them.

By this date a better feeling (for the time being) existed between the Maltese chiefs. This information was conveyed to Nelson in a confidential letter, under cover of that of the 10th December. The following is an extract thereof :—

[1] Brit. Mus. Add. MSS. 34908, f. 280.

Captain Ball to Lord Nelson.

H.M.S. *Alexander*, off Malta, 10th December 1798.[1]

. . . Upon the receipt of your letter I sent to the deputies of the island and recommended their hoisting the Neapolitan flag, which they have done. I have sent their letter to me upon that subject to Sir William Hamilton. The jealousies which existed between the Maltese chiefs have now subsided, and the business is carried on very well. . . .

The question of storming the lines at Cottonera had been discussed, but as it became known that there still existed in the city a party in favour of the French, the utmost caution had to be exercised. Moreover, Nelson had heard rumours of a contemplated landing in Malta of a body of Russian troops to assist in the siege, but with the intention eventually of asserting the right of sovereignty on behalf of the Czar.

Ball felt confident that this news would not be at all palatable to the Maltese leaders, and was most anxious that this information should be kept from them, as is evinced in the following extract of his dispatch to Nelson, dated the 26th December 1798:—

Captain Ball to Lord Nelson.

H.M.S. *Alexander*, off Malta, 26th December 1798.[2]

I communicated to Captain Drummond the necessary caution only, which your letter (of the 15th instant) stated, with a strict injunction to observe it most secretly. I shall do the same by Captain Foley. It is of great importance that the subject of your letter shall not be known to the Maltese, as there are many disaffected men among them, and I hope before it is publicly known to strike a blow and put an end to our tedious operations here. If it be possible to storm Cottonera with a prospect of success, we shall try it soon.

The 10-inch mortar which we are getting from the *Stromboli* bomb to put in the batteries will be ready for firing the 29th instant. Whenever the weather will permit, I shall make the *Perseus* bomb vessel try her sea mortar off the town.

Under these circumstances Nelson instructed Ball that should the rumour of a landing of Russian troops be confirmed, he was to protest against any infringement of existing compacts or encroachments on the rights of either the King of Naples or the blockading Power, England, and to threaten the closing of all Sicilian ports to Malta, should such an unfriendly act occur.[3]

Two other intercepted letters were taken during the month of December—one from the Commissary of Marine, Menard, to the Colonial Minister, dated the 2nd; the other of the 13th, from Commissary Doublet to the Minister for Foreign Affairs—together

---

[1] Brit. Mus. Add. MSS. 34903, f. 200.
[2] *Ibid.* 34908, f. 379.
[3] Nicolas, *Dispatches of Nelson*, vol. iii. p. 255 (edit. 1845).

with an official report on the situation of the garrison on the 21st, of which the following are copies :—

Commissaire de Marine, Menard, à Malte au Ministre de la Marine et des Colonies à Paris, en date du 12 Frimaire an 7ᵉ de la République (2nd December 1798).[1]

J'ai l'honneur de vous addresser l'état de situation des principales marchandises existantes au Port de Malte le 1ʳ Frimaire, vous remarquerès avec peine combien sont foibles nos moyens, tous les jours ils diminuent de manière à me faire craindre d'être sous peu obligé de vous annoncer que tout est consommé.

La partie des bois même sera bientôt épuissé. L'artillerie dont à present les besoins en grosses pièces sont immenses, ne prend plus que dans nos magazins, et le manque de bois de chauffage, m'obligera à donner toutes les petites pour le service de la garnison.

Si vous ne vous empressès Citoyen Ministre de venir à notre secours je serai forcé de renoncer à l'armament du vaisseau *Athénien*, ses mâts sont prêts pour son entière construction, il ne reste plus que quelques pièces de charpent à terminer. Je vais en donner la façon à l'enterprise ainsi que celle de la menuiserie et de la sculpture, je n'ai que ce moyen pour finir, les ouvriers du païs sont si lents que si je ne prenais ce parti, de six mois je ne serais guères plus avancé qu'aujourd'hui. Peut-être Citoyen Ministre vous trouverès mauvaises quelques unes de mes déterminations. Je sais que je devrais attendre vos ordres pour les mettre à execution, mais l'éloignement où nous sommes de vous faire parvenir mes lettres [sic]. Celle de recevoir vos ordres me forcent à agir comme je le fais. Soyès persuadé que rien n'égale mon zèle, pour le service de la République, c'est au seul désir de bien faire, que l'un doit attribuer les fautes que je pourrais commettre en ce genre.
(Signed) MENARD.

Commissaire Doublet pour les Îles de Malte et du Goze au Ministre des Relations Extérieures, 23 Frimaire an 7 de la Rép^(e.) (13th December 1798 (?)).[2]

Le citoyen Rapon n'ayant pas encore pu partir, je me fais un devoir d'ajouter à ce que j'ai eu l'honneur de vous [re]marquer dans ma première, sur la parte active que paroissoit prendre la Cour de Naples aux opérations des Anglais qui nous bloquent et nous assiègent par mer et par terre, qu'indépendamment de la frégate ou corvette Napolitaine entrée au Port St. Paul appartenant aux Anglo-Maltais, on a vu depuis deux autres frégates Napolitaines aussi rejoindre la Division Anglaise commandée par le Contre Amiral Nelson qui forme le blocus.

Je dois vous informer encore qu'un Parlementaire Anglais nous ayant amené 4 cit^(nes.) Françaises prises à bord d'un bateau sarde, l'officier Anglais sans qu'on le lui ait demandé, a donné pour nouvelles[3] :—

[1] Brit. Mus. Add. MSS. 34943.
[2] Ibid. f. 56.
[3] The Russian squadron combined with that of the Turks in September 1798, and proceeded, with the aid of some British ships, to blockade Corfu, greatly to the disgust of Nelson (see *Dispatches of Nelson*, vol. iii. p. 160), who maintained that the Russians ought to have helped their allies off the Nile, instead of furthering their own aims in the Adriatic.—J. H. R.

1°· Que Corfou s'était rendue à l'escadre Anglo-Russe qui la bloquait.
2°· Que les Anglais avaient pris Mahon.
3°· Que l'armée Napolitaine avait marché sur Rome. Nous n'avons rien cru de tout cela.

Mais ce dont nous ne pouvons pas douter c'est que le Pavillon Napolitaine a été arboré hier sur la citadelle de la Cité Vieille. Ce qui nous fait présumer que les Anglais paraissent dans le dessein de faire rentrer cette île sous la domination du Roi de Naples, et cela est sûrement un leure dont les Maltais seront aussi dupés qui les Napolitaines eux mêmes, car il n'est pas possible que les Anglais n'aient pas en cela un arrière pensée.

Jusqu'à présent nous n'avons pas encore eu de bombes, mais en revanche on nous envoye fréquemment des boulets de 24 à toute volée, plusieurs sont tombés sur le palais de l'ex-Grand Maître, où est logé le Général Vaubois, le Général Chanez, et une partie de l'État Major. Personne n'en a encore été blessé. Rien ne nous arrive de France ni d'ailleurs et nous manquons de deux objets bien essentiels—la viande et le vin. Hâtez-vous Citoyen Ministre de nous envoyer des secours efficaces, ou des provisions sans lesquelles, malgré tout le courage et le dévouement de la brave garnison nous ne pourrions conserver cette isle importante à la République. Si l'envoi de ces secours et provisions ne vous est pas possible, il n'y aurait qu'un moyen de sauver Malte, ce serait la paix. Je vous prie de communiquer cette lettre au Directoire. Salut et respect.

(Signed) Doublet.

État de Situation [1]

de la Division Militaire, commandée par le Général Vaubois à l'Époque du 1re Nivôse de l'an 7 de la République Française (21st December 1798).

Présens sous les armes	3822
Hôpitaux	172
Externes	70

L'artillerie de la division consiste en 552 pièces de canon depuis la calibre de 64 jusqu'à celui d'1 livre; 10 obusiers tant du calibre de 6^{srs}· que de celui de 6 P^{ces}· 69^n· et d'8 pouces; 48 mortiers de 5, 8, 9½, 11 et 12 pouces; et 36 perriers de 15 pouces.

Ville de Malte (St. Elme), et les Forts St. Ange, Ricasoli, Tigné, et Manoel.

Rapport des mouvemens opérés dans le courant du mois. On avoit formé ici par ordre du Général Bonaparte quatre compagnies de canoniers Maltais qui faisoient à peu pres 200 hommes.

Voyant qu'il désertoit chaque jour quelques uns de ces individus on s'avisa fort apropos de demander aux autres que ceux d'entre eux qui ni vouloient plus faire le service de canoniers et désiroient d'aller à la campagne pouroient sortir des rangs, ci qui firent 160 d'entre eux.

Bien loin de les envoyer pour rejoindre les rebelles on les arrêta, et ils furent mis en prison, où ils sont encore. On a réorganisé et formé une seule compagnie des hommes qui restaient fidèles, peut être encore en apparence.

---

[1] Brit. Mus. Add. MSS. 34943, f. 66.

CHAPTER XI

THE BRITISH BLOCKADE

(From the 5th January to the 3rd March 1799)

As already mentioned, an assault on the Cottonera lines was to be made by the insurgents. Sickness had already made its appearance amongst them, breeding discontent and insubordination, and it was consequently thought advisable no longer to delay the attempt.

On the 5th January, Captain Ball placed before the chiefs assembled at Citta Vecchia the following proposals[1] :—

1st. The chiefs of the island having met to take into consideration some plans for attacking the enemy, it is highly necessary that every member shall take an oath that he will not, directly or indirectly, divulge the business of the assembly.

2nd. A register is to be kept of the names of the chiefs and soldiers who have delivered their country from French tyranny, and when the Government is settled they are to be recommended in preference to any other persons to fill all places for which they are qualified.

3rd. There shall be in the cathedral an inscription in gold letters with the names of all those chiefs who by their bravery have expelled the French, and of all those who contributed money to support their countrymen during the critical period, with the sum each person respectively paid, that the country may never forget the services rendered. Their names shall likewise be inscribed in the same manner in the parish church to which they respectively belonged.

4th. The members of the assembly must report (as a ruse) that it is not our intention to attack the French until the arrival of four English regiments from Minorca, who are to be landed in the bay of Marsa Scirocco without the enemy's knowledge, and then the garrison is to be stormed.

5th. When the day is fixed for attacking the enemy, it must be signified in the morning that you have received intelligence the enemy intend making a sortie, and that every man must be at his post, and very vigilant; this may do away any suspicions of our motives.

6th. The chiefs and soldiers must be dressed in dark-coloured clothes, stockings, and cravat, and not to let their shirts be seen. Every chief to

[1] Brit. Mus. Add. MSS. 34909, f. 30.

have a speaking-trumpet. The soldiers must be cautioned to observe secrecy and silence, as the success of the enterprise greatly depends upon a strict observance of this.

7th. Great care to be taken in approaching the works, the enemy having thrown spikes and broken glass all round. It is recommended to have cotton bags thrown over these places.

8th. A parole and countersign to be given in English and Maltese, and a Maltese chief to be attached to each English party, to prevent mistakes.

9th. The sentinels to be doubled a day or two before the attack, and the greatest vigilance observed to prevent any intelligence going to the enemy.

10th. Each parish to have a rendezvous given, that they may know where to assemble upon the signal being made for alarm.

At one o'clock of the morning of the attack, an express to be sent to each parish to let them know it is expected the French will make an attack at four o'clock, and that every man must be armed at that time and ready to march when the alarm is given at St. John's, but the parishes are upon no account to sound an alarm until it shall be given from thence.

Captain Ball acquainted Nelson with these proceedings regarding the contemplated assault of the Cottonera lines in a dispatch of the 6th January 1799, of which the following is an extract:—

CAPTAIN BALL TO LORD NELSON.

H.M.S. *Alexander*, off Malta, *6th January* 1799.[1]

... I have the satisfaction to acquaint you that I have united all the chiefs in the most perfect harmony, and that our operations are in a train for a speedy and successful conclusion. ... The Maltese troops are getting sickly and discontented with their hard fare, and the moment is arrived when a bold stroke must be made. I have assembled all the chiefs and sworn them to secrecy, and to take into consideration a plan for storming the enemy's works, in which I have the most sanguine hopes of success, and I shall put it to the proof the 9th or 10th instant. The Maltese have an aversion to the Neapolitan Government, and wish to be under the English.

The chiefs have requested me, when we have driven the enemy out, to regulate and direct the management of all their concerns, from a conviction of the respect and deference which the Maltese pay to all orders which originate from the English. I shall have no objection to remain here a month or two for that purpose, if it shall meet your approbation, and you will do me a favour if you will let me go to England at the expiration of that time. From my observation of the disposition and manners of the people here, they require a person of good judgment and conciliatory manners, and the latter I conceive to be more essential than is generally imagined.

Before putting the projected plan of attack on the Cottonera

[1] Brit. Mus. Add. MSS. 34909, ff. 34, 36.

lines into execution, an attempt to seize the city of Valetta by stratagem was arranged for the night of the 11th January. Unfortunately the plot was discovered, the leaders arrested, and several shot on the palace square. The dispatches of Admiral Villeneuve to the Minister of Marine; Menard, Commissary of Marine, to the same; and of Adjutant-General Brouard[1] to Deputy Dubois-Dubay, all of the 17th January, give details of this conspiracy, which had been accidentally discovered.

General Brouard's animadversions on Regnaud's character, contained in the aforesaid letter, are additional proof of the dissensions which had existed between the civil and military authorities whom Bonaparte had appointed for the administration of the government.

Malte le 28 Nivôse an 7me (17th January 1799).[2]

Silvestre Villeneuve, Contre Amiral, au Ministre de la Marine et des Colonies.

CITOYEN MINISTRE,—Le génie qui veille sur les destinés de la République et de ses deffenseurs vient de faire avorter une des plus profondes conjurations qui ait été conçue et dont le résultat eût été le massacre de tous les français qui sont à Malte, et la perte pour la République de cette possession importante.

Le 22 je vous annonçais l'arrivée de la polacre *Galathée*, Capitaine Cavazza, expédiée de Gènes, par le Citoyen Belleville, chargée de vin, vinaigre, eau de vie, salaisons, &c. Nous apprîmes par ce bâtiment la défaite de l'armée Napolitaine[3] et l'entrée de nos troupes à Rome le 24 Frimaire; le Général Vaubois, en réjouissance de cet évènement, ordonna qu'à midi toutes les batteries qui font face à l'ennemi feroient une décharge de leurs artilleries; au moment où cette décharge eut lieu, une nuée de paysans armés se présenta sous les remparts de la Floriane et de la Cotonaire; ils crioient—ouvrès, ouvrès donc les portes; le feu de notre mousquetterie et des canons à mitraille les eut bientôt éloigné avec une perte d'hommes que l'on croit assez considérable. Dans la matinée le Général Vaubois avoit eu quelques indices qu'il se tramoit un complot. Cet évènement augmentat ses soupçons; toute la garnison eut ordre d'être en surveillance, à 8 heures. À 8 hours du soir le Citoyen Bovard, capitaine dans le 21me Demi-Brigade d'Infanterie légère et le Citoyen Roussel, sous lieutenant dans le même corps sortaient par la porte de Marsamusset pour se rendre au Fort Manuel [et] s'appercevoient qu'il y avoit du monde dans les magasins de la quarantaine qui sont attenant extérieurement à la dite porte; le Citoyen Bovard en arrivant au Fort Manuel donna une garde de 7 hommes à Roussel pour aller visiter ces magasins, il approche et reconnoît un rassemblement de 2 ou 300 hommes, il fait feu dessus; aussitôt ces gens prennent l'épouvante, s'échapent dans les fossés et dans une barquette qu'ils avoient, d'autres demandant grâce à genoux. Le

---

[1] I have omitted that of General Brouard as being a repetition of the others. See also the Journal of General Vaubois (Appendix, Part II *ad init.*).—J. H. R.

[2] Arch. Nat., AF III. 73.

[3] General Championnet speedily drove back the Neapolitan invaders, recaptured Rome, and marched on towards Naples.—J. H. R.

Citoyen Roussel fond dessus, une quarantaine sont arrettés et d'autres tués, il trouve dans les magasins, 200 fusils, des cartouches, des sabres et autres armes, une trentaine d'autres sont arrettés dans les fossés. On sçait par ces gens là qu'une conspiration étoit ourdie dans la ville pour leur ouvrir les portes et massacrer les français—qu'un nommé Guillelme fameux corsaire de ce pays en étoit le chef. L'agent de la santé chargé de la garde des magasins, un channoine, un commissaire de quartier étoient ses lieutenants. Au son des cloches de St. Jean que le channoine devoit faire sonner, tous les conjurés devoient se précipiter sur les postes français et ouvrir aux rebelles renfermés dans les magasins de la santé la porte de Marsamusset [Marsa Muscet], tous les ouvriers Maltais, presque tous les habitants, les forçats, tous étoient enrolés dans la conspiration. Le Conseil de Guerre a déjà fait justice du chef et de quelques autres. Les prisons du Fort St. Elme en sont remplies. Des sabres, des stylets, des cartouches avoient déjà été distribués; ils comptoient sur les fusils de la salle d'armes, et ceux des français qu'ils auroient surpris sans méfiance, et maîtres de la cité Valette où se trouvent tous les magasins, toutes les armes et toutes les munitions obligeois [sic] bientôt les différents forts de se rendre.

Tel étoit le plan de cette conspiration que la valeur des français eut sans doute déjoué, mais qui n'en étoit pas moins audacieuse.[1] Elle prouve encore combien nous avons à nous méfier de tous les habitants en général. On travaille à faire encore une évacuation considérable, mais on est obligé de garder des ouvriers tels que maçons, forgerons, menuisiers, boulangers, &c., et nous sommes assurés que ce sont autant d'ennemis. La première indice de la conjuration fut donnée au Général Vaubois par des gens qui habitent ce pays mais sans qu'ils ayent pu rien préciser. Depuis six jours toute la garnison et les marins sont sur pied, écrasés de fatigue, tous la supportent avec courage, mais ils ont à craindre que cette fatigue jointe à la mauvaise nourriture n'altère la santé du soldat et du marin. Nous avons un besoin urgent de renfort du garnison. Ne seroit-il pas possible d'expédier de Toulon la frégate, *La Boudeuse*, avec deux ou trois cents hommes, les vaisseaux Vénétiens avec quatre ou cinq cents hommes chacun et des vivres. De ces bâtiments expédiés isolément sans doute que quelques uns arriv[er]oient à bon port. Je me suis toujours tenu jusqu'au moment du bombardement en état d'appareiller pour protéger l'arrivée des bâtiments qui pourroient paroître, mais depuis ce moment les arrangements qu'il a fallu faire sur les vaisseaux et l'emploi de tous mes équipages à terre ne me laisse plus cet espoir.

Les Anglois croisent toujour autour de l'isle avec deux ou trois vaisseaux et des frégates; ils se tiennent moins devant l'entrée du port et nous restons quelque fois les deux ou trois jours sans les appercevoir.

Le 24 dans la nuit il nous est arrivé encore un brick, *L'Appolonie*, Capitaine Antoine Bigot, de 160 tonneaux venant de Marseille, ayant relâché à St. Tropés, chargé entièrement de vin et d'eau de vie. Nous avons à présent un approvisionnement assuré pour toute l'été pour la garnison, mais les habitants de la ville ne se nourrissent absolument qu'avec du pain qu'ils trempent dans l'huille. Aujourd'hui une tartanne française a été prise par deux frégates Anglaises par le travers de l'anse de St. Paul.

[1] For further details see the *Journal of the Siege of Malta* (Part II *ad init.*), by General Vaubois, in the Appendix.—J. H. R.

Du 3 Pluviôse :—Je termine ici cette dépêche que je vous adresse par voie de Gênes ; je vous adresserai un duplicata par la première occasion qui se présentera. Depuis deux jours les rebelles n'ont pas tirés sur la ville ; ici dans le port nous n'avons aucune nouvelle de ce qui se passe à la campagne depuis le moment que la conspiration a été découverte. Il n'y a qu'un seul vaisseau Anglois à l'entrée du port.   Salut & respect.

(Signed) VILLENEUVE.

Malte, le 28 *Nivôse* l'an 7 (17th January 1799).
Menard, Commissaire de Marine, au Ministre de la Marine et des Colonies.[1]

CITOYEN MINISTRE,—Depuis ma lettre du 8 Nivôse les rebelles sont parvenus à faire tomber le 15 une bombe sur la frégate *La Justice*, et le 18 une autre sur *La Diane* ; quoique elles ayent crevé à bord, elles n'ont fait aucun mal, ce qui nous donne parfaitement de la confiance dans le blindage qu'on y a établi.

Depuis aussi nous avons reçus trois nouveaux bâtimens, une polacre Génoise, Capitaine Cavazza, arrivée le 22, chargée de vin, d'eau de vie, viande salée, légumes et autres objets expédiés de Gènes pour compte de la République, un bâtiment impérial chargé de bled, parti de Triest depuis deux mois, expédié pour Livourne, est arrivé de relâche le 24, le Général a décidé de le garder ; le 25 il nous est entré un bâtiment français expédié de Marseille par la Maison Vranc et pour son compte, avec un chargement de vin et d'eau de vie.

L'arrivée de ces bâtiments nous a été avantageuse non seulement par les subsistances qu'ils nous ont apportés mais encore par l'évènement qu'a produit le premier.

Le Capitaine Cavazzo [*sic*] nous avoit apporté des lettres de Gènes, le C$^{en.}$ Belleville avoit écrit au Général Vaubois, le C$^{en.}$ L'Escalier m'avoit écrit à moy ; les deux lettres nous annonçoient la Révolution qui réunit le Piémont à la République [2] et les victoires de nos armées contre les Napolitains,[3] le Général en signe de réjouissance ordonna qu'il sera fait une salve de tous les canons dirigés sur l'ennemi. Elle fut faite à midy et demy mais à l'instant on apperçut de la Cotonerre 4 à 5,000 rebelles s'avancer vers cette partie, plusieurs d'entre eux étoient sans armes, d'autres portoient des haches ; tous s'approchoient avec confiance, en criant qu'on leur ouvrit la porte ; reçus par nos troupes d'une toute autre manière qu'ils ne s'attendoient, ils se rétirèrent avec une quantité considérable de morts et de blessés ; après cette expédition nous étions dans la sécurité la plus grande ; le soir par extraordinaire on joua la comédie, cet évènement si simple en luy même nous a sauvé du plus grand des dangers ; peut-être a-t-il conservé cette place à la République. Un des officiers de service au Fort Manuel au retour de la comédie se rendoit à son poste ; en sortant de la place de Marsa Mouchet [*sic*] il remarqua avec surprice qu'une des barrières du Lazaret qui étoit toujours ouverte

---

[1] Arch Nat., AF III. 73.
[2] Charles Emmanuel IV, King of Sardinia, abdicated on December 1, 1798, whereupon his realm was annexed to the French Republic, and underwent severe exactions.—J. H. R.
[3] The victories of Championnet over Mack and the Neapolitans. Ferdinand IV and Maria Carolina set sail from Naples on December 21, 1798, for Palermo.—J. H. R.

étoit à ce moment fermée ; sans y faire trop d'attention, il en parloit au battelier qui le passoit ; ce marin avoit cru appercevoir du monde dans les magazins du Quarantaine ; il communiqua ses craintes à cet officier qui, arrivé au fort, prit dans la barquette, 7 hommes qu'elle pouvait contenir et retourna pour s'assurer de la chose ; sans lumière, il s'introduit, les soldats ne sont pas longtems à s'appercevoir qu'ils sont au millieu d'une quantité ne rebelles, rien ne les arrete, ils frappent, ils tuent, les autres fuyent, se précipetent dans la mer. On en arrete quatorze ; des nouvelles troupes arrivent, on parcourt les établissements, on y trouve une quantité de fusils, de cartouches, d'échelles, et d'outils ; le reste de la nuit toutes les troupes sont sous les armes ; au point du jour on visite, on ramasse encore une quarantaine de rebelles repandus dans divers coins ou cachés dans des magazins de la douane situés à l'autre côté du pont. On ne doute plus que le complot denoncé la veille par un gru n'éxiste, on fait des perquisitions. Un serjent amène un porte-faix qui sait tout, qui dénonce le complot et nomme les conspirateurs. Des rebelles devoient être introduis dans la ville par les magazins de la Quarantaine, dont un conservateur de santé avoit donné les clefs ; d'autres devoient s'introduire dans la Floriane par la porte dite de la marine qui étant peu gardée ne donnoit aucune peine ; dans la ville les conjurés, au son convenu des cloches doivent le 23 à 7 heures du matin se réunir à ceux du dehors, s'emparer alors de la Porte Nationale, des Cavaliers et du Palais National, facilitant ainsi l'entrée de la ville aux habitans de la campagne, tous les français et leurs amis étoient égorgés. Le Capitaine Guilermi ancien corsaire de la réligion, et colonel au service de la Russie étoit le chef de la conjuration dans la ville, les personnes qui le secondoient avoient chacun leur poste marqué ; un employé du mont de piété devoit s'emparer de la Porte Nationale, un ex-officier municipal du Palais, les forçats n'étoient point oubliés, leurs armes étoient préparées.

De suite les principaux personages nommés par cet homme furent arrettés, l'instruction de la procédure a prouvé l'existence du complot, il devoit d'abord s'exécuter le 22 à huit heures du matin, on avoit en suite renvoyé l'exécution à trois heures de l'après diné, en suite à 7 heures du lendemain ; elle a aussi prouvé qu'il y avoit une communication entre la ville et la campagne. Quand le chef des rebelles voulait conférer avec les conjurés un pavillon rouge sur les batteries qui battent la ville et trois coups de canons le prévenaient et la nuit ils se rendoient, on ne sait encore guères comment, au lieu indiqué et rentroient le lendemain matin.

Les arrestations continuent et déjà le Cap[ne.] Guilermi d'autres conjurés et plusieurs paysans ont été fusillés, et bientôt nous serons débarrassés des traitres connus, mais nous aurons de la peine à nous débarrasser de tous ; pour le faire il faudrait nous défaire de tous les habitans de la ville, parmi lesquels on compte avec peine sept à huit familles attachées véritablement à la République. Salut & respect.

(Signed) MENARD.

PS.—Une bombe vient de tomber à l'instant sur le vaisseau, *Le Guillaume Tell*, il n'a reçu aucun dommage.

The discovery of this plot proved most calamitous to the besiegers: it damped the ardour of the insurgents, and the assault on the Cottonera lines had to be postponed.

The correspondence which took place between Captain Ball and Mr. Vincent Borg (one of the leaders in command of the insurgents from the villages of Lia and Birchircara), and that between General Vital and Captain Ball, of the 17th January, fully confirm the fact that the country levies had become sadly discouraged by the capture of the conspirators on the 11th, and the execution of several of them on the palace square between the 11th and 17th of January, the total number executed being forty-five.[1]

FROM CAPTAIN A. J. BALL TO MR. VINCENT BORG.[2]

H.M.S. *Alexander*, 17th January 1799.

SIR,—I cannot sufficiently express to you my vexation at seeing so great a change among the Maltese soldiers. They are so discouraged that I am strongly of opinion you ought not to press them to the assault until the chiefs can inspire them with courage to risk their lives for their religion and their country, for you may be persuaded that the French will never pardon them. The chiefs must show their zeal, otherwise I foresee great misfortunes. I have a great deal to say to you which I cannot write. I anchored here expressly to keep up a personal communication with you. I am just now so busy that I cannot leave my ship; it is against our rules for commanders to leave their vessels on a coast at this season without the greatest necessity; nevertheless I have done it often lately, at a great risk, with the hope of being useful to the Maltese, but as that has not succeeded I must remain on board. Generals Caruana and Vital, with the Abbé Savoia, have been on board the ship to-day, to whom I spoke very freely. I hope you will soon recover a good state of health. I shall not fail to pay you a visit when the weather permits. I have the honour, &c.

(Signed) ALEX. JOHN BALL.

VINCENT BORG, Esq.[3]

GENERAL VITAL TO CAPTAIN BALL.

Zabar, 8 o'clock p.m., 17th January 1799.[4]

SIR,—I have this instant received a letter from Captain Vivion, who has signified to me your opinion that the attack had better be deferred a few days, which appears to be founded on the backwardness and fears which the Maltese have shown. This was communicated to the troops, who unanimously declared they would not have the attack deferred, nor could they allow the English to lead in scaling the walls, as it would reflect an eternal disgrace on their character.

[1] Vassallo, p. 785.
[2] From V. Borg's *Appeals to the British Government*, p. 20.
[3] Vincent Borg afterwards became one of Ball's inveterate enemies, on the ground that he (Borg) had been inadequately recompensed for his services, and (as he claimed) unjustly persecuted. This will appear later. (Note of Mr. Hardman.)
[4] Brit. Mus. Add. MSS. 34909, f. 84.

I will not undertake to order an attack until I know your determination. The people in a body act as a strange machine, ever ready to go by the rule of contrary; pray honour me with an answer, and believe me, with respect, &c. (Signed) EMANUELE VITAL.

PS.—I have the honour to acquaint you that every arrangement is more perfect than we may be able to effect another time; however, if you have any other motives than what I have suggested, we will resist the general impulse of the people. (Signed) EM$^{L.}$ VITAL.

[Answer.]

H.M.S. *Alexander*, ½ past 9 o'clock p.m.,
17th *January* 1799.

SIR,—The only reason I have for deferring the attack of Cottonera is the backwardness which the Maltese troops have evinced. Several of the chiefs mentioned it to me. I would have you follow your own judgement. You shall have my suffrage. You are best acquainted with the character of your countrymen, and therefore ought to know when to seize the favourable moment to lead them to victory. Whenever Captain Vivion writes to me I shall land with my people to co-operate. God prosper you, my dear General. Your friend, &c. (Signed) ALEX$^{R.}$ JOHN BALL.[1]

Referring to the failure of this attempt to capture Valetta, Lord Nelson, basing his opinion upon the annexed copy of Ball's dispatch of the 29th January, informed Earl St. Vincent on the 3rd February as follows [2]:—

The *Incendiary* is just come from Ball off Malta, and has brought me information that the attempt of storming the city of Valetta had failed from (I am afraid I must call it) cowardice. They were over the first ditch, and retired, but I trust the zeal, judgment, and bravery of my friend Ball and his gallant party will overcome all difficulty.

[Extract.]

CAPTAIN BALL TO LORD NELSON.

H.M.S. *Alexander*, off Malta, 29th *January* 1799.[3]

MY LORD,—I had the honour of writing to Your Lordship the 6th inst. by the *Dorotea*, wherein I mentioned my expectation of soon making a successful stroke against the French. I enclose an account of the proceedings of the Maltese from the 5th to the 20th inst., with our co-operation, which will prove that had they possessed any spirit of enterprise or courage we could have forced the French to capitulate. We are to make another attempt to storm Cottonera as soon as General Vital has completed

---

[1] Captain Escoffier to the Minister of Marine, and ex-Consul Caruson, under date of the 23rd January, gave further details of the plot and the progress of the siege; but their letters are omitted, because they cover the same ground as the previous, and as Vaubois' *Journal of the Siege of Malta* (Part II), in the Appendix.—J. H. R.
[2] Nicolas, *Dispatches of Nelson*, vol. iii. p. 254 (edit. 1845).
[3] Clarke and MacArthur, vol. ii. p. 148; Brit. Mus. Add. MSS. 34909, f. 127.

the corps I recommended raising. I have the satisfaction to acquaint Your Lordship that the conduct of the captains, officers, and men under my command during the late land co-operation has given the Maltese the highest opinion of the character of the British nation. They wish very much to be under our Government, and have a general aversion to the Neapolitan one.

General Caruana informed me the day after the plot at Valetta failed that had the chief succeeded whose name is Guillaume Lorenzi, he would have hoisted Russian colours. I believe this Russian party extends in the country; two of the Russian deputies have been intriguing with the late Grand Master. The deputies have sent a letter to Your Lordship to request your intercession with His Sicilian Majesty to send them a supply of corn. If it be ordered them, I should recommend sending a small supply at a time.

I shall hope soon to find out the traitor in the Russian party. Nine-tenths of the people wish to be under the English Government.

By the end of January 1799 great scarcity of wheat was experienced, when the deputies implored Nelson to obtain a supply from the Neapolitan Government upon the hypothecation of their public and private property. Their petition (referred to by Ball) was dated the 26th January, as follows :—

[Translation.]

Malta, 26*th January* 1799.[1]

My Lord,—The entire Maltese nation very earnestly presents to Your Excellency the assurance of their most profound thanks for your efforts on their behalf in the past.

It is the fleet of His Britannic Majesty, which is under your orders, and that of the Portuguese, which was sent by you, my Lord, that has guarded the safety and the liberty of this people. During the five months in which we have defended our lines, our towers, and our shores against an obstinate garrison, which has caused such misfortune to this island, all private individuals have contributed towards maintaining this people under arms, as well as the immense number of emigrants and people driven from the blockaded cities, robbed even of their clothes. We have had recourse to His Majesty the King of Naples to supply us with the necessary provisions, both of war and for food. Orders have been given by this Sovereign, and victuals have been furnished us from Sicily, but after the past five months all our resources are now exhausted; all the funds belonging to the Maltese (who for the greater part are within the besieged cities) are not in our possession, and we now find ourselves in the most critical position. Our desolation is complete, and the urgency is inexpressible.

Our enemies, closed within the impregnable fortifications, the work of two centuries, obstinately resist; and they are in possession of wheat which will last for a long time.

Our industries, our forces, our provisions, have lasted until now.

[1] Brit. Mus. Add. MSS. 34943, f. 128.

What desolation, my Lord, if through the failing of food we shall have to capitulate to a perfidious nation, which has eluded its promises and violated all its treaties.

Our hope, my Lord, is in the protection of Your Excellency and the great Britannic nation. We venture to supplicate for your influence on our behalf with His Majesty the King of Naples, besides your personal interest, to obtain for us a supply of grain on credit, against the hypothecation of all our public and private properties. An Act for this purpose has been drawn up and signed by all the proprietors of Malta.

We beg you, my Lord, to come to our help and terminate a work so well commenced.

We pray, my Lord, that you will accept the assurances of respect from our nation, and particularly that of our own; and we have the honour, &c.

(Signed) COUNT SALVADORE MANDUCA.
,, COUNT FERDINANDO THEUMA.
,, MARCHESE VINCENZO DE PIRO.
,, EMMANUELE VITALE; also as Commandant.
,, CANON SAVERIO CARUANA.
,, VINCENZO BORG.

TO HIS EXCELLENCY LORD NELSON.

Notwithstanding Ball's admonitions, precautions, and sworn secrecy regarding the contemplated attack by assault on the Cottonera lines, it would appear from Admiral Villeneuve's dispatch to the Minister of Marine, under date of the 30th January, that the plan had been disclosed to the French authorities, and that in consequence due preparations were made for its repulse, should it ever be attempted :—

Malte, le 11 *Pluviôse* an $7^{\text{ème}}$ (30*th January* 1799).

Le Contre-Amiral Villeneuve au Ministre de la Marine et des Colonies.[1]

CITOYEN MINISTRE,—Le 2 de ce mois nous avons celébré ici l'anniversaire de la mort du dernier despote des français,[2] et le souvenir flateur de tous les évènements qui ont été la suite de ce grand acte, a remplacé, pendant cette journée, l'horreur des trahisons, des complots et des assassinats dont nous sommes environnées.

Le 5, le tems étant calme, j'ai fait sortir une felouque commandée par le Citoyen Aussety, lieutenant de vaisseau du *Guillaume Tell*, et armée de 30 hommes du même vaisseau pour intercepter quelques espéronares ou autres bâtiments que les rebelles employent le long de la côte ; elle s'est emparée en effet d'une espéronare chargé d'olive et fromage, ayant 6 hommes d'équipage et d'une felouque Napolitaine qui sortait de Marsa Siroco où elle avoit débarqué un chargement de bled. L'équipage de la felouque s'est jetté dans une embarcation et s'est sauvé à terre, et les deux prises sont rentrées dans le port malgré le feu des batteries de la côte qui tiroient sur elles de tous les côtés. Le même jour un enfant s'est échappé

---

[1] Arch. Nat., AF III. 73.
[2] Louis XVI was executed on January 21, 1793.—J. H. R.

de la campagne et est rentré en ville ; nous avons sçu par lui et par les matelots de l'espéronare pris que les rebelles, excités par les Anglais, au désespoir d'avoir vu entrer dans le port quatre bâtiments chargés de commestibles, désespérant de nous réduire par la famine se disposoient à nous donner un assaut général.

Toutes les mésures sont prises pour les recevoir ; les remparts sont garnis de monde pendant la nuit et s'ils osoient se présenter, il y a lieu de croire qu'il en seroit fait un exemple, qui les corrigeroit pour longtems. Nous n'avons à regretter que la fatigue que cette surveillance continue impose à la garnison et aux marins.

Trois vaisseaux Anglais se sont tenus plus rapprochés de nous depuis quelques jours, il est probable qu'ils veuillent prendre part à l'affaire et faire une diversion du côté du port. Salut et respect.

(Signed) VILLENEUVE.

On the 31st January the Maltese deputies addressed Lord Nelson for the purpose of soliciting the retention of Ball in command of the blockading squadron, as follows :—

[Translation.]

Malta, 31st January 1799.[1]

MY LORD,—We have the honour to confirm to Your Excellency the contents of our letter which we addressed your Lordship on the 26th inst.

We again beseech your protection, upon which we base all our hopes. Whilst asking for a supply of grain against the hypothecation of all our public and private properties, we have formulated another request which we supplicate Your Excellency to place before the eyes of His Majesty the King of Naples.

In the stores belonging to the Order of Malta in Augusta there exists a quantity of biscuit, which has been paid for by that Order. We have a legitimate right to make this demand, having regard to the considerable debt owing to our University [2] by that said Order. What more urgent occasion could our people have for such succour ?

We pray Your Excellency will use your influence so that His Majesty will issue orders for this biscuit to be delivered to us.

This is a favour which we beseech the King to grant, and we flatter ourselves that our demand presented through Your Excellency will be successful. Our second and main object in rendering you thanks is relative to the general officer to whom you have confided the command of the squadron stationed off our Island.

Monsieur the Commandant Ball, on whom we have frequently had occasion to call, and in whom we observe so much honesty of purpose, merits all our acknowledgment, nor can we find words daily to convey such to him. In repeating our thanks to Your Excellency, we beg you will not change the present arrangement, for on the contrary, we desire that the charge of the blockade and our victory should always be confided

---

[1] Brit. Mus. Add. MSS. 34943, f. 132.
[2] i.e. the corporation for the supply of corn, as before explained.—J. H. R.

to this respected chief, who has rendered us up to this time such signal services, and who so well understands the character of our nation.

We place great importance on this request, and we trust that Your Excellency would kindly add this to our occasions of gratitude.

We have the honour to avail ourselves of this occasion to repeat the assurances of the profound respect with which we remain, my Lord, Your Excellency's very humble and very obedient servants, the Deputies of the Maltese people.

>   (Signed) COUNT SALVADORE MANDUCA.
>   „ COUNT FERDINANDO THEUMA-CASTELLETTI.
>   „ MARQUIS VINCENZO DE PIRO.
>   „ EMMANUELE VITAL, and as Commandant.
>   „ CANON SAVERIO CARUANA.
>   „ VINCENZO BORG.

To HIS EXCELLENCY LORD NELSON.

Intrigues and jealousies amongst the representatives of the people once more reappeared, as may be gathered from Mr. Vincent Borg's letters to Ball, dated the 1st, 3rd, and 4th February 1799, as follows:—

> [Verbatim copy.]
>
> VINCENZO BORG TO CAPTAIN BALL.
>
> Birchircara, le premier jour de *Février* 1799.[1]

MONSIEUR,—Permettez-moi, Monsieur, de vous faire mille vives remerciemens de la bonté que vous avez faites voir d'avoir vers moi, quand vous êtes venus chez-moi, et de l'honneur que vous m'avez fait en y venant. Mes obligations sont très grandes, et je m'en souviendrais éternellement. Et ayès la satisfaction de savoir que la complaisance que vous avois [*sic*] eue pour moi a produit de très bons effets, s'étant [*sic*] tous mes adversaires humiliés, et mis dans la raison à ce qu'on montre dans leur manière d'agir.

Quant à moi je les traite avec toute la douceur, amitié, et prudence, communicant tant au Prevost, qu'aux autres prétendents au gouvernement du Casal, les affaires qu'on peut leur comuniquer, et les faisant qu'un corps. Mais s'il aura quelqu'un qui se montrera incorrigible, on tachera de trouver un paisible moyen pour l'éloigner de nous. Ce qui me déplait dans cette affaire, c'est que tous ceux qui avoient promis de s'en charger d'entretenir le camp, ont fort peu de substances, et en conséquence, il faut que je poursuis à m'écerveller pour trouver la manière de nourrir le camp pour ne le laisser pas perdre.

L'affaire duquel je vous ay écrit dans ma dernière lettre commence avec ma très grande satisfaction, et avec beaucoup de plaisir à se vérifier.

Je désire, Monsieur, avec beaucoup d'ardeur, d'avoir souvent des occasions de vous montrer que je suis vraiment tel que je me vante. Votre très humble, très obéissant et très obbligéant serv^r,

>   (Signed) VINCENZO BORG.

[1] Brit. Mus. Add. MSS. 34943, f. 106.

THE BRITISH BLOCKADE—1799

[Verbatim copy.]

VINCENZO BORG TO CAPTAIN BALL.

Le 3 *Février* 1799.[1]

MONSIEUR,—Je dois vous faire savoir qu'hier est sorti de la Valette un jeune homme de ceux qui avoit été au Marsamuscetto pour faire l'attaque de la ville, qui s'étoit tenu caché dans la même ville, et il nous a dit qu'on faisoit craindre pour fusiller des Maltois, mais que les éxécutions on les faisoint [sic] hors de la ville, tout près de la potence envers nous, que les Maltois s'étoint protestés qu'on ne vouloit plus voir fusiller ces patriottes, et comme les Français ont eu la complaisance de faire fusiller hors de la ville on peut conclure qu'ils craignent les Maltois qui sont au dedans, et qu'ils ne vouloient pas les aigrir. Il nous a encore dit ce jeune homme, qu'il y avait encore beaucoup de Maltois en prison, et encor 300 Français avec les Maltois, mais séparément à cause qu'ils s'étoint unis aux Maltois. Je dois encore vous faire savoir que les Français ont beaucoup renforcé la garnison du Fort Manoel, et moi de mon côté je montre de faire beaucoup de préparatifs pour les faire croire que je pense de les attacquer de ce côté, à fin qu'ils mettent beaucoup de soldats au Fort Manoel et Tigné, et que se diminuisent le nombre de soldats de la Cottonere, je fais tout ça croiant de vous plaire, et j'ai le plaisir de voir que mon idée réussit, car dans le Fort Manoel, on voit plus de monde, de ce qu'il y avoit, et ils nous tiroint beaucoup de coups de cannons et de bombes, et les nuits ils sortent avec de la lumière, pour voir jusque où arrivent nos gardes avancées, et nous de notre côté tenons nos gardes plus serrés, et plus renforcées, en cas que les Français désespérés s'aviseroient de faire quelque sortie.

On dit que hier les Français sont sortis au nombre du 150 du côté du Zabbar, et qu'on eu une petite attacque avec les Maltois, et que les Français ont eu, trois de tués et plusieurs blessés.

J'ai beaucoup de choses à vous faire savoir regardont la tranquillité de l'isle, mais je ne vous les comunique pas, avant d'être sûr, mais ils sont de choses qui se reparent facilement.

Je vous prie de pardoner la mauvaise facon d'écrire car je suis hors de chez moi, et je vous écris avec beaucoup de presse, laquelle néanmoins ne m'empêche pas de vous assurer d'être votre très umb^e, et très obéissant serviteur, (Signed) VINCENZO BORG.

[Verbatim copy.]

VINCENZO BORG TO CAPTAIN BALL.

Birchircara, 4 *Février* 1799.[2]

MONSIEUR,—Je ne saurois trouver des expressions adaptées pour vous remercier et vous expliquer ma reconaissance, pour la lettre de laquelle vous m'avait honoré hier, et en conséquence, je me réserve à vous la faire connoître par mon attachement à votre digne personne, et seulement je vous dis de n'avoir aucune affaire en Palerme, pour pouvoir me profiter de votre bonté.

Dans la lettre d'hier, je vous ai écrit que j'avois de choses à vous faire

[1] Brit. Mus. Add. MSS. 34943, f. 139.
[2] *Ibid.* f. 141.

savoir qui regardent la tranquillité publique, au présent que je me suis bien informé, et que j'ai fait des mures réflexions, je prends la liberté de vous mettre sous les yeux que nous avons besoin de deux choses pour être tranquillés.

Premièrement me semble nécessaire que vous vous donniez la peine de vous faire voir souvent à terre, à cause que tout le peuple ayant une grande estime pour vous, vous voyant souvent avec les chefs, il les obéissent plus facilement sans aucune peine, et l'envie qui regnoit contre les chefs entre les personnes qui voudroint se voir chefs eux mêmes, s'evanouisse au moment qu'on vous voit conférer avec eux, et nous avons eue l'expérience dans la cabale qu'on avoit formé contre moi, qui est cessé, et s'est évanouie aussitôt que vous avois eu la bonté de me faire l'honneur de venir chez-moi, et à present toutes les choses sont dans la plus grand tranquillité exécutant ce que vous avois ordonné, car tous les Maltais estiment beaucoup les Anglais et aiment particulièrement et vénèrent votre digne personne—et la plus part de nous en très grand nombre se proteste ouvertement qu'il ne désire rien autant que de ne voir l'isle dominée que par les Anglais et Maltais, et gouvernée par le Commandant Ball. Et le jour que vous étiois [sic] chez-moi, plusieurs personnes de la ville Notabile vouloint venir en corps à vous parler sur cette affaire, mais craignant de le faire sans vous prévenir au paravant, ils ont différé et remis à autre temps leur projet.

De tout ça, je suis été assuré entre autres par une dame des plus respectables, qui a beaucoup de crédit, mérite, et esprit.

L'autre chose nécessaire, Monsieur, c'est d'apporter remède à ce qui est souvent parvenu à vos oreilles régardant quelques partis qu'il peut y avoir, et se former, car j'ai su que pendant les dix ou onze mois que Hompesch à été Grand Maître, il avoit traité avec la Moscovie pour la faire entrer à particiter de la domination de Malte en exigeant une autre langue dans le Corps de la Religion pour les Muscovites, et on avoient déjà conclus toutes les conditions que je ne sais pas à present vous racconter, mais je les saurais en avant, mais sûrement elles etoient fort peu favorables aux Maltais, car la Religion et la Moscovie auroint fait des Maltais tout ce que leur auroit plût.

Tout ça s'est découvert par les écrits qu'on a trouvés dans l'occasion de l'expulsion du Grand Maître, comme m'a assuré de tout ça, la dite dame. Or comme le dit arrangement avec la Moscovie a été su par quelques Maltais attachés à la Religion, il y a cinque ou six d'entre eux qui sont en place, et qui voudroient (?) traiter de les rappeller, et faire venir de nouveau dans l'isle, et nous ne pouvons pas savoir çe que se fera alors.

Vous savois, Monsieur, qui sont telles personnes, et vous avois [sic] entre les mains leurs papiers, or toutes ces personnes qui inquiétoient l'isle, devroint ce me semble être totalement exclus du gouvernement, car des tels sujets ne doivent avoir aucune ingérance dans les affaires publics, autant plus qu'ils se trouvent en place accidentellement, non pas nommés par le peuple, mais mis par le Com$^{nt.}$ Vitale pour le soulager dans les affaires, ne connaissant pas leurs caractères, et ils sont actuellement très mal vus par tout le peuple, n'y a pas une seule personne qui se trouveroit contente d'eux, en sorte que s'il ne leur sera ôtée toute sorte d'ingérance dans le gouvernement, le peuple les chassera violennement, et il pourroit arriver quelque révolution, et soyez sûr que si le peuple viendra à savoir leurs intrigues il les massacrera tous certainement, car ils n'ont pas une personne qui soit de leur parti.

La nécessité de les exclure, et de les chasser est encore fort plus presante, à cause qu'étant eux seuls qui comme chefs écrivent hors de l'isle, ce qu'ils écrivent peut apporter la totale ruine de l'isle, car on croit que ce qu'ils écrivent soit la volonté de tout le peuple, quand en réalité, la volonté de tout les Maltais est toute contraire, or ce qu'ils leur manquoit étant des personnes qui ne c[h]erchent aucunement l'utilité du peuple, et l'avantage de la patrie, mais seulement leurs intérêts particuliers, et au contraire en les chassant et ne restant pas plus chefs, ce qu'ils écriront ne sera reçu hors de Malte comme volonté de tout les Maltais, mais comme une simple idée particulière d'eux seulement. J'ai eu, Monsieur, connoissance de tout ça en faisant des réflexions sur quelques mots, échappés de leur bouche, et par des informations qui m'ont étés données par un ami qui habite la ville Notabile, et je trouve que ça correspond à leur lettres, qui ont été interceptées, et sont parvenues dans vos mains, et en conséquence sans aucune difficulté je vous avance tout ce que je vous écris. Mais dans le même temps je vous prie d'être bien sûr que tout ce que je vous ai écrit du commencement de notre correspondance, et tout ce que j'aurais l'honneur de vous écrire jusque à ma mort n'a été, et ne sera jamais dicté d'aucun intérêt particulier, mais seulement inspiré par la vérité et la sincérité, et par le désir que je nourris dans mon sein de faciliter la défence de ma réligion, et de ma patrie, et de voir notre isle confiée à des bonnes mains.

Je me crois aussi obligé de vous faire savoir que toute l'Isle de Malte est très contente, et le peuple a une très grande joie de vous voir bloquer aussi étroitement le port, croiant que sur cela il puissent fonder une sûre espérance que vous n'êtes pas éloigné d'accepter nos veux et d'entreprendre notre protection.

Je suis, Monsieur, dans le cas de m'enhardir à vous supplier de vouloir bien accorder à un tel Cap^{n}· Mirabite, Maltais, la grâce qu'il vous demande, d'ordonner qu'on lui donnoit son brick ou cutter, avec son charge de vin, et je prends la liberté de vous prier cette grâce, non seulement à cause qu'il me semble selon son information, qu'il soit assisté, par la raison, mais encor parceque le dit cap$^{ne.}$ offre de nous prêter le montant du prix du vin pour l'employer à nourir notre battalion.

Mais avec tout cela, s'il ne mérite pas d'être reçu dans sa demande, je vous prie de ne lui pas accorder, et je vous prie ça, avec plus de ferveur de ce que je vous prie de la lui accorder. Pardonnez-moi, Monsieur, la liberté que j'ai pris, pardonnez-moi, aussi la longueur de cette lettre ; ne me privez jamais de votre protection, et permettez-moi de pouvoir toujours me vanter, Monsieur, votre très humble et très obéissant serv^{r}·,

(Signed) VINCENZO BORG.

PS.—Monsieur, soyez sûr que tout ce que je vous écris sont de sentiments bien mûrs que j'ai formés après des mûres réflexions que j'ai faites, et je puis assurer aussi de la fidélité de mon secrétaire, et de son silence, et pour nous assurer de ça, je vous écris de ma main.

(Signed) VINCENZO BORG.

The deplorable condition to which, by this time, the people had been reduced for want of food, and by the dissensions of their chiefs, were referred to by Ball in his dispatches to Nelson of the 4th and 5th February, of which the following are extracts :—

[Extract.]

H.M.S. *Alexander*, off Malta, 4th February 1799.[1]

. . . The Maltese chiefs have raised six hundred men on whom they can depend whenever they make an attack; they are to be supported by four thousand men, who, stimulated by our example, may act with vigour. They seem ashamed of their former conduct. They are to attack Cottonera in a few days. The chiefs express themselves much hurt at the treachery of Guillaume Lorenzi, the chief of the late plot, who with a few others would have hoisted Russian colours had he succeeded. The great body of the people were ignorant of it.

They have a great dislike to the Russians, and are so prepossessed in favour of the English that they are continually inviting me to hoist British colours all over the island. They pay such a deference to the English that it has enabled me, by a friendly interposition, to accommodate disputes between the chiefs, which otherwise would have terminated very seriously.

I enclose a letter which I have just received on that subject from a chief who supports a battalion at his own expense, and has shown more zeal and patriotism than any person on the island.

The Maltese begin to dread the want of bread. Last week they had not sufficient for one day, but fortunately a large Imperial ship laden with corn was brought-to off St. Paul's, and sent in there. I suspect she was bound to Valetta. She was from Girgenti, cleared out for Leghorn. We obliged the master to sell his cargo to the Maltese. I stopped a vessel the first of this month steering for Valetta with three hundred and fifty barrels of beef, fifty of pork, and fifty-three pipes of wine. I enclose her case, which I have drawn up, to be laid before the British Consul at Palermo. I intend having the hull and cargo adjudicated. . . . I am perfectly satisfied that the Russian party consists of a very few men who formerly were in places under the Grand Master. I am assured that the Maltese will never accept or listen to any terms which the Russians may hold out so long as the English protect them. . . . I have studiously endeavoured to attach the Maltese to the Neapolitan Government, and declared to them that I had not any authority to enter into any treaty with them, but whenever the French were driven from the Island I would give a passage to any of their Deputies who wished to consult Your Lordship. If we do not succeed in our attack of Cottonera we shall want a thirteen-inch mortar. We have twelve hundred shells which were sent with the two bad mortars, out of which we had not fired more than fifty before they were rendered useless.

[Extract.]

H.M.S. *Alexander*, off Malta, 5th February 1799.[2]

. . . The Maltese assure me they will be ready to storm Cottonera in a few days. They are in great distress for bread. I have this moment received a letter from Caruana, the Maltese chief, representing the necessity

---
[1] Brit. Mus. Add. MSS. 34909, f. 166.
[2] *Ibid.* f. 170.

of a speedy supply. *La Justice*, French frigate, has hauled out to the mouth of Valetta Harbour, and will push out the first favourable moment with the treasure of the Island. She is very deep.

The application for a supply of wheat, referred to in the deputies' dispatch of the 26th January, was at last favourably entertained by the Neapolitan Government, and Ball was ordered to send over to Girgenti or Licata a vessel of war, in order to secure the safe arrival of the corn in Malta. His instructions were as follows:—

Palermo, 4th February 1799.[1]

My dear Ball,—I have just received your letter with its several enclosures, and although I regret that the *malconduct* of the Maltese has caused the enterprise to fail, yet I trust that at a future day it will succeed. I am satisfied, my dear friend, that you and your brave companions have done all which was possible to do. Respecting the corn wanted for Malta, I wrote yesterday to General Acton, and received the answer, of which I enclose you a copy. This evening I saw the King, and he is exceedingly angry to think that his faithful Maltese subjects should want for any comforts or necessaries which it is in his power to bestow. I would wish you to send over to Girgenti or Alicata in order to secure the safe arrival of the corn in Malta. If ever Malta surrenders, the King of Naples is its legitimate Sovereign, and his flag must fly, and the British squadron will support it.

Should any party hoist the Russian or other flag, the King will not, and I will not, permit the extraction of corn from Sicily, nor from any other place. I trust you will be able to prevent all French vessels from entering the Port. I well know the difficulty of the task, but I am confident everything which an excellent officer can do will be done.

If I get hold of a Portuguese corvette she shall come to you. I have ordered a ship of the line of that nation to put herself under your command. If the commander objects, let it be in writing, and then recommend him to cruise in a particular place, so as not to annoy the Tunis cruisers, who are out against the French. In short, my dear Ball, use the Portuguese in some way or other. As to gunboats or any assistance from this Government, it is not [to] be expected, but you shall have every small vessel I can lay my hands upon. You will, with your usual discretion, tell the Deputies my opinion about the conduct of the Russians; and, should any Russian ships or admiral arrive off Malta, you will convince him of the very unhandsome manner of treating the legitimate Sovereign of Malta, by wishing to see the Russian flag fly in Malta, and also of me, who command the forces of a Power in such close alliance with the Russian Emperor, which have been blockading and attacking Malta for near six months. The Russians shall never take the lead.

Respecting stores and provisions, I have none here: all are at Syracuse, and Troubridge[2] authorised to make a distribution of them. Till the ships come from Egypt I cannot change any of your ships of the line, as they are older than yourself. The *Goliath* is to carry Sir William and Lady

---

[1] Nicolas, *Dispatches of Nelson*, vol. iii. p. 255.
[2] Captain Troubridge, of H.M.S. *Culloden*.—J. H. R.

Hamilton to England whenever they choose to go, but the time is not yet fixed.

Minorca calls for two sail of the line. *Minotaur* goes directly for Gibraltar; but the Earl tells me he will not send the *Foudroyant* till I send him two sail of the line. The exchange of Marine officers will suit Captain Cresswell, I hope; but many ships will, in my opinion, go down the Mediterranean before *Goliath*, as she is kept to attend our good friends. You will, my dear Ball, always act in such a manner as to do credit to yourself and country, and always to meet the approbation of your sincere and affectionate
(Signed) NELSON.

To THE DEPUTIES OF THE MALTESE PEOPLE.

H.M.S. *Bellerophon*, Palermo, 5*th February* 1799.[1]

GENTLEMEN,—I here enclose for your information the copy of a letter I have received from General Acton respecting the supply of corn wanted by the Maltese people. I am happy to have it in my power, and shall always be ready to yield you every assistance. Captain Ball, who commands before Malta, and of whose conduct and abilities I have the highest opinion, will also give you all the assistance in his power to get the corn over to Malta.

Wishing you every success against your enemies, and a speedy surrender of the capital again into your possession, I am, &c.

(Signed) NELSON.

Notwithstanding the promises of His Sicilian Majesty and Prime Minister Acton that a supply of wheat should be sent to Malta, the orders were not immediately obeyed. This delay drew from Canon Caruana the following pathetic appeal to Nelson, dated the 5th February 1799 :—

[Translation.]

From the Camp of St. Joseph, 5*th February* 1799.[2]

YOUR EXCELLENCY,—So long a time has elapsed since we appealed to His Majesty the King of Naples to supply us with the means of sustenance, that we have lost all hope of receiving his help.

We are reduced to the greatest straits, for the rich no longer exist, and the poor are dying of hunger. In all directions disease and death are rife for want of food. Foreign money cannot be found, and local money is also scarce. Trade of all kinds is impeded, and our produce no longer exported. We are consequently deprived of all aid which might to some extent sustain us. I am still confined to my bed with a feverish attack, and the anxiety of our situation increases my illness, and may be the cause of my death. As you are the hope of our salvation, I have at all times reposed my trust in Your Excellency, knowing the affection which you have assured me you possess for this unhappy population.

[1] Brit. Mus. Add. MSS. 34963, f. 63.
[2] *Ibid.* 34943, f. 145.

Your Excellency may remain assured that from present appearances we shall be compelled within a few days to lay down our arms and abandon our positions. Oh, what a misfortune! oh, what a disaster! if, after the endeavours we have made and sustained for so great a length of time, we should at last become a prey to our enemy for want of food.

In our present afflictions it is in Your Excellency alone that I can place any hope, and if at least you could give us some assurance it would sustain us in our many trials.

To have any trust in Sicily appears to be vain. This I gather from the complaints which are made to me by various Maltese, who find it difficult to obtain their cargoes, as they are detained in quarantine, and, moreover, are badly treated.

May Your Excellency be pleased to have commiseration upon us in our deplorable misfortunes, and cast upon us the benign glance of a generous English soul.

Your Excellency may be assured that my opinions are shared by all. All ask for your help—all firmly believe that you will become their liberator and common father.

I beg Your Excellency will pardon me, but the obligations which I owe to my country compels me to trouble you; and, whilst tendering you my warmest sentiments of gratitude, and full of sincerest esteem, I sign myself, &c.
CANON CARUANA.

In the Archives Nationales of Paris the following three extracts of Doublet's letters, written on the 8th, 13th, and 25th February, are to be found in Carton AF III. 73. They give an account of the situation of affairs within the city at those dates, with suggestions for the better government of the island when once the siege should be raised.

The same carton also contains a letter from Dejéan, chief of the 80th Demi-Brigade, dated Paris, 31st March 1799, but giving details of the besieged up to the 7th February, from a military point of view.

EXTRAITS DES LETTRES DU CITOYEN DOUBLET, COMMISSAIRE DU GOUVERNEMENT FRANÇAIS À MALTE.

Le 20 *Pluviôse* an 7 (8*th February* 1799).[1]

Le Citoyen Doublet établi à Malthe depuis 1779 a été premier Commis de la Secrétairerie d'État Française depuis 1781 jusqu'à la cession de l'isle aux Français. Il n'y a rien ignoré de la politique des Grands Maîtres Rohan et Hompesch avant et pendant la Révolution.

Rohan fut, jusqu'à sa mort, partisan de la Cause Royale et des Émigrés. Il en accueillit et pensionna plusieurs. Il laissa vexer à Malthe les amis de la Révolution, il souffrit après la prise de Toulon, que les Anglais fissent à Malthe une levée de matelots. Enfin le Citoyen Doublet assure que si dans l'exercise de sa place, il eut mis moins de prudence, d'adresse et de fermeté, il n'auroit pu ramener ce Grande Maître aux vrais principes de la

[1] Arch. Nat., AF III. 73.

neutralité et déjouer les intrigues qui tendoient à faire passer l'isle dans les mains des Anglais.

La proposition de se jeter entre leurs bras fut faite à cinq reprises différentes aux Grands Maîtres Rohan et Hompesch, mais toujours d'une manière indirecte, afin de sauver à Pitt en cas de non succès, la honte d'une tentative inutile.

La première de ces tentatives fut fait par le Ministre Anglais en Suisse, qui fit propose au Grand Maître de recevoir un subside du Roi d'Angleterre et de recevoir dans le port de Malthe tous les vaisseaux de guerre Anglais qui se présenteroient.

Cette proposition fut renouvellée par deux membres de l'Ordre, venus l'un d'Anspach et l'autre de Coblentz.

Le Vice-Roi éphémère de Corse, Elliot,[1] la fit faire de nouveau par un autre membre de l'Ordre, le Chevalier Sade.

Le Citoyen Doublet assure que, dans toutes ces occasions, ce fut lui qui empêcha Rohan d'accepter cette proposition et que de Sade quitta Malthe en le menaçant de toute la colère du gouvernement Anglais si jamais il tombait entre ses mains.[2] La cinquième tentative fut faite à Rastadt par le secrétaire de la Légation de l'Ordre au Congrès. Ce secrétaire nommé de Bray écrivoit au Grande Maître Hompesch (ses lettres originales ont été remises au Général Bonaparte) que les Français préparoient une expédition contre Malthe et contre l'Egypte, il le pressoit dans les termes les plus forts de confier la défense de Malthe aux Anglais en leur livrant le port, la place et les forts, et reservant pour l'Ordre la souveraineté sur les gens de la campagne.

Quelqu'-envie que Hompesch eut de régner, il se seroit peut-être décidé à recevoir les Anglais s'ils eussent paru, mais Bonaparte les prévint heureusement.

Il n'y avait pas un an que Hompesch étoit élu; il avoit acheté les suffrages, et ses dettes montaient à trois cent mille écus. La douceur et l'affabilité de son caractère, sa générosité, sa belle figure, l'avoient rendu l'idole du pays, en sorte que, malgré l'énormité de ses dettes, il trouvait encore les moyens d'emprunter. Il a emporté beaucoup d'argent aux Malthois indépendamment de celui que Bonaparte lui a fait compter. Il n'a du reste emporté d'autres papiers que les registres des protocoles de l'Ordre que le Général lui fit remettre.

Il avait engagé le Citoyen Doublet à le suivre en qualité de secrétaire en lui offrant des appointements considérables, mais le Citoyen Doublet lui répondit qu'il aimoit mieux rester à Malthe pour y servir la République.

Le Citoyen Doublet a sçu par le Général Bonaparte que le Directoire Exécutif avoit cru qu'il s'étoit formé entre les Grands Maîtres et la Russie des liaisons tendant à faire tomber l'isle entre les mains de cette puissance. Mais il assure qu'il n'a jamais été question d'un arrangement de cette nature, qu'il auroit été impossible de lui cacher.

---

[1] Sir Gilbert Elliot (afterwards Lord Minto) was Civil Commissioner for Corsica during the time of the British occupation from the early part of 1794 to the end of 1796. (See *Life of Lord Minto*, vol. ii. pp. 340–58.)—J. H. R.

[2] Nothing is known of this mission of De Sade to Malta.—J. H. R.

Pour le Directoire Exécutif.

25 *Pluviôse* an 7 (13th *February* 1799).[1]

Avec plus de prudence et de ménagements pour les habitans, avec plus de précautions et de surveillance on auroit conservé l'isle dans l'état où Bonaparte l'a laissée. Des changemens trop précipités ont disposé les habitans à la révolte et à faire cause commune avec nos ennemis.

Jusqu'à présent leurs attaques n'ont abouti qu'à écraser une centaine de maisons dans les parties de la ville, à l'est du pont, jadis appellées *La Sengle, Le Borgo* et *Bormola*. L'intention des Anglais étoit de brûler nos vaisseaux et frégates ainsi que l'arsenal et les magazins de la marine qui sont dans cette partie et qu'on ne peut placer ailleurs sans un plus grand danger.

Ils seront trompés dans leurs espérances; mais le garnison est extrêmement fatiguée. Les grandes chaleurs et la mauvaise nourriture peuvent produire des maladies et diminuer le nombre de nos soldats.

[The same to the same.]

7 *Ventôse* an 7 (25th *February* 1799).[2]

Les Anglais continuent à bloquer le port étroitement; le beautemps le favorise tellement que tout ce qui y seroit envoyé, n'impôrte de quel côté, tomberoit entre leurs mains. Le Général Vaubois continue à faire sortir de la ville toutes les bouches inutiles et tous les habitans sortiroient (tant est grande et leur misère et la peur qu'ils ont des bombes) si le Général ne retenait ceux dont les services sont nécessaires.

Une parfaite union règne entre les autorités civils et militaires. À dire vrai tous les pouvoirs sont à peu près réunis dans la personne du Général; rien ne se fait que par ses ordres, sa participation ou son approbation. Les attributions particulières peuvent en souffrir, ainsi que l'intérêt de quelques Maltais, mais les circonstances et le salut publique l'exigent pour conserver cette place, sans recevoir presque aucuns secours du dehors. Il faut user de toutes les ressources que le pays peut offrir, et ce n'est pas peu qu'elles ayent pu suffire. Au reste dans toutes les mesures de rigueur, telles que la vente des effets, engagés au mont de piété, la suppression ou la suspension du traitement d'invalides et du pain d'aumône, on a toujours excepté les mères, femmes et sœurs des Malthais embarqués pour l'expédition d'Egypte. Cependant les ressources s'épuisent et des secours en argent seroient bien nécessaires. Beaucoup de Malthais avoient avant l'arrivée des Français, fournis des objets ou des marchandises au trésor ou au Grand Maître de l'Ordre. Ils n'étoient point payés, ils ont réclamé leur payment. Dans le nombre il y en avoit qui étoient déjà pauvres et que le changement de gouvernement achevoit de ruiner.

Faute de moyens il a fallu ajourner leurs demandes. D'autres avoient engagé au mont de piété presque tous leurs effets qui ont été vendus pour servir aux besoins de la garnison. Tous ces hommes sont dans une situation très cruelle; il sera juste de les en dédommager, lorsque la République aura affermi sa conquête.

[1] Arch. Nat., AF III. 73.
[2] *Ibid.*

Cet évènement sera le résultat nécessaire ou de la défaite, ou de la lassitude des ennemis, ou de la paix générale.

Mais alors même il ne faudra pas songer à faire jouir tout d'un coup l'isle de Malthe des avantages de la constitution.

Le peuple Malthais n'est pas mûr pour la liberté,[1] il lui faudra des institutions préparatoires. L'ignorance, la superstition et le fanatisme sont la maladie universelle des habitants. Ce n'est qu'avec beaucoup de précautions et de soin qu'on parviendra à les en guérir. Ils sont, par habitude et par inclinaison sous le double joug des prêtres et des gens de loi, parmi lesquels on trouveroit difficilement une demi-douzaine d'individus capables d'avoir et d'inspirer aux autres l'amour de la liberté, de la République, et de ses lois.

L'Evêque, né sujet du Roi de Naples et ex-moine, est un homme bienfaisant. On lui doit d'avoir réformé les mœurs de son clergé et d'avoir rendu l'enseignement moins mauvais qu'il n'étoit avant lui. Mais cet enseignement n'en est pas moins déplorable ; peu d'écoles, point de société sçavante, point d'établissements de bienfaisance, point de manufacture ; tout est à créer dans ce pays. La première mésure à prendre sera de désarmer tous les habitants sans exception, et d'expulser tous auteurs et principaux soutiens de la rebellion. Ensuite il faudra tenir à Malthe une garnison assez forte, mais non pas celle qui s'y trouve maintenant, parceque, conservant le souvenir de ce qu'elle a souffert, elle ne pourroit voir de bon œil ni de sang froid les gens de campagne qui tous ont pris un part plus ou moins active à la révolte, et dans ce moment même, il résulte de cette disposition, beaucoup de désordre que tous les soins du Général en Chef ne peuvent prévenir.

Paris, le 11 *Germinal* an 7eme (31*st March* 1799).[2]

Déjean Chef de la 80eme ½ B$^{de.}$ d'Inf$^{rie.}$ de Ligne au Directoire Exécutif.

CITOYENS DIRECTEURS,—Atteint, depuis huit mois, d'un rumatisme qui avait paralisé une partie de mon corps, et dont les douleurs m'avaient encore renouvellé celles d'une ancienne blessure, j'avais obtenu en Vendémiaire dernier de la part du Général de Div$^{n.}$ Vaubois, command$^{t.}$ l'Isle de Malte, l'autorisation de passer en France, pour le rétablissement de ma santé. J'ai cru me devoir à moi-même l'honneur de rester, dans une place assiégée, dont le commandement m'avait été confié, par le Général Bonaparte ; croyant aussi que le tems diminuerait nos souffrances, et que les rigueurs de l'hiver se faisant sentir, obligerait non seulement les habitants de l'isle, insurgés contre nous, à rentrer dans l'ordre, et forcerait encore les Anglais à quitter le blocus de cette place ; mais trompé dans mes espérances, et sentant mon mal s'accroître tous les jours je n'ay pu me dispenser après cinq mois des plus fortes privations, de me déterminer à partir pour la France, où je retrouverai les secours nécessaires au rétablissement de ma santé.

C'est le 19e Pluviôse [7th February] dernier que le Général Vaubois me détermina de partir, chargé des dépêches pour le Gouvernement, et m'engagea après m'avoir donné connaissance de leur contenu, de prendre

---

[1] This is interesting in view of the excessive organisation of the island by the administration set up by Bonaparte.—J. H. R.

[2] Arch. Nat., AF III. 73.

des nottes [notes] particulières, desquelles je pourrais me servir en cas d'évènement en mer. Cette précaution n'a pas été sans succès, et le bâtiment sur lequel j'étais embarqué ayant été pris, j'ai cru qu'il était prudent de jeter les dépêches à la mer, *ne m'étant cependant déterminé à prendre ce partie, qu'à la dernière extrémité, et lorsque je me suis vu dans l'impossibilité absolue de pouvoir les sauver;* ce fait étant legalement constaté par le certificat de tous les passagers et officiers du bort [sic], sur lequel j'étais, croyant inutille de vous détailler tous les évènements qui nous sont survenus dans notre traversée, je me suis borné à avoir l'honneur de vous informer de l'objet principal qui est la situation de la place.

Malgré le blocus resserré, que faisait ordinairement dix vaisseaux ou frégates Anglais de la place; quatre battiments venus de Gennes [Gènes] et Marseille avai[en]t échappé à leur surveillance, et les approvisionnements qu'ils avait apportés, réunis à ceux qui existait, pouvait suffir aux besoins de la garnison pour dix mois, et un an en se génant un peu comm'on l'avait fait précédement.

Il est cependant des objets de première nécessité dont la place ne se trouve pas pourvu; la viande fraîche pour les malades manque totalement, ainsi que le bois ou charbon. Dans le cas il ne fut pas possible de faire parvenir le premier objet, il pourrait se remplacer par des tablettes de bouillon. L'hôpital, malgré les médicaments qui ont été envoyés, a un besoin absolu de quinquina. L'arsenal est dans un dépourvu total de charbon, ainsi que de bois de construction pour le rechange des affûts. Les bombes de huit et douze pouces ne sont guaire [guère] plus abondantes que les boulets de 12, 18, and 24. Il y aurait même à craindre, si le siège était soutenu et se faisait en règle, que la place ne peut pas empêcher l'établissement de certaines batteries qui lui nuirait sans doutte, si elle était privée de çes munitions.

Malgré qu'on aÿe utilisé toutes les ressources que nous avai[en]t procurées certaines établissements qui était dans la place, la solde de la trouppe commençait à être arrièrée, et son habillement était dans le plus pressant besoin.

Quatre mille combattants pour garder une place forte et assiègée de six milles d'arrondissement ne peut que bien fatiguer le militaire; aussi le Général Vaubois demandait il un supplement de garnison de quinze cents hommes.

Voilà, Citoyens Directeurs, quelle étoit la situation de la place lorsque ma triste situation m'a forcé d'en quitter le commandement et quellesque soyent les suittes des évènements qui semblait la ménacer, contès sur le courage et la persévérance des militaires qui la deffendent; ils sont déterminés à tout souffrir pour conserver à la République, un port duquel depent [sic] le sort de l'armée d'Egipte. Salut & respect.

(Signed) DÉJEAN.

PS.—À mon passage à Milan j'ai donné au Général en Chef de l'armée d'Italie, les instructions qu'il a paru désirer. J'ay aussi écrit au Ministre Belleville à Gennes [Gènes] pour que dans le cas il fit faire quelque expédition pour Malte, il ne manquât pas d'envoyer les objets manquants et desquels je lui aÿ aussi donné notte [note].

Five months' experience of the siege convinced Lord Nelson at last that Valetta could not be captured by assault, and that its eventual fall could only be assured, not by brilliant feats of arms, but by the pangs of famine, which a strict blockade must eventually secure, unless relief to the garrison in the meanwhile arrived. Possessed of this opinion he gave his views of the situation to Earl Spencer in the following dispatch :—

[Extract.]

7th February 1799.[1]

To EARL SPENCER,— . . . The enemy have only succeeded in getting two small vessels into the port during the whole winter, the others being all taken.[2] An *attempt* at assault has been made, but failed, not from the enemy, but from fear of the Maltese; 200 had got over the wall, and did not take possession of the gate to let in their comrades, but Captain Ball yet hopes to be more successful another time. I am sure nothing will be wanting on his part, or that of the English officers under him, but I own I build my hopes of success, more on the closeness of the blockade, than on the valour of the Maltese.   (Signed) NELSON.

On this same day a meeting of the Congress of all the Chiefs of Malta was held at Citta Vecchia, when it was unanimously agreed to dispatch a deputation to present to His Sicilian Majesty a humble petition, begging permission to appeal to His Britannic Majesty for his special protection until the close of the war, and further, to explain the critical position in which the island was placed, for want of the necessaries of life.

The deputation so appointed consisted of the Assessor Aguis, M. le Baron Fournier, and M. L'Abbé Savoye. The following is an extract of the deliberations of the Congress :—

[Translation.]

EXTRACT FROM THE RECORD OF THE DELIBERATIONS OF THE CONGRESS OF THE MALTESE CHIEFS.[3]

This 7th day of February 1799, at a meeting of the Assembly of all the Chiefs of Malta, held at Citta Vecchia, for the purpose of nominating three Deputies to proceed to Palermo, and there present to His Sicilian Majesty a petition relative to the present circumstances of this Island, it has hereby appointed for that mission the Assessor Aguis, Baron Fournier, and the Abbé Savoye, and the Congress has issued to them the following instructions :—

1st. The said Deputies will sign a petition to the King, wherein they will solicit His Majesty's permission for the Congress to appeal to His Britannic Majesty graciously to consent to grant them His Majesty's special protection.

---

[1] Nicolas, *Dispatches of Nelson*, vol. vii. p. clxxiii.
[2] Nelson here under-estimated the successes of the blockade-runners.—J. H. R.
[3] Brit. Mus. Add. MSS. 34943, f. 147.

2nd. They are authorised to make this petition, wherein they will explain the critical condition of the Island, the necessity of obtaining victuals, particularly on credit under the hypothecation of all public and private property.

3rd. That owing to these circumstances, the need of hoisting the flag of His Britannic Majesty.

4th. To request that a Governor shall be appointed who would conciliate and unite all parties.

5th. To do nothing without the permission of His Sicilian Majesty.

All which has been unanimously voted.

The original signed by all the members present at the Congress in conformity with the original.

The Maltese Deputies:
(Signed) The ABBÉ SAVOYE.
,, BARON FOURNIER.
,, ASSESSOR LOUIS AGUIS.

Captain Ball acquainted Nelson on the 9th and 10th of February of the appointment of these deputies, and the object of their Mission. The following are extracts of these letters:—

CAPTAIN BALL TO ADMIRAL NELSON.

H.M.S. *Alexander*, off Malta, *9th February* 1799.[1]

. . . The inhabitants have deputed three gentlemen of good character to present a petition to His Sicilian Majesty and Your Lordship, praying that they may be put under the protection of Great Britain during the war, and unless it takes place I have every reason to assert that it will soon fall into the hands of another nation. I can perceive by Your Lordship's letter of the 25th of last month that you foresaw the necessity of this measure, and of the great check this will give to the disaffected Jacobins in the Island of Sicily. Your Lordship will hear from many quarters of the strong attachment which the Maltese evince for the English, whom they esteem from principle, and whom they fear, knowing we have always the means of punishing them, and they are now more sensible of it than ever, from their having experienced what they would not believe before, that a British squadron can block them up and starve them in the winter months. . . . The Russians have not sent any proclamations here, and Your Lordship may depend upon my never allowing one of their ships to come in. Whenever any of them shall appear off the port I shall acquaint the commanders that the Russian plot formed last December in the Island, of which Guillaume Lorenzi was the chief, has occasioned the loss of a great many lives, which has so exasperated the Maltese that I could not answer for the safety of any of their ships.

With great deference I will venture to predict that Your Lordship is going to render your country a most essential service by annexing Malta to it, and it will give me an opportunity of proving your ideas, that by an economical government many islands would be a source of wealth to Great Britain; and I can answer you that Malta will pay fourfold the expense of maintaining it by making it a great depôt for the British manufactures,

[1] Brit. Mus. Add. MSS. 34909, f. 212.

which will be sent from thence to Tripoli, Tunis, Sicily, and the coast to the eastward.[1] Malta grows sufficient corn to support the inhabitants six months in the year, and their exports of cotton and salt would enable them to maintain the island, but they cannot keep a garrison to defend it against a vigorous attack. They have a sufficient number of men: all that is required of Great Britain will be to allow the expense of two thousand British soldiers, and a sufficient salary to me to support my rank with the smallest military staff that can be appointed. Four thousand a year would pay a builder, a master attendant, gunboats and crews with boats for warping ships in and out of port here. The first year money must be sent us, after which there will not be any difficulty in getting bills negotiated here. . . . I beg leave to observe to Your Lordship that it is absolutely necessary His Sicilian Majesty should send immediately five or ten thousand pounds, either on his own account or that of Great Britain; and I should strongly recommend not to send any British officers or soldiers here. I have already an officer of artillery and his party, with whom I am very well satisfied. The Maltese export a great deal of cotton to Spain, which can be carried on under the Tunisian flag. If the English were to keep Malta in the peace, they would take cotton in return for their goods, which they would carry to Spain and exchange for another cargo.

CAPTAIN BALL to ADMIRAL NELSON.

H.M.S. *Alexander*, off Malta, 10*th February* 1799.[2]

I shall attend the meeting to-morrow of the chiefs and principal inhabitants, which we call a Congress, at which I preside. It is held twice a week, and unless I am there they assure me it is not in their power to preserve sufficient order to proceed in business. I shall have great satisfaction in announcing to them His Sicilian Majesty's bounty in ordering so great a supply of corn, which I shall immediately have convoyed in safety here. I must beg leave to point out to Your Lordship that four thousand Maltese soldiers have been serving more than five months without pay or clothing, who are now so ragged as to make it impossible to do duty much longer without being clothed, and it is absolutely necessary that they should be taken into pay; without this is done the inhabitants foresee they shall be at the mercy of any nation who chooses to attack them. The Deputies will have the honour of representing these particulars to Your Lordship. . . . I shall enclose herewith a letter I have received from Vincenzo Borg, chef of Casal Lia and Birchircara, which I can assure Your Lordship is the language all over the Island. At the time the Maltese were in distress for bread their minds were in a great ferment, and they would have made an example of some of their chiefs had I not prevented it by visiting frequently the camps and acted with more energy and a greater dictatorial strain than usual. If His Sicilian Majesty will defray the expense of two thousand men on the footing which I pointed out in my letter of yesterday's date it may succeed, provided their trade can be protected, but I can assure Your Lordship that the most effectual way of securing this Island to

---

[1] See a somewhat similar Report on Malta, dated June 16, 1800, in the *Dropmore Papers*, vol. vi. pp. 248, 249.—J. H. R.

[2] Brit. Mus. Add. MSS. 34909, f. 224.

His Majesty will be to cede it for the war to Great Britain, and I cannot help being strongly impressed with the important consequences this will have in checking the plans of the Sicilian Jacobins, and it is probable the effect will reach Calabria.

Your Lordship will hear of the great antipathy the Maltese have to H.S. Majesty's Government, and of the great difficulty I had in making them hoist Neapolitan colours. They are more indifferent about the French leaving them, from the idea that we shall leave them the moment the business is over, and the great risk they run in being carried afterwards by a *coup de main*. I assured them that we should always have a naval force off here, and when I consented to their sending Deputies to His Sicilian Majesty and Your Lordship, and allowed for the present to unite English colours with the Neapolitan flag, it seemed to invigorate them, and occasioned a general joy throughout the Island. The chiefs promise me they will storm the French works in a very short time; they are now exercising the charge of bayonet, and seem more determined than ever. I am most particularly anxious that His Sicilian Majesty and Your Lordship may be assured that there has not been the smallest intrigue or indirect means to impress the Maltese with such an attachment to the English. They seem to feel as strong a partiality for them as the Minorcaeens do.

The petition to His Majesty the King of Naples was prepared in Malta, and although it bears no date it would appear from a letter addressed to Captain Ball by Vincenzo Borg to have been signed on the 9th February 1799.

This petition was severely criticised by the aforesaid Borg, who alleged that it did not accurately convey the people's desires, that it unnecessarily acknowledged rights of sovereignty over the Islands of Malta and Gozo, and, further, that by asking for permission to raise the British standard until the close of the war, it implied that when that event occurred the flag of another Power might be raised, which was in entire opposition to the wishes, desires, and aspirations of the population.

The petition, and Mr. Borg's letter referring thereto, are as follows :—

[Translation.]

9th February 1799.[1]

To His Majesty the King, our Sovereign.

SIRE,—The Representatives of the clergy and people of Malta, the most humble servants and faithful subjects of Your Majesty, with all reverence, approach the throne of Your Majesty to represent to what extent they the people have given the greatest proofs of their attachment and fidelity to Your Majesty's crown by having taken up arms against the French, who unlawfully have occupied the Islands of Malta and Gozo, and deprived Your Majesty of those rights Your Majesty possesses thereon, and

---

[1] Brit. Mus. Add. MSS. 34947, f. 96.

further, by having immediately appealed to Your Majesty's paternal protection for the purpose of obtaining the necessary aid both in food and munitions of war which are required in order to be able totally to expel the French now sheltered within the city and its fortifications.

Your Majesty has not failed to grant the wisest dispositions in this regard, so that from the near Island of Sicily food as well as munitions of war might be furnished to the Maltese.

This people have been able so far, notwithstanding the increased prices, and quarantine and other charges, to obtain the necessary provisions, but the military needs have been insufficiently received for the purpose required, inasmuch that although five months of active warfare have expired, the necessary means are still wanting to obtain an evacuation of the fortress, which delay has reduced the Maltese to the extremest misery and inertia, and they now find it impossible to continue further under such conditions.

Moreover, the country population is being daily increased, owing to the expulsion of the poorer classes from the four besieged cities, who have to be supported by the countrymen, who themselves are now no longer able to support the expense of maintaining the troops, carrying out the military works, such as trench-digging and various other duties; and as ready money has disappeared, they now find themselves in the most critical condition, either that of perishing by hunger or to lay down their arms and thus become French victims.

They have therefore to appeal to the paternal solicitude of Your Majesty in the belief that, owing to the troubled state of Italy and that of your kingdom of Naples, Your Majesty is unable to protect this Island by provisioning it with three months' stock under hypothecation of its public and private property, and further supplying it with all that is required for a decisive attack on their obstinate enemy. They, under such circumstances, beseech Your Majesty to allow them to appeal to an allied Power, the friend of Your Majesty, that of His Britannic Majesty, whose fleet continues to blockade the French, in order that they may obtain His Majesty's special protection and powerful co-operation.

And in order that His Britannic Majesty might be induced to take more interest in this matter, that permission should be granted to this people to hoist the British standard upon the public places and fortifications until the close of the war, should His Majesty be pleased to do so. That as deputies, and in the name of the most faithful Maltese clergy and people, they implore Your Majesty to have a pitiful commiseration for them and to grant them this prayer, for even at the risk of destruction they desire to make no arrangements without your Royal approval.

[Verbatim copy.]

VINCENZO BORG TO CAPTAIN BALL.

Birchircara, le 9 *Février* 1799.[1]

MONSIEUR,—Ce matin après onze heures, et après avoir envoyé l'autre lettre que je vous ai écrite ce matin, on m'a apporté pour signer la lettre qui doit être présentée au Roi de Naples, je l'ai signée avant que de la lire, à cause que je l'ai vue signée par tous ceux qui devoint la signer, car n'y

---

[1] Brit. Mus. Add. MSS. 34943, f. 152.

manquoit la signature que de trois ou quatre, tout au plus. Mais l'ayant après lue, il m'a fort déplue de l'avoir signée n'étant aucunement de mon goût et contraire aux sentiments de tous (si je l'ai bien comprise) ; les endroits qui m'ont le plus déplu sont deux, l'un dans son exorde, où sans aucune nécessité, se fait une protestation ou au moins une déclaration que le Roi de Naples aye le haut dominion et de droits sur les deux Isles de Malte et Gozo, et l'autre dans sa conclusion où on demandoint la permission d'arborer l'étendard Anglais, et de le tenir jusqu'à la fin de la guerre, de laquelle proposition on peut ce me semble inférer la conséquence, que la guerre finie on doit arborer tout autre étendard, proposition qui est diamètralement opposée aux plaisirs, désirs, et aux volontés universelles.

Ça étant, Monsieur, je vous prie autant que je puis et que je sais, de ne permettre que sorte de l'isle une telle lettre, au moins si elle fait sur vous, la même impression qu'elle a faite sur moi, en quel cas, je vous prie, encore une fois de l'arrêter dans son cours, pour en parler dans un congrès, et faire démasquer ceux qui veulent faire une double figure, et arranger les affaires dans la manière qui est uniforme à la volonté de tous les Maltais.

Je vous demande bien des excuses de la liberté que j'ai prise et l'attribuer seulement à mon zèle, à mon attachement, et à l'envie que j'ai de faire réussir ce que désirent tous les Maltais, au reste je me remets entièrement à tout ce que vous déterminerois, et plein d'estime, je me proteste pour toujours, Monsieur, votre très humble, très obéissant et très obligé serviteur, (Signed) VINCENZO BORG.

PS.—Je vous comunique une idée et c'est que je crois que la signature de tout a été faite pour cause, que personne ne vous paraisse singulier, et aucune ne vous l'opposer.

This appeal asking ' for the protection and powerful co-operation of Great Britain, and for permission to raise the British standard,' was due to the critical position of affairs on the Continent, and to the threatened destruction of the Neapolitan Government.

Naples had been captured by the French forces on the 22nd of the previous month, the flight of the Royal Family to Palermo had taken place, and the Parthenopean Republic in its stead had been declared on the 25th January.[1]

The people's Deputies were consequently in the deepest despair; there was a prospect of Sicily also falling into possession of the French,[2] when the garrison of Valetta would be immediately relieved, and if that event happened, they could easily conjecture what their fate would be. Their principal hope rested in Great Britain and Nelson. This extreme alarm, however, was soon appeased by the victories of Austria and Russia in Upper Italy and Switzerland (Bonaparte being still absent in Egypt), for by May, owing to the above-mentioned successes of the Allies, the French were compelled to evacuate Naples, and by this retreat the short-lived Parthenopean

---

[1] Really it was established on January 23, 1799 (see *Camb. Mod. History*, vol. viii. p. 653).—J. H. R.
[2] See Nelson's letter of 16th February 1799 to Mr. Stuart (*Dispatches of Nelson*, vol. iii. p. 267).—J. H. R.

Republic came to an end.[1] In the meanwhile, on the 13th February, the local committee of the Maltese chiefs forwarded a letter of thanks to Lord Nelson for having consented to grant their request of the 31st January by permitting Ball to remain at Malta as 'their protector and adviser.' This letter runs as follows :—

[Translation.]
THE DEPUTIES TO LORD NELSON.

Notabile, 13th February 1799.[2]

YOUR EXCELLENCY,—The weight of the many obligations we are under to Your Lordship is most sensibly felt by us, and to them must now be added the letter of the 5th instant, with which you have honoured us, for it is not only full of the most cordial expressions of good will, but it is dictated by a magnanimous heart, one that is actuated by humanity and generosity towards this Island and evincing great affection for its inhabitants.

All this kindness is increased by having granted us as our protector and adviser Captain Ball, a man not only of great merit and ability, but one who is full of goodness, and regard for this people, for we testify that by his beneficent conduct towards us he has acquired the universal love of us all without exception, and we desire above all that we may not be deprived of his valued presence, but that he may remain amongst us for our general happiness, which by his wise and prudent conduct we may confidently expect in the future.

At the same time there is nothing that we can greater desire than to see ourselves under the protection of Your Excellency, so that we may always be able and with much honour, &c., the Deputies of the Maltese People.

(Signed) COUNT FERDINAND THEUMA.
,, COUNT SALVADORE MANDUCA.
,, MARCHESE VINCENZO DE PIRO.
,, EMMANUELE VITALE; also as General Commanding.
,, LUIGI CARUANA, for my brother the Canon, now ill.
,, MICHELE CACHIA.
,, VINCENZO BORG.

On the 14th February 1799, Vaubois informed the Minister for War that 'the rebels persist in their enterprise. The chiefs have nothing else to do but to continue misleading them; they are at the mercy of the English, who threaten to blockade them, and starve them to death, if they lose courage.'[3]

---

[1] Suvórof's victories at Cassano (April 27), &c., placed Milan at the feet of the Allies, and a few days later General Macdonald withdrew the French garrison from Naples and retreated northwards. The forts at Naples (held by the local Republicans) surrendered to Cardinal Ruffo on June 19. Nelson appeared off Naples on June 24.—J. H. R.
[2] Brit. Mus. Add. MSS. 34943, f. 167.
[3] Arch. Nat., BB⁴ 136.

Hitherto the insurgents had governed the liberated portion of the islands by prominent and influential men, who styled their meetings an 'Assembly of Deputies.' Captain Ball, perceiving the wisdom of placing this body on a more authoritative and sounder footing, suggested they should add members duly elected by the various villages, and that it should henceforth be called a Congress.

Accordingly, at a meeting held at St. Antonio Palace on the 11th February 1799, when Captain Ball presided, the following attended, viz. the commanders of the various battalions, and the two generals, Caruana and Vitale.[1] It was then decided that in future the Congress should be composed of the deputy-lieutenant of the bishop, representing the clergy, one judge, and the representatives of the people to be elected by the heads of families in each village; that the election should take place during the following week; and that the judge should be elected at the next meeting of the Deputies; and further, that the two generals should have the right to attend all meetings, whenever so disposed.

At the next meeting of the 18th February, the Deputies of the villages presented their certificates of election, and were duly acknowledged. The following is a list of the elected members:—

LIST OF THE ELECTED DEPUTIES OR REPRESENTATIVES OF THE PEOPLE.

For Citta Vecchia, Rabbato, and Casali Dingli, Emmanuele Vitale; Zebbug, Notary Pietro Buttigieg; Siggeui, D. Salvatore Curso, parish priest; Micabiba, D. Bartolomeo Garaffa, parish priest; Crendi, Gregorio Mifsud; Zurico, D. Fortunato Dalli; Safi, Ch. Giuseppe Abdilla; Chircop, Enrico Herri; Gudia, Filippo Castagna; Axiach, D. Pietro Mallia; Zeitun, Capo Maestro Michele Cachia; Zabbar, Agostino Said; Tarscien, Giuseppe Montibello; Luca, Giuseppe Casha; Curmi, Stanislao Gatt; Birchircara, Vincenzo Borg; Gargur, Ch. Giovanni Gafà; Naxaro, Cav. Paolo Parisio; Musta, D. Felice Calbeja, parish priest; Lia, Salvatore Gafà; Balzan, Giuseppe Frendo; Attard, Notary Saverio Zarb.

One of the first acts of this newly constituted body was to elect Dr. Luigi Aguis Judge of the Assembly, and as secretaries, the Abbé Savoye and Giovanni Battista Aguis.

By H.M.S. *Vanguard*, which had left Malta for Palermo a short time previously, Messrs. Savoye, Fournier, and Aguis, the Deputies elected on the 7th February to present the petition to His Majesty the King of Naples, took passage, arriving there on the 13th of that month. Whilst these Deputies were anxiously waiting in Palermo for a reply to their petition, an effort was made by the French Commissioner in Valetta to appease the Maltese, by the issue of an enactment under date of the 19th February, for abrogating the obnoxious laws which had been promulgated by Regnaud de Saint Jean d'Angely, but it was attended with no success.

[1] Azopardi, p. 123.

The insurgents were determined to prosecute the war to the bitter end. The enactment was as follows :—

Enactment by Commission of the French Republic revoking previous enactments, abrogating or modifying the ancient laws of Malta, 19th February 1799.[1]

[Translation.]

Government Commission. Extract from the Registers of the deliberations of the Commission of Government, sitting of the 1st Ventôse an 7 (19th February 1799).

The Commission of Government, considering, that although it is true that the General Commander-in-Chief, Bonaparte, whilst granting to it the power of reorganising the Courts of Justice, he had expressly recommended their assimilation as nearly as possible to the French organisation; it is equally true, that all which he had prescribed in this respect has reference entirely to new forms to be introduced in the administration of justice, and that there is nothing which indicates or authorises the belief, that it was the intention of that General that the legislature of the country should be changed.

Considering also that it appears certain, that no one was invested by him with power to order such alterations, and that in consequence the Government Commissary Regnaud de Saint Jean d'Angely could not invest himself with such authority—therefore it decrees,

1st. That all the alterations which have been made in the laws of the country by virtue of published orders, emanating from the former Government Commissary Regnaud de Saint Jean d'Angely, either by establishing new laws, or by the abrogation or modification of the old laws, shall be regarded as if never made.

2nd. That commencing from this day all Acts or Judgments of whatsoever nature shall be based, as in the past, upon the ancient laws or legislation.

3rd. All Acts or Sentences, which have been passed in conformity with these innovations up to the present time, shall remain in force until such time as the French Corps Législatif shall order otherwise.

The President of the Commission, (signed) BOSREDON RANSIJAT.
Approved, (signed) GENERAL VAUBOIS.
The Secretary, (signed) BREUVART.

By a singular coincidence, on this same day (19th February) the following official answer to the Deputies' petition of the 9th February was graciously given by His Sicilian Majesty.[2]

[Translation.]

Palermo, 19*th February* 1799.[3]

Messieurs the Deputies of the Maltese People.

ILLUSTRIOUS SIRS,—With regard to the petition from the Maltese people which you, illustrious Sirs, as Deputies of the same, have presented to the

---

[1] Bandi, *Malta*, p. 173.
[2] On that same day Captain Ball sent Vaubois another summons to surrender, which he refused. See Vaubois, *Journal of the Siege of Malta*, Appendix, Part II.—J. H. R.
[3] Brit. Mus. Add. MSS. 34943, f. 188.

THE BRITISH BLOCKADE—1799

King, I am commanded to express and communicate to you what follows.

It has afforded His Majesty the greatest pleasure, and met with his approval, to hear of the efforts made by his beloved people to break the shackles by which a rapacious usurper by manifest treachery had sought to bind them, with the object of depriving them of all resources, to tread under foot the holy religion, and to make use of the Islands, the patrimony of His Majesty's Crown, as hostile posts, whence an easy attack might be made upon Sicily.

His Majesty again exhorts his faithful Maltese and Gozitans to redouble with the greatest energy every means in their power with which their native courage and the justice of the holy cause will inspire them, and for which they are fighting.

His Majesty declares that he will adopt, and efficaciously so, the measures which may be in his power to co-operate with effect in the efforts you are making to drive the French out of the fortifications, and so specially secure his people from later harm and calamity, which the common enemy is seeking to inflict.

From the petition advanced by the Maltese people, His Majesty observes, knows, and admits that the troubles which of late have afflicted his kingdom of Naples may have caused disquietude to some, and perhaps alarm to others, in the idea that owing to the necessary steps which are urgently required for the defence of his kingdom of the Two Sicilies, His Majesty might be less able or in a position to succour his Islands of Malta, and assist in the operations of his faithful people.

But in order to conciliate and tranquilise all who are discouraged on this point His Majesty invites all to the union and necessary concert which the case requires, and to avert any wavering which the circumstances might excite amongst a few individuals of that good populace.

His Majesty has further manifested his desire, that from Sicily Malta shall continue to receive, and with the greatest facility, every possible aid in the shape of food, and as far as possible in other respects, in conformity with what His Majesty has already expressed to the Deputies.

And whereas the military operations which are required to liberate Malta from the French, and defend it hereafter from future attempts of the enemy, are fortunately supported, thanks to the blockade, and opportune direction of him who commands the arms of His Britannic Majesty, the excellent, faithful, and worthy ally of the King, he His Majesty therefore willingly consents that the Maltese people should forward their entreaties to His Britannic Majesty through his brave admiral commanding in these seas, praying that His Majesty will continue efficaciously to protect that Island, and adopt for its defence every possible means under any denomination or exterior demonstration [1] which Admiral Lord Nelson may decide upon assuming in the name of His Britannic Majesty, so as to characterise in a greater measure the protection he grants to this Island. His Majesty is conscious of the loyalty of his praiseworthy ally, and is besides convinced of the views, sentiments, and experience of Lord Nelson, to whom His Majesty has confided, and confides, his most sacred and dearest interests.

[1] This must refer to the raising the British flag.—J. H. R.

Such is what the King has ordered me to convey to you, gentlemen, for the purpose of duly informing the good and beloved people of Malta. With the greatest esteem, I remain, &c. (Signed) JOHN ACTON.

The day following Sir John Acton acquainted Lord Nelson of the favourable result of the Maltese petition in the following letter:—

SIR J. ACTON TO LORD NELSON.

Palermo, 20th February 1799.[1]

MY DEAR SIR,—The Maltese Deputies have received this morning His Sicilian Majesty's answer to their formal demand; it is most evident that in the present most unhappy circumstances of the kingdom of Naples a kind of uneasiness in the mind of that people should arise on the fate even of Sicily, if these two kingdoms are not powerfully succoured, and before some months further do expire. They desire an assurance for their defence, and require it from His Britannic Majesty.

The King orders me to acquaint Your Lordship and Sir William Hamilton with the answer given to the Deputies, and to explain clearly his full confidence in the Court of St. James and in Your Lordship. If the Island of Malta cannot be sustained in its struggles and endeavours to expel the common enemy from those fortifications, and that poor people should be obliged to surrender, it would be of the utmost danger for Sicily in the numerous attacks that would partially be intended on the southern coasts, but even for the example and terror that would spread itself among the people of this Island, in part already seduced or affected with fears already spread, not without art, of such an enemy.

His Sicilian Majesty had openly expressed himself in the instructions sent to Marquis de Cirillo, for the stipulation of the treaty which afterwards was concluded in Naples.

The Islands of Corfu and even Malta were mentioned in those directions for the said Cirillo. The same intentions are, and shall ever be the same, towards His Britannic Majesty and the English nation.

You know that from his brave ally only does he expect relief and assistance; therefore in granting to the people of Malta provisions, and the other demands made upon His Majesty, in regard to warlike stores and ammunition, as well as for money wanted in Malta, His Majesty is obliged to provide first for the defence of this kingdom, and of Messina especially. When this serious care is completed, and the need properly fulfilled, Malta shall and must be completely provided with those wants. As to Captain Ball, who has the full confidence of those people, the King feels with a fine satisfaction that they do him such a justice which he desires most extensively.

If Your Lordship thinks his services better employed even on shore with that command and discretion, His Majesty will see it with gratitude settled in the manner that you shall think proper.

The rights of the King are known on that Island, but the British Colour, either conjointly or even alone, as belonging to the best ally, shall in every circumstance as the present be agreed upon, if Your Lordship thinks it proper. I am, with highest regard, &c. (Signed) J. ACTON.

[1] Brit. Mus. Add. MSS. 34909, f. 269.

The Maltese Deputies, upon the receipt of this favourable reply to their petition, requested Lord Nelson to appoint an English officer to take supreme command of the forces *on shore;* and, further, that if it were possible to allow Ball to land occasionally from his ship, with power to substitute another officer to serve on shore, that such grant would be esteemed an invaluable favour.

A written request to this effect was presented to Nelson on the 23rd February, as follows :—

[Translation.]

Palermo, 23rd *February* 1799.[1]

To His Excellency Lord Nelson, commanding His Britannic Majesty's Squadron.

MY LORD,—Having been authorised at a meeting of the congress, consisting of the Chiefs and Representatives of the Maltese clergy and people, held on the 7th instant, to present a petition to His Majesty our Sovereign, for the purpose of obtaining His Majesty's permission to have recourse to His Britannic Majesty as his allied Power, in order to obtain his special protection and powerful co-operation, whereby that people might be able to liberate themselves from the French, and further to solicit permission to raise the British standard until the close of the war ; we now beg to inform you that His Majesty has deigned to concede the petition of that people, and by a ministerial dispatch from His Excellency the Chevalier Acton, under date of the 19th inst., he has expressed his favourable intentions.

In consequence thereof we have the honour to approach Your Excellency in the name of the clergy and population of Malta, and to request that you will regard that Island as being placed under the special protection of His Britannic Majesty, and that you will be so good as to continue to adopt the most powerful and energetic co-operation for its safety.

And inasmuch as to obtain a successful result it becomes desirable that an English commander should be on shore, who would pacify the various and frequent dissensions which exist among the Maltese chiefs of battalions, and who would with his ability and military knowledge be able to advise such steps as would lead to a favourable result.

We are therefore charged by our constituents to pray that you will designate a commandant well known to Your Excellency, not omitting to state that the illustrious Captain Ball having gained the esteem of all, that the selection should fall upon him, and that he might be permitted to land on shore, whenever his services on board might allow him, and with power to substitute for service on shore a person well known to himself.

Such is what we have the honour to submit to Your Excellency ; and with our profound respect we sign ourselves, &c., the Maltese Deputies.

(Signed) RECTOR LUDOVICO SAVOYE.
,, BARON FOURNIER.
,, ASSESSOR LUIGI AGUIS.

[1] Brit. Mus. Add. MSS. 34943, f. 194.

On the 23rd February Ball was able to forward to Lord Nelson the following information, which had been obtained from within Valetta through the medium of spies.

[Extract.]

CAPTAIN BALL TO ADMIRAL NELSON.

H.M.S. *Alexander*, off Malta, 23rd February, 1799.[1]

... I have great satisfaction in observing that the Maltese have recovered from their panic, and now evince great intrepidity and firmness.

We had an occasion of trying them the other day, by making an attempt on Vittoriosa, but the French kept too good a look-out.

I enclose intelligence from the Maltese, which they assure me can be depended on. All the late accounts corroborate the discontents, distresses, and sickness of the French garrison, who cannot hold out much longer. They are endeavouring to brew beer, their beef is putrid, and their clothes very bare. The Maltese have stopped one of their vessels with 8,000 pairs of shoes, 6,000 shirts, some medicines, and a variety of other articles. The French are now endeavouring to bring about a counter-revolution in the country. They have many emissaries employed, circulating money among the Maltese : we very lately shot one of their spies. I have taken every precaution to guard against their plans, but the most effectual one would be for His Sicilian Majesty to clothe immediately three thousand Maltese, and take them into pay for Great Britain, which the British Minister could repay. I think this measure absolutely necessary, and would thus ensure the Island to His Majesty, for the Maltese would then cheerfully persevere in their duty, until the French shall be driven out. At present they are so ragged, and their families so wretchedly poor, that they are almost driven to despair. The sight of the English only, and the hope of relief from them, has kept them from desperate measures. They begin to want powder, and it will be necessary to send them two hundred barrels, and some lead for musket balls.

I have anchored the ships of the line in a position for blocking up Valetta, and I trust such efforts will be successful, but I am very sorry to acquaint Your Lordship that a corvette and a schooner have got into port, notwithstanding two line-of-battle ships and a frigate were stationed off the town, but the weather was such as to make it impossible for ships to keep to windward ; however, we have the consolation of knowing that their arrival occasioned a great gloom in the garrison, as they brought very little provisions, and acquainted them of the number of vessels which had sailed for their relief, which were either captured or had proceeded on to Alexandria on discovering the ships off here. The corvette was from Toulon, and the schooner from Ancona, with the news that Corfu had surrendered.

[Verbatim.]

INTELLIGENCE FROM PEOPLE WHO CAME OUT OF VALETTA THE 23RD FEBRUARY 1799.[2]

CONNAISSANCES,—Qu'ont donnez six personnes arrivez le 23 Février 1799 au Casal Birchircara en sortie de la Valette avec plusieurs autres

[1] Brit. Mus. Add. MSS. 34909, f. 282.   [2] *Ibid.* f. 286.

le 22 du dit mois en conséquence des 13 interrogations que leurs ont été faites dictiés par son excellence Mr. le Commandant Ball.

Il y a peu de jours que les Français ont placé dans une salle du Grand Hôpital les tableaux et portraits de Grand Maîtres de la Religion Gerosolimitaine qu'ils avoint ôtés auparavant il y a quelque temp.

Les Français ont dans la terrain Ferreira [?] remis dans leur place tout les maîtres Maltais qui anciennement y étoient, et qu'auparevent ils avait chassé. Dans le Château S. Ange ont renforcé la garnison.

Ont rempli tout les bastions de la Cottonere de pierres et de bombes pour s'en servir en cas d'attacque, les lancent même les bombes avec les mains sans mortiers.

Qu'une femme de quelque qualité a dit à une des dit six personnes sorties de la ville pour en faire rapport en campagne qu'il y a deux mois un officier Français de sa connaissance très honnêt homme lui avoit dit que les Français de la ville devoint sortir prenant avec eux tout ce qu'on auroint peu et qu'en sortant ils devoint attacquer le feu à la ville, et qu'il y a peu des jours il lui avoit ancor dit que les Français étoient dans l'intention de faire un puer [?] présent aux Maltais le premier jour du mois d'avril.

Le Général Vaubois s'étoit fait fere une petite poste pour y mettre les remèdes pour la playe qu'il porte say [?] sa mains de droite.

Des Maltais qui sont au service des Français les plus méchants sont le Conseiller Schembri, et le Baron Dorel, et l'Avocat Fenech, et au contraire le Vicomte Etien Maistre et Nicol Ebner sont les plus grands amis des patriots et qui cerchent de les soulager le plus qu'on peut, et dans ce jours passés ont eu l'abilité du faire exempter les moines et les prêtres du pénible exercice de transporter les pierres [?] auquel tous étoient éligés.

Que il y avoit environ 800 volontaires Français malads dans les deux hôpitaux, quelques uns estropiés, des autres qui avoint la gross verole, et d'autres aveugles. Qu'on ne faissoit pour les rations de soldats que 2,000 pains par jour et qu'au soldats on donnoit le pain un très petit morceaux de viande salée que leur avoit apporté la petite frégate, ou un petit morceau de thon salé, un très petite quantité d'eau de vie et de trois en trois jours du vin en fort petite quantité et de très mauvais qualité.

Que sur le commencement du blocq [?] on apportoit aux Français quelque peu de vivres, mais au présent on ne leur apporte rien.

Que les Français sûrement ont des espions [?] que les dits Maltais sortis de la ville ne conaissent pas, et que les Français savoint que en [on?] devoint attacquer l'isle et avoint renforcé les gardes de ces côtés.

La plus part des soldats et même des officiers se plaignent publiquement de leur chefs et généraux à cause qu'ils les retient dans Malte étant persuadés qu'un jour ou l'autre ils doiv^t être massacrés.

Que la frégate ou corvette arrivées dernièrement dans le grand port venoit de Toulon ont apporté aux Français des boulets de cannons de 18 et 24, viandes et thon salés, vin et eau de vie et le cutter venoit d'Ancone et qu'il n'avoit apporté aucun provision.

Qu'en conséquence du parlement de jours passés en avec les Anglais la nuit en avoit fait un grand congrès composé de tout les officiers et d'un sergeant, et d'un caporal de tout les compagnies le résultat duquel ne s'est pas répandu dans la ville et seulement en publié par la ville que les Anglais avoint pourcoup lues [beaucoup loués ?] les Français pour leur valeur et que les avoit priés de ne traiter mal les Maltais en cas de victoire, mais les Français ont répondu qu'ils le auroint tout massacrés mêmes qui étoint dans la ville.

Que les vaisseaux et frégates ne sont pas en état de sortir aussitôt à cause que ils ont tout leur mâts en caisse.

Que toute les portes sont peu garnis de soldats et que ceux pour la plus part sont de matelots très craintifs.

Qu'on peut espérer que la garnison viendra bientôt à une capitulation à cause du mécontentement de soldats qui sont arrivés à insulter par le rues le Général Vaubois avec de mots insultant et à cause que le Consul d'Espagne avoit dit secrètement à quelque qu'il ne devoit pas sortir de la ville, mais y rester car bientôt tout seroit fini.

On the 28th February and 2nd March further information was received through spies, of the condition of the beleaguered garrison, in the following report :—

[Verbatim.]

NOUVELLES VENUES PAR DES GENS SORTIES DE LA VALETTE
LE 23 FÉVRIER 1799.[1]

Les Français si misent tout sur les armes le 22 cour$^{te.}$ au soir et il restèrent en garde toute la nuit cregnant l'assaus de la campagne.

L'après dîné on fait une tumulte sur le vaisseaux, car le matelots et soldats réalistes commencèrent à chanté une chanson aristocratique et les Jacobins ne vouloient pas.

Le Général Vaubois, il est de nouveau malade.

NOUVELLE DU 2 MARS 1799.

Les fèves dans la Valette sont au but.

Vincent Abdilla il dit qu'il y a encore dans la Valette 2,400 salme de blé, 2,000 cafis d'huile peu près. Toutes personnes sorties dissent et assurent que la chair salée est puantée. Ils se préparent à partir Caruson et divers autres leur partissants et autres bastiments. Il doivent porter aussi deux autres bastiments avec le bien, e meubles des Maltais pour venir au Port de St. Paul.

Le Chef Magen nous a fait sentir par le Médecin Cassar d'être été appellé de Français pour former dans le Cottonera vis-à-vis à la mine nommée il Madlama une place pour pouvoir garder la musquetterie et les canons en outre, qui par la part due sauveur ont fait des fougades remplises de poudre. À la marine su le Couvent des P. Capucins où ont les Français une fosse, on dit qu'[ils] venait mettre un cannon, dans le Château St. Elmo portant toujours de la poudre et des provisions. Les deux Forts Cavaliere sont plein de poudre aussi à la moitié de passage au dedans ont fait une muraille comme une tranchée avec un canon qui garde la porte en ouerant [ouvrant ?] en cas de défense.

In response to the Deputies' request of the 23rd February, 'for the appointment of a British officer to land in Malta, to aid their

[1] Brit. Mus. Add. MSS. 34943, f. 201.

chiefs by his advice, and in other ways which might be in his power,' Lord Nelson, on the 28th February, issued the following order to Captain Ball, of H.M.S. *Alexander* [1] :—

Whereas the Deputies of the Maltese people have represented to His Excellency Sir William Hamilton and myself, that the distracted state of their Councils frequently renders it necessary to have some person of respectability to preside at their meetings, and that you had by your address frequently united the jarring interests of different chiefs, and it being also their wish that you should preside at their meetings, and knowing your conciliatory manners, judgement, activity and zeal, which renders you a fit person to assist and preside at their Councils, and it being also the desire of His Sicilian Majesty, you are therefore hereby permitted, whenever it may be necessary for you to be on shore to preside at the Maltese Councils, to leave your ship in charge of the First Lieutenant, directing him how to proceed, and you are at full liberty to be on shore with the Maltese Army, or on board your ship, whenever you may think it necessary. And His Sicilian Majesty having desired that the British flag should be hoisted on all parts of the Island, as well as the Sicilian flag, you are therefore, whenever a flagstaff is erected to hoist the Sicilian Colours, to erect another near it, and hoist the English Colours thereon, in order to mark that the Island is under the special protection of His Britannic Majesty; but whenever the British Colours are hoisted, the Sicilian Colours must also be hoisted, as the said Island is to be considered only as under the protection of His Britannic Majesty during the war.

From depositions made by people who had been expelled by Vaubois from Valetta, which are given below, and from other information received, Ball was led to believe that an early surrender of the French garrison might be expected, and on the 3rd March addressed Lord Nelson as below :—

H.M.S. *Alexander*, off Malta, *3rd March* 1799.[2]

My Lord,—I have the satisfaction to acquaint Your Lordship from the best intelligence that the French garrison at Valetta will capitulate very soon ; they have certainly fixed the time, which it is supposed is the end of the month, and it will be sooner if they hear of a counter-revolution at Naples. General Vaubois's brother and valet-de-chambre have embarked on board of a small vessel with a great deal of treasure, in which they will attempt to make their escape. The French sailors have torn the national cockades out of their hats, and have ventured to abuse their Government; Vaubois is insulted whenever he walks out ; the garrison is very sickly, the scurvy begins to spread among them, and they have not any medicines.

The General has turned out of the town a great many inhabitants and has employed every art to effect a counter-revolution, in which I trust he will be completely foiled. I have sent to Commino and Gozo every suspicious person, and formed the inhabitants into independent companies, at which they are much pleased. I have just intercepted some letters from

---
[1] Nicolas, *Dispatches of Nelson*, vol. iii. p. 272.
[2] Brit. Mus. Add. MSS. 34909, f. 327.

Trieste, which clearly prove that the Grand Master and Emperor are intriguing with some of the Maltese to get possession of the Island, in which I am sure they will never succeed if my plan can be put into immediate execution, and authority given me to take Maltese regiments into British pay. I shall send Your Lordship the original letters by the next conveyance; I shall not detain *La Bonne Citoyenne* for them, as the wind is so favourable. The *Alphonzo* joined the 12th, and the *Emerald* parted for Palermo the 20th ult. I have the honour, &c.

ALEX^R· JNO. BALL.

THE RT. HONBLE. HORATIO LORD NELSON, K.B.

TRANSLATION OF THE DEPOSITIONS GIVEN BY THE PEOPLE WHO CAME OUT OF VALETTA.[1]

Our enemies are always lamenting the sad effects of our strict blockade in this rigid winter; they are already without wine, that being finished. They have nothing but a little brandy, which is not distributed, and is not likely to be distributed, amongst the soldiers, but the real motive is not precisely known.

The bad condition in which the soldiers find themselves from being deprived of those things which are necessary for them makes them very discontented, a sign of their being of different minds; they very often quarrel amongst one another. A few days ago two soldiers having quarrelled together, one drew his sword and run it through the other's body. The new battery a few days ago having opened fire on Fort Ricasoli, has done a great deal of damage. The French, fearing an assault, are endeavouring to use all diligence and attention in every part that is possible, and they have sent a reinforcement of soldiers who will not stay, being very discontented on account of the consternation in which they find themselves.

They are at present preparing a speronara, in which is going away General Brouard, lately wounded by the Maltese in the neighbourhood of Bighi, the Engineer Fay, a commander of Engineers, another of the Artillery, and other officers, taking with them some boxes of diamonds; it is not exactly known to whom they belong, but we know that part belongs to the depositors in the Monte di Pietà.

Amongst the women that are come out there is one of the name of Gegnarda, wife of one Michael Tanti, who is also come out with her. This woman in the beginning of December 1798 found means to escape from the country into the city, and is again returned, together with the said husband, who was an artilleryman in the French service, and we have also noticed that he is of French extraction. These two we have sent into Citta Vecchia, that we may be able to ascertain from their own mouths the object of the escape of Gegnarda[2] from Valetta, and the reason of their returning again into the country.

The favourable result to the application for a supply of provisions and ammunition must be attributed to the efforts of Lord Nelson

[1] Brit. Mus. Add. MSS. 34915, p. 329.
[2] Contrast this with the description given by General Vaubois in the *Journal of the Siege of Malta* (Part II); also see letters of Lieut. Vivion of March 3, 1799, to General Vaubois, both in the Appendix.—J. H. R.

and Sir William Hamilton, who thus for the second time by their intervention saved the situation, as may be gathered from Sir William's dispatch to Lord Grenville of the 6th March, of which the following is an extract :—

SIR WILLIAM HAMILTON TO LORD GRENVILLE.

(Palermo) *6th March* 1799.[1]

... Three commissaries, Messieurs Rettore Ludovico Savoy, Barone Fournier, and Luigi Aguis, are come to this Court from the Maltese insurgents, to solicit a further supply of provisions and ammunition, *which by Lord Nelson's and my support has been immediately granted to them;* and as the Maltese were desirous for a demonstration of their fighting under the protection of Great Britain as well as that of the King of Naples, it has been agreed that the British flag should for the future be planted with that of His Sicilian Majesty in all the places recovered from the French in that Island.

Captain Ball, by desire of the Maltese and the consent of His Sicilian Majesty, has been appointed by Lord Nelson to the chief blockade of the port of Malta.

[1] Foreign Office Records, Sicily, 12.

CHAPTER XII

THE BRITISH BLOCKADE

(From the 4th March to the 18th November 1799)

On the 4th March it appears that a deputation, consisting of one Englishman and three Maltese, the latter styling themselves commandants of Maltese troops, sought an interview with Vaubois.

The manner of their reception, and the refusal of the rights of belligerents to the Maltese, are pithily given in Vaubois' letter to Captain Ball of the day following.

[Translation.]

LETTER FROM GENERAL VAUBOIS TO THE COMMANDANT OF THE ENGLISH NAVAL FORCES BEFORE MALTA.

Malta, the 15 *Ventôse* an 7 (5th March 1799).[1]

SIR,—I have had occasion to be astonished at the arrival yesterday, by land, of so-called *parlementaires*, charged with an unimportant letter. I cannot, nor should I, receive any emissaries but from you whilst in command of the British squadron before Malta. I will hold no communication with private officers, and more particularly when they style themselves commandants of Maltese troops. The Maltese troops are nothing more or less than an assembly of rebels, and he who commands them is not considered by me as an officer belonging to a Power with whom we are at war.

Curiosity alone can have occasioned such a deviation from the rules of war. It is my duty to treat these *parlementaires* as spies, and you must know what the penalty of such is; but, for the sake of humanity and out of generosity, I allow the Englishman to return to you, but I shall retain the three Maltese. I have the honour, &c. (Signed) VAUBOIS.[2]

In due course of time a favourable response to the Maltese Deputies' appeal for financial help was received from the King of Naples,

---

[1] Arch. Nat., AF III. 73.
[2] For other letters on this topic, see Vaubois' *Journal of the Siege of Malta* (Part II), in Appendix.—J. H. R.

who ordered the sum of oz. 7,000 (£3,500) should be remitted to Ball, with instructions ' to dispose of it to the best advantage for the cause.' This money, together with a supply of arms and ammunition, was to have gone forward in the *Thalia,* Captain Nesbit, together with the three Maltese Deputies, who were returning to Malta; but on the 10th March this order was cancelled, when the *Terpsichore,* Captain Gage, was substituted in her stead, taking over the specie.

March and April in this year (1799) proved to be most trying months for the besiegers. With poor prospects for the harvest, with an epidemic of fever decimating them, and famine at their doors, with the possibility of Sicily falling into the hands of the French (should Fortune once more favour them), from whence alone the supply of food was obtainable : all these circumstances induced them at this date seriously to contemplate an arrangement with the enemy, if favourable terms could be secured.

Fortunately, by the timely arrival at Messina from Port Mahon of the 30th and 89th British Regiments, under General Sir Charles Stuart, Sicily was secured for supplies. This fact, combined with the continued presence of the British blockading fleet, and Ball's indefatigable zeal, encouraged the Maltese to resist still further; but the rumour of a Russian occupation becoming public in April, the greatest alarm and excitement followed, and again opinions were entertained as to whether the French might not be preferable either to the Russians or to the Order.

Nelson, although informed that a landing of Russian troops in Malta was contemplated, was not aware in the month of March that such a step was owing to a secret agreement having been entered into between a section of the Order of St. John of Jerusalem (then at St. Petersburg) and the Czar of Russia, by which it was agreed that a body of Russian troops should be landed on the island to assist in the siege. It was only in the following month of April that he learned ' that at the request of the Grand Bailiff and other Dignitaries of the Order assembled in St. Petersburg in the previous October, the Czar Paul I had accepted the sovereignty of the Order, and established a Grand Priory in the capital of his Empire.' To this intervention on the part of Russia in Maltese affairs, owing to Paul I having first accepted the Protectorate, and finally the Magistracy of the Order, the opposition which Great Britain encountered in the negotiations for peace between England and France in 1801-2 was partly due; and as this circumstance has so much bearing on the eventual destiny of Malta, it is necessary to refer to it in a special chapter later on.

With Continental affairs in the critical state which has just been described, with local circumstances so distressing, through sickness and threatened famine, a meeting of the Congress was called for the 31st March at Citta Vecchia.

It was thereat decided, in view of the calamities which had overtaken the kingdom of Naples, to petition His Sicilian Majesty, 'that he would graciously deign to allow the sovereignty of Malta and the adjacent islands to be transferred to Great Britain.'

A copy of this petition (which follows) was sent on to Lord Nelson under the same date, with the following letter :—

[Translation.]

Malta, in the Hall of the Congress, the 31st March 1799.[1]

YOUR EXCELLENCY,—Whilst suffering the pain which our present extreme necessities impose upon us, we are nevertheless consoled by reflecting that they may be the eventual cause and the occasion, as we hope, of obtaining His Britannic Majesty for our Sovereign, under whose incorruptible and mild government all his subjects live happily.

From the enclosed copy of a petition which we are sending to His Sicilian Majesty, you will learn what our sentiments are.

We trust that, having regard to the calamities which the Kingdom of Naples is now undergoing, our prayers will not be disappointed.

We therefore appeal to Your Excellency with all respect; and in the event of His Majesty the King of Naples concurring in this cession—just and advantageous as it will be to us—that you will in such case forward by the quickest route possible the enclosed letter to His Excellency Lord Grenville, informing His Britannic Majesty of the same, and beseeching His Majesty to deign to accept the sovereignty, and to consider these two Islands as forming part of his kingdom of Great Britain. The almost paternal affection which you have exhibited for us in the few moments we were favoured with a personal interview, and also towards our Deputies in Palermo, convinces us that we may rely upon obtaining under these critical circumstances Your Excellency's protection.

In the hope of soon becoming subjects and vassals of that great British nation, by the valour of whose brave champions she has rendered herself formidable to all the world, we have the honour, &c.

(Signed) CANON SAVERIO CARUANA, Capitular Vicar of the country troops; STANISLAO GATT, Representative of Casal CURMI; SACERDOTE LORENZO TALIBA, do. Casal SIGGEUI; Parish Priest ALOISIO BARTOLOMEO CARAFFA, ALD$^{\text{re.}}$ GREGORIO MIFSUD, FORTUNATO DALLI, CHO. GIUSEPPE HADILLA, DR. ERRICO SCERRI, FELIPPO CASTAGNA, SACERD$^{\text{e.}}$ PIETRO MALLIA, SACERD$^{\text{e.}}$ GIUSEPPE CARUANA, MICHELE CACHIA, GIOVANNI AZZOPPARDI for Agostino Said, GIUSEPPE MONTEBELLO, VINCENZO BORG, GIUSEPPE FRENDO, SALVATORE GAFÀ, SAVERIO ZARB, GIOVANNI GAFÀ, PAOLO PARISI, Parish Priest FELICE CALLIJA, General EMMANUELE VITALE.

[Translation.]

Malta, in the Hall of the Congress, the 31st March 1799.[2]

TO HIS MAJESTY THE KING OUR SOVEREIGN.—Many and singular as are the favours which Your Majesty has deigned to grant to the humble

[1] Brit. Mus. Add. MSS. 34943, f. 229.   [2] Ibid. 34940, f. 227.

THE BRITISH BLOCKADE—1799

petitions made by our Deputies on behalf of this most faithful people, so do our most grateful thanks correspond.

To the above we have now to add another claim upon our gratitude by the timely arrival of a portion of the grain which Your Majesty has ordered to be supplied to us on credit, and which has reached us at a time when our people were perishing from hunger, and through which latter circumstance there were some fears of an insurrection.

We must further acknowledge that Your Majesty has graciously authorised Admiral Lord Nelson to allow Captain Alexander John Ball to govern us in the name of Your Majesty. With regard to the victuals, Your Majesty will, however, reflect that this providential supply was in a few days exhausted, and to continue this most justifiable siege, which has been protracted for fully seven months, other means must be adopted. The universal discontent has increased, due to the sufferings of this poverty-stricken people.

It will therefore be necessary to create out of the Maltese soldiers, properly organised and regular troops of the line, so as to maintain discipline in the defence of the Island and for attacking the French, still within the fortified cities; and, in order to continue and carry out our undertaking to a successful issue, much greater supplies of wheat and very large remittances of money are absolutely required.

But we imagine, Sire, that on account of the calamities occurring in Your Majesty's kingdom of Naples, and its need of defence, Your Majesty is not in a position to grant us such necessary aid. We therefore supplicate Your Majesty that you would be pleased to accord to us our request of transferring the sovereignty of these two Islands to His Britannic Majesty, Your Majesty's faithful ally, so that in the present critical circumstances we may be able to obtain the needed subsidies, and thus place Your Majesty in a better position to adopt the necessary measures for the preservation of your kingdom of Sicily.

Necessity alone compels us to make this proposal; and unless it be granted, this Island cannot be held.

We, the Representatives of this population, therefore humbly prostrate ourselves at Your Majesty's feet, in the hope that Your Majesty will not deny us this request, and will honour us with an early reply, as the circumstances of the case are so important that they will not suffer any delay.

With the most profound reverence, kissing the hands of Your Majesty, we declare ourselves Your Majesty's most humble, devoted, and obliged servants and subjects, &c.

Under the same date Captain Ball addressed Lord Nelson, acquainting him of the situation in Malta, as follows :—

CAPTAIN BALL TO ADMIRAL NELSON.

H.M.S. *Alexander*, off Malta, 31*st* March 1799.[1]

MY LORD,—I have the honour to acknowledge Your Lordship's letters of the 8th, 11th, and 21st instant by the *Terpsichore, La Bonne Citoyenne,* and *Thalia.*

[1] Brit. Mus. Add. MSS. 34910, f. 114.

Captain Caulfield of the *Aurora* will inform Your Lordship that I had not the power of writing by him. The 21,000 ducats which His Sicilian Majesty sent for the relief of the Maltese will be a great temporary succour, but to do it effectually, and enable them to carry on the war, the troops now embodied must be taken into pay and clothed—indeed, my Lord, my experience confirms the opinions and sentiments I offered in my former letters, on the necessity of this Island being ceded to Great Britain, and immediately granting the assistance required.

The Congress has written a letter to His Sicilian Majesty and Your Lordship on the subject. They are so prepossessed in favour of the English, that they will not be ceded to any other nation. They are totally against Russia.

If the Russians come here, and Your Lordship could be present at the same time, I am of opinion the French garrison would oblige General Vaubois to capitulate to you rather than fall into their hands, which they know would inevitably happen in a few weeks. At all events, I wish Your Lordship could come here for a few days, that you may witness the situation of the inhabitants and know their real sentiments. If Your Lordship cannot come, I beg you to send me instructions for my guidance with the Russians. If I do not receive your answer before the arrival of their squadron, I shall not allow them to land any troops, but I shall take care to act with such circumspection as will prevent any ground of jealousy or complaint.

The miseries and wretched poverty of the Maltese have caused a malignant fever to break out, which has swept off a number of the troops as well as inhabitants. All the Portuguese and Neapolitan officers are sick, and some in a very dangerous way. Out of eleven British artillerymen who were landed here, two are dead and three are dangerously ill. The infection got into my ship from having frequent communication with the inhabitants, and the sick list suddenly increased from five to twenty-seven, of which two only died, all the rest recovered, and the ship is now as healthy as ever, by taking precautions and fitting up a house in an airy situation on shore, where I sent every man who had the slightest symptom of the fever.

... With respect to the two mortars which are landed from the *Stromboli*, they are of use in keeping the French in constant check. The ships are in a disabled state—it would require five days to get them off, and if I were to take them away now, it would have such an effect on the Maltese as would drive them to despair, and give the French hope that we are going to evacuate the Island. I therefore request Your Lordship will be pleased to let them remain a short time longer. We have erected a battery which will command a part of the harbour, and I have landed two of my thirty-two pounders to assist. The extreme poverty of the Maltese, some of whom have died of hunger, has driven many to acts which they would not listen to if they could subsist themselves otherwise. I have great reason to believe that they carry fresh provisions to the French, and there are several spies in the country, who are circulating money, and endeavouring to bring about a counter-revolution. We shot a spy very lately, but could not make him confess who were concerned with him. The people of property are continually calling upon me to complain of the outrages and threats of the lower class, and my time lately has been very much taken up in visiting the different towns and enforcing a strict obedience to the laws and setting a better police, which has had a good effect. I enclose herewith the latest intelligence from Valetta.

'Intelligence received by the Head Apothecary and other respectable persons, lately come out of the City of Valetta, which is also corroborated by deserters and prisoners.

Allowance of provisions, &c. to the garrison.

' Three days in the week, salt meat—4 ounces each day.
' The intermediate days, two ounces of beans with one ounce of oil.
' One pound and a half of bread daily.
' One quart bottle of wine for ten days, with a wine glass of brandy twice in the same period.
' All the officers have double rations.
' Suppose there may be provisions in the garrison at the above allowance for about ten or twelve weeks.
' The garrison consists of about three thousand five hundred men, of whom there are in the different hospitals near seven hundred and fifty. Two and three die daily. The prevailing diseases are scurvy, venereal, and fever. Two or three hundred Maltese are enrolled in the French service, mostly for the service of the artillery, but they are fearful of trusting them, therefore only serve to consume the provisions.

' A considerable part of the salt provisions brought by the *Boudeuse* frigate, arrived about two months ago, was rotten and thrown aside as unserviceable. The enemy are very apprehensive of an attack from the Maltese, particularly on the Cottonera, the ramparts of which they have strewn with broken glass bottles, small iron instruments called cats, &c., and every night place loaded shells on the walls ready to set fire to, and roll over the moment of attack. A French frigate called the *Badine* is hourly expected from Toulon with all kinds of stores, &c. There has been a convulsion in the garrison among a number of the troops who wished to capitulate. Several officers have been sent away, and one bled to death in the hospital. This gave a check to the rest, and although there are great discontents among them, they certainly will spin out a longer time than was expected from the hope that Sicily will soon follow the fate of Naples.

' They have spies among the Maltese in the country who are circulating money and endeavouring to bring about a counter-revolution. The French soon expect a change in the sentiments of the country people, which will give them fifteen thousand men in arms on the Island.'

(Signed) ALEX^R. JNO. BALL.

H.M.S. *Alexander*, off Malta, 31*st March* 1799.

PS.—Intelligence just received that Vaubois lately got information of eighty thousand dollars which were put on board of a speronara by the Maltese in Valetta to send away, which he has seized.

Captain Ball on the 6th April further acquainted Sir William Hamilton of the miserable condition to which the inhabitants had been reduced for want of timely aid, and that when the last supply of wheat was received, they were within two days of absolute starvation.

CAPTAIN BALL TO SIR WM. HAMILTON.

H.M.S. *Alexander*, off Malta, 6*th April* 1799.[1]

I am much astonished at the Deputies appearing satisfied at the assistance they received from His Sicilian Majesty, for it is so short a respite from misery, that unless an immediate supply of money and clothes be sent for the troops, Malta will fall into the hands of the French or Russians.

The Congress has written to His Sicilian Majesty to urge the necessity of his ceding the Island to Great Britain, of whom they only require the assistance I mentioned to you in my letter of the 9th February. . . . When the corn arrived here, we had not two days' bread in the Island, the duties and freight on which have been paid by me, 8,331 ducats, because of the inability of the Maltese to pay. I expect to see the Russians this way, but I shall oppose their landing. . . . The Emperor Paul has offered a million to be put in possession of Malta. As His Sicilian Majesty cannot maintain this Island, I conceive it is for his interest that Great Britain should possess it. . . .

I hope, Sir, that you and my Lord Nelson will prevail on His Sicilian Majesty either to send some of his treasure here, or let the Maltese have the sovereignty of some Power that can raise them from their present miserable state.

Soon after the dispatch of the petition to His Sicilian Majesty, news reached the Island that an arrangement had been entered into between Russia, England, and Naples, whereby a joint occupation by their respective troops should be maintained until peace was secured.[2]

Under these circumstances the Deputies petitioned Lord Nelson to use his good offices for the retention of Captain Ball, in whom might be placed the government of the islands, and in whom they had implicit confidence. The following is the petition :—

[Translation.]

Malta, 11*th April* 1799.[3]

MY LORD,—We, the Deputies and Representatives of all the people in Malta, assembled in full Congress, most humbly state, that having received from you the intelligence that the Russians are actually embarking to succour this Island, and that the three Powers, viz. Russia, England, and Naples, should jointly dispatch troops to hold the Island until a general peace is declared, we hereby inform you that, on behalf of the Maltese people, we are preparing a petition addressed to the three aforesaid Powers, respectfully praying that the government of this Island may

---

[1] Foreign Office Records, Sicily, 12.

[2] A treaty signed by Whitworth at St. Petersburg in December 1798 bound Great Britain to hand over Malta to the Czar Paul, as protector of the Knights of St. John, when it should be recovered from the French. See my Introduction.—J. H. R.

[3] Brit. Mus. Add. MSS. 34944, f. 27.

THE BRITISH BLOCKADE—1799

be entrusted to the hands of Captain Ball, at present in command of the blockade of these Islands, in whom the entire population has the fullest confidence for his integrity, valour, and zeal.

Whilst waiting for the reply which these three Powers may deign to make to this request, we humbly pray that you will grant us the same favour by placing the reins of government in the hands of him who has proved himself so worthy. We address you this prayer, not only as a personal satisfaction, but in full conviction that nothing better could secure the tranquillity of this unfortunate Island, and conciliate the disorders which its misery produces. Permit us to tender you our humble thanks for the care with which you have watched over our interests, at a time when we were about to be abandoned in the extremity of our misfortunes.

> Canon SAVERIO CARUANA, Representative of the Maltese clergy; EMMANUELE VITALE, ALOISIO BARTOLOMEO CARAFFA, LORENZO TALIBA, GIUSEPPE CARUANA, PIETRO MALLIA, FELIPPO CASTAGNA, STANISLAO GATT, VINCENZO BORG, SALVATORE GAFÀ, SAVERIO ZARB, DR. ENRICO SCERRI, GIUSEPPE FRENDO, MICHELE CACHIA, JEAN BATTI AGUIS, Secretary of the Congress.

Lord Nelson was fully informed by Ball of the alarm entertained by the people upon hearing there was a possibility of the Island, contrary to their wish, being placed under the charge of three Powers, with a change in the officer supervising all. These letters were dated the 12th April, as follows :—

> CAPTAIN BALL TO LORD NELSON.
>
> H.M.S. *Alexander*, off Malta, 12th *April* 1799.[1]

MY LORD,—I have the honour of Your Lordship's letter of the 3rd instant, enclosing a copy of Sir Charles Whitworth's letter to Sir William Hamilton, and also a secret article of the treaty with His Sicilian Majesty, with a letter from Lord Grenville, and one extract from Lord Spencer's letter relative to Malta, also a sketch of a plan for the future government of Malta.[2]

I communicated to the leading men of the Island the treaty entered into between Great Britain, Russia, and His Sicilian Majesty, to guard Malta as a depôt jointly with their forces, until a general peace shall take place. They were much alarmed at the idea of having foreign troops of three different nations, from an idea that it would occasion party dissensions among the inhabitants, and be productive of the most melancholy consequences, and particularly so if they were to have a foreign governor a stranger to them at so critical a period. They therefore implored me to stay with them as their Governor until the end of the war, to which I shall consent if the Allied Powers approve of it, and Your Lordship will do me the honour to procure me an assurance that it will not break in hereafter upon my professional claims. I send herewith letters from the Congress to the three Allied Powers, and one to Your Lordship requesting that I may be permitted to remain their Governor.

[1] Brit. Mus. Add. MSS. 34910, f. 196.
[2] Sir Charles Whitworth was British ambassador at St. Petersburg. Lord Spencer was First Lord of the Admiralty.—J. H. R.

The whole of the inhabitants are so exasperated against the late Grand Master and the Knights, and the principles on which the government of the Island was administered by the Order, that I think it would be highly imprudent to touch upon the subject until the French are completely driven away. I will then introduce it with such modifications as will make it acceptable to the people, but I am sure they will revolt much at the idea of making eternal war on the Barbary States.

Their general object since their revolution has been to put themselves under the sovereignty of a power generally at peace with the Turks and Barbary States, for which reason they would have remained very contented under the French Government had their religion and laws been respected and they treated with kindness and humanity. The Island will only grow four months' corn for the inhabitants, consequently they are obliged to seek by commerce to supply themselves with sufficient for the remainder of the year, and as their capitals are small, they carry on their trade with speronaras and feluccas which are continually making passages to Sicily, &c., and when at war with the Barbary States, the merchants who occasionally cross and seafaring men are in constant dread of slavery. I think the Island may be kept at a very small expense by attaching the inhabitants to a form of government which would ensure their resisting the attack of any enemy, but I shall not at present trespass on Your Lordship's time. I have the honour, &c.

(Signed) ALEX$^{R.}$ JNO. BALL.

[Extract.]

CAPTAIN BALL TO LORD NELSON.

H.M.S. *Alexander*, off Malta, 12*th April* 1799.[1]

... I have the satisfaction to acquaint Your Lordship that we have opened an important battery which commands the length of the harbour of Valetta; the shot from the thirty-two pounders which I landed will reach the point of St. Elmo and Ricasoli. We struck one of the enemy's frigates stationed at the mouth of the harbour, and obliged her to take shelter with the rest of the French ships in the arm of the harbour called 'Porto delle Galere.' As the enemy's ships are now completely locked up both by sea and land, I trust that it will be considered the British squadron are solely entitled to them, notwithstanding we may be joined by a squadron of our allies at the surrender of the enemy. I could not open the battery sooner for want of battering cannons, and I did not think myself justified in landing my guns before, having intelligence of six sail of the line of the enemy's ships coming up the Mediterranean, and probably intended for the relief of Malta. I am extremely glad to hear that the Russian troops are coming here to drive out the French, for the Maltese troops are so reduced by sickness, and disheartened for want of pay, clothes, and sufficient nourishment, that it is with the utmost difficulty that I can rally them, and keep them at their posts. If the Russians do not come immediately, it is absolutely necessary that five thousand pounds be sent here for the troops. The number of Maltese officers is so reduced

[1] Brit. Mus. Add. MSS. 34910, f. 200.

by sickness and death, and the malignant fever rages still with such violence, that the Island is in a very critical state. I have slept on shore for these last ten days, and have had the Congress meet all this week to exert the whole energy of the Island, and I now hope we shall do very well for a short time, but money or troops must be sent very soon, or we shall be in a perilous state. The French are in so bad a state, that they do not like to risk the weakening their garrison by a sortie, or they certainly might have stood a good chance of succeeding. Whenever the Russians arrive off here, I shall treat the Commander-in-Chief with the most cordial attention. It would be more flattering to see English troops, and it would do away any jealousy respecting the right to the possession of the French ships. I have the honour, &c. (Signed) ALEX^R JNO. BALL.

The commander-in-chief, Lord St. Vincent, was likewise duly informed by Lord Nelson of the consternation existing in Malta upon receipt of the news that the Island would be probably occupied by the Russians, and of the deplorable state to which the population had been reduced by famine and sickness. An extract from his letter is as follows:—

[Extract.]

Naples, 17th April 1799.[1]

To EARL ST. VINCENT,— . . . The *Hyaena* is arrived from Malta, where she went with copies of Sir C. Whitworth's letters, and of the treaty between His Sicilian Majesty and the Emperor of Russia.

The account that the Russians are likely to become in any way masters of Malta has caused the greatest alarm in that Island. The distress of these poor people is terrible, and they are rapidly decreasing by an epidemic fever. This day brought me letters from Troubridge; he has been obliged to give all his flour to keep the inhabitants from starving.

(Signed) NELSON.

Towards the end of April the Neapolitan Government were able to make a further remittance of oz. 7,000 (£3,500), which was of considerable relief to the distressed Maltese;[2] its receipt was acknowledged in the following dispatch from Captain Ball to Lord Nelson on the 26th April.

CAPTAIN BALL TO LORD NELSON.

H.M.S. *Alexander*, off Malta, 26th April 1799.[3]

MY LORD,—Lieutenant Seargent, of His Majesty's cutter *St. Vincent*, has delivered to me seven thousand ounces which His Sicilian Majesty has been graciously pleased to send for the relief of the Maltese, which timely succour will very much alleviate their distresses, and I trust it will enable

[1] Clarke and McArthur, vol. ii. p. 157.
[2] Nelson's letter of 21st April to Captain Ball (*Dispatches of Nelson*, vol. iii. p. 332) shows that this sum was the gift of the Queen, Maria Carolina.—J. H. R.
[3] Brit. Mus. Add. MSS. 34910, f. 314.

us to continue the siege until the arrival of an effective force. The Maltese still continue extremely sickly, and a great many die daily; the news of a speedy reinforcement coming here keeps up their spirits, and I have now no doubt but the money you have sent us will make them cheerful and patient for some time. From very good intelligence the French garrison at Valetta are dying fast of the scurvy. I think they will capitulate soon after the arrival of a foreign force, and not await until we have made a breach for storming. We continue to harass them from our new battery, which I understand has given great uneasiness to General Vaubois, who would certainly make a sortie to destroy it if his garrison was not very weak.

I shall send Your Lordship an account of the corn the Maltese have received on credit. Your Lordship's humanity and ardour in procuring them these supplies has been the means of saving the lives of thousands, as well as relieving others from great distress. I have the honour, &c.

(Signed) ALEX$^{r.}$ J$^{N^o}$. BALL.

Owing to the departure of the French fleet from Brest on the 26th April, which was composed of nineteen sail of the line with frigates and smaller craft, Ball was suddenly called away from Malta on the 13th May, with orders to join Lord Nelson with his squadron off Maritimo and Marsala.

Lord St. Vincent had seen this formidable fleet pass Gibraltar on the 5th May, and it was again sighted off Minorca on the 12th, steering for Toulon.[1] Toulon and Genoa proving to be their destination, *immediate* danger of an attack or an attempt to relieve the garrison in Valetta passed away. Ball in consequence was ordered on the 28th May to return and blockade Valetta, taking with him the *Alexander, Audacious* (or *Goliath*), *Bonne Citoyenne, Stromboli*, and *Benjamin*,[2] but obedient to later orders had again to rejoin Nelson off Maritimo on the 18th June, accompanied by the *Goliath*, whence the entire fleet went on to Naples.

For reasons which are not given, Ball with his ship, the *Alexander*, was retained at Naples, and in his stead Captain Dixon, H.M.S. *Lion*, was ordered on the 26th June 'to proceed without loss of time, taking under his command the sloops *La Bonne Citoyenne, El Corso*, and *Benjamin*, then cruising off Malta, and closely blockade it, and to render all and any assistance in his power to the Maltese people.'

[1] Mr. Hardman's narrative does not bring out with sufficient emphasis the danger to the Allies of the entrance of Bruix with the Brest fleet into the Mediterranean. It numbered 25 sail of the line and 10 smaller vessels. Had not Lord Keith by bold and skilful seamanship prevented the union of this fleet with that blockaded in Cadiz, the result must have been disastrous. As it was, Lord St. Vincent had at once to order an immediate concentration of all British ships in that sea, and gather up the scattered squadrons round his own fleet. Fortunately Bruix did next to nothing except throw provisions into Genoa (then besieged by the Austrians), and then made for Carthagena, and ultimately passed out into the Atlantic. (For this threatening but ineffective raid see Mahan, *Influence of Sea Power*, vol. i. pp. 305-16; and *Camb. Mod. History*, vol. viii. pp. 630, 631; also my Introduction to this volume.)—J. H. R.

[2] The last-named was a Portuguese ship: see the list of the allied ships in the Mediterranean on 17th April in *Dispatches of Nelson*, vol. iii. pp. 331, 332.—J. H. R.

During the temporary absence from Malta of Captain Ball, Lieutenant Vivion, R.A., was left in charge of the land operations. Under date of the 31st May, 19th and 25th June, he made the following interesting reports to Lord Nelson, and a later one to Captain Ball of the 1st July :—

LIEUTENANT VIVION TO LORD NELSON.

Malta, 31*st May* 1799.[1]

MY LORD,—Having been left in this Island by Captain Ball, I consider it my duty, and am moreover urged by the Maltese chiefs, to represent to Your Lordship that ever since the departure of the British squadron the enemy have been complete masters of the seas in this neighbourhood, and have not only blocked up our two ports of St. Paul's and Marsa Scirocco, but interrupted and carried into Valetta every vessel and boat which has appeared in the offing. They have sent five or six speronaras armed, which apparently have gone over to the coast of Sicily, and besides these, have two half-gallies [*sic*] and two or three large launches, each carrying a gun, which cruise in the daytime near the Island, and at night close round the harbour's mouth.

I have been there ten days urging the Maltese to arm half a dozen speronaras and send out for the protection of their trade and to keep the enemy in check, which they might easily do, as calms at present prevail which will prevent any of their frigates from going out. I have at last, in some measure, succeeded, and last night dispatched three with orders to cruise in a line (in such a manner as to be able to support each other) about five leagues off, to board everything which approaches the Island, and as they are commanded and manned by experienced corsairs, I have great hopes they will be able to render themselves of great utility. I have written to the chief at Gozo to urge their sending two more to join the above. I consider it also an indispensable duty to state to Your Lordship that the Maltese are almost destitute of gunpowder; at the beginning of the blockade they were very improvident of that necessary article, and now have not above twenty barrels left in the whole Island. They are also in great distress for flints, not having one in reserve to replace those at present in their musquets. The inhabitants have been in the greatest despair ever since Captain Ball left them; the appearance, however, of the *Thalia* frigate, which returned off here for a day or two last week, afforded them a temporary relief, as they took it for granted she was the forerunner of the remainder of the squadron, her departure has again reduced them to their former despondency, but they flatter themselves that when their distressed state is made known Your Lordship will have the goodness to send one vessel at least, which will be competent to keeping the enemy's small cruisers in port. I trust I shall be pardoned for the liberty I have taken, and have the honour to remain, &c.

(Signed) J. VIVION.

[1] Brit. Mus. Add. MSS. 34940.

LIEUTENANT VIVION TO LORD NELSON.

St. Antoine, Malta, 19th June 1799.[1]

My Lord,—I feel myself highly honoured by the receipt of Your Lordship's letter of the 7th instant. The messenger I sent to Corfu the 20th last month with a letter from Captain Ball to the Russian Admiral having returned with his answer, I think it my duty to forward it to Your Lordship without loss of time. I have also the honour to enclose another letter which came by the same opportunity. The inhabitants of this Island are not yet aware of Captain Ball's having left them,[2] nor shall they know it, so long as I can possibly prevent it. To the many inquiries that are daily made after him, I reply, that he is cruising with the *Goliath* some leagues to the N.W. of Gozo. It is of some consequence that they should be kept in ignorance of this event at present, as I am sorry to observe to Your Lordship that they begin to show a very great indifference as to the event of this contest, the generality of the better sort beginning to relax very much in their exertions, both in their persons and their purses, for the general cause. Those even that are known to be people of property conceal it, and they endeavour by every possible means to draw the little money that remains in my possession from me, for so many different purposes, that were I not to persist in refusing their reiterated demands the whole would very soon be exhausted, and now that the troops have so long known what it is to be paid, it is not improbable that the war would terminate with the money. On the 15th instant, one hundred and fifty men, women, and children came out of the city. They state that General Vaubois not having been able to collect any but a very small portion of his late requisition of 3,000,000 livres, and suspecting that the inhabitants had concealed their money, had fallen upon a most barbarous plan to force them to contribute, which was to put a most enormous price upon the corn, which the Maltese have no other means of procuring than buying from the Republic. Thus they have no other alternative than giving their money or starving, as the respectable people are not allowed to come out. They all persist in the account, that the salt provisions are entirely exhausted, and that the hospitals are crowded with sick, of whom several die every day, but the garrison in general were in good spirits from the idea of relief very shortly from the combined French and Spanish fleets. A deserter came out on the 16th instant, but he told us so many circumstances that we knew to be false, that it would be giving Your Lordship unnecessary trouble to repeat them. In one particular, however, I have every reason to believe he deserves to be credited—the manner in which he accounts for their arming and preparing the men-of-war. He says they are so confident of the talked of relief that they are getting the ships ready to send off with the fleet that brings their saviours.[3]

I have no doubt but Captain Maling will report to Your Lordship the state of the French ships, which he is capable of doing in a much more correct manner than I possibly can; we took a near view of them yesterday. I entreat your Lordship to pardon this intrusion, and I have the honour, &c.

(Signed) J. Vivion.

---

[1] Brit. Mus. Add. MSS. 34940.
[2] Captain Ball with other ships returned to the Maltese station early in June, but Nelson again called them off. (See *Dispatches of Nelson*, vol. iii. p. 374.)—J. H. R.
[3] i.e. the fleet of Bruix.—J. H. R.

THE BRITISH BLOCKADE—1799

LIEUTENANT VIVION TO LORD NELSON.

St. Antoine, Malta, 25th June 1799.[1]

MY LORD,—On the 19th instant I did myself the honour of writing to Your Lordship, enclosing a letter from the Russian Admiral at Corfu in answer to Captain Ball's letter which I dispatched from hence the 20th May. In compliance with instructions given me by Captain Ball on his departure, I sent the above letters via Girgenti. Since that period some vessels have arrived from Messina with information of Your Lordship being cruising off Cape Marittimo with the squadron to intercept the French fleet, who are said to be out of Toulon. I have the honour to enclose a duplicate of my letter above mentioned.

I am now under the painful necessity of stating for Your Lordship's information, that the lower classes of Maltese are in a state of rebellion against their chiefs, whom they all accuse of being Jacobins and friends of the French. Yesterday afternoon a deputation of several hundreds came to me, and declared their independence of all command from them, and that they will only acknowledge and obey the orders of British officers. Some trivial events which I am bound to acknowledge had at first very much the appearance of treachery has [sic] led to all this unpleasant affair, and I have had very great difficulty in saving the lives of some of the chiefs, particularly the Canon Caruana, who is entirely fallen from the high situation in which he was considered by the army, and his life is as yet by no means in security.

In order to tranquillise the minds of all classes, I have been under the unpleasant necessity of receiving all the gunpowder and ammunition into the palace I inhabit, under my own immediate charge. I have thought it expedient on this occasion to dispatch one of our armed speronaras with my letter to Your Lordship in charge of Lieut. Cardona of H.S. Majesty's service, who is a very intelligent deserving young man and perfectly acquainted with every circumstance relative to the internal state of this island, being a native of Malta. I feel myself in a very new and embarrassing situation, but fortunately the natives are so much attached to the English Government that I have hitherto in some measure succeeded in pacifying them, even in their most intemperate conduct. I have not been without my fears of the Island (during these unpleasant contentions) falling entirely into the hands of the French again—though it is with great satisfaction I can inform Your Lordship that our enemies have been, and are, in as bad a situation as ourselves, and entirely ignorant, luckily for us, of what passes in the Island. Four days ago another deserter came out of the city, and yesterday three more, all of whom declare that the garrison has for many days past been nearly in a state of mutiny, threatening the General, if he did not find some speedy means of delivering them from their wretched situation, to open the gates, and allow the country people to enter the town. They have been under the necessity of taking another hospital, which makes the fourth, and that one day with another eight and nine die. They say that they are persuaded the garrison will insist on capitulating the moment they see a squadron of any force, as they will naturally suppose they have troops on board, and they are not in a condition

[1] Brit. Mus. Add. MSS. 34940.

to resist any attack. That nearly one half the sentinels on the ramparts at night are blind, occasioned as they suppose by the poorness of living. They also agree in stating that the *Boudeuse* French frigate has taken on board many valuables, and that she is to effect her escape the first blowing weather, with men just sufficient to navigate her, as she is reputed a very fast sailer. I have the honour, &c. (Signed) J. VIVION.

LIEUTENANT VIVION TO CAPTAIN BALL.

St. Antoine, 1*st July* 1799.[1]

MY DEAR SIR,—On the 25th ulto. I had the pleasure of writing you a long letter, which I hope has come safe to hand long ere this. I at the same time wrote to Lord Nelson, and sent one of the young Neapolitan officers in an armed speronara with my letters in order that His Lordship and yourself might have a full statement of the situation of affairs in this island. From a variety of channels we learnt that the whole of Lord Nelson's fleet was cruising off Marittimo, in which case the letter would reach you very soon. I am particularly anxious not only that you should be informed of our situation, but also to be relieved from the very responsible office in which I am at present placed.

The evening before last, a circumstance occurred which put me to the necessity of acting in such a decisive manner as will no doubt bring me a number of enemies, but I am so confident that I not only acted for the general good and the tranquility of the Island, but that you would have done the same thing had you been present. On Friday about three o'clock in the afternoon arrived in St. Paul's Bay, in a speronara, three of the Knights of Malta; two were baillies, and the third a commandant. They were last from Messina, but originally from Trieste, the residence of the late Grand Master; two of them were Germans, the other French. They were, however, all very popular with the Maltese of the country, on which account they no doubt were sent. One of them, Neveu, had commanded the regiment of chasseurs in the country, speaks Maltese perfectly well, and was particularly beloved by all classes. There are many of these chasseurs in every one of the villages, and the report was no sooner spread of his arrival, than the greatest joy was manifested by them, and all determining on going to St. Paul's (Bay) immediately to welcome his arrival. The opposite party likewise began to make a stir. Parnis put them into the church, until he received orders from me. They, however, told the Maltese about them ' that they had brought them money, and that a large quantity of provisions were to follow them.' The moment I heard what was going forward, I sent an order to Parnis to ask them what was their business, and that if they did not come in any public capacity with proper authority, to take all their papers, give them provisions sufficient to carry them to Sicily, and send them off. All this he complied with strictly. They said they were come for their own interests, and were savage at being turned out of their own country, as they called it. They were anchored off in the middle of the port all night, the wind being foul, but they went off at daybreak in the morning. They had many letters, all which I have perused—numbers without signatures—all from the Knights, and written many of

[1] Brit. Mus. Add. MSS. 34040.

them in very ambiguous terms, referring always to the bearers of them for information. In one expression they all seemed to agree—'that there were yet hopes.' They likewise brought which I have in my possession, the 'History of the Revolution of Malta,' written by a baillie in French—it is a vindication of the Grand Master and Knights in general, throwing the odium on, and accusing as the authors of the revolution, the French and Spanish Knights, in concert with the noblesse, bourgeois, avocats, and country people of Malta. I have not yet had time to read it through, but have seen enough of it to perceive the object.

These people arrived also at the most unfortunate moment that could be, when we were torn to pieces by a number of different parties, with all kinds of reports tending to create a general alarm and distrust.

In the morning of that day, upwards of one hundred and fifty persons came out of La Valette, every one of them with an account that a counter-revolution was to be effected in the country by the partisans of the French, that it was to take place during the great festival of St. Paul's at Citta Vecchia the next day, that they were to begin by destroying the English officers and all the Maltese chiefs, and that at the first signal the French were to make a sortie of seven or eight hundred to support them.

Although this story was so absurd, you can form no idea of the alarm it caused, as it appeared to combine with other reports that had been long about the country for something decisive on that day, and this was the moment that these men chose, or accident brought to this place.

I have not a doubt but that you will sanction and approve of what I have done in this business. On a poor old woman that came out on that day was found three copies of a printed paper, which I herewith enclose, entitled 'A Dialogue between Alexander Ball and the Marquis de Niza.' I also enclose Cutajar's translation of it. There is a great deal of deep policy in it, as it tends very much to depreciate the English character and our views on this Island. Vaubois is now reduced to his last resource, and begins to make war on us by these [sic] kind of publications.[1] I send you also another proclamation, which I could swear is written by the same hand as the other paper. Yesterday another deserter came out, which makes six the last ten days; he says another was stopped a few days ago in the act of desertion, and is to suffer death for it. He confirms all we have before heard, and says that if they do not surrender the moment a fleet appears (which he thinks they will do) that by landing a couple or three hundred soldiers to make false attacks every night for a week would send half the garrison to the hospital, and make the other half desert if Vaubois did not capitulate. Last week we made three false attacks, which kept the garrison on the ramparts all night, but we have not powder to go on. The last night of the three we attacked the advanced guard of Fort Manoel, drove them in in such haste that we took all their watch cloaks, the lanthorns in the guard-room, and everything that was there. The passage over the little bridge which we forced was strewn with such number of iron cats, that some of the Maltese got badly wounded in their feet, tho' none by the heavy fire of grape and musketry which they kept on us. On the Saturday, St. Paul's day, I was under the necessity of passing the day at Citta Veille [sic], and to receive all the honours in the church, procession

[1] See Vaubois' letter of June 28, 1799, in the Appendix (Part II *ad fin.*)—J. H. R.

&c., of commandant. You would, I am sure, have laughed to see me. Dr. Paigster will tell you all about it.

I suppose I am the first *heretick* that ever received these honours! We have heard of the surrender of Naples,[1] which affords us much pleasure—it appears, however, strange that we have no official accounts of it, as it is an event that so immediately concerns the Maltese. I have nothing more at present, but in the hope of seeing you back speedily, believe me, &c. (Signed) J. VIVION.

N.B.—I have got the hundred pounds belonging to your squadron, which I should be glad if possible to get rid of, for fear of accidents; it is the produce of the brig *Victoria*.

The prolonged absence of Captain Ball from Malta, which (with the exception of a brief visit early in June) was now approaching a period of six weeks, had been the cause of great anxiety to the leaders of the insurrection, when on the 5th July, Nelson ordered him to return to his former station at Malta.[2] This step was the more necessary, from the fact that, in addition to the question of the supply of food, it soon became *publicly* known that His Majesty the Czar of Russia contemplated interfering in any settlement of the Maltese question.

Owing to the schism which had arisen amongst the members of the scattered Order, and the protection given to it by the Czar, Lord Grenville, then Secretary of State for Foreign Affairs, on the 9th July addressed the Lords of the Admiralty to the following effect[3]:—

In consequence of a communication which His Majesty has received from Malta, and others which have been transmitted to me by Your Lordships, I have received the King's commands to apprise you:

That if the Island of Malta fell to any naval force employed by His Majesty separately, or in conjunction with other Powers, it should be restored to the Knights of St. John, who acknowledge the Emperor of Russia as Grand Master.

From the tenor of this dispatch it is evident that, even at this date, it was considered by those best competent to judge, that the anticipated fall of Valetta would be attributed to the naval forces blockading. There is no mention made of it falling to the Maltese insurgents. How then can it be maintained that the Maltese were the principals (as belligerents), and the British forces but auxiliaries?

The next event which has to be chronicled in point of date is Ball's arrival off Malta, and his dispatch to Nelson on the 17th July,

---

[1] Naples surrendered to the Royalists on June 23.—J. H. R.
[2] Captain Ball had recently been serving under Captain Troubridge, of H.M.S. *Culloden*, in the reduction of Fort St. Elmo at Naples. (See *Dispatches of Nelson*, vol. iii. p. 397.)—J. H. R.
[3] Pettigrew, *Nelson's Dispatches*, vol. i. p. 316.

wherein His Lordship is informed of another deputation having been sent to Palermo, with the object of petitioning for a further supply of wheat.

[Extract.]

CAPTAIN BALL TO LORD NELSON.

H.M.S. *Alexander*, off Malta, 17*th July* 1799.[1]

. . . Allow me to suggest to your Lordship that I think it of great consequence to the Russian cause to send here Le Chevalier Italinski[2] for a fortnight, that I may make him acquainted with the disposition and sentiments of the Maltese, and the political views of the different parties.

I have sent Colonel Cardona with some Maltese Deputies who are petitioning for more corn; he will return here with them. He can represent the state of the Maltese. I have the honour, &c.

(Signed) ALEX^R· JN^O· BALL.

The insurgents were by now inclined to believe that Vaubois might be more amenable to negotiations being opened for a surrender of the fortress, and in consequence requested Captain Ball to ask Lord Nelson for permission to open a parley with the French general.

This permission was awarded under the date of the 12th August, in the following words:—

The general is not to be regularly summoned, and if the capitulation followed, the garrison might be sent to France without being considered prisoners of war, provided their arms, and every colour of the place, as well as regimental, were surrendered. These favourable conditions, however, were only to be granted in the event of it saving fourteen days' labour, for the garrison in his opinion could never be succoured.[3]

Accordingly, on the 20th August Captain Broughton was sent to General Vaubois with the following letter:—

[Translation.]

19*th August* 1799.[4]

SIR,—I have been ordered by Admiral Nelson to forward you authentic information (as may be gathered from the gazettes herewith) which will prove to you that the French fleet is no longer in the Mediterranean,[5] and that serious insurrections have taken place at Toulon, Marseilles, and which are increasing daily, preventing any succour reaching you.[6]

[1] Brit. Mus. Add. MSS. 34912, f. 313.
There is an episode at this point to which Mr. Hardman does not refer, viz. the urgent request made by the Maltese to Captain Ball to be their governor. It is referred to in a letter of W. A. Miles to Captain Ball (in reply to one from him dated August 3, 1799), a portion of which I have quoted in the Introduction to this volume.—J. H. R.
[2] Italinski was the Russian envoy to the Neapolitan Court.—J. H. R.
[3] Nicolas, *Dispatches of Nelson*, vol. iii. p. 438 (edit. 1845).
[4] Lavigeri, *L'Ordre de Malte*, p. 201.
[5] Bruix sailed through the Straits for Cadiz early in July.—J. H. R.
[6] These tales of Royalist movements were grossly exaggerated.—J. H. R.

I have again to offer you terms for an honourable capitulation, which if you do not accept before the arrival of the Russian fleet and troops, which are assembling at Messina for that purpose, you will be deprived, you and your garrison, of the favourable conditions now offered you.

It is for this reason that I recommend you to no longer sacrifice the lives of your brave men by an obstinacy which deprives your country of their services.

I send you Captain Broughton, who will deliver you this letter. I have the honour, &c. (Signed) ALEXANDER BALL.

To this offer Vaubois made the following reply :—

Malte, le 2 *Fructidor* an 7 (19*th August* 1799).[1]

VAUBOIS, Général de Division, à MONSIEUR ALEXANDRE BALL.

La garnison de Malte est en trop bon état. Sa valeur est celle des Républicains aussi remplis de l'amour de leur devoir, que de courage. Je suis trop jaloux moi-même, de bien servir mon pays, et de conserver mon honneur, pour entendre vos propositions ; quel qu'ennemis qui la [se (?)] présentent nous les combattrons, avec la plus grande vigueur, et nous vous forcerons, ainsi que ceux qui pouroient venir, à nous estimer.

J'ai l'honneur d'être avec estime. (Signed) VAUBOIS.

Je suis fâché de n'avoir pu faire entrer en ville, l'officier que vous avez envoyé.

Captain Ball refers to this communication with Vaubois in his dispatch of the 20th August.

[Extract.]

CAPTAIN BALL TO LORD NELSON.

H.M.S. *Alexander*, off Malta, 20*th August* 1799.[2]

MY LORD—, . . . The Maltese armed peasants are so sickly that I ordered the Marines from the *Lion* and *Success* to be landed to strengthen the posts, previous to the receipt of Your Lordship's orders respecting them. I am informed that the French have not received the smallest supply of fresh provisions from this Island or Gozo these last four months ; they have nearly eaten all the cats, dogs, horses, and mules in the garrison. Mule's flesh sold for four shillings a pound a month ago, notwithstanding which General Vaubois keeps the garrison to their duty ; his great object is to procrastinate until the blowing weather will enable his troops to embark on board of the ships of war and make their escape. If Your Lordship would come off here for a few days it might greatly accelerate the surrender of the garrison. The language of the French soldiers has been that they will oblige their general to surrender whenever a force appears off. I beg leave to suggest that if the English troops

---

[1] Brit. Mus. Add. MSS. 34913, f. 148.
[2] *Ibid.* f. 146.

could be sent here from Messina with two thirteen-inch mortars, a few battering cannon, powder, &c., we could then carry on active operations and ensure a speedy surrender. I sent Captain Broughton with a letter to General Vaubois, and all the printed papers you sent me. I enclose his answer. The *Benjamin* is not yet arrived. I have the honour, &c.

(Signed) ALEX^R· JN^O· BALL.

PS.—I am just informed that Mr. de Alos[1] has talked to the Maltese armed peasants, evidently with an intention of stirring up an insurrection. The Maltese chiefs have written to the Prince of Luzzi complaining of his insults and calumny.

CAPTAIN BALL TO LORD NELSON.

H.M.S. *Alexander*, off Malta, 20th August 1799.[2]

MY LORD,—I have the honour to acquaint Your Lordship that on the 6th inst. a Mr. Christopher de Alos, his secretary and servant, appeared before me, and presented a paper signed by the Prince de Luzzi, a copy of which accompanies this, signifying that he is ordered by His Sicilian Majesty to enter [induce?] the French garrison of Valetta to execute a special commission; and the commander of the ships off Malta was requested to give him every assistance. As this gentleman did not bring any letter for me from Your Lordship or His Britannic Majesty's Minister, I expressed my doubts of his being employed by His Sicilian Majesty, as his Minister would certainly have previously obtained Your Lordship's approbation on a subject of such importance, otherwise it would appear to be offering an insult (which they are incapable of) to send a person to treat with an enemy without consulting Your Lordship, whose ships have blocked them up a year, and which has given the Maltese such a confidence as to encourage them to persevere in their long and arduous struggle, and to undergo the severest hardships in the most exemplary manner. I think it unnecessary to trespass on Your Lordship's time by mentioning the numerous inconsistencies in this gentleman's conduct, and the many reasons for distrusting him. Had he been really employed on this business, I beg leave to suggest my opinion that, so far from being attended with good consequences, it would be very prejudicial to our interest, as he must enter into La Valette without any passport, for if one were found about him he would be treated as a spy.

I enclose herewith his character sent to me and attested by the principal inhabitants, and as he is well known in La Valette the French would be prepossessed against giving credit to his being employed by His Sicilian Majesty to treat secretly with them. I think it very improbable that they would take his word for a million of money, and before any credentials could be brought a sufficient force might be sent here to oblige the French to surrender. The French General would probably turn this gentleman's arrival to his own advantage by threatening him with death if he did not immediately promulgate such news as would encourage the garrison to hold out until the blowing season sets in, that they might embark on board the ships of war and endeavour to effect their escape. They are now so

[1] Referred to in the next letter.—J. H. R.
[2] Brit. Mus. Add. MSS. 34913, f. 150.

reduced that, if Your Lordship were to come off here for a short time, it is the opinion of the most respectable men in La Valette that the French would surrender, which in every point of view would be better than risking the offering a sum of money, because this always gives a strong presumptive reason to believe that we are not provided with other means to compel it. It therefore stimulates a general who is above bribery to persevere to the last moment. To secure his person from any insult from the Maltese, I have ordered him to go to the *Alexander*, where he is to remain until Your Lordship's pleasure shall be known. I have the honour, &c.

(Signed) ALEX^{R.} JN^{O.} BALL.

Further correspondence from Ball to Nelson, dated the 28th August and 3rd September, is as follows :—

[Extract.]

CAPTAIN BALL TO LORD NELSON.

H.M.S. *Alexander*, off Malta, *28th August* 1799.[1]

Captain Hardy has delivered to me the money sent by His Sicilian Majesty for the Maltese. I shall soon forward to Your Lordship an account of the different sums I have received from His Majesty, with the expenditure, that it may be laid before His Sicilian Majesty's Minister. It is now under examination by a committee of the Congress, who will attest it before it is sent. . . . I enclose herewith an extract of a letter respecting the corn which is to be sent here from Sicily, which requires an order or permit for its being allowed to come here, otherwise there will be a delay which will occasion us great distress, as we have not ten days' corn in the Island.

General Vaubois intends making his escape with his ships whenever the weather will allow him. I have great hopes of preventing it by storming Ricasoli, or constructing a battery very near it. It may appear to Your Lordship that I have been much deceived in my intelligence relative to the actual state of the French garrison, which I thought would surrender very soon, six months ago. The report of the mutinous state of the garrison at that time induced the inhabitants who came out of La Valette to think so, but General Vaubois, whose life will be sacrificed whenever he returns to France, unless he can re-establish his character by the most vigorous defence, has shown himself full of resource. He has placed spies in every company to give him early notice of any intention to mutiny, that he may crush it in the bud, and he has the art to make the soldiers believe that the arms of the French Republic are victorious, and that Naples is still in their possession. The papers relating the successes of the Allied Powers, which we have given them, they declare to be fabricated at Malta. We have had frequent conversations with their soldiers, and made their deserters talk with them, but as yet with very little effect. The soldiers murmur, but they still remain at their posts. . . . I have the honour, &c.

(Signed) ALEX^{R.} JN^{O.} BALL.

[1] Brit. Mus. Add. MSS. 34913, f. 221.

CAPTAIN BALL TO LORD NELSON.

H.M.S. *Alexander*, off Malta, 28*th August* 1799.[1]

MY LORD,—Your Grace's[2] letter of the 10th inst. has contributed much to my happiness. I am truly grateful for what Your Grace has been pleased to say respecting their Sicilian Majesties' intentions towards me in the government of this Island, which I owe to your kind patronage, and I beg to be permitted to offer through Your Grace my tribute of thanks to Sir William and Lady Hamilton, and particularly to Her Ladyship, whose influence with the Queen can work miracles.[3] Colonel Cardona is a cunning old fox ; he has deceived me, but not the Maltese, who have a great dislike to him. I beg leave to trouble you to send one extract of his letter to me from Palermo, dated the 5th instant :—

' J'ai eu, Monsieur, l'honneur et le bonheur de me presenter chez Sa Majesté notre Reine, qui m'a reçu avec une bonté digne de lui même. En faisant le tableau de notre pays je n'ai pas manqué, mon cher Commandant, de lui dire que c'étoit la Providence qui vous avoit destiné à Malte pour nous soulager dans nos maux, et une seconde fois, dans la présence de deux députés de Malte. Je me suis acquitté de la commission dont mes compatriotes m'ont chargé avant que de partir. Ils m'ont chargé de prier Sa Majesté d'avoir en considération leurs peines et de leur accorder en récompense Monsr. le Commandant Ball pour gouverneur, comme, outre les vertus, [il] a encore la connaissance du pays. Je ne puis vous exprimer le plaisir que ma demande a fait à la Reine. Elle m'a répondu—c'est bon, ce soir même j'écrirai à Nelson, qui sans doute en sera très flatté.'

I will not trespass on Your Grace's time by making any comments on the Colonel's inconsistency. I was informed that Cristoforo, the young man who says he is employed by the Queen, was endeavouring to excite the Maltese armed peasants to revolt and probably to destroy me; he asked one of the soldiers what pay he had, and upon being informed of the sum, he said it was too little, that His Sicilian Majesty has an idea that they are better paid, as he sent money over on purpose for them. I am convinced that he must be employed by the Knights of Malta, to cause an insurrection and to prejudice the people against me.

If he be actually employed by the Queen he has betrayed her cause. I have therefore sent him to the *Alexander*, to be taken care of until Your Grace's pleasure can be made known. There are so many agents in the island, employed to cause a revolution, that nothing but utmost vigilance and circumspection will prevent it. At present the greatest tranquility and happiness reigns throughout the island, considering the difficulties we labour under. I have the honour, &c.

(Signed) ALEX. J^{NO.} BALL.

---

[1] Brit. Mus. Add. MSS. 34913, f. 219.
[2] Nelson had on August 16th received from King Ferdinand the title Duke of Bronte. Hence the title 'Your Grace' used by Captain Ball. Nelson did not, however, use the ducal title in England.—J. H. R.
[3] As is well known, the influence of Lady Hamilton at Court, and Nelson's infatuation for her, had terribly complicated affairs at Naples since the outbreak of war at the close of 1798.—J. H. R.

[Extract.]

CAPTAIN BALL TO LORD NELSON.

H.M.S. *Alexander*, off Malta, 3rd September 1799.[1]

Rear-Admiral the Marquis de Niza arrived here the 1st instant, and delivered me Your Lordship's order of the 21st ultimo, directing me to put the ships here under the command of the Marquis, and to take upon myself the command of all the Maltese people, with the seamen, marines, or others who may be landed from the squadron, and to co-operate with the marines for the good of His Majesty's service.[2] I beg leave to offer my sincere acknowledgements for this distinguished mark of additional favour with which Your Lordship is pleased to honour me. I regret very much not having the means of carrying on active operations with effect for want of men, mortars, guns, powder, flints, &c.; however, I shall attempt to get possession of an important post, which, if I can keep, will accelerate the surrender of the French garrison. I shall land from my ship both powder and guns, which I hope Your Lordship will approve. I have sent to Syracuse for some fascines; the moment they are brought over I shall rouse the enemy to attack me or capitulate. I applied some time since for two thirteen-inch mortars, which we are much in want of. Here are two nine-inch Neapolitan howitzers. If carriages and shells could be sent for them they would be very useful.

Four French seamen have lately deserted from Valetta, who confirm the report of the French ships being ready for sea, and the determination of General Vaubois to attempt to escape with his garrison.

Their forces amount to four thousand men, including seamen.[3]

The Maltese armed peasants are very sickly; there are fifteen hundred men capable of doing duty, and of that number may be selected six hundred men fit for an attack. I pay and feed weekly two thousand five hundred armed men, beside supporting one thousand poor and distressed families. I send Your Lordship the monthly expense of this Island as reported by the chiefs of the different towns.

There are many Maltese slaves in the Turkish fleet at Messina; the Maltese humbly solicit Your Lordship to relieve their unfortunate countrymen, that they may return to their disconsolate families. I have likewise received information of several Maltese boats being captured by the Algerine corsairs. The sufferers all look up to Your Lordship for a happy deliverance from their miseries. I have the honour, &c.

(Signed) ALEX. JN°· BALL.

In September the *Foudroyant* (lately selected as flagship) was sent from Palermo to join Ball's squadron for ten days, during which time it was suggested that her marines, as well as those from the other ships, should be landed and made use of at the advance posts,

---

[1] Brit. Mus. Add. MSS. 34913, f. 280.

[2] For the secret interview of Niza with Vaubois about September 6, see Vaubois' *Journal of the Siege of Malta* (Part III), in Appendix.—J. H. R.

[3] This is far in excess of the numbers given by Vaubois in his *Journal of the Siege of Malta*.—J. H. R.

as it was rumoured that the armed peasants allowed many articles to enter the town.

It would appear that Ball about this time proposed to Colonel Graham, then in command of the British troops stationed in the citadel of Messina, the advisability of transferring his force to Malta; for on the 3rd September Colonel Graham informed Lord Nelson, that without superior orders it was impossible for him to acquiesce.[1] His letter to Lord Nelson was to the following effect:—

COLONEL GRAHAM TO LORD NELSON.

[Private.]   Citadel of Messina, *3rd September* 1799.[2]

MY DEAR LORD,—Commodore[3] Ball seems to wish much that I would go to Malta for a short time with the troops of this garrison. However anxiously I should wish for such an opportunity for service, it is impossible for me *now* to stir a man from hence *without orders from Mahon*.

They have lately received three more regiments there, and I have sent Commodore Ball's letter to Sir James, saying that if he could spare another regiment, I might then leave of the three enough to keep possession of this place, and go south with something like a brigade of 11 or 12 hundred men, to which should be added some officers of Artillery and Engineers, with a small detachment of artillerymen from Mahon, and another from *hence*, where likewise some mortars and guns and a little ammunition might be procured.

Such a force might assist in getting possession of some of the detached works such as Fort Ricasoli, and then Vaubois, cut off from all hope of supplies from the sea, might think himself justified in surrendering. I cannot imagine that any less force would be of *real use*, and even this would only be as an experiment which in my mind, under the existing circumstances of the state of the garrison, and the season of the year, it would be well worth while to make. If it succeeded it would relieve a number of ships for other service, and it would more effectually secure Sicily from all chance of invasion than any other conquest, for while the French keep Malta it cannot be said to be *safe*, even though this place should remain in our hands. And on the other hand, if it failed, no disgrace or bad consequence would arise from the trial having being made. This is my sincere opinion, independent of all personal interest, though I own I should have a very strong one in being so employed, with a reasonable prospect of success, which would probably confirm my *temporary* rank in the Army, and by the means the most agreeable to me. There is no time to lose, however, as next month should be the active moment on account of the weather. Excuse my taking the liberty of writing to you in this haste with so much freedom. I have done the same in a private letter to Sir

---

[1] Thomas Graham was born at Balgowan, Perthshire, in 1748, but did not enter the army till 1793. He accompanied the Austrian army in Italy in 1796–7, and escaped from Mantua when besieged by the French. He helped Sir Charles Stuart to reduce Minorca. He afterwards served with distinction in the Peninsula, where he won the Battle of Barossa (1811). In 1815 he was raised to the peerage as Lord Lynedoch. He died in 1843.—J. H. R.

[2] Brit. Mus. Add. MSS. 34913, f. 284.

[3] This title is a mistake. Captain Ball is the correct title.—J. H. R.

James, but without much hope of being listened to unless strongly backed by Your Lordship. Perhaps he may never have heard from Government on the subject, but he cannot doubt of their anxiety to dispossess the French of such a fortress, and it should not be left, if possible, in their hands during the winter, when an active, enterprising enemy may throw in supplies. Adieu now, my dear Lord; best respects to Lady Hamilton and Sir William, and believe me ever most truly yours,

(Signed) THOS. GRAHAM.

About this time the Royal Commission, which had been appointed by the Neapolitan Government to superintend the shipment of cereals to the Maltese inhabitants, presented the following statement showing the quantity of wheat, barley, and vegetables shipped from Sicily during forty-nine weeks, from the 1st October 1798 to the 7th September 1799, inclusive.[1]

[Translation.]

Wheat	Quarters 31,281	6 3
Barley	,, 15,232	4 0
Pulse	,, 737	6 0
Beans	,, 1,630	0 0

Five months after the Maltese appeal to the Neapolitan Cabinet for the appointment of Captain Ball to the government of the island, a favourable reply was at last received.

This intelligence was conveyed to Captain Ball in the following very flattering dispatches from Sir John Acton, under date of the 11th September.

[Translation.]

Palermo, 11*th September* 1799.[2]

To CAPTAIN BALL, commanding the English line-of-battle ship *Alexander*.

His Sicilian Majesty having been fully informed of the valour, the great vigilance, and the most satisfactory manner in which the operations connected with the blockade of Malta have been conducted under Your Excellency, and more particularly with regard to the succour you have rendered the Maltese, and being desirous of testifying in a positive manner the faith which His Majesty reposes in Your Excellency's ability, and exact fulfilment thereof, has at the request of the Maltese, and with the consent of the worthy Admiral Lord Nelson, Duke of Bronte, confided to Your Excellency the command of the said Island until such time as other dispositions may be made, in accord with the two Courts who with His Majesty interest themselves in the felicity of the said Island.

His Majesty therefore has commanded me to convey to you notice of this appointment, and I fulfil the same with the greatest satisfaction, being fully aware that this marked proof of His Royal confidence in Your Excellency will induce you to exercise the zeal and activity which

---

[1] Brit. Mus. Add. MSS. 34946, f. 12. For lack of space I omit the details and give only the totals.—J. H. R.

[2] Brit. Mus. Add. MSS. 34946, f. 21.

characterises you even in a still higher degree in the Royal service of His Majesty, united to those which are similar, in the common cause, and which you have so gloriously fulfilled up to the present time, as well as on behalf of the Maltese, of whom you have been enabled to gain their fullest confidence, and through which, thanks to the bravery and knowledge of Your Excellency, and to the co-operation of the inhabitants of the said Island, the most advantageous results may be expected. I have the honour to be, Sir, (Signed) JOHN ACTON.

[Translation.]

[Private.] Palermo, 11th September 1799.¹
To Captain Ball, &c.

YOUR EXCELLENCY,—Having to forward to Your Excellency the enclosed Royal dispatch, whereby His Majesty the King, my Lord, confers upon you the command of the Island of Malta, I avail myself of the opportunity to express to you the extreme pleasure I have experienced in knowing that the selection has devolved upon you, which, whilst doing honour to the wise discrimination of His Majesty, is a most flattering acknowledgment of the excellent services you have rendered.

I therefore beg that Your Excellency will accept my heartiest congratulations, and have the honour to state, with extreme satisfaction, that I remain Your Excellency's most devoted and obedient servant,
(Signed) JOHN ACTON.

During this month of September, Deputies were again sent to Palermo imploring the Neapolitan Government to send further supplies of food and money. Ball acquainted Nelson under date of the 15th that the people were in the greatest distress for want of corn. His letter was as follows:—

CAPTAIN BALL TO LORD NELSON.

St. Antonio, Malta, 15th September 1799.²

MY LORD,—I am honoured with Your Lordship's letter of the 5th instant by the *Stromboli*, by which I am sorry to learn that the Maltese can only have a very small supply of corn from Sicily. Whatever it is, I hope that their Sicilian Majesty's [*sic*] Minister will order it to be sent so soon as possible, as we are in the utmost distress for that article.
If we had money we could get corn cheaper from the Levant than from Sicily. I am therefore to request Your Lordship to send monthly at the rate of fifty thousand crowns until the French shall surrender, as I presume the sovereign to whom this Island shall be ultimately ceded will repay their Sicilian Majesties for their generous assistance.

I am extremely mortified that I cannot assure Your Lordship that La Valette will very soon be carried by our operations, but I trust that when you reflect on the strength and resources of both parties you will be convinced that more cannot be effected. The French have 5,000 men.³

¹ Brit. Mus. Add. MSS. 34946, f. 22. ² *Ibid.* 34913, f. 380.
³ Probably Vaubois had not half that number of effectives.—J. H. R.

We have 500 English and Portuguese marines, and about 1,500 armed peasants; not 500 of the latter can be depended on for an assault.

I am going to take possession of an important post contrary to the general opinion of military men; if it can be maintained, which I have little doubt of, it will accelerate the surrender of the French garrison, and furnish a good pretext for their general to give up.

Lieut.-Col. Lord Blainey has been here for a few days, during which time he has been indefatigable, at the risk of his health and person, to ascertain the enemy's position and the best mode of attacking them; he will have the honour to detail the particulars of our situation to Your Lordship; he has seen a great deal of service, and appears to be a good soldier.

I sent the French prisoner who came by the *Stromboli* into La Valette. General Vaubois has put him in prison, and it is reported he is considered as a spy. I expected that he would be treated in this manner, but his report cannot fail having a very good effect.

I shall let Mr. Aloes return to Sicily; I am perfectly sensible that the good Queen did not employ him. The Prince de Luzzi has explained it, and I am now convinced that he was employed by the Knights of Malta to bring about a revolution in their favour, for which purpose he was holding the same language they did, and persuading the people that the chiefs and those holding places here were Jacobins and tyrants. I have the honour to be, my Lord, &c. (Signed) ALEX. J^{NO.} BALL.

The supply of wheat from Sicily at this period had become so reduced, that on the 30th September the Deputies at a plenary meeting held that day, whilst acknowledging their obligations to Lord Nelson, and attributing their salvation up to that time *entirely* to His Lordship's efforts on their behalf, had yet to deplore the scanty stock on hand.

[Translation.]

Congress Hall, Malta, 30*th September* 1799.[1]

To HIS EXCELLENCY LORD NELSON, Admiral of His Britannic Majesty's Fleet.

Numberless are the obligations of this faithful people to Your Excellency, nor indeed can we find words to properly express to you our everlasting gratitude.

It is alone to your valuable co-operation, My Lord, that we can attribute the arrival of the late supplies which His Majesty the King of the Two Sicilies has sent us, and we have further to thank you for having granted to us, as Governor of these two Islands, His Excellency Captain Ball, a most honest person, who has acquired the affections of this people, and whose conduct has been irreproachable, and as to his other merits, it is unnecessary to dilate upon them, the same being well known to Your Excellency.

We have received for the maintenance of our battalions fourteen hundred quarters of wheat; but what are these for so numerous a population?

[1] Brit. Mus. Add. MSS. 34946, f. 70.

THE BRITISH BLOCKADE—1799

We repeat, My Lord, our earnest solicitations, that under these critical circumstances you will not abandon us, and praying that you will accept the homage and most sincere respect of Your Excellency's most obedient and obliged servants, the Maltese Representatives.

(Signed) CANON SAVERIO CARUANA, THE CAPITAN DI VERGA BARON FRANCESCO GAUCI, COUNT SALVATORE MANDUCA, COUNT LUIGI MARIA GATTO, COUNT FERDINANDO THEUMA-CASTELLETTI, COUNT ROMUALDO BARBARO DEI MARCHESE DI S. GIORGIO, THE GENERAL COMMANDANT (EMMANUELE VITALE), LORENZO SALIBA, ALOISIO BART°· CARAFFA, FELICE CALLIJA, FELIPPO CASTAGNA, B^N· GREGORIO MIFSUD, N^{TO}· PIETRO BUTTIGIEG, PIETRO MALLIA, FORTUNATO DALLI, DR. ERRICO SCERRI, MICHELE CACHIA, VINCENZO BORG, GIUSEPPE FRENDO, DR. GIUSEPPE CASHA, GIUSEPPE MONTEBELLO, ADVOCATE GIUSEPPE HADILLA, FRANCESCO SAVERIO ZARB, SALVATORE GAFÀ, GIOVANNI GAFÀ, FRANCESCO PARISIO, AGOSTINO SAID.

Further correspondence from Captain Ball to Lord Nelson is as follows:—

[Extract.]

CAPTAIN BALL TO LORD NELSON.

[Private.] Malta, *2nd October* 1799.[1]

... The very important trust which their Sicilian Majesties have been pleased to confer upon me through Your Grace's intercession will be a lasting memorial of your goodness to me.

The Maltese have written to Your Grace a letter of thanks on the occasion.

I have just accomplished a plan which has rescued thousands of poor from misery, and is a great source of joy to almost the whole inhabitants, excepting a few wealthy merchants who had oppressed and borne down every class by the length of their purse. The Grand Master Rohan endeavoured to effect it, but did not succeed; this circumstance rewards me most amply for the many anxious nights I have passed here. . . . I have the honour to be, &c. (Signed) ALEX. J^N BALL.

CAPTAIN BALL TO LORD NELSON.

Malta, *2nd October* 1799.[2]

MY LORD,—I am honoured by Your Lordship's letters of the 14th and 19th of last month by the *St. Sebastian* with the dispatch from General Acton, for which I really feel overwhelmed by Your Lordship's unremitting friendship and goodness. I shall write by this conveyance to the General to express my sense of the honour conferred upon me.

The Deputies are not yet landed. In all their letters they expressed that their supplies have been obtained *entirely by Your Lordship's kind exertions*. Should the Russians come this way, I shall pay the strictest attention to Your Lordship's advice, and co-operate heartily with them, as well as execute the order respecting the colours.

[1] Brit. Mus. Add. MSS. 34914, f. 112. [2] *Ibid.* f. 110.

The *Alexander* is in Marsa Scirocco Bay, where she can remain at anchor until La Valette shall be surrendered. We are landing many of her guns for the different batteries, which must be defended chiefly by seamen. If a cable could be sent for the ship I should feel much easier for her safety. I sent my letters which went by the *St. Sebastian* to the Marquis de Niza, who gave them to Monsr. Talleyrand instead of Commodore Michele. This French gentleman came to Malta with the Marquis de Niza, who introduced him to me as his particular friend, and said he was patronised by the Queen, who sent him here, and desired I would give him an opportunity of distinguishing himself on shore. I have been very strict in preventing any foreigner or stranger coming to this Island unless fully authorised by their Majesties, because I am aware of the necessity of guarding against the numerous intrigues and views of different Powers to get possession of it, knowing that if they were to succeed in causing a counter-revolution or a serious disturbance, that my character and honour would materially suffer by it, and I should be thought undeserving the high trust which I have obtained through Your Lordship's patronage.

Nothing but a respect to Her Majesty's orders should have allowed me to receive Mr. Talleyrand, against whom I shall be guarded and take care that he does not intrigue or do any mischief. Lord Blayney will have the honour of explaining to Your Lordship the very many difficulties I have to encounter. I am now erecting batteries, and I shall strain every nerve to expel the French. The expence of making regular approaches is beyond our means. I have therefore given direction to take possession of posts which will put the enemy to the test. The engineer tells me I risk too much, but as there is not any other alternative, except remaining inactive, I have determined upon persevering my own plan, which I am sanguine enough to think will succeed. I have only sufficient money for three weeks' payment of the troops. I have therefore to request Your Lordship to urge His Sicilian Majesty to send another supply. I have mentioned the necessity of having it in my letter to General Acton. I shall make particular inquiry respecting Michel Durazzo, whose petition has been forwarded to me, which I shall answer by the next conveyance, as the ship which takes this sails immediately and will not allow time to do it now. I have the honour to be, &c.   ALEX. JN°· BALL.[1]

On the 7th October 1799 Lord Spencer, from the Admiralty, wrote to Lord Nelson as follows regarding Malta [2]:—

. . . You will receive a copy of a communication on the subject of this Island from the Secretary of State, which was left with Lord Keith, the new Commander-in-Chief, by his predecessor, Lord St. Vincent.[3] I have only to add to what you would collect from that paper, that the utmost importance is attached by His Majesty's Government to the object of

---

[1] Vaubois at this date appears to have held the besieging forces in great contempt. See his letter of the 6th October 1799 in his *Journal of the Siege of Malta* (Part III); also the summons to surrender sent by Niza on October 5th, in the Appendix.—J. H. R.

[2] Nicolas, *Dispatches of Nelson*, vol. iv. p. 116 (edit. 1845).

[3] George Keith (1746–1823) was born at Elphinstone Tower near Stirling. His chief naval services were in assisting the siege of Genoa and Malta in 1800, and the landing of Abercromby's force in Egypt. He was created Viscount Keith in 1814. See Allardyce, *Life of Lord Keith*.—J. H. R.

carefully avoiding to do anything which may raise any jealousies in the mind of the Emperor of Russia, who is particularly bent on the point of restoring, under some new regulations, the Order of Malta; and whose conduct even on this subject, though one on which he may perhaps have been suspected by the world of entertaining more ambitious views, has been, as far as we are enabled to judge of it, of the most disinterested and honourable kind.[1]

Further correspondence from Captain Ball to Lord Nelson is as follows:—

CAPTAIN BALL TO LORD NELSON.

Malta, 10th October 1799.[2]

MY LORD,—I am honoured with Your Lordship's letters of the 27th of last month and the 3rd instant, informing me of the intention of the Russians to assist in the reduction of the French garrison of La Valette, and directing me to co-operate in the most cordial manner. I beg leave to assure Your Lordship that I have been at infinite pains to prepare the minds of the Maltese to give the Russians a favourable reception.

They had many prejudices against them when I first landed, but from the moment I received Your Lordship's instructions respecting them, I employed people of confidence and influence to do away the bad impressions. I am perfectly aware that if the Maltese were to show any aversion to the Russians it would be ascribed to my intrigues. However, I trust that the utmost cordiality will appear, and that Your Lordship will not have any complaints.

I am very glad that the British troops are coming from Messina. I am much prepossessed in favour of General Graham's character, and I have not a doubt of our acting to the utmost for the public good.[3] We are very busy in constructing batteries close to the enemy's fortifications, which when completed will block up the port of La Valette, and make it very difficult for a ship to enter. These works are attended with very heavy expences, because we are upon a rock without soil, which we are obliged to bring from a great distance, and to send to Sicily for all our fascines, &c., &c.

If His Sicilian Majesty cannot send a small monthly supply of money to the Maltese, some other Power must do it, or thousands will die of hunger. When the Maltese revolted against the French, most of the wealthy inhabitants were in La Valette: the few who were in the country had most of their property in the town; the money which was in the country was soon drained by maintaining for the first three months eight thousand men. General Vaubois, to add to their distresses, turned all the poor out of the four towns which are within his fortifications, amounting to several thousands, which brought such an accumulated expence as would have driven the inhabitants to despair had not His Sicilian Majesty's bounty enabled them to extend a temporary relief, which must be continued until La Valette surrenders.

---

[1] In the Introduction I have shown that the trust of our Government in the Czar Paul I. was misplaced.—J. H. R.
[2] Brit. Mus. Add. MSS. 34914, f. 147.
[3] Colonel Graham was to hold the rank of Brigadier-General in Malta only.—J. H. R.

Whatever Power this Island shall be ceded to ought to refund the money His Sicilian Majesty has sent here.

There are likewise expences in the executive department of this Government which are unavoidable. I employ constantly one secretary, three clerks, and two aides-de-camp. The carriages and horses only, cost three hundred pounds a year. The Congress regularly examine the public accounts, who will witness that I shall leave this Island considerably poorer than I entered it, unless an allowance be given me when the business is over. I have the honour, &c.   (Signed) ALEX. J^{N°.} BALL.

CAPTAIN BALL TO LORD NELSON.

Malta, 14*th October* 1799.[1]

MY LORD,—I had the honour to write to Your Lordship the 11th inst. by *La Bonne Citoyenne*, since which I have received your letter of the 3rd inst. by the *Transfer*. General Graham informs me of his having been desired by His Sicilian Majesty to come here with five hundred men, which he cannot do without an order from his Commander-in-Chief at Minorca.

I am constructing batteries very close to the Palace at Bighi, where I hope we shall soon attempt to fix our post, it being highly important and well worth the risk. The military men think it untenable. I am aware it is irregular according to strict tactical rules to go there immediately, but I think if Your Lordship were to see it you would be apt to deviate from the regular progression. General Graham recommends my not attempting any attack until the arrival of succours, but if he delays coming I shall push for Bighi. I have prepared houses for the reception of the English and Russian troops, whose arrival will give great joy to the inhabitants, who know the critical state we are in. Very fortunately for us, General Vaubois is ignorant of it. The Maltese armed peasants are very sickly, caused by want of nourishment and clothing. I have the honour, &c.
(Signed) ALEX. J^{N°.} BALL.[2]

Captain Ball in his letter to Nelson of the 23rd October, whilst again acknowledging the gratitude of the Maltese people for His Lordship's past efforts on their behalf, lays great stress upon the urgent need of

---

[1] Brit. Mus. Add. MSS. 34914, f. 176.

[2] In the midst of all Vaubois' anxieties there appears to have been added to them that of the annoyance of internal dissensions between the civil authorities. This fact may be gathered from a dispatch, dated the 17th October 1799, which Doublet addressed to the Directory, wherein he accuses his colleagues of alleged encroachments upon the prerogatives of his office. He states that he had accepted most reluctantly the post of Commissioner of the Government of Malta, vacated by Regnaud de St. Jean d'Angely on his departure, but soon found that General Vaubois trenched on his functions. He referred the whole matter to the Directory at Paris. As this letter is long and unimportant, I have judged it best to omit it. The concentration of forces in the hands of General Vaubois is described in paragraph 7 of a very detailed report on the condition of Malta, the causes of the revolt against the French rule, the methods to be employed for preventing similar outbreaks, the possibility of adapting the French constitution to the islands, &c. The report (dated 19th October 1799) is too long to be quoted here, as it would interrupt the narrative of the siege. I have therefore relegated it to an Appendix.—J. H. R.

further remittances, which alone could prevent starvation amongst the poorer classes [1]:—

[Extract.]

CAPTAIN BALL TO LORD NELSON.

Malta, 23rd October 1799.[2]

... I have written to General Acton on the subject of sending over a small monthly supply of money to prevent the Maltese armed peasants and numerous poor families starving. I have already explained to Your Lordship the cause of the great distress and scarcity of money. I shall therefore not trespass on Your Lordship by repeating it.

The Maltese are sensible that they owe all the alleviations of their misfortunes to Your Lordship's kind exertions, and they once more implore your benevolent aid, with that of Sir William Hamilton, to extricate them from their deplorable state. I have the honour, &c.

(Signed) ALEX. J$^{no.}$ BALL.

Upon receipt of Lord Spencer's dispatch of the 7th October, referred to at p. 230, Lord Nelson acquainted His Imperial Majesty the Emperor of Russia with the proceedings which had taken place before Malta up to that date, in the following communication:—

Palermo, 31st October 1799.[3]

To His Imperial Majesty, the Emperor of Russia.

SIRE,—As Grand Master of the Order of Malta, I presume to detail to Your Majesty what has been done to prevent the French from re-possessing themselves of the Island, blockading them closely in La Valetta, and what means are now pursuing to force them to surrender. On the 2nd September 1798 the inhabitants of Malta rose against the French robbers, who, having taken all the money in the Island, levied contributions; and Vaubois, as a last act of villainy, said, as baptism was of no use he had sent for all the Church plate. On the 9th, I received a letter from the Deputies of the Island praying assistance to drive the French from La Valetta. I immediately directed the Marquis di Niza, with four sail of the line, to support the Islanders. At this time the crippled ships from Egypt were passing near it, and 2,000 stand of arms, complete with all the musket-ball cartridges, were landed from them, and 200 barrels of powder.

On the 24th October I relieved the Marquis from the station and took the Island of Gozo—a measure absolutely necessary, in order to form the complete blockade of La Valetta, the garrison of which at this time was composed of 7,000 French, including the seamen and some few Maltese; the inhabitants in the town, about 30,000; the Maltese in arms, volunteers,

---

[1] In reply, Nelson wrote to Ball from Palermo about 26th October 1799 that he had begged, almost on his knees, for money for the Maltese. He states that he hopes that at least 5,000 Russians will soon reach Malta. (*Nelson's Dispatches*, vol. iv. p. 68.)

By October 26, 1799, Nelson had come to see the extreme need of reducing Valetta, 'knowing the importance of possessing Malta to England and her Allies.' (*Ibid.* p. 69.)—J. H. R.

[2] Brit. Mus. Add. MSS. 34914, f. 237.

[3] Pettigrew, *Nelson's Dispatches*, vol. i. p. 325.

never exceeded 3,000.[1] I entrusted the blockade to Captain Alexander John Ball, of the *Alexander*, 74, an officer not only of the greatest merit, but of the most conciliating manners. From that period to this time it has fell to my lot to arrange for the feeding of 60,000 people, the population of Malta and Gozo; the arming the peasantry; and, the most difficult task, that of keeping up harmony between the Deputies of the Island. Hunger, fatigue, and corruption appeared several times in the Island, and amongst the Deputies. The situation of Italy, in particular this kingdom (the Two Sicilies), oftentimes reduced me to the greatest difficulties where to find food. Their Sicilian Majesties at different times have given more, I believe, than £40,000 in money and corn. The blockade in the expense of keeping the ships destined alone for this service (cost) full £180,000 sterling. It has pleased God hitherto to bless our endeavours to prevent supplies getting to the French, except one frigate and two small vessels with a small portion of salt provisions. Your Majesty will have the goodness to observe, that until it was known that you were elected Grand Master, and that the Order was to be restored in Malta, I never allowed an idea to go abroad that Great Britain had any wish to keep it. I therefore directed His Sicilian Majesty's flag to be hoisted, as I am told, had the Order not been restored, that he is the legitimate Sovereign of the Island.

Never less than 500 men have been landed from the squadron, which, although with the volunteers not sufficient to commence a siege, have yet kept posts and battery not more than 400 yards from the works. The quarrels of the nobles and misconduct of the chiefs rendered it absolutely necessary that some proper person should be placed at the head of the Island.

His Sicilian Majesty, therefore, by the united request of the whole Island, named Captain Ball for their chief director, and he will hold it till Your Majesty as Grand Master appoints a person to the office. Now the French are nearly expelled from Italy, by the valour and skill of your generals and army, all my thoughts are turned towards the placing the Grand Master and the Order of Malta in security in La Valetta, for which purpose I have just been at Minorca, and arranged with the English General a force of 2,500 British troops, cannon, bombs, &c., &c., for the siege. I have wrote to Your Majesty's Admiral, and His Sicilian Majesty joins cordially in the good work of endeavouring to drive the French from Malta.

In reply to another appeal for money, which was made this month, it was alleged by the Neapolitan Government to be out of their power to give any further pecuniary assistance beyond oz. 4,000 (£2,000), which was duly remitted towards the close of the month, when Nelson informed Ball 'that the larger sums required must now come from the three Allied Powers.'

During the following month of November, however, Nelson managed to prevail upon the Neapolitan Government to make another remittance, which will be referred to later on. The official advice of the intention of the Powers to restore the Order to the possession of

---

[1] The figures are inaccurate.—J. H. R.

the islands, under the Grand Mastership of the Czar, was now made public, and it was further added that His Majesty had been requested to be prepared to nominate his deputy to rule in the island immediately the fortress of Valetta should fall.

The former orders regarding the colours were cancelled, and, instead thereof, instructions were given for those of the Order to be hoisted the moment the French flag should be struck.

Meanwhile the condition of the inhabitants had become most deplorable, particularly of those who bore arms, who for some time had been not only without pay but also clothing, when fortunately, within six weeks, the first of the British contingent arrived in Malta, an event which had been vaguely referred to during the past month.

Minorca at this time was occupied by a British force, under the command of Major-General Sir James St. Clair Erskine, Bart. (afterwards Earl of Rosslyn, G.C.B.), and as Vaubois showed no signs of surrender, it was deemed advisable to apply for military aid, both from Minorca and from the British force which held the citadel of Messina. Erskine was requested to lend one or two regiments for a month or two; and, in order to secure this further assistance, Nelson determined upon visiting Minorca, sailing from Palermo on the 5th October, and arriving at Port Mahon before the 14th.

General St. Clair Erskine's command, however, was about to terminate, and his successor, General Fox, was daily expected. Under these circumstances Erskine felt disinclined to listen to Nelson's appeal, the more so as there was every probability that Fox would be the bearer of specific orders from the War Office, and desired that the question should remain in abeyance until Fox arrived.

Before sailing for Minorca, Nelson wrote from Palermo to Brigadier-General Graham, then commanding at Messina, under date of the 3rd October, informing him that he, Graham, would probably receive an application from His Sicilian Majesty to proceed to Malta with 500 men, part of the garrison of the citadel of Messina, and that the *Alliance*, on board of which there were two mortars and 700 shell for Malta, would sail [1] thence for Messina, for the embarkation of his troops.

On the same day Captain Ball, as chief of the Maltese, was made acquainted with the endeavour being made 'to obtain British troops from Messina, and was further advised that for this step to be successful it would be necessary for him to be as conciliatory as possible with General Graham in the divided command.'[2] It was further stated that 'whilst the British troops would naturally be under the exclusive command of the general, some of the Maltese insurgents might be added to the British regulars, if Ball so deemed it advisable.' Graham, however, did not feel justified in quitting his post until he received direct authority from his chief at Port Mahon.

[1] Nicolas, *Dispatches of Nelson*, vol. iv. p. 41 (edit. 1845).   [2] *Ibid.*

Nelson in due course informed the Admiralty of his arrival at Port Mahon, 'for the purpose of concerting measures with General Sir James St. Clair Erskine to force a surrender' of Malta; adding, 'It is of the very greatest importance to us and our Allies that a land force should be assisting our labours for its reduction.'[1] Five hundred English and Portuguese marines were the only help he had hitherto been able to give the islanders.

General Erskine was evidently desirous of rendering what assistance he could, for he expressly wished the *Dover* should be retained to carry the troops, if General Fox, his successor, upon arrival, approved of the measure.

During all this uncertainty in endeavouring to obtain British military aid, Nelson was informed that the Portuguese Government were most anxious to withdraw their squadron, and that instructions to that effect had been sent to Rear-Admiral the Marquis de Niza, commanding the Portuguese squadron off Valetta.

This called forth a spirited protest from Nelson, and the exercise of his authority as commander-in-chief, and counter-orders for them to remain were given.

Under these trying circumstances Nelson wrote to the general commanding the forces at Minorca, under date of the 26th October:[2]

I am in desperation about Malta; we shall lose it, I am afraid, past redemption. If Ball can hardly keep the inhabitants in hopes of relief by the 500 men landed from our ships, what must be expected when 400 of them and four sail of the line be withdrawn?

Nelson closed his letter with a fervent appeal that Graham should be permitted to proceed from Messina, and hold Malta until troops could be collected for attacking Valetta.

At this critical moment Lieut.-General the Honourable H. Fox,[3] who had been appointed to the command of the British troops in the Mediterranean, arrived at Port Mahon on the 10th November 1799, and as the question of reinforcing the troops then employed for the reduction of Valetta had to be immediately settled, he wrote on the 12th to the Right Honourable H. Dundas, then officiating as Secretary of State for the War Department, to the effect that 'he did not feel authorised to detach troops from Minorca for that purpose, but intended to remove the British garrison at Messina to Malta, under the command of Colonel Graham, with the rank of Brigadier-General.'[4] This dispatch was as follows:—

[1] Nicolas, *Dispatches of Nelson*, vol. iv. p. 41 (ed. 1845).
[2] *Ibid.* p. 69.
[3] Henry Edward Fox (1755–1811), brother of the statesman Charles James Fox, entered the army in 1770, served in America and Flanders, and commanded the British forces in Sicily in 1806-7.—J. H. R.
[4] This rank only held good during Graham's service in Malta, as appears from the following dispatch. See too *Memoirs of Lord Lynedoch* (London, 1877).—J. H. R.

Mahon, 12th November 1799.[1]

The Right Hon. Henry Dundas.

SIR,—Upon my arrival here on the 10th inst., Major-General Sir James St. Clair [Erskine] communicated to me several letters he received from Lord Nelson and Sir William Hamilton, and also made me acquainted with a conversation he had with Lord Nelson on the same subject.

As I did myself the honour of observing to you in my letter of the 3rd inst. from Gibraltar, that I did not consider myself authorised by my instructions to give troops to Lord Nelson from the Island of Minorca as a reinforcement for the purpose of reducing Malta, not knowing what might be His Majesty's intentions in respect to part of the force now here, I have written to His Lordship to that purpose, and have the honour to enclose a copy of my letter.

Major-General Sir James St. Clair [Erskine] will forward to you His Lordship's correspondence and his answers.

From the short time I have been here I cannot hazard an opinion formed upon my own observation, but must beg leave to refer you to that of Sir James St. Clair [Erskine] in his correspondence with His Lordship, and which from his long residence and knowledge of this part of the world, added to his good sense and professional abilities, I place every reliance on.

The 28th Regiment will embark in a day or two for Gibraltar.

I have conceived it necessary for His Majesty's service to give Colonel Graham the rank of Brigadier-General in the Island of Malta, with the annexed instructions in the event of Lord Nelson requiring the two regiments from Messina. I have the honour, &c.

(Signed) H. E. Fox.

On the same day definite instructions were given to Colonel Graham, as follows :—

Mahon, 12th November 1799.[2]

To Colonel Graham.

SIR,—I am directed by Lieut.-General Fox, commanding His Majesty's troops in the Mediterranean, to inform you that in case Rear-Admiral Lord Nelson shall require you to embark with the whole or any part of the British troops of your garrison for the Island of Malta, you are to comply with that requisition, His Lordship having provided means for your conveyance. The discretionary power for His Lordship to call upon you is in consequence of His Lordship's most urgent representation, and the object and purpose of the measure will be to co-operate with His Majesty's ships, and with the troops and ships of his allies, if there be any such in the blockade of Malta; and the Lieut.-General directs you will observe the following instructions.

You will have the command of His Majesty's forces serving on shore, and you will act in concert with Captain Ball, or the officer commanding His Majesty's ships on that station, and will do all in your power to preserve a good understanding and perfect harmony with him and the officers commanding any other troops who may be employed in the same service. You are not authorised to incur any expense for the provision of

[1] C.O.R. Malta, No. 1 (1799-1800). [2] Ibid.

stores, or, in fact, any extraordinary expense, except such as shall be in your judgment necessary for the subsistence, comfort, and health of your troops. The Assistant-Commissary-Genl. sent on this service will be instructed to provide the means of paying the troops their pay and allowances, and furnish them with provisions, according to the regulations of this army; and you are directed not to enter, on account of any operation against Malta, into any expenses which are not authorised under similar circumstances by your present instructions as Governor of the citadel of Messina. In the posts you take up, your object will be to secure your own troops, and to provide against the possibility of an attack from the enemy; and in every future operation your first duty is to avoid committing the small force under your command in any situation where they cannot make the most advantageous resistance that their numbers will permit to the attack of a superior enemy.

If upon your arrival off Malta you shall be of opinion, from such information as you may obtain, either from any reverse of circumstances, or other strong reasons, that it is unsafe or imprudent to land the troops under your command, you are empowered to decline doing so, and directed to return to Messina. Or if, after acquiring a full knowledge of the situation of the Island, the force and state of the enemy, and the disposition of the Maltese of all ranks, you shall be of opinion that the blockade cannot be materially assisted from the land side by the force under your command, or that your corps is in your judgment placed in an insecure position and exposed to the dangers of being cut off or surrounded, or in any other case in which upon mature deliberation you shall judge it to be for the essential interests of His Majesty's service that you should withdraw from the Island, you are hereby authorised and required so to do, and to call upon the commanding officer of His Majesty's ships to reimbark the troops under your command, when you will return to Messina.

You will take every opportunity of communicating to the Lieut.-General, not only the actual situation and progress of the operations carried on, but also your opinion of the probable result thereof, particularly respecting the numbers, character, and dispositions of the Maltese. I have the honour, &c. (Signed) R^D. STEWART, Adj^t.-Genl.

The instructions given to Brigadier-General Graham were communicated direct to Nelson by General Fox on the same date, as follows:—

Mahon, 12*th November* 1799.[1]

The Right Honble. Lord Nelson, K.B.

MY LORD,—Upon my arrival here, the 10th inst., Major-General Sir James St. Clair communicated to me your several letters, as well as those from Sir William Hamilton, and informed me of the conversation that had passed between Your Lordship and him; and I must confess I coincide in opinion with Sir James on this subject.

From the instructions I have received I do not conceive myself at liberty to detach troops from this garrison except by particular orders from home. But General O'Hara[2] having communicated to me at Gibraltar

---

[1] C.O.R. Malta, No. 1 (1799–1800).
[2] General O'Hara distinguished himself greatly at the siege of Toulon in 1793. He had long been Governor of Gibraltar.—J. H. R.

Your Lordship's letter of the 15th October, I wrote from thence to Mr. Dundas, enclosing an extract of your letter, requesting to be honoured with His Majesty's commands on that head as speedily as possible. But as it is stated in my instructions (an extract from which I have the honour to enclose) that for the expulsion of the French from Malta to send one or both, if they can be spared, of the British regiments in garrison at Messina, I think myself warranted in agreeing to those regiments, or a detachment from them, proceeding to Malta, should Your Lordship, after considering the nature of my instructions, still think it necessary for His Majesty's service. It will then rest solely with Your Lordship to determine how far their presence can be dispensed with in the Island of Sicily, and from the express purposes for which they were originally destined. It would be presumption in me to assure Your Lordship, whose very superior abilities and discernment have been so repeatedly displayed in the various and extensive services you have rendered His Majesty's arms, that I am confident you will not allow these troops to be employed where there is not a very great probability of success, and where a failure might deprive His Majesty of their future services. And I am also to observe that it depends upon Your Lordship to make the necessary arrangements for the providing the stores and supplies requisite for the troops from Messina (their subsistence excepted), as I cannot authorise Brigadier-General Graham to incur any sort of expense to Government on that account.

The British troops from Messina will be under the immediate command of Brigadier-General Graham, an officer of high reputation and known abilities, and who by his instructions (a copy of which I have the honour to enclose) is authorised to withdraw these troops should he conceive it to be absolutely necessary. I beg to assure Your Lordship that not a moment shall be lost, and that every exertion shall be made to have the troops in readiness to embark should I receive His Majesty's commands to that effect.

I am also to acquaint Your Lordship that the 28th Regiment, about 700 strong, are to embark immediately for Gibraltar, in consequence of orders I have received from home. I have the honour, &c.

(Signed) H. E. Fox.

Nelson received Fox's dispatch of the 12th November on the 25th, when Commodore Sir Thomas Troubridge was ordered to sail on that same day from Palermo for Messina, with his ship the *Culloden*, the *Foudroyant* following, and there embark the troops under Brigadier-General Graham, with stores, guns, ammunition, and provisions for Malta.

The restricted conditions regarding the necessary disbursements referred to in General Fox's dispatch were most disappointing and galling both to Lord Nelson and to Commodore Troubridge. The latter, fearing that delay would be the consequence, wrote to Nelson from Messina :

I have procured for Graham, my Lord, fifteen thousand of my cobs ; every farthing, and every atom of me, shall be devoted to the cause.[1]

[r] Brit. Mus. Add. MSS. 34915, f. 84.

Whilst Nelson on his part wrote:

> The cause cannot stand still for want of a little money . . . if nobody will pay it I will sell Bronté and the Emperor of Russia's box.[1]

Graham's departure with the troops from Messina was preceded by that of Lieutenant-Colonel Lindenthal from Port Mahon with orders to 'repair to Malta, and report on the position of affairs, and to render assistance to General Graham upon his arrival.' Lindenthal (an Austrian by birth) was an officer attached to the Minorca Regiment, and on the personal staff of General Fox.

The following letters of Ball to Nelson, dated the 3rd, 7th, 11th, and 18th November, refer to the great distress of the Maltese, for want of food and money, and consequent sickness, to the restoration of the Order, and to the contemplated withdrawal of the Portuguese fleet.

CAPTAIN BALL TO LORD NELSON.

St. Antoine, Island of Malta, *3rd November* 1799.[2]

MY LORD,—I beg leave to represent to Your Lordship the extreme necessity of a speedy supply of corn being sent for the inhabitants of this Island, otherwise they will be in the greatest distress. We have not yet received any of the corn which His Sicilian Majesty has been graciously pleased to order to be sent. I have the honour, &c.

(Signed) ALEX. JNº· BALL.

CAPTAIN BALL TO LORD NELSON.

Malta, *7th November* 1799.[3]

MY LORD,—I am honoured with Your Grace's letters of the 26th, 27th, and 28th of last month acquainting me that the Order of Malta is to be restored and their flag hoisted so soon as the French flag is struck, when the French shall surrender. I hope to prove myself deserving of the important trust Your Grace has been pleased to confide to me, by taking care of the honour of His Britannic Majesty, His Sicilian Majesty, and paying due respect to our faithful ally the Portuguese.

The four thousand ounces which His Sicilian Majesty has been pleased to send here for the support of the armed peasants arrived just in time to save this country from the most critical and perilous state. This is the second time that Your Grace and Sir William Hamilton have by your energetic measures rescued these poor islanders from famine, and all its dreadful consequences.

The British and Portuguese officers with their marines are sickly. The Maltese are equally so, one-third nearly unfit for duty owing to fatigue of service and occupying unhealthy posts. The Maltese are almost naked and totally unfit for winter service.

I shall derive great satisfaction in seeing Your Grace that you may witness the many difficulties I have had to stem.

---

[1] Nicolas, *Dispatches of Nelson*, vol. iv. p. 116 (edit. 1845).
[2] Brit. Mus. Add. MSS. 34914, f. 296.   [3] *Ibid.* f. 316.

The Marquis de Niza has conducted himself in a manner highly honourable, indeed I can never do sufficient justice to his merit and zeal, in disobeying such peremptory orders from his Court, which I believe is contrary to the opinion of most of his squadron, who quote General Graham refusing to come to our assistance, although solicited by His Sicilian Majesty and Your Grace. . . . I have the honour, &c.

(Signed) ALEX. JN⁰· BALL.

CAPTAIN BALL TO LORD NELSON.

Malta, 11th November 1799.[1]

MY LORD,—I have the honour to inform Your Grace that the four thousand ounces which H.S. Majesty was graciously pleased to send for the support of the Maltese armed peasants will only serve a fortnight, I am therefore under the necessity of requesting Your Grace to apply to the Ambassadors of those Sovereigns who guarantee the government of this Island to contribute their proportion for its support, otherwise famine and all its dreadful consequences will ensue. I have so repeatedly mentioned the cause of the great distress of these poor islanders that I conceive it unnecessary to enter into a detail. We are much in want of two thousand cartouch boxes, one thousand bayonets, and two thousand flints. I have the honour, &c. (Signed) ALEX. JN⁰· BALL.

CAPTAIN BALL TO LORD NELSON.

Malta, 18th November 1799.[2]

MY LORD,—I had the honour of writing to Your Grace by the *Foudroyant*, since which there has not been any particular occurrence.

The French permitted a great many Maltese to quit La Valette last week, one of whom informed me that he was commissioned to acquaint me that the enemy intend making a sortie in a few days, and that their ships will certainly sail the first favourable opportunity. I conceive the intention of the sortie is to destroy our guns and mortars, that the ships may escape without damage from our batteries. A few days ago we wounded the French Adjutant-General and some of his men, who came out to reconnoitre our new battery. The Maltese report that many were killed. Of this I have some doubt, but I am certain of the General being wounded. I am sorry that the *Minotaur's* marines were not landed according to the order of the Marquis, as their number would have eased the duty of the troops on shore.

The Marquis de Niza is extremely anxious to put into execution the orders of his Court. I can never sufficiently praise the zeal, and the desire he has of meriting your friendship. I hope the Emperor will give him the Grand Croix for his services here, I believe it would be highly gratifying to him. I hope for the honour of seeing Your Grace for a few days, and particularly if troops can be sent, as we shall then make a speedy finish of this tedious siege. I have put the Russian officer (who came here to serve in the squadron) on board of the *Audacious*, as I have already one on board of the *Alexander*. I have the honour, &c.

(Signed) ALEX. JN⁰· BALL.

[1] Brit. Mus. Add. MSS. 34914, f. 343.   [2] Ibid. 34915, f. 27.

CHAPTER XIII

THE BRITISH BLOCKADE

(From the 25th November 1799 to the 24th February 1800)

GENERAL FOX's permission for the embarkation of the Messina contingent of British troops was acknowledged by Lord Nelson, on the 25th November, in the following letter, which is not in the Nelson Dispatches :—

Palermo, 25th November 1799.[1]

His Excellency Hon. Gen. Fox.

SIR,—I am this moment honoured with Your Excellency's letter of November 12th, and I can assure you that on all occasions I shall co-operate most cordially with you on all points of public service, and in every situation to make your residence at Minorca as comfortable as possible.

If Malta can be held, of which I have strong doubts, till the arrival of the troops from Messina, and those of the Russians from Naples, it will very soon be taken, which will be a very great relief to our ships, and enable us the better to pay attention to Minorca, and the northern coast of Italy, for I believe [from] what I hear, that the French mean to try their strength again in Italy. The Russians, 2,400 grenadiers, were to sail from Naples on the 19th, therefore I hope by this day they are at Malta.

As the *Minotaur* is only standing into the bay to take this letter, I trust for your excuse in being so short. Ancona surrendered to the Austrians 14 days past. Believe me, &c.

(Signed) BRONTE NELSON.

Graham was also informed by Nelson on the 25th, that Commodore Sir Thomas Troubridge in his ship the *Culloden* would remain for some time co-operating with him for the reduction of Malta, and that Ball had been, by His Sicilian Majesty (the legitimate sovereign of the island), placed at the head of the Maltese, in both civil and (as he understood) military capacities, and that in any capitulation he thought Ball should sign. That it was further the desire of the British Government to gratify the Czar in every wish

---

[1] C.O.R. Malta, No. L.

about the Order of Malta, and concluded by saying, that if help in corn for the inhabitants should be required, it had been agreed by the ministers of Russia, Naples, and England to defray the expense by their respective Governments.[1]

Troubridge's instructions were dated the same day, and to the effect, That upon the departure of the Portuguese squadron from off Malta he was to assume command of the blockade. That in the event of the surrender of Malta the colours of the Order were to be hoisted, and that Government restored. That all public property should be valued, and the ships of war found in the harbours should remain at the disposal of the three allied Courts of London, St. Petersburg, and the Two Sicilies.

The question of victualling Malta continued to be a source of great anxiety to Lord Nelson, and upon the receipt of Ball's letter of the 11th November, already referred to, describing the destitution to which the Maltese had been reduced owing to the want of funds, he appears to have made a further urgent and successful application to His Majesty the King, for on the 28th November Sir William Hamilton received from the Prime Minister, the Chevalier Acton, the following communication:—

[Translation.]

Palermo, 28th November 1799.[2]

His Sicilian Majesty having foolishly consented to a remittance of eight thousand ounces (£4,000) being made to Captain Ball for the inhabitants of Malta, the Chevalier Acton, in informing Your Excellency the Chevalier Hamilton, Envoy Extraordinary and Minister Plenipotentiary of England, of this decision, begs that you will have the goodness to notify the same to Lord Nelson, and request His Lordship to issue the necessary orders, so that the said sum may be paid to him immediately.

The Chevalier Acton further requests his Excellency Sir William Hamilton to make his apologies for being unable, through stress of work at the present moment, to have the honour of addressing His Lordship direct, but he reserves that pleasure to some future time.

In the meanwhile the Chevalier Acton has the honour to confirm to the Chevalier Hamilton the sense of his high consideration.

The tone of this letter, the fact of its being written in the third person, and that it would have taken no more time to have addressed it direct to Lord Nelson, whom the subject more particularly concerned, than to write to Sir William direct, is convincing proof that the Chevalier Acton, probably owing to the Maltese having heartily expressed a wish to transfer the sovereignty of the islands to Great Britain, was opposed to this further grant of money.

[1] Nicolas, *Dispatches of Nelson*, vol. iv. pp. 108, 109 (edit. 1845).
[2] Brit. Mus. Add. MSS. 34946, f. 199.

Brigadier-General Graham acknowledged the receipt of General Fox's instructions of the 12th November in the following dispatch :—

Citadel of Messina, *4th November* 1799.[1]

Lt.-General the Honble. H. Fox, &c.

SIR,—I had the honour of receiving Your Excellency's dispatch of the 12th November, with the several enclosures mentioned on the 28th ulto., at the same time that Sir Thos. Troubridge brought me a letter from Lord Nelson, desiring me to lose no time in going to Malta.

The weather has been extremely unfavourable ever since, heavy falls from the S.E. with much rain. This has given time for receiving an answer from Palermo, where I thought it of consequence to send an express in order to know from Lord Nelson, to whose requisitions you referred me, whether the British were to go, and whether if any part were left under the care of a field officer, the command here would be intrusted to him, and I shall now carry the arrangement I wished to make into execution, an arrangement which, under all the contingent circumstances (provided for in the instructions contained in the Adjutant's letter to me) that may make it necessary to return, I hope you will approve of.

I shall embark about 800 rank and file, leaving Major Lockhart of the 30th Regiment with four other officers and the remainder of the men in this fortress, by which means, without any diminution of our force worth consideration, we shall move free from such encumbrance. The sick and convalescents will be much better accommodated, and quarters in good order will be secured for the men should we return here.

I have experienced considerable difficulty on account of the want of money, the English merchants here not being able to supply us as formerly, on account of the low course of exchange at Leghorn, where bills on London cannot be negotiated till the arrival of a convoy from England. Prince Cuto, the Governor of Messina, has very obligingly interfered, and a sum equal to the pay of the troops and their supply in the most material articles of provisions for two months has been raised by way of loan for three months on my bills.

I have availed myself of the power granted me by H.S.M. of taking ordnance stores from hence, and I hope we shall get one company of the Neapolitan Artillery, which would be a great addition to our force in *every* case, as they would meanwhile be useful in securing our post from insult. But I sincerely wish a considerable reinforcement may soon arrive from Minorca, under the command of an officer more capable than I am of judging of the expediency of adopting offensive operations, and of directing properly their execution.

Should all the Russian troops talked of arrive, the regular force will not be equal in numbers to the garrison. Much indeed may be expected from the Navy, but very little I doubt from the Maltese, so that unless some very favourable circumstances occur, there can be little hope of reducing one of the strongest fortresses in Europe with so small a force by any other means than by blockade. You may be assured, however, sir, that nothing in my power shall be wanting to endeavour to justify the favourable opinion you are pleased to express, but I beg leave to mention

[1] C.O.R. Malta, No. 1.

that it would be material assistance if you could spare me any officers of Engineers and Artillery. I imagine, notwithstanding the delays occasioned by the bad weather, the embarkation of the stores and provisions will be completed to-morrow or the following morning, then nothing will detain us but contrary winds and the want of the blankets and camp equipage, which are to be brought by the *Northumberland*, not yet arrived. I have the honour, &c. (Signed) THOS. GRAHAM, Governor, &c.

Sir William Hamilton, despairing of getting further help from the Neapolitan Government, informed Lord Grenville on the 6th November of the concerted measures which had been agreed upon by the representatives of England, Russia, and Naples for granting pecuniary aid to the distressed Maltese, but this agreement, so far as Russia was concerned, was of short duration.

[Extract.]

SIR WM. HAMILTON TO LORD GRENVILLE.

Palermo, 6th December 1799.[1]

. . . The poor, brave, and loyal inhabitants of Malta have often been at the point of surrendering to the French from extreme hunger and misery, and would have done so if they had not been prevented by the extraordinary efforts of Captain Ball, of H.M. ship *Alexander*, and the small sums of money, and some little provisions which Lord Nelson and I obtained for them from time to time *with the utmost difficulty from this Government*.[2] In order to prevent this inconveniency for the future, particularly as this Government refused to advance any more money or provisions solely on its own account, Lord Nelson, the Chevalier Italinski (the Russian Minister), and myself had a meeting with General Acton, when it was agreed by the end of the month that in future the expense of keeping the loyal Maltese from starving should be placed to the account of the three above-mentioned Powers.

Returning to the subject of active operations, it has to be recorded that in approaching Messina to embark the troops, the *Foudroyant* got on shore, but sustained little or no damage, and as the *Northumberland* (Captain Martin) had also arrived at Messina, she was ordered, with the *Culloden*, to receive the 30th and 89th Regiments. At 9 a.m. the 6th December, this force, in all 800 strong, marched from the citadel and embarked; and at 2 p.m. of the same day the *Culloden* and her consorts got under weigh, and by early morning of the 9th entered St. Paul's Bay, Malta.

After landing the troops, the ships were ordered round to Marsa Scirocco Bay to discharge their stores, &c., a fortified depôt having been established at that post. The *Culloden*, in going round to land cannon, ammunition, &c., unfortunately struck on a rock, resulting

[1] Foreign Office Records, Sicily, No. 12.
[2] See Nelson's note of about December 1, 1799, that he could not urge the King of Naples for more funds. (*Dispatches of Nelson*, vol. iv. p. 123.)—J. H. R.

in her rudder and greater part of the false keel being carried away. This was the second accident of the same nature which happened to the *Culloden*, the first having taken place at the battle of the Nile.

Upon the arrival of Commodore Troubridge, the Portuguese Admiral, Marquis de Niza, again notified to Nelson that he had received express orders from his Government to return to Lisbon with the fleet under his command without further delay—drawing attention to the fact that Generals Erskine and Graham had, on a former occasion, declined to disobey orders, even to save Malta, and that he ought not to be expected to do so. The circumstances being now entirely different from what existed when the first threatened withdrawal of the Portuguese squadron was made, and Nelson now having his intimate and valiant Troubridge in command of a reinforced blockading squadron with two British regiments, besides marines and sailors on shore, and with promised troops from Sicily shortly expected, he very willingly acquiesced in the Marquis de Niza's request, and under date of the 18th December, officially notified that he no longer considered the Portuguese Admiral and his fleet to be under his command.[1]

General Fox was duly informed of the safe arrival at Malta of the expedition by a dispatch from Brigadier-General Graham, as follows :—

St. Antonio, Malta, 10*th December* 1799.[2]

Lt.-General the Hon. Henry Fox, &c.

Sir,—I have the honour to inform your Excellency that the ships anchored in St. Paul's Bay yesterday, and that the troops disembarked this morning, and marched into cantonments in the villages of Birchircara and Nasciar in this neighbourhood.

As I have scarcely seen anything yet, and as Lt.-Colonel Lindenthal is to write by this opportunity, I will not say anything more about our situation here than I think it must remain a very critical one till reinforcements arrive, the more so as there is a necessity of separating so much these two regiments in order to occupy posts which are left by the Portuguese marines already ordered to embark. I have been reconciled to this temporary distribution of the force by the assurance from Colonel Lindenthal, in whose judgement and experience I have much confidence, that there is no risk, the advanced posts of the marines and Maltese being so well arranged that the enemy could not without much difficulty penetrate through them. Their not having attempted to do so for many months, when there were fewer troops on the Island, is a favourite argument with everybody here that they will never attempt it now.

I own I am not much convinced by it, for on the Island they seem to have lately undertaken several operations, which may render it almost necessary for the enemy to make a sortie, and which I am sure they could

---

[1] He added warm words of commendation to Niza for his activity and zeal. Nelson at that time could not get the Russian Admiral to sail from Naples to Malta. (See *Dispatches of Nelson*, vol. iv. pp. 144, 145.)—J. H. R.

[2] C.O.R. Malta, No. 1.

not have resisted so as to protect the works they have constructed. Having no engineer with me, I shall endeavour to keep Colonel Lindenthal as long as possible, and I shall direct his attention towards making some posts very sure, in case we should be obliged to fall back before the arrival of the Russians.

Citta Veccha will, I imagine, very easily be put in that situation, but the most interesting point I imagine will be the harbour of Marsa Scirocco at the eastern extremity of the Island, and which affords much better shelter for ships than St. Paul's, and is more convenient for the landing of stores, &c., near the posts. The 30th Regiment moves to-morrow from Birchircara to that side into the villages of Casal Asciak and Zeitun, and a part of the 89th replaces them, three companies remaining at Nasciar. If without opening the blockade altogether on this left side I can concentrate them more, I shall certainly be anxious to do it. I have the honour, &c. (Signed) THOS. GRAHAM.

Ball's dispatch to Nelson relative to the arrival of the British troops is as follows:—

CAPTAIN BALL TO LORD NELSON.

Malta, 10*th December* 1799.[1]

MY LORD,—I am honoured with Your Grace's letter of the 19th of last month acquainting me that the Chev^r Italinski will be here in a few days, at which I rejoice much, from the very high opinion which you and Sir William Hamilton have of his abilities and worth. I had the pleasure of being frequently in his company last year at Sir William's, where we formed rather an intimate acquaintance.

Your Grace may easily conceive the joy of the Maltese on the arrival of Sir Thomas Troubridge with the two regiments under the command of General Graham; they all disembarked this morning. Lieut.-Col. Lindenthal arrived here the 6th instant from Minorca, sent by General Fox as an experienced and intelligent officer, to examine and report upon the state of La Valette and the other works in possession of the enemy. He expressed his surprise at the enemy allowing us to advance our batteries so near, which, he says, cannot be better connected or more judiciously placed.

He does not think of any measures but what are defensive for the present. He is astonished that the French have not made a sortie, and although we are so strengthened, he does not think we are in a very safe situation. I understand General Graham's orders suggest great caution, and that if he thought his force not sufficient he had the power of returning to Messina. . . . I shall send to General Acton by this opportunity the account of the expenditure of the money sent here by His Sicilian Majesty. . . . I have the honour, &c.

(Signed) ALEX. JN^o BALL.

Colonel Lindenthal, who had preceded Graham's expedition, reached Malta on the 6th December, and on the 10th reported to General Fox from St. Antonio Palace, on the position, as follows[2]:—

[1] Brit. Mus. Add. MSS. 34915, f. 173.   [2] C.O.R. Malta, No. 1.

I avail myself of the earliest opportunity to report to you that I landed here the 6th instant, and Brig.-Gen. Graham with the two regiments arrived yesterday at St. Paul's Bay. I had just before seen sufficient of the different posts and their communication before Valetta to judge that the regiments may disembark in safety, which accordingly was effected to-day. Tho' in so short a time it would be impossible to give a perfect account of the state of affairs here, yet I will endeavour to answer such points in question of your instructions as may be of more consequence to be known immediately. The fortifications of Valetta and dependence are so strong that I do not suppose there will ever be sent here an army provided with the necessary artillery stores and provisions requisite for a regular siege. But there is every probability that the place might be forced to capitulate in less than two months if the blockade can be continued to that period, enforced at the same time by sending more troops and artillery to harass and frighten the enemy, who is by no means strong enough for such extensive works. But all what has been said of a speedy surrender of the place, in case we could make a show of regular troops, has no foundation whatsoever.

The garrison has still provisions for three months,[1] including the inhabitants, and tho' it will be difficult to ascertain the quantity of their ammunition, what I have seen of their useless firing could not make me suppose that they are afraid of want.

The forces forming the blockade by land at present consist of—

Two regiments of infantry . . .	800 men
Marines	400 ,,
Maltese soldiers	1,500 ,,

In case of a general attack we may depend upon 1,000 more armed Maltese. It is a pity we have not thought of forming this poor people into regiments; they are very much attached to us, and have really performed wonders.

The articles most wanted at present are a detachment of artillery, consisting at least of 3 officers and 50 men. There is at present only one officer here, Lieut. Vivion.

The guns are served by Maltese or sailors. There are no instruments for workmen here but what can be supplied from the Navy; no wood for making platforms. Some engineer officers, with about 20 artificers, are also wanted; as also a Power for paying the workmen and other accidental [sic] expences. As there is nobody here doing the duty of the Q.-M.-Gl.'s department, I should recommend Lieut. Vivion of the Royal Artillery, for our assistant, who during twelve months does here alone the duty for almost every department.

The extensive ground occupied by our small force makes the arrival of 3,000 Russian troops every day more necessary. The Portuguese squadron is returning to Portugal to-morrow. I have the honour, &c.

(Signed) LINDENTHAL.

On the 9th December, as already mentioned, His Majesty's ships *Northumberland* and *Culloden* arrived with Graham's contingent,

---

[1] It proved to be nine months. (Note of Mr. Hardman.)

consisting of the 30th and 89th Regiments, and anchored in St. Paul's Bay. On the 10th the troops disembarked and marched into cantonments at Birchircara and Nasicar, which permitted the Portuguese marines to re-embark. The head-quarters' staff was for the time being located at St. Antonio Palace, but by the end of the month it was removed to Gudia.

On the 11th December the 30th Regiment was ordered to proceed and occupy the villages of Asciak and Zeitun, so as to be nearer the harbour of Marsa Scirocco, which was found to be better sheltered, and more convenient for the landing of stores. Eighteen days later a further number of marines were landed from the *Culloden* and *Northumberland*, allowing the whole of the 30th Regiment to be concentrated at Zeitun, with charge of the advanced posts at Zabbar and the battery of Santo Rocco on the right, leaving the 89th Regiment at Gudia and Lucca to look after the post of Tarscien and the battery in front of it, the marines being left on the San Giuseppe road in charge of the advanced position and the battery at Samra. A considerable number of armed Maltese, all of whom, up to the end of December 1799, had been paid by His Sicilian Majesty, were placed in front of the line of communication, making frequent patrols, whilst to the left of the San Giuseppe road several strong Maltese posts were formed, to whom that part of the line of investment was entirely trusted.

Marsa Scirocco was made an intrenched post with a fortnight's provisions stored there, and in case of any reverse happening, a strong redoubt near the Torre della Grazia was further ordered, for the protection of the right, so as to secure a retreat from the battery of Santo Rocco towards Zeitun, should Zabbar be lost.

General Graham's dispatch to General Fox, dated the 10th December, notifying the safe arrival of the contingent of British troops in Malta, was forwarded for transmission to Lord Nelson, who sent it on, under a covering dispatch, dated the 14th, as follows:—

Palermo, 14*th December* 1799.

His Excellency Hon. Lt.-Gen. Fox.

DEAR SIR,—I send Your Excellency Colonel Graham's letters, both from Messina and Malta, where, thank God, he landed on the 10th. We shall now be able to hold our own till a sufficient force can be collected to attack La Valetta. Graham wants many stores, as I dare say he tells you, and I am sure Your Excellency will afford every assistance to get this very long business to a close. The Austrians are calling out for a naval co-operation on the coast of Genoa. It is my wish, for no man knows more the necessity than myself, having this war served with the Austrians when they were on that coast; they complain that the Russian ships never come near them. Our Government think that eleven sail of the line, frigates, &c., should do something. I find they do nothing. On the 17th November—at latest the 19th—the Admiral was to sail from

Naples with the troops for Malta; but also on the 19th December it was said it would be five or six days.

The troops are represented by those who have seen them as a very fine body of men, and as I feel confident that you will have orders to send more troops to Malta, we shall soon find our squadron liberated and on other service, for at this moment I have not a ship to send on the north coast of Italy. I send you Mr. Wyndham's letter and enclosures. I have directed the convoy for England to sail the moment the *Speedy* appears off Mahon with the trade from Messina. Captain Louis is directed to proceed to Malta with stores for our ships, which are in a truly miserable state.

In everything I shall be truly happy in meeting your wishes, my only desire is to know them, for believe me, with the greatest respect, Your Excellency's, &c. (Signed) BRONTE NELSON.

On the 15th December Captain Ball informed the Right Hon. Henry Dundas that the Maltese were anxious that he (Ball), upon the expected arrival of the Russian troops, should continue to hold the appointment of Governor, and that they had petitioned the Czar to that effect, but that he had thought proper not to give effect to the petition. Ball's dispatch was as follows:—

Malta, 15*th December* 1799.[1]

The Right Hon. Henry Dundas.

SIR,—I take the liberty of enclosing to you a brief account of the revenues and productions of the Islands of Malta and Gozo, conceiving it will be acceptable at this period.

As I have not the honor of being known to you, I beg leave to represent that in October /98, Lord Nelson gave me the command of the squadron blockading the French garrison in this Island.

In February /99, the Maltese, perceiving the necessity of having a chief to reside constantly with them, petitioned His Sicilian Majesty and Lord Nelson to give me that appointment, which was immediately granted, since which they applied to the Emperor of Russia to beg he will acquiesce in appointing me their Governor, but I have detained their petition from an apprehension that His Imperial Majesty might think it was procured by an improper influence. The Maltese are extremely attached to the English; they are more industrious, and have less vice than the inhabitants of any of the states in Italy; they have frequently expressed their wish to be under the sovereignty of Great Britain, and promised that they would defend the Island with their own troops, provided they were paid the expense of two full British regiments.

I am informed that some British officers have orders to raise two regiments in Albania for the garrison of this Island. This will be attended with many difficulties and great expense, and there is such a prejudice between the Albanians and Maltese that their arrival will create much disgust.

I beg leave to suggest to you, sir, that two regiments may be immediately raised here without bounty, but on condition that they are to serve only on the Island. They may be kept at one-fourth less expense

[1] C.O.R. Malta, No. 1.

than a British regiment. In time of war the Islands of Malta and Gozo would furnish many useful seamen for our Navy. I have the honour, &c.

(Signed) ALEX. JNO. BALL.

Revenue.[1]

The landed property of Government	£20,700
Customs	12,500
Excise	8,000
Tobacco	1,300
	£42,500

Productions Exported.

Spun cotton	£400,000[2]
Oranges	2,000
Salt	200
Stores, &c.	300
	£402,500

During the month of December 1799 famine again threatened the inhabitants, when the following urgent appeals for wheat were made by Ball to Nelson, under dates of the 21st and 22nd of this month:—

CAPTAIN BALL TO LORD NELSON.

Malta, 21st December 1799.[3]

MY LORD,—Sir Thomas Troubridge has just informed me of the arrival of the *Transfer*, and that he shall dispatch her immediately to Sicily. I write by her to General Acton and the Prince de Luzzi, to represent that unless an immediate supply of corn be sent here we shall experience all the horrors of famine.

The Deputies who went in the summer to implore of His Sicilian Majesty a credit of corn that they might have a provision for the winter could not obtain more than a *supply of six weeks* for the armed peasants; the individual inhabitants were too poor to purchase a large quantity for themselves.

I have sent to the States of Barbary for an immediate supply, and I have great hopes of getting some from the Levant, as I granted passports for four vessels which were to be here this month. I am to request that Your Grace will make use once more of your great influence with His Sicilian Majesty's Ministers to save these poor islanders from starving.

Sir Thomas Troubridge is going on with his usual zeal and perseverance; it requires all his abilities to manage the Naval business here at this critical juncture. We all like General Graham. The regiments behave remarkably well. There will not be any attack until we are reinforced. The General is taking all precautions to secure a retreat if the enemy's succours should arrive before ours. . . . I have the honour, &c.

(Signed) ALEX. JN°· BALL.

[1] C.O.R. Malta, No. 1.
[2] Thornton in his *Finances of Malta* (p. 35) gave £500,000 as the value of the cotton exported. See Chap. xxiv.—J. H. R.
[3] Brit. Mus. Add. MSS. 34915, f. 241.

CAPTAIN BALL TO LORD NELSON.

Malta, 22nd December 1799.[1]

MY LORD,—I had the honour of writing to Your Grace yesterday to represent that this Island is in the greatest distress for corn; if we have not a supply very soon, we shall experience all the horrors of famine. I have written very urgently on the subject to General Acton and the Prince de Luzzi. I have sent to Tunis and Tripoli for corn and bullocks, and I gave passports three months since for four vessels which are to bring corn from the Levant. Neither the Government nor the inhabitants possessed sufficient money in the summer to provide for the winter's consumption of corn. We endeavoured to obtain a sufficient quantity on credit from His Sicilian Majesty, *but as that could not be effected*, no blame can attach here for not making a greater provision.

I have the satisfaction to acquaint Your Grace that I feel particularly obliged to Sir Thomas Troubridge for his very cordial co-operation.

Brig^{r.}-Genl. Graham is equally attentive, his regiments behave in a manner highly to their credit. The General is throwing up a work to secure a retreat, and cutting traverses that we may not be surprised should the enemy's succours arrive before our reinforcements. He does not think it prudent to risk an attack with our present force. . . . I have the honour, &c. (Signed) ALEX. J^{No.} BALL.

Captain Ball's appeal for a further supply of corn so as to avoid all the horror of famine was fully confirmed by Captain Troubridge in his eloquent dispatches to Lord Nelson of the 22nd, 23rd, and 28th December, and of the 1st, 5th, and 6th January.

[Extract.]

SIR T. TROUBRIDGE TO LORD NELSON.

Marsa Scirocco, Malta, the 22nd December 1799.[2]

MY LORD,—The *Transfer* is arrived from Girgenti without any convoy, there being an order not to suffer corn to be shipped for exportation; if they do not except Malta, we may as well be off—the granaries are full at Girgenti, and the scarcity is all trick and villainy.[3] I am sorry to say, what I have long known, *the King* and Trabia have been in the habit of sending corn to Leghorn, (whilst) forbidding his subjects to send any, or what amounts to the same thing, not suffering them to do it, by refusing passports. The 20,000 tumoli of corn from Naples, which Your Lordship is told is intended for Malta, I much doubt. The same falsehoods were imposed on you [me ?] when I was at Procida, and no truth in it.

[1] Brit. Mus. Add. MSS. 34915, f. 249.
[2] *Ibid.* 34915.
[3] Nelson, in his reply of December 29, states that General Acton again denied that the granaries at Girgenti were full. (*Nelson's Dispatches*, vol. iv. p. 162.)—J. H. R.

[Extract.]

SIR THOMAS TROUBRIDGE TO LORD NELSON.

Malta, 23rd December 1799.[1]

MY LORD,— . . . Your Lordship must pardon me, but I really foresee that these poor inhabitants are to be sacrificed to the villainy of the Neapolitans.

If the ports are not opened immediately, both them and us [sic] must fly the country. I have little left in the *Culloden*, and hourly expect the General [Graham] will say, 'If the supplies are stopped from Sicily, take me and my soldiers off. I cannot leave them to be starved, tho' I shall have the painful task of leaving the inhabitants to their fate.' I know so well the system pursued about corn at Palermo, that I doubt every word they utter. The corn from Naples is an infamous falsehood. Why bring it so far when Girgenti has plenty? I beseech Your Lordship press them for a *yes* or *no*; the cries of hunger are now too great to admit of the common evasive answers usually given by the Sicilian Government. Do not suffer them to throw the odium on us. If they say we shall not or cannot be supplied, I see nothing for it but to retreat as fast as possible.

[Extract.]

SIR T. TROUBRIDGE TO LORD NELSON.

Marsa Scirocco, Malta, 28th December 1799.[2]

MY LORD,—I am sorry to dwell again on the hateful subject of provisions, but really it grows serious. I have not more than fourteen days' provisions at two-thirds allowance. The Island is without bread *in toto*. I have sent to smuggle or even seize any vessels laden with corn they may fall in with. The King of Naples ought *to recollect* that his flag is flying here. . . . If Your Lordship could see the distress of the people here, I am sure you would use such strong language as to induce His Majesty to permit corn to be shipped for this place.

[Extract.]

SIR T. TROUBRIDGE TO LORD NELSON.

Marsa Scirocco, Malta, 1st January 1800 (noon).[3]

. . . We *are dying* off fast for *want*. I learn from letters from Messina that Sir William Hamilton says Prince Luzzi refused corn some time ago, and he does not think it *worth while making another application*. If this is the case, I wish he commanded at the distressing scenes instead of me. Puglia has an immense harvest; near eighty sail left Messina before I did, to load corn. Will they let us have any of that? A short time will decide the business. We shall be obliged to leave the place for the want of

---

[1] Brit. Mus. Add. MSS. 34915, f. 256.
[2] *Ibid.* 34915.
  It must be admitted that the report which Brigadier-General Graham on that same day sent to General Fox paints the situation in far less dark colours. See below.—J. H. R.
[3] Brit. Mus. Add. MSS. 34916.

provisions. . . . Many happy returns of the day to you; I never spent a more miserable one. I am not *very tender hearted*, but really the distress here would, if he could see it, even move a Neapolitan.

[Extract.]

SIR T. TROUBRIDGE TO LORD NELSON.

Malta, *5th January* 1800.[1]

MY LORD,—I have this day saved 30,000 people from dying, but with this day my ability ceases, as the King of Naples, or rather the Queen and her party, are bent on starving us. I see no alternative but to leave these poor unhappy people to starve without our being witnesses to their distress. I curse the day I ever served the King of Naples—I, who know Your Lordship so well, can pity the distress you must suffer.

What must be our situation on the spot? If the Neapolitan Government will not supply corn, I pray Your Lordship to recall us, we are of no use. The Maltese soldiers must call on the French in Valetta, who have the *ability* to relieve them. The consequence will be, General Graham and his troops will be cut up to a man, if I do not withdraw them. I hourly expect him to apply to me for that purpose. . . . I foresee we shall forfeit the little we have gained before supplies can possibly come; many thousands must perish. Even if those supplies arrive in two days, the situation is worse than ever, there are not even locusts. Such is the fever of my brain this minute, that *I assure you on my honour*, if the Palermo traitors were here, I would shoot them first and then myself. . . . Oh, could you see the horrid distress I daily experience, something would be done! . . .[2]

SIR T. TROUBRIDGE TO LORD NELSON.

Malta, *5th January* 1800 (4 a.m.)[3]

MY LORD,—The business is drawing to a conclusion. As '*hunger knows no law*,' the Maltese seize the soldiers' bread. I hourly expect they will solicit supplies from Vaubois and destroy our troops. Nothing can possibly prevent it, if the General (Graham) stays; but the poor creatures knowing we are not the authors of their miseries, but rather their Sovereign, who they have a right to expect supplies from—they are not *soliciting corn* as a gift, but *for sale* to them, willing to give a good price.

Your Lordship must not be surprised to hear of my having embarked the troops and landed them at Messina, for the General says we cannot be expected to stay without provisions: 100,000 people will not quietly starve and see our troops eating.

I have taken some strong measures; if they do not succeed the game is up. We are acting with deceitful traitors of Sicilians, Neapolitans, and Russians. I trust Your Lordship will see me out of the scrape necessity has, or will draw me into. I cannot in this letter tell you the measures. If they succeed you will soon hear from Acton. Much, very much, of our

---

[1] Brit. Mus. Add. MSS. 34916.
[2] For the rest of this letter, see *Nelson's Dispatches*, vol. iv. pp. 166, 167 (notes).—J. H. R.
[3] Brit. Mus. Add. MSS. 34196.

distress is to be attributed to Sir William Hamilton *not thinking it necessary* to make a second application to Prince Luzzi, because he was refused three months ago to a similar application; the scarcity, if it exists in Sicily, is by the monopoly of Trabia, whatever is wanted his stores are *full* when he has *brought things to a high price*. I am truly miserable!

[Extract.]

SIR THOMAS TROUBRIDGE TO LORD NELSON.

Marsa Scirocco, Malta, 6th January 1800.[1]

. . . I have taken every method to secure supplies in future without depending on Sicily. If I can get the better of this famine created by the *monopolising trash of Sicilians*; however as hunger knows no law, I have sent the *Citoyenne* to Girgenti to *ask* and *demand* with *firmness*, supplies *agreeable* to *Treaty*—if refused, to seize on any vessels laden as far as 800 salms, and bring them to me, guaranteeing the payment by myself. I have also sent the *Stromboli* to Messina with directions to load corn and seize any he may meet coming from the Adriatic; the measures are strong, but necessity forced them. I have also doubly manned the *Arab*, and sent dollars of mine and Ball's to purchase if they will permit of it, if not to seize; I know I shall gain the displeasure of the King and all the petty merchants about his Court—nothing that could happen will give me less concern.[2]

Towards the end of December two intercepted dispatches were taken by the blockading fleet, one dated the 24th December from the Commissary of Marine, Menard, to General Vaubois, requesting authority for the Maltese quondam spy, Barbara, to proceed to France, and there submit plans which in his opinion might secure the success of the expedition of relief then being organised at Toulon.

Permission having been granted, Barbara sailed for France, but whilst *en route* was captured by the Bey of Tunis, and from a note attached to the above referred to dispatch, which is preserved amongst the 'Nelson Papers' in the British Museum (Add. MSS. 34950), it would appear that 'he was placed in the Bey's public works at Tunis, and a particularly large basket allotted to him to carry stores.' We hear no more of this renegade.

The other dispatch was dated the 27th of December, from Adjutant-General Brouard to the Minister of War, requesting permission to serve elsewhere after the relief of Malta. General Brouard was one of the prisoners of war captured on board the *Guillaume Tell* in the engagement of the 13th of March following.

These intercepted dispatches are as follows:—

[1] Brit. Mus. Add. MSS. 34916.
[2] See *Dispatches of Nelson*, vol. iv. p. 167 (note), for Troubridge's letter of January 8, 1799, accusing the Neapolitan Court of detaining the Russians.—J. H. R.

Le 3 *Nivôse* (24th December 1799).[1]

Menard, Commissaire de Marine, Ordonnateur, au Général Vaubois.

Général,—Le Citoyen Barbara, enseigne de vaisseaux qui dirigea la descente dans la partie de l'ouest de l'isle, a des nouvelles idées pour faire arriver des secours jusqu'à nous ; il me les a communiqués, elles me paroissent mériter quelque confiance. Veuillès les examiner il ne demande que d'aller en France pour s'embarquer sur l'expédition comme je puis me passer de lui dans la partie où il est employé, je ne mettrais aucune opposition à son depart si vous le jugiès nécessaire. Salut et considération.

(Signed) Menard.

Malte, 6 *Nivôse* (27th December 1799).[2]

L'Adjutant-Général Brouard au Ministre de la Guerre.

Citoyen Ministre,—Vous ne serez point surpris d'apprendre que l'esprit de la garnison de Malte est on ne peut meilleur, malgré les privations que les soldats suffrent, il n'y en a pas un qui ne préférât mille fois mourir, plutôt que d'avoir la douleur de voir rendre la place à ces trop orgueilleux Anglais, ou aux rebelles. Des raisons de santé m'avoient forcé de vous écrire pour être employé ailleure. Je vous prie de ne point perdre de vue ma demande et de me l'accorder, lorsque Malte sera entièrement dégagé des enemis qui l'entourent. Je vous avouerai franchement que tenant à l'honneur plus qu'à tout autre chose, je serai fâché de quitter un posté où il y a quelque danger à courir.   Salut et respect.

(Signed) Brouard.

Soon after his arrival in Malta, Brigadier-General Graham perceived that the means placed at his disposal were inadequate to accomplish the reduction of Valetta, and accordingly wrote to General Fox, urging him to send more troops and a senior officer, as quickly as possible, one better able (as he considered) to judge of the expediency of adopting offensive operations, and more capable than he was of properly directing their execution.

To this appeal for further reinforcements to be sent from Minorca, Graham received the following reply :—

Government House, Mahon, 28th December 1799.[3]

To Brigadier-General Graham, &c.

Dear Sir,—The day before yesterday I received your letters of the 4th instant from Messina, and of the 10th from Malta.

An answer from England is not yet arrived to my letters from Gibraltar, and from hence ; and I cannot till I receive orders for that purpose detach any troops from this Island. I have given directions to the Commissary-General to take proper steps to supply you with money. Colonel Lindenthal mentions the want of entrenching tools, which I am sorry to say I have not to send. I am aware of your critical situation, but I trust Lord Nelson will not require or ask of you contrary to your instructions

---

[1] Brit. Mus. Add. MSS. 34950. [2] *Ibid.*
[3] C.O.R. Malta, No. 1.

to remain on shore with the troops longer than your own opinion and prudence justify.

Colonel Lindenthal will stay with you as long as you may find his services necessary. As Lieut.-Colonel Boyle's regiment, the Tipperary Fencibles, are expected here every day, it will be necessary for him to repair here as soon as he hears of their arrival, or indeed, if he can be spared, I should wish him to come here immediately, as from the description of men that this regiment is composed of, the service of an active zealous officer will probably be wanted upon their landing. I have the honour, &c. (Signed) H. E. Fox.

Interesting details of the investment of Valetta are given by Graham to General Fox, and to the commander-in-chief, the Duke of York, under date of the 28th and 30th December respectively, as follows:—

Gudia, Malta, 28th December 1799.[1]

General Graham to Lieut.-General the Hon. Henry Fox, &c.

SIR,—I had the honour of writing to Your Excellency on the 10th instant to inform you of the arrival of the troops under my command in St. Paul's Bay on the preceding day, and of their having landed that morning, marched into cantonments, necessarily more dispersed than I liked. The marines already on shore, and those since landed from the *Culloden* and *Northumberland*, having been put under my command, I have been enabled to make a disposition of the troops so as to connect them better together, but I should be very glad to be able to concentrate them still more.

Colonel Lindenthal's plan which goes by this opportunity will explain our position. The 30th Regiment is at Zeitun with the care of the advanced posts, of Zabbar and the battery of St. Roque on the right; the 89th Regiment in Gudia and Luca have charge of the advanced post at Tarscien, with the battery in front of it. The marines are at St. Giuseppe with the care of the advanced post and battery at Samra.

Fornara, lying low at the head of what is called the Marsh,[2] is not occupied by any of our troops. During the night the advanced posts communicate with one another by advanced sentries or patrols.

In all these posts there are besides a considerable number of armed Maltese, who in the night occupy small houses rather in front of the line of communication, and make frequent patrols.

To the left of St. Giuseppe there are several strong Maltese posts, to whom that part of the line is entirely trusted. Indeed there is no risk of the enemy ever attempting to come out on that side unless they were in such force as to be able to possess themselves of the country, which it is quite certain they cannot do without great reinforcements. Citta Vecchia is in a respectable state of defence, and could not be taken by a *coup de main*, if tolerably defended. We therefore mean to get some provisions into it as soon as possible; after which time the marines, who would now retire to Luca, will have orders to fall back in case of a serious attack on Citta Vecchia, which by that means would become the rallying point for the Maltese, from whom little diversion could be expected, if all the

[1] C.O.R. Malta, No. 1 (1799–1800). [2] It is now drained and cultivated.—J. H. R.

British retired towards Casals Asciak and Zeitun—villages capable of being defended for some time, and behind which in the way to Marsa Scirocco the country offers a very favourable position for making a stand, at least so as to gain time and allow all the parties to join. Agreeable to what I mentioned in my last, an entrenched post is established at Marsa Scirocco, and a fortnight's provisions are already in store there. The next work to be undertaken immediately is a strong redoubt near the 'Torre de Grazia' for the protection of the right, and which will secure a retreat [sic] from the battery of 'St. Roque' towards Zeitun, though Zabbar should be lost.

As the soldiers have been much employed in landing stores, &c., the work is chiefly done by Maltese under the direction of Bonavia, a very zealous and intelligent inhabitant, bred in the line of an engineer; I have appointed him and his son to act as assistant engineers, and allowed him a dollar a day, and his son half a dollar with rations. I flatter myself that Your Excellency will not think that I exceed the bounds of my instructions by incurring the expense of these *purely defensive* works, without which I should consider the small force here exposed to too much risk, should the enemy determine to make a vigorous effort against us. From all I have now seen I think there is no danger of their attempting anything more than perhaps to spike the guns of some of the batteries which are found established so near to their works, and so little connected with one another, that it is justly matter of astonishment that they have never tried to destroy them; it seems to argue strongly a want of confidence in their own men. But notwithstanding, I consider it is my duty not to neglect any precautions for our security while our force is so small.

It is unlucky that the St. Roque battery was opened, as it has given the enemy a jealousy in that quarter. They fire frequently on it, and we know that the garrison of [Fort] Ricasoli, which consisted only of 250 men, has received lately a reinforcement of 100 men, and of course those greater precautions against surprise are now taken.

In my opinion nothing would so essentially assist the blockade as getting possession of that fort, for were it known to be in our hands, the French would scarcely think of sending reinforcements and supplies unless they could do it with a great armament, and meanwhile the effect on the garrison might perhaps be such as to create in M. Vaubois a disposition to treat, which without the loss of some important post he durst not think of; the men receive no wine or brandy, and only from four ounces to eight ounces of salt meat every ten days, but their daily rations of bread, beans, &c., is full, and they are healthy; the accounts of their force vary, but there is little reason to imagine that their numbers can be diminished by mortality, more than the [they (?)] increase by the crews of the ships from Egypt.

The enclosed authentic paper shows their original force—they still retain from 8,000 to 10,000 inhabitants, a strong proof that they are better provided with corn than is believed here. The Island is in much greater distress. We have all made such strong representations on that subject to Palermo that I hope positive orders will be sent to all the ports of Sicily to allow of the exportation of an ample supply. But the money furnished by the Court of Naples to Governor Ball for the use of the poorest inhabitants, and for other necessary expenses, will not last more than *one month*, and that Court has declared that no more will be sent until England and Russia furnish an equal proportion (£14,000).[1] At the end of that period, then, if money is not sent we shall probably lose all our Maltese soldiers, whose assistance is so material at present for our security, and even if reinforced, for the success of our operations.

Hitherto our men continue healthy, but the marines who were on shore some time before our arrival are far from being so. It is generally thought that their fevers were occasioned by the men lying on stone or earth floors; I have therefore sent to Sicily for a quantity of deal boards. When the Russians arrive there must be a change in the cantonments.

It would be desirable that the British troops should occupy this ridge from the sea at 'Torre della Grazia' to this place, in which line there will be room for more, if any come from Minorca. I need not repeat my anxiety on that point, but I may be allowed to mention, if you could spare the 90th Regiment (in case a larger corps under the command of a general officer cannot be sent), I should feel a particular satisfaction not only from the accession of numbers, but of quality of the troops, for I should be perfectly sure of their loyalty and attachment, and I am concerned to state that these two regiments, in which there are a great number of Irish of the worst description, cannot be so much relied on; three have already deserted—two of them last night from the advanced post of St. Roque—men who by their general good conduct had gained the esteem of the officers, never were punished, or had ever shown any signs of dissatisfaction. They have gone over from a mere principle of disaffection to the King's Government. Mr. Vivion writes to Lieut.-Colonel Cuppage for the clothing of the artillerymen landed from the *Bulldog* and *Perseus*, and Mr. Jamaison writes concerning hospital stores. Besides these very necessary articles I should be very glad to have a store of salt meat and biscuit sent, that there may be no risk of our being in want, whatever disappointments may happen from other quarters.

I shall have the honour of transmitting the monthly returns in a few days, meanwhile I enclose a report (No. 2) of the armed Maltese, &c., with a memorandum on the back concerning the marines and artillery. I have the honour, &c. (Signed) THOS. GRAHAM, A.B.G.

MEN

	Sergeants	Corporals	Privates
Birchircara	25	23	290
St. Joseph	23	14	192
Samra	27	14	182
Corradino	16	18	190
Tarscien	15	15	220
Zeitun	18	32	307
Zabbar	8	39	362
Citta Vecchia	8	4	136
St. Antonio	9	11	160
	149	170	2039

Mortars	32-Pdrs.	18-Pdrs.	12-Pdrs.	8-Pdrs.	4-Pdrs.
3	8	20	9	17	13

---

[1] This explains the reason for the refusal of the Neapolitan Court, then at Palermo, to send more supplies.—J. H. R.

Graham's letter of 30th December 1799 to the Duke of York has been printed in Delavoye's 'Life of General Graham' (p. 180), and need not be inserted here, as it traverses the ground already covered in the previous dispatch.

Colonel Lindenthal's second report to General Fox was dated the 31st December, as follows :—

To Lieut.-Gen. Fox.
Head-quarters, Gudia, 31st December 1799.[1]

SIR,—I hope you have received my first Report of the 10th December, of which I also send a duplicate. In another letter of the 28th of the same month I enclosed a map of the environs of Valetta, showing the position of the troops forming the blockade, and the several intrenchments.

The French Army in Valetta, according to our latest information, consists of—

- 2,500 soldiers,
- 1,500 sailors,
- 130 Garde Nationali, [sic]
- 70 Maltese.

4,200

of which they have at present 200 in hospital. 'Tis true, it is but a small force for such an extensive place, yet it is evident that it requires three times the number to act against them, with any hope of success, the ground all round the fortifications being solid rock, the approaches and necessary works are attended with more difficulty. The taking of one of the outworks does not essentially affect the others, and after being in possession of all the separate works together, it would be still necessary to besiege La Valetta in form. A bombardment would be attended with little success, there being no wood or timber in the houses to expect a sudden destruction. Therefore the probability of our getting at last possession of such a strong place originates more from the consideration of the enemy being already so long blockaded, and supposed to have lost the spirit of defence, and the soldiers unwilling of being [sic] so long reduced to short allowance will perhaps incline to mutiny; to hasten this epoque it is necessary that the Russian Corps should arrive soon, to enable us to harass the enemy on all sides, and to try to get some outwork by surprise. But until there be an absolute want of provisions I can only speak of probability.

So that the principal point in question is the continuation of the blockade to that period, which I am sorry to find is not so near at hand as mentioned in my first letter, as it did not occur to me at that time that the turning-out of town numbers of the inhabitants, and the supply of fish, and great quantities of garden stuff, materially lessens the quantity of the daily issue of provisions. We have been very glad, however, to hear from several Maltese deserted from town, that the wine and brandy is at an end.

I have as yet not been able to form an idea of the quantity of their ammunition. I hope to give you soon an exact account of the resources of

---

[1] C.O.R. Malta, No. 1.

the Islands, Malta and Gozo in particular. Brig.-General Graham probably has mentioned to you that the armed Maltese who have hitherto been paid and victualled by H.S. Majesty must necessarily be provided for by us, in case no more money should arrive from that quarter; otherwise it would be impossible to continue the blockade. I have not yet received any letters from you since my arrival, and am waiting your further orders concerning my return to Minorca. I have the honour, &c.

(Signed) LINDENTHAL.

From the correspondence which took place during the months of November and December, it will have been gathered that at the close of 1799 the condition of the Maltese outside the city walls had become more serious than that of the beleaguered garrison. The latter, as the event proved, had sufficient food to hold out until the following September, whilst famine already stared the villagers in the face. The wheat harvest in Sicily had been miserably poor, and the more distant Naples had to be resorted to for supplies. Three vessels at Palermo under convoy of a Neapolitan frigate, and one at Messina, all four laden with wheat at Naples for Malta, were alleged to be kept there windbound, but by Troubridge it was suspected to be treachery. Nelson, who was at Palermo at the time, declared that he was powerless to get the frigate and her convoy out of port.[1] Meanwhile the distress in Malta went on increasing. Not only food, but money also was wanted.

Besides threatened starvation (for not even locust beans remained) fever set in again, due to bad and insufficient food.

Under these sad circumstances Nelson, on the 8th January, authorised Troubridge to seize any vessels laden with corn, for the people could not be allowed to starve.[2]

Such a step, although in defiance of all international law, Troubridge had, as we have seen by his dispatches of the 28th December and the 5th and 6th January, already taken by dispatching His Majesty's ship *Stromboli* (Captain Broughton) to Girgenti, and there seizing two vessels laden with corn, and had brought them over to Malta, whilst the *Citoyenne* was sent to Messina on a similar errand. As was anticipated by Sir Thomas Troubridge, complaints were made by the Neapolitan Government at these high-handed and unlawful proceedings, and whilst Nelson expressed to Troubridge that such a measure was a strong one to take, diplomatically implying that his order of the 8th January had reference to seizure on the high seas, and not in port, he apologised to the Neapolitan Government by stating that the act was not to be considered as any intended disrespect to His Sicilian Majesty, but one of the most absolute and imperious necessity; for either he would have to deliver up the Island to the French or to anticipate the King's

---

[1] Clarke and MacArthur, vol. i. p. 240.
[2] Nicolas, *Dispatches of Nelson*, vol. iv. p. 173.

orders, as had been done in this instance. He concluded by expressing a hope that the Neapolitan Government would never again force His Britannic Majesty's servants to so unpleasant an alternative, from which may be gathered that should the occasion again arise, and 'necessity knowing no law,' the same remedy would be adopted.[1]

Owing to the success which of late had attended the Russian troops in the north of Italy, the apprehensions of the Neapolitan Government became allayed, and being thus encouraged, and aware of the necessity of reinforcements being sent on to Malta, it issued orders to prepare 2,600 Neapolitan mixed troops for embarkation, to be dispatched as soon as transport could be provided for them by the British authorities. The Neapolitan Court at this period continued to reside at Palermo, Sir William Hamilton being still attached thereto, as His Britannic Majesty's ambassador; whilst Nelson, notwithstanding the remonstrances from the Admiralty, persisted in making it his head-quarters.[2] Neither the hint from his friend Captain Goodhall, in November of 1799, nor the earnest request of Commodore Troubridge, which was to follow in February, nor (to anticipate a little further) the sympathetic letters from the First Lord of the Admiralty, Earl Spencer, dated the 25th April and 9th May 1800, had the slightest effect.[3] Nelson, on the plea of ill-health, would not move.

In the meantime the British Government, during the early part of the winter, appointed a senior officer in rank to the command of the Mediterranean Fleet, without recalling Nelson. Vice-Admiral Lord Keith was accordingly dispatched in the *Queen Charlotte*, with orders to take under his command such flag officers, ships, and vessels as he might find in the Mediterranean; and was expected to be at Minorca at the end of December or beginning of January, whilst Lord Nelson was required, so far back as the 30th November, to place himself under Lord Keith's command.[4]

Sir William Hamilton, by order of the Foreign Office, was superseded at the same time, although his successor, the Honourable Arthur Paget, did not arrive at Palermo until the following spring.

During the month of January the following important correspondence took place between General Graham and the Right Honourable H. Dundas, also between Nelson and General Fox:—

---

[1] Pettigrew, vol. i. p. 341.
[2] Already, at the end of 1799, the British Government had decided to recall Sir W. Hamilton and replace him by Mr. Paget, who left London on January 27, 1800, to proceed to Palermo. (See the *Paget Papers*, vol. i. pp. 170-77.)—J. H. R.
[3] Clarke and MacArthur, vol. i. p. 240.
[4] Nelson wrote at Leghorn on Jan. 23—'Lord Keith is now here, and I have only to obey':—a peevish reference; for Keith was a most considerate commander-in-chief.—J. H. R.

THE BRITISH BLOCKADE—1799-1800

[Private.] La Gudia, Malta, 6*th January* 1800.[1]
To the Right Hon. H. Dundas.

MY DEAR SIR,—No opportunity having occurred for sending the letter I wrote a few days ago until now, I am enabled to add a few lines on a subject which it seems to both Captain Ball and myself highly important His Majesty's Ministers should be made fully acquainted with, and as I write this merely as a private letter to you, I am sure you will not allow it to be supposed that I take this matter up as meddling with political arrangements which I have no business with. The Chevalier Italinski,[2] who came from Palermo lately, took occasion the other day to show Captain Ball his papers and instructions with regard to this place, and among others the disposition of the allied garrison, by which the Russians only are to be in La Valette, Floriana, and St Elmo, the Neapolitans within enceinte of the Cotonera, and His Majesty's troops to be in Ricasoli, Tigne, and Fort Manoel.

Captain Ball, in telling me this, asked me what I thought of it.

I said I thought it would have been better to have considered the means of getting possession than to have brought forward a disposition so disgraceful to His Majesty, that it was impossible for any officer to submit to put it in execution without positive orders, or being obliged to it, in consequence of superior force. Captain Ball said that, seeing it exactly in the same light, he had expressed his opinion so strongly and pointed out the absurdity and unfairness of an arrangement which, under a treaty of apparent equality, put everything of strength, consequence, and comfort into the hands of the Russians, completely separated the Neapolitans from the British, and condemned these to pass their time in casemates in three insulated and comparatively insignificant forts, in such a manner that the Chevalier Italinski had not a word to say, except that it had been agreed on between the two Courts (which both Ball and myself heard with equal surprise), but that, satisfied as he was of the purity of the Emperor's intentions, he would lose no time in writing to Petersburg and strongly urging that so improper an arrangement should be altered, and afterwards, on Ball asking him if he meant the conversation as an official communication, which he should inform me of, he said, ' By no means'; at the same time it certainly was brought forward as such. But he dropped in conversation an expression of surprise at hearing that it was seriously intended by the British Government to keep any garrison here at all.

Now, having told my story, I have only further to add, that if it is the intention to assist in giving Malta totally to the Russians (which, notwithstanding all that Whitworth says to the contrary, I am well convinced is the real object of the Court of Petersburg) it is all very well; but if there is no such intention, and that a fair and equal partition of the power and strength of the place is the object of the treaty, it is impossible that this arrangement should stand good. I need only refer to the plan of the fortress, which *now* must be in London, stating in explanation that St. Elmo, La Valette, and Floriana look into and command completely every one of the surrounding works. All the great magazines of every

[1] C.O.R. Malta, No. 1.
[2] Italinski, it will be remembered, was Russian envoy to the Neapolitan Court, then at Palermo.—J. H. R.

kind are in them; the others are mere outworks, dependent on the Valetta in every respect. I will not attempt to point out any suitable arrangement for a fair and safe military partition, well aware of the difficulties and objections that may occur in the execution of any that I have thought of, supposing a Russian Deputy Grand Master to be the Governor, and his instructions ever to be to seize on the place for his master. It is enough that I have fully explained the nature of the present arrangements, which in the opinion of all Europe, at least of everybody at all acquainted with this place, would be giving *Malta entirely to the Russians*. The Chevalier Italinski blames some of the Knights of Malta, who are about the Emperor, for having artfully brought forward this arrangement, which he is sure will be condemned at Petersburg when understood. It may not have been understood in London, but I can hardly believe it was not perfectly so there.

Meanwhile I have no doubt of Bonaparte, who knows its immense importance, making suitable exertions for relieving Malta and his friends in Egypt. There are three Russian battalions arrived at Corfu from the Black Sea, on their way to Naples. I shall try what can be done with Italinski and the Count of Palermo, to allow them to come here first, those with the 3,000 [Russians] coming from Naples (they are actually embarked by the last account) might enable us to get possession of the place before any succour can come. I have no doubt but that 10,000 or 12,000 men would take it in a few days, as so weak a garrison might be worn out by false attacks, and a real one at last would succeed.

Some accounts I have heard lately state their having a much larger quantity of grain in La Valetta than I heard at first; the truth cannot be known. I believe, in other respects, the account of their rations is true. I examined a prisoner taken this morning by the Maltese, and he confirmed exactly what we had heard before, and added that they begin to grow very sickly, and that a great many have been sent to the hospital within this fortnight for fevers. I am sorry to say we have appearances of a fever spreading fast in one of our quarters.

Adieu, my dear Sir. I recommend my packet particularly to Sir Wm. Hamilton, begging it may not go by the ordinary post, and I beg leave to recommend an enclosure to Mr. Butler, containing private papers of much consequence. With best respects to Lady Jane, I remain, &c.

(Signed) THOS. GRAHAM.

Palermo, *7th January* 1800.[1]

To Lt.-Gen¹. Fox.

DEAR SIR,—I am honoured with Your Excellency's two letters of December 28th, and return you the letter for the Captain-General of Catalonia. I have no doubt but your letter is a most proper one; I hope that you will have permission to assist in getting rid of this long, very long, business of Malta. The Russians, I hope, are there by this time; they arrived at Messina the 4th. As Graham wrote fully, he tells me, to you, by the *Princess Charlotte*, I shall not trouble you with any opinion of mine; all I trust will end well. This country has great calls upon it, and, unfortunately, has nothing to give.

[1] C.O.R. Malta, No. 1.

You may depend that Graham shall share the fate of the ships. I shall never suffer him to want if I can beg, borrow, or steal to supply him. Lord Keith is, I dare say, with you at this moment, and I am sure all matters will be much better arranged with him than I have ability of doing.[1] I have only the disposition to do what is right, and the desire of meriting your esteem, for believe me, with great respect, &c.

(Signed) BRONTE NELSON.

[Private.]   La Gudia, Malta, 12*th January* 1800.[2]
To Lt.-Gen. Henry Fox.

SIR,—The *Vincejo* not having sailed yesterday evening, I have the opportunity of returning Your Excellency my best thanks for the private letter which I had the honour of receiving from you.

I am much obliged by your allowing me to retain Lt.-Col. Lindenthal; his general knowledge of his profession, as well as his practice as a field engineer, makes his assistance very valuable to me. But we both hope for some officers of Artillery and Engineers, tho' no reinforcement should come from Minorca, as we do not hear of there being any with the Russians.

The dilatoriness of the Russian Admiral Usacoff is astonishing, considering the Emperor's anxiety about the success of the blockade. Chevalier Italinski seemed highly offended with him, and rather inclined to join in the suspicions against him of his being acted on by German influence, which his moral character by no means secures him from.

By letters I received from Naples, dated on the 28th ult., the troops were then embarking; their numbers will not exceed, including marines, 3,000 men—too few to be of much use in active operations; their arrival, however, would remove all grounds of apprehension, even if the French were to receive reinforcements; and indeed if circumstances prevented their ships going into La Valetta, and obliged them to attempt to land at a distance, I should hope there would be a good chance of our preventing them from making their way across this very difficult country. There is every reason to suppose that Bonaparte, now in power,[3] will attempt the relief of Malta and Egypt. The importance of this place to France is immense—impregnable for ever, if this opportunity is lost—giving them the entire command of the Adriatic and Levant, and the power of seizing Sicily whenever they choose. It is much to be regretted that the 10,000 or 12,000 regular troops could not have been employed on this service. Their success in a few days would have been certain against so weak a garrison.

I trouble you with a letter to my friend Lord Keith, whom I hope to

---

[1] This is one of the many bitter touches in Nelson's correspondence of this time, showing his resentment at Keith having been placed in supreme command in the Mediterranean over him. Nelson's neglect to obey Keith's orders to detach ships for the defence of Minorca led to much friction between them; and there are grounds for fearing that the excessive deference of Nelson to the interests of the Neapolitan Court sprang from the Hamilton connexion. See Allardyce, *Lord Keith*, pp. 170 et seq.; but Captain Mahan, *Life of Nelson* (vol. ii. pp. 5–12), has clearly brought out Nelson's anxiety that the siege of Malta should be pressed to the utmost.

[2] C.O.R. Malta, No. 1.

[3] i.e. as First Consul, by the Constitution of 1799.—J. H. R.

have the pleasure of seeing here. But it is impossible to be more fortunate than I think myself, in having such an officer as Sir Thos. Troubridge in the command of the naval force here, being certain of every co-operation and assistance that can be expected from superior abilities and the greatest zeal.

He has relieved the extreme distress of the Island, which the Court of Naples seemed inclined to starve, by sending to cut out corn vessels from Girgenti, and on this hint they have sent others. I shall appoint Lt. Vivion to be a Q.-M.-G., being persuaded nobody can be better qualified for that situation.

We expect some platforms from the citadel of Messina, and I shall write for some plank. But there is a difficulty to find any other than inch boards, which are brought from Calabria.

I have got a quantity of them for the men to sleep on, and am in hopes it will prevent their suffering from the cold and damp of the floors. The sickness, however, rather increases in the 89th, especially at Luca. I have diminished the night duty as much as possible, and shall take every means to check its progress. I have the honour, &c.

(Signed) THOS. GRAHAM.

PS.—Mr. Jamaison has written to Dr. Frank for hospital mates, and I hope they will be sent as soon as possible. Col. Lindenthal has only this moment received your letter, which he desires me to tell you, not now having time to write, as the Commodore has sent for the letters.

[Private.]   La Gudia, Malta, 12*th January* 1800.[1]

TO THE RT. HON. LORD KEITH, &c.—As the Commodore[2] has sent for my letters, I have [not ?] lost a moment, my dear Lord, to tell you how happy I am to hear of your return, and how much more so I shall be to see you here, if you can spare a few days. For God's sake don't take Troubridge away; he is invaluable to us, or to any service; his ship luckily can't go out, so that he is obliged to be near us, which I think very lucky—not that I am now under the least uneasiness about our situation, unless Bonaparte sends a reinforcement, but I trust you will be enabled to counteract any effort that may, and probably will, be made this way, and eastward. If you were to look in at Naples, *chemin faisant*, and shove out the Russians, you would do us a service. I hope the General will have leave from home to send up another regiment at least, and that it will be mine. When all collected, we must try *to do* something, otherwise this never can end till there is not a morsel of bread in La Valetta. When that may be, God knows. The accounts are very uncertain and contradictory, the last makes the quality of the bread very bad, and the garrison to be daily growing sick; they could not bear harassing long on bread and water.

Adieu. I wrote to you to London the other day to tell you of my being here, and something of our situation, and to beg you would bring me out some things. I desired my agent to throw my letter in the fire if you were gone. At all events, let me hear from you, and believe me ever most truly yours.   (Signed) THOS. GRAHAM.

[1] C.O.R. Malta, No. 1.
[2] i.e. Commodore Troubridge.—J. H. R.

PS.—Whatever becomes of this place afterwards, it is important beyond all calculation, I think, to get it out of the hands of the French, and *now* or *never*.[1]

By the 26th January, owing to the rigorous yet absolutely necessary steps which had been taken to secure a supply of corn from Sicily, sufficient was received for immediate requirements; but to add to the difficulties of the situation, sickness invaded the British troops. Graham had already informed Nelson that the troops under his command, numbering 1,500, combined with Ball's 2,000 Maltese, were totally inadequate for any serious attack on the enemy's works, and that he had been officially acquainted that the Russian Admiral was proceeding with his fleet and troops to Corfu. Thus ended all the negotiations and promised aid from Russia.[2]

The urgent need for further reinforcements was then strongly pleaded for by both General Graham, on the 1st, 8th, and 9th February, and Lord Keith, on the 5th February, in the following dispatches to General Fox, including an animadversion of the former on Ball's tactics :—

La Gudia, Malta, 1st February 1800.[3]

To Lieut.-Gen. Fox, &c.

SIR,—I have the honour to transmit to Your Excellency the monthly return, in which for your information the company and a half of Neapolitan Artillery are included.

The increase of the sickness in the 89th Regiment, and in the corps of marines, made the establishment of a general hospital necessary, and I appointed Dr. Jamaison to act as physician to it, and Mr. Price, assistant surgeon in the 30th Regiment, to do duty there. As the Neapolitan Artillery brought no surgeon, commissary, or any orders, but to put themselves under my command, I have been obliged to order that their sick should be received into the general hospital, and that they should all be supplied with rations meanwhile.

I lost no time, however, in writing to Sir William Hamilton and General Acton concerning them, and I understand from them that they, with some other Neapolitan troops, intended to be sent here, are to be maintained entirely at H.S. Majesty's expense.

As there have lately been some German and French deserters from the town who confirm the intelligence of the wants of the garrison, as well as of the increase of the sickness, I hope we shall not lose any more men by desertion. I have removed the companies of the 89th Regiment from Luca to Asciak, towards Tarscien and the Jesuits' battery, as there is little

---

[1] The spirits of the French garrison were raised by the arrival about this time of an *aviso*, with dispatches from the new Consular Government, and copies of the *Moniteur* up to the middle of December. The dispatches probably contained news of the relief expedition then being planned at Toulon, the fate of which will appear presently. We may note here the inaccuracy of James's assertion (*Naval History*, vol. ii. p. 437, edit. 1902) that after February 1799 no vessel slipped into the harbour of Valetta. This leaves out of count the events of May—June, as noted above.—J. H. R.

[2] The cause of this vacillating behaviour on the part of the Russian Government is explained in a separate chapter.   [3] C.O.R. Malta, No. 1.

doubt of the sickness originating from the bad air of the marsh at the head of the harbour, though from several instances there is reason to consider it likewise infectious.

I trust, however, from the extension of the hospital, and the great care taken not to allow men to do duty when they feel any of the first symptoms, nor till they are perfectly re-established, that the alarming progress of this fever will be stopped. I have desired Dr. Jamaison to write particularly to Dr. Franks concerning it, and I anxiously hope a supply of medicines, and particularly a large one of bark, will arrive soon.

The want of regular and well-supplied markets in this Island makes it impossible for the hospitals to be put on the footing directed by the King's regulations; the men cannot be provided otherwise than by drawing their rations from the A[ssistant]-Com[missary]-Gen[eral].

Referring to my letter to Your Excellency of the 28th December, wherein I expressed anxiety on account of the probable want of money to pay the Maltese, I am glad to be able to mention that Sir William Hamilton, pressed by the Governor and myself on that subject, has promised a supply, which is hourly expected. I have the honour, &c.

(Signed) THOS. GRAHAM, A.B.G.

Queen Charlotte, at Palermo, *5th February* 1800.[1]

To Lieutenant-General Fox.

SIR,—Your Excellency must have heard that in consequence of some sudden orders, the Russians have withdrawn[2] their troops from Malta for a time at least (and I hope so only), which has rendered our situation critical indeed, and distressing in point of risk and expense, but to abandon the Island is an object of too great importance for me to undertake without orders to that effect. I have therefore applied to this Government for such a number of troops as may put the Brigadier [Graham] out of risk from a sortie; but if the King could give me any number, I much fear that they [are (?)] so newly raised, as to be unfit for a *coup de main*, which seems the only means of getting possession of Malta, a place I well know to be extremely strong if it were well garrisoned. Perhaps Your Excellency may have had some orders from Britain ere this, and perhaps some troops.

It would be a waste of time to point out to you the consequences of some being sent for the service of Malta, and upon so pressing an occasion I think that Your Excellency may fairly construe the instructions, which you did me the honour of communicating, as a full sanction to detach all above the garrison, viz. five thousand men, and, in that case, I will either send some of the King's ships, or apply to the Russian Admiral for some of theirs to remain at or about Mahon, which shall contain more men than shall be sent from the Island; and the senior officer of His Majesty's ships at Minorca has my orders to embark such supplies as you can send as soon as possible. Major Duncan of the Artillery, who took the Island of Capri, would be of great use, as I have the idea of endeavouring the reconquest of that Island.[3] I have the honour, &c. (Signed) KEITH.

[1] C.O.R. Malta, No. 1.
[2] The word 'withdrawn' must, I think, be used here in the sense of 'withheld.'—J. H. R.
[3] Capri was not taken until the year 1806, by Sir Sidney Smith.—J. H. R.

Malta, 8th February 1800.[1]

To Lt.-Gen. Fox.

SIR,—I take the opportunity of the *Gorgon* to send my letter to Your Excellency, with the monthly return.

I have the satisfaction of being able to add that the sick seem to be doing better. As the Commodore could give no assurance of any other ship of war going soon to Minorca, I advised both Lt.-Col. Lindenthal and Lt.-Col. Boyle to go in the *Gorgon*, though she is ordered to go by Leghorn.

I did not consider myself at liberty to detain Lt.-Col. Lindenthal longer, as there seemed to be no chance of any active operation, and I thought that his services might be wanted elsewhere, and that, at all events, it might be material that he should have an opportunity of explaining more fully than can be done by letter everything about this place, both to Your Excellency and, if he should go home, to H.R.H.[2] and His Majesty's Ministers. Nobody can be more capable of satisfying every enquiry, as, fully aware of the great importance of the subject, he has taken great pains to investigate every point concerning it. These considerations determined me to give up the satisfaction I felt in having an officer of his merit near me. Everything remains very quiet.

In compliance with Governor Ball's wishes, we shall try to annoy the ships from two or three places,[3] and he means to amuse the Maltese with allowing them to go near the works in the night and fire their muskets. I am sure the French will not be much harassed by anything of the kind, as they know we cannot make a real attack, and as that kind of night duty would harass our men very much, I declined having anything to do with it. I have the honour, &c.

(Signed) THOS. GRAHAM, A.B.G.

[Private.]   La Gudia, 9th February 1800.[4]

To Lt.-Gen. Fox, &c.

SIR,—I should have been much inclined to detain Lt.-Col. Lindenthal according to Your Excellency's permission, but that I really think that it would be highly important that he could have an opportunity of talking to the King's Ministers, which might fix the views of Government concerning this place, of which, there is reason to think, their information has hitherto been very defective.

As we agree so much in opinion, it is needless for me now to add anything more on the subject. If there is any difference in our expectations, I think he is more sanguine than I am concerning the period of the surrender supposing nothing but *blockade* be attempted. In that case there is no saying when it will end.

Vaubois cannot give up such a place, without the loss of some outwork and the harbour, so long as there is a morsel of bread.

I think it is quite certain that Bonaparte, knowing well the immense advantages of holding this place, will make great efforts to relieve it.

[1] C.O.R. Malta, No. 1.
[2] i.e. the Duke of York.—J. H. R.
[3] i.e. the French ships, the *Guillaume Tell*, &c., in Valetta Harbour.—J. H. R.
[4] C.O.R. Malta, No. 1.

Shortening the term of the blockade therefore becomes of infinite consequence. I am so convinced of all this, that I regret not having the power of sending Colonel Lindenthal directly home from Leghorn. I have the honour, &c. (Signed) THOS. GRAHAM.

Thus, after a stay in Malta of a little over two months, Lt.-Colonel Lindenthal sailed from the Island for Minorca, via Leghorn, on the 9th February, and as a reward for his services was promoted to a colonelcy, and subsequently attached to Sir Ralph Abercromby's staff, when the latter in the following May was appointed commander-in-chief of the British forces in the Mediterranean.

In order to make the necessary arrangements for the transport of the Neapolitan troops Nelson sailed from Palermo on the 16th January in the *Foudroyant* for Leghorn, there to meet for the first time his chief, Lord Keith.

On the 25th the two flagships, the *Queen Charlotte* and *Foudroyant*, with their respective admirals, Lord Keith and Lord Nelson, sailed thence for Palermo, where they arrived on the 3rd February.

On the 9th February the King honoured Lord Keith's flagship with a visit, which compliment was also paid to Nelson on board the *Foudroyant* the following day, and three days later both these vessels sailed for Malta, carrying 1,200 troops, the first contingent of the 2,600 promised.

On the 15th Malta was reached, and the troops disembarked on the 16th at Marsa Scirocco, Lord Keith leaving to cruise off Valetta that same afternoon.

On the following evening the appearance of a small French squadron in the north-west quarter was reported. These ships proved to be the *Généreux* (74), flagship of Admiral Perrée, *Badin* (24), two corvettes, and the armed store-ship *Ville de Marseille*, in all carrying 4,000 troops for the relief of Malta; they had been at sea since the 7th of February. In the action which followed, the *Généreux* flagship and transport *Ville de Marseille* were captured with 2,000 of the troops, who were subsequently landed at Comino. Rear-Admiral Perrée was struck by a shot from the *Success*, and died of his wounds the following day.[1]

Lord Nelson's report to Lord Keith of this action was as follows:

Foudroyant at sea, off Cape di Corvo, eight leagues west of Cape Passaro, off shore 4 miles, 18th February 1800.[2]

MY LORD,—This morning, being in company with the *Northumberland*, *Audacious*, and *El Corso* brig, I saw the *Alexander* in chase of a line-of-

---

[1] For an account of this exploit and the plucky part played by the little *Success* (32 guns) in heading off and raking the *Généreux* (74 guns) see James's *Naval History*, vol. ii. pp. 438, 439 (edit. of 1902), and Captain Mahan, *Life of Nelson*, vol. ii. pp. 23-28.—J. H. R.

[2] *Nelson's Letters*, edited by Sir J. K. Laughton, p. 234.

battle ship, three frigates, and a corvette; at about eight o'clock she fired several shot at one of the enemy's frigates, which struck her colours; and leaving her to be secured by the ships astern, continued the chase.

I directed Captain Gould of the *Audacious* and the *El Corso* brig to take charge of this prize. At half-past one p.m. the frigates and corvette tacked to the westward, but the line-of-battle ship, not being able to tack without coming to action with the *Alexander*, bore up. The *Success* being to leeward, Capt[n.] Peard, with great judgment and gallantry, lay across his hawse, and raked him with several broadsides. In passing the French ship's broadside, several shot struck the *Success*, by which one man was killed, and the master and seven men wounded.

At half-past four, the *Foudroyant* and *Northumberland* coming up, the former fired two shot, when the French ship fired her broadside, and struck her colours. She proved to be the *Généreux*, of 74 guns, bearing the flag of Rear-Admiral Perrée, Commander-in-Chief of the French naval force in the Mediterranean, having a number of troops on board from Toulon, bound for the relief of Malta.

The *Généreux* was sent to Syracuse under care of the *Northumberland* and *Alexander*.

Lord Keith's dispatches to the Rt. Hon. Henry Dundas and General Fox, referring to this capture, were as follows:—

Malta, 19th *February* 1800.[1]

To the Rt. Hon. H. Dundas.

DEAR SIR,—Since my croaking letter of yesterday, I am happy to tell you the *Généreux* and *Ville de Marseille* are prizes; the three corvettes escaped, but I have sent every way to look for them, and shall continue most strictly to watch the port, so that they may not get in, if any are hardy enough to make the attempt (*it may be done*), which I doubt; if none of them get in, I am not without hopes Malta will offer to capitulate, and to make an opening, I have sent in all private letters which were *insignificant*.

Some of them mentioned an intended visit of the combined fleets to the Mediterranean;[2] those, of course, I did not send in.

I shall not release the prisoners without exchange, and parole only officers of rank. It is odd the ship cheered the English ships as they came up. They said they were glad to see them, we were a happy nation; all very well, perhaps not meant. I enclose you Graham's last letter. I hope he is more at ease. I have the honour, &c.

(Signed) KEITH.

Alluding to this effort of relief, which had been preparing for some considerable time at Toulon, the Minister of Marine, so far back as December 1799, informed Villeneuve that 'this expedition would be followed quickly by another, consisting of one Venetian battleship,

---

[1] C.O.R. Malta, No. 1.
[2] i.e. the combined fleets of France and Spain under Admiral Bruix, which had made so futile an attempt in the previous year.—J. H. R.

and two frigates, *La Carrère* and the *Muiron*, which would carry to Malta reinforcements in men, besides victuals and clothing.'[1]

If Perrée's expedition proved successful, Villeneuve was to return to France with the above-mentioned vessels, the *Guillaume Tell*, the *Athénien*, the *Diana*, and *Justice*, he in chief command, and Admiral Decrès as second in command, all the latter being then blocked in Valetta Harbour. The *Justice* was to be detached and sent on to Egypt with dispatches forwarded by the *Généreux*.

Queen Charlotte, off Malta, 20th February 1800.[2]

To His Excellency Lt.-Gen. Fox, &c.

SIR,—By the late attempt of the French, you will see the value which they set upon Malta, and I cannot always hope to be as fortunate in preventing their landing, which, if they effect, General Graham will certainly be made prisoner, unless we can get him off, and that must depend on the wind; besides there is an immense quantity of shipping and stores on or about the Island, which must fall into the hands of the enemy. Add to this, I am led to believe that the combined fleet is likely to look this way, in which case I must withdraw the ships. I am at a loss to account for the total silence of the Ministers on this subject, but I am still convinced the only means to save ourselves is by your sending 2,000 men before the French are reinforced. In that case I think we might succeed in an attack; if they are reinforced, 20,000 would be of no use whatever. I fairly think you may construe your orders so as to send all above 5,000 pointed out in Mr. Dundas's instructions. The consequence is great. General Graham talks of raising two regiments of Maltese and clothing them with the clothes taken in the prizes; that is doing something. Of Neapolitan troops I have plenty, but they are very bad. I have the honour, &c.   (Signed) KEITH.

Anticipating events a little, it may be mentioned here that to this dispatch General Fox replied on the 19th of March requesting Lord Keith 'to give immediate orders to the officer commanding His Majesty's ships at Malta to take such steps as may be requisite to re-embark the troops and to return to Messina.'[3] Fortunately this order was not obeyed.

On the 22nd and 24th of February Brigadier-General Graham addressed the following dispatches to General Fox:—

[1] Arch. Nat., BB⁴ 136.
The *Carrère* and the *Muiron* were the ships on which Bonaparte and his suite escaped from Egypt and made his way safely to Ajaccio and thence to Fréjus.—J. H. R.
[2] C.O.R. Malta, No. 1.
[3] Ibid.
This order of General Fox is inexplicable, save on the assumption that he had heard news portending the arrival of the Franco-Spanish fleet in the Mediterranean, and even that news would not have justified such an order. We may notice here that in the month of March British warships were engaged in the blockade of Savona by sea; and a month later we further aided our Austrian allies by helping to blockade Masséna and the French garrison of Genoa. Moreover, on March 17th H.M.S. *Queen Charlotte*, while reconnoitring towards the Isle of Capraja (near Elba), caught fire and was lost along with 673 of her crew.—J. H. R.

Gudia, Malta, 22nd February 1800.[1]

To Lt.-Genl. Fox.

Sir,—I had the honour of receiving Your Excellency's dispatch of the 2nd inst., with the enclosures Nos. 1 and 2 on the 18th inst., by the return of the *Vincejo*.

My last letters of the 1st and 8th inst. were sent by the *Gorgon*, which left this on the 9th to go by Leghorn.

As the Commodore said then, that there was no probability of a more direct opportunity, both Lt.-Colonels, Lindenthal and Boyle, went in her. Your Excellency will hear of the fortunate capture of the *Généreux*, and a large store-ship, which, with three corvettes, were near this with supplies, and 2,000 men to reinforce the garrison of La Valetta.

As I am well convinced the enemy will make other efforts for the relief of that fortress, which it is evident they set a true value on, I have determined to increase our armed force on the Island by a levy of Maltese. At first I thought of raising a regiment of 1,000 men, but Colonel Stewart of the 89th Regiment declining to undertake it, I mean to become answerable myself for all expenses, and to raise independent companies, each to be under the command of a British officer, appointed to do duty with it, from these two regiments. I understand that there are many of them willing to take the trouble of forming three companies, though I have expressly mentioned that I can give them no assurance of their obtaining any protection by it. But if we keep our footing in this Island, and should ever be fortunate to get possession of La Valetta, there can be no doubt of the necessity of such a corps, and therefore I should hope the voluntary services of the officers would be a strong recommendation in their favour.

Lord Keith having sent me notice this evening that he was sending off a vessel immediately to Leghorn, I had just time to write a note to Mr. Dundas, to mention my having ventured to take this determination without waiting for your orders.

Had the plan been digested, I should have written of it to H.R.H., and thinking it of consequence that no time should be lost, I begged of Mr. Dundas to mention it, and to state my reason for not laying it before him.

Governor Ball assures me that this levy may be carried to a considerable extent, without at all interfering with the battalions of armed peasants furnished by each village, or at least without diminishing their numbers, and there can be no doubt of their being much more useful and manageable than these are. I imagine that the rates of pay, including the ration, or value of it, must be fixed at 8*d*.; the armed peasants received 40 ounces of bread, valued at an average at two taris, and one tari in money; it will be necessary to give one tari more, and clothing to induce them to submit to the restraint of discipline and being absent from their families. The tari is reckoned here at present at 2*d*. st., but it is to be observed that dollars all pass for 5*s*. st., tho' the Spanish is only worth 4*s*. 6*d*., and the Sicilian worth 4*s*. 4*d*., at which rates they should be established.

The troops receive the Spanish dollars as at Messina at that rate, and the Sicilian at the same. As there are 30 taris in a dollar, 4 of them will not amount to so much as 8*d*. Arms, accoutrements, and clothing may be got immediately from the prizes; the material article is *that of their not*

[1] C.O.R. Malta, No. 1.

serving out of the Island—at present an *indispensable* one for the success of a *hasty levy*.

It may eventually expose me to a severe responsibility.

But being well aware of that, it is at least a strong proof of my conviction of the urgency of the case, and it is the only means in my power for increasing our force, and providing for our security in case the enemy should be enabled to act offensively. It is true I have the offer of more Neapolitans; five companies of one regiment are arrived, of which the enclosed is a return. I have written to Lord Keith to say that in the event of the arrival of Russian or more British troops, it would be useful to have Neapolitans, but not considering them to be depended on alone, either for offensive operations or effectual resistance, I thought at present they would rather be an embarrassment, and therefore advised him to desire that they should be assembled at Syracuse to be near if wanted. They are put under my command, and are to remain under that of the British officer commanding here, whatever the rank of any Russian officer may be.

Tho' Your Excellency has complied with my former request, and empowered me to advance money to pay the Maltese, I am extremely glad not to be called on, as I know nothing about the application of it. Sir William Hamilton has sent Governor Ball £4,000, and promises more. I must, of course, order meanwhile the A[ssistant]-C[ommissary]-G[eneral] to pay the expenses attending this levy, and the pay of these men afterwards, but without any pretention of covering myself from the responsibility under the authority of your letter, which could only apply to the payment of the armed peasants. I shall no doubt be very happy on every account to receive the sanction of your approbation to this measure, if you are satisfied of its necessity. I shall take the earliest opportunity of sending Your Excellency the particulars and of acquainting you of the progress of the levy.

I need not assure you of the caution with which I shall use the powers entrusted me by your warrant. I hope soon to receive the proceedings of the Court Martial.

I have appointed Mr. Gunson to act as Deputy Purveyor to the General Hospital. I enclose a state of the sick, and I have the honour, &c.

(Signed) THOS. GRAHAM, A.B.G.

Gudia, Malta, 24*th February* 1800.[1]

To Lt.-Gen. the Hon. Henry Fox, &c.

SIR,—Lord Keith having sent for me to come on board the *Queen Charlotte*, I had an opportunity of conversing with him.

He is fully persuaded of the anxiety of the British Government to obtain possession of La Valetta, and flatters me with the hopes that orders for reinforcements may be arrived by this time.

Meanwhile he waits the return of a cutter sent to Corfu, to know what dependence is to be had on the Russians. Till this answer comes I shall not proceed in the Maltese levy, and I should be very happy to think it was unnecessary for our security. I feel sincerely obliged by your attention to my requests, and the confidence placed in me, which it shall be my study to merit a continuance of.

[1] C.O.R. Malta, No. 1.

You will not be surprised at my anxiety to increase our force by every means, because you must be aware of the extreme unwillingness I should have to ask for, and the reluctance the officers of the Navy would have to grant, the means of embarking the troops after so long a blockade by sea. It must be imminent danger, and not merely the prospect of it, that could determine us to abandon all hope of reaping the fruits of it. For some little time we are probably more secure than ever, but I am very confident B.parté [sic] will not abandon the garrison here without risking some other trial; whether by single vessels repeatedly dispatched, or by some great effort I cannot pretend to guess.[1]

However, the Mediterranean seems to be the natural scene of their efforts this campaign; by relieving Genoa they may be enabled to carry on offensive operations from that quarter, as well as from the side of Switzerland, and it certainly must be a great object for them to attempt to get back into Italy, and to remove the theatre of war from their frontiers, especially if such advantages can be combined with the plan of relieving La Valette and their army in Egypt. It is very unlikely, however, that they should attempt any operation in the Mediterranean that would necessarily detain their fleet in one place, and, therefore, if we were reinforced, our risk would by no means increase in proportion to the magnitude of their armaments. They would most probably satisfy themselves with saving Valette, and would carry any troops they could spare on to Alexandria.

As all the officers, and indeed all the prisoners, were sent to Syracuse, there has been no opportunity of ascertaining whether Egypt was one of the objects of this expedition. There were many letters picked up at sea directed to people there, and it is said the quantity of medicines is very great, but Lord Keith has got no particulars from Captain Martin, who was sent with the *Alexander* in charge of the *Généreux*.

The French Admiral Perrée was killed by the fire of the *Success*, which fired a raking broadside into the *Généreux*.

They made no defence, but struck to the second shot from the *Foudroyant*; the *Northumberland* and *Alexander* were both near, all the ships having gone after the *Généreux*, by which means the others escaped easily.[2] The *Success* and *Phæton* were ordered to follow, but the latter was 24 hours behind them. The ships in the harbour, the *Guillaume Tell*, &c., are evidently in a great state of forwardness for sea. I should not be sorry to see them go, but we fire at them to please the Navy, hitherto without success. It brings a heavy fire from [Fort] Ricazoli or St. Roque but they have not done us any damage. Some private letters were sent in by way of letting them know of our success. We have had a sergeant and corporal (both French) deserters within these two days, and this morning about 200 inhabitants came out, the first for about a month past. I have the honour, &c. (Signed) THOS. GRAHAM.[3]

[1] The foregoing sentences show the sense of insecurity among the besiegers of Valetta, even after the capture of the *Généreux* and the transport. The fate of Malta really depended on the large Franco-Spanish fleet at Brest, under Admiral Bruix.—J. H. R.

[2] One of the French transports was captured a little later.—J. H. R.

[3] I have verified Mr. Hardman's copy of Sir Thomas Graham's letter from the original copy, which is in Mr. Broadley's collection of MSS. in the extra-illustrated edition of his and Mr. Bartlett's *Nelson's Hardy*.—J. H. R.

CHAPTER XIV

THE BRITISH BLOCKADE

(From the 24th February to the 30th June 1800)

TOWARDS the end of February, Lord Keith anticipated his withdrawal for a period from Malta.[1] He therefore instructed Lord Nelson to take command of the squadron, which was to remain; consisting of the *Foudroyant* (flagship), *Northumberland, Culloden, Lion, Success, Alexander, Bonne Citoyenne, Stromboli, Minorca, Penelope,* and *Vincejo,* and prosecute the necessary measures for the reduction of Malta, adding, that as the remoteness of Palermo from Malta rendered it an inconvenient place of rendezvous, it was to be discontinued, and Syracuse substituted, or, if he preferred, Augusta or Messina.[2]

Precise instructions were issued under date of the 24th February, as follows :—

LORD KEITH TO LORD NELSON.

Queen Charlotte, off Malta, *24th February* 1800.[3]

MY LORD,—In the event of any offer being made to surrender Valette to the forces of His Majesty and his Allies within one month from this date, or before the arrival of foreign forces, which may be expected daily, Your Lordship is hereby permitted and required to concur with His Excellency Governor Ball and Brigadier-General Graham and granting the most liberal terms to the French garrison in that place with respect to their persons, private property, and baggage, honours of war, swords to officers and permission to wear them, and also to consent to both officers and men being maintained while prisoners at the expense of His Majesty and his Allies, protected against all violence and insult which the inhabitants might be disposed to offer, and sent by the earliest opportunities which can be embraced to France, on the simple condition of not serving against any of the Allies till they are regularly exchanged. In this case, however, it is to be understood that all the ships of war, and others, and public

---

[1] Keith sailed for Leghorn in order to concert measures with the Austrians then operating on the Genoese riviera. He soon materially helped them to blockade Masséna at Genoa.—J. H. R.

[2] Nicolas, *Dispatches of Nelson,* vol. iv. p. 191.

[3] Brit. Mus. Add. MSS. 34916, f. 225.

stores, and property of every denomination, belonging to the French Republic, are to be honourably delivered up in their present state and condition to the Allied Powers.

These terms are in my opinion such as the Governor and General are perfectly disposed to acquiesce in, but should any others which relate to personal accommodation, or honorary concessions be insisted on, I leave Your Lordship at full liberty to agree to any terms to which the Governor and General may be disposed to accede. I have the honour, &c.

(Signed) KEITH.

EXTRACT FROM THE INSTRUCTIONS OF LORD KEITH TO LORD NELSON, 24TH FEBRUARY 1800.[1]

. . . In the event of the surrender of Valette, Your Lordship is to sign for His Majesty in conformity to the rank which you hold, as the General will do in his, and the Governor for His Majesty the King of Naples. And with respect to the garrisoning of the place, you are to be guided by His Majesty's instructions communicated by the Right Honourable Lord Grenville, one of His Majesty's principal Secretaries of State to the Lords Commissioners of the Admiralty, with copies of which, and their Lordships' directions thereon, you have been provided. Your Lordship is to use every means in your power for protecting and securing the property and effects belonging to the Knights of St. John, which nevertheless are to be inventoried and appraised, but not to be considered as booty or prize. You will most scrupulously preserve the property of the churches and the private effects of individuals, even of such inhabitants as may be reported to have favoured the French interest, and you will on no account consent to, or concur in, but on the contrary protest against every act of severe or cruel retaliation which would involve our national character in disgrace and excite the animosity of the inhabitants, and you are most expressly to prohibit the officers serving under your orders from so doing.

Your Lordship will in such event regard all the ships and vessels, stores, and effects of every description belonging to the French Republic, and all vessels having voluntarily traded with them, as booty or prize, and concur in directing the same to be proceeded against according to the Laws of Nations, and the subsequent determinations of the Sovereigns of the Allied forces. All which property should in the meantime be valued and put into the charge of commissioners till such determination of the respective Sovereigns whose forces have been employed in the reduction of the Island shall be made known.

But in case it should be judged requisite to equip and employ the ships of war that may be captured in the harbour, you may consent (the hulls, masts, yards, rigging, ordnance, ammunition, and stores of every denomination of each vessel having been first duly surveyed and separately valued) that the same be divided into lots, and be fairly drawn for in presence of the respective commanding officers of the Allies, and the value of the several lots so drawn, whatever the amount may be, should be charged against such proportion of each Power's share of the whole capture, as by the arrangement to be determined on by the several Sovereigns

[1] Brit. Mus. Add. MSS. 34916, p. 219.

as above mentioned may be thereafter allotted to the forces of each respectively. . . . Given on board His Majesty's ship *Queen Charlotte*, off Malta, the 24th February 1800. (Signed) KEITH.

The orders referring to Syracuse becoming the naval rendezvous for the future, instead of Palermo, caused Nelson the greatest chagrin, and two days after their receipt he wrote to his friend Lord Minto, British envoy at the Court of Vienna, as follows :—

'I have serious thoughts of giving up active service. Greenwich Hospital seems a fit retreat, after being evidently thought unfit to command in the Mediterranean.'[1]

During Nelson's stay off Malta (15th February to the 10th March) he received the following dispatches, from General Graham dated the 3rd March, from Captain Ball of the 5th March, and from Colonel Cardona of the 10th March :—

BRIG.-GEN. GRAHAM TO LORD NELSON.

La Gudia, Malta, *3rd March* 1800.[2]

MY DEAR LORD,—I have this moment received Your Lordship's letter of this morning's date. I have never doubted of the anxiety of the French Government to retain possession of this most important post, and I am quite convinced that every effort will be used to relieve it. On that account I have long sincerely regretted (and said so in all my letters) that a force adequate to some material offensive operation by which some post commanding the harbour might be gained, and thereby completing the blockade, was not employed on shore. There is no other means, no other chance in my mind of hastening the surrender one hour. I never considered the very trifling force under my command as capable of making and sustaining any such exertion. I am clear that nothing could be effected by regular approaches by it. The only possibility of success would be by surprise, and the critical situation we are in might justify a hazardous and desperate attempt in that way, provided on examination a place can be found that is accessible, and which would afford some probability of carrying the works. Of [*sic*] this I have been seriously occupied, and Captain Gordon has already been out one night to reconnoitre, and was to have gone again this evening, but was prevented by indisposition.

I hope he will be able to give me a final report to-morrow night.

If the thing can be attempted at all, very little preparation will be necessary, and there shall be no unnecessary delay (but the state of the weather must be consulted). I am convinced the enemy can never be more off their guard than they are now; they know our strength, or rather weakness, and they are satisfied we have at present no other object but blockade. I should be sorry, therefore, to awaken them to greater vigilance by any change in our conduct while there is any hope of being able to make a real attack.

Should that idea be necessarily given up as impracticable, I shall

---

[1] Laughton, *Nelson's Letters*, p. 235. [2] Brit. Mus. Add. MSS. 34916, f. 291.

have no objections to any trials of false attacks, &c., though I am convinced of their inefficacy—they will only laugh at our puny efforts.

Would any of us give up such a place without the loss of a post, as long as there was a morsel of bread to eat ? Impossible. Adieu, my dear Lord, &c.

(Signed) THOS. GRAHAM.

CAPTAIN BALL TO LORD NELSON.

St. Antonio, 5*th March* 1800.[1]

MY LORD,—I am very sorry to acquaint Your Lordship that a French corvette got into La Valette last night; she passed close along shore from the northward.

May I beg leave to suggest to Your Lordship that it is of great importance to station a ship 10 leagues N.W. of Gozo ? I have the honour, &c.

(Signed) ALEX. JN°· BALL.

MILORD,—Les fortifications et retranchemens des trouppes Maltaises sont sous les ordres de V[otre] E[xcellence] du moment qu'elle en a désigné le Chef, et qu'elles ont été dirigées d'après ses ordres. Je prends la liberté d'en addresser les plans à V. E. à laquelle ils sont dédiés comme un hommage qui lui est dû, et un gage du respectueux dévouement que je lui ay voué pour la vie. Je suis avec un très profond respect, &c.

(Signed) THÉODORE CARDONA.

Malte, le 10 *Mars* 1800.

The destruction of Admiral Perrée's relieving force on the 17th February did not destroy all hope in the gallant garrison of being eventually relieved. The spirit of the besieged rose to the occasion. They became convinced that the attacking force had renounced all idea of storming the fortifications, or of attempting capture by means of more regular siege works and approaches, and that it was evident that their intention was to starve the garrison into surrender. Under these circumstances Villeneuve proposed to dispatch the battleship *Guillaume Tell* to France, not only for the purpose of saving the ship, if possible, to the nation, but in order that she might, in company with other vessels, return to the rescue, promising to hold out for other three months, which term the valiant garrison increased to six months.

Villeneuve's proposal was placed by Vaubois before a council of war on the 1st March, and the suggestion unanimously approved. These particulars were forwarded to the Colonial Minister by Villeneuve, under date of the 4th March, in the following interesting dispatch :—

[1] Brit. Mus. Add. MSS. 34916, f. 302.
In all probability this was one of the three French corvettes which escaped the chase on February 17, as described in the Introduction, and in Sir Thomas Graham's letters of February 22 and 24 (Chap. xiii).

Malte, le 13 *Ventôse* an 8 (*4th March* 1800).[1]
Le Contre-Amiral Villeneuve au Ministre de la Marine et des Colonies.

CITOYEN MINISTRE,—Nous voici parvenus à une époque et dans une position qui ne me permet plus de me flatter que les mesures que vous aviés adoptées pour le ravitaillement de cette place et dont vous nous faisiés part au Citoyen Ménard et à moi, par vos lettres du 28 Thermidor[2] ayent leur exécution. Il nous paraît démontré par les rapports mêmes qui nous sont parvenus de l'ennemi qu'une partie des bâtimens que vous nous aviés expédiés sous le commandement de Contre-Amiral Pérée a été la proie de l'ennemi presqu'à l'atterrage de cet Isle. C'est ce qu'il résulte du moins d'une lettre que m'a écrit l'Amiral Nelson en m'envoyant des lettres particulières de ma famille qu'il a trouvé dit-il sur le vaisseau de cet Officier Général. Dans cet état de choses il ne nous reste plus qu'à ménager autant qu'il est possible, le peu de subsistances que nous avons encore pour prolonger notre deffense et donner le tems au Gouvernement de réparer cet échec.[3]

L'ennemi croit être sur le point d'arriver à ses fins ; il se borne à nous bloquer étroitement par terre et par mer ; il semble avoir renoncé à toute entreprise de vive force et encore plus à une attaque régulière ; la ville est presqu'entièrement évacuée de ses habitans et le soldat qui ne craint plus l'ennemi du dédans et qui connaît la force de la place, ne manifeste aucune inquiétude sur la possibilité d'y être assailli. C'est par ces considérations et attendant que les mesures que vous aviés ordonné le 28 Thermidor sont rompues par les évènements de la guerre, que j'ai proposé au Général Vaubois le départ du vaisseau *Le Guillaume Tell* pour France, qui [*sic*] parceque nous trouverions une économie de subsistance, que vu l'extrême modicité des rations ne pouvait se trouver que dans une réduction de consommateurs ; que la saison actuelle pouvait fournir des chances heureuses à ce vaisseau pour arriver à Toulon, impossible dans la saison où nous allons entrer prochainement. Enfin que ce vaisseau rémis à la disposition du Gouvernement pourait être employé encore efficacement à notre ravitaillement et remplacer les pertes que nous venons de faire.

Général Vaubois a cru devoir soumettre ma proposition à un conseil de guerre composé des Officiers Généraux et Ordonnateurs de terre et de mer, je joins ici une expédition de la délibération de ce conseil de guerre dont le considérant rélate les motifs qui ont fixé sa détermination.

Le Général Decrès d'après les vœux de ce conseil de guerre passe sur ce vaisseau ; personne mieux que lui peut vous faire connoîttre notre position et jusqu'à quel point il serait encore possible de venir à notre secour.

Voici le dix neuvième mois de siège et de blocus que nous soutenons, il y a près d'un an que nous n'avons reçu de bâtimens[4] et depuis trois mois il n'a été distribué à la garnison ni de la marée [?] ni du vin ni [de l']eau de vie, et précédement il n'en était distribué que trois fois la décade.

[1] Arch. Nat. BB⁴, 147.
[2] i.e. 15th August 1799.—J. H. R.
[3] The tone of this letter is more manly than that of Vaubois of March 4—a noteworthy fact in view of the censures lavished by the latter on the Admiral at a later time.—J. H. R.
[4] Strange to say, on that very night a corvette slipped in, as described in the PS.—J. H. R.

THE BRITISH BLOCKADE—1800

Depuis le mois de Vendémiaire, époque de l'arrivée de deux avisos par le retour desquels je vous ai écrit, nous n'avons reçu absolument aucune nouvelle de notre patrie et n'avons plus qu'un mois et demi de légumes et deux distributions de viande salée quoique depuis le commencement du siège la ration ait été réduite au tiers de l'ordonnance, l'huile pourait nous conduire jusqu'en Prairial.

En chargeant le Général Decrès d'aller presser l'envoy des secours qui peuvent nous être destinés, nous avons pris l'engagement de tenir au moins trois mois après son départ, j'espère que nous le tiendrons et que nous ne mettrons de terme à notre dévouement que l'abandon entier de nos forces physiques pour nous soutenir.

En expédiant le vaisseau, *Le Guillaume Tell*, il ne me reste plus sur les autres bâtiments qui restent dans le port qu'un simple garde. Tout le reste des équipages est employé dans les forts et batteries, je ne vous dissimule pas, Citoyen Ministre, que je conserve bien peu d'espoir de soustraire ces bâtiments au sort qui menace la place une fois la belle saison venuë. Les vaisseaux ennemis sont déjà mouillés à l'embouchure du port, nous sommes environnés de batteries et de postes ennemis qui observent nos moindres mouvements et lors même qu'une circonstance de tems favorable pour faire sortir quelque bâtiment se présenterait au moment où nous serions rendus à l'extrémité, je doute encore qu'on pût me rendre les équipages qui sont employés à terre et qui occupent des ouvrages essentiels ; soyez persuadé, Citoyen Ministre, que dans une circonstance aussi cruelle, mais qu'il devient impossible aujourd'hui de ne pas prévoir, je ne négligerai rien pour diminuer, s'il est possible, les pertes de la République. Salut et respect. (Signed) VILLENEUVE.

PS. du 15 *Ventôse* (6th *March* 1800).

Le navire *La Bellone* de Marseille du port de 150 t^x est arrivé ce matin avec un chargement de viandes salées, vins et eau de vie, la joie de la garnison a été inexprimable, l'arrivée de ce bâtiment nous procure les moyens d'adoucir le sort des soldats et des marins, et leur fait entrevoir la possibilité de voir arriver des secours plus puissants, il est fâcheux que des expéditions semblables et isolées n'ayent pas été faites pendant le cours de cet hiver, la place serait ravitaillée pour tout l'été ; le rassemblement d'un convoi éveille toujours l'attention de l'ennemi et il lui devient difficile d'échaper à sa surveillance. Le Général Vaubois prend la cargaison de ce bâtiment pour le compte de la République, il nous assure la possibilité de tenir tout le mois de Prairial.

Nous avons appris par ce bâtiment les premières nouvelles des évènements du mois de Brumaire et de la nouvelle Constitution acceptée par la nation ; l'assurance de retrouver à notre retour en France, une patrie, nos familles, nos biens, protégés par un gouvernement aussi ferme que juste et éclairé, ne peut que relever le courage, la persévérance et le dévouement des français dévoués à la défense d'une place aussi importante.

EXTRAIT DU REGISTRE DES DÉLIBÉRATIONS DU CONSEIL DE GUERRE.

Le dix *Ventôse*, an huitième (1*st March* 1800).

Les Généraux de Brigade Chanez et d'Hennezel [?], les Contre-Amiraux Villeneuve et Decrès, et les Ordonnateurs de la guerre et de la marine convoqués par le Général de Division Vaubois, Commandant en Chef dans les Isles de Malte et du Goze, pour la tenue d'un conseil de guerre, se sont assemblés au Palais National de la cité de Malte, partie de l'ouest.

Le Général Vaubois, après avoir fait lecture d'une lettre à lui écrite le 6 de ce mois par le Contre-Amiral Villeneuve, commandant les forces navales stationnées dans ce port et dont copie est cy-joint, a fait part au conseil des renseignements qu'il a eut de la prise par l'ennemi d'une partie du ravitaillement qui nous était annoncée ; de l'état de la place et de ses approvisionnements et a demandé qu'il soit délibéré sur la mesure proposée par le Contre-Amiral Villeneuve.

Le conseil, après avoir mûrement examiné les circonstances où nous nous trouvons et la proposition sus-enoncée—

Considérant :

Que les avis qui nous sont venus de l'ennemi, de la capture d'une partie des approvisionnements qui nous étaient destinés sont accompagnés de circonstances qui ne permettent pas de douter de cette vérité.

Que les magasins de vivres se trouvent dans ce moment, malgré les sévères réductions exercées depuis le commencement du siège, dans un tel état de pénurie, que le danger d'être forcés par la famine de capituler dans quelques mois, est devenu iminent.

Que dans cette position le parti le plus urgent à prendre est de diminuer le nombre des consommateurs ; qu'outre le devoir de tacher de soustraire ce qui sera possible de la Division Navale au sort qui ménace la place, le moyen le plus efficace d'opérer cette diminution de consommateurs serait d'expédier pour la France la partie des forces navales dont à toute rigueur on peut se passer ; sans compromettre nos points de deffense, d'où résulterait une économie dans les vivres tant par le départ des équipages que par celui des malades incurables, et des individus français dont les services sont actuellement inutiles, résultat qui prolongerait évidemment nos moyens de tenir plus longtems.[1]

Que bien que tous les équipages de la division aient étés nécessaires et seraient encore indispensables si la place était ménacée d'une nouvelle attaque régulière, l'état des forces de l'ennemi semble tel qu'il ne peut se porter avec succès à une semblable attaque et qu'il ne peut à l'avenir que continuer un blocus par lequel il espère arriver bientôt à ses fins.

Que dans cet état de choses, et après le dévouement énergique que montre la garnison, la place peut à toute force se passer de l'équipage du *Guillaume Tell*.

Considérant en outre tous les avantages qu'il y aurait à mettre ce vaisseau à la disposition du Gouvernement et enfin que bien que le salut de ce bâtiment expédié à travers les escadres ennemis qui nous bloquent, soit incertain, la mésure de son départ offre cependant plus de chances en faveur de sa conservation que n'en offrirait la prolongation de son séjour à Malte jusqu'à la saison très prochaine, où son départ commandé par les circonstances deviendrait impossible à raison de la brièveté des nuits, de la fréquence des calmes et de la continuelle présence de l'ennemi presque toujours mouillé à l'embouchure du port.

Le conseil par toutes ces considérations a unanimement délibéré que le

---

[1] As I have pointed out in the Introduction, this passage explains the discrepancy in the numbers of the crew of the *Guillaume Tell*. James (vol. ii. p. 443, edit. 1902) gives only 919 men ; Clarke and MacArthur (Bk. iii. pp. 249, 251) give 1,220 men.—J. H. R.

Contre-Amiral Villeneuve expédiera le vaisseau *Le Guillaume Tell* pour les ports de France aussitôt que la circonstance favorable se présentera et que le Contre-Amiral Decrès passera sur ce vaisseau pour se porter vers le Gouvernement lui rendre compte de notre situation actuelle et proposer ou hâter des nouveaux moyens de secours s'il en est tems encore.

Une expédition de la présente sera remise au Général Decrès et au Contre-Amiral Villeneuve. Suivent les signatures. Certifié conforme le Commissaire de la guerre faisant fonctions d'Ordonnateur.

(Signed) Dot.
„ Vaubois.

COPIE DE LA LETTRE DU CONTRE-AMIRAL VILLENEUVE AU GÉNÉRAL VAUBOIS.

GÉNÉRAL,—Les circonstances actuelles et le peu de renseignements qui nous sont parvenus de l'ennemi me ramènent à vous parler encore du départ de quelques bâtiments de la Division Navale qui se trouve ici. C'est sous le rapport de la conservation de cette place que j'en examine l'importance.

Il est certain que si après avoir considéré l'état de nos forces ici, celles de l'enemi qui vous assiège, vous trouvez qu'il est possible de vous départir d'environ quatre cents hommes de l'équipage du *Guillaume Tell* qui se trouvent actuellement employés au service de la place, il en résulterait que je pourrais expédier ce vaisseau pour la France, que vous y trouveriez sur le champ une grande économie en subsistances, que le vaisseau outre les 760 hommes de son équipage emporterait encore avec lui tous les malades de l'hôpital qui ne peuvent y espérer leur guérison et bien des bouches françaises inutiles qui sont dans la place et qui y reçoivent des rations, ce qui réduirait la consommation de vivres au moins du quart. Par cette mésure vous mettriez un bon vaisseau de plus à la disposition du Gouverne^t qui pourrait l'employer encore à notre ravitaillement.

Placé ici par le Gouvernement pour y diriger les opérations navales, et chargé de ses ordres, je ne me dissimule pas les inconvénients de cette mésure, mais dans la position où nous nous trouvons, mon principe est, qu'un Officier Général, privé de communication avec le Gouvernement, voyant les mesures qu'il avait adoptées rompues par des circonstances imprévues ou par les évènements de la guerre, j'ai (dis-je) pour principe qu'un officier général doit alors savoir prendre sur lui, les résolutions qu'il croit les plus avantageuses à la République et répondre aussi à la confiance qui lui est accordée.

Je sais qu'un vaisseau qui partirait d'ici a de grands dangers à courir pour se rendre dans un de nos ports, mais il est certain aussi que ces dangers sont bien moindres dans la saison où nous sommes, que dans trois mois d'ici, époque où la fin de nos vivres voudrait nous faire penser au salut de la Division pour la soustraire au sort dont la place soit ménacée. Ajoutez que les vaisseaux ennemis seront au moins aussi nombreux dans ces mers qu'ils peuvent l'être dans ce moment, qu'il viendront mouiller comme ils l'ont fait l'année passée devant l'entrée du port, que les calmes et la briéveté des nuits nous mettraient alors dans l'impossibilité d'espérer que rien ne puisse échaper.

Au reste comme suivant les ordres précis du Ministre, tout doit être sacrifié à la deffense de Malte. Je vous propose, Général, d'examiner si ce ne sera pas le moyen de prolonger la deffense que de faire partir le vaisseau

Le Guillaume Tell, je le répette, qui emportant avec lui toutes les malades incurables et les bouches françaises inutiles porterait une économie au moins d'un quart sur nos consommations ; et si les forces qui vous restent et celles qui pourraient être tirées encore des autres bâtiments de la République qui sont ici ne seraient pas suffisantes pour assurer la deffense de la place aussi longtems que la situation de vos vivres pourrait vous le permettre.

Si vous décidez pour l'affirmative, je vous engage alors à donner des ordres pour le remplacement des hommes de ce vaisseau qui sont employés à terre pour qu'il puissent rentrer à leur bord et le vaisseau sera prêt pour la première circonstance favorable. Salut et fraternité.

(Signed) VILLENEUVE.

By the Consular Constitution which was accepted by the people on the 24th December 1799, special laws were instituted for the regulation of colonial questions. Doublet, still officiating as Acting Commissary of Government, thereupon drew the attention of the authorities at Paris to various topics in this connexion which he considered worthy of their consideration. His opinions are interesting in that they emanate from an official who had then been twenty years resident in the island, and had occupied an important position in the Government of the Knights of St. John. But the report addressed to the Colonial Minister, under date of the 9th March 1800, is too long to be quoted here.

The dissensions between Lords Keith and Nelson were now evidently reaching a climax. On the 8th March, Nelson informed the commander-in-chief, from off Malta, that, owing to ill-health, he would be obliged to retire to Palermo for a few weeks, and that he intended to appoint Captain Troubridge to carry on the duties of senior officer during his absence. Accordingly, on the 10th March, Nelson sailed from Malta, arriving at Palermo on the 16th. On the 24th the *Foudroyant,* under Captain Edward Berry, was sent back to Malta, with orders to leave that island for Palermo on the 6th April, when Nelson would rejoin his ship.

During Nelson's stay at Palermo (16th March to 24th April) he received the following dispatches from Ball, dated the 16th and 25th March :—

CAPTAIN BALL TO LORD NELSON.

Malta, *16th March* 1800.[1]

MY LORD,—I have the honour to acquaint Your Lordship that a courier arrived here from Syracuse with three letters for you, which I send by him, to be forwarded to Palermo.

As Sir Thomas Troubridge is recovering his health, and will write fully to Your Lordship, I shall not repeat what belongs to him to detail.

[1] Brit. Mus. Add. MSS. 34916, f. 330.

A French deserter effected his escape the 14th from Fort Tigné; he had been only two days from the hospital. He says that sixty soldiers who are invalided had received orders to embark on board the *Guillaume Tell* the 15th inst., and that the French ships were to push out the very first opportunity. He reports the garrison to be in great misery and very sickly, and that the corn which they have left is much damaged, and that the bread which they get is very black and bad. We have not had any Maltese inhabitants from La Valette since the 24th of last month. . . . I have the honour, &c. (Signed) ALEX. JN°· BALL.

CAPTAIN BALL TO LORD NELSON,

Malta, 25*th March* 1800.

MY LORD,—When His Sicilian Majesty, through Your Lordship's recommendation and the solicitations of the inhabitants of Malta, did me the honour to appoint me chief of this Island, I was assured that a full compensation would be made to me for any expense or losses which I might sustain; I therefore beg leave to state as succinctly as possible my case, in the hope that through Your Lordship's protection I may meet the indemnification which may be deemed just and equitable. In October 1798 Your Lordship gave me the command of the squadron blockading the French ships in Malta. The inhabitants in the country revolted against the French in the preceding month, whom they were besieging in La Valette, and what will appear astonishing, 4,000 peasants with only 2,000 muskets kept in awe 6,000 regular troops.[1] I had to co-operate with these men, who had chosen for their chiefs a priest and an attorney; but as they did not receive any pay, and only a scanty allowance of provisions, they soon began to lose that energy which had roused them to vengeance; they were splitting into parties, and the two chiefs opposing each other in every business, which lost them the confidence of the people, who threatened their lives. Anarchy soon ensued; innocent men were put to death, and money extorted from individuals in a very unjust manner.

The inhabitants in the hour of terror and dismay implored me to assume an authority, and use my efforts to avert the miseries which awaited them. As early as January 1799 I directed the civil and military affairs of the Island; and the inhabitants were so sensible of its good effects, that they sent Deputies to His Sicilian Majesty, and to Your Lordship, praying that I might be appointed their chief, which has been graciously complied with. In May 1799 I was ordered off the station in consequence of the French fleet having entered the Mediterranean; I returned in a fortnight, and was called away a second time. During my absence the farmers and Jacobins held tumultuous meetings, and came to Sant Antonio, head-quarters, in a large body and declared they would not pay rent. The affairs of the Island were falling into the former anarchy, on account of which the people desired that an application might be made to Your Lordship to allow me to resume my command in the Island. Your Lordship was pleased to direct me to live on shore, and to leave the first lieutenant of the *Alexander* in charge of the ship, that I might receive the same advantages from her as if actually on board, particularly as I am

[1] These figures are inaccurate.—J. H. R.

acting on shore in a military as well as civil capacity. His Majesty's ship *Alexander* was lately in company with Your Lordship's ship, when she made the important and valuable capture of the French Admiral Perré's ship the *Généreux* and a French corvette, and it is now said that I cannot receive what would be my share of prize money, because I am employed on shore in a civil capacity; I have therefore to request Your Lordship's intercession with the Sovereigns who have entered into a treaty respecting this Island, that they may take it into their most gracious consideration. I beg leave to enclose two letters which I have received from the Congress of this Island and the Judges, as they will prove to Your Lordship that my services here, during a very critical and dangerous period, have gained me the confidence and attachment of these islanders. I have judged it good policy to live hospitably, and to entertain occasionally the principal inhabitants, which has had the best effect; but as this has incurred additional expenses, I shall hope that it will be duly considered. I have the honour, &c. (Signed) A. J. BALL.

On the 25th March, Admiral Villeneuve informed the Colonial Minister, in the following dispatch, that in accordance with the decision of the council of war held on the 12th of that month, the *Guillaume Tell* had been prepared for sea, but owing to the weather continuing unpropitious, and to the position and vigilance of the British fleet off the port, she had been unable to leave the harbour with any chance of escape:—

Malte, le 4 *Germinal* an 8 (25th March 1800).[1]

LE CONTRE-AMIRAL VILLENEUVE AU MINISTRE DE LA MARINE ET DES COLONIES.

Je joins ici, Citoyen Ministre, un duplicata de ma dépêche du 13 Ventôse et un extrait du procès verbal du conseil de guerre, dans lesquels vous verrès les motifs qui m'ont déterminés à expédier le vaisseau *Le Guillaume Tell* pour les ports de France. Les contrariétés du tems et la position des ennemis, ont retardé jusqu'aujourd'hui l'exécution de cette mésure, et peut la retarder encore. En effet nous sommes bloqués par quatre vaisseaux de ligne, plusieurs frégates et plusieurs corvettes, le port est environné de batteries et de postes ennemis.[2] Pourque le vaisseau *Le Guillaume Tell* puisse en sortir avec quelqu'espoir d'échaper à leur surveillance, il lui faut nécessairement un tems obscur tel qu'il puisse faire les mouvements et appareiller sans que l'ennemi en soit prévenu, ou du moins qu'il ne le soit pas assez tôt pour qu'il puisse venir l'attendre à la bouche du port, et enfin un vent assez frais pour que dans la nuit il puisse faire assez de chemin pour perdre de vue et l'Isle et l'escadre ennemie. Ces circonstances ne se sont pas encore présentées, mais tout est prêt pour profitter dès qu'elles se présenteront.

Le Général Decrès est à bord. Il instruit les équipages aux différentes exercises et rien ne sera négligé pour sauver ce vaisseau et le ramener dans nos ports; ou pour honorer son pavillon par une belle deffense s'il faut que la fortune se montre toujours contraire à nos expéditions maritimes.

[1] Arch. Nat., BB⁴ 147.
[2] Villeneuve here exaggerates the number of the blockading vessels.—J. H. R.

Je charge de cette dépêche le Capitaine Bennet du navire *La Bellone
du Ciotat* dont je vous ai annoncé l'arrivée dans ce port ; la petitesse de son
bâtiment peut le mettre à même d'appareiller par un tems qui ne le
permettrait pas au vaisseau *Le Guillaume Tell* ; et je désire que vous soyez
instruit de nos nouvelles par son arrivée en France, si elle précède celle du
Guillaume Tell.

Le chargement de ce navire a été un grand soulagement pour les
deffenseurs de cette place, le Général Vaubois l'a pris en entier pour le
comte de la République, il va se trouver à même de faire deux distributions
de vin par décade et quelques distributions de lard. Cette amélioration de
rations peut contribuer essentiellement à maintenir la santé du soldat et
du marin dans la saison du printems qui l'année dernière fut fatale à
un grand nombre ; et si le vaisseau *Le Guillaume Tell* part bientôt nous
esperons au moyen de ce surcroît de comestible de gagner tout le mois
de Messidor.

Il est de la justice du Gouvernement de satisfaire au plutôt aux lettres
de change qui ont été remises aux armateurs en payement de leur cargaison.
Le service qu'ils ont rendu leur donne droit à l'espérer et ce serait un
encouragement utile pour exciter de semblables expéditions. Si le sort
de Malte est de pouvoir être encore ravitaillé, la confiance que nous inspire
le Gouvernement nous fait espérer encore que deux ans de souffrance et de
privations ne seront pas terminés par une capitulation dont le mot seul
nous indigne. Salut & respect. (Signed) VILLENEUVE.

On the 31st March, Villeneuve was at last able to report to the
Minister of Marine that the *Guillaume Tell* had sailed with a fresh
south-east wind on the night of the 29th–30th.

Malte, le 10 *Germinal* an 8 (31*st March* 1800).[1]

CITOYEN MINISTRE,—*Le Guillaume Tell* a mis à la voile dans la nuit
du 8 au 9 par un vent de S.E. frais par grains. L'Amiral Nelson [2] venait
de mouiller sous le vent du port à deux portées de canons avec les vaisseaux
Le Foudroyant de 80, *L'Alexandre* de 74, *Le Lyon* de 64, deux frégates, trois
bricks étaient à la voile au vent et en face du port. Deux autres vaisseaux
étaient mouillés à Marsa Siroco ; quoique cette position rendit le départ
infiniment chanceux, il ne pouvait cependant être différé d'avantage. Les
ennemis avaient tirés pendant toute l'après midi du 8 des bombes et des
boulets sur ce vaisseau, et s'ils eussent pu continuer le lendemain ils
l'auraient assurement endommagé dans sa mâture et dans son grément
et mis dans l'impossibilité de pouvoir jamais partir, d'ailleurs étant
deblindé [*sic*] et ayant ses poudres à bord, il eut été un sujet de vive inquiétude pour lui même et pour le port s'il eût été atteint de quelque bombe.

C'est après nous être concertés sur cet état de choses, entre le Général
Vaubois, moi et le Contre-Amiral Decrès, que ce dernier a appareillé
à onze heures et demie du soir. Les batteries de terre l'ont signalé
aussitot qu'il a été sous voiles et ont tiré sur lui, les vaisseaux ennemis
ont répondu à ces signaux et ont aussi mis à la voile. Nous avons
apperçus des signaux en mer jusqu'à trois heures du matin. Au jour

[1] Arch. Nat., BB⁴ 147. [2] Nelson had sailed for Palermo on March 10th.

nous ne les avons plus apperçu et il n'est resté devant le port qu'un vaisseau (*L'Alexandre*) et une frégate. J'espère que par le vent qu'il a fait et les bonnes qualités du *Guillaume Tell* qu'il aura échapé à ce premier danger de traversée. La hardiesse de ce départ, la précision dans la manœuvre et dans son exécution honorent également et le Général Decrès et les officiers et marins de ce vaisseau.

Puisse leur dévouement être couronné par un succès complet par leur prompte arrivée dans les ports de la République. Salut et respects.

(Signed) VILLENEUVE.

As has been pointed out in the Introduction, the departure of the *Foudroyant* (80 guns) under Captain Edward Berry from Palermo on the 24th March enabled her to reach Malta just in time to take a prominent part in the capture, after a three-hours' most gallant resistance, of the last of the line-of-battle ships which had escaped from the battle of the Nile. Captain Ball and Sir Thomas Troubridge had become aware that an attempt would be made to save the *Guillaume Tell* (86 guns) to the Republic, and had taken the necessary precautions. Sir Thomas had kept his ships cruising close off the harbour's mouth, and had further placed a lieutenant and three good men every night after dark in a house called the Belvedere, close to the Cottonera lines, with a night-glass, to watch her movements.[1]

At midnight of the day on which the *Foudroyant* rejoined the British fleet the *Guillaume Tell* put to sea. Captain Blackwood in the *Penelope* (36 guns) soon descried the enemy, who had weathered the other ships, and under all sail was steering to the eastward; but soon after midnight he managed to get close up to her and subject her to several raking broadsides, which finally injured her sails and impaired her sailing powers. The *Foudroyant* in the meanwhile had slipped her cables, making all sail for the eastward. At dawn the *Lion* (64 guns, Captain Dixon), and *Penelope* were seen by the *Foudroyant* engaged with her in a crippled state, the main and mizen topmasts gone, shot away, as it proved to be, by the *Penelope*. The *Foudroyant* soon joined in the attack, and by ten minutes past eight of Sunday morning, the 30th, the enemy struck his colours.[2] Rear-Admiral Decrès proved to be on board, and was taken prisoner, wounded. The loss of life on board the *Foudroyant* was eight, whilst sixty-nine were wounded; that of the *Lion*, forty-six in killed and wounded.

The crew of the *Guillaume Tell* numbered 1,220[3]; the surviving officers and men were sent to Port Mahon in the *Champion*, which

---

[1] Clarke and MacArthur, vol. ii. p. 248.
[2] Other accounts, given by Clarke and MacArthur, represent the defence as far more desperate and prolonged. The *Foudroyant* suffered heavily. See James's *Naval History*, vol. ii. pp. 442–43 (edit. 1902).—J. H. R.
[3] Of these, as I have shown in the Introduction, a large number were invalids or "useless mouths."—J. H. R.

vessel had only just arrived from Gibraltar, escorting two transports laden with mortars, powder, shot, &c., for the use of the besiegers.

Instructions were sent by the *Champion* that these prisoners of war were not to be exchanged for the present.

The *Guillaume Tell* was towed to Syracuse, and subsequently named the *Malta*, and for many years was considered one of the finest ships in the British Navy. From a paper discovered on board it was learned that the garrison in Valetta and the Three Cities had wheat sufficient to last until the end of August. The following account of the capture is taken from the *Foudroyant's* journal:—

Sunday, 30th March 1800.—At 12 (midnight) saw a number of guns fired on shore, with signals; slipped cable, set all sail, saw and heard the report of several guns eastward, with signals. Made all sail, and stood for it. At daybreak, having all sail set, saw His Majesty's ships *Lion* and *Penelope* engaging a French line-of-battle ship with her main and mizen topmasts gone. At 6 a.m. came up with her, when Sir Edward Berry hailed her and desired him to strike, but received no answer. An officer shook his sword at him, and a broadside was fired from her, which was immediately returned from within half pistol-shot. Her first broadside cut our rigging very much, and the second carried away our foretopmast and maintopsail yard. At 6.30 a.m. shot away her main and mizen masts; saw a man nail the French ensign to the stump of the mizen mast. At 7 a.m. the *Penelope* again fired at the enemy whilst passing under her stern. At 7.30 spoke the *Penelope*.

At 8.05 a.m. shot away the enemy's foremast. At 8.10 a.m., all her masts being gone by the board, the enemy struck his colours and ceased firing. Sent a boat on board her. She proved to be the *Guillaume Tell*, of 84[1] guns, a ship that had come out of the harbour of Valetta, having on board Admiral Decrès, Captain Saunier, Adjutant-General Brouard, and 1,200 men.

The success of this engagement was mainly due to the *Lion* and the *Penelope* frigate, and more particularly to the latter, whose daring and brilliant manœuvring, and temerity in clinging to the enemy, notwithstanding the disparity in size and strength (36 guns to 86), crippled her, and gave time for the remainder of the squadron to come up and complete the victory.

Details of this engagement are graphically given in Captain Manley Dixon's official report of same to Commodore Sir T. Troubridge, and also in an extract from the log of the *Penelope*, which are recorded below:—

H.M.S. *Lion*, at sea off Cape Passaro, 31*st March* 1800.[2]

Sir,—I have the honour to inform you that yesterday morning at 9 o'clock, Cape Passaro bearing N. ½ E., distant 7 leagues, the French

---
[1] Really 86 in all.—J. H. R.   [2] Brit. Mus. Add. MSS. 34917.

ship of war *Le Guillaume Tell*, of 86 guns and 1,000 men, bearing the flag of Contre-Admiral Decrez, surrendered after a most gallant and obstinate defence of three hours and a half to H.M. ships *Foudroyant*, *Lion*, and *Penelope*.

To detail the particulars of this very important capture, I have to inform you that the signal rockets and cannonading from our batteries at Malta the midnight preceding, with the favourable strong southerly gale, together with the darkness which succeeded the setting of the moon, convinced me the enemy's ships of war were attempting to effect an escape, and which was immediately ascertained by that judicious and truly valuable officer, Captain Blackwood of the *Penelope*, who had been stationed a few hours before between the *Lion* and Valetta, for the purpose of observing closely the motions of the enemy. Nearly at midnight an enemy's ship was descried by him, when the *Minorca* was sent to inform me of it, giving chase himself, apprising me by signal that the strange ships seen were hauled to the wind on the starboard tack. I lost not one moment in making the signal for the squadron to cut or slip, and directed Captain Miller of the *Minorca* to run down to the *Foudroyant* and *Alexander* with the intelligence and to repeat the signal. Under a press of canvas I gave chase until 5 a.m., solely guided by the cannonading of the *Penelope*, and as a direction to the squadron, a rocket and blue light were shown every half-hour from the *Lion*. As the day broke I found myself in gunshot of the chase, and the *Penelope* within musket-shot raking her, by the effect of whose well-directed fire during the night were shot away the main and mizen topmasts and main yard; the enemy appeared in great confusion, being reduced to his head sails, going with the wind on the quarter.

The *Lion* was now close alongside, the yard-arms of both ships being just clear, when a destructive broadside of three round shot in each gun was poured in, luffing up across the bow, when the enemy's jibboom passed between the main and mizen shrouds. After a short interval I had the pleasure to see the boom carried away and the ships disentangled, maintaining a position across the bow, firing to great advantage.

I was not in the least solicitous either to board or to be boarded, as the enemy appeared to be of immense bulk and full of men, keeping up a prodigious fire of musketry, which with bow chasers she could for a long time only use. I found it absolutely necessary if possible to keep from the broadside of this ship. After being engaged about 50 minutes, the *Foudroyant* was seen under a press of canvas, and soon passed, hailing the enemy to strike, which being declined, a very heavy fire from both ships, broadside to broadside, was most gallantly maintained, the *Lion* and *Penelope* frequently in situations to do great execution; in short, Sir, after the hottest action that probably was ever maintained by an enemy's ship opposed to those of His Majesty's, and being totally dismasted, the French Admiral's flag and colours were struck.

I have not language to express the high sense of obligation I feel myself under to Captain Blackwood for his prompt and able conduct in leading the line-of-battle ships to the enemy, for the gallantry and spirit so highly conspicuous in him, and for his admirable management of the frigate; to your discriminating judgment it is unnecessary to remark of what real value and importance such an officer must ever be considered to

His Majesty's service. The termination of the battle must be attributed to the spirited fire of the *Foudroyant*, whose Captain, Sir Edward Berry, has justly added another laurel to the many he has gained during the war.

Captain Blackwood speaks in very high terms of the active and gallant conduct of Captain Long of the *Vincejo* during the night, and I beg to mention the services of Captains Broughton and Miller. The crippled condition of the *Lion* and *Foudroyant* made it necessary for me to direct Captain Blackwood to take possession of the enemy, take him in tow, and proceed to Syracuse. I received the greatest possible assistance from Lieutenant Joseph Patey, senior officer of the *Lion*, and from Mr. Spencer, the master, who, together with the other officers and ship's company, showed the most determined gallantry. Captains Sir Edward Berry and Blackwood have reported to me the same gallant and animated behaviour in the officers and crews of their respective ships.

I am sorry to say that the three ships have suffered much in killed and wounded, and that of the enemy is prodigious, being upwards of 200. I refer you to the enclosed reports for further particulars as to the state of His Majesty's ships, and have the honour, &c.

(Signed) MANLEY DIXON.

To COMMODORE SIR THOMAS TROUBRIDGE,
commanding His Majesty's ships at the blockade of Malta.

PS.—The *Guillaume Tell* is of the largest dimensions, and carries 36-pounders on the lower gun deck, 24-pounders on the main deck, 12-pounders on the quarter deck, and 32-pound carronades on the poop.[1]

The following account is taken from the log of the *Penelope*, kept by Lieutenant Charles Inglis[2]:—

On the night of the 30th March 1800 the *Guillaume Tell*, of 80 guns, taking advantage of a southerly gale and intense darkness, weighed and sailed out of the harbour.

As she passed the *Penelope* (36-gun frigate) Captain Blackwood immediately followed, and having the advantage of sailing, quickly came up with her, then, ' luffed under her stern and gave her the larboard broadside, bore up under the larboard quarter and gave her the starboard broadside, receiving from her only his sternchase guns. From this hour till daylight, finding that we could place ourselves on either quarter, the action continued in the foregoing manner, and with such success on our side that, when day broke, the *Guillaume Tell* was found in a most dismantled state.' At five o'clock the *Lion*, of 64 guns, and some little time afterwards the *Foudroyant*, of 80 guns, came up, and after a determined and gallant resistance the *Guillaume Tell* surrendered.

---

[1] It was these last which proved to be specially destructive at close quarters.—J. H. R.

[2] See Nelson's letter of congratulation to Inglis on the *Guillaume Tell* (*Nelson Dispatches*, vol. iv. p. 229). Inglis was made a Commander in October 1800, and Post-Captain in April 1802, he died in Feb. 1833.—J. H. R.

In this engagement the British loss was as follows :—

	Killed.	Wounded.	Total.
Foudroyant	8	69	77
Lion	8	38	46
Penelope [1]	2	2	4
			127
And in that of the capture of the *Généreux* on the 17th of the previous month, in killed and wounded			9
Total		.	136

General Vaubois, upon being made acquainted with the capture of the *Guillaume Tell* by the British, forwarded duplicates of the dispatches which that vessel was conveying to the French Government. These dispatches were committed by Admiral Villeneuve to the charge of Ensign Coulomb of the frigate *Diane*, who was to leave in a speronara, the smallness of which it was thought might escape the vigilance of the blockaders. Admiral Villeneuve's dispatch to the Minister of Marine is as follows :—

Malte, le 28 *Germinal* an 8 (18*th April* 1800).[2]

CITOYEN MINISTRE,—La contrariété des tems et la rigide surveillance de l'ennemi empêchent le navire, *La Bellone*, de partir et peuvent le retenir encore longtems. Le Général Vaubois, impatient de donner de ses nouvelles au Gouvernement, m'a demandé l'expédition d'un *esperonare* (barque du pays) avec un officier pour faire parvenir les duplicata des dépêches dont il avait chargé *Le Guillaume Tell* et de celles qu'il destine pour le navire, *La Bellone*, je joins ici également les miennes ; d'après les rapports de l'ennemi, il paraît que le vaisseau *Le Guillaume Tell* n'a pu échaper à la poursuite des vaisseaux qui l'ont chassé au moment de son départ, et qu'il a été pris à la hauteur du Cap Passaro après une deffense dont les Anglais eux-mêmes ne parlent qu'avec éloge. Si tel était le sort de ce vaisseau de tomber entre les mains de l'ennemi, il vaut mieux qu'il ait été pris de cette manière que de succomber avec la place de Malte sans deffense, ainsi qu'en sont menacés les bâtiments qui nous restent, si dans le courant des deux mois prochains nous ne recevons un puissant secours. Je me réfère à cet égard à mes dépêches du 13 Ventôse et 4 Germinal et à l'état de situation des magasins de vivres dont le Général Vaubois informe le Ministre de la Guerre.

S'il faut en croire les rapports de l'enemi le Général Decrès et tous les prisonniers du vaisseau *Le Guillaume Tell* auraient été transportés sur cet Isle ; et seraient à Marsa Siroco. Je regrette infiniment que le Général Decrès n'ait pas eu la faculté de se rendre immédiatement auprès de vous. Il eut pu vous informer de vive voix et avec toute connoissance de cause de la situation où nous nous trouvons. Il paraît qu'il n'a pas même la faculté de nous écrire et de nous donner de ses nouvelles personnelles.

[1] James, *op. cit.* (ii. 142), gives the loss of the *Penelope* as one killed and three wounded. Her losses were slight owing to her keeping astern and pouring in raking broadsides.— J. H. R.

[2] Arch. Nat., BB⁴ 147.

Les Anglais nous ont appris qu'il avait été blessé légèrement au genoux et le Capitaine Saunier à l'œuil. Puisse au moins cette dépêche vous parvenir et le Gouvernement sera persuadé que rien n'est négligé pour prolonger la deffense de cette place, qu'elle ne sera rendue que lorsque les moyens de subsister seront devenus physiquement insuffisants.

Le Citoyen Coulomb, enseigne de vaisseau sur *La Diane*, est chargé de ces dépêches, et le Général Vaubois lui prescrit de les porter lui-même au Gouvernement. C'est un officier actif et intelligent qui aura droit à la reconnaissance publique s'il parvient à sa destination, n'ayant aucun réfuge d'ici en France que la Corse. Il a à faire avant d'y arriver, une navigation longue et hazardeuse avec une frêle embarcation et dans une saison difficile. Salut et respect. (Signed) Villeneuve.

PS.—Les forces de l'ennemi devant le port sont de cinq vaisseaux; deux mouillés à l'embouchure et trois à Marsa Siroco, plusieurs frégates et corvettes à la voile.

Doublet, availing himself of the opportunity, thought proper to again address the Colonial Minister with one of his querulous letters, dated the 19th April.[1]

Doubtful whether Coulomb had succeeded in running the gauntlet of the blockading squadron on the 19th April, Rear-Admiral Villeneuve, at the suggestion of General Vaubois, dispatched Ensign Baste on the 21st with triplicates of the various documents which had been previously forwarded, and referred to in the dispatch of the latter date.

Malte, le 1ᵣ *Floreal* an 8 (21*st April* 1800).[2]

Au Ministre de la Marine et des Colonies.

Citoyen Ministre,—À la demande du Général Vaubois je vous expédie une nouvelle embarquation avec un officier, qui vous remettra les triplicata de mes dépêches du 13 Ventôse, 4 et 10 Germinal et un extrait de celle que je vous ai écrite le 28 Germinal par le Citoyen Coulomb, enseigne de V^{au}., parti avec un speronare le 29 Germinal au soir.

D'après les rapports de l'ennemi [here follows an exact repetition of the portion of the letter of the 28 Germinal an 8, beginning: '*il paraît que Le Guillaume Tell*,' and ending at '*physiquement insuffisants*,' and then continues as follows.]

Le Citoyen Baste, enseign de vaisseau, provenant de *La Diane* est chargé de ces dépêches et le Général Vaubois lui prescrit de les porter lui-même au Gouvernement.

Cet officier est un de ceux qui dans toutes les circonstances de ce long siège a montré le plus de zèle et d'ardeur et qui y a servi avec le plus de distinction; la garnison du Fort Chambray du Goze lui doit son salut dans les premiers jours de la révolte ainsi que j'en ai rendu compte dans ce tems. Et depuis lors il a commandé les marins en garnison au Fort Ricasoli, celui de tous les postes le plus convoité par l'ennemi. Il est susceptible par

---

[1] This letter, again, is so long and unimportant that I have judged it best to omit it.—J. H. R.

[2] Arch. Nat., BB⁴ 147.

l'ancienneté et le mérite de ses services des faveurs du Gouvernement. Salut et respect.

(Signed) VILLENEUVE.

PS.—Les forces de l'ennemi aujourd'huy devant ce port sont de 5 vaisseaux dont 3 mouillés à l'embouchure ou à la voile et deux mouillés à Marsa Siroco, plusieurs frégates et corvettes à la voile et quatre chaloupes canonières Napolitaines arrivées ici hier.

Delay in the arrival of further reinforcements induced Graham to carry into effect his proposal to raise a battalion of Maltese in British pay, to serve only in Malta and Gozo, a step which he had suggested so far back as the 22nd of the previous February.[1] His wishes were communicated by Captain Ball to the representatives of the people, who at once gave their assent to the measure. By the 2nd April two companies were completed with the exception of the officers, whom General Graham had no power to appoint. In the meantime, officers of the 30th and 89th Regiments were temporarily attached to the companies as they were formed, and by the middle of May four companies were completed, and four others in formation.

General Fox at Minorca, in the meantime, became somewhat alarmed at the protracted resistance of the besieged, and counselled Graham to run no risk beyond what discretion and prudence would justify. To this advice the brigadier-general replied:

that as no advantage could be obtained without some risk, he could never think of abandoning the Island, and losing all the fruits of the blockade, on the bare apprehension of eventual danger, and that he was in hopes nothing sinister would happen, unless it might be the arrival of a considerable reinforcement to the enemy; [continuing] that he would restrict himself to beleaguering the fortress only, saving as much as possible all unnecessary fatigue or danger to the troops, every individual being so valuable, and to keep them so cantonned as to be able to unite quickly, increasing the works of defence at the most important posts, and continuing the construction of new batteries in the best situations for effectually annoying the enemy whenever reinforcements arrived, but meanwhile confining all firing to the ships and fishing boats, the latter being an important factor in obtaining food for the garrison. Against the works no battery could be erected which could not be immediately overpowered by a tenfold fire. One regiment more would place the besiegers in security, and might even afford opportunities of successful enterprise which present weakness precludes all thoughts of profiting by, let the opportunities appear ever so tempting; for a check would be fatal.

Owing to the injury received during the action with the *Guillaume Tell*, the *Foudroyant* was detained at Malta longer than was at first anticipated, but by the 21st April she reached Palermo, when Nelson re-hoisted his flag, and on the 24th sailed for Syracuse and thence to Malta, taking Sir William and Lady Hamilton as passengers.

[1] Delavoye, *Life of Lord Lynedoch*, p. 188.

On the 4th May the *Foudroyant* anchored in St. Paul's Bay, where she remained a week, and then left for Marsa Scirocco Bay, finally quitting Malta with the same passengers on the 20th, after a stay of sixteen days.

Sir William Hamilton, having been relieved of his functions by the arrival at Palermo of the Honourable Arthur Paget during the previous month, was now on the point of leaving for London, and it was considered a good opportunity by General Graham to give a minute and detailed account of the position of affairs in the island, to be duly reported to the authorities in England.[1] This letter is dated the 19th May, the day before the *Foudroyant* sailed.

Head-quarters, Gudia, 19th May 1800.[2]

To Sir William Hamilton.

MY DEAR SIR WILLIAM,—As I see the *Foudroyant* is not under way, I hope I shall have time to write you some memoranda about our situation here, which will enable you to explain your plan more satisfactorily to my friends at home.

Every operation of war is as uncertain as the fate of those concerned, so that I am glad of this opportunity, whatever may happen. Though the name of such a command as this was much beyond my expectation, yet from the first I have strongly felt the disadvantage of being employed where such sanguine hopes had been so unaccountably raised with a force not only totally inadequate to any exertion that could contribute to realise them, but which in strictness, according to my instructions, scarcely justified my remaining here, for in my mind nothing can be more fallacious than the argument commonly used, that since the enemy never made a sortie last summer, when there were no regular troops on the Island, there is no probability of their making one at all.

There was no reason, then, for their losing a man—there was nothing to be gained. On the contrary, the complete success would have imposed on them the burden of maintaining the whole Island. They had then a large stock of the necessaries of life, and they had every reason to hope for effectual relief long before it was near exhausted.

The batteries erected against them might be said to be insulting to them under such circumstances, but they knew they could not be annoying, and must have felt it was in their power to destroy them whenever they chose to risk the loss of a few men ; but above all, the town was then full of inhabitants, many of whom had conspired against them, and who might rise against the guards left in the town were a sortie with a considerable force undertaken.

How different is their situation now! They have turned out all the inhabitants they wished to get rid of—those that remain add strength to the garrison; their resources are much diminished; their expectations of relief till after the summer must become every day less and less.

Whenever the combination of these circumstances shall render their

---

[1] For the annoyances to which Hamilton and Queen Maria Carolina subjected the Hon. A. Paget, see the *Paget Papers*, vol. i. pp. 174 et seq.—J. H. R.
[2] Delavoye, *Life of Lord Lynedoch*, p. 189.

situation desperate, then they must make a sortie. It is impossible the place should ever surrender to our force without their making an effort to drive us off the Island, or at least to seize on our magazines, and attempt to supply themselves from the nearest villages with the means of subsistence for some weeks longer.

They are sensible of the value of Malta, and know how much importance Bonaparte attaches to it. All the intercepted correspondence proves this, and every hour's delay of surrender becomes to them a matter of consequence, as relief may come in some shape or other. They probably know very accurately the state of our force; they may have been deceived formerly with regard to the number of the armed peasants, but they must know *that the enthusiasm which at first raised the whole country and rendered the inhabitants formidable is over,* and there is every reason to suppose, from the impossibility of watching such an immense extent, that they have frequent intercourse with people without the walls, and must be in possession of accurate information. Now, to enable you to judge of my real situation, compare the state of their force and of ours. From undoubted information they have 3,000 regular troops, about 1,000 sailors, about 600 National Guards, besides many cannoniers, and other Maltese formerly soldiers or sailors of the Order, employed on the batteries and in the arsenal.[1] The last weekly state, which I enclose, will show you that I have under my command only 2,092 rank and file fit for duty, of whom 400 are new raised Maltese, and above 700 are Neapolitans, on whom I cannot place much dependence. There are, besides, about 2,000 armed peasants under the Governor's command; half of them at least are allowed to go to work during the day, so that they are dispersed, and of course useless on a sudden emergency, and are tired and sleepy at night. They have no other officers but sergeants, and, though active, brave, hardy fellows, under no discipline nor restraint. It is a matter of doubt and accident whether they would act in case of a sortie so as to be of use even in the daytime; during the night I am sure they would only create confusion.

You have only to look at your plan to see what an extent of line is to be guarded by this trifling force. Beginning on the right, opposite to Ricasoli, and going round again to the sea on the left, opposite to Fort Tigné, the distance cannot be less than about eight miles were the best communications established, which we have not had time to do. Fortunately the country presents great obstacles; every field is an intrenchment, and it is only by the roads that an enemy could advance with any rapidity, and on the left, opposite to Tigné and Manoel, they are very narrow and bad; besides that, these two forts cannot afford to send out many men without receiving reinforcements which must pass the harbour of Marsamuscetto. There can never, therefore, be a sortie on that side for any other purpose but diversion or spiking our guns. It is necessary, however, to cover the great road from La Valetta to St. Antonio and Citta Vecchia, which obliges me to leave at Samra and San Giuseppe the whole of the marines for duty on shore: a very small detachment, it is true, but a very valuable one, from being admirably commanded and more *aguerri* than any other troops here. There is, besides, on that side at Birchircara all

---

[1] These figures are in excess of the actuality. See Vaubois' Reports in the Appendix.—J. H. R.

the Neapolitan infantry, who detach posts to assist the Maltese peasants opposite to Tigné and Manoel.

The post of the battery at the head of the great harbour is left to the Maltese peasants entirely; the marsh air rendered it so unhealthy for our people that I was obliged to remove them, and though by that communication with the marines is interrupted, I was not sorry to be forced to concentrate the two regiments towards the point of the greatest risk and importance opposite Cotonera and Fort Ricasoli, from which the enemy could have such facility of coming out in force in several columns, though direct roads have been blocked up and destroyed as much as possible. The batteries formerly erected, which cannot be defended from themselves, are in some degree protected by stone blockhouses in their rear.

The very exposed and important village of Zabbar, within musket-shot of the Cotonera, has been strengthened the same way. All the duty of the advanced part of this line is done by the Maltese, assisted during the night by some piquets and patrols of ours. These are merely for the purpose of alarm, for it is impossible to think of attempting to support any of these advanced posts on the batteries if vigorously attacked. Our stand must be made at Zeitun, on which everything depends. I have strengthened it in such a way that it will cost the enemy dear if they attempt it, and if all the troops behave well I should not be apprehensive of the issue of an attack by day. Were we to lose Zeitun, our intrenchments near Marsa Scirocco would only serve to cover our embarkation.

After this faithful account of our relative situation, you will not wonder at my anxiety. I have every reason to hope for a reinforcement of one regiment at least from Minorca, besides the expectation of positive security from the arrival of the Russians. Disappointed of these, the urgency of the case made me undertake a levy of Maltese independent companies entirely at my own risk for the expence of raising, clothing, and arming them; four are completed, and four more are going on.

I have written privately to Mr. Dundas on this subject, and hope the measure will be approved of. They are only to serve in the Island, and have no doubt of their doing well, as they will be much more manageable than the peasants, having British officers to command them.

Under these very discouraging circumstances, my command is far from an enviable one—no chance of gaining any credit, many of losing character, and increasing responsibility. At first I felt supported by Colonel Lindenthal's opinion (a confidential staff officer sent here by General Fox to report to him his opinions concerning this place) in fixing the troops on shore and stating that I should be able to maintain myself. General Fox has since been alarmed, and has repeatedly called on me not to risk the troops beyond what discretion and prudence would justify. My answer has been, that as no advantage can be obtained without some risk, I never could think of abandoning the Island and losing all the fruits of the blockade on the bare apprehension of eventual danger, and that I was in hopes nothing sinister could happen but by the arrival of a considerable reinforcement to the enemy, an event which I could not foresee, and which therefore might unavoidably prove fatal to us. My conduct in the management of our force has been guided by what I conceived the circumstances above described rendered not only prominent but necessary.

To save as much as possible from unnecessary fatigue or danger to the troops every individual being of so much value to us, and to keep them disposed so as to be able to unite quickly in the material points at all times; to increase as much as possible by works the defense of the most important posts; to go on with the construction of several new batteries in the best situation for effectually annoying the enemy whenever any increase of force would enable us to do so with propriety, but meanwhile to confine our firing to such objects as the common practice of war justify during a mere blockade without exposing ourselves to the ridicule of making puny efforts of a mock siege—we have therefore seldom or ever fired but at their ships and fishing boats; against the works we could erect no battery which they might not immediately overpower by a tenfold fire, though we might do some damage to the town by throwing shells—to make ourselves respected by the enemy as a blockade force by showing a readiness to resist any aggression of theirs, such as firing on them when they fire at the ships, but without wantonly irritating them so as to make it necessary for them to come out to attack our batteries, sensible we dare not risk defending them; to keep up the spirits of the Maltese by an equal attention to the security of their posts as well as our own—such have been the constant objects I have held in view.

Placed, as I have said, in a situation of great and unfounded expectations, and of course exposed to all the censure of disappointment, should it ever happen that the enemy choose to make a well-connected attack on any of our batteries or advanced posts, or even on the village of Zabbar, from which formerly the inhabitants repulsed them, I am much afraid an unpleasant discovery will be made. The Maltese will see that it is not my intention to commit the whole in defence of these advanced posts, and the enemy will find out that they may make such attacks without much risk, as the opposition will be feeble, and this may encourage them to attempt something more important, when the assistance to be expected from the Maltese will be less in proportion to what they conceive our neglect of their interests to have been.

Adieu, my dear Sir William; I did not mean to have detained you so long, but I have been led on by this subject, which gives me many sleepless nights. One regiment more would have put us in security, and might have even afforded opportunities of successful enterprise which my weakness precludes all thoughts of profiting by, let the opportunities appear ever so tempting, for a check would be fatal indeed to us. Thank God, this cannot last much longer; another month will clear the horizon of the mists that cover the seas, the squadrons, and the plans of our friends and foes.

I beg to recommend to your care some more letters, and, wishing you a happy voyage, remain, &c. (Signed) THOS. GRAHAM.

During this short stay in Malta, Nelson acquainted Lord Keith of his intention to return to Palermo in a few days, in order to fulfil a promise he had made some time previously to the Queen of Naples to convey Her Majesty and suite to the Continent, whenever she might determine to leave Palermo, and that, as it might be necessary to take another ship, he purposed selecting the *Alexander*.

Lord Keith (then engaged in the blockade of Genoa), upon receipt of this information, issued an order, dated the 5th June, directing Nelson to send the *Foudroyant* and *Alexander* to Malta *immediately*, and forbidding the King's ships to be employed on any other service than such as he had appointed. This order, however, was not received in time to stop the arrangements which Nelson had made.

The *Foudroyant* arrived at Palermo from Malta on the night of the 31st May, and on the 10th June she sailed with the Queen and family, Sir William and Lady Hamilton as passengers for Leghorn, accompanied by the *Alexander* and *Princess Charlotte*, where they arrived on the 14th June.[1]

Lord Keith was duly informed by Nelson of his movements, and on the 15th June, on the supposition that Nelson by that date would be at Leghorn (as was actually the case), ordered him to repair without a moment's delay to Genoa, with all the ships under his command, and join the commander-in-chief there.

Nelson only partially obeyed by sending the *Princess Charlotte*, promising the *Foudroyant* should soon follow, but the *Alexander* he would send back to Malta. In the meanwhile, news of the complete defeat of the Austrian army by Bonaparte on the 14th June at Marengo altered the destination of the *Alexander* to the Gulf of Spezia.

The disaster of Marengo caused considerable alarm amongst the Royal party at Leghorn, and Her Majesty the Queen contemplated returning to Palermo, believing it would be unsafe to cross Italy. The *Foudroyant* was accordingly retained for the conveyance of Her Majesty to the Sicilian capital. This proceeding on the part of Nelson caused the greatest annoyance to Lord Keith, who on the 19th June sent peremptory orders that in the event of Her Majesty not proceeding to Vienna, and wishing to return to Palermo, His Britannic Majesty's ships were not to be used for that purpose, and, to ensure obedience, proceeded to Leghorn, where he arrived on the 24th.

On the 28th, Nelson shifted his flag to the *Alexander*, the *Foudroyant* being sent to Mahon to be refitted.

During the early part of the following month of July the political state of Northern Italy became calmer, and Her Majesty then decided to venture upon the journey overland.[2] Nelson, who had been invited to join the party, struck his flag on the 11th, proceeding via Florence, Ancona, Trieste, and Vienna, finally reaching Yarmouth from Hamburg on the 6th November 1800, and London on the 8th, thus closing his personal and active participation in Maltese affairs, which island had then been two months in possession of the British forces.

[1] See *Dispatches of Nelson*, vol. iv. p. 251; also some of the previous letters, for his excessive deference to the King and Queen of Naples.—J. H. R.
[2] The calm was due to the armistice of June 15, by which General Melas, after his disaster at Marengo, tamely agreed to give up all the fortresses in Northern Italy held by the Austrians, on condition that their forces might retire to the east of the river Mincio. This of course sacrificed Genoa, which Keith had helped to reduce. (See Keith's indignant letter of June 20 to Paget, in the *Paget Papers*, vol. i. p. 232.)—J. H. R.

After this digression regarding Nelson's movements we return to the operations at Valetta. The fact has to be recorded of a French brig with a cargo of provisions having on the 8th June safely run the gauntlet and entered the Grand Harbour, followed by the *Penelope* to within gunshot of Fort St. Elmo.[1]

On the 9th June, Brigadier-General Moncreiff, of the 90th (General Graham's regiment), arrived in Malta on leave, to whom was offered the command of the Malta Fencible Corps, which he accepted pending instructions from Minorca. Until confirmation of the appointment was received, Captain Weir of the marines, to whom the Admiral gave the rank of major in his corps, took temporary command of the battalion.

On the 15th June, Captain Ball forwarded to Lord Grenville an account of the expenditure which had been incurred in Malta from March 1799 up to May 1800, for the subsistence of the 3,000 Maltese troops and 6,000 indigent poor, with other governmental expenses, amounting to £38,538 6s. The following is a copy of the dispatch and report :—

Malta, 15*th June* 1800.[2]

To the Right Hon. Lord Grenville.

My Lord,—I have the honour to enclose a few papers containing a succinct amount of the revenue of this Island, and the expenses, since it has been under my government. I take the liberty to send copies of letters to me from the Congress and judges of this Island, which will prove its very critical state when I landed to direct and restore to order its inhabitants.

I apprehend the French will not surrender La Valetta unless General Graham has the means of carrying on active operations. I have the honour, &c. (Signed) Alex. Jno. Ball.

Public Expenditure in Malta between March 1799 and May 1800.

Malta, 15*th June* 1800.

The expenditure of the public money is examined by the most approved characters, and the sum of £38,538 6s.[3] has been expended in paying and subsisting three thousand troops, six thousand poor, and all the expenses of the Government, except that of Governor-in-Chief, and a few employed, who have received the smallest salary. When I landed to direct the civil affairs of the Island, it was in the most dangerous state of anarchy, which is partly described in the letter from the judges to me, inclosed herewith. I deemed it politic to assemble a temporary congress of the people to sanction and give weight to the laws where the existing circumstances required. Each town elected a representative in the manner of Scot and Lot. The judges and Bishop, or in his absence the Grand Vicar, were admitted, at which I am President, and without my assent an Act

---

[1] Keith refers with just annoyance to this event in his letters of July 19 to Paget, and seems to connect it with with Nelson's dereliction of duty.—J. H. R.

[2] Foreign Office Records, Malta, 6.

[3] £91 per day.

cannot be passed. The number of the Congress amounts to twenty-five, whose labours have merited my confidence. *They know their functions will cease as soon as La Valetta is taken.* I presume it is unnecessary to comment on the many advantages I have derived from it.

(Signed) ALEX. JNO. BALL.

On the 14th June both Vaubois and Villeneuve acquainted the Minister of Marine with the timely arrival of the *Marguerite* with a supply of provisions.

Malte, le 25 *Prairial* an 8 (14*th June* 1800.)[1]

Le Contre-Amiral Villeneuve au Ministre de la Marine et des Colonies.

CITOYEN MINISTRE,—Le navire *La Marguerite*, Capitaine Barret, expédié du port de Toulon est entré ici le 19 de ce mois, il nous a apporté un chargement de vivres, qui ne pouvait arriver plus à propos ; il nous assure les moyens de tenir les mois de Messidor, Thermidor et Fructidor. Ce chargement qui a été calculé sur quinze jours de vivres pour 4,000 hommes, nous fera vivre trois mois. Les rations ici depuis deux ans étant réduites au dessous du quart de la ration ordinaire.

Pour prolonger la durée des grains qui nous restent, le Général Vaubois a ordonné la sortie de la ville de 2,000 personnes sur six mille qui en forment la population actuelle. Ces sorties doivent commencer à s'exécuter demain ; au moyen de cette nouvelle évacuation j'estime que nous pouvons avoir encore pour quatre à cinq mois de bleds ou de biscuit, mais malheureusement le bled qui reste est de fort mauvaise qualité et difficilement le pain qu'il produit pourrait servir seul d'aliment au soldat et au marin. Il importe donc, pour la conservation de Malte qu'il y soit expédié le plutôt possible des chargements de comestibles composés de farines et biscuits, huile, lard, ris et haricots, vinaigre, vin et eau de vie ; tel est l'ordre d'urgence des besoins de cette place, nous avons regretté infiniment de ne pas trouver de l'huile sur le dernier bâtiment arrivé quoiqu'il en ait été demandé instamment aux administrateurs de Toulon. Elle sert d'assaisonnement aux légumes que le soldat cultive et au produit de la pêche de nos marins, cette denrée serait si nécessaire ici qu'au besoin elle suppléerait à toutes les autres. Veuillez bien, Citoyen Ministre, donner des ordres pour que les bâtiments expédiés pour Malte soit à l'avenir chargés principalement en farines, huilles et lard, et que les autres articles ne composent au plus que le quart du chargement. Deux bâtiments ainsi chargés qui arriveraient à bon part ferait atteindre le cœur de l'hiver, époque à laquelle on pourrait espérer de ravitailler ce pays encore pour longtems par les moyens que j'ai toujours indiqué, je veux dire par des bâtiments expédiés isolement des differents ports, mais non pas par convoi qui éveille l'attention de l'ennemi qui dès lors ne néglige rien pour l'intercepter et dont la grande supériorité maritime leur donne toujours les moyens.

On ne peut dissimuler que dans cette saison l'arrivée de tout bâtiment expédié pour Malte ne soit très hazardeuse, l'ennemi bloque le port étroitement, il y occupe en ce moment deux vaisseaux, quatre frégates, une corvette et trois bricks ; plus de coup de vent qui puisse les éloigner,

[1] Arch. Nat., BB⁴ 147.

plus de tems couvert qui puissent leur dérober la vue des bâtiments qui peuvent s'en approcher la nuit. L'arrivée de ce dernier bâtiment commandé par le Citoyen Barret nous a été aussi agréable qu'inattendue ; ce capitaine mérite toutes sortes d'éloges par la manière dont il a manœuvré et dont il s'est conduit, après avoir tourné pendant huit jours dans le sud de l'Isle pour attendre un moment favorable il a profité d'une belle nuit, d'un vent frais et d'un tems brumeux. Il a été vivement canoné par toutes les batteries de la côte et par un vaisseau et une frégate et sans se détourner de la route il est parvenu à l'entrée du port, où il a été protégé par nos batteries qui ont fait lacher prise à un vaisseau[1] qui faisait sur lui un feu d'artillerie et de mousquetterie soutenu. Il est entré ainsi dans le port aux applaudissements de toute la garnison. Je ne saurais trop le recommander à la bienveillance du Gov$^{t.}$

Quoique la fortune n'ait pas favorisé la mésure du départ du *Guillaume Tell*, je ne puis regretter de l'avoir déterminé ; elle peut encore être le salut de Malte, par la diminution sensible des consommateurs qu'elle nous a procuré. Ce vaisseau a succombé après un combat glorieux ; en restant dans ce port il eût entraîné dans sa perte celle de cette place qui peut-être ne serait déjà plus en notre pouvoir.

Le Général Decrès doit être rendu auprès de vous ; il connoît notre manière d'être ici et nos besoins et personne ne peut mieux que lui vous donner des renseignements utiles sur les moyens qui peuvent être encore employés pour venir à secour. Salut et respect.

(Signed) VILLENEUVE.

[The same to the same.]

Malte, le 25 *Prairial* an 8 (14*th June* 1800).[2]

CITOYEN MINISTRE,—Le Général Vaubois ayant reçu officiellement par le Citoyen Remi, adjoint aux Adjutants-Généraux, arrivé sur le navire *La Marguerite*, Capitaine Barret, la Constitution de l'an[3] 8, elle a été proclamée à la tête des troupes auxquelles je me suis réunis avec tous les officiers civils et militaires de la marine et des détachements des marins de chaque bâtiment. Tous lui ont pretté avec transport le serment de fidélité préscrit par la Loi. J'ai profité de cette circonstance, pour assurer les marins que le nouveau Gouvernement entièrement occupé de l'amélioration de toutes les parties du service public travaillait particulièrement à ce qui concerne leur arme, que la marine désormais serait considérée comme une des branches essentielles de la force de l'État ; que leur service dans cette circonstance leur courage et leur dévouement dans la deffense de cette place au millieux des privations les plus pénibles leur serait comptés. Je ne saurais trop rendre hommage, Citoyen Ministre, au bon esprit, au zèle, au dévouement qui animent tous les officiers et les équipages des bâtiments de la République qui servent ici, aucune plainte, aucun murmure ne se fait entendre ; tous sentent l'importance de la conservation de ce port si interressant pour la navigation de la Méditeranée et tous sont résolus à le deffendre jusqu'à l'extinction de leur forces physiques.

[1] H.M. frigate *Penelope*.—J. H. R.
[2] Arch. Nat., BB⁴ 147.
[3] That of the close of the year 1799.—J. H. R.

Dans une canonade qui a eu lieu il y a quelques jours entre nos batteries et celles de l'ennemi, un canonier de *L'Athénien* a été tué et un matelot de *La Diane* a eu la jambe emporté. Salut et respect.

(Signed) Villeneuve.

Au Quartier Général le [no date] an 8 (*July* 1800 ?).[1]

Vaubois, Général de Division, au Ministre de la Marine.

Citoyen Ministre,—Les éloges que vous donnés par votre lettre du 28 Floréal à la brave garnison de Malte sont sa plus douce récompense, mes les efforts qu'elle fait seront ils couronnés du succès ?

Le Citoyen Baste, lieutenant de vaisseau, est entré dans le porte sur la félouque, *La Légère*, le 3 Messidor.[2] Quinze jours auparavent était arrivé le navire *Marguerite* chargé de vivres pour quinze jours pour quatre mille hommes. Suivant l'usage suivi ici depuis le premier jour du siège nous portons à trois fois autant de durée ce que nous avons. Après avoir passé le mois de Prairial avec du pain et un peu d'huile pour toutes rations, nous avons entamé ce chargement le 1er Messidor. Dans mes dernières dépêches, parties sur une félouque par le Citoyen Rémi, adjoint aux Adjudants-Généraux, j'ai promis la tenue de Malte pour Messidor et Thermidor, quoiqu'il y aura quinze jours de Thermidor pendant lesquels nous serons avec le pain seul. Arrivera-t-il quelque chose de ce qui nous est destiné pendant ce court espace de tems ? La saison est contre nous; les calmes et le blocus exact rendent cette chasse extrêmement douteuse. Il est vrai que les succès de la guerre peuvent aussi nous tirer d'embarras, et que nous nous persuadons que jamais le Roi de Naples ne sera admis à des conditions qu'il n'ait fait lever le siège et le blocus de Malte et fourni de vivres à cette isle.

Ne pourrait-on pas aussi nous expédier des félouques ? Tout est en faveur des bâtimens à rames. Cela porte peu mais cela entre plus sûrement. Les plus pressants articles sont le blé, la farine et l'huile. Par de nouvelles économies je prolongerai la durée du bled une partie de Fructidor à ce que j'espère; il est cependant de fort mauvaise qualité parcequ'il y a quatre ans au moins qu'il est en fosse. Telle est notre situation exacte.

Peignés-vous mes inquiétudes; le courage et la fermeté ne manquent pas, mais l'estomac les commande, nous sommes habitués à très peu, mais il le faut ce très peu.

La dissenterie se déclare, tout le monde est plein de vers et des maladies scrofuleuses se manifestent. La population offre un spectacle déchirant, ces misérables n'ont qu'un peu de mauvais pain et de l'eau, s'ils avaient de l'huile ils se croieraient heureux. Salut & respect.

(Signed) Vaubois.[3]

[1] Arch. Nat., BB⁴ 147.
[2] i.e. 22nd June, which fixes approximately the date of this letter. Vaubois' letter of 18th July to the Minister of War, as given in his *Journal of the Siege of Malta* (Part IV), in the Appendix, tallies very nearly with this one, but this is the fuller, and I therefore keep it here.—J. H. R.
[3] The most significant sentences of Vaubois' letter of July 18 to the Minister of War, referred to above (other than those which are almost identical with the tenour of the letter just cited), are these:—'L'ennemi ne nous fait rien. Ses cannonades, son bombardement, ne nous causent pas d'inquiétude. C'est notre peu de subsistance qui nous allarme.'—J. H. R.

The condition of the French garrison, notwithstanding the late succour received, was now becoming desperate, but to prolong the struggle, General Vaubois at this date began to expel from the city many of its inhabitants, who, being without dwellings and means of subsistence, had to be provided for by their countrymen in the villages.[1]

General Graham determined that this should be stopped, and accordingly, on the 17th June, the following notification was sent to General Vaubois:—

Malta, 17*th June* 1800.[2]

SIR,—I have the honour to inform you that henceforward it is my determination to prevent any intercourse with La Valetta for the purpose of any more of the inhabitants coming out. This measure, sanctioned and recommended to me by the Governor and the Congress of Malta, is so strictly conformable to the rules of war that the consequences resulting from it can never be reckoned severe by those who, having neglected the opportunities of such unusual indulgence, have shown their attachment to the French interest. I have the honour, &c.

(Signed) THO^{s.} GRAHAM.

To H. E. GENERAL VAUBOIS.

The lengthy reply of General Vaubois of 20th June 1800 will be found in his 'Journal of the Siege of Malta' (see Appendix). Graham felt disinclined to enter into a polemical discussion as to the duties and responsibilities of rival commanders, or to alter his decision regarding Maltese refugees from the besieged city, and closed the correspondence by a letter of the 21st June 1800, as follows:—

Head-quarters, Gudia, 21*st June* 1800.[3]

To General Vaubois.

SIR,—Without entering further into any reasoning concerning the duties of our respective situations than simply to state that the rules of war justify my resolution, and oblige you to provide for the inhabitants, I may be allowed to make one observation on your own statement. Surely, sir, those whom you have detained have an unquestionable right to your protection, and those who have chosen to remain so long within the walls can have none to any indulgence from me. But I revert to the general principle of the rules of war as the only one by which the conduct of an officer can be judged. If any inhumanity should result from this measure, the severe responsibility will fall on either of us, who, departing from that principle and acting in an arbitrary manner, shall break through those rules of war which civilised nations have established.

With regard, sir, to the complaint you make against the Maltese for murdering a prisoner, I can only assure you that it was reported at the

---

[1] See *inter alia* his Proclamation of June 19, 1800, in his *Journal of the Siege of Malta* (Part IV), in the Appendix.—J. H. R.
[2] Delavoye, *Life of Lord Lynedoch*, p. 197.
[3] *Ibid.* p. 199.

time that the French soldier was killed by the discharge of several muskets fired at him and his companions, from a very considerable distance; and I am inclined to believe this to be the truth, as I have not heard any instance since my arrival of prisoners or deserters having been treated with inhumanity by the Maltese. As they act under the orders of Governor Ball, I shall lose no time in informing him of your complaint, and I am sure he will not be less anxious than I am to prevent every wanton cruelty or excess.—I have the honour, &c.

(Signed) THOMAS GRAHAM.

PS.—From the report I have just received from the post of Samra you will not be surprised at my declaring that all intercourse by means of flags of truce between this town and the country is at an end.

Two days previously Graham published the following spirited address to the Maltese, in the hope of inducing a larger number of recruits to join and take a more active share in the operations. This address was the subject of a discussion in the House of Commons at a later date, which will be referred to in a subsequent chapter. It ran as follows:—

BRIGADIER-GENERAL GRAHAM TO THE MALTESE.[1]

BRAVE MALTESE,—You have rendered yourselves interesting and conspicuous to the world. History affords no more striking example. Betrayed to your invaders, deprived of the means of resistance, eternal slavery seemed to be your inevitable doom. The oppression, the sacrilege of your tyrants became intolerable. Regardless of consequences, you determined at every hazard to vindicate your wrongs.

Without arms, without the resources of war, you broke asunder your chains. Your patriotism, your courage, your religion, supplied all deficiencies. Your energy commanded victory, and an enemy formidable to the best-disciplined armies of Europe yielded in every point to your unexampled efforts, and hid their disgrace behind the ramparts. The gallant battalions of Casals have ever since confined them there, with a vigilance and patience worthy of the cause of freedom.

You called for assistance: the Powers acting in alliance for the support of civil society and of religion hastened to your relief; arms, ammunition, money, and corn have been supplied to you. Their ships have intercepted the succours of the enemy.

My master, the sovereign of a free and generous people, sent me with a handful of men to assist you till a powerful force could be prepared for the reduction of La Valetta. The circumstances of the war have hitherto retarded it, but this is a precious moment, and ought not to be lost. What is to be done to profit by this favourable conjuncture? I anticipate your answer.

You are ready again to unite in a mass, to complete the glorious work you began. To arms, then, Maltese! Let the universal cry through the Island be: 'For God and our country.' Who is there deaf to every sense of duty and of honour that will not gladly obey such a call? None, none

---

[1] Cobbett's *Register*, vol. iii. p. 774.

but traitors or time-serving cowards! We do not wish for such among our ranks. That unerring voice which will distinguish with the title of hero every man who exposes himself for his country, will equally stamp their names with indelible infamy.

Quit, then, your habits of industry for a few weeks; dedicate yourselves under the immediate direction of your own officers, and under the guidance of those whose professional skill and experience will direct your labours most beneficially, to the great and important object of the final conquest of your enemies. A weak and dispirited garrison, unequal to the defence of such extensive works, cannot withstand your efforts. Success will reward your toil, and you will soon return to the bosoms of your families, proud, justly proud, of having saved your country.

(Signed) Thos· Graham, Brig.-General.

Head-quarters, Gudia, 19*th June* 1800.

An irregular bombardment of the fortress of Valetta in the meanwhile continued, and on the 22nd June a shell exploded in the city, firing some ammunition, and causing great loss of life. Three small captures were made on the 1st July laden with brandy, wine, and flour. These losses had a most dispiriting effect upon the garrison, but still there were no signs of surrender.

It was now determined to send reinforcements to the British troops. Sir Ralph Abercromby,[1] who in May had been appointed to the supreme command of the British military forces in the Mediterranean, arrived at Gibraltar on the 6th June, and thereupon decided to visit Malta, after an interview with Keith and Nelson at Leghorn. As the result of their deliberations, and in accordance with instructions received from the home Government, further reinforcements were ordered to be dispatched to Malta from Minorca and Leghorn, together with a general in command to succeed Graham, who had already requested to be superseded.

Abercromby then sailed for Minorca, and the day following his arrival there, the 23rd June, 1,500 men were dispatched for Malta under the command of Major-General Pigot.[2]

---

[1] Sir Ralph Abercromby (1734–1801) had been employed with Pulteney in making fruitless attempts against Ferrol and Cadiz. It will be remembered that he proceeded finally to Egypt, and fell gloriously at the battle near Alexandria on March 21, 1801.—J. H. R.

[2] Keith had been very severe on General Fox, previously commanding at Minorca. On June 20 he wrote: 'There are 14,000 men in Minorca which cannot be used by reason there is no general, and Fox has not nerves to send a man on' (i.e. to Genoa, which Keith wished to defend). *Paget Papers*, vol. i. p. 232.—J. H. R.

CHAPTER XV

THE BRITISH BLOCKADE

(From the 4th July 1800 to the capitulation of the French Garrison, 4th September 1800)

THE difficulty of obtaining money, not only for the men under arms, but also for the Maltese population, went on increasing. The agreement which had been entered into between Sir William Hamilton, General Acton, and the Chevalier Italinsky was found to be unsatisfactory, and in consequence Mr. Paget on the 4th July asked Lord Grenville for specific instructions in this respect.[1]

HON. A. PAGET TO LORD GRENVILLE.

(Palermo) *4th July* 1800.[2]

I should be extremely happy to be furnished with Your Lordship's instructions upon the subject of granting money for the maintenance of the Maltese troops and inhabitants. Hitherto, in consequence of an agreement entered into by General Acton, Sir Wm. Hamilton, Chevalier Italinsky, the sum of £4,000 has been paid by them alternately for the above service; but I receive constant applications from Governor Ball for further remittances, which I cannot bring myself to grant without the consent of the other two Ministers to share the expense, and I meet with the greatest difficulty in the arrangement of this business.

Simultaneously with the request which had been made to the British Government for precise instructions regarding pecuniary aid, arrangements were also being made (as already recorded) for further British reinforcements in men being landed in the island.

---

[1] The reader should remember the facts which are dwelt on in the Introduction, viz. that on June 14 Bonaparte completely overthrew the Austrian army at Marengo, and on the next day signed with General Melas a convention whereby the latter agreed to give up all the conquests of Austria in Italy, and to withdraw her troops to the line of the river Mincio. This news became known at Palermo early in July (see *Paget Papers*, vol. i. pp. 238–48). It put an end to all chance of the Russian force (still at Naples) coming to help in the siege of Valetta, which Keith and Paget had lately been urging. In fact, by the month of June 1800 the Czar had broken off diplomatic connexions with England, and his attitude aroused the greatest suspicion at London. New light is thrown on this by documents printed in the MSS. of J. B. Fortescue (*Dropmore Papers*, vol. vi. pp. 250 et seq.)—J. H. R.

[2] Foreign Office Records, Sicily, 14.

Sir Ralph Abercromby, accompanied by General Hutchinson [Pigot?], arrived in Malta on the 17th July, and on the day following the 2nd Battalion of the 35th Regiment, which had sailed from Minorca on the 23rd June, reached the island, whilst on the 28th July part of the 48th Regiment from Leghorn joined them.[1]

At a review which took place a few days later, General Hutchinson was able to express his pleasure at the condition in which he found the Maltese Regiment, and complimented General Graham on the arrangements he had made, and on the disposition of the troops. On the 18th July, the day the 35th Regiment landed, Villeneuve in the following letter informed the French Colonial Minister of the straits the garrison were now being placed in by the advance of the English posts, and the closer blockade; that their stock of fuel was now also exhausted, and that the *Boudeuse* was being broken up for that purpose:—

Malte, le 29 *Messidor* an 8 (18*th July* 1800).[2]

CITOYEN MINISTRE,—De tous les bâtimens chargés de comestibles qui peuvent avoir été expédiés des différents ports de la République pour Malte la bombarde, *La Marguerite*, commandée par le Citoyen Barret, enseigne de vaisseau, est encore le seul qui soit arrivé à bon port. C'est pour informer le Gouvernement de cet état de choses que nous expédions une barque légère commandé par le Citoyen Bagot, enseigne de vaisseau.

Le Général Vaubois doit nous écrire lui-même et vous informer de notre situation en vivres.[3] Je me dispenserai donc de vous en entretenir. Il me paraît même, Citoyen Ministre, que vous m'en faites un devoir, lorsque pour toute réponse à mes dépêches des 13 Ventôse, 4, 10 & 28 Germinal et 1ᵉʳ· Floréal, que je vous ai fait remettre par les Citoyens Baste et Colomb, vous m'en faites accuser reception par le Général Vaubois, dans la lettre que vous lui avez écrite et que le Citoyen Baste lui a rapporté. Je ne vous cacherai pas, Citoyen Ministre, combien il m'a été pénible de n'avoir aucun témoignage de votre satisfaction à transmettre aux marins qui servent ici sous mes ordres, tandis que la garnison en a reçu d'éclatants de la part du Ministre de son département. Le mérite de la défense de cette place importante est au moins également partagé entre la garnison et la marine, et le bonheur d'avoir contribué essentiellement à sa conservation, nous sera toujours un dédomagement précieux et satisfaisant.

Je ne négligerai pas cependant de vous rendre compte de tout ce qui concerne ici nos affaires maritimes. Les Anglais continuent à bloquer étroitement ce port; ils employent en ce moment trois vaisseaux dont une de 74 et deux de 64 et plusieurs frégates, corvettes et bricks, les uns à la voile, les autres à l'ancre à portée et demi de cannon du port. Les ennemis ont démasqué depuis quelques jours trois batteries qui croisent le port de

---

[1] For the summons to surrender which General Pigot (not Hutchinson) sent to Vaubois on July 17, see Vaubois' *Journal of the Siege of Malta* (Part IV), in Appendix. —J. H. R.

[2] Arch. Nat., BB⁴ 147.

[3] See the letters of Vaubois of this date in his *Journal of the Siege of Malta* (Part IV), in Appendix.—J. H. R.

Marse Musceit en tous les sens, qui le rendent impraticable et nous privent de la resource de la pêche que nous en rétirions.

Ils travaillent toujours à renforcer leur ligne et à géner de plus en plus les mouvements dans le grand port; il paraît qu'ils ont reçu un renfort de troupes, et qu'ils se sont emparés de quelques bâtiments chargés de vivres pour nous; c'est sur ce motif qu'ils ont fondé une nouvelle sommation, qu'ils nous ont addressés hier, mais tous leurs efforts seront vains tant qu'il nous restera de quoi vivre. Puissent les succès des armées en Italie et le génie du chef de la République amener bientôt des circonstances qui puissent nous mettre à même de conserver ce poste important, c'est le prix le plus précieux que nous puissions recevoir de deux ans de travaux et de privations.

Nos ressources en bois à brûler étant terminés, la frégate *La Boudeuse* va être mise en démolition conformément à l'autorisation que nous en a donné l'Amiral Bruys pendant son ministère. Salut et respect.

(Signed) VILLENEUVE.[1]

Whilst the attacking forces were being strengthened, and whilst an effort was being made for better arrangements as to the supply of money and food for the troops, as well as the inhabitants in general, the tergiversations of Russia (referred to in another chapter of the work) were at last realised by the British Cabinet.[2] Their suspicions being aroused, Mr. Secretary Dundas found it necessary on the 1st August to issue the following instructions to Sir Ralph Abercromby:

EXTRACT FROM A DISPATCH FROM MR. SECRETARY DUNDAS TO GENERAL SIR RALPH ABERCROMBY, DATED 1ST AUGUST 1800.[3]

. . . In short, the object of this country in its views upon Malta being to secure to itself the advantage of a very important naval station in that part of the Mediterranean, you will understand that no exertion consistent with the other services in which you are engaged is to be spared on the one hand of expelling the enemy, and on the other, that every precaution, short of actual hostility, is to be taken to prevent our being deprived of this advantage by the interference or pretensions of another Power, whose late

---

[1] That Bonaparte took a keen interest in Malta appears from his letter of 18th July 1800, to the Senate, in which he announced the resolve of the garrison to hold out up to the last ounce of bread, and then to bury themselves under the ruins of the fortress. He proposed that Vaubois should be elected a member of the Senate.

It seems that 10 *tartanes* (or cutters) had been dispatched to Valetta, but only one succeeded in entering.—J. H. R.

[2] As will be pointed out in the notes appended to a later chapter, the situation in Italy had been entirely altered since the promise of the Czar Paul was first given with respect to help in the siege of Valetta; namely, firstly by the quarrels between the Austrians and Russians in the summer and autumn of 1799, which led to the detachment of Suvórof into Switzerland with disastrous results; and secondly, by the French victory of Marengo, which placed Italy once more at the disposal of Bonaparte. Moreover, the recent convention of Russia with Naples for her defence by 10,000 Russians now made that their first duty. (See *Paget Papers*, vol. i. pp. 240, 243.)

It must, however, also be remembered that in the summer of 1800 the Czar Paul began to show strong leanings towards a French alliance; and this it was which first determined the British Government not to allow Malta to become a Russian possession.— J. H. R.

[3] Foreign Office Records, Malta, No. 6 (1799-1800).

conduct justifies the apprehension that under its authority the Port of Malta would either be shut entirely against His Majesty's Fleets (and possibly open to those of his enemy's), or that the right of resorting to it, if granted to this country at all, would be so precarious and insecure, as to render it altogether nugatory and unavailable.

About this date, deserters from the beleaguered garrison informed General Pigot that the end was drawing near, and that, unless relieved, General Vaubois would have to surrender within a month.

This information was conveyed to Mr. Dundas by a dispatch of the 7th August.

Malta, *7th August* 1800.[1]

To the Right Hon. Henry Dundas.

SIR,—As Lieut.-Col. Stewart, who has been here as Adjt.-General, is going to England, I think it right, in case Sir Ralph Abercrombie should have left Minorca before he gets there, to inform you that nothing new has occurred here since Sir Ralph left this place about a fortnight ago, except that two vessels have been taken, going to the relief of Valetta, laden with wine, oil, brandy, and lard, all of which they are much in want of; of the three last articles, deserters tell us they have none left, and very little wine. They likewise say that 'they must surrender in a month, if not relieved.'

Without placing much faith in what deserters say, I should suppose from every information we can obtain, that it is most probable, if nothing gets in, in the course of six weeks or two months, that the place must surrender. I have the honour, &c.

(Signed) H. PIGOT, Maj.-Gen.

The French garrison had now become reduced to the direst extremities. On the 21st August, Rear-Admiral Villeneuve informed the Colonial Minister that, unless provisions were received before the 5th of the following month, they would be compelled on or about that date to surrender. He also expressed regret that the two frigates, the *Diane* and the *Justice*, still in harbour, would suffer the same fate as the garrison, unless they were able in the meanwhile to put to sea, which the season's prevalent calms and the lunar conditions had lately prevented.

Malte, le 3 *Fructidor* an 8 (21*st* August 1800).[2]

CITOYEN MINISTRE,—Le terme de nos moyens de résistance dans ce pays est prêt d'arriver et le 15 de ce mois, si aucune espèce de secours ne nous est arrivé, le Général Vaubois se trouve dans la nécessité d'entrer en pourparler avec l'ennemi ; nous n'avons plus de pain que jusqu'au 22 de ce mois et depuis quinze jours c'est la seule subsistance qu'ait reçu la garnison et les marins. C'est pour informer le Gouvernement de cette fatale circonstance que nous expédions une felouque pour France, pour arrêter toute expédition

---

[1] C.O.R. Malta, No. 1.
[2] Arch. Nat., BB⁴ 147.
See Vaubois' letter of 9th August 1800 to Villeneuve, in which he argued against the sailing of the frigates. (*Journal of the Siege of Malta* (Part IV), Appendix.)—J. H. R.

pour ce pays ultérieure à cette époque, si dans ces derniers jours rien n'a pu nous parvenir.

L'ennemi nous bloque très étroitement avec trois vaisseaux, trois frégates et nombre de petits bâtiments. Il est mouillé à l'embouchure du port et a constament des croiseurs dans l'est et dans l'ouest. C'est avec beaucoup de regret que je vois que les frégates *La Diane* et *La Justice* vont subir le même sort que la place. La faiblesse de la garnison n'a pas permis que leurs équipages qui sont employés à terre et que j'ai redemandé leur fussent rendus avant le dernier moment. Les frégates sont prêtes à les recevoir et à mettre à la voile avec 20 jours de biscuit mais les calmes continuels qui règnent et la clarté de la lune où nous entrons nous laisse aucun espoir qu'elles trouvent une chance favorable pour échaper. Salut et respect.

(Signed) Villeneuve.

Between the 21st and 24th August official correspondence passed between Vaubois and Villeneuve relative to the departure of these two vessels. It would appear that the former was at first averse from denuding the garrison to the extent required for the manning of these two ships; but at last he acquiesced, and at midnight of the 24th they were able to sail from Valetta Harbour.

Copy of this correspondence was forwarded by Villeneuve to the Colonial Minister on the 7th September, as follows:—

À Malte, le 20 *Fructidor* an 8 (*7th September* 1800).[1]

Citoyen Ministre,—Je n'ai cessé de vous informer par toutes les occasions des différentes circonstances dans lesquelles nous nous trouvions à Malte, je vous dois aujourd'hui un compte des derniers moments que nous y avons passés.

Je voyais le terme de nos moyens de subsistance approcher, et le 15 Fructidor fixé pour le jour où nous devions entrer en pourparler avec l'ennemie pour la reddition de la place. J'avais fait plusieurs tentatives auprès du Général Vaubois pour demander la rentrée à leur bord des équipages des bâtimens de la République, pour pouvoir les faire partir et tâcher de les soustraire au sort qui menaçait la place; mais la faiblesse de la garnison et les espérances dont le Gouvernement l'avait flatté, étaient toujours des motifs que le Général m'alléguait, et que je devais respecter.

J'entretenais toujours les bâtimens prêts à mettre à la voile. Enfin e 6 de ce mois, le vent s'étant établi à l'E.S.E. frais, cette circonstance, si rare dans cette saison et dans ce pays me détermina à renouveller mes instances pour avoir les moyens de faire partir au moins les frégates *La Justice* et *La Diane*. Le vaisseau, *L'Athénien*, de 64, n'étant pas doublé de cuivre et ayant une carène de plus de deux ans n'offrait aucun espoir d'échapper à la poursuite de l'ennemi qui était mouillé devant le port aux deux vaisseaux de 74, deux frégates et plusieurs petits bâtimens. Je fus chez le Général Vaubois et j'insistais pour qu'il me rendit les équipages des deux frégates, *La Justice* et *La Diane*, lui temoignant combien il serait honteux de rendre à l'ennemi dans le port deux bâtimens aussi importants sans avoir tenté tous les moyens de les sauver. Le Général parut douter

[1] Arch. Nat., BB⁴ 147.

de la possibilité du succès de l'entreprise et craindre qu'elle n'agravât les conditions de la capitulation à laquelle nous allions nous trouver obligés a recourrir ; il me représentait en outre que par le départ des deux frégates, les principaux postes de la partie de l'est allaient se trouver entièrement dégarnis de canoniers et exposés même à un coup de main, si l'ennemi osait l'entreprendre ; ne pouvant obtenir la totalité des équipages des deux bâtiments je me réduisis alors à lui demander seulement une quantité d'hommes nécessaire pour mettre les deux frégates en état de manœuvrer et que je lui laisserais les canonniers et un assez bon nombre de marins pour ne pas trop affaiblir les postes ; il fut ébranlé par cette dernière proposition et il fut convenu que je lui écrirais à ce sujet et qu'il me répondrait ; je rentrais donc chez moi et lui écrivis la lettre suivante :

'Le Contre-Amiral Villeneuve, &c., au Général Vaubois, &c.

'GÉNÉRAL,—Le vent qui s'est établi à partir de l'est nous fournit encore une chance pour faire échaper les deux frégates, *La Justice* et *La Diane*. En me rendant aux motifs qui vous obligent à retenir la presque totalité des équipages pour la sûreté de vos postes, je vous prie d'examiner s'il ne vous serait pas possible de vous départir de 40 hommes seulement au moyen desquels nous pourrions mettre ces deux frégates en état, non pas d'aller se mésurer avec l'ennemi, mais au moins d'être navigables, et d'échaper par la supériorité de leur marche. Ce sont bâtimens précieux, pour la conservation desquels rien ne doit être négligé et si vous consentés à ce mouvement d'équipage, peut-être de soir pourront elles courir ce hasard, le pis aller n'est-il pas de les rendre à l'ennemi dans le port sous dix jours ? J'ai l'honneur de vous saluer.'

Je reçus la réponse suivante :

'Le Général Vaubois, &c., au Contre-Amiral Villeneuve, &c.

'Vous sentés comme moi la nécessité de ne pas dégarnir des postes déjà très faiblement occupés, en même tems je m'intéresse aussi fort qu'on peut le faire à la conservation des deux frégates de la République. Je ne me connais pas en marine ; si vous croyez qu'elles peuvent échaper par la marche à l'ennemi en ne leur donnant pas [que] le monde nécessaire à les manœuvrer, l'inconvénient me paraît moindre que de les perdre sans ressource ; ça devient donc un devoir.

'À la vérité je comptais les demander par un article de la capitulation, mais je crois l'admission de cet article bien scabreux avec des Anglais. Vous pouvez donc tirer de La Victorieuse les quarante hommes que vous demandés, mais sans prendre les canoniers interressants qui se trouvent à d'autres postes essentiels. La chose me paraît encore très douteuse par ce parti mais presqu'infailliblement perdue autrement. Telle est le résultat de ma façon de voir, guidée par l'intérêt de la République que je m'imagine bien entendue. Salut et fraternité. (Signé) VAUBOIS.'

Avec tout *l'imbroglio* de cette lettre je me hâtais de donner tous les ordres nécessaires pour que le départ de ces frégates eût lieu le soir même ; il était onze heures du matin. Je répartis sur le champ les 40 hommes entre elles deux et je fis faire quelques échanges de marins plus capables qui étaient dans les forts, par ce moyen je réunis environ cent hommes de travail sur chaque frégate, le même jour, la chaîne du port fut ôtée, les poudres embarquées, du biscuit qui était à bord de *L'Athénien* reversé sur les frégates et à l'entrée de la nuit elles commencèrent à appareiller.

J'eus encore à vaincre la tiédeur de quelques hommes qui à bord de la frégate *La Justice* répugnaient à partir avec du biscuit et de l'eau, et qui craignaient après deux de blocus et de misère d'être encore jétés dans les prisons de l'Angleterre tandis qu'ils eussent espéré de jouir des avantages qu'on pouvait se promettre des articles de la capitulation; je fus à bord, je parlai, je ménaçai, je louai le zèle et l'énergie des braves qui ne voulaient pas de laisser prendre dans le port et j'ordonnai de mettre à la voile sous mes yeux; quelques amarres qui cassèrent à bord de *La Diane* retardèrent le départ jusqu'à 11 heures du soir que les deux frégates firent voile au même moment et sortirent du port.

Les batteries ennemis ne s'appercevaient pas de ce mouvement mais une chaloupe de bivouac qui était a portée de fusil en dehors donna aussitôt l'allerte; les deux frégates furent vivement canonées par les batteries ennemies de St. Roch et nous les perdîmes de vue; à une heure le vent calma: à deux il sauta au nord-ouest frais; au jour nous appercevions éloignement toute l'escadre ennemie qui chassait dans la partie de l'est.

Le chef de division, J. VILLENEUVE, Commandant.

The departure of these vessels from Valetta Harbour was observed by His Majesty's ship *Success*, which vessel on the 27th returned to her station off the island, towing the captured *Diane*, totally dismasted, the *Justice* having escaped.[1]

A postscript to Admiral Villeneuve's dispatch to the Colonial Minister of the 7th September gives an account of the capture of the *Diane* by the British frigate, and refers to the capitulation entered into two days previously.

[Postscript dated 20 *Fructidor* an 8 (7th *September* 1800)].[2]

La Justice a exécuté les ordres qui lui étaient donnés avec zèle et activité; le Citoyen Malingre, lieutenant de vaisseau, chargé du détail à bord de cette frégate a donné dans cette occasion des preuves de zèle et d'énergie digne des plus grandes éloges, les Citoyens Marc Aurelle et Taillefer, enseigns de vaisseau, se sont aussi très bien conduits. À bord de la frégate *La Diane*, j'ai trouvé dans le Capitaine Soleil, dans ses officiers et dans son équipage un unanimité de courage, de zèle et de dévouement qui les honore tous.

La République a dans le Capitaine Soleil et le Citoyen Chastellier, enseign de vaisseau, chargé du détail sur *La Diane*, deux officiers du plus grand mérite.

Le 9me *Fructidor* (27th *August*).

Nous avons vu revenir un des vaisseaux chasseurs ayant la frégate *La Diane* à la remorque, démâtée de tous ses mâts et perroquets.

---

[1] Why *La Justice* escaped 'under cover of darkness' (James, vol. ii. p. 444), while *La Diane* was captured, has never been explained. The latter was renamed *Niobe*.—J. H. R

[2] Arch. Nat. BB^4, 147.

Le 15me (*2nd September*).

Le conseil de guerre convoqué par le Général Vaubois a pris l'arrêtté ci-joint (Cotté A) qui autorise les généraux de terre et de mer d'entrer en pourparler avec l'ennemi pour la reddition de la place.

Le 17me (*4th September*).

Nous sommes entrés en pourparler avec l'ennemi et le 18 (5th September) nous avons signé la capitulation ci-jointe (Coté B) qui a eu son exécution.

Je m'occupe sans relâche de procurer le plutôt possible le transport des marins au port de Toulon. J'espère qu'il en partira dès demain une division.

Cet événement me laissant sans destination je vous prie, Citoyen Ministre, de m'addresser vos ordres au port de Toulon d'où je me propose de me rendre immédiatement à Paris pour vous rendre comptes particulier de toutes les circonstances dans lesquelles je me suis trouvé. Salut et respect. (Signed) VILLENEUVE.

From the crew of the *Diane* and from the papers found on board it was learned that unless succour in the meanwhile reached the defenders Vaubois would have to surrender in about a fortnight's time, but from Admiral Villeneuve's instructions to Captain Soleil of the *Diane*, which were also captured, there was every reason to expect that General Vaubois intended to treat for the surrender on or about the 2nd September. In fact on that day a council of war was held to discuss the situation, when it was unanimously decided that on the 4th September a *parlementaire* should be sent to the British commandant to open negotiations for a capitulation.

COUNCIL OF WAR.

Le 15 *Fructidor* an 8 (*2nd September* 1800).

Les Généraux, officiers supérieurs de terre et de mer, les commissaires ordonnateurs des guerres et de la marine, les commandans des forts, les officiers de tous grades qui se trouvent commander [?] les détachements des différens corps, convoqués par le Général de Division Vaubois, Commandant en Chef dans les Isles de Malte et du Goze, pour la tenue d'un conseil de guerre, se sont assemblés au Palais National de la cité de Malte, partie de l'ouest.

[Considérant] que le rapport du Général Vaubois, duquel il résulte que les magasins de subsistance de la place sont entièrement épuisés depuis plus d'un mois, que ceux des liquides le sont également; que le pain, seul aliment qui reste pour la nourriture de la garnison et de la population, doit avoir son terme au 22 de ce mois, le conseil considérant que la garnison de Malte, réduite au tiers de ration depuis deux ans a rempli avec honneur la tache qui lui était imposée de conserver cette place à la République jusqu'à la dernière extrémité; qui, après avoir repoussé toutes les attaques de vive force qui ont été tentées contre elle, a par sa contenance

---

[1] Arch. Nat., BB⁴ 147.

et son énergie, réduit l'ennemi à persévérer dans un blocus étroit qui ne permet plus d'espérer d'obtenir aucun secours du dehors.

Que les forces que l'ennemi employe pour assurer ce blocus et par terre et par mer, ne laissent à la brave garnison de Malte aucun moyen de s'en procurer par son courage et son dévouement, dans un pays stérile en lui même et hérissé de fortifications, que la nature, et l'art ont multiplié pour nous resserrer dans nos remparts; que d'ailleurs toute entreprise à cet égard serait sans succès par la précaution qu'a pris l'ennemi d'après le rapport de transfuges, de tenir ses bleds.

Que ce serait compromettre l'existence de douze mille âmes qui composent la population et la garnison de cette place, de différer d'avantage d'entrer en pourparler avec l'ennemi afin d'en obtenir une capitulation honorable et telle qu'elle est due à des braves militaires, qui ont aussi longtems souffert pour leur pays.

Que la marine a partagé avec honneur les travaux et les privations de la garnison, et qu'elle a cherché par le départ des deux frégates, *La Justice* et *La Diane*, d'épuiser tous les moyens de diminuer les pertes que va faire la République dans cette partie.

Que les lois de la guerre enfin, et celle de l'humanité autorisent suffisamment le Général Commandant en Chef à entamer une négociation avec l'ennemi.

À délibéré que le Général Vaubois enverra le dix-sept de ce mois un parlementaire au commandant Anglais, pour proposer la capitulation, et que le Contre-Amiral Villeneuve s'y réunira pour stipuler en faveur des marins, afin de les faire jouir des mêmes avantages qui pourront être accordés à la garnison.

Suivent les signatures.

Pour copie conforme le Commissaire des Guerres ff. d'Ordonnateur.

(Signed) DOT.

In anticipation of the surrender of the French garrison, General Pigot had received from Sir Ralph Abercromby precise instructions to hoist the British flag only when the fortress fell. Captain Ball having become aware of General Pigot's intention to treat with Vaubois direct, without reference to the representative of His Sicilian Majesty and chief of the Maltese people, felt constrained officially to resent this omission, and four days before the surrender of the French garrison, he addreed from Sant' Antonio Palace the following letter to General Pigot:—

[Extract.]

Malta, 1st *September* 1800.[1]

I consider the Maltese a distinct corps who have besieged La Valetta twelve months with unexampled bravery and perseverance without the aid of foreign troops. At present they have three thousand troops, who occupy the advanced posts, and they have three thousand militia enrolled ready to act; they have lately been maintained at the joint expense of

[1] C.O.R., Malta, No. 9.

England, Russia, and Naples, and if I am not allowed to sign the capitulation alluded to, I am apprehensive it will give much offence to the two latter Courts, as well as to the Maltese, who conceive that both in a civil and military point of view they are entitled to an important voice. I beg leave to acquaint you, that when Rear-Admiral Lord Nelson commanded in the Mediterranean, I received his order to hoist the colours of Saint John of Jerusalem whenever I enter Valetta, in conformity with an agreement between the Ministers of England, Russia, and Naples, since which I have been informed by Mr. Paget, the British Minister at Palermo, that he has not received counter orders; if there be any objection to the execution to that order, I trust there will not be any to the hoisting His Sicilian Majesty's colours with those of His Britannic Majesty.[1]

I shall only trespass one observation in support of His Sicilian Majesty's continued right to the sovereignty of this Island. In June 1798, the French invaded this Island without any previous declaration of war, and reduced the inhabitants to capitulate; three months after which the Maltese in the country, who are three-fourths of the population of the Island, revolted and besieged the French in Valetta and the adjacent posts; they then sent a deputation to His Silician Majesty, to renew their acknowledgements to him as their lawful sovereign, and to solicit his aid to expel the French, in which he was pleased to acquiesce, and from that period has contributed in troops, money, and ammunition to their support.

It will therefore be presumed that the English came here as an *ally* to His Sicilian Majesty, and cannot intend to dispossess him of the sovereignty of this Island by assuming an exclusive right to hoist British colours in Valetta.

I beg leave to express, Sir, the satisfaction I feel in having to discuss such subjects with an officer of your rank and character, as I am confident you will avoid as much as possible giving offence to the Allies of His Britannic Majesty. I have the honour, &c.

(Signed) ALEXR. JOHN BALL.

To this communication General Pigot on the same day from Casal Lia replied as follows [2]:—

I am honoured with your letter claiming a right, as chief of this Island, to sanction the terms on which the enemy in La Valette may be obliged

[1] Paget was in much perplexity (see his letters of July 21, 1800, and August 12, 1800, also that of Lord Keith to him on July 23, 1800, in *Paget Papers*, vol. i. pp. 255, 258, 265). Neither of them knew that the Czar Paul had practically severed his alliance with Austria in October 1799, owing to his annoyance with that Power for her treatment of Suvórof's army. The ill-success of the Anglo-Russian expedition in Holland in the autumn of 1799 annoyed him, as did also our siege of Valetta, and in February 1800 he demanded the recall of our ambassador, Sir C. Whitworth; in June he dismissed the *chargé d'affaires* who took his place. By this time the Czar was very friendly with Bonaparte, because the latter had sent back to Russia all the Russian prisoners taken from the army campaigning in Holland. Further, on July 4, 1800, Bonaparte recommended Talleyrand to draw up a letter offering to hand over Malta to the Czar in case the French garrison of Valetta were constrained to surrender (*Corres. de Nap. I*, vol. vi. p. 396). This offer clinched the resolve of the Czar to take the side of France, and was largely responsible for the formation of the Armed Neutrality League formed by him against Great Britain in the autumn of that year.—J. H. R.

[2] C.O.R. Malta, No. 9.

to submit, and to sign the capitulation. I hardly know an instance, except the one you mentioned to me, where the commanders of troops of different nations acting together have signed the capitulation; but where it has been done I believe you will find those officers have commanded *regular* troops, and that they have had commissions or letters of service, neither of which I have understood you to have. Though the Maltese have certainly made great exertions, and are entitled to a great deal of merit for their bravery and perseverance, yet with all their exertions they never could have compelled the French to surrender without the assistance of the British fleet and army.

It is impossible for me to say half what I think of the great service I consider you to have been of in this Island; your persevering attention to the service you have undertaken does you the highest honour, and is well deserving of being rewarded. At the same time, I must say I have always considered your office more as a civil than a military one, and as such, independent of other considerations, I cannot see what claim you can have to sign the capitulation. With regard to your having had an order from Lord Nelson to hoist the colours of the Order of Saint John of Jerusalem in the event of La Valette falling, I never heard of an instance of colours of different nations flying in a fortified town at the same time; but though La Valette, whenever it surrenders, is to be considered as falling to the British flag, yet no offence is intended thereby to the Courts of Russia or Naples, or to the Maltese.

From this correspondence it will be observed that Captain Ball faithfully and strenuously advocated the interests of His Sicilian Majesty, as he was bound in honour to do, for up to this date he had been that monarch's authorised and acknowledged representative in the island; but the altered circumstances in which Europe was now placed, and which had happened since Ball's original appointment, compelled the British Cabinet to modify their views with regard to the occupation of Malta, which had now become a question for settlement, when that of a general peace would have to be discussed.

These altered circumstances were, first, the ever-victorious progress of the French armies on the Continent; secondly, the inexplicable conduct of Russia; thirdly, the subjugation of the kingdom of Naples to the power and influence of France; and finally, the aspirations of the Maltese people, who no longer desired any connexion with what had become, and continued to be more or less, a dismembered kingdom, until its restoration fifteen years later.

Returning to the events which preceded the surrender of the French garrison, we must observe that it was on the 2nd September, with only one week's provision remaining, that General Vaubois summoned a council of war, when it was decided, as already recorded, to open negotiations with the British general for the capitulation of the garrison.

Nothing further occurred on that day, but on the 4th Brigadier-

General Graham was sent for by General Pigot, when upon arrival at head-quarters he found a letter had been received from General Vaubois proposing to treat. General Graham, with Captain Martin, of H.M.S. *Northumberland*, as senior naval officer afloat, thereupon entered Valetta, reaching there by noon, to discuss the articles of capitulation. During the negotiations Vaubois objected to Ball, as chief of the Maltese, signing the articles; some other difficulty also arose, which had to be referred to General Pigot, but on the morning of the 5th the articles of capitulation were duly signed by General Vaubois and Admiral Villeneuve on the one part, and by General Pigot and Captain Martin on the other.

The instructions given to General Graham by General Pigot, which were to be observed in treating with General Vaubois for the surrender of the fortress, were as follows [1]:—

You are to insist as long as possible upon the garrison remaining prisoners of war until regularly exchanged, and not to give up this point unless it should finally appear to you that no capitulation will be acceded to on that condition, in which case you may agree to their being at once transported to France, giving their parole, however, not to bear arms against His Majesty or his Allies, until they shall be exchanged for an equal number of such prisoners as may be in possession of the French.

Should the garrison surrender on the last-mentioned conditions, such a number are to be put immediately on board ship as Captain Martin may judge proper or has room for; the remainder will be accomodated on shore on what may be considered the most convenient situation; but you will endeavour to stipulate that their arms should be given up on a promise on our part to restore them when they are to sail for France.

Those on shore will receive provisions from us for the first few days, till an arrangement can be made for their supplying themselves. Those on board will receive the ship's provisions. If the French General should wish to stipulate that no Maltese should be allowed to enter the place till the French are gone, it should be confined to no armed Maltese, and the Maltese Corps should be excepted, which, being a regular corps, is under military discipline.

If medicines or medical assistance is required, it will of course be granted to them.

No arrangement is to be entered into with the enemy's garrison that can in any way prove an obstacle to the re-establishment of the Order of the Knights of St. John of Jerusalem as sovereigns of the Island.

Should the French General wish to stipulate for the three Langues of the Order, formerly belonging to his nation, not being abolished, it must be answered that no instructions having been received on that head, it is a matter that must be left for future consideration. All plans and writings which have any relation to the place and its fortifications to be faithfully delivered up. All the cannon, ammunition, and public property of every kind must be given up without reserve.

(Signed) H. PIGOT, M.-General.

To B.-GENERAL GRAHAM, &c.

[1] Delavoye, *Life of Graham*, p. 202.

The result of their deliberations was as follows:—

ARTICLES OF CAPITULATION between the General of Division, Vaubois, Commander-in-Chief of the Islands of Malta and Gozo, and Rear-Admiral Villeneuve, commanding the Marine at Malta, on one part, and Major-General Pigot, commanding the Troops of His Britannic Majesty and His Allies, and Captain Martin, commanding the British Squadron and that of the Allies before Malta.[1]

Art. 1. The garrison of Malta, its forts, and dependencies will march out to be embarked and conveyed to Marseilles, on such day and hour as may be appointed, with all the honours of war, viz. drums beating, colours flying, preceded by two four-pounders, with lighted matches, with tumbrils for artillery to serve them, and tumbrils for the infantry. The officers of the Marine, as well civil and military, the sailors and all persons belonging to that department, will in the same manner be conducted to Toulon.

Answer, Art. 1. The garrison shall receive the honours of war demanded, but as it is impossible the whole should be immediately embarked, the following arrangements will take place as soon as the Capitulation is signed. The forts of Ricasoli and Tigné will be delivered up to the British troops, and the British ships may enter the harbour. The Porte Nationale shall be occupied by a guard composed of French and English in equal numbers, until the vessels shall be ready to receive the first embarkation, when the whole garrison shall march out with the honours of war to the Marina, where they will lay down their arms.

Those who cannot be of the first embarkation will occupy the Island of Fort Manuel, having an armed guard to prevent anything that may happen towards the country. The garrison are to be considered as prisoners of war, and are not to serve against His Britannic Majesty or his Allies until exchanged, for which their respective officers will give their parole of honour. All the artillery, ammunition, and public magazines, of whatever description, shall be delivered to officers appointed to receive them, as well as inventories and public papers.

Art. 2. The General of Brigade Chaner, Commandant of the place and forts, the General of Brigade D'Henezal, commanding the Artillery and the Engineers, the officers, non-commissioned officers, and land troops, the officers, soldiers, and crews, and all other persons employed in the Marine, Citizen Pierre Alphonso Guyn, Commissary-General of Commercial Affairs for the French Republic in Syria and Palestine, accidentally at Malta, with his family, those holding civil and military employments, the Ordonnateurs and Commissaries of War and Marine, the officers of the Civil Administration, and other members of the constituted authorities, shall retain their arms, personal effects, and property of every description.

Answer, Art. 2. Granted, with the exception of the arms laid down by the soldiers. Agreeable to the First Article, the non-commissioned officers shall be allowed to retain their swords.

Art. 3. All persons having carried arms in the service of the

[1] C.O.R. Malta, No. 1.

Republic during the siege, of whatever nation, shall be considered as part of the garrison.

Answer, Art. 3. Granted.

Art. 4. The Division will be embarked at the expense of His Britannic Majesty, every officer, soldier, or person in public employment shall receive rations in proportion to their rank according to the French regulations. The officers and members of the Civil Administration who go to France shall enjoy the same advantages, they and their families being rated agreeable to that military rank which corresponds to the dignity of their situation.

Answer, Art. 4. Granted, as far as is conformable to the usage of the British Navy, which allows the same ration to every individual, of whatever rank or condition he may be.

Art. 5. The necessary number of carts and boats to transport and embark the personal effects of the Generals, their aides-de-camp, the Ordonnateurs and Commissaries, the Chiefs of Corps and officers, of Citizen Guyn, of the officers of the Civil and Military Administrations of Corps, those of the Commissaries of War by sea and land, of the Paymasters of the Division, and the other officers of the Civil and Military Administrations.

Their effects and papers are not to be subject to any search, under a guarantee given by the French Generals that they do not contain any public or private property.

Answer, Art. 5. Granted.

Art. 6. The ships belonging to the Republic that are fit to go to sea shall depart at the same time with the Division, to go to a port in France, after being furnished with the necessary provisions.

Answer, Art. 6. Refused.

Art. 7. The sick capable of being moved shall be embarked with their effects, and the surgeons necessary to their being taken care of during the voyage, at the same time with the Division, being furnished with provisions, surgical instruments, and medicine chests. Those who cannot be moved will be treated as their situation requires.

The General-in-Chief having at Malta a physician and surgeon who will take care of them, they shall be furnished with quarters gratis, if they should be moved from the hospital, and sent to France as soon as their situation admits of it, with everything that belongs to them, in the same manner as the garrison. The Generals-in-Chief by land and sea in evacuating Malta entrust them to the generosity and humanity of the English General.

Answer, Art. 7. Granted.

Art. 8. No individuals, of whatever nation, inhabitants of the Island of Malta, or otherwise, shall be in any manner molested for their political opinions, or for what they have done, or what has happened, during the time that Malta has been in the hands of the French Government. This Article applies principally, and in its full extent, to those who have taken arms or held employments, either civil, administrative, or military; they are not to be called to account or proceeded against for having done so, nor for what they may have done in the course of their employment.

Answer, Art. 8. This Article is not properly part of a military capitulation, but the inhabitants who wish to remain, or those who shall be permitted to remain, may be assured that they shall be treated with justice and humanity, and shall enjoy the full protection of the laws.

Art. 9. The French in Malta, and the Maltese of every description who wish to go to France, shall have permission to do so, with their property; those who have moveable or immoveable effects, that cannot be immediately sold, and intend going to France, shall have six months from the date of this Capitulation to sell their property. Their property shall be respected; they may act for themselves if they remain, or by regular attorneys if they sail with the Division. When their business shall be finished within the time stipulated, they shall be furnished with passports to go to France, carrying with them on board ship the moveables which they may choose to keep, as well as their capital in specie or bills of exchange, as may be most expedient.

Answer, Art. 9. Granted, referring to the answer of the last Article.

Art. 10. As soon as the Capitulation shall be signed, the English General shall leave it in the power of the General commanding the French troops, whenever he chooses, to send a felucca with the necessary crew, and an officer charged to carry the Capitulation to the French Government, for which the necessary safe-conduct will be given.

Answer, Art. 10. Granted.

Art. 11. The Articles of Capitulation being signed, the gate called Porte de Bombes will be delivered to the English General. It will be occupied by an equal guard of English and French, who will have it in charge, not to suffer any of the soldiers of the besieging army, or any of the inhabitants whatever of the Island, to enter until the French troops shall be embarked and out of sight of the harbour. By degrees, as the embarkation takes place, the English troops will occupy the posts which will give them the command of the place. The English General must be sensible that this precaution is indispensable, that there may be no subject of dispute, and that the Capitulation may be religiously observed.

Answer, Art. 11. Granted, according to the provisions contained in the answer given to the First Article. Every precaution will be taken that the armed Maltese shall not approach the posts occupied by the French troops.

Art. 12. All alienations, or sales of moveable or immoveable property whatsoever, made by the French Government while in possession of Malta, and all transactions between individuals, shall be held inviolable.

Answer, Art. 12. Granted, as far as they shall be just and lawful.

Art. 13. The agents of the Powers, Allies to the French, who shall be in Valetta at the reduction of the place, shall not be molested in their persons or property, but shall be guaranteed by this Capitulation.

Answer, Art. 13. Granted.

Art. 14. Ships of war or trading vessels coming from France under the national flag, and presenting themselves at the harbour to enter, shall not be considered as prizes, nor shall their crews be made prisoners, for the first twenty days after the date of the present Capitulation, but shall be sent back to France with a convoy.

Answer, Art. 14. Refused.

Art. 15. The General-in-Chief and the other Generals shall be embarked with their aides-de-camp and the officers attached to them, as well as the Ordonnateurs and suites respectively, who shall not be separated.

Answer, Art. 15. Granted.

Art. 16. The prisoners taken during the siege, including the crews of the ship *Le Guillaume Tell*, and the frigate *La Diane*, shall be restored, and treated as the garrison. Also the crew of the frigate *La Justice*, if she should be taken on her voyage to any of the ports of the Republic.

Answer, Art. 16. The crew of the *Le Guillaume Tell* is already exchanged, and that of *La Diane* shall be transported to Minorca, to be exchanged forthwith.

Art. 17. Every person in the service of the Republic shall be exempt from any act of reprisal, of whatever nature or under whatever pretext.

Answer, Art. 17. Granted.

Art. 18. If any doubt shall arise upon the terms of the Capitulation, it shall be interpreted in favour of the garrison.

Answer, Art. 18. Granted, according to justice.

Made and concluded at Malta the 5th day of September 1800.

In subsequent years it has been asserted that to the articles of capitulation General Pigot signed, as commanding the troops of His Britannic Majesty, *and his Allies*. This statement is incorrect, as may be seen by reference to the official copy of the capitulations certified as correct by Admiral Villeneuve, and forwarded by him to the Minister of Marine and Colonies on the 7th September. This copy of the capitulation is now deposited in the Archives Nationales of Paris (Marine Modern Section, Carton BB⁴ 147), wherein General Pigot, in accordance with the positive instructions received from His Britannic Majesty's Government, to the effect 'that it was not proposed to share with other parties the advantages to be derived from the conquest of Malta,'[1] simply signed the document as major-general.

The signatories to the deed are registered as follows:—

(Signed) 'THE GENERAL OF DIVISION, VAUBOIS.
" PIGOT, MAJOR-GENERAL.
" THE REAR-ADMIRAL VILLENEUVE.
" CAPTAIN MARTIN, commanding the ships of war of His Britannic Majesty, and of his Allies, off Malta.'

On the day the articles of capitulation were signed, Forts Ricasoli, Tigné, and Floriana were occupied by the British troops, and several of the British ships of war entered the Grand Harbour, and by early morning of the 8th September the greater portion of the French troops embarked for transport to Marseilles.

Information of the surrender of the French garrison was immediately dispatched to General Sir Ralph Abercromby and the Right Honourable Henry Dundas by General Pigot, under dates of the 5th and 6th September, as follows:—

[1] Foreign Office Records, Malta, 6 (1799—1800).

Malta, 5th *September* 1800.[1]

To the Right Hon. Gen. Sir Ralph Abercromby, K.B., &c.

SIR,—I have great satisfaction in acquainting you with the surrender of the fortress of Valetta, with all its dependencies, after sustaining a blockade of two years. The capitulation has been signed this day.

I had every reason to suppose that this most formidable fortress was likely soon to fall, from the circumstances of the two French frigates, *La Justice* and *La Diane*, going out of the harbour a few nights ago, one of which, *La Diane*, by the vigilance of the blockading squadron, was soon captured, and there are still some hopes that the other may have shared the same fate. Judging of how much consequence it may be that you should have the earliest intimation of this important capture, I have delayed until another opportunity sending returns of the stores, &c., found in the place, which could not yet be made up. In the short time you were here, you must have been sensible of the great exertions which Brig.-Gen. Graham must have made with the limited force he had previous to my arrival with a reinforcement. He has ever since continued these exertions, and I consider that the surrender of the place has been accelerated by the decision of his conduct in preventing any more inhabitants from coming out a short time before I came here.[2] He was sent to negotiate the terms of capitulation with General Vaubois, and I am much indebted to him for his assistance in that business.

I am happy to say that I have experienced every support from Brig.-Gen. Moncrieff, and the officers of the British and Allied troops, whose conduct in every respect has been most exemplary. The service of the Engineer Department, under Captain Gordon, has been carried on with great zeal and perseverance. I think it right to mention to you that Lieut. Vivion of the Royal Artillery, the Assistant Quarter-Master-General, has been of considerable service. He was landed here with his party from the *Stromboli* bomb at the commencement of the blockade, and for a long time did duty with these few men, without any other British or regular troops of any description.

I have great pleasure in acknowledging the constant and ready assistance and co-operation I have received from Captain Ball of H.M.S. *Alexander*, who has been employed on shore during the greater part of the blockade. His name and services are already well known to His Majesty's Ministers, and I am sure I need not say more than that what he has performed here does credit to his former character.

I herewith transmit to you the terms of capitulation.

I have derived great assistance from my aide-de-camp, Capt. Dalrymple, who has for some time been doing duty as Asst. Adjt.-General, and I should be happy if anything could be done for him.

I have the honour, &c.

(Signed) H. PIGOT, Maj.-Gen.

---

[1] C.O.R. Malta, No. 1.
[2] As I have pointed out in the Introduction, this proves that the resistance and the final surrender of Valetta turned essentially on the question of food supply.—J. H. R.

[Extract.]
MAJOR-GENERAL PIGOT TO SIR RALPH ABERCROMBY.

Malta, 5*th September* 1800.[1]

Captain Ball wanted to sign the capitulation for the Maltese. I, however, told him I could not admit of it, that I conceived the only two persons to sign the capitulation were Captain Martin and myself, as commanding the Navy and Army. Colonel Fardella wished to sign for the Neapolitans, but I gave him the same answer.

General Vaubois positively refused to treat with the Maltese or anybody for them. Captain Ball has remonstrated on my meaning to hoist British colours only, but 'till I receive any further instructions from you I shall not think myself justified in hoisting any other. If anything else is meant I hope I shall soon have directions about it. The instructions Captain Ball has on that head are totally different to what I understood it was your wish I should do, but I shall certainly abide by what you have instructed me to do.

Malta, 6*th September* 1800.[2]

To the Right Honourable Henry Dundas, &c.

SIR,—Conceiving that it may be of the utmost consequence that His Majesty's Ministers should be acquainted as soon as possible with the surrender of the important fortress of Valetta, I have desired Mr. Paget to dispatch a messenger to England, with a copy of my letter to General Sir Ralph Abercromby on the subject, and the articles of capitulation, which are herewith sent you.

We yesterday took possession of some of the works, and our ships entered the harbour, and I am in hopes the whole will be evacuated by the enemy to-morrow, except the Island of Manoel, where, agreeable to the capitulation, such are to remain as cannot be immediately sent to France for want of ships to take them. I have the honour, &c.

(Signed) H. PIGOT, Maj.-General.

Sir Alexander Ball in a letter to Lord Nelson confirms what has just been related regarding Vaubois' objections to Ball signing the capitulations on behalf of the Maltese. This letter is without a date, but it must have been written on or about the 7th September, and is to be found in Pettigrew, vol. i. p. 395. The following is an extract:—

I have just received a letter from General Graham, who conducted the business of the capitulations, saying that General Vaubois objected to my signing as chief of the Maltese. Major-General Pigot and I conduct business with great harmony, I have not had the slightest reason to be dissatisfied with him, he is very reserved, but I think he is a very friendly man.

Immediately Pigot was in possession of Valetta, Ball made another urgent application to the British Minister at Naples for money,

[1] C.O.R. Malta, No. 1.   [2] *Ibid.*

and on the 14th September Mr. Paget informed Lord Grenville that in consequence of an application from Governor Ball, General Acton and the Chevalier Italinsky having made the two last payments, he had sent 2,000 ounces to Malta (i.e. £4,533 6s. 8d.).[1]

On the vexed question of the colours which were hoisted when the evacuation of the fortress by the French garrison took place, as well as on the subject of declining to allow Colonel Fardella to sign the capitulations on behalf of the Neapolitan Government, General Fox, under date of the 18th September, wrote from Minorca to General Pigot, fully approving the decision of the latter.

Mahon, 18*th September* 1800.[2]

To Major-General Pigot.

SIR,—The *Mahon* brig, with your dispatches to General Sir Ralph Abercromby, arrived here on Monday morning, which according to his directions I opened, but had the opportunity of forwarding them to Gibraltar by the same brig that afternoon.

I most sincerely hope, and think it probable, that they may reach him before he quits Gibraltar. In the meantime I most perfectly coincide in opinion with you with respect to your situation with Captain Ball of His Majesty's Royal Navy, and that however highly you, as everyone must, respect his public and private character and admire the numerous and essential services he has rendered to the progress of His Majesty's arms, that you can acknowledge no order or control from him as Governor, unless authorised by our Government, and I am also to add that I conceive you have been perfectly correct in your answer to Colonel Fardella.

I am certain you have exactly followed General Sir Ralph Abercromby's orders in hoisting British colours only, and you will persevere in this conduct until you hear further from Sir Ralph Abercromby, or His Majesty's Ministers. I conclude you will have received long before this my letter of the 5th instant, by the *Transfer* brig, enclosing extracts of instructions from General Sir Ralph Abercromby, and of a secret dispatch from Mr. Dundas, but lest they should have miscarried, I now send duplicates.

I have given directions to the Commissary General to make arrangements for victualling La Valetta, according to Sir Ralph Abercromby's instructions, including forty days' provisions for 3,000 men, now supposed to be there. I have also communicated that part of your letter concerning ships and transports to Captain Lewis, the commanding officer of the navy in this port, who assures me he will take the necessary steps. It is unnecessary for me to explain to you that from the small force left here, the sending you a single soldier must be out of the question.[3] As there may be great delay in letters coming here, I must beg you will not have the least delicacy or hesitation in corresponding by the way of Italy, directly with His Royal Highness, the Captain General, or His Majesty's

---

[1] Foreign Office Records, Sicily, 14.
[2] C.O.R. Malta, No. 1.
[3] Most of the troops at Port Mahon had been withdrawn in order to strengthen General Abercromby's force destined for Egypt, but for the present were making an attempt on Cadiz.—J. H. R.

Ministers, when opportunities offer, and you think the matter of sufficient importance.

The Commissary General being of opinion that the duties of Assistant Commissary and Paymaster are more than can be well executed by one gentleman, and that there may be also some impropriety in those duties being concentrated in one person, you will have the goodness to appoint whoever you may think fit as Assistant Paymaster to the troops under your command. Mr. Feyers, the Paymaster General here, will inform you of the allowance that will be made him, and the necessary instructions to give him. I have the honour, &c. (Signed) H. E. Fox.

Ten days after the capture of the fortress General Graham obtained six months' leave of absence, sailing for England on the 15th September via Syracuse, Messina, and Trieste. From Syracuse, under date of the 19th of that month, he addressed to the Right Hon. Henry Dundas an important dispatch giving a full account of the position of affairs in Malta, advising for the future, and at the same time pointing out the grave dangers which would result from a Russian garrison, or the admission of a Deputy Grand Master of the Order. The following is a synopsis of this dispatch.[1]

If it continues to be the intention of the British Government to preserve such an interest in Malta as is described in your instructions, nothing short of the military command resting in the hands of one of His Majesty's officers can answer the purpose.

He then points out the antipathy existing between the country peasants and the people in Valetta:

. . . the simple inhabitants of the country being regarded by the citizens as an inferior race.

For the management of the Maltese too much praise cannot be given to Governor Ball; he has devoted himself to listen to their complaints, to relieve their distresses, to settle their disputes, to redress their grievances, and to administer equal justice to them with a degree of patience, address, and judgment that very few men are capable of.

Immediately on the surrender of La Valetta, Governor Ball, to put an end to his provisional revolutionary government, dissolved the Congress and disbanded the Casal battalions.[2]

General Graham closed his letter by saying:[3]

I think it fair to conclude that any mild well-regulated government would be more acceptable to the inhabitants than a restoration of the Order, tho' at present there may be a considerable party in its favour. The late Grand Master Hompesch borrowed large sums of money from many of the inhabitants to enable him to bribe the electors, all these look to his restoration as their only certain chance of payment.

[1] C.O.R. Malta, No. 1.
[2] In accordance with the agreement made when the Congress was formed (see Ball's dispatch to Lord Grenville, dated 15th June 1800).
[3] Foreign Office Records, Malta, No. 6.

THE BRITISH BLOCKADE 327

Sir Ralph Abercromby had also confirmed his instructions regarding the colours, as may be gathered from General Pigot's dispatch of the 24th September to the Right Hon. Henry Dundas.

La Valetta, 24th September 1800.[1]

To the Right Hon. Henry Dundas, &c.

SIR,—Having yesterday received information from Sir Ralph Abercromby that he was quitting the Mediterranean, by which I found he had not received my dispatches with an account of the surrender of this place, and there being an opportunity of writing to you by Colonel Hunter, who is going to England by land on account of the death of his father, I think it right to acquaint you (as the communication from hence so seldom occurs) that everything has gone on as quiet as possible here since we took possession; the people in general seem satisfied at being under the protection of the British; at the same time, though they are mostly glad that the French are gone, the minds of many are agitated to know in what way this place is to be considered. The British colours only are flying in Valetta and its dependencies, notwithstanding the many remonstrances I have heard to the contrary from Mr. Paget and Captain Ball, who thought that Sicilian colours should likewise be hoisted.[2]

I am, however, happy that Sir Ralph Abercromby confirmed, by a letter I received from him yesterday, what he had instructed me to do when he was here, which was to hoist British colours only.

I should not have presumed to have written to His Majesty's Ministers on this subject, but from the circumstances of knowing that Sir Ralph Abercromby has quitted the Mediterranean, and having this opportunity of acquainting you with the above particulars, which it may be necessary you should know, not being certain that Sir Ralph ever received the letters I had written to him on the subject previous to La Valetta surrendering.[3] I understand Captain Ball writes to Lord Grenville by this opportunity, acquainting him, as nearly as he is yet enabled to do, with the state of this Island.

I have received instructions from Sir Ralph Abercromby relative to the Russians should they come here, which I hope will not be the case. I shall in future communicate with Lt.-Gen. Fox, as I am instructed to do, but from particular circumstances I have thought it right to avail myself of this opportunity of acquainting you that the British have complete possession of the place, which you might not have heard.

There are about 1,200 French prisoners still remaining, 600 of whom will be sent off in three or four days; the remainder must occupy Fort Manoel till there is an opportunity of getting rid of them. I have the honour, &c. (Signed) H. PIGOT, Maj.-Gen.

The departure of General Graham from Malta was deeply regretted by the troops serving under his late command. This is

[1] Foreign Office Records, Malta, No. 6.
[2] See Paget's letter of protest to Pigot of 14th September 1800, in the *Paget Papers*, vol. i. pp. 269–70.—J. H. R.
[3] Sir Ralph Abercromby was with the force which made a futile attempt on Cadiz.—J. H. R.

testified by the following letter from the colonel commanding the 35th Regiment:

Malta, 4*th October* 1800.[1]

DEAR GENERAL,—I cannot omit the opportunity that offers to express my regret at losing the happiness of your society and the advantage of being under your command. Though apprehensive that this would be the case, I still hoped some fortunate accident would occur to detain you where your influence and advice, if followed, could not fail of being most useful in thoroughly establishing us in this Island. Our popularity does not, I believe, increase, and I fear it will be found very difficult to satisfy a fickle people, who value their services and sufferings at so high a rate. The Governor finds already that the distribution of those good things so eagerly looked forward to has made many discontented, and I fear it will be proved also that he has made *des ingrats*. The bigotry of the common people here will always afford to their chiefs a sufficient pretext to create disturbance and to complain of the government of damnable heretics. You will be surprised to hear that this and other inflammatory topics have been made use of by people who heretofore appeared most friendly to us. On the extensive works on our side it is inconceivable the mischief that has been done to the guns where there has been no sentries to protect them; many have been rendered unserviceable, and one howitzer carried away.

When such dispositions exist, and when the nature of the people is considered, it will require much vigilance and prudence in our chiefs to retain a quiet possession of the Island. I beg you to accept of my best wishes for your success on the more active service in which I understand you propose to engage, and at the same time assure you it will afford me much satisfaction at any future period to serve under your command. With every sentiment of respect and esteem, I remain, &c.

Colonel commanding 35th Reg$^{t.}$ (Signed) Jo$^{N.}$ OSWALD.

It would appear that the management of affairs in Malta by the British authorities gave great umbrage to the Neapolitan Government, which fact was communicated to the home Government by Mr. Paget, His Majesty's Minister at that Court. In justification of their action, Lord Grenville on the 17th October gave the following explanation:—

LORD GRENVILLE TO THE HON. A. PAGET.

Downing Street, 17*th October* 1800.[2]

SIR,—Your several dispatches to No. 13 inclusive have been received and laid before the King. The embarrassment which you have experienced in consequence of the variation existing between your instructions, dated as far as the 22nd January last, and those subsequently transmitted to Sir Ralph Abercromby relative to the Island of Malta, has been in a great measure inevitable; from the numerous delays and impediments to which the intercourse of Great Britain with Sicily has been exposed, and from the great delicacy of the subject in question, which did not admit of my

---

[1] Delavoye, *Life of Graham*, p. 212.   [2] *Paget Papers*, vol. i. p. 274.

explaining to you the various changes which have been made in this respect by the new situation in which the Court of Petersburg stands with respect to the present war. Since the date of the instructions which were given to you, the conduct of the Emperor of Russia has been totally repugnant to that system of concert and active co-operation which formed at once the object and the basis of the arrangement which was in question for the temporary and provisional occupation of Malta.

The Russian troops and ships, wherever employed, have been withdrawn; the Emperor's forces have in no degree contributed to the reduction of the Island of Malta, nor has he during the present campaign afforded to the Allies the smallest aid against the common enemy. He has even recently adopted measures hostile to the interests of this Court, and not content with declaring himself, by a memorial presented at Berlin,[1] in a state of neutrality as between Great Britain and France, he has taken such steps as must leave it doubtful whether his occupation of the whole or any part of the Island of Malta might not, under the influence of his present disposition, be converted to purposes essentially injurious to this country.[2] As the former agreement was by these circumstances wholly annulled, and as much the largest proportion of the land forces, and nearly the whole of the naval force, employed in this arduous service, have been furnished by His Majesty, it has followed, of course, that the British colours should be displayed on forts reduced by His Majesty's exertions, and garrisoned by His Majesty's troops.

You will, however, explain to the Neapolitan Ministers that it is by no means His Majesty's intention, by this temporary occupation of a military position during the war, to prejudge the question of the future disposition to be made of the Island at the conclusion of a general peace. . . .

The establishment of either Russia or France in that fortress might indeed give just cause of jealousy to His Sicilian Majesty, but no similar ground of apprehension could arise respecting Great Britain, which can have no view hostile to the security and independence of Naples. I am, &c. (Signed) GRENVILLE.

Anticipating animadversions in England on the terms of capitulation granted to the French garrison, Graham whilst *en route* wrote a supplementary letter to Dundas from Trieste, under date of the 28th November, as follows:—

BRIG.-GENERAL GRAHAM TO THE RIGHT HON. HY. DUNDAS.

Trieste, 28*th November* 1800.[3]

MY DEAR SIR,—I am obliged to trouble you with two lines more, having forgot to say that General Pigot was anxious to explain verbally to you on my arrival why the French troops were sent back to France. It was the best for all reasons that we did not know what else to do with them.

He desired me, too, to say that the directions of the instructions [*sic*]

---
[1] Haugwitz, the Prussian Minister, had helped in the formation of the Russo-French *entente*.—J. H. R.
[2] *Vide* chapter on the Preliminary Treaty of Peace.
[3] M.P.L. MSS. 441.

the issue of the struggle, it may be granted; but to state that they were the principals as belligerents is opposed to the facts of the case.

It must be apparent to everyone that the fall of Malta was *due entirely to the blockade* of the islands by His Majesty's fleet (aided for some time by that of the Portuguese), and that, without detracting in the least from the merit which the Maltese people deserve, it is none the less true that if the Maltese had not risen in revolt the French general, Vaubois, in the cause of humanity, would have had to capitulate within a very brief space of time, so soon as the blockade was effectively established. This was bound to follow in course of time, as the result of the British victory at the Nile. Sicily during this period depended for its existence as an independent nation (although dismembered for a time) upon the support and alliance of Great Britain.[1] With the neighbouring ports belonging to that kingdom closed to the island of Malta, an event which naturally would have arisen in the hypothetical case of the Maltese remaining faithful to the French, the only source of supplies to the island would have been closed, and with a vigorous blockade maintained the final result would have been achieved in six months. This is fully corroborated by Bosredon Ransijat, President of the French Commission of Government, one of the besieged, the best of all authorities, who at p. 17 of his 'Journal of the Siege of Malta' says: 'If the Maltese had not risen in revolt, the supplies of the garrison would have been exhausted by March 1799'—that is to say, in six months.

The capitulation of the 5th September 1800, which closed all Maltese participation in subsequent hostilities, did not constitute Malta a British colony or possession. It was not simply a question which interested England and France alone, and to be settled by the victorious occupation of the island at that time by either of these contending Powers, nor did its capture close the war between these two nations. There were too many international and conflicting interests involved in the settlement of its ultimate destiny and its final acquisition for it to be so summarily decided and confirmed.

There were the interests of the Maltese people, those of the Order of St. John, Russia, Naples, France, and England—all antagonistic to each other—which had to be considered and adjusted, and this was not to be accomplished without another desolating war of eleven years, during all which period the Maltese people, although the question of the final possession of Malta was the main cause of the war of 1803, enjoyed the blessings of peace at home, and not only so, but also laid the foundation of their future commercial

---

[1] Also to a less extent on that of Russia, which had recently been accorded by the Czar Paul.—J. H. R.

wealth, owing to the immense transit trade which continued, and obtained for that duration of time the appellation of *il tempo florido*.

The subsequent retention of Malta by the British could not depend *solely* upon the will and affection of the Maltese people, however great and sincere they may have been. Unless the Maltese, singly and alone, were capable of maintaining their national independence, they at the most (had they been asked) could only have assented to or have disapproved of the will of the European Powers in Congress, and their objection, if such had existed, would under the circumstances have remained a dead letter.

To what extent Great Britain defended Maltese interests and laboured on their behalf, both in diplomatic correspondence and in treaties, will be dealt with in the chapters which follow.

The British Government, had it been disposed to abandon the Maltese people and their cause, might have accepted for the sake of peace the proposal of Bonaparte, which he instructed his ambassador, Otto, to make to the British Government on the 22nd July 1801, ' to raze the fortifications and retire,' which in course of time, if adopted, would have placed the inhabitants socially, commercially, and intellectually on a level with, or little better than, the Lampedusans of the present day.[1]

So late as 1864, Mr. Cachia Zammit, a Maltese gentleman of influence, was in correspondence with the late Field-Marshal Sir John Burgoyne (who was present at the siege) with the view of demonstrating that the Maltese had recovered the island mainly by their own exertions, and without material assistance from the British, and elicited the following reply:—

War Office, London, 25*th July* 1864.[2]

My dear Mr. Cachia Zammit,—In reply to your request for my opinion on the conduct of the Maltese at the blockade in 1800, I can only give you reminiscences which, though of a general character, are vivid, for I was very young—under twenty—when I was sent to join the blockading force some six weeks or two months before the surrender of the place. It is true that the French troops could make sorties and penetrate into the country in any direction; but in doing so they could only hold the precise spot on which they trod, and had nothing of much service to them to obtain by such enterprises, in which they suffered, moreover, considerable losses; they were virtually shut up on the land side by the energy of the population.

On the first outbreak, however, French men-of-war from the harbour were enabled to interrupt the communication between the Island and Sicily, from which it was supplied with provisions, and the consequences would have been, no doubt, the subjection of the revolting population but for the arrival of a squadron under Captain Ball, R.N. (subsequently Sir Alexander Ball), which commenced the blockade of the French port and relieved the rest of the Island from its effects. Some British regiments of the line were

---

[1] Cobbett, vol. iii. p. 1192.   [2] Wrottesley, *Life of Burgoyne*, p. 7.

subsequently landed, with a general officer and staff, and the blockade of the fortress was more close, continuous, and systematic, the wild levies of the Maltese people, however, being still in force and active as ever. Finally the French garrison, without further struggle, yielded to a want of provisions, and surrendered to the British forces.

I do not quite understand the inference you would draw from the remark that 'the Maltese are said to have lost twenty thousand souls during the siege, while the British had not one single soldier killed by the enemy.' Without in the slightest degree detracting from the high courage of the Maltese, to which I would bear unreserved testimony, the twenty thousand loss, if assumed to be by the action of the enemy, must be a very great exaggeration, for the whole population, old and young, male and female, was only computed at one hundred thousand, and the actual contests could not have been many nor much prolonged. Regarding the small or no loss by the British, it was owing to the quiescent state of affairs during the later proceedings of the blockade, when only a shot or two was fired occasionally as a warning by either party; for assuredly from the time of their landing the British troops took the very front line in the operation of maintaining a very close blockade.—Yours faithfully,

(Signed) J. F. BURGOYNE.

This chapter cannot be more fittingly closed than by adding the following extracts from Miège's 'History of Malta'[1] (a writer not at all favourably disposed towards the English), and Botta's 'History of Italy under Napoleon,' both standard works. The former writes:

[Translation.]

Could the Maltese revolt have been suppressed by force? Most assuredly so, for General Vaubois had at his disposal 6,000 men, including the crews of the ships of war which had escaped from Aboukir, and such a force was more than sufficient for that purpose; and it is no less true that if the General had ordered 1,500 men to march on Citta Vecchia the moment he heard of the outbreak, order would have been restored; but what was feasible then became difficult as soon as time had permitted the insurgents to organise, arm, and intrench. With the inability to quell the rebellion, there remained but one means of preserving Malta to France, and that was to expel the whole of the inhabitants, without exception, from the four cities [Valetta and the three cities opposite] the moment the blockade was instituted, which would have enabled the General to hold the fortress for eight years. . . . The Maltese, or such amongst them who have pretended to write the history of that period (in the number may be mentioned Baron Azopardi), boast of having compelled the French to retire within the city walls, and to have defeated them every time a sortie was made.

If they had contented themselves so far only, it might have been considered as an assertion dictated by a puerile vanity unworthy of being noticed. . . . At the first signal of danger, the French withdrew within the four cities and fortress which surrounds them, as the possession of the Island depends upon their occupation. Military tactics required such a measure, and

[1] Miège, vol. iii. p. 343.

therefore it is untrue to state that the Maltese compelled them to retire therein. It is not denied that the French had to retreat at the sorties which were made by the garrison; but what was the reason? Only because they were much inferior in number. If, instead of dispatching men in columns, —the total number never exceeding seven hundred, who, immediately they were outside the fortifications, were surrounded by an armed population of twenty-two villages—General Vaubois had detached a body of 1,500 to 2,000 with artillery, what would have happened? The answer may be found in the attempts which the insurgents admit having made to arrange terms with the besieged at the time they despaired of receiving succour.

Moreover, if the losses experienced by both sides were to be recapitulated, it would be observed that the Maltese did not gain much glory in their pretended victories. . . . Finally, it was not the insurrection of the Maltese which wrested Malta from the French; such insurrection, on the contrary, was a fortunate circumstance in this sense, that it dispensed General Vaubois from the necessity of feeding the inhabitants in the country districts, and permitted him to prolong the period of his defence.

Famine was the only cause of its loss. It may be admitted that the first cause was the blockade by sea established by the English, which destroyed all hopes of success in the attempts made to revictual the garrison.

Botta also states: [1]

Glorious, certainly, was the conqueror Nelson, but not without glory was its defender, for neither greater courage, nor greater fortitude, nor greater ingenuity could have been displayed than what was found in Vaubois.

Deserted by all, he struggled for two years, and was at last overcome, not by the force of arms, but by that dreadful scourge, famine, which always takes from man the strength, and often, too, the will, to resist.

[1] Botta, *op. cit.* vol. i. p. 139.

CHAPTER XVI

CORRESPONDENCE FROM NOVEMBER 1800 TO JULY 1801

IN resuming the general course of the narrative, we may notice that General Sir Ralph Abercromby returned from Gibraltar to Malta on the 20th November 1800, and remained there until the 27th December, occupied with preparations for the expedition to Egypt. On the 10th of the latter month he issued the following instructions to Maj.-Gen. Pigot for his guidance in the affairs of Malta [1]:—

His Britannic Majesty's forces, with the assistance of the Maltese, having expelled the troops of the French Republic from the Island of Malta and its Dependencies, Great Britain takes the Maltese nation under its protection. Maj.-Gen. Pigot will not permit the pretensions of any other sovereign or body of men to be brought forward or discussed.

All the rights, privileges, and immunities in Church and State are confirmed to the Maltese people. The Bishop of Malta is the head of the Maltese Church. No inquisitorial powers emanating from the See of Rome can be admitted, and no ecclesiastical authority of any other sovereign can be acknowledged.

Maj.-Gen. Pigot will direct Captain Ball of the Royal Navy to take charge of the civil government of the country and of the revenue until His Majesty's pleasure shall be known. Captain Ball will keep regular accounts of the receipt and expenditure of all public money, and after defraying the expenses of the government the residue will be applied to the service of the public in paying for such repairs as may be necessary on the fortifications, and of such portion of militia of the country as shall be embodied, or for any other public use.

The port of Malta will be open to the ships of all nations in alliance or in amity with Great Britain; but the law of nations requires that no ship of war, privateer, or corsair which has been admitted into the port of Malta shall abuse the privilege thus granted by following, and taking within three leagues of that port, any vessel belonging to any nation not at war with Great Britain; and to the end that no ship belonging to Great Britain or her Allies may be deceived, the British colours will be hoisted in the Island of Gozo, and in all places in Malta where colours are usually displayed.

Maj.-Gen. Pigot will lose no time in putting in a state of repair the

[1] C.O.R., Malta, No. 4 (1801).

forts, towns, and batteries in the bay of St. Paul's and neighbourhood, and at Marsa Scirocco.

A detachment of British infantry will occupy Citta Vecchia, and send a detachment to St. Paul's if necessary. In like manner a detachment of British infantry will occupy Zeitun for the support of the batteries at Scirocco; a body of Maltese cannoniers and militia will do constant duty at St. Paul's and Marsa Scirocco; and a few non-commissioned officers and private men from the British artillery will be stationed at these bays to instruct the Maltese cannoniers and to take charge of the guns and ammunition. Maj.-Gen. Pigot will probably call out only a small part of the militia for this service in rotation. Maj.-Gen. Pigot will establish a plan of defence in case of the enemy landing either on the side of St. Paul's and St. Lucien in the bay of Marsa Scirocco, by calling out the whole force of the Island, or such part of it as he may judge necessary. General Sir Ralph Abercromby desires that Captain Vivion of the Royal Artillery may be appointed (with an allowance of ten shillings a day) inspector of the coast and of the Maltese cannoniers and militia employed there, in consideration of the services he rendered to his country during the blockade, and from his local knowledge of the Island. Maj.-Gen. Pigot will establish telegraphs and signals from Gozo to La Valetta.

The present state of the fortifications of La Valetta does not seem to require the incurring of any considerable expense; Maj.-Gen. Pigot will therefore not order any other repairs than such as are absolutely necessary on the principal and most essential parts of the works.

Maj.-Gen. Pigot will find it necessary to pay great attention to the re-arrangement of the artillery, which are [sic] of various calibres, so that each piece of ordnance may have its just proportion of ammunition allotted to it, and at hand; and if Maj.-Gen. Pigot should find from the report of Lieut.-Col. Bentham or officer commanding the Royal Artillery that there is not a sufficient quantity of shot suited to the different calibres of the ordnance, he will endeavour to procure it from the foundries in Sicily, Naples, or Sardinia. The gun carriages must be kept in a state of repair on such part of the works as shall be pointed out in the report of Brig.-Gen. Lawson and of the chief engineer now making out. The points chiefly to be attended to are the Cottonera, Ricasoli, St. Angelo, St. Elmo, Tigné, the two Cavaliers, and the interior parts of the works on the Florian side. Some few pieces of artillery ought certainly to be placed in the Florian.

It is recommended to Maj.-Gen. Pigot to dispose of, if possible, the materials of buildings on the Corradino, and he will take it into his consideration, with the assistance of the chief engineer, how the corn which these buildings afford can otherwise be best removed. Maj.-Gen. Pigot will pay all due attention to the accommodation of the troops, and will allow such public buildings as are best suited for barracks for their use, with as little expense to the public as possible.

All the public buildings belonging to the Order, as far as is necessary, should be set apart for this purpose, that the inhabitants may be relieved, and that as little expense as is possible may be incurred by the public. Until a barrack-master is appointed, the assistant-quarter-master-general will take charge of the barrack departments. The navy will occupy all the buildings in the dockyard, and probably will claim the house belonging to the Intendant of the Marine. This, in the present state of the port, will give them as much room as they can require, so that there can be no interference between the two services.

An assistant-quartermaster-general belonging to the army, under the immediate command of Sir R. Abercromby, will be left at La Valetta to take charge of all stores belonging to that army, and to forward the same as they may be wanted. Maj.-Gen. Pigot will allot to him such of the empty warehouses and magazines as he may require, and will give him every other assistance in his power. Particular instructions will be left in regard to the sick of that army, and the commissary-general will leave the resident assistant-commissary here instructions relative to that department.

Maj.-Gen. Pigot will forward all dispatches to Sir R. Abercromby with all possible expedition, and he requests that the General will correspond with him in such subjects as the public service requires.

Sir Ralph Abercromby most earnestly recommends the British troops serving at Malta to observe the strictest discipline, and to cultivate by every means in their power the good-will and confidence of the inhabitants.

(Signed) R. ABERCROMBY.

The day previous, Sir Ralph Abercromby conveyed to the Right Hon. Henry Dundas the reasons which had compelled him to transfer all authority from Ball to Pigot, in the following dispatch:

[Extract.]

La Valetta, *9th December* 1800.[1]

. . . It is necessary to explain the situation in which Captain Ball at present stands. On the revolt of the Island in September 1798, he was sent by Lord Nelson and the Court of Naples to attend to the interest of His Sicilian Majesty, and until the surrender of the town of La Valetta, every public act was in the name of the King of the Two Sicilies; the Sicilian colours were everywhere hoisted, and at this moment they are flying in most parts of the Island. If Captain Ball has received any salary, it was from His Sicilian Majesty. His table has been kept at the expense of the Island; having in obedience to Lord Nelson's orders given up his professional pursuits, he has reaped no benefit from prize-money, and has only received the bare pay as captain of the *Alexander;* his situation seems now incompatible with Maj.-Gen. Pigot's, and I hope that some decision will take place. I felt great delicacy in removing Captain Ball; at the same time I am obliged to place all authority in the hands of Maj.-Gen. Pigot, and to direct him to employ Captain Ball in the administration of the civil affairs of the Island until His Majesty's pleasure is known.

I trust that the honourable conduct of Captain Ball (who from every account has given general satisfaction to the inhabitants) will recommend him to some consideration for his services, and that any irregularity which may have taken place in his acting in the name of His Sicilian Majesty may not be imputed to him.

[1] C.O.R. Malta, No. 1.

The presence of Admiral Lord Keith in Malta during Sir Ralph Abercromby's visit gave the president of the courts of justice, the judges, and the magistrates an opportunity of offering him an address, to which on the 11th December he returned the following reply :—

[Translation.]

H.M.S. *Foudroyant*, Valetta, 11*th* December 1800.[1]

ILLUSTRIOUS SIRS,—I have had the honour to receive the letter which on behalf of the inhabitants of Malta you have been so kind as to address to me, and I observe with the warmest satisfaction these proofs of attachment towards my fellow-countrymen who have shown such distinguished regard for you.

As a private individual, I cannot but be touched with the signs of approval which you have manifested in such flattering terms; but what I have been able to do is due to my obedience to the orders of my beneficent Sovereign, who has taken such a lively interest in the fate of your celebrated Island, and who has commanded me to use all the power in my possession on your behalf, in the performance of which, duty and inclination has never been more strongly combined; and I can therefore state, in all sincerity and truth, that the capture of Malta has been an object which more than any other has occupied my attention and engaged my heartiest efforts.

I beg you will accept my sincerest congratulations on the happy deliverance of your Island from the usurpation under which it was held; and whilst I am irresistibly bound to agree to the honourable testimony with which you are pleased to acknowledge the merit of the forces engaged in the blockade, I am nevertheless obliged to express my conviction that the spirit of vigilance and perseverance which they showed was in a great measure due to the encouragement they received from the example of a virtuous people, independent and heroic, fighting against those who had attacked them without provocation, and who had despoiled them of all which they had venerated.

The Barbary States have been duly informed that you are now under the protection of the British nation, and that the passports which have been issued for the protection of your trade must be respected.

I am happy to know that the liberation from slavery of a number of your countrymen will soon be followed by the release of the remainder; and whilst I am in command of the naval forces in these seas, I shall not cease to adopt such measures as may be in my power to accomplish that object.—I have the honour, &c.

(Signed) KEITH.

To the Illustrious Sirs, the President of the Courts of Justice,
   the Judges, and Magistrates of the Island of Malta.

The substance of Sir Ralph Abercromby's instructions to General Pigot regarding Malta having reached the Neapolitan Government, further remonstrances were made to the British Minister at that Court, the Hon. A. Paget, then resident in Palermo, who at once

[1] MS. in the Malta Public Library (Marquis Aporp Testaferrata's papers).

communicated the same to the Ministry at Rome in a dispatch dated Palermo, 15th January 1801, worded as follows :—

HON. A. PAGET TO LORD GRENVILLE.

Palermo, 15th January 1801.[1]

MY LORD,—I have received complaints, both verbally and in writing, from His Sicilian Majesty's Ministers respecting certain transactions which have lately happened at Malta under the direction of the British Commanders.

The principal causes of complaint are that it has been declared to the magistrates in that Island by the persons exercising the English government, that His Britannic Majesty has put Malta under his protection; that the ecclesiastical tribunals are abolished; that the clergy were no longer to consider themselves as dependent upon their former metropolitan (who is a Sicilian archbishop); that Pratique house-boats were to hoist English instead of Neapolitan colours; that English governors and garrison were sent to Citta Vecchia and Gozo, hitherto occupied exclusively by Neapolitans; and finally, that corsairs from the coast of Barbary had been admitted into the ports and creeks of Malta, to the manifest prejudice of the interests and commerce of His Sicilian Majesty's subjects : that similar operations seemed to indicate nothing less than our effectual capture of the Island to the total exclusion of His Sicilian Majesty, a circumstance which had not failed to create the most unpleasant sensations in His Sicilian Majesty's mind.

The above is the substance of the notes I have received; the blame attached to these innovations is attributed to the officers commanding at Malta, His Majesty's Government being expressly exempted from any intention of giving any uneasiness to the King of Naples. In my answer I have briefly referred His Sicilian Majesty's Ministers to the explanations which I had already given them in obedience to the orders contained in Your Lordship's dispatch of the 17th October.

It was indeed impossible for me to enter into any detail upon the subject, having been kept in the most profound state of ignorance as to every arrangement which has been made at Malta. I know that His Sicilian Majesty feels himself extremely hurt upon this occasion, not so much in consequence of what has been done, as at the manner of doing it; for although it is indeed obvious that the facts complained of, and the conclusion drawn from them, bear no resemblance to the declaration I had made to his Ministers, namely, that it was not His Majesty's intention, by the temporary occupation of Malta as a military position during the war, to prejudge the question of the future disposition to be made of the Island at the conclusion of a general peace, yet I am authorised to say that His Sicilian Majesty would willingly have acceded to any arrangements whatever respecting Malta which might have been most agreeable to His Majesty, provided His Majesty's wishes had been made known to him; it is therefore clear that the mode which has been adopted of conducting the affairs in that Island is what has caused so much discontent and uneasiness to His Sicilian Majesty.   (Signed) A. PAGET.

[1] *Paget Papers*, vol. i, p 302.

It would seem that prior to this period Mr. Paget, probably influenced by the information he had received from the Neapolitan Government (which in the mean time had felt annoyed at the apparent change in the political views of the Maltese), or, it may be, by advice received from other sources, had not a very favourable opinion of the loyalty of the Maltese to the British Government; for, on the 16th November 1800, and again on the 25th January 1801, he addressed Lord Grenville as follows:—

[Extract.]
16th November 1800.[1]

I continually receive the most pressing demands from Governor Ball for money for the purchase of corn, a circumstance which at once proves the unaccommodating and unfriendly disposition of the monied people of that Island. I find, indeed, that the spirit of party there runs very high, and that the French have left a considerable number of friends behind them.

I have advanced money for procuring eight months' supply of corn for the garrison, and about two months' for the civil population. The Maltese will not cash bills; in a word, the Maltese seem unwilling to make the smallest sacrifice in order to insure their own existence.

[Extract.]
25th January 1801.[2]

It is a fact that the inhabitants of that Island (Malta) are a most troublesome, litigious, and capricious people, and that there are principal malcontents among them ready on every opportunity to augment their discontent, and to excite them to revolt.

Upwards of five months having now elapsed since the British occupied Valetta, the time had arrived for the withdrawal of Captain Ball from the government of the islands, in accordance with Sir Ralph Abercromby's views. This decision of the home Government regarding Captain Ball was conveyed to the Maltese people by a proclamation of General Pigot dated the 19th of February, as follows:—

TO THE INHABITANTS OF MALTA AND GOZO.[3]

In the act of addressing you for the first time, it is with the greatest pleasure I have to inform you that His Majesty takes the Maltese nation under his protection. He has authorised me, as his representative, to inform you that every possible means shall be used to make you contented and happy. Since I have been amongst you I have received the best impressions of your good dispositions and subordination to the laws; and of your gratitude to Divine Providence, by whose favour the fleets

---

[1] Foreign Office Records, Sicily, 14. [2] Ibid.
[3] Mitrovich, 1836, p. 8.

and army of the King were enabled to give an effective assistance to your brave exertions for the expulsion of your enemies, whereby peace and liberty have been restored to you. It shall be my constant care to ensure the continuance of this well-being. You will understand that this advantage can only be secured by a just and exact administration of the laws on the part of the Government, and on the part of the people by constant obedience and implicit trust in the protection the laws afford. This, with due reverence and respect for your religion and its ministers, and with reciprocal good faith, will constitute your happiness. The naval service, to which your chief belongs, and in which he has always been distinguished, does not permit him to remain longer with you; the unceasing care which he has always displayed for your interests entitles him to your warmest gratitude. You may rest assured, however, that his departure will entail no suspension of the laws, or of the administration of the civil government. The courts of justice now established shall continue. And it is my duty, as well as my inclination, to protect the Maltese nation, and to guarantee to them the full enjoyment of their religion, their property, and their freedom.

(Signed) HENRY PIGOT.

Palace, Valetta, 19*th* *February* 1801.

Before leaving Malta, Captain Ball addressed the following letter to the people he had so faithfully governed for two and a half years:—

[Translation.]

February 1801.

MY DEAR MALTESE,—By my Sovereign's order, and in accordance with the wise instructions of his Cabinet, I am called away on service from this beloved Island of Malta.

Before leaving, however, this happy country and separating myself from those whom I have watched over with loving and paternal care, I cannot refrain from expressing to you the warm admiration with which you have inspired me. I have seen you for the space of more than two years, resisting and defeating with intrepid courage our common enemy, and with equal valour attacking him in his trenches.

I have not been less surprised in observing the courage with which you have borne the sad consequences of war, and the fortitude you have evinced whilst suffering the scourge of famine, from the want of shelter and the inclemency of the seasons. So great is my admiration for all the virtues you have displayed that I shall never forget them, and it will be my privilege to recount them, which will gain the eulogium of the most enlightened nations.

It is further my duty to acknowledge with grateful thanks the affection you have always shown me, which is not less than that which I have entertained and still entertain for you. A proof of this is the sorrow I now suffer in parting from you for distant lands.

I am, however, comforted and encouraged not a little by reflecting that I am leaving you under the government of a most worthy General, possessing all the qualifications necessary to be beloved; of a General who for some portion of the siege has had you with the other troops under his command, thus giving him the opportunity of testing your valour, fidelity, and obedience.

You may therefore, without fear, rely upon enjoying under his government the perfect and tranquil happiness which I most ardently desire for you, assuring you at the same time that my love will only cease with my life.

Live happily, therefore, my dear Maltese, and ever keep in remembrance your affectionate father and friend,

(Signed) ALEXANDER JNO. BALL.

The universal esteem in which their late governor was held, and the regret at his approaching departure, were further attested in the following address from the Magistracies of the Five Cities, which was presented to him on the 11th February:—

[Translation.]

Malta, 11th February 1801.

YOUR EXCELLENCY,—The attachment which Your Excellency has shown for the Maltese nation, dating from the very commencement of the blockade up to the surrender of Valetta, and the no less tangible proofs of the same continued up to this present day, will not allow the sad news of your approaching departure from this Island to pass without an acknowledgement to Your Excellency of our sense of the gratitude due to a wise and beneficent Governor.

Your sagacious prudence and enlightened measures not only led this people happily through serious and dangerous circumstances, but also liberated them from the sad consequences and terrible straits to which they became exposed, by providing them first with arms, and secondly with what was required for their subsistence. For all these great and memorable benefits this nation will ever retain a loving remembrance of Your Excellency.

They further feel in duty bound, as it will be their privilege, to relate to their descendants how the courage and valour of the Maltese, as shown in the most critical and dangerous circumstances, were crowned with success, owing to the wise direction in which they were guided.[1]

They will have no less pleasure in reminding posterity that the result of your paternal care is the tranquillity and safe quietude which now reigns, and which they trust will continue under your worthy successor, endowed as he is with the same rare talents and noble qualities which adorn your own person. We therefore beg Your Excellency to accept this unworthy but sincere attestation of gratitude which this happy nation will eternally avow for you, proffering our most fervid thanks for the many marked favours received, and whilst wishing Your Excellency a most happy voyage, and the highest and best merited promotion that can be desired, we assure you of our everlasting acknowledgement and

[1] It is noteworthy that this address makes not the slightest reference to the services of the British fleet and land forces in reducing Valetta.—J. H. R.

gratitude, declaring ourselves, for all time, Your Excellency's most humble, devoted, and obedient servants,

The Magistracy of Città Notabile:
    (Signed) MARCHESE D. PADOLFO TESTAFERRATA.
    BARONE LORENZO GALEA.
    CONTE ROMUALDO BARBARO.
    DR. GIUSEPPE BONNICI.

The Magistracy of the Four Cities:
    (Signed) MARCHESE SAVERIO ALEOSI.
    MARCHESE GIRONIMO DELICATA.
    BARONE SAVERIO GAUCI.
    GIO. BATTISTA GROGNET

TO HIS EXCELLENCY MR. ALEXANDER JNO. BALL.
Governor of the Islands of Malta.

Captain Ball, upon relinquishing the government of Malta, rejoined his ship the *Alexander*, remaining for a short period in Maltese waters, and on the 6th March addressed the following important dispatch to the Right Hon. Henry Dundas:—

      H.M.S. *Alexander*, Malta, 6th *March* 1801.[1]
To the Right Hon. Henry Dundas, &c.

 SIR,—I had the honour to write to you on the 26th December by Captain Austen of the Navy, by whom I sent an account of the revenue of this Island with observations, a duplicate of which went by land in the charge of Mr. Morrison, and I now forward a triplicate by the *Speedwell*, armed schooner. In my different letters I have recommended a civil governor to be appointed here during the war, and I mentioned that Brig.-Gen. Graham would be an acceptable person to the Maltese. The inhabitants conceive their liberty insecure until the military and civil power be divided.

 They observe that a military governor cannot spare sufficient time from his garrison occupations to direct the civil administration of this Island without giving too much power to secretaries, who seek their own interest and not the happiness of the people; they are likewise apprehensive of experiencing similar oppressions to what they suffered under the government of the Order of St. John, as they are now placed in the second order of the State, the military being the first.

 I shall not trespass by entering into details of the necessary modifications to secure the affections of these islanders. I am aware that I risk incurring great displeasure by saying so much as I have done, but I should not discharge my duty if I failed giving you my opinion.

 I speak from a thorough knowledge of the character and sentiments of the inhabitants, and I now write under the fullest conviction of the necessity of this being attended to, otherwise we shall lose the affections and attachments of these brave islanders and risk serious consequences.

[1] C.O.R. Malta, No. 2.

I embarked on board the *Alexander* the 20th last month. I am happy to inform you that I leave this Island in a state which will make it independent of any great inconveniences which might have arisen from the necessity which His Sicilian Majesty is under of shutting all his ports against the English, and preventing any supplies coming here.[1] When I entered La Valetta there were only eight days' bread in the Island, and although the exportation of corn was prohibited in Sicily, and a great scarcity throughout Italy, I have procured sufficient to supply the inhabitants until next December, and I am convinced that by management and active exertion this Island can *now* be always abundantly supplied with every kind of provision. I am waiting the arrival of a gentleman from the Levant (whom I sent to purchase corn) to enable me to close my accounts.

I have consigned to Maj.-Gen. Pigot corn to the amount of more than one hundred thousand pounds, which when sold will nearly repay Government for the sums which have been drawn on the Treasury for the purchase of it; the very high price at which it was bought exceeded the ability of the inhabitants to purchase at that rate. I therefore consulted General Sir R. Abercromby, who agreed with me in opinion that it should be sold to them at a lower price. The former Government always did it in years of scarcity, which loss was generally indemnified the next year.

In the paper which I had the honour to send you of the sale of corn for the last twenty years, it appeared that Government had gained a clear profit of two hundred thousand pounds.

Soon after the surrender of La Valetta, I was desired by General Pigot to give in a list of the Maltese battalions, that they might share prize money for the capture of this place, which circumstances I made known to them. It is now said they are not entitled to share.

This change of opinion I cannot communicate, as it will occasion the most serious discontents. I will state some of their pretensions, in the hope that you will be induced to recommend them to His Majesty, that he may be graciously pleased to consider their services. These battalions amounted to nearly three thousand men, badly armed, besieged the French in one of the strongest fortifications in Europe whose force was seven thousand men, and continued it for fourteen months with the assistance of a lieutenant of the British artillery, five Neapolitan officers, and twenty privates. When the British regiments arrived they carried on the operations of the siege in conjunction with the Maltese; some of the advanced posts were so unhealthy that the English withdrew most of their troops from them, and left them to be defended principally by the Maltese. Another post was abandoned to the Maltese, because the British soldiers deserted from it to the enemy, and the Maltese, who were more to be trusted than our own troops, were the means of preventing our troops from deserting, and actually arrested one of our men close to the enemy's works. The Maltese have lost more than three hundred men killed and wounded. A lieutenant-colonel and two captains in the Neapolitan service had been actively employed under my command during the siege in the most unhealthy and

[1] The King of Naples had signed an armistice with the French on 18th February 1801, and was forced to agree to close his ports against English ships. This was ratified by the Treaty of Florence, signed on March 13. (See *Paget Papers*, vol. i. pp. 309 et seq.)—J. H. R.

exposed situations; when the English regiment landed they withdrew from these posts and acted as my aides-de-camp, reviewing and mustering the Maltese battalions. These officers are not allowed to share because they were not attached to particular corps, and from the landing of the English regiments my situation is considered purely civil. With respect to my own claims I shall only observe, that while I have been carrying on the service of this Island my brother captains of the Nile fleet have made from eight to sixteen thousand pounds—I mean those captains who have remained in the Mediterranean; and I suffer the inexpressible mortification of knowing that it is considered here, at Palermo, and at Naples, that I am disgraced, as I have not received any mark of His Majesty's pleasure; on that account I expressed a hope in my former letter that I should be created a baronet.

My health has suffered so much that I solicited to be a commissioner in the Navy, that I might have time to re-establish it. No other consideration could induce me to retire a moment from a service to which I! am most zealously attached, and in which I hope yet to be distinguished.

I have the honour, &c. (Signed) ALEX. JN^{o.} BALL.

[There follows here in Mr. Hardman's narrative a long report on the financial condition of Malta and Gozo, probably of date 26th December 1800. For lack of space it has been omitted.

The next two reports almost certainly emanated from Captain Ball. They are of sufficient importance to warrant their insertion here *in extenso*.

COMMERCIAL ADVANTAGES OF RETAINING POSSESSION OF MALTA.[1]

The impression which the surrender of La Valette has already made on the Barbary States evinces one considerable advantage which will result from our retaining possession of this Island.

These States have begun to give us supplies of corn and of cattle, and the Island becomes daily less dependent upon Sicily. The Maltese vessels with passports from Lord Keith are permitted to go into their ports, and to navigate all the neighbouring seas in security.

When English merchants and warehouses with English goods are established in La Valette, vessels from all the surrounding coasts of the Levant will come to Malta with their produce to barter them for these goods, and return with the woollens, cotton, hardware, &c., of England. The principal production of the Islands of Malta and Gozo is cotton. The quantity manufactured for their own consumption is very considerable, as nearly one hundred thousand inhabitants are clothed with it. But the quality is too coarse for any foreign market but the coast of Barbary. The exportation of cotton wool is prohibited, as spinning it is the chief branch of industry among the poor. They export annually into Spain cotton thread to the amount of nearly half a million sterling.

The oranges of Malta are of an excellent quality. They export

[1] From Stowe MSS. 918, p. 8; pages from 1 to 8 commence with a statement called Rendite de Beni, &c., amounting to sc. 346,607.

annually to the amount of £2,000 sterling, and a much greater quantity might be produced and exported without interfering with the lands now in cultivation.

The honey of Malta and Gozo is of a good quality, and might become an article of exportation. Anise and cummin seeds are so already. The Island produces the sugar-cane, red pepper, plantains, and guavas. The first is an article of food for the poor, but [the] other articles are not yet cultivated to any extent.

With these productions of hot climates the Island produces all the fruits, vegetables, and roots of cold latitudes, and in such abundance that the ships and troops on the expeditions commanded by Lord Keith and Sir Ralph Abercromby were plentifully supplied with these articles while they remained, and carried a sufficient stock with them to sea. The figs of Malta are delicious. They have a species of melon in appearance like the musk melon, but different in taste and superior in quality. It is in its greatest perfection in winter, and keeps for many weeks at sea. Their apples, pears, peaches, &c., are not equal to those of colder climates, but they are proofs that they may be greatly improved by cultivation, and their culinary vegetables of every kind are superior. The cultivation of potatoes is now introduced, and will prove of great advantage to the inhabitants.

The grape is only an article of food, but if they planted vines only along the walls which enclose their fields, they might have wine for their own consumption, and perhaps for exportation. There are few plains on the island; every rising ground is cultivated to the top. To prevent the torrents of rain which fall from washing away the soil, they bring the ground on the sides of every hill to a level by stone walls, and if the face of these walls alone were covered with vines, the quantity of wine that might be produced would add much to the wealth of the Island.

There is very little wood on the Island, and the whole face of it is a naked rock where the hand of industry has not covered it with soil. But the olive tree, the Indian fig, and the carube or locust tree push their most slender roots through the most solid rocks, and in course of time produce soil. The fruit of the two last are food for the inhabitants and their cattle, but cotton seed is the chief article of food for cattle, and the beef of the bullocks fattened with it is very fine.

There is reason to believe that the bread fruit tree would grow in Malta, and that the introduction of the guinea grass and the cedar tree would be very useful. A botanical garden is begun, in which it is supposed many curious exotics may be cultivated.

Works of this kind and public roads over all the Island are begun in order to employ the labouring poor, who would starve if they were not employed in this manner or maintained in idleness by the Government. The stones of Malta are easily wrought. They are exported to Sicily, the Adriatic, and the coast of Barbary for building and paving houses and making water conduits. By the help of the latter the inhabitants convey water to every garden and to almost every field over the Island. They are frugal, temperate, and industrious. They are good seamen, and gave signal proofs of personal courage during the siege. They rarely invent anything, but they are excellent imitators, and a master workman in iron or wood, particularly in the latter, can furnish any piece of furniture according to the model which is given to him.

The Maltese are great bigots in religion, and it is necessary to treat their prejudices with great indulgence. When betrayed and deserted by the Order they submitted to the French, and would not have revolted if their churches had not been plundered and if their religious prejudices had been respected. They are much influenced by their priests, on whom it is highly necessary to keep a watchful eye, as well as the emissaries and partizans of France and the adherents of the late Grand Master, Hompesch.

Observations on the Blockade of Malta, and the Defence it is capable of making.

From the smallness of the Island the port of La Valette is the most difficult to block of any naval port in Europe.

Ports situated on the Continent have only from a quarter to half a circle to guard, but to block Malta requires ships in the four quarters of the compass. Independant of those stationed directly off the port of La Valette, ships must be off Cape Bar, Cape Marittimo, Cape Passaro, and in the S.E. quarter from the Island, as well as 12 leagues westward of it. The weather during 4 months in the year is so stormy that it is almost impossible to prevent supplies getting in, particularly if they can be procured from Sicily and the Barbary States. Were even these ports shut against Malta, neutral vessels will always risk bringing supplies if well paid. An enemy would find a blockade so expensive, and attended with so much risk of having the detached squadrons cut off, that it is not likely to be attempted by the combined naval force whilst it is under the protection of Great Britain.

Should the enemy land a large force, 7,000 or 8,000 militia ready to be embodied according to the plan which is sent herewith, and whose services might be depended on, may be added to the regular force. The Government of the Order had this number.

It has been suggested that the inhabitants of Malta would starve if they could not draw their subsistance from Sicily. That Island from its vicinity is certainly convenient, but not absolutely necessary, as corn and oil can be procured from the Levant and the Barbary States cheaper than from thence. Malta, from its natural strength and its fortifications, may be considered as the most secure possession we have next to Gibraltar.

It has many advantages over Minorca, which is so vulnerable in many parts that it is not secure against a superior number to the garrison. The harbours of La Valette are equally capacious with and more secure than that of Port Mahon. The naval dockyard is small but complete. There are mast-houses, and a great many store-houses. There are six wateringplaces where water can be got without moving a cask out of the boat; it is very good, and a fleet can at any time complete from it most expeditiously.

At Minorca this summer it was so scarce that it was with great difficulty that a sufficient quantity could be procured for the Fleet, some of which was brackish and unwholesome. The harbours of La Valette are more accessible than that of Port Mahon, and the entrances are considered impregnable against any attack by sea. Malta can be defended by a much smaller force than Minorca by having the command of a militia force, which the other cannot have, the inhabitants having always refused to take part in the defence of their Island; and it can be kept at half the expense from having fewer troops, who are supplied with provisions at a cheaper rate. The Civil Establishment will not cost Government a shilling, the revenues of the Island being more than sufficient for its support. The situation of Minorca is preferable to Malta in some points of view from its being to the westward of Toulon and its vicinity to the coast of France and Spain, but Malta would have the advantage of protecting the British trade in the Levant, and destroying that of the enemy, and it may be an important post in checking the ambitious views of France and Russia in the Levant.

Gibraltar and Malta place the enemy as it were between two fires from their western and eastern situations, and, under this consideration, if it should be necessary to cede either Minorca or Malta to Russia, it might be political to cede the former in preference to the latter.

(Malta, 26th December 1800.)

Simultaneously with the organisation of the Government in Malta, efforts were made for obtaining the liberation of many Maltese held in slavery at Constantinople, Algiers, and the coast of Barbary. On the 19th March 1801 the following treaty with that object in view was agreed upon by His Britannic Majesty and the Dey of Algiers:—

TREATY BETWEEN HIS BRITANNIC MAJESTY AND THE DEY OF ALGIERS, DATED THE 19TH MARCH 1801.[1]

Whereas the Island of Malta in the Mediterranean Sea has been conquered by His Britannic Majesty's arms, it is now hereby agreed and fully concluded between John Falcon, Esquire, His Britannic Majesty's Agent-General and Consul-General for the city and kingdom of Algiers, and His Highness Mustapha Dey, Bashaw and Governor, &c., &c., of Algiers, that from the 7th day of December last, 1800, the inhabitants thereof shall be treated upon the same footing as the rest of His Britannic Majesty's subjects, and the said Island shall be considered in all respects like the other places subject to the Crown of Great Britain, and agreeable to the Convention made with His Britannic Majesty by Bracen Rais, Ambassador for His Highness the Dey. Confirmed and sealed in the warlike city and kingdom of Algiers in the presence of Almighty God the 19th day of March 1801, and in the year of the Hegira 1216, and the 6th day of the Moon Gelip. (Signed) JOHN FALCON.

Whilst on this subject it may be added that by the 5th February 1803 Mr. Cameron was able to announce by a public notification that His Britannic Majesty's ambassador at Constantinople had succeeded in obtaining the liberty of 164 Maltese, whose names are therein given, who had been detained in slavery for terms of from five to ten years, a few for twenty-five, twenty-six, twenty-eight, thirty-six, forty, and two for forty-eight years![2]

This liberation was due to Lord Keith's vigorous support of His

[1] Nicolas, *Dispatches of Nelson*, vol. vi. p. 43.
[2] M.P.L., Government Proclamations and Notices, CA 4.

Majesty's ambassador's efforts, as promised in his letter to the president of the Courts of Justice, judges, and magistrates of Malta, dated the 11th December 1800 (*vide* p. 339).

Meanwhile, on the 21st March 1801, Sir Ralph Abercromby was mortally wounded at the glorious victory near Alexandria, and on the 28th expired on board the flagship *Foudroyant*. It was decided by the authorities that no more fitting place than Malta could be selected for his body to rest. His remains were consequently removed to the frigate *Flora*, which sailed for Malta, arriving there on the 9th April 1801. Owing to quarantine regulations the funeral did not take place until the 29th April. The ceremony was most imposing. Maj.-Gen. Pigot was the chief mourner. The pall-bearers were :

    Lieut.-Col. Gordon, 48th Regt.
       „   „ Baylis, 35th Regt.
       „   „ Clay, 40th Regt.
       „   „ Oswald, 35th Regt.
       „   „ Bensham, R.A.
       „   „ Kemmis, 40th Regt.
       „   „ Brown, 35th Regt.
       „   „ Browne, 40th Regt.

Following him were Brig.-Gen. Moncrieff and Maj.-Gen. Villettes. Then came the officers of the regiments quartered in Malta, including those of the Maltese militia and the Neapolitan battalion.

Owing to the armistice concluded between the French Republic and the Neapolitan Government at Foligno on the 17th February 1801, it became necessary for the troops belonging to the latter Power to be withdrawn from the island, when general orders were issued by General Pigot on 4th May 1801, in which he thanked Colonel Fardella and his men for their services in suitable terms.

The time had now arrived for the home authorities to decide upon the future government of the Islands, and acting upon Sir Ralph Abercromby's advice, they recalled Captain Ball from the administration, but adopted the suggestion of the latter contained in his dispatch, already referred to, of the 6th March 1801, by appointing a civil commissioner to govern the islands in the person of Mr. Charles Cameron. Accordingly, on the 14th May, Lord Hobart, Secretary of State for War and the Colonies in the Addington Cabinet, delivered to Mr. Cameron the following instructions:—

          Lord Hobart to C. Cameron, Esq.

                Downing Street, 14*th May* 1801.[1]

Sir,—It being judged expedient that the direction and superintendence of the civil affairs and of the revenue of Malta should be separated from

---
[1] MSS. Malta Public Library, No. 388 ; C.O.R., Malta No. 2 (1801).

the duties of the commander of the forces in that Island, whose professional employments must necessarily require his more immediate attention ; but that in a military position of so much importance as Malta all measures of the former description should nevertheless be taken in concert with the person in whose hands are placed the safety and defence of the place; that they should be sanctioned with his concurrence and approbation previous to their being carried into execution ; His Majesty, from a confidence in your abilities and integrity, has been graciously pleased, with a view to the execution of this arrangement, to make choice of you for the management of the civil part of the service, and to direct that you should proceed to Malta, with the title of Civil Commissioner, to which will be annexed a salary of £2,000 per annum, to be paid out of the revenue of the Island. In pursuance of this arrangement, I have now to communicate to you, by His Majesty's command, such instructions as appear necessary under the present circumstances for your guidance in this important trust. The first object for your attention is to make yourself perfectly acquainted with the laws, customs, and privileges of the Maltese as they existed under the authority of the Grand Master and Order of St. John of Jerusalem, previous to the surrender of the Island to the French, and also with the different sources from which the public revenue was then derived, and the specific amount of the same under each of its different heads, together with the mode of collecting it, and generally to procure all the information possible on every point connected with the forms and detail of the administration formerly established in Malta. The inclosed report from Captain Ball, by whom the civil government was administered during the late blockade of the Island, and for some time after its surrender, will put you in possession of nearly everything that is known in this country on these interesting topics, and upon all points to which it may not refer, or respecting which it may not appear sufficiently minute and explicit, I can only at present observe, that you must trust to your own judgement, observation, and enquiries upon the spot to supply any deficiency of this nature.

It is of the more importance that you should apply yourself with the utmost diligence to acquire a knowledge of all the above-mentioned particulars, as the leading principle by which it is His Majesty's pleasure the government of Malta should for the present be regulated is, that in substance at least, and so far as circumstances will admit in form also, no alteration should be made in the modes, laws, and regulations according to which the civil affairs, and the revenue of the Island have been heretofore managed, unless the same shall appear to the officer commanding His Majesty's forces to be required for the safety and defence of the Island, or to be so evidently beneficial and desirable, as to leave no doubt of its expediency, or of its being generally acceptable to the wishes, the feelings, and even the prejudices of the inhabitants. You will therefore understand that the administration of justice and police is, as nearly as circumstances will permit, to continue to be exercised in conformity to the laws and institutions of the ancient Government of the Order of Saint John of Jerusalem, subject only to such directions as you may from time to time receive from this country, and to such deviations, in consequence of sudden and unforeseen emergencies, as may in the judgement of the Commander-in-Chief, render departure therefrom necessary and unavoidable, the occasion whereof, however, you will by the first opportunity report to me for His Majesty's information.

I observe by Captain Ball's report that the principal emoluments of the judges and officers of justice employed in the different Courts of Judicature arise from fees which it is His Majesty's pleasure they should for the present continue to receive upon their ancient footing; but you will take especial care to satisfy yourself with respect to the precise legal and established amount of the said fees in the different Courts, and you will cause a table thereof to be prepared in the English and Italian languages, and to be constantly hung up in some conspicuous place in each of the said Courts, for the information and guidance of all suitors therein, and others whom they may concern; and you will further make it your particular study to ascertain whether any practices contrary to the rules of the several Courts are inconsistent with the pure and impartial administration of justice as established and recognised by the laws of the Island, and the usages and practice of the said Courts are [sic] supposed to prevail therein, and in case your information should incline you to believe that abuses of this description do exist, you will apply yourself to frame such regulations as may appear to you adapted to correct and counteract their effects, and to ensure to all the Maltese indiscriminately the full protection and benefit of their laws, and of the tribunals under whose direction they are administered and carried into effect, and you will transmit the same to me by the earliest opportunity, for the purpose of their being laid before His Majesty previous to their publication.

The Courts called the *Consolato*, and of which the functions appear to correspond with those of our Court of Admiralty, cannot be continued; a Vice-Admiralty Court being the only authority by which, in conformity to the law of nations and the practice of this country, the jurisdiction now vested in the *Consolato* could be exercised in Malta, in its present situation as a dependence upon the Crown of the United Kingdom of Great Britain and Ireland. The expediency of granting a commission for the establishment of such a Court is reserved for further consideration.

With respect to the Revenue of the Island of Malta, the different sources from which it is derived, and the usual produce of each, are so distinctly stated in Captain Ball's report that I shall not find it necessary to go much at length into the subject. In strict conformity to the general principle already explained to you, it is His Majesty's pleasure that the public property, either in lands or buildings, as well as the different institutions and regulations from which a great part of the public revenue was derived under the Order of St. John of Jerusalem, should continue to be managed and enforced upon the former footing, with such alterations only as the change of circumstances by which the right of sovereignty formerly vested in that Order, but now exercised by His Majesty, have rendered obviously requisite.

For instance, the different descriptions of property which formerly belonged entirely to the Grand Master and Order of St. John of Jerusalem, or in which that Order had a beneficial [1] interest, must now be considered, as far as their rights existed, as belonging to the Crown, subject only to such charges and deductions as in justice to individuals having claims upon

---

[1] The term should probably be 'beneficiary.'—J. H. R.

them, or for the useful purpose either of charity or instruction to which some of the said property was appropriated, must continue to be allowed under His Majesty's Government. The property to which I allude is principally that which in Captain Ball's report is mentioned under the general head of *Beni Magistrali*, subdivided into the *Beni Rustici*, and the *Beni Urbani*.

Under the former description are included all the mesne lands and gardens belonging to Government. These he states as capable of considerable improvement; you will therefore feel it an early duty of your situation to make yourself acquainted with the regulations which have been established for their management, and to consider of the mode by which the proposed improvement can be most speedily and completely affected, and you will as soon as possible transmit to this country a full and explicit report upon these points, in order that you may receive from hence such further instructions as may be necessary thereupon. With respect to the *Beni Urbani*, or houses or warehouses in town or country, most of them appear at present to be occupied either for public or military purposes, or by officers of the Army, who are stated to hold them without paying any rent. This indulgence, as far as it accords with the established regulations for the accomodation of the King's forces in quarters, should be continued, but I am not aware of any circumstance that renders it necessary to introduce at Malta a system different in this respect from that which prevails in other foreign garrisons — Minorca or Gibraltar for instance—and you must therefore consult with the commander of the forces on this subject, and having in concert with him determined what description of officers are from their situation and from general usage entitled to be accomodated at the public expense, you will give notice to such others as may be in the occupation of houses belonging to Government, either to quit the same, or to pay for the future such rent as may appear reasonable, and may be agreed upon, they and you selecting for the occupation of the Civil Commissioner one house in the country and one other house in town, or such other accomodation in point of residence as may appear to you most suitable for the occasion without interfering with the established residence of the commander of the troops. The warehouses on the wharf for the accomodation of trade are represented by Captain Ball as extremely commodious for this purpose, and likely to produce a considerable revenue. I therefore trust that some other building may be found for the reception of the stores of the Commissary and quartermaster-general, by which they are now occupied, in order that the former may be reserved for the use for which they were originally intended.

The property formerly belonging to the Order of St. John of Jerusalem, and which in Captain Ball's report is described under the different heads of *Del Tesoro, Divisi Fondazione, Lingue et Collegio*, in as far as the same lies in the Island of Malta and its dependencies, do not appear to require any particular observation. The charges upon these different branches of the revenue will probably render their net proceeds payable to Government an object of small moment. Such of these charges as are specified by Captain Ball, namely, for allowances to invalid officers and men belonging to the Order, and for the education of the youth of the Island, are certainly proper, and must be continued.

If there be any other of a doubtful nature or any abuses, or any either in the administration of these different branches of the revenue or in the application of the allowances, though proper in themselves, you will consider of the best mode of remedying the same and report to me your proceedings for this purpose.

The duties of customs and excise may for the present be continued on their ancient footing and establishment. The Lords Commissioners of the Treasury will probably appoint a proper person to collect the former, and will furnish him with such instructions as they may think proper on the occasion. I must now come to one branch of the civil arrangement of Malta which, no less from its importance to the comfort of the inhabitants and the security of the Island, than from its connection with the revenue, will require great diligence and attention on your part, and must be under your immediate direction and control. I mean the mode by which the Island and its inhabitants are supplied with corn. However much at variance with general principles it may appear for a Government to retain in its own hands the exclusive privilege of buying and selling corn, and however dangerous and injurious to society such an attempt, if not impracticable, would prove in any country of greater extent or even in any island under different circumstances, I have no hesitation to give my opinion that in Malta the maintenance of the public authority, the defence of the Island, and particularly the care and comfort of the inhabitants themselves, all concur to require that the system which has been so long established in this respect should not be altered for the present.

If the limited number of inhabitants is considered, and consequently that the extent of the demand can be easily ascertained, that the Island depends for not less than three-fourths of its consumption upon importations from other countries, and how much in Malta, as in every country, the happiness of the great body of the inhabitants depends upon the price of corn—bearing a proper proportion to the earnings of their labour; that this proportion once ascertained and established (as in Malta I conceive it by long experience), any considerable or sudden fluctuation would be a great misfortune; that Malta from peculiar circumstances and its local situation would be liable to such fluctuations that any change in the habits of the people affecting them in a point that comes so immediately home to their feelings and daily wants is dangerous; and lastly, that the present system, at the same time that, upon an average of good and bad years, it produces a considerable revenue, may be considered as a constant and useful check over the people in the hands of Government, I am convinced that it ought to be adhered to as an arrangement no less politic on our part than provident towards the Maltese themselves.

For all these reasons it will become one of the most essential duties of your situation to make yourself thoroughly acquainted with every circumstance relative to the purchase and sale of corn at Malta, of which you will transmit to me a full detailed account, with such observations and suggestions as may occur to you upon the subject, together with the average amount of the imports and sale of grain during the ten years preceding the arrival of the French at Malta, and in the meantime this branch of the public service must be carried on through the medium of the Bank or University upon its present footing, but under your immediate superintendance and inspection.

Respecting the Monte di Pietà, I have no other observation to make than that it will be your duty to take care that the administration of it be placed in such hands, and under such checks and restrictions as may prevent as far as possible any fraud or abuse being practised, either to the prejudice of the Government or of the inhabitants. Several of the circumstances on which I have founded my opinion with respect to the exclusive privilege of buying and selling corn will equally apply to the regulations respecting windmills, which must therefore continue to be observed and enforced at least for the present.

With respect to the mode of keeping an account of the receipt and expenditure of the civil revenue of the Island, and transmitting the same to this country, you will receive particular instructions from the Lords Commissioners of His Majesty's Treasury.

Under the head of expenditure I have only to state [that] His Majesty's expectation that the revenue will be found fully adequate to defray all charges of the Civil Government, and to allow of a certain sum being appropriated annually to the repairs, first of the houses, warehouses, and buildings belonging to Government, and should any surplus remain, after providing for these services, then to the repairs of the fortifications of the Island.

As it appears that the emoluments attached to the civil employments in the Island are in most cases derived from fixed and established fees, which for the present are to be continued, of course a small part of the revenue will be sufficient to defray the charge of such civil employments as have salaries attached to them; but in order that it may be distinctly known in this country what are the offices of this description, and what proportion of the revenue is assigned to this purpose, I have to request that you will transmit to me as soon as possible a return of the Civil Establishment of Malta, specifying the name of each person holding an employment therein, the nature of that employment, and the salary derived from it. In Captain Ball's report I observe that the principal expense of the Civil Government under the Order of St. John of Jerusalem is stated to have been the maintenance of the hospitals, the charge of which, it would appear, amounted to ten thousand pounds per annum; the Captain, however, adds, that by reforming the abuses which prevailed in these establishments, the expense may be reduced one-half. As he does not, however, state the nature of these abuses, or suggest any plan for their reform, I must confine myself to call your attention generally to this subject, and to recommend to you to introduce into the administration of the hospitals, the utmost regularity, and to enforce a system of strict economy as far as may be consistent with justice to the persons employed in the service of the sick, and with a due attention to the relief and comfort of the latter.

With respect to the trade of Malta, His Majesty's confidential servants have it in contemplation to recommend to Parliament to grant to the Port of La Valetta all the advantages of a free port, and to make such regulations as may appear to them best calculated to encourage an extensive commercial intercourse between that port and the Mediterranean States; but under the present circumstances, and until this plan can be matured and completed, it is His Majesty's pleasure that the trade of Malta should continue to be carried on upon its present footing, subject, however, to such regulations and instructions as may be made and issued by the Lords Commissioners of the Treasury, or by the Lords of the Committee of

Council, for the consideration of all matters relating to the trade and foreign plantations. The chief article of the export trade at Malta consisting in cotton thread, the spinning of which is stated to be the principal branch of industry in the Island, it becomes necessary in order to tranquilise the minds of the people, which appear to have been artfully alarmed upon the subject, to assure them that every necessary protection and encouragement will continue to be given to this important object, and that notwithstanding the war now existing between this country and Spain, no interruption whatever will be given to the exportation in neutral bottoms to the Spanish ports of everything as may have been made in the Island of Malta or its dependencies from cotton *bonâ fide* of their own growth and produce.

As connected with the trade of Malta, I have now to advert to the lazzaretto situated on the Island in Marsamuscetto Harbour, and which I have every reason to believe is the most complete in the world, as connected with the views of His Majesty's Government to draw a great part of the trade of the Mediterranean, and particularly of the Levant, to Malta. It must be unnecessary for me to point out to you in detail how important and indispensable it will be found to render the service of this lazzaretto and the performance of quarantine as easy and commodious, and at the same time as efficient and secure, as possible.

The person to whom it is intended to confide the management and superintendance of this establishment is Mr. W. Eton, a gentleman who by his personal observations in several of the lazzarettos of Europe, and by his study of the subject, appears to have acquired a considerable degree of knowledge respecting the quarantine laws, and the different modes and precautions to be taken in observing and enforcing them according to the different degrees of suspicion which may attach upon the vessels, crews, and cargoes that are subjected to their operation.

I enclose to you such communications as have been received from him upon these points, and also the report of a Quarantine Committee appointed in this country, as it will be necessary that you should so far turn your attention to the subject as to be able to give every assistance in your power to Mr. Eton, and in some degree to judge of the expediency and propriety of the arrangements and regulations he may propose for the Quarantine Establishment at Malta.

Mr. Eton will proceed to Malta by the same opportunity with yourself, and on his arrival there, you will direct him to enquire minutely into every circumstance and regulation respecting the establishment of the lazzaretto under the government of the Order of St. John of Jerusalem, and also into the mode by which it has been managed and conducted since the expulsion of the French from the Island, and to make a full and detailed report upon each of these points, accompanied with a complete and methodical system of such regulations as in his judgment ought henceforward to be adopted and observed for the performance of quarantine at Malta and of the establishment that may be requisite for carrying these regulations into effect. In making this report it will be expected from Mr. Eton to accompany his proposals with a statement of the grounds on which they are recommended, and particularly in every instance of any deviation from the former regulations, or of any addition to the same.

This report having been submitted to the General commanding the troops, and to yourself, it will be your and his duty respectively to make such observations as may occur to you on the same, and to transmit the whole to me for the consideration of His Majesty's Government. In the meantime, Mr. Eton is from the period of his arrival at Malta to be placed in the superintendance and management of the lazzaretto, and the Quarantine regulations which he may find in force are to be observed, with such improvements and alterations as he may think it right to make with your sanction, and that of the General commanding the forces at Malta. His Majesty having been graciously pleased to determine that Mr. Eton should for the present receive a fixed salary at the rate of eight hundred pounds per annum, and that in consequence all the fees and perquisites that may be received at the lazzaretto are to be accounted for to Government.

All Proclamations or public Acts of the Government are to be signed jointly by the General commanding the forces, and by yourself as His Majesty's Commissioner for carrying on the civil administration of the Island.

Having already apprised you that the salary His Majesty had been pleased to assign to your office was two thousand pounds per annum, you will of course understand that no other advantage or emolument whatsoever is to be derived from your situation, and I must further observe to you, that it is considered by His Majesty as precluding you from engaging in any pursuits or speculations of commerce, which appear to His Majesty incompatible with a due attention to the functions of your office, and inconsistent with the rank and character to be maintained by the person placed in the immediate superintendance of the civil affairs of Malta. All the salaries charged upon the civil revenue of Malta should be paid quarterly, without any deduction or drawback whatsoever.

Having now stated to you such specific objects as will immediately require your attention, and the general nature of your appointment and authority, I have only at present to recommend to you in the strongest manner to act with the most unreserved confidence towards the officer commanding the forces on all points of a public concern, and to maintain a perfect good understanding, not only with him, but generally with the officers, both naval and military, in His Majesty's service at Malta; and with respect to the inhabitants, to use every endeavour, consistent with your public duty, to meet their wishes, to show yourself indulgent even to their prejudices, and to omit no fair opportunity of conciliating their affection and ensuring their fidelity to the Government under which they are now placed.—I am, Sir, &c. (Signed) HOBART.

The tenor of Lord Hobart's instructions to Mr. Cameron leaves the impression that the British Government at this date intended to retain possession of the island, and to assume its sovereignty. The time and current events appeared propitious. Firstly, the island had then been nine months in their possession. Secondly, there was the manifest desire of the inhabitants for annexation, which shortly found expression by the dispatch of a special deputation to the British Government, elected for that purpose. Thirdly, the removal of the principal obstacle to such a settlement of the question, by the death of the Emperor Paul, Grand Master and Protector of the Order of St. John, which had taken place two months previously—namely on the 24th March; and finally, Nelson's victory at Copenhagen on the 2nd April, which induced Russia to retire from the Northern Coalition, which six months previously had been formed against Great Britain.

But of these favourable circumstances the most promising was found to be delusive; for although Paul's successor, Alexander I, had declined the chief magistracy of the Order, yet nevertheless he promised to accord to it his protection, with the maintenance of its rights; and from that position he was not inclined to retire.

Great Britain in consequence was compelled to give way, and in the negotiations for peace between England and France, which were opened in London in the following October, she had to agree to the restoration of the Order, and to its reoccupation of Malta.[1]

In the meantime, Commissioner Cameron, immediately upon his arrival in the island, published the following proclamation, dated the 15th July 1801 :—

PROCLAMATION TO THE MALTESE NATION.[2]

Charged by His Majesty, the King of Great Britain, to conduct all the affairs (except the military) of these Islands of Malta and Gozo, with the title of His Majesty's Civil Commissioner, I embrace with the highest satisfaction this opportunity of assuring you of the paternal care and affection of the King towards you, and that His Majesty grants you full protection, and the enjoyments of all your dearest rights. He will protect your churches, your holy religion, your persons, and your property. His paternal care extends to the hospitals, and other charitable establishments, to the education of youth, to orphans, to the poor, and to all those who recur to his beneficence.

Happy people! whom the hand of God has saved from the horrible misery and oppression under which groan so many innocent nations, receive with gratitude all this goodness from a King who is the father of his subjects, who protects the weak against the strong, the poor against the rich, under whose dominion all are equally protected by the law.

Hitherto you have conducted yourselves with decorum and submission to the legitimate authorities, and your ancient fame in arms has not been tarnished by the defence which you lately made of your country. Commerce being now extended, the arts and sciences encouraged, manufactures and agriculture supported, and industry rewarded, Malta will become the emporium of the Mediterranean, and the seat of content.

To execute such gracious commands of my Sovereign is not less my ardent desire, than it is my sacred duty. My door shall be open to all;

[1] As I have pointed out in my *Life of Napoleon* (vol. i. p. 410), the Czar Alexander soon found out that Napoleon was bent on enticing him into Oriental schemes which he deemed to be dangerous. He thereupon changed his tone, and suggested to our ambassador that England had better keep Malta. But this was in December 1802. The Treaty of Amiens between Great Britain and France was signed on March 25, 1802.—J. H. R.

[2] *Bandi di Malta*, p. 67.

I will hear every one's plea; I shall be ready to render justice; to cause the law to be observed, tempering it with clemency; and to receive every information which shall have for its object the welfare of the Maltese; and above all, I shall devote myself to the means of promoting the cultivation of cotton, the manufacture of yarn, and of importing and maintaining an abundance of food in these Islands. (Signed) CHARLES CAMERON.
Palace, 15th *July* 1801.

Reports having reached the local Government that efforts would shortly be made with the object of creating an insurrection in the island in favour of the Order of St. John, a public notice, under date of the 23rd July, was issued to the following effect :—

The Palace (Valetta), 23rd *July* 1801.[1]

Whereas certain persons, not natives of these Islands, have had doubts respecting their being subject to the authority of the tribunals of this country, it has been thought necessary to inform such persons that every one, of whatever description or denomination, is, as the case may require, amenable to the laws of Malta now in force; it being His Majesty's order to continue in force the laws and to maintain the tribunals as heretofore practised, with the exception of such new laws and such regulations, as have been or shall for the future be established by His Majesty's command. (Signed) CHARLES CAMERON.

On the 29th, Lord Hobart was informed of the situation, as follows :—

Valetta, 29th *July* 1801.[2]
To the Right Hon. Lord Hobart.

MY LORD,—Advices from Messina and Trieste inform us that cabals are forming in this Island, in favour of the Order of St. John, by the French, that there are agents now here, one of whom is a nephew of the famous Poussielgue.

It is their project to cause an insurrection of the dissatisfied inhabitants, especially in the country, which is to be supported by 5,000 French to be landed. Mr. Eton and Mr. Macaulay[3] have both exerted themselves to procure information on this interesting subject, and I am sorry to say that they brought me in the same day, and from various and distinct sources, a strong confirmation of these reports. One of the reports spread by these emissaries is that the Grand Master will be here immediately. The alarm is so great that the University,[4] which used to give a horse race and other amusements to the people on the feast of St. Roch, wish this year to decline them, from an idea of danger in admitting so many people into Valetta from the country. I enclose Your Lordship a copy of an address to the Maltese, which I have reason to think has been useful in calming the minds of the people, irritated by the artful means above described. The respect which has been shown to their religion has greatly pleased them,

[1] C.O.R. Malta, No. 2.
[2] *Ibid.*
[3] Mr. Alex. Macaulay was public secretary to Mr. Cameron.—J. H. R.
[4] i.e. the Corporation for the supply of corn.—J. H. R.

but they are told by our enemies that Malta will be given up when a peace shall be made, the fear of which withholds many who would be active in our favour, as they fear the resentment of the French, should they become masters of the Island.

Perhaps no step would have a more favourable effect than His Majesty declaring the Bishop of Malta (who is also titular Archbishop of Rhodes, and a suffragan of Palermo) Metropolitan, and the Roman Catholic religion the Established Church, as is the case in Canada.

He is a most respectable character, and much looked up to by all ranks of people, and at the same time it would be attended with good effect, if I were empowered to declare that Malta was a part of the British dominions, and in all public Acts to permit that the King should be styled their Most Gracious Sovereign.

The attachment of the Maltese to their monasteries and public charities is very great, and some trifling pensions to the convents reduced to utter poverty, and really starving, have produced the strongest effects.

Every exertion is being made to discover those who are carrying on these intrigues, and Mr. Eton, without whose permission no vessel arriving in the port can have any communication, examines the letters. A correspondence is held with the people at Messina and Trieste. Three Spanish Knights are arrived from Barcelona in a neutral vessel; they will not be permitted to land. One of them is notorious. I am sorry to inform Your Lordship that some of the most respectable Baillis and Commandeurs who receive pensions from Government are suspected of being engaged in these cabals. I do not offer an individual opinion, but all those with whom I have talked on this subject, assure me that no security can be expected until all the foreign Baillis and Knights shall have left the Island. They are old and not numerous; perhaps it might be worth while to give them a comfortable pension on condition of their going to Sicily.

I have it in contemplation to propose to General Pigot another address to the Maltese.

Since writing the above, the enclosed letters, and many others of the same nature, have been intercepted. I have seen General Pigot on the subject, and shall send the most obnoxious persons away immediately. I have the honour, &c. (Signed) CHARLES CAMERON.

CHAPTER XVII

RUSSIA'S CONNEXION WITH THE ORDER OF ST. JOHN OF JERUSALEM

(From 1795 to 1801)

THE policy of Russia under Paul I concerning Malta during the two long years of its investment, a policy which his successor, Alexander I, for some time partly maintained, had the greatest influence on the destinies of the island. Whereas soon after the commencement of the siege Russia was in alliance against France, she soon after the fortress fell to England became one of the bitterest opponents of Great Britain.

The vacillation of Russian policy cannot be understood without reference to the general political condition of Europe at the time, and her own political connexion with the Order of St. John. Her close association with Malta and its government dates from the third partition of Poland in 1795, in which country since 1618 the Order of St. John had acquired property in the Ordination of Ostrog. At the said partition of Poland it fell to the lot of Russia.[1] During 1795 the Grand Master, De Rohan, appointed De Litta as Minister Plenipotentiary to the Russian Court, for the purpose of obtaining not only the restitution of the properties in question but also the arrears of revenue, of which the Order had been deprived, since 1788. De Litta presented his credentials to the Empress Catharine II on the 18th October 1795, but owing to her death, which occurred on the 17th November 1796, the negotiations were for a time suspended.[2]

Her son and successor, Paul I, who had always expressed great admiration for the glorious traditions of the Knights of St. John, showed every disposition to interest himself on their behalf. Negotiations were accordingly reopened, and so successful was De Litta, that by an agreement dated the 15th January 1797 the Grand Priory of Poland was merged into and styled the Grand Priory of Russia, with an establishment of one grand prior and ten commanderies. An annual endowment, payable in half-yearly instalments, amounting together to 300,000 Polish florins (£7,500), was

[1] Boisgelin, *History of Malta*, vol. iii. p. 37. [2] *Ibid.* p. 38.

allotted for their maintenance, to which were subsequently added three other commanderies, with a further annual income of 6,000 Polish florins (£150).[1] By a separate agreement, signed on the same day, it was stipulated that all the arrears since 1788 until the time when the estates and dependencies thereof were incorporated in the Russian dominions, together with 4,000 golden ducats, owing since the first foundation of the Order in Poland (in accordance with the treaty of 1775), should be comprised in the general debt of the Government, and be liquidated accordingly.

These agreements were signed on behalf of the Czar by Comte Alexandre de Bezborodoff,[2] Chancellor of the Empire, and Prince Alexander Kourakin, Vice-Chancellor, and on the part of the Grand Master by the Bailiff Fr. Jules Réné, Comte de Litta. The treaty was immediately dispatched by a special courier for the necessary ratification by the Grand Master and Council. Unfortunately, the route of Ancona was selected for his journey, where, owing to its occupation by a division of Bonaparte's army, he was immediately upon arrival arrested, and his documents seized.[3]

The information thus obtained had considerable influence upon Bonaparte who, during his stay at Ancona, in the early part of the year 1797, and subsequently strove to induce the Directory to take the necessary steps for the acquisition of Malta, in order, as he alleged, to prevent the Czar having in his power the means of interfering with the projected expedition to Egypt, which he (Bonaparte) was then contemplating. In the meanwhile a second courier, with duplicates of the treaty and of De Litta's dispatches, was more fortunate than his predecessor, and arrived in Malta just before the Grand Master, De Rohan, breathed his last (13th July 1797).[4] At the first meeting of the Council held by De Rohan's successor, Hompesch, the convention was ratified, and on the 7th August De Litta was again named Ambassador Extraordinary, for the purpose of presenting the ratifications which were carried to St. Petersburg by the Chevalier Raczynski with De Litta, who was further instructed to solicit His Majesty's protection over the Order.[5]

De Litta was received in public audience by Paul I on the 29th November 1797 when he delivered the following address :—

[Translation.]

Sire,—The Sovereign Order of Malta, eager to acknowledge its debt of gratitude, and to perform a duty, not only sacred but dear to the hearts

[1] Boisgelin's *History of Malta*, vol. iii. p. 3.
[2] This name should be Bezborodko.—J. H. R.
[3] These original documents are now to be found in the Archives Nationales, Paris, Carton AF. III. 73. Also see Boisgelin, vol. iii. p. 41.
[4] *Ibid.* pp. 41, 44.
[5] *Ibid.* p. 43.

All the documents which follow, and which were written in Russia, were dated in the Old Style, which is twelve days behind the New Style, used in the rest of Europe.—J. H. R.

of every one of its members, approaches the foot of your throne, to tender its grateful thanks. Your Majesty's benefactions are such as must ever remain deeply engraved on our memory.

The new establishment which the munificence of Your Imperial Majesty has secured to the Order of Malta in the Empire of Russia, has been sanctioned in that Island with the most lively enthusiasm, and with every sentiment of joy and gratitude. To give a still greater solemnity to our acknowledgments, and to express our homage still more forcibly, His Highness my Lord the Grand Master, together with the Supreme Council, have unanimously decreed an Extraordinary Embassy on the occasion.

Being chosen by my Order for this august mission, it is in quality of Ambassador Extraordinary, that I am charged to acquaint Your Imperial Majesty with the universal wish of the whole Order that you would deign to become chief of this establishment, and accept a title so dear, and so encouraging to us all; a title indeed which you, Sire, by your generous sentiments, and the favours bestowed upon us, have already so justly acquired, namely, that of *Protector of the Order of Malta*, and as such we trust we shall see Your Imperial Majesty invested with the ensigns of an Order equally ancient and illustrious, ever renowned for its exploits, and venerable from the sanctity of its institutions.

His Eminent Highness and the Supreme Council have, therefore, sent your Imperial Highness the Ancient Cross of the celebrated La Vallette, that invincible defender of our Island who bequeathed his name to a city which he alone has rendered impregnable. This cross has hitherto been religiously preserved in the treasury of our Cathedral Church, as a precious monument, which constantly recalled to our remembrance the glorious military exploits performed by a Grand Master of Malta, who might properly be termed the Hero of Christianity; and we now feel a pleasure in offering it to your Imperial Majesty, as a proof of our gratitude, as a mark worthy of his piety, and as a happy presage of the renewal of our prosperity.

This offer is accompanied by our most ardent vows for the glory of Your Imperial Majesty, and the happiness of your Empire. This august and revered ensign of our Order, together with the recollection of our ancestors, and the proofs of valour given by the Knights of Malta will, we doubt not, excite in the bosoms of the illustrious, brave, and faithful nobles of Your Majesty's Empire an enthusiasm and a spirit of emulation worthy the most glorious ages of chivalry; and the solemnity of this memorable day will constantly recall to posterity the remembrance of the munificence of Paul I, and the gratitude of the Order of Malta.

To this earnest appeal the Czar graciously acceded, but within seven months of His Majesty's acceptance of the protectorate, Malta had fallen into the possession of the French, her Grand Master had become an exile at Trieste, and her Knights were dispersed over Europe and Egypt.

Nine days after the fall of Malta a detailed account of its surrender was dispatched to De Litta, at St. Petersburg, wherein Hompesch was accused of treachery to the Order, of cowardice, and incapacity. This letter was alleged to have been written by the

Bailiff de Tigné, one of the most respected members of the Order, and it was not until the capitulation of the French garrison to the British in September 1800, during which time De Tigné was a captive within Valetta, that he was able to vindicate the honour of his chief, and to prove that the letter was not authentic.

This letter, although afterwards proved to be apocryphal, is inserted here for the important reason that in the meanwhile it served the purpose of the enemies and traducers of Hompesch. Being accepted by many members of the Order as a truthful version of what had occurred in Malta, it created a schism therein, and prevented the Grand Master's vindication being listened to by either the Austrian or the Russian Court.

According to Sir Morton Eden's dispatch to Lord Grenville, dated Vienna, August 1798, it is therein stated that 'M. Thugut, the Austrian Minister, strongly urged an emissary of Hompesch who had lately arrived in Vienna, *the expediency of not publishing the Grand Master's defence.*'[1] Why, is not stated, yet four months later Sir Morton Eden was able to inform Lord Grenville, on the 26th December, that the Chevalier O'Hara, lately Minister from the Court of St. Petersburg to the Maltese Government, and who is here (in Vienna) on his way back to St. Petersburg, has assured me that he has the fullest grounds to believe that the letter which appeared in the public papers under the name of the Bailli de Tigné is spurious. He supposes it to have been written by the Bailli de Loras, who is generally said to be a man of bad character.[2]

LETTRE DU BAILLI DE TIGNÉ, GRAND CROIX, DIGNITAIRE DE L'ORDRE DE MALTE, À MONSIEUR LE BAILLI DE LITTA À ST. PÉTERSBOURG.

À Malte, le 21 *Juin* 1798.[3]

MONSIEUR LE BAILLI,—Il est nécessaire que vous sachiés les véritables causes de la perte de l'Ordre que vous illustrés, que vous auriez défendu, que vous avés si bien servi et qui existeroit encore si nous avions eu un chef qui eut eu votre mérite et votre courage; je vais vous rendre compte des différentes raisons qui ont occasionné notre déshonorante destruction.

1°. Le Gouvernement faible et vacillant du feu Grand Maître Rohan avez [*sic*] laissé préparer les principes destructeurs de tout Gouvernement, il avoit dans presques toutes les places de l'administration des gens qui étoient hautement partisans des maximes Françaises et qui recevoient des gratifications des Tricolors.

2°. Nous élumes Ferdinand Hompesch parce qu'il fasoit paroître des sentimens nobles et courageux, mais nous pouvons [?] croire actuellement qu'il avoit fait son marché pour nous livrer, ce dont on sera persuadé

---

[1] Foreign Office Records, Austria, No. 51.
[2] *Ibid.* No. 53.
[3] This letter is reproduced with all its inaccuracies. Some words are illegible.—J. H. R.
Malta Public Library, MS. 421.

quand on connaîtra la conduit qu'il a tenu, de laquelle je vais rendre compte. C'est lui qui a perdu l'Ordre par son bêtise, par sa lâcheté et peut-être par sa perfidie.

3°. Nous avons été trahi par les membres de l'Ordre qui avoient la direction des finances, des fortifications et de l'artillerie, tels que Bosredon Ransijat, Toussard, Fay, et Bardonanche.

4°. Les riches habitans de Malte, barons, et négotians ont marqué la plus grand ingratitude, ils ont fait assasiner des Chevaliers en propageant le bruit que les Chevaliers les livroient aux Français.

5°. Le Roi d'Espagne, dont le devoir et l'intérêt étoit de protéger l'Ordre, l'a astucieusement livré aux Français au point que Mr Arnat, Ministre d'Espagne à Malte a signé l'arrangement de la reddition qui s'est faite sous sa médiation. Les Chevaliers étoient persuadés que Ferdinand Hompesch changeroit ceux qui gouvernoient sous le vieux Rohan, mais il a suivi servilement la manière de gouverner de son foible prédécesseur. Hompesch n'a eu de confiance que dans ceux qui étoient conûs par leur démocratie.

Au mois de Janvier de cette anné 1798, Le Directoire envia [sic] à Malte le nommé Poussielgue pour y organiser une insurection; cet envoyé se logea chez un parent de son nom qui reste à Malte, riche banquier, qui de plus étoit Capitaine de Port. Poussielgue voient publiquement et en secret les démocrates de ces pays, il donne l'ordre à Caruson, Consul de France à Malte, d'écrire la liste des Maltais qui vouloient un changement de Gouvernement et qui promettoient de se révolter lorsque la France leur en donneroit l'avis, il chargea ses agents d'engager les Maltais à aller se faire inscrire chez le Consul de France. Hompesch étoit instruit de ces menées qu'il laissa conduire et cela, malgré que même des Grands Croix lui en eussent rendu compte et lui . . . fait voir des lettres que Poussielgue avoit apportées. M. le Chevalier Ministre de Russie O'Hara en fut instruit dans le tems il peut en rendre compte.

Au commencement du mois de Mars de cette année l'amiral Brueys venant de Corfou avec une flotte de 12 vaisseaux de guerre parut devant Malte dont il vouloit connoître les côtes et il envoya dans le port un vaisseau qui avoit besoin de réparation et auquel l'Ordre accorda tous les secours dont il avoit besoin. L'escadre française re[connaissait?] pendant 8 jours les points où on pourrait faire un debarquement.

Les agents des Français essayèrent si les calomnies réussirent ils firent courir le bruit que les Chevaliers qui comandoient les postes le long de la mer les trahiroient [?], ce qui fut cru et ce qui ôta la confiance que les Maltais avoient dans les Chevaliers. Alors Mr Arnat, chargé d'affaires d'Espagne, aussi que les Chevaliers Espagnols trouvèrent mauvais les petites mesures de sûreté, qu'on avoit prises ce qui fit voir aux Maltais que les Chevaliers étoient divisés. Le Consul de France Caruson fit part à Bruyer qu'un grand nombre de Maltais se joindroit aux Français dès qu'il attaqueroient Malte. Toutes les nouvelles venant de Toulon des différentes ports de l'Italie annonçoient que les Français faisoient un grand armement maritime, qu'il y avoit beaucoup de bâtimens de transport et beaucoup d'artillerie. Les lettres de Paris disoient qu'un des objets de ce grand mouvement étoit de prendre Malte. La Chevalierie étoit inquiète et vouloit qu'on fit des préparatifs pour se deffendre; mais rien ne put tirer Hompesch de sa létargi.

La Congrégation de Guerre étoit composé du Bailli Frisari, Napolitain, égallement bête, avare et lâche, du Comandeur Neveu, Allemand, stupide et ivrogne, du Bailly Songa, Espagnol, tellement nul que le Council de l'Ordre lui avoit ôté l'administration de ses comanderies, et du Bailli de la Tour du Pin, bon officier, loyal, brave, et fort attaché à son Ordre, du Commandeur Bardonanche qui étoit directeur de l'artillerie, du Comandeur Toussard qui étoit directeur du génie, du Comand^r de Fay, qui étoit directeur des fortifications et des fontaines et des cisternes. J'ay déjà dit que ces trois derniers étoient d'accord avec Poussielgue en avoient reçu de l'argent et la promesse d'être attachés au service de France. Le Bailli de la Tour du Pin vouloit qu'on se mît en défense, qu'on pallisadât, qu'on fît des affûts, et tout ce qu'il faut pour manœuvrer le canon, qu'on chargeât les fougarres armes particulières à l'Isle de Malte qui est excellente pour émpêcher un débarquement, qu'on mît en état les fusils de rempart, qu'on exerçât les milices, qu'on y etablît la subordination, qu'on rentrât dans la ville les magasins à poudre qui étoient à la Cottoner, qu'on mît des vivres dans les forts, mais il ne put rien obtenir ni de la Congrégation ni du Grand Maître, qui seul avoit le droit de tout ordonner. Le Comandeur de Rosans, bon officier d'artillerie qui même avoit dirigé le dernier siège de Mahon a donné plusieurs excellent mémoires à Hompesch sur ces importants objets, mais il n'a jamais été écouté.

Hompesch ne sortoit de son palais que pour aller à des processions où il étoit extrèmement applaudi par le peuple, mais il n'a jamais été voir ni exercer les troupes de l'arsenal ni dans aucun fort, et il a toujours tenu cette conduit. Le mercredi 6 Juin paru devant Malte une partie du convoi Français composé de 70 bâtimens de transport et de quelques frégates qui attendoient le reste de l'armée que comandoit Bonaparte. L'inquiétude augmenta parmi les Chevaliers et Maltais qui n'étoient pas du complot, ils vouloient que l'on se hâtât de se mettre en défense.

En temps de paix différentes charges avoient le comandement. Le chef de la Langue d'Auvergne qu'on appelloit le Maréchal avoit le comandement de la ville et le Sénéchal des Milices de la campagne, mais quand l'Ordre étoit menacé, le Conseil nommoit un général ce qui n'a pas été fait, par conséquent le Sénéchal qui étoit le Prince Camille de Rohan homme très méprisable eut le comandement des milices, on mit sous ses ordres le Bailli Tomasi, homme de mérite, mais qui n'a jamais servi que sur mer et le Bailli de Clugni, brave homme viellard âgé de 72 ans, c'étoit avec des chefs pareils qu'on vouloit combattre les jeunes et entreprenants généraux Français.

Le jeudi 7 Mr Aidut [?] général français qui comandoit le convoit écrivit au Consul Caruson qu'il apprenoit que son apparition devant le Port de Malte y causoit de l'inquiétude, mais qu'il le chargeoit d'assurer le Grand Maître qu'il n'avoit aucune vue hostile contre Malte qui étoit amie de la République Française, cette assurance calma l'esprits. Effectivement l'Ordre étoit en paix avec la République Française dont les vaisseaux recevoient à Malte tous les secours dont ils avoient besoin.

Le même jour, 7, le vaisseaux et la frégate de l'Ordre venant de la Sicile travers. . . . paisiblement le convoi Française ce qui fit encore plus croire que la Paix ne . . . pas troublée.

Enfin le samedi 9 Juin, arrive le reste d'armée et escadre Français commandant par le célèbre Bonaparte qui fit demander verbalement à 4 heures de l'après midi par le Consul Caruson que l'on reçût dans le Port de Malte toute l'armée Française qui étoit composée de 18 vaisseaux de ligne de 90 autres bâtimens de guerre, corvettes, chaloupes canonières ou galiottes à bombes et de 300 bâtimens de transport qui portoient 60,000 hommes des meilleures troupes des France, cette immense flotte s'ettendoit depuis le Goze, jusqu'à Marsa Scirocco, et menaçoit en même tems tous les points attacables. Le Grand Maître assemble le Council qui répondit par une lettre dans laquelle on prioit Bonaparte de mettre par écrit la demande qu'il faisoit, lui faisant observer que les loix de l'Ordre, les règles de la neutralité, ne permettoient pas de recevoir plus de 4 vaisseaux à la fois, que la sûreté du port l'exigeoit, aussi le Council disoit enfin que l'Ordre avoit toujours été en paix avec la France qui l'avoit toujours assuré de son amitié.

Le Council remit cette espèce de supplique à 5 heures du soir au Consul Français Caruson qui la porta au Général Bonaparte abord du vaisseaux *L'Orient*, il lui remit aussi la liste des Maltais qui promettoient de se joindre aux Français et de massacrer les Chevaliers, s'ils se deffendoient, le signal devoit être le première bomb que Bonaparte feroit jetter sur la ville.

Le nombre des Maltais conspirateurs étoient de 4 mille Quand sur les 7 heures du soir on vit à Malte que Bonaparte ne envoyoit pas le Consul Caruson, alors seulement on se prepara ou l'on eut l'air de vouloir se préparer à se défendre ; on croyoit avec raison qu'on seroit attaqué le lendemain, l'on ordonna de faire prendre les armes aux milices, de pallasader et de transporter les poudres de la Cotoner dans la ville, chose qui auroit demandé au moins 8 jours dans des tems tranquils.

Comme il n'y avoit point général en chef, personne ne pouvoit donner d'ordre, et le Grand Maître ne sortait pas de son palais, on donna le comandement de l'enceinte de la Cotoner au Bailli de la Tour du Pin avec l'ordre de faire transporter les poudres dans la ville mais on [ne ?] lui donna personne pour faire ce transport, il y avoit cependant plus de $^{10}/_m$ barils de poudre à transporter à plus d'une demie lieue et le port à traverser. Le Grand Croix prit avec lui 16 Chevaliers qui rassemblèrent 200 Portfait, ils commencèrent cette périlleuse opération, voici quels étoient les comandants.

Le Prince Camille de Rohan, Sénéchal Comandant les Milices de la Campagne, ayant sous lui pour lieutenants Généraux les Baillis de Clugny et Tomasi. L'Isle du Goze étoit comandé par le Com^r de Megrigny Villebertin qui en étoit le Gouveneur. L'Isle du Comin par le Chevalier de Valin, La Tour Rouge par le C^r St Simon lequel voiant les Français débarquer déserta et passe de l'autre côté, La Melleha par le Comandeur de Bizieu, St. Paul par le Chev^r de la Perouse, St. Julien par le Chev^r de Preville, ces deux postes étoient sous le comandement du Capitaine de Vaisseaux St Felix. St. Tomas et Marsa Scirocco étoient comandés par le Chevalier du Pin de la Gueriviere. La cité Valette par le Bailli de Loras, Maréchal de l'Ordre. La Floriana par le Bailli de Belmont. Les forts Manuel et Tigné par les Baillis Courgeaux et La Tour St. Quentin. Le Fort Ricasoli par le Bailli d'Illiette. Le Château St. Ange par le Com^r de Castellan. Le Bourg par le Comand^r de Goudrecourt. L'Isle de la Sangle par le Bailli Suffran St. Troppez qui étoit comandant des vaisseaux. Burmola par le Capitaine de Vaisseau Subiras, l'enceinte de la Cotoner par le Bailli de la Tour du Pin, mais on n'y avoit placé aucun canon. Le Bailli Tomasi vouloit défendre les retranchement du Nasciar mais on eut l'attention de ne lui donner aucune pièce de canon de campagne ni d'autres.

Toutes ces dispositions se firent pendant la nuit pour défendre tous les points et 7 Lieues de côte à peine avoit-on $^7/_m$ hommes dont voici l'état :

Le Régiment de Malte	500
Les Gardes du Grand Maître	200
Le Bataillon des Vaisseaux	400
Le Bataillon des Galères	300
À peu près 100 vieux Canoniers	100
Un Corps de Milices appellés Chasseurs	1,200
1,200 Matelots de Galères et des Vaisseaux qui servoient de Canoniers	1,200
et $^3/_m$ hommes de très mauvaise Milices qui furent discipées dans la matinée du jour	3,000
	6,900

Mais le lendemain Dimanche, 10 Juin, Bonaparte débarqua à 4 heures du matin sur 7 points au Goze, au Cumin, à la Mulleta, au Selmun, à St. George, à St. Julien et à la Tombarella, il n'éprouva aucune difficulté. Le Comandant Bardonanche n'avoit fait charger aucune fourgasse, aussi elles furent inutiles.

Comme l'on n'avoit point de vivres dans les forts ni dans les tours, les Maltais ne voulurent pas s'y enfermer pour les deffendre. Bandonanche ne fit distribuer que 5 ou 6 cartouches par soldat dans lesquelles il n'y avoit pas de poudre, les affûts de canons étoient tellement pourris que quand on tira, la plupart se rompirent, il manquoit même des repouloir [sic] pour charger les canons.

Le découragement se mit parmi les Maltais attachées à l'Ordre, les conspirateurs en profitèrent pour leur dire que tous les Chevaliers les trahirent ce qui mit un grand désordre. Il est vrai que les chefs des atteliers et ceux qui avoient la confiance du Grand Maître trahisoient l'Ordre.

Que faisoit Hompesch, qui étoit aimé du peuple Maltais il ne fut voir aucune poste, aucune troupe, aucun fort, il resta dans son palais ayant pour aide-de-camp ou pour mieux dire pour secrétaire le Comandeur de St. Priest qui ne sortoit pas de palais lequel avoit probablement le plan de cette infâme intrigue et dirigeoit F. Hompesch. Il n'y avoit point de général en chef, ainsi de tous les postes on s'addressoit au Grand Maître; St. Priest répondit pour lui, il donnoit [des réponses] tellement contradictoires que le comandant du Fort Ricasoli ayant demandé de la poudre on lui donna l'ordre d'en prendre au fort Manoel et ce comandant du Château de St. Ange qui manquoit de poudre en demanda on donna ordre au comandant du Fort Ricasoli de lui en donner, et cela pendant que le Bailli de la Tour du Pin étoit occupé à debloyer le magazin à poudre de la Cotonère, d'ailleurs les Maltais fuyoient comme les lièvres. Cent Français qui avoient débarqués à St. Julien mirent en fuite le Régiment des Milices de Birchircara qui étoit de 1,200 hommes. Le Bailli Thomasi voulut défendre le retranchement du Nasciar, contre les Français qui avoient débarqués à la Melleha et à St. Paul, mais il fut tourné par un corps de Français qui avoient débarqués à St. George et à St. Julien, il fut abandonné par ses Milices Maltaises, et eut bien de la peine à se retirer dans la ville. Le Général Vaubois marcha tout de suite sur la Cité Vielle qui étant sans troupes, ni canons, ni vivres, ni comandants, lui ouvrit ses portes à 9 heures du matin et à 10 heures toute la campagne, toutes les tours, excepté celle de la Marsa Scirocco étoient au pouvoir des Français la pluspart des Chevaliers qui étoient dans ces différentes postes furent fait prisonniers, et conduits à Bonaparte qui leur dit comment pouviez vous croire qu'il fût possible de vous défendre avec des misérables paysans contre les troupes qui ont vaincu et soumis l'Europe.

Les Maltais massacr[èr]ent plusieurs Chevaliers, M. de Vallé Montazet, Dormis, et D'Endelard qui étoient de garde à la porte de la ville, ils en blessèrent plusieurs autres. Mais Ferdinand Hompesch ne sortoit pas de son palais et ne fit rien pour remettre l'ordre. À 11 heures du matin on fit sortir du port une galère, une chaloupe canonière et deux galliotes pour tâcher d'inquiéter le débarquement que faisoient les Français à St. Julien, on leur avoit donné 20 coups par canon quand ils leur eurent tiré ils rentrèrent dans le port on fit aussi une petite sortie du côté de la Pietà, mais les troupes ne tinrent pas un instant contre les tirailleurs Français elles se sauvèrent dans les fortifications de la Florian qui n'aiant pas de canons ne purent les protéger.

À midi il ne restoit au service de l'Ordre que 4/m hommes dont la plus part étoient de mauvaise volonté avec cela il falloit défendre la ville, le Fort Manoel, Tigné, Ricasoli, St. Ange, la Cotonère, le Bourg et L'Isle de la Sangle si on avoit voulu bien se défendre, il auroit fallu abandonner tous ces forts qui sont éloignés, les uns des autres et même séparés de la mer, rassembler les 4/m hommes dans la ville qui est très forte en chasser tous ceux des habitans qu'on suspectoit de cette manière on auroit pu tenir deux mois et attendre d'être secourru. La ville se remplit des fuyards, des femmes, ou d'enfants des paysans pendant le reste de cette journée les forts tirèrent les canons qui étoient en état de tirer ce qui faisoit du bruit mais peu de mal aux Français.

Sur les 9 heures du soir les portes étant fermés une terreur panique saisit le Bailli Suffren S^t· Tropez qui abandonna son poste de l'Isle de la Sangle, il se refugia avec ses officiers de vaisseaux dans la ville. Ils furent obliger de rester long tems à la porte jusque [à ce que] le Grand Maître eût ordonné qu'on ouvrit. Le Bailli Suffren S^t· Tropez étoit connu pour être lâche et méchant. C'est le seul Grand Croix qui dans cette dernière occasion se soit mal conduit. Il fut tellement aveuglé par la peur qu'il ne reflêchit pas, qu'il avoit en avant de lui Subiral à Burmola, et le Bailli La Tour du Pin à la Cotonère. Dans la ville il y avoit une telle confusion que les patrouilles se fusillent, il y avoit continuellement de fausses allertes. À minuit le Tribunal de la Rote, les barons, et les principaux habitans allèrent au palais, ils disoient à Ferdinand Hompesch qu'il falloit capituler sur leur demande il fit assembler le Conseil, il y fut décidé qu'on enverroit à Bonaparte les Barons Souza et Formosa le Consul d'Holland et qu'on ferroit une suspension d'armes pour traiter de la capitulation, pour faire une pareille demarche il étoit du [?] du Grand Maître d'assembler le Conseil complet, qui étoit composé de tous les Chefs des Langues, des Grand Croix et des deux anciens Chevaliers de chaque Langue ce qui ne fut pas fait. À ce conseil ne furent pas appelés les Baillis Gourgeos, la Tour S$^{t.}$ Quentin, Belmont, Du Dillert, La Tour du Pin, Glugni et Tigné; on connoissoit le courage de ces Grands Croix que se seroient opposés à une . . . . si humiliante.

Le lundi 11 Juin à 5 heures du matin on reçut dans tous les forts l'ordre de ne plus tirer qui étoit signé par S$^{t.}$ Priest. Le Chevalier du Pin de la Guiriviere se défendit à Marsa Scirocco jusqu'à 5 heures du matin, mais n'aiant pas de vivres, il fit une capitulation honorable, il rentra en ville avec sa garnison, il y apprit avec le plus grand étonnement que la ville se rendoit. Bonaparte ne fit point jetter de bombe ni tirer de canons contre la ville parceque les Maltais conspirateurs étoient convenus de massacrer les Chevaliers à ce signal et que Bonaparte n'a pas voulu permettre un pareil crime.

Bonaparte répondit au Bailli Souza et au Consul d'Hollande, qu'il entreroit dans la ville le mardi 12 Juin que pendant cet interval il régleroit la manière dont il vouloit traiter l'Ordre avec la médiation du Chargé d'Affaires d'Espagne M. Amut.

C'est aussi que la forte place de Malte a été soumise aux Français qui ont trouvé 1,800 canons, 30 mille fusils, 12,000 barils de poudre, des vivres pour 6 mois, deux vaisseaux, une frégate, 3 galères, et d'autres petits bâtimens de guerre et trois millions de livres en or et argent qui étoit dans la sacristie de St. Jean et qui auroit dû être emploié pour la défense de l'Ordre.

Ferdinand Hompesch n'a rien demandé pour l'Ordre ni pour les Chevaliers, il n'y avoit pas 11 mois qu'il étoit élu Grand Maître, mais il a obtenu pour lui un traitement considérable de 600,000 francs argent comptant et 300,000 francs de pension jusqu'à ce que la France lui ait fait avoir une souveraineté. On doit observer que les Francais ont déposedés beaucoup de petits souverains, ils n'en ont traité aucun aussi avantageusement que celui de Malte.

Les Chevaliers de Malte Français qui ont plus de 7 ans de résidence peuvent rentrer en France, tous les members de l'Ordre Français ont 700 francs de pension ceux qui ont soixante ans ont 1000 francs. Ce fut Bosredon Ransijat, le Bailli di Frisari, le Chargé d'Affaires d'Espagne et quelques Maltais qui ont fait et signé les arrangemens pour l'Ordre.

Le mardi 12 Juin avant que Bonaparte entre dans la ville Piccaut dut porter l'ordre à M$^{r.}$ O'Hara, Ministre de Russie de partir de Malte dans 3 heures, cet ordre regardoit les Chevaliers Russes. St. Priest a une comanderie en Russie, mais il eut la permission de rester auprès du Grand Maître, il avoit rendu trop de service pour n'en avoir quelque préférence.

Gardons-nous de faire le tort aux héros, Villers de la L'Isle Adam, de le comparer au misérable Hompesch. L'Isle Adam défendit une mauvaise place pendant six mois contre un grand conquérant, il ne parti de Rhodes que le dernier en menant avec lui tout l'Ordre, les reliques, les vases sacrées et les archives. Ferdinand Hompesch n'a pas défendu une excellente place seulement deux jours, il s'est sauvé comme un voleur, en portant le prix de la trahison, il est parti le dimanche 17 Juin, laissant les membres de l'Ordre à la discrétion du vainqueur, ainsi que le trésor de St Jean, et les archives de l'Ordre, et qui amène-t-il avec lui, le Com^r· St. Priest et le Nommé Gravagna qui étoit l'ami du Consul de France Caruson. Quelques personnes croient que St. Priest et Gravagna conduisoient cette infâme trame. Le Bailli Suffren S^t· Tropez celui qui le 10 au soir abandonna si lâchement son poste, le Comd^r· Boisredone qui est frère du traître Comm. Bosredon Ransjiat et quelques autres la récompense des traîtres a été de les placer au service de France. Bosredon Ransijat est president de la municipalité ayant pour secrétaire le nommé Doublet, démocrate connu, qui étoit secrétaire du Grand Maître Bardonanche qui comandoit l'artillerie de la place de Malte. Tousard qui étoit directeur du génie a été fait chef de brigade du corps du génie il a suivi Bonaparte. Je ne connois pas le marché qu'a fait Fay, peut-être aura-t-il quelque emploi en France. Bonaparte fit dire qu'il donneroit cet emploi à ceux des Chevaliers qui voulloient aller avec lui.

Quarante huit ont pris le parti sous ses enseignes, je vois dire que les 3 quarts sont des jeunes gens fort bons sujets ils se regardent [?] comme déshonnorés qu'il ne seroient reçus nullepart.

Le mardi 19 l'armée Française partit pour la grande expédition que nous ne conoissons pas et le lendemain la sortie du port fut permise. Je prie un Chevalier qui part demain de remettre cette lettre à un bureau de poste qu'il croira sûr pour qu'elle vous parvienne. J'écrirai par d'autres voyes po . . . [torn] Grand Empereur qui a voulu nous protéger, . . . sache [?] ce qui a occasionné notre destruction rien ne evit [?] et ne peut égaller mon chagrin ; mais la mort doit bientôt mettre fin à mes malheurs. Je suis témoin de la destruction de mon Ordre, j'entends briser les chefs d'œuvres en reliquaires d'or et d'argent, je vois démolir les armes de nos braves prédécesseurs chose que les Turcs n'ont pas fait à Rhodes. Mon oncle et moi avons travaillé et employé les talents que Dieu nous avoit donné pour l'Ordre qui m'en avoit grandement récompensé. J'ay plus de 80 ans et je suis accablé d'infirmité. J'avais demandé qu'on me portât sur la Bréege [?] pour au moins donner un . . . [torn]. Je n'ai pas vu les traités particuliers qu'a pu faire Hompesch.

S'il en a fait ils sont toujours tenus secrets, mais je rends compte de sa conduite ; on pourroit s'il y avoit une justice, l'interroger sur tout ce qu'il a fait et qui est de notoriété publique comme d'avoir conservé dans les places les personnes connus par leur attachement aux principes français, de n'avoir pas voulu qu'on chargeât les fourgasses, de n'avoir pas retirer les poudres dans la ville, de n'avoir pas fait mettre des vivres dans les postes. Il ne peut s'excuser de l'avoir oublié, attendu que plusieurs membres de l'Ordre le lui ont demandé par écrit, et d'être constament dans son palais. Il est nécessaire que cette lettre soit connue et qu'elle soit imprimée surtout dans le 'Courrier de Londres.'

Je désire d'autant plus que cette lettre soit rendue publique que je crois que ce sera la seule punition qu'auront les imbéciles, les lâches et les traîtres qui nous ont livrés. J'ay l'honneur &c.

(Signed) LE BAILLI DE TIGNÉE.

At the dispersion of the Knights from Malta by order of Bonaparte in June 1798, the Bailli de Tigné (on account of his great age, being then over eighty) remained in Valetta, and was there confined during the two years' siege, but in the month following that of the surrender of the French garrison, he embraced the first opportunity which had occurred, to deny the truth of the statements which had been made in his name to the prejudice of Hompesch, and on the 3rd October 1800 published the following repudiation in Italian, a translation of which appeared in the Bamberg Gazette, No. 325 of the 21st November 1801, under the following heading:—

Bamberg, 20*th November* 1801.[1]

We have been requested to publish the following declaration at full length. We have hesitated so much the less in doing so, as the imputations laid to the charge of the Grand Master Hompesch have been pointed out by the Vienna 'Court Gazette,' No. 33, as being '*false* and *calumnious*.'

'PROTEST.

'A letter of five sheets is in circulation at St. Petersburg dated the 21st June 1798, of which I am marked out as the author. It is full of the most atrocious calumnies against our lawful chief, the Grand Master of Malta.

'Though this document bears all the marks of improbability, it has yet acquired some credit, because the calumniators have had the assurance to publish it in print. My sorrow was inexpressible, when I learned that so dark a deception, and destitute of all credibility had nevertheless occasioned so unhappy a division in our Order. If every honest man is obliged to clear himself from a similar imputation which closely attacks his honour, this duty is the more strongly imposed upon an ecclesiastic to whom the editing of a libel against his superior is falsely attributed. I am persuaded that every one who is acquainted with me, has given no credit to such a calumny.

'Looking at its want of likelihood, and its absurdity, it would not have made any impression upon the public, if they did not so readily accept reports which tend to tarnish the reputation of any one, whosoever he may be. This is a sufficient reason for me to give the lie to the defamer, and to defend my own honour thus unjustly attacked. I might adduce numerous motives to remove the suspicion from myself that I could ever have been capable of composing such a libel. My years, my conduct, manners, and habits, sufficiently justify me; they would rather form my panegyric.

'It will suffice for me to observe that at the time when I am supposed to have written that document, I was on the point of death, suffering from a mortal complaint, and as a supposed dying man, had received the Holy Sacrament.

'Can any reasonable person suppose that in such a condition I could have thought of such calumnies, or could even have dictated them? What advantage could I expect to derive from so dark a proceeding, which was likely to expose me to the hatred and destation of every reasonable and honest man? I declare then to all my brethren, Ecclesiastics of my Order, and to all those to whom this justification shall come to hand,

---

[1] Cobbett, vol. ii. pp. 1077–1078; M.P.L. MSS. 418.

that I have not written, and that I could not have written that libel, which is circulated in my name.

'I call to witness all those who have known me and have had connexion with me, for they will acknowledge me incapable of having written it.

'I desire that this declaration signed by me, and duly attested by a notary, shall be set forth wherever it may be necessary, in order that the public may likewise have authentic proof of the truth, and of my innocence.

'Done in the city of Valetta, in the Island of Malta, the 3rd October 1800. (Signed) THE BAILLI DE TIGNÉ, Grand Prior of Champagne.'

The 'Bamberg Gazette,' however, does not give the attestation, which is as follows [1]:—

All that the venerable Bailli Renato Jacobo de Tigné has written in his defence is true, and we the undersigned, who know him well, declare on our oath that he is incapable of having written the letter attributed to him.

The serious illness which he was then suffering, during which he received the last rites of the Holy Sacrament, his decrepit age of 82, his unalterable moderation, his religious piety, and his uniformity in not only doing good, but of speaking well of all, with whomsoever he came in contact, still more so of his Superior, are sufficient for us to be assured that we are not mistaken in his character. In attestation of the truth herein expressed, we subscribe our names, in the place, and on the day above mentioned.

(Signed) LE BAILLI DE BARER, Grand Treasurer of the Order.
,, LE CHIOLE FRICOR, Commandeur.
,, GO. F. FRANCESCO, Fra Conventual Capucin.
,, FRA GIO LUIGI RIDOLI, Fra Conventual Capucin, formerly Secretary of the Italian Langue.
,, FRANCESCO ARENA, Administrator of the Valetta Granaries.
,, AGOSTINO CHIAPPE, Merchant of Valetta.
,, In the presence of Notary CRISTOPHER FRENDO, who received the solemn act.

Further proof of the Bailli de Tigné's innocence is to be found in the attestations of the Chevalier de Dienne, and of the Bailli des Barres, which were duly forwarded to Hompesch, under date of the 28th October 1800.

EXTRAIT D'UNE LETTRE DU BAILLI DES BARRES AU GRAND MAÎTRE.

Malte, 6 *Octobre* 1800.[2]

Vous recevrez, Monsigneur, le désaveu authentique du Bailli de Tigné, que j'ai adressé à M. le Chevalier de Dienne, pour vous le faire passer.

[1] M.P.L. MSS. 418.
[2] De Villeneuve-Bargemont, *Monumens des Grands Maîtres de l'Ordre de St. Jean de Jérusalem*, vol. ii. p. 446.

Ce bon viellard a été indigné d'un procédé digne de vos ennemis. Votre Eminence lui rend trop de justice pour le soupçonner d'avoir jamais été capable d'un pareil écrit contre elle.

EXTRAIT D'UNE LETTRE DU CHEVALIER DE DIENNE.

De Messine, 28 *Octobre* 1800.

Il paraît effectivement miraculeux que M. le Bailli de Tigné ait été conservé par le ciel, jusqu'au moment qu'il eut signé sa protestation. Il est mort le 16 du courant.

Il a fini avec cette résignation d'un véritable religieux ; il a emporté les regrets de tous ceux qui le connaissaient, continuant à protester contre l'act impie qu'on lui attribuait. Il a supplié, jusqu'à son dernier moment, ceux qui l'assistaient de rendre public, qu'il n'avait jamais fait ni même pensé à faire un acte aussi irréligieux ; que l'on pouvait le croire, puisqu'il était au moment de rendre compte à son juge suprême.

(Les Baillis de Clugny, d'Auray de Saint-Poix, de Belmont et de Rabastens, s'empressèrent de déclarer que la rétractation du Bailli de Tigné était véritable.)

The prolonged silence of the Bailli de Tigné due to his forced confinement within the beleaguered city of Valetta, until September 1800, was most unfortunate; for upon receipt of this spurious letter ascribed to him the Grand Priory of Russia at once issued a manifesto, dated the 26th August 1798, of which the following are the concluding passages [1]:—

It is to be observed, that in the infamous Treaty which yielded up Malta to the French, the interests of the Grand Master were alone attended to, and nothing stipulated in favour of the Order. The fact is explained by this simple reflection. Ferdinand Hompesch and his adherents have sold Malta, and they alone have received the price, in fact care alone was taken not to summon to the Council which decided on the surrender, the Sixteen Elders of the Complete Council, nor the Baillis Tigné, Gourgas, Clugny, Tillet, Bellemont, Loras, La Tour St. Quentin, La Tour du Pin, and others, who would have constituted more than half the Council, and without whose consent no decision could properly have been taken.

But they were certain that those brave Knights would have rejected with horror the dishonourable Treaty which they were anxious to conclude, and it was found more expedient to ignore, than to consult them. Equally inaccessible to the unjust prejudice which sees crimes everywhere, and to the culpable injustice that tolerates them, we have been guided in our enquiries into the events at Malta by those principles only which honour avows, and which equity prescribes, we have not advanced a fact without the proof before our eyes.

Throughout the whole proceedings, truth has demonstrated to us, that Ferdinand Hompesch is attainted and convicted of improvidence, cowardice, and perfidy, upon which considerations we, the Knights

---

[1] M.P.L., MSS. 420; *Annual Register*, 1798, pp. 275, 276.

of the Grand Priory of Russia, and others present at St. Petersburg, regard Ferdinand Hompesch as deposed from the rank to which we elevated him, and by virtue of our own laws we hold ourselves absolved from the obedience which we should owe him as our chief, and we invite our brethren of the other Grand Priories to unite with us in a proceeding which honour has rendered indispensable, and from which we could not abstain without participating in the opprobrium which Ferdinand Hompesch, Ransijat, St. Tropes, and others have so justly deserved.

We throw ourselves into the arms of our August and Sovereign Protector, Paul I, Emperor of All the Russias.

In the meantime, Hompesch, unaware of the machinations proceeding against him, took immediate steps to address his representative at St. Petersburg, and the Grand Priory of Russia there. of what had befallen the Order, never doubting their allegiance. These letters were written three days after his arrival at Trieste from Malta, whence he had sailed on the 17th June 1798.

[Translation.]

To the Venerable Bailli Count de Litta.

Trieste, 25th July 1798.[1]

The fatal circumstances, which have compelled us to abandon our residence of Malta, have profoundly afflicted our heart, but the hope, that with the consent of the Sovereigns our Protectors, the chief place of our Order may be found in some honourable and fixed abode, sustains and consoles us.

You will remit to the Venerable Grand Prior and Chapter of Russia the letter enclosed herewith, by which they are enjoined to attend to the affairs of the Grand Priory during the period prescribed by our statutes, and to fulfil with perfect exactitude and union the duties enjoined by our wise laws. With regard to the sums received and in your possession, and which you will continue to manage, we now order you to retain them in your own hands, as well as those which you may hereafter receive, in order that they may be available for the indispensable expenses which will be incurred during the negotiations which will soon be commenced for the maintenance of our Order.

Feeling perfectly assured of your zeal in its behalf, we rely upon you with perfect confidence.   (Signed) Hompesch.

Trieste, 25th July 1798.[2]

To the Venerable Grand Prior and Chapter of Russia.

You will have been profoundly afflicted upon hearing that an imperious necessity has compelled us to remove from Malta our residence and the chief place of our Order; but our mutual consolation in these misfortunes must be found in the maintenance of a perfect

[1] M.P.L. MSS. 421.   [2] Ibid.

union between the Chief of the Order and its members, and to attain that object our dearest efforts will be directed. On your side, you will attain this by your constancy, in drawing together more closely the ties of brotherhood by strictly performing your duties. You cannot have any doubt but that my paternal solicitude will be exercised, in obtaining as promptly as possible, through the medium of the Princes our protectors, a place where we may assemble, and where we may together recommence the exercise of our laws, and re-establish our statutory tribunals, but at the present moment it is impossible for us to fix a date, however dear to our heart will be the time for us to be found in the midst of our very dear and well-beloved friends, members of the Order.

In the meantime, and in virtue of the holy obedience which is your duty, we order you not to seek by the removal of the 'Common Mother' a pretext for the discontinuance of your assemblies, but on the contrary to continue as usual, and if possible with more zeal than ever, to attend to the affairs of your Priory.

(Signed) The Grand Master, HOMPESCH.

But all these efforts were of no avail; a scapegoat had to be found, and Hompesch was to be the victim; the spurious letter ascribed to De Tigné had succeeded in alienating not only the Grand Priory of Russia but also the ruling sovereigns of Russia and to some extent Austria. The only possible chance for the restoration of the Order was now deemed by the recalcitrant Knights to be that of placing themselves entirely under the sovereignty of the Czar. For this purpose, on the 26th of the following month, the Grand Priory of Russia issued the following protest:—

PROTEST OF THE GRAND PRIORY OF RUSSIA.

Thursday, 26th August 1798.[1]

We, the Baillies, Grand Cross, Commanders, Knights of the Grand Priory of Russia, and other Knights of St. John of Jerusalem at an Extraordinary Assembly, at the Priorial Palace of the Order, in the Imperial residence of St. Petersburg, being obliged to turn our attention towards Malta, what profound grief must we now feel in beholding that ancient and noble theatre of our glory, treacherously sold by a Convention as null in its principles as it was infamous in its effects. What indignation must we not experience in reflecting, that after an insignificant attack of some hours, the cowards who bore the name of Knights surrendered that bulwark of Christianity, which the example of their predecessors and the sacred laws of honour enjoined them to defend to the last drop of their blood, to banditti a hundred times more infidel than those against whom the duties of their profession armed them. In the course of a war of seven centuries, the Knights of St. John of Jerusalem experienced more than once the vicissitudes of fortune; more than once did the alarmed Christians behold the

[1] M.P.L., MSS. 420; *Annual Register*, 1798, p. 276.

Shield of Faith, if we may so call it, broken before its defenders, and the entire Order preserving no other refuge but in the hearts of its Knights. But the most noble always signalised their various successes, and their glory in the most disastrous reverses was as much respected as it was acknowledged to be splendid in their most brilliant exploits.

Since the origin of the Order and until now, the name of one traitor alone has sullied its annals; by what fatality do we now see it precipitated into the abyss of disgrace and ignominy, and by those very persons who were enjoined to preserve it?

If the speedy punishment of Amaret did not remedy the evils which his perfidy occasioned, it at least testified the principles of this illustrious corps.

Glory! glory! upon Villiers de l'Isle Adam, and opprobrium upon his infamous adversary. If it depends upon us at the present moment to wash off, in the blood of traitors, the crimes they have committed in shamefully bartering the ancient and superb inheritance of honour which our ancestors transmitted, let us at least show with energy the just resentment, hatred, and contempt, with which their felony inspires us; let us reject with horror the vile treaty which will dishonour them for ever, and devote them irrevocably to that remorse and infamy which will for ever be their portion. For ourselves, united under the glorious auspices of Paul I, the August Emperor of All the Russias, and the Protector of our Order, We protest in the face of God, and in the presence of all those with whom honour and fidelity are still regarded as virtues, against everything that perfidy has permitted to the detriment of our Order.

We solemnly disavow every proceeding contrary to the sacred laws of our Constitution. We regard as degraded from their rank and dignities all those who drew up, accepted, or consented to the infamous treaty that surrendered Malta, as well as all those who shall be convicted of having co-operated directly or indirectly in that work of iniquity. We renounce from this time all sort of connection with those unworthy, infected, and corrupted members. Finally, we will never acknowledge for our brethren but those who shall manifest the conformity of their principles with ours by adhering to the present protestation, whilst we reserve to ourselves the power of extending or renewing the same according to the exigency of the case. In the faith of which we have proposed the present act, we have unanimously accepted and stamped it with the seal of the Grand Priory of Russia.

Dated at St. Petersburg this day, Thursday, 26th August 1798.

This protest was immediately confirmed by Paul I, who issued the following declaration:—

DECLARATION OF THE EMPEROR OF RUSSIA.[1]

St. Petersburg, 26th *August* 1798.

Having attentively examined the acts presented to us by the Baillies, Knights of the Grand Cross, the Commanders and Knights of the Grand Priory of Russia, as well as the other Knights of the illustrious Order of

[1] *Annual Register*, 1798, p. 276.

St. John of Jerusalem, assembled in the Palace of the said Priory in our capital, acts which contain first, a protestation against the prejudicial conduct of the ci-devant Grand Master of the Order, Ferdinand Hompesch, and other Knights who have violated their engagements in surrendering, without any defence, their principal city and their whole State, and made a dishonourable capitulation with the chief of the French who attacked the Island of Malta, stipulating only for the personal advantage of the Grand Master and his adherents ; 2^{ndly.} the confidence of the members of that Order in us, as its protectors, marked by the desire that we should attend to its preservation, and an expression of readiness to submit to any arrangements which we might think necessary to make for its benefit.

We hereby confirm the said acts in their full force, and to testify our acknowledgements for the zeal of the members of the illustrious Order of St. John of Jerusalem we take all the well disposed of the corps under our supreme direction.

We promise, upon our Imperial word, not only to maintain it in all its institutions, privileges, and honours, but also to employ all means in our power for its re-establishment in the respectable state which it formerly held, and with which it contributed to the advantage of Christianity in general, and of every well-governed State in particular.

Not satisfied with obtaining the sanction of Paul I to their proceedings, the Russian Priory approached His Holiness the Pope, for the purpose of obtaining his approval of the steps they had taken.

Accordingly, on the 27th September, the Bailli de Litta forwarded a copy of the Czar's declaration, and that of the Priory's protest to His Holiness. Pius VI, who was then residing at the Carthusian Monastery of Cassini, near Florence, an exile from his dominions, at first appeared disinclined to condemn Hompesch, but finally replied on the 17th October 1798, as follows[1] :—

[Translation.]

The Monastery at Cassini, Florence,

17th October 1798.

Pius P. P. VI.

To my well-beloved Son,—Salutation and Apostolic Benediction.

By an extraordinary and singular coincidence we received your dispatch from St. Petersburg, dated the 27th ultimo, at the same time as another from the Chevalier Hompesch at Trieste. The latter asks us for a dispensation of the noviciate, and of the Carovane for the probationers, while you place before us, by a protest and by manifesto, the demerits of the said Hompesch, with regard to the Order.

To the latter, Hompesch, we have replied, that being, as he is, under censure and protestation of the Knights of the Russian Priory, he is not at present in a position to obtain from us the petition he has advanced, nevertheless as the Russian Priory so far is alone in this action, it is insufficient to declare him fallen from the magisterial dignity ; therefore it

[1] M.P.L., MSS. 420.

will be necessary to wait for the decision of the other Langues, to verify whether Hompesch is guilty of the crime which is laid to his charge by the said Priory.

But in order that whilst the investigation of the truth of the circumstances is being conducted, and that the Russian Priory should not be prejudiced in any extraordinary emergency which may arise, a Knight of the said Priory might be deputed, who would be furnished with the authority of the Grand Master, in accordance with the prescriptions of the Order.

Such is the answer we have sent to Hompesch at Trieste, and such is our reply to you, in order that you both may be instructed as to the course to be followed, and adapt yourselves thereto. Whilst we remain, &c.

(Signed) PIUS.

To THE BAILLI COUNT DE LITTA,
St. Petersburg.

His Holiness, on the same date, informed Hompesch that he had received copies of the manifesto and protest issued by the Grand Priory of Russia, and that in consequence thereof, he, His Holiness, was unable to accede to certain requests which Hompesch had made, until such time as he had answered satisfactorily the charges made against him, and had become repossessed of the authority of which he had been deprived. The letter ran as follows [1]:—

Ibid. 17th October 1798.

PIUS P. P. VI.

To MY WELL-BELOVED SON,—Salutation and Apostolic Benediction.

On the same day we received two letters, one from you, dated Trieste the 30th of the past month of September, wherein you petition us to grant a dispensation in favour of the probationers of your Order in Convent, and in the 'Carovane,' without prejudice to their seniority.

The other letter is one, from the Bailli Litta at St. Petersburg, under date of the 27th of the past August, covering a manifest and a protest issued by the Russian Priory, wherein we are told that you have been charged by the members of that Priory to acquaint us thereof.

In these documents it is alleged that, by unquestionable evidence, you have been found wanting in your duty towards the Order, and your personal honour; and that consequently you have forfeited the magisterial dignity, and all the rights appertaining thereto, and that such forfeiture must apply to all who have accepted, or consented directly or indirectly to the cession of the Island, and therefore they desire no longer to acknowledge, or have any connection or correspondence with unworthy and corrupt members, or acknowledge as brethren, those who do not accept the terms and principles contained in the protest they have forwarded to us.

In such state of the case, you can readily understand that we cannot grant your requests until you are cleared from the imputations laid to your charge, and restored to those rights from which they declare you have fallen.

[1] M.P.L., MSS. 420.

It is true that the deposition of a Grand Master cannot depend upon the vote of a single Priory, and that it should be necessary for the other Langues to adhere thereto.

In the meanwhile, for the government of the Russian Priory, they can depute one of their own body to administrate and provide for the needs which might occur, until such time as the facts have been heard and examined with all impartiality. We remain, &c.

(Signed) PIUS.

Whilst this correspondence was proceeding, Hompesch was, at last, made aware of the intrigues being conducted against him at St. Petersburg, and on the 12th October he accordingly published the following protest, appealing to the friendly Powers, more particularly to that of Naples, and forwarded a copy also to His Holiness the Pope.

PROTEST OF HIS HIGHNESS THE GRAND MASTER, ETC.[1]

The Grand Master of the Order of St. John of Jerusalem of the Holy Sepulchre and of St. Anthony of Vienna, in his own private name, as well as in that of the entire Order of which he is the legitimate Chief and Representative, protests before God, and all Sovereigns, and before the entire Universe, against the effects of the internal revolution which the French Republic brought about in the Island of Malta, also against the seduction, by means of which that Republic perverted some members of that Order, attracted a number of the inhabitants of the city, allured and deceived the fidelity of the people, and rendered vain the means of defence, and made futile all military dispositions.

Protests, further, against the hostile invasion by troops, at the very moment the Order was fulfilling towards them the duties of neutrality and of the most considerate hospitality; against their manifest and unjust usurpation of its property, rights, &c.

Formally protests against the document, maliciously called 'Convention,' conceived and dictated in the form and manner we have seen, by the Commander in Chief Bonaparte.

This document is nothing more than a violent law imposed by infamous traitors over whom the enemy prevailed to accomplish his designs by means of the French and Maltese Deputies and other rebels there, and then depriving the Grand Master and Council of the power to examine and refuse the said Convention.

Specially protests against his compulsory eviction and departure from the Island, to which he was subsequently forced, never having pretended, or could he pretend, to cede the Sovereignty to any Power, without the consent of His Majesty the King of the Two Sicilies, to whom alone the Sovereignty of the Island belongs, an acknowledgment which, as formerly, the Order always owes to His Majesty for a Principality over which he at all times preserves his rights.

The Grand Master energetically protests against all which personally refers to him in the Second Article of the Convention, believing it to have been maliciously invented and inserted, whether it regards the pecuniary

[1] De Villeneuve-Bargemont, vol. ii. p. 413; M.P.L., MSS. 420.

compensations, or that of the Sovereignty, which they (the Deputies) by means of French influence wished him to renounce, detesting and rejecting for ever all such, as having never been desired or solicited by him in any manner whatsoever.

The Grand Master further protests against all or any other Acts, whether private or public, made subsequently to the Convention, considering them as the result of undue and overwhelming violence, in defiance of public and international rights, and as such, absolutely null and void.

And finally, in order that the present formal and solemn protest, conceived and resolved from the first moments when, under the auspices of the August Emperor and King, the Order and its Chief regained the opportunity of freely expressing their sentiments and desire, in this city of Trieste; having previously made known and manifested to whom without controversy the Sovereignty of the Island of Malta belongs, and further to all the friendly Powers and Protectors of the Order.

The Grand Master in his own name, as well as in that of all the Order, respectfully submits this protest to His Majesty the King of the Two Sicilies, as he will also to all other Sovereigns.

(Signed) HOMPESCH.

Trieste, 12th October 1798.

On the 30th October, Hompesch addressed the following pathetic appeal to the Emperor Paul:—

LETTRE DU GRAND MAÎTRE À L'EMPEREUR PAUL I[er.]

30 Octobre 1798, de Trieste.[1]

SIRE,—Ma profonde douleur, la surprise causée par un événement inattendu, mon juste étonnement de me voir exposé aux plus atroces calomnies, qui ont pu égarer les membres du Prieuré de Russie, remplissent d'amertume mon âme, et empoisonnent tous les momens de ma vie. Mais ce qui finit de m'accabler et de m'anéantir, c'est l'opinion de Votre Majesté Impériale, déclarée dans le décret qui suit le manifesto imprimé du Grand-Prieuré de Russie ; c'est son courroux.

J'y succomberais sans doute, si la connaissance que j'ai de la justice et de l'équité de Votre Majesté Impériale ne m'inspirait et de l'espoir et de la force; si je ne savais pas que la grandeur d'âme de Votre Majesté Impériale, ne se laissant borner par aucune prévention, surmont[e] les entraves de l'opinion et embrasse généreusement la vérité. Ce sont, Sire, ces qualités respectables dans lesquelles je mets toute ma confiance.

Je ne rappellerai point à Votre Majesté Impériale sa clémence marquée envers moi, ni les bons grâces dont elle a daigné m'honorer. Je ne ferai pas mention de mon zèle, et de mon empressement pour m'en rendre digne en faisant tous les efforts pour seconder ses vues, efforts qui m'ont suscité des ennemis innombrables et qui sont peut-être la source de mon malheur.

Dans tout autre situation, les bontés de Votre Majesté Impériale envers

[1] De Villeneuve-Bargemont, Monumens des Grands Maîtres de l'Ordre de St. Jean, vol. ii. p. 410.

moi, et mon entier dévouement à ses désirs, pourraient me servir d'appui ; dans la présente, où je suis obligé d'implorer sa justice et son équité, éclairée de l'amour pur de la vérité, elles ne sauraient être d'aucun poids.

Un Prince, opprimé par un tissu horrible d'iniquités, est aux pieds du son trône et demande respectueusement *et vivement de pouvoir se justifier vis-à-vis d'elle*. Votre Majesté Impériale vaudra-t-elle, pourra-t-elle lui refuser ce bienfait ?

On a abusé, Sire, de la crédulité de beaucoup de membres du Prieuré de Russie et, qu'il me soit permis de le dire, on attente à surprendre la religion de Votre Majesté Impériale.

De vils calomniateurs se sont addressés au Prieuré de Russie, et, en forgeant les accusations les plus absurdes, ils l'ont amené à publier un manifeste diffamant qui base sur une fausse supposition, c'est-à-dire, celle qui fait accroire au monde que j'ai pu adhérer à un projet dicté et publié par les Français, et sans autre approbation que celle des traîtres et rebelles convenus secrètement avec les ennemis.

A peine arrivé à Trieste, je n'ai rien eu de plus pressant que de soumettre à Votre Majesté Impériale un projet de protestation contre cette pièce. Ce projet a été porté par le Courier Libérali au Bailli Litta, avec l'ordre de le présenter à Votre Majesté Impériale ; il m'est parfaitement inconnu si ce projet a eu le sort de passer sous les yeux de Votre Majesté Impériale.

Au reste, j'ose le dire, je me crois rassuré sur ma conduite, d'après les efforts inexprimables que j'ai faits contre le club gangréné que m'entourait, trop nombreux pour que je pusse m'en défaire et dont je ne pouvais pas éloigner les individus, la Constitution de l'Ordre ne me permettant point d'éloigner un dignitaire quelconque.

Comment mes ennemis ont-ils front de soutenir, et comment ceux qui me connaissent plus intimement ont-ils pu supposer un moment que moi, glorieux d'être le chef de l'élite de la Noblesse de l'Europe, j'ai pu avoir l'idée d'échanger cette destinée contre un avantage quelconque, même celui d'une couronne ? Et pourtant l'on voudrait fait accroire que j'ai été assez lâche de me laisser prendre par l'appât imaginaire d'une principauté en Allemagne.

Pardonnez, Sire, cette idée m'abîme, et rien que la justice connue de Votre Majesté Impériale sera capable de relever mon esprit ; j'espère tout de sa clémence.

Je m'y résigne tout entier ; un mot gracieux de Votre Majesté Impériale me fournira les moyens de me justifier vis-à-vis d'elle, me rendra la vie, et je ne vivrai dès ce moment que pour donner à Votre Majesté Impériale des preuves de ma plus vive reconnaissance et du plus profond respect avec lequel j'ai l'honneur d'être, Sire, &c. (Signed) HOMPESCH.

Assured of the Pope's sympathy, if not actual consent to their proceedings, the Grand Priory of Russia advanced a step further, and although aware that such would, in all probability, increase the schism then existing, they determined to offer the *Supreme Magistracy* to Paul I, and on the 27th October 1798 issued the following proclamation :—

[Translation.]

PROCLAMATION.

27th October 1798.[1]

We, the Bailiffs, Grand-Crosses, Commanders, Knights of the Grand Priory of Russia, and all other members of the Order of St. John of Jerusalem, present in this Imperial residence of St. Petersburg, reflecting on the disastrous situation of our Order; its total want of resources; the loss of its Sovereignty and chief place of residence; the dispersion of its members, wandering through the world without a commander, or any fixed spot of rendezvous; the increasing dangers by which it is threatened, and the plans formed by usurpers to invade its property, and ruin it entirely; being desirous, and in duty bound, to employ all possible methods to prevent the destruction of an Order, equally ancient and illustrious, which has ever been composed of the most chosen nobility, and which has rendered such important service to the Christian world; of an Order, the institutions of which were founded on such good principles, as must not only be the firmest support to all legitimate authority, but tend to its own preservation and future existence; animated by gratitude towards His Imperial Majesty, the Emperor of All the Russias, for the favours bestowed on our Order; penetrated with veneration for his virtues, and confidently relying on his 'sacred word,' that he will not only support us in our institutions, privileges, and honours, but that he will employ every possible means to re-establish our Order in its original respectable situation, when it contributed to the advantage of Christendom in general, and to every different State in particular.

Knowing the impossibility in our present circumstances (the members of our Order being generally dispersed) of preserving all the forms and customs prescribed in our Constitution and Statutes; but nevertheless desirous of securing the dignity and the power inherent to the Sovereignty of our Order by making a proper choice of a successor to D'Aubusson, L'Isle-Adam and La Valette, we, Bailiff and Grand-Crosses, Commanders, Knights of the Grand Priory of Russia, and all other members of the Order of St. John of Jerusalem, assembled at St. Petersburg, the chief place of residence of our Order, not only in our names, but in those of the other Langues, Grand Priories in general, and all their members in particular, who shall unite themselves to us, by a firm adhesion to our principles:
Proclaim His Imperial Majesty, the Emperor and Autocrat of All the Russias, Paul I, Grand Master of the Order of St. John of Jerusalem.

In virtue of the present Proclamation, we promise according to our laws and statutes, and that by a sacred and solemn engagement, obedience, submission, and fidelity to His Imperial Majesty, the most eminent Grand Master.

Done at St. Petersburg, the residence of our Order, this present Wednesday, the 27th of October 1798.

On the 5th November, Pope Pius VI addressed another letter to the Bailli de Litta, at St. Petersburg, which affords convincing proof that he had, at last, completely abandoned the cause of Hompesch; it runs as follows :—

[1] De Villeneuve-Bargemont, vol. ii. p. 426; M.P.L. MSS. 420.

[Translation.]

To our well-beloved Son, the Bailli de Litta,
St. Petersburg.

Monastery of Cassini, near Florence,
5th November 1798.[1]

Pius P. P. VI.

Beloved Son,—Our Salutation and Apostolic Benediction.

We were seized with horror upon the reception of your first dispatch, containing the protest and manifest of the Grand Priory of Russia upon the subject of the loss of Malta, and to learn that the Grand Master, in order to save his private interests, had had the unworthy weakness of sacrificing that of the entire Order.

His Majesty, the Emperor of All the Russias, who will use his utmost endeavours to re-establish the privileges and the honour of the Priory, being in possession of the facts of the case, has every reason to employ his great power to re-establish the said Priory in its primitive prerogatives and rights.

We shall co-operate with the authority which is needed, because in addition to the printed Act, signed by the Emperor, all the other Langues and Priories are invited, general and particular, to join in the said Act, so that the Order may be restored to its ancient splendour. And being aware that in a body composed of so many and divers nations, unless a preponderance of number intervened, nothing would be done obliging and compelling the individual members to observe the new law. Moreover it will be much more honourable and satisfactory for the Russian Priory to learn that the same ideas prevail among many of the brethren to vindicate the common honour. The crime, such as it has been represented, is enormous, indeed it could not be more atrocious, and having taken the measure against the Grand Master he so ignominiously deserves, it will be necessary to use the same against each of those Knights who, for a vile interest, were associated with him in this horrible scene.

We shall be desirous of knowing how many of the Knights of other Langues agree with the noble sentiments of the Emperor, and what may be the resolution which they may take, in order to sanction it, for the example of the others. Giving you, &c. (Signed) Pius VI, Pope.

On the 13th November, Paul I solemnly accepted the dignity and title of Grand Master of the Order,[2] the seventieth in rotation, when the standard of the Order was hoisted on the bastions of the Admiralty at St. Petersburg, and on that date published the following declaration :—

[Translation.]

Declaration.[3]

We, by the Grace of God, Paul I, Emperor and Autocrat of All the Russias, &c., in consideration of the wish expressed to us by the Bailiffs,

[1] De Villeneuve-Bargemont, vol. ii. p. 415; M.P.L. MSS. 421.
[2] Badger, *Description of Malta*.
[3] De Villeneuve-Bargemont, vol. ii. p. 428 M.P.L. MSS. 420.

Grand-Crosses, Commanders, Knights of the Illustrious Order of St. John of Jerusalem, of the Grand Priory of Russia, and other members assembled together in our capital, in the name of all the well-intentioned part of their Confraternity, we accept the title of Grand Master of this Order, and renew on this occasion the solemn promises we have already made in quality of Protector, not only to preserve all the institutions and privileges of this Illustrious Order for ever unchanged in regard to the free exercise of its Religion, with everything relating to the Knights of the Roman Catholic faith, and the jurisdiction of the Order, the seat of which we have fixed in our Imperial residence; but also we declare, that we will unceasingly employ for the future all our care and attention for the augmentation of the Order, for its re-establishment in the respectable situation which is due to the salutary end of its institution for assuring its solidity, and confirming its utility.

We likewise declare, that in taking this upon us, the supreme government of the Order of St. John of Jerusalem, and considering it our duty to make use of every possible means to obtain the restoration of the property of which it has been so unjustly deprived, we do not pretend in any degree as Emperor of All the Russias, to the smallest right or advantage which may threaten or prejudice any of the Powers, our Allies; on the contrary, we shall always have a peculiar satisfaction in contributing at all times everything in our power towards strengthening our alliance with the said Powers.

Our gracious and Imperial favour towards the Order of St. John of Jerusalem in general, and to each of its members in particular, shall ever remain invariably the same.

Given at St. Petersburg, the 13th November, in the year 1798, and in the third year of our reign.

(Signed) PAUL.
(Counter-signed) PRINCE BESBORODKO.

On the 16th November, Pius VI acknowledged the receipt of Hompesch's protest in the following dispatch:—

[Translation.]

BELOVED SON, FERDINAND DE HOMPESCH, OF THE ORDER OF ST. JOHN OF JERUSALEM, HIGH MAGISTRATE.

Ibid., 16*th November* 1798.

PIUS P. P. VI.[1]

OUR BELOVED SON,—Salutation and Apostolic Benediction.

The protest which you have thought proper no longer to withhold has duly reached us, but as protesting is not proving the falsity of what the Russian Priory advances, it is required of you to substantiate the truth of what you depose in the aforesaid protest. Of what proofs the Russian Priory possess, we know not, therefore we cannot re-establish the Langues in their former splendour, in order that those whom you believe rebels, may be punished, as if the principal point had been incontrovertibly

[1] M.P.L., MSS. 420.

decided. In the meanwhile we shall await from Russia what further they have to add, in order that we may be able to form an unbiassed judgement. We remain, &c. (Signed) PIUS VI.

Pius VI's treatment of Hompesch appears to have been sadly influenced by current political events. On the 17th October, His Holiness informed Hompesch that 'the deposition of a Grand Master could not depend upon the vote of a single Priory, and that it would be necessary for the other Langues to adhere thereto'; and on the 16th of the following month, 'that he would await to hear from Russia what further they have to add, on the subject of their indictment, in order that he might be able to form an unprejudiced opinion.' Whereas, in his dispatch to the Bailli de Litta, dated eleven days previously, he accepted the Russian Priory's statements (based on false information), and notwithstanding that he was in possession of Hompesch's protest of the 12th October, he informed that Priory on the 5th November, 'that he had taken note of the measures they had adopted against the Grand Master which he had so ignominiously deserved, and that it would be necessary to use the same against each of those Knights who, for a vile interest, were associated with him in this horrible scene.'

The question arises, was His Holiness in possession of Hompesch's protest of the 12th October, when he wrote to De Litta the referred-to letter of the 5th November? There appears no reason to doubt it, for at that period peace reigned on the mainland of the Continent of Europe, England (with her weak ally Portugal) alone remained at war with France, Bonaparte was in Egypt, and consequently there was no interruption in inland communication.

The distance from Trieste to Florence is about 220 miles, and there were three land routes open. On the authority of De la Jonquière, the couriers between Rome and Paris then occupied about nine days on their journeys, and, if we may assume the same mode of conveyance for correspondence was adopted in other directions, three days would suffice for transit between Trieste and Florence. Consequently Hompesch's protest would reach His Holiness on or about the 15th October, just three weeks prior to the dispatch of the 5th November addressed to De Litta.

Hompesch's protest is based upon five arguments:

1st. That the internal revolution brought about in Malta was due to the instigation of the French.

2nd. The perversion of members of the Order.

3rd. The adherence of a number of the inhabitants to the French invasion, and to republican ideas.

4th. Alluring and deceiving the people, working upon their fidelity, which rendered the means of defence vain, and made all military dispositions futile.

5th. The influence of the French over the Deputies who signed the Convention, the majority of whom were Maltese.

On all these points their truth has been amply verified in after years, but whence could the proof asked for by His Holiness *then* be obtained ?

The reliable sources were at that time blocked in the besieged city of Valetta, and two years had to elapse ere the Balli de Tigné could, in a measure, vindicate the honour of his chief by disavowing the apocryphal letter of the 21st June, whilst Hompesch in the meanwhile was living, according to Baron de Lavigerie, in absolute want.[1]

The following history of this transaction is taken from the 'Annual Register' for 1799, p. 78.

While His Russian Majesty exerted his whole authority and influence to rouse a general attack on the French Republic, he received into his protection those who had suffered from its tyranny and oppression. He extended his protection and munificent patronage to the dispersed and ejected Knights of Malta. The Grand Bailiff, the Grand Cross, and other distinguished members of this Order assembled at St. Petersburg in October 1798, elected the Emperor Grand Master of their Order. His Majesty, who is said to have solicited, accepted this dignity and exercised its prerogatives, in conferring with great pomp and solemnity the different degrees, titles, and offices of the Order on various persons of distinction. Count Litta, envoy extraordinary from the Pope, and the Prince Terra Capriola, envoy from Naples, were honoured with the Grand Cross. A new institution, under the name of a Grand Priory, was established at St. Petersburg in favour of the Knights of Malta, and endowed with an annual revenue of 216,000 roubles. This was to serve as a residence and rallying place for all the Knights.

The motives assigned by His Imperial Majesty for this act of munificence, were a regard to the common cause of Christianity and Christendom to which the illustrious Knights of Malta had been so eminently subservient, to preserve that Order, and to enable them to recover the possessions that had been ravished from them by injustice and violence, and to add a new incitement to the loyalty and bravery of the Russian nobles, by the hope of being admitted, in consequence of signalised merit, into the illustrious fraternity of the Knights of St. John of Jerusalem.

From this Order no person of noble descent and otherwise properly qualified according to the rules of the Order of any country in Christendom was to be interdicted. To the ancient and standing laws of the Order His Majesty added a number of regulations respecting his own new foundation.

The ukase for this establishment was accompanied by a proclamation, declaring that any gentleman of any Christian country, duly qualified, might be received as a Knight of St. John in the Imperial residence of St. Petersburg, and reside there, in that character, and enjoy the Emperor's favour and protection.

' We flatter ourselves (says His Majesty) that having through Divine

[1] Lavigerie, *Ordre de Malte*, p. 114.

Providence and hereditary right come to the Imperial throne of our ancestors, we have it in our power to protect, maintain, and even increase and extend the splendour of an Order so ancient and renowned among the orders of chivalry, convinced that by such a conduct we shall render an important service to the universe. The laws and regulations of this Order inspire a love of virtue, form good morals, strengthen the bonds of subordination, and present a powerful remedy against the present mania for innovation and the unbridled licentiousness of thought. Finally, this Order is a medium for augmenting the power, security, and glory of states.' The Emperor in February 1799 sent a note to all the foreign Ministers resident at St. Petersburg, requesting them to make known to their respective Courts, that he had accepted the title of Grand Master of the Sovereign Order of St. John of Jerusalem, of which St. Petersburg was henceforth to be the seat and the chief residence.

Orders were also issued to the Ministers of Russia not to receive any letters addressed to His Imperial Majesty, in which the title of Grand Master of the Sovereign Order of St. John of Jerusalem should be omitted.

On this new institution for the presentation of an ancient Order, although its patron and head was neither unmarried [n]or a Catholic, the aged, infirm, and unfortunate Pope, Pius VI, in the Monastery of Cassini near Florence, bestowed his approbation, sanction, and his paternal and apostolical benediction (in anticipation) on the 5th November 1798.

Sixteen days after Paul's acceptance of the Chief Magistracy of the Order, and in proof of his increased interest therein, he established an additional Priory for the benefit of the nobility in his dominions (who might be members of the Greek Church), and by virtue of a decree dated the 29th November 1798, he granted an annual allowance of 216,000 roubles (£23,400) in connexion with the Commanderies in his Empire; and in order to show his resentment against the Bavarian Government, who had been supporting the claims of Hompesch, he, at the same time, dismissed its Minister from the Russian Court. It must not be forgotten, that at this crisis in the affairs of the Island, Paul was in alliance with England, Austria and Turkey, against France, that Malta had then been in possession of the latter Power for five months, and had been blockaded for two months by the British and Portuguese squadrons, and invested by the Maltese insurgents since September. It is therefore from this date, and from his acceptance of the sovereignty by Paul, long before the capture of the Island from the French, that Russia laid claim to possession of the Island. Seven months after the event just recorded, i.e. in June 1799, and whilst the siege of Valetta was making slow progress, the Court of Vienna, to propitiate Russia, intimated to Hompesch (an Austrian subject) the necessity of his abdicating. This message was communicated by the Prévôt Maffei through the medium of his brother, who was then living at Trieste where Hompesch continued to reside.

Maffei wrote to his brother : [1]

It is necessary that the Grand Master should come to a prompt decision in the matter, it is neither the place nor the time for him to temporise or negiotiate. Whilst the Grand Master should formally declare his abdication to our Sovereign the Emperor of Germany,[2] it is necessary that he should in like manner inform the Emperor of Russia.

If he delays, or endeavours to evade the fulfilment of the desire of our Sovereign and the Ministry, he will then have to be considered as the Emperor's personal enemy, and will have to be treated as a prisoner of state.

He might make a protest for his action, by proceeding to some mineral bath resort for the benefit of his health.

Hompesch, of necessity, had to acquiesce, and addressed the following letters to the Emperors of Austria and Russia :—

LETTRE DU GRAND MAÎTRE À L'EMPEREUR D'AUTRICHE.

6th Juillet 1799.[3]

SIRE,—Courbé sous le poids des malheurs qui m'accablent, la conviction intime (autant que la nature et la marche rapide des événemens m'en ont laissé la faculté), que j'ai rempli religieusement les devoirs sacrés de mon état, peut seule m'empêcher de succomber à mon infortune, et me servir de quelque consolation.

Le même sentiment de mes devoirs envers l'Ordre, qui sous ma direction a éprouvé de si cruelles catastrophes, me porte aussi à me dévouer à son bien-être, à son rétablissement et à sa conservation dans ses anciens droits, statuts et privilèges, en me démettant volontairement de la dignité dont je suis revêtu, et dispensant par là même les Chevaliers de cet Ordre illustre des devoirs qu'ils avaient contractés envers leur malheureux chef.

Je supplie Votre Majesté Impériale et Royale de recevoir cette déclaration, d'y reconnaître l'attachement à mes devoirs et aux succès de la cause générale qui me l'a inspirée, et de daigner la faire valoir auprès de son intime allié, l'Empereur de toutes les Russies, sous les auspices puissans duquel l'Ordre de Saint-Jean de Jérusalem va renaître, dont j'ai été le premier à invoquer la protection, et dont je serai le premier à bénir les efforts généreux pour le bien de la Religion.

LETTRE DU GRAND MAÎTRE À L'EMPEREUR PAUL I$^{ER.}$

6 Juillet 1799.[4]

SIRE,—En daignant se rappeler que j'ai été le premier à mettre avec une respectueuse confiance l'Ordre de Saint-Jean de Jérusalem, dont la direction m'avait été confiée, sous la puissante protection de Votre Majesté Impériale, elle se persuadera aisément que j'ai été le premier aussi à bénir l'intérêt que Votre Majesté a témoigné à la Religion, depuis les malheurs qu'elle a

---

[1] De Villeneuve-Bargemont, vol. ii. (Appendix), p. 416.
[2] This title of course means 'the Emperor,' i.e. the head of the Holy Roman Empire.—J. H. R.
[3] De Villeneuve-Bargemont, *Monumens des Grands Maîtres*, vol. ii. p. 418.
[4] *Ibid.* p. 417.

éprouvés, que son infortuné chef a bien gémi de n'avoir pas pu empêcher, et dont il se serait estimé fort heureux d'être la seule victime. C'est l'attachement même à mes devoirs, Sire, et à la Religion de Malte, qui me fait la loi de tout sacrifier à son bien-être, et d'écarter les obstacles que ma personne pourrait porter à sa réunion et à son entier rétablissement, en me démettant volontairement de ma dignité du Grand Maître.

Ma conscience et l'approbation que j'attends de la justice de Votre Majesté Impériale seront mes seules consolations, et personne ne prendra une part plus vive aux avantages qui résulteront pour l'Ordre sous les glorieux auspices de Votre Majesté Impériale, que l'Europe entière reconnaît pour son défenseur et sauveur. Je la supplie d'être persuadée du profond respect, &c.

SECONDE LETTRE DU GRAND MAÎTRE À L'EMPEREUR D'AUTRICHE.[1]

6 *Juillet* 1799.

SIRE,—En implorant de Votre Majesté Impériale et Royale un asile pour mon Ordre et pour ma personne, après la catastrophe de Malta, j'étais prêt à me soumettre, dès-lors, à tout ce qu'il lui plairait d'ordonner pour le bien de la cause commune et pour celle du rétablissement de l'Ordre.

J'ai très-souvent renouvelé les mêmes assurances de cette parfaite soumission. C'est elle qui m'impose le sacrifice que le Prévôt Maffei m'a demandé de la parte de Votre Majesté.

Je la supplie d'être persuadée du profond respect, &c.

The information regarding Hompesch's abdication was immediately conveyed to the British Government on the 17th/28th July.

[Extract.]
WHITWORTH TO GRENVILLE.[2]

St. Petersburg, 17*th*/28*th July* 1799.

A messenger arrived two days ago from Vienna with the account that Baron Hompesch, late Grand Master of Malta, has formally renounced all pretensions to that dignity or title.

Your Lordship will recollect the circumstances which gave rise to this event.

The disasters which continued to follow the Allied Armies against France in 1799, combined with the misfortunes which attended the joint British and Russian expedition to Holland in October and November of that year, affected the mind of the Emperor Paul (who had already shown signs of mental aberration). In February 1800 he became so incensed against England that he demanded the recall of the British Minister, Lord Whitworth.

In the following June, the British Chargé d'Affaires at St. Petersburg was summarily dismissed; and Worronzow [Voronzoff],

---

[1] De Villeneuve-Bargemont, *Monumens des Grands Maîtres,* vol. ii. p. 419.
[2] Foreign Office Records, Russia, No. 60.

the Russian Ambassador, soon after was ordered to quit the Embassy in London, making the rupture complete.[1]

Upon the death of Paul, which occurred on the 23rd March 1801, his son and successor, Alexander I, moved, it was alleged, by parsimonious feelings, declined the honour of the Magistracy of the Order, whilst consenting to retain the Protectorate, and four days after his accession, he issued the following Proclamation :—

16th/27th March, 1801.[2]

'We, Alexander the First, by the Grace of God, Emperor and Autocrat of All the Russias. Inasmuch as we are desirous of affording a proof of our affection, and of our particular regard towards the Sovereign Order of St. John of Jerusalem, we therefore declare that we take it under our Imperial protection, and that we will employ our utmost means to reinstate it in all its rights, honours, privileges and immunities.

'To this end we command our Field-Marshal Bailli Count Nicholas Soltikoff to exercise the functions and authority of lieutenant or vicar of the Grand Master of the Order, and to convoke an assembly of the Great Council, and to make known to the same that it is our intention that this our imperial residence shall be considered as the capital of the Sovereign Order of St. John of Jerusalem, till circumstances shall admit of its having a Grand Master appointed according to its ancient forms and statutes. In expectation of that epoch, we command in our character of Protector that the same council shall maintain the Government of the Order; make known this our determination to all Nations and Prioriates, and invite them for their own advantage to submit to the decrees of the Council. We confirm by the present declaration our two Russian and Catholic Grand Prioriates, constituted within our Empire, in the enjoyment of all the properties, privileges, and administrations conferred upon them, and we ordain that they in our name as Protector, shall act in obedience to the directions of our Field-Marshal General Bailli Count Nicholas Soltikoff, vicar or substitute of the office of Grand Master. As soon as an agreement shall have been concluded with other Courts for appointing a proper place, and the necessary means, a general chapter of the Sovereign Order of St. John of Jerusalem shall be convened, and it shall be one of the first endeavours of our proclamation that such chapter shall proceed to the election of a Grand Master who is worthy to preside and capable of restoring to the Order its ancient constitution.'

(Signed) ALEXANDER.
(Countersigned) COUNT PAHLEN.

In the Memoirs of Prince Talleyrand, who was so closely associated with Bonaparte in the plans which preceded the conquest of the Island by the French, there is the following reference to these negotiations :—

---

[1] In the autumn a large number of British ships were detained by Paul I, and their crews were imprisoned—some of them in the interior. No hostilities, however, took place either there or at Copenhagen until April 1801 when the expedition of Parker and Nelson arrived in the Sound.—J. H. R.

[2] *Annual Register*, 1801, p. 241.

'After the taking of the island by the French, the Czar on the request of the Grand Priory declared himself Protector of the Order, and in November 1798, the place of Grand Master having become vacant, a fraction of the Order had an idea of offering it to the Czar. Paul solemnly accepted this new dignity. Bonaparte profited skilfully by these circumstances to conciliate Russia, and to detach it from Germany. It was then that he sent to the Czar the sword of La Valetta (the Grand Master) found at Malta, or according to another authority, the sword of the Grand Master, Villiers de L'Ile-Adam, that Leo X had given to that illustrious warrior, as a remembrance of his fine defence of Rhodes.

'When Malta was taken by the English, Paul claimed the island in the quality of Grand Master, but the English refused formally to cede this important post, and a rupture ensued.[1] The death of Paul in March 1801 terminated this curious episode. His successor, Alexander, did not claim the island and the matter ended there.'

Upon the death of Paul, Hompesch cherished the idea that he might be now reinstated in his dignity and possession; and in this hope he addressed to the Grand Prior Colloredo, the Prévôt Maffei, and the Austrian Minister Thugut, the following letters on the 7th May 1801 :—

AU GRAND PRIEUR COLLOREDO.

Porto di Fermo, le 7 *mai* 1801.[2]

La mort de S.M.I. Paul Ier, dont on avait surpris la religion, devait faire cesser la persécution que mes ennemis m'avaient suscitée, et, en ramenant un nouvel ordre de choses, remettre en exercice l'ancien gouvernement selon nos usages et statuts. La confiance respectueuse que j'ai toujours eue dans la haute protection de Sa Majesté Impériale et Royale, et que j'implore très-vivement dans ces nouvelles circonstances, me donne, M. le Grand Prieur, les espérances les plus flatteuses que, par la puissante protection de Sa Majesté Impériale et Royale, je pourrai exercer librement les fonctions de ma dignité, à l'exercice de laquelle S.M.I. Paul Ier s'opposait avec une invincible violence. Je prie Votre Excellence de vouloir, par vos bons offices, me rendre efficaces les magnanimes dispositions que Sa Majesté Impériale et Royale daigne manifester à mon égard. Le chevalier magistral Beker, que j'envoie exprès à Vienne, aura l'honneur de vous en donner des détails très intéressans. Je suis certain que Votre Excellence voudra bien seconder mon juste empressement de réunir tous les prieurés sous leur chef légitime, et de faire revivre le premier système de nos lois religieuses.

Il me reste à parler à Votre Excellence de mon existence et des dépenses que je suis obligé de faire pour le service de notre Ordre, surtout dans ces circonstances aussi intéressantes. J'ai une pleine confiance dans les

---

[1] The conduct of Great Britain was far more conciliatory than Talleyrand represented. Early in 1800 she offered to the Czar Paul, that British, Russian and Neapolitan forces should hold Malta conjointly during the war against France. This came to naught because the Russian troops did not come to Malta, but were withdrawn to Corfu, and because in the autumn of 1800 the Czar Paul came to an open rupture with us. (See *Paget Papers*, vol. i. p. 274; *Dropmore Papers*, vol. vi. pp. 199, 200; also ch. xviii. of this volume.)—J. H. R.

[2] De Villeneuve-Bargemont, *Monumens*, vol. ii. p. 445.

sentimens amicals que vous m'avez témoignés, persuadé que Votre Excellence voudra bien s'occuper des moyens de pourvoir à ma subsistance et aux dépenses que je suis obligé de faire pour l'Ordre. Veuillez, M. le Grand Prieur, être convaincu de l'assurance de ma vive reconnaissance, que j'ai chargé le chevalier magistral Beker de vous présenter de ma part. Avec ces sentimens je suis, &c. (Signé) HOMPESCH.

AU PRÉVÔT MAFFEI.

Porto di Fermo, le 7 *mai*, 1801.[1]

M. LE PRÉVÔT,—Les nouvelles circonstances m'ont engagé à faire partir le chevalier magistral Beker pour Vienne; j'aurais cru manquer à mes devoirs les plus sacrés et aux sermens que j'ai prêtés au moment de mon exaltation à la Grand-Maîtrise, si je n'employais les moyens les plus sûrs pour implorer efficacement la haute protection de Sa Majesté Impériale et Royale pour pouvoir exercer librement les fonctions de ma dignité. Tant qu'une violence invincible enchaînait toutes mes opérations, je ne pouvais que gémir sur le sort de mon Ordre. Libre de l'opposition violente que Sa Majesté Impériale feu l'Empereur Paul Ier faisait à l'exercice de ma dignité, je me rendrais responsable de tous les événemens qui pourraient arriver contre mon Ordre si je négligeais de réunir tous les prieurés sous leur chef légitime, et si je n'employais à cet effet l'appui des Puissances protectrices. Mais toute ma confiance est en la puissante protection de Sa Majesté Impériale et Royale. Vous savez, M. le prévôt, quel est mon parfait dévouement à la auguste Maison d'Autriche, et je suis certaine que vous ne manquerez pas de rendre efficaces par vos offices la bonne disposition que Sa Majesté Impériale et Royale daigne manifester à mon égard.

Non moins mon existence personelle que l'intérêt de mon Ordre exige que je réclame des moyens pour subsister et fournir aux dépenses nécessaires que je suis obligé de faire pour l'Ordre; je [ne] me mets point en doute que la recette du prieuré dont la régie vous est confiée ne me procure des secours qui fournissent des moyens pour veiller aux affaires de mon Ordre et pourvoir aux besoins de mon existence.

J'ai écrit à ce sujet à M. le Grand Prieur pour faciliter le résultat de ma demande. Il est inutile d'entrer dans les détails de ma position. Le chevalier magistral Beker s'est chargé de vous en faire le tableau ; il serait trop cruel pour moi de l'écrire.

Je saisirai toutes les occasions pour vous témoigner ma sensibilité ; en attendant je vous renouvelle l'assurance des sentimens sincères et invariables avec lesquels je suis, &c. (Signé) HOMPESCH.

À M. LE BARON DE THUGUT.

Porto di Fermo, le 7 *mai* 1801.[2]

Votre Excellence connaît quelle a toujours été la confiance que j'ai mise en votre amitié, et qu'elle est sans bornes ; elle n'a pas été l'effet des circonstances, mais elle est basée sur les sentimens sincères que je vous ai toujours témoignés. Je ne parle pas à Votre Excellence des persécutions que, pendant les dernières années du règne de Paul Ier, j'ai souffertes ; elles vous

[1] *Ibid*, p. 437.   [2] *Ibid*. p. 438.

sont connues : la mort de cet empereur aurait dû les faire cesser, et il n'aurait dû exister aucun obstacle pour le libre exercice de ma dignité. Mes ennemis, qui m'ont suscité la première persécution, mettent en mouvement tous les ressorts pour tâcher, sous d'autres formes plus masquées, de mettre des entraves à ce que je reprenne les rênes du gouvernement de mon Ordre.

Votre Excellence voudra bien permettre que je rappelle ici la violence avec laquelle S.M.I. Paul Ier, par les circonstances du moment et la position de l'Allemagne, a agi envers moi ; et ce parfait dévouement qu'en toutes les occasions je me suis empressé de prouver pour l'auguste maison d'Autriche personne mieux que vous, M. le baron, n'en connaît toutes les circonstances, et j'ose espérer en votre amitié que Votre Excellence trouvera bien un moyen efficace à faire parvenir aux pieds du trône de Sa Majesté Impériale et Royale tout ce qui a pu me mériter sa haute protection, et toutes les particularités qui peuvent faire constater la persécution, l'injustice et la violence.

Mes ennemis, qui se sont tous jetés dans le parti russe, se permettent tout pour parvenir à leur but. La puissante protection de Sa Majesté Impériale peut seule leur en imposer ; c'est par le puissant soutien de Sa Majesté Impériale que j'espère reprendre les rênes du gouvernement de mon Ordre ; c'est par sa haute protection que je pourrai réunir tous les prieurés et éviter le schisme, et c'est par son auguste médiation que j'ai une pleine confiance de récupérer Malte.

La cour de Rome croit être maîtrisée par les circonstances et gênée dans sa position.[1] La crainte de nuire à ses propres intérêts en se prononçant en ma faveur la retient. Les sentimens du Saint-Père me sont favorables, et de Rome même l'on me presse de solliciter l'appui des cours, en m'assurant que si Sa Majesté Impériale et Royale faisait connaître près de Sa Sainteté sa protection déclarée, Sa Sainteté ne balancerait plus à me reconnaître publiquement, parce qu'alors le Pape serait sûr d'être soutenu dans sa démarche.

Le chevalier magistral Beker, qui a déjà l'honneur d'être connu de Votre Excellence, et que dans ces nouvelles circonstances j'envoie exprès à Vienne, aura celui de vous présenter cette lettre, et il vous soumettra les détails des affaires qui me concernent. Je vous parle, M. le baron, avec l'épanchement de cœur d'un ami, et avec cette liberté et franchise avec laquelle je vous ai parlé depuis si longtemps. Je me rappelle avec une sensible satisfaction ce que je dois à votre amitié ; ma vive reconnaissance est gravée à jamais dans mon cœur. Avec ces sentimens et la considération la plus distinguée je suis, &c. (Signé) Hompesch.

No heed, however, was given to these appeals, nor to a similar application which Hompesch had made on the same day to King George III, begging His Majesty's intervention and support. The Emperor Alexander was in no way disposed to retire from the position he had taken on the 16th/27th March, when he confirmed his predecessor's action in the creation of two Russian Grand Priories, and when he further took the Order under his protection, promising to maintain its rights, and thereupon ordered Count Nicholas de Soltykoff

---

[1] i.e. dominated by French policy and the neighbourhood of French troops.—J. H. R.

to convene a sitting of the Sacred Council, in order that his intentions might be made known.

Hompesch was thus doomed to suffer disappointment and penury, but to the honour of Napoleon it must be recorded that two months after he (Napoleon) was raised to the throne of France he, in the month of July 1804, gave orders for the pension of 300,000 francs, which had been accorded Hompesch by the Convention of the 12th June 1798, to be paid.

This act of commiseration is acknowledged by the ex-Grand Master in a letter of thanks to His Imperial Majesty the Emperor Napoleon, dated at Città di Castello, the 2nd August 1804, which is now in the Archives Nationales, Paris (A.F. iv. 1685). This tardy fulfilment of an engagement was, however, destined to be of brief duration; Hompesch succumbed to an attack of asthma on the 12th May 1805.

The accusation of cowardice and treachery to the Order which was levelled against Hompesch cannot be sustained; the greatest reproach that may be made against his memory is that of having been feeble and incapable at the great crisis in the affairs of the Order; and from the documents and information published in this relation it is evident that he was more sinned against than sinning.

CHAPTER XVIII

THE PRELIMINARY TREATY OF PEACE BETWEEN ENGLAND AND FRANCE

(1st October 1801)

As has been noticed in previous chapters, the Second Coalition against France, formed by Great Britain, Russia, Austria, Naples, and Portugal, sustained severe shocks in the autumn of 1799 and during the campaign of 1800. Russia virtually retired from it in October 1799, and during the year 1800 she showed increasing dislike of Great Britain. The Pitt Ministry endeavoured to allay Russia's susceptibilities regarding Malta, notwithstanding her recent withdrawal from the coalition and her dubious behaviour. Accordingly, on the 22nd January 1800, Lord Grenville informed Mr. Paget, lately appointed Ambassador and Minister - Plenipotentiary to the Government at Naples, that it had been determined that the fortress of Malta shall be garrisoned by a force composed of English, Russian, and Neapolitans, to be held by them during the war as a deposit in trust for the Order of St. John of Jerusalem, which is to be re-established as soon as circumstances shall permit, agreeably to the system which shall be adopted by the Allied Powers. In the meantime the Emperor of Russia is recognised by His Majesty as Grand Master. The particular interest which that Sovereign takes in this favourite object is well known. Attempts have been made to excite in the Emperor's mind suspicions respecting the intentions of Great Britain. Paget was further ordered

to make it an object of study, to remove every subject of disagreement, and to conciliate the goodwill of the Russian Minister and commanders employed (in Southern Italy). His Majesty is of the opinion that the arrangement of the matter according to the plan proposed by the Emperor of Russia is advantageous to the interests of his (the King of Naples) dominions.[1]

[1] Foreign Office, Sicily, No. 14.
It should be remembered that the Czar had pledged himself to protect the Kingdoms of Naples and Sardinia. Of course the arrangement referred to above lapsed because the Russian troops did not come to Malta. This is stated in Lord Grenville's dispatch of 17th October 1800 to Paget, then at Palermo: 'The conduct of the Emperor of Russia has been totally repugnant to that system

THE PRELIMINARY TREATY OF PEACE

The British Minister at St. Petersburg, however, was not quite of this opinion, and felt it his duty to state his reasons in his dispatch of the 19th May to Lord Grenville as follows :

[Synopsis.]

LORD WHITWORTH TO LORD GRENVILLE.

St. Petersburg, 19th May 1800.[1]

Whitworth discusses the future of Malta at length ; distinguishes between the present position and that of two years ago. The framers of the arrangement which had been made, by allotting the exclusive defence of Valetta and the ports to the Emperor, designed to put the Island into his hands. A tacit assent was given to this arrangement on the idea that Russia could have no interest distinct from that of His Britannic Majesty. Experience has shown this not to be the case owing to the Emperor's caprice, and we must not think ourselves bound by any previous arrangement, and must not allow Russia to gain possession of La Valetta.

During the fruitless negotiations for peace between Austria and France which followed the disastrous battle of Marengo (14th June 1800), the former Power, loyal to its engagements with England, made it a condition that negotiations should simultaneously be opened with the British Government. Bonaparte in consequence demanded an armistice by sea as a preliminary to the negotiations with England. Malta and Egypt were then on the point of surrendering to the British, and it was believed that the object of the armistice was simply to gain time, in order to reinforce the garrisons which held them. England refused, and hostilities were resumed on sea and land.

Paul I, disappointed at the failure of the military operations in Holland and Switzerland, which, as noted earlier, he ascribed to the fault of England and Austria, became particularly angered against the former Power, which, at the exchange of prisoners with France, had refused to include those of Russia. Bonaparte, availing himself of this opportunity to gratify the fickle and capricious Czar, set at liberty 6,000 Russian prisoners without exchange, having first clothed them in new uniforms, returning them their arms and standards. This token of friendship on the part of the First Consul produced a great impression on the Czar, which soon afterwards was to ripen into an alliance between the two countries.

One of the first results of this *rapprochement* was the revival

---

of concert and active co-operation which formed at once the object and the basis of the arrangement which was in question for the temporary and provisional occupation of Malta (i.e. during the war). The Russian troops and ships wherever employed have been withdrawn, the Emperor's forces have in no degree contributed to the reduction of the Island of Malta, nor has he during the present campaign afforded to the Allies the smallest aid against the common enemy' (*Paget Papers*, vol. i. p. 274).—J. H. R.

[1] Foreign Office, Russia, 47.

of the 'Armed Neutrality League of the Northern Powers,' in opposition to the right of search claimed by England, which had been dormant since 1780. In May and June proposals were made by the Czar to Sweden and Denmark to join the coalition, which were accepted. In the meantime instructions had been sent to the commanders of all Danish ships of war to resist the right of search by British cruisers; and on the 25th July the commander of a Danish frigate, refusing to allow his convoy to be searched, his vessel was attacked and captured.[1]

Shortly afterwards Malta fell. News of the capture reached Vienna on the 25th September. During the following month it became known at that Court that Bonaparte had made an offer of that Island to the Emperor Paul, a move which, as has been noted previously, cemented the friendship of the Czar and the First Consul.

LORD MINTO TO LORD GRENVILLE.

Vienna, 7th November 1800.[2]

By letter from St. Petersburg, Baron Thugut has learned that Bonaparte has sent an offer of the cession of Malta to the Emperor Paul, who has received the offer very favourably. That a General Springporten, of whom your Lordship must have heard, was in consequence appointed Governor of Malta by the Emperor, and that this person is now sent to transact the release of the Russian prisoners in France, whom it was proposed to send as a garrison to Malta. A few days after this offer was received at St. Petersburg the Emperor learned the surrender of Malta, and was much dejected and affected by the intelligence, but afterwards recovered his spirits on the persuasion that His Majesty would not hesitate to make him a tender of the conquest.

The Russian Minister at Naples, the Chevalier Italinsky, confirmed this intelligence to the British Minister, Mr. Paget, on the 6th January 1801, in the following extract of his dispatch:[3]

His Imperial Majesty had ordered his General of Infantry, 'Monsieur le baron de Springporten, de se transporter à Malte avec des troupes, pour y mettre une garnison, conformément à ce qui a été arrêté par la Convention de l'année 1798 conclu entre SM. l'Empereur et leurs Maj^{tes} le Roi de la Grande-Bretagne et le Roi des Deux Siciles.'

Mr. Paget replied on the following day:[4]

Le soussigné demeure avec plaisir d'accord que la dite Convention (qu'il croit verbale) est l'effet des intentions droites et loyales de chacun des trois

---

[1] This capture had the effect of drawing still closer the bond of union between Russia, Sweden, and Denmark, which eventually resulted in a formal treaty between these Powers being signed on the 16th December, Prussia being compelled to accede on the 19th of the same month. (Note by Mr. Hardman.)
[2] Foreign Office, Austria, 61.   [3] Ibid. Sicily, 15.   [4] Ibid.

Puissances, mais il est évident en même tems qu'elle présuppose la coopération des mêmes trois Puissances pour la reddition des forteresses de l'isle de Malte, alors au pouvoir de l'ennemi.

He closed his dispatch by diplomatically adding—

That if it was the intention of the Sovereigns to put in garrisons of equal number of troops, this was based on the conviction that each would employ his means for seizing the fortress from the French. The object of the Convention would be the co-operation of the Powers for taking the Island, in which His Britannic Majesty has not had the advantage of Russia's assistance.

Disasters to the Austrian arms in the meanwhile continued, culminating in their total defeat at Hohenlinden on the 3rd December, whilst their military operations on the Adige and Brenta fared no better. The Hapsburg power was consequently compelled to abandon England and sue for a separate peace, which was finally signed at Lunéville on the 9th February 1801. To add to the British difficulties, it was rumoured that another attempt at an invasion upon India would be made. No sooner had peace been declared between Austria and France than a secret treaty, under date of the 28th February 1801,[1] was entered into between the latter Power and Russia, the text of which, according to Hardenberg, the Prussian Minister of Foreign Affairs, was as follows:[2]

A French army, 35,000 strong, with light artillery under the command of Masséna, shall be moved from France to Ulm, from whence, with the consent of Austria, it shall descend the Danube to the Black Sea. Arrived there, a Russian fleet will transport it to Taganrog, from whence it shall move to Taritzin, on the Volga, where it shall find boats to convey it to Astrakan. There it will find a Russian army of 35,000 men, composed of 15,000 infantry, 10,000 cavalry, and 10,000 Cossacks, amply provided with artillery and horses necessary for its conveyance. The combined army shall be transported by the Caspian Sea from Astrakan to Astrabat, where magazines of all sorts shall be established for its use. This march from the frontiers of France to Astrabat will be made in eighty days; fifty more will be requisite to bring the army to the banks of the Indus, by the route of Herat, Ferah and Candahar.

Paul afterwards agreed to increase the number of the Cossacks to 50,000, but his sudden death on the night of the 23rd of the following month put an end to the project.

The entire subjugation of Austria to French influence by the Treaty of Lunéville, on the 9th February 1801, left the Neapolitan Government completely at the mercy of the French Republic. Thanks partly to the friendly intervention of Russia, an armistice was arranged with the Neapolitan forces at Foligno on the 18th February 1801.

[1] Alison, vol. iv. p. 516.   [2] Hardenberg, vol. vii. p. 497.

Arriving at Vienna during the following month, the Queen of Naples there found the rumour of a friendship which the Czar entertained for France confirmed. In despair for the fate of her adopted country, as well as for that of her dynasty, she determined upon visiting St. Petersburg during the autumn, for the purpose of imploring the good offices of the Czar as mediator between France and Naples.

Paul, having just placed himself at the head of the Northern Confederacy against England, most willingly accepted the office. His Majesty's negotiations were completely successful, Bonaparte being too well pleased at the opportunity not only of ingratiating himself with the Czar, but also at being able to detach another Power from British influence.

The most important articles of the Convention were those which stipulated that all the ports of Naples and Sicily should be closed to England and Turkey, and prohibited the export of food of all kinds and munitions of war to England, Turkey, and especially to the Island of Malta. The armistice further provided that it should continue for thirty days, until a treaty of peace confirmed the Convention.

This treaty between the First Consul of the French Republic and the King of the Two Sicilies was signed at Florence on the 28th March 1801, by which Art. III provides for all ports in Naples and Sicily being closed to British and Turkish vessels of war and trade until the conclusion of peace, and until the settlement of all differences which have arisen between England and the Northern Powers, and specially between Russia and England. 'The said ports, on the other hand, will be open to all vessels of trade or war belonging to Russia and such States comprised in the Northern Maritime Neutrality, as well as to France and her allies.' After due ratification this treaty was published at Naples on the 28th April, and sanctioned by the French Corps Législatif on the 7th December 1801.

Thus, from having been at the head of a confederacy against France, England now found herself not only deprived of her allies but in actual conflict with the most powerful of them all, her quondam ally, Russia.

The Neapolitan Government, in the dilemma in which it had been placed, had previously sought the advice of His Britannic Majesty's Cabinet. The answer to this appeal, although dated ten days after the signature of the Convention at Foligno, conveyed the assurance that His Britannic Majesty's Government considered that any agreement which the Neapolitan Government would have to submit to would be one of necessity, and not construed as hostile to that of His Britannic Majesty. The dispatch was as follows:

THE PRELIMINARY TREATY OF PEACE

LORD HAWKESBURY TO THE HON. A. PAGET.[1]

Downing Street, 28*th February* 1801.

SIR,—In consequence of the indisposition of His Majesty, his confidential servants have not had it in their power for several days to receive his commands on any matters of business; but as the Neapolitan Minister has presented a memorial to me on the melancholy situation in which the King of the Two Sicilies is placed by the separate peace concluded between Austria and France, and as the answer to this memorial admits of no delay, I think it right to inform you that it is the decided opinion of His Majesty's confidential servants that, in the present state of the Continent, His Sicilian Majesty should use every endeavour to conclude a peace with the French Republic on the best terms he may be enabled to obtain, without any reference to his engagements with Great Britain; and that if he should find himself obliged to assent to the insertion of articles in the treaty which should prohibit to British ships the entrance of the ports of His Sicilian Majesty's dominions, His Majesty's confidential servants would consider this an act of necessity, and not as any proof of a hostile disposition in the King of the Two Sicilies towards this country.

In consequence of this treaty of peace between France and Naples an embargo was placed on all shipments of corn to Malta from the latter kingdom. This step of the Neapolitan Government became the more serious from the fact that Malta depended almost entirely upon obtaining her supplies from Sicily. So late as the previous October there remained in Malta but three weeks' consumption of wheat; but Captain Ball, anticipating events, had fortunately taken every precaution on the surrender of the French garrison to publish all over the Levant that the port of Valetta was now open to commerce. Agents were dispatched to Tunis and other foreign ports for the purchase of wheat, by which means he was able in March to report that he had succeeded in obtaining supplies to last until the following December.

Meanwhile the animosity of the Czar against England had increased, and Kalicheff was dispatched to Paris, where he arrived on the 6th March 1801[2] (seventeen days before Paul's death), charged with certain conditions—'that Russia and France should make no peace with England until Malta was given up, and that Piedmont and Naples should be left independent.'[3]

Notwithstanding the gloomy outlook, the new Addington Ministry began at once to consider the possibility of coming to terms with France. Within a week of its accession to office Lord Hawkesbury (afterwards second Earl of Liverpool) informed Monsieur Otto, then

---

[1] *Paget Papers*, vol. i. p. 315. Lord Hawkesbury was Minister for Foreign Affairs in the newly appointed Addington Cabinet, in which Lord Pelham took the Home Office, Lord Hobart that of War and the Colonies, and St. Vincent the Admiralty.—J. H. R.

[2] Lord Grenville had been informed by Mr. Whitworth, the British Minister at St. Petersburg since the 18th March 1800, 'that the Czar was literally not in his senses' (Note by Mr. Hardman).

[3] *Paget Papers*, vol. i. p. 330.

in London, representing France in the arrangement for an exchange of prisoners of war, under date of the 21st March,' that His Britannic Majesty was ready to send to Paris, or any other suitable place, a Minister fully authorised to give every explanation, as well as to negotiate and to conclude in the name of His Majesty a treaty between England and France.' Lord Hawkesbury, in the negotiations which followed, at first proposed that the French should evacuate Egypt, and that the English should *retain* Malta, Ceylon, Trinidad, and Martinique, relinquishing all other colonial conquests. This was refused.

During these discussions the death of Paul I became known, and by a Convention with England signed three months later (17th June), Russia, under Alexander I, withdrew from the Northern coalition, abandoning the principles of the Armed Neutrality League. Sweden and Denmark were obliged to follow Russia, an event accelerated by Nelson's victory over the Danes at Copenhagen on the 2nd April. As a further triumph of British diplomacy, Prussia, through the mediation of Russia, likewise withdrew from the coalition, and thus within six months from its foundation this formidable confederacy was dissolved.

These events materially assisted the efforts which were being made to arrange terms of peace between England and France, and on the 22nd of July 1801 the First Consul authorised Otto to state 'that he would agree to Malta being restored to the Order,' and if the King of England 'thought it conformable to his interests as a preponderating Power *to raze the fortifications, a clause to this effect should be admitted.*' And on the 7th of the following month added : '. . . but His Britannic Majesty having consented that the Island of Malta and its dependencies should be placed in such a position as to belong neither to France nor England, the sole obstacle (to peace) is removed, which the arrangements respecting the Mediterranean continued to offer.' [1]

At a later conference held between Lord Hawkesbury and Otto on the 6th September for the discussion of the preliminary treaty, it was mentioned [2]—

that so far as that which regarded Article VI, [concerning Malta,] it had not appeared to Lord Hawkesbury sufficiently explicit, as it did not contain the express condition under which His Britannic Majesty had determined to renounce the Island of Malta, viz. that the Order and the Island should be placed under the guarantee of another Power ; and he read to Monsieur Otto the article of the counter-project of the British Government, whereby Russia should be invited to take part in the arrangements which concerned Malta, and even to garrison the Island in quality of Protector of the Order of Saint John.

At this interview Monsieur Otto replied:

that the First Consul did not refuse to admit Russia to be guarantee, but that in the article proposed there were several clauses which would

[1] Cobbett's *Register*, vol. iii. p. 1192.   [2] *Ibid.* vol. iii. p. 1199.

produce delays, and retard not only the conclusion of the definitive treaty, but even its execution, in what related to the time that would there be stipulated for the evacuation; besides the Order of Malta appeared to exist in Russia; that consequently it would be useless to burden His Imperial Majesty with a protection which he had already formally avowed.

Lord Hawkesbury thought for his part that a schism existed in the Order of Saint John, and that it was important to determine clearly where and what this Order was, so as to prevent discussions which might take place after the conclusion of the treaty; that besides His Britannic Majesty would be making too great a sacrifice in renouncing Malta not to take every precaution in his power to prevent that important possession from coming eventually under the French Government; that the proposition made tended to do away with every motive of jealousy on the subject in leaving the Island under the protection of a strong third Government.

Talleyrand, in reply to these arguments, wrote to Otto under date of the 10th September as follows[1]:

It has been understood that Egypt, Naples, Malta, and Mahon shall be restored to the sovereigns who possessed them before the war. The Sovereign of Malta was the Order of Saint John of Jerusalem. This Order by its institution has been from time immemorial under the protection and immediate discipline of the Pope. If, then, it was found that the Order in its present situation has found itself given up to dangerous dissensions and to what the English Minister calls a schism, it is then to the intervention and the influence of the Holy See that it would consequently be most natural to recur, so as to cause them to cease whenever the restitution of the Island of Malta shall be in question, and the Order placed under the guarantee of a great Power. It cannot be understood that this Power will maintain troops in the fortress of Malta, because this Island is sufficiently understood to be in a situation to defend itself, and that any material occupation of it by a foreign Power would be an attempt at the sovereignty of the Order. In other respects, it was added, how can the re-establishment of peace between France and England be rendered subordinate to a condition which is found to be dependent on a third Power? The most proper mode will incontestably be to stipulate the pure and simple restitution of the Island of Malta to the Order of Saint John without a guarantee, and without a foreign protection. If there must absolutely be a guarantee, and that of Russia be admitted, such guarantee ought not to be attended with any military force nor any other protection than that which results from the treaty itself, just as it always took place in the system of politics in Europe; and if by the results there should be any points to decide with respect to Malta, the discussions should be referred to the negotiations for the definitive treaty, and then, without doubt, it will be perfectly acknowledged that the evacuation of Malta by the English forces cannot be delayed beyond the month agreed

---

[1] Cobbett's *Register*, vol. iii. p. 1205.

upon for the evacuations in Europe, without compromising even the benefit of the re-establishment of peace, and without announcing any essential pretensions opposed to what has been agreed upon as just up to the present period.

To the above Hawkesbury replied on the 22nd September:[1]

With regard to the arrangements relative to Malta, His Majesty has only consented not to occupy that Island on the express condition of its independence on France, as well as that of Great Britain. The only means to succeed in this would be to place it under the guarantee or protection of some Power capable of supporting it.

His Majesty will not persist in desiring to keep an English garrison in the Island till the establishment of the government of the Order of Saint John. He will be ready, on the contrary, to evacuate it in the time which shall be fixed on for taking measures of this sort in Europe, provided the Emperor of Russia, as Protector of the Order, or any other Power acknowledged by the contracting parties, will efficaciously take on itself the defence and safety of Malta.

To designate this Power was the subject of further discussions, but as they did not produce a final agreement, the article was framed in such a manner as to leave it to the definitive treaty to signify the guaranteeing Power.

These negotiations finally resulted in the preliminary treaty being signed in London on the 1st October 1801, to the following effect, so far as concerned Malta:

ART. IV.—The Island of Malta and its dependencies shall be evacuated by the troops of His Britannic Majesty, and restored to the Order of Saint John of Jerusalem.

For the purpose of rendering this Island completely independent of either of the two contracting parties, it shall be placed under the guarantee and protection of a third Power, to be agreed upon in the definitive treaty.

(Signed) HAWKESBURY.
,, OTTO.[2]

---

[1] Cobbett's *Register*, vol. iii. p. 1207.

[2] It is tolerably certain that the Pitt Ministry would not have agreed to give up both Minorca and Malta; Dundas was resolved to retain one of those islands, and clearly saw the great importance of Malta, as appears from his letter of the 20th April 1800 to Grenville. The latter did not at that time value Malta highly, as his reply shows (see *Dropmore Papers*, vol. vi. pp. 199, 200, 207). Possibly the 'Observations on Malta' sent to him by General Graham, and the urgent appeals of Wickham from Vienna in January 1801 to keep Malta (*ibid.* pp. 226, 248, 249, 421, 430), changed his opinion, for he spoke bitterly against the terms of the peace, as is seen by his speech in the House of Lords (Alison, vol. v. ch. xxxiv. pp. 166, 167). He censured especially the virtual abandonment of the Mediterranean to France.

The opinion of Pitt was far more favourable. On the 1st October 1801 he stated to Mr. Long that he thought the peace 'fortunate both for the Government and for the public'; and to Lord Mulgrave, that it was 'very advantageous,' though he regretted the retrocession of the Cape of Good Hope to the Dutch. In his speech in Parliament he even said that the gains to England—namely, Ceylon, Mysore, and Trinidad—were more glorious than those of Florida and Canada (!) by the Seven Years' War. He decried the importance of Minorca, but said, 'it is a matter of regret that we cannot retain so important an acquisition as Malta '.(Alison, vol. v. pp. 169, 171).—J. H. R.

CHAPTER XIX

THE MISSION OF THE MALTESE DEPUTIES TO ENGLAND

(October 1801—May 1802)

DURING the autumn of 1801 rumours reached Malta that negotiations were proceeding between England and France for the cessation of hostilities, and that in order to secure peace England, notwithstanding all the sacrifices she had made, would have to abandon Malta; and further, that there was a probability of the island being restored to the Order of St. John of Jerusalem under some modification of its statutes.

These rumours caused the greatest consternation among the inhabitants, who had already discovered the advantages they derived from their connexion with Great Britain. Public meetings were at once convened, denouncing the contemplated restoration of the Order to Malta, and beseeching the British Government to retain possession of the Island. On the 21st of October Mr. Eton addressed the following letter to the Civil Commissioner, Mr. Cameron, describing the state of feeling in the Island:

(Valetta), *October 21st* 1801.[1]

SIR,—I have the honour to enclose you a translation of a paper containing the sentiments of the principal Maltese, the Locotenenti and Representatives, &c., on the evacuation of this Island, and the delivering it up to the Order.

Since the arrival of the French cartel, I have had my house full of the most respectable people in the Island; they are too much agitated to sit down and draw up a fuller representation to His Majesty's Government.

The hasty departure of Sir Alexander Ball does not allow more time than for them briefly to state to you their sentiments and the desperate resolution they have taken, entreating you to lay it before His Majesty's Ministry. I have the honour, &c.   (Signed) WM. ETON.

Thereupon Mr. Cameron on the same day wrote to Lord Hobart:

Sir Alexander Ball, accompanied by Mr. Casolani, have accelerated their departure in order to be able to afford all the information that is

[1] Anderson's Journal, *Secret Expedition to Egypt*, p. 502.

needed. The people here are alarmed beyond description at the idea of the restoration of the Order, and I really believe they will never submit to it.[1]

The anguish of the people cannot be better described than by presenting a copy of the appeal, dated two days previously, which had been delivered to Mr. Cameron by Mr. Eton on the 21st October for the purpose of having it laid before His Majesty's Ministry:

[Translation.]

Representation by the Chiefs of the Villages, Representatives, Lieutenant-Governors, and Chiefs of the Battalions to the Royal Commissioner (Charles Cameron) in Malta on the 19th October 1801.

YOUR EXCELLENCY,—The sensation produced in Malta by the news which has reached us from France, to the effect that this Island is to be again delivered to the Order of Saint John of Jerusalem, is most intense and universal.

The conduct of the French captain and his officers, who landed immediately to communicate the tidings to their most notorious partisans, afford well-grounded reasons to suspect that Bonaparte has consented to this arrangement in order that he himself might repossess the Island on some future occasion. The Order has but few partisans, and these, since the expulsion of the Knights, have no influence among the people, yet attempt when occasion offers to excite odium against the existing Government under various false pretexts. The French are generally detested, and as the Maltese foresee that by placing the Order in possession of the Island it is virtually handing it over to the French, they for such justifiable fear are determined to oppose it. All those who have in the past made any resistance, either to the Order of Saint John or the French, will most certainly become victims, and they form the majority of the Maltese nation.

In the desperate situation of the nation by such an odd change of Government it must naturally be expected that the most obstinate resistance will be shown. The bravery and the high courage displayed in the past will be exhibited in the future. The Maltese have already begun to experience the advantages and enjoy the happiness of being governed by His Britannic Majesty; they have seen the trade of their islands flourishing, with every probability of their Island becoming the emporium of the Mediterranean, and, further, that the arts, sciences, and manufactures are protected. They begin to feel themselves of more importance through their becoming a portion of a vast Empire, and each individual experiences the consciousness that, having formerly been despised and vilified, he has become a respected member of society.

If in the future they are placed under the government of the Order or of that of the French, and as the importance of their Islands to these is due to its port and fortifications, they are convinced that they will return to a condition of things more deplorable than what existed in the past. Every merchant possessing means is determined to leave the place, persuaded

[1] C.O.R., Malta, No. 2.

that under the Order their trade will be restricted as formerly, if for no other than political reasons, cultivated for the purpose of creating jealousy amongst the Powers; and they further know well that under the French Government the ports of Marseilles and Toulon would have the preference. It is impossible to describe the fear of those who have taken up arms and fought the French and the traitorous Order with the greatest energy and rancour.

With regard to the ability of the Order to maintain its independence and neutrality it must be observed:—

First. That the other nations, having deprived the Order of its revenues, it would become dependent upon France, whose Government would not fail to support her own more numerous Knights, possessing as she does three Langues, so that without any declaration of war France will become mistress of Malta, and whenever she wishes to remove the mask she can raise her flag over this impregnable fortress.

Secondly. The garrison of Malta was formerly composed of Maltese; the Order would not, under existing circumstances, rely upon their fidelity, and would therefore engage foreign troops, and such would, without doubt, be selected from those nations which are in sympathy with the French, who, having the garrison in their pay and dedicated to their interests, would be in consequence masters of the Island.

Thirdly. The Maltese might have hopes that at some future time they would be able to dispossess the Order, as in the past, but would not the French provision the Island so as to endure a prolonged siege? A winter blockade is almost impossible. Would they not disarm the inhabitants? Would they not drive them out of the fortifications? Would they not, in fact, adopt every measure to ensure themselves against surprise?

Fourthly. Would the Maltese, after having been abandoned and sacrificed by the English, confide themselves a second time to their protection? From having been your most ardent friends, they would become your most implacable enemies.

Fifthly. If it is determined to withdraw the British troops from Malta, the people pray that they may be permitted to conduct their own affairs. The Maltese are determined not to submit to any other Power than Great Britain, preferring otherwise to perish under the walls of their city if they cannot maintain their liberty and independence.

After having received you as friends and liberators, after having been cordially united to you, the Maltese have reason to hope that you will not join their enemies in aiding to place them again in the bonds of slavery to masters whom they detest.

They will not yet believe you capable of such an act. They deeply deplore having been sacrificed in the Capitulations made with the French, and they have lately been provoked almost to the point of insurrection by the tyranny and insults of a military government, but the arrival of a Civil Governor has perfectly restored calm. From all this the better class of the Maltese nation is persuaded that the wrath of the people, on finding themselves abandoned by you, will be re-awakened, and that on no future occasion will you have the power to regain this Island.

Sixthly. They feel the great political importance of Malta to those who possess it; they know that in the hands of the French that nation can reconquer Egypt, and advance upon India with greater strength and experience. They know that Russia at this moment is anxious to see the Order of Saint John in Malta, which means France being mistress of the Island; that Russia (notwithstanding her projects against Turkey, which may be dormant for a reign) will be re-awakened, and that whosoever possesses Malta has the certain means of uniting with Russia, and that France, if she will but abandon the Turks, may rely on the co-operation of Russia in the annihilation of the British power in the Mediterranean.

They know that Russia united with France can obtain the entire and exclusive trade of the Levant, that France can procure from the Black Sea naval stores in safety, that Russia might march an army from the southern coasts of the Caspian Sea to the territories of Zaman Sera, and carry out the threats of the defunct Empress [Catharine] to expel you from India; in fact they are convinced that Malta is the key which opens the gates to India, and the link which binds the chain uniting Russia to France, for it will close the entrance of the English to the Mediterranean, impeding for all time the opportunity of counterbalancing French influence in Italy, creating a navy which some day will pass into the Atlantic, and there challenge the English fleets.

Whereas if England possesses Malta she will be Mistress of the Mediterranean, despite the enmity of the surrounding nations; and that which concerns England still more, and which the Maltese do not ignore, is the fact that their Island would become a commercial emporium and a grand depôt for British dry goods, where Italian, Turkish, and Russian produce would be abundantly poured in.

In the arsenal of Malta there exists every accommodation to build, equip, and maintain a fleet.

The granary of all Europe might be made in Malta importing grain from the Black Sea, from Egypt, and any other ports where it might be purchased at low rates, and re-shipped to the parts where scarcity prevailed, and particularly to Great Britain.

With regard to the Knights of the Order of Saint John of Jerusalem, we repeat that it is impossible that they can maintain their neutrality, for not only is internal strength wanting, but they are without the aid of neighbouring States. The only Power which could in such eventuality support them is the same which has in view the repression of the Island.

The Knights have violated their solemn oaths, made at the altar, by disgracefully surrendering the Island without making any defence, betraying their own religious and military institution; they have violated all codes of honour as knights and soldiers; they have sacrificed the Maltese people.[1]

Can such men ever be counted worthy of the Maltese confidence?

A large number of the Knights of the Order took service in the French army, accompanying it to Egypt. Nearly all have conducted themselves in a manner incompatible with their vows.

Only those Knights who were absent from Malta could allege innocence, but even such conducted themselves in a way no less reprehensible. Not one of them came, as was their duty, to reconquer their ancient seat.

---

[1] This is much exaggerated, for, as has been shown in this work, the Maltese were largely responsible for the surrender to the French.—J. H. R.

The road to honour was open to them. A national army was in the field, and there was a powerful co-operation of allies; in fact, there is not one single Knight who is not, according to the statutes of his Order, degraded and irreclaimable, and deprived of all pretensions to membership of that body.

The Order therefore exists no longer; it is annihilated in accordance with its own laws, and is despised and vagrant. They preferred taking refuge in Russia, where they were further from the place of danger, rather than in the campaign of Malta, and created for a morsel of bread, a schism in the Order, which was a violation of their obligations.

Yet this section of the Order may be considered the better portion among the infamous Knights, for *they* did not, like the majority of their brethren, prostitute their honour by opening the gates of Valetta to the French.

Until we have time to formulate a fitting representation to be sent by a national deputation to England we implore you, as the King's Commissioner, by all the attachment we have for your person, to the British Government, in honour of virtue, of religion, by the love we have for our wives and children, for our beloved Island, for the dignity of man, and for the sacred laws of justice, for the sake of humanity, generosity, gratitude, and for our sincere affection. We pray that you will be pleased to represent these sentiments and our deplorable situation at the throne of His Majesty, praying to the Almighty that Great Britain may ever remain the bulwark and asylum of liberty, fidelity, and religion.

If His Majesty absolutely wishes that the Order of Saint John should return to Malta, in such case the people beseech that all the fortifications remain in the possession of his said Majesty.

The day following the date of this appeal news was received in Malta that a preliminary treaty of peace between England and France had been actually signed on the 1st of October. How this news was received in Malta is further given in a dispatch from General Villettes to Lord Hobart, dated the 21st of October:

La Valette, 21st October 1801.[1]

The Right Hon. Lord Hobart, &c.

My Lord,—As your Lordship will receive from General Fox a report of the troops which have already arrived here from Egypt, I shall not trouble you at present with another.

The important news which we received yesterday by a French cartel, of a general peace having been signed in London on the 1st instant, is the only event of consequence that has occurred here since my last of the 9th instant. This intelligence has been announced to me by the Prefect Maritime of Toulon, in a letter which appears to be a circular (and of which I find Mr. Cameron proposes sending your Lordship a copy), but without mentioning any one of the articles of the treaty. We have, therefore, no other account of them but such as the French officers themselves are pleased to give us; and though very reasonable doubts may be entertained of its authenticity, it has not failed to excite the greatest

[1] C.O.R., Malta, No. 4 (1801).

agitation in the minds of the people of this Island. I shall not enter into any detail on this subject, as your Lordship will receive the fullest information upon it from Sir Alexander Ball, who is going home by this opportunity, and is better qualified than any other person to represent the alarm of the greater part of the population here on this occasion, and how sincerely they will lament any change likely to remove them from the immediate protection of His Majesty's Government.

I make no doubt but we shall soon receive more authentic information on this subject, and in the meantime I shall only beg leave to assure your Lordship that, whatever may prove the event, nothing shall be wanting on my part to fulfil His Majesty's wishes and instructions to the best of my abilities. I have the honour, &c. (Signed) W. A. VILLETTES.

Under these sad circumstances the leaders of the people deemed it advisable to prepare without further delay the petition to His Britannic Majesty which had been referred to in the last paragraph but one of their appeal to Mr. Cameron; and two days after reception of the news the following 'Representation' was prepared and ready for signature, namely, on the 22nd October 1801.

[Petitioners' own verbatim translation.[1]]

The humble Representation of the Deputies of Malta and Gozo, unanimously elected by the people, at the foot of the throne of His Britannic Majesty.

The Maltese first took up arms against the French and besieged them in Valetta; they afterwards received assistance from the Portuguese, the Neapolitans, and the British, who by their fleet blockaded the grand harbour and port of Saint Paul, while the Maltese guarded all other avenues to the island.[2]

The gates of Valetta were closed on the 2nd September 1798, and the city surrendered the 4th of September 1800 [this should be the 5th]; the foreign troops were only auxiliaries, as the proclamations of the British Government prove it; the Maltese were the principals. The Maltese had conquered the whole island except Valetta before they received any foreign assistance.

During the siege of Valetta the Maltese lost about 20,000 men; the British army had not one single soldier killed. The French garrison, reduced to the last extremity from want of provisions, offered to capitulate and to leave hostages for the payment of the large sums which they had taken from the public treasury, from the university, or public fund belonging to the Maltese for the furnishing the island with corn from the Monte di Pietà, where individuals pledged their effects, from churches, and by forced loans from private persons.

The situation of the French garrison was known to the British general, as well as to all the Maltese—that in two days it must surrender at discretion. There was found only five English quarters of wheat, and no

---

[1] C.O.R., Malta, No. 3 (1801).
[2] Of course this ridiculously underrates the importance of the British blockade. Several other statements are also incorrect—J. H. R.

other provisions in Valetta, when it surrendered. General Pigot, however, granted the garrison capitulations without consulting or even informing the Maltese, without naming them or stipulating one article in their favour, by which the French were allowed to carry away with them their effects; and accordingly before they gave up their posts they plundered the inhabitants of their remaining money, jewels, and effects, and carried them on board vessels, which conveyed to France the spoils of a victorious people. The British troops took possession of the place, and caused the Maltese to lay down their arms on the glacis before they entered the town.

The Maltese without suspicion, and relying on the good faith of the British nation, gave up their country into the hands of the British general without stipulation, obeying them with fidelity and submission, as ministers of the Sovereign their hearts had elected. They forbear to make any comment on the manner they have been treated, because they are fully persuaded that it will be discovered with horror and contempt by the King's Ministers.

The expenses of the war by land and the pay of the Maltese battalions were paid by the Maltese, and they mortgaged the lands of several villages to answer for debts which they had for that purpose contracted.

The Maltese therefore demand that if the island is not delivered up to them, that all expenses incurred for that share of the war which they took be paid to them, and the damages they suffered by the war be made good to them, and that they be indemnified for the plunder of the French.

They allege that they as principals in the war were the captors, that every public property is theirs, and that if by superior force it should be wrested out of their hands the mortgages on them should be paid.

They claim the island, therefore, by right of conquest from the French, who had by right of conquest acquired it from the Order of Saint John.

With respect to the claim of the Order of Saint John, they argue that the government of the island was ceded to them by the Emperor Charles the Fifth as a fief, and as a place for them to maintain their troops to make continual war against the infidels; as to the *property* they have acquired it is contrary to the stipulations, and it has been obtained by *usurpation* of private property; that a great part of the fortifications were built by taxes on the Maltese, as well as many of the best buildings.

The University,[1] the Monte di Pietà, and many other institutions were entirely Maltese private property.

That, however, whatever claim they might have had to the Island, they have lost it by an act more conclusive than that of being conquered, by the most disgraceful treason to their body, violating all the laws of honour, of religion, and the statutes of the Order, which they solemnly swore on the Gospels at the altar to maintain with the last drop of their blood.

By this act, according to their own laws they ceased to be members of the Order; they are degraded and '*become infamous,*' and the sound part of them, if any such had existed, were bound to put them to death. And then the Order was entire, embodied, assembled in the seat of their establishment (which had been witness of so many glorious actions), with

[1] As before noted, the University was the corporation for the supply of corn.—J. H. R.

every means of defence and without any wants. If, then, while their honour still had a name they were traitors and partisans of the French, what must they now be, vilified and disgraced, reduced to indigence and shameful dependency?

But the Maltese have other claims to the sovereignty of their own Island without recurring to the arguments made use of by some writers,[1] that when a throne is vacant the people have a right to name their own sovereign : they claim their own independency by having twice purchased the island, and paid the price stipulated to the Kings of Spain and Sicily.

King Alphonso (to whom they voluntarily submitted, after having bought the island), in his diploma of the 27th November 1397, declared that Malta composed a part of his dominions, but that if ever his successors alienated it from the Crown, under whatever title, even as a government or rectory, perpetual or temporary, to any person whatever, even though he should be of the royal blood of their sovereign reigning, and in the failure of the observance of this part he permitted the Maltese to resist ' *manu forti pro quo in nullum crimen delictum vel inobedientiam incurrere reputentur et aliquatinus censeantur* '; this was confirmed by King Ferdinand the 4th of January 1489, and it is considered by the Maltese as their Magna Charta, which last of all they expected would be ravished from them by the English, who hold their own Magna Charta so dear.

With these privileges they remained annexed to Sicily and treated by the Crown of Spain as a free people until Charles V ceded the Government to the Order of Saint John of Jerusalem after its expulsion from Rhodes. They submitted reluctantly, but with the express condition, however, that in the possession of the Order they should still enjoy their privileges and be considered as annexed and vassals to the Crown of Sicily ; that if the Order of Saint John went to another residence Malta should return as before under the Kings of Sicily. The submission of the Order of Saint John was voluntary, for they could have opposed it without being accounted rebels ; whence it evidently follows that the dominion belonged to the Maltese, and their subjection to Sicily or the Kings of Spain was not in consequence of any right in those Sovereigns to the islands, but by favour of the Maltese, who accepted them as sovereigns for the sake of protection against powerful enemies.

They were free allies, they elected their own sovereigns, the Kings of Sicily, and governed their own Island themselves. There are many documents existing which prove all this and much more.

Feeling their own political weakness, and putting a boundless confidence in the sincerity of the British Government and the faith of the British nation, they rather wished to become subjects of the King and enjoy all the advantages of free subjects to a monarch who is the father of all his people than to assert and maintain their own independence. But never did they suspect that, abusing their confidence and violating all the laws of justice, human and divine, they should be forcibly delivered over by their own auxiliary allies, as a conquered nation, or as vile slaves sold for a political consideration to new masters, and to masters whose tyranny, extortion, and sacrilege have rendered them the execration of every virtuous individual, and to whom, whatever misery may ensue, they

---

[1] e.g. by Locke, Rousseau, and others.—J. H. R.

never will submit. Excluded from the fortresses, almost without arms, without ammunition, without provisions, and absolutely without any foreign alliance or promise of assistance, our brave islanders resolved to perish or be free.

The whole country rose, armed mostly with utensils of agriculture; they expelled the French from every post out of the great fortifications and kept it blockaded, repulsing every sortie made by the enemy.[1]

They mortgaged their lands and procured corn from Sicily. The entrance of the great port they could not command; this object was accomplished by the British fleet, while the islanders defended every other inlet until Valetta surrendered.

Has the King of Great Britain ever declared himself in any public act in this island sovereign of it? No other term has been used but that of protector, ardently as the Maltese wished to be styled his subjects. Is it to be expected that such a people will deliver up their rights to such masters? They may be free, but they may perish. At whose door will their blood lie? The Maltese think it wholly unnecessary to recite how indignantly they were treated by the Order of Saint John under the government of the Grand Master: how they were held in vile subjection, treated as an inferior class of beings; every noble excluded from all pretensions to honour and distinction, every man of merit debarred from honourable employment; how their families were dishonoured or ruined whenever the caprice of a Knight fixed on his victim. What those men were, and what their government must have been, may easily be inferred from this one fact—*they betrayed their own Order, almost to a man.*

They pass over indignantly this point to prove that the delivering up Malta to the Order of Saint John is actually and in fact delivering it over to the French.

If the Order, in the possession of independent sovereignty and revenue, enjoying every ease and pleasure that luxurious imagination can frame, courted and bowed to as monarchs, if then the French could command them to go forth from their earthly paradise to wander in the wide world, could make them partisans of their cause, what must not the power of the French over them now be—dependent, degraded, vilified, and indigent beggars, in whom every spark of honour is extinct, and who have been guilty of the blackest and most infamous of crimes, treachery, and the most horrible infidelity towards their God, perjury of sacramental oath, and apostasy?

The French have three distinct *langues*, the Spaniards three others. The Spaniards are dependent on the French; they were so also when the Island was betrayed; there remain but two other *langues* which may anywise be called independent, the knights of Sicily and Naples. All those who from the Cis-alpine Republic and the parts of the French have been conquered, or subdued to virtual vassalage, will or must be of their party. Almost all the revenues of the Order and the great offices and places of trust are, according to the statutes of the Order, to be enjoyed by those who are now become creatures and dependent on France; in fine there is not, counting the new nation—Anglo-Bavaria—above one-

---

[1] As was shown by Vaubois in his letters to the Directory printed above, the French had few reasons for attempting sorties, as all the food from the open country had been removed by the Maltese.—J. H. R.

thirtieth part of the Knights' that will not be at the command of France, the public treasury being dissipated and the commanderies (supposing them to be everywhere restored) of any considerable value belonging to the French. On them the Order must depend for the expense of raising and maintaining an army to garrison the fortresses, ships and galleys, if not to cruise against infidels, at least to protect in some measure their commerce and the provisioning of the island.

If each langue (or nation) brings its own proportion, so great a majority will be of the same description that no apprehension will be entertained of the remainder by the French party.

To prove all this we need only refer to the list of his brother-traitors given by the Chevalier de St. Priest, and of the offices then in possession of the three French langues.

Many more proofs will be brought to prove the assertion that giving the island of Malta to the Order of Saint John is actually giving it up to the French. And can anyone doubt but that the principal object of the French in making peace with Great Britain was not to obtain possession of Malta? For on the possession of Malta depends the existence of India to Great Britain, her alliance with Russia, the safety of Sicily, the commerce of the Mediterranean, the Adriatic, and the whole Levant, and an uncontrolled power over every other country bordering on the seas. Sicily, as we too well know, must be an easy prey to the French when they are in possession of Malta. It would require a larger and a better-disciplined army of Neapolitan troops to guard all the numerous points where the island is assailable on this side than ever can be supported in that island by a king of Naples. We know the revolutionary progress those enemies to all Governments have made in creating a party in their favour, and in lowering in the eyes of the people the existing Government, and sowing discontent, the first step they always take. When the French were in possession of Malta, and never dreamed of being expelled, they declared without mystery the extent of their views, both in print, in letters, and in discourse, not those of the populace, but men in high office and command. They affirmed that from the Black Sea and the Adriatic a superabundance of naval stores could be procured cheaper than from the North. That the Russian fleets, and ports, and the more contemptible Turkish fleet were at their mercy, that they could dictate terms of vassalage to them. That Russia never would relinquish her project of expelling the Turks from Europe and erecting a Greek State.[1] That some unambitious sovereign might sleep at times over the project, but it was irrevocably resolved by the Council of the nation, from the time of the father of Peter the Great. That those only have been sincerely treated by Russia as allies who entered into the project. That in consequence France could easily detach Russia from Great Britain. The formidable navy in the Black Sea, joined to that which the Greek State would create, though alone unable to cope with the French fleet, joined to it, as it always must be by its independence, would far outvie the fleets Great Britain might detach to so great a distance from home, as she must always keep a sufficient force to guard her own coasts.

They [i.e. the French] concluded that the Mediterranean was exclusively

[1] The Czar Alexander I renounced this policy for a time, but recurred to it at Tilsit and Erfurt in 1807 and 1808.—J. H. R.

theirs. That from Egypt they could send an army to conquer India with ease, and even attack it in various points. They have plans of this invasion alone, and in conjunction with Russia, land to the south of Persia and to the north of Persia and the south of the Caspian joining the country of Zaman Shah. All the efforts of the House of Austria to have a commerce or a navy must be dependent on the will of France, [which has] the numerous sailors of the whole coast of Italy, and the Archipelago—Ragusa, which alone has some hundreds of vessels and the finest oak timber in the world, the copper mines, the hemp, masts from the Black Sea, the tar, pitch, iron, salpetre—in fine every product of naval armament or commerce. Egypt they now understand, and they have there, in spite of all their past tyranny, a party, which will increase. They have affirmed that the fleet which is, independently of their present means, to be created will be powerful enough to bid defiance to the navy of Great Britain, and to carry to England hundreds of thousands of men to invade her. They spoke of Ireland as theirs by showing themselves.

The French once established in Malta, it will be utterly impossible to expel them. There are no violent means that they will not take, such as turning the inhabitants out of the fortresses, disarming, putting to death, or banishing, all those whom they suppose enemies, having a large garrison, perhaps, as they once threatened, sending the whole population to France, and repeopling it with French families. And we have many reasons to think that this would have been put into execution as soon as they had got leisure. The island of Lampedusa, if cultivated, would produce very much more corn than the Island (Malta) and the largest garrison could consume.

With respect to the guarantee, which we have heard of to be given by other Powers—a war puts an end to it. If those Powers occupy some part of the fortresses the troops may be bribed, and the French will wisely sacrifice immense sums. The military posts are dependent one upon the other.

We can show the impracticability of occupying part without the whole. We can point out how they can and will obtain their ends. We can show that there will be no security but by an English garrison only, the inhabitants of the cities and country being governed by the English alone, and that the Knights cannot be admitted in any other shape than as a monastic fraternity, enjoying the credit of nobles and the respect due to birth, but not meddling with military or civil government.

They are now fit for neither. We do not enter into the profound views of Cabinets; but be it permitted to us merely to observe that, if France and Russia had no other intention than the re-establishment of the Order in its pristine splendour, why have they not chosen a place where they could be more independent? or why have they considered the possession of Malta by the Order as necessary to its re-establishment? This is but too clear to those who are in a position to see that Malta is not taken out of the hands of the English, to leave it in those of the Order of Saint John of Jerusalem.

A further meeting of the representatives of the various villages and districts was called for the 9th of the following month, when the annexed Declaration of the election of deputies to proceed to

England and present to His Majesty King George their formal protest to any transfer of the islands was submitted and approved :

[Translation.]

We the undersigned, of our own spontaneous desire, depute Messieurs Marquis Don Mario Testaferrata, Filippo Castagna, Lieutenant of the two cities Lenglea and Cospicua, Don Emmanuele Riccaud, Don Pietro Mallia, and Michele Cachia, to proceed to London in order to represent to His Majesty the situation and the needs of the inhabitants of these islands, Malta and Gozo, and to ask for the necessary provisions.

Relying on the said personages, who we are fully persuaded will endeavour to obtain all the advantages for our nation, and to whom we confide all the interests of the same, we do hereby sign with our own hands this 9th day of November 1801 :

GIUSEPPE CASHA, Lieutenant Vittoriosa.
DON FELICE CALLEJA, Representative of Musta.
PARROCO SALVATORE CORSO, Representative of Seggieni.
PARROCO CARAFA, Representative of Micabiba.
SACERDOTE DALLI, Representative of Zurrico.
PIETRO BUTTIGIEG, Representative of Zebbug.
GIUSEPPE FRENDO, Chief and Representative of Balzan.
EMMANUELE GELLEL, Lieutenant of Curmi.
ANGELO CILIA, Chief of Samra.
NICOLA CAMMILLERI, Lieutenant of Seggieni.
VINCENZO BORG, Representative of Birchircara.
SAVERIO ZARB, Representative of Attand.
GIOVANNI MARIA CHETANTI, Chief of Musta.
MICHELE VASSALLO, Lieutenant of Naxaro.
SALVATORE GAFÀ, Chief of Battalion, Lia.
GIUSEPPE MONTEBELLO, Representative of Tarscien.
GIORGIO BONNAI, Lieutenant of Gudia.
TOMMASO MALLIA, of the Committee of Asciak.
ENRICO SCERRI, Captain of the Port.
GAETANO FABRI, Lieutenant of Borgo Vilhena.
GIUSEPPE ABELA, Lieutenant of Zeitun.
ALESSANDRO DAMATO, Lieutenant of Zurrico.
FRANCESCO ZAMMIT, Lieutenant of Crendi.
DR. GREGORIO MIFSUD, Representative of Crendi.
GIOVANNI GAFÀ, Lieutenant of Gargur.
AGOSTINO SAID, Lieutenant of Zabbar.
CH. GIUSEPPE ABDILLA, Lieutenant of Safi.

The original *procès verbal* of the said election was legalised in the secretary's office the 26th November 1801.

(Signed) ALEXANDER MACAULAY, Secretary.
„ FELICE CUTAJAR, pro-Secretary.

On the same day a meeting took place at Gozo when the following election was made and certificate issued :

[Translation.]

We the undersigned, jurats and representatives of the magistracy of the island of Gozo and chiefs of the respective villages, having regard to the great benefits received during the late events, and those which we continue to receive by the clemency of His Britannic Majesty, of our own freewill depute Mr. Antonio Mallia, first jurat and lieutenant of said island, for the purpose of proceeding to London and representing at the foot of the throne of his beloved Majesty the condition, situation, and needs of the inhabitants of this island, and to beseech the granting of those opportune provisions and perpetual protection which up to the present time he has paternally bestowed.

Relying upon the said Mallia, whom we esteem capable to obtain for us all the advantages which the nation desires, we confide to him the protection of all the interests of the same.

In faith of which we subscribe our names to this present, with our own hands and seal of the said magistracy, this 9th day of November 1801.

(Signed) ANTONIO MALLIA, Jurat.
,, BARTOLOMMEO BUSUTTIL, Jurat.
,, MASSIMO DEBONO, Jurat.
,, ODOARDO BUSUTTIL DALLI, Jurat.
,, SACERDOTE HILI, Chief of Nadur.
,, FRANCESCO ZAMMIT, Chief of Xenchia.
,, SACERDOTE CAMILLERI.
,, MICHELE ANGELO CALLEJA, for Lorenzo Vella, Chief of Caccia.
,, MICHELE ANGELO CALLEJA, for Martino Asciach,
        Chief of Zebbug.
,, TOMMASO CASSAR, Chief of Garbo.
,, MICHELE ANGELO CALLEJA, for Giuseppe Muscat,
        Chief of Sannat.

Legalised at the secretary's office the 26th November 1801.

On the 13th November Mr. Cameron informed Lord Hobart that on the 5th of that month Malta had been declared a free port, amidst the wildest enthusiasm, and sent copies of the illuminated inscriptions which had appeared in the city of Valetta on that day.

[Translation.]

Freedom of Commerce
Given to Grateful Malta
By a Free and Powerful People,
the 5th November 1801.

George the Third, the Father of his People,
Gave to Grateful Malta
Freedom of Commerce,
the 5th of November 1801.

George the Third, King and Father,
Delivered grateful Malta
First from Slavery
Afterwards from exactions.

The following is Mr. Cameron's dispatch of the 13th November to Lord Hobart, above referred to :—

[Private and confidential.]
[Extract.]

Valetta, 13th November 1801.[1]

I do not think it will be easy to reconcile the Maltese to the return of the Order so as to make them act cordially together for the defence of the Island, and their general abhorrence of the French is not to be described.

Military force only can protect the Order, should it be found necessary to re-establish it. The attachment of the body of the people to His Majesty's Government is complete, but they are continually agitated by the acts of those who are employed by the different parties, who are not sufficiently enlightened to perceive how unavailing any efforts of theirs must be in deciding the future fate of this Island. Mr. Livingstone, who will be the bearer of this letter, will be able to inform your Lordship on many subjects to which your enquiries may lead; his experience and ability, as well as his firm attachment to His Majesty's Government, will, I trust, be accepted as an excuse for the confidence which I have reposed in him. He was there on the day the freedom of the port was declared, and witnessed the enthusiasm with which it was received by the Maltese. He will also tell you how cordially I have the good fortune to live with Lord Keith, Genl· Fox, Genl· Villettes, and in short, with all the officers of army and navy, as well as with the merchants, civil officers, and the Maltese generally.

I regret that this is not to be done without considerable expense, and I trust you will not think me mercenary in stating these circumstances to you. Pray allow me again to tell you how much I am flattered by your manner of expressing your approbation of my conduct, and how strongly I feel your Lordship's kindness to me. Believe me, &c.

(Signed) CHARLES CAMERON.

A further note to Lord Hobart of the same date is to the following effect :—

[Extract and synopsis.]

Malta, 13th November 1801.[2]

. . . I refused to assist in the expenses of the intended deputation to England, but at the same time I did not attempt to impede the journey. The spirit of party continues with redoubled violence, people are loud in their expressions of dislike to the Order, and adherents of the Order do not scruple to threaten those attached to the English Government.

To avoid all possibility of there being any doubt as to the unanimity of the election of the deputies to proceed to England, public notices appeared on the 16th November 1801, testifying to

[1] C.O.R. Malta, No. 3 (1801).   [2] Ibid.

the fact and empowering the deputies to speak on behalf of the Maltese people.[1]

In a private and confidential paper from the Royal Commissioner, Charles Cameron, dated the 15th November 1801, the personal character of the several deputies was given as follows [2] :—

Marquis Mario Testaferrata, of the first family in the Island. One of his ancestors was made Grandee of Spain. The Marquis has been distinguished for his moderation in practice and his prudent though manly conduct in the various trying situations he was placed in since the invasion of the French. He was so well thought of by all parties that he was appointed one of those who drew up the capitulations to the French. The French laid heavy contributions on the family, which is still one of the most opulent in the Island. He has always shown a great attachment to His Majesty's Government, and is at the same time esteemed a well wisher to his country, and consequently he is very popular. As to his talents, he is a man of sound judgment, and is well informed with respect to the ancient privileges, as well as the modern state of the Island.

Phil. Castagna, Luogotenente (or Lieutenant-Governor) of the two cities of Burmola and Senglea. A man of an excellent public character, exceedingly popular with every rank of the inhabitants. He distinguished himself at the siege of Valetta, and in the Congress, both by his courage, moderation, and wisdom. He took Gozo from the French with a handful of troops, and an address which raised him very high in the opinion of the military. He is very warmly attached to His Majesty's Government.

Don Pietro Mallia (Magister Theologiæ in the Public College), representative of Casal Asciak, a Maltese priest (not of the Order) and a man of very pure reputation, enjoying popular confidence, and is much attached to His Majesty's Government, as are all the Maltese priests, and the Monastic Orders.

Don Emanuel Riccaud, was first a Capuchin, but his health suffering by the rigour of the Order, he became a priest (not of the Order). He is a man in whom Governor Ball puts much confidence, he is very zealous in our cause and in that of his country. He is a respectable man and speaks French.

Michele Cacchia, military and civil engineer, representative of Casal Zeitun. He constructed all the batteries during the siege of Valetta, and contributed money towards the expense of the war. He is famed for his wisdom in counsel, and is the most popular man in the Island, his integrity and talents have acquired him a great reputation, and the entire confidence of the people of every description.

Antonio Mallia (Gozitano). In the beginning of the revolutions he stood forward. He is a gentleman, living on his income. He is the Lieutenant-Governor and first Provost of Gozo, and zealously attached to the British Government.

Although this movement commenced in October 1801, the memorial was not signed, certified, and legalised until the 20th,

[1] Lack of space compels us to omit these documents, which are of slight importance and of no interest.—J. H. R.
[2] C.O.R. Malta, No. 3 (1801).

23rd and 26th November respectively. As in the meantime the preliminary treaty of peace had been concluded (on the 1st October), the deputies upon their arrival in London on the 1st February 1802 found the negotiations for the definitive treaty so far advanced that there appeared little possibility of obtaining any modification of the stipulations so far agreed upon. In the *Annual Register* of the 5th February 1802, the arrival of the Maltese deputies is announced as follows :—

> A deputation from the principal inhabitants of Malta has arrived in London. The object of their mission is to put their country under the protection and government of His Majesty. No doubt can exist, but that this overture will be accepted by His Majesty's Ministers as some small equipoise to the Sovereignty of Italy, which the First Consul has acquired, since peace was signed.[1]

On the 4th February, three days after their arrival, the Maltese deputies addressed the following letter to Lord Hobart :—

London, *4th February* 1802.[2]

MY LORD,—We have the honour of announcing to your Lordship our arrival in this capital in the character of deputies from the Maltese Nation appointed as soon as the intelligence of the preliminary treaty of peace reached that Island. Happy shall we be, my Lord, in the opportunity of laying before your Lordship the truth and justice of the demands with which we are entrusted. It is this hope and the confidence we have in the equity of the British Government which have conducted us hither. We pray your Lordship to have the goodness to inform us in the course of three days from the date of this letter, when it will be convenient to your Lordship to receive the homage of the respectful attachment, with which we have the honour to be, &c., &c.   (Signed) THE DEPUTIES.

Although dated a month later, it will be well to insert here Mr. Eton's letter respecting these deputies, addressed to Mr. John Sullivan, His Majesty's Under Secretary of State, dated the 5th March 1802 :—

Valetta, *5th March* 1802.[3]

SIR,—I take the liberty of informing you, as you may not know the exact situation of the deputies from Malta, with respect to their finances, that all the money that was given them for their journey amounted to £700 sterling. Some of them have no private fortune and the others are much restricted in their circumstances, the French having taken from them all their cash and effects, and ruined their houses and lands. I therefore

---

[1] On January 22-25 Bonaparte succeeded in bending the will of the deputies of the Cisalpine Republic (assembled in a consulta at Lyons). He prescribed to them the form of their constitution, renamed it the Italian Republic, and became its first President. See my *Life of Napoleon I*, vol. i. pp. 348-351, for these events and the indignation they caused in England as a violation of the terms of the Treaty of Lunéville.—J. H. R.
[2] Cobbett, vol. iii. p. 679.
[3] C.O.R. Malta, No. 5.

have taken the liberty of making these particulars known to you, that you may not be surprised if they apply for some pecuniary assistance. I have the honour, &c. (Signed) WM. ETON.

Having been *officially* informed that the restoration of the Order was a *fait accompli*, the deputies nevertheless addressed the following remonstrance to Lord Hobart under the date of the 1st March 1802 :—

7 Berkeley Street, London, *1st March* 1802.[1]

YOUR EXCELLENCY,—It has been with the deepest pain, and greatest surprise, that the Maltese people have heard of the sad and unmerited lot to which they are destined, by the return of the Order of Saint John of Jerusalem, and its re-acquisition of the Islands of Malta and Gozo. The defection and treachery of which they (the Order) were guilty will be events in the annals of the world no less surprising than that which again throws us under its despotic government, after having delivered us over to an army unfaithful to its promises and engagements.

The sentence which posterity will pronounce will certainly not be one of eulogy worthy of the century in which we now live, and were we from any unworthy timidity to be silent, before the righteous and magnanimous tribunal, to which we have now the advantage to appeal, we should but anticipate the laments and reproaches of our children.

We would not wish to hide from your Excellency all that which justifies us in our resentments against the Order of Saint John of Jerusalem. The blood which has been shed, the death of about 20,000 of our citizens, following the most distressing misery, the expenses incurred during the early months of the Revolution for the support of the Battalions, the loss of 6,000,000 scudis (£500,000) are sufficient proofs to belie the atrocious calumnies which the author of the reply to the Manifesto of the Priory of Russia has sought to heap upon our heads.

The slander contains within itself its own condemnation, for it is well known that the plan for the invasion of Malta was conceived in Paris, and the secret confided to the most important Knights of the Order, resident in Malta.

Letters in cypher were continually arriving, without opening the eyes of either Grand Master de Rohan, or his successor Hompesch. Following such undeniable facts, of which we might cite without number, consider, your Excellency, whether the Maltese people can witness without horror, and in cold blood, the authors of their misfortunes regain possession of Malta, and have at their disposal the freedom of the nation. Nay indeed, for even if we wished to keep silence, the still warm ashes of those who gave up their lives to liberate and recover their native land would spur us on to better defend our rights, and give the greater prominence to truth.

Yes, your Excellency, we venture to say that the Knights of Saint John of Jerusalem cannot be re-established in Malta without injuring the legitimate rights of the august descendants of Charles V., the rights of

---

[1] Cobbett, vol. iii. p. 680.
This paper is also printed in the Papers relative to Discussions with France presented to Parliament.—J. H. R.

the Maltese, and without exposing the latter to fresh catastrophes. The fidelity of the Maltese people has always been acknowledged by its ancient Sovereigns, and they have shown in these later times that they are still the same, no less in energy, than in the love of justice.

They have willingly sacrificed their resentments, but they at the same time desire that the sacrifices that they have experienced should not be forgotten, and in proof of which we request your Excellency's permission to refer to the pacific resignation which the Maltese exhibited at the time of the capitulations between the English General and General Vaubois.

Our blood, our fatiguing labours, our rights, and all our interests were either forgotten or despised. We watched the French abandon their arms, in order to carry away what remained of our spoils, with a tranquillity without example, and worthy of the highest respect; and the Maltese faithful and virtuous were reduced to envy the lot and the treatment of Maltese rebels. Alas, how can we hide from our descendants the details of a capitulation which ruined our rights, and rendered us unhappy.

It is true that the presence, and the wisdom of Captain Ball, to whom we then made known our complaints, contributed not a little to make us forget the sacrifices we have made, but the vicissitudes which have followed have neither seconded our hopes nor our requirements. We cannot hide the fact, your Excellency, of the evil impressions which the preliminaries of peace have conveyed to us of a Government to which we incessantly desire to give proof of our attachment, our fidelity, and our preference.

We are aware, your Excellency, that it is not given to us to have influence in political matters. Nature has so formed Malta that she is to be regarded from the point of view of her situation, and according to her strength, and that she is not to dictate terms of arrangement, but it is the duty of politicians nevertheless to see that her numerous population is not forgotten. Russia, France, as well as the other nations of Europe, are too just and enlightened to censure the conduct of the Maltese, and their opposition to the re-establishment of the Order, which for its despotism, its faults, the corruption of its members, can never hope to inspire confidence, or reconcile our hearts.

Nevertheless, your Excellency, if by reason of the inevitable, imperious, and necessary circumstances, the Maltese people have to suffer the pain and misfortune to be detached from the Empire of His Britannic Majesty, and for the tranquillity of all Europe it is required that the Islands of Malta and Gozo should be placed in a state of neutrality, we beg your Excellency in the name of our constituents, and of all which is dearest and sacred among men, in the name of all human and divine laws, in the name of the rights of man and of justice, that you will supplicate His Britannic Majesty that he will deign to employ his efficacious and powerful mediation with the other Powers, to the effect that the Islands of Malta and Gozo should be left in their independence under the mutual guarantee of Great Britain and France, and not consider it as a conquered country, after its inhabitants have shed their blood and expended their substance.

Your Excellency will have seen that we as deputies could not be dispensed from bringing before your notice the views and intentions of our nation, and in mentioning some of the faults of the Order of St. John of Jerusalem it has not only been our intention to give vent to our feelings, but to justify ourselves before the world in our eternal opposition, and vigorous resistance if they dare to attempt to place their feet inside our forts, still wet with the blood they have caused to be shed.

We beseech your Excellency to employ your influence with His Britannic Majesty in favour of justice, truth, humanity, and of a nation worthy of a better fate, and be pleased to accept the homage of a resignation the most respectful, of which we have the honour to be. Yours, &c.

       (Signed) LE MARQUIS TESTAFERRATA.
         „ L'ABBÉ EMANUEL RICAUD.
         „ L'ABBÉ PIERRE MALLIA.
         „ PH. CASTAGNA.
         „ ANTOINE MALLIA.
         „ MICHEL CACHIA.

The following day the deputies addressed their constituents in Malta as follows :—

            London, *2nd March* 1802.[1]

MOST ILLUSTRIOUS SIGNORS,—We arrived here the 1st ultimo. The 4th February we wrote the enclosed letter (see ante) to Lord Hobart, the Minister, stating we were arrived in this capital in the character of deputies to represent the demands of our fellow citizens.

In consequence of this letter, the Minister made known to the deputation through the medium of Sir Alexander Ball that they would do well to procure their departure from London as soon as possible, adducing for reasons, that their remaining would give jealousy to France, and thereby impede the conclusion of the definitive articles of peace, and that he could not for reasons of State receive and hear them in his office, but that he would permit them to come in private to his house, where he would hear them.

We were received by the Minister on the 8th February, and he heard with patience all the reasons for which we were sent to London, particularly to protest to the British Government in the name of our nation against the cession of our Island to the Order of St. John, and all the reasons for which we do not recognise the right of the Order to the dominion of our Island and the firm and effectual resistance which we were resolved to make to oppose the return of the Order into our Mother Country. To this representation the Minister answered that the English Government would take care of the happiness of the Maltese, and that the result would prove to us that the return of the Order in Malta would be of advantage by the precautions which the English Government would take to guarantee the people of Malta.

Yesterday, with the approbation of Sir Alexander Ball, we presented the enclosed memorial (see ante), and await his answer. It is one day reported that there will be war, and the next that peace will be concluded, &c. We are, &c.

Lord Pelham, then Minister for Home Affairs, though defending most strenuously the action of the Ministry in signing the preliminary treaty so far as it related to Malta, yet protested against that

---

[1] Cobbett, vol. iii. p. 682.

portion of the proposed definitive treaty regarding the island being in the same terms; and he was thus instrumental in obtaining a revision in one or two important points, the principal being that of the incorporation of a Maltese Langue in the Order.[1] The Maltese deputies were duly informed that, under the existing circumstances, the utmost that could possibly be done for them was being attempted by His Britannic Majesty's Government, which drew from them their grateful acknowledgment in the following letter :—

[Translation.]

FROM THE MALTESE DEPUTIES TO LORD HOBART.

London, 2nd April 1802.[2]

MY LORD,—The deputies of the Islands of Malta and Gozo have the honour of presenting to your Excellency the warmest thanks for all that you have deigned to do in favour of their nation.

We are not ignorant, my Lord, of all that you must have had to overcome in order to insure the tranquillity and happiness of our country. The defence of it which you have been pleased to undertake is worthy the loyalty and magnanimity of your nation. Being unable to have the honour of forming a part of the Empire of his Britannic Majesty, by a faithful submission, we shall have that of being always united to it by an affectionate gratitude. In transmitting to our latest descendants the story of our revolution, we shall tell them, that without the assistance of Great Britain our ruin must have been inevitable ; and the date of our happiness will be the date of the protection with which your Excellency has honoured us.[3] We entreat you, my Lord, to permit us at a seasonable opportunity to lay before you that which would complete the felicity of the Maltese nation, and to tender you, if you please, the homage of the lively gratitude and respectful devotion with which we have the honour, &c.

(Signed) LE MARQUIS TESTAFERRATA.
„ L'ABBÉ MALLIA.
„ L'ABBÉ RICAUDE.
„ ANTOINE MALLIA.
„ PH. CASTAGNA.
„ MICHEL CACHIA.

Lord Hobart's reply was couched in the following words :—

LORD HOBART TO THE MALTESE DEPUTIES.

Downing Street, 20th April 1802.

GENTLEMEN,—I have the honour to forward you by order of the King a copy of the Xth Article of the definitive treaty of peace concluded in Amiens, from which you will learn of the new arrangement agreed

---

[1] i.e. in the Treaty of Amiens, signed March 27, 1801. For details respecting this treaty and the negotiations leading up to it, see the next chapter.—J. H. R.
[2] Cobbett, vol. iii. p. 867.
[3] The admission conveyed in this sentence disposes of the rodomontade in the other papers sent in by the Maltese deputies.—J. H. R.

upon by the Contracting Powers for the future government and trade of Malta.

From the time in which the abandonment of Malta became an indispensable sacrifice on the part of His Britannic Majesty in order to ensure a general peace,[1] one of the principal objects of his desire has been that of witnessing the happiness and prosperity of the Maltese nation increased and assured in such a manner as to render her able to participate in the authority through which her interests will have to be governed, as well as to avail herself of all the advantages relative to trade which her geographical position offers them in a manner so singular, and His Majesty experiences the most sincere and constant satisfaction, believing that these great and important advantages have been at last granted them by the Act of the Contracting Powers in the Treaty of Amiens.

I am now able to inform you that your letters of the 1st March, 2nd and 5th of the current April, have been received. With regard to the first, as its date is prior to that of the definitive treaty, you must be aware that I could not give you an earlier reply, seeing that it was delivered to me at a most critical moment of the negotiations, and I have deferred replying to this letter with less regret, knowing that the interests of the Maltese were being anxiously defended and considered by His Majesty's Government as far as the circumstances would permit.

In your letter of the 2nd instant I have had the satisfaction to receive the testimony which you offer for the success of the efforts made in favour of your compatriots, and with the most sincere pleasure I have to inform you that having placed this letter before the King, His Majesty has been graciously pleased to declare his great satisfaction at the expressions it contains. In reply to the letter dated the 5th instant, it will be sufficient for me to assure you in general terms, that His Majesty will employ all his influence to obtain a due execution of the treaty regarding Malta, according to the true intentions and true spirit of said treaty.

The fidelity, the attachment, and the good conduct of the people of Malta and Gozo, during the time in which these Islands have been connected with the British Government, have entitled them to any protection which [it] may lie in the power of His Majesty to grant.

I feel happy at being able to avail myself of this occasion to express to you my satisfaction, with regard to the prudent, discreet, and honourable conduct which you have observed during the whole period of your stay in this country. I have the honour, &c.   (Signed) HOBART.

Great efforts had been made both by Russia and that section of the Order resident in St. Petersburg to frustrate the mission of the deputies. On the 2nd April 1802, Lord St. Helens, the British Minister at St. Petersburg, was able to inform Lord Hawkesbury that a memorandum had been issued by the Provincial Council of State of the Order in that city, denouncing them as unrepresentative.

The Council had been informed by the Bailli Caraccolo de St. Erami, their Minister at Palermo, that they were not representative,

[1] See my *Life of Napoleon I*, vol. i. pp. 352–3, for the disputes at Amiens concerning Malta, which nearly ended the negotiations.—J. H. R.

and that the entire population of Malta had shown the most lively disquietude since the embarkation of the deputation. The despatch goes on to say [1] :—

> Jamais peut-être il n'y eut un gouvernement plus doux, plus modéré, plus paternal que celui des Grands Maîtres—nulle taxe, nulle imposition ; point d'injustices, ni de vexation[s] ; tribunaux composés par la noblesse et le tiers états du pays ; les habitans entretenus, soldés, nourris, défendus aux frais de l'Ordre. Tels étaient les avantages dont ils ont joués pendant près de trois siècles sans la moindre plainte de leur part. Les seules réclamations sont venues de deux classes privilégiés, celle des nobles et celle des prêtres.

The note closes by giving reasons for excluding Maltese nobles from the class of chevaliers, mainly because of the difficulties which would ensue if a Maltese knight were elected Grand Master !

The deputies had an interview with His Majesty the King at Kew on the 11th April, which is referred to in the 'Annual Register' in the following passage :—

> As His Majesty was coming out of church, he was met by several gentlemen from Malta, who had been waiting for some time to see the King. His Majesty was accompanied by Earl Morton. The King conversed a long time with the Maltese gentlemen. It must create some surprise that those gentlemen who attended as ambassadors from their State should not be admitted officially to a regular audience.
> Surely this did not proceed from any servile fear of the displeasure of Bonaparte to our Ministers.

It must be observed here that the arrival of the Maltese deputies during the interval between the preliminary and definitive treaties could not but be very embarrassing to the British Ministry. Whilst anxiously desirous of faithfully fulfilling the engagements they had entered into with France in the first treaty, and in their earnest wish for peace, they nevertheless could not but sympathise with the Maltese deputies, and deplore the sacrifice which had to be made, nor were they for this reason in a position to grant an official and regular audience to the deputation until the treaty had been signed.[2]

Soon after the receipt of Lord Hobart's letter of the 20th April, the deputies sailed for Malta, where they arrived at the end of May or beginning of June, when they presented to their constituents the following report :—

---

[1] Foreign Office, Russia, No. 50.

[2] Sir Alexander Ball and W. A. Miles (see his *Correspondence*, vol. ii. pp. 323–6) were anxious to further the aims of the Maltese deputies, and regretted the chilling reception given to them by Ministers. At Ball's request Miles drew up privately one of the memorials which the Maltese presented to our officials (see *post*), and Miles advised them that their Island could never be independent, because its food supply could support the population only for three months.—J. H. R.

[Translation.]

Dear Fellow Citizens,[1]—Upon our safe arrival in this our island it becomes our duty to report to you the manner in which we have performed the duties attached to the high office of representing you at the Royal Court of London, and the line of argument we adopted in supporting the rights of the Maltese our fellow citizens, and obtaining for them the utmost advantage.

At the first audience which we had with His Britannic Majesty's Minister, Lord Hobart (Minister for War and the Colonies) on the 8th of last February, and in obedience to the instructions communicated to us by you, previous to our departure, we expressed above all other things the ardent desire of the Maltese to become an integral part of the British dominions, from which Government they had already received signal proofs of its beneficence.

Such expression of our feeling would, we felt assured, be most gratifying to that Royal Court, rendering it most favourably disposed, and engage it in all eventualities to support the rights to which the Maltese nation is entitled. To this declaration of ours the Minister replied in feeling terms, assuring us on behalf of the Sovereign, of His Majesty's gracious acknowledgment, and informing us further, that what had been established in the preliminary articles of the treaty of peace was the result of the circumstances in which Europe was actually placed, and that Great Britain, having ratified these preliminaries, she was bound to keep them, and, therefore, compelled to relinquish the sovereignty of Malta.

Under these circumstances, we then considered it our duty, in accordance with the instructions received, to claim at least the protection of England, towards which Power the Maltese had given proofs of the greatest attachment, and in order that by her authority and influence Malta might obtain the most favourable conditions.

These most favourable conditions we conceived to be, freedom to return under the sovereignty of the Kingdom of the Two Sicilies, or independence under the protection of England or the United Powers. To this end tended all our expressions.

To strengthen our arguments, we mentioned that not only the natural rights which belong to all men justify us in demanding not only the above, but also those rights which result from privileges granted to the Maltese by our ancient sovereigns, demonstrating that such privileges had always been respected in the past by the Emperor Charles V. when granting the Island in fief to the Order of St. John of Jerusalem, and even by the French in the capitulations between them and the said Order, when Valetta was surrendered.

Not satisfied with an oral declaration of these views, advanced with all the zeal in our power, we repeated same in a written memorial addressed to the English Minister, and presented on the 1st March, in which we expressed the pain we had experienced in witnessing the unhappy lot which had befallen to our country in being prevented from becoming one of the signatory parties in the capitulations agreed upon between the British General and the French upon the surrender of Valetta.

[1] M.P.L., MSS. No. 380.

We further maintained that the treatment which the Maltese had received was that of a conquered people, whereas they ought certainly to have been considered, if not the sole conquerors of their own Island, at least as allies of England and the other Powers who had contributed to the capture of the city, and as a people who had shed their blood, as well as treasure, in the purchase of their liberty.

We further took the advantage of laying our case, with all the arguments we could bring to bear upon it, before all people of influence, who might aid our cause at Court.

Although our representations made no little impression upon the British Minister, nevertheless, he was not in a position to remedy the past. The ratifications of the preliminaries of peace, it was alleged, made it necessary to place the Island of Malta again under the dominion of the Knights of St. John of Jerusalem.

Knowing full well, that the whole object of placing Malta again in the possession of the Order of St. John was to secure its perfect neutrality, we expressed in the most positive manner the impossibility of the Order to maintain such pretended neutrality, that, in fact, the idea of neutrality was contrary to the secret constitution of the said Order. To add weight to our assertions, we gave an account of past events regarding the said Order, proving up to the hilt its absolutely necessary dependence upon one of the Powers of Europe, rather than that of any of the others. And we must not omit stating that we, with great warmth, defended our nation from the effects of the injurious accusations which the Order has circulated to our cost at the various Courts, describing us as rebels and traitors.

Owing to the circumstances we have related, we found ourselves at last compelled to dwell only on endeavouring, as far as possible, to mitigate the evil, and to improve the prospects of the Maltese about to be replaced under the sovereign dominion of the Order. For this purpose we adopted all the means at our disposal, which might in effect free the Maltese for the future from the vicissitudes they have suffered in the past, by giving to them also a voice in the government of their own country, in order that they might maintain by their influence and their additional strength that neutrality which the Powers required. If on these points all our demands have not been granted in full, the fault must be attributed to the political circumstances of the times.

It is a well known fact that, owing to the discussion which followed our representations, the conclusion of peace was delayed for a considerable time, and various couriers were successively despatched to the British Envoy (at Amiens) on this account, and we are persuaded that you will be fully convinced of our having, with every possible means, promoted the interests of our country, when you deign to compare Art. IV of the preliminary treaty of peace with the conditions of Art. X of the definitive treaty.

Our last efforts on your behalf were made for indemnity, for we remembered well with what warmth your instructions on this point were conveyed to us, and we, therefore, upon various occasions appealed most earnestly that such should be granted.

If these efforts have not been successful, the disappointment cannot be attributed to Great Britain, aided though she was by our co-operation. Nor will it be necessary to adduce any further reason to convince anyone, whosoever he may be, that England was not in a position to obtain for the Maltese such indemnity. On her part she had to abandon the Island, with the loss of considerable advantages, together with the expense incurred in acquiring its possession. These are sufficient reasons for her declining to support this claim—a claim which, without doubt, she would have paid (as on various occasions she proclaimed she would) had the Island remained under her dominion. It is, therefore, with great sorrow that we have to announce what the British Minister said to us in mitigation of the pain it gave us to hear, viz. : ' that if the Maltese do not succeed in obtaining such indemnity from the Order of St. John upon their arrival in Malta, the expenses they had been put to must become an indispensable sacrifice, for a sacrifice of much greater proportion each nation had to suffer, in their desire to obtain peace.'

But, in order that the sacrifice which had thus to be made should fall upon each individual Maltese in proportion to their means, we suggested to the English Minister that it would only be equitable that such expenses (in the event of their not being otherwise paid) be liquidated by Maltese possessors of property (landed or otherwise) in proportion to their rentals.

And, finally, our last effort was made by reminding the English Minister of the various difficulties which might arise after the Order had been re-established in the Island, and when the future civil administration had been decided upon, and which might, later on, be encountered in the execution of the conditions—difficulties which might unfortunately nullify the advantages gained by the Maltese in the definitive treaty, and we, therefore, demanded the adoption of those remedies which we considered applicable to the case. The English Minister promised that the assistance of England would be given to us, and he assured us further, that her good offices would be engaged with the other guaranteeing Powers in securing the independency of Malta, and that to such end the spirit of the definitive treaty should be faithfully observed.

Such also were the expressions of His Britannic Majesty when, in presence of the Royal Family, we were honoured with an interview, upon taking our leave to return to Malta.

In order to secure the fulfilment of all that had been promised, we deemed it expedient to demand that the Resident British Minister about to be appointed to Malta should be endowed with all those powers and qualifications which would inspire confidence amongst the Maltese, and maintain with force their rights.

We further on this occasion requested, for the security of our commerce, that the use of the British flag might be granted until the cessation of hostilities between the Order of St. John and the Barbary States, promised by the contracting Powers, had been verified. Nor did we omit, finally, to make the opportune entreaties that the widows, wounded, and well-deserving of the country should continue to receive the pensions which had been accorded them by the English Government, that all the battalions should participate equally with the English and the Neapolitans in the prize money of Malta, and that the Maltese slaves resident in Algiers should be liberated, as had been done with those in Constantinople, and other Ottoman dominions.

Having faith in all that has been done with regard to our Island, and relying upon the vigilance and power which our fellow citizens will for the future exercise in maintaining their ancient rights, as well as those lately acquired, by means of the Ministers of the guaranteeing Powers attached to the Order of St. John, we have not the slightest doubt but that Malta in the future will enjoy that good fortune, of which up to the present time she has been deprived.

This we desire from the bottom of our hearts; we have striven to obtain it for her, with all the zeal and fidelity we possess, in fulfilment of the commission entrusted to us. It remains for you and all our fellow citizens to support her, rendering her firmly established, and adding to the glory of the Maltese name. We trust that you will be able to approve of all that we have done regarding the commission you charged us with, in the like manner in which the Royal Court of London publicly approved our conduct during the whole time of our stay, giving proof of same by the manner in which we were hospitably received, and, further, by the last letter forwarded to us by the Minister under date of the 20th of April last. The satisfaction which results from having faithfully fulfilled our duty, and in having rendered some service to our country, leads us to forget all that we have suffered in its accomplishment, and we shall consider ourselves happily rewarded by obtaining your approbation.

(Signed) MARQUIS DON MARIO TESTAFERRATA, &c.

Some doubt has been raised as to which of two appeals prepared for presentation to His Majesty the King was *officially* delivered by the deputies, although it is a positive fact, that a copy of the representation, *prepared in Malta* in November, was forwarded to the *British Ministry* by Commissioner Cameron, and received by them, sixteen days *before* the deputies arrived in London.[1] On a printed copy of the memorial in question, preserved in the Public Library of Malta, numbered 1900, there is a MS. remark of the late Sir Ferdinand V. Inglott, Collector of H.M.'s Customs in that island, to the following effect:—' This document was deemed too libellous to be presented as a State Paper, and therefore *another Memorial* was drawn up by Mr. Miles, at the request of Sir Alexander Ball (then in England), a copy of which was sent to me.—F.V.I.' The Reverend Charles Popham Miles (editor of the 'Correspondence of William Augustus Miles') explains that 'the Memorial drawn up by his father (referred to above) was written in French, and is a document of some length, reviewing the position of the Maltese when under the government of the Order. It touches on the appearance of the French squadron off Valetta in June 1798, mentions the artifice of Bonaparte to effect a landing of his troops, and how, contrary to treaty, he succeeded through the treachery of the Order; and shows that in 1800 the Maltese militia, although undisciplined as soldiers, compelled the French to capitulate and retire, whereupon the English entered the harbour and took possession of the island, at the special desire of the inhabitants.'[2]

These latter statements, so at variance with the true facts of the

---

[1] C.O.R. Malta, No. 3. [2] Miles, *Correspondence*, vol. ii. p. 326.

case, induced the Reverend Mr. Miles to add :—'Internal evidence plainly indicates that portions of this document were dictated by the deputies themselves.' He proceeds, 'There is extant in Malta *the original Memorial* in Italian, brought over and signed by the deputies, Il Marchese Mario Testaferrata, Dr. Emmanuele Riccaud, Filippo Castagna, Michele Cachia Sacerdote, Dr. Pietro Mallia, and Antonio Mallia. The deputation was accompanied by Antonio Casolani as the confidential agent of the Government, and Eugenio Formosa as his clerk.'

'Why Sir Alexander Ball should have requested Mr. Miles to draw up another memorial after the deputies had arrived in London does not appear; but the fact is so.'[1]

A copy of the memorial prepared for the Maltese deputies by Mr. W. A. Miles is in the Malta Public Library.

[1] Miles, *Correspondence*, p. 327 (Note). See also pp. 323–6 for the whole of Miles's dealings with the deputies.—J. H. R.

CHAPTER XX

THE TREATY OF AMIENS

DURING the six months which intervened between the dates of the preliminary and the definitive treaties of peace, Russia proposed that if a Maltese Langue were added to the Order (one of the propositions then being discussed) it should only be granted provided that candidates for knighthood therein first presented proofs of their nobility, knowing well that in effect such a clause, if agreed to, would in most instances render the privilege nugatory.

This suggestion was doubtless instigated by that section of the Order then residing at St. Petersburg, who were violently opposed to the admission of Maltese to the Order under any condition.

Lord St. Helens was requested by the Russian Government to convey this proposal to the British Cabinet, which was accordingly done in the following letter to Lord Hawkesbury :—

[Synopsis.]

22nd December 1801.[1]

He states that the Russian Minister requests that in the arrangements being made relative to the future government of Malta the stipulation of the article which relates to the natives of Malta should be to the following effect, viz.,

'That the natives of Malta should be admissible to employments and offices within the Island, and be capable of becoming Knights of the Order *on their furnishing the proofs required by the statutes.*'

Later on, another difficulty arose as to who should bear the cost of the temporary garrison which it was proposed should be supplied by the King of Naples. A suggestion that the expense should be defrayed by England and France would have been approved by Russia, the Czar's Ambassador in London leading Lord Hawkesbury to believe that if France disagreed, England would, in such case, withdraw from the arrangement. On this point, Count Woronzow, Russian Ambassador at London, wrote to Lord Hawkesbury as follows :—

[1] F.O. Russia, 49.

THE TREATY OF AMIENS

[Synopsis.]

2nd February 1802.[1]

Referring to the subject of Malta, and the proposal that Malta should be garrisoned by the King of the Two Sicilies, and the cost of the garrison to be defrayed by England and France, this arrangement the Emperor of Russia will guarantee with pleasure. He proceeds to say that if, as Lord Hawkesbury had told him on that day, France was beginning 'à tergiverser,' the Britannic Government would compromise itself very much with the Russian Government if it abandoned on this account an arrangement which had been represented as vital. He suggests the putting into writing the article respecting Malta, submitting it with a note to the French Plenipotentiaries at Amiens, informing them that if they do not consent to it, the English troops will not abandon possession.

Before the negotiations could be brought to a close, and quite regardless of the interests of the Maltese people, the French Government proposed that 'the Order of Malta should be modified with respect to its composition, that instead of an order of Knighthood, it should become simply an Order of Hospitality, conformably to its primitive institution, and that the *Fortifications should be demolished*, and the Island converted into a great Lazaretto, appropriated to the equal accommodation of all the different nations which trade in the Mediterranean and the Levant.'[2]

The English Government, however, would not consent to this proposition, and when finally all difficulties, so far as England and France, together with her allies, Spain and the Batavian Republic, were concerned, were at last adjusted, the definitive treaty was duly signed at Amiens on the 27th March 1802. The tenth article, which concerned Malta, was to the following effect :—

Art. X. The Islands of Malta, Gozo, and Comino shall be restored to the Order of Saint John of Jerusalem, and shall be held by it upon the same conditions on which the Order held them previous to the war, and under the following stipulations.

1st. The Knights of the Order whose Langues shall continue to subsist after the exchange of the ratifications of the present treaty, are invited to return to Malta as soon as that exchange shall have taken place. They shall there form a general chapter, and shall proceed to the election of a Grand Master to be chosen from amongst the natives of those nations which preserve Langues, if no such election shall have been already made since the exchange of the ratifications of the preliminary articles of peace. It is understood that an election which shall have been made subsequently to that period shall alone be considered as valid, to the exclusion of every other which shall have taken place previous to the same period.

2nd. The Governments of Great Britain, and of the French Republic, being desirous of placing the Order of Saint John and the Island of Malta in a state of entire independence of each of those Powers, do agree that

[1] F.O. Russia. No. 50.
[2] Cobbett's *Weekly Political Register*, vol. iii. p. 1857.

there shall henceforth be no English nor French Langues, and that no individual belonging to either of the said Powers shall be admissible into the Order.

3rd. A Maltese Langue shall be established, to be supported out of the land revenues and commercial duties of the Island. There shall be dignities with appointments and an Auberge appropriated to this Langue. No proofs of nobility shall be necessary for the admission of Knights into the said Langue; they shall be competent to hold every office and to enjoy every privilege in the like manner as the Knights of the other Langues. The municipal revenue, civil, judicial, and other offices under the Government of the Island shall be filled at least in the proportion of one-half by native inhabitants of Malta, Gozo, and Comino.

4th. The forces of His Britannic Majesty shall evacuate the Island and its dependencies within three months after the exchange of the ratifications, or sooner if it can be done. At that period the Island shall be delivered up to the Order in the state in which it now is, provided that the Grand Master, or Commissioners fully empowered according to the statutes of the Order, be upon the Island to receive possession, and that the force to be furnished by His Sicilian Majesty as hereafter stipulated be arrived there.

5th. The garrison of the Island shall at all times consist at least one half of native Maltese, and the Order shall have the liberty of recruiting for the remainder of the garrison, from the natives of those countries only that shall continue to possess Langues. The native Maltese troops shall be officered by Maltese, and the supreme command of the garrison, as well as the appointment of the officers shall be vested in the Grand Master of the Order, and he shall not be at liberty to divest himself of it, even for a time, except in favour of a Knight of the Order, and in consequence of the opinion of the Council of the Order.

6th. The independence of the Islands of Malta, Gozo, and Comino, as well as the present arrangement, shall be under the protection and guarantee of Great Britain, France, Austria, Russia, Spain, and Prussia.

7th. The perpetual neutrality of the Order, and of the Island of Malta and its dependencies, is hereby declared.

8th. The ports of Malta shall be open to the commerce and navigation of all nations, who shall pay equal and moderate duties. These duties shall be applied to the support of the Maltese Langue in the manner specified in paragraph 3, to that of the civil and military establishments of the Island, and to that of a lazaretto open to all flags.

9th. The Barbary States are excepted from the provisions of the two preceding paragraphs until, by means of an arrangement to be made by the contracting parties, the system of hostility which subsists between the said Barbary States, the Order of Saint John, and the Powers possessing Langues, or taking part in the formation of them, shall be terminated.

10th. The Order shall be governed, both in spiritual and temporal matters, by the same statutes that were in force at the time when the Knights quitted the Island, so far as the same shall not be derogated from by the present treaty.

11th. The stipulations contained in paragraphs 3, 5, 7, 8, and 10 shall be converted into laws and perpetual statutes of the Order in the customary manner, and the Grand Master (or if he should not be in the Island at the time of its restitution to the Order, his representative), as well as his successors, shall be bound to take oath to observe them punctually.

12th. His Sicilian Majesty shall be invited to furnish 2,000 men, natives of his dominions, to serve as a garrison for the several fortresses upon the Island. This force shall remain there for one year from the period of the restitution of the Island to the Knights, after the expiration of which term, if the Order of Saint John shall not, in the opinion of the guaranteeing Powers, have raised a sufficient force to garrison the Island and its dependencies in the manner proposed in paragraph 5, the Neapolitan troops shall remain until they shall be relieved by another force judged to be sufficient by the said Powers.

13th. The several Powers specified in paragraph 6, viz. Great Britain, France, Austria, Russia, Spain and Prussia, shall be invited to accede to the present arrangement.

Anticipating adverse criticism of the treaty by the Russian Government, and in explanation of some alterations in details which the French Government insisted upon, Lord Hawkesbury instructed the British Ambassador at St. Petersburg to represent to that Government the motives which had induced his Court to give way on certain points. The substance of his dispatch was as follows:

[Synopsis.]

LORD HAWKESBURY TO LORD ST. HELENS.

Downing Street, 30th March 1802.[1]

[He announces the signature of the Treaty of Amiens on 27th March; on the subject of Malta (the 10th article) he writes at some length in explanation.]

The arrangement which has been made is slightly different from that proposed originally to Count Woronzow and the instructions to Lord Cornwallis, but very little variation in the spirit of the treaty is made by the alterations.

The election of the Grand Master, if it has already taken place in consequence of the declaration of the Emperor of Russia, is to be considered as valid; if not, this election should take place without further delay. The Knights should be summoned to meet on the spot. [With respect to the guarantee he trusts that the extension of the guarantee to the Great Powers will likewise be thought advantageous.] It is of the greatest importance that Your Excellency should use your best endeavours to represent this arrangement to the Russian Government in its true point of view, and you will urge them to induce those Knights over whom His Imperial Majesty may have influence to repair immediately to Malta, and to concur in the election of some independent and respectable person for the office of Grand Master.

The British Government was also anxious that it should be known by those whom it most closely concerned what had been the motives

[1] F.O. Russia, 50.

of her policy with regard to the arrangement respecting Malta, and issued the following memorandum :

The British Government have been governed by a desire to promote the fundamental and permanent interests of Malta. The geographical position of the Island and its political circumstances make it impossible that it should ever be annexed to any of those Powers unless in a state of things widely different from that in which the preliminary treaty took place. Since it was the sense of the European Powers to maintain the sovereignty of the Order of St. John in Malta, the first object sought for by the British Government was to destroy the bar by which the Maltese have been excluded from all share in the government of the Island. Let it not be forgotten that Great Britain has, while Malta was subject to the British Government, incurred expenses for the security, relief, and comfort of its inhabitants to an amount far exceeding the aggregate of all their losses ; for which expenses no other satisfaction is received than that which arises from the consideration of having first rescued the people from their condition of thraldom.

Although the interval of peace between England and France which followed this treaty was destined to be of short duration, the general opinion in England was one of satisfaction. But, as is well known, this feeling soon changed to one of grave concern when it was seen that the First Consul was bent on excluding British trade from France and from her vassal States, while he himself controlled the destinies of the Continent. His intervention in the affairs of Switzerland soon brought England and France to the verge of war ; and the mission to the Levant which he entrusted to Colonel Sebastiani aroused the fears of our Government.[1]

Equally disturbing was the attitude of Bonaparte towards the Maltese question. Mr. Drummond on the 19th April informed Lord Hawkesbury from Naples that he had seen a letter from the Neapolitan Ambassador at Paris, the Marquis di Gallo, who mentions therein what was said to him on the subject of the Treaty of Amiens by the First Consul, who called 'the new arrangement for Malta a romance, which could not be executed.'[2]

Notwithstanding the doubts which arose in the minds of the British Cabinet, they, faithful to their engagements, on the 30th April 1802, instructed Lieut.-General the Hon. H. E. Fox, then commanding the British forces in the Mediterranean, to withdraw the Malta garrison, in accordance with the Treaty of Amiens as follows :

LORD HOBART TO LIEUT.-GENERAL FOX.

Downing Street, 30th April 1802.[3]

SIR,—I herewith transmit to you a copy of the definitive treaty of peace, signed at Amiens on the 27th ultimo, the ratifications of which were

---

[1] See J. H. Rose, *Life of Napoleon I*, vol. i. cc. xvi., xvii.
[2] F.O., Sicily, 17.   [3] C.O.R. Malta, No. 8. (1802).

exchanged at Paris on the 18th instant, and in conformity thereto, I have the honour to enclose His Majesty's Royal Sign Manual directing you (provided that the Grand Master of the Order of Saint John of Jerusalem, or Commissioners fully empowered according to the statutes of the said Order to be upon the Island of Malta to receive possession of the same, and provided that the force of 2000 men to be furnished by His Sicilian Majesty be actually arrived thereon) to deliver within a period not exceeding three months from the date of the exchange of the ratifications of the treaty aforesaid the said Island of Malta and its dependencies to the Grand Master of the Order of Saint John of Jerusalem, or to Commissioners fully empowered as aforesaid, with the fortifications thereof, in the state in which they may have been at the time of the signature of the preliminary treaty, and as it is possible that some doubts may arise with regard to the artillery and ammunition belonging to the said fortifications, His Majesty is graciously pleased to authorise you to restore, together with the Island, all the artillery and ammunition found therein, at the time they were conquered by His Majesty's arms. Having carried these orders into execution it is His Majesty's pleasure that you do cause to embark such of His Majesty's troops or subjects as may be upon the said Island or its dependencies, together with all the artillery, stores, and other effects now there belonging to the King or any of His Majesty's subjects.

The Officer Commanding His Majesty's fleet in the Mediterranean is directed to co-operate with you in the evacuation of Malta and its dependencies, and instructions relative to the ultimate disposal of the troops under your command will be communicated to you by His Royal Highness the Commander-in-Chief. (Signed) HOBART.

A letter from Mr. Macaulay (Secretary to the Local Government) dated the 26th April, and two from Mr. W. Eton of the 17th and 18th May, describe how this treaty was received by the populace in Malta.

[Extract.]

ALEX. MACAULAY TO SIR ALEXANDER BALL.

Malta, 26th April 1802.[1]

. . . The Italian translation of the definitive treaty has arrived. The most judicious of (the population) acknowledge that the process they carried on against the Order for 200 years is now decided in their favour; at the same time they are apprehensive of the disadvantages under which they must labour for a length of time. How can this Island support their own Langue? and who are the individuals who can be elected who have ability, dignity, &c., enough to be proof against influence and intrigues, and to support with propriety and effect the interests of their country? The Pope is the only sovereign who has yet discovered an intention of returning their estates to the Order of St. John. I endeavour to reconcile to their fate the Maltese who converse with me about the situation and prospects. All the lower classes of people are attached to us, and wish that we should retain possession of the Island.

[1] F.O., Malta, 2.

[Private.]

MR. W. ETON TO MR. J. SULLIVAN.

Valetta, 17th May 1802.[1]

SIR,—We are but just this minute informed that a ship sails for England immediately. I take the liberty of mentioning to you that from private letters I have learnt it has been thought that I encouraged the Maltese deputation. I did not endeavour to resist what I could not prevent, but I can assure you that I promoted sentiments of moderation, and acted in general in such a manner as to gain their confidence and attach to me many of the leading people of the Island, so completely that I have information of every step they take and every resolution they form.

As a proof of this, I am now able to inform you that last night a Council of several of the nobility and popular characters was held at a private house in this city, when it was determined that the First Jurat, or President of the Senate of Città Vecchia should invite the different classes to elect representatives to form a Council, according to their ancient privileges, to consider of the interests of the nation, and how to put into effect the articles of the treaty so as to obtain the end proposed by the British Government. This Council representing the nation, they consider as necessary in order to consult with His Majesty's Commissioner and the Commander-in-Chief when affairs of the nation are to be treated of. They seem to be resolved to proceed immediately to the nomination of their Knights &c. to compose their Langue. I have no doubt but Marquis Mario Testaferrata will be the Grand Prior.

People are of opinion that the weight given to the Maltese in having a Langue has been entirely left to the Grand Master, who is as heretofore a despotic sovereign, with the whole legislative and executive authority in his own hands as Prince of the island, the Order never having had any interference in the government of the nation.

It will be necessary to quiet the minds of the people, that besides the French Knights and priests, all those Maltese who were naturalised Frenchmen, and as such possessed Commanderies or were canons in any of the French abolished Langues, should quit the Island. It will require great moderation and indulgence to prevent commotions. The dissatisfied with the treaty make the following observations:

That the Maltese will be more respected than they were before. That their vanity will be flattered and their consequence increased by having a Langue. That by the French Langues being abolished the Island will be in less danger of falling into the hands of France, but that, on the other hand, their revenues are reduced to a trifle by the want of the French Langues. The expense increased to the nation by the Maltese Langue. Commerce again annihilated by the abolishing of the free-port. The Grand Master, without any control, sole despotic sovereign, and besides nominates their officers.

Heretofore the whole troops, they observe, were Maltese, and the Militia trusted with arms, which in 1761 amounted alone to 16,000 men. The courts of justice and all offices which required learning, were always

[1] C.O.R. Malta No. 6 (1802).

occupied by Maltese. I hope the deputies who are satisfied will prevail on their countrymen to be so when they return—they are looked for with anxiety. I thought it would be interesting to you to learn how the treaty was received here. I have the honour, &c.

(Signed) WM. ETON.

[Private.]

SAME TO THE SAME.

Valetta, 18th May 1802.[1]

SIR,—Yesterday, 17th, by a ship I had the honor to write to you. The Council the Maltese proposed to elect from the different classes is not an innovation; they have had this right from time immemorial, and it was exercised during the reigns of all their Princes, the Grand Masters. It was called 'il Consiglio Popolare.'

If this Council is not permitted to be elected there will be a rebellion, I am fully persuaded. It may perhaps be managed so as to finish all matters smoothly, and may be a useful instrument. I know their present temper, but I will not be answerable that no violent resolutions will not hereafter be taken. They insist on electing their own Knights, and I believe there can be no objection to their so doing, as they submit to the Pope's confirmation. All the Order had to do in the nomination of Knights was to examine their claims to nobility. This with the Maltese is dispensed with; therefore the other Knights have no right of interference. They wish that the British Commander may raise the Maltese corps and appoint the officers. They insist on the Militia being again re-established to secure them from invasion. The taking from them the advantages of the free port, will reduce their commerce to its former insignificancy. They complain very loudly that there is no restraint on the power of the Grand Master, their Langue, as well as the others, having no concern in the government of the people. God send we may find means to quiet the fermentation that now exists, and probably will rise to a greater degree. I have the honour to be, &c. (Signed) WM. ETON.

PS.—Since writing the above Mr. Cameron has received a letter from the First Senator or Jurat of Citta Vecchia. I do not learn that there are many candidates for the Cross. What some years ago would have been a high gratification to the vanity of the Maltese is now held in contempt. By the English they have been treated with so much distinction and affability that, feeling no humiliation from a class of men who assumed no insulting superiority of rank, they had nothing to wish on the side of honour. It is too late an hour for Mr. Cameron to write on these subjects, but he will send a messenger in a few days. After all, I hope we shall get quietly out of the Island, and that is all we can expect. There has been no rejoicing here for the peace. I believe no one would venture to illuminate. I take the liberty of writing privately all these things, because I presume you wish to learn what the Maltese think.

(Signed) W. ETON.[2]

[1] C.O.R. Malta, No. 6 (1802).
[2] With regard to this last letter, it will be well to refer to the chapter which treats of Mr. Eton and the Consiglio Popolare. (Note by Mr. Hardman.)

CHAPTER XXI

DISCUSSIONS AND CORRESPONDENCE RELATING TO MALTA

(1802 to March 1803)

THE definitive Treaty of Amiens was severely criticised by the Opposition in both Houses of Parliament, led by Lords Grenville and Spencer in the House of Lords, and by Windham in the Commons. The attacks were principally directed against the re-establishment of the Order in Malta. Lord Grenville stated that 'the Order by the new regulations was impoverished in finance, it had become degraded in reputation, and that it must soon sink into a gang of low, needy, and unprincipled adventurers.'[1]

It was further stated that 'the independence of Malta was not safe in the hands of a Neapolitan garrison, whose monarch had become a vassal of France in all but the name at a time when the French Consul, Bonaparte, was President of the French Republic, with a French army constantly in the heart of Italy, and with Piedmont united to France.[2] Bonaparte was thus in a position to take Malta from His Sicilian Majesty at any time by demanding Malta or Naples. As for the six guarantors—France, Great Britain, Austria, Spain, Russia, and Prussia—four of these had no naval force, or were situated at an immense distance from the island, and the sixth, Prussia, in abject submission to France, then in possession of her arsenals, her fleet, and her armies.[3] Nor was it certain that Russia would agree to accept the responsibility to which she had been invited.' This proved eventually to be the case.

At the sitting of the 3rd May 1802, Windham (then member for Norwich) denounced the treaty in still more forcible terms. Referring to Malta Mr. Windham said:

By the preliminaries Malta was not to belong to France or England,

[1] See, too, Cobbett, vol. ii. pp. 512, 1239.
[2] Bonaparte by the *Senatus Consultum* of 21st September 1802 definitively annexed Piedmont to France. A little earlier he annexed Elba. For the alarm felt in England about Malta see a letter in Cobbett, vol. ii. pp. 838-844.—J. H. R.
[3] Prussian policy, then directed mainly by Haugwitz, was almost entirely subservient to France, which then helped her to gain very largely in the secularisation of clerical domains then being planned, and completed in February 1803.—J. H. R.

but to be restored to the Order, under the protection of a third Power, generally supposed to be Russia. It was originally conceived that Malta was not to be given up, but that would not now be a proper matter for discussion. We shall take it simply upon the condition of the preliminaries. Instead, however, of providing for Malta in the spirit of the preliminaries, a covered way has been devised by which England is completely ousted and France put into possession. That such at least will be the result I have no doubt. The first consideration that occurs is, how is the Order to be supported? We know the internal revenue of Malta does not exceed £30,000, a sum not more than equal to the support of the Grand Master, the various charitable institutions, and the supply of grain. These three objects absorb all the revenue of every description which the Island affords, so that for guards, garrison, and the defence of the place there will be no provision at all. Of the revenues that formerly belonged to the order, those in France, Bavaria, and different parts of Germany have been confiscated, and those which lay in Spain are on the eve of being so, making in the whole at least four-fifths of its ancient revenue, and reducing its revenue merely to that produced by the Island, to the amount of about £30,000, as I have already stated. Thus situated the Order must soon fall for want of support. I shall not dwell upon the disgraceful mode of modelling it upon the French regular or noble-democratic form. It is not of this I complain, but of putting it under the protection of Powers under the influence of France. For what is the Neapolitan garrison in fact but a French garrison? But supposing it is now under the influence of France, how is that influence provided against by the article which removes the hands of the Neapolitan Government. The plan is that we shall evacuate the Island in three months. *This stipulation is peremptory.* Then comes another clause, enjoining that it shall be delivered up generally, *but not attaching to the former clause and saving to the Order.* Next comes another clause, still more material, which says that the neutrality of the Order is proclaimed. What is meant by this it is difficult to understand, and may be variously interpreted. It may be neutrality to say that ships of war to any number belonging to the neutral nations may come in, or that they shall be all alike excluded. A third way may also be conceived—I mean the admission of an equal number of ships of all nations. Now see the effect of this neutrality in the event of a future war. In such a war France would have for her allies certainly more maritime Powers than England; she would at least have Spain and Holland, while we should probably not have one. Supposing, then, the number of vessels of each power admissible at Malta to be six, France would have these eighteen ships for our six, and so in the same proportion whatever should be the number. Had this stipulation been in the preliminaries, surely it would have been canvassed and set right in the definitive treaty.... If I wanted a voucher for all this, I find one in a French paper, ['Le Mercure de France,'] received this day, and which, if translated, I should have read as part of my speech. In it the writer talks of Malta as of a place that by the terms of the treaty *must eventually belong to France*.[1]

---

[1] Cobbett, vol. ii. pp. 1206, 1207. The passage above referred to comes from the *Mercure de France*, a publication appearing every ten days, not only under the

Lord Grenville on the day following (4th May 1802) spoke much to the same effect in the House of Lords.

At the sitting of the 13th of the same month Windham returned to the subject as follows:[1]

After the discussions that we have already had regarding the situation in which our interests in Malta are left by the treaty, it is unnecessary to enlarge upon the advantages which the French have gained by the stipulation of neutrality. It is clear that, including the force of their allies, Spain and Holland, they may have eighteen ships of the line in its neutral port while we have no more than six. But these points of detail are of inferior importance. The whole disposition of the island of Malta renders the stipulation of neutrality fictitious. The garrison must in fact be French. It is vain to talk of the mummery that there shall not be this Langue or the other Langue. The whole is French. If any man denies this to be the case, I shall be very happy to see his opinions and his reasons recorded, that they may be compared with the future result. So far from having restored the Order of Malta, we have by the arrangements of this treaty made war upon it in the very spirit of French principles. This little Order, which contained in itself the great characteristics and distinctive qualities of that which the French Revolution served to destroy, we have now concurred to overthrow. The little phial which contained the essence of the old principles Ministers have diluted, and not even with common water, but with water taken from the puddle. In this degradation, how can its ancient spirit be kept up? Nay, it is already understood that the German Knights refuse to serve in a body so degraded and fallen off from its original and peculiar character. As to the notion that Neapolitan troops can form any security for the independence of the Island of Malta, who does not see that the idea is wholly ridiculous?

The proceeding is a perfect syllogism. If Malta is put into the hands of Naples, and Naples is in the hands of France, Malta to be sure is in the hands of France. In truth the case of Malta is a virtual and total surrender, with a ridicule in the manner infinitely disgraceful to the reputation of our national counsels. Far better would it have been to have made an absolute cession of it, and thus have acquired a claim to compensation and equivalent, than to have formed a vain and futile pretence to establish its neutrality and independence. At present our footing and interest in the Mediterranean, which used to be reckoned of so much importance, are utterly abandoned. In this and in various other points there is a marked variation between the preliminaries and the definitive treaty, to the disadvantage of this country.

---

immediate patronage and influence of the French Consul, but also of the political department, which is actually conducted under the inspection of Lucien Bonaparte himself. 'In the conditions relative to Malta that important fortress, which the friends of England had so often assigned to her, everything is favourable to France, both in the provisional regulations and the definitive arrangements. As long as the island is Neapolitan it will be French, and to make it cease to be so, will require the concurrence of the Great Powers. If one day the Maltese Langue should become dominant, the position, the wants, the temper, the nature of that Langue would *bring it under the influence of the French Government*.' (Note by Mr. Hardman.)

[1] Cobbett, vol. ii. p. 1291.

This acrimonious debate in the House of Commons was continued the next day, when the opinion of many members was held 'that the effort to give a preponderance to the Maltese Langue would signally fail.' The Order, it was observed, 'was well known to pride itself upon its high nobility; that candidates for the new Langue would have to be accepted from individuals of inferior social rank, and that it might be received as a foregone conclusion that the Knights of the Order would not associate with such new members.

The insincerity of Bonaparte, however, was soon discovered, for a month to the day after the signature of the definitive treaty, viz. the 27th April 1802, there appeared in the 'Madrid Gazette' an edict of the King of Spain, by which he annexed in perpetuity to the royal domains the Langues and possessions of the Order of Malta in Spain, keeping the direction of the civil administration and leaving the spiritual to the authority of the Church and Holy See.[1] This action on the part of Spain was the more reprehensible as she was one of the signatory parties to the treaty, the chief object of which was to provide for and maintain the independence of the Order, but as an ally of France she was compelled to submit to the dictates of the First Consul.

Notwithstanding these provocations, the British Government in its desire of peace endeavoured to carry out faithfully the stipulations of the treaty. To the information conveyed by Monsieur Otto to Lord Hawkesbury, under date of the 23rd May, that the First Consul had nominated General Vial as Minister-Plenipotentiary to the Order, and Island of Malta, the British Government replied on the day following, that the King had appointed Sir Alexander John Ball as his Minister to the Order, who would at once proceed to Malta, and be instructed to concert with General Vial the necessary measures for carrying into effect the arrangements relative to that Island as stipulated in Article X of the Treaty of Amiens.

Accordingly, on the 9th June Ball was ordered to return to Malta, where he arrived on the 10th July; Vial followed from Paris, and arrived in Malta on the 21st August.

Before the period fixed for the British evacuation of the Island the Order of Malta (which, according to the terms of the treaty, was to consist of the Langues of Italy, Castille, Arragon, Germany, Bavaria and Malta) was materially curtailed and enfeebled by the suppression of the Langues of Castille and Arragon. More recently the Langue of Bavaria had been suppressed, and also that part of the Italian Langue comprised in Piedmont and the Duchy of Parma, which had become united to France. These measures reduced the Order to a mere skeleton, and rendered its sovereignty and independence a mere mockery.[2]

[1] Cobbett, vol. i. p. 663.   [2] Ibid. vol. iii. p. 440.

Russia made no official objection to the arrangement of the preliminaries, but with regard to the definitive treaty, whilst agreeing to the natives being admitted into the service of the Civil Government, she would not consent to the creation of a Maltese Langue, or the admission of natives to knighthood, unless her suggestion of the 22nd December 1801 were adopted, and further complained that her protectorate over the Order had been completely ignored in the treaty. She objected to rank merely as one of the six guaranteeing Powers, and refused, when invited to provide financially for Malta's defence and maintenance of the Order's independence, although agreeing to the neutrality of the Island, or its occupation by the King of Naples, until the restoration of the Order.[1]

The British ambassador at St. Petersburg sent the following letter to the Hon. A. Paget:

[Extract.]

St. Petersburg, 1st *May* 1802.

... I am afraid that the business of Malta is as much at sea as ever, notwithstanding all the pains and labour bestowed upon it by the plenipotentiaries at Amiens, who, by the way, seem to have acted somewhat injudiciously in giving to that subject a degree of apparent importance, which it by no means deserved, by placing in the body of the treaty a series of insignificant details, which would more properly have been reserved for a separate convention. Be that as it may, the Court of Russia appears determined to refuse its accession and guaranty to the said proposed arrangement, under the plea or pretext that in framing the clauses in Art. X which relate to this particular point sufficient attention was not paid to the Emperor's dignity; and besides this, the Russian Ministers either are or affect to be so much dissatisfied with the conduct of the contracting parties in appearing to set aside the move proposed from hence for the election of the new Grand Master of the Order, that they have seriously in contemplation the breaking off all connection between the Russian Priory and the body of the Order, by creating the former into an independent and separate community. There seems to be likewise great reason to believe that the conduct of Russia in this particular will be imitated by various other Powers concerned, and particularly by Austria. In these circumstances, therefore, how is it possible to suppose that the miserable remnants of the Order after being thus stripped of perhaps nine-tenths of the revenues that constituted its principal support, can be in a condition either three months hence, or at any future period, to take upon themselves the charge of maintaining and defending a possession like Malta, where the mere expense of repairing the fortifications would probably absorb more than the whole national revenue of the island.

Further, in a dispatch which Lord St. Helens sent to Lord Hawkesbury on 12th May 1802, he wrote:

It is impossible for His Imperial Majesty to subscribe to an arrangement which is so strongly in opposition with that which had been settled

[1] *Paget Papers*, vol. ii. pp. 50, 51, 56, 57.

between the Courts, and to lend himself in consequence to the guarantee that is asked from him.[1]

A further effort was made by Lord Hawkesbury to conciliate the Czar on the 3rd June through the medium of Lord St. Helens. Importance was laid upon the necessity of the two Imperial Courts (Russia and Austria) acceding to the guarantee required; but the Czar Alexander continued obdurate, as will appear from the following synopsis of Lord Hawkesbury's dispatch to Lord St. Helens:

[Synopsis].

3rd June 1802.[2]

He trusts that the Emperor of Russia will make no further difficulty in acceding to the invitation to guarantee. It must be equally the policy of His Majesty and the Emperor of Russia that Malta should become independent of France. . . . His Sicilian Majesty has agreed to furnish the force required from him by the 12 par. of the Article X. of the treaty. If the Emperor accedes, Lord St. Helens is to lose no time in communicating the intelligence to Sir Alex. Ball, whom His Majesty has appointed envoy to the Order of St. John. This communication is of importance, as the evacuation of the Island by His Majesty's troops will depend on the notification being made in the Island that the two Imperial Courts accede to the guarantee.

Notwithstanding all this uncertainty as to the future, Lord Hobart on the 9th June informed Mr. Cameron that Sir Alexander Ball was, leaving England to take up the appointment of His Majesty's Minister to the Order, in accordance with the treaty of the 27th March, and would relieve Mr. Cameron of his functions as Civil Commissioner in the Island. On the same day Lord Hobart issued the following instructions to Sir Alexander Ball:

Downing Street, 9th June 1802.[3]

. . . On your arrival in Malta you will take an early opportunity to inform General Vial that His Majesty being solicitous to fulfil, with the most scrupulous good faith, the engagements which he has contracted by the definitive treaty of peace, you are ready to concert with him the necessary measures for giving effect to the stipulations contained in the 10th Article of the treaty. You will take particular care that the two provisions (i.e. that the Grand Master or Commissioner duly authorised for the purpose be upon the Island to receive possession, and that the force of 2,000 men to be furnished by His Sicilian Majesty be actually arrived) should be literally effectuated; and should any difficulty or demur arise with respect to either of them, you will distinctly declare that His Majesty cannot consent to relinquish possession of the Island until they are effectuated conformably to the spirit and letter of the stipulations of the 10th Article of the treaty.

[1] Foreign Office, Russia, No. 50. [2] Ibid. No. 50.
[3] Foreign Office, Malta, No. 2.

The only substantial difficulties which are likely to occur relate to the election of the Grand Master, or to the Governments of Russia, Austria and Prussia accepting the invitation which has been made to them to become guarantees. His Majesty's Government is willing to consider as valid and to acknowledge as Grand Master the individual whom the Pope may select for that dignity from amongst the Knights (chosen for the office by their respective Chapters).

These preliminaries being carried out, you will signify to the Commander-in-Chief that he may proceed to execute his order for the evacuation of the Island. Finally, you will endeavour by all the means in your power to ensure the attachment of the native inhabitants of Malta to His Majesty's Government, and to frustrate the attempts of any foreign Power to acquire a predominant influence over the inhabitants, or over the government of the Order.

About this date the Russian Minister at the Court of St. James, Count Worontzow, angered at what he considered the neglect of Russia by England in the Treaty of Amiens, took a prolonged leave from his Embassy, and during his absence the Russian Chargé d'Affaires, Baron Nicolai, informed Lord Hawkesbury of the objections which the Czar had raised against certain dispositions contained in Articles X. and XIX. of the Treaty.

In reply to these strictures, Lord Hawkesbury on the 10th June informed the Hon. A. Paget, then British Minister at Vienna,

that Lord St. Helens had been instructed to explain that the principal objection urged by Russia, viz. that the election of a Grand Master which had taken place under the auspices of the Emperor of Russia was set aside, is evidently founded on a misconception of the Xth Article. The first paragraph stipulates that the Knights of the Order whose Langues shall continue to subsist after the exchange of the ratifications of the present treaty are invited to return to Malta as soon as that exchange shall have taken place. They shall there form a General Chapter, and shall proceed to the election of a Grand Master, to be chosen from amongst the natives which preserve Langues, *if no such election shall have been already made since the Ratification of the preliminary articles of peace.* These last words were intended to refer to the contingency of an election having taken place on the Continent in consequence of the proclamation of the Emperor of Russia, which election, if it should have happened, was to be considered as valid. His Majesty has, therefore, no hesitation in saying that he shall be ready to consider the proceeding as a valid election, and that any one of the individuals who were then named, and who may be selected by the Pope and confirmed as Grand Master, His Majesty will acknowledge, and will be ready to put him in possession of the Island of Malta, provided he will engage to carry into effect the stipulation of the Xth Article.

Lord Hawkesbury therefore hopes that the Emperor of Russia will be satisfied as to

the only objection of moment that has been offered, and will now readily accept the guarantee of the Island, and that the Emperor of Germany will make no further difficulty in acceding to the invitation,

which will be officially sent (in conjunction with the French Minister), to become one of the guaranteeing Powers.[1] . . . If the Emperor consents to become a guarantee to the arrangement respecting Malta, intelligence is instantly to be sent to Sir Alexander Ball, Minister-Plenipotentiary to the Order of St. John of Jerusalem 'as the evacuation of the Island by His Majesty's troops will depend on the notification being made in the Island that the two Imperial Courts accede to the guarantee.'

Notwithstanding all Lord Hawkesbury's efforts to induce the Czar to give way on the contested point, Lord St. Helens on the 9th July writes to say that he

regrets that he is unable to confirm his favourable expectation that the Emperor will consent to guarantee. Monsr. Kotschoubey is satisfied with the explanations of Great Britain on the subject of the Election of the Grand Master, but the Emperor is still inflexible; he (the Emperor) adhered to his former determination in this business, as expressed in his ostensible instructions to the Baron de Nicolay.[2]

In due course the provisional Act which Mr. Paget had concluded with the Court of Vienna, containing this latter Government's accession to and guarantee of the arrangements respecting Malta, was received by Lord St. Helens, and conveyed to the Russian Government; but all to no purpose. On the 1st August Prince Kourakin informed him 'that the fact of the accession of the Court of Vienna to the treaty is not a sufficient reason to make the Emperor change his resolution, because the two Courts are in different positions in the matter.' [3]

As there appeared to be little probability of an early solution of the difficulty, Lord St. Helens immediately acquainted Sir Alexander Ball with the hitch which had occurred in the proceedings, and on the 2nd August went on to say, 'that if the difficulty continues, a fresh concert of measures must necessarily be adjusted between the contracting parties previously to the evacuation of His Majesty's troops, and that he might look forward to the probability of their having to remain in the Island for several months to come.' [4] This proved to be the case, for the Czar continued to refuse his guarantee, as may be seen by Lord St. Helens' letter to Paget of 1st August 1802.[5]

Owing to the delay experienced in obtaining the guarantee of the Powers, matters with regard to Malta came to a deadlock.

On the 21st July 1802 Bonaparte informed Whitworth 'that on

[1] Both Germany and France subsequently acceded to the proposed guarantee.
[2] Foreign Office, Russia, No. 50.
[3] *Ibid.* No. 50.
[4] *Ibid.* I have omitted some extracts and details inserted here by Mr. Hardman, as being of slight importance.—J. H. R.
[5] See *Paget Papers*, vol. ii. pp. 58-60.

Malta depended the question of peace or war; that on no terms would England be permitted to retain Malta; that he would rather she should have the Faubourg St. Antoine than that Island.'[1] And on the 21st of the following month the French Government requested 'that facilities should be given to accelerate the removal of 2000 Neapolitan troops from Naples to Malta, which the British Minister at Naples had not been authorised to facilitate, the motive alleged being that the stipulations which ought to precede the evacuation by the British troops had not been fulfilled, and that, consequently, the evacuation could not yet take place.' Lord Hawkesbury replied on the 23rd August, 'that England was prepared to carry into effect the article respecting Malta the moment the other three Powers of Europe had guaranteed its execution.' The despatch was as follows :

Downing Street, *August* 23rd, 1802.[2]

The undersigned has the honour to acknowledge the receipt of Monsr. Otto's note of the 21st instant.[3] When the Neapolitan Government notified to Mr. Drummond, the King's Minister at Naples, that the 2000 troops which His Sicilian Majesty had selected to serve in Malta were ready to proceed to their destination, that gentleman declined taking any step to facilitate their embarcation till he should receive intelligence of the arrival of Sir Alexander Ball in that Island, and till he should be informed, that the Commander-in-Chief of the British forces had made suitable preparations for their reception.

By the last advices from Malta it appears that Sir Alexander Ball had arrived there on the 10th last month, and that after having conferred with General Fox upon the subject, he had written to Mr. Drummond that there was no impediment whatever to the immediate reception of the Neapolitan troops, and that their quarters would be prepared accordingly. The undersigned has the honour to state this to M. Otto as the most satisfactory answer which he can give to his note.

It is probable, therefore, that the troops of His Sicilian Majesty are already embarked and on their passage; but to prevent the possibility of any unnecessary delay or misconception the most explicit instructions will be immediately forwarded to Mr. Drummond on this subject. With regard to the other points in M. Otto's note, the undersigned can only repeat what he has before stated to him, that His Majesty is most sincerely desirous to see all the stipulations of the 10th Article of the definitive treaty carried into effect with the utmost punctuality and with the least possible delay. With this view he takes this opportunity of observing to M. Otto that, by the very last despatches from the English Ambassador at St. Petersburg, the French Minister at that Court had not even then received any instructions from his Government relative to the steps to be taken, in concert with Lord St. Helens, for inviting the Emperor to become a guarantee of the provisions and stipulations of the article in question.

[1] Mr. Hardman has antedated this conversation, which occurred on Feb. 21, 1803.—J. H. R.
[2] Cobbett, vol. iii. p. 1014.
[3] M. Otto was the French *chargé d'affaires* in London.—J. H. R.

DISCUSSIONS AND CORRESPONDENCE—1802-3

The French Minister at Berlin was in the same predicament. The undersigned therefore requests that M. Otto would have the goodness to represent these circumstances to his Government, and to urge them, if they have not already done it, to transmit without delay to their Ministers at those Courts the necessary instructions for bringing this part of the business to a conclusion. The undersigned requests M. Otto to accept the assurances of his high consideration. (Signed) HAWKESBURY.

Further correspondence of an acrimonious nature passed between the two Powers on other subjects than that of Malta, notably that of the right of hospitality shown to the French Royal Family and French *émigrés* resident in England, resulting in a refusal of the English Government to accede to the French demands, closing their despatch of the 28th August 1802 with the following words:

The French Government must have formed a most erroneous judgement of the disposition of the British nation, and of the character of its Government, if they have been taught to expect that any representation of a foreign Power will ever induce them to consent to a violation of those rights on which the liberties of the people of this country are founded.[1]

Late in September or early in October the rumour that the Bailli Rospoli had been appointed Grand Master of the Order of St. John by Pius VII on the 16th of the former month, reached Malta, which caused some disappointment in the Island. Intimation of this feeling was forwarded by Sir Alexander Ball to Mr. Drummond, on the 8th October, in the following note:[2]

The appointment of Chevalier Rospoli as Grand Master was totally unexpected here (Malta). He has no party whatever on the Island, and is by no means a favourite amongst the Maltese, who represent him as extremely avaricious. The adherents of Tomasi and the creditors of Hompesch are much disappointed. The latter I find owes from £30,000 to £40,000, which he contracted during the canvas for his election.[3]

These various difficulties which confronted the British Government compelled them at last to take a decisive step, and on the 17th October Lord Hobart instructed Sir Alexander Ball and General Villettes to postpone the evacuation of the islands until further orders. The dispatches are as follows :—

[Most Secret]. Downing Street, 17*th October* 1802.[4]
To Sir Alexander Ball, Bart.

SIR,—Circumstances having recently occurred which, in the consideration of His Majesty's confidential servants, have rendered it advisable

[1] Cobbett, vol. iii. p. 1013. It is further to be observed that not till September 16th or 17th 1802 did the French Envoy at St. Petersburg receive the instruction from Paris formally to invite the Czar to give his guarantee for the Maltese arrangement.—J. H. R.
[2] De Villeneuve-Bargemont, vol. ii. p. 447. [3] Foreign Office, Sicily, 18.
[4] C.O.R. Malta, No. 5 (1802). The circumstances referred to by Lord Hawkesbury were the French occupation of Switzerland and the probability of war arising between Great Britain and France on that subject. On October 7th Lord Hobart wrote urging the retention of the Cape of Good Hope by the British Forces.—J. H. R.

to suspend for the present all measures for evacuating the Island of Malta, I am directed by the King to signify to you His Majesty's commands that you do continue in the exercise of all the functions of Civil Commissioner upon the Island until his further pleasure upon that subject shall be communicated.

If any remonstrance should be made to you in consequence of your declining to proceed in the act of restitution upon the arrival of the Grand Master or of any Commissioner empowered by him to receive possession of the Island, you will refer to the paragraph of the 10th Article of the treaty, which specifies the Powers that were to be invited to become guarantees to the arrangement therein made; and in answer to such remonstrance you will declare, that as the Courts of St. Petersburg and Berlin have not yet acceded to the measure, you do not consider yourself authorised to terminate His Majesty's authority in Malta until you shall have received particular instructions to that effect from your own Court.

I shall explain myself more fully to you in my next despatch; in the meantime I confide entirely in your discernment, prudence, and ability for abstaining from such measures, as may be calculated to excite jealousy in consequence of His Majesty's troops remaining in the possession of Malta. And that whilst you cautiously avoid the disclosure of the object of these instructions, you will so direct your conduct as to do nothing that may have the effect of weakening your authority and influence under any circumstances. Enclosed I send you a copy of the orders which I have been directed by His Majesty to communicate to Major-General Villettes, or the officer in the command of the British troops in Malta.

(Signed) HOBART.

[Most Secret.]

Downing Street, 17th October 1802.[1]

To Major-General Villettes.

SIR,—Circumstances having recently occurred which render it advisable, that the former orders relative to the evacuation of Malta should be suspended, I am commanded by the King to signify to you His Majesty's pleasure that you do continue to occupy the said Island with his troops until his Civil Commissioner shall notify to you that the evacuation may take place; and if in the meantime any of His Majesty's land forces coming from Egypt shall arrive in the port of Malta, that you do require the officer who may be in the command of the said troops to land such part of them as can conveniently be accommodated, and direct him to proceed with the remainder to Gibraltar.

Enclosed I send you a copy of the instructions that have been sent to the Earl of Cavan. (Signed) HOBART.

The decision of the British Government to postpone the evacuation of the islands had its due effect on the French and Russian Governments. Great Britain felt unable to evacuate Malta until the French Government not only faithfully fulfilled all the stipulations

[1] Ibid.

of the Treaty of Amiens, but also those of Lunéville of the 9th February of the year previous. By Article 11 of this latter treaty the independence of the Batavian Republic was guaranteed, and upon the strict observance of this article the British Government laid stress.

Whilst matters were in this position, in November 1802 General Andréossy was sent to England as the representative of France.[1] On the 3rd of this month, the English and French Ambassadors at the Court of St. Petersburg had an interview with the Russian Chancellor, Woronzow, for the purpose of obtaining the Emperor's sanction and guarantee to the 10th Article of the Treaty of Amiens, without which it was held that either of the two Powers (France and England), upon the first difference between them, would look upon themselves at liberty to seize upon the Island.

As a result of this interview between the English and French Ambassadors with the Russian Chancellor, the latter on behalf of his Government addressed to the British Cabinet the following dispatch, dated the 12th November:

[Translation.]

St. Petersburg, 12th November 1802.[2]

The Chancellor of the Empire having received the orders of the Emperor relative to the invitation made to his Imperial Majesty by the two principal contracting parties to the Treaty of Amiens, to accede in quality of guarantee to this treaty so far as relates to the Order of St. John of Jerusalem and their restoration to the possession of the Island of Malta and its dependencies, is authorised to give to the communication of the 22nd October the following reply:

His Majesty the Emperor from the moment of his accession to the throne (23rd March 1801) has constantly shown so strong a desire to seize every opportunity which presented itself of giving to the two principal contracting parties to the Treaty of Amiens the most unequivocal proofs of his sincere desire to do whatever might be agreeable to both of them, and to contribute as far as was in his power to re-establish and to confirm the continuance of the peace existing betwixt them, that it cannot now be supposed that his invariable sentiments on this point can have suffered any change. On the other hand, the two Governments are too equitable not to acknowledge that it is beyond the power of the Emperor to yield to the demands made to him in virtue of the 10th Article of the Treaty of Amiens, which fixes the future establishment of the Order of St. John of Jerusalem, since it is under every consideration impossible for His Imperial Majesty to accede as a guarantee to stipulations which are not only contrary to wishes expressed relative to the Order, honoured by the interest he felt in their favour, and the protection he had pledged himself to give

---

[1] General Andréossy had distinguished himself in Italy and Egypt. Later on he was French Ambassador at Vienna in 1809. For his instructions and his conduct in England see P. Coquelle, *Napoleon and England* (1803–1813), Eng. edit., 1904.—J. H. R.

[2] Cobbett, vol. iii. p. 853.

them, but which would be inconsistent with what had been agreed upon anterior to that treaty betwixt His Imperial Majesty and one of the two contracting Powers with respect to the said Order, and relative to the independence and neutrality of the Island of Malta.

This consideration, as important in itself as it is necessarily supported by considerations of a different kind, has obliged the Emperor not to accede to the pressing requests which have been made to him on the point by the Court of London, in spite of the ardent desire of His Imperial Majesty to comply with the wishes expressed on this subject. The dispositions which that Court has manifested to accede to the wishes of the Emperor with respect to the Order and the Island of Malta, and the readiness expressed by the French Government to concert measures for promoting the same end, have not failed to be felt with corresponding sentiments of gratitude by His Imperial Majesty. But the obstacle which opposed his compliance with their wishes was not weakened, since the public and formal Act continued still contradictory to the known and expressed intention of His Imperial Majesty, and that it was for this Act that his guarantee was solicited.

Since, however, one of the principal difficulties is removed by the nomination and acknowledgement of the Grand Master, His Majesty the Emperor, desirous of giving to the contracting parties to the Treaty of Amiens the clearest proofs of his friendship, and wishing to omit nothing on his part which can tend to consolidate the general tranquility of Europe, has determined to propose to the two Governments the only plan which under existing circumstances can furnish the possibility of waiving the demand which they have mutually made, and this plan would be, that the two contracting Powers should form a convention or some other Act supplementary to the Treaty of Amiens, by which the 10th Article of the said treaty relative to the Order and the Island might be modified, altered, and completed with respect to several of its dispositions agreeably to the stipulations of the first arrangement agreed upon by His Imperial Majesty; which by this means being fully and formally re-established would receive the same sanction as the treaty of which they then would form an integral part. If the two Powers believed that such a supplementary article could be agreed upon, His Majesty the Emperor would hasten to accede to it in quality of guarantee, and to share the obligations attached to such a character with the Courts of Vienna, Madrid, Naples, and Berlin.

His Imperial Majesty would do this the more readily because, in complying with the wishes of the two Powers, he would only follow the impulse of his own feelings on this subject, from which he is desirous of giving them manifest and reiterated proofs of his good will by concurring in all possible cases with their wishes. The Chancellor by order of the Emperor, that in this affair no delay might be supposed to arise on the part of the Court of Russia, hastens to subjoin a project of the articles which may serve as the basis of a supplementary Act alluded to above, in case the two Powers should be inclined to accede to it. The Chancellor of the Empire, in communicating these instructions to General Hédouville, Minister-Plenipotentiary of the French Republic, which express the intentions of the Emperor in answer to the note of the 22nd of October, has the honour of repeating to him his high consideration.

(Signed) C. ALEXANDER DE WORONZOW.

[Translation.]

CONDITIONS UPON WHICH HIS IMPERIAL MAJESTY OF ALL THE RUSSIAS IS WILLING TO ACCEDE TO THE STIPULATIONS OF THE 10TH ARTICLE OF THE TREATY OF AMIENS, delivered to the British Ambassador at St. Petersburg on the 24th November 1802.

1. The acknowledgement of the sovereignty of the Order of St. John of Jerusalem over the Island of Malta and its dependencies; the acknowledgement of the Grand Master and of the civil government of the Order, according to its ancient institutions, with the admission into it of native Maltese. Upon this point, as well as upon every other that may relate to its interior organisation, the legal government of the Order shall have the power to enact and prescribe such regulations as it may judge best calculated to promote the future welfare and prosperity of the Order.

2. The rights of the King of the Two Sicilies, as Suzerain of the Island, shall remain upon the same footing as they were previous to the war, which is now terminated by the Treaty of Amiens.

3. The independence and the neutrality of the Island of Malta, its ports and dependencies, shall be secured and guaranteed by the respective and contracting Powers, who shall mutually engage to acknowledge and maintain that neutrality in all cases of war, whether between each other or between any of them and any other Power, not excepting His Sicilian Majesty, whose rights of suzerainty shall not extend so as to enable him to cause a departure from the neutrality of the Island as guaranteed by the present Act.

4. Until the Order shall be in a situation to provide by its own resources for the maintenance of its independence and neutrality, as secured by the preceding article, as well as for the defence of their principal residence, the different forts shall be occupied by His Sicilian Majesty's troops, who shall send a sufficient force for the defence of the Island and its dependencies, the number of which shall be agreed upon by his said Majesty and the two contracting Powers, who shall take upon themselves conjointly the expense of maintaining the whole of the said troops so long as the defence of the Island shall continue to be entrusted to them, during which period the said troops shall be under the authority of the Grand Master and his Government.

5. The present Additional Act shall be considered as forming an integral part of the Treaty of Amiens, the same as if it had been inserted therein word for word, and shall be executed in like manner.

6. Their Majesties the Emperor of All the Russias, the Emperor of the Romans, the King of Spain, the King of the Two Sicilies, and the King of Prussia, shall be invited to accede to this Act as guarantees.

(Signed) COMTE ALEXANDER DE WORONZOW.[1]

Before this dispatch of the Russian Government could reach England Lord Hawkesbury, on the 14th November, desired Lord Whitworth to be extremely cautious in his communications with the French Government, should the subject of the Island of Malta be introduced, as follows:—

[1] Papers presented to Parliament on May 18th, 1803, pp. 48, 49.

[Extract.]

LORD HAWKESBURY TO LORD WHITWORTH.

Downing Street, 14th November 1802.[1]

... If the French Government should enter into any conversation with you on the subject of the Island of Malta, it is of great importance that you should avoid committing His Majesty as to what may be eventually his intentions with respect to that island.

It is evident that the arrangement stipulated in the 10th Article of the definitive treaty cannot as yet be carried into effect; that neither the Government of St. Petersburg nor of Berlin[2] has given any decisive answer to the application that has been made to them to become guaranteeing Powers of the arrangement; that according to the article the Grand Master must be chosen before there can be any person properly authorised to receive possession of the Island; that Prince Ruspoli has declined the situation of Grand Master; and that it will be necessary, therefore, for the Pope to make some other selection.

I recommend you, however, to avoid saying anything which may engage His Majesty to restore the island, even if these arrangements could be completed according to the true intent and spirit of the 10th Article of the Treaty of Amiens. His Majesty would certainly be justified in claiming the possession of Malta as some counterpoise to the acquisition[s][3] of France, since the conclusion of the definitive treaty; but it is not necessary to decide in the present moment whether His Majesty will be disposed to avail himself of his pretension in this respect.

It would be better, therefore, that you should not bring the subject of Malta forward at present, unless it should be first mentioned by the French Ministers. You will therefore conform yourself to the instructions above stated, and you will be very particular in representing to me everything which may pass on this important subject. . . .

On the 18th November Sir John Borlase Warren[4] informed Lord Hawkesbury of the line of argument which the French Ambassador at the Court of St. Petersburg had adopted at the joint interview which they had had with the Russian Chancellor on the 3rd of that month:

[Extract.]

SIR JOHN BORLASE WARREN TO LORD HAWKESBURY.

St. Petersburg, 18th November 1802.[5]

On the 3rd instant I waited upon the Chancellor, with General Hédouville, when the note of invitation for His Imperial Majesty's

---

[1] Mr. O. Browning, *England and Napoleon*, p. 9.
[2] On 25th November Mr. Jackson, at Berlin, informed Lord Hawkesbury that Prussia took very little interest in the Maltese question, and had followed the lead of Spain.—J. H. R.
[3] e.g. Piedmont, Elba, and the renewed control over Switzerland.—J. H. R.
[4] Warren had just gone as Ambassador to the Russian Court; he had little ability.—J. H. R.
[5] Papers presented to Parliament on 18th May 1803, pp. 47, 48; also Cobbett, vol. iii. p. 1026.

guarantee of the 10th Article of the Treaty of Amiens was presented by each of us. General de Hédouville entered into various reasons to induce the Russian Government to grant the guarantee, the principal of which was to prove that without the guarantee of Russia either of the two Powers, upon the first difference between them, would look upon themselves at liberty to seize upon the Island, which was only important in a military point of view; and the only alteration he should make in his invitation was that the Island might be delivered up to the Neapolitan troops. He added that the Act of Guaranty would not be considered as affecting the arrangements of any particular Power with the Order, or of any alteration that Power might wish to make in the baillages, or that part belonging to itself, *as Spain had already done.*

On the 5th December Lord Whitworth informed Lord Hawkesbury that the Bailli Ruspoli had been earnestly requested to reconsider his refusal to accept the Magistracy of the Order of St. John, as follows:

[Extract.]

Paris, 5*th December* 1802.[1]

.... I think it necessary that your Lordship should know without loss of time that the Commander de Bussy, the person who some time ago went to England to notify to the Bailli de Ruspoli his election to the Grand Mastership of Malta, and who brought back his refusal, is now returned to him with a letter from the Cardinal Legate Caprara, urging him by the most forcible and personal arguments to accede to the nomination. He is given to understand that unless he does so he must expect to feel the utmost weight of the arrogance of the First Consul. This great solicitude of the French Government is an additional proof of its anxious desire to see us quit the Mediterranean.

In the meantime the anxiety in Paris, due to the delay in the evacuation of Malta by the British troops, went on increasing, and of this fact Lord Hawkesbury was informed by Lord Whitworth on the 7th January 1803:

[Extract.]

Paris, 7*th January* 1803.[2]

Although the subject has not been mentioned to me by M. Talleyrand, I nevertheless have reason to believe that the delay which has occurred in regard to the evacuation of Malta excites a considerable degree of anxiety at this moment. The person who suggested this to me may have been commissioned to sound me; and therefore I was not sorry to have an opportunity of saying to him what I should consider it as my duty to say to M. Talleyrand, should he think proper to introduce the subject. I told him, therefore, that the sole object which His Majesty's Government had in view in framing the articles of the Treaty of Amiens which related to Malta was to render that island as independent as it was possible to make it under the existing circumstances; that, had those stipulations been fulfilled by the accession of those Powers which were invited to guarantee,

[1] O. Browning, *England and Napoleon*, p. 20. [2] *Ibid.* p. 40.

and by the election of a Grand Master, the treaty would undoubtedly, with regard to Malta as in every other point, have been carried into effect without the smallest hesitation. It so happened, however, that none of these stipulations were complied with; Russia had not yet accepted the guarantee, and the person elected to the Grand Mastership had declined it. Under these circumstances there could be no question of giving up Malta.

Such, I told the Spanish Ambassador (for it was with him that the conversation took place), had been the intention of my Court; but how far events which had taken place, and others—very important ones indeed, both to his Court and mine, which were at this moment near their accomplishment—might operate on the counsels of His Majesty I could not undertake to foretell.

I professed to speak entirely from myself, being without instructions on the subject; but I said I would make no scruple to give him my private opinion, which was that Malta could not with any degree of prudence be given up whilst this country was making and meditating such acquisitions as could not but excite the utmost jealousy and justify the utmost precautions on the part of the other Powers of Europe. . . . .

At the end of January 1803 the negotiations between England and France assumed a most alarming aspect; the French encroachments in Switzerland, Holland, and Parma, notwithstanding the Treaty of Amiens, left no doubt in the minds of the British Ministry but that France desired war. Prussia still appeared disinclined to become one of the guaranteeing Powers, and, to crown all, an insulting official report of Colonel Sébastiani (who had been sent on a mission to Egypt) was published in the 'Moniteur' on the 30th January, which brought matters to a crisis.[1]

On the 27th January Lord Whitworth addressed the following letter to Lord Hawkesbury, describing his conversation with Talleyrand. The French Foreign Minister first complained of the abuse of France in the British Press:—

[Extract.]

Paris, 27th January 1803.[2]

. . . The second point related to Malta, and M. Talleyrand, with great solemnity, required of me to inform him, and this by the express order of the First Consul, what were His Majesty's intentions with regard to the evacuation of that Island. He again on this occasion made great professions of his sincere desire to set aside everything which could interrupt the good understanding between the two Governments, adding that it was absolutely necessary that the French Government should know what it was meant to do when the clause in the Treaty of Amiens which stipulates the cession of Malta should be fully accomplished. He said that another Grand Master would now very soon be elected; that all the Powers of Europe invited so to do, with the exception of Russia, whose difficulties it was easy

---

[1] On the significance of this famous report of Sébastiani, see my *Life of Napoleon*, vol. i. pp. 411–415.—J. H. R.

[2] O. Browning, *England and Napoleon*, p. 53.

to remove, and without whom the guarantee would be equally complete (as indeed I fear it would be), were ready to come forward; and that, consequently, the time would very soon arrive when Great Britain could have no pretext for keeping long possession. In answer to M. Talleyrand, I professed to be without instructions; that, therefore, I could not say what were His Majesty's intentions, or what His Majesty's opinion might be of the changes which had taken place in the relative state of Europe since the conclusion of the Treaty of Amiens; but that I would report to your Lordship, and would have the honour of communicating to him your Lordship's answer as soon as I should receive it.

After mature deliberation, the Chancellor Count A. Woronzow's dispatch of the 12th November, which covered the proposed articles, was replied to by Lord Hawkesbury on the 29th January 1803, and forwarded, enclosed in another dispatch, to the British Minister of the same date as follows:

Downing Street, 29th January 1803.[1]

SIR,—The undersigned, His Majesty's principal Secretary of State for Foreign Affairs, has laid before the King the Note of the Chancellor of His Imperial Majesty of All the Russias, together with the project of the articles enclosed in it, which was delivered to His Excellency Sir John Borlase Warren, in consequence of the invitation made by His Excellency and the French Minister, in the name of His Majesty and the First Consul of the French Republic, to His Imperial Majesty to accede as a guaranteeing Power to the 10th Article of the definitive treaty of peace signed at Amiens on the 27th day of March last. It has been His Majesty's sincere and constant desire that the stipulations of this article, as well as every other part of the definitive treaty of peace, should be carried into complete effect, and as circumstances have arisen since the conclusion of the treaty which render it impracticable to execute the 10th Article according to the terms of it, and which have made fresh stipulations necessary, that means should be found by amicable negotiation of accomplishing an arrangement which may be deemed conformable to the spirit of the treaty and to the intentions of the contracting parties at the time of concluding it. His Majesty attaches the greatest importance to the accession of the Emperor of Russia to the 10th Article of the definitive treaty, not only on account of the security which the guarantee of His Imperial Majesty would give to the independence of the Island of Malta, but likewise from a desire to obtain His Imperial Majesty's sanction and concurrence with respect to the arrangements stipulated in that article. His Majesty has invariably manifested the same disposition.

As soon as he learnt the proceeding which had been adopted at St. Petersburg in consequence of the proclamation of the Emperor of Russia for the election of a Grand Master, he proposed to the French Government to join with him in declaring that, as contracting parties to the Treaty of Amiens, they were ready to acknowledge that election to be valid, and to recognise the person who might be named by the Pope out of those who were chosen by the Priories in Russia, and whose names appeared in the list that was then published, to be Grand Master of the Order of St. John.

[1] Cobbett, vol. iii. p. 1140.

In conformity to the principles which governed His Majesty's conduct on that occasion, he is perfectly ready to adopt the suggestion of His Imperial Majesty for the conclusion of a supplementary convention to the 10th Article of the Treaty of Amiens, and he has no difficulty in declaring his entire acquiescence in the second, third, fifth, and sixth articles contained in the project delivered to Sir John Warren. His Majesty entirely concurs likewise in that part of the First Article which relates to the acknowledgement of the Sovereignty of the Order of St. John of Jerusalem over the Island of Malta and its dependencies.

With respect to the other part of the article, which refers to the advantages stipulated in favour of the Maltese, His Majesty is extremely anxious that means may be devised of reconciling the views of the Emperor of Russia relative to the Order of St. John with the attention which a regard for the honour of his Crown renders due to the interests and wishes of the Maltese inhabitants, and with the indispensable object of the 10th Article of the treaty of peace, that of providing effectually for the independence of the Island; and he trusts that such an arrangement may be found not inconsistent with the spirit of the original institution of the Order. His Majesty will lose no time in giving instructions to Sir Alexander Ball to take measures for obtaining the information which may be necessary for enabling His Majesty to form his determination on this subject.

His Majesty trusts that that part of the Fourth Article which relates to the number of Neapolitan troops will be judged unnecessary when it is understood that, with a view to the execution of the provisions of the Treaty of Amiens, measures have already been taken for raising a Maltese force of 2000 men, which, together with the 2000 at present in the Island, will form an adequate garrison for its defence. His Majesty, however, entirely agrees with the Emperor of Russia in the necessity of providing adequate funds for the support of this garrison; and as the property of the Spanish priories has been sequestered since the conclusion of the definitive treaty, to which treaty his Catholic Majesty was a party, he thinks it indispensable that the property of those priories should be restored, especially as the Portuguese Government have lately declared their intention of sequestrating the property of the Portuguese priory, as forming a part of the Spanish Langue, unless the priories of Spain are reinstated in their former possessions. As those sequestrations have been carried into effect since the conclusion of the treaty of peace, and as it is highly important to secure under any circumstance which may happen a revenue adequate to the maintenance of the civil and military government and of the independence of the island, His Majesty adopts, from a conviction of its necessity, the suggestion of the Emperor of Russia, that whatever sum may be requisite for that purpose beyond the ordinary revenue shall be provided by an equal contribution on the part of His Majesty and of the French Government, and in default of payment by either of the parties it shall be at the option of the other party to contribute the whole. His Majesty has thus stated without reserve to His Imperial Majesty his sentiments on every part of this important subject, and his readiness to agree in such modifications of the 10th Article of the Treaty of Amiens as may be found not inconsistent with the spirit of it, as may be compatible with the interests of all the parties concerned, and which, His Majesty trusts, will therefore prove satisfactory to the Emperor of Russia. (Signed) HAWKESBURY.

The British Minister for Foreign Affairs also sent to Sir John Warren the following dispatch:

Downing Street, 29th January 1803.[1]

SIR,—Your Excellency's dispatches to No. 21 inclusive have been received and laid before the King. I send you now inclosed the official answer to the Note of the Chancellor Count Woronzow relative to the 10th Article of the Treaty of Amiens. It has been delivered to Count Simon Woronzow, the Russian Ambassador at this Court. In communicating this Note you will express in suitable terms how sensibly His Majesty feels the friendship which the Emperor of Russia has manifested to him on this occasion in his disposition to concur in the arrangements relative to the Island of Malta, and how sincerely His Majesty regrets that it is not in his power to acquiesce without condition or explanation in everything that His Imperial Majesty has proposed on the subject. His Majesty, however, trusts that when all the circumstances are taken into consideration which bear upon this important subject the Emperor of Russia will be satisfied that the line of conduct which has been adopted by His Majesty is such as a regard to good faith and to the interest of his dominions have rendered necessary. The only material difference between the arrangement proposed by the Emperor of Russia for the Island of Malta, and that in which His Majesty is willing to concur, relates to the stipulations in favour of the Maltese inhabitants.

It is important that Your Excellency should impress the Russian Government with the conviction of the services rendered by the inhabitants of Malta to His Majesty and to the common cause at the time when the French were in possession of the island; that for nearly two years they maintained a state of constant and active hostility against the French; that several thousands of them perished in this state of hostility; and that these efforts were made at a time when they could receive assistance from no other foreign Power; that the attachment evinced by the Maltese to His Majesty during the blockade, and their loyalty to him since he has obtained possession of the Island, gives them a peculiar claim to his protection and a right to expect that in the future arrangements for the island some advantages should be stipulated in their favour; that, independent of every consideration of good faith, Your Excellency well knows that the Maltese inhabitants, if attached to their Government, are equal to the defence of the island, and that every motive of policy, therefore, as well as of justice, renders it expedient to endeavour to conciliate their affections.

These circumstances being premised, you will state that the objection which, it is conceived, has had most weight with His Imperial Majesty is that stipulation in the 10th Article of the Treaty of Amiens which at the time that it establishes a Maltese Langue requires no proof of nobility for admission into that Langue, that such a stipulation is considered as leading to the establishment of a plebeian Langue totally inconsistent with the spirit of the institution of the Order. His Majesty is extremely desirous of devising means by which this objection shall be obviated and the interests of the Maltese adequately consulted.

[1] Cobbett, vol. iii. p. 1138.

The proofs of nobility which have been required for other priories have been various, and the power of the Pope to grant dispensations has been admitted to exist; if, therefore, *actual nobility* was made the indispensable condition of admission into the Maltese Langue or priory, the objection which is at present made to this part of the arrangement would in a great degree, if not wholly, be removed. As, however, the number of persons who would be capable of admission into the Order in consequence of such a regulation would be very limited, it appears reasonable that some further stipulations should be made in favour of the inhabitants of Malta, and it may be proposed to revive, under such regulations and modifications as may be judged expedient, the National Council which formerly existed in that Island, which should form no part of the Order, but which should have a share in the government of the Island and a deliberative voice in all its internal concerns. A body of this description could not be considered as in any respect derogatory to the ancient institution of the Order, and would be conformable to what existed within the Island till within a very few years. It is for the purpose of obtaining information on these points that instructions will be sent to Sir Alexander Ball, it being impossible after all that has passed to bring the negotiation to an issue without some communication with the principal inhabitants of Malta. His Majesty relies on your zeal in giving effect to these instructions, and in your endeavours to reconcile the Russian Government to the objects of them.

The events which have happened since the conclusion of the definitive treaty; the unbounded ambition which has been, and still is, manifested by the French Government, might have justified His Majesty in bringing forward new demands, and in even claiming the appropriation of Malta as some counterpoise to the acquisitions made by France since the Treaty of peace; but the moderation with which His Majesty has been actuated in all his concerns with foreign Powers, and his anxious desire that the peace of Europe may, if possible, be effectually consolidated, has induced him to forego those claims which the increased and increasing power of France might have justified him in advancing; and as every stipulation in the Treaty of Amiens has been in a course of execution on his part, with the exception of the Xth Article, he is desirous of showing his disposition to concur in an arrangement which may be conformable to the spirit of the article, if such an arrangement can be rendered consistent with the honour of his Crown, and if it effectually provides for the object of the 10th Article—the independence of the Island of Malta. I am, &c.

(Signed) HAWKESBURY.

His Excellency Sir John Warren, &c.

At this crisis in the affairs of Malta it would be well for the better elucidation of what follows to refer to Russia's action in the election of the Grand Master of the Order. Two months after the signature of the preliminary treaty of peace (1st October 1801) the Russian Priory arranged for the election of a Grand Master at St. Petersburg on the 18th December 1801 without reference to the other Powers, but by a subsequent agreement between them the nomination of the Grand Master of the Order was referred to the Holy See, upon the representations of the Order, to which His Holiness the Pope and the Priors of the Order acceded.

This agreement was consented to by the British Government on the 8th June 1802, and on the 16th September His Holiness nominated the Bailli Barthélemy Ruspoli to that dignity. In connection with this appointment, Mr. Thomas Jackson, the British Ambassador at Rome, wrote to his colleague at the Court of Naples, the Hon. A. Paget, under date of the 30th October 1802 as follows :—

> On the election of the Grand Master of Malta the Pope sent a Knight and a messenger to England to inform the Bailli Ruspoli that the choice had fallen upon him. Upon their arrival at Paris they were told by Monsieur Talleyrand that their proceeding to London was unnecessary, as the First Consul would send a messenger of his own to inform the Bailli Ruspoli. The Knight of Malta and the Pope's Legate were at the same time told that they might write to the Grand Master by Bonaparte's courier and enjoin him to come without delay to Paris, from whence he might proceed to Toulon, where a French squadron was ready to convey him to his destination, and that he was above all to avoid having any communication with the British Ministers previous to his departure.[1]

Some opposition in the meantime arose in the British Parliament to any interference in the matter on the part of the Pope; but it was explained that Russia felt disposed to refuse her guarantee to Article X. of the treaty unless the steps which had been taken for the election of a Grand Master according to the mode suggested by Russia were considered to fulfil what was required on that head in part of the first paragraph in the Xth Article of the Treaty of Amiens, and that, consequently, no new election for that office should take place in the manner pointed out by the previous part of the same stipulation. The paragraph runs as follows :[2]—

> The Knights of the Order whose Langues shall continue to subsist after the exchange of the ratifications of the present treaty are invited to return to Malta as soon as that exchange shall have taken place. They shall there form a General Chapter, and shall proceed to the election of a Grand Master, to be chosen from amongst the natives of those nations which possess Langues, if no such election shall have already been made since the exchange of the ratifications of the preliminary articles of peace. . . .

The British Government was prepared to consider the mode of election of a Grand Master at St. Petersburg under the auspices of the Czar as valid, according to the stipulations of the 1st Article, and hopes were given by Lord St. Helens, then resident Minister at the Court of St. Petersburg, 'that if such were agreed to, Russia on her part would consent to guarantee.' These hopes, however, were not to be realised. A list of the suffrages obtained from several priories for the election of the Grand Master was forwarded to the

[1] *Paget Papers*, vol. ii. p. 65.   [2] Cobbett, vol. iii. p. 994.

British Government, with a notice that these priories had agreed amongst themselves that His Holiness the Pope should select (*pro hac vice*) from amongst the candidates there specified, who should fill the post of Grand Master, to which arrangement the French Government also agreed in accordance with their dispatch to the British Minister resident in Paris, Mr. Ant. Merry.

Lord Hobart, then Minister for War and the Colonies, had already declared in the House of Lords, on the 7th May 1802, that '*as we had won the island by force of arms*,'[1] we had consequently an indisputable right to arrange its government, but in order to meet as far as possible the views of Russia, and notwithstanding the fact that His Holiness Pope Pius VI had never acknowledged Paul I as Grand Master, nor had the Prior at Rome replied to that monarch's invitation, the British Government had decided to accept the election as proposed.[2]

The appointment of Prince Ruspoli to the Chief Magistracy of the Order was found on some points, however, contrary to its statutes, and was eventually declined by him on the grounds that, owing to age and infirmity, and the existing circumstances in which the Order was then placed, he felt unable to support the weight and responsibility of the office which His Holiness wished to confer upon him. His Holiness then nominated and appointed the Bailli Giovanni Tommasi by a brief dated the 9th February 1803, of which the following is a translation from the Latin:—

[Translation.]

CHER FILS,—Salut et bénédiction apostolique![3]

Notre cher fils Barthélemy Ruspoli, lequel, par toutes les raisons que vous devez connaître par notre bref du 16 septembre dernier, avait été nommé par nous Grand Maître de l'Ordre de Saint-Jean-de-Jérusalem, ayant répondu qu'il ne se sentait pas apte dans ces circonstances à soutenir un aussi grand poids, et ayant fait sa renonciation à la dignité magistrale et nous ayant envoyé sa déclaration par un acte signé d'un notaire ; nous ayant instamment supplié de ne pas le' contraindre à porter un si grand fardeau ;

Nous, considérant combien il est urgent de donner le plus tôt possible un chef à un Ordre qui nous est si cher, qui puisse lui rendre son ancienne splendeur ; mettant à part toutes considérations privées ; agréant les excuses de notre dit fils : nous avons aussitôt jeté les yeux sur vous qui vous êtes avantageusement distingué dans tous les emplois que vous avez exercés et qui avez été si digne d'être désigné par les prieurs.

À cette fin, pour ne pas différer cette élection, et pour vous donner une marque signalée de haute bienveillance et de l'estime que nous avons pour vos qualités qui vous rendent très digne de cette grande dignité, nous

---

[1] Cobbett, vol. ii. p. 1242. [2] *Ibid.* vol. ii. p. 1080.
[3] De Villeneuve-Bargemont, vol. ii. p. 548 ; De Lavigerie, *Order of Malta*, p. 94.

vous absolvons, suivant l'usage, et en virtu de la présente, de toute excommunication, interdit, et de toute censure ecclésiastique, peine directe ou infligée par les lois ou pour toute autre cause, de quelque manière que ce soit ou puisse être. Et pour que la présente ait son entier effet, nous vous élisons et nommons Grand Maître de l'Ordre de Saint-Jean-de-Jérusalem, avec toutes les charges et honneurs conformes aux statuts de l'Ordre et aux Constitutions ecclésiastiques, avec tous les honneurs, grâces, privilèges dont ont joui vos prédécesseurs, comme si vous eussiez été élu dans le chapitre de Malte, suivant les formes prescrites par notre prédécesseur Urbain VIII dans sa bulle du 21 octobre 1634; ordonnant à tous chevaliers, chapelains et autres, servants d'armes, &c., de vous garder l'obéissance due, de vous honorer et respecter comme Grand Maître souverain. Pour ce qui concerne ce que vous aurez à faire, aussitôt que vous aurez reçu le magistère nous vous remettrons un exemplaire du bref que nous avions adressé à notre cher fils Barthélemy Ruspoli. Nous vous prescrivons à vous-même tout ce que nous lui avions prescrit, ce que nous ne doutons point que vous n'observiez exactement et religieusement par suite de votre fidélité à notre personne. Nous prions Dieu qu'Il vous comble de prospérités et qu'Il soutienne votre carrière dans le magistère que vous allez remplir. Nous vous donnons affectueusement notre bénédiction apostolique.

Donné à Rome le 9 février 1803, l'an III de notre pontificat.

(Signed) PIUS VII.

On the 9th February Lord Hawkesbury replied to Lord Whitworth's important dispatch of the 27th January as follows:

[Extract.]

Downing Street, *9th February* 1803.[1]

... In answer to Your Excellency's dispatch [of 27th January,] relative to the enquiry made of you by the French Government on the subject of Malta, I can have no difficulty in assuring you that His Majesty has entertained a most sincere desire that the Treaty of Amiens might be executed in a full and complete manner; but it has not been possible for him to consider this treaty as having been founded on principles different from those which have been invariably applied to every other antecedent treaty or convention, namely that they were negotiated with reference to the actual state of possession of the different parties and of the treaties or public engagements by which they were bound at the time of its conclusion; and that if that state of possession and of engagements was so materially altered by the act of either of the parties as to affect the nature of the compact itself, the other party has a right, according to the law of nations, to interfere for the purpose of obtaining satisfaction or compensation for any essential difference which such acts may have subsequently made in their relative situation; that if there was a case to which this principle might be applied with peculiar propriety it was that of the late treaty of peace, for the negotiation was conducted on a basis not merely proposed by His Majesty, but specially agreed to in an official note

[1] Browning, *England and Napoleon*, p. 65.

by the French Government, viz. that His Majesty should keep a compensation out of his conquests for the important acquisitions of territory made by France upon the Continent. This is a sufficient proof that the compact was understood to have been concluded with reference to the then existing state of things; for the measure of His Majesty's compensation was to be calculated with reference to the acquisitions of France at that time; and if the interference of the French Government in the general affairs of Europe since that period; if their interposition with respect to Switzerland and Holland, whose independence was guaranteed by them [1] at the time of the conclusion of the treaty of peace; if the annexations which have been made to France in various quarters, but particularly those in Italy,[2] have extended the territory and increased the power of the French Government, His Majesty would be warranted, consistently with the spirit of the treaty of peace, in claiming equivalents for these acquisitions, as a counterpoise to the augmentation of the power of France.[3] His Majesty, however, anxious to prevent all ground of misunderstanding and desirous of consolidating the general peace of Europe, as far as might be in his power, was willing to have waived the pretensions he might have a right to advance of this nature; and as the other articles of the definitive treaty have been in a course of execution on his part, so he would have been ready to have carried into effect the true intent and spirit of the 10th Article, the execution of which according to its terms had been rendered impracticable by circumstances which it was not in His Majesty's power to control.

A communication to Your Lordship would have been prepared conformably to this disposition if the attention of His Majesty's Government had not been attracted by the very extraordinary publication of the report of Colonel Sébastiani to the First Consul.

It is impossible for His Majesty to view this report[4] in any other light than as an official publication, for, without referring particularly to explanations which have been repeatedly given upon the subject of publications in the *Moniteur*, the article in question, as it purports to be the report to the First Consul of an accredited agent, as it appears to have been signed by Colonel Sébastiani himself, and as it is published in the official paper with an official title prefixed to it, must be considered as authorised by the French Government. This report contains the most unjustifiable insinuations and charges against the officer who commanded his forces in Egypt, and against the British army in that quarter, insinuations and charges wholly destitute of foundation, and such as would warrant His Majesty in demanding that satisfaction, which on occasions of this nature independent Powers in a state of amity have a right to expect from each other. It discloses, moreover, views in the highest degree injurious to the interests of His Majesty's dominions, and

---

[1] i.e. by the Treaty of Lunéville in February 1801.—J. H. R.
[2] viz. Piedmont, Parma, and Elba.—J. H. R.
[3] Bonaparte had already admitted the justice of the principle of compensation as between England and France. See O. Browning, *England and Napoleon*, p. 7.—J. H. R.
[4] The original report is to be found in the Archives Nationales in Paris (Carton A. F. iv. 1687). It appeared in the *Moniteur* on the 30th January 1803, and on the 11th of the following June Napoleon wrote to Regnier from St. Cloud as follows: 'I beg you will hand 100,000 francs to Colonel Sébastiani for secret services.' (Note of Mr. Hardman.)

directly repugnant to and utterly inconsistent with the spirit and letter of the treaty of peace concluded between His Majesty and the French Government, and His Majesty would feel that he was wanting in a proper regard to the honour of his Crown and to the interests of his dominions if he could see with indifference such a system developed and avowed.[1] His Majesty cannot, therefore, regard the conduct of the French Government on various occasions since the conclusion of the definitive treaty, the insinuations and charges contained in the report of Colonel Sébastiani, and the views which that report discloses, without feeling it necessary for him distinctly to declare that it will be impossible for him to enter into any further discussion relative to Malta unless he receives satisfactory explanation on the subject of this communication. Your Excellency is desired to take an early opportunity of fully explaining His Majesty's sentiments as above stated to the French Government. I am, &c.

(Signed) HAWKESBURY.

During the month of February the following further correspondence passed between Lords Whitworth and Hawkesbury :—

[Extract.]

LORD WHITWORTH TO LORD HAWKESBURY.

Paris, 21st February 1803.[2]

... My last dispatch, in which I gave Your Lordship an account of my conference with M. de Talleyrand, was scarcely gone when I received a note from him informing me that the First Consul wished to converse with me, and desired I would come to him at the Tuilleries at nine o'clock. He received me in his cabinet with tolerable cordiality, and after talking on different subjects for a few minutes he desired me to sit down, as he himself did on the other side of the table, and began. ... He said it was a matter of infinite disappointment to him that the Treaty of Amiens, instead of being followed by conciliation and friendship, the natural effects of peace, had been productive only of continual and increasing jealousy and mistrust, and that this mistrust was now avowed in such a manner as must bring the point to an issue. He now enumerated the several provocations which he pretended to have received from England. He placed in the first line our not evacuating Malta and Alexandria, as we were bound to do by treaty. In this he said that no consideration on earth should make him acquiesce, and of the two he would rather see us in possession of the Faubourg St. Antoine than Malta. ... I do not pretend to follow the arguments of the First Consul in detail; this would be impossible from the vast variety of matter which he took occasion to introduce.

His purpose was evidently to convince me that on Malta must depend peace or war. ... I have the honour, &c. (Signed) WHITWORTH.[3]

---

[1] Among other statements were these, that 6000 French troops would suffice to conquer Egypt, and that the Ionian Isles (then a separate Republic) were ready to welcome the French back.—J. H. R.

[2] Browning, *England and Napoleon*, p. 78.

[3] The whole of this very long dispatch deserves perusal in Mr. Browning's volume, *England and Napoleon in 1803*, pp. 78–85.—J. H. R.

[Extract.]
LORD HAWKESBURY TO LORD WHITWORTH.
Downing Street, 28th February 1803.[1]

... With regard to that article of the treaty which relates to Malta, the stipulations contained in it (owing to circumstances which it was not in the power of His Majesty to control) have not been capable of execution. The refusal of Russia to accede to the arrangement except on condition that the Maltese Langue should be abolished, the silence of the Court of Berlin with respect to the invitation that has been made to it in consequence of the treaty to become a guaranteeing Power, the abolition of the Spanish priories, in defiance of the treaty to which the King of Spain was a party, the declaration of the Portuguese Government of their intention to sequestrate the property of the Portuguese priory, as forming a part of the Spanish Langue, unless the property of the Spanish priories is restored to them, and the non-election of a Grand Master—these circumstances would have been sufficient without any other special grounds to have warranted His Majesty in suspending the evacuation of the Island until some new arrangement could be adjusted for its security and independence. ... But after all that has passed His Majesty cannot consent that his troops should evacuate the Island of Malta until substantial security has been provided for these objects, which, under the present circumstances, might be materially endangered by their removal.

NOTIFICATION FROM THE CARDINAL LEGATE IN PARIS INFORMING LORD WHITWORTH OF THE ELECTION OF A GRAND MASTER OF THE ORDER OF MALTA.

Paris, le 4 Mars 1803.[2]

D'après le refus que Lord Whitworth connoît avoir été donné par le bailli Ruspoli de la Grande Maîtrise de Malte, à laquelle Sa Sainteté, suivant le convenu des Puissances, l'avoit nommé, le Pape est venu dans la détermination de nommer Grand Maître de l'Ordre de Malte le bailli Tommasi de Cortone. Le cardinal Caprara a l'honneur de faire part de cette nomination à lord Whitworth, ambassadeur de Sa Majesté Britannique, qu'il prie de la faire connoître au cabinet de St. James, et d'agréer l'assurance de sa haute considération.   (Signed) J. B. CARDINAL CAPRARA.

Towards the close of the month of February the Grand Master Tommasi (then at Messina) dispatched the Chevalier Buzi to Malta, as his Minister-Plenipotentiary, to arrange for the transfer of the Island to the Order of St. John, where he arrived on the 28th of that month. The day after his arrival he addressed the following letter to Sir Alexander John Ball:—

[Translation.]
Malta, 1st March 1803.[3]

MONS[r]. THE ENGLISH MINISTER,—I had the honour this morning of stating to Your Excellency the object of the mission with which I am charged; to

[1] *England and Napoleon in 1803*, p. 93.   [2] *Ibid.* p. 105.
[3] Cobbett, vol. iii. p. 555.

which you replied that you had no orders to evacuate Malta, and that gave me to understand that the Grand Master had better not repair hither. After having reflected upon this answer, which was not so satisfactory as His Highness expected, it seemed to me that it required further explanation. As Your Excellency's answer appeared to contain a refusal to restore Malta to the Order of St. John of Jerusalem conformably to the 10th Article of the Treaty of Amiens, and as such a violation of the treaty might lead to the most important consequences, and even the most fatal to the repose of Europe, I cannot remain satisfied with the verbal answer you have given me, and I therefore request you to state in a public and authentic manner the motives of this unexpected refusal. I have the honour to recall to the recollection of Your Excellency that, conformably to the 4th paragraph of the 10th Article of the Treaty of Amiens, the forces of His Britannic Majesty were to evacuate that Island and its dependencies within three months from the exchange of the ratification of the treaty, or sooner if possible. That period has expired some time.

The treaty adds that 'the Island shall be given up to the Order in its present state, provided the Grand Master or Commissaries fully authorised according to the statutes of the Order shall be in the Island to take possession, and provided the troops which His Sicilian Majesty is to furnish shall have arrived.' Those troops have arrived a long time, and the only condition remaining to be fulfilled was the arrival of the Grand Master or his Commissaries to take possession. This condition is now accomplished by my arrival. The Grand Master has deigned to appoint me 'his Ambassador Extraordinary and Plenipotentiary' to treat, conclude, accomplish and concert with the English and French Ministers-Plenipotentiary and with the actual English Governor in the Island upon all the articles relative to the restoration of the Order to the Island of Malta, as well as upon the restoration of the place.

Such are the terms of the full powers with which I am vested, and of which I have sent you a copy.

According to the tenour of these full powers, and the different stipulations of the Treaty of Amiens being accomplished for the restoration of the Island of Malta to the Order of St. John of Jerusalem, I demand formally the execution of the 10th Article, paragraph 4, of the said treaty, and I beg that I may receive a categorical answer. Accept the assurance, &c. (Signed) BUSSY.

To this communication Sir Alexander Ball sent the following reply:

Malta, *2nd March* 1803.[1]

SIR,—I have received the letter which Your Excellency did me the honour to write to me yesterday, in which some dissatisfaction is expressed at my verbal communication respecting the object of your mission, and in which it is demanded that I should detail in writing my reasons for refusing to deliver up the government of these isles on the arrival of His Eminence the Grand Master of the Order of St. John of Jerusalem.

---

[1] De Villeneuve-Bargemont, vol. ii. p. 450; Cobbett, vol. iii. p. 556; C.O.R. Malta, No. 9 (1803).

In reply I beg leave to observe that as some of the Powers invited by the terms of the 10th Article of the Treaty of Amiens to guarantee the independence of Malta have not yet acceded to that measure, I do not think myself authorised to put an end to the government of His Britannic Majesty here until I receive special instructions from my Court. Your Excellency will observe that I wish to dissuade the Grand Master from coming to reside here. Your Excellency may recollect that I spoke to you on that subject to the following purport.

On your observations that the Grand Master reckoned on having immediate possession of the Palace of Government at the Fort of Valetta, I informed you that under the present circumstances I could not accede to the desire of His Eminence, it being absolutely necessary that His Excellency General Villettes and myself should continue in the Palace for the purpose of transacting the official business of our respective departments. I request, however, to recall to Your Excellency's remembrance that I offered at the same time the Palace of Boschetto for the residence of the Grand Master, a situation which I conceived to be in every respect suitable to His Eminence, until the period when he might take upon him the direction of the Government. But as the Palace of Boschetto is not at present furnished, I took the liberty to suggest that it would be more suitable to remain some time in Sicily, and so much the more so as that residence of His Eminence would be but a day's voyage from this Island. As to anything further, His Eminence may be assured that the moment I think myself authorised to deliver up the government I will inform him of it. I have the honour, &c.

(Signed) ALEXANDER J. BALL.

On the 2nd March General Vial wrote to Sir Alexander Ball in support of the demands of the Chevalier Buzi, to which the following answer was returned:

SIR ALEXANDER BALL TO GENERAL VIAL.

Malta, 3rd March 1803.[1]

His Britannic Majesty's Civil Commissioner for the affairs of these Islands and Minister-Plenipotentiary to the Order of Saint John of Jerusalem has the honour to acknowledge the receipt of a note from His Excellency the Minister-Plenipotentiary of the French Republic to the above Order of the date 2nd instant.

In answer, the Civil Commissioner has the honour to refer His Excellency the French Minister to the Sixth stipulation of the Tenth Article of Amiens, and to observe that as some of the Powers to be invited in terms of that stipulation to become guarantees to the independence of these islands have not yet acceded to that measure, he does not consider himself authorised to terminate His Britannic Majesty's authority here until he shall have received particular instructions from his Court to that effect.

The reply being unsatisfactory, General Vial made the following

[1] C.O.R. Malta, No. 9 (1803).

peremptory demand for the prompt and entire execution of the 10th Article of the Treaty of Amiens:

[Translation.]

Malta, 5th March 1803.[1]

The Minister-Plenipotentiary of the French Republic at Malta has received the note which His Excellency the Minister-Plenipotentiary of His Britannic Majesty did him the honour to address to him the 3rd March, in answer to that which the undersigned transmitted to him on the 2nd day of that month. Before he specially replies to this note the French Minister thinks it proper to state to His Excellency the Minister of England that the Ambassador Extraordinary and Plenipotentiary of the Grand Master of the Order of St. John of Jerusalem has required, by a formal application to the French Republic, the interference of its Minister at Malta in order to induce the English Minister to forego his opposition to the immediate execution of the 10th Article of the Treaty of Amiens, and to concur in its accomplishment. The undersigned, in considering the note which he has received from the Minister Plenipotentiary of England, and also that which His Excellency has addressed to M. Buzi [sic], perceives that both these notes contain a similar refusal to accede to the immediate execution of the article in question, and that both in this refusal is [sic] grounded on the same pretexts. His Excellency alleges that the Powers invited under the article to guarantee the stipulated arrangements not having acceded to the measure, he does not think himself authorised to fulfil the article, and, further, that he has received no special instructions from his Court for resigning the government of these islands to the Grand Master of the Order of St. John of Jerusalem.

With respect to these two points the undersigned has the honour to represent to His Excellency the Minister of England:

I. That the independence of these islands and arrangements respecting them have been placed by 6th paragraph of Article X of the Treaty of Amiens under the protection and guarantee of six of the most independent Powers of Europe. France and Great Britain, who were the contracting parties, and who have solicited the other Powers to guarantee that clause of their treaty for peace, cannot, without giving scandal, be the first to refuse to execute these arrangements to insure that independence and to grant that protection and guarantee.

II. That the invitation set forth in the 13th paragraph of the said Article 10 to the other Powers to accede to the stipulations contained in that article is only a mark of politeness, or an honour which these Powers are at liberty to refuse; but it is otherwise with regard to France and Great Britain, who have promised their protection and accepted the guarantee by the very act of signing the treaty which contains the arrangements to be guaranteed, who thus have placed themselves at the head of the Powers to whom the invitation was addressed.

III. That the non-contracting Powers may refuse the guarantee because it is a burthen which these Powers are at liberty not to impose upon themselves, but how absurd it would be to believe the refusal could

[1] Miège, *History of Malta*, vol. iii. p. 634.

involve and effect the annulling of the treaty of peace, and exonerate from their engagements the Powers that have signed it.

IV. That an attempt to take advantage of so frivolous a pretext and so glaring a sophism in order to decline doing what they themselves have consented to do would be a breach of faith unworthy of a great Power, and with which England would not, most assuredly, sully the page of her history.

V. That this delay in the acceptation of an honourable duty, in the supposition that it exists on the part of the non-contracting Powers, cannot, above all, prove injurious to a third Power that has been acknowledged and solemnly established by the contracting parties, unless the latter be disposed openly to violate their own engagements, the faith of treaties, and the law of nations.

VI. That Russia, Austria, and Prussia, if they have not actually acceded, as the English Minister pretends, to the invitation made to them to accept the guarantee of the Island, were far from imagining that by this delay they would have prevented the re-establishment of the Order of Malta, the execution of the Treaty of Amiens, or compromised the tranquility of Europe.

The undersigned asks of His Excellency what these Powers will think when they find that their delay in acceding to the invitation has served as a pretext for the violation of so solemn a treaty of peace. As to the declaration made by the Minister of England, that he had no special instructions from his Court on the subject of the resignation of the government of the Island, or its surrender to the Grand Master, the undersigned has the honour of observing to His Excellency that in quality of Minister-Plenipotentiary of His Britannic Majesty the principal and immutable rule of his conduct is contained in the treaty itself, and such was so clearly the intention of his Court that in the full powers given him, and which he interchanged with the undersigned, it is positively said, 'You will on your arrival at Malta immediately inform General Vial that His Majesty, desirous of accomplishing with the utmost fidelity the engagement he contracted by the definitive treaty, wishes you to take in concert with him the necessary measures for giving effect to the stipulations contained in the 10th Article of the treaty.'

His Excellency might be invested with another character in that Island, but the French Republic does not recognise these contradictory qualities, these opposing duties, and the undersigned sees in the person of His Excellency nothing but the Minister-Plenipotentiary of His Britannic Majesty, charged with the execution and the maintenance of treaties. The English Minister has no doubt reflected duly on the consequences of an opposition which cannot fail to astonish all Europe. He ought to have seen that this refusal was a manifest violation of the treaty of peace, and that the British Government, to justify its intentions and to give a striking proof of its good faith, ought distinctly to disavow a conduct so little conformable to honour, and throw the whole odium on the Minister who had resorted to it without a positive order. For if, contrary to all appearances, this violation of a treaty which has given peace to the world was not disapproved of by His Britannic Majesty, the First Consul of the French Republic would be reduced to the necessity of appealing to the tribunal of Europe, and then he would find as many allies as there are

Powers friendly to peace and jealous of their dignity, the independence of the rights of sovereigns, and the rigorous observance of the faith of treaties.

The undersigned supports, therefore, in the most formal manner the demands made to the English Minister in the name of the Grand Master of the Order of Malta by his Extraordinary Minister Plenipotentiary M. Busi, and in consequence demands the prompt and entire execution of the 10th Article of the Treaty of Amiens. (Signed) VIAL.

Copies of this correspondence were forwarded to Lord Hobart by Sir Alexander Ball, with his comments thereon, under date of the 4th March, as follows:

Malta, 4th March 1803.[1]

To the Right Honourable Lord Hobart.

MY LORD,—I have the honour to acquaint your Lordship that on the 28th ultimo the Chevalier Buzi arrived here in the character of Ambassador Extraordinary and Minister-Plenipotentiary from the Bali Tommasi, who has been lately elected Grand Master of the Order of St. John of Jerusalem. The Chevalier has delivered to me letters from His Eminence notifying his nomination to this dignity, copies of which, with my answer, I have the honour to transmit for your Lordship's information. I beg leave to enclose the copy of a correspondence with the Chevalier Buzi, and also of one with the French Minister Vial, upon the subject of the restitution of Malta to the Grand Master, according to the Treaty of Amiens.

The partisans of the Order are actively employed in seducing the minds of the people, and their design is to prevail on them to sign a declaration expressing a wish to be again placed under the government of the Grand Master, in which, I am persuaded, they will not succeed. They have assured the inhabitants that the Grand Master will immediately reduce the price of bread; but the latter are nevertheless firm, and continue grateful to the British Government for having procured them, at a time of great scarcity, that essential article of life much cheaper than it was obtained in the neighbouring countries, and still bear in mind that on our entrance into Valetta they received corn at the low price of forty scudi the salm, when throughout Italy and Sicily it was sold at sixty, and during this last winter, while the inhabitants of those countries have received corn at fifty scudi, the Maltese have obtained it as low as thirty-seven.

Upon the whole, I can assure your Lordship that I have reason to believe there is not a people more loyally attached and zealously devoted to His Majesty's Government than the inhabitants of this Island, and whatever temptations may be devised to prejudice them in their fidelity must ever prove abortive and of no avail. The Maltese deputies have applied to me, entreating that in the event of the restoration of the Order no time may be lost to obtain the fulfilment of that part of the treaty which relates to the establishment of a Maltese Langue. And I think it right to acquaint your Lordship that I have merely assured

[1] C.O.R. Malta, No. 9 (1803).

them they may depend upon the solicitude of His Majesty's Government to support them in the attainment of this essential object.

The duplicate of this letter will be conveyed to your Lordship by the *Casher* sloop of war, which sails for England in the course of this day. I have the honour, &c. (Signed) ALEX. JNO. BALL.

On the 14th March Lord Whitworth acquainted Sir John Warren, British Ambassador at St. Petersburg, of the critical position of affairs in the following dispatch:

Paris, 14*th March* 1803.[1]

... You are not now to learn that it is on the subject of the evacuation of Malta that the two Governments are at issue. I have been instructed a fortnight ago to declare that until means are found to dissipate those alarms for the safety of Egypt which the conduct of the First Consul has excited, His Majesty does not think himself justified in giving up a point on which the safety of that country, and eventually that of his own possessions, so materially depends. In answer to this, assurances have been given that the First Consul has no present views on Egypt; that he has delayed his projects on that country, not because he does not wish for it, but because he is certain it must one day belong to him, either by a private agreement with the Porte or by the dissolution of the Turkish Empire. This the First Consul told me himself.

The question now became more acute. On the 15th March the French Ambassador, General Andréossy, received the following note from Lord Hawkesbury:

Downing Street, 15*th March* 1803.[2]

... Under these circumstances His Majesty feels that he has no alternative, and that a just regard to his own honour, and to the interests of his people, makes it necessary for him to declare that he cannot consent that his troops should evacuate the island of Malta until substantial security has been provided for those objects which, under the present circumstances, might be materially endangered by their removal. With respect to several of the positions stated in the Note, and grounded on the idea of the Tenth Article being executed in its literal sense, they call for some observations.

By the 10th Article of the Treaty of Amiens the Island of Malta was to be restored by His Majesty to the Order of St. John upon certain conditions. The evacuation of the island at a specified period formed a part of those conditions; and if the other stipulations had been in a due course of execution, His Majesty would have been bound by the terms of the treaty, to have ordered his forces to evacuate the Island.

But these conditions must be considered as being all of equal effect; and if any material parts of them should have been found incapable of execution, or if the execution of them should for any circumstance have been retarded, His Majesty would be warranted in deferring the evacuation of the Island until such time as the other conditions of the article could

---

[1] Browning, *op. cit.* p. 118.   [2] *Ibid.* p. 113.

be effected, or until some new arrangement could be concluded which should be judged satisfactory by the contracting parties. The refusal of Russia to accede to the arrangement, except on condition that the Maltese Langue should be abolished; the silence of the Court of Berlin with respect to the invitation that has been made to it, in consequence of the treaty, to become a guaranteeing Power; the abolition of the Spanish priories in defiance of the treaty, to which the King of Spain was a party; the declaration of the Portuguese Government of their intention to sequestrate the property of the Portuguese priory, as forming a part of the Spanish Langue, unless the property of the Spanish priories was restored to them—these circumstances would have been sufficient, without any other special grounds, to have warranted His Majesty in suspending the evacuation of the island.

CHAPTER XXII

DISCUSSIONS AND CORRESPONDENCE RELATING TO MALTA

(From April 1803 to July 1803)

DURING the month of April a final attempt at an amicable arrangement upon the points at issue was made by Lord Hawkesbury in his dispatch of the 4th of that month.[1] He therein authorised Lord Whitworth to present to the French Government a project 'which, under the present circumstances, would meet the ideas of His Majesty's Government, which would afford security for those objects which are considered as endangered by the unequivocal disclosure of the views of the First Consul, and which at the same time might entirely save the honour of the French Government.'[2] The project was as follows:

1st. Malta to remain in perpetuity in the possession of His Majesty.
2nd. The Knights of the Order of St. John to be indemnified by His Majesty for any losses of property which they may sustain in consequence of such an arrangement.
3rd. Holland and Switzerland to be evacuated by the French troops.
4th. The Island of Elba to be confirmed to France by His Majesty, and the King of Etruria to be acknowledged.
5th. The Italian and Ligurian Republics to be acknowledged by His Majesty, provided an arrangement is made in Italy for the King of Sardinia which shall be satisfactory to him.

The withdrawal of the French troops from Holland[3] and Switzerland was, however, a *sine quâ non* on the part of England, and to this France would not agree; but, before proceeding to extremities, Talleyrand, on the 8th April, in reply to Lord Hawkesbury's note of the 3rd April, wrote:

'The French Government would never consent to anything which

---
[1] That the British Government still wished for peace was the conviction of General Andréossy, who on April 4th warned Talleyrand that everything depended on France and the reasonable overtures she ought to make. See P. Coquelle, *Napoleon and England*, ch. vii.—J. H. R.
[2] Browning, *op. cit.* pp. 149, 151.
[3] For the importance of securing the actual neutrality of Holland see P. Coquelle, *Napoleon and England*, ch. viii.—J. H. R.

might prejudice the independence of the Maltese Order in their island, but that if the English Government could suggest an arrangement which should lead to the termination of the present difficulties, the French Government would have no objection to meeting them by some special agreement.

Whilst the difficulties between the two Cabinets appeared irreconcilable, those which were occurring locally could also not be satisfactorily arranged, for in the early part of this same month, Mr. A'Court, British Minister at Naples, informed Sir Alexander Ball that, notwithstanding the Grand Master's promise not to visit Malta until affairs wore a more favourable aspect, he contemplated leaving for that Island immediately, urged to that action by the French Minister, Vial, at Malta. An extract from this dispatch is as follows:

[Extract.]

[Private and Confidential.]

WILLIAM A'COURT TO SIR ALEXANDER BALL.

Naples, 8th April 1803.[1]

... Notwithstanding the assurance given by the Grand Master of the Order of St. John of Jerusalem to Captain Durban, that it was not his intention to attempt visiting Malta until affairs should wear a more favourable aspect, I find that he has changed his intention and means to proceed immediately to that island.

The aide-de-camp of General Vial has the address to engage the Grand Master to adopt this resolution, which is certainly contrary to his own wishes and inclination. He required, and obliged, this weak old man to write a letter to his Government requesting a Neapolitan ship of war to carry him to Malta. The letter was presented to General Acton by the French Ambassador at this Court, and although, as the General informed me, it was evidently written with coolness, and even with unwillingness, it was impossible for this Court to refuse its consent to the demand, when backed by the weighty and powerful arguments of the Consular Ambassador.

A frigate and corvette have absolutely sailed for Messina, though it is probable that they may be many days on their voyage, in order to offer a passage to the Grand Master. You may, therefore, expect him very soon at Malta. Early in the month of March an application was made by Gen. Andréossi to Lord Hawkesbury for the immediate evacuation of Malta. He received for answer that England would by no means consent to the evacuation of that Island until France should explain her conduct with regard to the Morea and her views upon the Turkish dominions in general.

A message was sent by His Majesty on the 9th March to his Parliament stating that 'great warlike preparations were making in France, intended, indeed, as was reported, for the recovery of her colonies, but which might be for any other purpose. That negotiations of the utmost consequence were pending between the two countries, and

[1] C.O.R. Malta, No. 9 (1803).

that in case of an unfavourable issue to them he hoped for the support of his Parliament.' The First Consul has already notified to this Government that in the event of another rupture he intends again to take possession of the Kingdom of Naples. He has also announced his displeasure at the continued supplies received from this country by the English at Malta. This last circumstance has thrown some obstacles in my way with regard to procuring supplies from Calabria, and I shall defer answering Your Excellency's official note upon that subject until I have arranged the business more satisfactorily with this Government.

(Signed) WILLIAM A'COURT.

Returning to the negotiations between London and Paris, we note that Lord Hawkesbury in the following dispatch of the 9th April was informed by Lord Whitworth that Bonaparte was resolutely determined to insist upon the evacuation of Malta :

[Extract.]

LORD WHITWORTH TO LORD HAWKESBURY.

Paris, 9th April 1803.[1]

. . . If [said M. Talleyrand] the English Government insists absolutely on breaking the Treaty of Amiens, the First Consul is determined to go all lengths to maintain it. If the English Government is determined to keep possession of Malta, the First Consul will suffer himself to be cut in pieces rather than consent to it.

In response to Talleyrand's invitation of the 8th April, Lord Hawkesbury, on the 13th, went further into details in expressing the views of the British Government in the following dispatch addressed to Lord Whitworth :—

[Extract.]

LORD HAWKESBURY TO LORD WHITWORTH.

Downing Street, 13th April 1803.[2]

. . . With respect to the assertion so often advanced, and repeated in your last conversations, of the non-execution of the Treaty of Amiens relative to Malta, I have only to observe again that the execution of that article is become impracticable from causes which it has not been in the power of His Majesty to control; that the greatest part of the funds assigned to the support of the Order, and indispensably necessary for the independence of the Order and the defence of the Island, have been sequestrated since the conclusion of the definitive treaty, in direct repugnance to the spirit and letter of that treaty; and that two of the principal Powers who were invited to accede as guarantees to the arrangement have refused their accession, except on the condition that the part of the arrangement which was deemed so material relative to the Maltese Langue should be entirely cancelled.

[1] Browning, op. cit. p. 164. [2] Ibid. p. 170.

'I observe in the *note verbale* of M. Talleyrand he makes use of the expression the *independence* of the Order of Malta. If this is meant to apply to the Order exclusively, His Majesty would be willing for the preservation of peace that the civil government of the Island should be given to the Order of St. John, the Maltese enjoying the privileges which were stipulated in their favour in the Treaty of Amiens, and that, conformably to principles which have been adopted on other occasions, the fortifications of the Island should be garrisoned for ever by the troops of His Majesty. In the event of either of these propositions being found unattainable, His Majesty might be disposed to consent to an arrangement by which the Island of Malta would remain in his possession for a limited number of years, and to waive in consequence his demand for a perpetual occupation, provided that the number of years was not less than ten, and that His Sicilian Majesty could be induced to cede the sovereignty of the Island of Lampedusa for a valuable consideration. If this proposition is admitted, the Island of Malta should be given up to the inhabitants at the end of that period and it should be acknowledged as an independent State.'

In the event of non-compliance to these demands, Whitworth was instructed under date of the 23rd April to present to the French Government in the form of an ultimatum the following proposals :— First : The possession of Malta by the British for ten years, during which period the authority, civil and military, was to remain solely in His Majesty, and that at the expiration of that term it was to be given up to the inhabitants, and not to the Order; provided also that His Sicilian Majesty shall be induced to cede to His Majesty the Island of Lampedusa. Secondly : That Holland shall be evacuated by the French troops within a month after the conclusion of a convention by which all these provisions shall be secured. Thirdly : That His Majesty would consent to acknowledge the new Italian States provided stipulations were made in favour of His Sardinian Majesty and of Switzerland.[1]

A crisis in the negotiations had now been reached; the British ultimatum had been delivered, and unless France gave way, war was inevitable. It may be desirable here to refer to some of the letters written by General Andréossy to Napoleon and Talleyrand, which were published by Monsieur Coquelle.[2] Andréossy, soon after his arrival in England, became convinced that the British people were anxious to maintain peace, and that the question of peace or war rested entirely with France, for on the 2nd April 1803 he addressed Bonaparte as follows :—

London, 2nd *April* 1803.

CITIZEN PREMIER CONSUL,—The English Cabinet have been distressed by the Note which I forwarded to the Secretary of State, and I have not yet received an answer.

[1] Browning, *op. cit.* pp. 182-183.
[2] See P. Coquelle, *Napoleon and England*, Engl. edit., pp. 52-55.

Being persuaded that you desire peace, and are in need of it, I am acting in accordance with that principle, but you afford the English Cabinet no means of escape from the unfortunate position in which they have become involved, and however serious the consequences, it is certain that they will take up any challenge they may receive.

It is true that the age and infirmities of the King make him look with an anxious eye on the prospect of being harassed in his latter days by a terrible war, and by the stress of work which such a situation necessarily entails, but the responsible statesmen feel bound to try to secure a peaceful opening for the next reign, which under the happiest conditions must be a stormy one.

The prayers, the needs, and the wishes of this country are for peace. God forbid that I should for a moment think that France ought to forego the least of her advantages, and certainly my regard for this country is not likely to lead me astray, but I am morally certain that by appearing not to exert pressure on England you could easily obtain all which is necessary to secure the safety of the French Government, and preserve the advantages it derives from the countries under its control; you might thus effect the consolidation of that fine edifice which your hands have raised, but which arouses the jealousy of certain Frenchmen, who are perhaps more treacherous foes than the London journalists.

There is ample material for another rising in the Vendée country, and the chief Powers on the Continent could easily be combined into a coalition against France.

I have learnt on the most excellent authority that designs have been formed on South America. St. Domingo will be a prey to insurrection. Puisaye has just returned from Canada; he has sent to tell me that he will not associate himself with any scheme that may be formed against us.

I have considered it my duty, Citizen Premier Consul, to bring to your notice some of the evils that would be the inevitable result of war, and the means by which you may easily preserve peace. The loyalty of my intentions and my devotion to your person will prompt you to pardon my outspokenness.

(Signed) F. ANDRÉOSSY.

In confirmation of the above he wrote officially two days later to the Minister of Foreign Affairs as follows:—

ANDRÉOSSY TO TALLEYRAND.

(London) *4th April* 1803.

Lord Hawkesbury's note (of the 3rd April) still leaves the French Government the alternative of peace or war. *It is not a secret desire of the British Government to keep Malta*, as Lord Hawkesbury has actually told a person of my acquaintance in these words: 'We cannot evacuate Malta until we find ourselves in a position to assure Parliament and the nation, that the discussion has assumed a fairly peaceful aspect; but we do not say, "either Malta or war!"'

Andréossy concludes thus:

Everything depends on the French Government; if it is willing to give an explanation, a satisfactory compromise will easily be arrived at between the two Powers; if it refuses, war is inevitable, and will be popular in England. If the French Government discusses the matter in a generous spirit, Europe will attribute it to the magnanimity of the First Consul, and to his desire to preserve peace among all the Powers, for no one will dare to suggest weakness as a motive; in these circumstances peace will be preserved, and England will be persuaded to make a free surrender to the First Consul of anything which he is justified in asking of her.

On the same day Andréossy concluded a dispatch to Bonaparte as follows:

Never, I believe, in any circumstances were Englishmen more generally agreed on the desirability of keeping peace, and you are now in a most favourable position to decide the world's destiny for all time.[1]

The English proposals of the 23rd April (see *ante*) were not, however, acceptable to the First Consul. He had decided to retain possession of Holland, but although bent on war, he was desirous of gaining time to complete his preparations.[2]

The dispatch of the 23rd April was crossed by another of the same date from Lord Whitworth to Lord Hawkesbury, from which an extract is here given:

Paris, 23rd April 1803.[3]

... M. Talleyrand told me that if I had called upon him sooner he should, two days ago, have communicated to me the First Consul's answer,[4] which was, that no consideration on earth should induce him to consent to a concession in perpetuity of Malta in any shape whatever, and that the reestablishment of the Order was not so much the point to be discussed as that of suffering Great Britain to acquire a possession in the Mediterranean.[5]

The British proposals of the 23rd April were presented to Talleyrand on the 26th, and on the 4th May the following counter-proposition was returned by the French Government:—'That the Island should be garrisoned by one of the three Powers who had guaranteed its independence—either Austria, Russia, or Prussia, instead of Neapolitan troops.'

The day previous Lord Whitworth received from M. Huber the following interesting communication:

[1] Archives Nationales (A.F. iv. 1672).
[2] See further proofs of this in my *Life of Napoleon*, ch. xvii., ad fin.—J. H. R.
[3] Browning, *op. cit.* p. 183.
[4] i.e., to the proposals contained in Lord Hawkesbury's dispatch of the 13th April. See *ante*.
[5] This last admission is of the highest significance; it probably clinched the resolve of the Addington Ministry to risk war rather than give way respecting Malta.—J. H. R.

[Extract.]

M. HUBER TO LORD WHITWORTH.

Paris, *3rd May* 1803.[1]

... On every such occasion the few men who have in vain laboured to prevent a renewal of the war now will vigorously and constantly exert themselves to determine and operate an accommodation. Your Lordship knows that, combining together character, situation, and abilities, they form a very strong phalanx and a very desirable association. Joseph Bonaparte (the best of his family) has, on account of his morality and good conduct, a constant, and *at times* successful, influence on his brother.[2] Regnault de St. Jean d'Angely, his intimate friend and confidant, and a Councillor of State, is a man of excellent unsullied character and eminent abilities, and under the several points of view a man of real importance, as well as a very rising man, being high in the favour of the First Consul. M. Malouet, a man whose moral character and talents are well known in England, and are here in high and general estimation—he is an essential member of this little phalanx. Fouché, senator, a very different man from those just named in point of morality, stands notoriously high in point of abilities, energy, and independence of mind; he has on this occasion been a bold and loud advocate for peace, and alone has dared repeatedly to combat the Consul's mistaken pride and ambition. ... These different men (each of whom I have thought it right for your Lordship's recollection hereafter to place in his true light), knowing my political creed, and relying on me in every respect, seem earnestly desirous that I should continue to be a medium between England and them. In the course of my co-operation with them I have found such unanimity in principles, opinion, and action (I mean essentially Joseph Bonaparte, Regnault, and Malouet) as to be seriously encouraged and justified in my confidence in their public views, and looking upon them collectively (as long as the Bonaparte family retains the power) as the decided and sure channel to peace whenever the moment arrives, I am very ready to remain in any auxiliary situation, provided I am placed in a convenient and safe post. ...

To the counter-proposals of the French Government of the 4th May Lord Hawkesbury on the 7th gave his final instructions to Lord Whitworth, as follows:

LORD HAWKESBURY TO LORD WHITWORTH.

Downing Street, *7th May* 1803.[3]

... The French Government propose that His Majesty should give up the Island of Malta to a Russian, Austrian or Prussian garrison. If His Majesty could be disposed (which, under the present circumstances, he deems impossible) to waive his demand for a temporary occupation of

---

[1] Browning, *op. cit.* p. 210.
[2] Joseph Bonaparte had negotiated the Treaty of Amiens, and felt a personal interest in upholding it.—J. H. R.
[3] *Ibid.* p. 224.

the Island of Malta, the Emperor of Russia would be the only Sovereign to whom in the present state of Europe he could consent that the Island should be assigned, and his Majesty has certain and authentic information that the Emperor of Russia would on no account consent to garrison Malta. Under these circumstances His Majesty perseveres in his determination to adhere to the substance of his third *project* as his ultimatum.

PROJECT.

1. The French Government should engage to make no opposition to the cession of the Island of Lampedusa to His Majesty by the King of the Two Sicilies.

2. In consequence of the present state of the Island of Lampedusa, His Majesty shall remain in possession of the Island of Malta until such arrangements shall be made by him as may enable His Majesty to occupy Lampedusa as a naval station; after which period the Island of Malta shall be given up to the inhabitants, and acknowledged as an independent State.

3. The territories of the Batavian Republic shall be evacuated by the French forces within one month after the conclusion of a Convention founded on the principles of this *project*.

4. The King of Etruria and the Italian and Ligurian Republics shall be acknowledged by His Majesty.

5. Switzerland shall be evacuated by the French forces.

6. A suitable territorial provision shall be assigned to the King of Sardinia in Italy.

Articles 4, 5 and 6 may be entirely omitted, or must all be inserted.

(*Secret Article*). His Majesty shall not be required by the French Government to evacuate the Island of Malta until after the expiration of ten years.

If the French Government will not consent that the occupation of Malta by His Majesty's forces for ten years should be inserted in the body of the treaty, the Secret Article must be considered as an indispensable part of the arrangement.

The French Government declined to accept the British final proposals, which were presented on the 10th May, a result which Lord Whitworth on the day previous had led Lord Hawkesbury to expect.

[Extract.]

LORD WHITWORTH TO LORD HAWKESBURY.

Paris, 9th May 1803, 9 p.m.[1]

Joseph Bonaparte has been with me, and I have communicated to him the nature of the project I have to propose. Were I to judge from his language I should consider the business as desperate. He repeatedly assured me that the First Consul would never consent to our possession of Malta unless it were on the ground stated in that part of the project which is meant to be public, and by which such a possession is to be considered as

[1] Browning, *op. cit.*, p. 230.

dependent on the works to be carried on at Lampedusa, and not to exceed a year or two.

To this Lord Whitworth refused to assent, and stated that the last word had been uttered by the British Government on this topic. The negotiations consequently failed, Lord Whitworth demanded his passports, and at 10 p.m. of the 12th May left Paris for London.[1]

Although the rupture appeared now quite complete, Talleyrand on the following day was ordered by Bonaparte to convey to Andréossy these further instructions, dated the 13th May 1803:[2]

You will employ Citizen Schimmelpenninck (the Dutch Minister at the Court of St. James', and partisan of Bonaparte) or any indirect means to suggest to the British Cabinet that if they absolutely refuse to cede Malta to one of the Powers who are acting as guarantors, we might be willing to permit England to remain in the Island for a further period of ten years on condition that France should for the same number of years occupy Tarentum, Otranto, and all the positions she occupied in the Kingdom of Naples on the occasion of the signature of the Treaty of Amiens.

If this suggestion is favourably received, then let it be known that you are authorised to sign an agreement couched in the following terms:—

(1) The British troops shall be permitted to occupy Malta for ten years.

(2) For the same period of time the French troops shall occupy, as they did at the time of the signature of the Treaty of Amiens, the positions of Tarentum and Otranto, which they only evacuated in pursuance of Article II. of the said treaty.

You must realise, General, that if you have the slightest reason to believe that the proposal will not recommend itself to them you must be careful to leave no trace of it, so that it may always be possible to deny that the French Government ever agreed to these terms. The First Consul leaves it to your discretion to decide what use you will make of the authorisation he now gives you.

As will be seen by reference to the valuable work of M. Coquelle, 'Napoleon and England' (ch. ix.), nothing came of this overture, which may be regarded as an attempt by the First Consul to delay the rupture, which his decision and that of the Council of St. Cloud had rendered inevitable. War against France was consequently declared by England on the 16th May, and on the same day notification thereof was conveyed to Sir A. Ball by Lord Hobart in the following dispatch:

[1] See Mr. Browning, *op. cit.* pp. 233-8, for Whitworth's final attempt to come to an understanding with Talleyrand, who (along with Joseph Bonaparte) advised strongly for the acceptance of the British terms in a council held at St. Cloud. Five others voted against them, and they carried the day. Bonaparte's final resolve was strengthened by the arrival of news that the Czar Alexander I. now offered his intervention between the disputants.—J. H. R.

[2] French Foreign Office Supplement, vol. xxxii. fol. 76. Coquelle, *Napoleon and England*, p. 66.

Downing Street, 16th May 1803.[1]

To Sir Alexander Ball.

SIR,—I have received the King's commands to acquaint you that in consequence of the termination of the dissensions lately depending between His Majesty and the French Government (of the probability of which result I gave you notice in my secret letter of the 7th instant) His Majesty's Ambassador at Paris has quitted that capital, and the French Ambassador at this Court will likewise leave London to-morrow morning.

In consequence of this event, I am to signify to you His Majesty's commands that you do immediately take preparatory measures for the conveyance of the Neapolitan troops from Malta, and that you acquaint the officer who may be in chief command of the said troops that a Neapolitan garrison having only been received into Malta in conformity to the provisions of the Treaty of Amiens, the interruption given to the final execution of that treaty by the conduct of France has induced His Majesty to instruct his Minister at Naples to signify to that Court that the continuation of the said troops at Malta is no longer necessary.

I am also to signify to you His Majesty's further pleasure that you do immediately require General Vial and all persons connected with the French Mission to quit the Island of Malta without delay. And I am further to desire that you will proceed immediately with the formation of the Maltese corps directed in my secret letter of 6th November, according to the instructions therein contained. In regard to the appointment of British officers, either to command these Corps or to serve in them with the native officers, you will receive special instructions in the course of a very few days. His Majesty has been graciously pleased to appoint you to be his Civil Commissioner to the affairs of Malta and its dependencies, with a salary annexed of £2,000 a year, in the room of Charles Cameron, Esquire, whose salary is to cease from this date. I am desired that you will communicate the contents of this letter to Major-General Villettes.

(Signed) HOBART.

Two days later, namely, on the 18th May, the following justification of their action was made by the British Cabinet in the House of Commons:

His Majesty's earnest endeavours for the preservation of peace having failed of success, he entertains the fullest confidence that he shall receive the same support from his Parliament, and that the same zeal and spirit will be manifested by his people, which he has experienced on every occasion when the honour of his Crown has been attacked or the essential interests of his dominions have been endangered. . . . His Majesty has, unfortunately, had too much reason to observe and to lament that the system of violence, aggression, and aggrandisement which characterised the proceedings of the different Governments of France during the war has been continued with as little disguise since its termination.

They have continued to keep a French army in Holland against the will and in defiance of the remonstrances of the Batavian Republic, and in repugnance to the letter of three solemn treaties. They have in a period

[1] C.O.R. Malta, No. 9.

of peace invaded the territory and violated the independence of the Swiss nation in defiance of the treaty of Lunéville, which had stipulated the independence of their territory and the right of the inhabitants to choose their own form of Government. They have annexed to the dominions of France Piedmont, Parma, and Piacenza, and the island of Elba, without allotting any provision to the King of Sardinia, whom they have despoiled of the most valuable part of his territory, though they were bound by a solemn engagement to the Emperor of Russia to attend to his interests and to provide for his establishment. . . .

His Majesty was called upon to evacuate the Island of Malta. His Majesty had manifested from the moment of the signature of the definitive treaty an anxious disposition to carry into full effect the stipulations of the Treaty of Amiens relative to that Island. As soon as he was informed that an election of a Grand Master had taken place under the auspices of the Emperor of Russia, and that it had been agreed by the different priories assembled at St. Petersburg to acknowledge the person whom the Court of Rome should select out of those who had been named by them to be Grand Master of the Order of St. John, His Majesty proposed to the French Government, for the purpose of avoiding any difficulties which might arise in the execution of the arrangement, to acknowledge that election to be valid; and when in the month of August the French Government applied to His Majesty to permit the Neapolitan troops to be sent to the Island of Malta, as a preliminary measure for preventing any unnecessary delay, His Majesty consented without hesitation to this proposal, and gave direction for the admission of the Neapolitan troops into the Island. His Majesty had thus shown his disposition not only to throw no obstacle in the way of the execution of the treaty, but, on the contrary, to facilitate the execution of it by every means in his power.

His Majesty cannot, however, admit that at any period since the conclusion of the Treaty of Amiens the French Government have had a right to call upon him in conformity to the stipulations of that treaty to withdraw his forces from the Island of Malta.

At the time when this demand was made by the French Government several of the most important stipulations of the arrangement respecting Malta remained unexecuted; the election of a Grand Master had not been carried into effect.

The 10th Article had stipulated that the independence of the Island should be placed under the guarantee and protection of Great Britain, France, Austria, Russia, Spain, and Prussia. The Emperor of Germany had acceded to the guarantee, but only on condition of a like accession on the part of the other Powers specified in the article. The Emperor of Russia had refused his accession, except on the condition that the Maltese Langue should be abrogated, and the King of Prussia had given no answer whatever to the application which had been made to him to accede to the arrangement.[1]

But the fundamental principle, upon the existence of which depended the execution of the other parts of the article, had been defeated by the changes which had taken place in the constitution of the Order since the

---

[1] This omission of the Prussian Government is very curious, considering that it was then very Gallophile in policy.—J. H. R.

conclusion of the treaty of peace. It was to the Order of St. John of Jerusalem that His Majesty was, by the first stipulation of the 10th Article, bound to restore the Island of Malta. The Order is defined to consist of those Langues which were in existence at the time of the conclusion of the treaty, the three French Langues having been abolished and a Maltese Langue added to the institution. The Order consisted therefore at that time of the following Langues, viz. of Arragon, Castile, Germany, Italy, Bavaria, and Russia.

Since the conclusion of the definitive treaty the Langues of Arragon and Castile have been separated from the Order by Spain, a part of the Italian Langue has been abolished by the annexation of Piedmont and Parma to France. There is strong reason to believe that it has been in contemplation to sequestrate the property of the Bavarian Langue, and the intention has been avowed of keeping the Russian Langues within the dominions of the Emperor. Under these circumstances the Order of St. John cannot now be considered as that body to which according to the stipulations of the treaty the Island was to be restored, and the funds indispensably necessary for its support, and for the maintenance of the independence of that Island have been nearly, if not wholly, sequestered.[1]

Even if this had arisen from circumstances which it was not in the power of any of the contracting parties to the Treaty to control, His Majesty would nevertheless have had a right to defer the evacuation of the Island by his forces until such time as an equivalent arrangement had been concluded for the preservation of the independence of the Order and of the Island. But if these changes have taken place in consequence of any acts of the other parties of the treaty, if the French Government shall appear to have proceeded upon a system of rendering the Order, whose independence they had stipulated, incapable of maintaining that independence, His Majesty's right to continue in the occupation of the Island under such circumstances will hardly be contested.

It is indisputable that the revenues of the two Spanish Langues have been withdrawn from the Order by his Catholic Majesty; a part of the Italian Langue has, in fact, been abolished by France through the unjust annexation of Piedmont and Parma and Piacentia to the French territory.

The Elector of Bavaria has been instigated by the French Government to sequestrate the property of the Order within his territories, and it is certain they have not only sanctioned but encouraged the idea of the propriety of separating the Russian Langues from the remainder of the Order.

As the conduct of the Governments of France and Spain has therefore in some instances directly, and in others indirectly, contributed to the changes which have taken place in the Order, and thus destroyed its means of supporting its independence, it is to those Governments, and not to His Majesty, that the non-execution of the 10th Article of the Treaty of Amiens must be ascribed. Such would be the just conclusion if the 10th Article of that treaty were considered as an arrangement by itself. It must be observed, however, that this article forms a part only of a treaty of peace, the whole of which is connected together, and the

[1] This argument is weighty when it is remembered that the properties of these Langues had supplied the funds by which alone the great expense of maintaining the fortress of Valetta could be met.—J. H. R.

stipulations of which must, upon a principle common to all treaties, be construed as having a reference to each other.

His Majesty was induced by the treaty of peace to consent to abandon and to restore to the Order of St. John the Island of Malta on condition of its independence and neutrality. But a further condition, which must necessarily be supposed to have had considerable influence with His Majesty in inducing him to make so important a concession, was the acquiescence of the French Government in an arrangement for the security of the Levant by the 8th and 9th Articles in the treaty, stipulating the integrity of the Turkish Empire and the independence of the Ionian Islands. His Majesty has, however, since learnt that the French Government have entertained views hostile to both these objects, and that they have even suggested the idea of a partition of the Turkish Empire. These views must now be manifest to all the world from the official publication of the report of Colonel Sébastiani, from the conduct of that officer and of the other French agents in Egypt, Syria, and the Ionian Islands, and from the distinct admission of the First Consul himself in his communication with Lord Whitworth.

His Majesty was therefore warranted in considering it to be the determination of the French Government to violate those articles of the treaty of peace which stipulated for the integrity and independence of the Turkish Empire and of the Ionian Islands, and consequently he would not have been justified in evacuating the Island of Malta without receiving some other security which might equally provide for these important objects.

His Majesty accordingly feels that he has an incontestable claim in consequence of the conduct of France since the treaty of peace, and with reference to the objects which made part of the stipulations of that treaty, to refuse under the present circumstances to relinquish the possession of the Island of Malta. Yet, notwithstanding this right, so clear and so unquestionable, the alternative presented by the French Government to His Majesty in language the most peremptory and menacing, was the evacuation of Malta or the renewal of war. . . .[1]

In the debate in Parliament on Friday, the 20th May 1803, four days after the declaration of war against France, Lord Hawkesbury, referring to Malta and Maltese affairs, said it had been asserted, and had been even introduced into periodical publications, that a remonstrance had been made by the Maltese deputies in which they brought forward a grave subject of complaint against the Government of this country for indifference to their just rights and privileges in the arrangement of the definitive treaty.

[1] A further topic not referred to in the documents collected by Mr. Hardman was the sailing from Brest of a French expedition to the East Indies on 6th March. This undoubtedly made the British Government more nervous about its communications with India. As our troops had evacuated the Cape of Good Hope and Egypt, Malta was the only point left where we could hinder the French in their movements towards India. For the secret instructions issued by Bonaparte to General Decaen commanding the expedition to India, and the prospect which he held out of war against England in September 1804, see Rose, *Life of Napoleon*, vol. i. pp. 374, 375.—J. H. R.

This was a charge which he felt it necessary on his part to repel in the strongest terms. With this view, he could not do better than direct the attention of the House to a letter written by the deputies subsequent to the Treaty of Amiens, in which they expressed their perfect satisfaction with the conduct held towards them by Ministers, and their gratitude for the exertions which had been resorted to in their favour.

Their great object, he did not mean to deny, was the privilege of being under the direct protection and government of His Britannic Majesty, but if this could not be obtained, the arrangement made in their behalf was one which they thought demanded a warm expression of gratitude. Here the noble Lord read a part of the letter which fully justified his statements. The deputies declared that they considered it their highest honour to be admitted to the privileges of British subjects. As this, however, was impracticable, they could not without the most affectionate gratitude reflect ôn the efforts made by Ministers to secure their privileges. These efforts they should communicate, with the history of their country, to the latest posterity, and while they gloried in the continuance of their privileges, they would tell that to the British Government was their protection to be ascribed.

At the climax of the negotiations which preceded the declaration of war Mr. William Eton, a discredited official of the Malta Government (who has been accused of promoting discontent among the people of Malta), arrived in England, furnished with copies of correspondence which had passed between the Maltese deputies and the British Government.

This correspondence, consisting of the Petition of the Maltese People to His Majesty the King, and the so-termed 'Remonstrance' of the 1st March 1802 (which have appeared in another chapter of this work), were published in Cobbett's weekly Opposition paper of the 7th May (vol. iii. page 679).

Owing to this publication General Gascoyne, at the sitting of the Commons held on the 20th May (four days after the declaration of war), moved for the production of papers respecting 'Representations which had been made to the British Government by the Maltese people from October 1801 to March 1802,'[1] and of the Proclamation issued to the Inhabitants of Malta by Colonel Graham (the future Lord Lynedoch), then member for Perthshire. The motion, being opposed by Lord Hawkesbury and others, was negatived, Colonel Graham observing that so far as the Proclamation which he had issued to the inhabitants of Malta was concerned, he could assure the House, that the production of a copy of it would be altogether useless, and this on a very simple ground. He had issued the Proclamation on his own private opinion of its expediency, and

[1] Cobbett, vol. iii. p. 1637.

not on the authority of any orders which he had received from Government.¹

Thereupon Cobbett, having been provided by his coadjutors, the agitators from Malta, with a copy of the Proclamation which had been moved for and negatived, immediately published it in his next issue of the 28th May, together with other papers reflecting on General Pigot's character.²

Five days later Mr. Canning moved again for copies of all 'Maltese remonstrances made by the natives of Malta,' and all other papers respecting the intended restoration of the Order of St. John,³ and during the debate which followed on the next day, the 3rd June 1803, Colonel Graham remarked that 'about two hours before he came down to the House, General Pigot called upon him, with Mr. Cobbett's Registers, which probably contained the same papers which had been moved for by an honourable gentlemen (Mr. Canning) yesterday concerning Malta; and he was particularly requested to say from General Pigot that these papers contained the most gross misrepresentations and charges against his character.'⁴

Meanwhile General Pigot addressed the following letter to Lord Hobart:

Hertford Street, 31st May 1803.⁵

MY DEAR LORD,—I was yesterday honoured with your Lordship's letter, for which I return you many thanks, I shall be exceedingly obliged to you if you will take the trouble of reading the extracts of letters herewith sent you, which passed between Mr. Paget, Sir Alexander Ball, and myself relative to Malta. By these you will see the difficult card I had to play, and that if I had listened to their pressing solicitations of hoisting Sicilian colours, or those of the Order of St. John of Jerusalem, and had not been firm and acted as I did, Malta never would have been considered as a *conquest* made by the British, or as exclusively belonging to the King of Great Britain; at the same time, I have not a doubt that the advice they gave was with the best intention. I have the honour, &c.

(Signed) H. PIGOT.

To the Right Honourable Lord Hobart.

At the discussion on the Address, which took place three days later in the Upper House, Lord Melville⁶ gave the following cogent reasons for voting in its favour:

Now indeed was he (Lord Melville) at liberty to contemplate the possibility of realising an object of so much importance as the settlement of Malta under British protection. Well did he remember the melancholy moments he had passed, when, after reading the definitive treaty, he found Malta exposed to so much danger of falling into the hands of a Power that would employ it for our destruction. The importance of that Island

---

¹ Cobbett, vol. iii. p. 1642. ² *Ibid.* vol. iii. pp. 769 - 774.
³ *Ibid,* vol. iii. p. 870. ⁴ *Ibid.* vol. iii. p. 1751.
⁵ C.O.R., Malta, No. 9.
⁶ Formerly the Rt. Hon. Henry Dundas —J. H. R.

had long appeared to him to be very great, and Europe had in the most decisive instances witnessed it.

By means of Malta it was that the French had attacked and made themselves masters of Egypt. By Malta it was that we had been enabled to recover that possession. If Malta remained in our hands it was impossible that all the efforts of France, that all the armaments she could send forth, could obtain possession of Egypt while we with a superior navy had the opportunity of availing ourselves of the harbours of Malta. Malta, therefore, was to be considered as of infinite importance to the strengthening and security of our Empire in India. He considered it as a great tower erected in the Mediterranean, on which the flag of Great Britain, displayed and floating, would hold forth an invitation to the people of the Mediterranean, of the Adriatic, and of the Levant seas to rally round it, and to avail themselves of the protection of this country. As we were now going to war, and as Malta formed one of the main objects of the war, he wished that its value should be fully understood, and that we should likewise keep in view the necessity of availing ourselves of its advantages to the utmost. It was evident how great interests depended upon the retention of Malta. Were we, then, to give up that possession, which was so essential to those interests? If, then, we were going to war for Malta, it was our object to animate the courage and reward the achievements of our fleets and armies. We should go to war therefore on this ground as a broad question both of right and of general policy. In this view it was a matter of congratulation that Malta was to be considered as a British object.

It was to be considered that we went to the aid of the Maltese, previously engaged in the reduction of the French. We ought, therefore, to secure to the Maltese a wise and suitable form of civil government, to be enjoyed by them under the protection of the British power. This object ought to be prosecuted and settled without any delay, so that whenever any new negotiation should be set on foot, we might be enabled to say that the people of Malta, under a form of government agreeable to their wishes, were now established under the protection of Great Britain.

He wished it to be understood that he considered the retention of Malta for ever to be a most essential object, and one which in the relative circumstances of France and this country we were fully entitled to prosecute by war. In voting for the Address we therefore voted our concurrence in the war, of which that was the principal object. The attainment of it would be of the utmost benefit to all the States of the Levant, and under our protection alone Malta could be rendered independent and happy.

Lord Pelham spoke in similar terms, pointing out also that the British Government had honestly striven to carry out the terms of the Treaty of Amiens respecting Malta and had admitted a small body of Neapolitan troops as part of its garrison. He then continued as follows:

It was about the 27th January that the French Government began to press in a very peremptory manner the evacuation of Malta, and it was about that period that Ministers thought themselves bound to demand some satisfactory explanations of the pretensions advanced and the views disclosed by the French Government. Circumstances then existed which rendered it necessary to refer back to what had been the conduct of the First Consul from the period when the treaty was concluded. In the course of this review the plain, the irresistible inference was that the conduct of the French Government had been one constant series of acts totally inconsistent with a sincere desire of preserving the peace of the two countries. . . . In a formal conference with the ambassador of an independent Power the First Consul had not hesitated to declare that Egypt must sooner or later be in the possession of France. He would put it to the candour and the feelings of their Lordships whether Ministers were not entitled to demand from the French Government some security for its future views relative to Egypt, beyond what the Treaty of Amiens provided.

In the continued possession of Malta Ministers conceived that this security could be found, and hence originated the discussions which this subject had created and the importance which the possession of the island afterwards assumed. Malta in the hands of this country could only be viewed as a security; it could afford to France or any other Power no reasonable ground of jealousy or alarm. No other place was so liable to so little objection, and on this ground Ministers rested their claims to its possession. . . .

Turning for a moment from these discussions in Parliament to what was happening about the same time in Malta, we notice that during the month of May General Vial made another attempt to induce Ball to order the evacuation of the garrison and to restore the Island to the Order of St. John, alleging that he had received official intimation that the Courts of Vienna, St. Petersburg, and Berlin had consented to guarantee the arrangement made by the 10th Article of the Treaty of Amiens. Ball's reply and report to Lord Hobart thereon, dated the 18th and 24th May respectively, were as follows :

SIR ALEXANDER BALL TO GENERAL VIAL.

Malta, 18*th May* 1803.[1]

SIR,—I am honoured with your Excellency's letters of yesterday, stating that you had received official advice from your Government that the Courts of Vienna, St. Petersburg and Berlin have formally consented to become guarantees to that part of the Treaty of Amiens which relates to the Island of Malta and the Order of St. John of Jerusalem.

Your Excellency is pleased to add, that as the acceptance of all the guaranteeing Powers leaves no longer any apparent reason for delaying the restitution of this Island to the Order of St. John, you desire to know what measures I think proper to take for the accomplishment of the treaty. In answer I have the honour to observe that as I have not yet received any official advice from my Court on the subject of Your Excellency's communication, I must decline to act upon any other authority. I have the honour, &c. (Signed) ALEX. JNO. BALL.

[1] C.O.R. Malta, No. 9 (1803).

SIR ALEX. JOHN BALL TO LORD HOBART.

Malta, 24th May 1803.[1]

MY LORD,—I have the honour to acquaint your Lordship that the French Minister called on me a few days ago to inform me that he had received official advice from his Government, of the Courts of Vienna, St. Petersburg and Berlin having formally consented to guarantee the arrangement made by the Tenth Article of the Treaty of Amiens with respect to the Island.

Enclosed I have the honour to transmit to your Lordship the copy of a letter which the Minister addressed to me on that subject, together with my answer. I could perceive that General Vial had on this occasion two objects in view. The first was to induce me to consent to the evacuation of the garrison upon the ground of every obstacle being now removed, and to effect this he argued that as the authenticity of his information was unquestionable I ought to consider this official communication as a sufficient authority to take immediate measures for the completion of the treaty. Finding that I was not disposed to yield to his arguments, the Minister's next endeavour was to persuade me that I might expect to receive orders from my Court to evacuate the Island, hoping, no doubt, that this would certainly operate to detain the fleet under the command of Rear-Admiral Sir Richard Bickerton, which was then under sailing orders

The Minister acknowledged that the dispatches alluded to were of an old date, and that they had come by way of Naples and Messina.

By an order from the Viceroy of Sicily the ports of that Island are shut against all vessels coming from Malta. A malicious and totally unfounded report that the army from Egypt had shown symptoms of the plague during the performance of quarantine in this lazaretto has served for a pretext for this extraordinary measure.

Having requested His Majesty's Chargé d'Affaires at Naples to remonstrate on the injustice of this proceeding, I am now in daily expectation of hearing that all restrictions on our intercourse with Sicily are removed.

It appears that the French Secretary of Legation at the Court of Naples has been for some time at Messina, for the avowed purpose of examining the fortifications at that place ; and I must observe to Your Lordship that the above mandate from the Viceroy was issued soon after his arrival there.

From a variety of circumstances, indeed, there is every reason to believe that, should hostilities commence, the French will instantly endeavour to possess themselves of Sicily. Under this impression, Sir Richard Bickerton has taken a position which will, he trusts, enable him to frustrate the designs of France on that valuable Island without detriment to any other objects which His Majesty's Ministers may have in view. I have the honour, &c. (Signed) ALEX. JNO. BALL.

The Rt. Hon. Lord Hobart, &c.

Upon the declaration of war Lord Nelson was appointed Commander-in-Chief of the British naval forces in the Mediterranean,

[1] C.O.R. Malta, No. 9 (1803).

arriving in Malta for a brief visit of thirty-six hours on the 15th June. On the 28th of that month he addressed to the Prime Minister a dispatch, from which the following is an extract:

[Extract.]

H.M.S. *Amphion*, 28th June 1803.[1]

To the Rt. Honble. Henry Addington.

I arrived at Malta on the 15th June in the evening. The French Minister, General Vial, had left in a Ragusa vessel in the morning. The Maltese are in the highest spirits, and sincerely hope that they will now never be separated from England.

. . . I consider Malta as a most important outwork to India; that it will ever give us great influence in the Levant, and indeed all the southern part of Italy. In this view I hope we shall never give it up. I carried out orders from Lord Hobart that General Villettes was to hold 2,000 men at my requisition, if they could be spared from the defence of Malta, for the service of Sicily. The language of General Villettes was natural. The garrison appointed for Malta is not more than on the most economical number of men was judged sufficient, and, looking to the assistance of the Maltese in case of a siege, that these numbers of British troops were only sufficient for the ordinary duties, and that when the Neapolitan troops went away (and he was ordered to send them away) the duty would be very severe, that the addition of Maltese troops when trained and formed would be little better than a well-formed Militia, and however much they undoubtedly would assist, yet they would not be counted as British troops. However, that he should not hesitate in providing 1,200 men and a corps of artillery, to be under the command of General Oakes, a most excellent officer, for the service of Messina whenever I might call for them, and the General wished that I should mention this conversation when I had any opportunity of communicating with Ministers (but which opportunity I never can have but in this private and confidential way) . . . . . . On the 17th, at daylight, I left Malta.

(Signed) NELSON.

The departure of General Vial from Malta, which Lord Nelson mentions, and that of the Chevalier Buzi, was communicated to Lord Hobart by Sir Alexander Ball, in the following dispatch, dated the 26th July 1803.

Malta, 26th July 1803.[2]

To the Right Hon. Lord Hobart.

MY LORD,—I have the honour to acknowledge the receipt of your Lordship's letter of the 16th May last in duplicate; the original has not yet reached me. The Neapolitan troops sent to this Island in terms of the late treaty of peace were on the 14th instant embarked on board of British transports, at the request of His Sicilian Majesty, and conveyed to Syracuse and Messina, at which places they are now in garrison. It is with much satisfaction that I have the honour to inform you that General

---

[1] Nicolas, *Dispatches of Nelson*, vol. v. p. 507.   [2] C.O.R. Malta, No. 9.

Vial and all persons connected with the French Mission quitted Malta on the 15th ultimo, a few hours previous to the receipt of your Lordship's letter. The Bailli Buzi likewise retired from the Island about the same time.

I must observe with regret that it will not be possible to complete at present the Maltese corps to the number proposed in the plan I had the honour to transmit to your Lordship on the 13th August last. This difficulty of raising men is partly to be ascribed to the great loss sustained by the Island during the blockade in consequence of the prevalence of an epidemic disease, which proved fatal to many thousands of the inhabitants of the country; but it is probably no less owing to the great increase of trade occasioned by the arrival here of English merchants from Italy, and the constant employ thus afforded to the lower order of people.

I trust, however, that the measure I have now adopted of requiring each officer to raise a certain proportion of soldiers before he can receive pay will effect the completion of the corps in the course of the ensuing winter. Permit me to express to your Lordship the deep sense I entertain of His Majesty's gracious condescension in having conferred on me so distinguished a mark of his favour as that of appointing me to fill the important station of his Civil Commissioner for the affairs of these Islands. I have the honour, &c. (Signed) ALEX. JNO. BALL.

CHAPTER XXIII

THE BRITISH ADMINISTRATION OF MALTA UP TO THE 30TH MAY 1814

WE now turn to the narration of the principal events which occurred in Malta from the commencement of Sir Alexander Ball's second period of administration up to the treaty of peace signed at Paris on the 30th May 1814, and confirmed by that of the 20th November 1815.

This period of his administration, including the ten months when also acting as Minister-Plenipotentiary to the Order of St. John, lasted from the 10th July 1802 to the day of his death, the 25th October 1809. During the early portion of this period he not only had to contend with intrigues of emissaries of the Order, who still had partisans in the Island, but had also to defend himself later on against unscrupulous attacks on his character by a Government employé, William Eton, who in 1807 published a work entitled 'Materials for an Authentic History of Malta.'[1] William Eton, for some time previous to his appointment to an official position in the Government of Malta, had acted as Civil Commissary at Guernsey, to hear complaints and adjust all differences between the Russian troops and His Majesty's subjects;[2] and when, in October 1800, the British authorities were seeking for a competent person to officiate as a Commissioner to re-establish the ancient regulations for quarantine in Malta, he applied on the 28th of that month to the Right Honourable Henry Dundas for the situation.[3] He based his

---

[1] In later years this work has been referred to as an authority in support of the alleged grievances of the Maltese, more particularly with regard to the pretended suppression of the 'Consiglio Popolare,' a privilege which they asserted had been in their enjoyment since the most remote times, and of which they had been arbitrarily deprived by Sir Alexander Ball and the British Government. In a copy of Mr. Eton's book which is to be found in the Malta Public Library there is the following annotation:—
'Little credit is to be placed in the statements of this writer or faith in his opinions; he wrote a history of the Turkish Empire, and I have been told that the object of it was to serve the political purposes of Russia; he had a place under the Government of Malta, and did not give satisfaction, and held it for a short time, and was not esteemed there. I have heard him spoken of with great disrespect.' Athough much importance is not to be placed upon the statements of anonymous writers, nevertheless they are the opinions of a contemporary, to be either confirmed or refuted. (Note by Mr. Hardman.)

[2] The Russian troops serving in Holland in 1799 wintered in the Channel Islands.— J. H. R.

[3] C.O.R. Malta, 2.

application on the grounds that he had been a resident in that Island for three months (fifty days of which he had lodged in the lazaretto), that he had been in favour with the late Grand Master De Rohan, and that he had been sent there on a mission by Prince Potemkin on behalf of the Russian Government.

His mission had been for the purpose, so he asserted:—To examine the state of Malta; to discover the disposition of its inhabitants and the causes of the rebellion which (in 1797) had nearly expelled the Order; to give Prince Potemkin an account of the cabals among the Knights; to examine the lazaretto, and to examine the Island of Lampedusa.[1]

Mr. Eton's application for the appointment as Superintendent of the Lazaretto was successful, and in May 1801 he was ordered to accompany Mr. Charles Cameron to Malta, to which Island the latter had been nominated His Majesty's Civil Commissioner.

Upon his arrival in Malta, Mr. Eton's appointment as Superintendent of the lazaretto and Supervisor of the quarantine regulations was duly made public by a Government notice dated the 14th July 1801.

The exigencies of the time required a most rigorous application of these regulations (the breaking of which entailed the penalty of death without benefit of clergy), not so much for the preservation of the public health as for political reasons, by preventing the landing of French emissaries or of partisans of the Order of St. John. For this purpose correspondence and printed matter had to pass through the lazaretto for examination, and the information so obtained, when found detrimental to the public weal, was acted upon without scruple. This system of espionage was a necessity of the times, and the Superintendent of the lazaretto (who, if tradition does not belie him, was also a spy in the Russian service) was selected for its administration.

In Mr. Henry Dundas's letter, dated the 14th May 1801, acquainting Mr. Cameron with Mr. Eton's appointment, there is sufficient evidence to prove that the latter was to hold the post he was about to occupy independent of the Commissioner, who was only 'in some degree to *judge* of the expediency and propriety of the arrangements Mr. Eton might propose.'

This independence, which could only create misunderstanding and friction, was further aggravated by the reprehensible permission to correspond direct with the Ministry in London, which gave him undue importance in the eyes of the people and to their deputies, who later on were to proceed to England for the purpose of presenting their petition to the King.

---

[1] I keep the details as they are given by Mr. Hardman, but doubt their accuracy. Eton had earlier been in the employ of the Russian Government; but Prince Potemkin, who desired to seize Constantinople in the war of 1787-91, died in 1791.—J. H. R.

Within *five* days of his arrival in Malta he addressed a letter to Mr. J. Sullivan (Under-Secretary of State) which at once stamps the character of the man; for, in that short space of time, he felt himself qualified to form an opinion of and indicate his antipathy to Captain Ball (which soon developed into bitter enmity, for reasons hereafter related), and declare himself competent to stigmatise a prominent member of Captain Ball's staff.

The following is a synopsis of the letter :—

[Synopsis.]

[Private.]   MR. ETON TO MR. J. SULLIVAN.

Malta, 5th July 1801.[1]

He informs him of his arrival with Mr. Cameron on the Island, and of his having re-established the lazaretto and quarantine according to the ancient regulations in force during the Grand Mastership of Rohan, and he goes on to say: 'I cannot refrain from informing you that Mr. Cameron has been received as a Messiah. Mr. Cameron is formed to regain and to secure the affection of a good and grateful people. It is the opinion of everyone, without a single exception, with whom I have spoken, of every description, natives or British, that had Mr. Cameron not arrived an insurrection would very shortly have taken place. The joy of the people, which was extravagant, has been somewhat damped by the resolution unexpectedly taken by a certain person [Ball] to remain here, and retain near his person a man (Macaulay) abhorred for every species of vexation and insult. General P. (Pigot) everyone who knows him says is himself a good man.'

As much of the controversy which has arisen in regard to Maltese affairs has its foundation in Mr. Eton's acts and writings, it is well to ascertain what at the present day can be learnt respecting him. Three months after his arrival in Malta a petition to His Britannic Majesty was prepared, beseeching His Majesty to retain possession of the Island, and a deputation was nominated to proceed to England and present it. Although the primary object of the deputation may have been laudable in itself, it nevertheless embarrassed the Government, then deep in negotiations for peace with France.

It soon became reported in England not only that Mr. Eton had encouraged, but that with him had originated the idea of electing a deputation to proceed to the British Court, and that the meetings in connection with the petition and its drafting took place at his house. Five years later Mr. Eton admitted that such meetings had taken place at his house, but added, 'they were held only for the election of the deputies.' Of his intimate relations with these latter whilst they were in England it is sufficient to quote his letter to the Under-Secretary of State dated the 5th March 1802, wherein he pleads for financial help on their behalf.

[1] C.O.R. Malta, 4.

THE BRITISH ADMINISTRATION UP TO MAY 1814

Owing to the decision of the Powers met at Amiens that Malta should again revert to the Order of St. John, Sir Alexander Ball returned to Malta, where he arrived on the 10th July 1802, as Minister-Plenipotentiary thereto, relieving Mr. Cameron from his functions as Civil Commissioner on that same day. This dual position and authority Sir Alexander was to possess until the arrival of the Grand Master.

So complete a change in the settlement of Maltese affairs, as well as in the Chief Administrator, was not congenial to Mr. Eton, whose disappointment was further accentuated by personal dislike of the Public Secretary, Mr. Alexander Macaulay; and two months after the arrival of Sir Alexander Ball, Mr. Eton, although retaining the appointment and emolument of his office, withdrew from the Island.

Aware of the rumours which were current, laying to his charge that of being an unprincipled agitator, promoting discontent and encouraging unfounded pretensions, he looked for his vindication not to Mr. Cameron or Sir Alexander Ball, but to certificates of character obtained from the coterie with whom he was associated.

These certificates were dated the 18th August and the 8th September 1802, and appear at p. 223 of his book, and among the signatories there are the following names:—Marchese Don M. Testaferrata, Fil. Castagna, Luogotenente of Senglea and Cospicua, Michele Cachia, representative of Zeitun, and Ant. Mallia, Lieut.-Governor of Gozo, four out of the six gentlemen who, according to Mr. Eton's statement, had been elected at his house as deputies to the British Government. With a knowledge of these facts it is reasonable to assume that he had succeeded in inculcating in the minds of these gentlemen opinions which for his personal advantage he intended to promulgate.

Soon after obtaining the certificates Mr. Eton sailed for England, and on the 24th December of the same year (1802) there were issued from the press, *but not published*, Parts I and II of his book entitled 'Materials for an Authentic History of Malta.' In the following May Mr. Eton proposed to Lord Hobart, then Minister for War, that he should return to Malta viâ Southern Russia, and buy 40,000 quarters of wheat on account of the Malta Government, to be consigned to His Majesty's Commissioner there. This offer was not immediately accepted, but on the 27th September 1803 he was dispatched on this mission, with orders to buy only 2,500 quarters and sundry stores Sir Alexander Ball being duly informed of what had been done. This wheat was shipped to Malta from Odessa on the 28th July 1804, *ten* months after Mr. Eton left London.

Commissioner Ball in the meantime, having no great confidence in Mr. Eton, dispatched an officer of his own direct to Odessa with an order to purchase 40,000 quarters of wheat. This officer, with the vessels necessary for transport of the wheat, arrived at Odessa during Mr. Eton's stay in Russia, who, not having been consulted or engaged in the purchase, felt it a personal affront, and returned to England imbued with a desire of revenge.

Accordingly, no sooner had he arrived in England than he prepared for printing (in 1805) Part III of his work, severely criticising Sir Alexander Ball's administration of the Government of Malta. But for reasons unexplained, which Mr. Eton called 'uninteresting to the public,' this part (No. III), like the preceding Parts I and II, *was not published until two years later*, when Part IV was added, and the book published in its entirety in 1807.

So great a portion of this book is devoted to a description of the 'Consiglio Popolare' and its attributes, and so much has been said on the same subject in later years up to the present day, that it will be interesting to trace its history from the time it was sought to invest it with legislative power, which Mr. Eton endeavoured to establish in his letter to the Under-Secretary of State (Mr. Sullivan), dated the 18th May 1802.

Of the existence of the 'Consiglio Popolare' from remote times there has never been any doubt; the only question has been, what were its attributes ? Whilst, on the one hand, it was alleged that its functions were simply municipal, it was stated by Mr. Eton and his adherents that the whole legislative authority resided in the 'Consiglio Popolare.' They maintained also that Sir Alexander Ball had confirmed the fact by convoking an Assembly of Notables, which he termed a Congress, in whose hands lay the power of government during the blockade of 1798–1800. To this assertion Sir Alexander Ball gave a flat denial, as appears from a letter to Mr. Miles dated Malta, the 2nd August 1807, as follows [1]:—

Mr. Eton and Mr. Dillon have lately published two books on Malta tending to prejudice me in the public mind and to get me removed from the situation, that *they* and their friends may come here and direct the administration under the Duke of Sussex. I have answered Mr. Eton's charges, and His Majesty's Ministers have been pleased to express in handsome terms their confidence in me. Mr. Eton complains of the discontent of the Maltese because they are deprived of their Popular Assembly, and he says that the moment they revolted against the French their first act was to convene the 'Consiglio Popolare,' at which I was made President on my landing. This is the most impudent falsehood that ever was asserted. The fact is, Lord Nelson gave me the command of a squadron to blockade the French in La Valetta, and to assist the Maltese in the country who were in arms. On my arrival I found the inhabitants split into parties—the former refusing to pay rent, the lower classes going in bodies at night to commit every kind of devastation and plunder. In this state the chiefs were continually applying to me for advice and assistance, and after five months' experience they found themselves under the necessity of requesting me to land and direct the civil and military departments.

[1] Miles, *Correspondence of W. A. Miles*, vol. ii. p. 353.

THE BRITISH ADMINISTRATION UP TO MAY 1814   499

At this period the Maltese had never thought of convening an assembly. I perceived the advantages to be derived from having a congress, and I drew up a plan of one, which was immediately formed, and at which I was President, and I can positively declare this, it was entirely a suggestion of my own, and done with the view of making the assembly bear the odium of the necessary regulations for restoring order.

The dispatch from Mr. Windham (the Secretary for War and the Colonies), to which Sir Alexander Ball refers, is as follows:

[Extract.]

THE RT. HON. W. WINDHAM TO SIR ALEXANDER J. BALL.

(London), Downing Street, 6*th January* 1807.[1]

SIR,—. . . I have now to advert to your private communication of the 10th September, on the subject of which I herewith enclose copies of several documents which have been laid before me, conveying such serious charges against your administration, as call for immediate investigation.

The favourable sentiments, however, which your meritorious services and established reputation were calculated to produce in the minds of His Majesty's Ministers still remain unshaken, and I have the fullest reliance on your being enabled to effectually refute those aspersions which have thus been thrown upon your character, and to prove that your conduct has been invariably guided by such principles as fully justify the high opinion which Government have hitherto entertained of you, and the confidence which His Majesty has condescended to repose in your zeal and abilities. I have the honour, &c.   (Signed) W. WINDHAM.

In the copy of Mr. Eton's book which is to be found in the Malta Public Library there is, at p. 82, the following annotation by the late Sir Ferdinand Inglott, a Maltese gentleman well versed in the history of Malta: 'Not a single historical document can be produced to prove the assertion that in the "Consiglio Popolare" resided the whole legislative authority; not one law among the minutes of this body can be found in the Archives. See report of the Royal Commissioners which sat in 1812. These Commissioners append to their report a most valuable document (which will be referred to later on), drawn up by Mr. Dolci, a lawyer of considerable ability, who proved that the "Consiglio Popolare" was neither legislative nor deliberative.'

The publication of Mr. Eton's 'Materials for an Authentic History of Malta' was deferred from 1802 to 1807. Although the cause of this delay cannot now be ascertained, it can, nevertheless, from what followed, be readily surmised. During this interval of five years Mr. Eton retained his appointment in Malta, with the emolument attached to it, but was absent from his post; and it was not until the latter year that the period became ripe for the

[1] Malta Pub. Library, MS. No. 388.

publication of strictures on Sir Alexander Ball's Administration. By this means he trusted to supplant Sir Alexander in the government of the island.

In Part III of the said work, at p. 144, whilst criticising the judicial procedure then in force (1802), Mr. Eton says, 'It may seem somewhat strange that Captain Sir Alexander Ball should have chosen the "Code Rohan" (1782) in preference to that of Vilhena (1721), but it must be remembered that in the latter the "Consiglio Popolare" and the privileges of the Maltese have a place,' insinuating that it was thus evidently the desire of Sir Alexander Ball to trample upon the alleged privileges of the Maltese. Nevertheless, a few pages further on (p. 176) he is compelled to admit that the 'Code Rohan' does refer to the 'Consiglio Popolare,' and with characteristic inconsistency recommends that, in the event of a new scheme or constitution being adopted, a constitution which he was then advocating for the island (at a period, 1805, be it remembered, when its future destiny was still uncertain), the 'Code Rohan' should be admitted as the 'Lex Scripta' (p. 192) until a new code was promulgated, and that no older laws should be valid.

This new scheme or proposed constitution is mentioned by Mr. Eton at p. 178 'as a form of government for Malta and Gozo uniting the essential parts of the privileges of the island with the functions of a British governor, and (said to be) drafted in 1802 by some of the first lawyers and some of the nobility and others, which would perfectly satisfy the people.'

As, however, it was therein stipulated that, beyond the governorship of the islands, the only other appointment to be left to His Majesty should be that of the Superintendent-General of the quarantine, the post which he (Mr. Eton) then occupied, and that such appointment should be independent of the Civil Government, it would appear that in the compilation of this scheme Mr. Eton's advice was sought for, if not voluntarily given.

Mr. Eton's defence of his publication, written in 1807, runs as follows :—

In 1802, when I wrote and printed the first and second parts of these materials (the publication of which was, for reasons uninteresting to the public, deferred), I endeavoured to do justice to Sir Alexander Ball, who had presided with great applause in the Congress composed of the Popular Council ('Consiglio Popolare') and the chiefs of battalions or colonels, and the Maltese generals. That same year I had brought with me from Malta the matter contained in the third part, which I was anxiously requested to translate and publish, as the facts were notorious in every country but this, which they most concern. However, still hoping that those who professed so much attachment to the Maltese would have represented their grievances, I deferred printing them three years, and now only, in the fifth year after I had announced them, I lay them before the public.

THE BRITISH ADMINISTRATION UP TO MAY 1814

He further acknowledges having been accused of promoting discontent among the people of Malta, of instigating them to demand the restoration of their ancient rights and privileges ('Consiglio Popolare'), and assuring them of success if they persevered, and added, by the publication of a certificate to be found at p. 233, 'that it was at the instance of the representatives of the people that these political meetings were held at his house, but for the sole object of proceeding to the election of the deputies sent to London.' Such undeserved and unfounded attacks were keenly felt by Sir Alexander Ball, who, in the words of a contemporary,[1] 'was as a master, a parent, or a husband, a model for all; nor were the Maltese slow to show that they thoroughly appreciated his many virtues, and it is not too much to say that they idolised him. To him they exclusively attributed their emancipation, and in him they rested their hopes for the future.' Mr. Eton, as already stated, published these charges in 1807, and on the 5th May of that year Sir Alexander Ball wrote from Malta to his intimate friend, Mr. Miles, as follows:—

I have not written to you as often as I wished lately, having been extremely hurried by a multiplicity of business, occasioned by the explosion of two powder magazines within eight months; the first was caused by shameful neglect, and the second by mismanagement. I have likewise been attacked by a most unprincipled fellow of the name of Eton, who has a place here of £800 a year, which he has enjoyed during an absence of four years, but as his conduct and plans have at last been fully developed at the Secretary of State's office, I trust that he will be dismissed.[2]

It is difficult to understand why Mr. Eton, although absent from the Island, should have been permitted to retain his appointment in the Malta Civil Service from 1802 to 1807 (which was to continue until September 1811), enjoying its emolument in the meanwhile; and the surprise would be greater still when, after the publication of his book in the latter year, charging Sir Alexander Ball in the manner we have seen, we learn that he was still retained, were it not that an explanation is given in a dispatch from the Under-Secretary of State to Sir Alexander Ball on the subject, dated Downing Street, 5th April 1808, as follows[3]:—

SIR,—I received the honour of your letter, returning the anonymous letters and papers which had been sent from Malta to Mr. Eton, and which he communicated to Government with a view of raising suspicions against your conduct. His view, as well as the views of the writers, have been entirely frustrated, and every justice is done to your character, which accusations of such a nature can never reach. There may, however, have

---

[1] S. T. Coleridge, *The Friend*, pp. 352, 374.
[2] Malta Public Library, MS. No. 392.
[3] *Ibid.* Supplemental Append., C.A. Case on the Marriage Question, page 209.

arisen a natural feeling in your mind that the attempts made by Mr. Eton ought not to be passed unpunished, and it must appear as disgusting to the authority of a governor if any officer within his command shall have preferred accusations against him which he has not been able to substantiate, and still be allowed to retain his situation, and this view of the case is certainly just. At the same time, you will permit me *privately* to state that there are many difficulties in the case. Mr. Eton's defence is that he has not brought charges against you, but that he has merely been the channel of transmitting to Government complaints from the Maltese, which complaints it was his duty not to suppress. If he should be dismissed on account of these communications so made, he will endeavour to inflame the public upon the point of his dismissal, and to combine their feelings with the situation of the Maltese, the government over whom is carried on at present necessarily on garrison principles rather than under any regular form of constitution. If, therefore, any delay has taken place in removing Mr. Eton, or if it should be found advisable not to remove him at present, you will attribute [it] rather to the policy of preventing any artful misrepresentations being played off against the Maltese than [to] what is due to your character and authority. I have the honour, &c. (Signed) E. COOKE.

There may have been another reason for the leniency displayed towards Mr. Eton during this period, which the Colonial Minister was not then in a position to disclose, and that was Mr. Eton's former connexion with the Russian Government, making the British Cabinet doubtful of his fidelity at a time when the strained political relations between the two Powers had at last culminated in Russia declaring war against England since the 31st of October previous,[1] and that consequently, in the effort to retain his loyalty, he was kept in the service of the State. In the absence of documents on this point at the disposal of the present writer, this, however, can only be a matter of surmise.

It may possibly be considered by many that undue importance has been given to Mr. Eton in this portion of the volume; but whoever will meditate upon the conduct of the Maltese deputies when in England, their grateful acknowledgment to the Colonial Minister, Lord Hobart, the report of their mission which the deputies rendered to their constituents upon their return to Malta, and contrast the same with their demeanour after consultation with Mr. Eton, Mr. Vincent Borg, and other malcontents, will admit that much of the ensuing agitation had its origin in Mr. Eton's iniquitous proceedings, and must be laid to his charge.

We may remark here, although the topic is not in chronological order, that from the date of Mr. Cooke's letter of the 5th April 1808 until 1811 Mr. Eton, who remained absent from Malta, was yet retained on its Civil Service List, but owing again to his unwarrantable interference in local politics, he was summarily

[1] In pursuance of the secret Franco-Russian Treaty of Tilsit.—J. H. R.

dismissed, and the information conveyed to Lieut.-General Oakes by Lord Liverpool, Secretary of State for the Colonies, in the following despatch:

Downing Street, 18th September 1811.[1]

SIR,—I have to acquaint you that in consequence of the very improper conduct of Mr. Eton, Superintendent of the Quarantine Establishment at Malta, His Royal Highness the Prince Regent has been pleased to remove him from that situation, which is conferred upon William Pym, Esquire, at present Deputy-Inspector of Hospitals at Gibraltar. Mr. Eton's salary is to be paid to him up to the 25th of the present month, when Mr. Pym will be considered to succeed to the office, and the latter gentleman will be directed to repair to Malta with the least possible delay. I have the honour, &c. (Signed) LIVERPOOL.[2]

Foremost among the many subjects which caused anxiety to Sir Alexander Ball was that of the ecclesiastical rights and pretensions of His Sicilian Majesty and the jurisdiction of the Papal Government in the affairs of the Island. We learn from Captain Ball's report[3] of the 26th December 1800 (within five months after the capture of Valetta) that

the former claimed the right of nominating a bishop, with the prerogative of appeal in ecclesiastical cases to the Court of the Metropolitan at Palermo, called 'La Tribunale della Monarchia.' The archbishop desired to have a resident Minister in the Island, but this was always resisted by the Grand Masters. The Popes having constituted themselves Superiors of the Order of St. John, had also supreme jurisdiction over the ecclesiastical courts, from whence all cases might be carried to Rome by appeal. If the plaintiffs would not agree which of the two courts, Palermo or Rome, should decide the appeal, the first inhibition from either of the courts determined it.

The Pope's Minister, under the name of the 'Grand Inquisitor,' resided in Malta, and held supreme jurisdiction; he could distribute patents by virtue of which the patentee was out of the reach and power of the Grand Master. It was not necessary that the patented person should wear a clerical dress, and he was not known to be sheltered by the ecclesiastical court until called on by the civil court. A great number of Maltese sought their protection. The only check of the abuse of it was that the number of the patented persons, though very considerable, was limited, and that men engaged in trade could not be protected by these patents.

While Sir Alexander Ball was in England, 1801–02 (after relinquishing his first administration), the Colonial Office again sought his advice on this subject, and in reply he addressed the following letter :—

[1] Crown Advocate's Case, Mixed Marriages, p. 280.
[2] The Earl of Liverpool was the Minister whose acquaintance we have already made as Lord Hawkesbury.—J. H. R.
[3] Colonial Office Papers, Malta, 1801. Ball's report, 26th December 1800.

23rd January 1802.[1]

To John Sullivan, Esq., Under-Secretary of State, &c.

SIR,—On considering the subject of His Sicilian Majesty's ecclesiastical rights in the islands of Malta and Gozo, I conceive that by the original grant of the Island to the Order he has only the power of nominating the bishop. He has asserted a right to the jurisdiction over the ecclesiastical courts at Malta, from which an appeal may be made to the Court of the Archbishop of Palermo, which is called 'La Tribunale della Monarchia,' but this has not always been admitted by the Grand Masters. The Archbishop of Palermo wished to have a resident Minister there, in which he was strongly supported by His Sicilian Majesty, who sent the Minister in one of his frigates; but the Grand Master Pinto sent to the captain of the frigate to inform him that if he landed the Minister he would sink his ship; this was considered by His Majesty as an insult; he therefore shut all his ports against Malta. Pinto sent word that, if the ports were not opened to his subjects on the same footing as before, he would make peace with the Barbary States and admit their cruisers into his port. This caused His Sicilian Majesty to open his ports to the Maltese, and not trouble the Grand Master any further on the subject of ecclesiastical rights.

During my government the Archbishop authorised a Minister to sell indulgences at Malta, the produce of which would have amounted to three thousand pounds, and was to be sent to him; as this was a great drain, as well as a tax on the poor, I would not allow it unless the sum would be appropriated to support the poor. The Archbishop will try this every year, but I am of opinion that he should not be allowed to interfere in the ecclesiastical affairs at Malta. The Maltese deputies will be enabled to explain very fully the subject. I have the honour, &c.

(Signed) ALEX. JNO. BALL.

Having thus referred to ecclesiastical affairs we may indicate here the various reforms which the British Government were desirous in the interests of the inhabitants to introduce. These consisted of: 1. The right of the Government (on behalf of the Maltese) to nominate one of their own people to the bishopric, which hitherto had been very seldom so bestowed. 2. Rendering the See of Malta perfectly independent of the Metropolitan of Palermo. 3. The abolition of the right of sanctuary. 4. The removal from the ecclesiastical court of the cognisance of all matters in dispute in relation to debts, contracts, and inheritance, subjecting such to the ordinary civil tribunals of the island; and 5. Abolishing the exemption of ecclesiastics from lay jurisdiction in all matters not spiritual.

Whilst many of these proposals had to remain in abeyance for a considerable time, that of the succession to the bishopric might be expected to arise within a few years. Upon the death of Bishop Labini, a native of Bitonto, near Bari, which occurred on the

[1] C.O.R. Malta, No. 5.

THE BRITISH ADMINISTRATION UP TO MAY 1814   505

30th April 1807, the British Government was desirous that Canon Caruana, who had deserved so well of his country, should obtain the vacant see, but as the claim of the Neapolitan Government to the nomination of the bishop, as well as that of his subjection to the Metropolitan of Palermo, had not then been definitely abrogated, His Holiness Pius VII settled the question by raising Monsignor Ferdinand Mattei to that dignity on the 27th September 1807.

Before this prelate, however, could take possession of the see a rearrangement of the patrimony attached thereto was considered necessary, and on this subject Viscount Castlereagh on the 1st April 1808 addressed Sir Alexander Ball as follows:—

[Extract.]

VISCOUNT CASTLEREAGH TO SIR ALEXANDER J. BALL.

Downing Street, *1st April* 1808.[1]

SIR,— . . . His Majesty has directed me to convey to you his royal commands that you should take the necessary measures for causing Mons. Mattei to be received into the vacant See of Malta. At the same time, I am to signify to you His Majesty's approbation of the suggestions submitted by you in your dispatch of the 7th May last, wherein you state that the annual revenue of the Bishop of Malta should be reduced to an income of £2,000 a year, and that the remainder of the proceeds of the bishopric, amounting to £1,800 a year, should be applied partly to the seminary for educating the clergy, partly for the amelioration of the condition of the parochial priests, and the remainder to other pious uses. As you have stated that an arrangement of this nature would be highly satisfactory to the clergy and the people, I have no doubt that in your arrangement of this business you will take care not to fail in producing the beneficial result you so fully expect, and I am to desire you will take an early occasion of transmitting to me the detail of the measures you adopt.

Bishop Mattei died on the 14th July 1829, whereupon His Majesty's Government took the necessary steps to obtain the appointment of Canon Francesco Saverio Caruana to the vacant see, who, as Capitulary Vicar and Archdeacon, had ruled the Church since the 20th July 1829; and in February 1831, all difficulties having been overcome, he was reported by the Pope's Consistory as qualified for the dignity (preconizato), duly appointed Bishop by Gregory XVII, consecrated on the 15th May 1831, and from that time the British nominee in the person of a Maltese, and in accordance with the desire of the people, has always been adopted.

Another subject which Sir Alexander Ball had at heart, and which he strenuously urged upon the attention of the Home Government, was that of a fitting compensation, to which he considered the Maltese insurgents were entitled. It will be remembered that in

[1] Malta Public Library, MS. No. 388.

his dispatch to Mr. Henry Dundas, then Secretary of State for War and the Colonies, dated the 6th March 1801, he referred to a rumour then current in the Island that their share of the prize money for the capture of Valetta, which had been promised to them, was not to be granted. As a result of his remonstrance, he had the satisfaction on 3rd March 1803 to inform them by a public notice issued on that date that His Majesty had been graciously pleased to order 'that the sum of one hundred and sixty-seven thousand scudi, equivalent to £13,916 13s. 4d., should be distributed amongst the brave Maltese who had served in the battalions.'[1]

This beneficent gift was subsequently increased by an additional grant of £8,786 7s. 2d., making in the aggregate £22,703 0s. 6d.; its distribution was acknowledged by Marquis Mario Testaferrata and Count Francesco Sant (who had been appointed auditors of the accounts) in their report to His Excellency of the 3rd December 1805.[2]

Notwithstanding the general popularity which Sir Alexander Ball enjoyed in the Island, he had many adversaries, who, either from disappointment at what they alleged were unrequited services rendered to the Government during the blockade, or for other reasons, became his bitterest opponents; and it is not surprising to hear that anonymous letters and papers were sent to Sir Alexander's inveterate enemy, Mr. Eton, for presentation to His Majesty's Cabinet, for the purpose of defaming him and obtaining his recall.

None were more assiduous in this direction than Mr. Vincent Borg. Mr. Borg, who had been elected in 1798 Chief of the Birchircara contingent of insurgents, and who, as we saw, asserted that he was actuated by the purest and most disinterested patriotism, yet, nevertheless, on the 20th March 1799, during the siege of Valetta, accepted the guardianship of the harbours of St. Paul and Marsa Scirocco with the promise of that of Valetta when captured, and within a fortnight after the fall of that city he was appointed one of the administrators of public property, and further, on the 1st of the following November, nominated Lieutenant of Birchircara, with the emoluments attached to these offices.

Referring to Mr. Borg's appeal to the British Government, which he published in 1810, it would appear that for some reason which he does not give [3] he was on the 11th January 1804 deprived of his official employments and told to consider himself under arrest, with a sentinel placed at the door of his abode, and not allowed out of the city for two months, after which he was only permitted to proceed into the country to look after his property and affairs upon obtaining permission on each occasion from the Secretary's office, this surveillance continuing for close upon two years.

[1] Government Proclamations and Notices, M.P.L., C.A. 4.
[2] *Raccolta di Vani Cose*, p. 268.   [3] M.P.L.

THE BRITISH ADMINISTRATION UP TO MAY 1814

Mr. Borg admits that he was called upon to refund several sums which, he asserts, had been borrowed for the service of the camp he had commanded, that he had to refund crowns $\frac{3875}{£337}$ (*i.e.* £337) to stop a *procedure* which was threatened; also 1,000 crowns to the Countess Manduca; and finally to vacate a store which he occupied, a decision communicated to him by a colleague-administrator of public property, whilst maintaining that he had a claim against the Government of 24,000 crowns. There is no desire to enter into the merits of the question, but it is necessary to give this outline of the case in order to explain the bitter animosity which Mr. Borg subsequently displayed against Sir Alexander Ball and his Administration.

It is somewhat singular that within a month of the liberation of Mr. Borg instructions were forwarded to Mr. John Richards, a so-termed political agent of the Maltese, to represent to the British Government the alleged grievances of the people, instructions which resemble in form and diction (presumably by the same authors) the complaints which were subsequently embodied in the violent and scurrilous petition forwarded to the King in Council in July 1811, hereafter referred to.

In the meanwhile Mr. Eton, who, according to Sir Alexander Ball, had Mr. Borg for an accomplice, completed his work, 'Materials for the History of Malta,' including Part III, which so strongly criticised Sir Alexander Ball's Administration, and published the same in 1807. These accusations and attempts to damage Sir Alexander's character in the estimation of the Home Government, however, proved quite harmless; and as Sir Alexander stated at the time, His Majesty's Minister expressed the greatest confidence in his government of the islands.

It is no doubt true that various reforms in the government were advisable, and would have been introduced earlier than they were, but at the time they were impracticable; for it must be remembered that at this date (1806-7) the European political outlook was dark in the extreme; an attempt to arrange peace between England and France had failed;[1] that both the Prussians and the Russians had been severely defeated at Jena and Friedland; and that, consequently, it was impossible to say at this period what the future fate of Malta was to be, and whether the detested Order might not after all be reinstated in possession of the island. The *desire alone* of the Maltese to remain British subjects could but have small weight or influence in the ultimate decision.

In the midst of all this turmoil and agitation Sir Alexander Ball died. This sad occurrence took place at San Antonio Palace at 3.17 p.m. of Wednesday, the 25th October 1809, when Edmond

[1] viz. during the negotiations of the summer of 1806. For the Maltese question as then discussed see Coquelle, *Napoleon and England*, pp. 113 *et seq.*—J. H. R.

Francis Chapman, at the time Public Secretary and Treasurer, assumed the reins of government until instructions were received from England.[1]

Amidst the almost universal sorrow which Sir Alexander's death occasioned, a desire was evinced to erect a monument to perpetuate his memory, and within two months of his demise a committee was formed, consisting of sixteen 'deputies of the nation,' who by the 22nd December presented to the Acting Commissioner, Mr. Chapman, a design of the proposed monument and the following letter [2]:—

[Translation.]

YOUR EXCELLENCY,—Having rescued us from the heavy hand of France, having calmed our excited spirits, lacerated by the jealousy of political and conflicting factions, substituting a just and paternal Government in the place of a revolutionary regency, bringing from the farthest coast of the Black Sea abundant supplies of wheat in times of direst necessity, protecting our merchandise on the high seas, compelling our honour on shore to be respected, whilst respecting our religion and our customs, beautifying our Island with gardens, edifices, roads, and planting immense numbers of all sorts of trees.

These and many other were the works performed in our country by the late Sir Alexander John Ball. We consider that we should deserve to be branded with the name of ingrates were we to omit after death this acknowledgment of our gratitude, which we had so often proffered to him whilst living.

Therefore, having decided to perpetuate his memory amongst us, the memory of this Father of the Maltese, by erecting a mausoleum, which will proclaim to foreigners his public worth, and will remind our children of the benefits which we have received at his hands and attest eternal proof of our gratitude,

We therefore beg to present to you herewith the design of this proposed monument, and to express a hope that you will be pleased to select a site for it. We flatter ourselves that you will deign to accede to this request, for we have reason to know that you second all our honest undertakings, and, moreover, that you have at all times proved to be a friend of the Maltese people.

(Signed) THE DEPUTIES OF THE NATION.

This monument now stands in the centre of the Lower Baracca. Upon hearing of the death of Sir Alexander Ball His Majesty's Cabinet nominated Sir Richard Keats as Civil Commissioner in succession to Ball, but he was no sooner appointed than he resigned. Lord Liverpool, Secretary of State for the Colonies, thereupon, on the 14th April 1810, selected Major-General Hildebrand Oakes (who at the time was in command of the troops stationed in the island) to be Civil Commissioner, which news reached Malta by the cutter *Black Joke* on the 11th of the following month, the proclamation

---

[1] Brochure, M.P.L., No. 463. [2] Ibid.

THE BRITISH ADMINISTRATION UP TO MAY 1814   509

announcing Sir Hildebrand's assumption of office appearing on the 12th May.[1]

No sooner had death removed Sir Alexander Ball than renewed agitation followed, in furtherance of the views held by Mr. Eton, and on this occasion championed by Nicolo Capo di Ferro, Marchese Testaferrata. A petition to the Throne was prepared, dated the 10th July 1811, embodying the alleged grievances of the Maltese, particularly the continued obeyance of the 'Consiglio Popolare,' and worded as follows :—

> TO HIS MAJESTY THE KING OF THE UNITED KINGDOM OF
> GREAT BRITAIN AND IRELAND IN HIS COUNCIL.[2]

We, natives of Malta, faithful subjects of Your Majesty, our elected and gracious Sovereign, induced by several transactions which have taken place in these Islands of Malta and Gozo for the last ten years (directly contrary to that high idea which public fame, and the experience we had during the siege of Valetta, had caused us to entertain of the magnanimous English nation), we take the liberty humbly to represent at the foot of Your Majesty's throne that—

The full confidence and entire submission with which the Maltese demonstrated their inviolate attachment to the British Government, submitting themselves to the arrangements of Your Majesty's officers, notwithstanding the full authority which rested with the Maltese, gave to us the strongest motives to hope a friendly and just return on their part. Nevertheless, the Maltese saw themselves fatally deluded in their hopes, and their most sacred rights and greatest interests sacrificed to a sordid policy. A misused capitulation stipulated by Your Majesty's Officers with the French garrison, without the least participation of the Maltese, unjustly, and without necessity sacrificed our property; persuaded to lay down our arms in the country at the same time that our enemies laid down theirs in the surrendered cities, we saw with the most lively chagrin these our enemies, under our eyes, loading themselves with the plunder of almost the whole nation, and insulting our universal ruin, after we had for two years under the walls of Valetta endured mortality, famine, and sufferings and labour indescribable.

The privileges of the 'Consiglio,' after the surrender of Valetta suddenly suspended and suppressed, though with the flattering promise made by Sir Alexander Ball to the representatives, that they should be assembled in future, when the case required, increased the infelicity of our condition. We began from that time to feel the fatal effects of this suppression. Perhaps the most honourable and respectable of the country [were] unjustly oppressed. Just and reasonable petitions often remained without a sentence, besides several violences, injurious to the free exercise of the jurisdiction of the Magistrates; sudden removals of entire magistracies made at the caprice of His Excellency Ball, without any formality of judgment.

Some deputations (assumed by a few persons, among whom were even

[1] Brochure, M.P.L., No. 463.   [2] C.O.R., Malta, No. 20 (1812).

foreigners, for private purposes without any formality of legitimacy) printed in the name of our nation, approving of some late Royal Commissioners; the occupation of public places for the exercise of piety [*sic*], and the education of youth, by our ancestors solemnly consecrated; grievances and insults of which both the distance from Your Majesty's throne and the terror which the despotism of His Excellency Ball inspired, obstructed for a long time our just appeals. By false imputations it was endeavoured to stain the character of the faithful Maltese by representing them as a turbulent people. All which the language of our most ample privileges, granted by our most ancient Sovereigns, our patience, submission, and confidence in the justice of Your Majesty during ten years gave our fidelity the strongest argument of facts, and not of words, and ought to confound our calumniators. Finally, numerous other acts of injustice of which our prudence imposed on us silence, but a part of which documents are with our elected agent, Mr. John Richards, filled the measure of our misfortunes and sufficiently justified our suspicions and distrust in respect to future times.

To dissipate, therefore, our fears and mistrust, and to further augment the bonds of the warm attachment of our countrymen to Your Majesty's Crown in a manner inseparable, we supplicate Your Majesty to take into consideration the state in which we find ourselves placed, and to look with benignity on our supplications, that we may at length obtain the restitution of our dearest ancient rights, so often promised to us, which will fill the hearts of a whole people with gratitude, fidelity, and love. And Your Majesty will have a people the most faithful, and attached to your Crown to defend our Islands.

The supplications may be reduced in general terms to the restitution of our ancient sacred rights, violated by the latter Grand Masters of the Order of St. John; enjoyed by us during the siege of Valetta, expressly stipulated, when with unlimited confidence we delivered up our Islands to Your Majesty's officers; afterwards taken from us by the late Sir Alexander Ball, and again solemnly promised to us in the name of Your Majesty by the representative of Mr. Cameron:—

FIRST. The principal of these our rights are a free representation of the People or 'Consiglio Popolare,' with the right of sending deputies or memorials to Your Majesty in Council whenever our rights are found to be violated.

SECOND. Independent tribunals.

THIRD. A free Press, but not licentious in matters, and where our Catholic religion shall not be offended.

FOURTH. A jury either in the manner practised in England, or according to our ancient usage, with the right of appeal in every case from the sentence of the judges to the 'Consiglio Popolare.'

In fine, a Constitution which shall unite the spirit of our ancient, free, and only legitimate government with that of the English Constitution, our religion being always kept inviolate.

To obtain our ancient rights we elected by acclamation Your Majesty for our Sovereign. We therefore supplicate Your Majesty, in the name of justice, of humanity, and by all laws, divine and human, and by the lives of twenty thousand persons lost during the siege of Valetta, to be pleased to restore to us our rights and privileges, by which the Maltese were

THE BRITISH ADMINISTRATION UP TO MAY 1814

authorised by their most ancient Sovereigns to give their legitimate consent in every change of Government, which consent cannot be dispensed with without offending justice, which we do not expect from the Government of Your Majesty, whom we cordially elected.

The natives of Malta, Your Majesty's petitioners (as in duty bound), will never cease to pray. And we profess ourselves the most faithful subjects of Your Majesty.

Malta, 10th July 1811.

The tenour of this petition was so offensive that General Oakes considered it his duty to rebuke the signatories in a public notice of the 23rd August as follows:

Palace, Valetta, 23rd August 1811.[1]

The King's Civil Commissioner observes with regret that some weak and inconsiderate persons, deceived under specious pretexts, have suffered themselves to become the instruments of a few turbulent and factious individuals. They have been seduced to subscribe a paper purporting to be an application to the King for certain changes in the existing form of the government of these Islands, but which is in fact a scandalous libel upon that Government as hitherto administered, and the vehicle of private malignity.

The acts of His Majesty's former representatives are grossly and insidiously perverted, facts are misrepresented, and the revered memory of one whose long administration, marked as it was by wisdom and mildness, and by the most distinguished benefits to these Islands, had been sanctioned by the gracious approbation of his Sovereign, is ungratefully and vindictively traduced by an unfeeling and disappointed faction.

Whilst His Excellency feels himself called upon thus to animadvert upon a proceeding no less dishonourable to the parties concerned than it is disrespectful to the Government, he reflects with peculiar satisfaction that so small a number of individuals, and of those so very few of any respectability, have been seduced by the insidious arts so long and so industriously practised to mislead them. This consideration, added to the well-grounded confidence which the King's Civil Commissioner reposes in the loyalty and attachment of the Maltese at large, whose happiness has long been dear to him, and whose real interests His Excellency shall ever be solicitous to promote, enables him to exercise more generally towards a misguided few the lenity and forbearance which have ever characterised His Majesty's Government in these islands. Few indeed and prejudiced must those Maltese be who are insensible to the superior advantages they possess under the auspices of Great Britain: but if such there are, let them learn from the victims of French oppression, who daily crowd to these shores, as to an envied asylum, how much they ought to appreciate the prosperity and security, which, under the powerful protection of His Majesty's fleets and armies, they so liberally enjoy.

If His Excellency has hitherto delayed publicly to notice this extraordinary Memorial, he has been actuated by the desire of affording to those who might have been deceived an opportunity of acknowledging

[1] Government Proclamation, M.P.L., C.A. 4.

their error, and several have accordingly come forward and avowed in writing the gross delusion under which their subscriptions were obtained to the document, and their total ignorance of its contents.

The paper in question, such as it is, His Excellency is determined to transmit by the first opportunity to His Majesty's Ministers.

By Command of His Excellency.

(Signed) F. LAING, Acting Public Secretary.

Marquis Testaferrata, nothing daunted, proceeded to London to support the views of his adherents by personal interviews, if possible, with Earl Bathurst. These views are recapitulated in his two letters to the latter under date of January and 21st April 1812, which are given below.

THE MARCHESE TESTAFERRATA TO EARL BATHURST.

Duke Street, No. 24 Piccadilly, London,
January 1812.[1]

SIR,—Commissioned by some of the most noble and respectable families of Malta to lay before His Majesty the situation of that Island, I take the liberty of submitting the following facts for the consideration of your Lordship and the information of His Majesty in Council. From time immemorial the Islands of Malta and Gozo enjoyed the rights and privileges of a free people. As far back as the year 1397 King Martin confirmed these rights and privileges. In 1425, on account of the urgent necessities of the kingdom, these islands were mortgaged for the sum of 30,000 florins of gold. Our ancestors, not submitting to be governed by a person unsceptred, sent ambassadors to the King to repurchase the Island for the same sum, and we returned under the Royal Demanium [*sic*] with our former and additional rights and privileges, as is fully to be seen in the deed of King Alphonsus of the 3rd January 1427.

The administration of the Government, civil and military, was and remained entirely in our hands; our liberties were preserved to us and jealously guaranteed by a free representation of the people, or 'Consiglio Popolare' of the Island. When the Emperor Charles the Fifth assigned Malta and Gozo to the Grand Masters and Knights as a noble feud with limited powers, he guaranteed and preserved our ancient Constitution, and the Maltese, our forefathers, before they permitted the infeudation, stipulated by their deputies elected by the 'Consiglio Popolare,' and by the procurators of the Grand Master and Knights for the confirmation of their privileges, customs, and for that state of freedom which we then enjoyed; and our countrymen, not content, sent for greater security ambassadors to Syracuse, where the Grand Master then resided, for the ratification of their privileges, the deed respecting which was executed in 1530; and no Grand Master was acknowledged Prince of the Island by reclamation until he had taken before the first senator, at the outer gate of the capital, a solemn oath on the Gospel to maintain inviolate all our ancient rights and privileges. And although several Grand Masters, notwithstanding their

[1] Colonial Office Papers, Malta, No. 20 (1812).

THE BRITISH ADMINISTRATION UP TO MAY 1814   513

oath, at various times attempted to limit our rights and privileges, yet such attempts were uniformly resisted by the Maltese.

This form of government with the 'Consiglio Popolare' was in force until 1782, when the Grand Master Rohan Soubise, supported by the French party, published his ill-judged and despotic code, under which, however, we had still more privileges than we have at this day.

Until 1798 the Knights were masters of the fortresses, when *they delivered them up to the French* [sic], who, soon after committing acts of injustice and violence, the whole Maltese people (except the city, which had been disarmed by the French) took up arms, beat the French in the field, and shut them up in Valetta. All this was done by themselves, without the assistance of or communication with any other Power.

Some time after the ports were blockaded by the Portuguese, and finally by the English. During the space of fifteen months the war was carried on at the sole expense of the Maltese. They afterwards received some assistance from Sicily, mortgaging their lands for that purpose.

During two years that the war lasted we lost by sickness and the sword of the enemy about 20,000 persons, while our handful of auxiliaries lost not one soldier killed by the enemy. Three days after revolution had taken place we re-established a free government upon the basis of our ancient Constitution, every town or *borg* (*casale*) choosing its head or representative, and the people elected four senators, who formed the chief political body and representation, and these united directed all affairs, civil and military.

Two months afterwards, during which time the French made several sorties and were repulsed by the Maltese, who, having shut them up more closely in Valetta, we had more leisure to establish a more systematic form of government, and the people in every town (*casal* or *burgh*), having elected representatives, these with the aforesaid senators formed the Congress.

Sir Alexander Ball, then commander of the blockade by sea, was by the spontaneous will of the Maltese elected President of the Congress, without whose vote he had no authority whatever; and though afterwards he was by the King of Sicily appointed his governor, the full power of legislation remained with the Congress. The public Acts existing in the registers furnish proofs of this fact. The French garrison, reduced to extremity by famine, were forced to demand a capitulation, and their own council of war determined, in case it was required, to leave hostages, to indemnify the Maltese for all the damages, forced contributions, plunder of the University and *Monti di Redenzione e Pietà*, and all other property, public and private, which they had extorted during the siege.

At this juncture the English, who styled themselves our military auxiliaries [sic], without our knowledge granted to the enemy a capitulation by which, without our consent, we had the mortification of seeing the spoils, even of us their conquerers, carried to France in British ships. The gates of Valetta being opened, the Maltese laid down their arms, and the Congress being dissolved, but with promises that the 'Consiglio Popolare' should be assembled, we permitted the King's officers to occupy the fortresses and to have the administration of the public property, and by acclamation we elected the King of Great Britain for our sovereign; but with the express stipulation that our ancient, sacred and only legitimate rights should be continued without any kind of interruption. We accepted this compact in the confidence we had, and still have, in the honour of the English Government, and what we assert we consider to be incontestably proved by the letter of Sir Alexander Ball to Mr. Secretary Windham, printed at the Government Press in Malta, in which he says: 'You are aware, Sir, that when the British first took possession of the Island it was stipulated that the privileges of the Maltese should be preserved and their ancient laws continued in force.' But notwithstanding this, from the year 1800, when we remained fully masters of our own cities, until this day, the 'Consiglio Popolare' has not been assembled nor have our rights and privileges been in vigour, but we are governed in such a manner that we cannot raise the voice of appeal against any tyranny, however oppressive.

During ten years we have not ceased to demand a remedy for the grievances under which we groan. Our deputies sent to London in 1802 demanded it; my Lord Melville proposed it in the House of Lords; the Secretary of State, Mr. Windham, was favourable to our cause; but the Ministry being changed, it was left undone.

From that time certain persons who were, and now are, interested in maintaining that despotic form of government under which we groan, have constantly, by intrigues and misrepresentations, misled His Majesty's Government from doing us that justice which otherwise they would have done.

When we sent instructions to our agent, Mr. Richards, to solicit the restitution of our stipulated and hereditary rights, signed by almost all the respectable persons in Malta, he obtained an audience of your Lordship, who only objected to the form, and directed that the petition should be addressed to His Majesty in Council, and signed as the other had been, and delivered to General Oakes, His Majesty's Civil Commissioner and Commander-in-Chief of the troops in Malta, to be by him transmitted to London.

Having received this answer from our agent, we altered the form as directed by your Lordship, and we began to sign it. On the 26th July we acquainted the Governor with the instructions we had received, upon which we were informed that no answer could be given without first knowing the contents of the petition. We again wrote to the Governor, enclosing a copy of the petition, on the receipt of which His Excellency, by letter of the 3rd August, ordered the original petition to be immediately sent to him with the signatures already put to it. Upon receiving these orders, which we felt obliged to obey, it was delivered to His Excellency, with the express condition that it should be returned to us to add the remaining signatures; or in case he resolved otherwise that, imperfect as it was, it should be sent to His Majesty in Council.

The Governor, relying on his power and ascendancy over those who had offices or employments, the next day called such individuals, and by persuasion or menace obliged several to retract what they had signed and to sign other papers prepared for or dictated to them. Terror of a power without limit and the promise of preserving a salary induced some to this dishonourable step. All those who refused were deprived of their offices.

A counter-declaration was procured by the Government from persons in the same dependent situation, and this being signed by a few only, notwithstanding that it was proposed by the Government itself, we may reasonably conclude that the remaining Maltese have the same sentiments as those in the humble petition to His Majesty in Council, and would, had they not been prevented by the strong hand of Government, have expressed them by their signatures.

A proclamation was afterwards issued in which we are styled little better than rebels, and the Governor is pleased to say that few persons have signed the petition, when he himself stopped the signing of others; and he also says that few of these were of any respectability, though they form the principal part of the nobility of Malta. I request the favour of your Lordship to confront the respectability of these few with that of the others who, induced by promises or menaces, made counter declarations, and to recollect that the one was voluntary, the other forced. By this proceeding the internal state of the Island was exposed to the knowledge of the whole world at a most critical moment, a most loyal people, its nobility, and everything that is respectable in Malta, defamed and insulted.

The universal surprise of the whole nation, and even that of the English themselves, can scarcely be imagined at seeing a petition addressed to the Sovereign, as directed by the Minister of His Majesty, to whom alone appertained the approval or condemnation, suppressed by the sole will of the Governor. I cannot conclude without expressing to your Lordship that the most anxious wish of my countrymen is to know whether His Majesty's Government considers us as appertaining to the United Kingdom of Great Britain and Ireland, or whether it is His Royal pleasure that we be considered as an independent nation. I have the honour, &c.

(Signed) NICOLO CAPO DI FERRO, MARCHESE TESTAFERRATA.

THE MARCHESE TESTAFERRATA TO EARL BATHURST, SECRETARY OF STATE, WAR, AND COLONIES.

Duke Street, Piccadilly, London, 21*st April* 1812.[1]

MY LORD,—I had the honour to receive your Lordship's letter of the 3rd instant, informing me that there does not appear to the Prince Regent's Government sufficient grounds for considering the papers which I presented to be, what they profess to be, authorised declarations of the wishes and opinions of the people of Malta, and that I can be considered here only as a private individual, but that it nevertheless was in contemplation to send Commissioners out to Malta in order to examine fully into the circumstances of the Civil Government and its laws, and for which information I beg leave to express to your Lordship my most grateful acknowledgments.

Ignorant as I necessarily must be of what may be considered here 'as authorised declarations of the wishes and opinions of the people of Malta,' I can only say that the persons whose numerous signatures I had the honour to submit to your Lordship are to be found amongst the most eminent for rank, for talent, and for property in the Island, and would

---

[1] Government Proclamation, M.P.L., C.A. 4.

have been followed by the signatures of the whole population but for the interference of the Governor, the circumstances respecting which I have already had the honour to state to your Lordship, and that your Lordship will find that these persons have only spoken the genuine wishes and opinions of my countrymen at large.

That your Lordship, however, and the Commissioners who may be sent there may be the better able to judge of the fidelity of my representation as to those wishes and opinions, I take the liberty to subjoin these their following requests, with a copy of the authority under which I act and some of the ancient privileges and rights of the Maltese, as a justification of what I have presented to your Lordship on the 16th January, which they are desirous of having recognised:

That the ' Consiglio Popolare,' composed of the nobility and of a representative elected in every casale, shall be restored, in order to form together the first or chief representative body; that the *Università*, or Public Bank, shall be put on its former footing, its debts paid, and credits called in and realised; that the powers of the King's Commissioner shall be defined; that courts of justice shall be established and rendered independent in giving their sentences; that the suitors shall not be obliged for the institution of their suits to obtain any licence from the Governor; that the judges shall not be displaced unless guilty of improper conduct; that juries shall be established as the basis for the administration of justice; that the Intendant of Police (an employ of the most delicate nature for public security and tranquility) shall be entrusted to a Maltese gentleman of honour and ability; that the Casa Santa shall be restored for retirement and exercises of piety; that the Press shall be free; that the property of individuals shall be respected; that the expenses of the war and of the present Mission shall be discharged out of the revenues of the Island, and that such of the grievances of individuals as have been hitherto suppressed shall be heard.

For these purposes the Maltese most humbly request that His Royal Highness the Prince Regent will be graciously pleased to appoint Commissioners who, with Commissioners to be elected in a general Congress of the Island, may form a plan of government for His Royal Highness's approval, with powers for hearing the complaints of aggrieved individuals.

In a word, that measures may be adopted for putting the Maltese under the protection of a Constitution which will render them happy, and for ever unite them to the Crown of His Britannic Majesty. I have the honour, &c.

NICOLO CAPO DI FERRO, MARCHESE TESTAFERRATA.

Lord Liverpool (then Premier), however, on the 3rd of April had informed Marquis Testaferrata that he could only receive him as a private individual, and refused to place before the Privy Council the documents of which he had been the bearer. The Marquis was also informed that the Prince Regent contemplated sending to Malta a Special Commission to inquire into the alleged abuses 'and to establish a system calculated to ensure the happiness and prosperity of the Maltese nation.'

This information was also conveyed to General Oakes by a letter

THE BRITISH ADMINISTRATION UP TO MAY 1814 517

from Lord Liverpool under date of the 5th May 1812, of which the following is an epitome :

[Epitome.]

He informs General Oakes of the appointment of a Commission to make ' a full and immediate enquiry into all matters touching the civil government, laws, judicial proceedings, revenue, &c. of the Island of Malta.' The Commissioners were to be A'Court, late Chargé d'affaires at Palermo ; Burrows, late Chief Justice of Dominica ; General Oakes, Governor of Malta.

The arrival in Malta of two members of the Commission was duly announced in the public Press as follows : [1]

On Monday, the 29th June (1812), arrived in this port of Valetta, in six weeks from England, a convoy under the protection of His Majesty's frigate *Ganymede*, on board of which were Messieurs A'Court and Burrows, Commissioners entrusted, with His Excellency the Lieut.-General H. Oakes, Civil Commissioner in these Islands, by H.R.H. the Prince Regent to enquire into the laws, revenue, and civil government of these Islands, and to report their investigations to the Government in London. The Commissioners are accompanied by Mr. Meyer as secretary, and Lord Herbert as assistant secretary.

The result of the labours of this Commission appeared in a very able report dated the 30th August 1812 / 16th October 1812. This report has never been made public in its entirety, but extracts have occasionally appeared, notably one in a return asked for by the House of Commons and ordered to be printed on the 17th June 1846.

The extracts which have been made public treat upon the ' Consiglio Popolare,' Papal jurisdiction, ecclesiastical establishments, Representative Assembly, and are as follows [2] :

CONSIGLIO POPOLARE.

An enquiry into the claims of the Maltese with respect to a Representative Assembly, with rights of discussion and appeal and with powers of legislation, having been particularly prescribed to us in our instructions, we have not failed to give to so important a subject all that attention to which it is so justly entitled.

The result of our enquiries has been the most firm conviction that these claims, so loudly urged by turbulent and interested individuals, are totally without foundation, and that at no period of their history did the Maltese ever possess the slightest pretension or right to a deliberative and legislative assembly. To enter into a long historical detail in order to disprove the truth of the assertions which have been so confidently advanced upon the subject would be foreign to the nature of this report. From the variety of papers, however, which the consideration of these

[1] Extract from *Il Giornale di Malta*, No. 26, of the 1st July 1812, which paper preceded the *Government Gazette*, and was the first and only newspaper then published in Malta.
[2] C.O.R. Malta, No. 21 (1812).

claims has brought more immediately under our notice we have selected one which is particularly entitled to attention from the number of authentic documents upon which it is founded. It will be found in the Appendix to this Report. It was drawn up by a Mr. Dolci, a lawyer of considerable ability, and it may be considered as a refutation of every claim, founded upon the supposition of the former existence of a deliberative and legislative assembly. The 'Consiglio Popolare' never did, and never pretended to, possess any deliberative or legislative authority. It was simply an assembly of the people summoned by order of the Crown for the nomination of certain jurats of the *Università*, which nomination was afterwards submitted to the Sovereign for his approbation. The *Università* of Citta Vecchia (which, with some alterations in its functions, exists to this day) was a municipal body, charged with the superintendency of the markets, the supply of provisions, the weights and measures, the roads, and public edifices. From this body members were, indeed, occasionally sent to Palermo in order to lay before the Sovereign, or his viceroy, any complaints or representations respecting the affairs within its immediate jurisdiction, but never upon any occasion did it arrogate to itself the right of legislation, nor in any way presume to interfere with the uncontrolled exercise of the executive power.

The meetings from whence these deputations were sent were denominated 'Consiglio dell' Università,' and were totally distinct from the Electoral or 'Consiglio Popolare.'

The early periods of the Maltese history are so extremely confused that it is difficult to trace the origin of these different assemblies or to fix the precise time of their establishment.

The first mention of a 'Consiglio Popolare' is in the year 1420, when King Alphonso appears to have mortgaged the Islands of Malta and Gozo to Antonio Cardona for the sum of 30,000 florins. An Assembly was at that time convened under this appellation, by order of the procurator of Cardona, for the purpose of electing two Syndics, who might take the oath of allegiance to the new Lord in the name of the people.

But the 'Consiglio Popolare' (properly so called) appears to have been assembled so rarely as to induce Mr. Dolci to speak with some degree of doubt even of its power of electing candidates for the office of Jurats, conceiving it rather in those early times to have been an assembly of the people ordered by the Sovereign for some extraordinary occasion like that to which we have just referred.

It appears also that the 'Consiglio Popolare' and 'Consiglio dell' Università' are occasionally confounded by historians, though nothing can be more distinct than their characters of *electors* and *elected*. It is, however, to this remote period of history that we are referred by the advocates of a legislative assembly for the proofs both of its existence and of its powers; but although the obscurity in which it is involved is particularly favourable to the advancement of such or any other pretensions, still there is a sufficient degree of light thrown upon the transactions of this period to enable us to pronounce with the greatest degree of certainty that these claims are without foundation and totally unwarranted by the history of the times to which we are referred. From the time of the expulsion of the Saracens in the year 1090 the Islands of Malta and Gozo belonged to the Crown of Sicily by right of conquest. From that period until the year 1428 they were commonly conferred upon different subjects as feudal tenures without any particular restrictions whatsoever.

In fact it is in no way reconcilable to reason to suppose that these Islands could have been given and taken away three times in little more than a year by the sole *fiat* and authority of Martin, King of Sicily, without any opposition on the part of the 'Consiglio Popolare,' supposing it to have been possessed of those powers of deliberation and legislation with which fancy has been pleased to invest it.

The very circumstance of the mortgage of these Islands by King Alphonso in 1420, and again in 1425, proves beyond a doubt that they were considered as a property that might be alienated, sold or mortgaged at pleasure, and the existence of such a power in the Crown appears to us so totally incompatible with the existence of a popular deliberative body as to lead us at once to the conclusion that an assembly so constituted never did nor could exist. In the year 1428 the *Università*, in the name of the people, advanced a sum of 30,000 florins in order to enable the Crown to redeem these Islands from the hands of Gonsalvo di Monroi, and the reasons which led to the offer afford additional grounds for the belief that the master of these Islands (whoever he might be) was absolute and uncontrollable. They (the inhabitants) had experienced so much inconvenience from the frequent change of masters that they were desirous of being attached to the Crown of Sicily as an unalienable fief, in order to avoid the heavy contributions and vexatious services which each possessor in succession had never failed to exact. The existence of an absolute despotism can scarcely be more plainly proved. From henceforward these Islands were never alienated from the Crown until the final cession to the Order of St. John in the year 1530.

The 'Consiglio Popolare' comes frequently under our notice whilst tracing the history of the Island from the period of its occupation by the Knights, but here it is admitted, even by the most strenuous supporters of its ancient privileges and authority, to have been nothing more than an assembly for the purpose of electing four candidates, from amongst whom the Grand Master selected one to go to Sicily in order to treat for the purchase of corn, and four others from whom he also selected one to be the depositary of the monies of the *Università*.

Although this assembly bore the name of 'Consiglio Popolare,' it was more properly speaking a 'Consiglio dell' Università,' for it was composed only of the different members of the *Università*, persons holding certain fiefs, and others holding those offices, a list of which is to be seen in the Code of Vilhena. It met every year, and had no other powers whatsoever than the election of these candidates, from whom, however, the Grand Masters did not always select the persons to be employed. In the later periods of the existence of the Order of St. John these assemblies were discontinued.

Some stress has been laid upon an assembly of the different heads of *casals* convened by Sir Alexander Ball, at the time of the blockade, for the purpose of giving more ready effect to the orders which he found it necessary to issue.

This has been ingeniously construed into an acknowledgment of the former existence of a deliberative body. Nothing can be more gratuitous than such a deduction. The meeting was convened for the sole purpose before mentioned, and was a representative rather than an electoral body, such as we know the 'Consiglio Popolare' to have been. Indeed, so little attention was paid at that time to the existence of any former assembly that it met under the simple title of *Congresso*.

[Recently an attempt to substantiate the assertion that the ancient 'Consiglio Popolare' possessed legislative power has again been made by certain local politicians.

This opinion has been based upon arguments presented by counsel in the case 'In the matter of the validity of certain mixed and unmixed marriages in Malta,' which was argued before the Privy Council in 1891. It would appear, however, that such opinion was derived from Eton's 'Materials for the History of Malta,' a work pronounced by the highest local legal authority as that of a discredited official.

In reply to such attempts and observations it is only necessary to state that Sir Joseph Carbone (who at the time was Crown Advocate in the aforesaid judicial case) fully confirmed the opinion of the Commissioners of 1812, and at p. 7 of his case answers:

With regard to the constitutional history of Malta, it would appear that from 1190 to 1530 that Island was (as part of Sicily) subject to the laws of Sicily. Malta had a local municipal institution, known as the 'Consiglio Popolare,' which was much less authorised to exercise powers of legislation than is a county council or a vestry in modern times.]

Papal Jurisdiction.[1]

The Papal jurisdiction in these Islands is restricted to the receiving of appeals in all ecclesiastical causes, the nomination alternately with the bishop to about sixty small benefices, and the investiture of the bishop at the period of his election with the usual insignia of his office.

. . . .

Ecclesiastical Establishments: Papal Authority.[2]

In order to comply in the most satisfactory manner with that part of our instructions by which we are directed to enquire into the ecclesiastical establishments and revenues and the extent of the Papal authority, we judged it advisable to apply directly to the bishop himself (Monsignor Mattei) for information upon these subjects.

The statement he was pleased to prepare will be found in the Appendix to this Report, and, with the exception of some unfounded claims to the possession of the Church of St. John, it may be considered as entitled to the character of fidelity and accuracy. It will be seen by this paper that there exist in these Islands three ecclesiastical courts for the trial of causes in which the Church is immediately concerned. The first, which is fixed in Valetta, comprises a vicar-general, two judges denominated assessors, an advocate fiscal, an advocate for the poor, and some other inferior officers. The second, which is in Citta Vecchia, and the third,

[1] C.O.R. Malta, No. 21 (1812).   [2] *Ibid.*

which is in Gozo, are perhaps rather to be considered as branches of the first than as separate and distinct tribunals. They are in everything dependent upon the superior Court of Valetta, and are presided over by two pro-vicars, to whom a very limited authority is accorded.

The appeal from the decrees of these tribunals lies either to the Metropolitan Court of Palermo (of whose archbishop the Bishop of Malta is a suffragan) or directly to the See of Rome. But on account of the difficulty which at present exists of obtaining access to the Roman Pontiff,[1] a permission has been by him granted to the Bishop of Malta to appoint judges, to whom all appeals may be made in the first instance. The advantage resulting from this arrangement is that, in cases which involve any questions of property, the transfer or payment is immediately made whenever the judge of appeal confirms the original sentence.

This, however, is not considered as abrogating the right of the suffering party to appeal to the Roman See, as the two concurring sentences, though they authorise the immediate transfer of the property in dispute, may subsequently be set aside by a decision obtained from Rome. The judges receive fees, but on account of the paucity of the business their amount is inconsiderable, and they all receive additional salaries from the bishop.

It is impossible not to perceive that every abuse existing in the secular tribunal of Malta prevails to an equal extent in the ecclesiastical courts. Yet, although we have ventured to recommend their summary abolition in the one case, so many difficulties and impediments present themselves in the other that we are reluctantly obliged to confess that they appear at present to be insurmountable.

Every act of the British Government with regard to ecclesiastical matters is viewed with so jealous an eye that an infringement of the long-established rights and privileges of the Church (however beneficial to the community) would undoubtedly draw down the indignation of an angry priesthood, and, through their means, create a considerable degree of discontent even amongst the people themselves. In these countries it seems to be an established axiom of the Church that no change can possibly prove an amendment; and it must be recollected that previous to the introduction of any innovation whatever we have not only to obtain the consent of the ecclesiastical authorities on the spot, but also the concurrence and approval of the Romish Church.

It may therefore be more prudent for the present to abstain from any material alteration, either in the jurisdiction or administration of the ecclesiastical courts.

The causes which come under their cognisance are not so numerous or important as to call for an immediate interference of the legislature, and we may indulge [in] the hope that, after the clergy shall have witnessed the good effect which we are persuaded will result from the proposed alterations in the secular courts, much of the jealousy and mistrust which at present exist will be removed, and that we may look forward to the time when, even here, innovation will not always be considered as a folly, nor the attempt to improve upon the imperfect establishments of our forefathers as a wild and presumptuous experiment.

[1] The Pope was then detained by Napoleon at Fontainebleau.—J. H. R.

REPRESENTATIVE ASSEMBLY.

[The enquiry into the claims of the Maltese with respect to a representative assembly, with rights of discussion and appeal and with powers of legislation, ascribed to the ancient 'Consiglio Popolare' having proved such pretensions to be futile, the Commissioners of 1812 proceed with their Report, adding the following remarks upon the consequences which they conceived would be the result of the introduction of a deliberative assembly:—]

The inhabitants of Malta (they say) are quiet and well disposed under laws they have been accustomed to reverence; they are by nature possessed of the most ardent minds, and inflammable passions.

A word unguardedly dropped, or an accusation artfully made, might at any time be sufficient to rouse them to acts of the most ungovernable fury; but in the composition of a numerous body chosen by the suffrages of the people there would also be found individuals capable to discover, and to turn to their own profit, the credulity and violence of their associates. Of these two materials the 'Consiglio' would inevitably be composed. The great majority would consist of the illiterate and fanatic; but these, so far from being any counterpoise to the smaller number of another description, would, on the contrary, offer the readiest and most effective instruments that could be presented to their hands. The nature and functions of this assembly are still, however, to be ascertained. Even the few discontented persons who are the loudest in their cries for its appointment, the most zealous in their assertions of its former existence as a deliberative body, are unable to give any definition of its duties, its prerogatives, or its jurisdiction. Whether its powers supersede those of the existing Government; whether the chief magistrate has any check upon its deliberations; whether its decrees have at once the validity of laws—these are questions which no one is prepared to answer; and this inability (where a pretence has been advanced of its having been made a subject of study) argues clearly that there are no precedents by which we can be guided, no experience of former transactions to which any reference can be made.

But on what is this 'Consiglio Popolare' to deliberate when assembled? On taxes? With the exception of a small duty on carriages there are none imposed. On laws? The limited community of this Island cannot certainly require the annual interference of the legislative power, as in countries of greater extent. On commercial matters? These must necessarily depend upon the arrangements of the mother country.

Little, therefore, remains for the deliberation of this deliberative assembly, unless in the plenitude of its power it should proceed to the discussion of the acts of the executive Government so to interfere in the arrangements of the State.

Should this concession be made, we will not say to the wishes of the Maltese, but to those of an insignificant and turbulent party, the consequences are obvious but unavoidable. Every chimerical project that folly, ignorance, or ambition can frame will be brought forward and discussed. The fury of superstition and the influence of priesthood will be set in motion. The leaders of the assembly must either be bought at the price that vanity may attach to its own importance, or they will oppose the Government in every measure. The elections will be the source of continual tumult and intrigue in the *casals*, and the assembly itself productive of every species of disorder in the capital. In a word, it will be the focus of sedition radiating from the centre to the extremities, and paralysing all the efforts of government.

So firmly are we persuaded of the mischievous effects that would result from entrusting any portion of political power to a people so singularly unfitted to enjoy it, that with a view to the real happiness of the Maltese we have no hesitation in saying, that, were the pretensions to a former existence of a deliberative and legislative assembly as clear and incontestable as they really are obscure and groundless, we should still feel it our duty to recommend most earnestly a positive refusal of its re-establishment, as a measure fraught with the greatest danger and involving the most ruinous consequences.—Extract from the Report of the Royal Commissioners of 16th October 1812.[1]

At the close of the investigations made by the Commissioners, the Marquis Testaferrata appears to have been somewhat anxious as to the nature of their Report, and evidently feared that he had been unable to substantiate his charges or to convert the members to his opinions, for on the 2nd November he addressed the following letter to Earl Bathurst:—

[Translation.]

THE MARCHESE TESTAFERRATA TO EARL BATHURST.

Malta, *2nd November* 1812.[2]

It is rumoured here that the Commissioners before leaving this Island had formed their opinion upon the demands made in the name of the Maltese nation.

It is also publicly understood that several English gentlemen (we do not know if on political grounds, or from a spirit of contradiction) had greatly busied themselves in discrediting and offering every impediment to the very moderate propositions of the Nationalists. But what has most displeased the discreet part of the people is that to the above-mentioned English gentlemen, who have shown themselves so inimical to the rights and privileges of the nation, and to its happiness, there have been communicated all the representations that were made by the Nationalists for the information of His Royal Highness the Prince Regent in Council; while, on the other hand, they were not made acquainted with any of the many difficulties said to have been advanced by the opposite party, whose conduct in the affairs of government, particularly what interests the country, has contributed not a little to oblige the Maltese to appeal to their Sovereign.

Under these impressions the undersigned, together with all persons jealous of the honour and happiness of their country and attached to the Government and to British honour, are fearful that the representations that have been made to their Sovereign, and the signal favour conferred upon them by His Royal Highness the Prince Regent in sending his

[1] Return ordered by the House of Commons to be printed, 17th June 1846.
[2] C.O.R. Malta, No. 20 (1812).

Commissioners, will be of no avail if the secret opposition of these gentlemen, who have proved themselves so ill-affected towards the nation, should be presented to the Council without there appearing any answer to their baneful representations, and more particularly if these have had any weight on the minds of the Commissioners; which is by no means unlikely, as they did not permit any explanation or reply on the part of those who had made their demands, and it cannot be supposed to be in the power of the Commissioners to get unaided the necessary knowledge of the ancient constitution of Malta, and to distinguish legitimate right from despotism, by which former Governments have often nearly subverted the privileges of the nation.

Therefore, if the Commissioners' Report should blindly pass approved, without giving the Maltese an opportunity of knowing its contents, in order that they may deliver such reflections and such documents as may be necessary to dissolve the difficulties that may have been raised to the prejudice of their national appeal, it is much to be feared that it will occasion a very different result to that intended by H.R.H. the Prince Regent, who certainly was more inclined to favour the Maltese nation than to encumber their rights with new shackles and add greater degradation to their civil and political existence.

From what is rumoured here it would appear that it is intended either never to re-establish or greatly diminish the privileges of the people, while others report that the unlimited power formerly enjoyed and still held by the Royal Commissioner over the nation and its magistrates, certainly much more extensive than that exercised by the King in his dominions, will be checked; and it is said that several Englishmen will be appointed for the purpose of counteracting and resisting every act of despotism.

Should this be the case the nation will certainly not be ameliorated by the change; on the contrary, it will be more degraded than it actually is. These rumours occasion just fears that by the introduction of new authority in the persons of Englishmen every shadow of national influence will vanish with regard to the civil government, and instead of the magistrates being dependent on the nation and on the sole authority of a representative and of his Council, composed of elected Maltese, they will be dependent on and influenced by persons not natives, and consequently their authority will be greatly degraded, and in all decisions of the Government which may interest the nation entirely taken away. They will be thus prevented from counteracting such acts of despotism as may take place, either in consequence of false information or from the want of a perfect knowledge of the privileges of the laws of the Maltese, evils that must necessarily emanate from persons not natives being invested with public authority.

We flatter ourselves that after the representations made by us to the Commissioners shall have been laid before the Prince Regent in Council so great a misfortune will not befall the nation, which would give a final blow to all its civil liberty.

But as it is the duty of everyone to endeavour to avert so unfortunate an event, I take the liberty of submitting these ideas to Your Excellency, begging you will communicate to the persons who have made the present representations all the difficulties the Commissioners have had to encounter

THE BRITISH ADMINISTRATION UP TO MAY 1814

in not adhering altogether or in part to the proposed projects for the re-establishment of the ancient privileges of the country; also to acquaint them of the nature of the opposition that may have been made by the disaffected to the Maltese nation, men who certainly can care but little for the honour of the British Government.

I cannot forbear stating to Your Excellency that amongst the Maltese, in common with all other nations, are to be found individuals deprived of every sentiment of honour and love of their country, who are easily corrupted by any person invested with the least character to second his desires, although injurious to the interests and to the honour of their native country. The representations of such men ought, therefore, to make no impression on the Sovereign and his Ministers, should they present a memorial subscribed by a number of Maltese opposing the demands made in favour of the nation, as it will be very easy for me to demonstrate the absurdity of such opposition, and the little confidence that should be placed in their propositions, which under the authority of the abovementioned persons tend to destroy the interests and the honour of the very people who incautiously subscribed to them. I have the honour, &c.

(Signed) NICOLO CAPO DI FERRO, MARCHESE TESTAFERRATA.

During the three months and a half, in which the Commission was occupied in drawing up their Report (i.e. from the 29th June to the 12th October), there occurred the most momentous of all events in connection with the incorporation of Malta in the dominion of the British Crown.

This was the declaration of war by Russia against France, preceding peace with England, which latter was signed on the 18th July 1812. By this act Russia was compelled to recede from the position she had taken up with regard to the Order of St. John of Jerusalem and its return to Malta.

This circumstance, combined with the disasters which subsequently befell Napoleon, enabled Great Britain to declare her determination to recognise the people of Malta and Gozo as subjects of the British Crown, and to take the necessary steps to introduce various reforms in the government, which Sir Thomas Maitland was shortly to be instructed to carry out. The nature of these reforms was foreshadowed in Lord Bathurst's despatch to General Oakes of the 15th May 1813, of which the following is an Extract:—

[Extract.]

LORD BATHURST TO LIEUT.-GENERAL OAKES.

War Department, London, 15th May 1813.[1]

After referring to the work of the recent Commission upon the affairs of Malta the despatch proceeds:

In the meantime you may consider yourself authorised to intimate in

[1] Crown Ad. Case, Mixed Marriages, p. 10.

a private manner to the principal individuals in Malta that, while His Majesty's Government thus publicly mark the incorporation of Malta with the dominions of the British Crown, it is not their intention to destroy the laws which at present exist in the Island, or to make any other changes in the establishment and practice of the courts of justice than such as appear necessary to keep pace with the improved condition of the inhabitants, and as may effectually give to His Majesty's Maltese subjects the fullest security in their persons and property.

General Oakes's Administration was now drawing to a close. He had already expressed a desire to be relieved, but owing to the terrible epidemic of plague which had afflicted the Island since the 16th April he felt bound to remain at his post until the scourge showed some signs of diminution. Meanwhile His Majesty's Government selected Lieut.-General Sir Thomas Maitland to fill the appointment, no longer as Royal Commissioner, but as Governor of the Island of Malta and its dependencies. This appointment was made on the 15th July 1813, and on the 28th of that month, the following copious and precise instructions were given to Sir Thomas, with unlimited power granted for their due execution :—

EARL BATHURST TO LIEUT.-GENERAL SIR THOMAS MAITLAND.

War Department, *28th July* 1813.[1]

SIR,—Since the Island of Malta and its dependencies came under the protection and dominion of His Majesty in the year 1800 no permanent or defined system has been laid down for their government. They appeared at first to be valuable only as affording a secure naval station, from which the enemy's designs upon Egypt or the Levant might be watched and counteracted, and the state of Europe rendered it probable that Great Britain might withdraw her pretensions to the sovereignty of those islands in the event of peace.

The circumstances of the present war have occasioned a material change in the actual value of Malta, as well as in regard to the importance of our holding a permanent station in the Mediterranean.

As a military post, as a naval arsenal, as a secure place of depôt for the British merchants, there is no spot in the South of Europe which appears so well calculated to fix the influence and extend the interests of Great Britain, as the Island of Malta.

To these weighty considerations must be added that the Maltese people have (with an inconsiderable exception) attached themselves enthusiastically to the British connection, and offer to His Majesty a wealthy and concentrated population of 100,000 persons, whose active industry is most satisfactorily attested by the astonishing increase which has taken place in the trade and general affluence of the Island within the last few years.

In proportion as the circumstances of Malta have improved, the inconveniences resulting from an undefined mode of government, from

[1] C.O.R. Malta, No. 21 (1813).

defective laws, and an inadequate judicature, have become more obvious, and the anxious desire which the Maltese were understood to possess of being acknowledged publicly as subjects of the British Crown has favoured the disposition of His Majesty's Government to establish the civil authorities of the Island upon a permanent footing, and to introduce such improvements in the Maltese law and in the practice of the courts as the improved state of society and the extended relations of the people appear to demand.

Commissioners were accordingly sent to Malta in the summer of last year, with powers and instructions to enquire into and to report upon all the circumstances connected with the civil government, the laws, tribunals, revenues and commerce of Malta, in order that His Majesty's Government might be enabled to decide upon the system which it would be expedient to introduce with a view to the lasting prosperity of the Maltese as subjects of Great Britain, and to connect their interests more closely with those of the United Kingdom.

You have perused the very able Report which has been made to His Majesty's Government by the Commissioners, and a copy is transmitted herewith for your occasional reference. In most of the opinions expressed by the Commissioners His Majesty's Government are inclined to coincide, as it has been resolved to act (with certain modifications) upon several of their suggestions.

At the moment when measures were in preparation for putting in execution the proposed arrangements circumstances have enabled His Royal Highness the Prince Regent to commit the government of Malta to your charge, and I esteem myself particularly fortunate in being able to profit by your abilities and experience to carry these measures into effect.

I have now to communicate to you the intentions of His Majesty's Government respecting Malta, and shall proceed to state them separately under principal heads, viz. :
1. Office and Authority of the Governor.
2. Principal Civil Officers.
3. Suzerainty and Ecclesiastical Affairs.
4. Laws and Courts of Justice.
5. Revenue and Local Interests.

The chief authority is vested in the person of the Governor. This officer will hold the King's commission as such, and also as Vice-Admiral of Malta and its dependencies. It is the opinion of His Majesty's Government that it is highly advantageous to unite the civil and military authorities in the same person, and you will hold the chief command of His Majesty's land forces upon the Island.

The authority of the Governor is limited only by the orders of the King. He is responsible to His Majesty and to his country for his conduct ; but his discretion is not to be shackled by any person or by any body of persons resident in Malta. If, however, you shall see fit (either for the better transaction of public business or for other sufficient reasons) to form a Council for the investigation and discussion of such matters relating to the civil interests of the Island as you may think proper to lay before it, you are authorised to do so ; observing that the number of members shall not exceed six, exclusive of the Governor, and that the Bishop of Malta, the President of the High Court of Appeal, the Public Secretary, and the

Treasurer of the Island shall sit in this Council, the other members to be named at your discretion.

No business shall be discussed in this Council but what shall have been brought before them by the Governor himself. The members shall not vote, but merely deliver their opinions and advice, and in case any member shall, after the discussion, disapprove of the course which the Governor may pursue, he shall be at liberty to transmit in writing within twenty-four hours a statement of his reasons for dissenting, and if the member requires it the Governor shall be obliged to send home this protest to the Secretary of State. Having thus detailed the principal civil offices which are to be filled by British subjects, I proceed to point out the objects to which it is necessary you should give your earliest attention upon assuming the government.

In the first place, it is advisable that you should issue a Proclamation announcing publicly the benevolent intentions of the Prince Regent with regard to the Maltese subjects of His Majesty. That it has been His Royal Highness's object to inform himself fully of their real interests, and to consider maturely what system it would be most advisable to adopt in order to secure and extend the prosperity of these Islands, at the same time that he united them more closely and permanently with the British Empire. That His Royal Highness, acting in the name and on the behalf of His Majesty, thus publicly recognises the people of Malta and Gozo as subjects of the British Crown, and as entitled to its full protection. That the free exercise of their religion is secured to them, and the ecclesiastical establishment will subsist as heretofore.

That in regard to the laws by which the Maltese have been accustomed to be governed, and the proceedings of the courts of judicature, the Prince Regent has commanded that such alterations only should be introduced as appear to be imperiously called for by the improved circumstances of the Island, and to be necessary for ensuring to all classes of the inhabitants an equal dispensation of justice and for guarding against abuses and delays in the proceedings of the courts. Finally, that His Royal Highness has given to you full powers and instructions to carry into effect such changes as may appear indispensable, and to take the necessary measures for improving the revenue, extending the commerce, and securing to the Maltese people those articles of primary necessity which must be derived from other countries.

I am inclined to believe that a declaration of this nature will be productive of very beneficial effects, and that the boon the Maltese receive in their annexation to the British dominion will outweigh the considerations of any partial shock, which the first introduction of British principles might occasion to one or other of the classes of society. Immediately after the issuing of a Proclamation to this effect you will cause the arms or emblems of the Order of St. John to be removed from all the public buildings, and likewise the armorial bearings of the different Langues and Grand Masters, and you will cause His Majesty's arms to be affixed, with due ceremony, to the Governor's Palace, and to any other edifices, when you may think it advisable.

Sovereignty of the Islands.

Lord William Bentinck has been instructed to take the first favourable opportunity of calling upon the Court of Palermo to renounce, by a public

THE BRITISH ADMINISTRATION UP TO MAY 1814 529

declaration, all the ancient pretensions to the suzerainty of Malta which have been dormant in the Crown of the Two Sicilies.

I have no reason to doubt that this request will be readily complied with ; but, in case of any demur, you will embrace every opportunity of marking unequivocally that Malta is to be considered as a possession of His Majesty, totally independent in all its relations of the Crown of Sicily and of every other foreign country.

Ecclesiastical Affairs.

In regard to the ecclesiastical affairs of Malta it is not the intention of His Majesty's Government to propose any material alteration. The nomination to the bishopric, whenever it may become vacant, is to rest with the King, subject to the final approbation of the Pope. Upon the demise of the Bishop the Governor will make provision for the due administration of the episcopal functions during the interval and will immediately report the event for His Majesty's information. The Governor will, at the same time, submit the name of such ecclesiastic (being a native of Malta) as he may consider most fitting to fill this high situation.

It appears that upon the appointment of the present Bishop he agreed to relinquish a considerable portion of the episcopal revenue, and that this portion remains in the hands of Government. You will be best able to judge, when upon the spot, whether any and what augmentation to the actual revenue of the Bishop is advisable under present circumstances ; and you will also turn your attention to the question of redeeming the debt charged by the Sicilian courts upon the Maltese estates at Lentini, or of exchanging these estates for that which is possessed in Malta by the Benedictine Convent of Catania.

The system and practice of the ecclesiastical courts of Malta are manifestly defective ; but until the minds of the inhabitants shall become more enlightened it appears advisable not to propose any essential alteration. In one respect, however, a variation from the course of proceedings is indispensable.

It seems that appeals from the decisions of the courts lay, in the first instance, to the Court of the Archbishop of Palermo, as Metropolitan of Malta as well as of Sicily.

The supremacy of this Prelate over the ecclesiastical affairs of Malta must be denied as positively as the pretensions of the King of Sicily to the Sovereignty of the Island.

The practice of appealing to the Archbishop, therefore, must be set aside, and appeals from the judgments of the ecclesiastical courts may be brought at once before two judges nominated by the Bishop.

I come now to the laws of Malta, and, defective and inadequate as they may be in many respects, it still appears inadvisable to make any sudden or radical alteration in the code. A correction of the vices which are but too manifest in the constitution and practice of the courts is more immediately requisite, and will be productive of more practical benefit to the people under their present circumstances. The removal of these abuses and the gradual progress of information may prepare the way for the future introduction of a more liberal and refined system of law. The power of inflicting torture shall be formally and publicly abolished.

An Order in Council will be framed without delay, conveying to you a general authority to carry into effect the alterations in the practice and constitution of the Maltese courts; to suppress the Consolato del Mare and the Court for the Administration of Public Property, and to annul the privilege of sanctuary in cases of sacrilege, treason, murder, or assassination.

The instructions previously given to Cameron in 1801, and those to Maitland in 1813, afford ample proof of the earnest desire of the British Government to ameliorate the condition of the Maltese people and to fulfil the promises made to them on its behalf since the commencement of the occupation, namely :

The full protection, and enjoyment of all their dearest rights in their persons and property ;
The free exercise of their religion ;[1] and
The maintenance of their ecclesiastical establishment.

During the autumn the plague showed signs of abatement, which permitted Maitland to sail for Malta, where he arrived on Sunday, the 3rd October 1813.

Upon his arrival he wrote to his friends: 'We breathe very much through a medium of arsenic and brimstone at present, but I am told when I get accustomed to it, it will be quite delicious.' On the 5th Maitland assumed the reins of government, when he issued the following Proclamation and Minute :[2]

PROCLAMATION.[3]

The Right Honourable Thomas Maitland, Governor and Commander-in-Chief of the Island of Malta and its dependencies, Lieutenant-General in His Majesty's army, &c.

This day His Royal Highness the Prince Regent's commission appointing the Right Honourable Thomas Maitland Governor and Commander-in-Chief of these Islands, having been read in the Palace, before such of the public functionaries as could with convenience be assembled under present circumstances [the existing plague epidemic] and His Excellency having taken the oaths of office, he is henceforth to be obeyed as such.

Palace, Valetta, 5th October 1813.

[1] In connexion with this subject the following extract from Governor O'Ferrall's address laid before the Council of Government on the 10th August 1849 may be given:
'Religious liberty is maintained alike by the law and concurrent practice of Malta, whilst the established Catholic religion of the Island' (of which faith he was a member) 'enjoys all its rights, privileges, and property, under a Protestant State, with less of lay interference, than is to be found under Catholic sovereigns.' (Note of Mr. Hardman.)
[2] Lord's Life of Maitland, p. 142.
[3] C.O.R. Malta, No. 26 (1813-14).

MINUTE BY HIS EXCELLENCY THE GOVERNOR.[1]

His Excellency on assuming the government of these Islands is most happy to find that the severe calamity with which Malta has been afflicted is rapidly decreasing, and he is firmly persuaded that a steady, rigid, and uniform adherence to those wise and salutary restrictions enjoined by His Excellency's predecessor will, within a very limited period, completely eradicate the plague now, and he trusts for ever, from this Island.

Until that desirable object be attained it will be impossible for His Excellency to enter upon any of those measures he has been charged by His Royal Master to carry into effect, with a view to consolidate and establish on a firm and permanent basis the happiness and prosperity of these Islands. His Excellency, however, cannot refrain from stating to the Maltese, even thus early, the greatest interest His Royal Highness the Prince Regent, acting in the name and on behalf of His Majesty, has been graciously pleased to take in their welfare—the deep consideration he has given to their hitherto uncertain and unsettled state—and His gracious determination henceforth to recognise the people of Malta and Gozo as subjects of the British Crown, and as entitled to its fullest protection. It will be His Excellency's duty, in carrying into effect His Royal Master's benevolent instructions on this head, to secure to the Maltese in the fullest manner the free exercise of their religion; to maintain their ecclesiastical establishment; to introduce such amelioration in the proceedings of the courts of law as will secure to everyone the certainty of speedy and effective justice; to make such improvement in the laws themselves as past experience or change of circumstances may have rendered necessary and advisable; and, in short, to adopt every measure that may be requisite to secure to the inhabitants a full share of that happiness, wealth, security, and prosperity fortunately enjoyed by all the subjects of the British Empire in every part of the world.

Until His Excellency can with propriety enter upon this course of proceedings he expects from the public functionaries of all descriptions a steady and energetic adherence to those measures so wisely laid down by his worthy and excellent predecessor, and from the people the calm and temperate endurance of those privations, absolutely necessary to be tolerated under the afflicting circumstances in which they have been placed—circumstances which no human wisdom could avert—but which may gradually be subdued by the energy of Government and the acquiescence of all ranks in the measures, however painful, yet absolutely necessary to be adopted to that effect.

Palace, Valetta, 5th *October* 1813.

By the end of January 1814 the Island was considered to be free from the epidemic, which had raged for close upon ten months,[2] and on the 4th February, Sir Thomas Maitland issued the following Proclamation and Minute, wherein His Excellency expressed his desire ' now to carry into effect the measures of Government with

[1] C.O.R. Malta, No. 26 (1813-14).
[2] The first case was reported 16th April 1813. (Note of Mr. Hardman.)

which he had been charged by his Sovereign,' and defined a system for the conduct of public business.

PROCLAMATION AND MINUTE OF SIR THOMAS MAITLAND.

Proclamation.

4th February 1814.

His Excellency the Governor from the cessation of the plague is at length fortunately enabled to commence carrying into effect those measures with which he is charged by his Sovereign.

In his Minute of the 5th October, when he assumed the government of these Islands, he explained to the people of Malta and Gozo that it was His Royal Master's gracious intention to recognise them as subjects of the British Crown, and that in consequence he had assumed the sovereignty of these possessions.

His Excellency therefore directs that all the armorial bearings and other emblems of sovereignty of every kind, wherever they may be found, be removed, but with that degree of observance and decency due to an Order of great antiquity and much well-deserved celebrity, and that in their place His Majesty's arms be substituted as soon as they can be prepared.

His Excellency further directs that all the courts of law within these possessions be hereafter styled His Majesty's Courts of Justice; that the judges be denominated in all petitions and on all occasions His Majesty's judges, and that in every part of the legal process in these Islands, where the name of the Grand Master may have heretofore been used, the name of His Majesty be in future substituted.

Palace, Valetta, *4th February* 1814.

Minute by His Excellency the Governor.

His Excellency having signified in his Proclamation of this date that he is now about to commence those measures with which he is charged by his Sovereign, it becomes necessary in order to do this with effect, that all the departments of Government should have a fixed and invariable rule laid down for their guidance relative to the orders they are to receive, and the applications they may have occasion to make.

His Excellency the Governor therefore signifies that in future all orders, of whatever kind, will be given to every department by Government alone, and that such orders will be issued, as occasion may require, either by the Governor himself or through the office of the Chief Secretary to Government, and that no other office whatsoever has any other power or authority to issue orders of any kind.

From this general rule are excepted the Administrators of Public Property, who will receive their instructions and orders from the Government through the medium of the Treasurer.

All applications are in like manner to be made from the different departments direct to Government. When the application attaches to a general concern, it is to be made invariably to the Chief Secretary to Government. When it applies to an individual concern it may be made to the Governor himself or to his private Secretary.

THE BRITISH ADMINISTRATION UP TO MAY 1814

His Excellency having observed that in several instances an acquiescence to a proposition made verbally has been deemed sufficient grounds for supposing that Government has approved of such proposal, it is to be clearly understood that no such acquiescence is to be deemed any authority, and that invariably after such acquiescence the proposition must be submitted in writing, through the proper channel, to be regularly and systematically laid before Government, when an answer will be given to such proposition in writing.

It is further clearly to be understood that all applications, letters, and reports of every kind are to be directed to the Chief Secretary to Government, and above the direction is to be stated, 'On His Majesty's Service,' and every application, letter, or report, not having this direction will be considered null and void.

In consequence of the abdication of Napoleon on 11th April 1814, an assembly of the representatives of the Powers took place in Paris for the purpose of arranging terms of peace. By the 30th May the Ministers of Austria, Russia, Great Britain, and Prussia on the one part, and France on the other, were able to complete the treaty, whereby Malta became *unconditionally* a British Colony in the following words :—

Art. 7. 'The Island of Malta and its dependencies shall belong in full right and sovereignty to His Britannic Majesty.'

Art. 32. 'Within two months all the Powers who have been engaged in the present war will send Plenipotentiaries to Vienna to complete at a general Congress the arrangements and dispositions of the present treaty.'

Thus did Malta finally become a British possession. But at what cost ! Not only had Great Britain to bear heavy sacrifices in treasure prior to the treaty of 1802, but also those experienced during the war of eleven years which followed the rupture of that treaty, a war, so far as England and France were concerned, waged *principally* on account of Malta. In that period the British casualties in Europe amounted to from 25,000 to 30,000 men *annually*. In the year 1813 her expenditure for the army amounted to £37,000,000, for the Navy £22,000,000, for advances to Continental States £10,000,000 (of which latter sum £316,666 was paid to the Neapolitan Government), and her total expenditure to the enormous sum of £117,000,000. All this by 1814 (from 1803 only) had increased her National Debt by £421,000,000.

But this was not all. By the terms of the Treaties of Paris (1814 and 1815) Great Britain relinquished to France all the conquests she had made in the continents or in the seas of America, Africa, and Asia since the 1st January 1792, including Cayenne and Martinique captured in 1809, Guadeloupe and Bourbon in 1810. Also to Holland, in accordance with Articles 6 and 9 of the Treaty of the 30th May 1814, and by a Special Convention ratified in London on the

30th August 1814, all British conquests were restored, with the exception of the Cape of Good Hope (captured in 1806), Demerara and Berbice, and for these, with other engagements, she paid as compensation the sum of £6,000,000.[1] The British conquests so restored to Holland were Surinam, captured in 1804, Curaçoa and St. Eustatius in 1807, Amboyna, Banda and Ternate in 1810, the Moluccas, together with Batavia and her other possessions in Java, captured in 1811.

At the Congress of Vienna, when Austria, Spain, France, Great Britain, Portugal, Prussia, Russia, Sweden and Norway were represented, and which closed on the 9th June 1815, the Treaty of Paris of the 30th May 1814 was fully confirmed.

In consequence of the events of the year 1815 a second meeting of Plenipotentiaries was held at Paris, and on the 20th November 1815 it was enacted by Article VIII, and agreed to by Austria, Great Britain, Prussia, and Russia on the one part, and France on the other, that 'all the dispositions of the Treaty of Paris of the 30th May 1814 relative to countries ceded by that treaty apply equally to the different territories and districts ceded by the present treaty.'

[1] Martens' *Recueil de Traités*, vol. x. pp. 57-60 and 715.

CHAPTER XXIV

A RETROSPECT AND COMPARISON

In order correctly to appreciate the benefits which the Maltese people have derived from their connexion with Great Britain, in the limited sense of their commercial and financial prosperity, reference may be made to the following statistical tables, which relate to trade and revenue, population, &c., as they existed in 1798, and Savings Bank accumulations since the opening of the Bank in 1834. A comparison will be made with the returns for 1905, and intermediate years.

TRADE AND REVENUE.

In submitting a comparative statement of the trade of Malta and Gozo as it existed in 1798 with that of 1905, it is well to remember that, although these islands have always been cultivated most industriously wherever soil could be found on the rocky surface, their produce at the former period was restricted to cotton, cereals, and oranges—and all three to a very limited extent.

According to a MS. in the British Museum, cotton was the chief production of the islands at the close of the eighteenth and beginning of the nineteenth centuries. Enough was spun to clothe the inhabitants, but the quality of the material was too coarse for any market but Barbary. Spinning was the chief business of the poor. The exportation of the raw cotton was prohibited, but the thread was exported to Barcelona to the value of £500,000 per annum; oranges for export to about £2000.[1]

The produce in wheat and barley at the same period, at a time when the population was not very much greater than half its present number, was only sufficient for nine months' consumption, and the imports in consequence consisted of wheat, barley and wine, all three of which were obtained chiefly from Sicily.

That the import trade was insignificant is proved by the Customs returns for 1792 to 1796, which are given by Mr. Thornton, late Auditor-General in the Malta Government Civil Service.[2] During

---

[1] Brit. Mus. MSS., Stowe's, No. 102.
[2] *Finances of Malta*, p. 35. Captain Ball, in his letter of 15th December 1799 to Dundas, gave £400,000 as the value of the cotton exported. See Chap. xiii.—J. H. R.

these five years, the average annual Revenue derived from the Customs was as follows :—

Indirect tax on bread through the corn monopoly	£3,650
Wine	£5,800
Duties levied on other articles imported, including tobacco	£7,800
	£17,250

The manufactured articles or goods for export appear also to have been almost nil, and were comprised of Malta stone, cut for building purposes, cheap cigars, filigree work, and coral.[1]

During a debate in the House of Commons on the 'Affairs of Malta' held in May 1802, a Return of the Territorial Revenues and Commercial Duties collected within the Islands of Malta, Gozo, and Comino previous to the French Occupation of the Islands in the year 1798, was called for. This Return was presented by order on the 12th of that month, and is evidently taken from Captain Ball's elaborate Report of the 26th December 1800, detailed in Chapter xvii. of this work, and for the purpose of comparison is briefly repeated here :[2]

	£	s.	d.
1. Estates allotted to the Grand Master	8,175	13	5½
2. Estates belonging to the Treasury, or Common Tesoro	972	3	3¼
3. Estates of different foundations, become the property of Government	7,832	17	2
4. Estates belonging to the respective Langues	1,088	8	9
5. Estates belonging to the College of the Jesuits	618	19	4
6. Interest of money lent by Government upon mortgage	175	12	2
7. Customs	10,000	0	0
8. Excise on wine	5,000	0	0
9. 3½ per cent. on the sale of real property	800	0	0
	£34,663	14	2

Two days later, during a continuation of the debate, Sir William Young, member for St. Mawes, Cornwall, stated 'that he had recently resided for ten weeks in that island, and was able to affirm that there were not five men there who could be called merchants,' nor under the circumstances could it be otherwise.[3]

We are further told by Lieutenant Æneas Anderson, of the 40th Regiment, who was quartered in Malta for twelve months, 1800-01, whose 'Journal of the Secret Expedition to Egypt' was published in 1802, that 'the Customs prior to 1798, exclusive of

---

[1] See an interesting account of the resources of Malta, dated Malta, 16 June 1800 (probably by Sir Thomas Graham), in the *Dropmore Papers*, vol. vi. p. 249.—J. H. R.
[2] Brit. Mus. Newspaper Dept.
[3] Cobbett's *Weekly Register*, vol. ii. p. 1325.

A RETROSPECT AND COMPARISON

the bread tax, gave £10,000 as the revenue of Malta, whilst wine yielded £5000 annually, and that the largest income in the island, with the exception of that of the Bishop, was £400 per annum.'[1]

These details indicate the general poverty of the inhabitants.

With the advent of a British garrison and a large fleet at the close of the year 1800 trade soon developed, and owing to Bonaparte's Berlin Decree of November 1806, which closed most European ports to British trade, Malta became an important emporium, whence Italy and Central Europe, through the Adriatic, became supplied with goods of British origin. As a result of this action on the part of France some thirty to forty eminent British firms established commercial branches in the island, which laid the foundation of trade that for a century has continued to expand in various directions.

The Crimean war (1854–1856) left immense sums of money in the islands; and in later years the opening of the Suez Canal has been of immense benefit to the general trade, owing to the position of Malta and the introduction of steam navigation, which made it a convenient coaling station.

Returning to the closing years of the government of these islands by the Knights of St. John, we are informed by Auditor-General Thornton in his work already quoted, 'Finances of Malta,'[2] that the revenue of the islands under that Government was derived from three sources, viz. (a) the General Treasury; (b) the Magisterial Receipt; (c) Municipal Services.

The income received under the first of these sources, namely (a) the General Treasury, was obtained from dues, imposts, and fees laid upon the dignitaries and commanderies *abroad*, and therefore for the purpose of this comparative statement cannot be included.

From the information obtained through official documents, the average result of the second source, (b) or Magisterial Receipt, consisting of revenue derived from rents of landed property and Customs dues, for the period 1778 to 1788 amounted annually to £20,132
whilst that obtained from (c) Municipal Services reached . 8,203

Total . . . £28,335

From 1815 to 1827, under British rule, the gross revenue, according to the same authority, amounted annually to about £100,000.[3]

From Martin's 'Statistics of British Colonies,'[4] we gather that the revenue of Malta for the years 1828 to 1831 was as follows:

[1] Anderson, *op. cit.* p. 178.
[2] Thornton, *op. cit.* pp. 29, 31.
[3] *Ibid.* p. 65.
[4] Martin, *op. cit.* p. 583.

538   A HISTORY OF MALTA

```
1828   .   .   .   .   .   .   £104,034
1829   .   .   .   .   .   .    103,072
1830   .   .   .   .   .   .    102,030
1831   .   .   .   .   .   .    103,086
```

and for the years 1832, 1833 and 1834, as given by Thornton,[1] we have this result:

	1832.	1833.	1834.
Customs and port dues	£10,511	£11,283	£13,324
Excise on wines and spirits	14,485	16,107	16,751
Grain department	35,346	37,314	37,898
Quarantine	7,762	4,212	3,718
Chief Secretary and dependent offices	1,747	1,954	1,965
Land rent and taxes	27,102	25,827	26,571
Judicial departments	3,506	3,363	3,306
Interest of capital	171	376	376
Incidental	472	1,274	132
	(1) £101,102	(2) £101,710	(3) £104,041

In 1835, owing to the removal of duties upon sixty articles of import, besides a reduction in other duties and taxes, the net amount of revenue was reduced to £95,558.

In 1837 the Royal Commissioners who, in September of the year previous, had been appointed by the Home Government to investigate and report on the desirability of reforming the administration of the island informed Lord Glenelg, then Secretary of State for the Colonies, that the revenue of the Government was obtained from the following sources, the annual produce of each of which was stated, in round numbers, to be as follows:

1. Rents of the Crown lands £23,000
2. Small internal taxes (chiefly licences for exercising trades, also a tax on the transfer of landed property, and an auction duty) . 2,400
3. Fees of Court and Government offices, postage, receipts of Government printing office, fines, &c. 5,200
4. Duties on imports, tonnage dues, and quarantine dues . . 65,000

£95,600

From 1840, the following quinquennial returns, extracted from official reports and Blue Books, are given below:—

RETURN OF LIVE STOCK IN MALTA AND GOZO
EXTRACTED FROM OFFICIAL RECORDS AND BLUE-BOOKS

	1830	1835	1840	1845	1850	1855	1860	1865
Horses, mules and asses	4,905	5,022	4,390	3,878	4,034	4,249	4,374	4,842
Horned cattle	6,457	6,501	5,372	5,096	3,783	4,897	5,258	6,134
Sheep	13,948	12,535	10,605	10,513	10,846	7,889	9,257	9,197
Goats	4,729	6,981	3,050	3,641	3,595	2,895	3,658	3,706

[1] Thornton, op. cit. pp. 65, 73.

A RETROSPECT AND COMPARISON

	1870	1875	1880	1885	1890	1895	1900	1904–1905
Horses, mules, and asses	4,427	4,217	4,937	6,125	6,978	7,153	10,510	10,426
Horned cattle	4,312	7,293	8,570	9,005	8,134	7,605	7,877	7,851
Sheep	9,053	10,621	10,478	10,529	10,930	14,800	14,323	18,529
Goats	3,169	4,334	5,233	5,245	8,463	11,663	15,924	18,419

POPULATION.

It has been justly observed that one of the most convincing proofs of the prosperity of a country is that of the regular and continuous increase of its population. That of Malta and Gozo, notwithstanding the extremely high rate of mortality amongst infants and children up to five years of age, may be considered satisfactory.

Although for the present purpose it is necessary only to commence with the estimated number of the inhabitants at the time of the French conquest in 1798, it may nevertheless be interesting to observe that when Malta and Gozo were ceded by Charles V to the Order of St. John of Jerusalem in 1530, the number of the inhabitants, as given by Bosio, the historian of the Order, was 25,000.

In the Malta Public Library[1] there is a copy of a Report prepared in 1572 by the Apostolic Vicar resident in Malta, Monsignor Gaspare Visconti, for the information of Gregory XIII, from which it would appear that owing to some unexplained cause the number of inhabitants had fallen at that period to 18,000. But by 1590 again, according to Bosio, whose historical work was published four years later, the number had increased to 32,500, of which 3,500 were Knights, soldiers, slaves, and prisoners.

For the purpose of computing the number of inhabitants prior to 1842 reliance has been placed upon information derived from the registers of the various parish priests, and therefore such estimates can only be deemed approximate; but in that year a regular census was taken, although the decennial returns on modern lines, as prepared by Giglio, were not introduced until the year 1861.

Various authorities, including Bonaparte, Ransijat, and Coleridge, give 100,000 as the number of inhabitants in Malta and Gozo in 1798, of whom, according to General Regnier's report on the capture of Gozo, dated the 11th June 1798, there were from 13,000 to 14,000 in that island. The following tabular statement is given, with the source whence the information is derived:

[1] M.P.L. MSS. No. xxiii.

540 A HISTORY OF MALTA

Year	Source of Information	Number	Increase
1798	Various authorities	100,000	
1806	Old almanack	92,824	
1808	,, Miscellanea, M.P.L., No. 463	93,011	
1813	Dr. Burrell, in his report on the plague of that year, returned as the probable number of the population for Malta as . . . . . 96,403 and for Gozo. . . . 14,400	110,803	
1823	Official records	112,204	
1826	,,	119,736	
1828	As per statement in Census report of 1901	115,945	
1836	Official records	123,148	
21st March 1842	Census	114,499	
31st March 1851	,,	123,496	Nine Years Annual 8,997 999
31st October 1861	,, as compiled by Giglio (exclusive of Garrison and Navy, but including Malta Fencibles Artillery)	134,055	Decennial 10,559 1,055
3rd May 1871	,,	141,775	7,720 772
3rd April 1881	,,	149,782	8,007 800
5th April 1891	,,	165,337	15,255 1,525
31st March 1901	,,	184,742	19,705 1,970
1st April 1906	Estimated	205,062	Quinquennial 20,320 2,032

SAVINGS BANKS.

The Malta Savings Bank, established by proclamation on the 27th November 1833, was opened for business on the 4th January 1834, whilst that for Gozo was opened on the 1st June 1853. The following statement shows the number of deposits, and the amount to the credit of depositors, at the end of each of the following years, from 1840:

	MALTA.				GOZO.			
Year	Number of Deposits	Increase	Amount	Increase	Number of Deposits	Increase	Amount	Increase
			£ s. d.	£ s. d.			£ s. d.	£ s. d.
1840			9,391 17 0					
1845			23,004 12 9	13,612 15 9				
1850			32,180 7 5	9,175 14 8			Returns not available	
1855			47,639 2 0	15,458 14 7				
1860	1201		55,568 5 3	7,929 3 3				
1865	2058	857	110,009 15 0	54,441 9 9	219		8,580 18 4	
1870	2730	672	157,332 18 3	47,323 3 3	196	{ 23 decrease	7,082 15 7	{1,498 2 9 decrease
1875	2944	214	173,669 6 6	16,336 8 3	195	{ 1 decrease	8,258 12 6	1,175 16 11
1880	3751	807	250,906 7 8	77,237 1 2	257	62	12,066 19 5	3,808 6 11
1885	4411	660	323,366 17 10	72,460 10 2	394	137	19,715 8 1	7,648 8 8
1890	5116	705	428,321 0 8	104,954 2 10	578	184	39,026 11 3	19,311 3 2
1895	5401	285	426,995 8 8	{1,325 12 0 decrease	662	84	46,047 0 11	7,020 9 8
1900	6207	806	480,912 16 11	53,917 8 3	753	91	54,658 13 10	8,611 12 11
1905–6	7315	1108	515,874 10 9	34,961 13 10	1056	303	69,994 17 1	15,336 3 3

A RETROSPECT AND COMPARISON

During the seventy-three years of this bank's existence in Malta two runs upon it have occurred, brought about by unprincipled political agitators. The first took place in 1895, when about £50,000 were withdrawn, the second in 1904, when about £44,000 were withdrawn, but in both instances they were met by the bank without any inconvenience.

NOTE.

This chapter cannot be more fittingly brought to a close than by giving an extract from Sir William Thornton's 'Memoirs on the Finances of Malta' (p. 62), which affords the amplest proof of the practical sympathy which the British Government has displayed towards the inhabitants of these islands since the time of their acquisition. From this extract it will be seen that between September 1800 and December 1829 the net amount of £668,666 7s. 2d. sterling was supplied out of the revenues of the United Kingdom, in aid of the civil revenue of these Islands. This sum went towards the re-establishment of the Municipal Grain Institution, the sale of wheat to the public at moderate prices during times of dearth, the construction of granaries, the liberation of Maltese held in slavery in the Bagnio at Constantinople, charitable dispensations to the inhabitants during the plague of 1813 and 1814, and other assistance, as follows :—

		£	s.	d.
1800. Sept.	Value of 6,000 Sicilian ounces furnished through the Hon. Arthur Paget, Minister at Palermo	4,444	8	10
Nov.	Amount of a draft drawn by Sir A. J. Ball on the Hon. Arthur Paget at Palermo, who reimbursed himself by means of his own drafts drawn on the Lords Commissioners of His Majesty's Treasury	2,571	15	0
1801.	Value of 40,000 Sicilian ounces furnished through Commissary-General Motz . .	25,417	14	5
1800–01.	As much of the value of wheat purchased in Greece in three years, through the agency of Mr. John Tyson, as was discharged by his draft drawn on their Lordships . . .	39,954	12	10
	Amount of drafts drawn on their Lordships by Sir A. J. Ball	20,634	11	4
1801–02.	Amount of drafts drawn on their Lordships by Charles Cameron, Esquire	22,185	16	8
1800–03.	As much of the value of wheat purchased in Turkey through the intervention of the Earl of Elgin as was settled for in his account with their Lordships	27,561	16	1
1802.	Expenses incurred at Constantinople by the Earl of Elgin for the redemption of Maltese from slavery, and charged by him, in account with their Lordships	3,783	14	3
1805.	Value of 32,000 ounces silver retained by the Government of Malta out of a larger sum received from England by H.M.S. *Aurora*, *Renommée*, and *Aimable*	8,400	0	0
	Carried forward . . £154,954	9	5	

		£	s.	d.
	Brought forward	154,954	9	5
1807.	Value of 200,000 Spanish dollars received by the said Government from on board H.M.S. *Thames*	46,666	13	4
1802–09.	Amount of drafts drawn on their Lordships by and under the authority of Sir Alexander John Ball during his second administration	225,273	1	1
1814.	Net amount derived from fees received on licences to trade with enemies' ports, commencing in 1808, and ending at the peace of 1814, which funds, although a perquisite of the British Treasury, as bearing the charge of the war, were applied in aid of the civil revenues of Malta	37,910	3	7
1814.	Amount of money received over from the military chest during the year ending the 30th September 1814	155,875	0	0
1811.	Surplus of the grant of £18,000 made by their Lordships to indemnify those individuals whose property was destroyed by the explosion of a powder magazine in 1806 . . . £18,000 0 0 *Less* amount expended in liquidation of the claims. . . 15,909 15 1½	2,090	4	10½
1815–29.	Balance of the money furnished by their Lordships to the agent in London from the 1st January 1815 to the 31st December 1829. Amounts furnished . . £297,230 8 0 Less amounts refunded by the local Government at various periods 267,944 6 1	29,286	1	11
1827.	Amount of money received from the military chest in 1827 to enable the withdrawal from circulation of the copper coinage left by the Government of the Order	16,610	12	11½
		£668,666	7	2

In addition to the evidence which these statistical tables exhibit of the advantages derived by the Maltese people from their connection with Great Britain, there must also be mentioned the substantial help rendered by the Mother Country in times of great distress, as, for example, during visitations of cholera, or in aid of great public works such as the Grand Harbour extension, drainage, water, roads, &c. These latter expenditures have been justified before British Parliamentary constituents on the ground that the British garrison and Navy were benefited by them. Nevertheless, in wealthier colonies it may safely be assumed that the cost of such works would have gladly and exclusively been borne by them, in view of the benefits which accrue to the people by the presence of a garrison and fleet, and consequent increased trade.

A RETROSPECT AND COMPARISON

Statement of Expenditure incurred by Great Britain for the Military Protection and in aid of the Civil Establishment of Malta, *exclusive* of the Disbursements for Military Works (Fortifications, Barracks, or Stores) or for Naval Expenditure on the Fleet, or Naval Works, such as Dry Docks, Breakwater, &c. :—

Year(s)	Source	Amount
1829. 1832.	From 'Martin's Colonial History' vol. v. p. 280.	£101,181 0 0 / 100,462 0 0
1900. 1901. 1902. 1903.	From Malta.	615,613 16 0 / 637,318 19 4 / 719,383 0 0
1903. 1904. 1904. 1905.	Blue Books.	699,057 0 0 / 720,788 0 0

It is to be regretted that the statements of amounts expended by the Army upon fortifications, &c., or by the Admiralty on behalf of the Navy, or for naval works, such as dry docks, breakwaters, &c., which of late years have been enormous, are not available.

COMPARATIVE YEARLY STATEMENT OF MALTA REVENUE,

	1840	1845	1850	1855	1860	1865
	£ s. d.	£ s. d.	£ s. d.	£ s. d.	£ s. d.	£ s. d.
Rent and dues of land revenue	25,188 5 4	23,101 1 5¾	28,033 4 8¼	27,975 7 1½	33,937 6 6½	36,362 17 7¼
Customs	—	—	—	—	—	—
Transfer duty on immovable property	1,175 11 0	498 0 4¼	—	—	—	—
Auction duty	126 4 1¾	174 9 2¼	—	—	—	—
Miscellaneous land taxes and dues	1,594 15 0	—	—	—	—	—
Import duty on goods . .	54,678 19 1	60,670 13 5	85,587 19 5	85,692 9 7	94,659 5 9	113,759 5 3
Store rent on bonded goods .	520 19 8	902 16 8	—	—	—	—
Tonnage dues on shipping .	3,084 5 0	4,124 18 0	—	—	—	—
Office fees of the Customs .	77 10 0	—	—	—	—	—
Quarantine dues . . .	3,003 14 2	2,282 14 10	1,608 0 5	30 19 6	—	479 6 3
Fees Chief Secretary's office .	122 15 6	—	509 14 0	521 10 5	585 0 5½	766 18 3
Postage of letters . . .	170 9 2	87 3 11	79 8 7	73 4 4	26 17 11	79 2 10
Licences, court fines, &c. .	—	—	—	—	—	—
Printing office with Gazette .	39 3 3	—	—	—	—	—
Public registry of contracts .	127 13 4	148 1 3	—	—	—	—
Dues and fees of Court Justice	2,802 1 4	2,198 1 0¼	—	—	—	—
Dues of the Charity Institution	114 16 5	190 18 6	—	—	—	—
Fines and forfeitures . .	285 11 11½	—	—	—	—	—
Stoppage of salaries of civil officers on leave . . .	126 10 8¼	—	—	—	—	—
Proceeds of art manufacture, home of industry . .	127 17 7	—	—	—	—	—
Salaries for separate charity funds	928 6 8	680 0 0	—	—	—	—
Money received for convicts' labour	91 13 4	—	—	—	—	—
Money received through confessional	—	—	—	—	—	—
Export duty on coal . .	—	826 18 8	—	—	—	—
Licences	—	1,642 5 0	1,519 0 0	1,374 5 0	1,949 15 0	2,168 5 0
Incidental receipts . . .	—	579 2 0¼	—	—	—	—
Land sales	—	—	162 10 6¼	370 16 3¾	328 16 9½	604 2 8¼
Fines, forfeitures, and fees of Court	—	—	6,075 18 8¾	5,519 17 2¼	4,991 19 0½	5,198 11 4¼
Sale of Government property	—	—	1,425 6 2¼	182 15 6½	76 3 9½	629 2 8½
Reimbursement	—	—	414 5 11	759 13 3½	1,031 7 5¾	1,290 3 5¼
Special receipts	—	—	3,877 18 2¼	4,237 10 1½	6,647 13 10	7,036 2 0½
Miscellaneous	—	—	—	—	—	—
Interest	—	—	—	—	—	—
Railway	—	—	—	—	—	—
Water service	—	—	—	—	—	—
Stamps	—	—	—	—	—	—
Electric lighting	—	—	—	—	—	—
Totals	94,387 2 8	98,107 4 3¾	129,293 6 8½	126,738 8 5	144,234 6 6½	168,373 17 5

EXTRACTED FROM OFFICIAL REPORTS AND BLUE-BOOKS.

1870	1875	1880	1885	1890	1895	1900	1904–1905
£ s. d.	£ s. d.	£ s. d.	£ s. d.	£ s. d.	£ s. d.	£ s. d.	£ s. d.
35,701 9 10½	36,598 7 9½	36,970 6 4½	37,910 8 1½	39,386 3 11½	44,583 4 1½	44,567 18 2½	45,053 18 5
—	—	—	—	—	168,729 3 7	193,367 19 2	267,733 7 7
—	—	—	—	—	—	—	—
—	—	—	—	—	—	—	—
—	—	—	—	—	—	—	—
97,029 9 2	109,497 1 1	120,496 19 2	135,907 11 3	160,162 5 8	—	—	—
1,622 9 2	—	—	—	—	—	—	—
5,791 0 6	—	—	—	—	—	—	—
—	—	—	—	—	—	—	—
148 14 0	534 15 0	407 13 9	360 10 3	704 13 7	8,905 14 2	9,331 13 3	8,493 13 8
769 6 6	986 7 7	1,188 10 2	1,758 12 8	4,421 18 11	—	—	—
93 7 4	122 6 5	129 5 9	7,976 18 9	10,452 1 2	13,337 17 9	15,219 18 4	22,547 0 11
—	—	—	—	—	5,605 5 5¼	5,519 5 10½	8,002 13 7¾
—	—	—	—	—	—	—	—
—	—	—	—	—	—	—	—
—	—	—	—	—	—	—	—
—	—	—	—	—	—	—	—
—	—	—	—	—	—	—	—
—	—	—	—	—	—	—	—
—	—	—	—	—	—	—	—
—	—	—	—	—	—	—	—
—	—	—	—	—	—	—	—
—	—	—	—	—	—	—	—
—	—	—	—	—	—	—	—
1,529 15 0	2,914 15 0	2,968 15 0	3,115 5 0	4,153 14 11	—	—	—
—	—	—	—	—	—	—	—
62 8 9½	1,000 10 1	218 4 2½	—	—	—	—	—
5,353 12 3	5,540 6 1½	6,380 8 3½	5,317 1 8½	6,927 4 2½	—	—	—
105 2 0	412 17 9½	164 7 8¾	—	—	—	—	—
1,379 8 3¾	4,467 19 9½	2,943 8 4¾	3,180 19 3¾	4,454 17 2¾	22,623 1 4¾	24,604 8 8	28,650 15 5
9,044 13 7¾	10,892 16 0½	11,926 17 3¾	17,784 2 2½	30,591 5 10¼	—	—	—
—	—	—	—	—	—	—	2,773 1 10
—	—	—	—	—	27,376 6 0½	29,390 1 1½	34,223 10 6¾
—	—	—	—	—	5,963 2 0	7,735 9 7½	9,929 0 7
—	—	—	—	—	8,316 19 9	11,898 3 4½	18,701 3 4
—	—	—	—	—	—	1,811 3 9½	4,706 14 0
—	—	—	—	—	—	13,312 5 6	17,020 9 5
158,630 16 6	172,968 2 8½	183,794 16 1½	213,311 9 3½	261,254 5 6½	305,440 14 3¾	356,758 6 10¾	467,835 9 4½

APPENDIX I

THE FINANCIAL CONDITION OF THE ORDER OF ST. JOHN AND THE REVENUE OF THE ISLANDS IN 1798

THE finances of the Order during the economical government of the early portion of De Rohan's Magistracy (1775–97) had been most satisfactory, but in 1792, the Decree of the French Government abolishing the Order in French territory, with the confiscation of its property therein, was a death blow to its prosperity.

Bosredon Ransijat, former Treasurer of the Order, in his work entitled 'The Siege and Blockade of Malta,' gives the following statement of the revenue in 1788, as an average of the previous ten years:—

LANGUES AND PRIORIES

			livres	(francs)
France	Langue de Provence		477,395	
	" d'Auvergne		172,756	
	" France		742,823	
				1,392,974
Spain	" d'Aragon		276,137	
	" de Castille		375,355	
				651,492
	Priory of Portugal	. . .		220,503
	" Poland	. . .		15,880
	Langue d'Italie	. . .		564,802
	" d'Allemagne	. . .		98,221
	" de Bavière	. . .		5,175
	In the Island of Malta	. .		207,602
	Total Income	.		3,156,719
	" Expenditure		.	2,967,503
	Surplus		.	189,216 *Livres*

Mr. Thornton, who held the appointment of Auditor of Accounts in the early years of the British occupation, in his valuable memoir on the 'Finances of Malta,' takes exception to the above statement, but the result of his investigations does not appear to make any very appreciable difference. Mr. Thornton gives as the annual average income for the same period, ... £136,417
and that of the expenditure 128,533

Leaving a surplus of   £7,884

As the next decennial Report would have been rendered in 1798, the year of the invasion and capture of the island by the French, it is improbable that such a statement was ever presented; none has been published. Thanks however to a Report which had been called for in the House of Commons during a debate, and presented on the 12th May 1802 (referred to later on), we learn that the total Revenue of the islands prior to their occupation by the French, amounted to £34,663 14s. 2d.

It will thus be observed that owing to the French confiscations and other European troubles the Revenue had fallen from £136,417 in 1788 to £34,663 14s. 2d. in 1798, or to about one-fourth.[1]

From Bosredon Ransijat we learn that in 1777 a Religious Order of Hospitallers (created in 1590 for the relief of sufferers from a species of leprosy, then called ' St. Anthony's fire ') was constrained to join the Order of St. John of Jerusalem, as being the nearest in affinity, and after long negotiations its property, known as the 'Antonine Estates,' was eventually conveyed to the Knights of Malta, subject to various life pensions, charges, and conditions.

These charges upon the property became eventually exceedingly burdensome, for by 1788 the Order had expended upon it £85,675, which by 1792, it was calculated, had been increased to £100,000. These large amounts were disbursed in the expectation that by 1794 a refunding might reasonably be expected to commence. Unfortunately these anticipations were not to be realised, for owing to the French Republican Government in 1792 confiscating the estates held by the Order in France, their annual income was reduced by close upon £50,000. Three years later a Financial Report was furnished to Grand Master De Rohan, dated the 9th December 1795, showing the loss which this spoliation had entailed to its annual income, amounting to £47,178, in addition to the loss of its aforesaid Antonine Estates, and the £100,000 expended thereon. Although by the strictest economy the expenditure in the following year was reduced by £14,689, there was a deficit of £34,249 in 1796, which, there was every reason to expect, would be constant and permanent, unless the negotiations already commenced between the Grand Master and the Empress Catherine II of Russia were brought to a successful issue.

Prior to the dismemberment of the Kingdom of Poland, there were various ' Commanderies' therein, of some considerable value, belonging to the Order, which had fallen to Russia in the third and final partition of that Kingdom in 1795.[2]

De Rohan considered the occasion a favourable opportunity, in view of their exhausted exchequer, to dispatch a special envoy, beseeching Catherine II to become Protectress of the Order. The Bailiff de Litta was selected for the office, as a *persona grata*, being at the time in the naval service of Russia, but the death of Catherine II in 1796 delayed the negotiations, which were continued under her son and successor, Paul I. These negotiations gave great umbrage to the French Republican Government, which, since the commencement of the Revolution in 1789, and its consequent foreign wars, had been ever on the alert to discover violations of neutrality, for which an account sooner or later would have to be rendered. The Grand Master and his Council were fully aware of the peril thus incurred, but their financial position had become desperate, and although feeling the step taken was hazardous, they knew from sad experience that clemency was not to be expected from France, whilst Russia might become their salvation.

Details of these negotiations for placing the Order under the protection of

---

[1] See for some of the economies effected by slave-labour, and the neglect of the works and artillery of Valetta, the details given in the *Note sur Malte*, of Vaubois, printed in full in Chap. x of this work.—J. H. R.

[2] See Talleyrand's *Memoirs*, vol. i. p. 210.

Russia, together with the original agreement between Russia and the Order of St. John to form a Russian Langue, which had been signed at St. Petersburg, 4/15th January 1797, by Alexandre Besborodko, and Prince Alexandre Kourakin on the one part, and Fr. Jules René Bailli Comte de Litta, on the other, fell into the hands of Bonaparte at Ancona where he captured the courier bearer of the dispatch.[1]

This step was considered by the French Government opposed to their interests, and an offence further aggravated by the appointment of the Prince of Condé as Grand Prior to the Russian Priory, whilst several commanderies of this new Langue were conferred upon other French political *émigrés* and gave occasion to the Directory to avail itself of the first opportunity, not only to suppress the Order, but to endeavour to possess itself of the island.

With the finances of the Order in this hopeless condition, unless a foreign power at once intervened and rendered prompt assistance, with disaffection growing amongst the people, owing to the impoverished state of the island, and discontent fostered by a local Republican party, which yearly increased in number and influence, nothing appeared wanting to favour the designs of Bonaparte, who saw in the possession of Malta a favourable *point d'appui*, in the direction of either Egypt, the Two Sicilies, or Greece, as circumstances might require.

[1] Arch. Nat., AF III 73.
See on this topic the information given in the Introduction to this volume, also *Corres. de Nap. I*, vol. iv. p. 16; and De la Jonquière, *Expédition d'Egypte*, vol. i. p. 657.—J. H. R.

APPENDIX II

REPORT ON THE REVENUE OF MALTA, WITH SOME OBSERVATIONS.

(*26th December* 1800?)

NOTE.—A copy of this report is found in the Manuscript Department, British Museum (Stowe MSS. Collection, 918).

This document is without signature or date, but from the references made to it in Lord Hobart's instructions to Commissioner Cameron of the 14th May 1801 (who was on the point of proceeding to Malta), it is undoubtedly proved to be that of Captain Alexander Ball, and should be dated the 26th December 1800. The financial portion of this report was presented to the House of Commons by order, on the 12th May 1802, entitled a 'Return of the Revenue of the Islands of Malta and Gozo, prior to the French occupation of 1798.'

This report is of the greatest interest and importance, owing to it being the first authentic and reliable statement of the affairs of Malta and Gozo which had been forwarded to the British Government, and by which, Lord Hobart, as Secretary of State for the Colonies, was guided in framing his instructions to the Royal Commissioner (as above referred to) for the future government of the islands. The report further treats of the past administration of the government of the islands under the Order of St. John, and the judicature and commerce.

STATEMENT OF THE PUBLIC REVENUE OF THE ISLANDS OF MALTA AND GOZO PRIOR TO THE FRENCH OCCUPATION IN 1798.

		SC.	T.	G.	SC.	T.	G.
Beni Magistrali							
Rustici	.	81,279	8	13			
Urbani .	. . .	477	0	0			
					81,756	8	13
Del Tesoro							
Beni Rustici . .	. . .	418	0	19			
Molini . . .	. . .	294	0	0			
Case . . .	. . .	6,020	6	6			
Camere e Botteghe	. . .	122	0	0			
Magazzini . .	. . .	2,867	0	0			
					9,721	7	5
Fondazione Paula							
Beni Rustici . .	. . . .	10,994	10	0			
Case . .	. . . .	183	0	0			
					11,177	10	0
Lascaris							
Beni Rustici . .	. . .	21,496	10	0			
Case . . .	. . .	1,493	6	0			
Camere e Botteghe	. . .	5,478	6	0			
Magazzini . .	. . .	5,275	0	0			
					33,743	10	0
	Carried forward				136,399	11	18

APPENDICES

		sc.	T.	G.	sc.	T.	G.
Brought forward					136,399	11	18
	Cottoner						
Beni Rustici		3,449	7	0			
Urbani		2,165	0	0			
Case		5,402	9	0			
Camere e Magazzini		2,587	11	0			
					13,605	3	0
	Perrellos						
Beni Rustici		10	4	0			
Molini		822	0	0			
Camere e Magazzini		3,704	8	0			
					4,537	0	0
	Villhena						
Beni Rustici		2,472	10	14			
Molini		2,940	0	0			
Case		3,719	0	0			
Cammere e Botteghe		185	0	0			
Magazzini		1,423	8	19			
					10,740	7	13
	Carnero						
Beni Rustici					210	0	0
	Passalacqua						
Beni Rustici		405	10	0			
Urbani		1,322	7	0			
					1,728	5	0
	Fondazione Marulli						
Beni Rustici					312	5	0
	Lomellino						
Beni Rustici		195	0	0			
Urbani		298	0	0			
					493	0	0
	Marradas						
Beni Rustici					476	6	0
	Caraffa						
Magazzini					250	0	0
	Gironda						
Beni Urbani					88	0	0
	Varie Commende						
Beni Urbani					966	3	0
	Collegio						
Beni Rustici		5,094	2	0			
Urbani		1,095	6	0			
					6,189	8	0
Partite Bollati					1,756	1	1
	Lingue						
Di Provinza	Beni Urbani				1,754	1	0
Alvernia	do.				1,410	0	0
Francia	do.				1,449	9	12
Italia	do.				1,605	6	0
Arrago e Navarra	do.				1,369	0	0
Alemagna	do.				114	0	0
Castiglia	do.				3,182	0	0
Dogana					100,000	0	0
Sisa sopra il vino					50,000	0	0
Sisa sopra i Beni stabili					8,000	0	0
[Say £34,663 12s.]	Totale				346,635	6	14

Varj dei suddetti Beni sono soggetti a pesi ed oblighi.

Or in other words the different foundations in Malta are the bequest of pious individuals. They are burdened with certain annual donations to churches and to convents. The precise sum is not ascertained, but the payment must be continued.

Accounts are kept in Maltese denominations, scudis, taris, and grains. Twenty grains make one tari, twelve taris one scudo, and ten scudi make one pound sterling according to the present rate of exchange.

Beni Rustici mean lands and gardens belonging to Government. The lands are capable of considerable improvement. The leases which have fallen in during the siege have been renewed for four years only, and the rents raised one-third more than before, without occasioning the smallest discontent.

Beni Urbani are houses and warehouses in town or country belonging to Government. They will not immediately yield the estimated rents. Many houses were damaged during the siege and revolution, and will require expensive repairs.

Almost the whole of the houses belonging to Government in town are now occupied by British and Neapolitan officers who do not pay rent. The warehouses situated in the *marina* or wharf are extremely commodious, and will yield a high rent when trade is in a flourishing state. At present the British and Neapolitan commissaries and quartermasters-general have engaged many of them, who do not pay rent.

Summary

	SC.	T.	G.
1. Beni magistrali	81,756	8	13
2. Del Tesoro	9,721	7	15
3. Delle diverse fondazioni	78,328	7	5
4. Lingue	10,884	4	12
5. Collegio	6,189	8	0
6. Partite Bollati	1,756	1	1
7. Dogana	100,000	0	0
8. Sisa sopra il vino	50,000	0	0
9. Sisa sopra i beni stabili	8,000	0	0
[Say £34,663 14s.] Totale	346,637	1	6

This abridged statement of the public revenue may require an explanation of the terms employed:

No. 1. *Beni magistrali* means lands and houses allotted for the expenses of the Grand Master's household.

No. 2. *Del Tesoro*. This is a property which accrued from legacies and from what was called the *dépouille* or *spoglie* of deceased Knights. The Order was heir to every deceased knight, and the funds arising from the sale of their effects, after paying the expenses of funeral and wages of servants, were sometimes employed to purchase houses or lands. The rents of these houses and lands were administered for the general use and expenditure of the Order by a Board called Commun Tesoro. These rents are now the property of Government.

The Commun Tesoro, besides the management of this separate fund, had the superintendence of all the receipts and expenditure of the Order. The Prieurs and Commandeurs who had the management of the estates of the Order in foreign countries were accountable to the Commun Tesoro in Malta, and obliged to remit a fifth, often a fourth, and sometimes a half, and even the whole of their receipts, according to the orders they received from the Chapter-General of the Order in Malta.

This was called the Responsions. But the real property of the Commun

APPENDICES 553

Tesoro, or the lands and houses which were sometimes purchased with a part of the *dépouilles*, is all that concerns the present Government.

No. 3. *Diverse Fondazioni.* These foundations now become the property of Government, who support out of it all the officers and men invalids who had pensions granted by the Order, and some baillies, commandeurs, and chevaliers, who, on account of their age and infirmities, were permitted by the French to remain on the island. They were not accomplices in the treason which delivered the island over to the French, and they lived in convents in La Vallette during the Maltese revolution.

No. 4. *Lingue.* The several languages or tongues into which the Order was divided had each a distinct and separate property here which they could divide among themselves or apply to the purposes of their particular nation.

No. 5. *Collegio.* On the estate which the Order of the Jesuits preserved in Malta; it was appropriated by the Order of St. John for the support of a college for the education of young men. It is now re-established.

No. 6. *Partite Bollati.* Means the interest of money lent by the late Order on mortgages, which the mortgager may repay whenever he pleases, but the mortgagee cannot demand his money if the interest be regularly paid.

Nos. 7 and 8. *Dogana e Sisa.* The Customs and Excise will produce a much larger sum when the trade of the island is encouraged and protected. The duties were low, and the sums in 7 and 8 are the annual average estimate of their produce when even trade was neglected, and the revenues of the Customs and Excise diminished by exemptions from duties, which were granted to the dignitaries of the Order and by their connivance to individual merchants. When the Customs House was established in the country during the revolution, the duties were lowered, and it would be injudicious to raise them to their former rate until the price of bread is fallen.

No. 9. *Sisa sopra i beni stabili* means $3\frac{1}{2}$ per cent. upon the sale of real property.

University, Monte Pietà, Corn and Windmills.

Four magistrates called Jurats had the management of a Public Bank called University. It was permitted to every one to place his money in this bank, for which he received 3 per cent. interest, and he might demand his money whenever he pleased.

The object of this bank was to supply the island with corn, and to accomplish it this bank or university had the exclusive privilege of purchasing and selling corn. The government of the Order of St. John conceived it necessary to have always a year's corn in La Vallette, and not to allow any quantity to be kept in the country, lest the internal or foreign enemy should derive an advantage from it, and unless this article is under the immediate and special direction of Government, it is impossible to be secure against the combination or treachery of merchants and the emissaries of hostile powers.

The safety of the island in time of war and the maintenance of the labouring poor in time of peace are inseparably connected with it. The Island only produces three months' corn for the consumption of its inhabitants. The monthly expenditure amounts to four thousand salms, consequently thirty-five thousand salms must be imported annually. Were this trade left to the merchants, they would reap the profit of it in years of great plenty, but in years of scarcity the labouring poor would starve if Government did not support them, which the late Order always did, and sometimes at a considerable loss.

It deserves to be remarked that a company of Genoese merchants once offered to contract with the Order of St. John to supply the Island with corn at a fixed price, obliging themselves never to add but one scudo or two shillings sterling to the price of the tumulo in times of the greatest scarcity. But the Government rejected this proposal for the reasons that have been mentioned, and whatever the wisdom of an administration may determine hereafter, it is absolutely necessary to continue this system at present, for supposing no danger could be apprehended from allowing individuals to trade in corn, there are not merchants now on the island who are willing or able to undertake it.

Since the surrender of La Vallette corn has been purchased at forty-five scudi and sold at forty, which is one-fourth more than the inhabitants usually paid. The labouring poor are distressed, and the great body of the people regret that this Government will not entirely adopt the regulations established by the Order of St. John. It is now established in part, as much as scanty resources will permit, and the people are assured that it will in time be followed up in all its shapes. This and the putting the Monte di Pietà on its former footing are amongst the most popular acts of this Government.

Monte di Pietà is an establishment of the government for lending money on goods at 6 per cent., the profits of which netted three hundred pounds a year. When the French arrived here, they plundered this bank of all the pledged articles. It is now re-established, but it will require a capital of five thousand pounds.

The French seized upon all the money that existed in the chest of the University likewise. The sufferings of individuals by that act, and the uncertainty in which the inhabitants are in regard to the future fate of the island, prevent the monied men from placing their money in the bank of the University as they used to do under the government of the Order.

Windmills throughout the island are the property of the Government. The following is an extract from a report made by the French administrators to the Ministry of Finance:—

Les moulins au vent sont d'un gros produit en égard au peu de valeur de leur bâtise et de l'emplacement qu'ils occupent, et suivant l'usage sous l'ancien gouvernement il n'étoit pas permis à aucun particulier d'en construire. En réservant ces moulins pour un establissement public, nous leur conservions leur valeur qu'ils auroient perdue, s'ils avoient été mis en vente, parceque du moment qu'ils seroient entrés dans la classe des biens particuliers, il auroit été possible à tout propriétaire d'en faire construire dans les fonds.

Cette idée d'un privilège exclusif en faveur du gouvernement pour pouvoir posséder des moulins à vente et y édifier de nouveaux, n'est peut-être pas bien d'accord avec les principes consacrés par notre législation, cependant ce privilège est une suite de celui que les localités et le salut de la place et de la population exigent. Suivant la commune opinion d'entretenir en faveur du Gouvernement pour l'approvisionment et la vente exclusif des grains.

Administration of the Estates belonging to Government.

The Grand Master's estates were under the direction of a magistrate called Segret, who had authority to hold a court of justice to examine all causes relative to his administration; his income arising from fixed fees amounts to £300 a year. The other foundations belonging to Government are administered by agents called Œconomes, who are paid for the money they collect from 2 to $3\frac{1}{2}$ and even 4 per cent. according to the distance of places and trouble in collecting.

Civil Government.

The expense of civil government in the Islands of Malta and Gozo is inconsiderable, as judges, magistrates, and officers are paid by fixed fees with no expense to government. There is no abuse, as the annual amount of fees is regulated and publicly known.

APPENDICES

The annual amount of fees depends upon the number of causes which come before a judge, and upon the business which the officers of the customs, &c., transact. The officers of the Health Office alone receive salaries, and these salaries with sundry expenses amount to £200 a year. The principal expense of the civil government is the maintenance of hospitals. The expense of the hospital for men amounted to £8000 a year, and for women to £2000. They may be reduced to nearly half these sums, as there were great abuses. The expense of a foundling hospital, or more properly speaking, a hospital for poor bastard children, amounted to £600 a year.

The Island of Gozo contains twelve thousand inhabitants, it is totally dependent upon this island. All vessels bound there must come to the port of La Vallette to pay the customs and get pratique from the Health Office, and all vessels outward bound must do the same. The governor's income amounts to £200 a year. There is a court of justice and university, similar to that in Citta Vecchia.

Laws.

In Malta they have their civil law, statute law, common law, and canon law. They adhere to the last in all their ecclesiastical concerns. Their common law is the usages of the country; their statute laws are the ordinances of the Grand Masters; but the Roman law is the rule of their procedure in civil and criminal causes.

All their statute or municipal laws are comprised in one folio volume, and form a clear and well-digested system of laws.

Capital crimes are seldom committed. There was not a prisoner sentenced to be executed for four years before the revolution.

Auditors.

The governor has four assistants called auditors, some of them at least must be lawyers. They are the governor's counsellors in matters of justice and equity, and sign all the decrees relating to such causes. They assemble for that purpose twice a week. All memorials and petitions are laid before this board. They sometimes order a revision of a cause when litigants complain of the sentence of the courts of justice.

Courts of Judicature.

The grand court of judicature is held in the city of La Vallette (the capital of the island) and is composed of a president and four judges whose incomes arise from fixed fees paid to the Court. In Citta Vecchia, situated in the centre of the island, there is held a court of justice at which the Captain di Verge (who is lieutenant-governor of that place, and all the country) is president with a judge, who try all the civil and criminal causes relative to the country. But the civil causes with the consent of the parties may be tried in the court in La Vallette. The president's and judges' incomes arise from fixed fees paid to the court.

There is a court called the Consulato, for deciding all maritime causes, composed of a judge and two or three merchants, whose incomes arise from fixed fees.

There are five cities and twenty-one casals in the island, each having a chief magistrate, who receives certain fees, amounting to £10 a year, and a salary from Government of £20. He has the power with the consent of the parties to try all causes under twenty shillings.

APPENDIX III

GENERAL VAUBOIS' 'JOURNAL OF THE SIEGE OF MALTA'

[From Les Archives Nationales, AF III 73.]

PART I—FROM SEPTEMBER 1798 TO DECEMBER 1798

IN the National Archives in Paris, there is to be found General Vaubois' original report entitled 'Journal du Siège de Malte,' with a dedicatory letter to the First Consul Bonaparte, dated Paris, the 10th November 1800. From a memorandum attached to this report, it appears that the First Consul issued orders for brief and succinct extracts to be published in the *Moniteur*. These extracts appeared in the issues of that paper on the 15th, 16th, and 17th of that month. Beyond these extracts, and two or three others which appeared in the military periodical, *Sabretache*, the 'journal' has hitherto never been published in its entirety.

The appearance of these extracts in the *Moniteur* aroused the indignation of Villeneuve, who had arrived in Paris from Malta and Port Mahon (after performing quarantine at Toulon), about the end of October 1800.[1]

JOURNAL OF THE SIEGE OF MALTA.

... On ne pouvait pas se dissimuler que le clergé ne pouvait qu'être très aigri contre le nouvel ordre de choses, et l'on n'ignoroit pas sans doute que l'ascendant prodigieux des prêtres sur un peuple superstitieux s'accroît de toutes les misères de ce peuple. Eh! bien on disoit sans cesse d'eux et à eux des choses propres à les mettre au désespoir, et à force de repéter qu'on n'auroit jamais de repos qu'on ne les eut déportés, qu'on ne les fusillat, ils sentirent qu'ils n'avoient plus rien à ménager; les revers qu'éprouva notre escadre en Egypte, en établissant les Anglais maîtres de la mer, rendoit les communications presqu'impraticables entre la France et Malte, et entre Malte et l'Egypte.[2] Les prêtres et les nobles comprirent dès lors que nous [ne] en serions longtems reduits à la faible garnison qui occupait la ville, et leurs projets sédicieux appuyés par la cour de Naples et les Anglais, ils rallièrent à leur parti celui des mécontens qui étoient composé d'une grande partie des habitans de l'isle; on faisoit courir le bruit que les Anglais ne tarderoient pas à paroitre, qu'ils

---

[1] Mr. Hardman had included in this Appendix copies of the letters respecting the dispute between Vaubois and Villeneuve, but as the charges of the former are vague and are largely met by the details given above in chaps. xiv, xv, I have judged it well to omit them; also the first part of Vaubois' Journal of the Siege in which he seeks to account for the revolt of the Maltese by blaming the French civil authorities in Valetta, for which see chap. viii.—J. H. R.

[2] This admission is noteworthy.—J. H. R.

devoient bombarder la ville, et sur ce prétexte beaucoup de personnes alloient s'établir à la campagne. On ne peut pas douter que le foyer de la conspiration ne fut dans la ville et il est clair que ses chefs, qui la conduisoient avec beaucoup de dextérité, n'attendoient qu'une occasion favorable pour la faire éclater partout en même tems. Heureusement un incident hâta le moment de l'exécution et tout échoua par le défaut d'ensemble. Un agent du commissaire se transporta le 16 Fructidor an 6me Rep^e· à la Cité Vieille pour y mettre à l'encan l'emplacement du couvent des Carmes qui avoit été réuni à celui de la ville. Une miserable tapisserie qu'il voulut faire enlever de l'Église fit naître des murmures dans la foule : quelques propos imprudens les accroissent. L'agent s'echappe avec peine, et retourne précipitemment en ville, où il rend compte de l'émeute, en finissant par assurer qu'à son départ tout étoit rentré dans l'ordre. Cependant les têtes s'étoient tellement montées à la Cité Vieille, que le peuple court aux armes, enfonce les portes et massacre la foible garnison qui défendoit ce poste. On n'eut dans le jour aucun rapport officiel sur cet événement. Le surlendemain matin on envoia l'accusateur public pour informer sur ce fait : il étoit précédé de deux compagnies de carabiniers qui devoient lui prêter main forte au besoin. À peine le détachement est-il arrivé à St. Joseph qu'il est entouré d'une multitude de paysans armés ; et il est obligé de se rétirer en se faisant jour avec la bajonette : il rentra en ville après avoir eu un officier et quelques hommes de blessés.[1] Depuis ce moment on vit des rassemblements sur toutes les avenues, et les insurgés se sont rétranchés dans les points principaux, comme le chemin derrier le fort Manuel, St. Joseph, la Montée du Cazal Luca, l'entrée du Zabbar, &c.

Peu de tems après l'insurrection il parut une éscadre portugaise composée de quatre vaisseaux et deux frégattes, qui établirent leur croisière devant le port. Le commandant ne tarda pas à envoyer sommer la ville de se rendre. Le Général répondit à cette bouffonnerie comme il le devoit.

La lettre du commandant portugais étoit accompagnée d'une autre dépeche signée par deux individus qui s'intituloient *deputés du peuple maltais*. Elle étoit en tout sens digne de ses auteurs, *Le Chanoine Caruana et l'avocat Vitale*. Le Général n'y fit point de réponse.

Plusieurs personnes sont allées à la campagne dans l'intention de prendre des informations, des Capucins sont sortis par le même motif, quatres notables de la ville sont partis dans la même vue ; aucuns de tous ces gens-là ne sont rentrés.

On voit par tout ce qui vient d'être dit que la conduite du Commissaire civil avoit fortement contribué à aliéner les esprits ; à la ville, à la campagne son nom n'étoit prononcé qu'avec indignation et tandisque le Général employait tous les moyens pour faire aimer le gouvernement français, que l'habillement, les vivres, et la solde des troupes étoient les objets de ses solicitudes perpetuelles, on eut dit que l'autre se faisoit une étude de tout désorganiser, et de porter le découragement dans tous les cœurs.[2] Il affectoit surtout de repeter que le gouvernement ne nous enverroit aucun secours. La ville étoit en état de siége, toute l'autorité étoit passé entre les mains du Général, et le Commissaire civil avoit cessé ses fonctions. Ce dernier ne parloit d'abord qu'à mettre tout à feu et à sang ; mais dès qu'il vit le caractère sérieux que prenoit l'insurrection, toute cette puérile jactance fit place à des craintes qu'il cherchoit vainement à dissimuler, et sous prétexte de stimuler l'insouciance du gouvernement, il montrait le plus vif désir de repasser en France. Partagé entre la crainte d'être pris par les rébelles s'il restoit à Malte, et celle de leur être livré si le bâtiment

---

[1] This may be compared with the Maltese account of the same skirmish given in chap. ix of this work.—J. H. R.

[2] In the previous part (which has been omitted) Vaubois charged the *commissaire civil* (Regnaud de St. Jean d'Angely) with folly in carrying off the silver from the churches, and other acts, which (he said) were the cause of the Maltese rising. For these questions see chap. viii.—J. H. R.

qu'il devoit monter étoit pris par les Anglais, sa tête n'y étoit plus pendant tout le temps qu'il passa en tergiversations sur son départ.

Le Général avoit assemblé un conseil de guerre où l'on s'occupoit des mesures à prendre dans la situation allarmante où l'on se trouvoit. Il n'ignoroit pas qu'un rassemblement de plusieurs personnes peut être bon pour discuter et non pour agir, de sorte qu'après avoir pris ce qu'il pouvoit y avoir d'utile dans les avis de ceux qui composoient le Conseil, il jugea à propos de le dissoudre lorsqu'il se vit persuadé lui même que son existence nuiroit à la célerité et à l'ensemble des opérations. Avant d'entrer dans le détail des événements relatifs au siège et au blocus, il est indispensable de jetter un coup d'œil rapide sur la situation de la place.

Malte est une place très forte sans doute, mais dont les ouvrages sont d'une étendue immense, et multipliés à l'infini, dont plusieurs sont imparfaits, tandis que des autres ont éprouvés des dégradations qu'on n'avoit point eu le tems de réparer. Indépendemment du corps de la place, il existe des forts, tels que Manuel, Tigné, Ricazoli, St. Ange, les deux sites de la Victorieuse et de la Sengle, les deux Cotoners[1] qui en sont séparés, les uns par le port de Marsamucet, les autres par le grand port. La grande Cotoner surtout n'est qu'ébauché, elle n'a point de fossé, le terre plein n'est achevé nulle part et dans plusieurs endroits, des plus essentiels, il n'en existe point, enfin elle ne peut être considerée que comme un vaste rétranchement susceptible de résister à un simple coup de main, en supposant qu'on ait assez de monde pour l'occuper. Il étoit d'autant plus important d'empêcher l'enemi de s'en rendre maître, que l'enceinte de la S$^{te.}$ Marguerite qui est derrière n'est pas plus rassurante, et que l'on devoit supposer que les Anglais employeroient tous les moyens que dépendroient d'eux pour s'en emparer, puisque c'étoit un moyen assuré de détruire l'arsenal et les bâtimens de guerre qui étoient dans le port.

L'artillerie étoit dans un état de délabrement dont on ne peut pas se faire une idée. Une très grande partie des affuts exposés à un soleil brulant étoient hors de service, ou le seroient d'autant plus vite que toutes les plattes formes sont en pierre. Non seulement il n'y avoit point d'affuts de réchange, mais il s'en falloit de beaucoup que l'armement des pièces fut au complet.

Dans cet état de choses, il falloit tout le zèle et l'intelligence de Général de l'artillerie soutenue par l'activité et les talens du Citoyen Raulot chargé des travaux de l'arsenal, pour se mettre dans un état de deffense respectable. Au reste la sureté de la ville ne fut pas plutôt menacée, que tous les moyens, toutes les volontés, tous les efforts se réunirent pour sa deffense.

Généraux, officiers, troupes de terre et de mer, artillerie, tous jurèrent de conserver Malte à la République ou de s'ensevelir sous ses ruines.

L'insurrection des habitans fournit au Général des moyens de subvenir aux frais de l'habillement de la troupe, à ceux des effets de casernement, à sa solde, et aux dépenses qu'exigoient les rafraichissemens qu'il se procuroit malgré le blocus, de Sardaigne et de Barbarie, en attendant que le gouvernement peut venir à son secours sur ce sujet.[2]

La première mesure qu'il prit pour satisfaire à ces besoins importans, fut d'établir sur les gens aisés, un emprunt forcé en raison de leurs facultés, et en se rendant caution pour la République, pourvû que leur conduite ne fut souillée par aucun acte d'incivisme.

Le Général s'est encore emparé de la caisse de l'Université, de celle des dépôts, et du Mont de Piété, ainsi que de toutes les créances de ceux qui sont à la campagne, et il n'y aura que les personnes qui n'auront point pris part à la revolte qui pourront un jour être remboursés.

C'est par de semblables dispositions que le Général s'est éfforcé de mériter

---

[1] i.e. Cotonera.—J. H. R.
[2] This sentence is very noteworthy. The revolt enabled Vaubois to exact money and supplies which he could not have done from a loyal population.—J. H. R.

les suffrages de la brave garnison qui est sous ses ordres. Ses solicitudes trouvent la plus flateuse des récompenses dans le zèle infatigable qui anime tous les cœurs. Dans une place d'aussi grande étendue, bloquée par mer, assiegée par terre, en proie aux séditions intestines, depuis cinq mois la garnison est nuit et jour sous les armes, elle a été plus de deux mois sans vin et sans eau de vie, et personne ne se plaint.

Les vaisseaux *Le Guillaume Tell* et *Le Dégo* [sic] les frégattes *La Diane, La Justice* et *La Carthaginoise*, ne pouvant sortir du port à cause de l'escadre Anglais dont il est bloqué, on les a mis à l'abris des bombes par un solide blindage. Leurs équipages ont été employés au service des forts. Leur conduite est la même que celle des troupes de terre, c'est à dire audessus de tout éloge. Sans ce renfort il eût été impossible d'occuper la grande Cotoner, à moins de s'affaiblir prodigieusement sur tous les points. Les munitions de guerre ne manqueront pas de sitot. Il seroit seulement à désirer qu'on ait une plus grande quantité de boulets de 24 et de bombes surtout de celles de 8 pouces.

À l'egard des subsistances, il y a du bled pour un an et des autres provisions comme : vin, eau de vie, lard, fèves, riz, et viande salée pour 8 à 9 mois.

Le nombre des malades augmente. Beaucoup de soldats éprouvent une incommodité très facheuse, qu'on attribue à l'air vif et salin, et surtout au serein pénétrant des nuits. Dès que le jour baisse ces malheureux sont dans un état de cécité absolue, et ne recouvrent la vue qu'au lever du soleil.

EXTRAIT LITTÉRAL DU REGISTRE D'ORDRES ET DE LA CORRESPONDANCE DU GÉNÉRAL VAUBOIS.

Ordres.

16 Fructidor an 6 Rep$^{e.}$ (2nd September 1798).

Deux compagnies de Carabiniers de la 23eme demie Brigade d'infanterie legère ont ordre de se rendre demain au matin à la Citté Vieille. L'accusateur public, qu'elles doivent protéger en cas d'événement, doit les suivre pour informer sur l'emeute qui a eu lieu aujourd'hui.

17 Fructidor (3rd September 1798).

Les deux compagnies de Carabiniers parties ce matin, ont trouvé à St. Joseph un si grand nombre de paysans armés qu'elles ont été obligées de rentrer en ville après avoir eu un officier et deux homme blessés.

Ordre au Capitaine du Vaisseau *Le Dégo* de s'embosser près du magazin à poudre du Coradin pour en faciliter l'évacuation.

Ordre à la garde nationale de s'assembler sur la place pour y être désarmée, ce qui est executé.

Ordre au Contre-Amiral Villeneuve d'embosser le vaisseau *Le Guillaume Tell* et la frégatte *La Diane*, mouillés dans le port de Marsamuscet, de manière à battre la ville et la campagne du côté de la Piéta.

Ordre à l'Adjudant-Général Brouard de faire fusiller sur la place de Bourmola un rebelle pris les armes à la main, ce qui est exécuté sur le champ.

Les insurgens de la campagne pénetrent dans la Cotoner [sic], et enlèvent quelques barils de poudre, tandis qu'un de leurs partis entre à Bourmola.

Ordre à l'Adjudant-General Brouard de se rendre à la Citté de l'est avec la 80° demie Brigade pour y reduire les rébelles. Il a un latitude de pouvoir qui le met à même d'agir selon les circonstances. Il donne ordre au Commandant du vaisseau *Le Dégo*, mouillé à l'Arsenal, de s'entraverser sur Bourmola, menace de détruire la ville si les rébelles ne déposent pas les armes, et en cas de refus donne vingt minutes aux femmes et aux enfants pour sortir. Cette mésure vigoureuse ramène la tranquilité. Cependant un bruit court que l'Adjutant-Général doit être attaqué dans la nuit : Le Général l'en fait prévenir et lui récommande la plus grand surveillance. La nuit se passe dans le plus grand calme.

Ordre au Commandant des Armes de faire sortir une chaloupe cannonière pour observer ce qui se passe sur la côte.

Ordre au Contre-Amiral Villeneuve de faire appareiller une frégatte afin d'empêcher que rien ne sorte de l'isle, et même d'envoyer au grand port tout bâtiment qui tenteroit d'y aborder.

18 Fructidor (4th September 1798).

Ordre au Général Chanez de Commander des Officiers de ronde qui se succederont pendant la nuit, et d'ordonner que tout le monde ait du feu à dix heures et que la ville soit illuminée.

Ordre au Chef du Génie de faire murer solidement toutes les ports de la Cotoner.

Ordre au General d'Artillerie d'envoyer des cannoniers des munitions de guerre pour le service de deux pièces situées près d'un magazin à poudre de la Cotoner dont les rébelles cherchent toujours à s'approcher.

On envoye une barque soutenue par une chaloupe cannonière pour exécuter la retraite du détachement qui est au fort St. Thomas.

19 Fructidor (5th September 1798).

Ordre au Commandant du Génie de faire évacuer les personnes qui habitent dans l'enceinte de la Cotoner, et les autres fortifications.

Ordre au Commandant des differents forts de ne pas consommer leurs munitions inutilement.

Ordre au Commandant des Armes de prendre des précautions les plus séveres pour empêcher qu'aucun bâtiment ne sorte du port.

21 Fructidor (7th September 1798).

Le Général écrit au Citoyen Belleville chargé d'affaires de la République à Gênes. Il lui donne part de la révolte des Maltais, et le prie de lui envoyer plusieurs objets de première nécéssité, comme vin, charbon, &c.

22 idem (8th September 1798).

Ordre au Contre-Amiral Villeneuve de jetter 300 hommes et trente cannoniers dans le fort Manuel.

Ordre qui réforme les officiers et sous officiers des Chasseurs Maltais, et leur enjoint de quitter l'uniforme, motivé sur ce que les soldats de ce corps, sans exception ont pris part à la révolte.

Ordre au Contre-Amiral Villeneuve d'envoyer une chaloupe cannonière sur la côte du Goze, pour découvrir si le pavillon national flotte encore sur le château et sur le fort Chambraÿ.

27 idem (13th September 1798).

On apprend que la garnison du Goze est en possession des forts, et on ne perd pas un moment pour lui envoyer des sécours en hommes, vivres et munitions.

28 idem (14th September 1798).

Le Conseil de guerre arrete :

1°. Qu'il sera embarqué sur les vaisseaux de la République des matelots Maltais dans la proportion d'un quart des équipages français.

2°. Que les troupes Maltaises faisant le service de la Marine seront embarqués comme garnison sur les vaisseaux.

3°. Que les deux vaisseaux et trois frégattes établissent une crosière sur la côte.'

APPENDICES

30 idem (16th September 1798).

Plainte au Contre-Amiral Villeneuve contre l'officier qui commandat la chaloupe cannonière qui a laissé entrer à St. Paul un bâtiment.

1 Jour Complem$^{re.}$ (17th September 1798).

Ordre au Contre-Amiral Villeneuve de faire partir deux chaloupes cannonières pour aller enlever ou bruler le bâtiment qu'on dit être entré hier à St. Paul.

Le Général adresse au Conseil de guerre la lettre suivante :[1]

'... Quel parti prendre dans cette position? Voici mes vues que j'expose au Conseil de Guerre. Comme je suis persuadé que rien ne peut mettre à couvert ma responsabilité, je lui en fais part et je la prie de le faire consigner sur les régistres du Conseil. Je demande qu'il soit expédié des avisos qui fassent parvenir en France et en Italie notre situation ; que nos demandes soient les plus instantes pour obtenir des forces, des munitions de guerre et des comestibles. Cette mésure doit être renouvellée jusqu'à ce que nous ayons des reponses rassurantes de notre gouvernement. Je demande que les puissances barbaresques soient extrêmement ménagées. Je demande que notre marine protège nos côtes jusqu'à ce que des forces supérieures l'oblige de rentrer. Ces forces maritimes doivent consister en deux ou trois frégattes, deux galiottes et quatre speronares. Les chaloupes cannonières resteront dans le port prêtes à être employées au besoin, mais je préfere les autres bâtimens legers comme plus propres au service exigé. Je demande que la ville soit armée le plus formidablement, et suivant tous nos moyens, surtout qu'on mette du canon en batterie plus qu'il n'y en a, principalement à la Sengle et à la Victorieuse, de manière que si la Cotoner étoit emportée, on peut arreter l'ennemi dans sa course.

'Je demande que l'on presse extrêmement la confection des cartouches, et qu'il soit fait une visite exacte pour se procurer tout le plomb qui est dans le pays. Je remarque que dans le cas où le port seroit bloqué, et que les frégattes et autres embarcations soient rentrées, nous pouvons augmenter nos forces de terre au moins de douze cents hommes.

'Je n'ai pas de répugnance à employer quelques Maltais et je crois au contraire qu'il seroit extrêmement politique d'armer le peuple contre le peuple, mais il faut que ce soit dans une proportion qui ne laisse rien à craindre, et qu'ils soient divisés de manière à ne pouvoir nuire. Dès ce moment je pense qu'on peut mettre deux cannoniers Maltais sur six Français à différens postes.

'J'invite le Chef du Genie à ne rien épargner pour assurer les parties foibles de la fortification, et à se concerter avec le Général Chanez pour déterminer le service le plus sûr et le plus propre à tenir les troupes dans la plus grande surveillance. Je demande qu'en cas d'attaque sur un point quelconque, il y ait toujours des troupes de la reserve commandées et prêtes à marcher sur le lieu indiqué. Je ne vois aucune utilité aux sorties. Les postes attaqués réculeront en fusillant, le soldat se livrera, le pillage sera impossible à arreter. Celui qui est forcé à prendre les armes sera victime comme le malintentionné. On tuera peu de monde et le soldat egaré sera assassiné. Les sorties me paroissent donc inutiles, nuisibles même pour le moment.

'Quant aux subsistances, point essentiel, mais qui cependant n'a rien d'effrayant pour nous par rapport à la quantité de bled que nous possédons, je pense qu'entre les demandes que nous devons faire en France et en Italie, nous devons expédier le plus qu'il nous sera possible de bâtimens neutres pour nous en procurer. C'est le plus grand objet d'utilité qu'ils puissent remplir. Nous n'avons besoin de ces bâtimens que pour cela, du reste nous ne devons pas songer

---

[1] I omit the first part of this lengthy letter, namely, that which describes the opinions of the general and his officers on the origin of the Maltese revolt.—J. H. R.

à nous en servir pour nous. Nous devons ici triompher ou mourir sur les remparts.

'Je demande qu'on surveille ceux-là qui pourroient être nos ennemis dans l'intérieure et que tout crime découvert soit puni sur le champ. Mais qu'en même temps on acceuille les habitans tranquilles, qu'on ait l'air de leur témoigner de la confiance, qu'on leur fasse parler, et qu'on employe enfin tous moyens de decouvrir ce qui pourrait se trainer, chaque membre du Conseil de Guerre ayant ses mouches pour obtenir des renseignements sûrs.'[1]

3me Jour Complem$^{re.}$ (19th September 1798).

Il paroit deux frégattes et l'on fait sortir un vaisseau et une frégatte pour s'en emparer. Bientôt on s'appercoit qu'elles sont suivies de quatre vaisseaux, et les nôtres sont obligés de rentrer.

4me Jour Complem$^{re.}$ (20th September 1798).

Invitation au Contre-Amiral Villeneuve d'armer des petits bâtimens pour intercepter ce qui pourroit venir de Sicile aux rébelles.

Ordre au Général Chanez de se concerter avec le Général d'Artillerie pour faciliter l'évacuation des pièces qui sont dans l'ouvrage avancé de la Florianne, qu'on ne sauroit occuper à cause du peu de monde qu'il y a dans la place.

Invitation au Commissaire du Gouvernement de faire mettre tous les bœufs en réquisition pour le service de l'hôpital.

2me Vendémiaire an 7eme (23rd September 1798).

Invitation au Commissaire du Gouvernement de faire acheter des vins d'Alicante et de Malaga pour les convalescens, le vin d'ordinaire étant excessivement rare.

Ordre au Général Chanez de faire arreter et conduire au fort St. Elme le nommé Dom Annibal prêtre et Anglois d'origine.

Ordre au Général Chanez d'expulser de la ville tous les hommes en état de porter les armes, dont les noms sont inscrits sur les listes jointes à cet ordre. Il y aura autant de détachemens commandés qu'il y a de feuilles. Au présent ordre est annexée la liste des officiers publics qui doivent conduire cette expédition, et dont un ou deux doivent se trouver à la tête de chaque détachement. Pareil ordre est donné pour l'évacuation de la Florianne. On battera à cet effet la générale à cinq heures et demie du matin.

Le Citoyen Fournier frère d'un des chefs des rébelles doit être expulsé en même tems que les autres. Sa famille restera en ville.

4 Vendémiaire (25th September 1798).

Le Général écrit au payeur de la division, pour le prevenir qu'il va exiger des habitans des cités de l'est et de l'ouest un emprunt forcé, qui doit être versé dans sa caisse.

La garnison du fort Chambray après avoir repoussée plusieurs assauts, manquant de vivres, s'empare des barques qui sont au port du Miggiaro et se rend à la Valette le même jour.

Ordre au Général Chanez:

'1°. De faire passer dans le jour au fort St. Ange le détachement de la 6me demie Brigade qui est à Ricazoli, dès qu'il sera rélevé par les troupes des vaisseaux qui doivent occuper ce dernier fort.

'2o. Il ordonnera au détachement de la 6me Brigade qui a évacué le fort Chambray, et qui est maintenant au fort Manuel de se rendre au fort St. Ange.

'3°. Il donnera ordre au Battaillon de la 19eme demie Brigade qui est à

For Vaubois' letters of 18th September to the Directors see chap. x. *ad init.*—J. H. R.

APPENDICES

St. Ange de passer à la Sengle pour se réunir au Battallon qui s'y trouve déjà. Par cet arrangement les forts de Ricazoli et Manuel seront occupés par les troupes et cannoniers des vaisseaux, sur lesquels il restera encore une reserve de 400 hommes et cent cannoniers prêts à se porter où le besoin l'exigera.

'Le Contre-Amiral Decrès est nommé commandant des forts Ricazoli, Manuel et Tigné.'

7 Vendémiaire (28th September 1798).

Le Général écrit aux habitants de l'est et de l'ouest la lettre suivante :

Les atroces délits commis par vos concitoyens de la campagne, et plusieurs personnes des cantons de l'est et de l'ouest, me mettent dans le cas d'avoir recours à un emprunt pour payer la troupe. Il faut que le soldat soit exactement payé pour pouvoir arreter son juste ressentiment et contenir dans la plus exacte discipline des hommes qui ont vu leurs compagnons lachement égorgés dans Bourmola et dans la campagne.

Je vous ai donc compris dans cet emprunt pour la somme de . . . que vous voudrés bien payer dans le delai de vingt quatre heures à compte du moment où vous recevrés la présente. Je vous garantis votre argent, et je me rends responsable au nom de la République sur la loyauté de laquelle vous pouvés compter. Le moindre refus me deviendroit suspect, puisque je suis informé de vos moyens. Je crois agir avec beaucoup de modération d'autant plus que les lois de la guerre m'autorisent à vous demander une contribution ; les intérêts vous seront payés à raison de trois pour cent par an.

10 Vendémiaire (1st October 1798).

Lettre au Commissaire du Gouvernement pour l'engager à acheter de bled des bâtimens Grecs qui sont dans le port.

Ordre au Commandant de l'est de faire sortir les personnes nommés dans la liste qu'on lui fait passer.

13 Vendémiaire (4th October 1798).

Ordre au Général Chanez :

'Demain 14 du courant il sera fait une sortie par la Cotoner sur le Cazal Zabbar à la pointe du jour.

'Quatre cent hommes armés des vaisseaux se porteront pendant la nuit sur la Cotoner pour garnir le rempart. Le Chef de Bat$^{on.}$ Pouvreau donnera des ordres pour qu'on les y place.

'Huit cents hommes de la garnison de l'est, sans rien tirer de Ricazoli, joints à deux cents hommes de la 17eme demie Brigade dont une compagnie de Carabiniers et qui passeront pendant la nuit seront rassemblés par le Chef de Battalion Pouvreau pour éffectuer la sortie sous ses ordres par la porte du Salvator.

'Ces mille hommes se mettront en marche à la pointe du jour et se dirigeront sur le Cazal Zabbar. À portée du Cazal le Command$^{t.}$ Pouvreau divisera sa troupe en deux pour le tourner et éviter le feu de trois pièces qui s'y trouvent. Cela fait, il fera garder par des forces suffisantes les avenues du Cazal Zeiton et celles du côté de Marsa Scala. Il détachera une partie de la troupe pour réduire le cazal, enlever tous les commestibles, les munitions de guerre et les canons. Il recommandera aux soldats de ne traiter comme ennemis que ceux qui portent les armes contre nous.

'Avant d'arriver au Cazal Zabbar, il sera jetté des bombes et tiré du canon jusqu'à ce que les troupes soient à portée.

'La sortie durera le moins de tems possible.

'Pour faire diversion il sortira en reconnoissance cinquante hommes par la porte des Bombes et cinquante hommes par le fort Manuel qui se montreront sans s'engager au dela de la portée de notre canon. Toutes les troupes seront en alerte pendant la sortie.'

Nota :—On trouva toutes les avenues du Cazal tellement rétranchées qu'il fût impossible d'y pénétrer. Le détachement fut contraint de revenir après avoir eu un officier et quelques soldats de blessés.

14 Vendémiaire (5th October 1798).

Lettre du Général au Consul de la République Française à Cagliari :
' Depuis trente deux jours Citoyen Consul, les paysans de l'isle sont révoltés. Quatres vaisseaux portugais et deux autres petits bâtimens sont devant le port. Envoyés nous du lard, du vin, de l'eau de vie, du fromage, des legumes secs : nous avons du bled abondamment. Vous savés que ce sont des français qui sont dans Malte et qu'on n'en vient pas à bout aisément. Des vivres et tout ira bien. Je vous récommande instamment cette belle conquête de la République. Faites le prix de chaque chose et des notes et nous payerons.'

Ordre au Commissaire Ordonateur de Terre de faire enlever toutes les toiles de fil et de coton propres à faire des chemises et de les payer sur estimation faite par des experts.

Ordre au Contre-Amiral Villeneuve de faire partir la frégatte *La Justice* pour porter des dépêches au Gouvernement. Le Commissaire Regnaud de St. Jean d'Angely en sera le porteur.[1]

15 Vendémiaire (6th October 1798).

Au Général Chanez :
' Vous voudrés bien, Général, instruire la garnison qu'il a été réquis pour son usage, du fromage, des salaisons, de la graisse et du beurre. Les proprietaires de ces comestibles ne peuvent ouvrir leur vente au public qu'après huit jours, époque à laquelle il faut que les militaires soient pourvus. Ces objets se gatent en magazin. Je ne peux en retarder plus longtems la vente. La Municipalité donnera l'adresse des marchands.

' Je propose aux officiers de leur donner les mêmes rations de vivres qu'aux soldats. Je compte sur la discretion de ceux qui se trouveroient ne pas en avoir encore besoin. J'aime à croire qu'ils partagent mes sentiments sur la grande économie qu'il faut employer dans la consommation de nos commestibles. Comme moi, ils connoissent la position de la place, ils sauront vivre au milieu des privations dont la perspective nous est offerte.'

Ordre au Général d'Artillerie de faire transporter six pièces de 24 et deux mortiers sur le Bastion des Capucins de la Florianne et une pièce de moindre calibre destiné à battre le chemin. Il sera aussi transporté une pièce de 24 près les deux mortiers qui sont à la Sengle, et quatre pièces de 24 à la courtine du Bastion de St François de Paul. L'objet de ces dispositions est d'empêcher l'ennemi de s'établir sur le Coradin.

16 Vendémiaire (7th October 1798).

Supplément à la lettre du 15 au Directoire exécutif :
' Les mêmes causes produisent les mêmes éffets, j'ai éprouvé la guerre civile en Corse ; j'en ai triomphé. Je l'ai vu inévitable avant qu'elle n'éclatat, j'en ai averti. Ici mêmes causes, mêmes effets, ordres sages de la part du Général en Chef ; abus d'un autre côté, mésures mal prises, innovations précipitées, intérêts compromis, préjugés attaqués avec imprudence, dans un pays dont la conquête n'est point consolidée, sans faire attention que ce point est l'appui d'une armée éloignée. Enfin défaut de politique, de conduite, jamais la moindre démarche pour se faire un parti, injustices, formes rébutantes, tout cela a amené la guerre civile.

' Si jamais j'approche de Paris, je verrai le gouvernement, je lui parlerai à cœur

[1] I have omitted this letter as it is published in chap. x. of this work.—J. H. R.

ouvert, en vrai, sincere et imperturbable Républicain, je lui ferai connoître que sa sollicitude est souvent paralysée par des individus qui n'aiment pas la République, et qui l'exposent parcequ'ils ne la servent que pour eux. Mais quoiqu'il arrive, mes dévoirs seront remplis avec un zèle que les obstacles ne feront qu'augmenter.

'Les deux Contre-Amiraux Villeneuve et Decrès sont ici, le premier commande la Marine, . . . [?] fournit du monde, et m'est très utile.[1] Le second ne l'est pas moins, il a remis le commandement de sa frégatte à son capitaine. Je lui ai donné le commandement de trois forts qui ont des commandants particuliers. Son activité, son intelligence ont multipliés les moyens de deffense.

'Le malheur de l'escadre les a amenés ici, et leur présence m'est d'autant plus utile que je manque de chefs.'

18 Vendémiaire (9th October 1798).

Invitation au Commissaire du Gouvernement de se procurer tout ce qui peut servir à l'habillement de la troupe.

19 Vendémiaire (10th October 1798).

Invitation à la Municipalité de l'ouest de faire délivrer cent trente paillasses et autant de couvertures pour le fort Ricazoli.

Lettre à la Commission du Gouvernement:

'Je vous prie, Citoyens, de vouloir bien ordonner aux administrateurs du Mont de Piété de suivre scrupuleusement l'administration telle qu'elle existoit, jusqu'à ce que j'ai santionné quelque espéce de changement que les circonstances exigeroient.'

Au Commissaire du Gouvernement :—

'Le Gouvernement, quand il existe des tribunaux, ne peut d'autorité obliger les parties à un arbitrage, et quand ce seroit une manière de terminer les affaires avantageusement pour ces parties, il faudroit qu'elles consentissent, et qu'elles ai [sic] choisi respectivement et avec liberté leurs arbitres. Les affaires qui n'ont pas été jugées ainsi excitent des réclamations qui me paroissent fondées, je ne puis m'empêcher de les prendre en considération, et rien ne peut empêcher qu'elles soient rapportées devant les juges compétens.'

22 Vendémiaire (13th October 1798).

Ordre à l'Adjudant-Général Brouard de faire passer à la Municipalité la lettre ci-jointe pour qu'elle avertisse ceux qui y sont portés de se trouver demain à quatre heures après midi sur la place de l'Égalité pour organiser une campagnie de cannoniers.

Il écrira au Général d'Artillerie pour lui en donner avis et l'inviter à s'y trouver. Il le priera en même tems de faire préparer sur la ditte place, les moyens d'instruction, afin que leur zèle à apprendre ce métier soit vu de leurs concitoyens. Des pièces legères seront disposés en conséquence. Il écrira au Contre-Amiral Villeneuve d'avertir tous les Français des navires marchants qui sont dans le port de s'y trouver pour entrer dans cette organisation.

Lettre au Directoire exécutif dans laquelle le Général lui donne part que le départ du Commissaire Regnaud a été rétardé par les vents contraires. Il réitere ses sollicitations pour des ravitaillemens.

Ordre au Commissaire ordonnateur de terre de payer aux veuves Attard et Trigame les modiques appointemens de leurs maris qui ont été massacrés par les rébelles le jour de la révolte, étant de service à la campagne. Ils étoient chefs du corps des Chasseurs. L'un laisse dix enfans, l'autre sept.

[1] In view of the accusations subsequently brought by Vaubois against Villeneuve, this statement should be noted.—J. H. R.

24 Vendémiaire (15th October 1798).

Ordre au payeur de faire passer à la monoye tous les lingots qu'il a entre les mains.

Lettre au Commiss^{re.} Regnaud:

'Des officiers de chaque corps qui sont chez moi, exigent que je vous écrive pour vous engager à laisser les fonds qui se trouvent entre vos mains, ainsi que ceux de vos campagnons de voyage. J'ai plaidé pour le respect dû aux propriétés, mais ils m'ont repondus, qu'après en avoir agi ainsi vis-à-vis d'un étranger, ce seroit négliger mal à propos un sécours que des Français pourroient procurer dans cette circonstance, et ils comptent d'advance sur votre empressement à venir à leurs sécours. Je délivrerai la reconnoissance.'

25 Vendémiaire (16th October 1798).

Au Commissaire Ordonnateur de la Marine:

'J'apprends qu'il se brule du bois neuf fourni par la marine pour la troupe. Je vous prie de concerter avec l'ingénieur le dépécement de quelques vieux pontons dont la valeur sera infiniment moindre. Le bois neuf nous deviendra indispensable pour l'entretient des affuts qui sont hors de service dès les premiers coups.'

Ordre au Général Chanez de faire exécuter dans les vingt quatre heures un jugement de la Commission Militaire qui condamne à la peine de mort le nommé Dumont convaincu d'embauchage.

26 Vendémiaire (17th October 1798).

Au Commissaire du Gouvernement Regnaud:

'J'ai reçu hier soir la lettre que vous m'avés écrite, et par laquelle vous demandés que les malles des voyageurs, et même la vôtre qui se trouve sur la frégatte *La Justice* soient visitées. Pourquoi prendrai-je d'autorité cette mésure, quand des officiers sont venus hier matin et m'ont dit que leurs désirs étoient seulement que si quelques uns de ceux qui se proposent de passer en France avoient des fonds excédant les besoins de la route, ils croyent trouver chez eux la volonté de laisser pour le service de l'armée le surplus de ce qui leur est nécessaire en leur remettant une reconnoissance pour être payés en France.'

Au Commandant des Forces Angloises devant le port de Malte:

'Le Bais Assés de Tunis me demande, Monsieur, à sortir du port si vous lui garantissés son passage. Il a un passeport qu'il vous manifestera. Si vous n'y trouvés pas de difficulté et que vous et Messieurs les portugais lui assurés son voyage, je lui permettrai de sortir. Je vous prie de vouloir bien me faire connoître vos intentions.'

27 Vendémiaire (18th October 1798).

Au Commandant du Génie:

'L'inquiétude que l'on a sur les cavaliers m'a suggeré une idée dont je vous fais part et que j'ai communiqué à Fay, pour que vous vous concertiés avec lui pour l'exécution à son attelier. C'est de mettre les herses sous la voûte audessous de l'entrée des magazins à poudre, ce qui formera une double cloture et expose l'attaquant à être pris entre deux feux. La plus prompte exécution je vous prie.'

Sommation de l'amiral Portugais:

'Les evénements politiques et militaires survenus depuis un mois, les sentimens d'humanité qui me préscrivent d'employer tous les moyens possibles pour ménager la vie des hommes, m'engagent à faire de nouveaux efforts pour faire ouvrir les yeux à la garnison française sur l'inutilité et le danger d'une plus grande résistance.

'La réponse faite à la première sommation en datte du 25 Septembre a pu flatter l'orgueuil mais elle blesse la raison: la garnison française doit réfléchir sur les motifs qu'elle à d'être persuadée qu'il ne lui reste aucun espoir d'être secouru.

'Elle saura que cinq vaisseaux Russes sont devant Alexandrie réunis aux forces navales du Grand Seigneur, que les troupes françaises laissées en Egypte ont été battues trois fois par les Mameloucks réunis aux troupes du Grand Seigneur venues de la Sirie, qu'après la dernière action le Général Bonaparte et le reste de ses troupes étoient entourées sans espoir de retraitte, et que les troupes laissées à Alexandrie avoient refusé de marcher à son secours: que le Grand Seigneur ayant fait enfermer aux sept tours à Constantinople l'envoyé des français a fait publier un Divan par lequel il invite tous les Musulmans à faire main basse sur les Français, à les traiter comme traîtres et parjurés, qui sous l'apparence d'amitié et d'alliance sont venus piller et dévaster ses états. Tripoli, Tunis, et Alger ont reçu et mis à exécution cet ordre. Un bâtiment français venant de Tripoli, pris devant Malte il y a huit jours, en étoit parti sur son lest et à la hâte pour éviter le sort d'être massacré ou fait esclave.

'L'isle de Corfou est en insurrection contre les français et une escadre Anglaise qu'elle y a appellé y est maintenant. Une escadre croise sur les côtes de la Provence, devant le port de Toulon, dont on ne peut rien faire sortir depuis longtems, ainsi que le mande le Sieur Najac dans une lettre au Sieur Escoffier à Malte. Il y a environ six semaines que cette lettre a été interceptée. Le port de l'isle de Malte ne cessera pas à être bloqué ainsi qu'il a été jusqu'à présent.

'Il est donc certain qu'il n'existe aucun espoir pour la garnison française de recevoir aucun secour, soit militaire soit d'approvisionnements. La tentative faite par sa garnison contre les habitans de l'isle a dû lui prouver qu'ils sont amplement pourvus d'armes et de munitions en même tems qu'elle a pû servir à lui faire connoître l'esprit de vengeance qui anime le peuple.

'La conséquence, nous, Marquis de Nizza, Chef d'Escadre Commandant le Vaisseau de sa Majesté très fidelle, *Le Prince Royal*, réunis à une division de vaisseaux de sa Majesté Britannique, au noms de leurs Majestés, la Reine de Portugal et le Roi d'Angleterre sommons la garnison française de remettre en notre pouvoir la ville et port de l'isle de Malte et dépendances, comme ainsi tous vaisseaux, frégattes et bâtimens quelconques qui peuvent s'y trouver afin que les habitans de l'isle de Malte puissent rentrer en possession de leurs biens et jouir de leurs droits et propriétés ; nous engageant aux noms de leurs Majestés de laisser à la garnison française la liberté de rétourner en France, de fournir les moyens de l'y transporter avec sureté sous la condition que la garnison française ne servira dans aucune armée jusqu'à qu'elle ait été reguliérement changée contre des sujets des deux souverains dénommés ou de ceux de leurs alliées.

'On entrera en pourparler sur les conditions et arrangemens qui pourront avoir lieu pour éffectuer l'evacuation de la place et le transport de la garnison.

'À bord *Le Prince Royal* le 18 Oct$^{re.}$ 1798.

(Signé) le Marquis de Nizza, Chef d'Escadre.'

Reponse du Général Vaubois à la Sommation du Marquis de Nizza :

27 Vendémiaire (18th October 1798).

'Je viens de recevoir, Monsieur, votre seconde sommation. J'y reponds comme à la première. Malta est une ville des plus fortes, nous avons des vivres, des munitions de guerre et du courage. Avec ces moyens des français ne craignent ni les bombes, ni les boulets, ni les efforts d'un peuple rébelle passé sous les lois de la France par un acte authentique.

'PS.—Votre vaisseau, Monsieur, s'est approché ce matin trop près des forts. Un vaisseau ne peut se présenter en parlementaire. J'ai l'honneur de vous prévenir que je serai obligé de faire tirer dessus si une autre fois il venait à une pareille distance.'

28 Vendémiaire (19th October 1798).

PROCLAMATION.

Nous, Général de Division, Commandant en Chef les isles de Malte et de Goze ordonnons ce qui suit :

ART^{e.} 1er.

Tout citoyen des cittés de l'est et de l'ouest est obligé d'être muni d'une carte de sûreté.

ART^{e.} 2me.

Ne sont point excepté de cette mésure les fonctionnaires publics. Les militaires, la Commission du Gouvernement et les administrations de l'armée sont seuls exceptés mais ils seront toujours en uniforme.

ART^{e.} 3me.

Il y aura trois bureaux établis pour y aller prendre les cartes de sûreté.
Un au palais pour la citté de l'ouest et de Florianne. Un à la Victorieuse chez le Commandant de l'est pour la Victorieuse et la Bourmola.
Un à la Sengle chez le Chef de Battaillon de la 7me Brigade.

ART. 4.

Il sera proclamé dans chacun de ces chefs lieu, le jour et l'heure de l'ouverture des bureaux par les Municipalités.

ART. 5.

La distribution des cartes de sûreté faite, il est ordonné à toutes les gardes des troupes françaises d'arrêter tous ceux qui ne seront pas munis de cette carte. Ils seront détenus dans les corps de garde jusqu'à ce que d'après le compte qui en sera rendu au Général Chanez, il prononce sur les individus suivant les instructions qui lui seront remises par le Général en Chef.

ART. 6.

Tout fonctionnaire public, ou individu français qui sauroit qu'un homme n'est pas muni d'une carte de sûreté et qui ne la feroit pas connoître sera poursuivi comme complice de projet contre-révolutionnaire dont on pourroit convaincre le désobéissant à cette loi.

ART. 7.

Tout citoyen qui prêteroit sa carte à un autre seroit puni comme rébelle.

ART. 8.

Toute personne arrêtée dans un mouvement séditieux y prenant part, sera puni de mort dans les vingt quatre heures.

ART. 9.

Tout attroupement au dessus de trois personnes est defendu.

29 Vendémiaire (20th October 1798).

Ordre au Général d'Artillerie :

' Des renseignemens vrais ou faux m'annoncent des entreprises hardies de la part des habitans et de l'Amiral Nelson attendu de jour en jour.

' Il doit y avoir suivant ce que l'on dit à la compagne une attaque générale par mer et par terre la même nuit. Sans m'arrêter au plus ou moins de vraisemblance d'un pareil bruit, je veux prendre des précautions comme s'il étoit fondé, et si Nelson est un homme à entreprises ou il risque le tout pour le tout, il faut être en garde contre tout ce qu'il peut tenter. En conséquence vous voudrés bien prendre les mesures nécessaires pour [que] les batteries de St. Elme, de Ricazoli, de la Sengle, de la Barraque soient dans le meilleur état de service.

' Vous ferés faire des paniers à pierriers, je ferai distribuer aux batteries où cela conviendra des boulets inflammables qui sont à bord des vaisseaux. Je vous prie d'avoir toujours l'œuil sur la Pietà, c'est à mon avis l'endroit que l'ennemi doit choisir pour établir des batteries de bombes contre la ville. Si nous avions plus de petites pièces, je les préféreroit pour la deffense des flancs.

' Faites dépêcher, je vous prie, les affûts à la gomer.

' Les cannoniers Maltais inspirent peu de confiance et doivent être employés aux travaux et non au service des pièces.'

30 Vendémiaire (21st October 1798).

Ordre aux Commissaires ordonateurs de terre et de mer de prendre les mesures les plus promptes et les plus efficaces pour assurer l'habillement des troupes et des matelots.

2 Brumaire (23rd October 1798).

Ordre au Payeur de la Division de payer aux officiers le mois de Floréal que le Général en Chef Bonaparte leur a accordé en gratification.

Le Général previent le payeur qu'il vient d'établir un supplément d'emprunt de 80,000$^{fr.}$ sur les cittés de l'est.

3 Brumaire (24th October 1798).

Ordre au Général d'Artillerie pour accroître les moyens de deffense du port de Marsamuscet, de disposer les boulets incendiaires partout où il convient d'en avoir, et d'ordonner qu'aux forts de Tigné, St. Elme, et Ricazoli on tire sur tout vessau qui s'en approcheroit.

Ordre du jour :

' Suivant les rapports que j'ai eu de la campagne, on doit attaquer cette nuit ou la nuit prochaine par terre et par mer. Les troupes recevront en conséquence l'ordre d'être prêtes à marcher. Il est ordonné de surveiller à Tigné à St. Elme et à Ricazoli, l'approche des vaisseaux et de tirer dessus à boulets rouges. Tout doit être disposé en conséquence, et le Général d'Artillerie a l'ordre de disposer des boulets incendiaires partout où ils peuvent être utiles. Si quelques vaisseaux avoient la hardiesse d'entrer dans le port, de l'infanterie doit filer le long de la courtine de l'hôpital pour fusiller.

' Il faut augmenter le talud [sic] de la batterie de salut, afin que les pièces ayent plus de plongée.

' Les pièces de la barraque des esclaves seroient disposées de manière à faire effet sur le port.

' On disposera le transport des cartouches d'infanterie pour les differens postes.

' Le Commandant du Génie fera murer de suitte l'entrée du magazin situé à côté de l'ancienne auberge de Baviere.

' Tout français attaché aux administrations de terre ou de mer, ceux qui font les fonctions de secrétaires, ou de domestiques, viendront se faire inscrire dans les vingt quatre heures chez le Général Chanez pour être employés au service de la place en cas d'attaques.'[1]

Lettre au Commandant de la partie de l'est dans laquelle le Général se plaint amèrement des pillages qu'on laisse commettre à la troupe, et finit par lui dire : ' qu'une telle conduite nous mène à notre perte, et que vous êtes responsable des désordres que commettent les militaires qui sont sous vos ordres.'

[1] There follows here the third summons to surrender, viz. that made by Nelson on October 25th, 1798, for which see chap. x. and *Nelson's Dispatches*, vol. iv. pp. 155, 156. The reply of General Vaubois is also given in chap. x.—J. H. R.

4 Brumaire (25th October 1798).

Au Contre-Amiral Villeneuve :
' Je crois, mon cher Général, vous faire une chose qui vous est agréable en vous associant au service de la place pendant qu'elle est bloquée, je ne puis mieux faire que de mettre à profit votre zèle et votre intelligence. En conséquence je vous prie de vous charger de la surveillance du fort St. Ange et des batteries de l'extrémité de la Sengle. La proximité des forces navales que vous commandés exige que ces deux points d'appui soient réunis à votre deffensive dans le port.'

9 Brumaire (30th October 1798).

Ordre au Général d'Artillerie d'inquiéter et de détruire l'établissement que l'ennemi paroit toujours vouloir faire au Coradin.

12 Brumaire (2nd November 1798).

Ordre au Commandant de la place de se transporter à l'hôpital avec un aide de camp du Général pour vérifier, lors de la distribution la quantité de viande que l'on consomme par jour, afin de mettre un frein aux intollerables abus qui se commettent sur cet important objet.

Lettre au Commandant de l'est contenant d'iteratives plaintes sur l'indiscipline de la troupe, et par laquelle on lui préscrit dans les termes les plus forts de reprimer ces desordres par les moyens les plus sévères.

13 idem (3rd November 1798).

Ordre au Contre-Amiral Villeneuve de remplacer par 40 boulangers Français les 40 Maltais qui sont employés à la munitionnaire, parce que la mauvaise qualité du pain autorise à leur croire le projet de nuire à la garnison.

16 Brumaire (6th November 1798).

Ordre au Général d'Artillerie de continuer à inquiéter les travaux de l'ennemi sur le Coradin.

À la Commission du Gouvernement :
' Les circonstances impérieuses dans lesquelles nous nous trouvons, la résolution inébranlable de conserver Malte à la République ou de nous ensévelir sous les murs de la ville, m'obligent à prendre des mesures extraordinaires de l'exécution desquelles je charge la Commission du Gouvernement, mais tout en me portant à ces actes que la nécessité exige, je veux conserver et suivre les principes de l'équité la plus scrupuleuse, convaincu que Malte restant à la République le Gouvernement Français remplira réligieusement les obligations contractées par ses agens.' [1]

19 Brumaire (9th November 1798).

Lettre au Commissaire Ordonateur de la Marine dans laquelle le Général l'informe qu'il a été instruit qu'on vendoit dans la ville des bois neufs provenant des magazins de la Marine. Il lui enjoint de prendre des informations sur cet objet, et si le delit est prouvé d'en livrer les auteurs au Conseil de Guerre.

20 Brumaire (10th November 1798).

Lettre aux membres de la Municipalité :
' Aussitot la présente reçue, faites un inventaire exact de tout ce qui se trouve à la municipalité provenant ou de marchandises données en payement de l'emprunt, ou des séquestres, ou de toute autre manière quelconque. Vous m'enverrés un double de cet inventaire pour disposer ultérieurement des objets utiles à la République. Vous ne pouvés mettre trop de célérité dans la mesure que je vous demande.'

---

[1] Items follow respecting the supply of clothing to the troops.—J. H. R.

21 idem (11th November 1798).

Lettre à la Commission de Gouvernement dans laquelle le Général approuve la choix qu'elle vient de faire du Citoyen Doublet pour le Citoyen Regnaud de St. Jean d'Angely dans l'emploi de Commissaire du Gouvernement.

Lettre au Citoyen Bertis par laquelle le Général accepte sa démission de la place de président de la Municipalité de l'est.

À la Commission du Gouvernement :
'Je vous fais passer, Citoyens, copie de la démission du Citoyen Bertis, président de la municipalité de l'est. Je l'ai accepté avec empressement, vous en ferés sûrement de même, quand vous saurés qu'il est indigne de la confiance publique, un patriotisme qui n'existe qu'en démonstrations verbales et que la cupidité souille, est mille fois plus à craindre pour la chose publique que l'aristocratie même.'

22 Brumaire (12th November 1798).

Le Citoyen Regnaud de St. Jean d'Angely m'a laissé en partant une note des ressources en argent pour le payement des troupes et pour celui de quelques agens civils qui ne pourroient vivre si on differoit leur payement. Je vous fais passer copie de cette note pour en vérifier l'exactitude, et que vous vous occupiés sans delai du versement de ces fonds dans la caisse du Payeur de la Division sauf les articles que des raisons majeures empêcheroient d'y comprendre.

	fr.
Dans la caisse du Gouvernement, en argent, lingots et bijoux provenant d'un leg	45,588
Au Mont de Piété	17,000
À la caisse de la redemption	17,000
À la caisse des depôts, argenterie comprise	120,000
Total	199,588

L'Université n'ayant aucun achat à faire, tous les deniers provenans de la vente du bled aux habitans, frais d'administration des cittés de l'est et de l'ouest présents, argent monoyé ou bijoux d'or et d'argent doivent être exactement versés dans la caisse du payeur.

Je vous fais passer des livres de commerce dans lesquels il se trouve des billets payables par des habitans du pays à un nommé françois Calleja de Bourmola. Les livres et billets de la valeur de 72,000$^{fr.}$ environ m'ont été remis par le Citoyen Bertis ci-devant président de la municipalité de l'est. Le dit Calleja est à la campagne, et il est présumable qu'y ayant été de son propre mouvement, et que se trouvant du Cazal Zebbug presque entièrement rébelle, il est du nombre des insurgés, circonstances qui rendroient les créances propriétés de la République. Vous voudrés bien examiner cet objet et me transmettre vos réflexions.

24 Brumaire (14th November 1798).

Lettre à la Municipalité de l'est pour l'autoriser à faire cultiver les terrains de l'enceinte de la Cotoner qui appartiennent à des particuliers qui sont à la campagne :
'Je compte sur la sagesse de votre administration pour tirer le parti le plus avantageux des terrains abandonnés ; et même pour exciter le travail des habitans qui sont présens et qui en possèdent.'

26 Brumaire (16th November 1798).

Lettre Circulaire aux Consuls de France à Cagliari, Gênes et Livourne :
'Vous ne pouvés ignorer, Citoyens, que depuis trois mois, les habitans revoltés de l'isle nous bloquent par terre, tandis que les Anglois nous bloquent par mer.

Ces ennemis ne sont pas en état de forcer nos remparts, mais notre salut dépend des subsistences ; vous êtes placés avantageusement pour nous en procurer. Faites donc tout ce que vous est humainement possible pour nous faire parvenir des bœufs le plus que vous pourrés. Vous sentez que l'hôpital a besoin de viande fraîche. Il faut du lard, du vin et de l'eau de vie pour la troupe—nous avons du bled.

'Cette conquête est d'un si grand avantage, qu'il ne faut pas regarder aux pertes que l'on pourroit faire, le bénéfice des armateurs doit être en raison des risques, et quand même il ne nous parviendroit que la moitié des chargemens, cela seroit toujours très heureux.

'Vous pouvés annoncer qu'on sera bien payé à Malte, et même je m'occupe en ce moment de vous faire passer des traites sur Livourne et Gênes. Les démarches que je vous engage à faire sont d'une telle importance pour la France que je compte sur votre zèle et je suis persuadé que vous vous empresserés de saisir cette nouvelle occasion de bien mériter de la patrie. Les payemens sont sûrs, ainsi que les récompenses pour les capitaines, et fallut-il répondre des bâtimens après estimation faite je n'hesiterai pas. Un vent frais du nord-ouest fait dériver les Anglois et pourroit ammener en peu de tems les objets que je vous demande. C'est une occasion de gros gains pour les marins et de gloire pour vous. Je vous la repette ; nous ne craignons pas la force, et en nous procurant les subsistances nous rébuterons nos ennemis, et nous consérverons à la France ce superbe port. Notre patrie compte sur notre courage ; elle n'aura rien à nous réprocher. Vous savés que le Roi de Naples depuis notre entré ici, nous a tout refusé et tout accordé aux Anglois. La Sicile, par conséquent, nous est interdite.'

27 Brumaire (17th November 1798).

À la Commission de Gouvernement :

'Les rues sont pleines de mendians qu'il est nécessaire d'envoyer à la campagne pour diminuer d'autant la consommation du pain. En conséquence vous voudrés bien prendre un arrêté pour que le pain de charité soit retranché aux pauvres, excepté—

'1º. Aux mères et épouses des Maltais qui sont partis avec le Général en Chef Bonaparte.

'2º. Aux vétérans à qui l'on ne paye pas la pension en ce moment.'

Au Général Comm$^{t\cdot}$ en Corse :

'Vous savés, mon cher Général, que nous sommes à Malte bloqués par mer et par terre. Le courage des soldats qui s'y trouvent renfermés garantit cette place des efforts de l'ennemi ; mais cela ne suffit pas, il faut des subsistances pour conserver cette belle conquête à la République. Je vous fais passer cette lettre par un officier de marine nommé Sardaigne pour cet objet. Faites donc tous vos efforts, mon cher Général, pour l'aider de tous les moyens qui sont en votre pouvoir, soit par des embarcations que la Corse pourroit fournir, et même par des cargaisons de bois, de charbon, de vin, d'eau de vie, &c. Votre amour pour la République est la Baze [sic] de mes espérances.'

Au Vice-Roi de Sardaigne :

'Vous n'ignorés pas la situation où se trouve la place de Malte. Je ne puis me rappeller la Corse où je commandois l'année passée, sans me ressouvenir encore de toute l'utilité que nous rétirions du voisinage de la Sardaigne, et de vos bons offices. L'amitié doit rapprocher les distances. Assuré par mon expérience de trouver ce sentiment dans le réprésentant d'un souverain qui a marqué le plus d'attachement et de confiance au Directoire exécutif, je n'hésite pas à faire connoître à V. E. nos besoins ; besoins cependant qui ne sont pas au gré de nos ennemis, puisque nous sommes approvisionnés pour longtems des commestibles les plus essentiels.

'Le citoyen qui aura l'honneur de vous remettre la présente, sous les auspices de notre consul, est chargé des achats et des expéditions successives des articles dont vous trouverés ci-joint l'énoncé. Il devra s'en occuper pendant le cours de l'hiver qui doit favoriser ses opérations. Je suis encore plus certain du succés qui peut dépendre de vous. Votre amitié active aplanira sans doute les obstacles de localité qui pourroient s'opposer à la sortie des articles qu'il nous importe de recevoir. On n'a pas oublié en France que l'un de vos prédécesseurs en 1789 nous fit avoir avec célerité des secours considérables en grains. On doit se promettre encore plus de la part de V. E. et je puis l'assurer d'avance de toute la gratitude du Directoire exécutif.

'État des différens commestibles et autres articles de première nécessité dont le gouvernement de Malte désireroit d'obtenir l'extraction des ports de Sardaigne, en ayant commis l'achat et l'éxpédition au Citoyen Vital Coste qui a reçu des ordres à cet effet, sçavoir—

'500 bœufs ; 500 quintaux de lard ; 1,000 moutons ; 4,000 pintes d'eau de vie ; 10,000 pintes de vin ou deux mille quartiers, mesure de Sardaigne ; 2,000 salmes d'orge ; un fort chargement de charbon ; deux chargemens de bois ; du thon salé.'

28 Brumaire (18th November 1798).

À la Commission de Gouvernement :
'La nécessité des circonstances me détermine à vous prier de prendre des dispositions pour que provisoirement il ne sorte aucuns fonds de la caisse des dépôts, sous quelque prétexte que ce puisse être.'[1]

2 Frimaire (22nd November 1798).

PROCLAMATION.

ART. 1ᴱᴿ.

Les habitans de l'est et de l'ouest ne pourront monter sur le rempart. Il n'y aura que les troupes et les employés au service militaire qui pourront y monter. Il est enjoint aux gardes d'arrêter ceux qui contreviendront à cette deffense.

ART. 2.

Les commandants militaires dans chaque partie donneront des ordres pour qu'on laisse l'usage des terrasses aux habitans. Il n'y a qu'autant qu'on en mesureroit d'une façon quelconque qu'on puniroit sévèrement les coupables.

ART. 3.

Voulant détruire la mendicité, et envoyer les personnes qui mendient dans les rues à la campagne, le pain de charité est rétranché à tous, excepté aux mères et épouses de ceux qui sont partis avec l'escadre française, soit comme matelots soit comme soldats.

ART. 4.

Les gardes n'arrêteront dans les rues que les pauvres qu'ils verront demander l'aumone, et ils seront de suite mis hors de la ville.

ART. 5.

Le Général renouvelle l'ordre de respecter les propriétés. Les possessions des traîtres et des parjures envers la République française ne peut (sic) devenir la proie d'aucuns particuliers, mais appartient de droit à la République, et doit servir au besoin de tous.

[1] For Vaubois' letter of Nov. 19, 1798, which follows, see chap. x.—J. H. R.

Art. 6.

Les femmes dont les maris sont absens, les filles qui ne restent point avec leurs pères et mères, et les veuves qui n'ont pas été representées seront tenus de se faire inscrire au bureau de l'État Major de la Division. Celles dont le domicile est à la Sengle, à la Victorieuse, ou à Bourmola se feront inscrire chez le commandant de la citté de l'est. Les bureaux seront ouverts depuis huit heures du matin jusqu'à midi, et depuis deux heures jusqu'à huit heures du soir.

Art. 7.

Il est fait la plus expresse deffense aux habitans d'acheter chose quelconques soldats sans le consentement de leurs commandans. Les acheteurs seront arrêtés et mis en prison et condamnés à 30$^{fr.}$ d'amende avec confiscation des objets achetés.

3 Frimaire (23rd November 1798).

Au Payeur de la Division :

'Les circonstances impérieuses dans lesquelles nous nous trouvous nous font un devoir d'user de tous les moyens possibles pour conserver Malte à la République. De tous ces moyens le plus infaillible est de nous procurer des subsistances, et nous sommes sûrs en y réussissant d'assurer cette conquête et d'être approuvé par le gouvernement. Pour cet effet j'expédie différens individus en Sardaigne et à Tripoli, je m'adresse à tous les agents de la République qui se trouvent dans les ports d'Italie ; mais cette mesure pourroit devenir infructueuse si nous ne fournissions pas des moyens d'achat. Je prends dont le parti de livrer aux agens que j'employe des lettres de change jusqu'à la concurrence de cent cinquante mille écus. J'ai trouvé ici un banquier, le Citoyen Mattei, qui par patriotisme, et pour nous aider à triompher du blocus que nous éprouvons veut bien nous aider de son crédit et endosser ces lettres de change. Vous voudrés donc bien, et le salut de Malte en dépend, tirer ces lettres de change sur la trésorerie nationale, jusqu'à concurrence de cent cinquante mille écus. J'approuverai par ma signature sur ces lettres de change votre action sur la trésorerie, et le Citoyen Mattei les endossera. Je suis si convaincu que nous faisons une action qui sera approuvée par le gouvernement, et qui est si impérieusement demandée par les circonstances, que vous pouvez regarder cette lettre comme un ordre positif.'

Au Citoyen Belleville, Chargé d'Affaires pour la République à Gênes :

' Vous pensiés peutêtre, mon cher ami, que mon séjour à Malte seroit exempte d'orage : vous vous êtes trompé : nous sommes depuis trois mois bloqués par terre par les habitans de la campagne en pleine insurrection, et les Anglois nous bloquent par mer.

'L'insurrection des habitans est bien criminelle, mais n'a-t'elle pas été provoquée ? a-t'on fait ce qu'on devoit pour l'éviter ? n'a-t'on point outre passé les ordres du Général Bonaparte ? a-t'on eu une conduite politique commandée par les circonstances ? Les principes de l'équité et de la justice ont-ils été suivis ?

'Non, mon sort est d'avoir des co-opérateurs qui gatent toujours les affaires et d'être chargé ensuite du rédressement des torts énormes qu'ils se donnent. Rappellés-vous la Corse ; c'est ici le second volume de cette histoire, et si vous connoîssés le fameux Regnaud de St. Jean d'Angely dont le patriotisme a tant brillé à l'assemblée constituante, vous ne serés point étonné que cet être qui rivalisoit de pouvoir avec moi ne m'ait ménagé des contrariétés si préjudiciables à notre chère patrie. Je n'ai été employé qu'une fois à ma satisfaction. C'est à Livourne avec mon ami Belleville. Nos ames ont la même trempe quoique douées de moyens bien différens. La supériorité de Belleville fournissoit des moyens d'exécution aux intentions qui me dictoit mon zèle. Il s'en est ensuivi que la République par la réunion de deux êtres qui l'aiment, a été bien servie.

Les mêmes dispositions ne m'ont point quittés ; mais des coquins d'arristocrates anéantissoient tout mon travail. Mes peines sont perdues et la conquête de Malte est compromise. Cette place restera à la République, et, en dépit des malveillans ce beau port sera un jour l'entrepôt du commerce du Levant.

'L'infaillible moyen de conserver ce poste important est de nous procurer des subsistances. J'attends beaucoup de la sollicitude du Gouvernement ; mais je ne ferois pas mon devoir si je ne faisois pas moi-même les plus grands efforts pour assurer notre ravitaillement. En conséquence j'envoye au Sardaigne un négociant juif nommé Coste accompagné d'un autre nommé Secone. Je l'ai muni de lettres de change tirées sur la trésorerie nationale et endossées par un banquier nommé Mattei, riche et dévoué à la France.

'Peut-être Coste aura t'il de la peine à les négocier à Cagliari. Je lui enjoins de s'adresser à vous, et je suis persuadé, mon cher ami, que par vos soins, votre credit, et même par des fonds, s'il ne peut placer son papier, vous l'aiderès dans cette mission. C'est un coup de partie, nos remparts ne seront point forcés ; le canons y grondent continuellement, et les braves volontaires qui sont dessus sont les mêmes que dans les plaines d'Italie, et sur les bords du Rhin. Des vivres, quoiqu'il en coute, des bombes, des boulets de 24, du vin, des bœufs pour l'hôpital, des salaissons pour les bien portants et ça ira. Le courage est au comble, mais il faut le soutenir par des alimens. Je ne me suis point contenté d'envoyer en Sardaigne, j'expédie encore à Tripoli pour le même objet.'

4 Frimaire (24th November 1798).

Au Contre-Amiral Villeneuve :

'Par une lettre écrite au Commissaire Ordonateur de la Marine au Commissaire Ordonateur de Toulon qui lui mande qu'un convoi de vivres qui doit partir de Toulon sera escorté par trois vaisseaux et *La Boudeuse*, ne seroit-il pas à propos de tenir prêt *Le Guillaume Tell* et une frégatte au moins pour porter secours et dégager le convoi s'il se présente devant l'isle. Il peut se faire que nous ayons une chance favorable ; les vaisseaux ennemis pourroient être séparés et par là nous donner plus beau jeu.

'Disposés donc ces bâtimens pourqu'au premier avis, tout ce qui leur appartient se trouve abord, et que nous puissions réaliser cette idée.'

5 Frimaire (25th November 1798).

Au Consul de la République à Cagliari :

'Je vous ai écrit dernièrement, Citoyen Consul, par une barque de Sardaigne, et un officier de marine qui est passé dessus, vous aura remis mes depêches, si la traversée a été heureuse comme je l'espère. Je vous instruisois des moyens que j'employe pour tirer des commestibles de Sardaigne. Les Citoyens Coste et Secone que j'employe comme agens de la République dans cette affaire vous manifesteront leurs pouvoirs. Ils sont munis de lettres de change sur la trésorerie nationale, endossées par un banquier riche. Mettés vous, je vous prie, à la tête de cette entreprise et faites la réussir : elle est de la plus haute importance. Si par hazard il se rencontroit des difficultés à placer ce papier à Cagliari, j'écris à Belleville, chargé de la Legation de France à Gênes, de vous aider de tout son crédit, de tout son pouvoir, et même de fonds s'il le faut. Je suis assuré de ses bons offices.

'Vous pouvés mettre notre confiance dans les Citoyens Coste et Secone : ils m'ont été donnés comme en étant digne à tous les égards. Ils sont munis de l'état des commestibles qui nous sont indispensables. Je ne doute pas qu'ils se trouvent aisement en Sardaigne. Ils vous mettront au fait de vive voix de la situation exacte de la ville de Malte.

'J'écris par duplicata au Vice Roi au nom de l'amitié qui existe entre les deux nations de vous aider de son pouvoir même de fonds s'il est nécessaire. Je suis persuadé aussi que vos rélations avec des négociants à Cagliari aplaniront toutes les difficultés qui pourroient se rencontrer. Il est superflu que je cherche à exciter votre activité et votre zèle, c'est le cas de rendre à la République un service des plus signalés.'

Au Vice-Roi de Sardaigne :
'Il pourroit se faire, Monsieur, que malgré la protection que j'ai reclamé auprès de vous pour mes comissionnaires ils éprouvaient des difficultés dans le placement des lettres de change dont ils sont porteurs. Ne pourrois-je pas me flatter, vu les circonstances qu'ils obtiendront de vous même des avances pecuniares ? Vous devés être convaincu de l'empressement de la trésorerie nationale à satisfaire à cette dette sacrée, et je suis bien persuadé que l'amitié que règne entre nos deux nations vous y portera si vous n'y trouvés aucune difficulté.'[1]

7 Frimaire (27th November 1798).

Lettres aux deux municipalités de l'est et l'ouest par laquelle on les invite à mettre le séquestre sur des marchandises appartenantes à des habitans qui sont passés chez les rébelles.

10 Frimaire (30th November 1798).

Au Gouverneur de Souza :
'J'ai apris par le Citoyen Conseil, agent pour la République française, le gracieux accuil que vous lui avés fait dans son premier voyage à Souza. Il ne m'a pas laissé ignorer, non plus vos sentimens pour la République, et cela m'engage à réclamer votre appui pour sa personne et votre interêt pour l'accomplissement de la mission dont je l'ai chargé. Il m'importe infiniment qu'il s'en acquitte le plus promptement possible. C'est d'acheter et d'expédier à Malte de la manière dont il aura l'honneur de vous l'expliquer, les objets d'approvisionnemens nécessaires à la place de Malte que je commande, et sur laqu'elle le Roi de Naples, l'ennemi de toutes les puissances barbaresques, a d'injustes prétentions.

'Le Citoyen Conseil m'a fait le plus grand éloge des dispositions amicales qui vous animent pour la République. Je ne doute pas que vous ne le recevés avec bonté et que sa commission ne soit remplie avec succès et célérité. Vous sentés combien il importe aux princes Africains que Malte soit aux français plutôt que de rester sous la domination du Roi de Naples. Cette considération n'a sûrement pas échappée à votre haute sagesse.

'Je vous prie d'être persuadé que de mon côté je saisirai toujours avec bien du plaisir les occasions de vous assurer de toute mon estime et de mon amitié.'

Au Bey de Bengazi :
'Les marques de prédiliction et d'attachement que votre illustre maison et V.E. elle même n'ont pas cessé de donner à la nation française, la jalousie et le désespoir du Roi de Naples, notre commun ennemi, de ce Roi qui a violé les traités les plus sacrés envers la République, et qui est l'ennemi le plus acharné à vos sujets, me porte à m'adresser à vous avec la plus grande confiance dans un tems où nos ennemis font de vains efforts. Je sais que dans le pays où vous regnés, la viande est très abondante et excellente. Je prie V.E. de permettre au Citoyen Conseil, agent pour la République, qui aura l'honneur de vous présenter ma lettre, d'acheter dans vos états et de faire embarquer pour Malte, non seulement la plus grande quantité de bœufs et de moutons qu'il pourroit se procurer mais aussi de la volaille et autre objets utiles à la consommation de ce pays-ci.

'V.E. est trop éclairée pour ne pas sentir qu'il est bien plus avantageux pour elle, et pour les peuples qu'elle gouverne de voir l'isle de Malte rester à la France que de tomber entre les mains du Roy de Naples notre ennemi naturel, et qui acquereroit encore plus de moyens de vous nuire si jamais il possédait Malte.

[1] For Vaubois' letter of November 26, 1798, to the Directory, see chap. x.—J. H. R.

'J'ai tout lieu de croire que son éspérance à cet égard sera déçu, de même que celle des Anglois. J'ai heureusement assez de bled et de denrées de première nécessite pour garder longtems cette place très forte pour avoir jamais rien à craindre des foibles ennemis qui l'environnent.

'Le Directoire de la République française qui voit dans votre Excellence un de ses vrais amis, lui saura bon gré de la protection et des facillités qu'elle accordera au Citoyen Conseil pour l'accomplissement de la mission dont je l'ai chargé. Je la prie d'en agréer d'avance mes remercimens et l'assurance de mon respect.'

Au Général d'Artillerie :
'Le Général d'Artillerie donnera des ordres pour que les postes de la Cotoner soient garnies des chausses-trappes qui y soit destinées, et que les remparts soient aussi munis de beaucoup de grénades chargées à jetter à la main, on chargera encore les pierriers. Vous ferés aussi distribuer des tourteaux pour éclairer en cas d'attaque de nuit.'

Lettre circulaire aux gouverneurs de Gerbi, Monestir et Sfax pour leur recommander le Citoyen Conseil et les prier de lui faciliter les moyens de se procurer les objets nécessaires à l'approvisionnement de Malte.

Au Citoyen Beaussier, Consul à Tripoli :
'Je crois devoir vous prévenir secrètement, Citoyen Consul, que ne connoissant pas assez le Citoyen Conseil pour savoir s'il est doué de toutes les qualités qu'exige la mission importante qu'il a sollicitée, je l'appui essentiellement sur vous, comme vous l'avez déjà connu dans son premier voyage en Barbarie, il vous sera plus facile qu'à moi d'apprécier son véritable mérite. Le zèle qu'il peut avoir pour servir la République, et le mémoire qu'il m'a présenté annonçant de l'intelligence et des connoissances sur la Barbarie, m'ont décidé à accepter ses offres ; mais bien entendu qu'il ne doit rien faire d'essentiel sans vous consulter et dans le cas où sa conduite vous feroit juger qu'il ne mérite pas votre confiance, vous pourrés ne lui accorder que celle qui vous paroitra convenable, car, je vous le repette, c'est vous seul qui par votre place devés avoir toute la mienne, et sur qui par conséquent, je me repose essentiellement du soin de faire réussir la mission importante pour laquelle s'est offert le Citoyen Conseil, et qui peut concourrir si efficacement au salut de cette isle.'

Extrait d'une autre lettre au même datte :
'J'ai pensé que pour faire réussir vos opérations, il convenoit de faire un présent au pacha, et qu'un petit bâtiment armé en guerre seroit celui qui conviendroit le mieux à son goût. J'ai en conséquence destiné pour cet objet le cutter sur lequel est embarqué le Citoyen Conseil et je vous prie de le lui présenter de ma part.'

Au Bacha de Tripoli :
'Illustre et magnifique Seigneur, la bonne intelligence qui a toujours regné entre la France et votre excellence, me donne lieu d'espérer qu'à ma prière vous voudrés bien autoriser le Citoyen Beaussier, résident auprès de vous en qualité de consul de ma nation, et le Citoyen Conseil, agent de la République, de faire exporter de vos états les objets qu'ils auront l'un et l'autre l'honneur de vous demander de ma part pour l'approvisionnement de cette place.

'Si comme j'ose m'en flatter vous avés la bonté d'acquiescer à ma demande, la République y sera d'autant plus sensible, que les objets que vous pourrés m'accorder dans cette circonstance me sont très essentiels.

'Je prie votre excellence d'agréer, au nom de la République, le petit cutter qui vous sera présenté par le Consul Beaussier, et d'être bien convaincu de la plus haute considération et la sincere amitié que j'ai pour vous, illustre et magnifique Seigneur.'

Au Directoire exécutif :

'Citoyens Directeurs,—J'ai eu l'honneur de vous écrire il y a quelques jours avec un chiffre qu'avoit ici le chargé d'affaires de France à Malte qui lui a été envoyé en 1778 esperant qu'on en trouveroit la clef dans les bureaux et que je pourrois être lu. Aujourd'hui je me sers d'une chiffre plus récent dont le Citoyen Sibon ci-devant chargé d'affaires de Malte à Paris a la clef. Le blocus de Malte par mer et par terre continue toujours. Comptés sur notre résistance et notre courage ; mais les subsistances, les munitions de guerre et de tout espéce s'épuisent. Je sais par un avis qui vient d'arriver quels sont les moyens que vous prenés pour me ravittailler. Ce bâtiment est le seul des cinq expédiés de Toulon qui soit parvenu à sa destination. J'ai cru qu'il étoit de mon devoir d'assossier (sic) encore des entreprises aux vôtres pour rendre notre ravittaillement plus sûr. Ce qui est arreté venant d'une part se trouve remplacé venant de l'autre et notre salut en dépend. J'ai trouvé ici un banquier qui a endossé des lettres de change tirées sur la trésorerie nationale pour cent cinquante mille livres.

'Je depèche à Cagliari, en Sardaigne et à Tripoli des agens à qui je crois devoir donner ma confiance pour nous expédier de ces endroits de la viande fraîche et des salaisons. Ce que vous faites au grand, Citoyens Directeurs, et ce que je peux faire de mon côté conservera Malte à la France. Le courage des Républicains est au comble, mais des vivres, du vin, de l'eau de vie, des bombes de huit pouces et de douze, des boulets de 24, et tout ira bien.

'Que le Roi de Naples expie les echecs de la Méditerrannée, il est cause de notre misère. Pour nous, nous mourrons s'il le faut, toujours digne de notre patrie. L'argent nous est nécéssaire : tout est presque épuisé, et ce qui reste est à des prix incroyables.

'Après le malheur qu'a éprouvé l'escadre il est heureux pour nous d'avoir réceuilli *Le Guillame Tell*, *La Diane*, et *La Justice*, sans l'arrivée de ces bâtimens il m'eut été impossible d'occuper l'ouvrage immense de la Cotoner. Leur garnison et une grande partie des matelots, qui ne cesse s'exercer aux armes, me deffendent le fort Manuel, le fort Ricazoli, le fort Tigné et celui de St. Ange.

'J'ai donné des commandemens aux Contre-Amiraux Villeneuve et Decrés, leur conduite est pleine de zèle, d'activité et d'intelligence.'[1] Les soldats sont un jour sur les remparts et un jour sur la paille. Ils sont extrêmement fatigués. L'enceinte est immense et il faut tout deffendre.

'Tout est commun pour notre nourriture entre la terre et la mer. L'eau est notre unique boisson. Nous prenons le plus grand soin de l'hôpital dont les malades sont nombreux, mais malgré nos épargnes, la viande fraîche va nous manquer. Cet état ne nous abbat pas cependant. Pensés à nous. Nos regards sont tournés vers la République.'

13 Frimaire (3rd December 1798).

Ordre du jour :

'Le 21 courant les trois compagnies de la 23me et la 41me demi Brigade réléveront la 6me demi Brigade et la 80e demi Brigade. Une campagnie de la 20me occupera le Salvator. Trente hommes commandés par un officier, deux sergents, et quatre caporaux occuperont le fort St. Ange. Le reste de la 23me et de la 41eme occuperont la Victorieuse et feront le service dans cette place et à la Cotoner jusqu'à la Porte de Zabbar.

'Cette partie de gauche sera commandé par le chef de Battaillon Noblot ainsi que la droite.

'La 7me demie Brigade d'inf^{rie} legere fera le service de la Sengle et de la droite jusqu'à la porte de Zabbar, chaque officier et chaque corps qui font des changemens, est obligé de remettre aux municipalités de l'ouest et de l'est tous

---

[1] For the letters of Villeneuve to the Directory, of this same date, see chap. x.—J. H. R.

les effets qu'ils ont reçu. Cet ordre est de rigueur. Les officiers et les corps en répondent.

'La 8me rélevera la 41eme à la Florianne, et la 6me rélevera les compagnies de carabiniers de la 23me dont une sera placée à l'auberge de Castille, et le reste aux cazernes de la porte nationale.

'Il est ordonné à toutes les troupes de vivre dans la meilleure discipline dans es endroits qu'ils vont occuper.

'Les chefs instruiront ceux qui les remplacent du service. Il leur est expressement recommandé, et on met sous leur responsabilité de ne point laisser consommer des munitions inutilement. Ils examineront soigneusement les fortifications dont la deffense leur est confiée. Ils en chercheront le fort et le foible, et combineront leur deffense en conséquence.'

Lettre du Commandant des forces Angloises navales devant Malte au Gén$^{l.}$ Vaubois :

4 X$^{bre.}$ 1798.

'MONSIEUR,—'J'ai grand satisfaction de vous envoyer les femmes des officiers qui ont été conduites à St. Paul. Les Maltais m'ont sollicités de les rétenir comme une garantie des bons traitements de leurs compatriottes que vous avés emprisonnés.

'Comme j'ai promis à ces dames que leur captivité seroit très courte, je ne voudrois pas ajouter à leur malheur le severe désagrément de les tenir separées de leurs maris, mais, monsieur, je dois vous avertir que je serai dans la nécessité de détenir tous ceux qui pourroient être pris pour tranquiliser les esprits des Maltais dont vous aves emprisonnés les parents. J'ai l'honneur d'être, &c. ALEXANDRE BALL.'

14 Frimaire (4th December 1798).

Reponse du Général Vaubois à la lettre ci-dessus :

'Les femmes que vous avés envoyé, Monsieur, sont arrivées à la satisfaction de leurs maris. Vous pouvés agir comme il vous plaira vis-à-vis des prisonniers qui tomberont à l'avenir entre vos mains, les loix de la guerre a (sic) ses réprisailles. J'ai l'honneur d'être, &c. LE GENERAL VAUBOIS.'

Sommation faite au Général Vaubois par le Commandant des forces navales Angloises devant Malte :

7 Décembre.

'MONSIEUR,—Je juge à propos de vous informer qu'il est arrivé ici des bâtimens chargés de mortiers, canons, et de toutes choses nécessaires pour réduire le poste que vous commandés et comme la France n'est point en état de vous porter du secours j'espère que par humanité vous ne voudrés pas me mettre dans la nécessité de détruire la ville sans autre motif que de pouvoir dire que vous ne l'avés rendue que lorsqu'elle a été réduite en cendres. Je vous offre encore les mêmes termes de capitulation que l'Amiral Nelson vous offrit il y a six semaines, mais si je suis obligé de jetter des bombes j'y ferai certainement une grande différence.

'Pour vous prouver que vous n'avez aucun motif d'attendre des secours, je vous informe qu'une escadre Angloise ayant plusieurs regimens à bord est entrée dans la Méditerrannée et s'est emparée de l'isle de Minorque,[1] et que notre escadre ayant rencontré une escadre française ayant six mille hommes à bord, les a pris ou coulés bas, excepté trois frégattes. Le vaisseau appellé Le Hoche est du nombre des vaisseaux pris, vous connoissés déjà le sort de Corfou et des vaisseaux qui s'y trouvoient. Je sais que tout est embarqué à bord des vaisseaux prêts à mettre à la voile mais si pareille chose étoit tentée j'espère que l'événement prouveroit que c'est sacrifier nombre de braves gens pour l'amour des formes. J'ai l'honneur d'être, &c. ALEXANDRE BALL.'

[1] Minorca was occupied by the force under General Fox.—J. H. R.

17 Frimaire (7th December 1798).

Reponse du Général Vaubois :
'J'ai repondu aux diverses sommations qui m'ont été faites comme je le devois ; faites, monsieur, ce que vous croyés devoir faire. La garnison française qui est à Malte est prête à supporter vos attaques, elle justifiera à vos yeux l'idée que vous devés avoir de brave gens. J'ai l'honneur d'être, &c.
LE GENERAL VAUBOIS.'

20 Frimaire (10th December 1798).

PROCLAMATION.

L'ennemi ménace de bombarder la ville. Cela ne fait aucune sensation aux français accoutumeés aux bombes et aux boulets. Si cela détruit les maisons, ce sera un service de plus que les Maltais rendroient à leurs concitoyens. Ceux et celles qui craignent les bombes peuvent se présenter pour sortir de la ville chez le chef de l'État Major de la Citté Valette, et chez les commandans dans les autres endroits.

Le Chef de l'État Major et les Commandans en enverront les listes au Général en Chef avant de les mettre dehors. Une seule bombe tirée sur la ville, personne n'aura plus la liberté de sortir.

Au Général en Chef Bonaparte :
'Je profite de l'envoi que je fais d'un nommé Conseil à Tripoli pour vous écrire avec le chiffre que le Citoyen Doublet vous a remis. Si cette lettre vous arrive, vous serés informé exactement de notre situation.

'L'insurrection de la campagne de Malte à éclaté le 2 Sep$^{re.}$ vieux style. Elle a été préparée par le Roi de Naples qui sous le pretexte d'une quarantaine, nous a tout refusé depuis notre arrivée et qui faisoit même maltraiter les Maltais qui se présentoient en Sicile. Le malheur de l'escadre a déterminé les chefs à s'adresser au Roi de Naples et aux Anglais. Au millieu d'une tranquilité apparente l'explosion a eu lieu dans les deux isles en même tems.

'La garnison de la Citté Vieille a été égorgé dès le premier instant, le fanatisme étant le moyen avec lequel les chefs ont enflammé le peuple, il s'est porté à des actes de Barbarie.

'Depuis ce tems nous sommes bloqués par terre par les habitans et quelques jours après nous le fûmes par mer par les Portugais et les Anglois. Les paysans qui du premier instant se sont glissés de l'autre côté du port à la Bourmola, et ont agi en même tems que ceux de la campagne. Nous les avons repoussés et chassés. La révolte avoit ses partisans en ville ; il a fallu se garder devant et derrière par notre vigueur, quelques punitions, quelques fusillades, et par l'expulsion et l'arrestation d'un grand nombre, nous nous sommes mis à l'abri des mouvemens intérieurs. La ville est armée formidablement. Nous nous deffendons avec courage. Nous faisons de tems en tems des sorties que les habitans reçoivent avec acharnement, et qui n'aboutissent qu'à leur tuer quelques hommes. La multitude de murs dont cette isle est couverte diminuant pour le danger.

'La vive force jusqu'à présent ne peut donc, à ce que je pense, triompher de nous ; mais les subsistances sont allarmantes. Nous avons du bled, mais tout le reste nous manque : vin, eau de vie, salaison, viande fraîche pour l'hôpital. Le peu qui se trouve est portée à un prix exorbitant. J'ai vû une lettre du Ministre de la Marine qui annonce que l'on pense à notre ravittaillement ; moi-même j'envoye en Sardaigne et à Tripoli avec des lettres de change du Citoyen Mattei qui se montre assez bien. Puissent mes emissaires passer et nous faire avoir quelque chose.

'Nous n'avons pas reçu un écu du Gouvernement. Je prends partout pour payer la troupe et soutenir sa valeur en la contenant, d'ailleurs en m'emparant de la propriété des Maltais je les attache à la République par leur fortune, car si la France perdoit cette isle la fortune de beaucoup seroit compromise et ma conduite est tracée par la nécessité et la politique. L'arrivée du *Guillaume Tell*, *La Diane* et de *La Justice* nous rend un service des plus grands, une grande partie des équipages et des cannoniers font le service de terre. Les Contre-Amiraux Villeneuve et Decrés ont des commandemens de forts qui sont bien armés, et qu'ils deffendent avec le plus grand zèle et la plus grande intelligence. Sans eux je n'aurois jamais pû garnir nos immenses remparts et les mettre en deffense. Nous manquons de quelques objets en munitions de guerre, comme cartouches d'infanterie, bombes et boulets de 24. Tel est notre situation. Des vivres surtout et Malte tiendra longtems. Comptés d'ailleurs que nous ferons notre devoir. Si on est heureux en Italie, on ne manquera pas de nous fournir de quoi triompher des rébelles.'

Au Commissaire Ordonateur de Terre :
'Par arrangement pris avec la commission de Gouvernement et pour que le traitement des habitans qui se trouvent à l'hôpital civile soit le même que celui des militaires français on continuera à donner la même quantité de viande par jour que j'ai autorisé précédemment.
'On fournira à raison de six cartouches de vin par jour. Les autres vivres doivent être livrés suivant le nombre de malades en mêmes rations et mêmes quantités, et les administrateurs de l'hopital civil ne pourront sous aucun prétexte rendre le traitement de ces malades meilleur que celui des militaires.'

22 Frimaire (12th December 1798).

À l'Adjudant-Général Brouard :
'Après avoir murement réfléchi aux circonstances je m'arrête décidemment au parti de ne laisser sortir aucun individu riche, homme ou femme. Ils craignent extrèmement le bombardement et ils ont à la campagne des parens qui le craignent pour eux. Il est donc certain que tous ceux qui sont absens gemiront sur leur sort, et que eux mêmes malgré leur arristocratie ne peuvent qu'être très fachés de l'évenement. Je comprends dans les gens riches les chanoines, les ex-barons et enfin tous ceux qui passent pour avoir quelque fortune et des propriétés à la campagne. Je vous prie en ne précipitant rien de suivre exactement cette marche qui est certainement très-politique.'

23 Frimaire (13th December 1798).

Ordre au Chef de Bataillon Noblot :
'Je confie au Chef de Bataillon Noblot, le commandement de la partie de l'est sous les ordres du Général Chanez. Le premier soin que le Citoyen Noblot doit se donner est de visiter et reconnoître toutes les parties de son commandement, de distinguer les parties foibles, peu escarpées dont le fossé n'est pas fini ; pour prendre ses précautions en conséquence. De fixer l'emplacement de ses troupes de manière qu'en cas d'attacque ses dispositions soient promptes. De déterminer aussi la destination de la réserve des vaisseaux. D'avoir bien attention dans le cas d'un attaque à la Cotoner aux mouvements intérieurs, de faire deffense expresse à qui que ce soit, s'il n'est employé au service militaire ou dans des fonctions publiques, de sortir de chez lui pendant que l'on se bât. D'ordonner qu'en cas de combat, tout usage de cloches doit cesser dans les églises, jusqu'à ce que l'affaire soit terminée et la défense levée. Le Commandant Noblot doit observer que les fortifications de la Victorieuse et de la Sengle sont des points d'appui qui doivent rendre nulle la prise de la Cotoner, si on la perdoit. Ces fronts doivent donc toujours être exactement gardés et armés formidablement, d'après la visite la plus exacte, il sera fait au général d'artillerie la demande de tout ce qui est necessaire.
'Il ne faut pas non plus négliger la partie d'enceinte de la Victorieuse et de la

Sengle sur les bras de mer qui les prolongent. Faire l'examen le plus scrupuleux de tous les passages qui étoient autrefois ouverts pour reconnoître s'ils sont fermés d'une façon sûre. Exciter la surveillance du fort St. Ange et du petit bastion de la Sengle, et sur les points voisins en cas d'attaque.

'Il reste à recommander au Commandant Noblot de surveiller la partie civile avec fermeté, mais avec justice ; de ne point ménager les mal-intentionnés ; mais faire respecter les personnes et les propriétés de l'homme tranquille, d'avoir des espions bien choisis, de se concerter avec la municipalité sur laquelle je crois pouvoir compter jusqu'à présent de maintenir la plus exacte discipline, moyen le plus sûr d'être victorieux.'

24 Frimaire (14th December 1798).

Au Citoyen Astor, membre de la Commiss^n de Gouvernement :

'Je vous charge, citoyen, de faire la recherche la plus exacte chez les marchands, et autres personnes de tout ce qui appartient en fonds ou autres objets aux chefs des révoltés ou aux revoltés eux-mêmes. Je mets cette recherche sous votre responsabilité, et en cas d'empêchement apporté par des notaires ou par quelque autre que ce soit, vous voudrés bien m'en instruire pour que j'agisse avec rigueur contre les opposans à cette perquisition, et je les traiterai comme partageant les sentimens de ceux dont ils veulent épargner la fortune.'

26 Frimaire (16th December 1798).

À la Commission de Gouvernement :

'Il est extrêmement essentiel, citoyens, de faire tout ce que nous pourrons pour mettre les vaisseaux à l'abri des boulets. En conséquence je vous prie d'inviter les municipalités de faire avec promptitude la recherche de toutes les balles de coton qui se trouvent dans la ville pour les bastinguer. Le Citoyen Ciantar doit en avoir beaucoup. Après la conservation de la ville, les vaisseaux sont ce qui nous intéresse le plus, et nous serions très-coupables si nous apportions la moindre négligence à les sauver.'

PROCLAMATION.

Vaubois, Général de Division, Commandant, &c.

Considérant qu'il est très à propos de faire partir de la ville toutes les bouches inutiles, ordonne ce qui suit :

ART. 1er.

Toutes les femmes dont les maris sont absens, les veuves et les filles faisant le métier de tricoteuses, fileuses, blanchisseuses ou coutourières, se rendront demain à une heure après-midi avec leurs effets, savoir celles de la citté de l'ouest (dont la Florianne fait partie) sur la place de la liberté, et celles de la citté de l'est chez le commandant, elles seront conduites de suitte aux portes et mises dehors.

ART. 2.

Toutes celles qui ne se présenteront pas seront arrêtées en campagne sans leurs effets.

ART. 3.

Sont exceptées les femmes vivans de leurs rentes et plus particulièrement les mères et femmes de ceux qui sont partis avec l'armée, qui seront toujours sous la protection des français.

ART. 4.

Les citoyens qui auroient connoissance que quelques unes de ces femmes sont restées en ville, sont invités à les faire connoître.

APPENDICES

Art. 5.

Les cazemates, les voûtes, les magazins, les souterrains et autres endroits à l'épreuve de la bombe, devant être occupés par des français et les citoyens employés au service de la République, tous les autres individus qui s'y seroient placés, ou qui s'y mettroient sans ma permission, en sortiront sur le champ.

Art. 6.

Le Commandant du Génie et les Commandants de place sont chargés de veiller à l'éxécution de l'article précédent.

Art. 7.

Il sera désigné des endroits sûrs, où les fonctionnaires publics pourront se retirer.

28 Frimaire (18th December 1798).

Je viens de reconnoître l'ouvrage qui se fait au Coradin : pour la détruire il faut chercher dans les ouvrages de la Florianne, de la Sengle, de la Bourmola, de la Cotoner, les points les plus rapprochés. C'est en vain qu'on se flatteroit de ruiner un ouvrage en maçonnerie qui a beaucoup d'épaisseur, à une distance de huit, sept, ou six cent toises, lors même qu'on y employeroit le plus gros calibre.

À l'inspection du plan, si les ouvrages que je vais indiquer sont assez élevés, je pense que les capucins et ouvrages ajacens offrent déjà un emplacement de choix.

À la Sengle au Bastion de St. Michel	460 toises
À la Cotoner au Bastion de Valperga	320 toises
Au Bastion St. Paul à la Cotoner	410 id.
Au Bastion St. Paul à la Bourmola	350 toises

Le Général d'Artillerie et le Commandant du Génie se concerteront et feront les plus grands efforts pour armer ces différens endroits en pièces de dix-huit au moins, et me feront connoître s'il y a possibilité d'exécution, ou s'il se trouve des inconveniens majeurs.

3 Nivôse (23rd December 1798).

Au Commandant du fort Manoël :

'Je suis instruit, Citoyen, qu'au mépris des ordres que j'ai donné, l'on communique toujours avec les rébelles. Le rapport vient de m'être fait qu'on se disposoit de revenir aujourd'hui au rendez-vous. Je vous charge d'interrompre un tel commerce, vous rendant responsable des évenemens ; mon intention est de traduire devant le conseil de guerre le premier des officiers qui contreviendroit à mes ordres. Ayés pour cette nuit la plus grande surveillance ; observés jusqu'au moindre mouvement.'

6 Nivôse (26th December 1798).

À la Commission de Gouvernement :

'Il est tems, Citoyens, de chercher une ressource dans l'or et l'argent qui se trouvent au Mont de Piété. Fidèle aux principes de justice que je cherche à pratiquer imperturbablement, je vous soumets mon projet sur cette opération. Mon but est d'envoyer à la monoye tous les objets qu'on peut convertir en numéraire, de vendre les bijoux qui ne sont pas susceptibles d'être fondus sans perdre de leur valeur ; on pourroit aussi permettre de racheter certains gages dont les intérêts n'ont point été payés, et qui par là acquerreront plus de valeur que par une simple vente. Je ne veux faire aucun tort aux propriétaires, qui sont au service de la République, à ceux qui lui sont restés fidèlles dans cette occasion. Aux uns leurs effets leur seront rendus moyennant rachat ; aux autres ils seront payés ; à d'autres enfin ils seront dûs par la République qui les remboursera lors que la paix sera rétabli.

'Il faut une loi pénale contre ceux qui présenteroient des polices qui ne leur appartiendroient pas. Enfin il faut que les rébelles perdent absolument tout ce qu'ils ont dans cet établissement.

'Je pense que les Citoyens le Brun et Appap peuvent être choisis comme estimateurs, ainsi que le Citoyen Chartier, et je crois que lorsqu'une partie sera estimée, qu'on aura distingué ce qu'il faut envoyer à la monoye, ce qui peut être vendu avantageusement et ce qui peut être racheté, nous pourrons de suitte procéder aux ventes, et sur l'argent qui en proviendra rembourser les privilégiés à juste titre.'

8 Nivôse (28th December 1798).

Au Ministre de la Guerre :

'CITOYEN MINISTRE,—Le Citoyen Dejean, Chef de Brigade de la 80eme demi Brigade se trouvant incommodé au point de ne pouvoir continuer son service se rend à Paris pour y rétablir sa santé.

'C'est une perte, surtout à la tête d'un corps qui a reçu beaucoup de recrues à Toulon, et qui a besoin d'un homme ferme en opinion, et qui ait des talens militaires.

'Il vous rendra compte de vive-voix de notre position, mais cela ne peut me dispenser de vous en entretenir et je vous prie d'en faire part au Directoire exécutif.

'Nous faisons notre devoir, vous pouvez y compter. Nous bravons les bombes et les boulets, mais nous ne voyons pas de termes aux attaques de l'ennemi, et au blocus par mer. Notre resistance sera celle de vrais Républicains ; mais sa durée et notre triomphe dépendent du gouvernement. Nos vivres consistent en bled pour six mois au moins, à calculer la consommation sur le nombre que nous sommes.

'Il vient d'arriver un petit navire français et un autre expédié par Backri de Marseille qui donnent du vin pour l'hôpital pour six mois, si le nombre de malades n'augmente pas. Le dernier nous a apporté un peu de viande salée dont nous manquons absolument. Nous avons pour quelques mois d'eau de vie en en donnant deux fois par décade. Nous avons très-peu de legumes secs, et il ne nous reste qu'une vingtaine de bœufs pour l'hopital. Nous manquons des boulets de 24 et de bombes de 8 et de 12 pouces. Vous voyés, Citoyen Ministre, qu'à l'exception du bled nous manquons de tout.

'Nous sommes même réduits à craindre en quelque façon la fin de la guerre avec la population révoltée, car alors il faudroit faire périr les chefs et nourrir la multitude, ce qui nous exposeroit à manquer du bled cet été.

'Les habitans de la ville manquent de tout et si nous n'avions expulsé au moins douze mille personnes, ils périroient de faim. La mesure prise pour notre sûreté a donc un double avantage.

'Je manque de Chefs. La troupe est excédée de fatigues par son petit nombre et l'immensité des fortifications.

'Jusqu'à présent le soldat et l'officier ont été payés mois par mois, sans avoir pu liquider l'arriéré. J'ai pris toutes les caisses publiques, les révenus de l'université, et le Mont de Piété. Cela étoit indispensable pour soutenir la troupe dans son excellent esprit, mais ces ressources sont épuisées. J'ai procédé dans les emprunts et dans la prise des caisses et du Mont de Piété avec justice et équité, de sorte que d'après les procés-verbaux et les estimations, la République pourra un jour rembourser ceux qui sont restés fidèles, et se trouvera en possession de tout ce qui appartient aux rébelles.

'La Marine qui s'est rendue ici, me rend les plus grands services en hommes et en commandans. Les Contre-Amiraux Villeneuve et Decrès, et les autres officiers sont tout entiers à la besogne. Comme on jette des bombes sur leurs bâtimens, ils sont bastingués à six pieds de hauteur en coton, en bois, en liban, et nous les croyons à l'abri. Enfin d'après tout ce détail, il s'en suit que pour nous délivrer, et assurer toute la campagne prochaine il nous faut beaucoup de vivres, des munitions de guerre, en boulets de 24 et bombes de 8 et de 12 pouces, des cartouches d'infanterie dont nous manquons, du plomb en saumon, des médicamens qui sont presque épuisés, et enfin six à huit mille hommes qui débarquent dans cette isle pour joindre leurs efforts aux nôtres et écraser cette maudite engeance.

'Le plus grand ordre regne dans toutes les parties. Ces moyens envoyés, l'affaire finira. Si notre patrie ne peut le faire nous ne nous deffendrons pas moins jusqu'à l'extremité.'

9 Nivôse (29th December 1728).

Lettre à la Commission du Gouvernement pour l'inviter à faire mettre le sequestre sur les cotons filés dont les proprietaires sont à la campagne.

11 Nivôse (31st December 1798).

Au Consul de Naples à Malte :

'J'ai reçu, monsieur, la lettre que vous m'aves fait l'honneur de m'écrire. Vous doutés de (*sic*) la République Française soit en guerre avec Naples. Mais moi, je ne puis douter que le pavillon Napolitain ne flotte sur la Citté Vielle chef lieu des rébelles, qu'il ne flotte sur les batteries ennemis qui tirent sur la ville ; que la Sicile et Naples, qui nous ont tout réfusé depuis notre entrée dans Malte, ne fournissent aux rébelles Maltais des vivres et munitions de guerre ; que deux frégattes avec pavillon Napolitain ne soient venues se joindre à l'escadre Angloise, et insulter nos forts bloqués par terre et par mer. Ne pouvant communiquer avec mon gouvernement, ne dois-je pas m'en rapporter à cette évidence, et ne dois-je pas prendre contre l'agent d'un roi notre ennemi les mesures que la sûreté des Français et la ferme résolution de conserver cette place à la République exigent ?

'Voilà ce qui m'a décidé à vous ordonner une réclusion exacte chez vous, et à vous interdire toute communication avec les mal intentionnés ; cette mesure est commandée par les circonstances, et j'en prendrois de plus séveres si j'apprenois que vous y manquiés.'

PART II—FROM 1ST JANUARY 1799 TO 28TH JUNE 1799

23 Nivôse (12th January 1799).

À la Commission Militaire :

'Il vient d'être découvert un complot horrible qui ne permet pas de douter que les rébelles qui vouloient surprendre des postes cette nuit ont des complices dans l'intérieur des cittés. C'est à votre sagesse de démêler cette trame et à purger la ville des criminels contre lesquels vous aurés des preuves d'intelligence. Des rébelles, suivant le rapport que l'on m'a fait, ont été pris les armes à la main au millieu de deux cents autres près la porte de Marsamuscet. C'est à la valeur du brave Roussel et de sept de ses compagnons d'armes qui ont affrontés ce danger avec le plus grand courage que nous devons l'évanouissement du projet.[1]

'Déjà j'avais eu des indices, et j'avois ordonné la surveillance pour cette nuit ; mais sans Roussel nous n'aurions pas su que l'ennemi étoit si près de nous.

'Interrogés longuement ces rébelles pris les armes à la main. Retournés

[1] See too the letters of Villeneuve and Menard describing this plot in chap. xi. of this work.—J. H. R.

les de toutes les façons pour savoir quel étoit leur projet, quels étoient leurs complices ici, et ce qu'ils se proposoient de faire cette nuit. Des grecs m'avoient déjà donné l'éveil sur quelque chose. J'ai donné ordre d'arrêter deux personnes qui m'ont été dénoncées pour tremper dans cette conjuration intérieure liée avec l'extérieure.

'Le Commandant de la 7eme doit aussi avoir fait arrêter un homme qui a donné quelques renseignements. Faites la perquisition la plus sévere, et que les coupables périssent. Les personnes qui jusqu'à présent sont arrettées ou qui doivent l'être, sont : *Guilliemi* et *Pulis* parfumeur de la quarantaine, la mère de *Guilain*, nommée Babot Zammit.'

Au Général Chanez :
'Il sera fait de suitte une visite domiciliaire dans les Cittés, par un officier major et la municipalité ; on cherchera soigneusement les armes et les munitions de guerre : il faut que la perquisition se fasse même dans les citernes.'

24 Nivôse (13th January 1799).

Au Comm^{re}· Ordon^{rs}· de la Marine :
'Je suis informé, Citoyen, que tous les forçats sont armés de couteaux et de stylets qui leur ont été distribués. Faites tout de suite la plus stricte perquisition.'

Au Général Chanez :
'Il n'y a point de doute que les batteliers et autres de la partie de l'est qui étoient passés à la côte et qui ne sont point retournés chez eux avant la nuit, étoient du complot, et devoient nous égorger. Il faut donc les arretter, pour cela il faut lever la consigne qui les empêche de sortir et les saisir lorsqu'ils se présenteront pour sortir.'

26 Nivôse (15th January 1799).

Au Ministre de la Guerre :
'CITOYEN MINISTRE,—Je profite du retour d'un bâtiment génois qui nous a été expédié par le Citoyen Belleville, chargé d'affaires à Gênes pour vous donner des nouvelles de Malte. Malte est toujours à la République : Malte restera à la République. Déjà quelques bâtimens sont arrivés. Trois nous ont apportés du vin, de la viande salée, un peu d'harricots et de l'eau de vie. Nous sommes assurés de la sollicitude du Directoire. Nous avons encore quelques bœufs pour l'hôpital. Tout est economisé, l'orde régne, et cela durera longtems. Nous nous battrons jusqu'à l'extermination, il nous arrivera encore des subsistances et des secours en hommes : nous triompherons et vive la République.

'Nous venons d'échapper au plus sinistre des complots. Malgré notre surveillance, une conjuration étoit tramée dans l'intérieur. Le plus grand nombre des habitans en étoit instruit. Nous ne savions rien : les poignards étoient levés. Le projet étoit concerté avec l'extérieur : l'avis d'un grec, et la superbe action du Lieutenant Roussel nous ont sauvés.

'Les conjurés nombreux et leurs sattelites devoient égorger l'État Major dans le palais, de là se porter à la porte de Marsammuscet, égorger le poste et ouvrir cette porte, s'emparer ensuitte de la porte nationale, autrefois dite porte réale, prendre un des cavaliers, et finir par nous massacrer dans la ville, en nous coupant toute communication avec la Florianne, et avec les villes de l'est, situées de l'autre côté du grand port. Pendant ce temps, un grand nombre des rébelles de l'isle, passés par des barques à la faveur d'un nuit obscure et d'un grand vent, et cachés dans des magazins extérieurs ouverts par un nommé *Pulis* parfumeur de la Santé, et d'un des chefs de la conjuration, devoient entrer par la porte de Marsammuscet. Je crois qu'ils n'auroient pas réussi ; mais il y auroit eu beaucoup de sang répandu et cela nous auroit affoibli. Toute la surveillance des gardes et des sentinelles n'avoit pas découvert ces barques à cause de l'obscurité : elles sont d'ailleurs pendant le jour dans un endroit où nous ne pouvons les appercevoir, situé derrière la Piéta. Vous sentés que pendant ce trouble intérieur nous devions être occupés partout sur les remparts par les attaques des rébelles de la campagne. C'étoit dans la nuit du 22 au 23 que cela devoit s'exécuter.

'J'avois reçu un avis le matin par un grec (il est cependant presque sûr qu'il y a eu des individus de cette nation de compromis) nous tenions le fil. Cet avertissement nous avoit mis sur nos gardes. Tout étoit sous les armes et la surveillance : mais nous ne nous doutions pas de rassemblement à la porte de Marsamuscet. Le brave Roussel, qui, à neuf heures du soir, passoit de la ville au fort Manoël, vit de sa barque rémuer quelque chose contre le rempart. Cela l'inquiétat ; de rétour au fort Manoël, il demande quelques hommes de la garde pour aller examiner. Il prend sept hommes de la garde, va droit au magazin de la Santé, et se trouve au millieu de ces rébelles. Il fait feu dessus, il en tue, il en blesse : les uns se rembarquent, d'autres se jettent à la mer, enfin ces huit braves gens nous sauvent par l'action la plus valeureuse et la plus intelligente. Roussel fait dix prisonniers. J'ai fait courir après le reste, et l'on en a pris encore une trentaine. J'invoque la gratitude nationale en sa faveur et pour ses braves compagnons d'armes.

'Un événement très heureux arrivé aussi ce jour-là, c'est l'entrée dans le port d'un bâtiment génois. Comme il m'a apporté de Belleville une lettre qui m'apprenoit l'affaire du Roi de Sardaigne et de la fuite des Napolitains, j'ai mis ces bonnes nouvelles à l'ordre, et j'ai ordonné en rejouissance une salve générale de toutes les batteries sur celles des ennemis.[1] Je crois que ces imbécilles se sont trompés en prenant cette canonade pour une preuve de réussite en ville de la part des conjurés ; ils se sont approchés très près en colonne, les uns armés, d'autres avec des haches, des pelles ; la mittraille et la fusillade en ont fait raison.

'Maintenant la commission militaire moissonne les conjurés ; il en périt un certain nombre tous les jours, et ça ira longtems. Les arrestations se continuent avec activité. Telle est notre situation présente : en bonne posture contre l'extérieur, et purgeant l'intérieur. Jugés, Citoyen Ministre, si nous aurions pu échapper à ce dernier danger, si je n'avois réduit à douze mille une population qui passoit trente mille. Je vais encore purger de deux manières, par la glaive de la loi, et par l'expulsion. Il est constant que nous n'avons pas ici ,vingt-cinq habitans portés pour nous. Le chef du Génie a une malaise grave qui me prive de ses services. Il ne se trouve qu'un jeune de ses frères à la tête de ce service le plus essentiel. Heureusement pour moi que j'ai trouvé ici faÿ [?] un de mes anciens camarades dans l'artillerie, rempli de talens, qui par rapport à ses opinions a éprouvé de la part du ci-devant ordre, toutes les persécutions qu'un patriote peut supporter. Ce faÿ sans titre depuis le commencement du siège me rend les services les plus grands. Pour récompenser ce zèle utile, je viens de l'assimuler provisoirement au grade de Chef de Battaillon de Génie, ce qui a un peu allarmé l'ambition des deux frères le Blanc. Je n'ai point été content de cela. Toute la garnison temoin des soins qu'il se donne a vu avec plaisir ce bon republicain revêtu d'une autorité momentanée.

'J'ai aussi ici un frère Diaco dans l'ordre que l'on a mis sur la tête des émigrés, qui cependant est parti de Paris au commencement de la Révolution avec un passeport de la municipalité, n'ayant d'autre objet que de n'être point à charge à sa famille. Il m'aide avec zèle ; si j'ai le bonneur de réussir, comme je l'espère, je demande sa radiation, comme un acte de justice. Cette fausse

---

[1] The flight of the Neapolitans before Championnet's force ; also the abdication of the King of Sardinia on Dec. 8, 1798.—J. H. R.

émigration a fait vendre tout ce que j'avois, tout cela n'est rien, erreur n'est pas compte. Si on veut je le prendai pour aide de camp, je repondes de lui. S'il n'étoit pas republicain je le tuerois. Tout va bien. Tout ira bien. Des vivres, des hommes, nous sommes sur les dents, des boulets de 24, des bombes de huit et de douze pouces.'

Au Ministre de la Guerre :
'CITOYEN MINISTRE,—Outre la lettre que je vous ai écrite par le retour d'un bâtiment génois, je crois à propos de vous rendre compte de mes opérations politiques, dont j'éprouve journellement de la satisfaction, et qui seront, je l'espère approuvées par le Directoire. J'ai pensé que l'officier ne pouvant se procurer sa subsistance qu'à un prix excessif, que le soldat payé servoit avec plus de satisfaction, que l'espionage étoit couteux, que le Maltais cupide ne pouvoit être retenu qu'en mettant une partie de sa fortune entre les mains de la République, que cela seul pouvoit l'assurer à la France : que d'ailleurs ce qui appartenoit aux Maltais rébelles étant de droit acquis à la France, j'ai dirigé mes démarches en conséquence de ces observations. J'ai procédé avec ordre et justice et je vous rends compte de mes opérations.

'La première a été de faire verser dans la caisse du Payeur de la Division, différentes caisses peu considérables à la verité, mais dans lesquelles les rébelles avoient des capitaux.

'Ma seconde opération a été de faire un emprunt chez les habitans en état de payer, et j'ai pensé que cela les empêcheroit de trahir parce que cela seroit perdu pour eux s'ils ne se conduisoient pas bien.

'Pour dernière ressource, je suis tombé sur le Mont de Piété, opération que j'ai fait dans la plus grande régle. Tout s'estime, une partie se vend, et nous procure quelque argent. Une partie va à la monoye pour faire des écus, une partie se rachète. On rembourse celui dont on n'a point à se plaindre et qui reste fidèlle à la République. Je fais quelques grâces à ces pauvres gens qui ont leurs enfans et leurs maris avec le Général en Chef Bonaparte. Je m'empare de tout ce que appartient aux rébelles. Je fais au moins contracter avec la République les riches aristocrates. Voilà mon plan, voilà ma conduitte. Tout est prouvé, tout est en régle, tout se fait par la voye de la commission du Gouvernement, qui prend des arrettés sur les différentes opérations qui sont enregistrés. Des procès verbaux détaillés, des états justes représentant les intérêts du chacun. La consommation ne se fait qu'après la loi. Les voleurs n'auroient pas beau jeu ici.

'Voilà ce que j'ai cru devoir vous détailler, et ce que je vous prie de mettre sous les yeux du Directoire. Mon but n'a point été totalement rempli, puisque les coquins conspirent encore, mais cela nous fait vivre. Au surplus ces ressources sont epuisées et je ne crois pas pouvoir payer le mois de Pluviôse ; mais vous songez à nous, nous manquons de charbon pour la monoye et des creusets.'

NOTA.—L'opération du Mont de Piété nous a produit aussi du linge pour l'hôpital et quelques habits pour la troupe.

Au Citoyen Belleville Chargé d'Affaires à Gênes :
'Il est donc bien prouvé que tout ce qui parle italien a de la fourberie jusqu'au bout des ongles : nous venons de l'echapper belle, malgré la purgation que j'ai fait de quinze mille âmes au moins de cette ville, il se trouvoit encore assez de traîtres pour essayer de nous égorger. Le complot étoit ourdi avec les brigands du dehors. Tout est découvert. Ils subiront maintenant la peine due à leurs forfaits. Des gens comblés de nos faveurs se trouvent du nombre des conjurés. La commission militaire les moissonne et ils recueillent le fruit des instigations angloises. Ce que la force n'a pu faire jusqu'à présent, ils l'essoyoient par la ruse et la perfidie. Il seroit trop long de vous faire le détail

de ces infames complots. Je finis seulement par une petite réflection, c'est que le principal chef, qui est déjà fusillé, étoit un ancien forban, Corse d'origine.

'Le bâtiment de Cavassa est arrivé à bon port; il nous a fait un plaisir inexprimable, et il est en partie cause de la découverte de la conspiration. Il est entré le jour même que cela devoit éclater. J'ordonnais en réjouissance que l'on fit feu de toutes nos batteries sur celles de nos ennemis. Je fis jouer la comedie, car j'aime que mes braves compagnons d'armes oublient de manger en entendant chanter. Un officier du fort Manoël en y retournant a tout découvert. Il est tombé dehors du rempart lui septième sur deux cent hommes armés, les a culbuté dans la mer, en a tué plusieurs et en a pris dix. Nous en avons pris d'autres en les poursuivant. Cette action a empêché ceux de l'intérieur de faire jouer les couteaux, et nous a fait tout decouvrir. Qu'ils meurent tous, voilà ce qu'ils méritent.

' Continués à nous expédir des bâtiments. Nous ne sommes pas au bout de nos trauvaux, mais nous réussirons à ce que j'espère. Je m'attends à un dernier coup de désespoir, c'est à dire à un assaut, et nous sommes prêts à les recevoir, la mitraille, les balles, les grénades, tomberont comme la grêle. Nous avons bastingué nos vaisseaux à six pieds de hauteur. Des bombes sont tombés dessus sans y faire le moindre mal. Enfin nous faisons notre devoir. J'ai expédié en Tripoli et Sardaigne pour avoir de la viande fraiche pour notre hôpital. Je ne sais pas si je réussirai, cela seroit bien à souhaiter.

' Quant à vous, mon cher Belleville, du vin, du lard, des légumes secs. Je vaudrais bien aussi quelques bâtimens pour les habitans. Ils meurent de faim. Le premier bâtimen qui entreroit, je lui permettrois de vendre et il feroit un argent immense. J'imagine que le Roi de Naples est serré de près.[1] C'est lui qui est l'auteur de tous nos maux; qu'on les lui fasse expier. J'attends de ses nouvelles avec impatience. N'oubliés pas surtout de lester les bâtimens que vous nous enverrés avec du plomb. Je ne connois d'autres moyens de nous débarrasser ici qu'en faisant débarquer des troupes dans l'isle. Alors nous les corrigerons, mais l'immensité de nos remparts ne permet pas qu'on fasse des sorties. Quand cela m'est arrivé, je leur ai tué du monde, et ils m'en ont tué. Je diminuerois mes forces plus sensiblement qu'eux.'

27 Nivôse (16th January 1799).

Au Général d'Artillerie:

' J'ai vu hier, Général, à la Florianne différentes embrasures battant le chemin de la Carcare qui peuvent être garnies de petites pièces. Il y en a deux audessus du magazin à poudre et une peut-être à gauche de la batterie des Capucins. Il y a dans les fortifications de la droite de la Florianne des pièces non montées: la marine peut fournir les affûts. N'ayant point assez de cannoniers pour les garnir, ils doivent avoir une instruction pour passer d'une batterie à l'autre, par exemple si la Carcare étoit attaquée de vive force, il faut qu'à la première connoissance qu'on auroit de l'approche de l'enemi, que les pièces qui battent le chemin de la Carcare soient servies vivement. Il faut que des pièces de la Barracque et du Salut le soient également.

' Ce qui me tient encore extrêmement à cœur, c'est l'armement formidable et complet de la Victorieuse, et surtout qu'on n'oublie pas des pièces placées à quelques flancs bas, qui battent le fossé en avant de la porte du Salvator. Il faut encore que du Salvator il y ait des feux croisés avec Ricazoli. Le Salvator est un endroit à tenir, lors même que la Cotoner seroit prise. Il doit donc être armé avec le plus grand soin. Le pont de communication avec la Cotoner doit être détruit, et l'on fera un pont volant avec des madriers. Le fort sera garni de grénades. Il faut aussi des traverses à la Cotoner partout où le feu de l'ennemi peut nuire. Les vaisseaux fourniront en canon et affûts tout ce qu'il faudra.'

[1] i.e. by the march of Championnet on Naples.—J. H. R.

28 Nivôse (17th January 1799).

PROCLAMATION.

Vaubois, Général de Division, Commandant, &c., ordonne :

ART. 1ER.

Aucun habitant Maltais ne pourra jouir d'un jardin situé dans l'intérieur des fortifications, excepté les personnes que l'on jugera sûres, et qui répondront des ouvriers qu'ils y entretiendront.

ART. 2.

Il est défendu sous peine de la vie d'avoir chez eux, non seulement des armes blanches ou à feu, mais encore des stylets ou des couteaux pointus.

ART. 3.

Tous ceux qui en ont sont tenus de les apporter au bureau de la place, chez le Général Chanez.

ART. 4.

Il·leur est également deffendu d'avoir chez eux des munitions de guerre, comme balles, plomb et poudre. Ceux chez qui ou sur qui on en trouveroit seront punis de mort.

ART. 5.

Toute charette entrant dans la ville sera visitée par la garde des portes, et s'il se trouve dessus des armes ou des munitions de guerre, le conducteur sera fusillé.

ART. 6.

Il est défendu à tout coutelier ou marchand de vendre des couteaux pointus ou autres armes. On ne pourra plus vendre que des couteaux émoussés.

ART. 7.

Tout fendeur de bois sera tenu d'apporter ses masses, hâches et instrumens tranchans au bureau de la place. On ne les délivera que pour le travail qu'aux personnes sûres, lesquelles seront tenues de les rapporter tous les soirs.

ART. 8.

Enfin toute personne quelle qu'elle soit qui attenteroit à la vie des français ou qui machineroit contre la République, sera mise à mort, ses biens confisqués et sa famille exilée. Les Maltais qui entreront dans les fortifications subiront la même peine.

29 Nivôse (18th January 1799).

La Commission Militaire :

'Je viens de recevoir, citoyens, votre lettre, je partage vos soupçons sur les prêtres. Si vous en connoissés quelques uns de coupables, ou même qui soient prévenu du crime de rebellion, il faut qu'ils soient arrêtés de suitte. Quelle autre conduitte pourroit-on tenir ? une accusation générale ou le renvoi à la compagne de tous les prêtres sont des mesures, qui politiquement, peuvent être bonnes ou mauvaises. Il me semble que les jugemens des coupables, ou la réclusion des prévenus vaudroient mieux.

'À l'exception de Xerri, je ne connois encore personne de cette robe de chargé. Je les soupçonne mais cela ne suffit pas. Si une mesure de rigueur générale m'offre une sûreté d'un côté, de l'autre, je vois un fanatisme exaspéré, qui m'otera tous moyens de réconciliation avec le peuple égaré, dont on ne pourra venir à bout que par des forces de plus arrivant à Malte. Cela donneroit donc pour le moment de nouvelles armes aux puissances étrangères qui influent ces ignorans.

C'est une mesure à bien réfléchir et qui a son pour et son contre ; mais ce qui est parfaitement du ressort de la justice, c'est de tomber sur tous ceux sur qui on a prise par les renseignemens que vous recevés.'

30 Nivôse (19th January 1799).

Au Général Chanez :
' Il y a beaucoup de monde, général, à expulser de la Citté Valette. Cela vous regarde particulièrement ayant la responsabilité de la ville. Il est nécessaire de faire cette expulsion avec connoissance de cause, et de conserver ici les gens indispensables, comme boulangers, maçons, charpentiers, charretiers, &c. Vous ne pouvés mieux faire cette opération qu'en vous servant du régistre dressé par ordre de Chef de l'État Major pour reconnoître les gens inutiles, en joignant à cette liste tous ceux que des gens bien intentionnés vous feront connoître pour être suspects, vous parviendrés par cette opération à assurer la tranquilité intérieure.'

6 Pluviôse (25th January 1799).

Instruction au Citoyen Chartier rélativement à la vente des effets du Mont de Piété :
' Tous les gages d'un écu et audessous seront rendus pour rien. Tous les gages de dix écus et audessous jusqu'à un écu seront rendus en payant les quatre cinquièmes.
' Tous les gages de vingt écus et audessous jusqu'à dix seront rendus en payant toujours les quatre cinquièmes.
' Les gages de vingt écus et audessus seront rendus en payant toujour les quatre cinquièmes.
' Les gages des personnes notées sur les registres comme pauvres seront rendus en payant moitié.
' Sont exceptés de cette diminution les officiers, les fonctionnaires publics, et ceux qui leur sont attachés comme sécretaires, ou de toute autre manière. Ceux-là ont la liberté de dégager leurs effets en payant les intérêts.'

7 Pluviôse (26th January 1799).

À la Municipalité de l'Est :
' Je vous prie, Citoyens, de faire la recherche dans les maisons de ceux qui sont à la campagne de tous les agrès en voiles, avirons, &c., des speronares, barques, ou bâtimens qui leur appartiennent, pour être mis à la disposition du commissaire ordonateur de la marine. Je vous prie de vouloir bien ne pas perdre un instant pour l'exécution de cette mesure.'

8 Pluviôse (27th January 1799).

Circulaire aux Municipalités :
' Vous voudrés bien, Citoyens, faire proclamer dans votre arrondissement qu'à commencer de Lundi prochain, 9 Pluviôse, tous les pères, mères, épouses des Maltais qui se trouvent à l'armée d'Egypte, ainsi que ceux qui se trouvent au service militaire de la République peuvent se présenter au Mont de Piété pour dégager les effets qu'ils y ont avec le soulagement que j'ai déterminé.'[1]

13 Pluviôse (1st February 1799).

INSTRUCTION AU CITOYEN CHARTIER SUR LA VENTE DES EFFETS DU MONT DE PIÉTÉ.

ART. 1ᴱᴿ.

Trouvant qu'il est plus avantageuse de laisser retirer en payant les intérêts, tout ce qui s'appelle vêtemens, vous êtes autorisé à laisser, dégager tous ces objets.

[1] There follow two unimportant letters which I have omitted.—J. H. R.

Art. 2.

Il n'est point dérogé à la première instruction qui vous a été donné pour les pères, mères, épouses, frères et sœurs de ceux qui sont à l'armée d'Egypte ou au service de la République à Malte.

Art. 3.

Les cannoniers Maltais soldés, les ouvriers de l'arsenal, ceux du flanc, les marins employés, tout ceux généralement qui tiennent au service de terre et de mer peuvent rétirer ce qu'ils ont au Mont de Piété avec le bénéfice d'un cinquième, excepté pour les officiers, mais comme les personnes indiquées ci-dessus n'ont pas pour la plupart l'argent nécessaire pour payer les intérêts, il faut séparer leurs effets, et leur rendre comme il est convenu plus haut à mesure qu'ils ont l'argent pour satisfaire aux intérêts, et si par hazard quelqu'uns de leurs meubles ont été pris pour le service de la République, il faut leur tenir compte du prix de ces effets en compensation des intérêts qu'ils doivent pour les autres objets.

Art. 4.

Les états de police présentés par les fonctionnaires publics paroissant très-forts, et soupçonnant qu'ils veulent faire acquitter des polices qui ne leur appartiennent pas, soupçonnant aussi que ceux mêmes que je regardois comme pauvres, ont, malgré les deffenses, des polices qui leur sont étrangères entre les mains, vous voudrés bien fait prêter serment à tous ceux qui se présenteront pour dégager des effets, que toutes les polices presentées sont à eux et si j'ai la moindre connoissance de leur infidelité à cet égard vous pouvés les assurer que j'en ferai un exemple, et que la punition sera rigoureuse.

14 Pluviôse (2nd February 1799).

Au Citoyen Mestra, Chef de la Police :

' Le Général Vaubois arrête que l'expulsion qui va avoir lieu se fera de la manière suivante :

' Les maquerelles, les filles de joie, les gueux, les misérables qui ne sont point attachés par des parens à l'armée d'Egypte ou au service de la République à Malte. Les gens suspects, qui ne peuvent nuire étant dehors. Les autres personnes suspectes doivent être surveillées et même arrêtées s'il est nécessaire. En général ce seroit une mauvaise politique d'envoyer en campagne des gens riches, et capables d'entreprises ; il vaut mieux s'en assurer si l'on a des motifs pour le faire, et en tout tems suivre leur conduite de près.'

15 Pluvoise (3rd February 1799).

Au Citoyen Beaussier Consul de Tripoli :

' La tartanne le St. Esprit est arrivée fort heureusement. Nous sommes dans l'attente de chargemens de viande fraîche, et tout ce que nous recevrons, en ce genre ainsi qu'en vin, eau de vie, légumes et fromages nous fera grand plaisir. Nos bras deffendent Malte ; mais la République ne vous devra pas moins pour sa conservation, si vous nous faites parvenir des comestibles. . . .'

16 Pluviôse (4th February 1799).

À la Municipalité :

' Je viens, Citoyens, de donner ordre au Commissaire ordonateur, de vous faire passer trente couffes de dattes. Vous ferés vendre au peuple cette denrée à raison de quatre tarins douze grains la rotte. Cette distribution ne sera faite qu'en détail pour que les pauvres puissent avoir la faculté de se pourvoir de préférence. L'argent que produira cette vente sera versé dans la caisse du payeur de la Division.'

17 Pluviôse (5th February 1799).

À la brave garnison de Malte :
' Je vous fais part avec le plus grand empressement, mes braves camarades, des heureuses nouvelles que la frégatte *La Boudeuse* vient de nous apporter. Nos ennemis n'ayant plus le courage de se présenter devant les Républicains vouloient nous détruire par les assassinats : en Belgique la conjuration étoit des plus sérieuses, les troupes Républicaines ont tué tous ces lâches.

'En Piémont le tiran faisoit égorger tous les François,[1] le tiran est détroné. Les braves volontaires, les patriotes piémontais ont moissonné les traîtres, et actuellement ce peuple devenu libre fait la guerre avec les Français. Le Roi de Naples a voulu faire le rodomont. Il a marché sur Rome, comme vous le savés, le brave Championnet à l'approche de 8,000 hommes avoit été obligé d'évacuer cette ville ; mais rassemblant bien vite le peu de troupe qu'il avoit près de lui, il a marché sur ces audacieux qu'il a massacré. Une fuite honteuse en a sauvé un petit nombre.

'Poursuivant ses succès, le brave Championet a marché sur Naples avec ses héros, et s'est emparé de cette grande ville. Le Roi de Naples n'a eu que le tems de se sauver en Sicile avec sa famille. Il a perdu un fils dans la traversée. L'Amiral Anglois Nelson s'est bien vite échappé et rassemblant à la hâte sa pacotille, il a fui avec ses proscrits. On dit que le Roi a été fort mal reçu eu Sicile. Des lettres de ce pays nous apprennent qu'il y existe un parti nombreux pour la République, qui n'attend que l'arrivée de l'armée française.

'Dans peu nos frères d'armes seront nos voisins les plus près : ils nous enverront tout ce dont nous avons besoin, il en viendra se joindre à nous pour exterminer les rébelles. Redoublés, s'il est possible, mes camarades, de zèle et de courage. Le Directoire et votre patrie entière satisfaits de votre conduite, de votre courage et de votre ferme résolution à garder ce poste si utile à la République reconnoitront les services essentiels que vous leur rendés. J'ai de quoi vous nourrir avec discrétion. J'ai des munitions de guerre en abondance. Je fais mon possible pour que vous ne manquiés pas d'argent. Tout le monde est à son devoir, tout le monde me seconde, et de tems en tems les conjurés périssent. Une corvette française de 20 canons et de 150 hommes d'équipage venant des colonies a rencontré une frégatte Angloise de 40 canons et de 300 hommes d'équipages. Les Français qui montoient la corvette ont sauté à l'abordage et pris celle belle frégatte.

'Vive la République, notre patrie est partout triomphante et les héros de Malte sont des enfans qu'elle chérit.'

18 Pluviôse (6th February 1799).

PROCLAMATION.

Vaubois, Général de Division, Commandant, &c., voulant assurer à la République une juste indemnité des frais de la guerre qu'occasionne la révolte, et pourvoir en même tems à la conservation des propriétés des absens, qui n'auront point pris part à la Rébellion,

Ordonne, sous peine de désobéissance, à toute personne qui occupe dans la ville de Malte des maisons, appartemens, magazins, boutiques et autres immeubles appartenants à des établissemens, corps, communautés, corporations, associations, ou particuliers résidens dans les villes, villages de l'intérieur de l'isle de Malte et de celle du Goze, d'en faire leur déclaration à la commission chargée de l'administration des biens nationaux des dites isles, au lieu ordinaire de ses séances dans le délai de huit jours.

La même chose est ordonné à toute personne qui seroient en comptables envers les dits établissemens, corps et individus, de toute somme de deniers ou

---

[1] This charge is of course false.—J. H. R.

prestations quelconques, tant en capitaux qu'intérêts et arrérages à quelque titre que ce puisse être.

Les contrevenants seront poursuivis devant les tribunaux pour le payement de toutes les sommes appartenantes aux dits établissemens, corps et individus dont ils seront découverts être débiteurs ou dépositaires, et condamnés personnellement, et sans répétition aux frais des instances et procés auxquels leur contravention aura donné lieu.

Tous les notaires de la ville de Malte sont tenus de remettre à la commission des domaines nationaux, dans le même délai, une notice des minutes de ceux de leurs actes qui auroient rapport aux immeubles situés en ville, et aux capitaux, intérêts, sens, et rentes dûs en ville, dont les dits établissements corps et individus seroient propriétaires à peine d'interdiction.

23 Pluviôse (11th February 1799).

À la Commission de Gouvernement:

'J'ai reçu, Citoyens, trois lettres de vous des 20, 21, et 22 du courant, j'y reponds.

'Je crois indispensable, et je persiste, à ce que le juge de paix, qui n'a pas beaucoup d'affaires maintenant par la diminution de la population, assiste avec vous aux différentes opérations dont vous êtes nouvellement chargés par rapport aux communes rébelles et individus absens qui se trouvent à la campagne. Quant aux droits à percevoir pour sentence à rendre ou pour tout autre opération qui auroit un rapport direct aux intérets de la République, rien ne sera payé par anticipation; mais on tiendra une note exacte de tous les frais, et il lui sera alloué par la suitte ce qu'il est convenable qu'il recoive comme officier public.

'Dans les circonstances où nous nous trouvons, j'ai cru devoir continuer l'ouverture du théâtre, parceque cela procure un délassement à des braves militaires, qui ont d'ailleurs tant d'occupations. Mais je vois que les intérêts de l'entrepreneur sont compromis, parceque la diminution de la population diminuent ses ressources. Il seroit impossible qu'il se soutient si l'on exigeoit de lui ce qu'en tout autre tems on devroit lui faire payer. En conséquence je pense qu'il faut lui faire grace de trois cent écus, comme nous l'avons fait pour ceux qui viennent de quitter.'

24 Pluviôse (12th February 1799).

Ordre du jour:

'Des indices me sont donnés et me font connoître que malgré la punition exemplaire des conjurés, il se trame encore quelque horreur en ce genre contre les Français. L'accord est fait à entretenir entre les monstres qui peuvent encore se trouver dans l'intérieur et ceux de la campagne, par le moyen de ceux que l'on expulse coutinuellement. Rédoublons de zèle, mes camarades; ayons les yeux sans cesse ouverts. Faisons le service le jour et la nuit avec un zèle infatigable, et que le moment de l'insurrection de qui que ce soit, soit celui de son extermination. Ne provoquons rien, agissons sagement, mais prenons garde à nous. Ne prenez pas cette tranquilité apparente de la campagne pour une preuve de lassitude et pour les approches de la paix. Ils trament dans l'ombre, des projets contre nous. Les Anglois, fertiles en trahisons, leur fournissent des idées; mais ils sont foibles et lâches. Quelqu'action qu'ils tentent, elle les ménera à leur perte. Il ne s'agit que de veiller et de ne pas quitter les armes.'

26 Pluviôse (14th February 1799).

Au Ministre de la Guerre:

'CITOYEN MINISTRE,—Dans ma dernière lettre je vous rends compte de l'affreuse conspiration formée dans la ville de concert avec les rébelles du dehors; nous l'avons découverte à tems et une commission militaire en a fait périr les auteurs avec justice. Sa marche imposante intimidera ceux que la haine porte à de pareilles atrocités. J'espére que vous aurés reçu les détails que je vous faisois dans la lettre que je vous ai adressée par le retour d'un petit bâtiment venant de Marseille. Malte est deffendue avec un courage porté au dernier terme. Nous triompherons, c'est un espoir qui ne m'a jamais abandonné. Nos travaux deffensifs acquièrent de jour en jour de l'accroissement. Les idées font naitre les idées. Nous suppléons à la foiblesse de nos moyens par l'art et une surveillances des plus actives. Déjà nous avons reçu des bâtimens qui nous assurent pour quelques mois de subsistances.[1] Ma spéculation sur Tripoli nous a déjà rendu un petit bâtiment. J'en attend de jour en jour de la viande fraîche pour notre hôpital. Lorsque la tartane qui est venue, est sortie de Tripoli; le pacha conservoit pour nous de la bonne volonté. Il soit que l'arrivée du chedout du Grand Seigneur n'ait rien changé à ses bonnes dispositions. J'ai aussi des agens en Sardaigne munis de lettres de change, mais je n'entends pas parler d'eux. Ces agens se nomment Coste et Seconde : on peut compter sur eux.

'Une chose vraiment aff[l]igeante c'est que la population de la ville meurt absolument de faim. Je désire que le commerce amène quelques bâtimens de comestibles dont on puisse disposer pour les habitans. Quant à nos magazins, je n'en peux rien extraire pour eux ; je compromettois la salut de la place.

'Les troupes sont excessivement fatiguées. Deux raisons me font désirer un renfort ; pour les soulager et pour mieux garnir nos deffenses : elles sont immenses, et ce qui m'afflige le plus c'est que beaucoup de volontaires perdent la vue, et n'y voient point de tout pendant la nuit : d'ailleurs le nombre des malades augmente. Les dissenteries surtout nous privent de beaucoup de monde. Tous nos vœux se portent vers la Sicile. Que nos frères d'armes y arrivent, une partie nous tendra les bras et nous rejoindra.

'Les rébelles persistent dans leurs entreprises, les chefs n'ont d'autre partie à prendre que celui de continuer à les tromper. D'ailleurs ils sont à la merci des Anglois qui les ménacent sûrement de les bloquer eux même et de les faire mourir de faim s'ils se découragent.

'La frégatte La Boudeuse est arrivée à bon port : jugez comme elle a été accœuillie. Une chose malheureuse est que je n'ai pas encore reçue une syllabe depuis mon arrivée à Malte, ni de vous, Citoyen Ministre, ni du Directoire, ni d'aucun autre Ministre, ni du Général Bonaparte. Toutes les depeches qui m'ont été adressées ont eues [sic] un malheureux sort. Je cherche à diviner les intentions du gouvernement ; celle qui n'est pas douteuse, c'est de nous bien deffendre, et elle sera remplie. Mais je vous en conjure, des vivres pour nous et pour les habitans de la ville et un renfort de troupes. Je crains l'augmentation des maladies déjà nombreuses ; des habillemens pour deux mille hommes au moins, des bombes de 12 et de 8 pouces surtout, des saumons de plomb, et de l'argent, car toutes les ressources dont j'ai usé s'épuisent : mais le Directoire apprendra sans doute avec plaisir, qu'étant depuis sept mois à Malte, sept mois ont été payés aux troupes et à la Marine. J'ai payé aussi des sommes considérables aux navires marchands, arrivés ici à bon port, avec des cotons filés pris aux rébelles. La possession de Malte n'a pas encore couté un sol au gouvernement. À la verité, j'ai pris au nom de la République des engagemens avec ceux qui sont, je n'ose dire, fidèlles mais qui du moins ne nuisent pas. Vous pensés bien que cela sera couvert par le sequestre des biens appartenans aux rébelles, enfin, je rendrai le compte le plus exact de mes travaux. Puissent ils obtenir l'approbation de mon gouvernement, c'est la recompense où j'aspire.

'Malheureusement pour moi, l'air salin de ce pays a fait une révolution sur mon individu. Je suis couvert de dartres vives, et je crains quelques dépôts d'humeurs ; cela n'empêche pas l'exécution de mes devoirs. Je songerai à moi quand la chose publique sera sauvée. Les ennemis que nous avons en présence

---

[1] This fact is very noteworthy.—J. H. R.

ne nous auront [?] pas, mais des Russes, des Turcs peuvent paroître. Cela nécessite d'autant plus le renfort que je sollicite.

'Le dehors, le dedans, le port, tout est surveillé et deffendu. Si les traîtres se levent encore, ils seront écrasés. Comptés sur mes braves frères d'armes de tous les grades ; ils méritent le regard de leur patrie. Vaincre ou mourir pour la République—telle est la volonté générale.

'Je n'ai pas assez de chefs, hereusement que la marine, qui ne fait qu'un avec la terre, y supplée. Je vous previens que si elle étoit destinée à quelque expédition par le gouvernement nous ne pourrions garder tous nos remparts, qu'autant que nous recevrions, non seulement les renforts demandés, mais un supplément qui remplaceroit le nombre de soldats qu'elle fournit.

'PS.—Cette lettre étant faite depuis plusieurs jours et l'occasion de la faire partir étant retardée j'ai encore à vous instruire que les Anglois ont déterminé les insurgés à nous livrer l'assaut. Le 27 du courant ils sont venus avec des embarcations du fond de la marse nous attaquer et appliquer des échelles contre nos murs. Leur principale attaque étoit dirigée sur un point à la verité la plus foible, à l'extremité de la Sengle où commence l'enceinte de la Bourmola. Ils ont été reçu républicainement : tout a été mis en fuite, on s'est sauvé à la nage. Il en a sûrement péri beaucoup. D'autres se sont noyés. Nous avons pris les échelles et les barques. C'est la 19ème demie Brigade de ligne qui leur a fait cet acceuil. Nous n'avons rien perdu. Seulement quelques blessés légèrement. Leur bombardement continue, ce qui est à remarquer c'est qu'ils ne touchent pas des français, s'il y a quelques victimes, ce sont des Maltais.

'Si vous faites attention à notre immensité de remparts, ainsi que le gouvernement, nous verrons arriver un renfort puissant. Je ne doute point que cela n'entre dans vos vues. Puisse le génie de la liberté les faire entrer dans le port, puisse aussi la Sicile être occupée par les républicains ; tout alors deviendra bien plus facile.'

30 Pluviôse (18th February 1799).

Au Vice-Amiral Pleville :

'La goëlette partie d'Ancona est arrivée à bon port et est venue augmenter nos ressources. Nos magazins de vivres commencent à me rassurer pour un peu de tems. Mais il nous faut un renfort de troupes accompagné de vivres, à raison de leur nombre. L'immensité de nos remparts exige un service audessus de nos forces, les maladies augmentent et deviennent plus sérieuses de jour en jour.

'Beaucoup de volontaires sont frappés d'une cécité absolue pendant la nuit et cela diminue d'autant le nombre des combatans, c'est sans doute l'air vif et salin qui occasionne cette cruelle infirmité. Ceux qui en sont atteints trouvent quelque soulagement à l'hôpital par l'usage de bains de vapeurs. Toutes nos affaires vont aussi bien qu'elles peuvent aller. Le tems presse d'augmenter nos troupes, et les vivres en conséquence. La population que j'ai conservée et qui est extrêmement diminuée meurt absolument de faim. Je ne pourrois m'empêcher de lui laisser acheter une partie de ce qui pourroit entrer pour le compte du commerce, quoique je diminue journellement le nombre des bouches, en sorte qu'il ne reste n'a plus absolument que du pain et de l'huile.

'L'hiver s'avance, le tems des calmes s'approche, rien n'est plus pressant que les secours. Si malheureusement Corfou succombait, ce qui n'arrivera pas, je l'espère, ne verrions-nous pas tous les efforts de la terre et de la mer se diriger contre nous ? La prise de possession de la Sicile par les Français mettroit fin à nos inquiétudes. J'espère et je desire que cela entre dans le plan du Directoire. Les Anglois nous bloquent avec beaucoup plus de précaution depuis que *La Boudeuse* et la goëlette sont entrées ; malgré cela, ceux qui savent naviguer, profitant de la nuit, connoissant l'entrée du port, qui ne prennent pas les fanaux ennemis de St. Paul et de Marsasiroc pour le nôtre qui le trouve au milieu, réussissent presque toujours ; faire passer trois mille hommes au moins, voilà le plus difficile, et cela est le plus indispensable. Vous connoissés sûrement Malte, c'est une place des plus fortes, mais immense, les forts et les enceintes des deux côtés du grand port demanderoient beaucoup plus de bras que nous n'en avons. Des vivres et des hommes je le repette encore. Contribués à ces envois de tout votre pouvoir.

'Le courage ici est au comble, la surveillance est continuelle, toute est pratiqué pour la deffense ; si nos ennemis sont acharnés, les deffenseurs ne le sont pas moins. Nous nous attendons à les voir augmenter, que l'on profite donc du tems qui reste pour nous secourir, et surtout que les républicains arrivent en Sicile, cela applanira bien des difficultés. Si vous nous envoyés quelque chose d'Ancône ou de tout autre endroit d'où on puisse se procurer des boulets de 24, des bombes de 12 et de 8 et du plomb en saumons, que le bâtiment se leste avec [?] nous en avons besoin. Le 28 l'ennemi nous a livré un assaut, il a été repoussé vigoureusement et a perdu ses échelles et ses barques.'

Au Général Command^{t} l'expédition de Naples :
'Des transfuges venus de chez nos ennemis nous ont appris que Naples étoit entre les mains des Républicains, mais rien d'officiel. Jugés combien il seroit agréable pour vos frères d'armes bloqués et assiégés depuis sept mois d'apprendre de vous même vos brillans succès. Ce n'est pas assez pour vous d'avoir mis le Roi de Naples en fuite, c'est en Sicile qu'il faut terminer son sort, alors vous serés rapproché de nous, et malgré les Anglois, vous pourrés nous faire passer des secours en hommes et en vivres. Vos frères d'armes de Malte sont dignes de vous, et ils deffendent cette précieuse conquête avec tout le courage dont ils sont capables. Les assiégeans sont repoussés, les conjurations intérieures sont dejouées, et leurs auteurs fusillés. Le 28 du courant encore, l'assaut que nous ont livré les rébelles s'est terminé par leur fuite et par la prise des échelles et des barques qui les avoient amenés sous nos murs ; mais rien ne les rebute.

'Il est extrêmement à souhaiter qu'il nous arrive un secours puissant d'hommes et de vivres pour leur consommation. L'immensité de nos remparts, le nombre de forts que nous deffendons tient notre petit nombre continuellement de service, et les maladies augmentent par suite de fatigues. Une fatalité, c'est que beaucoup de soldats perdent la vue pendant la nuit, effet sans doute de la vivacité de l'air. Nous avons aussi beaucoup de scorbutiques.

'Nous sommes informés que le gouvernement prend le plus grand intérêt à Malte. Cela ne peut être autrement, puisque ce port et cette forteresse acquerrent un nouveau dégré d'importance depuis notre établissement en Egypte. Nous les deffendrons avec le dernier courage : mais qu'on fasse tout [ce] qu'il est possible pour augmenter nos moyens, et surtout que les ports de Sicile soient occupés par les républicains.

'Vous entretenir de notre position, c'est exciter votre zèle pour nous être utile, et je suis convaincu que vous ferés pour nous tout ce qu'il vous sera possible, et que je ne serai pas longtems sans recevoir de vous des nouvelles interessantes, et que [nous] aurons à réjouir de vos nouveaux succès.'

Au Citoyen Mestre Chef de la Police :
'Toutes les cartes de sûreté de la citté de l'ouest sont entre mes mains, il faut que vous les examiniés toutes, et que d'après des informations exactes vous me fassiés connoître :
'1°. Les gens dangereux qu'il faut éloigner de la ville parce qu'on ne peut point s'y fier.
'2°. Les gens inutiles qu'il faut aussi renvoyer pour diminuer la consommation de vivres.
'3. Les gens honnêtes et paisibles qu'on peut conserver sans inconvénient.
'4. Les gens riches qui pourroient être utiles par leurs moyens à la campagne, et qui le seront à nous même sans être à craindre.

'5. Les gens riches qui ne sont pas méchans et qui n'ont pas les moyens de vivre ici faute d'argent.

'Vous voudrés bien vous occuper de ce travail sans interruption, et pour que vous ne perdiés pas un instant, je vous fais passer cent cartes de sûreté que vous examinerés tout de suitte, et il n'en sera délivré d'autres que sur des renseignemens positifs que vous donnerés.'

Sommation du Commandant des forces navales Angloises devant Malte :
19 Février 1799.

'Monsieur,—Les dernières nouvelles que vous avés reçu avec le peu d'approvisionnement qui vous est arrivé pour votre garnison doivent vous avoir convaincu à present que vous ne pouvés avoir aucune esperance de secours de France ni de l'Espagne. Je suis donc induit à obéir à la voix de l'humanité en vous offrant les mêmes termes de capitulation qui ont déjà été offerts à votre brave garnison.

'Vous avés déjà prouvé que vous éties digne de la confiance que l'on a placée en vous, en faisant usage de toute espèce de stratagème pour entretenir le courage de vos soldats et les disposer à persévérer dans leurs devoirs dans la plus dure situation.

'Mais, Monsieur, cela ne peut durer plus longtems. Ils connoissent à present leur situation et si vous êtes encore déterminé à trainer en longueur plus longtems cela ne peut tendre qu'à les convaincre ainsi que le monde entier que vous sacrifiés la vie de nombre de personnes pour enrichir quelque peu d'individu ce qui ne peut qu'ajouter à la haine implacable des Maltais qui ne cesseront jamais de faire tous les efforts qu'on peut attendre d'un brave peuple pour recouvrer leur isle. Ile se sont mis sous la protection de sa Majesté Brittanique. J'ai l'honneur d'être, &c. Alexandre Ball.'

Reponse du Général Vaubois à la Sommation du Commandant Anglois :

'J'ai l'honneur de vous prévenir, Monsieur, que la garnison qui est dans Malte étoit décidée de périr plutôt que de rendre la ville ; je n'ai pas besoin d'uzer de stratagême pour encourager les républicains qui la deffendent. Nous ne manquons absolument de rien, et nous attendons de pied ferme tels ennemis qui viendroient nous attaquer. J'ai l'honneur d'être, &c. General Vaubois.'

Au Citoyen Belleville, chargé d'affaires à Gênes :

'Nous avons eû, mon cher Belleville, pendant plusieurs jours un vent du N.O. qui me faisoit espérer des bâtimens et de vos nouvelles ; rien n'a paru. Nous n'avons pas à nous plaindre parce qu'il nous est arrivé plusieurs bâtimens en peu de tems cependant il ne faut pas se relacher. Non ennemis peuvent prendre beaucoup de navires, mais il en échappe toujours quelques uns qui sont précieux, et Malte vaut bien tous les sacrifices que l'on peut faire.

'Les Anglois continuent à soutenir la sotte entreprise des insurgés. Ces imbéciles ne voient pas que leur ruine se consomme, et que la victoire même ne pourroit l'empêcher. Après l'issue sanguinaire de la conjuration interne et externe dont je vous ai parlé dans ma dernière, ils ont échauffé les esprits au point de les déterminer à un assaut.

'Toutes leurs échelles et leurs barques sont restées en notre pouvoir. Ils sont retournés plus vite qu'ils n'étoient venus et avec perte, sans que nous ayons à régretter un seul homme. C'est le 27 Pluviôse qu'ils ont fait cette belle équipée.

'Nous espérons que toute autre tentative aura le même résultat. Ils continuent à nous bombarder. Chacun de nos bâtimens de guerre en a eu sa part ; mais ils sont si bien blindés, qu'ils n'ont point été endommagés ; les maisons ne sont pas blindées et ces gens-là sont si bêtes qu'ils se détruisent eux mêmes. Les trois quarts des habitans de la ville sont à la campagne, et s'ils excitent le bombardement eux seuls en souffrent.

'Nos travaux, mon cher Belleville, sont inconcevables, et notre courage porté au dernier terme. Ne recevant aucune lettre, la situation de l'Europe nous est absolument inconnue. Va-t-on prendre la Sicile ? C'est ce que nous désirons le plus ardemment ; alors de quelle manière que nous soyons bloqués, il nous arrivera toujours quelque chose de cette isle. Achève-t-on le Roi de Naples ? traite-t-on avec lui ? il nous faut absolument les ports de la Sicile pour que les Anglois n'en aient plus dans ces parages. . . .'

2 Ventôse (20th February 1799).

Au Général d'Artillerie :
' J'ai été hier à la Sengle, et j'ai observé que l'endroit par lequel les brigands se proposoient d'entrer est le plus foible de tous les points de la fortification. J'ai remarqué que pour murer la porte du seul mur qui existe, on a détruit un autre mur qui fermoit le fossé, ce qui auroit mis l'ennemi après avoir franchi le premier mur, à même et sans difficulté de se jetter dans la Bormola et d'entreprendre d'ouvrir la porte, qui est fort peu éloignée, et à laquelle ils auroient travaillés en dedans conjointement avec ceux du dehors. J'ai remarqué encore que le poste qui occupe la demie lune qui couvre le Bastion St. Michel (poste dans lequel on est obligé de monter avec une échelle) est tout à fait à découvert, et très exposé au feux de la Batterie du Cazal Tarsien. J'ai résolu en conséquence de mettre cette partie de deffense en meilleur état et pour ne point déranger les travaux de la Cotoner, que je trouve si importans, j'ai jugé convenable que le battaillon que est à la Sengle, et qui a des ouvriers de différens genres, se charge de ces travaux de maçonnerie faciles à faire, en payant 16 sols par jour aux ouvriers qui y seront employés, et dont on vous présentera le controle. C'est fort peu de chose, et l'intérêt qu'ils y mettent pour leur sûreté ménera ce travail plus vite. Le poste de la demie lune de droitte dont il est aussi question plus haut sera mis en sûreté.
' Il sera fait une porte à l'ouvrage avancé de gauche, on placera aussi, s'il est possible, la petite pièce de canon qui est au haut de St. Michel dans une casematte au dessous. Les coups seront moins fichans. En pratiquant tous les moyens, cet endroit sera à l'abri de toute surprise, et la troupe sera plus tranquille.
' Il est à remarquer que cet enfant transfuge qui nous est venu dernièrement avoit précisement indiqué cet endroit pour celui où les rebelles devoient livrer leur assaut, et qu'il nous avoit fait connoître que l'intention de l'ennemi était de pénétrer par le fossé de Bormola.'

5 Ventôse (23rd February 1799).

Au Commissaire Ordonateur de la Marine :
' Il m'est impossible de me passer d'avoir un état de situation de tous les comestibles qui se trouvent dans les magazins de la marine. Je vous prie de mettre en observation à chaque article la bonne ou mauvaise qualité afin que si des objets courroient le risque de se détériorer promptement, je puisse les faire consommer avant que cela n'arrive.'

8 Ventôse (26th February 1799).

Au Commissaire Ordonateur de Terre :
' D'après la connoissance exacte de la situation des magazins de vivres, à commencer de la seconde decade de Ventôse il ne sera plus distribué du vin que deux fois par décade, la décade est le quintidi. Deux fois de l'eau de vie les tridi et septidi. Le lard et le bœuf salé continueront à être distribués comme auparavant, avec l'attention de faire manger le lard le premier parce qu'il n'est pas en aussi bon état que le bœuf. Il ne sera plus donné de ris à la troupe ; il est réservé pour l'hôpital. Pour remplacer le ris, on distribuera du porc frais une fois par décade ; les autres fois seront remplacées par des fèves. Il est à propos de calculer ce qui couteroient les pâtés pour suppléer à quelques contributions de fèves.

'Le Commissaire ordonateur de la Marine est chargé de nous remettre tous les comestibles qu'il a en magazin.

'Vous les ferés recevoir au grand magazin de la terre et il faudra faire consommer d'abord les comestibles et le vin dont la conservation n'est pas possible.'

9 Ventôse (27th February 1799).

Au Ministre de la Guerre :

'Dans la vue, Citoyen Ministre, de soulager la trésorerie nationale, j'ai payé le peu de vivres qui nous sont arrivés par des navires marchands, avec des cotons filés et en laine pris aux rébelles Maltais. Ces sortes de marchandises restent encore prohibées en France, je vous prie de vouloir bien faire excepter de cette régle générale des négociants qui ont pris ces cotons en payement, et qu'il leur soit permis de les entrer à Marseille. Il ne me paroitroit pas juste que ces négociants ne pussent pas faire usage dans leur pays d'une marchandise que la République leur donne en payement. Le Capitaine Murat que je charge de cette lettre se trouve dans le cas de l'exception que je sollicite. Il a chargé de ces cotons pour une somme assez considérable sur le navire L'*Appollonie*, Capitaine Bigaud.

'Au moment où je vous écris nous avons le désagrément de voir perdre sous nos yeux un bâtiment génois, qui nous arrivoit, et qui a eu la lâcheté de se rendre lorsqu'il pouvoit entrer dans le port sans rien craindre, et hors de portée des vaisseaux ennemis dont les boulets n'alloient qu'à moitié chemin.

'Aucune espérance de réconciliation avec les rébelles de l'isle : la force seule peut en triompher ; n'ayant que peu de troupes pour la deffense de la place et du port, je ne puis leur faire une guerre de campagne. Ils se sont mis sous la protection des Anglois, dont le pavillon flotte dans l'intérieur de l'isle. La position dans laquelle nous nous trouvons exige donc impérieusement des troupes, des vivres et de l'argent.

'Quant à la ville de Malte, soyés convaincu que les ennemis ne l'auront qu'en nous détruisant sur les remparts. Leurs tentatives jusqu'à présent ont toujours tourné à leur désavantage. Le courage des troupes de terre et de la marine me garantissent de nouveaux succès contre tout ce qu'ils tenteront. Les assauts ne réussissent pas mieux que les conjurations ; mais ces pauvres troupes sont sans cesse sous les armes. Si les ports de la Sicile étoient entre les mains des Républicains, cela apporteroit sûrement une grande changement. Il y a une grande différence d'entreprendre la petite traversée de Syracuse à Malte, ou de venir des côtés de France, d'Italie, ou du golfe Adriatique.

'Les tems n'ont point favorisé tous les envois qu'on nous à fait. Pas un coup de vent sérieux pendant tout l'hiver dans ces parages. La sollicitude du gouvernement nous est connue, et vous pouvés l'assurer, Citoyen Ministre, que notre resistance y répondra parfaitement.'

10 Ventôse (28th February 1799).

Au Général d'Artillerie :

'D'après les avis que j'ai sur le projet des rébelles, il faut absolument que deux pièces de 8 ou de 6 soient placées à une courtine du Bastion de St. Paul qui bat le port dit des Français et dont l'emplacement pourra d'ailleurs être indiqué plus précisément par le Citoyen Caissel, Commandant à la Sengle ; il n'y a pas un moment à perdre et j'espère que cela sera prêt ce soir.'

Au Contre-Amiral Villeneuve :

'Des avis reitérés, les cris des rébelles, le remuement que l'on entend pendant la nuit, les différens transports qui ont lieu en même tems autour de la ville, tout fait presumer que les rébelles vont effectuer quelque projet.

'Donnés des ordres, je vous prie, pour que les barques de garde, que vous fournissez soient en grande surveillance surtout à la pointe de la Sengle.'

APPENDICES 601

11 Ventôse (1st March 1799).

À la Commission du Gouvernement:
'Le Commissaire ordonateur de la Marine vient de me remettre un jugement du Tribunal Consulaire qui m'étonne, et qui me porte à croire que les citoyens qui la composent, ont, non seulement fait preuve de faiblesse, mais même se sont mis dans le cas d'appeler le soupçon sur leur conduite.

'Le Commissaire ordonateur avoit cru de son devoir de s'adresser au Tribunal Consulaire pour avoir une sentence sur la prise faite d'une speronare chargé de comestibles, d'un petit bâtiment napolitain. Aucun doute que ces bâtimens étoient de Marsa Siroc pour se rendre à St. Paul. Par le jugement intervenu au sujet de la speronare, les juges ont l'air de reconnoître le Tribunal de Santé établi par les rébelles au Zeiton, et ce qui peut devenir criminel pour eux, c'est qu'ils paroissent douter que les campagnards soient leurs ennemis, et ils les traitent comme ils seroient dans le cas de faire de puissance à puissance. Il faut que ces fonctionnaires publics sachent que des rébelles ne sont que des rébelles, qu'on ne doit leur reconnoître aucune pavillon, et que toutes affaires avec eux sont hors de la classe ordinaire même avec les puissances ennemis.

'Vû la sentence mentionnée ci-dessus le Général Commandant en Chef, considérant que les juges qui l'ont prononcée se sont écartés de leur dévoir, non seulement en ayant l'air de reconnoître comme puissance ennémi les rébelles Maltais, mais encore en s'écartant des loix de la République qui déclarent de bonne prise tout bâtiment qui sort d'un port ennemi pour se rendre dans un autre, et tout bâtiment à bord duquel il n'est trouvé aucune expédition, facture ou connoissement, ordonne que la présente sentence, en ce qui concerne la barque speronare n'aura aucun effet et que la vente du dit bâtiment et des marchandises qui composent sa cargaison aura lieu conformément aux loix, pour le produit en être reparti aux équipages preneurs. L'ordonateur de la marine est chargé de l'exécution du présent arrêté.'

12 Ventôse (2nd March 1799).

Au Commissaire Ordonateur de la Marine:
'J'ai de continuelles réclamations de la part des gens employés à la marine que vous avés supprimé depuis quelque tems. Cela occasionne un mécontentement dont nous voyons journellement les suites. Les plus acharnés de la campagne sont les marins qui ont perdu leur existence. Si dans ce moment d'anciens serviteurs (et même de jeunes comme le fils d'Attard Pilote) tel qu'un nommé Testa Grossa, vieux et bon sujet, parmi ceux qui par un long service ont gagné du pain, perdent aussi ce qui les faisoit vivre, nous ne pouvons plus nous flatter de conserver un seul individu, attaché à la République. Je vous prie de prendre cette lettre en grande considération.'

Au Citoyen Muscat, President du Tribunal Civil:
'Je suis parfaitement informé que vous avés tenu des propos qui peuvent nuire aux opérations du gouvernement. Observés vous sur vos actions et vos discours. S'il me revenoit sur votre compte la moindre chose à l'avenir, je vous ferai sentir la justice nationale, en faisant de vous l'exemple le plus terrible.'

13 Ventôse (3rd March 1799).

Ordre du Général Chanez:
'Vous ferés mettre sur le champ dans les prisons St. Elme trois Maltais qui, sous le nom de parlementaire, ne sont rien moins que des espions.'

Lettre d'un Officier Anglois Command$^{t.}$ les forces de terre Brittaniques, du Cazal Zeiton:
'Monsieur,—Votre dernière réponse au commandant de l'escadre Brittanique employé au blocus de la Citté Valette, lui ayant ôté la possibilité d'entrer avec

vous dans aucune sorte de négociations pour la rédition des postes que vous commandés, je pense qu'il est de mon devoir de vous faire savoir que les habitans et nous même avons été informés que plusieurs bâtimens dans le port sont dans ce moment occupés à charger leurs propriétés et que des officiers et autres personnes prennent actuellement les moyens de cacher des effets de valeur, appartenant à des Maltais dans l'intention de les faire passer parmi leurs bagages. Il est donc nécessaire que vous et votre garnison sachent que si quelqu'un de ces bâtimens (desquels nous avons description exacte), quitte le port qu'aucun officier ni particulier n'aura jamais la faculté de quitter l'isle sans qu'il soit visité strictement tant dans leur personne que dans leur propriété.

En égard à la possibilité que quelque bâtiment ou autre vaisseau parvienne à s'echapper, je dois vous informer qu'une tartane partie de la Citté Valette avec un cargaison considérable et un trésor tant en or qu'en argent caché dans différentes parties du bâtiment a été prise et conduite à Tunis, et qu'il est actuellement impossible à aucun de vos bâtimens d'échapper à la vigilence de nos nombreux croiseurs et de ceux des Tunisiens qui environnent l'isle.

'Une petite reflexion, Monsieur, doit vous convaincre qu'il seroit beaucoup plus de votre intérêt et de celui de votre garnison de vous confier à une capitulation, que d'exporter ainsi les propriétés de la manière que vous l'avés fait, et que vous vous proposés encore de faire, ce qui ne peut manquer de souiller le caractère d'un peuple militaire.

'Pour vous prouver que vous n'avés aucun espoir de côté de Naples, permettés que je joigne ici une lettre contenant des nouvelles qui a été reçu ici de Sicile par un des plus respectable habitant de l'isle, et je vous donne ma parole d'honneur, Monsieur, que cette nouvelle est généralement accrédité et qu'elle n'a pas été fabriquée dans l'intention de vous être envoyée ni de tromper personne. J'ai l'honneur d'être, &c.

VIVION, Commandant les Troupes Brittanniques à Malte.'[1]

15 Ventôse (5th March 1799).

Ordre du jour:

'Braves soldats de terre et de mer, nos ennemis ne pouvant triompher par la force, employent les subterfuges. Ils envoyent des parlementaires sans nécessité pour examiner la force des postes, pour tacher de reconnoître notre situation. Ils ne savent plus comment s'y prendre. Redoublons d'exactitude dans le service. Craignons toutes les ruses qu'ils peuvent employer au deffaut de la force, et ne perdons point de vûe que leur situation doit les porter à quelque coup de désespoir. Ils se presenteront encore, soyons en sûrs. Que les bayonettes soient bien aiguisées, et qu'ils sachent ce que c'est d'avoir affaire à des Républicains, vainqueurs de l'Europe.

'Surtout que le service se fasse dans les postes avec la plus grande exactitude; que personne ne s'en eloigne, que l'on ait toujour la vue sur les armes. Beaucoup de gens du dedans, valent peut-être encore moins que ceux du dehors. Je recommande toujours de bien ménager les munitions de guerre, et de n'en user que dans les besoins réels.

'Il me reste encore à vous parler d'un grand désordre et je m'adresse aux soldats pour qu'ils l'empêchent eux mêmes. On pille les jardins des français, qui les font cultiver à grands frais. On vole les propriétés de la République. La maison de Guillielmo en est un exemple. Je ne soupçonne personne; mais si quelqu'un a le malheur de déshonnorer l'habit republicain, j'en appelle aux braves militaires qui souffrent de ces actions, et je suis persuadé qu'ils me les feront connoître et j'en ferai justice.'

[1] Vaubois' letter of March 5, 1799, in reply to *parlementaires* sent by the Maltese will be found (in a translation) in chap. xii. *ad init.*—J. H. R.

Au Général Chanez :
'Vous voudrés bien, mon cher Général, faire conduire par l'Adjudant Major Beaulieujus qu'à la première sentinelle du poste avancé de la Carcare, l'Anglois venu ici hier en parlementaire. Il aura les yeux bandés à son départ du palais.

'Le service s'étant fort mal fait hier à la poste de la Carcare lors de son arrivée, il sera consigné à ce poste de ne se jamais laisser approcher par les Maltais de l'intérieur à la distance de cent pas. L'Anglois sera conduit avec les formalités prescrittes par le réglement de campagne, et s'il s'en présente jamais d'autres à quelque poste que ce soit, j'espère qu'on se comportera mieux, et qu'on ne permettra jamais dans telle circonstance que ce soit au peuple de s'assembler, quand il y a une proclamation qui dit que trois Maltais ne doivent jamais se trouver ensemble.'

17 Ventôse (7th March 1799).

Au Commissaire Ordonateur de la Marine :
'Le bois est de nécessité absolu pour les troupes et pour les fours. J'observe seulement que la consommation en est exhorbitante, quoique j'ai réduit les rations au moins possible pour le moment. Je ne conçois par comment le Citoyen Martin, munitionnaire, peut, ainsi qu'il me la dit, consommer cinquante quintaux de bois par jour. Il faut cependant en trouver, et n'avoir recours qu'à la dernière extrêmité au demolissement de la frégatte *La Boudeuse*. Prenez donc les vieux bâtimens français. Lorsqu'ils seront consommés il faudra bien avoir récours aux bâtimens maltais.

'Je ne saurois trop vous recommander de faire surveiller scrupuleusement à ce que tout le bois provenant de ces démolitions soit entièrement conservé à la fourniture des troupes. J'ai de grands indices de malversation dans cette partie ; tous les particuliers de la ville sont approvisionés du bois destiné aux troupes ; je crois bien que malgré les deffenses, le soldat en vend, mais il est difficile de penser que cela puisse subvenir au besoin de tout le monde, faites donc, je vous prie strictement surveiller les sous ordres.'

19 Ventôse (9th March 1799).

Ordre du jour :
'La garde nationale fera un service journalier pour soulager la troupe et se rendre utile à la conservation de Malte.

'En cas d'alerte, toute la garde nationale s'assemblera devant le palais, et de là sera envoyée aux différens postes qu'elle doit occuper.'

20 Ventôse (10th March 1799).

À la Commission des Domaines Nationaux :
'Les jugemens de la Commission Militaire ne portant pas confiscation, il est juste que les biens des personnes justiciées par rapport à la dernière conjuration retourne à leurs heritiers lorsqu'ils sont présens et que le jugement est antérieur à la proclamation du [?] par laquelle je prononce que les biens des traîtres au gouvernement seront confisqués. Je vous prie d'agir en conséquence, parce que cette proclamation ne peut avoir d'effet rétroactif, et que je ne l'ai fait que dans la vûe d'enrayer d'avantage ceux qui auroient des dispositions à se rendre coupables du même crime.'

Lettre du Comm^t des forces Navales Angloises devant Malte :

15 Mars [15th March] 1799.

'MONSIEUR,—J'ai reçu votre lettre dattée du 15 Ventôse [5th March], accompagnée de Monsieur Vivion Officier Commandant les troupes Brittanniques à Malte, que je joins ici pour que vous la lisiés. Je ne puis m'empécher de considérer votre conduite à l'egarde des parlementaires qui vous a été envoyé par Monsieur Vivion comme une violation des loix de la guerre qui jettera une tâche indélible sur votre caractère.

'Vous parlés d'humanité et de générosité dans votre lettre, mais je pense que votre conduite y est diamétralement opposée, et que vous provoqués par tous les moyens qui sont en votre pouvoir toutes les calamités de la guerre.

'Je demande que ces hommes que vous aves si injustement retenu me soient rendus, ou j'userai de reprisailles envers tous les français que j'ai pris.

'En égard à ce que vous ne voulés pas reconnoître un officier Anglois commandant des troupes Maltaises comme un ennemi, d'une nation avec laquelle vous êtes en guerre, veuillés bien vous rappeler le langage que tenoit les français, quand ils faisoient la guerre avec les Americains, que la Grande Bretagne avoit déclaré rébelles, et vous apprendrés que les français qui furent faits prisonniers de guerre furent traités avec les égards usités.

'Mais, Monsieur, je ne puis m'empêcher d'observer que vous rejettés tous les usages qui ne conviennent pas à vos dessein. Vous semblés sentir que votre situation personnelle est désesperée et vous désirés d'y enveloper tout le monde au même degré. J'ai l'honneur d'être, &c. ALEXANDRE BALL.'

6 Germinal (26th March 1799).

PROCLAMATION.

Le Capitaine Cavazza, génois, a vendu une pacotille que la cupidité a porté à un prix extraordinaire. Le capitaine qui rend un service essentiel à la République à ses risques et perils, tire naturellement parti des circonstances et ne peut se réfuser aux propositions des accapareurs qui spéculent sur le besoin public. Voulant mettre un terme à leur insatiabilité, j'ordonne ce qui suit:

ART. 1ᴱᴿ.

Les acheteurs de la pacotille dont le prix de chaque objet vendu est connu, ne pourront excéder en le revendant le bénéfice de cinq pour cent.

ART. 2.

Ils rendront compte journellement à la municipalité de ce qu'ils auront vendu et à qui.

ART. 3.

S'ils excèdent les cinq pour cent de bénéfice, ils seront condamnés à deux mille écus d'amende et enfermés à St Elme pour six mois.

ART. 4.

Tout dénonciateur qui prouvera qu'ils ont enfreint cette deffense et gagné d'avantage, recevra une récompense de cent écus pris sur l'amende.

ART. 5.

Six tonneaux de vin de onze barils et demie chacun ou environ seront destinés aux officiers de la garnison et ne pourront être vendus à d'autres.

ART. 6.

Les officiers auront une décade à partir du jour de la publication de cette proclamation pour se pourvoir.

ART. 7.

Toute falsification faite au vin, pour en augmenter la quantité, sera punie, et les marchands seront condamnés à payer ce qu'ils auroient pu dérober par cette fraude, qui se connoîtra aisement par les essais qui seront conservés. La municipalité est surveillante et responsable de l'éxécution de cette proclamation.

APPENDICES

9 Germinal (29th March 1799).

Au Citoyen Belleville, chargé d'affaires de la République à Gênes :
 'C'est toujours mon cher Belleville qui vole avec le plus d'ardeur au secours des Républicains. À vous seul nous devons la moitié et plus de nos provisions. Cavazza est arrivé pour la seconde fois à bon port, et il n'a pas perdu ses peines. La pacotille lui a valu bien, de l'argent, mais il le mérite pour sa hardiesse et par son zèle pour les Républicains.
 'Voila des vivres pour longtems, mon cher ami, mais les maladies nous privent de bien du monde, et écrasent ceux qui sont sur pied. Nous manquons de viande fraîche pour l'hôpital et mes émissaires à Tripoli ne nous envoyent rien. Je m'attends à la prise de la Sicile. Pourra-t-on de là nous faire passer du monde et augmenter les vivres en conséquence ? C'est mon vœu et j'espère qu'il sera exaucé. La Sicile prise, tous les efforts de l'ennemi rétomberont sur nous. J'ai une garnison excellente. Il existe ici la plus grande union et l'envie de triompher est égale chez tous. Avant qu'on emporte nos remparts nous y périrons, les armes à la main.
 'Dépuis quelque tems les campagnards sont plus tranquilles ; les boulets ont cessé. Peut-être que l'affaire Sicile les inquiète. Peut-être aussi nous préparent-ils quelque coup vigoureux. Nous sommes toujours prêts. Cette misérable isle se ruine tout à fait et si nous la conservons à la France comme je l'espère, il faut qu'on s'attend à y jetter bien de l'argent : mais elle sera si utile par la suitte qu'il ne faut pas le regretter. Quel plaisir me feroit des troupes qui arriveroient ici ! Je donnerai[s] à ces campagnards une leçon de laquelle ils se souviendroient. Je n'y peux songer avec ce que j'ai de monde : l'ennemi est de tous côtés et la ville est immense . . .'

12 Germinal (1st April 1799).

Au Commissaire Ordonateur de la Marine :
 'Veuillés bien, Citoyen Ordonateur, me faire passer l'état nominatif des Maltais employés à la Marine pour lesquels vous m'avés dernièrement la subsistance. Comme j'ai fort à cœur d'économiser nos ressources, je ne veux accorder des rations de vivres qu'à de gens d'une utilité indispensable. Vous me dirés en même tems quel est l'emploi de chacun.'

Au Ministre de la Guerre :
 'CITOYEN MINISTRE,—Nous avons reçu depuis la dernière lettre que je vous ai écrite un second chargement de vivres envoyé de Gênes par le Citoyen Belleville, chargé d'affaires. Nous avons des vivres pour un certain nombre de mois pour la garnison. Le peuple n'est pas plus avancé ; il est dans une détresse affreuse. Je ne peux subvenir à ses besoins sans exposer Malte. La population est cependant réduite à moins du tiers de ce qu'elle étoit.
 'Les maladies augmentent considérablement, et il s'en suit deux maux incalculables. Ceux qui sont sur pied éprouvent des fatigues qui vont toujours en augmentant. La cécité de beaucoup de volontaires est un autre fléau désespérant. À mesure que les uns récouvrent la vue, d'autres la perdent. Comment arrêter les progrés de cette incomodité, due aux fatigues et à l'humidité des nuits, lorsqu'on est de toutes parts environné de l'ennemi, et qu'on est si clair sémés sur des fortifications immenses ?
 'L'ardeur ne diminue pas ; une parfaite union regne, et l'envie extrême de conserver Malte se trouve chez chaque individu. Nous pensons que la conquête de la Sicile ouvrira les yeux des insurgés, puisqu'ils tirent toute leur nourriture de cette isle. Mais je ne peux me dissimuler que nos ennemis succombant en Sicile se porteront sur l'isle de Malta ; le blocus déviendra encore plus exact et l'ardeur des insurgés reprendra de l'activité à l'arrivée de quelques troupes Angloises, ils n'en seront, j'espère, pas plus avancés ; mais les maladies peuvent nous affaiblir au point de ne pouvoir faire face partout.

'Ce que je vous expose, Citoyen Ministre, doit vous faire sentir l'extrême nécessité de secours en vivres et en hommes que je sollicite.

'Peut-être sera-t-il bien difficile de les faire arriver. Mais vous pouvés toujours compter sur la résistance la plus opiniâtre et la plus vigoureuse. Nous avons travaillé et nous travaillons continuellement à renforcer nos deffenses par des ouvrages extrêment utiles. Le désir de conserver cette possession est si prononcé chez le militaire, que les peines les plus excessives n'ont pas encore excité la moindre plainte, et il regne un esprit des plus satisfaisant. Comptez sur nous; mais que les moyens soient employés pour nous soulager et pour augmenter nos forces.

'J'ai crée une garde nationale composé de français attachés à la division et de quelques Maltais. Elle est peu nombreuse; mais cela soulage quelques soldats dans le service intérieur. . . .[1]

'Une réflexion bien juste qui ne nous est échappé est que sans l'insurrection des habitans nous étions perdus. Les Anglois bloquant l'isle, il auroit fallu nourrir une population de près de cent mille âmes : ils auroient épuisés nos greniers, surtout la Sicile nous étant interdite.

'Enfin, Citoyen Ministre, notre position est telle que nous sommes foibles, extrêmement foibles, et diminués de plus d'un quart par les maladies. Nous n'avons que pour cinq à six mois de vivres au plus.

'Nous avons fait et faisons en travaux deffensifs tout ce qui supplée au nombre. L'ésprit des troupes est parfait; mais l'enceinte est d'une étendue effrayante; le soldat est nuit et jour sur pied.'

17 Germinal (6th April 1799).

Au Commissaire Ordonateur de Terre :

'Le Capitaine Cavazza ayant remis pour l'hôpital vingt-huit moutons et deux chevres, vous voudrés bien, Citoyen, en ordonner le payement. Il demande cinq louis par mouton et quinze louis par chevre. Voyés si vous pouvés diminuer le prix de gré à gré.'

20 Germinal (9th April 1799).

Au Commandant de l'Est :

'Sur l'information que vous m'avés donné d'un travail de mine fait par l'ennemi, et qui doit être dirigé sous le bastion de droite de la porte Zabbar, ou sur la porte elle même, vous ferés sortir cette nuit cinquante grenadiers qui s'embusqueront dans les environs de la petite maison où se trouve l'entrée de cette mine et qui enleveront les ouvriers lorsqu'ils y seront entrés. Récommandés le silence et la plus grande attention pour ne pas manquer le coup.'

21 Germinal (10th April 1799).

Au Général d'Artillerie :

'Il est clair, Général, que la nouvelle batterie des ennemis établie à la pointe du Kortin seroit des plus génantes si nous ne venions à bout de la détruire : elle a d'abord eu pour objet de détruire la frégatte *La Boudeuse* puisqu'elle tiroit dessus à boulets rouges; mais il faut prendre garde que les ennemis ne travaillent à côté comme j'ai cru m'en appercevoir hier. Je suis bien satisfait du feu de nos batteries dessus, elle est toute demantibulée. Ils ne manqueroient pas de rendre notre communication avec la partie de l'est très difficile. Cela m'engage à vous prier de faire mettre du calibre de 18 et un mortier au bastion du magazin à poudre sous les Capucins, si une batterie se demasque à l'endroit que je vous indique elle sera foudroyée par un feu croisé de cette batterie et de celle des Capucins. Si notre attente étoit trompée, il

---

[1] Personal details of little interest follow, but the next sentence should be noticed.—J. H. R.

faudroit absolument l'enlever. Je l'aurois déjà fait si je n'avois les plus fortes raisons de menager les hommes.'

Au Général d'Artillerie :
' Les projets que les ennemis manifestent de faire des mines exigent une précaution qui nous facillite la surveillance de ce qui se passe au dehors. On croit entendre des travaux souterains du côté du Bastion de St. Paul que nous sommes occupés à fermer. En conséquence vous donnerés les ordres les plus prompts pour que l'on ouvre la poterne située vis-à-vis de St. Jean l'aumonier. Il faut aussi ouvrir un guichet à la porte du Salvador. Toutes les précautions doivent être prises pour que ces points soient fermés de la manière la plus résistante. Le Citoyen Blanc suivra ces travaux sans interruption.'

30 Germinal (19th April 1799).

Au Commissaire Ordonateur de Terre :
' On vient de mettre sous mes yeux du biscuit de fort mauvaise qualité : une partie n'est pas assez cuite. L'autre provient à coup sûr d'une farine dont on a extrait la fleur, cela ne me paroit pas étonnant, si c'est un faiseur de pâtes qui en est chargé. Il est sûr qu'il tire la fine fleur pour ses pâtes, et qu'il convertit le reste en biscuit. Y-aura-t-il donc toujours des abus dont je doive me plaindre ?

' Je suis déterminé à faire des examples. En attendant l'occasion qui sûrement ne tardera pas à se présenter, refusés tout le biscuit de mauvaise qualité, laissés-le aux frais de celui qui l'a fait, et qu'on ne perde pas de tems pour en avoir un approvisionnement de trois mois à raison de six mille rations par jour. Je viens de voir un compte rendu à la marine de la situation de l'hôpital. Rien n'est si affreux. Les salles sont mal-propres. On ne donne pas le vinaigre nécessaire. Le jardin livré à l'hôpital est de toute nullité, si ce n'est peut-être pour le jardinier, qui doit faire sa fortune.'

5 Floréal (24th April 1799).

PROCLAMATION.

Le Gouvernement paye avec des lingots d'or et d'argent. La valeur intrinsèque en est fixée avec la plus grande exactitude. Ils sont préférables à la monoye, puisqu'il ne se trouve aucune valeur idéale ni de fabrications. Cependant la cupidité s'éveille, et déjà l'on a hésité à les changer pour les discréditer et les avoir audessous de la valeur intrinsèque ; voulant arrêter ce désordre, et empêcher les spéculations odieuses j'ai pris les déterminations suivantes :

ART. 1.

Les lingots sont reçus comme monoye suivant la valeur fixée par l'empreinte qui se trouve dessus.

ART. 2.

Tout habitant qui refuse de les prendre pour leur valeur, qui proposera un rabais, ou qui refusera de rendre le surplus de ce qui sera dû, sera condamné à une amende de la valeur du lingot refusé.

ART. 3.

Les lingots seront reçus par toutes les caisses publiques pour le compte de la République par ses débiteurs.

ART. 4.

Les corps administratifs et judiciaires prêteront la main à l'exécution de ces differens articles.

10 Floréal (29th April 1799).

Au Commissaire Ordonateur de Terre :
' Les lenteurs qu'éprouvent le service sont insupportables. Hier j'ai écrit au Commissaire Ordonateur de la Marine au sujet de la démolition des bâtimens. Il me repond que cela regarde la terre, que quand il a livré le bâtiment, son devoir est rempli. Le fait est que le bois manque, et que le soldat ne peut faire sa soupe, tandis qu'il y a plus de huit jours que j'ai désigné quatre bâtimens qui doivent fournir plus d'un mois.
' Cet économie de l'hôpital n'a point encore fait préparer l'auberge de Bavière. L'évacuation de l'hôpital qui auroit dû être terminée promptement traine. Usez donc de votre autorité. Faites marcher tout le monde avec le zèle et la célérité qui convient. On ne fait pas la guerre sans se donner de continuels mouvemens. Je ne peux me le dissimuler, l'administration en général va on ne peut pas plus mal.'

17 Floréal (6th May 1799).

Au Général Chanez :
' Les maladies nous affoiblissent journellement. La perte est considérable, et il faut menager les hommes le plus qu'il est possible. Le service doit donc être ordonné de manière à ce que personne ne redouble. Il faut d'ailleurs observer que cette place n'a rien à craindre de l'ennemi tant que les forts et ouvrages avancés ne sont pas emportés. Simplifiés donc le service. Diminués le en soldats, et en officiers.
' Que pouvons-nous craindre de l'intérieur ? Je vais encore dans quelques jours expulser du monde. La diminution de cinquante hommes au moins sur la garde peut contribuer à conserver la santé du soldat. Tachons d'éviter d'être forcés à une diminution plus sérieuse.
' La garde nationale n'est point exacte. Je sais que plusieurs quittent leurs postes pendant la nuit. Le conseil de discipline a tué le service. Je le suprime, ce n'étoit pas le cas de l'établir. Quand la Garde Nationale ait le service de guerre, elle doit être à la discipline ordinaire, et dans une place assiégée elle doit être encore plus forte que lorsqu'on se met en campagne. Je ne me doutoit pas que cela en détruiroit le nerf, mais sitot que ce conseil a été affoibli par des actes inutiles, il est devenu illusoire. En tems de siège, chez un peuple conquis et non gouverné par la constitution, nos circonstances n'ont rien de commun avec l'intérieur de la France. C'est un objet tout-à-fait manqué. Vous voudrés bien, Général, vous conformer au contenu de cette lettre.'

20 Floréal (9th May 1799).

À la Commission du Gouvernement :
' Les fonds destinés à la solde des troupes, aux dépenses des hôpitaux, ainsi que pour la partie civile, s'épuisent.
' Nous ne pouvons nous exposer aux besoins de tous genres sans nuire à la République, et cette malheureuse guerre que nous font les habitans doit nécessairement rétomber à leur charge. L'humanité cependant m'a dicté la mesure de prendre à titre d'emprunt tout ce que je tirerai des habitans, afin que, cette guerre terminée, on puisse rembourser les citoyens tranquilles qui n'ont point méconnu le gouvernement légitime de la France ou qui aident les Français dans cette circonstance à triompher des brigands.
' Je vous prie en conséquence, Citoyens, d'assembler à jours différens les citoyens aisés de l'une et de l'autre partie ; vous leur férés sontir qu'une partie de leurs moyens étant entre les mains de la République, ils ne peuvent les sauver que par le succès des Républicains et qu'en conséquence ils doivent contribuer au soutien de cette guerre. Vous leur dirés que la République est digne d'une confiance que ses ennemis seuls feignent de méconnoître. Vous

leur ferés sentir que le gouvernement français seul leur convient, que les Anglois par rapport à leur commerce des Indes détruiroient les manufactures dont l'industrie et le succès ont besoin d'être perfectionnés par les secours paternels d'une grande nation. Vous leur dirés que je ne puis croire que leur aveuglement aille au point de ne pas appercevoir que déjà un nombre assez considérable de millions seroient perdus irrémissiblement pour eux si les Français ne restoient possesseurs de ce pays réduit à l'infortune par la criminelle ambition de quelques uns de leurs compatriotes. . . .'

22 Floréal (11th May 1799).

Ordre :
Vaubois, Général de Division &c. ordonne qu'après demain 24 du courant on mette dehors les habitants, qui par leur misere ou leur mauvaise santé demandent à aller en campagne.

Il est deffendu de laisser sortir aucuns négociants, aucuns prêtres, aucuns ci-devant nobles, à moins que l'état de leur santé, ou des raisons particulières d'utilité publique n'engage à faire quelques exceptions.

Un adjud^t.-major de la place et un officier municipal accompagneront le Citoyen Mestre, Chef de la Police.

24 Floréal (13th May 1799).

Au Général d'Artillerie :
'L'ennemi travaille à placer une pièce que je juge un peu à la droite de la porte du Coradin dans le mur de cloture qui regarde la Marse. Cette pièce bat le poste de la Carcare et celui des Capucins, elle incommodera fort : elle ne peut manquer d'être vû des Capucins. On y travaille encore à présent. Il faut tacher de la démonter. Reglez le nombre de coups afin que l'on ne consomme pas trop de munitions. Il est nécessaire de leur répondre aussi à la batterie de la Sambre et à celle des Jesuites ; mais il faut aussi un nombre de coups déterminé, bien pointés, lentement, et quand on est sûr qu'ils sont au travail ou en batterie. Réglés tout cela avec parcimonie et avec votre prudence ordinaire. Vous avés à l'arsenal le Citoyen Mollard sous-garde dont je voudrois que vous puissiés vous passer pendant quelque tems. Il nous seroit utile pour parfumer les hopitaux. Faites lui délivrer, je vous prie, la poudre avariée qui lui est nécessaire pour cet objet.'

25 Floréal (14th May 1799).

Ordre du jour :
Français, vous n'êtes plus sur vos gardes. Les volontaires aux postes perdent de vue leurs fusils et se promenent trop éloignés. Les propos recommencent comme avant la conspiration de Guiglielmo. Les Bastases se rassemblent, tandis qu'il est ordonné de dissiper tous les grouppes de plus de trois personnes. Des habitants montent sur la fortification quoiqu'il est consigné de les en empêcher. Les forcats ne sont point enchainés. Prenés garde à vous : il se machine quelque chose.

Le Général Chanez renouvellera l'ordre de ne pas s'éloigner des postes, et à tout militaire de chaque grade de ne plus sortir sans armes, et punira même ceux qui négligeront cette précaution que la circonstance commande impérieusement.

Il ordonnera aux gardes de dissiper les grouppes de plus de trois personnes, aux sentinelles et aux postes des fortifications de ne laisser aucun habitant monter dessus. Il enjoindra au Commissaire Ordonateur de la Marine de faire enchainer tous les forçats. Ayés les yeux ouverts braves francais et empêchés par les moyens les plus fermes tous les malveillans de nous nuire. Que la plus grand surveillance soit renouvellée, que quiconque attenteroit à la sûreté et à la vie des français soit puni de mort par la Commission Militaire.

26 Floréal (15th May 1799).

PROCLAMATION.

Vaubois Général de Division &c. Depuis quelques jours il paroît dans la citté Valette des personnes qui n'y habitoient pas. Leur changement de domicile doit avoir un motif juste ou doit être dirigé par la malveillance. Pour en être informé avec exactitude, laisser en paix les bons, et sévir avec rigeur contre les méchans. Il est ordonné ce qui suit :

ART. 1.

Tout habitant de Bourmola, de la Victorieuse, de la Sengle, de la Valette et de la Florianne, qui ayant son domicile dans un de ces endroits, la quitte pour habiter dans un autre, doit se présenter à la Municipalité pour lui faire connoître qu'il passe d'un endroit dans l'autre, et s'il change de municipalité, il doit aussi venir se faire inscrire à la nouvelle ; et décliner les motifs de son changement. Cet article aura un effet retroactif jusqu'à l'époque de la rébellion.

ART. 2.

Tout individu qui ne se conformera pas à la première article sera puni comme mal intentionné et avec une sévérité reglée par les circonstances.

ART. 3.

Tout transfuge passant à la Campagne dans une des Municipalités et qui passera vint-quatre heures sans se présenter à l'Etat Major du lieu sera puni de mort.

ART. 4.

Les Grecs sont tenus d'être rentrés chez eux à huit heures du soir. Tous ceux qui seront arrêtés dans les rues, ou qu'on trouvera chez quelqu'autre habitant passé cette heure seront conduits à la Castellaine, et on recherchera les motifs de leur desobéissance pour y appliquer la peine convenable.

ART. 5.

On renouvelle la deffense sous peine de mort à tout habitant, excepté à la garde nationale, et à quelques fonctionnaires publics qui ont des permissions particulieres, d'avoir des armes ou des munitions de guerre.

ART. 6.

Les autorités militaires et civiles tiendront la main à l'exécution la plus stricte de ces articles.

6 Prairial (25th May 1799).

Au Commissaire Ordonateur de la Marine :

' Les prises faites hier offrent un objet d'utilité qu'il faut qu'elles remplissent sans nuire aux preneurs.[1] Le Charbon est utile à la République, et elle payera ce que de droit. Les harengs salés ne sont point une nourriture convenable aux soldats, il faut donc que le public en profite ; mais si on les vendoit sans précautions, les accapareurs s'en saisiroient et le public payeroit trop cher.

---

[1] See for these prizes taken by *speroneras* from Valetta the letter of Lieut. Vivion of May 31, 1799, in Chap. xii. The British blockading force was withdrawn for a time owing to the incursion of the fleet of Bruix.—J. H. R.

Emparés vous en, qu'un prix raisonable y soit fixé, et que des distributeurs les portent chez les habitans, et les répartissent suivant la force des ménages, surtout que les misérables ne soient pas oubliés. Je crois que le prix de deux tarins [8 sols] le hareng sera assez considérable.'[1]

10 Prairial (29th May 1799).

A la Municipalité de l'Ouest :
Vous voudrés bien proclamer que les pêcheurs ne pourront vendre leur poisson aux habitans que deux tarins de plus [8^s] que le tarif fixé pour l'hopital, le plus beau poisson est porté à vingt tarins [4 ff] il ne pourra donc excéder vingt deux tarins et ainsi de suitte pour les autres espéces. C'est un gain considérable pour les pêcheurs et il faut empêcher qu'ils ne fassent une fortune trop rapide au depens de leurs concitoyens.

1 Messidor (19th June 1799).

Ordre :
On vient de me rendre compte que la garnison réfusoit le pain. L'Adjudant-Général le Commissaire Ordonateur s'y sont transportés ; le pain est jugé bon. Les troupes ont donc tort de le réfuser. Il y avoient des Volontaires qui le jugoient mauvais avant de l'avoir vû. J'observe à mes freres d'armes quand on prend autant de peine pour qu'il ne leur manque rien, un réfus aussi mal fondé a l'air d'une insurrection, et c'est faire triompher nos ennemis, en leur donnant un spectacle qui leur plait tandis qu'ils ne doivent voir que de l'union. J'ordonne qu'à dix heures on aille prendre le pain. Les quartiers maîtres qui l'ont reconnu bon eux-mêmes, conduiront en ordre les corvées.

4 Messidor (22nd June 1799).

Proclamation :
Quand j'ai demandé de l'argent aux habitans et que le nouvel emprunt a été reparti, je ne m'attendois pas que la rentrée en seroit aussi lente. Les personnes aisé sont celles dont il est le plus difficile de tirer des secours. Combien même s'en trouve-t'il dans cette classe qui ne peuvent pas alléguer la gêne que leur a cause le premier emprunt, puisqu'elles ne l'ont pas payées.[2]
Les maux que le siége entraine n'empêchent pas qu'il n'y ait une quantité considérable de numeraire dans la ville. Une telle conduite est le produit de la mauvaise volonté seule, car je ne pense pas qu'on puisse douter du triomphe de la République dans cette isle. Il faudroit être ou bien stupide, ou ennemi bien acharné pour croire, ou feindre de croire, que des Républicains vainqueurs de la plus grande partie de l'Europe abandonneront cette place à une poignée de vagabonds ou à quelques vaisseaux qui n'ont jamais conçu l'espoir de s'en emparer.
Il ne faut pas de grandes lumiéres en politique pour sentir que l'objet des Anglois est de ruiner la population et le pays précisement parce qu'ils n'espérent pas s'en rendre maîtres. Ils détruisent parcequ'un autre doit réparer. Voilà l'unique but d'une entreprise à laqu'elle la vanité et l'ambition de beaucoup de vos concitoyens se sont aussi sottement que criminellement associés. Ils ont voulu faire la guerre. Nous la ferons avec une fermeté et une constance inébranlable ; et pour triompher de la mauvaise volonté de ceux qui réfusent les moyens de la soutenir, rejettant toujours l'idée de m'emparer de l'argenterie des Eglises, quoique j'y sois suffisamment autorisé par les circonstances, je déclare que ceux qui ne satisferont pas de suite ou en prenant des termes peu

---

[1] For an account of the situation in Valetta, as stated by deserters, see Vivion's letter of June 19, 1799, to Nelson in Chap. xii.—J. H. R.
[2] For these exactions see Vivion's letter, referred to in the previous note.—J. H. R.

éloignés pour le payement du nouvel emprunt, auront leur mobilier saisi juridiquement et vendu ou fondu pour subvenir au besoin des troupes, des hopitaux, et des dépenses civiles.

Aux Chefs des Corps :

Je ne vous assemble point, Citoyens, parceque la dernière fois que cela m'est arrivé, il s'est tenu des propos dans la ville. Il paroit toujours aux yeux des gens mal intentionnés ou pusillanimes que l'on ne s'assemble que pour déterminer la reddition de la place.[1] Ce mot seul révolte un républicain.

Je prends donc le parti de vous écrire sur un objet de la plus grande importance. L'histoire du pain, des indiscrétions, ces fausses et insipides gazettes ramassées dehors pas des soldats avec une lettre d'envoi écrite en français par l'officier Anglois dont j'ai déjà une lettre qui me prouve parfaitement que c'est la même écriture. Ces absurdités sont le fruit de la perfidie des Anglois puisqu'elles sont en pleine contradiction avec une lettre de Calabre du 13 May qui a été apportée ici par la premiere prise que nous avons faite. Mais toutes ces menées pourroient inquiéter les republicains si on ne leur montroit la verité dans tout son jour et combien notre situation doit nous inspirer de confiance.

Détruisés cette idée fausse sur le pain. Si l'on en faisoit de deux espèces, c'étoit sans mes ordres. Cela pouvoit entrainer des abus et augmenter la consommation, ce qui est contraire à la loi ; cette espèce d'insurrection n'a donc aucun motif fondé, et elle a été soufflée. Assemblés vos officiers. Faites leur sentir que la moindre indiscrétion fait le plus mauvais effet sur l'esprit d'un peuple aussi ignorant que foible de caractere, et dont la plus grande partie est mal intentionnée. Je compte et je me repose entiérement sur votre énergie, votre vertu, et votre patriotisme.

6 Messidor (24th June 1799).

Au Commissaire Ordonateur de Terre :

Vous donnerés des ordres pour que l'habillement soit délivré aux corps suivant les quantités déterminés par l'état ci joint.

Ordre :

Des personnes au moins indiscrettes, et qui ne savent pas ce qui existe, font courrir le bruit que les medicamens manquent aux hopitaux, ce qui est faux. C'est d'après ces préjugés que les Volontaires malades se livrent à des remedes et aux soins de gens hors d'état de les traiter et qui leur font le plus grand tort, malgré leurs bonnes intentions.

Que les malades aillent donc aux hopitaux : il y a des rémedes ; les soins sont portés au dernier point, et les medecins apperçoivent un grand changement que la saison améliorera encore.

Je recommande aux Volontaires de se baigner souvent parce que la propreté influe beaucoup sur la santé, de manger des legumes et de faire réflection que dans les pays chauds, le tems des chaleurs est le plus sain, et que les épidemies cessent toujours dans cette saison.

Au President de la Municipalité de l'Est :

L'orge recueilli pour la République ne se bât point. La récolte des particuliers doit nous procurer de la paille en payant. Elle ne vient point au magazin. Faites exécuter promptement les mésures qui ont été prises à ce sujet.

---

[1] For this insubordination of part of the garrison, see Vivion's letter of June 25th, 1799, in Chap. xii.—J. H. R.

10 Messidor (28th June 1799).

Au Ministre de la Guerre :
Citoyen Ministre,
Depuis dix mois révolus vous savés que nous sommes assiégés par terre et bloqués par mer. Une cruelle épidémie, un scorbut terrible nous enlève une partie de nos camarades. Une maladie d'un autre genre nous prive d'un grand nombre de deffenseurs qui sont absolument aveugles, pendant la nuit. L'étendue immense de nos remparts est foiblement gardée. Nous n'entendons parler de rien ; mais nous croyons à l'existence d'une escadre dans la Méditeranée. Combien j'en désire l'arrivée avec ardeur ! principalement pour triompher de la lassitude qui commence à se manifester et qui me desespére. Pendant neuf mois la volonté unie au courage s'est montré de la manière la plus satisfaisante : mais je vois de l'abbatement, des indiscrétions, des propos imprudens qui font un mauvais effet. Je tache de remonter la machine tant que je peux. Je suis secondé par bien des Braves ; mais combien d'autres manquent de la fermeté nécessaire pour supporter les privations et les travaux d'un long siége.

Les ennemis usent de toutes les fourberies imaginables. Ils jettent des fausses gazettes devant les postes avancés. Quelque précaution que l'on prenne, le soldat reçoit des impressions facheuses qui influent sur un certain nombre. Des Officiers mêmes ont une insouciance condamnable. S'ils s'occupoient à élever l'ame du soldat, la volonté et la Bravoure se soutiendroit mieux.

J'ai ménagé les vivres avec toute l'économie possible. J'ai toujours fait payer partout, et je n'ai pu y parvenir qu'en faisant des emprunts, qui doivent me procurer le double avantage de soutenir l'ardeur du soldat, et obliger les Maltais de désirer que nous restassions ici, puisque leur fortune est en partie entre les mains de la République. Nous ne comptons pas ici six amis sincéres. Une partie de la population ne remue pas parceque si nous quittions Malte sa fortune seroit perdue, et cest où ma politique vouloit les amener. L'autre partie est tranquille, parcequ'elle n'a point d'armes et surtout de courage.

D'ailleurs la population de la ville est tellement réduite, que nous n'aurons, je crois, jamais rien à craindre de l'intérieur. Elle fait pitié, cette population par rapport aux besoins extrêmes qu'elle éprouve.

On ne voit que des cadavres ambulans. Il meurt environ vingt personnes par jour, et souvent plus. Les moyens de subsistence, les médicamens sont épuisés, un œuf coute seize sols, une poule vingt cinq écus. Tout est extrêmement rare. J'ai même été obligé d'empêcher qu'on ne tuât des chevaux et des mulets, n'en ayant qu'un petit nombre indispensable au service, et prévoyant la nécessité où l'on sera peutêtre de s'en servir pour l'hopital. Depuis plusieurs mois nous perdons par maladie 100, 120, et 130 hommes par mois. Qu'elle playe pour une aussi foible garnison. . . . Vous pensés bien assi, [sic] que depuis dix mois que cela dure, les munitions de guerre ont été consommées. On ne répousse pas une multitude d'attaques, on n'est pas obligé de tirer sur Beaucoup de Batteries inquiétantes sans diminuer les approvisionnements. Si j'avois reçue des lettres du gouvernement, elles auroient sûrement augmenté le courage des Troupes : mais par une fatalité désolante, tout ce qui m'a été adressé a été pris. Je n'ai rien reçu du tout, et plusieurs ont pris pour de l'abandon ce qui n'étoit que l'effet naturel de la guerre.

Quel Bonheur pour nous que le vaisseau *Le Guillaume Tell*, les fregattes *La Diane* et *La Justice* se soient rendus ici ! Le courage et le zèle des Contre-Amiraux Villeneuve et Décrés dérigeant l'emulation de ce qui est sous leurs ordres ont opéré le plus grand effet. Sans ces forces qui servent à terre, nous n'aurions jamais pu embrasser une aussi grande deffense, et nous aurions été obligés en nous resserant d'abandonner des fortifications à l'ennemi.

PART III—FROM 6TH JULY 1799 TO 25TH DECEMBER 1799.

18 Messidor (6th July 1799).

Aux Administrateurs de l'Université :

Il y a plusieurs mois, citoyens, que je fis faire le recensement des huiles qui se trouvoient alors dans les deux parties de l'est et de l'ouest.[1] On me rendit compte qu'il existoit chez les marchands et à l'Université cinq mille cafis d'huile, Supposant que bien des particuliers en étoient pourvus pour leur consommation, je jugeai que nous ne devions avoir aucun inquiétude sur cette denrée ; mais d'après les renseignements particuliers il me paroit que la cupidité cherche à s'exercir sur cet objet de premiere nécéssité. Nous devons donc prendre les moyens convenables, non seulement pour assurer l'approvisionnement nécéssaire au siége, mais même apporter des obstacles, si nous pouvons, aux spéculations de ces êtres vils qui veulent accroitre leur fortune par la misère publique. En conséquence vous tiendrés à la disposition de la République, et par réquisition spéciale, non seulement ce qui reste des mille cafis dont le Commissaire Ordonateur peut disposer, mais les dix-neuf cent qui restent des trois mille, dont il est fait mention plus haut.

Je vais faire une recherche nouvelle de tout ce qui existe. Je ferai enlever tout dépôt un peu considérable, et si je reussis a en faire entrer une certaine quantité dans nos magazins, je rendrai une service au public, la place pourvue, de lui en faire distribuer à un prix convenable et au bénéfice des propriétaires. Gardés, je vous prie, le secret sur cette dernière mesure.

23 Messidor (11th July 1799).

Au Commandant de la partie de l'Est :

Nous celebrons la fete du 14 Juillet à la Valette. Vous êtes, ainsi que les troupes que vous commandés aussi empressé que nous à donner à ce grand jour des preuves de votre patriotisme. Comme il est nécéssaire que personne ne s'éloigne de son poste, celebrés la fête sur la place de la Victorieuse avec la musique, et des detachements des différens corps. L'ordre de la Division vous informera du nombre des salves d'artillerie qui doivent être faites. Chantez de toutes vos forces les belles hymnes patriotiques et croyés que ça ira.[2]

29 Messidor (17th July 1799).

Au Commissaire Ordonateur de la Marine :

La position de nos finances exige forcement une épargne de fonds. Les travaux du port étant diminués, et le nombre des employés étant réduit à un point considérable, j'ai cru que je pouvois, sans nuire au service le plus essentiel de votre partie vous rétrancher dix mille livres par mois, et vous faire compter quinze mille (15,000) au lieu de 25,000. Cette mesure est forcée. L'excessive cherté des denrées ne nous permettroient pas de suffir aux depenses des hopitaux sans des réductions dont je vais m'occuper sur les différentes parties.

30 Messidor (18th July 1799).

A l'Adjudant Général Brouard :

Vous ordonnerés de ma part au Commissaire des Guerres auquel vous adjoindrés des officiers intelligens de commencer demain la vérification exacte de chaque espéce de comestibles ; et le jaujage précis de tous les liquides. Ces

---

[1] i.e. of the city of Valetta. For the repulse of the French at Fort Manoel see Vivion's letter of July 1, in Chap. xii.—J. H. R.

[2] A popular song of the Revolution.—J. H. R.

opérations doivent être suivies sans rélâche. Vous me rendrés compte de chaque objet aussitôt qu'il sera terminé.

9 Thermidor (27th July 1799).

A la Commission de Gouvernement :
Je viens de faire verser chez le trésorier Saut la somme de trois mille écus pour faire face aux depenses civiles de Messidor. L'état de la caisse militaire me force à reduire la solde et les appointemens des militaires de tout grades [sic], ainsi que des administrations à moitié. A datter du premier Thermidor la partie civile ne sera plus payée que par trimestre. Cet arrangement est subordonné aux circonstances. Si des fonds rentroient je m'empresseroit de remettre tout le monde au courant. Cet ordre est général pour tous les corps constitués et pour tous les salaires. Les hopitaux seuls exceptés. La rentrée de l'emprunt est même nécéssaire pour soutenir cette depense diminuée. Avertissés donc les habitans que forcé par les circonstances je vais user de rigueur puisque leur mauvaise volonté est si manifestée. Donnés promptement cet avis afin que j'agisse.

La compagnie qui garde le fort Tigné mérite les éloges dûs à de braves Republicains. Peu d'hommes ont mis en fuite beaucoup de Brigands. Il est recommandé au Citoyen Pepin commandant cette compagnie de se défier des embuscades de ces Bandits, qui n'approchent qu'à la faveur des murs et des maisons, de prendre toutes les précautions militaires, et de ne laisser sortir du fort qui que ce soit le matin qu'on ne soit sûr de ce qui se passe dans les environs. Un fort de l'espéce de celui de Tigné est imprénable quand il est garde par des Braves gens commandés par des officiers Républicains jusqu'au fond du cœur.

15 Thermidor (2nd August 1799).

Au Citoyen Delafeufs [?] Garde Magazin des Subsistances :
D'après la vérification que j'ai fait faire de vos magazins, j'ai lieu d'être satisfait de vos services. Tout est en régle et prouve une gestion suivie et exacte. Rédoublés d'attention et de surveillance, la conservation de Malte tient à la stricte administration des comestibles. Les abus naitront bien vite si vos sousordres n'étoient pas examinés de prés ; choisissés les donc à la probité et à l'intelligence.[1]

8 Fructidor (25th August 1799).

Au Général Décres :
Mécontent à l'excés, Général, de la conduite d'une partie de la garnison du fort Ricasoli qui s'expose journellement en allant marauder dans la campagne, je vous prie d'ordonner qu'elle soit toute consignée jusqu'à nouvel ordre, et de recommander aux officiers de surveiller exactement leurs subordonnés, afin de prévenir les suites facheuses de ces sorties que la cupidité occasionne.

9 Fructidor (26th August 1799).

Ordre du jour :
La tranquilité des Brigands ne doit point nous tenir en sécurité, et apporter aucune négligence dans le service. Ils méditent peutêtre quelques sottes attaques comme celles qu'ils ont déjà faites. L'approche de l'hiver tourmente les Anglois et les vagabonds armés. Qu'on soit toujours prêt à les bien récevoir.

L'envie de gagner de l'argent, la cupidité, cette passion si dégradante pour un brave militaire, nous a fait perdre quelques hommes qui se sont éloignés sans armes des remparts pour enlever quelques denrées. Il est ordonné à tous les

[1] For Ball's summons to Vaubois to surrender (August 19), and the reply of the latter on the same day, see Chap. xii. of this work.—J. H. R.

chefs de poste et officiers quelconques d'empêcher que personne ne s'écarte. Je ferai traduire au conseil de guerre et punir comme maraudeur, et même comme deserteur tous ceux qui s'écarteront des remparts. Il est deffendu à toutes barques de porter sous un prétexte quelconque quelque personne que ce soit hors de l'enceinte des villes et forts; de sorte que nul ne pourra être débarqué autre part qu'à l'entrée des forts ou dans les villes de l'est et de l'ouest. Tout patron ou matelot qui debarqueroit du monde autre part seront punis, les barques saisies, et les militaires qui les auront portés à cette désobéissance seront aussi sévèrement punis. Les commandants des villes se concerteront avec les Municipalités et les officiers du port pour l'execution du dernier article.

14 Fructidor (31st August 1799).

Au Contre-Amiral Villeneuve:

Un des objets le plus essentiel pour les malades et pour le reste de l'armée, c'est le vinaigre, et c'est celui dont nous sommes le moins pourvus. Vous avés à Bord des Batimens, Beaucoup de Barriques de vin de Sicile. Si le compte que l'on m'a rendu est exact, il n'est point de parti plus avantageux à tirer de ce vin de mauvaise qualité, et dont peutêtre une partie est déjà gatée, que de la transformer en vinaigre. Quel service cela ne nous rendra-t'-il pas dans la saison scabreuse de l'automne, si les maladies se manifestent? Mettés donc ce vin à la disposition du garde magazin des approvisionnements de siége. J'en surveillerai exactement la scrupuleuse conversion en vinaigre.

16 Fructidor (2nd September 1799).

À la Commission de Gouvernement:

Des vues d'utilité publique, m'engagent à faire faire un nouveau dénombrement des habitans qui n'a point été fait avec assez d'exactitude la premiere fois. Vous voudrés bien inviter les municipalités de l'est et de l'ouest de s'en occuper sans delai.

Lettre de l'amiral portugais le Marquis de Nizza au Général Vaubois:

5 Septembre 1799.

Je pense, Monsieur, qu'il est également intéressant pour vous et pour moi que nous ayons incessemment une entrevûe.

Je désire fort que vous acceptiés cette proposition, et vous prie de me faire savoir vos intentions. Je suis très parfaitement, &c.

LE MARQUIS DE NIZZA.

Réponse du Général Vaubois à la lettre du Marquis de Nizza.

19 Fructidor (5th September 1799).

S'il vous convient, Monsieur, de vous trouver dimanche de onze heures à midi, au fort Manoël, je m'y rendrai. Votre canot pourra entrer par le port de Marsamoucette pour venir au dit fort. Je suis, &c., GÉNÉRAL VAUBOIS.

22 Fructidor (8th September 1799).

Ordre du jour:

La garnison est avertie que le Commandant Portugais m'a demandé une entrevue. Je regarde cette démarche comme une marque de foiblesse de la part de nos ennemis. J'ai cru devoir la lui accorder, et lui parler en présence de mon Etat Major. S'il ouvre la Bouche pour parler capitulation, je la fermerai sur le champ en lui repondant en vrai Républicain, si c'est pour autre chose, je le laisserai dire. Quand des enemis cherchent à parlementer, c'est qu'ils connoissent leur foiblesse. Il y a l'apparence que l'hiver leur fait peur.

2eme Jour Complem^{re} (18th September 1799).

Au Commissaire Ordonateur de Terre :
Tous les bois neufs et vieux existans dans les magazins des particuliers des trois villes seront mis à la disposition du Commissaire Ordonateur de la Division sur la demande qu'il est autorisé d'en faire aux propriétaires. Les démolitions seront faites aux frais de la République.

Les bois seront pésés et il sera délivré à chaque particulier une reconnoissance dans la qu'elle seront mentionnés exactement la quantité des bois qui auront été fournis.

5me Jour Complem^{re} (21st September 1799).

Ordre du jour :
La garnison française de l'est et de l'ouest célébrera la fete de la naissance de la République. Les batteries feront feu sur les batteries ennemis comme la précédente fête. L'autel de la patrie sera dressé sur la place d'armes à la Citte Valette, et sur la place de la Victorieuse. . . .

13 Vendémiaire an 8 Rép^e (5th October 1799).

Au Ministre de la Guerre :
Par ma dernière lettre en datte du 10 Messidor que vous devés avoir reçue par le Citoyen Fouques Officier de Marine, s'il est arrivé à bon port, j'ai dû allarmer le gouvernement. Nous étions effectivement dans une situation affreuse ; en proye à un scorbut contagieux qui nous enlevoit journellement beaucoup de monde, les troupes étoient effrayées, la lassitude se manifestoit. Mais les chaleurs ont affoibli cette espéce d'épidémie, et le nombre des malades est réduit à 280 au moment ou je vous écris, c'est à dire à moitié. Nous avons perdu beaucoup et ce qui nous reste éprouve de grandes fatigues à cause de l'étendue de ce que nous avons à deffendre. Voici d'ailleurs l'automne saison dangereuse.

Notre situation est toujours la même. Bloqués par quatre vaisseaux portugais, trois vaisseaux anglois, deux frégattes, deux corvettes et deux bricks. Quelques troupes angloises et portugaises jointes aux habitans nous assiegent par terre. Ils ont beaucoup ralenti leur feu ; cependant ils jettent encore de tems en tems des bombes et des obus dirigés principalement sur les vaisseaux qu'ils cherchent à détruire, et qui n'ont encore reçue aucune dommage, graces aux précautions que nous avons prises. Les maisons voisines du port sont écrasées.

Nous avons ajouté aux fortifications des ouvrages qui rendent le service le plus sûr en même tems qu'il le diminue. L'arsenal a fait un travail surprenant en reparations et en constructions neuves, et je ne puis trop louer à cet égard les soins du Général d'artillerie D'hennezal, et l'activité du Capitaine Raulot faisant fonctions de Sous-Directeur.

La cessation des maladies a produit sur le soldat un effet le plus marqué. Son ardeur et son désir de conserver Malte sont au comble, c'est j'ose vous l'assurer une garnison impayable, à l'exception de quelques officiers dont la résolution m'a paru quelque fois affoiblie : mais j'ai juré que je ferois périr celui à qui il echapperoit une indiscrétion. Le soldat admireroit cette justice, et le petit nombre de malveillans n'est pas en état de l'ébranler. Il s'est glissé dans cette expédition des gens de tout genre, et les opinions de quelques uns sont peut-être criminelles.

Malheur à eux si je les connois bien.

Monsieur le Marquis de Nizza chef d'escadre portugais et Alexandre Ball capitaine de vaisseau anglois, commandant les Anglois à terre, m'ont assommé de sommations. Je leur ai répondu en Républicain : enfin ils m'ont demandé une entrevue. Après y avoir bien réfléchi je n'ai vû de leur part qu'une marque de foiblesse, une envie de me séduire et de nous raconter mille absurdités sur la guerre qu'ils disent avoir lieu en Italie. J'ai cru pouvoir faire tourner cette circonstance à leur honte, en les recevant au milieu de mon Etat Major dans un fort où ils ne verroient rien, porte ouverte, leur empêcher de prononcer le mot Capitulation, de raconter aucune nouvelle, de leur faire voir des gens résolus, de leur faire essuyer la bordée des propos Républicains, les expressions du courage et du patriotisme et de fatiguer leurs oreilles des acclamations du soldat qui crioit, *Malte ou la Mort, plutot perir sur les remparts jusqu'au dernier que de capituler.*

Enfin j'ai réussi parfaitement ; ils n'ont pu proférer une parole de ce qu'ils vouloient dire, beaucoup de politesse ; mais ils sont partis avec la honte d'une demarche absurde, marchant au milieu d'une haie de soldats qui crioient à tue tête, qui les invitoient à venir à l'assaut.

La garnison de la ville répondit à ces cris par un mouvement spontané, les tambours battoient *ça ira*. Tout cela sans être arrangé et par pur enthousiasme. Ils ont je crois renoncé au projet de me séduire, s'ils en ont eu l'envie.

Je passe à l'article le plus interressant de ma lettre. Le gouvernement compte surement nous ravitailler, en hommes, en vivres, et en argent : cela est indispensable. J'ai menagé les vivres tant que j'ai pû. Les administrations ont été surveillées avec scrupule. Les rations n'ont été pour bien des choses que la moitié de ce qu'elles devoient être par la loi. Le vin ne s'est distribué à tiers de pinte pour tous les grades que trois fois par decade. Je vais en rétrancher une. Il me reste sur le pied où nous sommes, et suivant la médiocrité des rations

Bled pour	8 Mois.
Lard et Bœuf salé	4 Mois.
Vin pour	3 Mois.
Vinaigre	2 Mois.
Haricots	5 Mois.
Eau de Vie	4 Mois.

Il nous faudroit, en comptant sept mille parties prenantes, à cause de tous ceux qui sont employés au service et qui n'ont rien pour vivre, du vin au moins pour un an au tiers de pinte par ration pour tous les jours et suivant les grades.

Lard surtout et Bœuf salé qui ne se conserve pas bien ici, pour un an.

Vinaigre en assez grande quantité comme antiscorbutique.

Eau de vie suffisemment.

Haricots et autres légumes secs pour un an.

Graisse, huile, beurre salé, saindoux, ris, pruneaux, sucre, miel, linge pour l'hopital, tous ces articles nous manquent absolument.

Des moutons pour l'hopital.

Un assortiment de médicamens en tous genres.

Un habillement. Nous n'en avons que de toile, et nous manquons de chapeaux, de souliers et de chemises.

La quantité de ces différens objets doit être augmentée en raison en proportion du nombre des troupes qu'on nous enverra.

Nous n'avons plus d'argent, et vous allés voir la détresse où se trouve l'officier, qui est a demie solde, ainsi que le soldat depuis deux mois, par le tarif du prix des comestibles :—

Une Poule 60 fr.; Une paire de Pigeons 24 fr.; Un Lapin 12 fr.; Un Œuf 16 sols; Une Laitue 16 ou 18 sols; Viande de Cheval 2fr. la livre; Un Rat 1 fr. 10 c. jusquà 2 fr.; Poisson 6 fr. la livre. Ces articles sont en petite quantité et le reste manque.

Le bled sera peut-être difficile à renouveller, et il aura un terme. La farine ne se conserve pas bien ici, et si l'occasion de faire la paix avec les habitans se présentoit, il faudroit les nourrir. Les ennemis ne leur font parvenir que le necessaire du jour. C'est un article d'une grande considération. La population de la ville qui se montoit au moins à quarante mille ames est réduite à neuf mille, dont un tiers de femmes et un tiers d'enfants. Il est mort environ trois mille personnes dans la ville. Il y a beaucoup de spectres ambulans. Leur situation est affreuse. On ne peut se dispenser de penser aux habitans qui restent. L'argent est très-necessaire. On ne peut vivre qu'en achetant, et vous voyés que tout est hors de prix. Les hopitaux militaires et civils coutent horriblement, On nourrit les malades avec du poisson et des œufs. Les membres des autorités constituées périssent de faim.

Telle est notre situation. Nous tournerons continuellement les yeux vers la France en brumaire et en frimaire. Songés à nous, je vous en conjure, et comptés toujours sur notre vigoureuse résistance. La faim peut devenir notre plus cruel ennemi et nous sommes excédés de fatigue.

J'allois finir cette lettre et la faire partir avec un de mes aides de camp, lorsqu'il est arrivé un aviso.

Nous savons donc qu'on nous prépare à Toulon ce qui nous est nécéssaire ; Vive la République. Je ne change rien à ma lettre, seulement, je vous observe, Citoyen Ministre, que l'objet seul de l'habillement ne me paroit pas aussi etendu que les autres. Un article non moins essentiel ce sont des couvertures. Nous n'en avons point, et il est impossible de s'en procurer ici. Elles sont indispensables. S'il est difficile d'en trouver à Toulon, on pourroit surement nous en envoyer de Gènes, pour le peu qu'on reveille la sollicitude de Belleville. C'est un Républicain qui n'est jamais en rétard. Nous avons appris les désastres de l'Italie en frémissant. Ils ne font qu'exciter notre courage et la garnison de Malte crie comme tous les Républicains, vengeance du crime sans exemple de Rastad. Je vous ferai passer par le retour de l'escadre mon journal que je vous prie de communiquer au gouvernement. Vous y verrés nos travaux et ma conduite ; puisse t'elle être digne de notre République adorée et impérissable.

Sommation faite au Général Vaubois par l'Amiral Portugais :
5 Octobre 1799.

La constance et la perseverance avec la qu'elle vous vous êtes maintenu, monsieur, dans la place de la Valette depuis plus d'une année, mérite assurement des éloges et est fait pour vous mériter l'estime de l'ennemi ; mais il est un terme à tout et passé le quel, ce qui étoit nommé vertu devient imprudence et temérité.

Jusqu'au moment où vous avés eu des espérances raisonnables d'être secouru et dégagé, votre conduite annonce une fermeté estimable, mais lorsque vous ne pouvés plus avoir aucun espoir de secours, que la situation actuelle de l'Europe vous annonce un abandon absolu, votre persévérance à ne vouloir pas entrer *en pourparler* peut être à juste titre taxée d'obstination, aussi contraire aux lois de l'humanité, qu'à celle de la justice, puisque c'est vous opposer à faire obtenir aux troupes que vous commandés un sort honorable et avantageux.

Je sais bien que vous pouvés m'opposer la raison de n'être pas attaqué, que nul ouvrage n'a encore été fait pour battre vos murailles et qu'il n'est pas naturel d'évacuer une place par l'effet d'un simple blocus. Cette raison seroit sans réplique, sans doute, si vous étiés enfermé dans votre place seulement depuis quelques mois et que la situation des affaires politiques, le succes de vos armées vous donnaient lieu d'espérer de voir triompher votre parti, et avant l'epoque actuelle peutêtre eussiés vous pû être taxé de manquer de perseverance ; mais actuellement que vous savés positivement que vos escadres ont été forcées de quitter la Méditerrannée, que l'Italie entiere et la Sicile sont rentrées sous la domination de leur legitime Gouvernement, que toutes les nations barbaresques sont devenues vos ennemis, vous êtes abandonné sur un point isolé au millieu de la Méditerrannée sans espoir de recevoir aucun secours. L'espoir de sortir de la place sur les vaisseaux que vous avés ne peut être raisonnable ; des escadres Angloises, Portugais Russes et Turques vous ferment tous les chemins. . . . Jai l'honneur d'être &c., Le Marquis de Nizza.

Reponse du Général Vaubois à la sommation de l'Amiral Portugais :
Je vous ai fait connoitre mes intentions, Monsieur, je suis, et tous ceux que j'ai l'honneur de commander, dans les mêmes dispositions qui sont de nous deffendre avec tout le courage dont des braves gens sont susceptibles. Nous avons reçue des nouvelles aussi, il y a quelques jours. Nous savons la position de l'Europe, et nous sommes assurés que la Victoire se fixera à nos drapeaux dans le courant de l'hiver. J'ai l'honneur d'être, &c.,

GÉNÉRAL VAUBOIS.

14 Vendémiaire an 8eme Rep^e (6th October 1799).

Au Ministre de la Marine :
J'ai récue, Citoyen Ministre, votre lettre du 18 Thermidor, par la qu'elle vous me faites connoître les opérations du Gouvernement rélativement à nous. Je m'y attendois, et j'étois bien persuadé qu'on s'occuperoit des deffenseurs de Malte. Mon seul desir est qu'on ne précipite rien et qu'on attende un tems fait ; alors il n'y aura rien contre, malgré les quatres vaisseaux portugais, deux anglois, deux fregattes, deux corvettes et deux bricks occupés au blocus de Malte.

J'ai vû avec plaisir l'état detaillé de l'envoi, qui cependant ne porte pas les quantités. Une partie seule essentielle m'a paru foible, et nous en avons grand besoin, c'est celle de l'habillement et de l'équipement. Nous manquons aussi des couvertures et nous ne pouvons nous en procurer. Votre lettre secrette m'est arrivée trop tard. Tout ce qui se trouvoit de plus suspect est dehors de la ville. Cependant je donnerai encore quelque effet à vos ordres. Nous n'avons rien à craindre de l'intérieur. Il est trop peu nombreux, et la crainte est trop grande. Cette population ne nous manifeste aucun attachement mais c'est en grande partie le sentiment de ses souffrances qui dirige ses motifs. Si elle recouvrait la paix, elle auroit de suite l'air de se vouer à la République ; cependant il est un grand nombre dont il faudra absolument se defaire.

Je rédige un mémoire, qui à ce que j'espère fera connoître au Gouvernement bien des choses que je juge extrêmement essentielles.

Je le ferai parvenir lorsqu'il sera fini.

Je serai à même aussi dans le tems de donner une infinité de détails.

L'esprit militaire est excellent parmi nous. Le courage et l'envie de triompher sont au comble. . . . Malte ou la mort telle est notre volonté.

Le ministre de la guerre reçoit de moi des détails sur notre situation actuelle.

17 Vendémiaire (9th October 1799).

Au Commissaire Ordonateur de Terre :
Je voudrés bien, Citoyen Ordonateur, mettre des bornes à la dégustation scandaleuse du vin qui a lieu à l'hopital, et qui porte jusqu'à huit pintes par jour. L'officier de police qui fait journellement la visite de l'hopital a le droit de gouter le vin, mais il n'en faut pour cela qu'une très petite quantité, et il y a loin de cette consommation à huit pintes.

24 Vendémiaire (16th October 1799).

Ordre du jour :
Par l'aviso arrivé ce matin, mes braves Camarades, j'ai reçu les nouvelles les plus satisfaisantes et je m'empresse de vous les transmettre. Le Général Masséna a remporté en Helvétie la victoire la plus eclatante sur les Austro-Russes.[1]

Cette intrépide armée a tué, pris, et blessé suivant les détails, trente deux mille hommes, pris tout le train d'artillerie, beaucoup de drapeaux et la caisse de l'armée.

[1] That of Zürich (Sept. 25-26, 1799).—J. H. R.

En Hollande des Russes et des Anglois ont débarqués en nombre considérable, ils ont été battus de la bonne maniere, les restes se sont embarqués comme ils ont pû.

En Egypte une armée composé de Turcs, de Russes et d'Anglois est débarquée à Abukir.[1] Le Général Bonaparte à la tête des troupes les a pris, tués ou noyés.

Nous avons eu des avantages sur le Rhin. La victoire est donc à l'ordre du jour, et les efforts des Républicains vont surement aneantir les efforts des fourbes coalisés qui excitent notre vengeance pour le crime horrible de l'assassinat de nos plenipotentiaires à Rastad. Le gouvernement, convaincu de votre courage, compte que Malte sera conservé.

Il attache à la possession de cette isle la plus haute importance. Il va nous envoyer sécours, vivres, et argent, et il ne cessera de s'occuper de nous, ainsi que le Ministre me le mande.

Vous acquerrés comme il me le dit une réputation impérissable. Vive la République.

Au Ministre de la Guerre :

L'aviso que je renvois en France, retardé par le vent contraire, Citoyen Ministre, me donne encore le tems de joindre une dépêche à celle dont je l'ai chargé.

Le Citoyen Fouques arrivé ce matin, m'a remis votre lettre. J'y vois avec plaisir ce que le Gouvernement fait pour nous. Soyés persuadé, Citoyen Ministre, que nous meritons qu'il s'en occupe. Les Volontaires à Malte sont autant de héros. Ce n'est qu'en passant sur nos corps qu'on pourra pénétrer dans cette ville. Mais surtout, je vous en conjure, que l'attention du Gouvernement se fixe sur la quantité de bled. Tout a un terme en subsistance, et cet article est plus difficile à remplacer. Il en faut pour la population et pour l'armée. Ce pays ne subsiste que par ce qu'il tire tout de l'étranger, sa sureté tient donc principalement à un amas de provisions de premiere necessité. . . . Nous avons toujours devant nous six vaisseaux, deux fregattes, deux corvettes, et deux bricks.

Nous avons grand besoin d'habillement, de chapeaux, de souliers, de chemises et de couvertures, tout va bien, tout ira bien, je me flatte de triompher, et ' Vive la République.'

26 Vendémiaire (18th October 1799).

Au Payeur de la Division :

Je sais que vous avés entre les mains 18290 francs, que le Citoyen Regnaud de St. Jean d'Angely vous à déposé à son depart ; il me dit alors qu'il me laissoit de l'argent dont nous pouvions user au besoin. Il est venu, ce besoin, et il est des plus urgent. Versés donc dans votre caisse cette somme et employés la au service. Ma lettre vous mettra à l'abri de toute responsabilité. Regardés la comme un ordre positif nécessité par les circonstances.

27 Vendémiaire (19th October 1799).

Circulaire à plusieurs Citoyens :

Personne plus que moi ne prend par [sic] à la misére du peuple, mais je distingue celui qui souffre de celui que la mauvaise volonté eloigne de faire ce qui est indispensable. D'après les renseignemens que j'ai pris, vous êtes dans le cas de payer l'emprunt auquel vos concitoyens ont jugés que vous pouviés être assujeti. Si sous peu de jours vous ne vous présentés pas à l'université pour payer, j'employerai des voyes séveres auxqu'elles les circonstances m'obligent impérieusement. C'est la dernière fois que je vous avertis.

[1] This was solely a Turkish force.—J. H. R.

28 Vendémiaire (20th October 1799).

Aux Citoyens Bonnario et Mallia:
Afin de tirer parti des effets qui nous reste au Mont de Piété, j'ai ordonné au Citoyen Chartier de faire une lotterie. Si des fonctionnaires publics ne surveillent point cette opération, la confiance pourroit, avec raison, s'allarmer. J'ai jetté les yeux sur vous pour être un des Commissaires qui en garantisse la fidelité. Vous voudrés bien vous concerter avec le Citoyen Chartier pour l'exécution la plus prompte de cette mesure.

30 Vendémiaire (22nd October 1799).
Proclamation:
C'est avec douleur que je vois la population manquer de tout. L'ingratitude et l'infidelité même ne détruisent pas l'humanité d'une nation genereuse. Pouvés vous douter que la France n'eût déjà beaucoup fait pour vous sans l'insurrection criminelle de vos concitoyens, qui plus ambitieux encore qu'ignorants, ont plongé cette malheureuse nation dans un abîme de malheurs?[1] Si les chefs survivent à cet événément, quels réproches n'aurés-vous pas à leur faire sur cette inepte et coupable entreprise? Qui ne leur redémandera des parens péris de misére? Qui ne les accusera pas de la perte de sa fortune? Mais la masse infortunée, la masse entrainée par des suggestions perfides, a encore la voye du répentir qui lui est ouverte. Ne se trouvera t'il donc personne parmi vous qui ait des idées saines en politiques qui vous instruise sur l'absurdité de l'indépendance dont on vous berce, sur la dureté du gouvernement anglois, sur les vûes perfides de cette nation, qui a toujours sacrifié les possessions eloignées aux intérêts de la Métropole? Sur la foiblesse du Gouvernement Napolitain, hors d'état de soutenir et de deffendre ce rocher élevé au millieu de la mer?[2] Sur le rétablissement des fortunes qui ne peut avoir lieu que par les remboursemens faits par la République.

Affecté par votre position, touché de votre denûement absolu des commestibles indispensables à la vie, ne pouvant vous en fournir, puisque je dois tout conserver pour les deffenseurs de cette forteresse, persuadé que la campagne vous fournira plus de secours que vous ne pouvés en trouver ici, je vous engage

1° A vous faire inscrire pour aller en campagne.

2° Je vous préviens que si le nombre de ceux qui seront inscrits, ne se porte pas à la quantité que je juge nécessaire, je serai forcé de faire une liste considerable de Citoyens que j'obligerai à sortir à une époque déterminée.

1er Brumaire (23rd October 1799).
Au Ministre de la Guerre:
Par ma dernière lettre du 28 Vendemiaire [20th October] je vous ai instruit, Citoyen Ministre, des forces navales ennemis qui nous bloquent. On doit en être positivement informé à Toulon. Ces bâtimens se tiennent presque toujours à la hauteur de St. Paul au nord ouest du port de la Valette. L'ennemi a construit une batterie à la pointe de St. Georges dont les boulets viennent à toute volée à l'entrée du port. Je fais avertir à Toulon de ne point trop ranger la cote pour entrer, parceque les vaisseaux seroient exposés au feu de cette batterie, qui d'ailleurs est très aisée à voir. Vous sentés, Citoyen Ministre, combien nous désirons le mauvais tems pour voir arriver ce qui nous est destiné.

En lisant l'état de ce qui sera expédié, je n'ai trouvé qu'un article qui m'a paru oublié, c'est celui de l'habillement et de l'équipement.

Les nuits sur les remparts sont dures; il fait un vent et un froid extrêmement pénétrant.

[1] This may be compared with Vaubois' admission given above that the insurrection had much benefited the French defence.—J. H. R.
[2] It is strange that the British Government did not realise this fact.—J. H. R.

Nous avons un très grand nombre de Volontaires qui ont passés aux hopitaux.

Epargnons à ces braves des maladies bien plus à craindre que le feu de l'ennemi.

N'ayant point de paille pour faire des paillasses, je fais faire beaucoup de hamacs ; mais il nous faudroit des couvertures.

Ce que je ne cesserai de recommander au gouvernement c'est de songer au Bled. C'est l'approvisionnement que je trouve le plus difficile à faire. Que de bâtiment ne faut-il pas pour un grand transport de bled!

C'est cependant en grand qu'on doit s'en occuper de cet objet. Les troupes et la population paissent dans les mêmes gréniers ; vous sentés, Citoyen Ministre, quelle doit être la force de cet approvisionnement. . . .

Nous sommes dignes de votre sollicitude. Les Généraux d'Hennezel, Chanez et les Généraux de la Marine me secondent avec une égale ardeur. Il y a long-tems que nous éprouvons des privations, mais elles nous paroissent douces à supporter puisque c'est pour la République.

5 Brumaire (27th October 1799).

Au Chef de Bataillon Noblot :

Demain six du courant il sera faite une sortie sur Bichi pour enlever du bois. L'objet qu'on se propose est que l'ennemi s'en apperçoive, et qu'étant occupé depuis longtems a demolir les mêmes maisons il lui prenne envie de venir chercher ce qui reste pendant la nuit. Il sera en consequence formé différentes embuscades qui iront prendre poste à l'entrée de Muet et surprendront surement les brigands qui auront envie de ne pas perdre tout ce qu'ils ont laissé. Soixante carabiniers, leurs Officiers et Sousofficiers, seront chargés de cette expédition. L'Adjudant Général Brouard dirigera l'opération, et donnera les ordres nécessaires pour l'exécution.[1]

9 Brumaire (31st October 1799).

Au Commandant du Genie :

Les dix sept cent espagnols qui doivent venir logeront 600 hommes à la Bormula, les 1100 hommes restant au grand quartier de St. Elme. La 80eme demie Brigade logera dans le Fort de St. Elme. Ce qui se trouve de la 7eme. ira loger à la Florianne. Les 2200 hommes seront distribués ainsi qu'il suit : 400 hommes à Ricazoli, 300 hommes au Fort Manoël, 200 hommes au Fort St. Ange, 400 hommes à la pointe de la Sengle, 600 hommes à la Victorieuse, 300 idem destinés pour l'artillerie seront disposés dans les postes. Le Génie est chargé de faire préparer les emplacemens pour le logement de ces troupes.

14 Brumaire (5th November 1799).

[On precautions to be taken against the introduction of the plague.]

Ordre du jour :

Des plaintes m'ont été portées sur différentes mauvaises actions commises pendant la nuit. Je n'imagine pas que des Républicains puissent se dégrader à ce point, et pour écarter tous les soupçons à l'égard des Français, ou connoitre les mauvais sujets capables de ces indignités et les punir au gré de leurs braves camarades, il est ordonné ce qui suit :

Le Général commandant la place réglera les heures des appels et prendra avec les chefs des corps les mésures ordinaires pourqu'aucun soldat ne puisse s'évader la nuit, et fera surveiller aussi particulierement les gardes et les piquets dans les forts. Le Contre Amiral Villeneuve est invité de donner l'ordre à tous les officiers de la marine de rétirer les permissions qu'ils auroient pu

[1] There is nothing in the letters of the British officers to show that this sortie was at all important (see Chap. x.)—J. H. R.

donner aux marins de demeurer en ville, afin qu'ils ne puissent s'absenter à nuit. Le Commissaire Ordonateur de la marine s'assurera de la fermeture de la prison pendant la nuit. La Commission chargée de la police de l'hopital Militaire ordonnera la fermeture des portes de maniére à ce qu'aucun soldat ne puisse sortir après souper jusqu'au lendemain. . . . [Precautions against the plague follow.]

21 Brumaire (12th November 1799).

Aux fournisseurs du pain :

Quand vous vous êtes chargés de faire le pain de l'hopital, à la place du Citoyen Galt, je m'attendois qu'il seroit meilleur ; on vient de m'en apporter qui est mal travaillé et qui n'est pas cuit. Si à la premiere livraison il n'est pas bon, je viens d'ordonner qu'on vous retienne mille livres sur votre marché. J'ai déjà reçu plusieurs plaintes à ce sujet.

Aux Municipalités de l'Est et de l'Ouest :

Je suis entièrement décidé de permettre la sortie des personnes qui ont demandées à aller à la campagne. Proclamés en conséquence que le 23 et le 25 on ouvrira les portes. Engagés le peuple à se faire inscrire, sans quoi je formerai une liste ainsi que je l'ai annoncé.

28 Brumaire (19th November 1799).

Ordre du jour :

L'épuisement de la caisse met dans l'impossibilité de payer la demie solde et les demis appointemens. J'espère que cela ne sera pas long. La garnison a dû s'appercevoir de tous les efforts qui ont été faits pour prolonger le payement jusqu'à ce jour. Elle est d'ailleurs si brave, si bien intentionné, et si attachée à sa patrie qu'elle supportera sans peine un délai forcé par les circonstances. Les officiers qui en ont extrèmement besoin, doivent être convaincus que je vais remuer ciel et terre pour leur faire tomber dans le courant du mois prochain, la moitié des appointemens d'un mois dont ils sont arrierés sur la troupe.

30 Brumaire (21st November 1799).

Au Contre-Amiral Villeneuve :

La nouvelle batterie des ennemis, me cause aussi la plus grand inquietude pour les bâtimens de la République. Nul doute à mon avis, que s'il nous arrivoit un convoi et quelques troupes qu'il ne fallut marcher dessus toute de suite ; mais dans la circonstance où nous sommes, cela demande beaucoup de prudence.

La garnison de Malte se trouve composée en ce moment de 2200 hommes sous les armes. Les forces que vous y joignés sont un puissant soutien, mais des ordres peuvent nous en priver d'un instant à l'autre.

Je ne doute point que si on attaquoit cette batterie l'ennemi ne s'y réunit au nombre de mille hommes. Trois ou quatre cent des notres l'emporteront ; mais avec perte sûrement, et nous n'en avons point à faire. Les localités sont diaboliques par rapport au couvert que les murs donnent à ceux qui les deffendent, et à la tour qui est derriere.

Un jour qu'on ménaçoit la batterie de Farchien, je me suis apperçu qu'en se couvrant par les murs, ils fournissoient un bon feu.[1]

Je me persuade que cette opération nous feroit perdre des hommes. Que seroit-ce si on ne réussissoit pas ?

S'il nous arrivoit du monde, non seulement je pense qu'on pourroit l'enlever, mais s'y établir le tems qu'on voudroit, sans cela, ce seroit une demarche inutile. Le lendemain on y placeroit un nouveau mortier et d'autres piéces, et ce seroit à recommencer. Au reste, si vous voulés venir demain avec

---

[1] As I have pointed out in the Introduction, this may explain, in part, the failure of the French to make any effective sorties.—J. H. R.

le contre-amiral Decrés, à dix heures du matin chez moi, nous nous entretiendrons de cette entreprise, qui n'est à discuter que par rapport aux circonstances.

3 Frimaire (24th November 1799).

Ordre du jour :
Les braves deffenseurs de Malte de toutes les armes ne recevant plus de solde, ni les officiers d'appointemens à cause de l'épuisement de la caisse, je m'empresse de venir à leur secours et de les faire jouir, autant que le devoir me le permêt, de ce que leur courage et leur bonne conduite méritent. Bien entendu cependant que la consommation de plus que j'ordonne aujourd'hui sera compensée par une diminution égale dans la consommation du public à laqu'elle les militaires avoient part. En conséquence, à dater du 5 frimaire [26th November], la ration de pain sera de 28 onces, et cette quantité de pain étant suffisante pour la nourriture d'un homme, il est deffendu sous les peines les plus graves à tout militaire qui prend ses rations en nature d'en acheter ni d'en faire acheter chez les boulangers ou sur le marché public.

Tout militaire ne pourra se présenter sous quelque prétexte que ce soit chez les boulangers ni au marché pour acheter du pain pour la consommation de quelque personne que ce soit, puisque ces personnes peuvent elles mêmes acquérir celui qui leur est nécéssaire. Par la diminution de la quantité de bled delivré à la population la consommation restera la même. Les officiers de tout grade, a dater de la même époque jouiront d'une once d'huile de plus par jour.

8 Frimaire (29th November 1799).

Aux Municipalités de l'est et de l'ouest :
N'ayant pu fournir aux troupes les couvertures nécessaires dans cette saison, vous voudrés bien faire une proclamation par laqu'elle vous obligerés chaque chef de famille d'en fournir ; ceux qui pourront le faire et qui s'y réfuseront y seront obligés par la voie du rigueur ; la santé du soldat commande cette mesure.

15 Frimaire (6th December 1799).

Ordre du jour :
Malgré les deffenses réiterées de consommer sans fruit les munitions de guerre, differentes batteries font un feu inutile sur les ouvrages ennemis, trop éloignés et trop peu garnis de monde pour qu'on puisse y causer du dommage. Nous devons surtout ménager les bombes dont nous sommes peu pourvûs. En conséquence, le général d'artillerie, que je rends responsable de cette enorme et inutile consommation qui peut compromettre le salut de la place, voudra bien sévir contre les officiers qui contreviendront aux ordres existans.

19 Frimaire (10th December 1799).

Au President de la Municipalité de l'Est :
Je vous ai entretenu la dernière fois que je vous ai vû de la nécessité de rassembler des masets [?] pour le service public. Cela est trans-urgent [sic], et l'on ne m'a point rendu compte de ceux que vous avés trouvé ; cependant il est sorti bien de boulangers, et il se trouvent d'autres habitans qui en ont aussi. Mettés les de suitte en réquisition. Ils seront estimés, nourris, entrêtenus, et employés au service public.

Je compte sur tous vos soins pour la prompte exécution de cette mesure.

20 Frimaire (11th December 1799).

À la Municipalité de l'Ouest :
Nos entrepreneurs des fours ont la plus grande peine à se procurer la farine nécessaire pour la fabrication journalière du pain. Dans quel embarras ne se trouveroient-ils pas s'il arrivoit une augmentation de troupes ? Il

afut donc apporter le rémede le plus prompte à cet inconvénient, et pour y parvenir je vous demande, au nom de la République, huit moulins que vous requerrerés en vingt quatre heures. Je ne doute point, vûe la diminution de la population, que sans nuire à la fabrication du pain qui lui est nécessaire vous ne les trouviés chez les habitans absens ou présens. Vous mettrés ces moulins à la disposition du citoyen Faÿ qui a disposé l'endroit pour les reçevoir. Mettés, je vous prie, la plus grande célérité dans cette affaire.

22 Frimaire (13th December 1799).

Proclamation :

En permettant aux habitans qui ne peuvent vivre ici de sortir en campagne, je dois veiller à ce que cette acte d'humanité ne nuise point à la sureté de la place.

Il est en conséquence deffendu :

Art^e 1^{ier}.

à toutes personnes, même aux fontionnaires publics, ou autres employés aux sorties de passer le dernier rateau.

Art^e 2.

Les habitans qui sortent et à qui l'on permet de sortir avec eux quelques effets, seront tenus de les sortir eux-mêmes.

Art^e 3.

Les petites voitures dont ils se servoient sont deffendues parce qu'elles occasionnent de la lenteur et de l'embarras. On ne pourra sortir en effet que ce que l'on peut porter.

Art^e 4.

Si la quantité des effets que des personnes emportent fait soupçonner qu'il peut y en avoir qui appartiennent à des absens, les commandants et employés aux sorties sont autorisés à les faire visiter, et à retenir ceux qui n'appartiennent pas aux personnes sortantes.

Art^e 5.

Ceux qui sont dans l'intention d'aller en campagne doivent se présenter de suitte. Dans peu il ne sera plus permis d'ouvrir les portes.

Au Contre-Amiral Décres :

Les ouvrages que l'ennemi a construit au dessus de Ricazoli peuvent avoir deux objets, celui de battre l'entrée du port au cas qu'il entre quelque batiment, et celui de faciliter et soutenir les approches du fort au cas qu'on voulut l'assiéger.

Je ne doute pas que s'il arrivoit des troupes à l'ennemi, ce poste important ne devient l'objet de sa convoitise. C'est dans cette idée que je l'ai déjà renforcé hier, et que je le ferois encore au besoin. Un coup de main me paroit peu à craindre, si l'on se garde bien, comme j'en suis convaincu. Cependant, s'il devoit avoir lieu, je pense que ce seroit sur l'ouvrage non-achevé à l'extrêmité gauche du front qu'on le tenteroit. Il faut prendre des précautions à cet égard, et je crois qu'une essentielle seroit d'établir un poste sur la demie lune de gauche. Si l'ennemi tentoit quelque chose sur Ricazoli, peut être favoriseroit t'il son attaque par une cannonade de mer. Les parapets de ce côté n'ont point assez d'élévation et cet inconvénient facheux est irréparable à cause de l'extreme rareté des ouvriers. Il faut donc se déterminer d'occuper sur ce front les points qui sont les plus avantageux pour battre les vaisseaux ennemis en s'exposant le moins possible à leur feu.

Suitte . . . Il est encore essentiel de s'occuper des moyens de pouvoir occuper promptement la fausse braye en cas d'attaque. Peutêtre même seroit-il nécessaire d'y établir quelques postes fixes, surtout à l'extrêmité du coté de la mer, afin de pouvoir deffendre de près l'ouvrage non fini.

29 Frimaire (20th December 1799).

Au Contre-Amiral Décres [sic] :

Je vous préviens, Général, que toujours occupé du fort de Ricazoli que l'ennemi pourroit attaquer un jour, je fais faire une quantité considérable de sacs-à-terre qui vous seront livrés incessement.

Cela vous mettra à même de couvrir les deffenseurs au rempart, de réparer promptement toutes les dégradations que le feu de l'ennemi pourroit faire aux merlons peu solides de cette ancienne fortification.

30 Frimaire (21st December 1799).

A l'Adjudant Général Brouard. Ordre:

Le peu de vin qui reste étant nécessaire pour l'hopital, mettés à l'ordre aujourd'hui qu'à commencer de demain, premier nivôse [22nd December] on cessera d'en donner à la troupe. L'eau de vie, se trouvant réduite à une petite quantité, ne se délivrera desormais que pour des travaux extraordinaires, et d'après un ordre particulier.

PART IV—FROM 28TH JANUARY 1800 TO 4TH SEPTEMBER 1800

8 Pluviôse (28th January 1800).

Au Contre-Amiral Villeneuve :

J'ai la plus grande envie, Général, d'écrire encore au Ministre et de lui peindre de nouveau notre situation pour engager le Gouvernement à nous envoyer des secours. Il n'est question que de savoir si vous pouvés me donner quelques matelots : il en faut peu. Il seroit même possible de mettre le batiment à l'abri des barbaresques en lui faisant porter le pavillon de Dannemarck au moyen d'une vente simulée faite au Consul de cette nation.

9 Pluviôse (29th January 1800).

Au Contre-Amiral Villeneuve :

En me demandant de faire partir la marine, vous voulés, sûrement, Général, être à même de justifier de cette démarche dans l'occasion pour n'être plus responsable des batimens de la République. J'ai à cœur comme vous de ne lui porter aucun dommage.

Cela est d'une conséquence majeure, et si je croyais succomber à Malte et que le moment de cette perte soit prochaine, je n'hésiterois pas ; mais pouvons-nous donner le moindre accès à cette idée désespérante ? Voyons nous donc cet évenement si prochain pour songer déja à des retraites ? Je me garde de mettre sous les yeux d'un conseil de guerre cette proposition affligeante. L'objet qui nous rassembleroit seroit surement connu. Je vous prie, au nom de votre patriotisme si éprouvé de n'en parler à qui que ce soit. Pour vous mettre à découvert ma façon de penser, je vous dirai que je suis convaincu que le gouvernement va manifester par une grande opération que l'armée d'Egypte, composée de tant de héros, ne lui est pas indifférente. Malte qui est son point d'appuy entre naturellement pour quelque chose dans le projet.¹ Remettons donc à un tems désesperé le soin de sauver les vaisseaux. Mais éloignons toute pensée sinistre. Votre monde est indispensable, je dois faire attention aux moindres choses, et si j'en crois ce transfuge d'hier, l'ennemi a encore des idées d'attaque. D'ailleurs l'ordre du Gouvernement est formel. La marine doit partir quand le convoi sera arrivé. Vous devés tout sacrifier au salut de Malte. D'après tout ce que cet ordre a de positif, notre devoir n'est il pas fixé ? telle est ma façon de penser. Peut-être la votre y reviendra t'elle. D'ailleurs cette lettre pourra vous paroitre une piéce suffisante pour vous mettre à l'abri. Pour moi j'ai une régle de conduite qui ne varie point. C'est de ne rien craindre quand toutes mes idées, toutes mes actions ont pour but le triomphe de la République. Ce n'est pas que je n'accueille avec empressement tous les avis qu'on me peut me donner.

Je me connais assez pour apprecier la foiblesse de mes moyens. Je suis faché que vous ne puissiez me donner quelques matelots. C'étoit pour obéir aux ordres du Ministre qui me mande de l'informer souvent de notre situation que je voulais faire partir un aviso.²

27 Pluviôse (16th February 1800).

Au Général Chanez :

Je vous préviens, Général, que l'ennemi paroit faire des mouvemens, que l'on a vu plusieurs batimens passer de la rade St. Paul à celle de Marsa Siroc, portant, à ce que l'on presume, des troupes.³ En consequence tous les postes seront avertis de se tenir dans la plus grande surveillance et personne ne doit s'en écarter.

7 Ventôse (26th February 1800).

Ordre du jour :

L'Adjudant Général Brouard est suspendu de ses fonctions à datter de ce jour et gardera les arrets de rigueur jusqu'à nouvel ordre. Cet officier supérieur méconnoissant l'autorité qui m'est confié n'a cessée de donner des preuves d'insubordination depuis quelque tems, et hier encore malgré ma deffense, a adressé aux corps et détachemens qui forment la garnison une imprimé signé de lui qui n'a pour but que d'échauffer les esprits et inculper des militaires tout entier à leur devoir. Le Général Chanez est chargé de faire exécuter cet ordre.

12 Ventôse (3rd March 1800).

Au Commissaire Ordonateur de Terre :

Il est de nécessité absolu que nous convertissions quinze cent pintes de vin en vinaigre. Nous ne pouvons laisser manquer cet objet sans nous exposer aux plus grands maux, et faire tomber la culture des jardins, principale nourriture dans cette circonstance critique.

Au Ministre de la Guerre :

Vous avés connu, Citoyen Ministre, la situation exacte de Malte par ma lettre du 13 Vendémiaire [5th October] dernier. Vous la croyés surement désesperée, si nous ne recevons pas promptement un secours en vivres et en hommes.

Qu'elle affreuse nouvelle pour nous que celle de la mort du Contre Amiral

---

[1] In a fortnight's time the French squadron, headed by the *Généreux*, sought to succour Valletta. For the battle which ensued with Nelson's squadron see Chap. xiii. near the end.— J. H. R.

[2] There follow several letters dealing with a theft of diamonds at Valetta in which General Brouard and Captains Gastinel and Ricard were implicated. Vaubois arrested them all.— J. H. R.

[3] This movement may have arisen from the appearance of the French squadron, the *Généreux*, &c. (see Chap. xiii.).—J. H. R.

Perré, et la prise du *Généreux*, de la *Badine*, et du *Commerce de Marseille*.[1] Nous ignorons si les deux autres batimens sous ses ordres sont au pouvoir de l'ennemi. Cette catastrophe est arrivée à peu de distance de l'isle, puisque nous avons appris par l'ennemi, qui a mis bien de l'empressement à nous l'annoncer, qu'ils étoient en vûe de Malte. En vain nous nous efforçons de douter ce malheur, il est trop détaillé pour n'y pas croire.

Voila donc Malte compromis et le fruit de dix-huit mois de siége et de blocus peut-être perdu sans ressource. Si le vent nous eut secondé encore quelques instants, tout étoit sauvé. Les privations sans nombre, le dévouement la plus courageux, la plus parfaite intelligence, le zèle infatiguable des Généraux de terre et de mer, le service penible de la garnison composée de ces deux armes est digne des plus grands éloges. Tout cela devient donc inutile et perdu pour la patrie si dans le courant de Floréal il ne nous arrive rien. Nous ne mangeons depuis le commencement du siége, que pour exister. L'espérance nous a toujours soutenue. Les diminutions des rations, le service excessif, rien ne pouvoit détruire l'harmonie. L'Adjudant Général Brouard seul a violé les loix de discipline et s'est porté a des excés. Je vous en entretiens dans un autre paquet, et je vous en demande justice.

Je finis cette triste lettre en vous exposant l'état exact de nos magazins, vous en frémirés ; à notre secours au plus tot, ou nous sommes perdus.

ETAT EXACT DES MAGAZINS AU 12 VENTÔSE.

Vivres en Magazin	Consommation par mois y compris le dechec	Observations
Vin . . . 9000 Pintes	3050 Pintes	Sur la quantité de vin on va être forcé d'en prendre pour le vinaigre qui est indispensable. Il faut observer que l'hopital seul en consomme et que la garnison en est privé depuis plus de 4 mois. La consommation en huile et ris va devenir plus forte, parce qu'il faut suppléer à la viande salée qui manque.
Vinaigre . . 1342 ,,	2977 ,,	
Eau de Vie . 1855 ,,	Suivant le besoin	
Huile . . . 275 Quinx.	107 Quintaux	
Bis . . . . 218 ,,	50 ,,	
Fèves . . . 123 ,,	150 ,,	
Haricots . . 96 ,,	65 ,,	
Bœuf salé et lard . . .	fini	
Bled . . . 8000 Salmes	1500 Salmes	Il faudra remplacer les vivres qui manquent par des pâtes, ce qui augmentera la consommation du bled.

Sur tous ces articles, la consommation sera diminuée par le depart du *Guillaume Tell*, mais il faut faire les vivres pour son voyage.[2]

[He then accuses General Brouard and others of fomenting discontent.]

14 Ventôse (5th March 1800).

Au Ministre de la Guerre :

La corvette *La Bellonne*, arrivée hier de Marseille a amélioré un peu notre situation, mais nous ne nous consolons pas de la perte du convoi du Contre-Amiral Perret [*sic*]. D'après cette reception je compte tenir tout le mois de Prairial. Cela est extrêmement difficile, mais les dispositions de la garnison sont si bonnes que j'en conçois de grandes espérances.

Le Contre-Amiral Decrés vous donnera des détails exacts sur notre position.[3]

Faites, je vous prie, attention, Citoyen Ministre, aux récits d'un Général dont je regrette infiniment les lumiéres et l'infatigable zèle. Sa mission est tres

---

[1] Taken by Nelson's ships in the fight of February 18th, 1800 (see Chap. xiii ; also Villeneuve's letter of March 3rd in Chap. xiv).—J. H. R.

[2] It was Villeneuve who proposed to Vaubois to send off this ship (see his letter of March 3rd, 1800, Chap. xiv).—J. H. R.

[3] Decrès was to sail on the *Guillaume Tell* now preparing for sea.

importante et cela seul me console de son depart. Je le regrette ; à notre secours en Floreal ou au plus tard commencement de Prairial. Que tant de peines et de soucis ne soient pas perdu pour la France. A l'époque que je vous désigne nous serons réduits à la famine la plus inevitable.

25 Ventôse (16th March 1800).

Au Ministre de la Guerre :

Je vous ai rendu compte, Citoyen Ministre, dans ma lettre du 14 Ventose [5th March] de l'arrivée de la corvette *La Bellonne* de Marseille, qui nous a apporté une cargaison dont le prix est effrayant. Aussi n'ais-je voulu rien conclure qu'en présence des Généraux, des Commissaires Ordonateurs, et de la Commission du Gouvernement. Tous ont sentis que les périls de la mer, et que l'encouragement à donner au commerce pour nous sécourir devoit faire passer par dessus toute autre considération. Aussi cette cargaison coute t'elle cinq cent quatre vingt mille livres. Je ne vous fais point le detail de ce qu'elle contient, celui qui vous remettra cette lettre peut vous mettre au fait.

J'ai donné pour environ 200,000fr. de coton. Le reste est en traites sur la Tresorerie Nationale, à l'exception d'une somme de quinz à seize mille livres en argent qu'ils ont exigés, et pour laqu'elle quelques autres et moi avons boursillés, en nous privant du nécéssaire en vendant et en nous exposant à ne pouvoir vivre dans une circonstance aussi chere ; mais avec l'espoir que cela sera envoyé à nos femmes et à nos enfans qui en ont besoin. Je vous en donnerai les détails par le retour de la corvette *La Bellonne*.

J'intercède pour les armateurs, pour que les traites soient payées, vous sentés, Citoyen Ministre, que quelque chers que soient ces approvisionnemens, ils nous sont d'une utilité si grande qu'on ne peut que savoir gré à ceux qui nous les ont procurés.

Le payement deviendra un stimulant pour le commerce qui peut nous sauver.

Le Citoyen Goyon, un des armateurs, qui vous remettra cette lettre nous promet un autre chargement s'il est satisfait.

Au Général Chanez :

Vous voudrés bien, Général, donner des ordres pour que l'on conduise à Bord du Vaisseau *Le Guillaume Tell*, l'Adjudant Général Brouard, et le Capitaine Gastinel, consignés prisonniers au Contre-Amiral Decrés. Vous sentés qu'ils doivent être transférés d'une maniere sûre et sans leur permettre d'entrer nulle part.[1]

8 Germinal (29th March 1800).

Au Général Chanez :

Le Général Chanez fera commander cinquante hommes de la garnison de La Valette, commandés par deux officiers, un Capitaine et un Lieutenant, qui se rendront à la nuit faite au Chateau de Bichi. Il sera expressement ordonné à l'officier Comm$^{t.}$ de ne laisser sortir personne du Chateau, de s'y garder dans le plus grand silence, de maniere à ce que l'ennemi ne puisse découvrir ce détachement. L'objet est d'empêcher si l'ennemi s'appercevoit du depart du vaisseau, que l'on vienne couper les amarres sous Bichi.

12 Germinal (2nd April 1800).

Au Ministre de la Guerre :

L'ennemi vient de m'instruire par un parlementaire que le vaisseau *Le Guillaume Tell*, qui étoit sorti du port à la demande du Contre-Amiral Villeneuve et d'après la décision d'un Conseil de Guerre venoit d'être pris.

---

[1] Long letters follow on a theft of diamonds which had taken place ; also further charges against General Brouard.—J. H. R.

C'est un malheur auquel nous sommes extrêmement sensibles. Les raisons principales qui nous ont déterminés étoient de le sauver en cas de l'événement qui nous menace si nous ne sommes pas secouru dans peu ; de diminuer le nombre des bouches, afin de nous mettre à même de tenir plus long-tems, et par là fournir au gouvernement le moyen de nous ravitailler. D'ailleurs le vaisseau [a] été assailli de bombes tous les jours, ce qui le mettoit dans le cas d'être détruit sous nos yeux d'un instant à l'autre. Enfin tout bien pesé pendant trois Conseils de guerre consécutifs, nous nous étions décidés pour le départ.

Ce qui me fache encore extrêmement, c'est qu'il étoit porteur de beaucoup de dépeches qui contenoient des détails essentiels. Je regarde celle-ci comme très peu assurée sur le petit batiment qui s'en charge. Si elle vous arrivoit, vous sauriés qu'en epargnant excessivement, c'est à dire en ne mangeant que pour exister, nous tiendrons, sauf d'autres causes malheureuses que je ne puis prévoir, Germinal, Floréal et Prairial, je ne puis me flatter d'aller plus loin, quelque soit notre bonne volonté.[1]

La garnison de Malte a fait, et fera jusqu'à à la derniere bouchée de pain, ce qu'on devoit attendre de braves gens qui ont toujours supporté toutes les privations sans se plaindre et qui dans toutes les occasions a montré le plus grand courage. Ce sera un desespoir général si toutes ces peines sont perdues pour la République ; mais vingt deux mois de blocus et de siége doivent assez faire connoître les sentimens qui n'ont cessé de nous animer.

[He then refers again to the insubordination and complicity in theft of General Brouard and two subordinates.]

22 Germinal (12th April 1800).

Au Ministre de la Guerre :

J'ajoute encore une lettre qui me permet d'écrire le retard occasionné par le vent à la corvette *La Belonne*. Que vous dirai-je de plus ? Si le mois de Prairial se passe sans qu'il arrive rien, nous voyons la perte de Malte inévitable.

Le vaisseau *Le Guillaume Tell*, suivant le rapport de l'ennemi s'est bien battu, et a été dématé ; mais à quoi cela nous sert il ? il n'en est pas moins perdu. J'ai résisté long tems à consentir à son départ. Il pouvoit être coulé bas dans le port, et son équipage acceleroit notre perte en augmentant la consommation. Enfin j'étois seul à mon avis, tant on espéroit qu'il pourroit nous apporter quelque chose. Quand les ressources s'épuisent on employe tous les moyens.

Le Contre-Amiral Decrès, le Citoyen Saunier, Capitaine de Vaisseau, et l'Adjudant Général [Brouard] que j'envoyais en France, avec les piéces justificatives de sa deshonnorante affaire, sont à Marsa Siroc. Le Général de Division Dug[u]a s'y trouve aussi ; mais nous ne savons comment. L'ennemi paroit vouloir retenir plus long-tems les officiers supérieurs.

Quoique l'arrivée de la petite corvette *La Bellonne* de Marseille nous ait fait du bien par sa cargaison, il n'en est pas moins vrai que le prix de chaque chose, surtout des objets de détails, autres que le vin, l'eau de vie, les légumes secs, sont d'une excessive cherté. J'ai même la preuve que différens objets de pacotille de même nature ont été vendus aux particuliers à beaucoup meilleur compte. Je vous en informe, Citoyen Ministre, parceque le marché passé avec eux ne peut avoir lieu qu'avec votre approbation.

Je finis le désespoir dans le cœur de voir que la conduite admirable des troupes et les peines que j'ai prises vont être perdues si le plus prompte secours ne nous arrive. Ce qui augmente mes sollicitudes, c'est que le bled devenant le

---

[1] This would be up to the 17th of June. The arrival of *La Marguerite* on 19th Prairial (8th June) enabled the garrison to hold out up to September 2nd. See Villeneuve's letter, 14th of June, in Chap. xiv.—J. H. R.

principal objet, qui va nous manquer comme tous les autres, demande de gros chargemens qu'il sera peut-être impossible de se procurer.

27 Germinal (17th April 1800).

Au Contre-Amiral Villeneuve :

Je dois tout risquer, Général, pour faire parvenir mes lettres en France. Je ne vous démande que huit hommes de bonne volonté. J'ai deux Maltais bien capables de gouverner et d'orienter les voiles d'une spéronare. Ils me répondent de sa réussite et ne craignent point le gros tems, sachant où se tirer à terre en Sicile ou ailleurs sans rien craindre.

Le Citoyen Ervaux marchera, rien ne peut donc empêcher cette entreprise. La trahison des Maltais n'est point à craindre puis qu'ils ne peuvent paroitre à la campagne, où ils sont fortement compromis. J'espére que vous adopterés mon idée.

28 Germinal (18th April 1800).

Au Ministre de la Guerre :

Vous verrés par ce triplicata, Citoyen Ministre, s'il vous parvient, qu'il y a long-tems que je desire que vous soyés informé de notre cruelle situation ; mais tout nous est contraire. Ou l'exactitude du blocus nous enléve toutes les expéditions, ou les vents contraires retardent les departs. La prise du *Guillaume Tell* me fait une peine extrême, elle a suivie de trop près celle du convoi expédié de Toulon, pour n'être pas désespérante. J'étois seul dans le conseil de guerre opposé à son départ.

Je ne pouvois cependant me dissimuler que son séjour ici hâtoit notre perte ; enfin ne connoissant rien à la marine, il a fallu céder, surtout lorsqu'on m'assuroit que son arrivée étoit si probable. Je n'ajouterai rien à ce triplicata. Vous y verrés que sans un prompt secours nous sommes perdus. Nous n'avons plus que pour deux mois. Je ferai cependant les plus grands efforts pour que nous tenions jusqu'à ce que l'inaction justifie aux yeux de toute l'Europe notre courage.

1er Floréal (21st April 1800).

Au Contre-Amiral Villeneuve :

Nous ne pouvons être assurés de faire parvenir nos dépêches au Gouvernement qu'en multipliant les envois, et cela est indispensable pour se mettre à l'abri de tout reproche. Il existe à l'arsenal une petite felouque en bon état et parfaitement propre à cette nouvelle mission.

Un pilote du ci-devant ordre ayant la réputation d'être habile, et qui me sollicite depuis un an, la montera en second. Il fournira deux autres Maltais, et il ne faudra plus que six matelots. Il faudroit que cela partit ce soir s'il est possible.

22 Floréal (12th May 1800).

Au Commissaire Ordonateur de Terre :

Voulant donner un écu à chaque soldat et sous officier sans distinction de grade dans les premiers jours de Prairial,[1] il est nécéssaire que dans les derniers jours de ce mois une revue soit passée. Je mettrai ensuite à l'ordre du jour que les états de solde devront être formés et porter en titre, à compte de la solde arrierée.

16 Prairial (5th June 1800).

Au Commandant dans la partie de l'est :

J'ai un projet dans le quel il faut que vous m'aidiés. On prend actuellement une assez grande quantité de poisson entr'autres de l'espéce appelé *Vopi*.

[1] i.e. from 20th May onwards.—J. H. R.

Ce poisson est propre à être salé. Mais je ne réussirai qu'autant que les barques de pêche viendront à la consigne, et qu'on leur achêtra ce qui sera propre à la salaison. Il faut donc une consigne severe à St. Ange pour qu'il ne passe aucune barque de pêche sans un billet du Citoyen Lot, qui fasse connoitre qu'elle a passé à la consigne. Si mes ordres sont bien executés, je suis sûr que nous aurons bientôt plusieurs tonnes de poisson salé.[1]

21 Prairial (10th June 1800).

Au Commandant du fort Tigné :
Il nous seroit nécéssaire pour des besoins particuliers de la Division de faire du sel. Vous êtes à même au fort Tigné puisqu'il se trouve des endroits destinés pour cela. Engagés les Volontaires de s'en occuper de suite, et il sera réglé un prix pour les payer au quintal.

22 Prairial (11th June 1800).

[Lettre à l'administration de l'Université pour la prevenir qu'on l'accuse de malversation, et lui enjoindre de justifier authentiquement sa conduite.]

Lettre aux deux municipalités pour faire afficher la proclamation suivante :
'Ayant pris connoissance des personnes inutiles qui se trouvent dans les cittés de l'ouest et de l'est, les municipalités sont chargées de les faire avertir que Samedi prochain à 7 heures du matin, la porte des Bombes sera ouverte, et qu'elles seront tenues de sortir de la place pour se rendre à la campagne. Cette mesure n'a été déterminée que par le seul motif de soulager la place, et d'en assurer la possession à la République francaise, et persuadé d'ailleurs que les habitans trouveront plus de ressources à la campagne. Cet ordre sera exécuté avec rigueur, et j'espère qu'aucun contrevenant n'obligera d'employer la force armée contre lui. La présente proclamation sera lue et affichée dès sa réception.'[2]

27 Prairial (16th June 1800).

Au Ministre de la Guerre :
Je vous addresse, Citoyen Ministre, les procés-verbaux d'acceptation de la Constitution de l'an huit,[3] par les troupes de terre et de mer qui sont à Malte, et de la prestation du serment décrété. L'unanimité prouve combien nous sommes pénétrés de l'idée que notre patrie assure son bonheur.

Par mes dernieres lettres que j'ai envoyé en quadruplicata, et qui sont parvenues, je vous instruisois de la situation exacte de Malte. Je vous annonçois qu'avec les privations les plus grandes, nous tiendrons Floréal et Prairial. Je pouvois dire les plus grandes, puisque Prairial devoit se passer avec du pain pour toute nourriture, trois rations de vin par décade, trois rations d'eau de vie, et deux rations de vinaigre. Un jour sur les dix avec du pain seul sans boisson. Le petit batiment porteur de l'adjoint aux Adjudants Généraux, le Citoyen Remi, est entré par miracle au millieu des batimens ennemis, et vient de prolonger un peu notre existence. Voici l'effet exact qu'il produit. Il se trouve dessus 120 quintaux de lard et 116 de haricots. Avec notre parcimonie ordinaire nous ferons dix huit prises de chacun des ces comestibles, à deux onces par rations ; ce qui fait pour les deux mois Messidor et Thermidor que nous voulons absolument tenir, 36 jours. Il en restera donc 24 au pain seul.

[1] There follows a letter from Brig.-General Graham to Vaubois, stating that he will send back all persons who came out from Valletta. See the original (dated June 17th) and Vaubois' reply in Chap. xiv.—J. H. R.
[2] It was evidently this measure which led to Graham's letter of June 17th referred to above.—J. H. R.
[3] That of December 15th, 1799, which inaugurated the Consulate.—J. H. R.

Par le moyen du vin et de l'eau-de-vie que nous avons reçu, il y aura quatre rations de vin par décade, quatre d'eau de vie et deux de vinaigre.

Mais ce n'est pas le plus effrayant encore. C'est que le bled finit exactement à la même époque; il y a même strictement parlant un peu moins de bled de ce qu'il en faudroit pour la consommation de Messidor et Thermidor; mais je supporterai à ce qui me manquera par quelques quintaux de biscuit qui me restent. Alors la denrée d'absolue nécéssité sera entierement consommée.[1]

29 Prairial (18th June 1800).

Ordre au Général d'Artillerie de faire évacuer les magazins du cavalier de gauche occupés par la 6eme afin de pouvoir y déposer les farines pour les mettre à l'abri de la bombe.

30 Prairial (19th June 1800).

Proclamation:

Le deux du mois prochain a six heures du matin tout ce qui ne doit pas recevoir du pain, c'est-à-dire tous ceux qui n'ont pas une carte de la municipalité doivent sortir des places. Ceux de l'est par la porte du Salvator, et ceux de l'ouest par la porte des Bombes et celle de la Carcare. Ceux de l'est doivent être au nombre de douze cent et ceux de l'ouest quinze cent, à moins qu'il se trouve des habitans de ceux notés pour sortir, qui ayant des ressources pour vivre sans recevoir ni pain ni bled, car décidement ils n'en auront plus des Magazins de l'Université.

1 Messidor (20th June 1800).

Lettre du Général Vaubois au Général Anglois Graham:

Je ne peux me persuader, Monsieur, que vous ayés pris la résolution de ne pas recevoir à la campagne des habitans qui désirent retrouver leurs parens et leurs amis. Si des affaires particulières à règler les ont retenu jusqu'à présent, ils ont toujours pensé que la liberté de sortir existeroit jusqu'au moment où ils pourroient effectuer leur rapprochement.

Tout devoit les persuader, et j'ai l'honneur de vous observer qu'ils seroient seuls victimes de ce changement. Ma consommation est reglée, et je ne m'en départirai pas. Dans tous les cas la dureté ne retombera pas sur moi. Si le congrès de l'isle est composé au moins en partie de Maltais, j'ai lieu d'être bien surpris de ce manque de bienveillance pour leurs concitoyens, dont un grand nombre a été rétenu ici par mes ordres. Au reste leur reflexion ne se porte pas bien loin dans l'avenir.

Etant donc convaincu que vous ne persisterés pas dans ce parti, je fais sortir, bien persuadé que vous ne ferés pas tirer dessus. Ce sera réduire au desespoir leurs parens et amis du dehors. Je me trouverois parfaitement à l'abri du reproche d'inhumanité, et des nations civilisées comme la votre et la mienne, étant incapable de toute espéce de barbarie, je ne doute nullement qu'ils ne puissent se rendre tranquillement auprès de leurs proches.

Il s'est commis, Monsieur, auprès du Cazal Zabber une atrocité qui sûrement a excité votre indignation si elle est parvenu à votre connoissance. Des soldats étoient descendus du rempart malgré la deffense, et s'étoient mis dans le cas de recevoir des coups de fusils ou d'être pris; un d'eux, entouré, se rendant a été massacré inhumainement. Vous sentés combien cet infame action excite le courroux du soldat. Puis-je promettre de règler sa fureur si l'occasion d'une action extérieure se présente? Cet homme étoit sans armes et sans aucun moyen de deffense. J'ai l'honneur d'être, &c.

Le Gen$^{l.}$ Vaubois.[2]

[1] The rest of the letter is similar to that of July 18, 1800, quoted in Chap. xiv.—J. H. R.

[2] The reply of General Graham of date 21st June 1800 will be found in Chap. xiv. near the end.—J. H. R.

Au Général Chanez :
Vous savés, Général, que le Général ennemi m'a écrit qu'il ne recevrait plus les habitans que nous voulons faire sortir de la place. Il est cependant de la dernière importance de diminuer encore la population. Je prends donc le parti d'effectuer encore des sorties—peut-être que l'ennemi tirera sur ceux qu'on mettra dehors et la peur pourra les faire retourner.
Pour remplir plus aisément notre objet, et peut-être dissuader de tirer, il ne faut pas faire ouvrir la porte et evacuer par la poterne. Cela sera plus long : mais c'est plus sûr. Pour s'assurer encore que tout ce qui se présentera sortira, il faut consigner qu'on ne laisse rentrer en ville aucun baggage qui sera sorti. Alors les sortants seront obligés de prendre leur parti. Il faut aussi tacher d'obtenir qu'aucun militaire ne se montre sur le rempart. Les hommes commandés peuvent se tenir à couvert au bas du rempart, et n'attireront point sur eux l'attention de l'ennemi. Au reste venez à onze heures avec les autres Généraux, nous discuterons ces objets.

Aux Medecins de l'Hopital Civil :
Ce n'est pas par cause de mécontentement d'aucune espèce, Citoyens, qu'on a réduit à un plus petit nombre les officiers de santé de l'hopital. Il n'est pas dans mon caractere de meconnoitre les bons services de gens recommandables comme vous, mais vous avés dû penser que cela entroit dans un plan de réforme générale qui concourt à la conservation de Malte. Cette raison seule, qui est la plus forte pour moi, me met souvent en guerre avec moi-même.
Je voudrois soulager tout le monde dans ce tems de misère ; mais je fais tous mes efforts pour faire triompher mon devoir de la sensibilité de mon ame. Je sers ma patrie de toutes mes forces et de tous mes moyens. Je crois être bien différent de ces ambitieux Maltais qui ont égaré ce peuple en appellant les nations étrangères. Ils ont consommé la ruine totale de cette isle. Puisse la France un jour cicatriser ces playes ! Je ne peux qu'applaudir à votre zèle charitable qui vous porte à soulager les pauvres sans intérêt.

4 Messidor (23rd June 1800).

[Invitation au Contre-Amiral Villeneuve de tenir des embarcations prêtes, pour aider les batimens annoncés par le gouvernement et qui pourroient se présenter pour entrer dans le port.]

9 Messidor (28th June 1800).

[Invitation à la Municipalité de l'est de mettre en réquisition le sel qui se trouve chez les citoyens qu'on lui indique.]

15 Messidor (4th July 1800).

Proclamation :
N'ayant pû parvenir encore malgré tous mes efforts, à avoir un dénombrement exact des habitans, étant d'ailleurs assuré que les cartes distribuées pour le pain porte la population plus haut qu'elle n'est réelment, et voulant connoitre exactement qu'elle est sa force,
Il est ordonné ce qui suit :
Le 18 du courant les habitans sans exception, de quelque sexe et de quelque âge qu'ils soient sont tenus de rester chez eux jusqu'à ce que la vérification soit faite.
Tous ceux qui ne s'y trouveront pas sont dans le cas d'être arrêtés, et de n'avoir plus de part à la distribution du pain.
Des Français ayant chez eux des Maltais ou des étrangers à leur service sont assujeties [sic] à ces visites domiciliaires.
Un nombre suffisant de Commissaires Maltais et Français sera nommé pour faire ces visites en même tems, afin que cela soit prompt et que les habitans redeviennent libres de vaquer à leurs affaires.

À l'entrée des Commissaires dans chaque ménage, les chefs de famille ou les personnes habitantes seules présenteront la carte du pain qui leur a été donnée précédemment.

Ils feront paroitre aux yeux des Commissaires tous les individus qui jouissent du pain porté sur cette carte.

Les Commissaires seront munis de feuilles divisées en colonnes qu'ils rempliront comme il est indiqué au dessus de chaque colonne. L'opération finie, les Commissaires rapporteront les feuilles à la Commission du Gouvernement.

16 Messidor (5th July 1800).

Instruction qui doit être lue aux Commissaires chargés du recensement avant de commencer leurs opérations.

L'objet des opérations que vous allez faire, Citoyens n'est pas seulement de procurer le recensement exact de la population, ce qui facilitera une juste distribution du pain, mais de connoitre ce que les habitants peuvent avoir chez eux de bled, farine, huile et sel, principalement chez les meuniers et les boulangers où vous devés trouver de la farine.

Il n'est pas juste que les habitans qui ont des provisions en tirent du magazin commun. Faites donc la perquisition la plus exacte sans distinction de personne. Tenés une note de ce que vous aurés trouvés de ces objets et des personnes à qui ils appartiennent. Si c'est du bled ou de la farine, retenés la carte de distribution de pain à ceux qui en ont, et écrivés au dot de cette carte ce qu'ils possédent. Nous parviendrons ainsi à diminuer la consommation.

25 Messidor (14th July 1800).

Au Citoyen Dubelet, Recteur du College :

Pénétré, Citoyen, de la situation malheureuse de plusieurs exchevaliers, je n'ai cessé depuis la pétition que vous m'avés présenté de chercher le moyen de venir à leurs sécours, enfin j'ai pû me procurer cinquante louis que vous voudrés bien remettre aux dénommés ci-dessous : Clugni, Belmont, Rabastens, Vinson, Rayberti, Watour, Leaumons, Latour, Pestelle et Bellet. Ces cinquante louis vous seront remis par le Citoyen Chartier. Ils serviront de payement aux vingt cinq écus qu'ils recevoient par mois pour ceux de Prairial et Messidor.

Sommation du Gen$^{l.}$ Comm$^{t.}$ les troupes Angloises dans l'isle :

17 Juillet 1800.

Monsieur,—Je me fais l'honneur de vous annoncer que j'ai eu ordre de prendre le commandement des troupes formant le blocus de la Valette. J'ai emmené avec moi un renfort considérable et je suis d'heure en heure dans l'attente d'être joint par un corps de troupes Brittanniques encore plus considérable que les circonstances de la guerre n'avoient pas permis d'envoyer ici. Il est inutile de vous représenter combien la flote du Roi mon maitre bloque completement votre port et empêche les approches d'aucun sécours. La Division de petits batimens dont elle s'est emparée si récemment, vous en est une preuve suffisante, et la misère de vos gens doit vous le mettre à chaque instant sous les yeux.

C'est par amour de l'humanité que je vous presse de ne pas imposer plus long-tems des malheurs accumulés sur votre garnison et sur les habitans en les exposant aux désastres inévitables qui doivent s'en suivre si vous persistés à rester en possession de la Valette.

Vous avés déjà rempli completement vos devoirs envers votre pays et vous avés mérité sa reconnoissance. Ne négligés pas ce titre par vos efforts à une courte prolongation de blocus en sacrifiant les troupes en les livrant ultérieurement à la misere et à la destruction.

La conséquence est telle que vous ne pouvés vous flatter d'obtenir à l'avenir des conditions telles qu'elles pourroient vous être accordées en ce moment.

Si par ces considérations vous êtes porté à entrer en quelques négociations pour la rédition de la place et des forts qui sont sous votre commandement, moi de mon coté je vous enverrai un officier de marque pour établir des termes tels qui puissent conduire cette affaire à une favorable conclusion.
Je suis, Monsieur, &c.   PIGOT, MAJOR GÉNÉRAL.

29 Messidor (18th July 1800).

Réponse du Général Vaubois à la Sommation du Gén¹· Commᵗ· les Troupes Angloises dans l'isle :
J'ai reçue, Monsieur, la sommation que vous m'avés fait l'honneur de m'envoyer hier 28 Messidor. Nous ne pouvons nous rendre aux propositions que vous nous faites. Vous croyés que nous avons satisfait à ce que le service de notre patrie exige. Nous sommes bien éloigné de partager votre sentiment. Nous croyons avoir encore beaucoup à faire. L'attaque de Malte exige une grosse armée. Notre situation peut se prolonger bien loin, et nous ne commettrons pas le crime de l'abréger un instant. Notre résistance nous acquerra surement votre estime. J'ai l'honneur d'être, &c.
GÉNᴸ· VAUBOIS.

Au Ministre de la Guerre :
Le Citoyen Baste, lieutenant de vaisseau porteur de vos dépêches du 4 Prairial est entré dans ce port avec la felouque *La Legere* le 3 Messidor....
[A great part of this letter is very like that of July 18th to the Minister of Marine quoted near the end of Chap. xiv. The last parts of it contain new matter and are as follows.]

Un autre fléau, c'est que l'eau commence à devenir rare. Il en est peu tombé cette année. La culture que fait le soldat est indispensable pour la nourriture et pour éviter les maladies.

Il faut cependant y apporter beaucoup de reserve pour ne pas epuiser nos citernes, car il n'en tombera pas encore de long-tems.

Enfin, Citoyen Ministre, je suis à tout autant qu'il est en moi. Si nous triomphons, le souvenir de nos peines déviendra une source de satisfaction. Si nous succombons toute ma vie est empoisonnée.

Au 15 Thermidor nous serons au pain avec un peu de vin et d'eau de vie, en Fructidor au pain seul, et à la fin de ce mois il ne nous restera plus rien de tout. La pauvre population périt de misère. Les dissenteries se déclarent. Tout le monde, militaires et habitans est rempli de vers. Comment pourroit résister ce pauvre peuple qui n'a qu'un peu de mauvais pain et de l'eau ? S'il avoit de l'huile il s'estimeroit heureux. Joignés à cela la peur extrême que les femmes ont des bombes ce qui occasionne des maladies scrofuleuses que les medecins attribuent aux suppressions occasionnées par la frayeur. Ah ! Citoyen Ministre qu'elle situation déchirante !

Au premier Consul de la République française :
Subervie,[1] Aide de Camp du Général Lannes qui a été retenu ici par une cruelle maladie, n'a pû après son rétablissement passer en Egypte à cause du blocus, et m'a servi d'aide de camp pendant le Siége. Il est chargé de vous remettre cette dépêche. Il a servi avec moi avec distinction, et si son Général n'eut été en pleine guerre, j'aurais eu de la peine à le lacher. C'est un de ces bons sujets d'ont l'avis a toujours été de conserver Malte ou de périr....

... Par des economies poussées encore plus loin, le bled durera une grande parti de Fructidor, et peutêtre même tout Fructidor ; mais le peu de population qui reste périt d'inanition et de maladie. Cette misère vous feroit horreur....

[1] Subervie afterwards had a successful career. At Waterloo, as general, he commanded a light cavalry division, which checked the advance of Bülow's corps.—J. H. R.

... Si par bonheur pour nous, une escadre venoit nous ravitailler et nous jetter du monde, il ne faudroit pas que les vaisseaux entrassent dans le port. Les bombes en couleraient nécéssairement quelques uns. Mais en mettant trois à quatre mille hommes à terre au dela de la ligne de circonvallation de l'ennemi, on détruiroit toutes les batteries qui environnent le port. C'est à mon avis, derrière les ouvrages faits entre Ricazoli et Marsa Scala qu'il faudroit effectuer cette descente. En me concertant avec le commandant, j'aiderois l'opération par des sorties, qui, je crois ne seroient pas bien difficiles. Alors les vaisseaux entreront sans rien craindre. De l'autre coté du port l'opération seroit trop long et trop penible à exécuter.

Je change d'avis, Citoyen Consul, et ne vous envoye pas Subervie. Le bruit court que nous avons une escadre dans la Méditerrannée, que beaucoup de batimens sont expédiés pour nous ravitailler, j'attends qu'il nous arrive quelque chose d'heureux pour vous l'envoyer, et vous faire l'amélioration de notre sort.

Le tems presse : je vois s'approcher l'instant du mauvais pain seul, et je crains l'épidemie causée par les vers : elle commence à se manifester.

Au Citoyen Bertin Comissaire Ord^{r.} de la Marine à Toulon :

Je vous remercie bien sincèrement et des bonnes nouvelles que vous nous avés donnés et des Moniteurs que vous m'avés envoyé. Depuis vos lettres des 28 Floréal, 7 et 19 Prairial arrivées par le Citoyen Baste sur la felouque *La Legère*, dont les deux premieres étoient des duplicata, je n'en ai point recue d'autres.

Le seule petit batiment, *La Marguerite*, étoit entré peu de tems avant la consommation de son chargement jusqu'au 10 ou 12 Thermidor. Passé ce terme il ne nous restera que du pain.

Jugés combien je suis pressé d'en voir arriver d'autres. C'est la farine et l'huile qui doivent composer la plus grande partie des chargemens. Ces objets sont de nécéssité absolue. Quand on manque d'autres comestibles, on fait la soupe avec de l'huile, on fait cuire les légumes que l'on cultive, et s'il nous en arrivoit en quantité suffisante on pourroit soulager la population qui périt de misere et de maladie.

Quoique des felouques portent peu, je serois bien d'avis d'en multiplier l'envoi : Tout est en faveur des batimens à rames dans cette saison des calmes. Le sort de Malte est toujours bien precaire, puisque nous n'avons de subsistance qu'au jour le jour.

L'objet doit être de gagner le mois de Brumaire. Pour y parvenir il faudroit environ 8000 quintaux de farine, 500 quintaux d'huile, du vin, du lard, des légumes calculés à raison de 5000 rations par jour. Il est sur qu'en nourrissant des hommes comme nous le faisons depuis deux ans, à moins du tiers de ration on épargne beaucoup ; mais la nature succombe. D'ailleurs ce qui existoit dans la ville est tout consommé, et le peu qui reste est d'un prix à étonner toute l'Europe. Ah, mon cher ordonateur, il faut avoir été assiégé deux ans pour savoir ce que c'est. Tout le monde ici a le corps rempli de vers. Jugez des craintes que cela me donne qu'une fièvre vermineuse ne se déclare. Notre disette sera peutêtre suivie d'une épidémie. Nous en avons déjà éprouvé deux. Un scorbut destructeur qui enlevoit une partie de nos braves, et une optalmie qui rendoit une partie de la garnison aveugle. Mais notre détermination a toujours été de sauver Malte ou de périr. Son salut ne dépend plus de nous. Reçevons de quoi subsister et Malte est à la République.

Depuis vos lettres reçues nos armées ont surement continuée [*sic*] de vaincre ; mais nous ne savons rien. Pourquoi ne pas nous envoyer quelques petits bateaux comme l'esperonare que nous avons expédié, pour porter des lettres et des nouvelles ? Nous nous en nourrissons. Cela soutient notre courage. Nous n'entendons plus les bombes et les boulets quand nous savons que la République triomphe. Comptés sur la reconnoissance des deffenseurs de Malte qui se joindra a celle de la République.

Au Commandant des Armes à Toulon :
J'ai reçue, Général, votre lettre du 19 Prairial qui m'a été remise le 3 Messidor par le Citoyen Baste, lieutenant de vaisseau arrivé ce jour là. Je n'ai point reçue la précédente. De tout ce qui a pû être expédié pour notre ravitaillement, il ne nous est arrivé que *La Marguerite*.[1]
Nous avons commencé la consommation de son chargement le 1er Messidor. Il étoit tems.
Le mois de Prairial s'étoit passé sans autres comestibles que le pain. Cette cargaison, en la faisant durer trois fois autant qu'elle le devroit d'après la loi, nous menera jusqu'au millieu de Thermidor. Jugés a qu'elle extrêmité nous sommes réduits. Le blocus exact et les calmes rendent l'entrée des batimens bien scabreuse. Cependant nous espérons que le genie de la République en amenera une partie à bon port. Que faut-il, mon cher Général, pour nous sauver ? Six batimens qui réussiroient à l'hiver, saison des grandes espérances. Mais ce qui soutient notre espoir, c'est la marche triomphante des armées. Par arrangement ou par conquêtes n'occuperons-nous pas la Sicile ? Le premier Consul veut la paix, mais il ne l'accordera surement qu'avec des grandes sûretés, surtout avec le Roi qui est cause de notre détresse.[2]
Tous les chargemens qu'on nous destine doivent être composés d'huile et de farine. Ce sont les deux articles les plus importans. Avec du pain et de l'huile pour faire la soupe, et pour cuire les légumes que nos soldats cultivent, on peut exister. Nous nous embarrassons fort peu des bombes et des boulets. Qu'il nous arrive de quoi subsister et nous nous deffendrons.

[He then refers to the diseases now prevalent at Valetta.]

Au Ministre de la Marine :
Les éloges que vous donnez, Citoyen Ministre, à la garnison de Malte sont sa plus douce récompense mais seront-ils couronnés par le succès ? . . . Par de nouvelles économies, je prolongerai la durée du bled une partie de Fructidor, à ce que j'espére. Il est cependant de fort mauvaise qualité par ce qu'il y a quatre ans au moins qu'il est en fosse.
Telle est notre situation exacte. Peignés-vous mes inquiétudes. Le courage et la fermeté ne manquent pas, mais l'estomac les commande. Nous sommes habitués a très peu, mais il faut ce très peu.

2 Thermidor (21st July 1800).

Au Général Chanez :
Le fort Manuel étant géné pour tirer ses vivres pendant le jour par la nouvelle batterie qui tire sur les barques employées à les transporter, je vous prie de donner des ordres pour qu'il puisse les reçevoir à neuf heures du soir. La porte de Marsa Muscet s'ouvrira en conséquence, et les vivres passés elle sera refermée.

3 Thermidor (22nd July 1800).

Invitation au Général d'Artillerie d'activer les travaux à faire au front de Ricazoli qui régarde la terre, afin de ménager le moyen d'éteindre par un feu vif les batteries de l'ennemi situées de manière a inquiéter les batimens qui pourroient se présenter pour entrer dans le port.

---
[1] It is difficult to reconcile this with the statement that two other small vessels had arrived, except on the supposition that they came from different ports.—J. H. R.
[2] He had heard of Marengo (June 14th) and the re-conquest of N. Italy ; and stated at the close of his letter that he hoped the French were at Naples.—J. H. R.

Ordre au Commissaire Ordonateur de la Marine de fournir au fort Ricazoli les objets nécessaires pour y établir des signaux de jour et de nuit, afin d'avertir le fort Salvator des batimens qui se présenteroient pour qu'ils puissent diriger son feu sur les batteries ennemis.

Le Général informe l'accusateur public, que des mulets ont été tués dans la partie de l'est malgré la deffense qui en a été faite. Il l'invite à prendre des informations sur ce délit et à poursuivre les auteurs.

9 Thermidor (28th July 1800).

Ordre du jour :

Il vient de m'être rapporté que de mauvais sujets indignes du nom Francais, et de porter l'habit militaire faisoient courir le bruit qu'on alloit diminuer la ration de pain. Cela est de toute fausseté. Jamais cette pensée n'est venue au Général qui se fait un si grand honneur de vous commander. L'ordre du Gouvernement est de soutenir Malte jusqu'à la dernière once de pain ; mais je sens que puisqu'il n'est pas possible de vous donner d'autre nourriture, il seroit cruel de diminuer ce qui est indispensablement nécéssaire. Courage, braves soldats. Faisons tout ce que l'honneur et le service de notre patrie exigent. La France et l'Europe ont les yeux ouverts sur vous.

Continuons de prouver jusqu'à la fin que nous sommes de courageux Républicains.

Faites moi connoître les laches qui cherchent à émouvoir les esprits. Quelque soit leur grade, qu'ils soient deshonnorés, et punis en criminels ; l'honneur nous en fait un devoir.

Le Citoyen Roujeol de la 41eme demie Brigade se trouvant à l'hopital par suite des ses exces, y sera consigné tout le tems qu'il y demeurera.

10 Thermidor (29th July 1800).

Ordre du jour :

Le tems des privations est arrivé. Celui du courage et du patriotisme ne fait qu'augmenter. Des secours nous sommes promis ; il [sic] ne le sont pas en vain. L'ordre précis du Gouvernement est de tenir jusqu'à la dernière once de pain. Les deffenseurs de Malte, couverts d'honneur aux yeux du monde entier ne savent qu'obéir à la voix de la patrie.

Les rations des deux dernieres décades de Thermidor seront distribuees ainsi qu'il suit :

Pain, une livre et douze onces. Biscuit une once de plus c'est à dire 4 onces. Vin trois fois par décade. Eau de vie une fois par décade. Vinaigre deux fois par décade. Du lard le 15 de la seconde décade seulement. Deux fois des pâtes cette seconde decade seulement.

13 Thermidor (1st August 1800).

Invitation à la Municipalité de faire des recherches exactes chez certains particuliers que l'on soupçonne avoir de l'huile en assez grande quantité et qui ont déférré jusqu'à présent de la vendre, malgré le prix excessif où elle est.

21 Thermidor (9th August 1800).

Au Contre-Amiral Villeneuve :

Vous m'avés fait part il y a quelques jours, Général, du projet de faire partir les frégattes La Diane et La Justice.[1] Qu'elle n'a été ma surprise d'apprendre que ce projet été [sic] devenu public ?

Il faut que ceux à qui vous êtes obligé de donner vos ordres d'exécution ne sachent pas garder le secret. Au reste j'ai beaucoup réfléchi sur cette affaire depuis notre entretien et voici le résultat de mes réflexions : Ce n'est pas une vaine démonstration de devoirs remplis que nous cherchons, C'est de sauver

---

[1] See the letter of Villeneuve of August 21st, 1800, in Chap. xv.—J. H. R.

réelement ces batimens à la République ; si nous sommes dans le cas de céder ce pays à l'ennemi faute de vivres. L'ordre de tenir et l'espoir du gouvernement de nous voir prolonger la deffense de cette place autant qu'il est possible est un devoir qu'accompagne toujours l'espérance.

Tout doit donc suivre la même marche. Si les deux frégattes partent, nos feux sont éteints sur une grande partie des fortifications. Nous ne sommes plus en deffense. Vous savés en outre qu'on ne peut pas déblinder les fregattes et les préparer sans que cela soit vû de la campagne. Les précautions se prendront donc de la part de l'ennemi en conséquence. Il n'y a donc qu'un coup de vent qui pourroit assurer le succes de ce départ. L'évenement du *Guillaume Tell* nous le prouve. D'après ces considérations, je pense qu'on ne peut fixer le départ de ces batimens avec sagesse qu'à l'époque où nous aurons totalement perdu l'espoir d'être secourus, c'est-à-dire au 15 Fructidor.

Je vous soumets mon avis, il est la suite de beaucoup de réflexions.

1 Fructidor (19th August 1800).

Au Ministre de la Guerre :

Citoyen Ministre,—Jusqu'à ce jour, les précautions prises par le Gouvernement pour nous ravitailler ont été infructueuses. Nous sommes au pain seul depuis le 15 Thermidor, et ce pain va nous manquer. Nous n'en avons plus que jusqu'au vingt du courant : il faudra donc que j'entre en négociations le 15[1] si rien ne nous arrive. Vous ne pouvés vous peindre le désespoir de cette brave garnison qui ne voit aucune fruit des travaux et des privations qu'elle a supportée pendant deux ans, sauf la gloire qui ne peut leur être enlevée. Je partage sa façon de penser et il ne faut rien moins que l'impossibilité physique pour me résoudre à capituler : mais nulle espéce de ressource : L'ennemi n'a point de magazin : il tient sur des batimens le peu de subsistance qu'il fournit à l'isle. Il n'est donc aucun moyen de résister à la plus entiere famine. C'étoit pendant le premier hiver surtout qu'il falloit nous fournir de quoi lasser l'ennemi. Dès les premiers jours du siége nous avons su nous réduire à très peu de chose. Nous espérons tous que la France rendra justice à notre conduite ; mais cela ne satisfait pas de braves gens moins occupés d'eux que de leur patrie.

Je compte demander qu'on nous conduise à Marseille, si nous obtenons, comme je l'espère de rentrer en France, nous pensons que vous voudrés bien donner des ordres pour que nous y trouvions des à comptes d'appointemens de solde.

Que deviendroient ces pauvres officiers à qui il ne reste aucun moyen d'existence, et qui ne sont pas vêtus ? La troupe aussi n'a sur le corps que des habits de toile. L'entrée de la saison rigoureuse leur rend nécessaire des habits de drap à son arrivée. Si nous obtenons toutes les conditions honorables que je demanderai, il vous restera une troupe qu'on peut conduire partout contre les ennemis de la République, quoiqu'elle ait grand besoin de repos.

Recevez les respects d'un Républicain désolé.

2 Fructidor (20th August 1800).

Au Citoyen Bertin Comm$^{re.}$ Ordonateur de la Marine à Toulon :

Aucun des batimens qui nous ont été destinés, et que vous m'annonciés par votre lettre du mois de Prairial ne sont arrivés. Depuis le 15 Prairial nous sommes au pain pour toute nourriture. Ce pain, notre dernière ressource, va finir. Je serai obligé d'entrer en pourparler le 15 du courant. Il ne me restera du bled que pour cinq jours au plus. Il me faut au moins ce tems pour terminer les articles et ne pas exposer la garnison à mourir de faim. Si vous avés encore quelque batiment qui nous soit destiné, calculez sur cette époque.

[1] i.e. on September 2nd. On that day he summoned a council of war, and opened negotiations with General Pigot on September 4th.—J. H. R.

Si d'ici au 15 il entre quelque chose, nous continuerons nos travaux et nos efforts. Si Malte est perdu c'est ma désolation.

6 Fructidor (24th August 1800).

Au Contre-Amiral Villeneuve:

Vous sentés comme moi, Général, la nécessite de ne pas dégarnir des postes déjà très foiblement occupées. En même tems je m'interesse aussi fort qu'on peut le faire à la conservation des deux fregattes de la République. Je ne me connois pas en marine : Si vous croyés qu'elles puissent échapper par leur marche à l'ennemi, en ne leur donnant que le nombre d'hommes nécessaire à la manœuvre, l'inconvenient me paroit moindre que de les perdre sans ressource : cela devient donc un devoir.[1]

Je comptais les demander par des articles de la Capitulation ; mais je doute qu'on ne les accorde. Vous pouvés donc tirer de la Victorieuse les quarante hommes que vous me demandés ; mais sans prendre les cannoniers qui se trouvent à des postes essentiels.

La chose me paroit de très difficile exécution mais en restant dans le port elles seroient infailliblement perdues. Tel est le résultat de ma façon de voir ; elle est guidée par l'intérêt de la République que j'imagine bien entendu.

9 Fructidor (27th August 1800).

Au Payeur de la Division:

Il est tems de songer au secours que je pourrai donner à des fonctionnaires publics qui se refugient en France. Le mois dernier nous avions envie de donner un écu aux soldats. Vous deviés déjà avoir entre les mains un à compte conséquent : il est aisé de calculer ce qui reste à venir : mais pour plus de régle je crois qu'il vaudroit mieux qu'ils reçussent de l'Université que de vous. Leurs mandats ne seront peut-être pas des piéces comptables pour vous.

14 Fructidor (1st September 1800).

Au Général Chanez :

Vous voudrés bien, Général, convoquer le Conseil de Guerre de la Division qui devra s'assembler demain 15 du courant chez moi à dix heures du matin. Il doit être composé des Généraux et officiers supérieurs de terre et de mer, des commandants des corps, des commandants des forts quelques grades qu'ils ayent, et des deux Commissaires Ordonateurs des deux services.

17 Fructidor an 8 Rep^e (4th September 1800).

Au Commandant des troupes Angloises dans l'isle de Malte :

Par votre lettre dattée du 17 Juillet dernier, vous me proposés, Monsieur, d'envoyer à la Valette un officier de marque pour traitter. L'honneur me permet de le recevoir si vous persistés à ce qu'il se présente. Je vous garantis qu'il sera reçu et respecté comme doit l'être un officier revêtu du caractère qu'il aura. Entrant dés ce moment en négociation pour capituler, je vous préviens que je viens de donner ordre pour qu'on cesse toutes hostilités. J'espére que vous voudrés bien en donner de semblables. J'ai l'honneur d'être &c.

VAUBOIS.

---

[1] This admission should be noted, as it bears on the subsequent dispute between Vaubois and Villeneuve. See ' Journal du Siège ' Pt. 1 ad init.—J. H. R.

APPENDIX IV

[NOTE.—The *italics* in this appendix are those of Mr. Hardman. They have been made for the purpose of emphasising such passages as have been refuted by official documents.]

NOTE BY THE LATE MR. HARDMAN ON MALTESE HISTORIES

WHAT is the *fons et origo* of the agitation which has existed for so long a period amongst a certain class of Maltese inhabitants, an agitation which continues to this day, notwithstanding the admitted benefits which the people have derived from their connection with Great Britain for now more than a century?

We are told by those who profess to be leaders of public opinion—

1st. That having regard to General Graham's (Lord Lynedoch's) proclamation of the 19th June 1800, and the subsequent agreement between the English and French commanders at the capitulation of the French garrison on the 5th September 1800, the British Government has broken faith with them as a people who had fought for and won their independence.

2nd. That the Islands of Malta and Gozo were not British military conquests, for the reason that in the operations which resulted in the capture of the fortress the Maltese as belligerents were the principals, the British but auxiliaries.

3rd. That by their own military exploits they have gained the right of self or home government, although acknowledging that the importance of Malta is due to it being a military and naval station which must necessarily be dependent upon and in possession of a foreign European power.

4th. That such self-government existed during the occupancy of the islands by the Knights of St. John of Jerusalem in the form of a 'Consiglio Popolare,' which the British Government arbitrarily abolished, and have since declined to restore.

Three generations having now almost passed away since the events referred to occurred, local politicians of the present day derive their information on the subject and rely exclusively upon *fragmentary* writings of contemporary *partisans* or of those who immediately followed them.

In this category there may be named Eton, Dillon, Marchese Testaferrata, Monsignor Bres, Mitrovich, Baron de Piro, Baron Azopardi.[1]

[1] Much of the controversy which has arisen on this subject is due to the political writings of the two individuals last named, the one an aspirant to the government of the islands, the other a paid advocate of a faction. (Note by Mr. Hardman.)

In order more clearly to define the alleged grievances, it will be well to submit the following extracts from these writers, and by subsequent references the student will be able to form a correct judgment as to their accuracy or otherwise.

MR. W. ETON.

In 1807 Mr. Eton, an ex-Government employé, published a work entitled 'Authentic Materials for a History of the People of Malta,' which appears to have had great influence at the time in creating a strong anti-Government feeling in the islands, and on this account it deserves a special reference, which is devoted to it in connection with the 'Consiglio Popolare.' See Chap. xxiii.

DILLON'S MEMOIR, 15TH MAY 1807.

PAGE 6.—' Whatever rights the Order of St. John possessed to the sovereignty of the Island, so far as they concerned the relations between the Order and Great Britain, they have passed to us (the British) through the medium of the French, who had *legally* acquired them by reason of the surrender which the Order made to them. The Order voluntarily abandoned the Island, and has certainly no legal right to be re-established in Malta, which it had voluntarily surrendered.

' It might have defended the Island, and did not do so.'

PAGE 8.—' The French garrison was driven by the Maltese within the lines of the fortifications, and were on the point of dying of famine, *and would have had to surrender to the Maltese if the combined fleets had not appeared, or if they had delayed their arrival.*'

PAGE 10.—' It must be remembered that Sir A. Ball is the person who from the beginning induced the Maltese to accept the British protection, *and suspended the form of Government which they had established for themselves*, and further that he is the person who reintroduced the Code promulgated in 1782 by the Grand Master De Rohan, which destroyed the franchises of the Island, *and suppressed the " Consiglio popolare,"* as dear to this people as our Chamber of Commons is to us.'[1]

MARCHESE TESTAFERRATA.

LETTER TO EARL BATHURST, DATED JANUARY 1812.[2]

'. . . *The administration of the Government, civil and military, was, and remained entirely, in our hands, our liberties were preserved to us, and jealously guaranteed by a free representation of the people, or " Consiglio popolare" of the Island.*

'. . . Until 1798, the Knights were masters of the fortresses, when they delivered them up to the French party, who soon after committing acts of injustice and violence, the whole Maltese people (except the city which had been disarmed by the French) took up arms, beat the French in the field, and shut them up in Valletta. All this was done by themselves without the assistance of or communication with any other Power. Some time after the ports were blockaded by the Portuguese, and finally by the English.

' *During the space of fifteen months the war was carried on at the sole expense of the Maltese.*

' They *afterwards* received some assistance from Sicily, mortgaging their lands for that purpose.

' *During two years that the war lasted we lost* by sickness and the *sword* of the enemy about 20,000 persons, while our handful of auxiliaries lost not one soldier killed by the enemy.

'. . . The French garrison, reduced to extremity by famine, were forced to demand a capitulation, and their own Council of War determined, in case it was required, to leave hostages to indemnify the Maltese for all the damages, forced contributions, plunder of the University and Monti di Redenzione e Pietà, and all other property, public and private, which they had extorted during the siege.

' At this juncture the English, who styled themselves our military auxiliaries, without our knowledge granted to the enemy a capitulation by which, without our consent, we

---

[1] For Sir Alexander Ball's vindication on this point, see Chap. xxiii.
[2] Colonial Office, Malta, No. 20.

had the mortification of seeing the spoils, even of us their conquerors, carried to France in British ships.

'The gates of Valletta being opened, the Maltese laid down their arms, and the Congress being dissolved, *but with promises that the " Consiglio Popolare " should be assembled,* we *permitted* the King's officers to occupy the fortresses and to have the administration of the public property; and by acclamation we elected the King of Great Britain for our Sovereign, but with the express stipulation that our ancient and sacred and only legitimate rights should be continued without any kind of interruption.

'We accepted this compact in the confidence we had, and still have, in the honour of the English Government, and what we assert we consider to be incontestably proved by the letter of Sir Alexander Ball to Mr. Secretary Windham, printed at the Government press in Malta, in which he says : " You are aware, Sir, that when the British first took possession of the Island it was stipulated that the privileges of the Maltese should be preserved and their ancient laws continued in force."

'But notwithstanding this, from the year 1800, when we remained fully masters of our own cities, until this day, the " Consiglio Popolare " has not been assembled, nor have our rights and privileges been in vigour, but we are governed in such a manner that we cannot raise the voice of appeal against any tyranny, however oppressive.'

MONSIGNOR BRES.

[Translation.]

EXTRACT FROM A LETTER ADDRESSED TO THE COMMISSIONERS, MESSRS. OAKES, A'COURT, AND BARROWS, DATED 8TH JULY 1812.[1]

'Nobody can have the impudence to deny that the *Maltese alone, by their own efforts,* broke the French thraldom, made themselves independent, forming their own government, and spontaneously elected as their Sovereign the King of England, and being seconded by the Auxiliary Powers (England, Portugal, and Sicily) as allies, drove the French out of the principal fortifications of Malta.'

GEORGE MITROVICH.

31st July 1835.

'THE CLAIMS OF THE MALTESE.'

PAGE 3.—'On the breaking out of the insurrection against the French Republicans in September 1798, the first measure of the Maltese was to *re-establish this Council (Consiglio Popolare), which had been despotically suspended by the latter Grand Masters of the Order of St. John of Jerusalem, to which they then gave the name of " Congress."* This Congress was composed of representatives of the clergy, and of the people of the whole country freely elected, and had appointed as President Sir Alexander John Ball, then commanding His Majesty's naval forces in the blockade of Valletta.

'When the British troops took possession of the fortifications in September 1800, the Congress was suspended *by Sir A. Ball, the very man who had stipulated with the Maltese, and promised its preservation.* He established a system of government entirely arbitrary and despotic, contrary to the expectations of the Maltese, and instead of allowing them to be governed by their ancient laws, conformably to the spirit of the British constitution, he adopted the detested code of Rohan, which had already destroyed some of their privileges, and which code is in force in the island to this day.'

ADDRESS BY GEORGE MITROVICH TO THE MALTESE.

November 1835.

'Immediately the English troops took possession of the fortifications, the Congress was dissolved by Sir A. Ball, *who had promised to maintain it.*

'General Pigot, who took up the reins of government after Ball's departure, promised to the Maltese by means of a proclamation "the enjoyments of their liberty."

'The well-beloved Chevalier Charles Cameron, upon his arrival soon afterwards, took occasion, in his noble and interesting proclamation to the Maltese, to express himself as follows : " His Majesty accords you his full protection and the enjoyment of all your dearest rights." '

[1] MS., M.P.L. 385.

BARON GIUSEPPE DE PIRO.

From De Piro's 'Squarci di Storia,' published in 1839.

[Translation.]

PAGE 7.—'*Malta was gained by the English, not by the expenditure of millions, not by lengthy negotiations or bloody battles*, for not even the life of a single soldier was lost, but owing to the heroic efforts of the Maltese *and their voluntary submission to England.*'

PAGE 9.—' It is true that the assistance rendered in the first instance by the Portuguese,[1] then by the King of Sicily, and also the British blockade, *contributed largely in completing the glorious work of the Maltese, of whom 20,000 perished by the labours and disasters of the war.*

'... Further, if the fortune of war had not favoured the British fleet at Aboukir, *would not all the consequences of the hostilities commenced* and sustained by the Maltese have fallen upon them exclusively ? If such a calamity (as a British defeat) had happened, they would have had to support all the evils consequent on the step (the insurrection) which they had taken. Why then, when successful, should they be deprived of the consoling idea that they themselves had been the principal factors in procuring their emancipation ? '[2]

PAGE 11.—' It was in the interest of Great Britain to obtain an island of so much importance without costing her the slightest sacrifice.'

PAGE 27.—' That in the political catastrophe of the fall of Malta to the French, *no treachery existed either on the part of the Knights or the Maltese.*'

PAGE 32.—' Poussielgue must have reported to the Directory that there would be nothing to fear from the Knights, but only from the people, *who had an affection for the Order, and who were much averse to Republican maxims.*'

PAGE 37.—' *The Maltese were deeply attached to their Government.*'

PAGE 41.—' *There never was a population more affectionately attached to its Government than that of the Maltese towards the Order.*'

PAGE 45.—' *That in addition to the riches which the Maltese drew from the abundant revenues of the Order, they were generally governed with benevolent consideration, and on occasions when individual Knights committed an abuse the offended parties received due protection, and their cause was vindicated by the Grand Master.*

' Moreover, all were treated according to their merit and condition of life, *promenading wherever they wished*, participating in the sport of pursuit of game, whilst the educated civilians were received in their circle by the Knights in the most friendly manner, entering together into all the amusements and pastimes which the island afforded.

' *The weaker sex were approached by the Knights with all the respect due to their position or respectability*, but as in all places and at all times there have been women and families of doubtful reputation, it is certainly no wonder that there were such who received the attentions of such members of the Order who did not observe the sanctity of their vows, of whom it must be admitted there were not a few, particularly during the latter days of their rule.'[3]

---

[1] The Portuguese Fleet under Admiral Marquis de Nizza formed part of Nelson's command, and their arrival off Valletta and participation in the blockade was due to Nelson's express orders to that effect. (Note by Mr. Hardman.)

[2] The reader must here be reminded that the above statement is founded upon the grossest distortion of an historical fact. The Maltese insurrection against the French was directly due to the British victory at the Nile; it did not occur *previously* to the event, as the above paragraph implies. The battle and annihilation of the French fleet at Aboukir took place on the 1st and 2nd August, and the Maltese insurrection broke out on the 2nd September 1798, *five days after the information was received in Malta* by one of the escaped battleships, the ' Guillaume Tell ' (Admiral Villeneuve), which took refuge in Valletta harbour together with the frigates ' Diane ' and ' Justice ' on the 28th August. (Note by Mr. Hardman.)

[3] De Piro, at page 10, eulogises Samuel Taylor Coleridge's work entitled ' The Friend,' a few chapters of which treat of Maltese affairs. We refer the reader to a quotation therefrom, concerning the profligacy of the Knights, which will be found in Chap. ii. of this book, entitled ' The social condition of the Maltese people at the close of the eighteenth century.' (Note by Mr. Hardman.)

APPENDICES

PAGE 57.—De Piro denies the fact that Bonaparte ridiculed the desire of a Maltese member of the deputation, who signed the Convention on board *L'Orient*, and who wished the insertion of an Article therein, guaranteeing rights and privileges to the Maltese people, and goes on to say : '*Bonaparte's hilarity had reference to the Chevalier Frisari's protest safeguarding the suzerain rights of His Sicilian Majesty.*' Whereas according to the memoirs of the Grand Master's Secretary Doublet (published subsequently to De Piro's 'Squarci '), who was present at the Convention in an official capacity, it is distinctly stated at pages 207 and 215 'that *it was* the Ex-Auditor Muscat, *a Maltese,* who desired an article to be inserted granting to the Maltese the exceptions and privileges of his nation, to which Bonaparte, much amused, remarked that privileges no longer existed nor corporations, and that the law was the same for all.'

PAGE 58.—' *The English commanders, military and naval, found themselves at the head of an armed and victorious people, provided with every need as to munitions of war, as well as food,* guarded by formidable fleets, and no other enemy before them than a small and discouraged garrison closed within the walls of Valletta, reduced to the lowest straits by famine, which in a few days they would have had to surrender at discretion ; and yet such commanders placed in this advantageous position signed the most shameful capitulation, one not dared to be hoped for by the French, without seeking for the intervention of any of the chiefs of the Maltese, and bartered away arbitrarily *the blood of 20,000 Maltese who fell in the war, absolving the French Government from any indemnity for all the waste, destruction, extortion, and many damages committed by them against the Maltese.*'

BARON GIUSEPPE DE PIRO.

MS. No. 359 in the Malta Public Library.

[Translation.]

AN ABRIDGED HISTORY OF THE ISLAND OF MALTA AND ITS DEPENDENCIES.

Extract.—' Notwithstanding the many reasons which the Maltese had for complaining of the government of the Knights Hospitallers, nevertheless the compensations which they enjoyed under the Order were many, and, speaking generally, they sincerely loved the Knights, out of gratitude for the many benefits which their country had received during their rule.'

PAGE 9.—' *But neither they (the English) or the Neapolitans took part in the hostilities up to May 1800.*'

BARON AZOPARDI.

COLLECTION OF VARIOUS ANNALS, ANCIENT AND MODERN, USEFUL AND INTERESTING, CONCERNING MALTA AND GOZO. COMPILED BY THE LATE BARON AZOPARDI, AND PUBLISHED IN 1843—WHICH MAY BE ACCEPTED AS THE COMMON AND ACCEPTED OPINION HELD IN THE ISLANDS.

PAGE 350. [Translation.]—' Regarding the Treaty of Paris, 1814, the Maltese may well congratulate themselves upon the fact that, in virtue of this treaty, Malta and its Dependencies belong from this date to Great Britain, *she being then in possession of the Islands, due to the voluntary donation made her of them by the Maltese in 1802,* and for the retention of which Great Britain declared war against France, after the rupture of the Treaty of Amiens.'

Such is the literature, and such are the malicious misstatements, and none other, which are at the disposal of the Maltese youth, illustrating this period of their country's history. Is it therefore surprising that the Maltese people entertain the opinions which the majority of the local Press, from interested motives, do their utmost to disseminate ? These writers, it will have been observed, attribute the acquisition of Malta by the British nation to the expulsion of the French in 1800, when, as they assert, it became a spontaneous gift on the part of the inhabitants.

This view is quite erroneous; the capitulation of the French garrison, be the cause thereof what it may have been, was only the prelude of the final possession. The subsequent destiny of Malta was a question beset with international difficulties, and its eventual acquisition by Great Britain was the result of a long, protracted, and bloody war of twelve years (1803–1815) waged by Great Britain on account of Malta, a war which cost the mother country many thousands of her sons' lives and increased her national debt by £421,000,000, the burden of which is being paid by the British people to this day, and will have so to be paid for many generations to come.

The Author, who for fifty years has made Malta his second home, and counts amongst the Maltese many valued and esteemed friends, would sincerely regret if, owing to the publication of the result of his researches, he should wound their pardonable susceptibilities; but his sole object has been to learn the truth for the benefit of those most interested in the question, and to ascertain whether Great Britain can justifiably be accused of the offences which have been laid to her charge. There is no desire to excite political discussion upon disputed points, which have been rendered controversial from the lack of reliable information, but by supplying original and official papers referring thereto, which until lately have been either inaccessible or unknown to the general public, this effort is made, to make clear what in many instances partisan malevolence has distorted.

INDEX

ABDILLA, Chev. G., 191, 416
Abdilla, V., 198
Abela, G., 115, 416
Abercromby, Sir R., 306, 308, 310, 315, 322, 325, 326, 336, 350
   Dispatches from, 338
   Dispatches to, 309, 323, 324
A'Court, M. W., 475, 517
Acton, Gen., 36, 43, 110, 137, 177, 178, 193, 227, 230, 233, 243, 251, 267, 325
Addington Ministry, 401
Aguis, G. B., 191, 209
Aguis, L., 184, 191, 195, 200
Aleosi, Marchese S., 344
Algiers, 41, 91, 349
Allos, M. C. de, 221, 227
Amati, Chev. de, 60, 61, 66, 71
Amiens, Treaty of, 432–439
Ancona, 242, 362
Andréossy, Gen., 451, 472, 477, 478, 482
Anglo-Bavarian Langue, 56
Arena, Francesco, 373
Armed Neutrality League, 398
Army of the East, 29–31
Arnault, M., 79
Astor, C., 80, 582
Attard, T., 115, 191
Aussety, L. de V., 170
Austria, 34, 399
   Maltese afraid of, 22
   and Knights of Malta, 154, 200, 389
Axiach, 191
Azzopardi, G., 115, 204, 643

BALL, Sir A. J., 38, 130, 133, 137, 139, 140, 141, 153, 157, 158, 161, 167, 168, 171, 172, 173, 176, 177, 178, 184, 185, 186, 187, 188, 190, 191, 194, 195, 196, 197, 199, 201, 205, 207, 208, 209, 211, 212, 213, 214, 216, 218–224, 225, 229, 231, 235, 247, 250, 251, 263, 269, 276, 279, 284, 288, 300, 315, 323, 324, 325, 326, 327, 341, 401, 405, 419, 423, 426, 437, 449, 475, 483, 490, 491, 492, 497, 501, 519, 598, 604, 617
   Commander of Malta, 242, 337

Ball, Sir A. J.—cont.
   His position, 338
   Retirement of, 341–346
   Reports on Malta, 346–349
   Minister to the Order, 443, 444, 447, 448, 466, 467, 471
   Administration of Malta, 494–507
   Opposition to, in Malta, 506–507
   Denies Eton's allegations, 498
   Death of, 507
Balzan, 191
Bamberg Gazette, 372
Banca di Ginati, 62
Barbara, 7, 11, 14, 17, 32, 51, 255
Barbaro, Romualdo, 51, 52, 229, 344
Bardonenche, 7, 69, 70
Barer, Bailli de, 373
Barker, Capt., R.N., 130
Barras, 67, 68
Barres, Bailli des, 373
Baste, E. de V., 293, 303, 308, 637
Batavian Consul, 56, 64, 71
Bathurst, Earl, 512, 515, 523, 525, 526
Beaufort, 69
Beauharnais, Eugène de, 13
Beaussier, 148, 151
Belleville, M., 183, 574, 588
Belliard, Gen., 45
Belmont, Bailli de, 374
Bennet, Capt., 287
Berry, Sir E., 38, 288, 291
Berthier, Gen., 59, 66, 74, 80, 81, 111
Berthollet, 74, 81
Bezborodko, Comte A. de, 362 and n., 385
Bezzina, P. P., 114, 115
Bickerton, Adm. Sir R., 491
Bighi, 232
Bigot, Capt. A., 166
Birchircara, 191, 196, 247, 249, 259, 296
Blackwood, Capt., R.N., 288, 290
Blaymey, Lt.-Col. Lord, 228, 230
Blerus, 121
Bonaparte, Joseph, 481
Bonaparte, Napoleon, 32, 35, 39, 42, 45, 64, 66, 68, 69, 71, 72, 76, 77, 92, 100, 101, 112, 128, 144, 157, 180, 260, 265,

Bonaparte, Napoleon—*cont.*
320 *n.*, 362, 367, 370, 380, 395, 397, 400, 426, 460, 463, 467, 621
Dispatches on importance of Malta, 8, 12
Dispatches to, from Malta, 89, 90, 564, 580
At Passeriano, 10, 68
Commands Army of the East, 30
Arrives off Malta, 33
Sends ultimatum to Grand Master, 46
Draws up convention of surrender, 60
Lands in Valetta, 64
Orders inventory of treasures, 74
Orders concerning government of Malta, 79–88
Offer to cede Malta to Russia, 398
Attitude towards Maltese question, 436
Dispatches to, 477, 479
Abdication of, 533
Bonici, G., 52, 344
Bonnai, G., 416
Bonnani, 58, 60, 61, 62
Bonnvita, G., 70
Borg, V., 167 *n.*, 170, 172, 173, 186, 187, 190, 191, 204, 209, 229, 416, 502, 506, 507
Bourdé, Capt., 76
Bourgeois, B., 70
Bourrienne, 72
Bovard, Capt., 163
Boyle, Lt.-Col., 257, 273
Bray, de, 180
Bres, Monsignor, 643
Breuvart, 69, 192
Briffa, 110
Brouard, Adj.-Gen., 121, 163 and *n.*, 200, 255, 559, 565, 581, 614, 627, 629, 630, 631
Broughton, Capt., 261, 291
Brueys, Adm., 10, 11, 14, 16, 31, 102
Bruno, 57, 60
Bugeja, L., 115
Burgoyne, Sir J., 333
Burmola, Fort, 62, 64, 559, 610
Burrows, Mr., 517
Busuttil, B., 417
Buttigieg, P., 191, 229, 416
Buzi, Chev., 466, 467, 492

Cachia, M., 190, 191, 204, 209, 229, 416, 419, 422, 424, 431, 497
Caffarelli, Gen., 72
Calbeja, F., 191, 571
Callija, F., 204, 229, 416
Callija, M. A., 417
Cameron, C., 350, 358, 405, 409, 417, 418, 419, 430, 439, 444, 495, 497
Proclamations by, 358–359
Dispatches from, 359, 404
Camilleri, N., 110, 416
Camilleri, S., 417
Capefigue, 7
Capo Maestro, 191
Caprara, Cardinal, 466
Caraffa, A. B., 191, 204, 209, 229, 416
Cardona, Lt., 215, 279
Cardou, Col., 154
Carovane, 6 and *n.*
Caruana, F. S., 80, 115, 117, 131, 135, 138, 153, 167, 169, 170, 172, 176, 178, 190, 191, 204, 209, 215, 229, 505, 557
Caruana, G., 204, 209
Caruana, L., 190
Caruana, V., 70, 80
Caruson, 7, 14, 16, 19, 46, 56, 70, 80, 163 *n.*, 198, 365
Casalani, A., 405, 431
Casal Asciak, 247, 249, 257, 267
Casal Attard, 33
Casal Dingli, 191
Casal Lia, 33, 186, 191, 315
Casal Nadur, 47
Casal Sciara, 47
Casal Zabar, 118, 167, 173, 191, 257, 259, 297, 563
Casha, G., 191, 229, 416
Cassar, Dr., 198, 417
Castagna, F., 191, 204, 209, 229, 416, 419, 423, 424, 431, 497
Castlereagh, Viscount, 505
Caulfield, Capt., 206
Cavalieri, Forts, 198
Cavazza, Capt., 163, 165
Chambray, 47
Chanez, Gen., 121, 160, 281, 560, 562, 563, 564, 581, 586, 591, 601, 603, 608, 628, 630, 635, 639, 642
Chapman, E. F., 508
Chetanti, G. M., 416
Chiapi, A., 373
Chircop, 191
Ciantar, P., 80
Cibon, 149
Cilia, A., 416
Cirillo, Marquis de, 194
Citta Vecchia, 30, 33, 51, 52, 64, 78, 106, 114, 115, 117, 119, 120, 122, 135, 138, 160, 161, 175, 184, 191, 200, 203, 217, 247, 257, 259, 296
Clugny, Bailli de, 374
Cockades, 94
Coleridge, S. T., 2
Colleredo, Grand Prior, 392
Commenda, 6
Commino, 199
Cooke, E., 502
Corfu, 159 *n.*, 194, 196, 214
Corradino, 259
Corso, P. S., 416
Cospicua, 115, 135
Coste, V., 150, 151
Coulombe, E. de V., 293, 308
Crendi, 191
Cresswell, Capt., R.N., 140
Curmi, 191
Curso, S., 191

INDEX 651

Curtis, Sir R., 40
Cutajar, F., 416

DACLA, 69
Dalli, F., 191, 204, 229
Dalli, O. B., 417
Dalli, S., 416
Damato, A., 416
D'Angely, R. St. Jean, 5, 77, 80, 89, 91, 92, 103, 104, 105, 121, 123, 125, 126, 142, 143, 150, 151, 154, 191, 565, 566, 571
Debono, M., 417
Decrès, Adm., 31, 101, 145, 149, 272, 280, 281, 286, 288, 302, 563, 564, 578, 615, 626, 627, 629, 631
Dejean, M., 121, 179, 182
Delicata, M. G., 63, 344
De Piro, Marchese V., 113, 115, 117, 135, 138, 170, 172, 190, 643
Desaix, 32, 33, 46, 49, 75
d'Henngel, 121
d'Hennezel, Gen., 281, 319
d'Hilliers, B., 32, 34, 46, 48, 49, 77
Dienne, Chev. de, 373
Dillon, Mr., 643
Dixon, Capt. M., R.N., 212, 288, 289
Dolomieu, Chev., 58, 59, 68, 70
Dommartin, Gen., 52
Dorell, F., 63, 64, 80, 197
Dorrail, Baron, 70
Dot, 121, 283, 315
Doublet, M., 7, 53, 69, 70, 148, 150, 158, 179–182, 232, 284, 293
  His book on Malta, 53–58, 60–63
Drummond, Capt., R.N., 158
Drummond, Mr., 436, 448
Duchayla, Adm., 31, 33
Dugua, Gen., 76
Duncan, Major, 268
Dundas, H., 4, 236, 250, 263, 271, 309, 322, 324, 325, 326, 327, 329, 337, 344, 488, 494
Du Pin, Bailli La T., 45, 51, 366
Durazzo, M., 230

EBNER, N., 197
Eden, Sir M., 9, 154, 364
Elliot, Sir G., 66, 180
Erskine, Major-Gen. Sir J. St. C., 235, 237, 246
Escoffier, Capt., 168 n.
Estève, P. M. G., 75, 91
Eton, W., 356, 405, 420, 437, 487, 494–503, 507, 509, 643
Eynaud, 7

FABIN, G., 416
Fardella, Col., 325
Farrugia, 110
Fay, 7, 69, 70, 200, 366, 566
Fermech, 197
Ferroni, 115

Fim, 69
Fione, F., 63
Foley, Capt., R.N., 158
Foligno Convention, 400
Foote, Capt. E. J., 76
Formosa, E., 431
Fournier, Baron, 103, 185, 191, 195, 200
Fox, Gen. H. E., 235, 236, 242, 243, 246, 249, 264, 271, 272, 273, 294, 325, 409, 436
France—
  Directory: Dispatches to, 8, 67, 76, 77, 91, 93, 100, 101, 103, 104, 119, 121, 123, 125, 130, 132, 142, 143, 148–152, 155, 159, 170, 179–183, 232 n., 279–284, 286, 287, 292–294, 301–303, 308, 310, 311, 564, 565, 578, 584, 586, 588, 594, 601, 605, 617, 619, 621, 622, 628, 630, 631, 632, 633, 637, 639, 641
  Dispatches from, 13, 14, 256
  Minutes of, 67
  Proposals concerning Malta, 463–482
  War declared against, 482
Francesco, Fra, 373
Fremeaux, de. See Batavian Consul
Frendo, G., 191, 204, 209, 229, 373, 416
Frendu, C., 80
Fricor, 373
Frisari, Bailli, 60, 62, 65, 365

GAFÀ, Chev. G., 191, 204, 229, 416
Gafà, S., 191, 204, 209, 416
Gage, Capt., R.N., 108, 113, 130, 203
Gaivoard, E. de V., 151
Galea, L., 344
Galea, P., 63, 115
Gallo, Marquis di, 137, 141, 436
Ganteaume, Adm., 31
Garat, 65
Gargur, 191
Gatt, S., 191, 204, 209
Gatto, Count L. M., 229
Gauchi, F., 63, 229
Gauchi, S., 344
Gavino, E., 63
Gellel, E., 416
Godoy, 8 and n.
Goodhall, Capt., R.N., 262
Gordon, Capt., 323
Gourgaud, Gen., 35
Gozo, 34, 45, 46, 47, 74, 111, 120, 132–134, 140, 156, 199, 213 (Also under Malta)
Graham, Gen., 4, 231, 235, 236, 240, 242, 243, 252, 276, 294, 305, 308, 318, 323, 324, 326, 328, 487, 634
  Dispatches from, 225, 246, 249, 256, 259, 264, 266, 268, 269, 273–275, 278, 295–298, 304, 326, 329, 633 n., 634 n.
Gras, 69
Greicher, 69
Grenville, Lord, 36, 113, 129, 141, 154, 200, 204, 209, 218, 244, 300, 307, 325, 328, 339, 364, 390, 397, 398, 440

Grognet, B., 344
Grumier, Jurat, 63
Grungo, Judge, 80
Gudia, 191, 249
Guido, 7, 56, 57, 60, 63, 70
Guilermi, Capt., 166
Guipony, 121
Gunson, Mr., 274
Guye, 148

HADILLA, C. G., 204, 229
Hamilton, Lady, 177, 223 and n., 294
Hamilton, Sir Wm., 35, 36, 37, 43, 110, 113, 129, 137, 141, 158, 177, 194, 199, 200, 207, 208, 209, 223, 238, 243, 244, 245, 247, 253, 262, 267, 294
Hardenberg, 399
Hardy, Sir T. M., 41, 222
Hawkesbury, Lord, 401, 402, 404, 425, 432, 435, 436, 443, 444, 445, 448, 453, 455, 456, 462-465, 466, 476, 479, 480, 481, 487
Herri, E., 70, 191
Hili, S., 417
Hobart, Lord, 350, 405, 409, 417, 418, 420, 421, 424, 427, 436, 445, 449, 462, 471, 483, 488, 492, 502
Hompesch, Ferdinand, 8, 9, 20, 45, 50, 52, 54-58, 60, 68, 69, 71, 72, 77, 78, 100, 154, 174, 180, 326, 362, 363, 365, 372, 373, 375, 376, 378, 379, 380, 381, 383, 385, 389, 390, 392-395, 421
Hood, Capt., R.N., 108
Hoste, Lt., R.N., 108
Huerel, A., 115

INGLIS, Lt. C., R.N., 291
Italinsky, Chev., 245, 247, 263, 265, 307, 325, 398

JAMAISON, Dr., 266, 267
Junot, Gen., 45, 59, 60

KEATS, Sir R., 508
Keith, Lord, 230 and n., 265, 266, 270, 284, 298, 306, 331 n., 349
  Dispatches from, 268, 271, 272, 276, 339
  at Malta, 270, 274, 339
Knights of St. John—
  Causes of the ruin of, 1-6
  Death of de Rohan, 8
  Election of Hompesch, 8-9
  Poussielgue's report on, 19-28
  Income of Grand Master, 27
  Secret correspondence code, 53
  Conduct of, during attack on Valetta, 54
  French charges against, 65
  Certain Knights expelled, 69, 80
  List of traitors, 70

Knights of St. John—cont.
  Debts of, 100
  Hopes of restoration, 129, 228, 318, 358
  Russia's protection of, 154, 203, 208 n., 218, 242, 378
  Russia's connexion with, 361-395
  Attempts to return to Malta, 216, 359
  Czar of Russia Grand Master of, 235, 358, 363, 383-385, 387, 391-392
  and the Pope, 378-380, 385-386, 462-463, 505
  Opposition to restoration of, 405-431
  Restoration under Treaty of Amiens, 433
  Finances of, 546-549
Kornan, Baron de M., 68
Kourakin, Prince A., 362

LABINI, Bishop, 3, 51, 64, 94, 182, 504
Lachaise, 104
Langues, of the Order of St. John, 6 and n., 318, 433-435, 443
Lannes, Gen., 33, 49
Lascaris, 69
Leoben, Preliminaries of, 72
Lewis, Capt., R.N., 325
Ligondez, 54, 55
Lindenthal, Lt.-Col., 246, 247, 257, 260, 265, 266, 269, 273, 297
Litta, Count de, 361, 362, 364, 375, 378, 379, 382, 383
Liverpool, Lord, 516
Lochey, Lt.-Col., 140
Long, Capt., R.N., 291
Lorenzi, G., 169, 176, 185
Luca, 191
Lunéville, Treaty of, 399
Luzzi, Prince de, 221, 227, 251, 253

MACAULAY, Alex., 359 n., 416, 437
Maddalena, 33
Maffei, Prévôt, 388, 389, 392, 393
Magen, 198
Maistre, Count E., 197
Maitland, Sir T., 525, 526, 530, 532
Maling, Capt., 214
Mallia, A., 417, 419, 423, 424, 431, 497
Mallia, P., 191, 204, 209, 229, 416, 419, 423, 424, 431, 622
Mallia, T., 416
Malta—
  Ammunition supplied to insurgents, 109, 138
  Arrêté referring to, 30
  Arrival of Nelson off, 135
  Assembly of Deputies, 191
  Ball's summons to surrender, 219-220
  Bonaparte's attack on, 29-73
  Bonaparte's reorganisation of government, 79-88
  British blockade of, 125-335

INDEX

Malta—*cont.*
British expenditure in, 300
British plans for government of, 209, 336–338, 494–534
  Complaints concerning, 340
British protection for, 199
British reforms in, 525–530
Bruey's visit to, 17–18
Capitulation of, 74
Captain Ball lands in, 199
Causes of conquest of, 67
Civil Commission of, 351
Civil marriage introduced, 89, 93
Commission of Government, 85
Commission sent to, 517
  Report of, 517–523
Convention of surrender, 60–63, 71
Congress of the chiefs, 184–189, 203, 208, 211
D'Angely's reports on, 144–149, 155–157
Deputies' report on, 427–430
Discussions in Parliament on, 440–443, 483–490, 536
Ecclesiastical troubles in, 503–505
Education in, 86–87
Election of Hompesch, 8
Eton's book on, 494–503, 645
Exposé of conduct of, 65–66
Finances of, 541
Food supply, importance of, 142 *n.*, 145, 169, 171, 176, 178, 193, 207, 226, 228, 240, 243, 252, 253–255, 261, 323 *n.*, 401
Forged report on, 364–371, 372–374
French garrison at, 76, 105, 109, 112, 125, 135, 145, 160, 196, 199, 200, 207, 215, 222, 258, 260, 310
French government of, 74–106
French preparations against, 29–31
Health laws, 82, 86
Histories of, 643–648
Hospitals in, 86, 88
Importance of, 8, 12, 32, 129, 130 *n.*, 153 *n.*, 185, 233 *n.*, 272, 294
Inventory of treasures in, 74–75
Jealousies among the insurgents, 153, 158, 161, 172, 176, 215
Judicial Courts of, 352
Maltese Regiment, 24, 76, 103, 294, 326, 345, 368
  Compensation for, 505–506
Methods of assault, 23
Monasteries in, 84, 88
National Guards in, 83, 115, 119
Naval apprentices in, 83
Naval conscription in, 83
Need of money in, 230, 231, 233, 234, 241, 243, 258, 274, 307, 325
Negotiations for evacuating, 404
Nelson's questions on, 132–134
Nelson's memoranda on, 137
Population of, 539
Post Office in, 86

Malta—*cont.*
Poussielgue's report on, 19–28
Production and revenue of, 250, 352, 535–539, 544–545, 550–555
Public Library of, 53, 68, 71
Religious bodies in, 84, 85, 87, 88
  Regulations affecting, 93, 97
Repeal of unpopular laws, 192
Reports concerning, 135, 295–298
Republican Party in, 7
Revolt of the Maltese, 76, 106 *et seq.*
  Reasons for, 77–100
  Nelson informed of, 108, 112
Savings-banks in, 540
Sickness among troops, 264, 266, 267, 268
Slavery abolished in, 81, 349
Social condition of, 1–6
Surrender to the English, 318–335
  Conditions of, 319–322
Suspension of arms, 59
Summonses to surrender, 109, 139, 308 *n.*, 566, 579, 598, 619, 636
  Replies to, 109, 140, 566, 621, 636
Taxes and imposts, 85
Tribunal of Commerce, 93
Vaubois' notes and reports on, 126–129, 130–131, 556–642
Volunteer corps in, 82
Manduca, S., 52, 113, 115, 117, 135, 138, 170, 172, 190, 229
Manoel, Grand Master, 5
Manoel, Fort, 24, 33, 45, 62, 64, 118, 145, 149, 160, 163, 165, 177, 263, 296, 319, 558, 560, 563, 583
Marchese, S., 63
Marchese, V., 63
Marengo, 299 and *n.*
Marsa Muchetta, 145, 164, 165, 173, 309, 356, 587
Marsa Scirocco, 45, 46, 50, 75, 112, 155, 157, 170, 213, 230, 245, 247, 249, 257, 292, 297, 337
Martin, Capt., R.N., 245, 275, 318, 322
Masson, 114
Master, Mr. (British Consul), 41
Mattei, Bishop, 505
Mauritius, 32
Mayer, de, collection of MSS., 68, 72
Mechain, 144 and *n.*, 147
Medicis, 69
Mélan, Chancellor B., 58, 64
Melleha Bay, 34
Melville, Lord. *See* Dundas
Menard, 121, 158, 159, 163, 165, 255
Mesgrigny, Chev. de, 45
Metrovitch, 643
Miari, Cav., 58, 59
Micabiba, 191
Mifsud, G., 191, 204, 229, 416
Miles, W. A., 426 *n.*, 430
Miller, Capt., R.N., 290, 291
Minto, Lord, 278, 398
Mirabite, Capt., 175

Moncrief, Brig.-Gen., 300, 323
Monge, 74, 80
Montebello, G., 191, 204, 229, 416
Mornaa, P. de, 7, 48 *n.*, 68, 70
Muscat, Dr., 56, 60, 61, 63, 70, 417
Muscat, J., 63
Muscat, V., 115
Musci, G., 115
Musta, 191

NAPLES, King of, 60, 103, 111, 131, 134-135, 137, 141, 142, 158, 169, 171, 176, 178, 184, 188, 191, 192, 204, 208, 211
Naples, Nelson at, 110, 141, 190 *n.*
Naples, Queen of, 211 *n.*, 400
Narbonne, Fritzlar, Count de, 65
Nasicar, 249
Naxaro, 191
Nelson, Adm. Lord, 37, 38, 40, 103, 108, 109, 110, 112, 130, 132, 141, 157, 158, 159, 184, 189, 193, 200, 205, 212, 236, 242, 244, 256, 261, 270, 276, 278, 284, 294, 298-299, 306
   Dispatches from, 133, 139, 168, 177, 178, 184, 199, 211, 233, 235, 236, 240, 241, 249, 265, 270, 492
   Dispatches to, 153, 157, 158, 161, 168, 169, 171, 178, 185, 186, 190, 194, 195, 196, 199, 204, 205, 208, 209, 210, 211, 213-216, 218, 220, 221, 222, 223, 225, 227, 228, 229, 231, 232, 238, 239, 240-241, 247, 251, 252, 253, 276, 284, 285, 324
   Deputations to, 135, 185
   Memoranda concerning Malta, 132-134, 135, 137, 492
   Command in the Mediterranean, 491
Neven, Chev., 216, 366
Nile, Battle of the, 100-106, 129 *n.*
Nisbet, Capt., R.N., 130, 203
Nizza, Adm. de, 108, 113, 126, 131, 224, 230, 236, 241, 246, 567, 616, 617, 619
Noblot, 121
Notabile. *See* Citta Vecchia

OAKES, Major-Gen. H., 508, 511, 517, 525, 526
O'Hara, Chev., 364, 365
Olivier, G. B., 63
Oswald, Col. J., 328
Otto, M., 401, 402, 443, 448

PAGET, Hon. A., 295, 307, 315, 325, 327, 328, 339, 396, 398, 401, 444, 446
Parisio, P., 191, 204, 229
Parnis, 216
Passeriano, 10, 68
Patey, Lt. J., R.N., 291
Peace of Campo Formio 10
Peard, Capt., R.N., 271

Pelham, Lord, 423, 489
Pennes, Bailli de, 45, 59
Perrée, Adm., 270
Petitions of Deputies, 57, 405, 512
Pigot, Major-Gen., 306, 308, 315, 319, 322, 329, 345, 350, 488
   Dispatches from, 310, 316, 323, 324, 327, 637
   Dispatches to, 315, 325, 336
Pinto, Grand Master, 504
Pius VI, Pope, 378-380, 383, 385-386
Pius VII, Pope, 462-463, 505
Ponsonby, Sir F., 53
Porte des Bombes, 115, 117
Portelli, Dr. M. A., 63
Portuguese fleet, 108, 113, 137, 177, 224, 236, 243
Poussielgue, 7, 14, 32, 59, 68, 70, 80, 365
   Report on Malta, 19-28
Preville, Chev. de, 48 *n.*
Preziosi, L., 63

RABASTENS, Bailli de, 374
Rabato, 47, 114, 191
Raczynski, Chev., 362
Ragusa, 12
Ragusa, Duke of, 29, 33, 48, 49
Ramla, 34
Rampon, L. de V., 152
Ransijat, Bosredon, 3, 7, 51, 59, 60, 61, 65, 69, 70, 77, 80, 89, 90, 92, 192, 365
Rapon, Capt., 150, 159
Rastadt, Congress of, 44, 61, 71, 180
Regnaud. *See* D'Angely
'Representation,' the Maltese, 63, 410
Réunion, 32
Reveau, A. V., 63
Reynier, Gen., 32, 33, 46, 47, 49
Riband, Consul, 99, 103, 104
Ricasoli, Fort, 24, 33, 45, 55, 62, 64, 118, 120, 145, 149, 160, 200, 210, 222, 225, 258, 263, 275, 293, 296, 297, 318, 322, 337, 558, 563, 626
Riccaud, E., 416, 419, 423, 424, 431
Ridoli, Fra, 373
Rights of belligerents refused, 200
Rohan, de, Grand Master, 8, 179, 180, 361, 362, 421, 495
Rohan, Fort, 50
Rospoli, Grand Master, 449, 461, 462
Roussel, Lt., 80, 163
Rouyer, 54, 55, 69
Russia, 129, 154, 189, 206, 208, 218, 231, 316 *n.*, 444, 445, 446, 460
   Bonaparte's jealousy of, 85 and *n.*
   Conditions concerning Treaty of Amiens, 451-453
   Declares war against France, 525
   Fleet in Mediterranean, 159 *n.*, 246 *n.*, 264, 329
   Grand Mastership of the Czar, 235, 358, 363, 383-385, 387

INDEX 655

Russia—*cont.*
  Grand Priory of, 376, 379, 382
  Intrigues in Malta, 169, 174, 176, 177, 185, 203, 208, 263, 309 and *n.*
  Nelson's dispatch to Emperor of, 233
  Policy of, in Malta, 361–395
  Treaty with Malta, 76
  Troops in Malta, 158, 203, 210, 231, 250, 268, 329

SACHET, 70
Sade, Chev., 180 and *n.*
Safi, 191
Said, A., 191, 204, 229, 416
St. Angelo, Fort, 62, 64, 71, 120, 145, 149, 160, 197, 337, 558, 562
St. Antonio, 118, 191, 214, 259, 296
St. Elmo, Fort, 24, 45, 55, 62, 64, 120, 145, 149, 160, 163, 198, 210, 263, 562
St. Erami, Bailli C. de, 435
St. Helens, Lord, 425, 435, 441, 445, 447, 461
St. Ildefonso, 66
St. Joseph, Fort, 259
St. Julian, 33, 46, 52, 60
St. Michele, Fort, 115
St. Paul's Bay, 46, 47, 48, 112, 213, 216, 245, 247, 257, 294, 337
St. Poix, Bailli de, 374
St. Priest, 7
St. Roque, 257–258
St. Tropez, Chev. de, 45, 71
St. Vincent, Lord, 35, 37, 39, 40, 108, 134, 210, 212
Saliba, L., 229
Samra, 259
Sandelleau, 69
Sapiano, M., 115
Saumarez, Sir J., 38, 107, 109, 110, 113, 131 *n.*, 135
Savoye, Abbé, 167, 184, 185, 191–195, 200
Scebberas, Baron C., 126
Scerri, Dr. E., 204, 209, 229, 416
Schembry, B., 56, 57, 60, 63, 70, 80, 197
Scherer, Gen., 148 and *n.*
Schoenau, Bailli de, 44
Scifo, B., 63
Scifo, S., 63
Sea power, influence of, 212 and *n.*
Ships, names of—
  Alceste (Fr.), 34, 47
  Alerte (Fr.), 14
  Alexander, 38, 39, 107, 110, 130, 137, 140, 141, 153, 157, 158, 161, 167, 168, 176, 185, 186, 199, 205, 209, 211, 212, 218–224, 230, 241, 245, 270, 271, 275, 276, 285, 287, 290, 297, 299, 323, 338, 344
  Alfonso de Albuquerque, 108
  Alliance, 235
  Alphonzo, 200
  Anemone (Fr.), 99
  Appolonie, 164

Ships, names of—*cont.*
  Aquilon, 107
  Artemise, 14, 15, 66
  Assaillante, 100, 101, 152
  Athénien, 159, 272, 303, 311, 313
  Audacious, 40, 107, 134, 135, 139, 141, 212, 241, 270, 271
  Aurora, 206
  Badine, 207, 270, 629
  Bellerophon, 40, 107, 178
  Bellone (Fr.), 281, 287, 292, 629, 630, 631
  Benjamin, 212, 221
  Black Joke, 508
  Bonne Citoyenne, 38, 107, 110, 130, 200, 205, 212, 232, 255, 261, 276
  Boudeuse, 164, 207, 216, 309, 593, 595, 603
  Bulldog, 259
  Carrère, 272
  Carthaginoise, 101, 131, 559
  Causse, 102
  Champion, 288, 289
  Cisalpine, 39
  Commerce de Marseille, 629
  Conquérant, 107
  Cornish Hero, 16
  Culloden, 40, 107, 110, 239, 242, 245, 248, 249, 253, 257, 276
  Defence, 40, 107
  Dégo, 115, 131
  Désirée, 126, 151
  Diane (Fr.), 100, 101, 107, 108, 131, 133, 139, 149, 165, 272, 293, 303, 310, 311, 312, 313, 315, 322, 559, 578, 581, 640
  Diego (Fr.), 101, 559
  Dorotea, 168
  Dover, 236
  Dubois, 11, 16
  Earl St. Vincent, 108, 211
  El Corso, 212, 270, 271
  Emerald, 38, 200
  Etoile, 47
  Falcao, 108
  Flora, 38
  Fortune, 16
  Foudroyant, 178, 224, 239, 245, 270, 271, 275, 276, 284, 287, 288, 289, 290, 291, 292, 294, 298, 299, 339, 350
  Franklin, 107
  Frontin, 17, 18
  Galathée, 163
  Ganymede, 517
  Généreux, 104, 107, 270, 271, 273, 275, 292, 330, 629
  Goliath, 40, 133, 135, 139, 141, 177, 178, 212, 214
  Gorgon, 269, 273
  Guillaume Tell, 16, 100, 104, 107, 108, 131, 133, 139, 149, 166, 170, 255, 269 *n.*, 272, 275, 279, 280, 282, 283, 286, 287, 288, 289, 290, 291, 292, 302, 322, 330, 559, 578, 581, 629, 630, 631, 632, 641
  Hoche, 579

Ships, names of—*cont.*
Hyæna, 211
Incendiary, 130, 139, 141, 168
Justice (Fr.), 14, 15, 17, 66, 100, 101, 107, 108, 126, 133, 139, 149, 165, 176, 272, 310, 311, 312, 313, 315, 322, 559, 566, 578, 581, 640
Leander, 41, 42
Légère, 637, 638
Lion, 212, 220, 276, 287, 288, 289, 290, 291, 292
Mahon, 325
Majestic, 40, 107
Malta (formerly *Guillaume Tell*), 289
Marguerite (Fr.), 301, 308, 631 *n.*, 638
Minorca, 276, 290
Minotaur, 40, 107, 135, 141, 178, 241, 242
Muiron, 272
Mutine, 41, 42, 43, 108, 135
Niobe, 313 *n.*
Northumberland, 245, 248, 249, 257, 270, 271, 276, 318
Orient (Fr.), 32, 46, 58, 60, 61, 64, 71, 103, 367
Orion, 38, 107, 109, 110
Penelope, 276, 288, 289, 290, 291, 292, 300
Perseus, 158, 259
Phæton, 275
Pierre, 39
Pluvier, 47
Princess Charlotte, 264, 299
Principe Real, 108, 567
Queen Charlotte, 268, 270, 272, 274, 276
Rainha de Portugal, 108
Retuza, 157
St. Giovanni, 133
St. John (Fr.), 77
St. Maria, 133
St. Sebastian, 108, 229
Seahorse, 76, 79
Sensible (Fr.), 15, 76, 79
Sérieuse, 48
Sirène, 157
Souverain Peuple, 107
Spartiate, 107
Speedy, 250
Stromboli, 158, 206, 212, 227, 228, 261, 276, 323
Success, 220, 270, 271, 275, 276
Swiftsure, 40
Terpsichore, 38, 109, 113, 130, 139, 141, 203, 205, 207
Thalia, 110, 203, 205, 213
Theseus, 40, 107
Tonnant, 107
Transfer, 232, 252, 325
Vanguard, 38, 39, 42, 107, 110, 135, 141, 191
Vaubois, 153
Victoria, 218

Ships, names of—*cont.*
Victorieuse, 312
Ville de Marseille, 270, 271
Vincejo, 265, 273, 276, 291
Zealous, 40, 108
Sicily, 78, 179, 185, 186, 189, 193, 203, 210
Siggeui, 191, 204
Soleil, Captain, 313, 314
Soltikoff, Bailli, Count N., 391
Songa, Bailli de, 365
Spain, 65, 66, 71, 443
Spencer, Lord, 37, 184, 209, 230, 440
Spencer, Mr., R.N., 291
Spiteri, A. P., 63, 114
Spiteri, G., 114
Stendardi, 69
Stewart, Lt.-Col., 310
Strickland, Sir G., 71
Stuart, Sir C., 4, 203
Sulkowski, 49-50
Suspension of Arms Act, 59
Switzerland, 29, 189
Syracuse, 137, 176

TABONE, S., 52
Taliba, S. L., 204, 209
Talleyrand, 9, 143, 154, 155, 230, 391, 403, 455, 456, 465, 477, 478, 479, 482
Views on Malta, 12, 13
Tanjore, Sultan of, 32
Tanti, M., 200
Tarscien, 191, 259, 267
Testaferrata, G. L., 63
Testaferrata, Baron M., 56, 60, 63, 416, 419, 423, 424, 430, 431, 438, 497
Testaferrata, N. C. di F., 509, 511, 515, 523, 643
Testaferrata, Pietro P., 63, 344
Teuma-Castelleti, F., 52, 113, 115, 117, 135, 138, 170, 172, 190, 229
Thompson, Capt. T. B., 41
Thugut, Baron, 154, 364, 393, 398
Tigné, Bailli de, 364, 370-375, 376
Tigné, Fort, 33, 45, 52, 62, 64, 160, 173, 263, 285, 296, 318, 322, 337, 558, 563, 615, 633
Tippoo Sahib, 32
Tolentino, Treaty of, 29
Tommasi, Bailli, 45, 59, 366
Elected Grand Master, 466
Torregiani, Dr., 54, 56, 60, 63
Toussard, 7, 69, 70
Treaty of Amiens, 432-439
Treilhard, 123
Trigance, 115
Tripoli, 91, 104, 127, 148, 149, 151, 186, 577
Troubridge, Sir T., 40, 42, 177, 211, 239, 242, 244, 246, 247, 251, 252-255, 261, 265, 284, 288, 289
Tunis, 41, 91, 104, 120, 127, 148, 151, 177, 186, 401

INDEX

Turkey, 81, 210
Tuscany, Grand Duke of, 41

UDINE, Conference at, 11
Udney, Mr. (British Consul), 37
University of Valetta, 56, 86 and n., 89, 92, 359, 411 and n., 614, 633
Usacoff, Adm., 265

VALETTA, 17, 24, 33, 45, 48, 49, 80, 106, 108, 115, 135, 176, 184, 191, 196, 199, 210, 212, 213, 217, 218, 227, 256, 264, 300, 306, 325, 337, 355
  Blockades of, 113, 163–166, 168, 231, 257–260
  Carmelite church in, 54
  Central school of, 86–87, 99
  Events in, 52–58
  Instructions on surrender of, 277–278
  Occupation of, by French, 64
    Reports on, 196–198, 200, 207, 247–248, 281–284, 345
  Surrendered to Graham, 318–335
Vargas, Bailli, 46
Varisi, P., 63
Vassallo, M., 66, 114, 416
Vatanges, 115
Vathier, C. de V., 151
Vaubois, Gen., 32, 33, 46, 48, 49, 64, 75, 77, 89, 90, 92, 103, 109, 111, 113, 114, 120, 125, 126, 130, 132, 140, 142, 148, 152, 160, 163, 165, 182, 190, 192, 197, 198, 201, 214, 218, 231, 255, 279, 283, 287, 292, 301, 311, 312, 314, 317, 322
  Journal of the Siege, 556–642

Vence, Gen., 152
Venice, 13
Verga, Capt. di, 229
Vial, Gen., 443, 468–471, 490, 491, 492
Villeneuve, Adm., 16, 31, 101, 104, 126, 140, 145, 148, 149, 151, 163, 170, 272, 279, 281, 286, 301, 308, 311–314, 322, 560, 561, 562, 564, 570, 575, 600, 616, 622, 632, 635, 640, 642
Villeneuve, Capt., 101
Villettes, Gen., 409, 450, 492
Vitale, Gen. E., 113, 114, 115, 117, 131, 167, 170, 172, 174, 190, 191, 204, 209, 229, 557
Vitale, Gaetano, 115
Vivion, Lt. J., 167, 213–218, 248, 259, 266, 323, 337, 602, 603

WARREN, Sir J. B., 454, 459, 472
Whitworth, Sir C., 208 n., 209, 263, 390, 397, 401, 447, 453, 455, 456, 463, 465, 466, 472, 476, 479, 480, 481
Williams, Mr. (British Consul), 72
Windham, Mr., M.P., 440–442, 499, 501
Woodhouse, Mr. J., 135
Woronzow, Count, 432, 435, 446, 457

ZAMMIT, F., 416, 417
Zammit, G. N., 63
Zarb, S., 191, 204, 209, 229, 416
Zebbing, 191
Zeitun, 191, 247, 249, 257, 259, 297, 563
Zurico, 191

THE END

www.ingramcontent.com/pod-product-compliance
Lightning Source LLC
Chambersburg PA
CBHW071352300426
44114CB00016B/2028